University Casebook Series

November, 1992

ACCOUNTING AND THE LAW, Fourth Edition (1978), with Problems Pamphlet (Successor to Dohr, Phillips, Thompson & Warren)

George C. Thompson, Professor, Columbia University Graduate School of Business.
Robert Whitman, Professor of Law, University of Connecticut.
Ellis L. Phillips, Jr., Member of the New York Bar.
William C. Warren, Professor of Law Emeritus, Columbia University.

ACCOUNTING FOR LAWYERS, MATERIALS ON (1980)

David R. Herwitz, Professor of Law, Harvard University.

ADMINISTRATIVE LAW, Eighth Edition (1987), with 1993 Case Supplement and 1983 Problems Supplement (Supplement edited in association with Paul R. Verkuil, Dean and Professor of Law, Tulane University)

Walter Gellhorn, University Professor Emeritus, Columbia University.
Clark Byse, Professor of Law, Harvard University.
Peter L. Strauss, Professor of Law, Columbia University.
Todd D. Rakoff, Professor of Law, Harvard University.
Roy A. Schotland, Professor of Law, Georgetown University.

ADMIRALTY, Third Edition (1987), with 1991 Statute and Rule Supplement

Jo Desha Lucas, Professor of Law, University of Chicago.

ADVOCACY, see also Lawyering Process

AGENCY, see also Enterprise Organization

AGENCY—PARTNERSHIPS, Fourth Edition (1987)

Abridgement from Conard, Knauss & Siegel's Enterprise Organization, Fourth Edition.

AGENCY AND PARTNERSHIPS (1987)

Melvin A. Eisenberg, Professor of Law, University of California, Berkeley.

ANTITRUST: FREE ENTERPRISE AND ECONOMIC ORGANIZATION, Sixth Edition (1983), with 1983 Problems in Antitrust Supplement and 1992 Case Supplement

Louis B. Schwartz, Professor of Law, University of Pennsylvania.
John J. Flynn, Professor of Law, University of Utah.
Harry First, Professor of Law, New York University.

BANKRUPTCY, Second Edition (1989), with 1992 Case Supplement

Robert L. Jordan, Professor of Law, University of California, Los Angeles.
William D. Warren, Professor of Law, University of California, Los Angeles.

BANKRUPTCY AND DEBTOR–CREDITOR LAW, Second Edition (1988)

Theodore Eisenberg, Professor of Law, Cornell University.

COMPARATIVE LAW, Fifth Edition (1988)

Rudolf B. Schlesinger, Professor of Law, Hastings College of the Law.
Hans W. Baade, Professor of Law, University of Texas.
Mirjan P. Damaska, Professor of Law, Yale Law School.
Peter E. Herzog, Professor of Law, Syracuse University.

COMPETITIVE PROCESS, LEGAL REGULATION OF THE, Revised Fourth Edition (1991), with 1991 Selected Statutes Supplement

Edmund W. Kitch, Professor of Law, University of Virginia.
Harvey S. Perlman, Dean of the Law School, University of Nebraska.

CONFLICT OF LAWS, Ninth Edition (1990), with 1992 Supplement

Willis L. M. Reese, Professor of Law, Columbia University.
Maurice Rosenberg, Professor of Law, Columbia University.
Peter Hay, Professor of Law, University of Illinois.

CONSTITUTIONAL LAW, Eighth Edition (1989), with 1992 Case Supplement

Edward L. Barrett, Jr., Professor of Law, University of California, Davis.
William Cohen, Professor of Law, Stanford University.
Jonathan D. Varat, Professor of Law, University of California, Los Angeles.

CONSTITUTIONAL LAW, CIVIL LIBERTY AND INDIVIDUAL RIGHTS, Second Edition (1982), with 1992 Supplement

William Cohen, Professor of Law, Stanford University.
John Kaplan, Professor of Law, Stanford University.

CONSTITUTIONAL LAW, Twelfth Edition (1991), with 1992 Supplement (Supplement edited in association with Frederick F. Schauer, Professor, Harvard University)

Gerald Gunther, Professor of Law, Stanford University.

CONSTITUTIONAL LAW, INDIVIDUAL RIGHTS IN, Fifth Edition (1992), (Reprinted from CONSTITUTIONAL LAW, Twelfth Edition), with 1992 Supplement (Supplement edited in association with Frederick F. Schauer, Professor, Harvard University)

Gerald Gunther, Professor of Law, Stanford University.

CONSUMER TRANSACTIONS, Second Edition (1991), with Selected Statutes and Regulations Supplement

Michael M. Greenfield, Professor of Law, Washington University.

CONTRACT LAW AND ITS APPLICATION, Fourth Edition (1988)

Arthur Rosett, Professor of Law, University of California, Los Angeles.

CONTRACT LAW, STUDIES IN, Fourth Edition (1991)

Edward J. Murphy, Professor of Law, University of Notre Dame.
Richard E. Speidel, Professor of Law, Northwestern University.

CONTRACTS, Fifth Edition (1987)

John P. Dawson, late Professor of Law, Harvard University.
William Burnett Harvey, Professor of Law and Political Science, Boston University.
Stanley D. Henderson, Professor of Law, University of Virginia.

CONTRACTS, Fourth Edition (1988)

E. Allan Farnsworth, Professor of Law, Columbia University.
William F. Young, Professor of Law, Columbia University.

CONTRACTS, Selections on (statutory materials) (1992)

UNIVERSITY CASEBOOK SERIES—Continued

CONTRACTS, Second Edition (1978), with Statutory and Administrative Law Supplement (1978)

Ian R. Macneil, Professor of Law, Cornell University.

COPYRIGHT, PATENTS AND TRADEMARKS, see also Competitive Process; see also Selected Statutes and International Agreements

COPYRIGHT, PATENT, TRADEMARK AND RELATED STATE DOCTRINES, Third Edition (1990), with 1991 Selected Statutes Supplement and 1981 Problem Supplement

Paul Goldstein, Professor of Law, Stanford University.

COPYRIGHT, Unfair Competition, and Other Topics Bearing on the Protection of Literary, Musical, and Artistic Works, Fifth Edition (1990), with 1991 Statutory and Case Supplement

Ralph S. Brown, Jr., Professor of Law, Yale University.
Robert C. Denicola, Professor of Law, University of Nebraska.

CORPORATE ACQUISITIONS, The Law and Finance of (1986), with 1992 Supplement

Ronald J. Gilson, Professor of Law, Stanford University.

CORPORATE FINANCE, Third Edition (1987)

Victor Brudney, Professor of Law, Harvard University.
Marvin A. Chirelstein, Professor of Law, Columbia University.

CORPORATION LAW, BASIC, Third Edition (1989), with Documentary Supplement

Detlev F. Vagts, Professor of Law, Harvard University.

CORPORATIONS, see also Enterprise Organization and Business Organization

CORPORATIONS, Sixth Edition—Concise (1988), with 1992 Case Supplement and 1992 Statutory Supplement

William L. Cary, late Professor of Law, Columbia University.
Melvin Aron Eisenberg, Professor of Law, University of California, Berkeley.

CORPORATIONS, Sixth Edition—Unabridged (1988), with 1992 Case Supplement and 1992 Statutory Supplement

William L. Cary, late Professor of Law, Columbia University.
Melvin Aron Eisenberg, Professor of Law, University of California, Berkeley.

CORPORATIONS AND BUSINESS ASSOCIATIONS—STATUTES, RULES, AND FORMS (1992)

CORRECTIONS, SEE SENTENCING

CREDITORS' RIGHTS, see also Debtor-Creditor Law

CRIMINAL JUSTICE ADMINISTRATION, Fourth Edition (1991), with 1992 Supplement

Frank W. Miller, Professor of Law, Washington University.
Robert O. Dawson, Professor of Law, University of Texas.
George E. Dix, Professor of Law, University of Texas.
Raymond I. Parnas, Professor of Law, University of California, Davis.

CRIMINAL LAW, Fifth Edition (1992)

Andre A. Moenssens, Professor of Law, University of Richmond.
Fred E. Inbau, Professor of Law Emeritus, Northwestern University.
Ronald J. Bacigal, Professor of Law, University of Richmond.

CRIMINAL LAW AND APPROACHES TO THE STUDY OF LAW, Second Edition (1991)

John M. Brumbaugh, Professor of Law, University of Maryland.

CRIMINAL LAW, Second Edition (1986)

Peter W. Low, Professor of Law, University of Virginia.
John C. Jeffries, Jr., Professor of Law, University of Virginia.
Richard C. Bonnie, Professor of Law, University of Virginia.

CRIMINAL LAW, Fourth Edition (1986)

Lloyd L. Weinreb, Professor of Law, Harvard University.

CRIMINAL LAW AND PROCEDURE, Seventh Edition (1989)

Ronald N. Boyce, Professor of Law, University of Utah.
Rollin M. Perkins, Professor of Law Emeritus, University of California, Hastings College of the Law.

CRIMINAL PROCEDURE, Fourth Edition (1992), with 1992 Supplement

James B. Haddad, late Professor of Law, Northwestern University.
James B. Zagel, Chief, Criminal Justice Division, Office of Attorney General of Illinois.
Gary L. Starkman, Assistant U. S. Attorney, Northern District of Illinois.
William J. Bauer, Chief Judge of the U.S. Court of Appeals, Seventh Circuit.

CRIMINAL PROCESS, Fourth Edition (1987), with 1992 Supplement

Lloyd L. Weinreb, Professor of Law, Harvard University.

DAMAGES, Second Edition (1952)

Charles T. McCormick, late Professor of Law, University of Texas.
William F. Fritz, late Professor of Law, University of Texas.

DECEDENTS' ESTATES AND TRUSTS, See also Family Property Law

DECEDENTS' ESTATES AND TRUSTS, Seventh Edition (1988)

John Ritchie, late Professor of Law, University of Virginia.
Neill H. Alford, Jr., Professor of Law, University of Virginia.
Richard W. Effland, late Professor of Law, Arizona State University.

DISPUTE RESOLUTION, Processes of (1989)

John S. Murray, President and Executive Director of The Conflict Clinic, Inc., George Mason University.
Alan Scott Rau, Professor of Law, University of Texas.
Edward F. Sherman, Professor of Law, University of Texas.

DOMESTIC RELATIONS, see also Family Law

DOMESTIC RELATIONS, Second Edition (1990), with 1992 Supplement

Walter Wadlington, Professor of Law, University of Virginia.

EMPLOYMENT DISCRIMINATION, Third Edition (1993)

Joel W. Friedman, Professor of Law, Tulane University.
George M. Strickler, Professor of Law, Tulane University.

EMPLOYMENT LAW, Second Edition (1991), with 1992 Statutory Supplement and 1992 Case Supplement

Mark A. Rothstein, Professor of Law, University of Houston.
Andria S. Knapp, Visiting Professor of Law, Golden Gate University.
Lance Liebman, Professor of Law, Harvard University.

FAMILY PROPERTY LAW, Cases and Materials on Wills, Trusts and Future Interests (1991)

Lawrence W. Waggoner, Professor of Law, University of Michigan.
Richard V. Wellman, Professor of Law, University of Georgia.
Gregory Alexander, Professor of Law, Cornell Law School.
Mary L. Fellows, Professor of Law, University of Minnesota.

FEDERAL COURTS, Ninth Edition (1992)

Charles T. McCormick, late Professor of Law, University of Texas.
James H. Chadbourn, late Professor of Law, Harvard University.
Charles Alan Wright, Professor of Law, University of Texas, Austin.

FEDERAL COURTS AND THE FEDERAL SYSTEM, Hart and Wechsler's Third Edition (1988), with 1992 Case Supplement, and the Judicial Code and Rules of Procedure in the Federal Courts (1991)

Paul M. Bator, Professor of Law, University of Chicago.
Daniel J. Meltzer, Professor of Law, Harvard University.
Paul J. Mishkin, Professor of Law, University of California, Berkeley.
David L. Shapiro, Professor of Law, Harvard University.

FEDERAL COURTS AND THE LAW OF FEDERAL–STATE RELATIONS, Second Edition (1989), with 1992 Supplement

Peter W. Low, Professor of Law, University of Virginia.
John C. Jeffries, Jr., Professor of Law, University of Virginia.

FEDERAL PUBLIC LAND AND RESOURCES LAW, Third Edition (1993), with 1990 Statutory Supplement

George C. Coggins, Professor of Law, University of Kansas.
Charles F. Wilkinson, Professor of Law, University of Oregon.
John D. Leshy, Professor of Law, Arizona State University.

FEDERAL RULES OF CIVIL PROCEDURE and Selected Other Procedural Provisions, 1992 Edition

FEDERAL TAXATION, see Taxation

FIRST AMENDMENT (1991), with 1992 Supplement

William W. Van Alstyne, Professor of Law, Duke University.

FOOD AND DRUG LAW, Second Edition (1991), with Statutory Supplement

Peter Barton Hutt, Esq.
Richard A. Merrill, Professor of Law, University of Virginia.

FUTURE INTERESTS (1970)

Howard R. Williams, Professor of Law, Stanford University.

FUTURE INTERESTS AND ESTATE PLANNING (1961), with 1962 Supplement

W. Barton Leach, late Professor of Law, Harvard University.
James K. Logan, formerly Dean of the Law School, University of Kansas.

GENDER DISCRIMINATION, see Women and the Law

GOVERNMENT CONTRACTS, FEDERAL, Successor Edition (1985), with 1989 Supplement

John W. Whelan, Professor of Law, Hastings College of the Law.

GOVERNMENT REGULATION: FREE ENTERPRISE AND ECONOMIC ORGANIZATION, Sixth Edition (1985)

Louis B. Schwartz, Professor of Law, Hastings College of the Law.
John J. Flynn, Professor of Law, University of Utah.
Harry First, Professor of Law, New York University.

UNIVERSITY CASEBOOK SERIES—Continued

HEALTH CARE LAW AND POLICY (1988), with 1992 Supplement

Clark C. Havighurst, Professor of Law, Duke University.

HINCKLEY, JOHN W., JR., TRIAL OF: A Case Study of the Insanity Defense (1986)

Peter W. Low, Professor of Law, University of Virginia.
John C. Jeffries, Jr., Professor of Law, University of Virginia.
Richard C. Bonnie, Professor of Law, University of Virginia.

IMMIGRATION LAW AND POLICY (1992)

Stephen H. Legomsky, Professor of Law, Washington University.

INJUNCTIONS, Second Edition (1984)

Owen M. Fiss, Professor of Law, Yale University.
Doug Rendleman, Professor of Law, College of William and Mary.

INSTITUTIONAL INVESTORS (1978)

David L. Ratner, Professor of Law, Cornell University.

INSURANCE, Second Edition (1985)

William F. Young, Professor of Law, Columbia University.
Eric M. Holmes, Professor of Law, University of Georgia.

INSURANCE LAW AND REGULATION (1990)

Kenneth S. Abraham, University of Virginia.

INTERNATIONAL LAW, see also Transnational Legal Problems, Transnational Business Problems, and United Nations Law

INTERNATIONAL LAW IN CONTEMPORARY PERSPECTIVE (1981), with Essay Supplement

Myres S. McDougal, Professor of Law, Yale University.
W. Michael Reisman, Professor of Law, Yale University.

INTERNATIONAL LEGAL SYSTEM, Third Edition (1988), with Documentary Supplement

Joseph Modeste Sweeney, Professor of Law, University of California, Hastings.
Covey T. Oliver, Professor of Law, University of Pennsylvania.
Noyes E. Leech, Professor of Law Emeritus, University of Pennsylvania.

INTRODUCTION TO LAW, see also Legal Method, On Law in Courts, and Dynamics of American Law

INTRODUCTION TO THE STUDY OF LAW (1970)

E. Wayne Thode, late Professor of Law, University of Utah.
Leon Lebowitz, Professor of Law, University of Texas.
Lester J. Mazor, Professor of Law, University of Utah.

JUDICIAL CODE and Rules of Procedure in the Federal Courts, Students' Edition, 1991 Revision

Daniel J. Meltzer, Professor of Law, Harvard University.
David L. Shapiro, Professor of Law, Harvard University.

JURISPRUDENCE (Temporary Edition Hardbound) (1949)

Lon L. Fuller, late Professor of Law, Harvard University.

JUVENILE, see also Children

JUVENILE JUSTICE PROCESS, Third Edition (1985)

Frank W. Miller, Professor of Law, Washington University.
Robert O. Dawson, Professor of Law, University of Texas.
George E. Dix, Professor of Law, University of Texas.
Raymond I. Parnas, Professor of Law, University of California, Davis.

LABOR LAW, Eleventh Edition (1991), with 1991 Statutory Supplement and 1992 Case Supplement

Archibald Cox, Professor of Law, Harvard University.
Derek C. Bok, President, Harvard University.
Robert A. Gorman, Professor of Law, University of Pennsylvania.
Matthew W. Finkin, Professor of Law, University of Illinois.

LABOR LAW, Second Edition (1982), with Statutory Supplement

Clyde W. Summers, Professor of Law, University of Pennsylvania.
Harry H. Wellington, Dean of the Law School, Yale University.
Alan Hyde, Professor of Law, Rutgers University.

LAND FINANCING, Third Edition (1985)

The late Norman Penney, Professor of Law, Cornell University.
Richard F. Broude, Member of the California Bar.
Roger Cunningham, Professor of Law, University of Michigan.

LAW AND MEDICINE (1980)

Walter Wadlington, Professor of Law and Professor of Legal Medicine, University of Virginia.
Jon R. Waltz, Professor of Law, Northwestern University.
Roger B. Dworkin, Professor of Law, Indiana University, and Professor of Biomedical History, University of Washington.

LAW, LANGUAGE AND ETHICS (1972)

William R. Bishin, Professor of Law, University of Southern California.
Christopher D. Stone, Professor of Law, University of Southern California.

LAW, SCIENCE AND MEDICINE (1984), with 1989 Supplement

Judith C. Areen, Professor of Law, Georgetown University.
Patricia A. King, Professor of Law, Georgetown University.
Steven P. Goldberg, Professor of Law, Georgetown University.
Alexander M. Capron, Professor of Law, University of Southern California.

LAWYERING PROCESS (1978), with Civil Problem Supplement and Criminal Problem Supplement

Gary Bellow, Professor of Law, Harvard University.
Bea Moulton, Professor of Law, Arizona State University.

LEGAL ETHICS (1992)

Deborah Rhode, Professor of Law, Stanford University.
David Luban, Professor of Law, University of Maryland.

LEGAL METHOD (1980)

Harry W. Jones, Professor of Law Emeritus, Columbia University.
John M. Kernochan, Professor of Law, Columbia University.
Arthur W. Murphy, Professor of Law, Columbia University.

LEGAL METHODS (1969)

Robert N. Covington, Professor of Law, Vanderbilt University.
E. Blythe Stason, late Professor of Law, Vanderbilt University.
John W. Wade, Professor of Law, Vanderbilt University.
Elliott E. Cheatham, late Professor of Law, Vanderbilt University.
Theodore A. Smedley, Professor of Law, Vanderbilt University.

UNIVERSITY CASEBOOK SERIES—Continued

LEGAL PROFESSION, THE, Responsibility and Regulation, Second Edition (1988)

Geoffrey C. Hazard, Jr., Professor of Law, Yale University.
Deborah L. Rhode, Professor of Law, Stanford University.

LEGISLATION, Fourth Edition (1982) (by Fordham)

Horace E. Read, late Vice President, Dalhousie University.
John W. MacDonald, Professor of Law Emeritus, Cornell Law School.
Jefferson B. Fordham, Professor of Law, University of Utah.
William J. Pierce, Professor of Law, University of Michigan.

LEGISLATIVE AND ADMINISTRATIVE PROCESSES, Second Edition (1981)

Hans A. Linde, Judge, Supreme Court of Oregon.
George Bunn, Professor of Law, University of Wisconsin.
Fredericka Paff, Professor of Law, University of Wisconsin.
W. Lawrence Church, Professor of Law, University of Wisconsin.

LOCAL GOVERNMENT LAW, Second Revised Edition (1986)

Jefferson B. Fordham, Professor of Law, University of Utah.

MASS MEDIA LAW, Fourth Edition (1990)

Marc A. Franklin, Professor of Law, Stanford University.
David A. Anderson, Professor of Law, University of Texas.

MUNICIPAL CORPORATIONS, see Local Government Law

NEGOTIABLE INSTRUMENTS, see Commercial Paper

NEGOTIABLE INSTRUMENTS AND LETTERS OF CREDIT (1992) (Reprinted from Commercial Law) Third Edition (1992)

Robert L. Jordan, Professor of Law, University of California, Los Angeles.
William D. Warren, Professor of Law, University of California, Los Angeles.

NEGOTIATION (1981) (Reprinted from THE LAWYERING PROCESS)

Gary Bellow, Professor of Law, Harvard Law School.
Bea Moulton, Legal Services Corporation.

NEW YORK PRACTICE, Fourth Edition (1978)

Herbert Peterfreund, Professor of Law, New York University.
Joseph M. McLaughlin, Dean of the Law School, Fordham University.

OIL AND GAS, Sixth Edition (1992)

Richard C. Maxwell, Professor of Law, Duke University.
Stephen F. Williams, Judge of the United States Court of Appeals.
Patrick Henry Martin, Professor of Law, Louisiana State University.
Bruce M. Kramer, Professor of Law, Texas Tech University.

ON LAW IN COURTS (1965)

Paul J. Mishkin, Professor of Law, University of California, Berkeley.
Clarence Morris, Professor of Law Emeritus, University of Pennsylvania.

PENSION AND EMPLOYEE BENEFIT LAW (1990), with 1992 Supplement

John H. Langbein, Professor of Law, University of Chicago.
Bruce A. Wolk, Professor of Law, University of California, Davis.

PLEADING AND PROCEDURE, see Procedure, Civil

POLICE FUNCTION, Fifth Edition (1991), with 1992 Supplement

Reprint of Chapters 1–10 of Miller, Dawson, Dix and Parnas's CRIMINAL JUSTICE ADMINISTRATION, Fourth Edition.

TAXATION, FEDERAL INCOME, OF BUSINESS ORGANIZATIONS (1991), with 1992 Supplement

Paul R. McDaniel, Professor of Law, Boston College.
Hugh J. Ault, Professor of Law, Boston College.
Martin J. McMahon, Jr., Professor of Law, University of Kentucky.
Daniel L. Simmons, Professor of Law, University of California, Davis.

TAXATION, FEDERAL INCOME, OF PARTNERSHIPS AND S CORPORATIONS (1991), with 1992 Supplement

Paul R. McDaniel, Professor of Law, Boston College.
Hugh J. Ault, Professor of Law, Boston College.
Martin J. McMahon, Jr., Professor of Law, University of Kentucky.
Daniel L. Simmons, Professor of Law, University of California, Davis.

TAXATION, FEDERAL INCOME, OIL AND GAS, NATURAL RESOURCES TRANSACTIONS (1990)

Peter C. Maxfield, Professor of Law, University of Wyoming.
James L. Houghton, CPA, Partner, Ernst and Young.
James R. Gaar, CPA, Partner, Ernst and Young.

TAXATION, FEDERAL WEALTH TRANSFER, Successor Edition (1987)

Stanley S. Surrey, late Professor of Law, Harvard University.
Paul R. McDaniel, Professor of Law, Boston College.
Harry L. Gutman, Professor of Law, University of Pennsylvania.

TAXATION, FUNDAMENTALS OF CORPORATE, Third Edition (1991)

Stephen A. Lind, Professor of Law, University of Florida and University of California, Hastings.
Stephen Schwarz, Professor of Law, University of California, Hastings.
Daniel J. Lathrope, Professor of Law, University of California, Hastings.
Joshua Rosenberg, Professor of Law, University of San Francisco.

TAXATION, FUNDAMENTALS OF PARTNERSHIP, Third Edition (1992)

Stephen A. Lind, Professor of Law, University of Florida and University of California, Hastings.
Stephen Schwarz, Professor of Law, University of California, Hastings.
Daniel J. Lathrope, Professor of Law, University of California, Hastings.
Joshua Rosenberg, Professor of Law, University of San Francisco.

TAXATION OF CORPORATIONS AND THEIR SHAREHOLDERS (1991)

David J. Shakow, Professor of Law, University of Pennsylvania.

TAXATION, PROBLEMS IN THE FEDERAL INCOME TAXATION OF PARTNERSHIPS AND CORPORATIONS, Second Edition (1986)

Norton L. Steuben, Professor of Law, University of Colorado.
William J. Turnier, Professor of Law, University of North Carolina.

TAXATION, PROBLEMS IN THE FUNDAMENTALS OF FEDERAL INCOME, Second Edition (1985)

Norton L. Steuben, Professor of Law, University of Colorado.
William J. Turnier, Professor of Law, University of North Carolina.

TORT LAW AND ALTERNATIVES, Fifth Edition (1992)

Marc A. Franklin, Professor of Law, Stanford University.
Robert L. Rabin, Professor of Law, Stanford University.

TORTS, Eighth Edition (1988)

William L. Prosser, late Professor of Law, University of California, Hastings.
John W. Wade, Professor of Law, Vanderbilt University.
Victor E. Schwartz, Adjunct Professor of Law, Georgetown University.

TORTS, Third Edition (1976)

Harry Shulman, late Dean of the Law School, Yale University.
Fleming James, Jr., Professor of Law Emeritus, Yale University.
Oscar S. Gray, Professor of Law, University of Maryland.

TRADE REGULATION, Third Edition (1990), with 1992 Supplement

Milton Handler, Professor of Law Emeritus, Columbia University.
Harlan M. Blake, Professor of Law, Columbia University.
Robert Pitofsky, Professor of Law, Georgetown University.
Harvey J. Goldschmid, Professor of Law, Columbia University.

TRADE REGULATION, see Antitrust

TRANSNATIONAL BUSINESS PROBLEMS (1986)

Detlev F. Vagts, Professor of Law, Harvard University.

TRANSNATIONAL LEGAL PROBLEMS, Third Edition (1986), with 1991 Revised Edition of Documentary Supplement

Henry J. Steiner, Professor of Law, Harvard University.
Detlev F. Vagts, Professor of Law, Harvard University.

TRIAL, see also Evidence, Making the Record, Lawyering Process and Preparing and Presenting the Case

TRUSTS, Sixth Edition (1991)

George G. Bogert, late Professor of Law Emeritus, University of Chicago.
Dallin H. Oaks, President, Brigham Young University.
H. Reese Hansen, Dean and Professor of Law, Brigham Young University.
Claralyn Martin Hill, J.D. Brigham Young University.

TRUSTS AND ESTATES, SELECTED STATUTES ON, 1992 Edition

TRUSTS AND WILLS, See also Decedents' Estates and Trusts, and Family Property Law

UNFAIR COMPETITION, see Competitive Process and Business Torts

WATER RESOURCE MANAGEMENT, Third Edition (1988), with 1992 Supplement

The late Charles J. Meyers, formerly Dean, Stanford University Law School.
A. Dan Tarlock, Professor of Law, IIT Chicago-Kent College of Law.
James N. Corbridge, Jr., Chancellor, University of Colorado at Boulder, and Professor of Law, University of Colorado.
David H. Getches, Professor of Law, University of Colorado.

WOMEN AND THE LAW (1992)

Mary Joe Frug, late Professor of Law, New England School of Law.

WILLS AND ADMINISTRATION, Fifth Edition (1961)

Philip Mechem, late Professor of Law, University of Pennsylvania.
Thomas E. Atkinson, late Professor of Law, New York University.

WRITING AND ANALYSIS IN THE LAW, Second Edition (1991)

Helene S. Shapo, Professor of Law, Northwestern University.
Marilyn R. Walter, Professor of Law, Brooklyn Law School.
Elizabeth Fajans, Writing Specialist, Brooklyn Law School.

University Casebook Series

LEGAL REGULATION

OF THE

COMPETITIVE PROCESS

Cases, Materials and Notes

on

Unfair Business Practices, Trademarks,
Copyrights and Patents

REVISED FOURTH EDITION

By

EDMUND W. KITCH
Joseph M. Hartfield Professor of Law
The University of Virginia

HARVEY S. PERLMAN
Dean and Professor of Law
The University of Nebraska

Westbury, New York
THE FOUNDATION PRESS, INC.
1991

Library of Congress Cataloging-in-Publication Data

Kitch, Edmund W.

   Legal regulation of the competitive process : cases, materials, and
notes on unfair business practices, trademarks, copyrights, and
patents / by Edmund W. Kitch, Harvey S. Perlman. — Rev.4th ed.

     p.   cm. — (University casebook series)

  Includes index.

  ISBN 0–88277–887–0

  1. Competition, Unfair—United States—Cases. 2. Trade
regulation—United States—Cases. I. Perlman, Harvey S., 1942–   .
II. Title. III. Series.

KF1608.K56 1991

343.73'072—dc20

[347.30372]   91–10241

     Kitch & Perlman Rev.4th Ed. UCB
     1st Reprint—1993

ACKNOWLEDGMENTS

We remain indebted to those teachers and students who have used the earlier editions and have provided us with helpful suggestions for improvements.

Dean Perlman acknowledges the support of the University of Nebraska College of Law's faculty and staff who in many ways made his participation in this revision possible. His contribution is dedicated to Susan, Anne, and Amie (a.k.a. Amy).

Professor Kitch acknowledges the support of the University of Virginia School of Law and of the University of Virginia Law School Foundation. His contribution is dedicated to Alison.

E.W.K.
H.S.P.

May, 1991

*

ACKNOWLEDGMENTS

SUMMARY OF CONTENTS

SUMMARY OF CONTENTS

SUMMARY OF CONTENTS

*

TABLE OF CONTENTS

TABLE OF CONTENTS

TABLE OF CONTENTS

Page

TABLE OF CONTENTS

*

TABLE OF CASES

Principal cases are in italic type. Non-principal cases are in roman type. References are to Pages.

TABLE OF CASES

TABLE OF CASES

LEGAL REGULATION

OF THE

COMPETITIVE PROCESS

*

Chapter I

THE PROBLEM OF ENTRY

A. THE COMMON LAW

TUTTLE v. BUCK

Supreme Court of Minnesota, 1909.
107 Minn. 145, 119 N.W. 946.

This appeal is from an order overruling a general demurrer to a complaint in which the plaintiff alleged: That for more than ten years last past he has been and still is a barber by trade, and engaged in business as such in the village of Howard Lake, Minn., in said county, where he resides, owning and operating a shop for the purpose of his said trade. That until the injury hereinafter complained of his said business was prosperous, and plaintiff was enabled thereby to comfortably maintain himself and family out of the income and profits thereof, and also to save a considerable sum per annum, to wit, about $800. That the defendant, during the period of about 12 months last past, has wrongfully, unlawfully, and maliciously endeavored to destroy plaintiff's said business and compel plaintiff to abandon the same. That to that end he has persistently and systematically sought, by false and malicious reports and accusations of and concerning the plaintiff, by personally soliciting and urging plaintiff's patrons no longer to employ plaintiff, by threats of his personal displeasure, and by various other unlawful means and devices, to induce, and has thereby induced, many of said patrons to withhold from plaintiff the employment by them formerly given. That defendant is possessed of large means, and is engaged in the business of a banker in said village of Howard Lake, at Dassel, Minn., and at divers other places, and is nowise interested in the occupation of a barber; yet in the pursuance of the wicked, malicious, and unlawful purpose aforesaid, and for the sole and only purpose of injuring the trade of the plaintiff, and of accomplishing his purpose and threats of ruining the plaintiff's said business and driving him out of said village, the defendant fitted up and furnished a barber shop in said village for conducting the trade of barbering. That failing to induce any barber to occupy said shop on his own account, though offered at nominal rental, said defendant, with the wrongful and malicious purpose aforesaid, and not otherwise, has during the time herein stated hired two barbers in succession for a stated salary, paid by him, to occupy said shop, and to serve so many of plaintiff's patrons as said defendant has been or may be able by the means aforesaid to direct from plaintiff's shop. That at the present time a barber so employed and paid by the defendant is occupying and nominally con-

1

ducting the shop thus fitted and furnished by the defendant, without paying any rent therefor, and under an agreement with defendant whereby the income of said shop is required to be paid to defendant, and is so paid in partial return for his wages. That all of said things were and are done by defendant with the sole design of injuring the plaintiff, and of destroying his said business, and not for the purpose of serving any legitimate interest of his own. That by reason of the great wealth and prominence of the defendant, and the personal and financial influence consequent thereon, he has by the means aforesaid, and through other unlawful means and devices by him employed, materially injured the business of the plaintiff, has largely reduced the income and profits thereof, and intends and threatens to destroy the same altogether, to plaintiff's damage in the sum of $10,000.

ELLIOTT, J. (after stating the facts as above). It has been said that the law deals only with externals, and that a lawful act cannot be made the foundation of an action because it was done with an evil motive. * * *

We do not intend to enter upon an elaborate discussion of the subject, or become entangled in the subtleties connected with the words "malice" and "malicious." We are not able to accept without limitations the doctrine above referred to, but at this time content ourselves with a brief reference to some general principles. It must be remembered that the common law is the result of growth, and that its development has been determined by the social needs of the community which it governs. Necessarily its form and substance has been greatly affected by prevalent economic theories. For generations there has been a practical agreement upon the proposition that competition in trade and business is desirable, and this idea has found expression in the decisions of the courts as well as in statutes. But it has led to grievous and manifold wrongs to individuals, and many courts have manifested an earnest desire to protect the individuals from the evils which result from unrestrained business competition. The problem has been to so adjust matters as to preserve the principle of competition and yet guard against its abuse to the unnecessary injury to the individual. So the principle that a man may use his own property according to his own needs and desires, while true in the abstract, is subject to many limitations in the concrete. Men cannot always, in civilized society, be allowed to use their own property as their interests or desires may dictate without reference to the fact that they have neighbors whose rights are as sacred as their own. The existence and well-being of society requires that each and every person shall conduct himself consistently with the fact that he is a social and reasonable person. The purpose for which a man is using his own property may thus sometimes determine his rights. * * *

Many of the restrictions which should be recognized and enforced result from a tacit recognition of principles which are not often stated in the decisions in express terms. Sir Frederick Pollock notes that not many years ago it was difficult to find any definite authority for stating as a general proposition of English law that it is wrong to do a willful wrong to one's neighbor without lawful justification or excuse. But neither is there any express authority for the general proposition that men must perform their contracts. Both principles, in this generality of form and conception, are modern and there was a time when neither was true. After developing the idea that law begins, not with authentic general principles, but with the enumeration of particular remedies, the learned writer continues: "If there exists, then, a positive duty to avoid harm, much more, then, exists the negative duty of not doing willful harm, subject, as all general duties must be subject, to the necessary exceptions. The three main heads of duty with which the law of torts is concerned, namely, to abstain from willful injury, to respect the property of others, and to use due diligence to avoid causing harm to others, are all alike of a comprehensive nature." Pollock, Torts, (8th Ed.) p. 21. He then quotes with approval the statement of Lord Bowen that "at common law there was a cause of action whenever one person did damage to another, willfully and intentionally, without just cause and excuse." In Plant v. Woods, 176 Mass. 492, 57 N.E. 1011, 51 L.R.A. 339, 79 Am.St.Rep. 330, Mr. Justice Hammond said: "It is said, also, that, where one has the lawful right to do a thing, the motive by which he is actuated is immaterial. One form of this statement appears in the first headnote in Allen v. Flood, as reported in [1898] A.C. 1, as follows: 'An act lawful in itself is not converted by a malicious or bad motive into an unlawful act, so as to make the doer of the act liable to a civil action.' If the meaning of this and similar expressions is that, where a person has the lawful right to do a thing irrespective of his motive, his motive is immaterial, the proposition is a mere truism. If, however, the meaning is that where a person, if actuated by one kind of a motive, has a lawful right to do a thing, the act is lawful when done under any conceivable motive, or that an act lawful under one set of circumstances is therefore lawful under every conceivable set of circumstances, the proposition does not commend itself to us as either logically or legally accurate."

* * *

It is freely conceded that there are many decisions contrary to this view; but, when carried to the extent contended for by the appellant, we think they are unsafe, unsound, and illy adapted to modern conditions. To divert to one's self the customers of a business rival by the offer of goods at lower prices is in general a legitimate mode of serving one's own interest, and justifiable as fair competition. But when a man starts an opposition place of business, not for the sake of profit to himself, but regardless of loss to himself, and for the sole purpose of driving his competitor out of business, and with the intention of himself retiring upon the accomplishment of his malevolent purpose, he is guilty of a wanton wrong and an actionable tort. In such a case he would not be exercising his legal right, or doing an act which can be judged separately from the motive which actuated him. To call such conduct competition is a perversion of terms. It is simply the application of force without legal justification, which in its moral quality may be no better than highway robbery.

Nevertheless, in the opinion of the writer this complaint is insufficient. It is not claimed that it states a cause of action for slander. No question of conspiracy or combination is involved. Stripped of the adjectives and the statement that what was done was for the sole purpose of injuring the plaintiff, and not for the purpose of serving a legitimate purpose of the defendant, the complaint states facts which in themselves amount only to an ordinary everyday business transaction. There is no allegation that the defendant was intentionally running the business at a financial loss to himself, or that after driving the plaintiff out of business the defendant closed up or intended to close up his shop. From all that appears from the complaint he may have opened the barber shop, energetically sought business from his acquaintances and the customers of the plaintiff, and as a result of his enterprise and command of capital obtained it, with the result that the plaintiff, from want of capital, acquaintance, or enterprise, was unable to stand the competition and was thus driven out of business. The facts thus alleged do not, in my opinion, in themselves, without reference to the way in which they are characterized by the pleader, tend to show a malicious and wanton wrong to the plaintiff.

A majority of the Justices, however, are of the opinion that, on the principle declared in the foregoing opinion, the complaint states a cause of action, and the order is therefore affirmed.

Affirmed.

JAGGARD, J., dissents.

SORENSON v. CHEVROLET MOTOR CO., 171 Minn. 260, 214 N.W. 754 (1927). [The plaintiff had an agency contract with the defendant, Chevrolet, terminable by either party after adequate notice. Plaintiff had a successful business and advertised extensively. Defendant Sander was plaintiff's competitor. The complaint charging a conspiracy to destroy plaintiff's business alleged that "Sander knew of plaintiff's contract with the corporation and defendants agreed to acquire plaintiff's business for Sander. Pursuant to this plan and the agreement between defendants, the corporation wrongfully repudiated its contract with plaintiff without giving the notice therein required for cancellation. Plaintiff's business was thereby destroyed by the wrongful acts of defendants. This was done with actual malice toward plaintiff and such malice of the two defendants was well known to each and adopted by both of them." In reversing the lower court which sustained demurrers, the court noted:]

Every act done by a businessman in diverting trade from a competitor to himself is an act intentionally done, and when successful is an injury to the competitor because to that extent it lessens his profits. But it is not wrongful. Trade must be free and unrestricted but the competitor should operate within the zone of fair dealing. Competition justifies the use of all lawful and fair means to gain the trade that would otherwise go to a competitor in business.

*　　*　　*

Under his contract with the corporation, plaintiff had built up a valuable business. His relations with the company were mutually satisfactory. Sander, a stranger to the contract, wished to put an end to the business relations between plaintiff and the company and induced the company to repudiate the contract. If he had done this for no other purpose than to deprive plaintiff of the benefits of the contract and of his established business, under all the cases Sander would be liable for his wrongful interference in the contract relations between plaintiff and the company. But, according to the complaint, Sander had another motive. Not only did he wish to deprive plaintiff of his business, but he also desired to appropriate the business to himself. It cannot be said that this desire furnishes an excuse or justification for an act which would otherwise be unlawful. On the contrary, it accentuates the inherent wrongfulness of Sander's conduct. Under these circumstances, it would be contrary to the decided weight of authority to hold that Sander was serving his legitimate interests, or that his conduct was free from wrong, or that, since plaintiff has a cause of action against the company for breach of contract, Sander should go scot-free. It seems clear that elementary principles of business ethics demonstrate the unlawfulness of Sander's conduct, and the law ought to insist on as high a standard of business morality as prevails among reputable business men.

*　　*　　*

When one has knowledge of the contract rights of another, his wrongful inducement of a breach thereof is a willful destruction of the property of another and cannot be justified on the theory that it enhances and advances the business interests of the wrongdoer.

*　　*　　*

WITTE TRANSPORTATION CO. v. MURPHY MOTOR FREIGHT LINES, INC., 291 Minn. 461, 193 N.W.2d 148 (1971). [Plaintiff and defendant were competing motor common carriers who both used "routing letters" as an integral and important part of their business. A "routing letter" is a letter from a consignee requesting a shipper to ship goods only by a specified carrier. Salesmen for each carrier sought to obtain "routing letters" from its customers, oftentimes preparing the letters in advance for their signatures. The defendant had several letters prepared in the process of soliciting new business, but they were never signed by the consignees. However, copies of the unsigned letters were delivered to the consignors. The Minnesota Supreme Court framed the issue: "Does the evidence sustain the trial court's finding in substance that defendant intentionally, maliciously, and wrongfully interfered with the business relationship between plaintiff and its customers?"]

This court has long recognized that there lies an action for the wrongful interference with noncontractual as well as contractual business relationships. Tuttle v. Buck, 107 Minn. 145, 119 N.W. 946 (1909). Other courts that have considered this question have likewise held, almost universally, that the tort of interference with contractual rights should be extended to include noncontractual business relationships. Annotation, 9 A.L.R.2d 228, 255. Prosser, Torts (4 ed.) § 130.

Defendant argues that, even if there was an interference with the business relationship of the plaintiff and its customers, there was not sufficient malice or intent to bring the present case within the scope of tortious interference with a business relationship. Although it is true that the basis of liability in Tuttle v. Buck, supra, was predicated upon an intentional, malicious attack upon the business of another, in subsequent cases we have explained that malicious intent of the kind found in Tuttle is not a prerequisite to a finding of liability. The scope of the tort encompasses a broader legal area than the narrow limits of the facts in Tuttle. For example, we later held that an action could be based on "the intentional doing of a wrongful act without legal justification or excuse, or, otherwise stated the wilful violation of a known right * * *, malice in the sense of ill-will or spite not being essential." Carnes v. St. Paul Union Stockyards Co., 164 Minn. 457, 462, 205 N.W. 630, 631 (1925). See, also, Joyce v. G.N. Ry. Co., 100 Minn. 225, 110 N.W. 975 (1907).

However, we have never allowed a recovery for negligent wrongful interference with a business relationship. The wrongful act of interference must have been intentionally done. The courts generally have not recognized a negligent wrongful interference with a business relationship as an actionable tort. Cf. Prosser, Torts (4 ed.) § 130, p. 952.

[The court concluded that an administrative failure resulted in the delivery of the letters and that there was no evidence to support a finding that the letters were prepared or delivered with intent to deceive. A judgment for the plaintiff was reversed.]

NOTES

1. Compare the action of the New York Secretary of State who denied a license to a woman barber who planned to wear a see-through uniform and serve cocktails. N.Y. Times, July 10, 1969. What result if Buck had resorted to such devices to destroy plaintiff's business?

2. Product markets vary in the degree to which they are competitive or monopolistic. As a given product market moves closer to competition, the interests of the individual competitors become less important. The common law is designed to resolve disputes between individuals. Although the common law could not ignore the broader impact of decisions on society in general, the litigant's individual interests were more immediate and apparent. Thus when the common law with its traditional dislike for monopoly intervened to regulate business practices, it was forced to resolve the conflict between the interests of individual competitors and the interest of maintenance of competition. This conflict runs continuously throughout this material. The student should be alert for the adjustments required in the common law arising from this conflict.

3. The Minnesota Supreme Court observed in *Sorenson* that the nature of competition requires a businessman to attempt to inflict injury on his competitors by appropriating his customers and thereby his profits. This is the competitive process resulting in better products and services at lower prices. Which of the opinions, *Tuttle, Sorenson,* or *Witte* best adjusts common law doctrines to take this observation into account? In *Witte* do you suspect that the competitive relationship between the parties will be considered in determining "legal justification or excuse"? Can *Tuttle* and *Sorenson* be distinguished? Does the court lose sight of the distinction in *Witte?* Consider Justice Traynor's dictum in Imperial Ice Co. v. Rossier, 18 Cal.2d 33, 36, 112 P.2d 631, 633 (1941):

> Whatever interest society has in encouraging free and open competition by means not in themselves unlawful, contractual stability is generally accepted as of greater importance than competitive freedom. Competitive freedom, however, is of sufficient importance to justify one competitor in inducing a third party to forsake another competitor if no contractual relationship exists between the latter two.

4. If you were a Minnesota consumer which of the competing rules announced by the court in the three cases would you prefer?

5. The issue of compensable competitive injury is a difficult one and arises in a variety of situations. Consider Brunswick Corp. v. Pueblo Bowl-O-Mat, Inc., 429 U.S. 477 (1977) where a manufacturer of pin setting equipment acquired several failing bowling centers that had defaulted on payment for bowling equipment. The plaintiffs, three bowling centers that had competed with those acquired by the manufacturer, alleged the acquisition violated section 7 of the Clayton Act which prohibits mergers substantially lessening competition and sought damages on the theory that in the absence of the acquisition the acquired bowling centers would have failed and plaintiffs would have accordingly increased their own profits. The jury returned a verdict for $2,358,000, a figure based on the lost profits resulting from the continued competition with the acquired centers and the court trebled the verdict. On appeal, should the Supreme Court affirm? It did not!

Is this Tuttle v. Buck in different costume? What if the banker in *Tuttle,* solely for the purpose of injuring plaintiff, had subsidized the losses of a competing barber by making an unsecured loan at a low interest rate?

6. *The English Cases.* The conflict posed by Tuttle v. Buck—the intrusion of tort law into the marketplace—has its historical antecedents and contemporary contrasts in the English common law. The famous House of Lords Trilogy and its progeny provide useful counterpoints to the development of the American doctrines. The Trilogy consists of three cases: Mogul Steamship Co. v. McGregor, Gow & Co., 23 Q.B.Div. 598 (1889); aff'd [1892] A.C. 25 (1891); Allen v. Flood, [1898] A.C. 1; and Quinn v. Leatham, [1901] A.C. 495.

In *Mogul,* shipowners formed an association to regulate the number of ships sent by members to loading ports, the division of cargoes, and the freight charges. A rebate of 5 per cent was allowed to all shippers who exclusively used association members. Plaintiffs were shipowners excluded from the association. The association underbid plaintiffs and reduced freights so low that plaintiffs were unable to show a profit. Plaintiffs brought an action for damages against the associated owners alleging a conspiracy to injure plaintiffs. Held, for defendants.

The opinion of Bowen, L.J. contains the statement of the correlative rights of competitors:

What, then, are the limitations which the law imposes on a trader in the conduct of his business as between himself and other traders? * * * No man, whether trader or not, can, * * * justify damaging another in his commercial business by fraud or misrepresentation. Intimidation, obstruction, and molestation are forbidden; so is the intentional procurement of a violation of individual rights, contractual or other, assuming always that there is no just cause for it. The intentional driving away of customers by shew of violence; * * * the obstruction of actors on the stage by preconcerted hissing; * * * the disturbance of wild fowl in decoys by the firing of guns; * * * the impeding or threatening servants or workmen; * * * the inducing persons under personal contracts to break their contracts; * * * all are instances of such forbidden acts. But the defendants have been guilty of none of these acts. They have done nothing more against the plaintiffs than pursue to the bitter end a war of competition waged in the interest of their own trade. To the argument that a competition so pursued ceases to have a just cause or excuse when there is ill-will or a personal intention to harm, it is sufficient to reply * * * that there was here no personal intention to do any other or greater harm to the plaintiffs than such as was necessarily involved in the desire to attract to the defendants' ships the entire tea freights of the ports, a portion of which would otherwise have fallen to the plaintiffs' share. I can find no authority for the doctrine that such a commercial motive deprives of "just cause or excuse" acts done in the course of trade which would but for such a motive be justifiable. So to hold would be to convert into an illegal motive the instinct of self-advancement and self-protection, which is the very incentive to all trade.

Lord Justice Bowen decided also that to impose a standard of reasonableness on commercial conduct would be to "impose a novel fetter upon trade * * *. A man is bound not to use his property so as to infringe upon another's right * * *. If engaged in actions which may involve danger to others, he ought, speaking generally, to take reasonable care to avoid endangering them. But there is surely no doctrine of law which compels him to use his property in a way that judges and juries may consider reasonable * * *. If there is no such fetter upon the use of property known to the English law, why should there be any such fetter upon trade?"

7. Should the existence of a conspiracy or combination of competitors alter the thrust of Tuttle v. Buck?

8. The Restatement (Third) of Unfair Competition § 1 (Tent. Draft No. 1, 1988) provides that a person causing harm to another's commercial relations by competitive acts is not liable unless the acts constitute deceptive marketing, trademark infringement, appropriation of trade values, or are "determined to be similarly actionable as an unfair method of competition, taking into account the nature of the conduct and its likely effect on both the party seeking relief and the public". The Restatement places the burden of proof on the person alleging injury to "establish facts sufficient to subject the actor to liability." Comment *a*. Do you think a general catch-all provision that permits courts to determine which methods of competition are "unfair" is a wise policy?

B. REGULATION

AMERICAN FINANCIAL SERVICES ASS'N v. FEDERAL TRADE COMMISSION

United States Court of Appeals, District of Columbia Circuit, 1985.
767 F.2d 957.

[The American Financial Services Association and the South Carolina Department of Consumer Affairs seek review of a Federal Trade Commission rule that prevents a lender from including in a loan or installment sales contract a provision which results in a wage assignment by the debtor in the event of default on the loan or which provides for a nonpossessory security interest in household goods such as furniture other than a purchase money security interest. A wage assignment allows a creditor to require the debtor's employer to pay all or part of the debtor's wages to the creditor and the security interest ("HHG security interest") allows the creditor, on default, to seize the debtor's household goods without judgment or court order. Section 5 of the Act conferring authority on the Commission permits it to regulate "unfair or deceptive acts and practices". The petitioners contend the FTC went beyond its statutory authority both in adopting the rule and in attempting to preempt state laws which permit these remedies.

The court first reviewed the history of the rulemaking authority of the Commission and the pattern of Congressional delegation to the Commission to determine what acts or practices are "unfair". The Commission had adopted a policy statement in 1964 identifying three criteria used to determine whether a given practice was unfair: whether the practice (1) was against public policy, (2) was immoral, unethical, oppressive, or unscrupulous, and (3) caused substantial injury to consumers. This policy was approved by the Supreme Court in Federal Trade Commission v. Sperry & Hutchinson, 405 U.S. 233 (1972). After substantial Commission activity, much of it controversial, Congress requested and received in 1980 a clarification of the Commission's views of its unfairness jurisdiction. The 1980 Policy Statement provided the following standard for identifying unfair practices: "To justify a finding of unfairness the injury must satisfy three tests. It must be substantial; it must not be outweighted by any countervailing benefits to consumers or competition that the practice produces; and it must be an injury that consumers themselves could not reasonably have avoided." It is against this standard that the court evaluates the Commission's rule.]

WALD, CIRCUIT JUDGE:

C. *The FTC's Exercise of Unfairness Authority Under Section 5(a)*

Applying the three-part consumer unfairness standard, the Commission found that HHG security interests and wage assignments were unfair creditor remedies because they caused substantial, unjustified consumer injury. Our analysis begins with a review of the Commission's reasoning with respect to each of the three criteria set out in the consumer unfairness standard.

1. *Substantial Injury*

In elaborating the term "substantial injury" in its Policy Statement, the Commission stated that in most cases substantial injury would involve monetary harm and that "ordinarily" "emotional impact and other more subjective types of harm" would not make a practice unfair. See Policy Statement at 36. The Commission further clarified that it "is not concerned with trivial or merely speculative harms." Id. "An injury may be sufficiently substantial, however, if it does a small harm to a large number of people, or if it raises a significant risk of concrete harm." Id. at n. 12. With these guidelines in mind, we turn to the specific injuries found to result from HHG security interests and wage assignments.

[The court accepted the Commission's findings that both HHG security interests and wage assignments caused substantial injury. Because the value of household goods on the market is generally low whereas the cost of replacement and the value to the owner is high, the seizure represents a cost disproportionate to any benefit the creditor might enjoy. Also the need for basic household goods makes consumers vulnerable to threats of seizure which may result in them accepting additional terms that are not to their financial advantage or lead to them giving up defenses. Wage assignments are harmful because they can be invoked without due process procedural requirements and they interject the creditor into the employment relationship. The threat of a wage assignment again may coerce consumers to act to their own disadvantage.]

2. *Countervailing Benefits*

The Commission recognizes that most business practices entail a balancing of costs and benefits to the consumer. Therefore the Commission "will not find that a practice unfairly injures consumers unless it is injurious in its net effects." Policy Statement at 37. To make this cost-benefit determination, the Commission examines the potential costs that the proposed remedy would impose on the parties and society in general. In the present case, the Commission made the following assessment:

> The potential costs of most significance in this proceeding include increased collection costs, increased screening costs, larger legal costs and increases in bad debt losses or reserves. Increased creditor costs generally would be reflected in higher interests to borrowers, reduced credit availability, or other restrictions such as increased collateral or down payment requirements.

49 Fed.Reg. at 7744 (footnotes omitted).

[The Commission minimized the benefits of HHG security interests and wage assignments because of the presence of a wide variety of other permissible creditor remedies.]

* * * Based on record evidence, the Commission concluded that the Rule would have only a marginal impact on the cost or availability of credit, and that this marginal cost was clearly overshadowed by the much greater risks to consumers resulting from the use of HHG security interests and wage assignments. Thus we find that the Commission satisfied the second prong of the three-part consumer injury test set out in its Policy Statement.

3. *Injury is Not Reasonably Avoidable*

The requirement that the injury cannot be reasonably avoided by the consumers stems from the Commission's general reliance on free and informed consumer choice as the best regulator of the market. "Normally we expect the marketplace to be self-correcting, and we rely on consumer choice—the ability of individual consumers to make their own private purchasing decisions without regulatory intervention—to govern the market." Policy Statement at 37. As long recognized, however, certain types of seller conduct or market imperfections may unjustifiably hinder consumers' free market decisions and prevent the forces of supply and demand from maximizing benefits and minimizing costs. In such instances of market failure, the Commission may be required to take corrective action. Such corrective action is taken "not to second-guess the wisdom of particular consumer decisions, but rather to halt some form of seller behavior that unreasonably creates or takes advantage of an obstacle to the free exercise of consumer decisionmaking." Id. at 37.

[The Commission found that consumers could not avoid the two remedies because of market imperfections evidenced by (1) the use of standard form contracts which gave consumers no leverage to bargain over terms; (2) the wide-scale use of similar forms in those parts of the industry providing credit to high-risk consumers; (3) the lack of consumer understanding of the technical language used in contracts that made it difficult for consumers to shop for better terms; (4) the lack of incentive on the part of creditors to compete on the basis of remedial terms given the consumers' lack of understanding of the consequences; and (5) the observation that default by consumers resulted largely from forces outside the control of the debtor.]

D. *Challenge to the FTC's Exercise of Unfairness Authority Under Section 5(a)*

Although the Commission has identified a substantial consumer injury, which is not offset by countervailing benefits, and which cannot be reasonably avoided by consumers, petitioners nonetheless challenge the ban on HHG security interests and wage assignments as outside the scope of the Commission's unfairness authority.

* * *

In essence, petitioners ask the court to limit the FTC's exercise of its unfairness authority to situations involving deception, coercion, or withholding of material information. As noted earlier, despite considerable controversy over the bounds of the FTC's authority, neither Congress nor the FTC has seen fit to delineate the specific "kinds" of practices which will be deemed unfair within the meaning of section 5. Instead the FTC has adhered to its established convention, envisioned by Congress, of developing and refining its unfair practice criteria on a progressive, incremental basis. * * *

While we agree with petitioners that the Commission cannot be allowed to intervene at will whenever it believes the market is not producing the "best deal" for consumers, we nonetheless believe that this court would be overstepping its authority if we were to mandate, as petitioners urge, that the Commission's unfairness authority is limited solely to the regulation of conduct involving deception, coercion or the withholding of material information. As previously discussed, the Commission's consumer injury test, set forth in its Policy Statement, while not specifically defining the "kinds" of practices or injuries encompassed, is the most precise definition of unfairness articulated to date by either the Commission or Congress. Upon reviewing it, Congress has not seen fit to enact any more particularized definition of unfairness to limit the Commission's discretion. Indeed, the most significant congressional response to the Policy Statement has not been criticisms or rejection, but proposals to enact the Commission's three-part consumer injury standard into law. Thus, the Commission has, for all practical purposes, been left to develop its unfairness doctrine on an incremental, evolutionary basis. At this juncture, it is not for this court to step in and confine, by judicial fiat, the Commission's unfairness authority to acts or practices found to be deceptive or coercive.
* * *

IV. PREEMPTION OF STATE LAW

Petitioners AFSA and, in particular, SCDCA, claim that the FTC has exceeded its rulemaking authority by "preempting" or "supplanting" the "carefully wrought consumer protection statutes" of those states that either allow or regulate the use of HHG security interests and wage assignments. Although the Magnuson-Moss Act contains no explicit preemption provision, "[i]t has long since been firmly established that state statutes and regulations may be superseded by validly enacted regulations of federal agencies such as the FTC." Katharine Gibbs, 612 F.2d at 667 (citing Free v. Bland, 369 U.S. 663 (1962); Spiegel, Inc. v. FTC, 540 F.2d 287, 293 (7th Cir.1976)). The legislative history of the Magnuson-Moss Act and predecessor bills indicate that while Congress did not intend the Commission's regulations to "occupy the field," it did intend FTC rules to have that preemptive effect which flows naturally from a repugnancy between the Commission's valid enactments and state laws. * * *

In *Katharine Gibbs*, the Second Circuit found the preemption provisions of the Vocational Schools Rule overly broad and thus beyond the Commission's power. 612 F.2d at 667. The preemption provision of the Vocational Schools Rule decreed preemption of any state law or regulation which frustrated the purpose of the Rule's "inadequately spelled out provisions," thereby potentially preempting "an indefinite variety of state laws and regulations governing the contractual relations between vocational schools and their students." Katharine Gibbs, 612 F.2d at 667. The court noted that "[i]f the Commission had defined with specificity the acts or practices it deemed unfair or deceptive, questions of preemption could be answered with relatively little difficulty." Id. This court in *American Optometric Ass'n,* found that the Commission had at least approached the outer boundaries of its authority where "the Commission's proposed pre-emption of state law [was] almost as thorough as human ingenuity could make it." 626 F.2d at 910. In *American Optometric,* the Commission proposed to preempt the whole field of ophthalmic advertising. These cases recognize only that Congress did not intend for the Commission's regulations "to occupy the field." Hence they do not support petitioners' challenge to preemption in this case, since the Commission has made explicit that "the rule is not intended to occupy the field of credit regulation or to preempt state law in the absence of requirements that are inconsistent with the rule." 49 Fed.Reg. at 7783.

In the Statement of Basis and Purpose for the Credit Practices Rule the Commission states:

> The rule has been drafted to be as consistent with existing state laws as possible. Indeed, state laws served as the model for several rule provisions. The rule prohibits practices that are authorized by statute or common law in at least some states. However, none of the rule provisions *preempts* state law by creating an irreconcilable conflict. That is, creditors will be able to comply with both state law and this rule.

Id. at 7782 (footnote omitted) (emphasis in original). The Commission further included in the Rule an exemption provision whereby states that offer protections equal to or greater than the Rule can obtain an exemption from the Rule. See 16 C.F.R. § 444.5. * * *

The Commission in this proceeding considered and modified the Rule to be as consistent with state laws as possible, explicitly expressed its intent not to occupy the field, and included a provision which allows states providing equal or greater protections to obtain an exemption. Under these circumstances, we cannot agree with petitioners that the Commission has exceeded its authority.

* * *

TAMM, CIRCUIT JUDGE, dissenting:

The Commission's decision to ban security interests in household goods and future earnings is in excess of its statutory authority to regulate unfair trade practices. Although rationalized in terms of "market imperfection" and "consumer choice," the Commission's action reflects nothing more than its paternalistic judgment that lenders should not extend credit to low-income consumers. Such a judgment not only violates the approach to consumer protection outlined in the

Policy Statement but also will have the practical effect of forcing needy consumers out of the credit market. I therefore dissent.

* * *

Because no market responds perfectly to consumer choice, any market could conceivably be subject to wholesale Commission regulation. The reviewing court's first task, therefore, is to ensure that the Commission's intervention is a genuine response to a market failure "which prevents free consumer choice from effectuating a self-correcting market," Maj. op. at 981, and not a disguised attempt to impose a paternalistic purchasing decision upon consumers. To perform this task adequately, the court must insist that the Commission sufficiently understand and explain the dynamics of the marketplace. Furthermore, unless the Commission manifests an understanding of how the market responds to consumer choice, it cannot measure the costs and benefits of Commission intervention.

If the Commission has identified with sufficient clarity the impediment that blocks the market's natural allocation, it *may* be appropriate for the Commission to intervene. Whether intervention is appropriate, and if so, what form it should take, can only be answered by weighing the costs and benefits of the Commission's action.

III. APPLICATION OF THE UNFAIRNESS TEST

A. *Market Failure or "Reasonably Avoidable Injury"*

The Commission discusses market failure in terms of what the consumer can "reasonably avoid"; if the consumer can "reasonably avoid" the practice, there is no market imperfection and, hence, no justification for intervention. The most common example of an injury consumers cannot "reasonably avoid" occurs when a seller has failed to disclose a risk involved in the exchange. Although the Commission states that the consumer's ability to shop and bargain for credit remedies is constricted by fine print and technical language, it found not only that consumers generally understand the consequences of default, but that more information would not lead to different consumer decisions. 49 Fed.Reg. at 7746–47. Moreover, while it is true that creditors present standard form credit contracts on a take-it-or-leave-it basis, everyone in this proceeding recognizes that such contracts are the only efficient method of conducting loan transactions. * * * Creditors, therefore, do not unfairly take advantage of a market imperfection by imposing upon consumers hidden risks. Discussion by the Commission and the majority about standard form contracts and fine print is thus empty rhetoric, completely irrelevant to the market analysis.

Lacking any evidence of inadequate or undisclosed information that would distort consumer choice, the Commission alternatively concludes that consumer choice is restricted because consumers do not have access to standard form contracts that do not contain the provisions in question. This conclusion rests on one of two premises—one factually incorrect, the other theoretically bankrupt.

First, the Commission could mean that consumers generally do not have access to loan contracts without these provisions. This is wrong as a matter of fact. Millions of consumers acquire credit each year without pledging any collateral. Millions more, forced to do business with pawnbrokers or loan sharks, do not even have access to loan contracts *with* these provisions. It is not simply common sense and everyday experience, however, that refutes the Commission's finding. The Presiding Officer found that "[i]t was generally agreed that consumers shopping among different classes of creditors *would find differences in terms* offered by banks as opposed to finance companies." J.A. at 404 (emphasis added).

Second, the Commission could mean that *high-risk* consumers do not have access to loan contracts that do not contain these provisions. Some consumers, to be sure, cannot avoid these provisions in loan contracts, an "obstacle to the free exercise of consumer decisionmaking." *Policy Statement* at 7. This phenomenon reflects a market failure, however, only if one is willing to accept the proposition that the high-risk consumer should be free to choose the same credit as the credit-worthy consumer. Under the Commission's reasoning, since not every driver can choose the lowest insurance premium, by selling more expensive automobile insurance to the high-risk driver, the insurer takes advantage of an "obstacle to free choice." The only obstacle to free choice identified by the Commission is the level of risk the borrower, like the insured, brings to the transaction.

* * *

B. *The Cost-Benefit Analysis*

* * *

The Commission makes two fatal errors in its cost-benefit analysis of security interests in household goods. First, in measuring the costs of these security interests, the Commission fails to separate the injury *caused by* these creditor practices from the financial and emotional hardships that inevitably accompany default. Second, in evaluating the offsetting benefits of these provisions, the Commission never squarely addresses the single critical question: the extent to which the intended beneficiaries of the Rule depend upon the ability to pledge household goods and future earnings to acquire credit.

* * *

The economic hardships that inevitably accompany indebtedness and default will remain despite the prohibition of these creditor remedies. The Commission, therefore, grossly exaggerates the beneficial impact of the Rule. The Rule does not eliminate the need for credit, does not provide debtors with any more cash with which to discharge obligations, does not make default a less likely occurrence, does not relieve the financial and emotional hardships that accompany default, does not insulate household necessities from forfeit, does not protect consumers from unscrupulous lenders intent in any event upon breaking the law, and does not lessen the compounding burden unpaid debts place upon debtors.

* * *

2.   Offsetting Benefits

Security interests in household goods benefit consumers to the extent that they enable consumers to acquire credit without resorting to the pawnbroker or the loan shark. The Commission, however, never squarely addresses whether any consumers' access to credit depends upon their ability to pledge household goods as collateral. Instead, it evaluates the impact of the Rule—not upon the high-risk consumer it purports to protect—but upon the credit-worthy consumer who needs no protection from these "abusive" credit practices in the first instance.

* * *

The problem with the Commission's analysis is that the Rule unfortunately does not make the poor rich, or the high-risk consumer credit worthy. The Commission proves only that security interests in household goods cost the high-risk consumer more than they benefit the credit-worthy consumer.

NOTES

1.   The principal case involved a regulation designed to protect consumers. Tuttle v. Buck was brought to protect competitors. Are the approaches to the problems necessarily different? What is the consumer interest in *Tuttle?* What is the competitor interest in *American Financial?*

2.   *Anti-trust Laws.* The federal anti-trust laws are designed to preserve and foster a competitive economy. Section 1 of the Sherman Act declares illegal contracts, combinations, or conspiracies in restraint of trade and § 2 prohibits a person or combination of persons from securing or attempting to secure a monopoly. Section 4 of the Clayton Act authorizes a private action by any person "injured in his business or property by reason of anything forbidden in the anti-trust laws * * *." The anti-trust laws may be regarded as background context for the material considered in this course. In the development of the laws of unfair competition and in fashioning administrative regulations, it may be well to remember that the anti-trust laws provide protection and relief from at least the most egregious "market imperfections".

3.   There has been some uncertainty as to what extent acts regarded as unfair competition at common law should subject the violator to actions under the anti-trust laws. See George R. Whitten, Jr., Inc. v. Paddock Pool Builders, Inc., 508 F.2d 547 (1st Cir.1974), cert. denied 421 U.S. 1004 (1975). See generally, Hutter, "Dirty Tricks" and § 1 of the Sherman Act: Federalizing State Unfair Competition Law, 18 B.C.Indus. & Com.L.Rev. 239 (1977).

4.   The authority of the Federal Trade Commission to define unfair and deceptive practices has taken on new significance with the adoption in many states of model legislation proposed by the Commission to prohibit unfair and deceptive practices. In many instances these statutes incorporate Commission regulations and holdings into state law. Both criminal and private remedies are provided. These statutes have been interpreted broadly and may emerge as one of the more significant legal regimes facing competitors in the marketplace. We consider this development in Chapter 2.

C. THE REGULATION OF PUBLIC GOODS

INTERNATIONAL NEWS SERVICE v. ASSOCIATED PRESS

Supreme Court of the United States, 1918.
248 U.S. 215, 39 S.Ct. 68, 63 L.Ed. 211.

MR. JUSTICE PITNEY delivered the opinion of the Court.

[Associated Press is a news gathering organization. Local newspapers become members and are thus entitled to purchase access to news collected from around the world. Member newspapers agree not to use AP supplied news in any way other than in their newspaper. Each member is also obligated to gather local news and supply it to AP. International News Service is a competing organization with similar operating methods. AP brings this action to enjoin INS from taking published AP news stories and distributing them to INS member papers for publication.]

The only matter that has been argued before us is whether defendant may lawfully be restrained from appropriating news taken from bulletins issued by complainant or any of its members, or from newspapers published by them, for the purpose of selling it to defendant's clients. Complainant asserts that defendant's admitted course of conduct in this regard both violates complainant's property right in the news and constitutes unfair competition in business. And notwithstanding the case has proceeded only to the stage of a preliminary injunction, we have deemed it proper to consider the underlying questions, since they go to the very merits of the action and are presented upon facts that are not in dispute. As presented in argument, these questions are: (1) Whether there is any property in news; (2) whether, if there be property in news collected for the purpose of being published, it survives the instant of its publication in the first newspaper to which it is communicated by the news-gatherer; and (3) whether defendant's admitted course of conduct in appropriating for commercial use matter taken from bulletins or early editions of Associated Press publications constitutes unfair competition in trade.

The federal jurisdiction was invoked because of diversity of citizenship, not upon the ground that the suit arose under the copyright or other laws of the United States. Complainant's news matter is not copyrighted. It is said that it could not, in practice, be copyrighted, because of the large number of dispatches that are sent daily; and, according to complainant's contention, news is not within the operation of the copyright act. Defendant, while apparently conceding this, nevertheless invokes the analogies of the law of literary property and copyright, insisting as its principal contention that, assuming complainant has a right of property in its news, it can be maintained (unless the copyright act be complied with) only by being kept secret and confidential, and that upon the publication with complainant's consent of uncopyrighted news of any of complainant's members in a newspaper or upon a bulletin board, the right of property is lost, and the subsequent use of the news by the public or by defendant for any purpose whatever becomes lawful.

* * *

In considering the general question of property in news matter, it is necessary to recognize its dual character, distinguishing between the substance of the information and the particular form or collocation of words in which the writer has communicated it.

No doubt news articles often possess a literary quality, and are the subject of literary property at the common law; nor do we question that such an article, as a literary production, is the subject of copyright by the terms of the act as it now stands. * * *

But the news element—the information respecting current events contained in the literary production—is not the creation of the writer, but is a report of matters that ordinarily are publici juris; it is the history of the day. It is not to be supposed that the framers of the Constitution, when they empowered Congress "to promote the progress of science and useful arts by securing for limited times to authors and inventors the exclusive right to their respective writings and discoveries" (Const. art. 1, § 8, par. 8), intended to confer upon one who might happen to be the first to report a historic event the exclusive right for any period to spread the knowledge of it.

We need spend no time, however, upon the general question of property in news matter at common law, or the application of the copyright act, since it seems to us the case must turn upon the question of unfair competition in business. And, in our opinion, this does not depend upon any general right of property analogous to the common-law right of the proprietor of an unpublished work to prevent its publication without his consent; nor is it foreclosed by showing that the benefits of the copyright act have been waived. We are dealing here not with restrictions upon publication but with the very facilities and processes of publication. The peculiar value of news is in the spreading of it while it is fresh; and it is evident that a valuable property interest in the news, as news, cannot be maintained by keeping it secret. Besides, except for matters improperly disclosed, or published in breach of trust or confidence, or in violation of law, none of which is involved in this branch of the case, the news of current events may be regarded as common property. What we are concerned with is the business of making it known to the world, in which both parties to the present suit are engaged. That business consists in maintaining a prompt, sure, steady, and reliable service designed to place the daily events of the world at the breakfast table of the millions at a price that, while of trifling moment to each reader, is sufficient in the aggregate to afford compensation for the cost of gathering and distributing it, with the added profit so necessary as an incentive to effective action in the commercial world. The service thus performed for newspaper readers is not only innocent but extremely useful in itself, and indubitably constitutes a legitimate business. The parties are competitors in this field; and, on fundamental principles, applicable here as elsewhere, when the rights or privileges of the one are liable to conflict with those of the other, each party is under a duty so to conduct its own business as not unnecessarily or unfairly to injure that of the other. * * *

Obviously, the question of what is unfair competition in business must be determined with particular reference to the character and circumstances of the business. The question here is not so much the rights of either party as against the public but their rights as between themselves. See Morison v. Moat, 9 Hare, 241, 258. And, although we may and do assume that neither party has any remaining property interest as against the public in uncopyrighted news matter after the moment of its first publication, it by no means follows that there is no remaining property interest in it as between themselves. For, to both of them alike, news matter, however little susceptible of ownership or dominion in the absolute sense, is stock in trade, to be gathered at the cost of enterprise, organization, skill, labor, and money, and to be distributed and sold to those who will pay money for it, as for any other merchandise. Regarding the news, therefore, as but the material out of which both parties are seeking to make profits at the same time and in the same field, we hardly can fail to recognize that for this purpose, and as between them, it must be regarded as quasi property, irrespective of the rights of either as against the public.

* * *

The question, whether one who has gathered general information or news at pains and expense for the purpose of subsequent publication through the press has such an interest in its publication as may be protected from interference, has been raised many times, although never, perhaps, in the precise form in which it is now presented.

Board of Trade v. Christie Grain & Stock Co., 198 U.S. 236, related to the distribution of quotations of prices on dealings upon a board of trade, which were collected by plaintiff and communicated on confidential terms to numerous persons under a contract not to make them public. This court held that, apart from certain special objections that were overruled, plaintiff's collection of quotations was entitled to the protection of the law; that, like a trade secret, plaintiff might keep to itself the work done at its expense, and did not lose its right by communicating the result to persons, even if many, in confidential relations to itself, under a contract not to make it public; and that strangers should be restrained from getting at the knowledge by inducing a breach of trust.

In National Tel. News Co. v. Western Union Tel. Co., 119 Fed. 294, 56 C.C.A. 198, 60 L.R.A. 805, the Circuit Court of Appeals for the Seventh Circuit dealt with news matter gathered and transmitted by a telegraph company, and consisting merely of a notation of current events having but a transient value due to quick transmission and distribution; and, while declaring that this was not copyrightable although printed on a tape by tickers in the offices of the recipients, and that it was a commercial not a literary product, nevertheless held that the business of gathering and communicating the news—the service of purveying it—was a legitimate business, meeting a distinctive commercial want and adding to the facilities of the business world, and partaking of the nature of property in a sense that entitled it to the protection of a court of equity against piracy.

Other cases are cited, but none that we deem it necessary to mention.

Not only do the acquisition and transmission of news require elaborate organization and a large expenditure of money, skill, and effort; not only has it an exchange value to the gatherer, dependent chiefly upon its novelty and freshness, the regularity of the service, its reputed reliability and thoroughness, and its adaptability to the public needs; but also, as is evident, the news has an exchange value to one who can misappropriate it.

The peculiar features of the case arise from the fact that, while novelty and freshness form so important an element in the success of the business, the very processes of distribution and publication necessarily occupy a good deal of time. Complainant's service, as well as defendant's, is a daily service to daily newspapers; most of the foreign news reaches this country at the Atlantic seaboard, principally at the city of New York, and because of this, and of time differentials, due to the earth's rotation, the distribution of news matter throughout the country is principally from east to west; and, since in speed the telegraph and telephone easily outstrip the rotation of the earth, it is a simple matter for defendant to take complainant's news from bulletins or early editions of complainant's members in the eastern cities and at the mere cost of telegraphic transmission cause it to be published in western papers issued at least as early as those served by complainant. Besides this, and irrespective of time differentials, irregularities in telegraphic transmission on different lines, and the normal consumption of time in printing and distributing the newspaper, result in permitting printed news to be placed in the hands of defendant's readers sometimes simultaneously with the service of competing Associated Press papers, occasionally even earlier.

Defendant insists that when, with the sanction and approval of complainant, and as the result of the use of its news for the very purpose for which it is distributed, a portion of complainant's members communicate it to the general public by posting it upon bulletin boards so that all may read, or by issuing it to newspapers and distributing it indiscriminately, complainant no longer has the right to control the use to be made of it; that when it thus reaches the light of day it becomes the common possession of all to whom it is accessible; and that any purchaser of a newspaper has the right to communicate the intelligence which it contains to anybody and for any purpose, even for the purpose of selling it for profit to newspapers published for profit in competition with complainant's members.

The fault in the reasoning lies in applying as a test the right of the complainant as against the public, instead of considering the rights of complainant and defendant, competitors in business, as between themselves. The right of the purchaser of a single newspaper to spread knowledge of its contents gratuitously, for any legitimate purpose not unreasonably interfering with complainant's right to make merchandise of it, may be admitted; but to transmit that news for commercial use, in competition with complainant—which is what defendant has done and seeks to justify—is a very different matter. In doing this defendant, by its very act, admits that it is taking material that has been acquired by complainant as the result of organization and the expenditure of labor, skill and money, and which is salable by complainant for money, and that defendant in appropriating it and selling it as its own is endeavoring to reap where it has not sown, and by disposing of it to newspapers that are competitors of complainant's members is appropriating to itself the harvest of those who have sown. Stripped of all disguises, the process amounts to an unauthorized interference with the normal operation of complainant's legitimate business precisely at the point where the profit is to be reaped, in order to divert a material portion of the profit from those who have earned it to those who have not; with special advantage to defendant in the competition because of the fact that it is not burdened with any part of the expense of gathering the news. The transaction speaks for itself, and a court of equity ought not to hesitate long in characterizing it as unfair competition in business.

The underlying principle is much the same as that which lies at the base of the equitable theory of consideration in the law of trusts— that he who has fairly paid the price should have the beneficial use of the property. Pom.Eq.Jur. § 981. It is no answer to say that complainant spends its money for that which is too fugitive or evanescent to be the subject of property. That might, and for the purposes of the discussion we are assuming that it would, furnish an answer in a common-law controversy. But in a court of equity, where the question in one of unfair competition, if that which complainant has acquired fairly at substantial cost may be sold fairly at substantial profit, a competitor who is misappropriating it for the purpose of disposing of it to his own profit and to the disadvantage of the complainant cannot be heard to say that it is too fugitive or evanescent to be regarded as property. It has all the attributes of property necessary for determining that a misappropriation of it by a competitor is unfair competition because contrary to good conscience.

The contention that the news is abandoned to the public for all purposes when published in the first newspaper is untenable. Abandonment is a question of intent, and the entire organization of the Associated Press negatives such a purpose. The cost of the service would be prohibitive if the reward were to be so limited. No single newspaper, no small group of newspapers, could sustain the expenditure. Indeed, it is one of the most obvious results of defendant's theory that, by permitting indiscriminate publication by anybody and every-body for purposes of profit in competition with the newsgatherer, it would render publication profitless, or so little profitable as in effect to cut off the service by rendering the cost prohibitive in comparison with the return. The practical needs and requirements of the business are reflected in complainant's by-laws which have been referred to. Their effect is that publication by each member must be deemed not by any means an abandonment of the news to the world for any and all purposes, but a publication for limited purposes; for the benefit of the readers of the bulletin or the newspaper as such; not for the purpose of making merchandise of it as news, with the result of depriving com-plainant's other members of their reasonable opportunity to obtain just returns for their expenditures.

It is to be observed that the view we adopt does not result in giving to complainant the right to monopolize either the gathering or the distribution of the news, or, without complying with the copyright act, to prevent the reproduction of its news articles, but only postpones participation by complainant's competitor in the processes of distribu-tion and reproduction of news that it has not gathered, and only to the extent necessary to prevent that competitor from reaping the fruits of complainant's efforts and expenditure, to the partial exclusion of com-plainant, and in violation of the principle that underlies the maxim "sic utere tuo," etc.

It is said that the elements of unfair competition are lacking because there is no attempt by defendant to palm off its goods as those of the complainant, characteristic of the most familiar, if not the most typical, cases of unfair competition. Howe Scale Co. v. Wyckoff, Sea-mans, etc., 198 U.S. 118. But we cannot concede that the right to equitable relief is confined to that class of cases. In the present case the fraud upon complainant's rights is more direct and obvious. Re-garding news matter as the mere material from which these two competing parties are endeavoring to make money, and treating it, therefore, as quasi property for the purposes of their business because they are both selling it as such, defendant's conduct differs from the ordinary case of unfair competition in trade principally in this that, instead of selling its own goods as those of complainant, it substitutes misappropriation in the place of misrepresentation, and sells complain-ant's goods as its own.

Besides the misappropriation, there are elements of imitation, of false pretense, in defendant's practices. The device of rewriting com-plainant's news articles, frequently resorted to, carries its own com-ment. The habitual failure to give credit to complainant for that which is taken is significant. Indeed, the entire system of appropriating complainant's news and transmitting it as a commercial product to defendant's clients and patrons amounts to a false representation to them and to their newspaper readers that the news transmitted is the result of defendant's own investigation in the field. But these ele-ments, although accentuating the wrong, are not the essence of it. It is something more than the advantage of celebrity of which complainant is being deprived.

The doctrine of unclean hands is invoked as a bar to relief; it being insisted that defendant's practices against which complainant seeks an injunction are not different from the practice attributed to complainant, of utilizing defendant's news published by its subscribers. At this point it becomes necessary to consider a distinction * * * between two kinds of use that may be made by one news agency of news taken from the bulletin and newspapers of the other. The first is the bodily appropriation of a statement of fact or a news article, with or without rewriting, but without independent investigation or other expense. * * * This practice complainant denies having pursued and the denial was sustained by the finding of the District Court. It is not contended by defendant that the finding can be set aside, upon the proofs as they now stand. The other use is to take the news of a rival agency as a "tip" to be investigated, and if verified by independent investigation the news thus gathered is sold. This practice complainant admits that it has pursued and still is willing that defendant shall employ.

* * *

As to securing "tips" from a competing news agency, the District Court (240 Fed. 991, 995), while not sanctioning the practice, found that both parties had adopted it in accordance with common business usage, in the belief that their conduct was technically lawful, and hence did not find in it any sufficient ground for attributing unclean hands to complainant. The Circuit Court of Appeals (245 Fed. 247, 157 C.C.A. 436) found that the tip habit, though discouraged by complainant, was "incurably journalistic," and that there was "no difficulty in discriminating between the utilization of tips and the bodily appropriation of another's labor in accumulating and stating information."

We are inclined to think a distinction may be drawn between the utilization of tips and the bodily appropriation of news matter, either in its original form or after rewriting and without independent investigation and verification: whatever may appear at the final hearing, the proofs as they now stand recognize such a distinction; both parties avowedly recognize the practice of taking tips, and neither party alleges it to be unlawful or to amount to unfair competition in business. In a line of English cases a somewhat analogous practice has been held not to amount to an infringement of the copyright of a directory or other book containing compiled information. * * *

There is some criticism of the injunction that was directed by the District Court upon the going down of the mandate from the Circuit Court of Appeals. In brief, it restrains any taking or gainfully using of the complainant's news, either bodily or in substance from bulletins issued by the complainant or any of its members, or from editions of their newspapers, *"until its commercial value as news to the complainant and all of its members has passed away."* The part complained of is the clause we have italicized; but if this be indefinite, it is no more so than the criticism. Perhaps it would be better that the terms of the injunction be made specific, and so framed as to confine the restraint to an extent consistent with the reasonable protection of complainant's newspapers, each in its own area and for a specified time after its publication, against the competitive use of pirated news by defendant's customers. But the case presents practical difficulties; and we have not the materials, either in the way of a definite suggestion of amendment, or in the way of proofs, upon which to frame a specific injunction; hence, while not expressing approval of the form adopted by the District Court, we decline to modify it at this preliminary stage of the case, and will leave that court to deal with the matter upon appropriate application made to it for the purpose.

The decree of the Circuit Court of Appeals will be affirmed.

MR. JUSTICE CLARKE took no part in the consideration or decision of this case.

MR. JUSTICE HOLMES, dissenting.

When an uncopyrighted combination of words is published there is no general right to forbid other people repeating them—in other words there is no property in the combination or in the thoughts or facts that the words express. Property, a creation of law, does not arise from value, although exchangeable—a matter of fact. Many exchangeable values may be destroyed intentionally without compensation. Property depends upon exclusion by law from interference, and a person is not excluded from using any combination of words merely because some one has used it before, even if it took labor and genius to make it. If a given person is to be prohibited from making the use of words that his neighbors are free to make some other ground must be found. One such ground is vaguely expressed in the phrase unfair trade. This means that the words are repeated by a competitor in business in such a way as to convey a misrepresentation that materially injures the person who first used them, by appropriating credit of some kind which the first user has earned. The ordinary case is a representation by device, appearance, or other indirection that the defendant's goods come from the plaintiff. But the only reason why it is actionable to make such a representation is that it tends to give the defendant an advantage in his competition with the plaintiff and that it is thought undesirable that an advantage should be gained in that way. Apart from that the defendant may use such unpatented devices and uncopyrighted combinations of words as he likes. The ordinary case, I say, is palming off the defendant's product as the plaintiff's, but the same evil may follow from the opposite falsehood—from saying whether in words or by implication that the plaintiff's product is the defendant's, and that, it seems to me, is what has happened here.

Fresh news is got only by enterprise and expense. To produce such news as it is produced by the defendant represents by implication that it has been acquired by the defendant's enterprise and at its expense.

When it comes from one of the great news collecting agencies like the Associated Press, the source generally is indicated, plainly importing that credit; and that such a representation is implied may be inferred with some confidence from the unwillingness of the defendant to give the credit and tell the truth. If the plaintiff produces the news at the same time that the defendant does, the defendant's presentation impliedly denies to the plaintiff the credit of collecting the facts and assumes that credit to the defendant. If the plaintiff is later in Western cities it naturally will be supposed to have obtained its information from the defendant. The falsehood is a little more subtle, the injury a little more indirect, than in ordinary cases of unfair trade, but I think that the principle that condemns the one condemns the other. It is a question of how strong an infusion of fraud is necessary to turn a flavor into a poison. The dose seems to me strong enough here to need a remedy from the law. But as, in my view, the only ground of complaint that can be recognized without legislation is the implied misstatement, it can be corrected by stating the truth; and a suitable acknowledgment of the source is all that the plaintiff can require. I think that within the limits recognized by the decision of the Court the defendant should be enjoined from publishing news obtained from the Associated Press for ___ hours after publication by the plaintiff unless it gives express credit to the Associated Press; the number of hours and the form of acknowledgment to be settled by the District Court.

MR. JUSTICE MCKENNA concurs in this opinion.

MR. JUSTICE BRANDEIS, dissenting.

* * *

No question of statutory copyright is involved. The sole question for our consideration is this: Was the International News Service properly enjoined from using, or causing to be used gainfully, news of which it acquired knowledge by lawful means (namely, by reading publicly posted bulletins or papers purchased by it in the open market) merely because the news had been originally gathered by the Associated Press and continued to be of value to some of its members, or because it did not reveal the source from which it was acquired?

* * *

News is a report of recent occurrences. The business of the news agency is to gather systematically knowledge of such occurrences of interest and to distribute reports thereof. The Associated Press contended that knowledge so acquired is property, because it costs money and labor to produce and because it has value for which those who have it not are ready to pay; that it remains property and is entitled to protection as long as it has commercial value as news; and that to protect it effectively the defendant must be enjoined from making, or causing to be made, any gainful use of it while it retains such value. An essential element of individual property is the legal right to exclude others from enjoying it. If the property is private, the right of exclusion may be absolute; if the property is affected with a public interest, the right of exclusion is qualified. But the fact that a product of the mind has cost its producer money and labor, and has a value for which others are willing to pay, is not sufficient to ensure to it this legal attribute of property. The general rule of law is, that the noblest of human productions—knowledge, truths ascertained, conceptions, and ideas—become, after voluntary communication to others, free as the air to common use. Upon these incorporeal productions the attribute of property is continued after such communication only in certain classes of cases where public policy has seemed to demand it. These exceptions are confined to productions which, in some degree, involve creation, invention, or discovery. But by no means all such are endowed with this attribute of property. The creations which are recognized as property by the common law are literary, dramatic, musical, and other artistic creations; and these have also protection under the copyright statutes. The inventions and discoveries upon which this attribute of property is conferred only by statute, are the few comprised within the patent law. There are also many other cases in which courts interfere to prevent curtailment of plaintiff's enjoyment of incorporeal productions; and in which the right to relief is often called a property right, but is such only in a special sense. In those cases, the plaintiff has no absolute right to the protection of his production; he has merely the qualified right to be protected as against the defendant's acts, because of the special relation in which the latter stands or the wrongful method or means employed in acquiring the knowledge or the manner in which it is used. Protection of this character is afforded where the suit is based upon breach of contract or of trust or upon unfair competition.

The knowledge for which protection is sought in the case at bar is not of a kind upon which the law has heretofore conferred the attributes of property; nor is the manner of its acquisition or use nor the purpose to which it is applied, such as has heretofore been recognized as entitling a plaintiff to relief.

First. Plaintiff's principal reliance was upon the "ticker" cases; but they do not support its contention. The leading cases on this subject rest the grant of relief, not upon the existence of a general property right in news, but upon the breach of a contract or trust concerning the use of news communicated; and that element is lacking here. * * *

Second. Plaintiff also relied upon the cases which hold that the common law right of the producer to prohibit copying is not lost by the private circulation of a literary composition, the delivery of a lecture, the exhibition of a painting, or the performance of a dramatic or musical composition. These cases rest upon the ground that the common law recognizes such productions as property which, despite restricted communication, continues until there is a dedication to the public under the copyright statutes or otherwise. But they are inapplicable for two reasons: (1) At common law, as under the copyright acts, intellectual productions are entitled to such protection only if there is underneath something evincing the mind of a creator or originator, however modest the requirements. The mere record of isolated happenings, whether in words or by photographs not involving artistic skill, are denied such protection. (2) At common law, as under the copyright acts, the element in intellectual productions which secures such protection, is not the knowledge, truths, ideas, or emotions which the composition expresses, but the form or sequence in which they are expressed; that is, "some new collocation of visible or audible points— of lines, colors, sounds, or words." * * *

Third. If news be treated as possessing the characteristics not of a trade secret, but of literary property, then the earliest issue of a paper of general circulation or the earliest public posting of a bulletin which embodies such news would, under the established rules governing literary property, operate as a publication, and all property in the news would then cease. * * *

Fourth. Plaintiff further contended that defendant's practice constitutes unfair competition, because there is "appropriation without cost to itself of values created by" the plaintiff; and it is upon this ground that the decision of this court appears to be based. To appropriate and use for profit, knowledge and ideas produced by other men, without making compensation or even acknowledgement, may be inconsistent with a finer sense of propriety; but, with the exceptions indicated above, the law has heretofore sanctioned the practice. Thus it was held that one may ordinarily make and sell anything in any form, may copy with exactness that which another has produced, or may otherwise use his ideas without his consent and without the payment of compensation, and yet not inflict a legal injury; and that ordinarily one is at perfect liberty to find out, if he can by lawful means, trade secrets of another, however valuable, and then use the knowledge so acquired gainfully, although it cost the original owner much in effort and in money to collect or produce. * * *

It is also suggested that the fact that defendant does not refer to the Associated Press as the source of the news may furnish a basis for the relief. But the defendant and its subscribers, unlike members of the Associated Press, were under no contractual obligation to disclose the source of the news; and there is no rule of law requiring acknowledgement to be made where uncopyrighted matter is reproduced. * * *

Fifth. * * *

The rule for which the plaintiff contends would effect an important extension of property rights and a corresponding curtailment of the free use of knowledge and of ideas; and the facts of this case admonish us of the danger involved in recognizing such a property right in news, without imposing upon news-gatherers corresponding obligations. * * *

A Legislature, urged to enact a law by which one news agency or newspaper may prevent appropriation of the fruits of its labors by another, would consider such facts and possibilities and others which appropriate inquiry might disclose. Legislators might conclude that it was impossible to put an end to the obvious injustice involved in such appropriation of news, without opening the door to other evils, greater than that sought to be remedied. * * *

Or legislators dealing with the subject might conclude, that the right to news values should be protected to the extent of permitting recovery of damages for any unauthorized use, but that protection by injunction should be denied, just as courts of equity ordinarily refuse (perhaps in the interest of free speech) to restrain actionable libels, and for other reasons decline to protect by injunction mere political rights; and as Congress has prohibited courts from enjoining the illegal assessment or collection of federal taxes. If a Legislature concluded to recognize property in published news to the extent of permitting recovery at law, it might, with a view to making the remedy more certain and adequate, provide a fixed measure of damages, as in the case of copyright infringement.

Or again, a Legislature might conclude that it was unwise to recognize even so limited a property right in published news as that above indicated; but that a news agency should, on some conditions, be given full protection of its business; and to that end a remedy by injunction as well as one for damages should be granted, where news collected by it is gainfully used without permission. If a Legislature concluded (as at least one court has held, New York and Chicago Grain and Stock Exchange v. Board of Trade, 127 Ill. 153, 19 N.E. 855, 2 L.R.A. 411, 11 Am.St.Rep. 107) that under certain circumstances newsgathering is a business affected with a public interest; it might declare that, in such cases, news should be protected against appropriation, only if the gatherer assumed the obligation of supplying it at reasonable rates and without discrimination, to all papers which applied therefor. If legislators reached that conclusion, they would probably go further, and prescribe the conditions under which and the extent to which the protection should be afforded; and they might also provide the administrative machinery necessary for insuring to the public, the press, and the news agencies, full enjoyment of the rights so conferred.

Courts are ill-equipped to make the investigations which should precede a determination of the limitations which should be set upon any property right in news or of the circumstances under which news gathered by a private agency should be deemed affected with a public interest. Courts would be powerless to prescribe the detailed regulations essential to full enjoyment of the rights conferred or to introduce the machinery required for enforcement of such regulations. Considerations such as these should lead us to decline to establish a new rule of law in the effort to redress a newly disclosed wrong, although the propriety of some remedy appears to be clear.

NOTES

1. *Historical Note.* International News Service's troubles began in 1916 when the British government banned the Hearst owned INS from using the Official Press Bureau and all other facilities for the transmission of news from Great Britain. The ban arose from stories published in American newspapers and attributed to an INS correspondent in London, about the battle of Jutland and air raids over London. The dispatches indicated that the British navy had admitted an "overwhelming defeat" by the German navy. Since news transmission at the time was officially censored by the British government, the Home Secretary was asked in the House of Commons whether the censor had passed such news accounts. He replied that no such dispatches were sent from Britain and that they must have been composed in the New York offices of INS. This "garbling" of news accounts was cited as the reason for the ban. The New York American, a Hearst newspaper, published the reply of the manager of INS which read in part: "The English censors have been threatening for many months to deny the International News Service the privilege of the mails and cables because the International News Service did not print the kind of news that the English desired to have printed in this country. * * * It is the intention of the International News Service to continue printing the news, all the news, and nothing but the news." N.Y. Times, October 11, 1916, at 11, col. 4.

The following story was carried by the New York Times on Jan. 25, 1918, at 3, col. 7:

The United Press Association announced yesterday that the International News Service, against which The Associated Press recently secured an injunction to prevent the pirating of news, had walked straight into a trap set by The United Press to show that the International News was pirating the news of that organization. The International News incidentally brought into newspaper fame a hitherto unknown official, "Under Foreign Secretary Nelotsky," whose name, spelled backwards, reads "stolen" with the "ky" thrown in for "Russian camouflage."

Early in the day The United Press inserted "Nelotsky" in a dispatch from Petrograd, but soon "killed" this name for all its papers. Within a short time, The United Press says, papers receiving the International News Service appeared with "M. Nelotsky" figuring prominently in an alleged dispatch from London recounting in a general way the same facts set forth in The United Press cable from Petrograd. The United Press says it made sure that the Nelotsky story was sent over the wires of the International News.

The story was printed in papers receiving the International News Service in Boston, New York, Pittsburgh, Detroit, Chicago, Kansas City, San Francisco, and elsewhere.

The New York Times commented editorially that "[t]raps of this sort are rather cruel, but of their efficiency there is no doubt, and when one really wants a hide to nail up on one's barn door—well, one uses the trap that will supply the hide, as in this instance." N.Y. Times, Jan. 26, 1918, at 12, col. 5.

2. *Acceptance of the INS Doctrine.* The majority opinion in *INS* stands as the foundation for development of the "misappropriation" doctrine of unfair competition. Its checkered career will be repeatedly explored throughout much

of this material. The case, read in its broadest sense, was a dramatic departure from the existing tort concepts regulating business practices. The opinions of Holmes and Brandeis reveal the more traditional analyses.

Although the decision was potentially upsetting to the existing precedent, it was met in lower federal and state courts with disinterest. It was approved in dictum in a number of decisions and applied in some cases where it was unnecessary. E.g., Coca-Cola Co. v. Old Dominion Beverage Corp., 271 Fed. 600 (4th Cir.1921) (trade mark infringement).

Some early decisions read the majority opinion narrowly. In Harvey Hubbell, Inc. v. General Elec. Co., 262 Fed. 155 (S.D.N.Y.1919) various manufacturers including plaintiff and defendant were marketing different types of electric plugs and wall receptacles for electric appliances making interchangeability impossible. Many of the manufacturers sought to standardize the dimensions and forms of these plugs and receptacles but plaintiff refused. The other manufacturers, including defendants, standardized using plaintiff's measurements as the standard. Plaintiff brought an action for unfair competition. The court denied relief. "No court has ever gone to the extent of permitting the establishment of a monopoly of proportions or measurements, in the absence of some patent protection. To do so would be practically to engross the particular business. * * * To do so would be to stifle competition." The court interpreted *INS* as based on acts amounting to fraud and bribery. "The Supreme Court stated that the complainant had a property right in the news which it secured in the conduct of its business, and restrained the defendant from bribing the employes of the complainant to release the news to the defendant. There is no question of fraud, or palming off by the defendants in this issue, nor is there any claim of deception advanced upon this theory of the case."

In Meyer v. Hurwitz, 5 F.2d 370 (D.Pa.1925) the plaintiff designed and manufactured a post card vending machine. He sold the machine at cost and made his profit by selling cards. Defendant produced cards designed to be sold through plaintiff's machine and priced the cards below what plaintiff charged. There was some evidence defendant's cards caused the machines to jam. The court, without citing *INS* held for the plaintiff because defendant "appropriated to himself the plaintiff's system and organization for the purpose of underselling him * * *."

Some early cases did read the decision broadly. In National Telephone Directory Co. v. Dawson Mfg. Co., 214 Mo.App. 683, 263 S.W. 483 (St. Louis Ct. App.1924) the plaintiff published a telephone directory and sold advertising therein. The best advertising space was on the outside covers of the directory. The defendants manufactured covers to fit over the directory and sold advertising space thereon. The covers were put on all directories in the defendants' hotel. The court granted an injunction in reliance on *INS:*

> The petition discloses that the defendants' purpose to pass off their own advertising medium as the advertising medium of the plaintiff, not merely by simulating the plaintiff's medium, but by actually tacking their own medium upon that of the plaintiff. By this unfair means, the defendants purpose to place their advertising business in competition with that of the plaintiff. A more flagrant case of unfair competition is nowhere disclosed by the books. In fact, the scheme is more than unfair competition; it amounts to an actual appropriation

of the plaintiff's property by the defendants to their own business purposes.

INS was read to grant relief against all "schemes and inventions of the modern genius bent upon reaping where he has not sown".

Such an inauspicious beginning did not promise a lively career for the misappropriation doctrine. And in 1929, Judge Learned Hand attempted to seal the grave. In Cheney Bros. v. Doris Silk Corp., 35 F.2d 279 (2d Cir.1929) he wrote of *INS:*

> While it is of course true that law ordinarily speaks in general terms, there are cases where the occasion is at once the justification for, and the limit of, what is decided. This appears to us such an instance; we think that no more was covered than situations substantially similar to those then at bar. The difficulties of understanding it otherwise are insuperable. We are to suppose that the court meant to create a sort of common-law patent or copyright for reasons of justice. Either would flagrantly conflict with the scheme which Congress has for more than a century devised to cover the subject-matter.

Whatever binding effect *INS* might have had was removed by Erie R.R. Co. v. Tompkins, 304 U.S. 64 (1938) since *INS* was a diversity case decided on the basis of federal common law no longer applicable to such actions after *Erie.* However, subsequent decisions involving a variety of factual situations breathed new life into the doctrine. These are considered throughout the remainder of this material.

3. Would your view of the principal case differ if Associated Press had by-laws which in addition to prohibiting members from selling AP dispatches to non-members also gave member publishers veto power over the application of competing newspapers for membership in the organization? Such by-laws were in existence in various forms from 1900 until 1943 when they were struck down as violative of the Sherman Act. United States v. Associated Press, 52 F.Supp. 362 (S.D.N.Y.1943), affirmed 326 U.S. 1 (1945).

4. What was "misappropriated" in *INS?* How would the various judges in *INS* have ruled in Tuttle v. Buck? Is the issue the same in both cases? We have noted that trade practice cases can involve the interest of consumers as well as those of the two competitors. How did the consumer's interest fare in *INS?* What about the interest of the advertisers in Associated Press affiliated newspapers who bear a large part of the cost of newspaper production through the price of advertising? Was their interest considered by any of the Justices? Assume you were interested in establishing a competing news gathering agency. Which opinion would most encourage you to make a large investment in such an operation?

5. Consider Brandeis' discussion of the copyright and patent statutes. Why are they relevant to the factual situation? Likewise, what is Hand's concern in the quote from *Cheney?* Consider also Clipper Belt Lacer Co. v. Detroit Belt Lacer Co., 223 Mich. 399, 194 N.W. 125 (1923). Here the plaintiff held a patent on a belt-lacing machine which was used to insert hooks which plaintiff also manufactured and sold. The hooks were bound together in such a way that they could be utilized in the machine. The machine was sold without regard to profit; the sale of hooks being the major source of plaintiff's business. Defendant also manufactured hooks and began making them in such a way as they would fit into plaintiff's machine. Plaintiff contended that the spacing of the hooks was a nonfunctional feature and appropriated by the defendant solely

for the purpose of obtaining part of the plaintiff's market. Defendant argued that they found the spacing functional because of certain economies in production. Plaintiff sued for an injunction on a theory of unfair competition. The court denied the injunction. After finding that there was no "passing off", that the defendant did not attempt to deceive customers into thinking that the hooks made by the defendant were made by the plaintiff, the court concluded:

> * * * The profits on refills or replacements constitutes the principal profit in various kinds of business. Except as protected by patents, the question is to what extent and by what methods other dealers may, in the ordinary course of trade, compete for the increased demand and good will of consumers so developed within the field of fair competition. * * *

> Plaintiff avoids the Clayton Act (38 Stat. 730) against monopolistic methods of creating a demand on an unpatented commodity by selling its lacing tool outright, without binding the purchaser to use its lacing hooks; but if it can prevent dealers in lacing hooks from putting on the market ganged hooks spaced the same as those it sells, it is as well or better off than if its spacing was a monopoly legalized by a patent. An injunction such as asked for here would have the practical effect of putting plaintiff in as good a position with a longer period of absolute control of its arbitrarily selected spacing than as though it were protected by a patent, which must eventually expire.

Is *Clipper Belt* consistent with Meyer v. Hurwitz? Does the patent in *Clipper Belt* affect the result?

6. How would the various Justices in *INS* solve the following problems:

PROBLEMS

1. Plaintiff owns a television station in Salt Lake City, Utah. Its programming can be received within a fifty-mile radius of Salt Lake. Ten per cent of the programming is produced locally by the plaintiff; ninety per cent is purchased from a national network. Defendant establishes a cable television enterprise which receives plaintiff's programming and rebroadcasts it to subscribers of defendant's service. The subscriber pays an installation fee to have the cable connected with the home set and a monthly rental charge which basically covers the maintenance of the equipment plus a modest profit for the defendant. Plaintiff sues defendant for damages and an injunction. What result if the following were true:

a. Defendant's subscribers were all located within the fifty-mile radius of Salt Lake.

b. Defendant's subscribers were all located outside the fifty-mile radius.

c. Defendant had subscribers within and without the fifty-mile radius.

Would any of the above cases be different if defendant carried the plaintiff's programming but substituted its own commercials for those carried on plaintiff's station?

What result if a third station, located in Twin Falls, Idaho, which is more than fifty miles from Salt Lake, sued defendant to prevent him from bringing Salt Lake programming into the Twin Falls broadcasting area?

2. Plaintiff is a dress designer and manufacturer who produces for each season numerous new dress designs. Only a few will attract the attention of

department stores and ultimately the consuming public and for those that are successful significant sales will last for only one season. After the designs selected by buyers for the department stores appear in the stores, it is relatively easy for defendant, a discount clothing manufacturer, to manufacture and distribute to its discount outlets copies of plaintiff's successful designs to be sold at a price below that of the plaintiff's dresses. Plaintiff sues to enjoin the copying of its dress designs. What result? Would it affect the result if defendant advertised its discount dresses as "copies of plaintiff's originals"?

3. A commodity exchange, unconnected with Dow Jones, wishes to develop a futures contract based on the "Dow Jones Average of 30 Industrials." Can the Dow Jones Company object on the basis of *INS?* See Board of Trade v. Dow Jones & Co., 108 Ill.App.3d 681, 64 Ill.Dec. 275, 439 N.E.2d 526 (1982); Standard & Poor's Corp. v. Commodity Exch., Inc., 683 F.2d 704 (2d Cir.1982).

See generally, Baird, Common Law Intellectual Property and the Legacy of International News Service v. Associated Press, 50 U.Chi.L.Rev. 411 (1983).

SEARS, ROEBUCK & CO. v. STIFFEL CO.
Supreme Court of the United States, 1964.
376 U.S. 225, 84 S.Ct. 784, 11 L.Ed.2d 661, rehearing denied 376 U.S. 973,
84 S.Ct. 1131, 12 L.Ed.2d 87.

MR. JUSTICE BLACK delivered the opinion of the Court.

The question in this case is whether a State's unfair competition law can, consistently with the federal patent laws, impose liability for or prohibit the copying of an article which is protected by neither a federal patent nor a copyright. The respondent, Stiffel Company, secured design and mechanical patents on a "pole lamp"—a vertical tube having lamp fixtures along the outside, the tube being made so that it will stand upright between the floor and ceiling of a room. Pole lamps proved a decided commercial success, and soon after Stiffel brought them on the market Sears, Roebuck & Company put on the market a substantially identical lamp, which it sold more cheaply, Sears' retail price being about the same as Stiffel's wholesale price. Stiffel then brought this action against Sears in the United States District Court for the Northern District of Illinois, claiming in its first count that by copying its design Sears had infringed Stiffel's patents and in its second count that by selling copies of Stiffel's lamp Sears had caused confusion in the trade as to the source of the lamps and had thereby engaged in unfair competition under Illinois law. There was evidence that identifying tags were not attached to the Sears lamps although labels appeared on the cartons in which they were delivered to customers, that customers had asked Stiffel whether its lamps differed from Sears', and that in two cases customers who had bought Stiffel lamps had complained to Stiffel on learning that Sears was selling substantially identical lamps at a much lower price.

The District Court, after holding the patents invalid for want of invention, went on to find as a fact that Sears' lamp was "a substantially exact copy" of Stiffel's and that the two lamps were so much alike, both in appearance and in functional details, "that confusion between them is likely, and some confusion has already occurred." On these findings the court held Sears guilty of unfair competition, enjoined Sears "from unfairly competing with [Stiffel] by selling or attempting to sell pole lamps identical to or confusingly similar to" Stiffel's lamp and ordered an accounting to fix profits and damages resulting from Sears' "unfair competition."

The Court of Appeals affirmed.[1] 313 F.2d 115. That court held that, to make out a case of unfair competition under Illinois law, there was no need to show that Sears had been "palming off" its lamps as Stiffel lamps; Stiffel had only to prove that there was a "likelihood of confusion as to the source of the products"—that the two articles were sufficiently identical that customers could not tell who had made a particular one. Impressed by the "remarkable sameness of appearance" of the lamps, the Court of Appeals upheld the trial court's findings of likelihood of confusion and some actual confusion, findings which the appellate court construed to mean confusion "as to the source of the lamps." The Court of Appeals thought this enough under Illinois law to sustain the trial court's holding of unfair competition and thus held Sears liable under Illinois law for doing no more than copying and marketing an unpatented article.[2] We granted certiorari to consider whether this use of a State's law of unfair competition is compatible with the federal patent law. 374 U.S. 826.

1. No review is sought here of the ruling affirming the District Court's holding that the patent is invalid.

2. 313 F.2d, at 118 and nn. 6, 7. At least one Illinois case has held in an exhaustive opinion that unfair competition under the law of Illinois is not proved unless the defendant is shown to have "palmed off" the article which he sells as that of another seller; the court there said that "[t]he courts in this State do not treat the 'palming off' doctrine as merely the designation of a typical class of cases of unfair competition, but they announce it as the rule of law itself—the test by which it is determined whether a given state of facts constitutes unfair competition as a matter of law. * * * The 'palming off' rule is expressed in a positive, concrete form which will not admit of 'broadening' or 'widening' by any proper judicial process." Stevens-Davis Co. v. Mather & Co., 230 Ill.App. 45, 65–66 (1923). In spite of this the Court of Appeals in its opinions both in this case and in Day-Brite Lighting, Inc. v. Compco Corp., 7 Cir., 311 F.2d 26, rev'd 375 U.S. 234, relied upon one of its previous decisions in a tradename case, Independent Nail & Packing Co. v. Stronghold Screw Products, 205 F.2d 921 (C.A.7th Cir.1953), which concluded that as to use of trade names the Stevens-Davis rule had been overruled by two subsequent Illinois decisions. Those two cases, however-

er, discussed only misleading use of trade names, not copying of articles of trade. One prohibited the use of a name so similar to that of another seller as to deceive or confuse customers, even though the defendant company did not sell the same products as the plaintiff and so in one sense could not be said to have palmed off its goods as those of a competitor, since the plaintiff was not a competitor. Lady Esther, Ltd., v. Lady Esther Corset Shoppe, Inc., 317 Ill.App. 451, 46 N.E.2d 165 (1943). The other Illinois case on which the Court of Appeals relied was a mandamus action which held that under an Illinois statute a corporation was properly denied registration in the State when its name was "deceptively similar" to that of a corporation already registered. Investors Syndicate of America, Inc., v. Hughes, 378 Ill. 413, 38 N.E.2d 754 (1941). The Court of Appeals, by holding that because Illinois forbids misleading use of trade names it also forbids as unfair competition the mere copying of an article of trade without any palming off, thus appears to have extended greatly the scope of the Illinois law of unfair competition beyond the limits indicated in the Illinois cases and beyond any previous decisions of the Seventh Circuit itself. Because of our disposition of these cases we need not decide whether it was correct in doing so.

Before the Constitution was adopted, some States had granted patents either by special act or by general statute,[3] but when the Constitution was adopted provision for a federal patent law was made one of the enumerated powers of Congress because, as Madison put it in The Federalist No. 43, the States "cannot separately make effectual provision" for either patents or copyrights.[4] That constitutional provision is Art. I, § 8, cl. 8, which empowers Congress "To promote the Progress of Science and useful Arts, by securing for limited Times to Authors and Inventors the exclusive Right to their respective Writings and Discoveries." Pursuant to this constitutional authority, Congress in 1790 enacted the first federal patent and copyright law, 1 Stat. 100, and ever since that time has fixed the conditions upon which patents and copyrights shall be granted, see 17 U.S.C. §§ 1–216; 35 U.S.C. §§ 1–293. These laws, like other laws of the United States enacted pursuant to constitutional authority, are the supreme law of the land. See Sperry v. Florida, 373 U.S. 379 (1963). When state law touches upon the area of these federal statutes, it is "familiar doctrine" that the federal policy "may not be set at naught, or its benefits denied" by the state law. Sola Elec. Co. v. Jefferson Elec. Co., 317 U.S. 172, 173, 176 (1942). This is true, of course, even if the state law is enacted in the exercise of otherwise undoubted state power.

The grant of a patent is the grant of a statutory monopoly;[5] indeed, the grant of patents in England was an explicit exception to the statute of James I prohibiting monopolies.[6] Patents are not given as favors, as was the case of monopolies given by the Tudor monarchs, see The Case of Monopolies (Darcy v. Allein), 11 Co.Rep. 84 b., 77 Eng.Rep. 1200 (K.B.1602), but are meant to encourage invention by rewarding the inventor with the right, limited to a term of years fixed by the patent, to exclude others from the use of his invention. During that period of time no one may make, use, or sell the patented product without the patentee's authority. 35 U.S.C. § 271. But in rewarding useful invention, the "rights and welfare of the community must be fairly dealt with and effectually guarded." Kendall v. Winsor, 21 How. 322, 329 (1859). To that end the prerequisites to obtaining a patent are strictly observed, and when the patent has issued the limitations on its exercise are equally strictly enforced. To begin with, a genuine "invention" or "discovery" must be demonstrated "lest in the constant demand for new appliances the heavy hand of tribute be laid on each slight technological advance in an art." Cuno Engineering Corp. v. Automatic Devices Corp., 314 U.S. 84, 92 (1941); see Great Atlantic & Pacific Tea Co. v. Supermarket

---

3. See I Walker, Patents (Deller ed. 1937), § 7.

4. The Federalist (Cooke ed. 1961) 288.

5. Patent rights exist only by virtue of statute. Wheaton v. Peters, 8 Pet. 591, 658 (1834).

6. The Statute of Monopolies, 21 Jac I, e. 3 (1623), declared all monopolies "contrary to the Laws of this Realm" and "utterly void and of none Effect." Section VI, however, excepted patents of 14 years to "the true and first Inventor and Inventors" of "new Manufacturers" so long as they were "not contrary to the Law, nor mischievous to the State, by raising Prices of Commodities at home, or Hurt of Trade, or generally inconvenient * * *." Much American patent law derives from English patent law.

Equipment Corp., 340 U.S. 147, 152–153 (1950); Atlantic Works v. Brady, 107 U.S. 192, 199–200 (1883). Once the patent issues, it is strictly construed. United States v. Masonite Corp., 316 U.S. 265, 280 (1942), it cannot be used to secure any monopoly beyond that contained in the patent, Morton Salt Co. v. G.S. Suppiger Co., 314 U.S. 488, 492 (1942), the patentee's control over the product when it leaves his hands is sharply limited, see United States v. Univis Lens Co., 316 U.S. 241, 250–252 (1942), and the patent monopoly may not be used in disregard of the antitrust laws, see International Business Machines Corp. v. United States, 208 U.S. 131 (1936); United Shoe Machinery Corp. v. United States, 258 U.S. 451, 463–464 (1922). Finally, and especially relevant here, when the patent expires the monopoly created by it expires, too, and the right to make the article—including the right to make it in precisely the shape it carried when patented—passes to the public. Kellogg Co. v. National Biscuit Co., 305 U.S. 111, 120–122 (1938); Singer Mfg. Co. v. June Mfg. Co., 163 U.S. 169, 185 (1896).

Thus the patent system is one in which uniform federal standards are carefully used to promote invention while at the same time preserving free competition.[7] Obviously a State could not, consistently with the Supremacy Clause of the Constitution,[8] extend the life of a patent beyond its expiration date or give a patent on an article which lacked the level of invention required for federal patents. To do either would run counter to the policy of Congress of granting patents only to true inventions, and then only for a limited time. Just as a State cannot encroach upon the federal patent laws directly, it cannot, under some other law, such as that forbidding unfair competition, give protection of a kind that clashes with the objectives of the federal patent laws.

In the present case the "pole lamp" sold by Stiffel has been held not to be entitled to the protection of either a mechanical or a design patent. An unpatentable article, like an article on which the patent has expired, is in the public domain and may be made and sold by whoever chooses to do so. What Sears did was to copy Stiffel's design and to sell lamps almost identical to those sold by Stiffel. This it had every right to do under the federal patent laws. That Stiffel originated the pole lamp and made it popular is immaterial. "Sharing in the goodwill of an article unprotected by patent or trade-mark is the exercise of a right possessed by all—and in the free exercise of which the consuming public is deeply interested." Kellogg Co. v. National Biscuit Co., supra, 305 U.S. at 122. To allow a State by use of its law of unfair competition to prevent the copying of an article which represents too slight an advance to be patented would be to permit the State to block off from the public something which federal law has said

---

7. The purpose of Congress to have national uniformity in patent and copyright laws can be inferred from such statutes as that which vests exclusive jurisdiction to hear patent and copyright cases in federal courts, 28 U.S.C. § 1338(a), and that section of the Copyright Act which expressly saves state protection of unpublished writings but does not include published writings, 17 U.S.C. § 2. 17 U.S.C. § 2 [of the 1909 Copyright Act, no longer in effect].

8. U.S.Const., Art. VI.

belongs to the public. The result would be that while federal law grants only 14 or 17 years' protection to genuine inventions, see 35 U.S.C. §§ 154, 173, States could allow perpetual protection to articles too lacking in novelty to merit any patent at all under federal constitutional standards. This would be too great an encroachment on the federal patent system to be tolerated.

Sears has been held liable here for unfair competition because of a finding of likelihood of confusion based only on the fact that Sears' lamp was copied from Stiffel's unpatented lamp and that consequently the two looked exactly alike. Of course there could be "confusion" as to who had manufactured these nearly identical articles. But mere inability of the public to tell two identical articles apart is not enough to support an injunction against copying or an award of damages for copying that which the federal patent laws permit to be copied. Doubtless a State may, in appropriate circumstances, require that goods, whether patented or unpatented, be labeled or that other precautionary steps be taken to prevent customers from being misled as to the source just as it may protect businesses in the use of their trademarks, labels, or distinctive dress in the packaging of goods so as to prevent others, by imitating such markings, from misleading purchasers as to the source of the goods.[9] But because of the federal patent laws a State may not, when the article is unpatented and uncopyrighted, prohibit the copying of the article itself or award damages for such copying. Cf. G. Ricordi & Co. v. Haendler, 194 F.2d 914, 916 (C.A.2d Cir.1952). The judgment below did both and in so doing gave Stiffel the equivalent of a patent monopoly on its unpatented lamp. That was error, and Sears is entitled to a judgment in its favor.

Reversed.

COMPCO CORP. v. DAY–BRITE LIGHTING, INC.

Supreme Court of the United States, 1964.
376 U.S. 234, 84 S.Ct. 779, 11 L.Ed.2d 669, rehearing denied 377 U.S. 913,
84 S.Ct. 1162, 12 L.Ed.2d 183.

MR. JUSTICE BLACK delivered the opinion of the Court.

As in Sears, Roebuck & Co. v. Stiffel Co., 376 U.S. 225, the question here is whether the use of a state unfair competition law to give relief against the copying of an unpatented industrial design conflicts with the federal patent laws. Both Compco and Day-Brite are manufacturers of fluorescent lighting fixtures of a kind widely used in offices and stores. Day-Brite in 1955 secured from the Patent Office a design patent on a reflector having cross-ribs claimed to give both strength and attractiveness to the fixture. Day-Brite also sought, but was refused, a mechanical patent on the same device. After Day-Brite had begun selling its fixture, Compco's predecessor [1] began making and

---

9. It seems apparent that Illinois has not seen fit to impose liability on sellers who do not label their goods. Neither the discussions in the opinions below nor the briefs before us cite any Illinois statute or decision requiring labeling.

1. The sales of which Day-Brite complained in this action had actually been

selling fixtures very similar to Day-Brite's. This action was then brought by Day-Brite. One count alleged that Compco had infringed Day-Brite's design patent; a second count charged that the public and the trade had come to associate this particular design with Day-Brite, that Compco had copied Day-Brite's distinctive design so as to confuse and deceive purchasers into thinking Compco's fixtures were actually Day-Brite's, and that by doing this Compco had unfairly competed with Day-Brite. The complaint prayed for both an accounting and an injunction.

The District Court held the design patent invalid; but as to the second count, while the court did not find that Compco had engaged in any deceptive or fraudulent practices, it did hold that Compco had been guilty of unfair competition under Illinois law. The court found that the overall appearance of Compco's fixture was "the same, to the eye of the ordinary observer, as the overall appearance" of Day-Brite's reflector, which embodied the design of the invalidated patent; that the appearance of Day-Brite's design had "the capacity to identify [Day-Brite] in the trade and does in fact so identify [it] to the trade"; that the concurrent sale of the two products was "likely to cause confusion in the trade"; and that "[a]ctual confusion has occurred." On these findings the court adjudged Compco guilty of unfair competition in the sale of its fixtures, ordered Compco to account to Day-Brite for damages, and enjoined Compco "from unfairly competing with plaintiff by the sale or attempted sale of reflectors identical to, or confusingly similar to" those made by Day-Brite. The Court of Appeals held there was substantial evidence in the record to support the District Court's finding of likely confusion and that this finding was sufficient to support a holding of unfair competition under Illinois law.[2] 311 F.2d 26. Although the District Court had not made such a finding, the appellate court observed that "several choices of ribbing were apparently available to meet the functional needs of the product," yet Compco "chose precisely the same design used by the plaintiff and followed it so closely as to make confusion likely." 311 F.2d, at 30. A design which identifies its maker to the trade, the Court of Appeals held, is a "protectable" right under Illinois law, even though the design is unpatentable.[3] We granted certiorari. 374 U.S. 825.

To support its findings of likelihood of confusion and actual confusion, the trial court was able to refer to only one circumstance in the record. A plant manager who had installed some of Compco's fixtures later asked Day-Brite to service the fixtures, thinking they had been

made by the Mitchell Lighting Company. However, by the time the complaint was filed, Mitchell had been acquired by Compco, which was therefore the defendant in the action and is the petitioner here. For simplicity we shall throughout the opinion refer only to Compco even though the transactions for which Compco was sought to be held liable were those of the predecessor company, Mitchell.

2. The Court of Appeals also affirmed the holding that the design patent was invalid. No review of this ruling is sought here.

3. As stated in Sears, Roebuck & Co. v. Stiffel Co., 376 U.S., at p. 228, n. 2, we do not here decide whether the Court of Appeals was correct in its statement of Illinois law.

made by Day-Brite. There was no testimony given by a purchaser or by anyone else that any customer had ever been misled, deceived, or "confused," that is, that anyone had ever bought a Compco fixture thinking it was a Day-Brite fixture. All the record shows, as to the one instance cited by the trial court, is that both Compco and Day-Brite fixtures had been installed in the same plant, that three years later some repairs were needed, and that the manager viewing the Compco fixtures—hung at least 15 feet above the floor and arranged end to end in a continuous line so that identifying marks were hidden—thought they were Day-Brite fixtures and asked Day-Brite to service them.[4] Not only is this incident suggestive only of confusion after a purchase had been made, but also there is considerable evidence of the care taken by Compco to prevent customer confusion, including clearly labeling both the fixtures and the containers in which they were shipped and not selling through manufacturers' representatives who handled competing lines.

Notwithstanding the thinness of the evidence to support findings of likely and actual confusion among purchasers, we do not find it necessary in this case to determine whether there is "clear error" in these findings. They, like those in Sears, Roebuck & Co. v. Stiffel Co., 376 U.S. 225, were based wholly on the fact that selling an article which is an exact copy of another unpatented article is likely to produce and did in this case produce confusion as to the source of the article. Even accepting the findings, we hold that the order for an accounting for damages and the injunction are in conflict with the federal patent laws. Today we have held in Sears, Roebuck & Co. v. Stiffel Co., 376 U.S. 225, that when an article is unprotected by a patent or a copyright, state law may not forbid others to copy that article. To forbid copying would interfere with the federal policy, found in Art. I, § 8, cl. 8, of the Constitution and in the implementing federal statutes, of allowing free access to copy whatever the federal patent and copyright laws leave in the public domain. Here Day-Brite's fixture has been held not to be entitled to a design or mechanical patent. Under the federal patent laws it is, therefore, in the public domain and can be copied in every detail by whoever pleases. It is true that the trial court found that the configuration of Day-Brite's fixture identified Day-Brite to the trade because the arrangement of the ribbing had, like a trademark, acquired a "secondary meaning" by which that particular design was associated with Day-Brite. But if the design is not entitled to a design patent or other federal statutory protection, then it can be copied at will.

As we have said in Sears, while the federal patent laws prevent a State from prohibiting the copying and selling of unpatented articles, they do not stand in the way of state law, statutory or decisional, which requires those who make and sell copies to take precautions to identify their products as their own. A state of course has power to impose

4. The only testimony about this incident was given by a sales representative of Day-Brite, who said that the plant manager had climbed up on a forklift truck to look at the fixtures. The manager was not called as a witness.

liability upon those who, knowing that the public is relying upon an original manufacturer's reputation for quality and integrity, deceive the public by palming off their copies as the original. That an article copied from an unpatented article could be made in some other way, that the design is "nonfunctional" and not essential to the use of either article, that the configuration of the article copied may have a "secondary meaning" which identifies the maker to the trade, or that there may be "confusion" among purchasers as to which article is which or as to who is the maker, may be relevant evidence in applying a State's law requiring such precautions as labeling; however, and regardless of the copier's motives, neither these facts nor any others can furnish a basis for imposing liability for or prohibiting the actual acts of copying and selling. Cf. Kellogg Co. v. National Biscuit Co., 305 U.S. 111, 120 (1938). And of course a State cannot hold a copier accountable in damages for failure to label or otherwise to identify his goods unless his failure is in violation of valid state statutory or decisional law requiring the copier to label or take other precautions to prevent confusion of customers as to the source of the goods.[5]

Since the judgment below forbids the sale of a copy of an unpatented article and orders an accounting for damages for such copying, it cannot stand.

Reversed.

MR. JUSTICE HARLAN, concurring in the result.[*]

In one respect I would give the States more leeway in unfair competition "copying" cases than the Court's opinions would allow. If copying is found, other than by an inference arising from the mere act of copying, to have been undertaken with the dominant purpose and effect of palming off one's goods as those of another or of confusing customers as to the source of such goods, I see no reason why the State may not impose reasonable restrictions on the future "copying" itself. Vindication of the paramount federal interest at stake does not require a State to tolerate such specifically oriented predatory business practices. Apart from this, I am in accord with the opinions of the Court, and concur in both judgments since neither case presents the point on which I find myself in disagreement.

NOTES

1. The sweep of the language in *Sears* and *Compco* seemed for awhile to auger revolutionary change in the American law of unfair competition. See, e.g., Callmann § 60.4(a): "These startlingly disappointing companion decisions so revolutionized our thinking with respect to the law of unfair competition that almost every one of its previously accepted premises must now be reexamined." See also Derenberg, Product Simulation: A Right or a Wrong?, 64 Colum.L.Rev. 1192 (1964): "The roof had seemingly fallen in on a vast structure

5. As we pointed out in Sears, Roebuck & Co. v. Stiffel Co., 376 U.S., at p. 232, n. 9, there is no showing that Illinois has any such law.

* This opinion also applies to Sears, Roebuck & Co. v. Stiffel Co., 376 U.S. 225.

of federal and state precedents laboriously built up since the days of the Court's famous decision in the *International News* case."

2. *Sears* and *Compco* must be viewed in the context of Erie R.R. v. Tompkins, 304 U.S. 64 (1938). Prior to *Erie* unfair competition was an area in which the power of the federal courts to announce common law rules played an important role. The last of those cases, was Kellogg Co. v. National Biscuit Co., 305 U.S. 111 (1938), infra page 235. See note 1 of the *Kellogg* opinion. Although the federal unfair competition cases did not rely on a preemption doctrine, the opinions showed an awareness of the need to announce unfair competition law compatible with the patent and copyright statutes. As long as the federal courts were in a position to make the accommodation themselves, it was unnecessary to develop a preemption theory. But *Erie* ended the power of the federal courts to declare rules of federal common law in diversity cases and in the 1950's state unfair competition law particularly in the important states of New York and California began to depart significantly from the earlier federal law.

3. Is unfair competition law an area where there is a need for substantial uniformity? Is product simulation an area where there is need for substantial uniformity?

4. The Court in *Sears* and *Compco* could have relied on a narrower version of the preemption theory to reach the same result. In Singer Mfg. Co. v. June Mfg. Co., 163 U.S. 169, 185 (1896), the Court said:

> It is self evident that on the expiration of a patent the monopoly created by it ceases to exist, and the right to make the thing formerly covered by the patent becomes public property. It is upon this condition that the patent is granted. It follows, as a matter of course, that on the termination of the patent here passes to the public the right to make the machine in the form in which it was constructed during the patent.

The Court could have simply extended that position to designs covered by invalid as well as expired patents on the theory that the act of obtaining a patent constituted a dedication of the disclosure of the patent to public use. But the Court in its discussion put no weight on the fact that there was an invalid patent covering the pole lamp. Rather the Court relied on the existence of the patent system itself without regard to whether the particular design had been patented. This broad use of the preemption doctrine is the radical element of the opinions—although it is not altogether clear that Mr. Justice Black was aware of the implications of this approach.

Further complications are created by the fact that the Court did not make any distinction in its discussion between the mechanical and design patent statutes and the fact that it simultaneously relied on the copyright statute. The Court did not specify whether its preemption theory was based on an interpretation of the legislation, or was a constitutional doctrine interpreting the constitutional copyright and patent power as exclusive.

BONITO BOATS, INC. v. THUNDER CRAFT BOATS
United States Supreme Court, 1989.
489 U.S. 141, 109 S.Ct. 971, 103 L.Ed.2d 118.

[Florida enacted legislation that prohibited use of the direct molding process to duplicate boat hulls. The statute made it unlawful to use the process or to knowingly sell boat hulls duplicated by that process. Direct molding contemplates using an original hull as a "plug" and spraying it with fiberglass to create a mold from which additional hulls can be made. Bonito claimed that Thunder Craft used the process to copy Bonito's successful Model 5VBR hull. The 5VBR was unpatented and had been on the market five years before the statute was enacted. The Florida Supreme Court denied relief on the basis that the statute was preempted under *Sears* and *Compco*. In an earlier case the Federal Circuit had upheld a similar California law. Interpart Corp. v. Italia, 777 F.2d 678 (1985). The Supreme Court, in a 9–0 opinion, strongly reaffirmed *Sears* and *Compco* and invalidated the statute.

The moral underpinnings of the misappropriation doctrine are strong and in the 25 years between *Sears* and *Bonito* (as the student will soon discover) doubts were cast on the scope or continued viability of preemption. A unanimous court and a broadly worded opinion renewed the vigor of the preemptive force of the patent and copyright laws.]

JUSTICE O'CONNOR delivered the opinion of the Court.

* * *

The attractiveness of [the patent system's grant of monopoly in return for disclosure] and its effectiveness in inducing creative effort and disclosure of the results of that effort, depend almost entirely on a backdrop of free competition in the exploitation of unpatented designs and innovations. The novelty and nonobviousness requirements of patentability embody a congressional understanding, implicit in the Patent Clause itself, that free exploitation of ideas will be the rule, to which the protection of a federal patent is the exception. Moreover, the ultimate goal of the patent system is to bring new designs and technologies into the public domain through disclosure. State law protection for techniques and designs whose disclosure has already been induced by market rewards may conflict with the very purpose of the patent laws by decreasing the range of ideas available as the building blocks of further innovation. The offer of federal protection from competitive exploitation of intellectual property would be rendered meaningless in a world where substantially similar state law protections were readily available. To a limited extent, the federal patent laws must determine not only what is protected, but also what is free for all to use.

* * *

The pre-emptive sweep of our decisions in *Sears* and *Compco* has been the subject of heated scholarly and judicial debate. See, e.g., Symposium, Product Simulation: A Right or a Wrong?, 64 Colum.L.

Rev. 1178 (1964); Lear, Inc. v. Adkins, 395 U.S. 653, 676 (1969) (Black, J., concurring in part and dissenting in part). Read at their highest level of generality, the two decisions could be taken to stand for the proposition that the States are completely disabled from offering any form of protection to articles or processes which fall within the broad scope of patentable subject matter. See id., at 677. Since the potentially patentable includes "anything under the sun that is made by man," Diamond v. Chakrabarty, 447 U.S. 303, 309 (1980) (citation omitted), the broadest reading of *Sears* would prohibit the States from regulating the deceptive simulation of trade dress or the tortious appropriation of private information.

That the extrapolation of such a broad pre-emptive principle from *Sears* is inappropriate is clear from the balance struck in *Sears* itself. The *Sears* Court made it plain that the States "may protect businesses in the use of their trademarks, labels, or distinctive dress in the packaging of goods so as to prevent others, by imitating such markings, from misleading purchasers as to the source of the goods." *Sears,* supra, 376 U.S., at 232 (footnote omitted). Trade dress is, of course, potentially the subject matter of design patents. See W.T. Rogers Co. v. Keene, 778 F.2d 334, 337 (CA7 1985). Yet our decision in *Sears* clearly indicates that the States may place limited regulations on the circumstances in which such designs are used in order to prevent consumer confusion as to source. Thus, while *Sears* speaks in absolutist terms, its conclusion that the States may place some conditions on the use of trade dress indicates an implicit recognition that all state regulation of potentially patentable but unpatented subject matter is not *ipso facto* pre-empted by the federal patent laws.

* * *

At the heart of *Sears* and *Compco* is the conclusion that the efficient operation of the federal patent system depends upon substantially free trade in publicly known, unpatented design and utilitarian conceptions. In *Sears,* the state law offered "the equivalent of a patent monopoly," 376 U.S., at 233 in the functional aspects of a product which had been placed in public commerce absent the protection of a valid patent. While, as noted above, our decisions since *Sears* have taken a decidedly less rigid view of the scope of federal pre-emption under the patent laws, e.g., *Kewanee,* supra, 416 U.S., at 479–480, we believe that the *Sears* Court correctly concluded that the States may not offer patent-like protection to intellectual creations which would otherwise remain unprotected as a matter of federal law. Both the novelty and the nonobviousness requirements of federal patent law are grounded in the notion that concepts within the public grasp, or those so obvious that they readily could be, are the tools of creation available to all. They provide the baseline of free competition upon which the patent system's incentive to creative effort depends. A state law that substantially interferes with the enjoyment of an unpatented utilitarian or design conception which has been freely disclosed by its author to the public at large impermissibly contravenes the ultimate goal of public disclosure and use which is the centerpiece of federal patent policy. Moreover, through the creation of patent-like rights, the States could essentially redirect inventive efforts away from the careful criteria of patentability developed by Congress over the last 200 years. We understand this to be the reasoning at the core of our decisions in *Sears* and *Compco* and we reaffirm that reasoning today.

III

We believe that the Florida statute at issue in this case so substantially impedes the public use of the otherwise unprotected design and utilitarian ideas embodied in unpatented boat hulls as to run afoul of the teaching of our decisions in *Sears* and *Compco*. It is readily apparent that the Florida statute does not operate to prohibit "unfair competition" in the usual sense that the term is understood. The law of unfair competition has its roots in the common-law tort of deceit: its general concern is with protecting consumers from confusion as to source. While that concern may result in the creation of "quasi-property rights" in communicative symbols, the focus is on the protection of consumers, not the protection of producers as an incentive to product innovation. * * *

With some notable exceptions, including the interpretation of the Illinois law of unfair competition at issue in Sears and Compco, the common-law tort of unfair competition has been limited to protection against copying of nonfunctional aspects of consumer products which have acquired secondary meaning such that they operate as a designation of source. The "protection" granted a particular design under the law of unfair competition is thus limited to one context where consumer confusion is likely to result; the design "idea" itself may be freely exploited in all other contexts.

In contrast to the operation of unfair competition law, the Florida statute is aimed directly at preventing the exploitation of the design and utilitarian conceptions embodied in the product itself. * * * To accomplish this goal, the Florida statute endows the original boat hull manufacturer with rights against the world, similar in scope and operation to the rights accorded a federal patentee. Like the patentee, the beneficiary of the Florida statute may prevent a competitor from "making" the product in what is evidently the most efficient manner available and from "selling" the product when it is produced in that fashion. The Florida scheme offers this protection for an unlimited number of years to all boat hulls and their component parts, without regard to their ornamental or technological merit. Protection is available for subject matter for which patent protection has been denied or has expired, as well as for designs which have been freely revealed to the consuming public by their creators.

* * *

That the Florida statute does not remove all means of reproduction and sale does not eliminate the conflict with the federal scheme. See

Kellogg, 305 U.S., at 122. In essence, the Florida law prohibits the entire public from engaging in a form of reverse engineering of a product in the public domain. This is clearly one of the rights vested in the federal patent holder, but has never been a part of state protection under the law of unfair competition or trade secrets. * * *

Moreover, as we noted in *Kewanee,* the competitive reality of reverse engineering may act as a spur to the inventor, creating an incentive to develop inventions which meet the rigorous requirements of patentability. 416 U.S., at 489–490, 94 S.Ct., at 1889–1890. The Florida statute substantially reduces this competitive incentive, thus eroding the general rule of free competition upon which the attractiveness of the federal patent bargain depends. The protections of state trade secret law are most effective at the developmental stage, before a product has been marketed and threat of reverse engineering becomes real. During this period, patentability will often be an uncertain prospect, and to a certain extent, the protection offered by trade secret law may "dovetail" with the incentives created by the federal patent monopoly. See Goldstein, Kewanee Oil Co. v. Bicron Corp.: Notes on a Closing Circle, 1974 Sup.Ct.Rev. 81, 92. In contrast, under the Florida scheme, the would-be inventor is aware from the outset of his efforts that rights against the public are available regardless of his ability to satisfy the rigorous standards of patentability. Indeed, it appears that even the most mundane and obvious changes in the design of a boat hull will trigger the protections of the statute. Given the substantial protection offered by the Florida scheme, we cannot dismiss as hypothetical the possibility that it will become a significant competitor to the federal patent laws, offering investors similar protection without the quid pro quo of substantial creative effort required by the federal statute. The prospect of all 50 States establishing similar protections for preferred industries without the rigorous requirements of patentability prescribed by Congress could pose a substantial threat to the patent system's ability to accomplish its mission of promoting progress in the useful arts.

Finally, allowing the States to create patent-like rights in various products in public circulation would lead to administrative problems of no small dimension. The federal patent scheme provides a basis for the public to ascertain the status of the intellectual property embodied in any article in general circulation. * * *

The Florida scheme blurs this clear federal demarcation between public and private property. One of the fundamental purposes behind the Patent and Copyright Clauses of the Constitution was to promote national uniformity in the realm of intellectual property. * * * This purpose is frustrated by the Florida scheme, which renders the status of the design and utilitarian "ideas" embodied in the boat hulls it protects uncertain. Given the inherently ephemeral nature of property in ideas, and the great power such property has to cause harm to the competitive policies which underlay the federal patent laws, the demarcation of broad zones of public and private right is "the type of regulation that demands a uniform national rule." Ray v. Atlantic Richfield Co., 435 U.S. 151, 179 (1978). Absent such a federal rule, each State could afford patent-like protection to particularly favored home industries, effectively insulating them from competition from outside the State.

*   *   *

Nor does the fact that a particular item lies within the subject matter of the federal patent laws necessarily preclude the States from offering limited protection which does not impermissibly interfere with the federal patent scheme. As Sears itself makes clear, States may place limited regulations on the use of unpatented designs in order to prevent consumer confusion as to source. In Kewanee, we found that state protection of trade secrets, as applied to both patentable and unpatentable subject matter, did not conflict with the federal patent laws. In both situations, state protection was not aimed exclusively at the promotion of invention itself, and the state restrictions on the use of unpatented ideas were limited to those necessary to promote goals outside the contemplation of the federal patent scheme. *   *   *

The Florida statute is aimed directly at the promotion of intellectual creation by substantially restricting the public's ability to exploit ideas which the patent system mandates shall be free for all to use. Like the interpretation of Illinois unfair competition law in Sears and Compco, the Florida statute represents a break with the tradition of peaceful co-existence between state market regulation and federal patent policy. The Florida law substantially restricts the public's ability to exploit an unpatented design in general circulation, raising the specter of state-created monopolies in a host of useful shapes and processes for which patent protection has been denied or is otherwise unobtainable. It thus enters a field of regulation which the patent laws have reserved to Congress. The patent statute's careful balance between public right and private monopoly to promote certain creative activity is a "scheme of federal regulation . . . so pervasive as to make reasonable the inference that Congress left no room for the States to supplement it." Rice v. Sante Fe Elevator Corp., 331 U.S. 218, 230 (1947).

Congress has considered extending various forms of limited protection to industrial design either through the copyright laws or by relaxing the restrictions on the availability of design patents. See generally Brown, Design Protection: An Overview, 34 U.C.L.A.L.Rev. 1341 (1987). Congress explicitly refused to take this step in the copyright laws, see 17 U.S.C. § 101; H.R.Rep. No. 94–1476, p. 55 (1976), U.S. Code Cong. & Admin.News 1976, pp. 5659, 5668, and despite sustained criticism for a number of years, it has declined to alter the patent protections presently available for industrial design. See Report of the President's Commission on the Patent System, S.Doc. No. 5, 90th Cong., 1st Sess., 20–21 (1967); Lindgren, The Sanctity of the Design Patent: Illusion or Reality?, 10 Okla.City L.Rev. 195 (1985). It is for Congress to determine if the present system of design and utility patents is ineffectual in promoting the useful arts in the context of industrial design. By offering patent-like protection for ideas deemed unprotected under the present federal scheme, the Florida statute conflicts with the "strong federal policy favoring free competition in ideas which do not merit patent protection." *Lear, Inc.,* 395 U.S., at 656. We therefore agree with the majority of the Florida Supreme Court that the Florida statute is preempted by the Supremacy Clause and the judgment of that court is hereby affirmed.

A. ALCHIAN & W. ALLEN, EXCHANGE AND PRODUCTION THEORY IN USE
251–53 (1969).*

There is a class of goods known as "public goods," wherein the amount of use of the good or service by one person does not reduce the amount available to others *if* the good has been produced. Classic examples are melodies, poems, ideas, and theories. Anyone can use them without in any way reducing someone else's supply. If I hum a new tune, you can hum it too. *Once the good is produced,* any restriction on its use by some person, say by charging a price for each use, would be "inefficient"—in the sense that the restriction reduces the total utility of the members of the community. Someone has less utility and *no one* else thereby gets more. (It is not a *free* good once it is produced, for even more of it might be desired; but, it is a public good in the sense that no actual or potential user supplants some other possible user.)

Exclusion of any potential user would be undesirable if we accept the simplest ethical criterion that more for some people, if it does not mean less for anyone else, is certainly desirable. However, accepting this criterion creates a conflict of goals. We want to encourage the invention of new ideas, melodies, and literature, and we want them fully used. But to charge for their use in order to provide incentive for development and invention will restrict their use. How can we induce people to create public goods if we prohibit charging for their use?

Examine the example of a lighthouse. All shipowners benefit, and they would like more light. If the lighthouse builder were able to control the light rays so that any nonpaying shipowner could not see the light, beneficiaries could induce him to provide as much more of the service as it was worth. Barring this possibility, some shipowners will not voluntarily pay for their value of service received—pro-rated share (say, $100) of the light they otherwise would get free, plus an amount (say, $10) to cover the cost of a larger light that they each might prefer. They would have to share payment for all the light ($110), but the worth of the additional light they get by cooperating is only the marginal increment ($10). As far as any one user is concerned, the

* From EXCHANGE AND PRODUC-TION, THEORY IN USE by Armen A. Alchian and William R. Allen. © 1969 by Wadsworth Publishing Co., Inc., Belmont, California 94002. Reprinted by permission of the publisher.

choice is between paying the pro-rata share of the total cost of $110 to get a $10 gain in value of light, or paying nothing and still getting some (or hoping others will provide) lighthouse service. Obviously, it will benefit him not to pay at all. And almost everyone will hope to get a "free ride." Too few lighthouses would be built too late. The consequence arises from the "unwillingness" of the nonexcludable beneficiaries to induce the provider of the service to provide more. Yet, *once the lighthouse is built,* exclusion of anyone could be wasteful (except that it is a very reliable means of ascertaining the value of the service for guiding production).

The landlubber counterpart is television. If all who wanted the program were to pay, the program would be available, but no one person is willing to bear the full cost of an "optimum" amount of service if he can view for nothing. Each person holds back in the hope that someone else will act.

If, fancifully, there were a way to measure the benefit obtained by each user and then have each pay not more than that amount to the producer, the problem would be solved. The user would pay a nonrestrictive lump-sum, and all who paid could use as much of the public good as was available. The lump-sum payment is not restrictive, because it is not a price for more use of the public good. It is an entry fee that one pays, once and for all, and thereby does not restrict the extent to which he makes use of the public good.

How to determine for each person what the appropriate lump-sum payment is and how to collect it? Everyone would want to conceal the real value to him while someone else paid to get the good produced. An excellent current example is the community television antenna for relatively isolated towns. Once the antenna is installed everyone can tap it with no loss of signal to anyone else. So why should anyone pay? And to prohibit its use by nonpayers is to restrict needlessly the extent of viewing—needlessly, in the sense of maximizing total utility *once the antenna is installed.* But if, in the absence of pricing and restricting, the antenna were not constructed (not enough volunteer to cover the costs), then pricing may be desirable to *get* the antenna *constructed.* Is it better not to restrict (and have no antenna) or to restrict and have an antenna? Clearly, the latter is superior.

But there is another alternative. Let the government tax everyone on a lump-sum basis and, with the proceeds, build the antenna. Then do not restrict the number who use it. But this solution also has flaws. (1) The tax is compulsory even on those who do not want an antenna. (2) It, too, is exclusionary, for failure to pay taxes will "exclude" you. (3) Who decides what ideas and programs shall be produced by the tax proceeds? Without a price per unit of use, viewers have no means of directly rewarding producers of more desirable programs. The control of production passes to the political arena and is more controlled by group political competition than decentralized market competition. For those who are strong in political competitive power, this may seem desirable. The choice is not determinable by some simple or even any known ethical criterion.

*   *   *

The problem of public goods is a relatively new one in economic analysis. Perhaps in a few more decades, more definitive analyses can be accomplished and rigorous implications perceived. The problem is covered here to warn against blind carryover of principles from private goods to public goods as if there were no difference.

We can summarize the problem of "external effects." Some potential uses of resources also benefit people other than the current owners. Those "external" benefits can be made influential by paying the resource controller to adjust his use of the good. "External effects are thus internalized, or social effects are made private." For some goods this is prohibitively expensive; there then exists a disparity between social and private benefits and costs. For any good heavily loaded with the "public goods" characteristic, *once the good is produced,* there is no allocating or rationing problem, since no one user will deprive any other user. Hence, charging a price for its use would restrict use unnecessarily. But a means of defraying the costs of production and of discovering how much to produce is necessary. The conflicting objectives for "public" goods are (1) to induce beneficiaries to reveal their values of services and to pay for the production of the service and (2) the "unnecessary" restriction on use if any fee restricts use. Various devices were mentioned that have been adopted to meet partially both objectives of inducing appropriate production and of not restricting use once production has occurred. Some involve group action via private markets and some via government taxing or production.

NOTES

1. Does the economic analysis of Alchian and Allen highlight the problem faced by the Court in *INS, Sears, Compco* and *Bonito?* The opinion in *INS* has a heavy moral undertone, i.e., "endeavoring to reap where it has not sown"; Justice Black in *Sears* and *Compco* explores the technical doctrines of federal preemption. Does the Court in each case also attempt, either explicitly or implicitly, to solve the economic dilemma of "public goods"?

There has been a traditional view that "inventive genius" or artistic talent were largely immune from economic incentives. The struggling painter or novelist laboring to beautify or civilize society without regard to his own personal fortune is an enduring vision. It is more romantic to contemplate Newton accidentally confronting an apple or Franklin enjoying the thrill of kite flying than the plodding pursuit of knowledge or discoveries by corporate research and development departments.

More systematic analysis, however, suggests that inventive activity is motivated by personal gain. A study based on data derived from the patent system concluded that "invention is largely an economic activity which, like other economic activities, is pursued for gain. * * *" J. Schmookler, Invention and Economic Growth 206 (1966).*

Despite the popularity of the idea that scientific discoveries and major inventions typically provide the stimulus for inventions, the historical record of important inventions in petroleum refining, papermaking, railroading, and farming revealed not a single, unambiguous instance in which either discoveries or inventions played the role hypothesized. Instead, in hundreds of cases the stimulus was the recognition of a costly problem to be solved or a potentially profitable opportunity to be seized; in short, a technical problem or opportunity evaluated in economic terms. In a few cases, sheer accident was credited. Id. at 199.

INS, Sears, Compco and *Bonito* affect the extent to which the common law can allow an innovator to appropriate the gains derived from his effort. As Alchian and Allen make clear, the economic problem is not one of allocation but one of incentives. More specifically, the social problem is allowing the innovator the right amount of return on his activity to insure the *optimum* amount of innovative activity.

Of course, legal protection against misappropriation is not the only method of capturing gains from innovative activity. See, Schmookler, id. at 37–38:

Large concerns will ordinarily introduce neither a new product in the market nor a new process in the plant until the "bugs" have been substantially eliminated, that is, until much of the necessary "know-how" has been developed. Generally so far as processes are concerned, and often in the case of products, rivals will remain at a disadvantage for some time after the invention is introduced, even in the absence of patents.

Since many results of corporate research today are apparently unpatented, it seems probable that this period of initial advantage is both a necessary and, usually, a sufficient condition for a large part of present-day corporate research. In its absence, any one firm would be better off to engage in no research at all. It would need merely to copy its competitors' inventions. Its own research would presumably help its rivals as much as itself, and under these conditions, little or no industrial research would occur. Since the magnitude of industrial research today is enormous, it is clear that this situation does not obtain. One may surmise that it is either the advantage of being first or the necessity for catching up which motivates corporate invention. Once one firm in an industry engages in research, its rivals are perforce obligated to follow suit to maintain their own relative standing. Thus Frederic M. Scherer et al. concluded that

the prospect of exclusive patent monopoly is normally not necessary before investment in technical advance will take place. Of far greater everyday importance are reward structures related to the necessity of retaining market positions, of attaining production more efficient than competitors, of securing the corporation through diversification against disastrous product obsolescence, and of gaining short-term advantages which can be exploited by advertising and well-developed sales channels. [Scherer, Patents and the Corporation 136–38 (1959)].

All these motives presuppose the advantage of the early start.

Moreover, corporations have engaged in research chiefly since science has grown to a stage where it can be immediately useful in industry. One consequence of the growth of science seems to have been an increase in the number of alternative solutions to a given industrial problem. Hence once a given result is achieved, other men can often discover an alternative means for accomplishing the same result. One outstanding example of this, out of many possible ones, is the multiplicity of catalytic cracking processes developed in petroleum refining following the Houdry process. A patent cannot protect a firm against such responsive inventions. The firm's only protection then is to remain ahead, or at least not too far behind, in the race. In other words, the ability of researchers to find alternative means, an ability resulting from the growth of science, implies that even with patent protection the initial inventor in a scientific field is likely to have only the advantage of the early start—an advantage which he has without a patent.

It should be recognized that the foregoing is a description of tendencies, not of absolutes. There are obviously many occasions on which firms, large and small, still take out patents.

The lead time monopoly without subsequent copyright protection has been suggested to be a sufficient incentive for the production of written material. Breyer, The Uneasy Case for Copyright: A Study of Copyright in Books, Photocopies, and Computer Programs, 84 Harv.L.Rev. 281 (1970).

There are, of course, limits on the extent of a lead time monopoly. See W. Nordhaus, Invention, Growth, and Welfare 61 (1969):

There are two powerful forces that tend to reduce any technological lead. First, other firms tend to catch up by performing parallel or identical research and narrowing the difference in the stock of technological information. A second and perhaps more important force comes from the inappropriability of scarce knowledge. The mobility of labor, industrial spying, disclosure in patents, and the inability to seal off the research and productive processes tend to erode the differential level of knowledge among firms.

See also, Plant, The Economic Theory Concerning Patents for Inventions, 1 Economica 30 (N.S.1934). It should not be assumed that reverse engineering of a competitor's innovation is a costless or low cost activity. To the extent an innovation can be commercially exploited in secrecy, the lead time monopoly may be extensive and the costs of piercing the secrecy (including overcoming any legal barriers to doing so) may be high. Even where the costs of transmitting the knowledge is low, the ability to absorb and utilize what is acquired is in many instances conditioned on having developed a base of basic knowledge, skilled employees, and capital equipment. But see, R. Nelson, M. Peck, & E. Kalachek, Technology, Economic Growth and Public Policy 159–60 (1967): "The costs of imitating relative to the cost of the original R & D obviously varies from case to case, as does the lead time of the innovator. However, if a head start defended by secrecy were the only advantage, in many instances there would be little incentive for invention and innovation."

2. The economic analysis of public goods is greatly complicated once one considers that utilization of the public good itself has costs (or to put it another way, requires the use of additional resources) and attention is shifted to the problem of creating incentives for the efficient timing of the utilization of these additional resources. See Barzel, The Optimal Timing of Innovations, 50 Rev. Econ. & Stat. 348 (1968). These problems are discussed in connection with the patent system in Kitch, The Nature and Function of the Patent System, 20 J.L. & Econ. 265 (1977). The lighthouse problem discussed by Alchian and Allen is further explored in Coase, The Lighthouse in Economics, 17 J.L. & Econ. 357 (1974).

3. Does a manufacturer have a duty to help other persons to profit from his original efforts? In Berkey Photo, Inc. v. Eastman Kodak Co., 603 F.2d 263 (2d Cir.1979), cert. denied 444 U.S. 1093 (1980), the district court found that Kodak had violated the antitrust laws when it withheld information on its newly developed cartridge film until it was ready to market its own cartridge camera. The simultaneous introduction of camera and film delayed competition by other camera manufacturers and competing photofinishers. The Court of Appeals reversed:

> * * * a firm may normally keep its innovations secret from its rivals as long as it wishes, forcing them to catch up on the strength of their own efforts after the new product is introduced. * * * It is the possibility of success in the market place, attributable to superior performance, that provides the incentives on which the proper functioning of our competitive economy rests. If a firm that has engaged in the risks and expenses of research and development were required in all circumstances to share with its rivals the benefits of those endeavors, this incentive would very likely be vitiated.
>
> Withholding from others advance knowledge of one's new products, therefore, ordinarily constitutes valid competitive conduct. Because * * * a monopolist is permitted, and indeed encouraged, by § 2 [of the Sherman Act] to compete aggressively on the merits, any success that it may achieve through "the process of invention and innovation" is clearly tolerated by the antitrust laws.

603 F.2d at 281.

See also California Computer Products, Inc. v. International Business Machines Corp., 613 F.2d 727 (9th Cir.1979), where a manufacturer of peripheral equipment for computers unsuccessfully argued that IBM committed an antitrust violation by redesigning its computers to make production and sale of peripheral equipment more difficult. "IBM, assuming it was a monopolist, had the right to redesign its products to make them more attractive to buyers— whether by reason of lower manufacturing cost and price or improved performance. It was under no duty to help CalComp or other peripheral equipment manufacturers survive or expand." 613 F.2d at 744.

In Telex Corp. v. International Business Machines Corp., 464 F.2d 1025 (8th Cir.1972) the court dissolved a temporary injunction that had prohibited IBM from making advance public announcement of new products. Telex had argued that the announcements, long in advance of actual marketing, chilled the market for competitors' products.

4. A policy issue in these cases is how to establish a legal regime that will tend toward an efficient level of innovative activity. See, Demsetz, The Private Production of Public Goods, 13 J.L. & Econ. 293 (1970); Samuelson, Contrast

Between Welfare Conditions for Joint Supply and for Public Goods, 51 Rev. Econ. & Stat. 26 (1969); Oakland, Public Goods, Perfect Competition and Underproduction, 82 J.Pol.Econ. 927 (1974). This social question is central to the consideration of material in this book.

For an examination of this issue in another context suggesting that legislative rather than judicial action is more appropriate see Perlman & Rhinelander, Williams & Wilkins Co. v. United States: Photocopying, Copyright, and the Judicial Process, 1975 Sup.Ct.Rev. 355. See generally, E. Mansfield, The Economics of Technological Change (1968).

D. THE REGULATION OF ADVERTISING

FRIEDMAN v. ROGERS

Supreme Court of the United States, 1979.
440 U.S. 1, 99 S.Ct. 887, 59 L.Ed.2d 100.

MR. JUSTICE POWELL delivered the opinion of the Court.

Texas law prohibits the practice of optometry under a trade name. It also requires that four of the six members of the State's regulatory board, the Texas Optometry Board, be members of the Texas Optometric Association, a professional organization of optometrists. A three-judge District Court sustained the constitutionality of the statute governing the composition of the Texas Optometry Board against a challenge based on the First and Fourteenth Amendments. But it held that the prohibition of the practice of optometry under a trade name ran afoul of First Amendment protection of commercial speech. 438 F.Supp. 428 (E.D. Tex.1977). These appeals and cross-appeal bring both of the District Court's holdings before the Court.

I

The Texas Legislature approved the Texas Optometry Act (the Act) in 1969, repealing an earlier law governing the practice of optometry in the State. Section 2.01 of the Act establishes the Texas Optometry Board (the Board) and § 2.02 prescribes the qualifications for Board members. The Board is responsible for the administration of the Act, and has the authority to grant, renew, suspend, and revoke licenses to practice optometry in the State. The Act imposes numerous regulations on the practice of optometry, and on several aspects of the business of optometry. Many of the Act's business regulations are contained in § 5.13, which restricts fee splitting by optometrists and forbids an optometrist to allow his name to be associated with any optometrical office unless he is present and practicing there at least half of the hours that the office is open or half of the hours that he practices, whichever is less. Section 5.13(d), at issue here, prohibits the practice of optometry under an assumed name, trade name, or corporate name.[6]

6. Section 5.13(d) provides in part:

"No optometrist shall practice or continue to practice optometry under, or use in connection with his practice of optometry, any assumed name, corporate name, trade name, or any name other

The dispute in this case grows out of the schism between "professional" and "commercial" optometrists in Texas. Although all optometrists in the State must meet the same licensing requirements, and are subject to the same laws regulating their practices, they have divided themselves informally into two groups according to their divergent approaches to the practice of optometry. Rogers, an advocate of the commercial practice of optometry and a member of the Board, commenced this action by filing a suit against the other five members of the Board. He sought declaratory and injunctive relief from the enforcement of § 2.02 of the Act, prescribing the composition of the Board, and § 5.13(d) of the Act, prohibiting the practice of optometry under a trade name. [Rogers used the trade name "Texas State Optical" or "TSO".]

[Section 2.02 of the Act required four of the six members to be affiliated with the Texas Optometric Association (TOA). Commercial optometrists were ineligible for membership. Rogers claimed this statutory scheme deprived him of equal protection and due process. The TOA intervened to support the statute; the Texas Senior Citizens Association intervened on behalf of Rogers claiming their membership was deprived of Fourteenth Amendment rights by the restrictions on commercial optometrists. In part of the opinion omitted below, a unanimous Supreme Court affirmed the District Court's ruling sustaining the constitutionality of § 2.02 as reasonably related to a valid state interest in regulating optometrists.]

II

In holding that § 5.13(d) infringes First Amendment rights, the District Court relied primarily on this Court's decisions in Bates v. State Bar of Arizona, 433 U.S. 350 (1977), and Virginia State Board of Pharmacy v. Virginia Citizens Consumer Council, 425 U.S. 748 (1976). A trade name is a form of advertising, it concluded, because after the name has been used for some time, people "identify the name with a certain quality of service and goods." It found specifically "that the Texas State Optical [TSO] name has come to communicate to the consuming public information as to certain standards of price and quality, and availability of routine services," and rejected the argument that the TSO name misleads the public as to the identity of the optometrists with whom it deals. Balancing the constitutional inter-

than the name under which he is licensed to practice optometry in Texas * * * " The scope of the prohibition in § 5.13(d) is limited by various provisions in § 5.13 that make it clear that the Act does not proscribe partnerships for the practice of optometry, or the employment of optometrists by other optometrists. Regarding partnerships, counsel for the defendant Board members indicated at oral argument that § 5.13(d) does not require that the names of all partners be included in the name used to identify the office of an optometrical partnership. Tr. of Oral Arg., at 28. With respect to employees, § 5.13 provides that "[o]ptometrists who are employed by other optometrists shall practice in their own names, but may practice in an office listed under the name of the individual optometrist or partnership of optometrists by whom they are employed."

ests in the commercial speech in question against the State's interest in regulating it, the District Court held that the prohibition of the use of trade names by § 5.13(d) is an unconstitutional restriction of the "free flow of commercial information."   438 F.Supp., at 430–431.

A

A review of *Virginia Pharmacy* and *Bates* shows that the reliance on them by the court below, a reliance reasserted here by Rogers and the TSCA (the plaintiffs), was misplaced. At issue in *Virginia Pharmacy* was the validity of Virginia's law preventing advertising by pharmacists of the prices of prescription drugs. After establishing that the economic nature of the pharmacists' interest in the speech did not preclude First Amendment protection for their advertisements, the Court discussed the other interests in the advertisements that warranted First Amendment protection. To individual consumers, information about prices of prescription drugs at competing pharmacies "could mean the alleviation of physical pain or the enjoyment of basic necessities." Id., at 764, 96 S.Ct., at 1827. Society also has a strong interest in the free flow of commercial information, both because the efficient allocation of resources depends upon informed consumer choices and because "even an individual advertisement, though entirely 'commercial,' may be of general public interest." Ibid. The Court acknowledged the important interest of the State in maintaining high standards among pharmacists, but concluded that this interest could not justify the ban on truthful price advertising when weighed against the First Amendment interests in the information conveyed.

In the next Term, the Court applied the rationale of *Virginia Pharmacy* to the advertising of certain information by lawyers. After weighing the First Amendment interests identified in *Virginia Pharmacy* against the State's interests in regulating the speech in question, the Court concluded that the truthful advertising of the prices at which routine legal services will be performed also is protected by the First Amendment. Bates v. State Bar of Arizona, supra.

In both *Virginia Pharmacy* and *Bates*, we were careful to emphasize that "[s]ome forms of commercial speech regulation are surely permissible." Virginia Pharmacy, supra, at 770, Bates, supra, 433 U.S., at 383. For example, restrictions on the time, place, or manner of expression are permissible provided that "they are [imposed] without reference to the content of the regulated speech, that they serve a significant governmental interest, and that in so doing they leave open ample alternative channels for communication of the information." Virginia Pharmacy, supra, 425 U.S., at 771. Equally permissible are restrictions on false, deceptive, and misleading commercial speech.

"Untruthful speech, commercial or otherwise, has never been protected for its own sake. Gertz v. Robert Welch, Inc., 418 U.S. 323, 340 (1974); Konisberg v. State Bar, 366 U.S. 36, 49, and n. 10 (1961). Obviously, much commercial speech is not provably false, or even wholly false, but only deceptive or misleading. We foresee no obstacle to a State's dealing effectively with this problem. The First Amendment, as we construe it today, does not prohibit the State from insuring that the stream of commercial information flows cleanly as well as freely." *Virginia Pharmacy,* supra, at 771–772; accord, *Bates,* supra, 433 U.S., at 383.

Regarding the permissible extent of commercial speech regulation, the Court observed in *Virginia Pharmacy* that certain features of commercial speech differentiate it from other varieties of speech in ways that suggest that "a different degree of protection is necessary to insure that the flow of truthful and legitimate commercial information is unimpaired." 425 U.S., at 771–772 n. 24. Because it relates to a particular product or service, commercial speech is more objective, hence more verifiable, than other varieties of speech. Commercial speech, because of its importance to business profits, and because it is carefully calculated, is also less likely than other forms of speech to be inhibited by proper regulation. These attributes, the Court concluded, indicate that it is "appropriate to require that a commercial message appear in such a form * * * as [is] necessary to prevent its being deceptive. * * * They may also make inapplicable the prohibition against prior restraints." Ibid. (citations omitted); see id., at 775–781, 96 S.Ct., at 1832–1835 (concurring opinion of Mr. Justice Stewart).[9]

B

Once a trade name has been in use for some time, it may serve to identify an optometrical practice and also to convey information about the type, price, and quality of services offered for sale in that practice. In each role, the trade name is used as part of a proposal of a commercial transaction. Like the pharmacist who desired to advertise his prices in *Virginia Pharmacy,* supra, the optometrist who uses a

---

9. The application of First Amendment protection to speech that does "no more than propose a commercial transaction," Pittsburgh Press Co. v. Human Relations Comm'n, 413 U.S. 376, 385 (1973), has been recognized generally as a substantial extension of traditional free-speech doctrine which poses special problems not presented by other forms of protected speech. Jackson & Jeffries, Commercial Speech: Economic Due Process and the First Amendment, 65 Va.L.Rev. 1 (1979); Note First Amendment and Misleading Advertising, 57 B.U.L.Rev. 833 (1977). Cf. Note, First Amendment Protection for Commercial Advertising: The New Constitutional Doctrine, 44 U.Chi.L.Rev. 205 (1976). By definition, commercial speech is linked inextricably to commercial activity: while the First Amendment affords such speech "a limited measure of protection," it is also true that "the State does not lose its power to regulate commercial activity deemed harmful to the public whenever speech is a component of that activity." Ohralik v. Ohio State Bar Assn., 436 U.S. 447, 456 (1978). Because of the special character of commercial speech and the relative novelty of First Amendment protection for such speech, we act with caution in confronting First Amendment challenges to economic legislation that serves legitimate regulatory interests. Our decisions dealing with more traditional First Amendment problems do not extend automatically to this as yet uncharted area. See, e.g., id., at 462 n. 20 (overbreadth analysis not applicable to commercial speech). When dealing with restrictions on commercial speech we frame our decisions narrowly, "allowing modes of regulation [of commercial speech] that might be impermissible in the realm of non-commercial expression." Id., at 456.

trade name "does not wish to editorialize on any subject, cultural, philosophical, or political. He does not wish to report any particularly newsworthy fact, or to make generalized observations even about commercial matters." 425 U.S., at 761. His purpose is strictly business. The use of trade names in connection with optometrical practice, then, is a form of commercial speech and nothing more.

A trade name is, however, a significantly different form of commercial speech from that considered in *Virginia Pharmacy* and *Bates*. In those cases, the State had proscribed advertising by pharmacists and lawyers that contained statements about the products or services offered and their prices. These statements were self-contained and self-explanatory. Here, we are concerned with a form of commercial speech that has no intrinsic meaning. A trade name conveys no information about the price and nature of the services offered by an optometrist until it acquires meaning over a period of time by associations formed in the minds of the public between the name and some standard of price or quality. Because these ill-defined associations of trade names with price and quality information can be manipulated by the users of trade names, there is a significant possibility that trade names will be used to mislead the public.

The possibilities for deception are numerous. The trade name of an optometrical practice can remain unchanged despite changes in the staff of optometrists upon whose skill and care the public depends when it patronizes the practice. Thus, the public may be attracted by a trade name that reflects the reputation of an optometrist no longer associated with the practice. A trade name frees an optometrist from dependence on his personal reputation to attract clients, and even allows him to assume a new trade name if negligence or misconduct casts a shadow over the old one. By using different trade names at shops under his common ownership, an optometrist can give the public the false impression of competition among the shops. The use of a trade name also facilitates the advertising essential to large-scale commercial practices with numerous branch offices, conduct the State rationally may wish to discourage while not prohibiting commercial optometrical practice altogether.

The concerns of the Texas Legislature about the deceptive and misleading uses of optometrical trade names were not speculative or hypothetical, but were based on experience in Texas with which the legislature was familiar when in 1969 it enacted § 5.13(d). The forerunner of § 5.13(d) was adopted as part of a "Professional Responsibility Rule" by the Texas State Board of Examiners in Optometry in 1959. In a decision upholding the validity of the Rule, the Texas Supreme Court reviewed some of the practices that had prompted its adoption. Texas State Bd. of Examiners in Optometry v. Carp, 412 S.W.2d 307, appeal dismissed and cert. denied, 389 U.S. 52 (1967). One of the plaintiffs in that case, Carp, operated 71 optometrical offices in Texas under at least 10 different trade names. From time to time, he changed the trade names of various shops, though the licensed optometrists practicing in each shop remained the same. He purchased the practices of other optometrists and continued to practice under their names, even though they were no longer associated with the practice. In several instances, Carp used different trade names on offices located in close proximity to one another and selling the same optical goods and services. The offices were under common management, and had a common staff of optometrists, but the use of different trade names facilitated advertising that gave the impression of competition among the offices.

The Texas court found that Carp used trade names to give a misleading impression of competitive ownership and management of his shops. It also found that Rogers, a party to this suit and a plaintiff in *Carp,* had used a trade name to convey the impression of standardized optometrical care. All 82 of his shops went under the trade name "Texas State Optical" or "TSO," and he advertised "scientific TSO eye examination[s]" available in every shop. 412 S.W.2d, at 312. The TSO advertising was calculated as well, the court found, to give "the impression that [Rogers or one of his brothers] is present at a particular office. Actually they have neither been inside nor seen some of their eighty-two offices distributed generally over Texas." Id., at 313. Even if Rogers' use and advertising of the trade name were not in fact misleading, they were an example of the use of a trade name to facilitate the large-scale commercialization which enhances the opportunity for misleading practices.[13]

It is clear that the State's interest in protecting the public from the deceptive and misleading use of optometrical trade names is substantial and well-demonstrated.[14] We are convinced that § 5.13(d) is a constitutionally permissible state regulation in furtherance of this interest. We emphasize, in so holding, that the restriction on the use of trade

13. Although the individual defendants and the TOA (collectively, the defendants) rely primarily on *Carp* to establish the history of false and misleading uses of optometrical trade names, some evidence of such practices also was included in the deposition testimony presented to the District Court. A former associate of Carp's testified to some of the trade name abuses that had occurred in their business. Shannon Deposition, at 8. Rogers' testimony showed that the "Texas State Optical" name was used by offices wholly owned by him, partly owned by him, and by offices in which he had no ownership interest. The dissenting opinion states that the "Rogers organization is able to offer and enforce a degree of uniformity in care at all of its offices * * *." Post, at 900. This was not Rogers' testimony. He stated that he exercised "no control whatsoever" over "office policy routines" in those TSO offices in which he owned no interest. Rogers' Deposition, at 16. It appears from Rogers' testi-

mony that his primary business relationship with such offices was their participation in the TSO advertising and their purchase of materials and equipment from his supply house. Id., at 16–18, 22–23.

14. The plaintiffs argue that the fact that the public might be subject to similar deception by optometrists who do not use trade names but practice in partnerships or with numerous employees shows that the State actually was not concerned with misleading and deceptive practices when it enacted § 5.13(d). The plaintiffs have not attempted to show, however, that any of the demonstrated abuses associated with the use of trade names also has occurred apart from their use. Tr. of Oral Arg., at 29. There is no requirement that the State legislate more broadly than required by the problem it seeks to remedy. See *Williamson v. Lee Optical Co.,* 348 U.S. 483, 489 (1955).

names has only the most incidental effect on the content of the commercial speech of Texas optometrists. As noted above, a trade name conveys information only because of the associations that grow up over time between the name and a certain level of price and quality of service. Moreover, the information associated with a trade name is largely factual, concerning the kind and price of the services offered for sale. Since the Act does not prohibit or limit the type of informational advertising held to be protected in *Virginia Pharmacy* and *Bates*, the factual information associated with trade names may be communicated freely and explicitly to the public. An optometrist may advertise the type of service he offers, the prices he charges, and whether he practices as a partner, associate, or employee with other optometrists. Rather than stifling commercial speech, § 5.13(d) ensures that information regarding optometrical services will be communicated more fully and accurately to consumers than it had been in the past when optometrists were allowed to convey the information through unstated and ambiguous associations with a trade name. In sum, Texas has done no more than require that commercial information about optometrical services "appear in such a form . . . as [is] necessary to prevent its being deceptive." *Virginia Pharmacy,* supra, 425 U.S., at 771–772 n. 24.

*   *   *

IV

*   *   * The case is remanded with instructions to dissolve the injunction against the enforcement of § 5.13(d).

So ordered.

MR. JUSTICE BLACKMUN, with whom MR. JUSTICE MARSHALL joins, concurring in part and dissenting in part.

*   *   *

I do not agree with the Court's holding that the Texas Optometry Act's § 5.13(d), which bans the use of a trade name "in connection with" the practice of optometry in the State, is constitutional. In my view, the Court's restricted analysis of the nature of a trade name overestimates the potential for deception, and underestimates the harmful impact of the broad sweep of § 5.13(d). The Court also ignores the fact that in Texas the practice of "commercial" optometry is *legal.* It has never been outlawed or made illegal. This inescapable conclusion is one of profound importance in the measure of the First Amendment rights that are asserted here. It follows, it seems to me, that Texas has abridged the First Amendment rights not only of Doctor Rogers but of the members of the intervenor-plaintiff Texas Senior Citizens Association by absolutely prohibiting, without reasonable justification, the dissemination of truthful information about wholly legal commercial conduct.

I

*   *   *

In 1976, Texas had 934 resident licensed optometrists divided almost evenly between "professional" and "commercial" factions. Rogers is the leader of the commercial forces. He and his associates operate more than 100 optometry offices. Before the enactment of § 5.13(d) in 1969, and where still allowed by a grandfather provision, § 5.13(k) (which, but for the decision of the District Court, would have expired on January 1, 1979), their offices use the name Texas State Optical, or TSO. An optometrist who agrees to participate with Rogers in his organization must obey an elaborate set of restrictions on pain of termination. He must purchase all inventory and supplies from Rogers Brothers; do all laboratory work at their laboratory; abide by their policies concerning the examination of patients; take patients on a first-come-first-served basis rather than by appointment; and retain Rogers Brothers at 4% of net cash to do all accounting and advertising. App. A71–A98. As a result of these and other rules, the Rogers organization is able to offer and enforce a degree of uniformity in care at all its offices along with other consumer benefits, namely, sales on credit, adjustment of frames and lenses without cost, one-stop care, and transferability of patient records among Texas State Optical offices.[2] The TSO chain typifies commercial optometry, with its emphasis on advertising, volume, and speed of service.

The Court today glosses over the important private and public interests that support Rogers' use of his trade name. For those who need them, eyeglasses are one of the "basic necessities" of life in which a consumer's interest "may be as keen, if not keener by far, than his interest in the day's most urgent political debate." Virginia Pharmacy Board, 425 U.S., at 763–764. For the mobile consumer, the Rogers trade name provides a valuable service.[3] Lee Kenneth Benham, a professor and economist whose studies in this area have been relied

2. Rogers owns some Texas State Optical offices; in others he is merely a partner; and in still others he has no financial interest other than licensing the TSO trade name and selling optical supplies and services to the "associated" optometrist. The Court, ante, at 13 n. 13, relies on Rogers' deposition testimony to suggest that he exerts no control at all over associated offices. The representative contract introduced into evidence, however, requires that, as a condition of using the TSO trade name, the licensee must operate the office in accord with TSO policy and purchase all optical material from Rogers Brothers Laboratory. App. A82–A83. See Brief for Appellee *Texas Optometric Association, Inc.,* in No. 77–1164, pp. 16–18. The parties do not question the District Court's factual finding that the TSO trade name is associated with certain standards of quality. See infra, at 900–901 [Casebook page 61].

3. Trade names are a vital form of commercial speech. It has even been suggested that commercial speech can be defined as "speech referring to a brand name product or service that is not itself protected by the first amendment, issued by a speaker with a financial interest in the sale of the product or service or in the distribution of the speech." Note, First Amendment Protection for Commercial Advertising: The New Constitutional Doctrine, 44 U.Chi.L. Rev. 205, 254 (1976).

upon by the Federal Trade Commission,[4] testified in a deposition which is part of the record here:

> "One of the most valuable assets which individuals have in this large mobile country is their knowledge about trade names. Consumers develop a sophisticated understanding of the goods and services provided and the prices associated with different trade names. This permits them to locate the goods, services, and prices they prefer on a continuing basis with substantially lower search costs than would otherwise be the case. This can perhaps be illustrated by pointing out the information provided by such names as Sears, Neiman Marcus or Volkswagen. This also means that firms have an enormous incentive to develop and maintain the integrity of the products and services provided under their trade name: the entire package they offer is being judged continuously by consumers on the basis of the samples they purchase." App. A–336.

And the District Court found in this case that "the Texas State Optical name [TSO] has come to communicate to the consuming public information as to certain standards of price and quality, and availability of particular routine services." 438 F.Supp. 428, 431 (ED Tex.1977).

The Rogers trade name also serves a distinctly public interest. To that part of the general public that is not then in the market for eye care, a trade name is the distinguishing characteristic of the commercial optometrist. The professional faction does not use trade names. Without trade names, an entirely legal but regulated mode of organizing optometrical practice would be banished from that public's view.

* * *

II

The Court characterizes as "substantial and well-demonstrated" the state interests offered to support suppression of this valuable information. Ante, at 897. It first contends that because a trade name has no intrinsic meaning, it can cause deception. The name may remain unchanged, it is pointed out, despite a change in the identities of the optometrists who employ it. Secondly, the Court says that the State may ban trade names to discourage commercial optometry while stopping short of prohibiting it altogether. Neither of these interests justifies a statute so sweeping as § 5.13(d).

---

4. The Federal Trade Commission has promulgated a rule pre-empting certain state laws that restrict advertising of ophthalmic goods and services. 43 Fed. Reg. 24006 (1978). The Commission's statement of basis and purpose characterize the Benham studies as "reliable." Id., at 23995. See Benham, The Effect of Advertising on the Price of Eyeglasses, 15 J.Law & Econ. 337 (1972); Benham & Benham, Regulating Through the Professions: A Perspective on Information Control, 18 J.Law & Econ. 421 (1975).

A

Because a trade name has no intrinsic meaning, it cannot by itself be deceptive. A trade name will deceive only if it is used in a misleading context. The hypotheticals posed by the Court, and the facts of Texas State Bd. of Examiners in Optometry v. Carp, 412 S.W.2d 307 (Tex.Sup.Ct.), appeal dis'd and cert. denied, 389 U.S. 52 (1967), concern the use of optometric trade names in situations where the name of the practicing optometrist is kept concealed. The deception lies not in the use of the trade name, but in the failure simultaneously to disclose the name of the optometrist. In the present case, counsel for the State conceded at oral argument that § 5.13(d) prohibits the use of a trade name even when the optometrist's name is also prominently displayed. Tr. of Oral Arg. 39. It thus prohibits wholly truthful speech that is entirely removed from the justification on which the Court most heavily relies to support the statute.

The Court suggests that a State may prohibit "misleading commercial speech" even though it is "offset" by the publication of clarifying information. Ante, at 895 n. 11. Corrected falsehood, however, is truth, and, absent some other regulatory justification, a State may not prohibit the dissemination of truthful commercial information. By disclosing his individual name along with his trade name, the commercial optometrist acts in the spirit of our First Amendment jurisprudence, where traditionally "the remedy to be applied is more speech, not enforced silence." Linmark Associates, Inc. v. Willingboro, 431 U.S., at 97, quoting Whitney v. California, 274 U.S. 357, 377 (1927) (Brandeis, J., concurring). The ultimate irony of the Court's analysis is that § 5.13(d), because of its broad sweep, actually encourages deception. That statute, in conjunction with § 5.13(e), prevents the consumer from ever discovering that Rogers controls and in some cases employs the optometrist upon whom the patient has relied for care. In effect, the statute conceals the fact that a particular practitioner is engaged in commercial rather than professional optometry, and so deprives consumers of information that may well be thought relevant to the selection of an optometrist.

B

The second justification proffered by the Court is that a State, while not prohibiting commercial optometry practice altogether, could ban the use of trade names in order to discourage commercial optometry. Just last Term, however, the Court rejected the argument that the States' power to create, regulate, or wind-up a corporation by itself could justify a restriction on that corporation's speech. See First National Bank v. Bellotti, 435 U.S. 765, 780 n. 16 (1978). Moreover, this justification ignores the substantial First Amendment interest in the dissemination of truthful information about legally available professional services. See Bigelow v. Virginia, 421 U.S. 809, 822–825 (1975).

It is not without significance that most of the persons influenced by a trade name are those who, by experience or by reputation, know the quality of service for which the trade name stands. The determination that banning trade names would discourage commercial optometry, therefore, necessarily relies on an assumption that persons previously served thought that the trade name practitioner had performed an acceptable service. If the prior experience had been bad, the consumer would want to know the trade name in order to avoid those who practice under it. The first and second stated purposes of § 5.13 are "to protect the public in the practice of optometry," and to "better enable members of the public to fix professional responsibility." These purposes are ill-served by a statute that hinders consumers from enlisting the services of an organization they have found helpful, and so, in effect, prevents consumers from protecting themselves.

The Court repeatedly has rejected the "highly paternalistic" approach implicit in this justification. See First National Bank v. Bellotti, 435 U.S., at 791, n. 31. There is nothing about the nature of an optometrist's services that justifies adopting an approach of this kind here. An optometrist's duties are confined by the statute, § 1.02(1), to measuring the powers of vision of the eye and fitting corrective lenses. See Williamson v. Lee Optical Co., 348 U.S. 483, 486 (1955) (defining terms). The optometrist does not treat disease. His service is highly standardized. Each step is controlled by statute. § 5.12. Many of his functions are so mechanical that they can be duplicated by machines that would enable a patient to measure his own vision. Patients participate in the refraction process, and they frequently can easily assess the quality of service rendered. The cost per visit is low enough—$15 to $35—that comparison shopping is sometimes possible. See App. A420. Because more than half the Nation's population uses eyeglasses, 43 Fed.Reg. 23992 (1978), reputation information is readily available. In this context, the First Amendment forbids the choice which Texas has made to shut off entirely the flow of commercial information to consumers who, we have assumed, "will perceive their own best interest if only they are well enough informed." Virginia Pharmacy Board, 425 U.S., at 770.

NOTES

1. *Virginia Pharmacy*, cited in the principal case, was the first case to abandon the commercial speech exception to first amendment protections. The reaction to *Virginia Pharmacy* among commentators has been mixed. Some are unable to locate any first amendment value advanced by protecting statements that merely "propose a commercial transaction." BeVier, The First Amendment and Political Speech: An Inquiry into the Substance and Limits of Principle, 30 Stan.L.Rev. 299 (1978); Bork, Neutral Principles and Some First Amendment Problems, 47 Ind.L.J. 1 (1971). These authors generally limit the protections of the first amendment to political speech—speech essential to representative democracy—and to speech necessary for individual self-fulfillment, i.e., educational speech, artistic expression. *Virginia Pharmacy*, in their view, unnecessarily withdraws from the political process and majoritarian

control the power to regulate one element of the economic marketplace when it is generally conceded that other elements are subject to regulation. For example, it is argued that if the government can completely prohibit the sale of cigarettes, why should it be precluded from taking the less drastic step of prohibiting cigarette advertising? Presumably Virginia could have set the price at which prescription drugs were sold.

The abandonment of the commercial speech exception is defended in Coase, Advertising and Free Speech, 6 J. of Leg.Stud. 1 (1977), printed in Advertising and Free Speech 1 (Hyman & Johnson ed. 1977). Professor Coase supports *Virginia Pharmacy* on economic grounds because it reduces governmental regulation of the marketplace. He argues that the first amendment is not limited to political expression since "Nude dancing is now covered, or uncovered, by the first amendment and it would be difficult to argue that this activity * * * is vital to the working of a democratic system." 6 J.Leg.Stud. at 13. If "self-fulfillment" is the appropriate value, in Coase's view, individual consumer choices in the marketplace are, for most people "more important than much of what is protected by the First Amendment." Id. at 14. For the simple view that commercial speech is "speech" and thus protected see Countryman, Advertising Is Speech, in Advertising and Free Speech 35 (Hyman & Johnson ed. 1977).

In Board of Trustees of the State University of New York v. Fox, 109 S.Ct. 3028 (1989) the Court made clear that notwithstanding the language of *Central Hudson*, the government did not have to adopt the "least restrictive means of achieving the governmental interest" when regulating commercial speech but must only show a reasonable fit between the government's ends and the means adopted. The Court upheld a state university's prohibition against commercial activity in dormitories as applied to the sale of housewares at a party held for that purpose in a student's room.

2. In Central Hudson Gas & Elec. Corp. v. Public Service Comm'n of New York, 447 U.S. 557, 566 (1980) the Court invalidated a Commission rule that prohibited a regulated electric utility from engaging in promotional advertising. In doing so the court adopted a four-part analysis for commercial speech cases:

> At the outset, we must determine whether the expression is protected by the First Amendment. For commercial speech to come within that provision, it at least must concern lawful activity and not be misleading. Next, we ask whether the asserted governmental interest is substantial. If both inquires yield positive answers, we must determine whether the regulation directly advances the governmental interest asserted, and whether it is not more extensive than is necessary to serve that interest.

Justice Rehnquist, in Posadas de Puerto Rico Associates v. Tourism Company of Puerto Rico, 478 U.S. 328 (1986), purported to apply this analysis in upholding a Puerto Rico statute and regulation which prohibited legal gambling casinos in Puerto Rico to advertise in media directed at Puerto Rican residents. Only advertisements directed at tourists was permitted. Rehnquist, writing for a 5 member majority, found the interest in reducing demand for casino gambling among residents substantial, the advertising ban "directly advanced" that interest, and that it was not more extensive than necessary. Most significantly the Court holds that the "greater power to completely ban casino gambling necessarily includes the lesser power to ban advertising of casino gambling * * *." Does this do away with any protection for commercial speech? Is there any economic activity that government could not prohibit? See, e.g., P. Kurland, Posadas de Puerto Rico v. Tourism Co., 1986 Sup.Ct. Rev. 1.

3. Even though the Supreme Court freed commercial speech from some governmental regulation, it has emphasized in all of the cases that deceptive or false speech may still be prohibited. In *Friedman* the Court follows its view announced in Bates v. State Bar of Arizona, 433 U.S. 350 (1977), that the advertisement of professional services must be examined with particular care because of the vulnerability of those to whom it is addressed. "[B]ecause the public lacks sophistication concerning legal services, misstatements that might be overlooked or deemed unimportant in other advertising may be found quite inappropriate in legal advertising." In Ohralik v. Ohio State Bar Ass'n, 436 U.S. 447 (1978) the Court found that in-person solicitation by lawyers of accident victims was particularly susceptible to deception and could thus be prohibited. See also In re R.M.J., 455 U.S. 191 (1982) striking down certain regulations regarding attorney advertisements in Missouri.

4. Does Justice Powell convince you that a trade name is "a significantly different form of commercial speech" from advertised prices? Do either convey information unless attached to underlying goods or services? Can advertised prices be used deceptively? Consider bait and switch schemes or the relevance of the automobile sticker price to the price likely to be paid by a consumer. Would Justice Powell protect against government regulation an advertisement that read: "Buy one at regular price and get one free"?

5. See generally Reich, Preventing Deception in Commercial Speech, 54 N.Y.U.L.Rev. 775 (1979) proposing two categories of commercial speech regulation: that which is presumptively inefficient in that it prohibits speech which facilitates comparison shopping (price advertising and, he argues, trade name use) and that which is presumptively efficient in that it regulates forms of solicitation (door-to-door sales) that discourage comparison shopping and are not subject to competitive pressure.

6. One of the major precedents upholding price advertising regulation by states was Head v. New Mexico Board of Examiners in Optometry, 374 U.S. 424 (1963) (a prohibition against advertising the price of eyeglasses). On July 3, 1978, a Federal Trade Commission rule became effective making it an unfair practice for any state or local government or any governmental official or private group to enforce any rule that prohibits the advertising of the price of ophthalmic goods and services. 16 C.F.R. § 456 (1978).

State statutes present a crazy-quilt pattern of regulations affecting the advertising of price. See generally, Annot., 89 A.L.R.2d 901 (1963).

THE ECONOMICS OF ADVERTISING

The debate on the impact of advertising stems primarily from disagreement on its role in the economy. One view asserts that advertising simply provides the consuming public with information necessary to make market decisions. Under this view consumers retain control of the kind and quality of goods produced by exercising an informed choice in purchasing decisions. Viewed as information commercial speech takes on an emotionally neutral mask, and, if one of the values of the first amendment is to reduce ignorance and to seek truth then this type of information is both worthy and entitled to dissemination. From an economic perspective, the informational content of advertising promotes efficiency and should be encouraged.

The critics of advertising, on the other hand, minimize the informational value of commercial advertising, arguing that its major role is not to inform but to persuade. Under this view, the advertiser acquires power—the psychological power to dictate the tastes and wants of consumers and the economic power to escape the rigors of a competitive market. Resources expended to acquire this power are thought to represent waste. Henry Simon, an avowed libertarian economist, wrote:

> It is a commonplace that our vaunted efficiency in production is dissipated extravagantly in the wastes of merchandising. This economic system is one which offers rewards, both to those who direct resources into industries where the indirect pecuniary demand is greatest and to those who divert pecuniary demand to commodities which they happened to be producing. Profits may be obtained either by producing what consumers want or by making consumers want what one is actually producing. The possibility of profitably utilizing resources to manipulate demand is, perhaps, the greatest source of diseconomy under the existing system. If present tendencies continue, we may soon reach a situation where most of our resources are utilized in persuading people to buy one thing rather than another, and only a minor fraction is actually employed in creating things to be bought. Simons, Economic Policy for a Free Society, (1948) p. 71.

If one thinks that advertising is largely a waste of resources, one is encouraged, or at least not restrained, to make the legal requirements for its use complex and demanding. These requirements will raise the costs of advertising and reduce the amount accordingly. Viewed as a manipulative technique, it is easier to construct a societal interest in regulating the scope and content of commercial messages. Conversely if one thinks that advertising provides information and promotes efficiency one is likely to approach regulation of commercial speech with the same skepticism as one approaches regulation of political speech.

One of the difficulties in reviewing the economic impact of advertising is that the subject matter encompasses widely disparate phenomena. Commercial speech includes a range of media from the classified section of a newspaper to the commercial message on television to the front yard "for sale" sign. Presumably the promotional activities of the showroom salesman and the label on the product are also included. And advertising impacts on a variety of different purchasing decisions—from an impulsive purchase of a candy bar to the deliberate acquisition of a new automobile.

The result of an analysis of advertising has equally wide-ranging import. Both the common law and legislation have in recent years greatly expanded the regulation of the speech of merchants in response to the perceived "consumer revolution." These developments are considered in Chapter II.

The relationship of trademark law to advertising is indirect but important. The trademark is the legal device that enables the advertiser to capture the returns from advertising. It is unlikely to be profitable to expend resources touting the advantages of "George's Pizza" if any other firm is free, once the world has heard of its merits, to also market a "George's Pizza." And while no one seriously argues that the law ought not protect merchant identification in the example posed, trademark law is presented with many less central issues as we shall see in Chapter III.

The economic case against advertising emanates primarily from Chamberlain, The Theory of Monopolistic Competition (5th ed. 1946); Bain, Barriers to New Competition (1956); Bain, Industrial Organization (1968). Advertising allows a merchant to differentiate his product from those of other producers. To the extent that consumer preference values this differentiation, the advertiser can raise his price above competing producers. This gives the advertiser some control over price, as distinguished from the producer in a purely competitive market who cannot raise his price above the market. This differentiation has monopoly characteristics—to the extent a consumer wants a "George's Pizza" as distinguished from any other pizza, he has only a single source of supply.

Professor Bain argues in addition that product differentiation also serves as a barrier to the entry of new firms into a market and to that extent detracts from a competitive model. As he states it:

> The established firms in an industry may enjoy a product-differentiation advantage over potential entrants because of the preference of buyers for the products of established firms over new ones. If so, any potential entrant may be unable to secure a selling price as high (relative to average costs) as established firms can when selling their products in competition with the entrant.

> The resulting disadvantage to the entrant can be reflected in three alternative ways. First, it may be that established firms can charge prices above minimal average costs and the competing entrant would be able to charge only a lower price that does not cover his average costs. Second, it is possible that to secure a comparably favorable price, the entrant would have to incur sales-promotion costs per unit of output greater than those of established firms, again having average costs greater than his price. Finally, even if neither of these disadvantages is incurred so long as the entrant supplies a limited fraction of the market, he might be unable, at comparable prices and selling costs, to secure a sufficiently large market share to enable him to support an economically large production and distribution organization. Excluded from realizing

available economies of large scale production and distribution, he might again find his average costs above his selling price, even though established firms were receiving prices in excess of minimal average costs. Bain, Industrial Organization, 255–56 (1968).

Proponents of limited trademark protection have used Chamberlain's and Bain's theories. See Brown, Advertising and the Public Interest: Legal Protection of Trade Symbols, 57 Yale L.J. 1165 (1948); Muellen, Sources of Monopoly Powers: A Phenomenon Called "Product Differentiation", 18 Amer.U.L.Rev. 1 (1968); Alexander, Honesty and Competition (1965). Comanor and Wilson, Advertising and Market Power (1974), is an ambitious statistical study that finds evidence that industries with high rates of advertising enjoy higher profitability, among other things. The authors read the evidence as supportive of the barrier to entry hypothesis.

The opponents of advertising also deplore the "waste" of resources devoted to changing the tastes and wants of consumers. This assumes, of course, that changing tastes is bad, per se, or that the change resulting from advertising is in the wrong direction. See Galbraith, The New Industrial State (1967). But see, Nelson, The Economic Consequences of Advertising, 48 J.Bus. 213 (1975) ("We economists have no theory of taste changes, so this approach leads to no behavioral predictions.") and Coase, Advertising and Free Speech, 6 J.Leg. Studies 1, 11 (1977) ("It is not easy to gauge the effect of advertising on taste, in part because it is obviously not great, but judging by the emphasis in advertisements on convenience, cleanliness, and beauty, such effect as it has is presumably generally in the right direction."). See also J. Simon, Issues in the Economics of Advertising 205–206 (1970) discounting the extent to which advertising affects a consumer's propensity to consume rather than to save.

A second line of analysis, first developed in George J. Stigler, The Economics of Information, 69 J. of Pol.Econ. 213 (1961), reprinted in George J. Stigler, The Organization of Industry (1968), has argued that advertising is primarily informative and contributes to efficiency. Stigler's analysis is built around a simple and admittedly atypical case: a market of undifferentiated products emanating from numerous sellers with different prices. The problem for the buyer is to find the correct price at which to buy. You might think that the answer is obvious: the lowest. But it is not. Assume that a buyer finds a seller and, inquiring of his price, is told it is twenty-five dollars. What does the buyer do? He must weigh the expected gain from finding a seller with a lower price against the costs to him in time and travel of further search. His decision whether to accept or engage in further search will be determined by his estimate of the likely dispersion of prices, the relation of the price asked to his estimate of the averages and ranges of that dispersion, and of his own costs of further search. If he thinks the price dispersion small (and hence any gain from further search small) and the price quoted in the lower part of the range, he will tend to accept. If his costs of further search are high (requiring, for instance, a long car ride) he will tend to accept. If he thinks them low (requiring perhaps, only a few more phone calls) he will tend to search further.

The advertising of prices lowers the buyer's cost of search. The advertising communicates to him information about the market that he would otherwise have to acquire through his own search costs. The seller is providing a service to the buyer, which reduces the real cost of the purchase to him because the real cost of the purchase is the cost of the product plus the cost of the search for the right price. The buyer may be willing to pay a higher price for an advertised product because the advertised product may in real terms, when search costs are considered, be cheaper. It is this consumer willingness to pay more that makes advertising profitable for the seller.

Stigler's approach views the consumer as needing not one, but two, products—the thing he wants to buy and information about the price at which he can purchase. More generally, the consumer has a demand for utility satisfying products and services and a demand for information about what may satisfy those utilities. Every transaction can be viewed as the sale of a product or service and the provision of information about that product. The resources necessary to produce that information will be provided by both the seller and the buyer. The seller will have to hold himself out for business, offer descriptions or samples of the product, and perhaps, depending on the product, provide additional information. The buyer will have to take the time to identify sellers in the market and learn something about the relative quality of their goods and prices. The extent to which the seller provides the resources as compared to the buyer will be determined by their relative efficiency in providing the information. The seller has many advantages—he is constantly in the market, he knows the product intimately, and he will know much about the previous (and hence about likely future) buyers of his product. The seller who reaches his prospect in his living room easy chair with a brief interruption of an entertainment program reduces the costs the prospect must incur to learn about the products.

A notable trend during the period of the trademark cases in this book—approximately 1850 to the present—has been the emergence of goods marketed with national trademarks and advertising and a reduction in the expenses and hence price markups of retail merchants. The modern supermarket with its branded and advertised products is able to function with a relatively low labor cost (as a percentage of sales) because consumers arrive at the store themselves equipped to pick out what they will buy. In this process, expenditures for advertising have reduced both the costs of buyers in obtaining comparative product information and the costs of retailers in acquiring and distributing the information. This has produced a less costly distribution system. The emergence of a strong national law of trademarks has paralleled this development. It will be interesting to see whether the last preserves of the non-branded supermarket product—the produce and meat departments—will survive. Already there are incursions.

One might argue, however, that much of advertising contains little perceptible information. What is the informational content of a television commercial depicting the magical appearance of a crown on the head of a taster of margarine, or the evaluations of the relative merits of automatic coffee makers by a former sports figure, or the demonstration that a particular brand of shaving cream can shave sandpaper? The most extensive analysis of advertising's informational role has been by Phillip Nelson: The Economic Consequences of Advertising, 48 J.Bus. 213 (1975); Advertising as Information, 82 J.Pol.Econ. 729 (1974); The Economic Value of Advertising in Advertising and Society (Brozen ed. 1974); Information and Consumer Behavior, 78 J.Pol.Econ. 311 (1970).

Nelson divides goods into "search" goods and "experience" goods. Search goods are those in which most of the information relevant to the purchasing decision can be acquired by examining the product itself prior to purchase. Experience goods are those for which the relevant qualities are not observable—the life expectancy of a television set, the taste of a can of tuna, or the skills of a lawyer. It would be expected that regarding search goods, advertising would be objective and readily informative since the consumer can determine the accuracy of the advertisement prior to purchase. No amount of advertisement will persuade a consumer that a two wheel bicycle is really a tricycle. With regard to experience goods, Nelson contends that the basic information a consumer gains from advertising is the fact that a given seller advertises: "Their [advertisements for experience goods] total informational role—beyond the relation of brand to function—is simply contained in their existence. The consumer believes that the more a brand advertises the more likely it is to be a better buy. In consequence, the more advertisements of a brand the consumer encounters and remembers, the more likely he is to try the brand." Nelson, The Economic Value of Advertising, supra at 50. Nelson suggests that this reaction to advertising is not irrational since "advertised brands are better * * *. Simply put, it pays to advertise winners rather than losers." The seller who has the incentive to advertise the most is the seller who satisfies the highest percentage of the consumers who examine or try the product.

Consider the situation of a customer who wishes to select a product and a price from the array of products and prices confronting him. How should he proceed? The consumer must have a strategy for sampling the available goods. His strategy must give him guidance on two questions: what to search or sample first, second, and so on; and how to know when to stop. The heart of Nelson's approach is the assumption that consumer tastes tend to cluster around a mean, and that therefore the best search strategy (assuming no other information) is to start at the mean. In other words, the best working rule (until disproved by experience) is that the consumer will want what most other consumers want. Advertising makes the use of this rule cheaper for the consumer because the consumer's rough sense of the relative frequency of advertising is his cheapest guide to where that mean lies.

Why is advertising a good guide to the mean? Advertising pays only to the extent that it results in sales. The advertiser of a product whose qualities are not satisfactory will experience a rapid drop off in repeat customers. You may buy that supposedly great tasting mouthwash once, but not twice. The advertiser of the product that satisfies a high percentage of customers will obtain a string of repeat purchases from a single ad, but the advertiser of the unsatisfactory product will not. The advertiser of the satisfactory product will obtain a higher return from each dollar expenditure of advertising than the seller of the unsatisfactory product, and will, therefore, advertise more. This force will, over time, make the frequency of advertising a reliable guide to the mean, and hence a reliable guide to an efficient search process.

Thus viewed, much that has bothered economists and others about advertising becomes explicable. Sellers are clamoring for our attention so that we might perceive their relative importance in the market. The superstar testimonial, the slogans, and the demonstrations are not really designed to persuade us of anything. Rather, they are designed to capture our attention and a bit of our memory, much as we might find it easier to remember Mr. Perlman's name if, upon introduction, we paused to think of an oyster.

The real life consumer, of course, does not start the search without any information. He may know much about his own preferences—and indeed that in many product areas he prefers to purchase goods with characteristics quite different from the mean—think for instance of clothing, jewelry, furniture, and art. But how does he find a seller who purveys to his special tastes? Why not start with the seller whose advertising he likes? The analysis does not mean that because Sears advertises hardware supplies extensively everyone will start the search at Sears. A buyer may prefer a neighborhood store, or a seller aiming at the professional, not the do-it-yourself market, and start his search elsewhere. And of course there are many other consumer strategies that do not rely on advertising—the observation of the behavior of others, inquiries of friends who have already searched, and so on.

Nelson uses his analysis to explore a number of interesting questions about advertising. He predicts that the amount of advertising space dedicated to goods whose qualities are principally experience would exceed that dedicated to goods whose qualities are principally search on the ground that search information can be communicated in words while superior experience qualities can only be effectively communicated by leaving the consumer with an impression of a higher advertising intensity. The first takes words, the second space. An analysis of advertising in *New Yorker* magazine in 1965 led him to the finding that as the volume of advertising by brand increased, the physical size of the advertisements increased more for experience than for search goods. 82 J.Pol.Econ. at 740–43, supra.

Nelson used his analysis to explore other interesting questions. Why are advertising expenditures per sales dollar higher for small, repeat purchase non-durables than for large durables? Id. at 747–49. Will *Consumer Reports* report more on experience goods or search goods? 78 J.Pol.Econ. at 321–323, supra. Will sellers of search goods tend to cluster more than sellers of experience goods? Id. at 323–325. And what is the impact of advertising on industry structure. 48 J.Bus. at 213, supra.

Neither Stigler nor Nelson provide direct quantitative estimates of the relative importance of advertising for consumer welfare. Are the effects trivial or significant? That question was illuminated in Lee Benham, The Effect of Advertising on the Price of Eyeglasses, 15 J. of Law & Econ. 337 (1972). As its use by the United States Supreme Court in *Bates* and *Virginia Pharmacy* attests, the article has had an unusual impact on public policy, partly because its results were replicated in a series of studies undertaken by the Federal Trade Commission. Benham's study made use of the fact that some states—as part of the regulation of the "profession" of eyeglass dispensing—prohibit advertising of the service. He was able to obtain data providing the actual purchase price of eyeglasses in all states—both those that permitted advertising and those that did not. He found that the mean price paid for a pair of eyeglasses in states with complete restrictions was $33.04 and in states with no advertising restrictions was $26.34. Table I. 15 J. of Law & Econ. 342. In other words, consumers saved $6.70 (or 25%) a pair from advertising.

Neither the direction nor magnitude of this difference is predicted by the Stigler-Nelson analysis. That theory only predicted that the consumer would be better off with advertising net of price and search costs. Even if the price were higher, the consumer would be better off because his search cost would be less by more than the higher price. But the Benham results suggest that advertising has a second effect. Because search costs are lower, consumers search more, and this added search (in terms of useful information obtained) makes competition more effective. For instance, if it is cheaper for the consumer to search, he will search more firms, and thus more firms will effectively be in the market. This increased competition will put more pressure on firms to be efficient, and the overall cost structure of the industry will be affected. Thus Benham found that in states that permitted advertising, commercial sellers had a relatively larger, and eye doctors a relatively smaller, share of the eyeglass market. Table 4, Id. at 351.

Two works conclude that advertising tends to stimulate rather than inhibit competition. J. Simon, Issues in the Economics of Advertising (1970) and J. Lambin, Advertising, Competition and Market Conduct in Oligopoly Over Time (1976). The latter is an econometric analysis of advertising in nine Western European countries using 16 product classes, 170 brands, and a 10-year observation period. Both works contain extensive and useful bibliographies.

In recent years the economic literature has reflected a rough consensus on a number of basic issues. First, many industries behave differently with advertising than they would if advertising did not exist, and some of these differences are probably large. Second, any effort to weigh the net benefit or loss of advertising is plagued by the complexity of the multiple interacting factors. Third, even if the net social effects of advertising are negative, it is difficult to formulate responsive regulatory policies that would clearly improve the situation. Surveys include Comanor and Wilson, Advertising and Competition: A Survey, 17 J. of Econ.Lit. 453 (1979) and Albion and Farris, The Advertising Controversy: Evidence on the Economic Effects of Advertising (1981).

Chapter II

DECEPTIVE PRACTICES

A. COMPETITORS' REMEDIES

(1) FALSE ADVERTISING AT COMMON LAW

ELY–NORRIS SAFE CO. v. MOSLER SAFE CO.
United States Circuit Court of Appeals, Second Circuit, 1925.
7 F.2d 603.

Suit in equity by the Ely-Norris Safe Company against the Mosler Safe Company. From decree of dismissal, plaintiff appeals. Reversed.

The jurisdiction of the District Court depended upon diverse citizenship, and the suit was for unfair competition. The bill alleged that the plaintiff manufactured and sold safes under certain letters patent, which had as their distinctive feature an explosion chamber, designed for protection against burglars. Before the acts complained of, no one but the plaintiff had ever made or sold safes with such chambers, and, except for the defendant's infringement, the plaintiff has remained the only manufacturer and seller of such safes. By reason of the plaintiff's efforts the public has come to recognize the value of the explosion chamber and to wish to purchase safes containing them. Besides infringing the patent, the defendant has manufactured and sold safes without a chamber, but with a metal band around the door, in the same place where the plaintiff put the chamber, and has falsely told its customers that this band was employed to cover and close an explosion chamber. Customers have been thus led to buy safes upon the faith of the representation, who in fact wished to buy safes with explosion chambers, and would have done so, but for the deceit.

The bill prayed an injunction against selling safes with such metal bands, and against representing that any of its safes contained an explosion chamber. From the plaintiff's answers to interrogatories it appeared that all the defendant's safes bore the defendant's name and address, and were sold as its own. Furthermore, that the defendant never gave a customer reason to suppose that any safe sold by it was made by the plaintiff.

Before HOUGH, MANTON, and HAND, CIRCUIT JUDGES.

HAND, CIRCUIT JUDGE (after stating the facts as above). This case is not the same as that before Mr. Justice Bradley in New York & Rosendale Co. v. Coplay Cement Co. (C.C.) 44 F. 277, 10 L.R.A. 833. The plaintiffs there manufactured cement at Rosendale, N.Y., but it did not appear that they were the only persons making cement at that place. There was no reason, therefore, to assume that a customer of the defendant, deceived as to the place of origin of the defendant's cement, and desiring to buy only such cement, would have bought of the plaintiffs. It resulted that the plaintiffs did not show any necessary loss of trade through the defendant's fraud upon its own customers. We agree that some of the language of the opinion goes further, but it was not necessary for the disposition of the case.

American Washboard Co. v. Saginaw Mfg. Co., 103 F. 281 (C.C.A.6), 43 C.C.A. 233, 50 L.R.A. 609, was, however, a case in substance like that at bar, because there the plaintiff alleged that it had acquired the entire output of sheet aluminum suitable for washboards. It necessarily followed that the plaintiff had a practical monopoly of this metal for the articles in question, and from this it was a fair inference that any customer of the defendant, who was deceived into buying as an aluminum washboard one which was not such, was a presumptive customer of the plaintiff, who had therefore lost a bargain. This was held, however, not to constitute a private wrong, and so the bill was dismissed.

* * *

We must concede, therefore, that on the cases as they stand the law is with the defendant, and the especially high authority of the court which decided American Washboard Co. v. Saginaw Mfg. Co., supra, makes us hesitate to differ from their conclusion. Yet there is no part of the law which is more plastic than unfair competition, and what was not reckoned an actionable wrong 25 years ago may have become such today. We find it impossible to deny the strength of the plaintiff's case on the allegations of its bill. As we view it, the question is, as it always is in such cases, one of fact. While a competitor may, generally speaking, take away all the customers of another that he can, there are means which he must not use. One of these is deceit. The false use of another's name as maker or source of his own goods is deceit, of which the false use of geographical or descriptive terms is only one example. But we conceive that in the end the questions which arise are always two: Has the plaintiff in fact lost customers? And has he lost them by means which the law forbids? The false use of the plaintiff's name is only an instance in which each element is clearly shown.

In the case at bar the means are as plainly unlawful as in the usual case of palming off. It is as unlawful to lie about the quality of one's wares as about their maker; it equally subjects the seller to action by the buyer. * * * The reason, as we think, why such deceits have not been regarded as actionable by a competitor, depends only upon his inability to show any injury for which there is a known remedy. In an open market it is generally impossible to prove that a customer, whom the defendant has secured by falsely describing his goods, would have bought of the plaintiff, if the defendant had been truthful. Without that, the plaintiff, though aggrieved in company with other honest traders, cannot show any ascertainable loss. He may not recover at law, and the equitable remedy is concurrent. The law does not allow him to sue as a vicarious avenger of the defendant's customers.

But, if it be true that the plaintiff has a monopoly of the kind of wares concerned, and if to secure a customer the defendant must represent his own as of that kind, it is a fair inference that the customer wants those and those only. Had he not supposed that the defendant could supply him, presumably he would have gone to the plaintiff, who alone could. At least, if the plaintiff can prove that in fact he would, he shows a direct loss, measured by his profits on the putative sale. If a tradesman falsely foists on a customer a substitute for what the plaintiff alone can supply, it can scarcely be that the plaintiff is without remedy, if he can show that the customer would certainly have come to him, had the truth been told.

Yet that is in substance the situation which this bill presents. It says that the plaintiff alone could lawfully make such safes, and that the defendant has sold others to customers who asked for the patented kind. It can make no difference that the defendant sold them as its own. The sale by hypothesis depended upon the structure of the safes, not on their maker. To be satisfied, the customer must in fact have gone to the plaintiff, or the defendant must have infringed. Had he infringed, the plaintiff could have recovered his profit on the sale; had the customer gone to him, he would have made that profit. Any possibilities that the customers might not have gone to the plaintiff, had they been told the truth, are foreclosed by the allegation that the plaintiff in fact lost the sales. It seems to us * * * that if this can be proved, a private suit will lie.

Decree reversed.

MOSLER SAFE CO. v. ELY–NORRIS SAFE CO.
Supreme Court of the United States, 1927.
273 U.S. 132, 47 S.Ct. 314, 71 L.Ed. 578.

MR. JUSTICE HOLMES delivered the opinion of the Court.

* * *

At the hearing below all attention seems to have been concentrated on the question passed upon and the forcibly stated reasons that induced this Court of Appeals to differ from that for the Sixth Circuit. But, upon a closer scrutiny of the bill than seems to have been invited before, it does not present that broad and interesting issue. The bill alleges that the plaintiff has a patent for an explosion chamber as described and claimed in said Letters Patent; that it has the exclusive right to make and sell safes containing such an explosion chamber; that no other safes containing such an explosion chamber could be got in the United States before the defendant, as it is alleged, infringed the plaintiff's patent, for which alleged infringement a suit is pending. It then is alleged that the defendant is making and selling safes with a metal band around the door at substantially the same location as the explosion chamber of plaintiff's safes, and has represented to the public that the said metal band was employed to cover or close an explosion chamber by reason of which the public has been led to purchase defendant's said safes as and for safes containing an explosion chamber, such as is manufactured and sold by the plaintiff herein. It is alleged further that sometimes the defendant's safes have no explosion chamber under the band but are bought by those who want safes with a chamber and so the defendant has deprived the plaintiff of sales, competed unfairly and damaged the plaintiff's reputation. The plaintiff relies upon its patent suit for relief in respect of the sales of safes alleged to infringe its rights. It complains here only of false representations as to safes that do not infringe but that are sold as having explosion chambers although in fact they do not.

It is consistent with every allegation in the bill and the defendant in argument asserted it to be a fact, that there are other safes with explosion chambers beside that for which the plaintiff has a patent. The defendant is charged only with representing that its safes had an explosion chamber, which, so far as appears, it had a perfect right to do if the representation was true. If on the other hand the representation was false as it is alleged sometimes to have been, there is nothing to show that customers had they known the facts would have gone to the plaintiff rather than to other competitors in the market, or to lay a foundation for the claim for a loss of sales. The bill is so framed as to seem to invite the decision that was obtained from the Circuit Court of Appeals, but when scrutinized is seen to have so limited its statements as to exclude the right to complain.

Decree reversed.

NOTES

1. American Washboard Co. v. Saginaw Mfg. Co., 103 Fed. 281 (6th Cir. 1900) cited in *Mosler* retains its vitality as a landmark decision primarily because of the eminence of the judges involved—Taft, Lurton, and Day. Defendant sold a washboard which purported to have a rubbing face of aluminum which in fact was zinc. Plaintiff was the only manufacturer of a genuine aluminum washboard. The Sixth Circuit upheld a lower court demurrer. It held that the complaint did not allege "passing off" of the defendant's washboard as that of the plaintiff and was therefore deficient. The court also could see no relevance in the fact that plaintiff had a monopoly in aluminum washboards.

> It [the complaint in analogizing to the passing off cases] loses sight of the thoroughly established principle that the private right of action in such cases is not based upon fraud or imposition upon the public, but is maintained solely for the protection of the property rights of complainant. It is true that in these cases it is an important factor that the public are deceived, but it is only where this deception induces the public to buy the goods as those of complainant that a private right of action arises * * *. It is doubtless morally wrong and improper to impose upon the public by the sale of spurious goods, but this does not give rise to a private right of action unless the property rights of the

plaintiff are thereby invaded. There are many wrongs which can only be righted through public prosecution, and for which the legislature, and not the courts, must provide a remedy.

2. In Pillsbury-Washburn Flour Mills Co. v. Eagle, 86 Fed. 608 (7th Cir. 1898), cert. denied 173 U.S. 703 (1899) defendant was restrained from falsely designating his flour as coming from Minneapolis, Minnesota, in a suit brought by various flour mills manufacturing flour in that city. The court found that flour coming from Minnesota had built up a reputation of quality although the use of the geographic term could not be exclusively appropriated by plaintiffs as against others who in fact produced flour in Minnesota. The court observed:

> * * * to still say that the court has no jurisdiction or power to grant relief is to fly in the face of the well-grounded principle running through all the cases that fraud accompanied by damages is actionable at law, and that, where one person has so dressed out his goods as to deceive the public into the belief that they are really the goods of another person, and so put them upon the market, to the manifest injury of that person and of the public, an action of law will lie for the deceit, and, to save a multiplicity of suits, and prevent irreparable injury, equity will restrain such unfair and fraudulent competition. This rule is so well established, is so general and elastic in its application, and so consonant to the general principles of equity jurisprudence, that it would be difficult to frame a case coming fairly within its spirit and meaning in which a court of chancery will not find a way to afford the proper relief.

The *Pillsbury* case was decided before *American Washboard* and *Mosler*. In Grand Rapids Furniture Co. v. Grand Rapids Furniture Co., 127 F.2d 245 (7th Cir.1942) the defendant owned a furniture store in Chicago and falsely advertised that the furniture it sold was manufactured in Grand Rapids, Michigan. Plaintiffs were several furniture manufacturers in Grand Rapids and the Furniture Manufacturers Association of Grand Rapids. The court found that furniture manufactured in Grand Rapids was considered by the purchasing public to be of superior quality and the furniture sold by the defendant was inferior to that of the Grand Rapids manufacturers. Plaintiffs sought an injunction prohibiting defendant from utilizing references to Grand Rapids. The court characterized the complaint as a class suit and affirmed the lower court's determination that the complaint stated a cause of action and a preliminary injunction should issue. See also, Anheuser-Busch Brewing Ass'n v. Fred Miller Brewing Co., 87 Fed. 864 (E.D.Wis.1898).

Compare the *Grand Rapids* decision with the Second Circuit's decision in California Apparel Creators v. Wieder of California, 162 F.2d 893 (2d Cir.1947). The defendants were New York wearing apparel dealers using the names "California" or "Californian" in connection with their business. The plaintiffs were an incorporated trade association and 75 named California wearing apparel manufacturers. The named plaintiffs sought to represent themselves and all other California manufacturers similarly situated. The association was a non-profit corporation organized three months before the institution of the suit and included as members 17 associations of wearing apparel manufacturers and their respective members composed in the aggregate of hundreds of firms manufacturing wearing apparel within the metropolitan area of the County of Los Angeles. The parties stipulated that there were "upwards of 4,500" wearing apparel manufacturers in California. Thus, plaintiffs represented "less than 2 per cent of the potential number". Plaintiffs demanded an injunction, an accounting for profits, and damages from the defendants.

The district court granted defendants' motion for summary judgment preserving for trial the claim of one plaintiff, California Sportswear Co., against one defendant, California Sportswear, Inc. because of the similarity of their trade names and another claim by the same plaintiff against another defendant because of a similarity in label. Held: Judgment affirmed, L. Hand dissenting. The court denominated the action a "spurious" class action noting that the rights of the absent wearing apparel manufacturers could not be finally determined. "We stress this point because at times there appear to be suggestions that the representative character of this suit may aid in recovery. Of course where there is a true class suit * * * the consequences are otherwise; but in this situation there is no safety in potentially greater numbers of property claimants. Indeed, it but serves to accentuate the fundamental weakness of plaintiffs' claim here that the rights claimed are so diffused and attenuated that they do not show convincing reality as to any particular persons."

The circuit court distinguished the *Grand Rapids* case by noting that here the number of potential plaintiffs was greater, the various goods involved from men's and women's wearing apparel to jewelry had "no apparent or obvious connection with the locality", and there were no "definite standards of quality or grading" for goods produced in California. The court then found the *Mosler* doctrine compelling:

> It is nowhere claimed that there is, or will be, available any proof of specific customers diverted from specific plaintiffs through the actions of these defendants. The only possible suggestion of injury is by a strained process of inference, as by the suggested conclusion that the general effect of defendants' actions must have diverted customers from the plaintiffs. Here we are met with the direct difficulty found insurmountable by Justice Holmes in the Ely-Norris Safe Co. case, that there is no reason to assume that defendants' customers, deceived as to the place of origin, would otherwise have bought of these plaintiffs. Not only are these plaintiffs a small portion of the total California manufacturers, but they do not even appear to be large manufacturers themselves or to control any considerable portion of the California business. The reasons which led the Supreme Court to dismiss the bill in that case on its allegations are therefore more pertinent here, where the limited extent of the plaintiffs' share of the total business definitely appears and is not merely a matter of inference, as there.
>
> True, the complaint here contains, in addition to the general allegations of superiority of the California clothes, certain general allegations that the inferior character of the defendants' clothes injures the reputation of California clothes. But no attempt is made to support these conclusory statements in the affidavits and it is clear that they cannot be supported. Some of the various affiants do make the general claims of superiority of manufacture of the California goods which we have noted, but they also show the absence of definite standards of quality and assert only a group pressure to produce goods of high quality. By the very form of their statements they show that there are necessarily deviations in quality in their own group which are more natural sources of injury to the other manufacturers in California than this distant and only potential New York competition.

Were such injury by deleterious quality directly charged by specific and comparative facts, we would still be thrown back, however, on the question of lack of showing of loss to these particular plaintiffs, out of all the California manufacturers who conceivably might be injured. In other words, the difficulty found in the Ely-Norris case still exists in much more pointed fashion than it did there.

Judge Hand in his dissent agreed that the trade association had no standing to sue but disagreed with reference to the individual plaintiffs.

* * * there are seventy-five individual merchants who have joined as plaintiffs; and it well may be that collectively they could prove that some of them must have lost, or were losing, customers by the advertisements, although they could not identify the individual sufferers. That would be enough to my mind to support an injunction in favor of all the seventy-five against the defendants; and my justification is this. By hypothesis the defendants are injuring some one or more of the group; and he or they would get an injunction, if they could be ascertained; the others are not so entitled only because they have not been able to prove that they do not as yet need one. Faced with a choice between denying any remedy to those to whom a remedy is due, and extending it to those who do not need it, I should not hesitate.

3. *The Position of the American Law Institute.* The first edition of the Restatement of Torts published in 1939 contained the following provision:

§ 761. False Advertising—Liability to Competitor

One who diverts trade from a competitor by fraudulently representing that the goods which he markets have ingredients or qualities which in fact they do not have but which the goods of the competitor do have is liable to the competitor for the harm so caused, if,

(a) when making the representation he intends that it should, or knows or should know that it is likely to, divert trade from the competitor, and

(b) the competitor is not marketing his goods with material fraudulent misrepresentations about them.

When the proposed section was before the Institute, arguments were raised over the meaning of *Mosler* and what appeared to be an extension of that doctrine to allow any competitor to sue regardless of whether he was a monopolist. Opponents of the section argued that there was no precedent to support the extension. Judge Hand, in defending the proposal reminded the Institute that the language "One who diverts trade" imposes on the plaintiff in the case "what is ordinarily an insuperable objection, how can he prove that the goods which sold by the defendant diverted trade from him if there are a number of people who are engaged in that particular business." Noting that "under modern procedure * * * you can gather into one suit all the persons who would be affected whose trade collectively could be damaged and, therefore, has been damaged" Hand viewed the section as requiring that plaintiffs "show, as the text reads, that they have lost the bargain and it is difficult for me to see how that differs from any other case when by improper means a customer has been diverted." A motion to strike the entire section was defeated 37 to 51. The following day a motion to reconsider that action was defeated 55 to 70. 16 ALI Proceedings 130 (1938–39).

In 1963, the Institute reviewed a proposed revision which, read: "One falsely markets goods or services * * * if, in the marketing process, he makes any material false representation which is likely to induce persons to purchase, to the commercial detriment of another, the goods or services which he markets." Restatement, Second, Torts § 712 (Tent.Draft No. 8, 1963). The tentative draft was approved with the condition that the commentary reflect with appropriate comments that the section may go slightly beyond the reported decision. 40 ALI Proceedings 152 (1963). Causing particular difficulty in the debate was the meaning of "commercial detriment" and the appropriateness of an illustration which read: "*A* manufactures solid walnut furniture. *B*, a competitor, manufacturers veneer furniture which he falsely represents to be solid walnut. *B* is subject to liability to *A*." Illus. No. 9.

A similar hypothetical bothered the Institute during debate on the 1939 provision:

> Mr. Shulman: * * * when a merchant falsely advertises that furniture, for example, is solid mahogany and it turns out to be mahogany veneer, the reputation of solid mahogany furniture is destroyed in the market and dealers who sell solid mahogany furniture are injured in exactly the same way under these circumstances as in the other case [passing off].

> Judge Tuttle: I cannot agree with that argument because the reason they are going to be dissatisfied is that they have found out that what they bought from that chap was not solid mahogany and he is the one who risks his reputation and it is not injuring the reputation of solid mahogany at all.

16 ALI Proceedings 135 (1938–1939).

If in fact Illustration No. 9 is the law, would there be a different result in the following case: *A* manufactures veneer walnut furniture. *B*, a competitor, manufactures veneer furniture which he falsely represents to be solid walnut. *A* sues *B?*

The debate in 1963, however informative, proved futile. The American Law Institute removed all sections relating to unfair competition from the final version of the Restatement, Second, Torts on the theory that it had developed into an independent field and was no longer controlled by tort principles. Letter from John Wade, Reporter for Restatement, Second, Torts to Harvey Perlman (June 23, 1977).

In 1988 the ALI began consideration of a new Restatement of the Law of Unfair Competition. The first tentative draft proposes liability for "[o]ne who makes a representation relating to the goods or services that it markets, which is likely to deceive or mislead prospective purchasers to the likely commercial detriment of another. . . ." Restatement, Third, Unfair Competition § 2 (Tent. Draft No. 1, 1988). There is a "likely commercial detriment" when a representation is "material" and there is a "reasonable basis for believing that the representation has caused or is likely to cause a diversion of trade from the other or harm to the other's reputation or good will." Id. at § 3. Does this draft go beyond the earlier drafts and the common law?

4. What justification is there for distinguishing between false indications of regional origin and false representations as to the quality or ingredients of a product? See Lanham Act § 4, 15 U.S.C. § 1054, which provides for federal registration and protection of "indications of regional origin." Does a Grand Rapids furniture maker have a greater interest to protect than the maker of an

explosion chamber safe? Would a class action on behalf of all manufacturers of explosion chamber safes succeed? Are the interests of the consumers of safes and furniture protected in these cases? Or can we expect that the consumers will protect their own interests if deceived?

5. Why does the common law appear to be reluctant to give competitors a remedy for false advertising? If the advertisement is false and capable of misleading consumers, why should it matter that the competitor cannot show direct injury?

6. Consider 35 U.S.C. § 292. The statute prohibits false indications that a product is patented and provides a fine of $500 for each offense. Subsection (b) allows "any person" to sue for the penalty, half of which is retained by the person bringing the action.

7. For a critical discussion of the *Mosler* doctrine see Handler, False and Misleading Advertising, 39 Yale L.J. 22, 34–37 (1929); Callmann, False Advertising as a Competitive Tort, 48 Colum.L.Rev. 876 (1948). Both articles have had distinguished careers.

8. What action, short of further litigation, should Ely-Norris now take? Should it advertise to inform potential customers that Mosler's safes do not have explosion chambers? What are the incentives and disincentives operating on that decision? Does it make a difference if Ely-Norris is the only producer of genuine explosion chamber safes? What if an explosion chamber is not worth what it costs? What if only a very few consumers base their decision between competing safes on the presence of an explosion chamber? Are you convinced by the argument that competition alone will produce truth in advertising without legal intervention?

(2) DISPARAGEMENT

Early in its history, the common law provided a remedy for false statements that attacked the personal integrity and reputation of the plaintiff. The action for personal defamation grew to involve a number of technical distinctions, one of which divided the offending statements into per se defamations and those statements requiring proof of special damages. The question in all of these cases was essentially whether the statements of the defendant had injured the reputation of the plaintiff. Those statements which would obviously cause that result were classified as libel per se or slander per se. In such cases, the plaintiff was entitled to recover damages for the dignitary harm without the necessity of showing actual economic loss. However, in those cases where the statements were such that their injurious effect was in doubt, the plaintiff was required to prove "special damages" as an element of his cause of action. The special damage rule required the plaintiff to show some specific economic harm resulting from the defendant's statement. A further distinction between statements made in writing (libel) and those made orally (slander) was also considered crucial and resulted in differing rules and results. The student might find a quick review of the doctrines of defamation helpful at this point. See, Prosser & Keeton, Torts Ch. 19 (5th ed. 1984).

The developing doctrinal content of personal defamation had an impact on other cases confronting early common law courts. In these cases the statements of the defendant were directed at the property of the plaintiff rather than at his reputation or integrity. For example, the defendant would spread the false rumor that the plaintiff did not have valid title to the property plaintiff was then attempting to sell. Plaintiff would contend that the false statement of the defendant resulted in his inability to market the property with resulting damage. It is also easily seen that by implication the defendant's statement also attacked the integrity of the plaintiff by alleging that plaintiff was fraudulently attempting to sell property to which he did not have title. The analogy to personal defamation was compelling and around 1600 the common law devised a cause of action for "slander of title" to compensate plaintiff for his injury. This action was subsequently extended to protect against statements calling into question the title to personalty and eventually to statements denouncing the quality rather than the title of the plaintiff's property. As the following material will demonstrate, the cause of action for false statements directed against property remains in search of a comfortable name. It has been variously denominated as "slander of title", "trade libel", "disparagement", and "injurious falsehood". The last reference was apparently coined by Sir John Salmond in his treatise on torts, was subsequently adopted by Prosser and was adopted by the American Law Institute to refer to any false statement harmful to the interests of another. See Restatement, Second, Torts § 623A (1977). "Disparagement" will be utilized in this material as a narrower term used generally to describe injurious falsehoods in a commercial context.

SYSTEMS OPERATIONS, INC. v. SCIENTIFIC GAMES DEVELOPMENT CORP.

United States District Court, District New Jersey, 1976.
414 F.Supp. 750.

CLARKSON S. FISHER, DISTRICT JUDGE.

[Plaintiffs and defendants were lottery consulting firms or lottery ticket manufacturers who competed with each other to provide tickets to state lotteries. The plaintiff Systems Operations contracted with the city of Omaha, Nebraska, to provide lottery tickets for the city's lottery. Dr. Koza, chairman of the defendant, Scientific Games, called the Omaha lottery director and was "very outspoken about the security of [the plaintiff's] tickets" and suggested they could be easily "broken". To effectively "break" a lottery ticket requires a fast moving and inexpensive system to penetrate the cover of the ticket to read the numbers in order to find a winning ticket and at the same time keeping all of the tickets saleable. Koza and other Scientific Games representatives suggested the Omaha ticket was insecure but never explained the basis for their claim. Omaha proceeded with plaintiff's tickets and the Omaha lottery functioned as expected.

Plaintiffs were retained by Delaware to implement its state lottery. Defendants' representatives met with the Delaware lottery director, Peter Simmons, and indicated that plaintiff's Omaha tickets were insecure and were invited to make an investigation of plaintiffs' Delaware tickets. The Delaware lottery was to begin February 10th. At a meeting on February 2nd, defendant's representative, Bower met with Simmons to report.]

* * * While Bower was able to predict approximately 65 of 66 numbers on 13 tickets submitted to him by Simmons, Simmons testified that only some of the tickets remained salable. Apparently most of these tickets were "noticeably changed" and could not be considered to have been "broken." (cf. T.—I, p. 150, 165). *Moreover, when asked how it was done, Bower refused to explain, except to say that it was easy and did not take long. Simmons placed another "hold" on plaintiffs' production.*

On February 5th Simmons met again with Bower and also with Gilbert Bachman, President of Dittler Brothers. Both gentlemen informed Simmons that they could have a Delaware instant lottery game in three to four weeks if he should place an order with Scientific Games. On the same date, Simmons lifted the "hold" on Delaware ticket production.

It must be noted that this Court also finds the instant lottery industry to be a growing field with rapidly expanding markets. The sizable contracts with certain states are not permanent, and competitive bidding is often involved when a contract is to be awarded. Moreover there are presently a mere handful of states now actively engaged in or pursuing instant lottery games, but the national market is potentially enormous. Two contracts were up for bids during the course of the hearings in this matter. In short, these parties are almost constantly negotiating or bidding on contracts or urging other states to enter the market. In light of all the foregoing discussion, the Court now examines the law.

B

CONCLUSIONS OF LAW

The plaintiffs' complaint alleges disparagement of their product by the defendant. Unfortunately, disparagement, sometimes called "trade libel" as well, is not a clearly defined tort.[12]

"Because of the unfortunate association with 'slander,' a supposed analogy to defamation has hung over the tort like a fog, concealing its real character, and has had great influence on its development."

W. Prosser, Law of Torts 916 (4th ed. 1971). "Trade libel" is concerned with interests in property and should be called "disparagement" to avoid confusion with defamation (libel and slander) which concerns interests of personality. This approach should make it clear:

---

12. This Court could find no significant legal differences among the states in the area of disparagement. This is truly a developing area of the law and my references are general, guided only in part by New Jersey and Third Circuit authorities.

" * * * that the action for disparagement of property has a place of its own in the law; and is not a mere branch, or special variety, of the action for defamation of personal reputation or of the action for deceit."

Black & Yates v. Mahogany Ass'n, 129 F.2d 227, 236 (3rd Cir.1942), cert. denied 317 U.S. 672 (1942).

A problem developed from the early confusion with the old dogma that "equity will not enjoin a continuing libel or slander." To avoid this problem in cases where a competitor's goods were disparaged, some courts characterized the matters before them as unfair competition actions and enjoined disparaging statements under that heading. See Id., at 235; Royer v. Stoody Company, 192 F.Supp. 949, 951, 952 (W.D. Okl.1961); *Prosser,* supra at 917. This Court need not bother with such characterizations, for the United States Court of Appeals for the Third Circuit faced the problem head-on in *Black & Yates,* supra, and recognized that disparagement stands on an entirely different footing than libel and slander.

"Assuming that the plaintiffs here have pleaded nothing more than an action for disparagement of goods, that is to say, a 'pure' trade libel, * * * [t]he need for granting equitable relief in cases like the present, where there are involved genuine proprietary interests of great social and commercial significance to the parties affected, is urgent."

Black & Yates, supra, at 236. The plaintiff having pleaded disparagement, this Court will view the law in this light.

It being clear that disparagement can be enjoined when a proper case is presented, and that no special damages need be shown or alleged for such relief, the task now becomes one of defining the cause of action. In Paramount Pictures v. Leader Press, 106 F.2d 229, 231 (10th Cir.1939) the court described disparagement as follows:

"One without privilege so to do, has no right to issue and publish an untrue or deceptive statement of fact which has a disparaging effect upon the quality of another's property, under circumstances which would lead a reasonable person to foresee that it will have such effect. The making of such a statement in such circumstances is tortious."

* * *

Testing Systems, Inc. v. Magnaflux Corp., 251 F.Supp. 286 (E.D.Pa. 1966) provides an excellent analysis of the type of statements which are considered actionable. In that case the defendant was alleged to have published a "false report to the effect that the United States Government had tested plaintiff's product, and found it to be only about 40% as effective as that of the defendant." Id., at 288. In addition, the defendant's agent had stated to plaintiff's customers that plaintiff's "stuff was no good" and that "the government is throwing them out." Id. The court noted:

" * * * that a statement which takes the form of an unfavorable comparison of products, or which 'puffs' or exaggerates the quality of one's own product is not ordinarily actionable."

Id. Supporting this view is the old English case of White v. Mellin, A.C. 154 (1895), where the defendant had advertised his product was more healthful than the plaintiff's product. That court's decision that such unfavorable comparisons were not actionable, was based:

" * * * on the near impossibility of ascertaining the truth or falsity of general allegations respecting the superiority of one product over another. To decide otherwise, * * * would turn the courts 'into a machinery for advertising rival productions by obtaining a judicial determination [as to] which of the two was better.' "

Testing Systems, Inc., supra. On the other hand:

"[t]he tradesman must be assured that his competitors will not be suffered to engage in conduct which falls below the minimum standard of fair dealing."

Id., at 289. The court concluded:

"[t]here is a readily observable difference between saying that one's product is, in general, better than another's * * * and asserting, as here, that such other's is only 40% as effective as one's own. The former, arguably, merely expresses an opinion, the truth or falsity of which is difficult or impossible [to ascertain]. The latter, however, is *an assertion of fact,* not subject to the same frailties of proof, *implying that the party making the statement is fortified with the substantive facts necessary to make it.*" (emphasis added).

Id.

In addition to the general description of disparagement outlined above, two other more difficult aspects of the cause of action must be examined—the issues of malice and burden of proof.

As to malice, there is much disagreement. The view taken in the Restatement of the Law of Torts, § 629, is that if a disparaging statement is made or reasonably understood as such, it is immaterial that the person making it did not intend to be understood in that manner. This strict liability approach is sharply criticized by Professor Prosser as predicated on a false analogy to cases of personal defamation. See Prosser, Injurious Falsehood: The Basis of Liability, 59 Colum.L.Rev. 425 (1959); Prosser, Law of Torts, supra at 921. Prosser points out, however, that malice can be sufficiently established when the defendant acts "for the purpose of doing harm to [or affecting] the interests of the plaintiff in a manner in which he is not privileged so to interfere." Id. This Court need not decide which of these two views is the better, for even under Prosser's approach the Court finds that defendant, Scientific Games, its officers and agents, acted with the intent to affect, if not harm the plaintiffs' interests. Of this there can be little doubt when one considers the nature of the statements of defendants' agents in both initiating and pursuing conversations with the lottery directors using plaintiffs' tickets.

The most difficult aspect of a disparagement action involves the issue of the burden of proof. Prosser, in his discussion of this tort discloses two views on this issue. In Law of Torts, supra at 920, Prosser states:

> " * * * the plaintiff must plead and prove not only the publication and its disparaging innuendo, as in defamation, but something more. There is no presumption, as in the case of personal slander, that the disparaging statement is false, and the plaintiff must establish its falsity as a part of his cause of action."

Five pages later, in examining the role of privilege in disparagement cases, Prosser states:

> "The privilege of competition for future business, as distinguished from the protection of an existing interest, has been recognized only to a limited extent. *False statements of fact disparaging the quality of a competitor's goods,* or the conduct of his business, are regarded as 'unfair' methods of competition, and *are never privileged.* The defendant who violates the rules of business ethics against disparaging attacks upon the business of a competitor *must be prepared to prove that his assertions are true* * * * " (emphasis added).

In resolving this conflict, it is important to keep in mind that allocating the burden of proof is a function of policy rather than dogma.

In stating that plaintiff has the burden of proving falsity of the disparaging statement, Prosser cites five cases in support. It is important to note that all of these cases are "slander of title" actions. In this type of case:

> "[the] rival claimant is privileged to disparage another's property [title] in land * * * by an honest assertion of an inconsistent legally protected interest in himself."

Restatement of Torts, Sec. 647, pp. 364–365 (1938). * * *

As a matter of policy in the disparagement of quality cases, it would appear eminently fair and reasonable to place the burden of proving the truth of the disparaging statement upon the speaker. In this context a competing trader's disparaging statements to another's current or potential customers do not involve any type of protection of the former's title in his own goods. (e.g., "the protection of an existing interest" which Prosser distinguishes from competing for future business). He makes such statements to decrease the others sales and to increase his own. This Court can see no reason why one disparaging the quality of another's goods should be given prima facie protection in making such statements. To require the plaintiff to prove the falsity of a defendant-competitor's disparaging remarks would place an incredible burden upon him especially in situations where the facts are likely to be within the knowledge of the defendant. Considering the unfair competition aspects of such cases and the modern view that all businessmen "play by the rules of the game," placing the burden on the defendant is justified. Such approach will be all the more reasonable and appropriate where the courts are diligent in examining whether the statements under consideration are merely unfavorable comparisons, puffing or opinion, or whether they are statements of fact. In this way the constitutional and competitive interests of all parties and the public will be adequately protected. For the foregoing reasons, this Court concludes that the defendants have the burden of proving that any disparaging statements made regarding the plaintiffs' product were true.

In view of the foregoing discussion and an evaluation of the facts, this Court concludes that the defendant, Scientific Games, its officers, agents and employees, made false and disparaging statements about plaintiffs' instant lottery ticket to their current and potential customers. The statement to the Omaha lottery director regarding the New Jersey State Police findings was never proven to be true. In fact, the defendant offered no evidence at all on this point. References to the Michigan lottery, while not completely false, were certainly misleading. Plaintiffs' original Michigan ticket was apparently secure, but there was another problem with the ticket which plaintiffs could not rapidly remedy without forfeiting some security. Insecurity was not the sole reason for plaintiffs losing the Michigan contract. Moreover, the Omaha ticket was not the same as the Michigan ticket.

Statements to the effect that ticket agents in Omaha were "ripping off" the public by breaking the ticket were clearly false, for plaintiff established that there were no problems with the Omaha instant lottery. Moreover, to the extent that rumors were spread about the above activity, where the rumor is known to be false or is spread to harm another it can be said to be disparaging.

Another statement which was made to lottery officials by several individuals connected with Scientific Games was that plaintiffs' tickets, both Delaware and Omaha, were insecure or could be broken. Considering the circumstances under which such statements were made, it is clear and any reasonable person could foresee that they would have a disparaging effect upon the quality of plaintiffs' product. In addition such statements are statements of fact in the context of this case.

* * *

The defendant's explanation to the lottery directors for its refusal to reveal how the tickets were allegedly broken was to the effect that it did not wish to disclose trade secrets or educate plaintiffs on how to improve their ticket. Whatever justification this may be for defendant's failure to explain to the lottery directors, it is no justification for defendant's failure to explain or demonstrate to this Court how the tickets could be broken. * * *

While this Court concludes that several statements made by Scientific Games' representatives were false and disparaging, there remains the question of whether preliminary injunctive relief is proper, and, if so, what form it should take. The plaintiff has established a reasonable probability of success upon a trial on the merits, and, in view of the rapid and continuing expansion of instant lottery business, the Court concludes that plaintiffs will suffer irreparable injury *pendente lite*. Considering the actions taken by the defendant, there is little possibility of harm to it from a properly drawn order. The most important consideration for this Court in granting injunctive relief is a consideration of the public interest. The defendant would have this Court deny injunctive relief altogether for it views its activities as service in the public interest. This Court disagrees. * * *

It cannot be denied, however, that important questions of public interest are present in the case, and, as just noted, must be considered in shaping injunctive relief.

In view of the strong public interest which must be protected by the lottery directors and this Court, injunctive relief must be tailored to grant greater latitude in certain circumstances. When a lottery director makes an *unsolicited request for ticket evaluation* by the defendant, the public interest would not be served by an injunction which might hinder an open and factually accurate response. On the other hand, as this case makes clear, statements regarding insecurity without explanation of how a ticket is broken serve no purpose at all. Considering that trade secret information given to the lottery director by way of explanation will be protected if given in confidence, there is little reason why defendant should not relate how a ticket was broken. Moreover, if defendant truly desires to act in the public interest, it should be willing to explain how a ticket was broken in any event. * * *

An order has issued.

ORDER
* * *

It is on this 22nd day of March 1976

ORDERED that defendant Scientific Games Development Corporation, its officers, agents, employees and any other persons acting in concert with the above, be and are hereby enjoined from making, uttering or publishing false and disparaging statements, whether direct or indirect, regarding plaintiffs' instant lottery tickets, this to include statements that plaintiffs' instant lottery tickets are not secure or can be "broken"; statements relating to rumors of ticket selling agents taking advantage of the alleged insecurity of plaintiffs' instant lottery tickets; and other similar statements or innuendo regarding the security of plaintiffs' instant lottery tickets; and

* * *

It is further ORDERED that the defendants Scientific Games Development Corporation and Dittler Brothers, Inc., their officers, agents, employees and those acting in concert with them, shall not be held to be in violation of the aforesaid orders as they relate to statements regarding ticket security, when responding to an unsolicited written request for assistance in ticket evaluation from a state, local or commercial lottery director, except that such responses as relate to ticket security must be accompanied by a full explanation as to how the ticket was determined to be insecure.

* * *

CLARIFICATION and MODIFICATION OF THE COURT'S ORDER

From the post hearing motion papers and briefs of both defendants, it has become apparent to the Court that there is some misunderstanding of the March 22nd order. Accordingly, the Court will now make an attempt at clarification.

First and foremost, the order enjoins only those statements regarding plaintiffs' lottery tickets which are *both false and disparaging.*
* * *

The portion of the order which has created the greatest misunderstanding is that dealing with communications between the defendants and lottery directors. The order states that the defendants:

"* * * *shall not be held to be in violation of the aforesaid orders* as they relate to statements regarding ticket security, when responding to an unsolicited written request for assistance in ticket evaluation from a state, local or commercial lottery director, except that such responses as relate to ticket security must be accompanied by a full explanation as to how the ticket was determined to be insecure * * *" (Emphasis added).

This is not to say that this is the only manner in which the defendants may communicate with lottery directors regarding the plaintiffs' lottery ticket. * * * Where *true* statements of fact are made, the defendants do not contravene this portion of the order.

* * *

Upon further reflection and consideration of the latter portion of the March 22nd order and upon consideration of the affidavits on file and portions of the testimony as both relate to the practices in the industry, this Court has, on its own initiative, decided to modify this portion of the order by striking from it the word "unsolicited". * * *

By removing the word "unsolicited", the Court seeks to provide for a less restricted flow of *substantiated* factual information from which lottery directors and the public can benefit. As was noted above and is clear from this Court's earlier opinion, when lottery directors have objectively verifiable facts before them, they are in the best possible position to determine the security or insecurity of a given ticket for their purposes. This Court does not wish to disrupt the acquisition of these facts or oversee a director's determination. * * *

Thus, when the defendants are responding to written requests for assistance in ticket evaluation from a lottery director and such responses as relate to ticket security are accompanied by a full and factual explanation of how a ticket was determined to be insecure, the defendants' statements are privileged. This qualified privilege is brought about in these circumstances because of the strong public interest in the security of lottery tickets. Said statements will not be actionable absent a showing by the plaintiffs that defendants knew they were false or made said statements in reckless disregard for their truth or falsity. As this Court's original opinion makes clear, however, statements such as those found to have been made in Omaha and Delaware (e.g. "plaintiffs' ticket is insecure"; "it can be easily broken"; "a child could break it"; "ticket agents are ripping off the public") which go unexplained and unsubstantiated are not privileged, and the defendants must be prepared to prove these assertions are true.

*   *   *

Submit an order.

NOTES

1. The parties were again before Judge Fisher in System Operations, Inc. v. Scientific Games Development Corp., 425 F.Supp. 130 (D.N.J.1977) to determine whether subsequent conduct by the defendant regarding the Ohio lottery was a violation of the earlier order. Plaintiff had a contract to provide Ohio with lottery tickets. Defendant developed a technique to "break" plaintiff's tickets. Defendant also began negotiations with Ohio officials seeking to become the supplier of tickets for the next Ohio lottery. During these negotiations defendant sent a letter to Ohio officials indicating it had become aware of "certain information * * * vitally important" to the lottery in progress in Ohio. The letter offered to demonstrate the "clear significance of our discovery" and was accompanied by a two page explanation of the order of the court rendered in the prior case. The bait worked, and an auditor for the Ohio lottery submitted a written request for a demonstration which was subsequently performed before various Ohio officials. Plaintiff argued that the written request did not come from the "lottery director" and was thus in violation of the court's order. The court found no "wilful violation" but made clear that "the public interest would [not] be served by contacts with and demonstrations for other state officials who have no authority over or understanding of lottery operations."

Subsequent to this development the Third Circuit decided the appeal from Judge Fisher's first decision. 555 F.2d 1131 (3d Cir.1977). The court reversed and remanded and held according to New Jersey law that the plaintiff must bear the burden of showing that disparaging statements were false and must prove the existence of special damages in order to obtain injunctive relief in a disparagement action. The court observed that it did not need to reach several "interesting issues" such as: "Does a preliminary injunction against a competitor's product disparagement necessarily violate the constitutional prohibition against prior restraints on speech? Does the constitution require that a plaintiff in a product disparagement action prove 'actual malice' on the part of the defendant within the meaning of New York Times Co. v. Sullivan * * * ?"

2.   One of the difficulties in these cases is distinguishing between disparagement of property, personal defamation, and puffing.   One of the categories of per se personal defamation involves statements affecting the plaintiff in his trade or profession.   What implicit statements are being made about the personal reputation of officials of Systems Operations in the principal case?

National Refining Co. v. Benzo Gas Motor Fuel Co., 20 F.2d 763 (8th Cir. 1927), cert. denied 275 U.S. 570 (1927) provides a classic formulation of the categories of disparaging speech:

> (1) Those where, though the alleged libelous statement is made in reference to goods or product, there are also included libelous words in reference to the vendor or producer, which impute to him, in connection with the goods or product, fraud, deceit, dishonesty, or reprehensible business methods.   *   *   *

> (2) Those where the alleged libelous statement is made merely as to the quality of the goods or product of another.   In those cases special damage must be alleged and proved, or no recovery can be had.

> *   *   *

> (3) Those where the alleged libelous statements amount to no more than assertions by one tradesman that his goods are superior to those of his rival.   Here no recovery can be had, though the statements are false and malicious, and though special damage is alleged.   *   *   *

The owner of the only service stations selling Benzo gasoline, a gasoline containing a coal derivative, complained of statements in a pamphlet distributed by the defendant, a seller of White Rose gasoline products.   The pamphlet in addition to promoting the benefits of White Rose gasoline, proclaimed that gas with benzo was affirmatively harmful to automobiles, and urged consumers to purchase White Rose, "an honestly made gasoline."   The court found the statements to be in category 2 requiring proof of special damages.

In Tex Smith, The Harmonica Man, Inc. v. Godfrey, 198 Misc. 1006, 102 N.Y.S.2d 251 (1951) Arthur Godfrey during radio and television appearances compared the plaintiff's $2.98 ukulele to more expensive ones and proclaimed it unsuited for either study or performance and "to sell the instrument as a ukulele might not be contrary to law but that people who did it should be jailed."   The court denied defendant's motion to dismiss.   "It is sometimes difficult to say whether words impeach the product or the sale of it.   This is particularly true where, as here, they assert the marketing of inferior merchandise.   It is, however, clear that in this statement the method as well as the goods are within the field of the remarks.   Their intendment is that a purchaser is duped into buying a worthless article by grossly unfair advertising.   It is not only that plaintiff is inept, unskillful, or ignorant in manufacture, but that it is unethical.   This is actionable.   If the words are regarded purely as a reflection on the instruments, the same result would be reached."

For an unusual situation where the plaintiff was advantaged by claiming disparagement of property rather than personal defamation see Menefee v. CBS, Inc., 458 Pa. 46, 329 A.2d 216 (1974).   Robert Menefee was the host of a controversial radio talk show and was fired by the station.   The station announced poor ratings as the reason for the firing, but it was subsequently discovered it resulted from Menefee's unpleasant remarks about the Veterans of Foreign Wars.   Menefee died one day before the trial.   His executrix avoided a statutory provision preventing the survival of actions for slander or libel by arguing that the statements injured Menefee in his ability to secure employment and was thus a disparagement of his services. The court agreed that a cause of action for disparagement of the intangible property interest in his broadcasting personality survived his death.

3. *Puffing.* Does the discussion of *Testing Systems* and White v. Mellin in the principal case help you draw a line between "puffing" and actionable disparagement? What is the underlying basis for the puffing privilege? Is such a privilege constitutionally required? How would you formulate the rule that separates puffery from actionable disparagement? See Prosser & Keeton, Torts §§ 109, 128 (5th ed. 1984): "The 'puffing' rule amounts to a seller's privilege to lie his head off. So long as he says nothing specific, on the theory that no reasonable man would believe him, or that no reasonable man would be influenced by such talk." In Smith-Victor Corp. v. Sylvania Electric Products, Inc., 242 F.Supp. 302, 308 (N.D.Ill.1965) the court applied the rule as follows:

> Both parties agree that advertising which merely states in general terms that one product is superior is not actionable. Statements such as "far brighter than any lamp ever before offered for home movies," and "the beam floods an area greater than the coverage of the widest wide angle lens," fall in this category. * * *

> Nevertheless, statements which ascribe absolute qualities to the defendant's product, such as 35,000 candlepower and 10-hour life, could give rise to a legal liability if they were not true. These exceed the traditional bounds of puffing.

The Restatement, Second, Torts § 647 (1977) provides a competitor a conditional privilege to make unfavorable comparisons "if the comparison does not contain false assertions of specific unfavorable facts regarding the rival competitor's things." Is the Restatement attempting to draw a distinction between statements of fact and statements of opinion? Would the statement "In my opinion our product has a longer life expectancy than X's product" be one of fact or opinion?

For a book length treatment of puffing see Preston, The Great American Blow-up: Puffery in Advertising and Selling (1975). The author concludes that false or unsubstantiated puffing should be prohibited arguing that it deceives consumers and provides a legally protected method of advertising for producers who otherwise would provide more information in their advertising. Do you agree?

4. *Intent, Malice and Knowledge of Falsity.* What intent on the part of the defendant was found to be sufficient to incur liability in the principal case? Did the plaintiff prove that the defendants knew the statements made about the plaintiff's tickets were false?

The precise elements of a prima facie case in disparagement remains unsettled and the experience of the American Law Institute's attempt to restate the law is instructive. A leading article of its time, Smith, Disparagement of Property, 13 Colum.L.Rev. 13, 121 (1913), concluded that in the absence of privilege, liability would result from innocent and negligent misstatements as well as those which were intentionally uttered to cause harm. Smith's position dramatically influenced the drafters of the first Restatement of Torts which announced liability for unprivileged disparagement regardless of the intent or knowledge of the defendant.

The drafters of the second Restatement, including William Prosser, concluded that Smith "missed the point of the English cases." In 1967 Dean Prosser proposed to the Institute a provision that required the plaintiff to show the defendant should have recognized his statements would likely result in harm to the plaintiff and that:

(a) The publisher is motivated by ill will toward the other, or

(b) He intends to interfere with the interests of the other in a manner which he is not privileged to do, or

(c) He knows the matter to be otherwise than as stated, or that he has not the basis for knowledge or belief professed by his assertion.

Restatement, Second, Torts § 623A (Tent. Draft No. 13, 1967).

The membership of the Institute did not challenge the essential thrust of Prosser's change when the draft was considered in 1967. See 44 ALI Proceedings 188 (1967). No mention was made of the United States Supreme Court's decision in New York Times v. Sullivan that had applied first amendment limitations to common law defamation actions. However, when the Court in 1974 in Gertz v. Robert Welch, Inc., 418 U.S. 323 (1974), explored the extent to which the law of defamation must be reexamined and in 1975 in Bigelow v. Virginia, 421 U.S. 809 (1975), began the full scale assault on the "commercial speech" exception, the implications for the law of disparagement became clearer. In 1976 the Institute was presented with a new draft, produced by Dean John Wade, the purpose of which was to "state as law those constitutional restrictions which were clearly applicable and those common law rules which were expected to be held constitutional, and to express the others in terms of caveats." See Restatement, Second, Torts, (Tent. Draft No. 22, 1976). After amendment by the Institute the provision as it appears in Restatement, Second, Torts (1976) is as follows:

§ 623A. Liability for Publication of Injurious Falsehood—General Principle

One who publishes a false statement harmful to the interests of another is subject to liability for pecuniary loss resulting to the other if

(a) he intends for publication of the statement to result in harm to interests of the other having a pecuniary value, or either recognizes or should recognize that it is likely to do so, and

(b) he knows that the statement is false or acts in reckless disregard of its truth or falsity.

Caveats:

The Institute takes no position on the questions of:

(1) Whether, instead of showing the publisher's knowledge or reckless disregard of the falsity of the statement, as indicated in Clause (b), the other may recover by showing that the publisher had either

(a) a motive of ill will toward him, or

(b) an intent to interfere in an unprivileged manner with his interests; or

(2) Whether either of these alternate bases, if not alone sufficient, would be made sufficient by being combined with a showing of negligence regarding the truth or falsity of the statement.

Does the Institute's analysis of the constitutional limitations on the cause of action of injurious falsehood also call into question the validity of Tuttle v. Buck? Could you draw a distinction between the constitutional limitation on a cause of action for disparagement and those that might be applicable to one for false advertising?

5. The extent to which constitutional limitations apply generally to product disparagement actions depends on the Supreme Court's ultimate view of four issues: (1) Is a commercial enterprise to be regarded, because of its participation in the marketplace, as a "public figure"? (2) Are statements made about goods and services to be regarded as matters of "public concern"? (3) Do constitutional limitations on defamation and disparagement apply to non-media defendants? (4) Do constitutional limitations developed in personal defamation actions apply with equal force to "commercial speech"? For the most part the cases that hint at an answer to some of these issues have involved media defendants (or defendants who are not directly in competition with the plaintiff). See Bose Corporation v. Consumers Union of United States, Inc., reprinted later in this Chapter.

6. Do you agree with Judge Fisher's analysis of the burden of proof requirement in disparagement or with the reversal on appeal? Is there any reason why a firm should be given *prima facie* protection in making statements about its competitor's goods forcing the competitor to prove the statements are false? In Philadelphia Newspapers, Inc. v. Hepps, 475 U.S. 767 (1986) the Supreme Court held in a personal defamation action (a newspaper accused a chain of stores which sold beer and snacks of having mafia connections) that because the stories were of "public concern" the first amendment required the plaintiff to bear the burden of proof that the statements were false.

TESTING SYSTEMS, INC. v. MAGNAFLUX CORP.
United States District Court, E.D. Pennsylvania, 1966.
251 F.Supp. 286.

JOHN W. LORD, JR., DISTRICT JUDGE. This is an action for trade libel or disparagement of property. Jurisdiction is predicated on diversity of citizenship and the requisite amount in controversy. The matter is now before this Court on the defendant's motion to dismiss for failure to state a claim upon which relief can be granted.

Essentially the facts are these. Both plaintiff, Testing Systems, Inc., and the defendant, Magnaflux Corp., are engaged in the manufacture and sale of equipment, devices and systems, including chemical products, for use in the nondestructive testing of commercial and industrial materials. The allegedly actionable statements concern similar chemical products of the parties; that of the plaintiff being known as "Flaw Finder", and that of the defendant identified as "Spotcheck". The complaint contains allegations that both written and oral statements disparaging plaintiff's product were circulated by the defendant's agents to plaintiff's current and prospective customers. * * *

[The description of the statements and the portion of the opinion on liability for unfavorable comparison are quoted at length in *Systems Operations* and are omitted here.]

* * *

DAMAGES

However, there remains for consideration the equally important matter of damages. In his complaint, plaintiff states merely that as a result of the defendant's disparagement, he has suffered a loss of customers, current and prospective. No attempt is made to specify which customers, nor is there any effort to even approximate their value to him. He asserts merely that the amount of his loss exceeds the minimum jurisdictional requirements of this Court.

After careful examination of the authorities on the question, it is apparent that plaintiff has failed to set forth his damages with the required particularity. The necessity of pleading and proving special damages has been an integral part of the action of disparagement of property since it first developed as an extension of slander of title. See Note, 77 Harv.L.Rev. 888, 890 (1964); Comment, 65 Dick.L.Rev. 145 (1961). It arose as a result of the friction between the ecclesiastical and common law courts of England when the common law courts sought to assume jurisdiction over actions for defamation. "Since slander of any kind was a sin, church courts alone could punish unless temporal damage could be shown to have resulted from the defamatory words." See Note, 41 Ill.L.Rev. 660, 662 (1947).

Until the 19th Century the requirement did not impose any untoward burden on the litigant. The early business community was devoid of the complexities that characterize the modern market place, and it was the rule, rather than the exception, that tradesmen knew their customers well. It was not too difficult, therefore, to determine just when and why one's customers began to favor a competitor.

As is so often the case, however, the rule respecting special damages continued in force long after its *raison d'être* had passed. Today, in the vast majority of States, including Pennsylvania, a plaintiff in a disparagement of property action must both plead and prove special damages. See Comment, 7 Vill.L.Rev. 271 (1962); 1 Harper & James, Torts § 474 (1956); Annot., 150 A.L.R. 716 (1944): Smith, Disparagement of Property [13 Colum.L.Rev. 121 (1913)]. The inflexibility of most courts in demanding strict compliance with the rule has hampered the effectiveness of the action and contributed to its unpopularity. One can appreciate the plight of the small metropolitan retailer whose patrons are, for the most part, unknown to him by name. Here, however, we are not dealing with small retailers. Both the defendant and the plaintiff in this action are business organizations of some substance who are well aware of their present and potential sources of business. The rule requiring some showing of damage, while perhaps harsh in some cases, is entirely reasonable under the circumstances as presented here.

[The court then noted it was required to follow the law of Pennsylvania which required a specific pleading of special damages.]

Thus to avoid the necessity of specially pleading his damages, the plaintiff must show that the defendant's statements constituted libel per se. * * * Here the defendant falsely reported that the United States Government had found plaintiff's product to be so ineffective in comparison with defendant's that it chose to discontinue dealing with plaintiff. However unethical this may be from a business standpoint, it does not amount to libel per se. It does not accuse the plaintiff of fraud or otherwise attack his character personally, nor does it by reasonable inference draw into question the solvency of his business. Under these circumstances libel per se did not materialize, and this argument must be dismissed accordingly.

* * *

The complaint in this action was filed almost immediately after the disparagement occurred. Nine months have expired since the cause of action arose. It may now be possible for plaintiff to plead over with the requisite degree of specificity. For this reason, the complaint will not be dismissed unless the plaintiff fails to so plead within the period specified below.

NOTES

1. "In cases where 'special damages' must be shown, the courts require that the pleader identify the particular loss with a definiteness which is not ordinarily requisite in pleading damages. Here the standard practice is to require that the lost contract, employment, sale, or other valuable thing be identified in pleading and proof by name, date, and place. A mere general statement that the plaintiff has lost patronage or business of a given amount, or that he would have derived profits to a certain amount, are not enough where, so far as appears, these specific details would be known by the plaintiff, and could be furnished. * * * But where the plaintiff can, under the circumstances, only know that the flow of his business as a whole is diminished and it would be impossible to point to any specific customers or orders which have been lost, then it is sufficient to plead and prove the total loss generally." McCormick, Damages § 115 (1935).

2. Restatement, Second, Torts § 633 (1977) defines the pecuniary loss recoverable in an injurious falsehood case to include, in addition to directly resulting pecuniary losses, "the expense of measures reasonably necessary to counteract the publication, including litigation to remove the doubt cast upon vendibility or value by disparagement." How would a plaintiff counteract a disparagement of the quality of his goods? See, Big O Tire Dealers, Inc. v. Goodyear Tire & Rubber Co., 561 F.2d 1365 (10th Cir.1977).

3. What role is the concept of "special damages" designed to play in the law of disparagement? Is the absence of special damages the rationale behind *Mosler*? If the defendant in *American Washboard* had disparaged aluminum washboards would the result have been different? Or could it be argued that calling a zinc washboard aluminum when aluminum is superior does in fact disparage aluminum washboards at least with reference to a consumer who purchases a zinc board thinking it is aluminum? Is proof of special damages constitutionally required by analogy to Gertz v. Robert Welch, Inc., 418 U.S. 323 (1974) which held that "the States may not permit recovery of presumed or

punitive damages at least when liability is not based on a showing of knowledge of falsity or reckless disregard for the truth?" Id. at 349.

4. The analogy to personal defamation produced the traditional rule that injunctive relief is unavailable to a plaintiff in a disparagement suit. The most often cited decision for the rule is Marlin Firearms Co. v. Shields, 171 N.Y. 384, 64 N.E. 163 (1902). In *Marlin* the plaintiff manufactured Marlin repeating rifles and for a time advertised in defendant's magazine. When defendant's rates increased, plaintiff withdrew his advertising whereupon defendant published letters, purporting to be from correspondents, reflecting unfavorably on plaintiff's rifles. A number of the letters compared the plaintiff's rifle to other brands and recommended the other brands over that of the plaintiff. The letters were in fact written and published by the defendant. Plaintiff's request for an injunction was based primarily on the theory that he had no adequate remedy at law because he could not prove special damages. Held: For defendant.

> This brings us to the real question of the case,—whether an injust and malicious criticism of a manufactured article, for which the manufacturer has no remedy at law because of his inability to prove special damage, is the subject of equitable cognizance. The constitutional guaranty of freedom of speech and press, which in terms provides that "every citizen may freely speak, write, and publish his sentiments on all subjects, being responsible for the abuse of that right; and no law shall be passed to restrain or abridge the liberty of speech or of the press" (Const.N.Y. art. 1, § 8), has for its only limitations the law of slander and libel. Hitherto freedom of speech and of the press could only be interfered with where the speaker or writer offended against the criminal law, or where the words amounted to a slander or libel of a person or corporation or their property, and the guaranteed right of trial by jury entitled the parties accused of slander or libel to have 12 men pass upon the question of their liability to respond in damages therefor and to measure such damages. But the precedent which the plaintiff seeks to establish would open the door for a judge sitting in equity to establish a censorship not only over the past and present conduct of a publisher of a magazine or newspaper, but would authorize such judge by decree to lay down a chart for future guidance in so far as a plaintiff's property rights might seem to require, and, in case of the violation of the provisions of such a decree, the usual course and practice of equity would necessarily be invoked, which would authorize the court to determine whether such published articles were contrary to the prohibitions of the decree, and, if so found, punishment as for a contempt might follow. Thus a party could be punished for publishing an article which was not libelous, and that, too, without a trial by jury.

Other courts, including those in New York, have not viewed the *Marlin* decision with total approbation. The decision may stand for no more than if you cannot prove a prima facie case for disparagement you are not entitled to relief on the disparagement issues. It is not entirely clear from the opinion what the court would have done with the injunction question if special damages had been proven.

The landmark decision rejecting the traditional rule is Black & Yates, Inc. v. Mahogany Ass'n, Inc., 129 F.2d 227 (3d Cir.1942) upon which Judge Fisher in *Systems Operations* relies. The court placed great weight on Pound, Equitable Relief Against Defamation and Injuries to Personality, 29 Harv.L.Rev. 640

(1916) and his conclusion that "the traditional doctrine puts anyone's business at the mercy of any insolvent malicious defamer who has sufficient imagination to lay out a skillful campaign of extortion." Id. at 668. The court added its own observation that the "irrelevance of 'free speech' and of 'a libel is for a jury' are patent. Freedom of discussion of public issues does not demand lack of 'previous restraint' for injury to private individuals. Disparagement of goods presents no confusing or complicated matter of personality requiring the sympathetic attention of one's peers." 129 F.2d at 231.

Should the availability of injunctive relief depend on whether the plaintiff and defendant are in competition with each other? In *Marlin*, the defendant did not sell rifles directly. In *Black & Yates* competition was present. Or should a showing of coercion or intimidation in addition to the disparagement overcome objections to injunctive relief? In Emack v. Kane, 34 Fed. 46 (C.C. N.D.Ill.1888) the parties both manufactured muffled writing slates for school children under different patents. The defendant threatened plaintiff's customers that the defendant would bring patent infringement suits against them if they continued to buy from plaintiff. Plaintiff lost substantial business. In granting the injunction the court noted that while a "mere personal slander or libel * * * can [not] wholly destroy a man's reputation * * * statements and charges intended to frighten away a man's customers, and intimidate them from dealing with him, may wholly break up and ruin him financially, with no adequate remedy * * *." Id. at 51. Other courts enjoined defamatory statements when utilized in conjunction with acts of coercion, intimidation, and conspiracy. Vegelahn v. Guntner, 167 Mass. 92, 44 N.E. 1077 (1896).

5. Many courts and litigants frustrated by the restricted relief available in disparagement have searched for different rhetoric with some success. In New York, the Court of Appeals in Advance Music Corp. v. American Tobacco Co., 296 N.Y. 79, 70 N.E.2d 401 (1946) adopted the "prima facie tort" doctrine which provided damages for intentional infliction of injury without justification. However, subsequent decisions required proof of special damage under this heading also. Rager v. McCloskey, 305 N.Y. 75, 111 N.E.2d 214 (1953); Eversharp, Inc. v. Pal Blade Co., 182 F.2d 779 (2d Cir.1950).

Some plaintiffs were more successful if the cause of action was denominated as "unfair competition." In Royer v. Stoody Co., 192 F.Supp. 949 (W.D.Okl. 1961), affirmed 374 F.2d 672 (10th Cir.1967), the court held that if the plaintiff sued for unfair competition, he must allege and prove the publication complained of was false and was intended to deceive, but that the special damage rule would be inapplicable. ("Even in trade libel cases, the trend is toward doing away with the necessity of alleging special damages.") See also H.E. Allen Mfg. Co., Inc. v. Smith, 224 App.Div. 187, 229 N.Y.S. 692 (1928) which avoided the *Marlin* result by awarding injunctive relief on a claim of unfair competition.

6. *Disparagement by consumers.* Would you develop different rules governing a suit by the seller of a product against a consumer for disparagement? In Menard v. Houle, 298 Mass. 546, 11 N.E.2d 436 (1937) the defendant, unhappy with the automobile he purchased from plaintiff, outfitted the vehicle with signs reading in part "Don't believe what they say, this car is no good; I tried to have it fixed but they can't fix it and they will do nothing about it * * * this car was no good when I got it; don't be a sucker, this car is no good but it looks all right." Apparently, the defendant also tied lemons to the automobile. Thus attired, the automobile was driven around the city and left parked on the public streets. The court in granting plaintiff an injunction

noted past precedent which had held that equity jurisdiction does not extend to disparagement but relied on later cases which had "held that equity will take jurisdiction where there is a continuing course of unjustified and wrongful attack upon the plaintiff motivated by actual malice, and causing damage to property rights as distinguished from 'injury to the personality affecting feelings, sensibility and honor' * * * even though false statements and false announcements are the means or are among the means employed, and that in such cases there is no adequate remedy at law. * * * Neither conspiracy nor unfair competition need appear."

Compare Willing v. Mazzocone, 482 Pa. 377, 393 A.2d 1155 (1978) in which the appellant had been a client of appellee attorneys and thought the attorneys had misallocated $25 of a $150 expense item recovered in a workmen's compensation case. The court described the appellant's activities, conducted on a well traveled pedestrian pathway, as follows:

> While engaged in this activity, which lasted for several hours each day, appellant wore a "sandwich-board" sign around her neck. On the sign she had hand lettered the following: "LAW—FIRM of QUINN—MAZZOCONE *Stole money from me*—and Sold-me-out-to-the INSURANCE COMPANY." As she marched back and forth, appellant also pushed a shopping cart on which she had placed an American flag. She continuously rang a cow bell and blew on a whistle to further attract attention.

393 A.2d at 1156.

The lower court awarded an injunction against appellant's activity arguing that, in the present case, a damage action was an inadequate remedy because the appellant was indigent. The Pennsylvania Supreme Court reversed, holding the injunction was a prior restraint violative of the state constitutional right to speech and further that "the insolvency of the defendant does not create a situation where there is no adequate remedy at law." Id. at 1158.

7. In Organization for a Better Austin v. Keefe, 402 U.S. 415 (1971) the defendants, OBA, a racially integrated community association accused Keefe, a real estate broker of "panic peddling" and "blockbusting." The OBA distributed leaflets in Keefe's own neighborhood describing his activities and requesting recipients to call Keefe and urge him to cease his activities. The Illinois courts enjoined the distribution of the leaflets because they were intended to be coercive and to invade Keefe's privacy. The Supreme Court, 8–1, found the injunction to be a prior restraint and violative of the first amendment.

See also Matter of National Service Corp., 742 F.2d 859 (5th Cir.1984) where Turner Advertising Company furnished outdoor billboard advertising pursuant to a contract with NSC. When NSC filed for voluntary bankruptcy, Turner proposed to superimpose on the billboards in large black letters the phrase: "Beware, This Company Does Not Pay Its Bills." The bankruptcy court enjoined TAC on the grounds that the action was an illegal attempt to harass the debtor. The Fifth Circuit held the posting was not "commercial speech" but "pure speech" and thus the injunction was a prior restraint and invalid. "TAC's message is not a solicitation for the sale or purchase of a product or service * * *. Rather, the message more closely resembles a public service message, and one for which TAC is not being remunerated."

KEMART CORP. v. PRINTING ARTS RESEARCH LAB., INC.
United States Court of Appeals, Ninth Circuit, 1959.
269 F.2d 375, cert. denied 361 U.S. 893, 80 S.Ct. 197, 4 L.Ed.2d 151.

[This case culminated a long history of litigation involving two photoengraving processes employed and licensed respectively by Kemart Corp. and Printing Arts. Printing Arts held the Marx patent No. 2,191,939 on a photoengraving process. The patentee was the "actual operating head" of Printing Arts. On October 6, 1948, Albert McCaleb, President and Director of Printing Arts, and also their patent attorney, rendered a written opinion to Printing Arts that the process employed and licensed by Kemart was infringing the Marx patent. The written opinion advised that "all users of the Kemart process, insofar as you are able to identify them, be notified of the existence of your aforesaid patent * * * its nature and coverage, and their infringement thereof." On October 7, 1948, Marx displayed the letter to the President of Kemart and other individuals attending the national convention of photoengravers. On November 10, McCaleb sent a letter to Kemart which read in part: "I have now been instructed to institute suit for infringement of the above identified patent against a representative user of the Kemart process, and intend so to do just as soon as certain prerequisite information can be obtained." On November 23, 1948, Kemart instituted a declaratory judgment action to declare its right to use and license the Kemart process without interference from Printing Arts, to declare the Marx patent void, for an injunction precluding Printing Arts from threatening Kemart's licensees with infringement suits, and for damages resulting from Printing Arts' "wrongful acts and doings". On the same day, Kemart sent a letter to its licensees advising them of the litigation and that it had been instituted "for the purpose of protecting you and ourselves against a series of threats by * * * Printing Arts * * *." The letter also indicated that Printing Arts' threats were false and contrary to fair competition. This letter was subsequently printed in a photoengraving trade journal at the request of Kemart. On March 28, 1949, the lower court denied Kemart a temporary injunction precluding Printing Arts from bringing a patent infringement suit against Kemart's licensees. This fact was subsequently printed in the trade journal at the request of Printing Arts and in addition, that Printing Arts would "when it is legally advisable" bring an action against a licensee.

Kemart received several letters from its licensees during 1949, some cancelling their license agreement and others demanding that Kemart take steps to protect them against infringement suits by posting bonds.

In opinions preceding the one reproduced below, the court held that Kemart did not infringe the Printing Arts patents. The remaining issue concerned Kemart's suit for damages against Printing Arts for "unfair competition and trade libel". The lower court found that prior to the litigation Printing Arts reasonably believed its patent valid and infringed, that this belief was based on advice of experienced although interested counsel and not upon careless ascertainment of their rights. The lower court concluded that Ohio law granted a privilege in this situation as defense to trade libel.   Kemart appealed.]

BONE, SENIOR JUDGE.

Regardless of the applicable state law, the problem presented by the facts shown here must be handled in essentially the same manner. It is clear from the record (and is not challenged by the parties) that all the publications attributable to Printing Arts were disparaging either to the "person" or the property of Kemart.   The lower court found that, with regard to each of these publications, Printing Arts acted without malice in an effort to protect what it reasonably believed to be its valid and existing property rights.   These efforts were reasonably calculated to adequately protect its claimed rights without *unnecessary* damage to the parties concerned.   In this manner the elements of the defense of privilege were brought into the record.[10]   *   *   *

It is the general rule in the United States that a qualified privilege is recognized in cases where the publisher and the recipient of the publication have a common interest which might be reasonably believed to be protected or furthered by the publication and the publication is made reasonably and in good faith.   Prosser, Handbook of the Law of Torts (2d ed., 1955) pp. 606, 618–619.   This privilege has been recognized in Ohio, De Angelo v. W.T. Grant, Ohio App., 111 N.E.2d 773; McKenna v. Mansfield Leland Hotel Co., 55 Ohio App. 163, 9 N.E.2d 166.   Though these cases involve disparagements made by an employer concerning an employee, the *privilege* involved is the same as that involved in the instant case.   Both Printing Arts (the publisher) and the recipient members of the photoengraving industry attending the convention had an interest (in this case a pecuniary interest) in the subject matter of the publication.

The second and apparently most important publication by Printing Arts was made in the May 1949, issue of the Photoengraver's Bulletin, a trade journal which circulates to "everyone in the industry".   Subsequent publications were also made, one in the June, 1950, issue of the

---

10. Appellant challenges the finding of the trial court that the charges were published in good faith and without malice on the ground that the charge was based upon the advice of interested counsel.   Appellant asserts that "advice of counsel" is *not a defense* in a libel action.

However, the basis of Printing Arts' defense, as indicated by the record, is that of "privilege" rather than advice of counsel. As will be discussed later in this opinion, the absence of "actual malice" is one of the elements of this defense (privilege).   Proof of "advice of counsel" was introduced in testimony and exhibits by Printing Arts to indicate its lack of "actual malice" in the

present case.   If appellee believed its charge of infringement to be true, and if it was reasonable for it to so believe, there was no "actual malice" on its part, hence one of the required elements of the defense of "privilege" was established.   The fact that McCaleb informed Marx of his (McCaleb's) belief that the Kemart process infringed that Marx Patent and that McCaleb was an experienced and otherwise qualified patent attorney, was merely evidentiary of the fact that Marx believed the charge to be true, and further, that since at least one qualified patent attorney believed it to be true, it was reasonable for Marx to so believe.

aforementioned Bulletin and a second in the National Lithographer for the same month. This latter magazine is the equivalent trade journal for lithographers.

*   *   *

[The court notes that the latter publication was nation-wide and "must be regarded as 'multi-state' in nature without an easily locatable situs of applicable law." California is determined to have the closest relationship to the parties and the litigation and is therefore applied as the substantive law governing the second publication.]

The law of California is clear in respect to privileged publications of claimed defamatory material. Section 47 of the California Civil Code provides:

"A privileged publication or broadcast is one made—

*   *   *

"3. In a communication, without malice, to a person interested therein, (1) by one who is also interested *   *   * "

In the instant case, the publisher of the claimed defamation (Printing Arts) is the holder of a competing patent. The recipients of the claimed defamatory publications were the present and the prospective licensees of the here competing patent owners. Both are financially interested in the subject matter of the claimed defamation and thus clearly come within the terms of the stated privilege. It is unnecessary to determine whether the tort involved in the instant case is one for unfair competition or one for libel since the California courts have applied the above statutory privilege to both types of wrongs.

Since the claimed defamations appearing in the Bulletin and the other "trade" journals were privileged, it was necessary for Kemart, in order to prevail, to show "actual malice" as distinguished from malice inferred from the false communication in and of itself. Cal.Civil Code § 48; Brewer v. Second Baptist Church of Los Angeles, 32 Cal.2d 791, 197 P.2d 713; Miles v. Rosenthal, 90 Cal.App. 390, 266 P. 320. The "actual malice" required to overcome the statutory privilege is to be distinguished from that sometimes inferred from the intentional doing of a wrongful act without justification. Snively v. Record Pub. Co., 185 Cal. 565, 198 P. 1; Harris v. Curtis Pub. Co., 49 Cal.App.2d 340, 121 P.2d 761. In the instant case, the trial court made a specific finding that no such malice existed on the part of Printing Arts and that the said Printing Arts had reasonable cause to believe that its charge of patent infringement by the Kemart process was true. The only conclusion which this court can reach is that Printing Arts was qualifiedly privileged in making the complained-of publications and that this privilege was not overcome by an adequate showing of malice. Printing Arts cannot, therefore, be held liable for the damage flowing from those publications.

*   *   *

NOTES

1. For a similar case in which the defendant was unsuccessful in establishing a privilege see International Industries & Developments, Inc. v. Farbach Chemical Co., 241 F.2d 246 (6th Cir.1957). Here it was shown that the defendant did not subject the plaintiff's product to a readily available chemical analysis prior to sending out 8000 letters to the trade alleging plaintiff's product infringed defendant's patent. The Sixth Circuit found the "record supports the conclusion of the trial court that the issuance of the notice of infringement was done in implied malice in law, if not in actual malice, and in bad faith constituting unfair competition." Note should be made that 35 U.S. C.A. § 287 provides that a patent holder may not recover damages for infringements occurring before he has fixed a notice on the patented object or has specifically notified the infringer of his claim to patent rights.

2. Can you sort out (1) the role of privilege in allocating the burden of proof (*Systems Operation*), (2) the role of privilege in requiring "actual malice," and (3) the level of intent generally required in a disparagement case? Should the privilege announced in *Kemart* have equal applicability to a case in which the disparagement relates to the quality of a competitor's goods? Could Scientific Games have asserted the *Kemart* privilege requiring Systems Operations to prove "actual malice." How would you apply the privilege across three possible cases: (1) disparagement by a competitor; (2) disparagement by a consumer; and (3) disparagement by an independent third party. Does *Kemart* suggest that as your interest in the subject matter of the controversy increases you have greater leeway in commenting? Could it also be that where your interest is apparent, the credibility of your statement and the potential damage it might cause decrease? The protection of the first amendment seems at least primarily directed at independent commentators like the press. Have these two different legal threads—common law privileges and first amendment protections—now been woven together to provide a relatively uniform restriction on liability for disparaging statements? Or could it be said that the common law had worked out, at least in disparagement cases, some first amendment-like protections for commercial speech long before the Supreme Court entered the area.

3. For a review of disparagement doctrines and the potential first amendment problems they create see Note, Corporate Defamation and the Product Disparagement: Narrowing the Analogy to Personal Defamation, 75 Colum.L. Rev. 963 (1975); Note, The Tort of Disparagement and the Developing First Amendment, 1987 Duke L.J. 727.

(3) INTERLUDE: FEDERAL–STATE TENSIONS: THE SEARCH FOR UNIFORMITY

The purpose here is to explore again the tension between state and federal authority regarding the general law of unfair competition with emphasis on the regulation of market-place deception. In Chapter I against a landscape of common law tort principles, we saw the potential intrusion of Federal anti-trust laws, the influence of the Federal Trade Commission, and the limiting features of the federal patent and copyright statutes. In the regulation of market-place deception, the battle has been waged on many fronts with mixed results and continues today as claims of state authority conflict with the interest in uniform regulation.

a. Common Law Application

The major cases studied thus far have been federal cases, i.e., *INS, Mosler,* and *American Washboard.* All were decided prior to Erie R.R. Co. v. Tompkins, 304 U.S. 64 (1938). During the reign of Swift v. Tyson, 41 U.S. (16 Pet.) 1 (1842), which authorized a federal common law in diversity cases, much of the law of unfair competition was developed by federal courts because diversity of citizenship and a large amount in controversy were more likely to coexist in suits between business enterprises. It should be noted that neither *Swift* nor *Erie* were trade practice cases, *Swift* involving the issue of whether a preexisting debt constituted valuable consideration in the law of negotiable instruments and *Erie* involving the question of whether a person on a commonly used footpath which ran for a short distance alongside the tracks of the defendant's railroad was a licensee or trespasser. In *Erie* Justice Brandeis recognized the dilemma of federalism: "In attempting to promote uniformity of law throughout the United States, the doctrine [of Swift] had prevented uniformity in the administration of the law of the state."

Is there any reason why *Erie* should not be equally applicable to a case involving unfair competition? Or trademark infringement? Or the type of deception in *Mosler?* Consider the applicability of *Erie* to the factual situation of the *INS* case. What problems would Associated Press and International News face? Assume that Justice Holmes' opinion reflected California law.

It has been assumed by the Supreme Court that *Erie* applies to cases of unfair competition and common law trademark infringement. In Kellogg Co. v. National Biscuit Co., 305 U.S. 111 (1938) involving both causes of action Justice Brandeis noted that the case was governed by local law although "no claim has been made that the local law is any different from the general law on the subject, and both parties have relied almost entirely on federal precedents". See also Pecheur Lozenge Co. v. National Candy Co., 315 U.S. 666 (1942) where the court remanded a lower court's decision involving unfair competition and common law trademark infringement "to afford [the Circuit Court of Appeals] opportunity to apply the appropriate local law."

Failing to carve out an exemption from the *Erie* doctrine for unfair competition cases, litigants turned to the federal trademark registration act and pendent jurisdiction which had been announced in Hurn v. Oursler, 289 U.S. 238 (1933) and codified in 28 U.S.C. § 1338(b) and which allowed federal subject matter jurisdiction without diversity over an unfair competition claim "when joined with a substantial and related claim under the copyright, patent or trademark laws". Pendent jurisdiction is likely to be available in many unfair competition cases.

For a lively debate on whether federal law should apply see pro: Zlinkoff, Erie v. Tompkins: In Relation to the Law of Trademarks and Unfair Competition, 42 Colum.L.Rev. 955 (1942) (E.g., most states do not have modern body of local law and national character of commercial activity requires uniform rule); con: Wyzanski, J. in National Fruit Prod. Co. v. Dwinell-Wright Co., 47 F.Supp. 499 (D.Mass.1942) (Massachusetts does have a large modern body of precedents and "the point that national commerce requires a national rule of unfair competition is peculiarly appropriate for consideration by the legislative rather than the judicial branch"); rebuttal: Zlinkoff, Some Reactions to the Opinion of Judge Wyzanski in National Fruit Products Co. v. Dwinell-Wright Co., 32 Trademark Rep. 131 (1942). Five years later, Judge Wyzanski's colleague Judge Sweeney accepted Zlinkoff's position: "On more careful consideration, I feel that there is a strong policy in favor of interstate uniformity in the field of unfair competition. There is the dilemma between a checkerboard result in the automatic application of Klaxon * * * to multi-state unfair competition on the one hand, or a return, on the other, to the evils of choice of forum if local law is to govern the interstate as well as local aspects of the tort." Bulova Watch Co. v. Stolzberg, 69 F.Supp. 543 (D.Mass.1947). See also Neal v. Thomas Organ Co., 325 F.2d 978 (9th Cir.1963) (federal law); Moore's Federal Practice ¶ 0.60 at 661 (federal law); Maternally Yours, Inc. v. Your Maternity Shop, Inc., 234 F.2d 538 (2d Cir.1956) (state law); Hart and Wechsler, The Federal Courts and the Federal System 809 (1953) ("The view has occasionally been expressed that a district court * * * is free to decide [the pendent claim] according to pre-Erie 'general law'. * * * There isn't anything in this notion, is there? See the answer in National Fruit. * * * ").

b. *Model and Uniform State Legislation*

States have developed informal mechanisms designed to promote uniform laws, one of which is the National Conference of Commissioners on Uniform State Laws whose stated purpose is to develop uniform laws for enactment by state legislatures. The Uniform Commercial Code is a major achievement for which it is in part responsible. The wide acceptance of the UCC illustrates the potential for uniformity through state legislation. In the trade regulation area the Commissioners have promulgated the Uniform Deceptive Trade Practices Act, 7A Uniform L.Ann. 35 (1978), and the Uniform Consumer Sales Practices Act, 7A Uniform L.Ann. 1 (1978). See generally, Dole, Uniform Deceptive Trade Practices Act: Another Step Toward a National Law of Unfair Trade Practices, 51 Minn.L.Rev. 1005 (1967).

With the assistance of the Federal Trade Commission, the Council of State Governments has recommended for adoption by the states the Unfair Trade Practices and Consumer Protection Act. Council of State Governments, 1970 Suggested State Legislation 141. The act provides both public enforcement and private remedies and is often referred to as a "little FTC Act." See Lovett, State Deceptive Trade Practice

Legislation, 46 Tul.L.Rev. 724 (1972) (reporting that 36 states have adopted legislation similar to the Act.) These enactments are considered in a subsequent section of this Chapter.

c. Federal Legislation

The interest in national uniformity in regulating business activity was enhanced by several Congressional legislative efforts. Of course the authority for federal regulation of interstate commerce is recognized in the Constitution. One of the most pervasive results of that power was establishment in 1914 of the Federal Trade Commission to give nationwide content to the anti-trust laws. The Commission also attempted to deal with market-place deception and was given express authority to do so in 1933.

In a number of instances Congress has legislated against deception in particular industries. The Automobile Information Disclosure Act, 15 U.S.C. § 1231 et seq. requires a label to be affixed to new automobiles disclosing identifying information such as the make, model, and serial number of the vehicle and other items such as the suggested retail price and other costs. Willful failure to comply is a criminal offense subject to a $1,000 fine. In 1972, Congress enacted the Motor Vehicle Information and Cost Savings Act, 15 U.S.C. § 1901 et seq., subchapter IV of which provides liability of 3 times the amount of damage or $1,500, whichever is greater, in addition to attorneys fees and costs for falsifying odometer readings on automobiles. In the Interstate Land Sales Full Disclosure Act, 15 U.S.C. § 1701 et seq. Congress required land developers in interstate commerce to furnish prospective purchasers with a statement containing the description of the land, conditions affecting access to the property, availability of sewage disposal and utility service, and any encumbrances on the property. False statements or omissions constituting a material misrepresentation subjects the developer to a private cause of action by the injured purchaser. And in 1977 Congress passed the Fair Debt Collection Practices Act, 15 U.S.C. § 1692 et seq. which provides a civil remedy for persons injured by false, deceptive or misleading representations in connection with the collection of debts.

Congress has responded to the need for a law of general applicability governing private causes of action for unfair competition although in each instance, the provision has been incorporated into a bill designed to accomplish other more publicized purposes. For long periods of time they went unnoticed. In 1920, Congress amended the federal trade mark registration act of 1905 in order to implement certain international conventions. The amendments contained a provision for a limited federal law of unfair competition. Section 3 of the Act of 1920 provided:

> That any person who shall willfully and with intent to deceive, affix, apply, or annex, or use in connection with any article or articles of merchandise, or any container or containers of the same, a false designation of origin, including words or other

symbols, tending to falsely identify the origin of the merchandise, and shall then cause such merchandise to enter into
interstate or foreign commerce, and any person who shall
knowingly cause or procure the same to be transported in
interstate or foreign commerce or commerce with Indian
tribes, or shall knowingly deliver the same to any carrier to be
so transported, shall be liable to an action at law for damages
and to an action in equity for an injunction, at the suit of any
person, firm, or corporation doing business in the locality
falsely indicated as that of origin, or in the region in which
said locality is situated, or at the suit of any association of such
persons, firms, or corporations. Act of March 19, 1920, ch. 104,
§ 3, 41 Stat. 534.

The section created a general federal cause of action for deception
of a particular type and was available to persons regardless of whether
they had a federally registered trademark. However, three limitations
made the section an ineffective tool against false advertising. First, it
applied only to false designations of origin; second, it applied to
merchandise and not services; and third, it required a showing of an
intent to deceive. Immediately after passage of the 1920 act, various
groups began developing plans for total revision of the federal trademark laws. Most of the revisions included a provision for federal
control of unfair competition in various degrees.

In 1946 Congress replaced both the acts of 1905 and 1920 with the
Lanham Act, a complete revision of the federal trademark statutes.
Sections 43(a) and 44 of that enactment became the foundation upon
which some sought to build a uniform law of unfair competition.

One of the themes that runs throughout the remainder of this
course is the resolution of these federal-state tensions as they affect
business practices. One of the questions which should be asked about
any of the issues raised hereafter is whether it is an issue more
appropriately handled by federal or state law. It is hoped the student
will continually posit that question wherever the authors have failed to
do so.

(4) THE LANHAM ACT

LANHAM ACT § 43(a) (1946–1989)

§ 1125. False designations of origin and false descriptions forbidden

(a) Any person who shall affix, apply, or annex, or use in connection with any goods or services, or any container or containers for
goods, a false designation of origin, or any false description or representation, including words or other symbols tending falsely to describe or
represent the same, and shall cause such goods or services to enter into
commerce, and any person who shall with knowledge of the falsity of
such designation of origin or description or representation cause or

procure the same to be transported or used in commerce or deliver the same to any carrier to be transported or used, shall be liable to a civil action by any person doing business in the locality falsely indicated as that of origin or in the region in which said locality is situated, or by any person who believes that he is or is likely to be damaged by the use of any such false description or representation.

LANHAM ACT § 43(a)
as amended by the
TRADEMARK REVISION ACT OF 1988
Effective November 16, 1989

SEC. 132.　Unregistered marks, descriptions, and representations.

(a) Any person who, on or in connection with any goods or services, or any container for goods, uses in commerce any word, term, name, symbol, or device, or any combination thereof, or any false designation of origin, false or misleading description of fact, or false or misleading representation of fact, which—

(1) is likely to cause confusion, or to cause mistake, or to deceive as to the affiliation, connection, or association of such person with another person, or as to the origin, sponsorship, or approval of his or her goods, services, or commercial activities by another person, or

(2) in commercial advertising or promotion, misrepresents the nature, characteristics, qualities, or geographic origin of his or her or another person's goods, services, or commercial activities,

shall be liable in a civil action by any person who believes that he or she is or is likely to be damaged by such act.

JOHNSON & JOHNSON v. CARTER–WALLACE, INC.
United States Court of Appeals, Second Circuit, 1980.
631 F.2d 186.

MANSFIELD, CIRCUIT JUDGE.

* * *

Johnson's claim arises out of Carter's use of baby oil in NAIR and its advertising campaign regarding that inclusion.　In 1977, Carter added baby oil to its NAIR lotion and initiated a successful advertising campaign emphasizing this fact.　NAIR is sold in a pink plastic bottle with the word "NAIR" written in large, pink letters.　A bright turquoise-blue banner, open at both ends, contains the words "with baby oil."　In addition to its packaging of NAIR, Carter's television advertisements emphasize that NAIR contains baby oil.[2]

2. The court has viewed samples of Carter's television advertisements.　Carter's commercials all featured several young women dancing and singing while dressed in clothing that revealed their legs.　A typical audio portion of these commercials is as follows:

"Who's got Baby Oil?

Nair's got Baby Oil.

If you're a baby goil, Nair with Baby Oil.

Nair with Baby Oil.

It takes off the hair * * * so your legs feel baby smooth.

And Nair's baby-soft scent * * * smells terrific, baby.

Alleging (1) that Carter is making false claims for NAIR with baby oil and (2) that it is packaging and advertising NAIR so as to give consumers the false impression that NAIR is a Johnson & Johnson product, plaintiff filed the instant suit for injunctive relief under § 43(a) of the Lanham Act, 15 U.S.C. § 1125(a), and under New York's common law of unfair competition. Section 43(a) of the Lanham Act provides for two separate causes of action: one is for "false designation of origin," the other for a "false description or representation, including words or symbols tending falsely to describe or represent" the product. Johnson's false representation claim alleges that Carter's "NAIR with baby oil" campaign falsely represents to consumers that the baby oil in NAIR has moisturizing and softening effect on the skin of the user. While recognizing that Carter's advertising makes no explicit claims for its product, Johnson alleges that this claim is implicit in the manner in which NAIR has been marketed. It contends that these false claims have unfairly dissuaded consumers from using its products in favor of NAIR with baby oil.

*   *   *

At the close of plaintiff's case, the trial court granted defendant's motion to dismiss the action. Plaintiff appeals from the dismissal of its false advertising claim under § 43(a). The propriety of the dismissal of its false designation of origin claim is not raised on appeal.

In dismissing Johnson's false advertising claim, the trial court did not reach either the question of whether Carter advertises or implies in its advertising that baby oil as an ingredient in NAIR has a moisturizing and softening effect, or the issue of whether such a claim is false. Instead, its dismissal was "granted on the ground that [Johnson] failed to carry its burden of proving damage or the likelihood of damage." Just what that burden is and what evidence will satisfy it, are the central issues in this appeal.

DISCUSSION

Prior to the enactment of § 43(a) of the Lanham Act, false advertising claims were governed by the common law of trade disparagement. Under the common law, liability was generally confined to "palming-off" cases where the deceit related to the origin of the product. Ely-Norris Safe Co. v. Mosler Safe Co., 7 F.2d 603 (2d Cir.1925), revd. on other grounds, 273 U.S. 132 (1926); 2 McCarthy, Trademarks and Unfair Competition, § 27:1 at 242 (1973). In these cases the offending product was foisted upon an unwary consumer by deceiving him into the belief that he was buying the plaintiff's product (normally an item with a reputation for quality). Other instances of false advertising were safe from actions by competitors due to the difficulty of satisfying the requirement of proof of actual damage caused by the false claims. In an open market it is normally impossible to prove that a customer,

Who's got Baby Oil?   Soft-smelling Nair with Baby Oil.
Nair's got Baby Oil.   Nair, for baby-smooth legs."

who was induced by the defendant through the use of false claims to purchase the product, would have bought from the plaintiff if the defendant had been truthful.

The passage of § 43(a) represented a departure from the common law action for trade disparagement and from the need to prove actual damages as a prerequisite for injunctive relief. This departure marked the creation of a "new statutory tort" intended to secure a market-place free from deceitful marketing practices. L'Aiglon Apparel v. Lana Lobell, Inc., 214 F.2d 649, 651 (3d Cir.1954); Bose Corp. v. Linear Design Labs, Inc., 467 F.2d 304, 311 (2d Cir.1972). The new tort, as subsequently interpreted by the courts, differs from the common law action for trade disparagement in two important respects: (1) it does not require proof of intent to deceive, and (2) it entitles a broad range of commercial parties to relief. See, Alfred Dunhill Ltd. v. Interstate Cigar Co., Inc., 499 F.2d 232, 236 (2d Cir.1974); L'Aiglon Apparel, supra, 214 F.2d at 651.

The broadening of the scope of liability results from a provision in § 43(a) allowing suit to be brought "by any person who believes that he is or is likely to be damaged by the use of any false description or representation." 15 U.S.C. § 1125(a). Whether this clause is viewed as a matter of standing to sue, see, Potato Chip Institute v. General Mills, 333 F.Supp. 173, 179 (D.Neb.1971), affd., 461 F.2d 1088 (8th Cir.1972), or as an element of the substantive claim for relief, certain bounds are well established. On the one hand, despite the use of the word "believes," something more than a plaintiff's mere subjective belief that he is injured or likely to be damaged is required before he will be entitled even to injunctive relief. See, Chromium Industries v. Mirror Polishing & Plating, 448 F.Supp. 544, 554 (N.D.Ill.1978); D.M. Antique Import Corp. v. Royal Saxe Corp., 311 F.Supp. 1261, 1269 n. 6 (S.D.N.Y. 1970). On the other hand, as the district court in this case recognized, a plaintiff seeking an injunction, as opposed to money damages, need not quantify the losses actually borne. What showing of damage in between those two extremes will satisfy the statute is the subject of the instant dispute.

Johnson claims, in effect, that once it is shown that the plaintiff's and the defendant's products compete in a relevant market and that the defendant's ads are false, a likelihood of damage sufficient to satisfy the statute should be *presumed* and an injunction should issue "as a matter of course." The district court, in contrast, drew the line as follows: "Of course, J&J [Johnson] need not quantify its injury in order to obtain injunctive relief. But J&J must at least prove the existence of some injury caused by Carter." The court had said that "J&J has failed to prove that its loss of sales was in any way *caused* by NAIR's allegedly false advertising."

Both the case law and the policy behind § 43(a) indicate that the district court's construction of the statute placed too high a burden on the plaintiff in this case. To require a plaintiff to "prove the existence of some injury caused by" the defendant, is to demand proof of actual loss and specific evidence of causation. Perhaps a competitor in an open market could meet this standard with proof short of quantified sales loss, but it is not required to do so. The statute demands only proof providing a reasonable basis for the belief that the plaintiff is likely to be damaged as a result of the false advertising. The correct standard is whether it is *likely* that Carter's advertising has caused or will cause a loss of Johnson sales, not whether Johnson has come forward with specific evidence that Carter's ads actually resulted in some definite loss of sales. * * * Contrary to Johnson's argument, however, the likelihood of injury and causation will not be presumed, but must be demonstrated. If such a showing is made, the plaintiff will have established a reasonable belief that he is likely to be damaged within the meaning of § 43(a) and will be entitled to injunctive relief, as distinguished from damages, which would require more proof. We believe that the evidence offered by Johnson, though not overwhelming, is sufficient to prove a likelihood of damage from loss of sales.

Initially, we find that Johnson has shown that it and Carter are competitors in a relevant market. Although Johnson's Baby Oil and Lotion do not compete with NAIR in the narrower depilatory market, they do compete in the broader hair removal market. NAIR is used for hair removal by depilation. Johnson's Baby Lotion has been promoted as a substitute for shaving cream and is used for removal of hair by shaving. Also, both of Johnson's products are used as skin moisturizers after shaving or after the use of depilatories. Such indirect competitors may avail themselves of the protection of § 43(a); the competition need not be direct. Moreover, Carter's advertising campaign itself, by its emphasis on baby oil, directly links the depilation and the moisturizer markets. Johnson's stake in the shaving market gives it a "reasonable interest to be protected against the alleged false advertising." 1 R. Callman, Unfair Competition, Trademarks and Monopolies, § 18.2(b) at 625 (3d ed. 1967).

To prove a likelihood of injury Johnson must also show a logical causal connection between the alleged false advertising and its own sales position. This it has done with specific evidence. It has shown that large numbers of consumers in fact use its baby lotion for shaving and its baby oil as an after-shave and after-depilation moisturizer. Carter's "NAIR with baby oil" campaign affects both markets. First, NAIR's share of the hair removal market has increased since its baby oil advertising began. For each new depilatory user, a corresponding decline in the use of shaving products such as oils and lotions appears probable. Second, the use of baby oil after depilation is likely to be reduced if, as Johnson contends, Carter's advertising conveys to consumers the idea that NAIR's baby oil has a moisturizing and softening effect and leads the consumer to believe that use of a second, post-depilation, moisturizer is unnecessary. Of course, if Carter's ads are truthful, then its gains at Johnson's expense are well earned. If false, however, the damage to Johnson is unfair.

Johnson's case is supported by more than just the above logic. First, sales of its baby oil have in fact declined. Second, a consumer witness testified at trial that she switched from use of baby oil by shaving to NAIR because it was advertised as containing baby oil. Third, Johnson introduced surveys indicating that some people, after viewing NAIR ads, thought they would not have to use baby oil if they used NAIR. Together, Johnson's evidence was enough to prove a likelihood of competitive injury resulting from the NAIR advertising.

That much of the decline in Johnson's Baby Oil sales may be due to competition from lower priced baby oils, does not save Carter. * * * Further, the possibility that the total pecuniary harm to Johnson might be relatively slight does not bar injunctive relief. See Ames Publishing Co., supra, 372 F.Supp. at 13.

Finally, Johnson's inability to point to a definite amount of sales lost *to Carter* (a failure which would bar monetary relief) does not preclude injunctive relief. Likelihood of competitive injury sufficient to warrant a § 43(a) injunction has been found in the absence of proof of actual sales diversion in numerous cases. * * *

Sound policy reasons exist for not requiring proof of actual loss as a prerequisite to § 43(a) injunctive relief. Failure to prove actual damages in an injunction suit, as distinguished from an action for damages, poses no likelihood of a windfall for the plaintiff. The complaining competitor gains no more than that to which it is already entitled—a market free of false advertising.

While proof of actual diversion of sales is not required for a § 43(a) injunction to issue, proof that the advertising complained of is in fact false is essential. This issue, though briefed by parties in this case, is not before the court at this time. The district court did not reach the question for purposes of determining whether permanent relief should issue. Since the action was dismissed at the close of the plaintiff's case, Carter was afforded no opportunity to introduce additional evidence answering the plaintiff on this point. Johnson, having shown that it is likely to be damaged by Carter's advertising, must prove that the NAIR advertising was false before being entitled to injunctive relief under the Lanham Act. Should the district court find that the defendant's advertising conveys a false message, irreparable injury for the purpose of injunctive relief would be present for the very reason that in an open market it is impossible to measure the exact amount of Johnson's damages. * * *

Accordingly, this cause is reversed and remanded for further proceedings in conformity with this opinion. We retain jurisdiction.

COCA COLA v. TROPICANA PRODUCTS
United States Court of Appeals, Second Circuit, 1982.
690 F.2d 312.

[Tropicana showed a television commercial with the renowned American Olympic athlete Bruce Jenner squeezing an orange while saying "It's pure, pasteurized juice as it comes from the orange," and then shows Jenner pouring the fresh-squeezed juice into a Tropicana carton while the audio states "It's the only leading brand not made with concentrate and water." Plaintiff Coca–Cola Company (Coke, Coca–Cola), maker of Minute Maid orange juice, claimed the commercial is false because it incorrectly represents that Premium Pack contains unprocessed, fresh-squeezed juice when in fact the juice is pasteurized (heated to about 200° Fahrenheit) and sometimes frozen prior to packaging.]

Perhaps the most difficult element to demonstrate when seeking an injunction against false advertising is the likelihood that one will suffer irreparable harm if the injunction does not issue. It is virtually impossible to prove that so much of one's sales will be lost or that one's goodwill will be damaged as a direct result of a competitor's advertisement. Too many market variables enter into the advertising-sales equation. Because of these impediments, a Lanham Act plaintiff who can prove actual lost sales may obtain an injunction even if most of his sales decline is attributable to factors other than a competitor's false advertising. Johnson & Johnson v. Carter–Wallace, Inc., 631 F.2d 186, 191 (2d Cir.1980). In fact, he need not even point to an actual loss or diversion of sales. Id. at 190–91. The Lanham Act plaintiff must, however, offer something more than a mere subjective belief that he is likely to be injured as a result of the false advertising, id. at 189; he must submit proof which provides a reasonable basis for that belief, Vidal Sassoon, Inc. v. Bristol–Myers Co., 661 F.2d 272, 278 (2d Cir.1981). The likelihood of injury and causation will not be presumed, but must be demonstrated in some manner. Johnson & Johnson, 631 F.2d at 190. Two recent decisions of this Court have examined the type of proof necessary to satisfy this requirement. Relying on the fact that the products involved were in head-to-head competition, the Court in both cases directed the issuance of a preliminary injunction under the Lanham Act. Vidal Sassoon, 661 F.2d at 227; Johnson & Johnson, 631 F.2d at 189–91.[2] In both decisions the Court reasoned that sales of the plaintiffs' products would probably be harmed if the competing products' advertising tended to mislead consumers in the manner alleged.[3] Market studies were used as evidence that some consumers were in fact misled by the advertising in issue. Thus, the market studies supplied the causative link between the advertising and the plaintiffs' potential lost sales; and thereby indicated a likelihood of injury.

Applying the same reasoning to the instant case, if consumers are misled by Tropicana's commercial, Coca–Cola probably would suffer

2. In Vidal Sassoon it was assumed that two different shampoos competed for the same market, but in Johnson & Johnson the element of competition had to be proven because the two products, baby oil and a depilatory containing baby oil, were not obviously competing for the same consumer dollars.

3. In Vidal Sassoon consumers were allegedly misled to believe that Body on Tap shampoo was an all-around superior product. In Johnson & Johnson consumers were allegedly misled into thinking that using NAIR depilatory with baby oil would obviate the need for using baby oil alone to moisturize the skin after shaving.

irreparable injury. Tropicana and Coca–Cola are the leading national competitors for the chilled (ready-to-serve) orange juice market. If Tropicana's advertisement misleads consumers into believing that Premium Pack is a more desirable product because it contains only fresh-squeezed, unprocessed juice, then it is likely that Coke will lose a portion of the chilled juice market and thus suffer irreparable injury.

Evidence in the record supports the conclusion that consumers are likely to be misled in this manner. A consumer reaction survey conducted by ASI Market Research, Inc. and a Burke test, measuring recall of the commercial after it was aired on television, were admitted into evidence, though neither one was considered by the district court in reference to irreparable injury. The trial court examined the ASI survey regarding the issue of likelihood of success on the merits, and found that it contained various flaws which made it difficult to determine for certain whether a large number of consumers were misled. We do not disagree with those findings. We note, moreover, that despite these flaws the district court ruled that there were at least a small number of clearly deceived ASI interviewees. Our examination of the Burke test results leads to the same conclusion, i.e., that a not insubstantial number of consumers were clearly misled by the defendant's ad. Together these tests provide sufficient evidence of a risk of irreparable harm because they demonstrate that a significant number of consumers would be likely to be misled. The trial court should have considered these studies on the issue of irreparable injury. If it had, we think that it would surely have concluded, as did this Court in Vidal Sassoon and Johnson & Johnson, that the commercial will mislead consumers and, as a consequence, shift their purchases from plaintiff's product to defendant's. Coke, therefore, demonstrated that it is likely to suffer irreparable injury. * * *

III

Likelihood of Success on the Merits

* * *

Coke is entitled to relief under the Lanham Act if Tropicana has used a false description or representation in its Jenner commercial. When a merchandising statement or representation is literally or explicitly false, the court may grant relief without reference to the advertisement's impact on the buying public. American Home Products Corp. v. Johnson & Johnson, 577 F.2d 160, 165 (2d Cir.1978); American Brands, Inc. v. R.J. Reynolds Tobacco Co., 413 F.Supp. 1352, 1356 (S.D.N.Y.1976). When the challenged advertisement is implicitly rather than explicitly false, its tendency to violate the Lanham Act by misleading, confusing or deceiving should be tested by public reaction. American Home Products, 577 F.2d at 165.

* * * We find, therefore, that the squeezing-pouring sequence in the Jenner commercial is false on its face. The visual component of the ad makes an explicit representation that Premium Pack is produced by

squeezing oranges and pouring the freshly-squeezed juice directly into the carton. This is not a true representation of how the product is prepared. Premium Pack juice is heated and sometimes frozen prior to packaging. Additionally, the simultaneous audio component of the ad states that Premium Pack is "pasteurized juice as it comes from the orange." This statement is blatantly false—pasteurized juice does not come from oranges. Pasteurization entails heating the juice to approximately 200° Fahrenheit to kill certain natural enzymes and microorganisms which cause spoilage. Moreover, even if the addition of the word "pasteurized" somehow made sense and effectively qualified the visual image, Tropicana's commercial nevertheless represented that the juice is only squeezed, heated and packaged when in fact it may actually also be frozen.

* * *

ALPO PETFOODS, INC. v. RALSTON PURINA CO.

United States Court of Appeals, District of Columbia Circuit, 1990.
913 F.2d 958.

CLARENCE THOMAS, CIRCUIT JUDGE:

In this case, Ralston Purina Co. and ALPO Petfoods, Inc. two of the leading dog food producers in the United States, have sued each other under § 43(a) of the Lanham Act alleging false advertising. ALPO asserts that Ralston has violated § 43(a) by claiming that its Puppy Chow products can lessen the severity of canine hip dysplasia (CHD), a crippling joint condition. Ralston, for its part, attacks ALPO's claims that ALPO Puppy Food contains "the formula preferred by responding vets two to one over the leading puppy food."

[The trial court found that Ralston's CHD related claims were false because they lacked sufficient empirical support and that the claims materially increased Ralston's sales at the expense of ALPO and other competitors. The court also found that ALPO had no basis for its veterinarian preference claims. These findings were affirmed with the exception that the Court of Appeals reversed a finding that Ralston's violation was wilful and in bad faith.]

B. Monetary Award in Favor of ALPO

Besides challenging the district court's conclusion that its CHD-related advertising violated section 43(a), Ralston attacks the monetary remedy for that violation: a $10.4 million judgment in favor of ALPO under section 35(a) of the Lanham Act. Ralston concentrates its attack on the court's decision to use Ralston's advertising costs as a measure of monetary relief, a method derived from U-Haul, Int'l, Inc. v. Jartran, Inc., 793 F.2d 1034, 1042 (9th Cir.1986). Ralston argues that the court made an error of law in adopting *U-Haul*, and that the court incorporated clearly erronous findings of fact into its *U-Haul* analysis. Reviewing the court's decision on monetary relief for abuse of discretion we agree that the award against Ralston must be vacated.

The district court's opinion states that Ralston's false advertising caused ALPO financial harm, and describes the $10.4 million award to

ALPO as damages. * * * The two-part analysis supporting the amount of the monetary relief, however, shows that the court actually awarded Ralston's profits to ALPO. In deciding the amount of relief, the district court first adopted the reasoning in *U-Haul*, 793 F.2d at 1042. In that case, the Ninth Circuit affirmed an unprecedented $40 million award to a competitor injured by a section 43(a) violation. * * * The district court here, after using the *U-Haul* approach to calculate Ralston's profits at $10.4 million [assuming that a firm's profits are at least equal to its advertising expenditures], confirmed that figure by comparing it with "the 11 million dollar adjusted net profits Ralston earned from the sales of its Puppy Chow products during the period of its CHD advertising program." *ALPO*, 720 F.Supp. at 215; see id. at 212, 215 ("adjusted net profits" figure equals Ralston's nationwide pre-tax profits, multiplied by ALPO's percentage share of non-Ralston puppy food market).

Leaving aside whether the *U-Haul* standard [9] or the district court's alternative calculation [10] accurately measures the profits that Ralston derived from its false advertising, we hold that this case does not justify an award of profits. Section 35(a) authorizes courts to award to an aggrieved plaintiff both plaintiff's damages and defendant's profits, but, as this court noted in [Foxtrap, Inc. v. Foxtrap, Inc., 671 F.2d 636, at 641 (D.C.Cir.1982)] courts' discretion to award these remedies has limits. Just as "any award based on plaintiff's damages requires some showing of actual loss," id. at 642; an award based on a defendant's profits requires proof that the defendant acted willfully or in bad faith. Proof of this sort is lacking. Ralston's decision to run CHD-related advertising that lacked solid empirical support does not, without more, reflect willfulness or bad faith. * * *

In [Reader's Digest Ass'n v. Conservative Digest, Inc., 821 F.2d 800 (D.C.Cir.1987)] we "left open the possibility that a court could properly award damages to a plaintiff when the defendant has been unjustly enriched." 821 F.2d at 807–08 (citing *Foxtrap*, 671 F.2d at 641 & n. 9). The unjust-enrichment theory, which emerged in trademark cases in which the infringer and the infringed were not competitors, holds that courts should divest an infringer of his profits, regardless of whether

---

9. The Ninth Circuit has already noted the limitations of the *U-Haul* rule. See Harper House, 889 F.2d at 209 n. 8 (justification for *U-Haul* rule weakens in cases that do not involve passing off or direct comparative advertising). Commentators, too, have criticized the decision. See, e.g., Comment, *Money Damages and Corrective Advertising: An Economic Analysis*, 55 U.Chi.L.Rev. 629, 638–42 (1988) (refuting premise that defendants' advertising costs reflect value of plaintiffs' lost reputation and good will); Comment, *Monetary Relief for False Advertising Claims Arising Under Section 43(a) of the Lanham Act*, 34 UCLA L.Rev. 953, 955 n. 6, 973–74 (1987) (large awards under *U-Haul* give firms incentives to attack rivals, particularly new entrants, with false-advertising suits). But cf. Best, *Monetary Damages for False Advertising*, 49 U.Pitt.L.Rev. 1, 18–22 (1987) (praising U-Haul for easing plaintiffs' burden of proving actual damages, but noting that the U-Haul surrogate measure itself can lead to overcompensation). * * *

10. As Ralston points out, the alternative calculation "assumes that (1) all of Ralston's Puppy Chow profits were attributable solely to its advertising and (2) all the profits attributable to advertising were due to the CHD claims." Brief of Appellant at 47 (emphasis deleted).

the infringer's actions have harmed the owner of the infringed trade-mark. Awards of profits are justified under the theory because they deter infringement in general and thereby vindicate consumers' inter-ests. * * * As we state below, however, we doubt the wisdom of an approach to damages that permits courts to award profits for their sheer deterrent effect.

Relying on *W.E. Bassett [Co. v. Revlon, Inc.*, 435 F.2d 656 (2d Cir. 1970)] at 664 and *Monsanto Chemical [Co. v. Perfect Fit Prods. Mfg. Co.*, 349 F.2d 389 (2d Cir. 1965)] at 396, ALPO proposes such an approach. Indeed, at oral argument, counsel for ALPO claimed that because *Foxtrap*, 671 F.2d at 641, cites *W.E. Bassett*, this circuit has "adopted the Bassett theory for [profits awards based solely on] deterrence in an egregious case." *Foxtrap*, however, cites *W.E. Bassett* to suggest that courts can award profits only when they find "a relatively egregious display of bad faith." *Foxtrap*, 671 F.2d at 641. Indeed, this court in *Foxtrap* advised a district court to make an award that would "deter the defendant, yet not be a windfall to plaintiff nor amount to punitive damages." Id. at 642 n. 11 (emphasis added). Based on *Foxtrap*, as well as our concern that deterrence is too weak and too easily invoked a justification for the severe and often cumbersome remedy of a profits award, see Koelemay, *Monetary Relief for Trademark Infringement Under the Lanham Act*, 72 Trademark Rep. 458, 493–94, 536–37 (1982), we hold that deterrence alone cannot justify such an award.

Since this case lacks the elements required to support the court's award of Ralston's profits, we vacate the $10.4 million judgment in favor of ALPO. We do not mean, however, to deny ALPO all monetary relief for Ralston's false advertising. Because the district court has so far focused on awarding Ralston's profits it has not yet decided what actual damages ALPO has proved. On remand, the court should award ALPO its actual damages, bearing in mind the requirement that any amount awarded have support in the record, as well as the following points about the governing law.

In a false-advertising case such as this one, actual damages under section 35(a) can include:—profits lost by the plaintiff on sales actually diverted to the false advertiser;—profits lost by the plaintiff on sales made at prices reduced as a demonstrated result of the false advertis-ing;—the costs of any completed advertising that actually and reasona-bly responds to the defendant's offending ads; [11] and—quantifiable harm to the plaintiff's good will, to the extent that completed corrective advertising has not repaired that harm.[12]

11. See also Best, 49 U.Pitt.L.Rev. at 23 ("For this approach to be effective, the plain-tiff's responsive marketing campaign must be found to have been a reasonable response to the defendant's conduct."); Comment, 55 U.Chi.L.Rev. at 633 ("Although courts should make available the defense that the counter-advertising performed was unreasonable or wasteful, most courts are willing to accept counter-advertising costs as recoverable busi-ness losses.").

12. The thin body of case law on actual damages for successful false-advertising claims reflects the fact that litigants, who best understand their real losses, almost always settle these cases once a court has given its view of the merits. See Com-ment, 55 U.Chi.L.Rev. at 631.

When assessing these actual damages, the district court may take into account the difficulty of proving an exact amount of damages from false advertising, as well as the maxim that " 'the wrongdoer shall bear the risk of the uncertainty which his own wrong has created.' " Otis Clapp & Son v. Filmore Vitamin Co., 754 F.2d 738, 745 (7th Cir.1985). At the same time, the court must ensure that the record adequately supports all items of damages claimed and establishes a causal link between the damages and the defendant's conduct, lest the award become speculative or violate section 35(a)'s prohibition against punishment. * * *

Section 35(a) also authorizes the court to "enter judgment according to the circumstances of the case, for any sum above the amount found as actual damages, not exceeding three times such amount." Lanham Act 35(a). This provision gives the court discretion to enhance damages, as long as the ultimate award qualifies as "compensation and not [as] a penalty." Id.; see Koelemay, 72 Trademark Rep. at 516–19, 521–25 (discussing interplay of damages enhancement provision and antipenalty clause); see also Getty Petroleum Corp. v. Bartco Petroleum Corp., 858 F.2d 103, 112–13 (2d Cir.1988) (in trademark infringement case, interpreting section 35(a) to ban any awards of punitive damages), cert. denied, 109 S.Ct. 1642 (1989). Given this express statutory restriction, if the district court decides to enhance damages under section 35(a), it should explain why the enhanced award is compensatory and not punitive.

C. Denial of Monetary Relief in Favor of Ralston

[The trial court had denied Ralston relief even though it found ALPO's advertising false because "[t]he magnitude of the wrongdoing by Ralston in comparison to that of ALPO is so much greater that a damage award would not be justified," because ALPO, but not Ralston, had shown remorse, and because the court considered Ralston's counterclaim "an afterthought." The Second Circuit held that a denial of damages was not proper on this basis. "Since section 35(a) expressly provides for compensation, rather than punishment, courts dealing with offsetting meritorious claims must let the degree of injury that each party proves, rather than the degree of opprobrium that the court attaches to each party's conduct, determine the monetary relief."

The Second Circuit also reversed the lower court's award of attorneys fees to ALPO because Ralston's behavior was not wilful or in bad faith.].

NOTES

1. *History of § 43(a).* Although § 43(a) became effective in 1947 with passage of the Lanham Act, early decisions narrowed its impact. In California Apparel Creators v. Wieder of California, 162 F.2d 893 (2d Cir.1947) the Second Circuit in dictum suggested and in Chamberlain v. Columbia Pictures Corp., 186 F.2d 923 (9th Cir.1951) the Ninth Circuit specifically held that the *Mosler* doctrine applied to § 43(a) cases. See also Samson Crane Co. v. Union Nat.

Sales, Inc., 87 F.Supp. 218, 222 (D.Mass.1949), affirmed mem. 180 F.2d 896 (1st Cir.1950) (§ 43(a) applies only to activities akin to trademark infringement and does not "bring within its scope any kind of undesirable business practice . . ."). These decisions sparked great disappointment in several commentators. See Callmann, False Advertising as a Competitive Tort, 48 Colum.L.Rev. 876, 885 (1948): "Instead of welcoming the new law and using its language and sweep as a basis for bypassing an unhappy precedent, the court's dictum [in California Apparel] apparently accepts the devitalizing interpretation that the new provision merely codifies the doctrine of Grand Rapids * * *."

The first broad interpretation of § 43(a) came in L'Aiglon Apparel v. Lana Lobell, Inc., 214 F.2d 649 (3d Cir.1954) (defendant advertised its $6.95 dress by using a picture of plaintiff's $17.95 dress). The Third Circuit rejected the claim that § 43(a) was merely declarative of existing law (*Mosler*) and held that the section created a new statutory tort of broad scope. Most courts quickly accepted the Third Circuit's view, and the section became widely used in false advertising, unfair competition and trademark cases. Although a number of issues of interpretation arose in the implementation of the section significant amendments to the section did not occur until the Trademark Revision Act of 1988.

2. *The Trademark Revision Act of 1988—§ 43(a).* Students should make a careful comparison of the old and amended § 43(a).

The amended version applies to four categories of statements: (1) word, name, symbol, or device, or any combination thereof; (2) false designation of origin; (3) false or misleading description of fact; and (4) false or misleading representation of fact. The first category mirrors the definition of "trademark" in § 45 of the Lanham Act. In the trademark context these words are broadly interpreted to include packaging, colors, sounds, etc. that function to identify the origin of goods (the source that produced the goods or provided the services). By incorporating a second category, "false designation of origin" did Congress intend a different meaning to "origin". Under the old section "origin" was interpreted to mean both geographic origin and origin of manufacture. See Federal–Mogul–Bower Bearings, Inc. v. Azoff, 313 F.2d 405 (6th Cir.1963). What does the phrase add to categories (3) and (4)? And what is the difference between a "description" of fact (category (3)) and a "representation" of fact (category (4))?

There are two substantive prohibitions in the amended version. The statement to be actionable must either (1) likely cause confusion as to the relationship between the speaker and another or their goods, or (2) misrepresent the "nature, characteristics, qualities, or geographic origin" of goods or services. Presumably statements in categories (1) and (2) would primarily fit prohibition (1) and statements in categories (3) and (4) would primarily fit prohibition (2). In this view the section appears to provide for causes of action analagous to trademark infringement and separately for actions for false advertising.

The last phrase of the amended version is a standing provision that permits any person who "is or is likely to be damaged" to bring a civil action.

Under the first prohibition, who must likely be confused? Consumers? Potential consumers? Reasonable persons? Competitors? Is there a connection between these persons and the persons authorized to bring suit? The second prohibition requires that the statement "misrepresents" the listed features of the goods or services. Because the second prohibition does not require confusion, mistake, or deception, does it mean Congress intended to prohibit any false statement regardless of whether consumers take it seriously? Does the misrepresentation have to be "material"? Or reasonably relied upon?

Does the amended version attach penalties to innocent misrepresentations?

The original section provided that the goods or services about which the statements were made must be placed in interstate commerce by the person making the statements. The amended version requires that the statements themselves be used "in commerce". Section 45 of the Lanham Act defines "commerce" broadly. What is the consequence of the amendment to § 43(a)? See Burger King of Florida, Inc. v. Brewer, 244 F.Supp. 293 (W.D.Tenn.1965) which held that a "purely intrastate business is in interstate commerce for purposes of § 43(a) of the Lanham Act if it has a substantial economic effect on interstate commerce." Under the amended version, are statements made by the salesclerk of an interstate department store actionable? Is a misrepresentation in a classified advertisement actionable under the amended version if copies of the newspaper are in interstate commerce?

The original section applied to statements regarding goods or services. The amended version uses the phrase "goods, services, or *commercial activities*" in the prohibition phrases but not in the phrase describing the categories of statements? What might be included in "commercial activities"? What is the consequence of omitting the phrase in the first part of the section?

In the amended version the false advertising prohibition, but not the trademark prohibition, is limited to "commercial advertising or promotion". Do either of the prohibitions protect a non-profit association? A charity? A governmental entity? Do they both apply to a classified advertisement by a non-merchant seller?

3. Why should the law prohibit false advertising only if someone is likely to be injured? Don't you agree with the claim by Johnson & Johnson that if it is shown that the two products compete in a relevant market, likelihood of injury should be *presumed*? Does the court convince you that its requirement of a "logical causal connection" differs from a presumption arising from direct competition?

Does the holding in *Coca Cola* that survey proof of deception can supply the causal link do nothing more than require that the plaintiff must prove deception and competition to satisfy the § 43(a) requirements?

4. Both versions of § 43(a) authorize a "civil action". Under the original version there was a question about what remedies applied. The 1988 amendments to the Lanham Act make it clear that the remedies provided in § 34(a) (injunctions), § 35(a) (profits which may be a sum the court determines to be "just", damages including the possibility of treble damages, costs, and in "exceptional cases" reasonable attorneys fees), and § 36 (destruction of infringing articles) apply to § 43(a) violations. The more onerous penalties in § 34(d) and § 35(b) are reserved for registered marks.

5. Can the monetary remedies fashioned for trademark infringement be easily applied to a false advertising case? How can we be certain in *Alpo Petfoods* that Ralston's gains came at the expense of Alpo or that any loss of sales Alpo may be able to show was caused by Ralston's advertising? In the *U-Haul* decision, referred to in *Alpo*, the advertisement at issue was comparative and the court found that a substantial segment of the consuming public understood the defendant's advertisements referred to the plaintiff and that after defendant entered the market with the false statements, the plaintiff's

revenues declined. But in *Alpo,* Ralston's statements are made about its own product. Does it matter whether the amount sought by the plaintiff represents its own proven damages or the defendant's profits? In *Alpo,* the court, after observing that profits are awarded in trademark cases where there is a purposeful attempt to trade on the good-will of the trademark owner, held that in broader false advertising cases " 'willfulness' and 'bad faith' require a connection between a defendant's awareness of its competitors and its actions at those competitors' expense." Do you see why something like this is required? If *A* makes an intentionally false statement about its own goods, how many of *A's* competitors could recover its profits?

6. The scope of § 43(a) and the patience of a federal judge were both tested in Rare Earth, Inc. v. Hoorelbeke, Inc., 401 F.Supp. 26 (S.D.N.Y.1975). The case involved an incorporated rock group who performed under the trademark "Rare Earth." When the group split into two factions, a controversy arose over which group had the controlling shares in the corporation and thus the right to perform as the "Rare Earth." The action was brought in federal court under § 43(a) to prevent deception and palming off by unauthorized use or interference with the "Rare Earth" mark, but the resolution of the controversy depended almost exclusively on the validity of the title to corporate shares asserted by the competing members and this in turn depended on construction of the Michigan Business Corporation Act and Article 8 of the Michigan Uniform Commercial Code. The court recognized federal subject jurisdiction under the Lanham Act

> despite gnawing reservations. * * * However, in this age of congested court calendars—"a time when our dockets are burgeoning with matters peculiar to federal courts"—litigants who seek to advance primarily state law claims are well advised to proceed in the state courts and, thereby, permit other litigants, who have no other forum available to them, an opportunity to advance exclusively federal controversies before federal courts. The present, somewhat discursive endeavor is well concluded with the following words of the modern poet and popular singer Bob Dylan:
>
> > * * * goodbye's too good a word, gal
> > So I'll just say fare thee well
> > I ain't sayin' you treated me unkind
> > You could have done better but I don't mind
> > You just kinda wasted my precious time
> > But don't think twice, it's all right.

AMERICAN HOME PRODUCTS CORP. v. JOHNSON & JOHNSON

United States Court of Appeals, Second Circuit, 1978.
577 F.2d 160.

OAKES, CIRCUIT JUDGE.

Comparative advertising in which the competing product is explicitly named is a relatively new weapon in the Madison Avenue arsenal. These cross-appeals by two of the leading manufacturers of analgesics—pain relief tablets—raise questions regarding the permissible boundaries of this novel approach to consumer persuasion.

* * *

I. THE FACTS

AHP's product, Anacin, is a compound of aspirin (ASA), its analgesic component, and caffeine. McNeil's product, Tylenol, affords analgesia through the ingredient acetaminophen (APAP). Anacin advertises more heavily than the other leading aspirin brands. It took over the Number One pain reliever spot from another aspirin-based product, Bayer Aspirin, a few years ago. Since the summer of 1976, however, Tylenol has replaced Anacin as the largest selling over-the-counter (OTC) internal analgesic product. Anacin remains the largest selling aspirin-based analgesic.

The lawsuit arose out of two Anacin advertisements initiated shortly after Tylenol became market leader. The first is a thirty-second television commercial initially aired by CBS in late November, 1976, and by NBC in early December, 1976. It commences with the phrase: "Your body knows the difference between these pain relievers * * * and Adult Strength Anacin," and asserts its superiority to Datril, Tylenol and Extra-Strength Tylenol.[3] The second advertisement was introduced in national magazines in late January, 1977. It carries a similar theme, stating that "Anacin can reduce inflammation that comes with most pain," "Tylenol cannot."

The controversy began when McNeil protested the television commercial to the networks and the magazine advertisement to the print media on the ground that they were deceptive and misleading. McNeil also complained to the National Advertising Division of the Better Business Bureau. These protests were, for the most part, unsuccessful. CBS, NBC and the print media continued to carry the two advertisements without alteration. As a result of the protests, AHP filed a declaratory judgment action under 28 U.S.C. § 2201 and sought to enjoin McNeil from interfering with the dissemination of the commercial and the printed advertisement. McNeil counterclaimed under Section 43(a) of the Lanham Act, 15 U.S.C. § 1125(a), urging that the following claims contained in AHP's advertisements were false: (A) that Anacin is a superior analgesic to Tylenol, (B) that Anacin is an efficacious anti-inflammatory drug for the conditions listed in the advertisements, (C) that Anacin provides faster relief than Tylenol, and (D) that Anacin does not harm the stomach. It sought declaratory relief and an injunction prohibiting AHP from continuing to make false claims which disparaged Tylenol.

3. The "story board" of the television commercial is printed in Judge Stewart's opinion below, 436 F.Supp. 785, 788 (S.D. N.Y.1977). The script for the commercial reads as follows:

SPOKESMAN: Your body knows the difference between these pain relievers [showing other products] and Adult Strength Anacin. For pain other than headache Anacin reduces the inflamma-

tion that often comes with pain. These do not. (SFX: MUTED KETTLE DRUM.) Specifically, inflammation of tooth extraction[,] muscle strain (SFX BUILDS)[,] backache (SFX BUILDS)[,] or if your doctor diagnoses tendonitis[,] neuritis. (SFX FADES.) Anacin reduces that inflammation (SFX OUT) as Anacin relieves pain fast. These do not. Take Adult Strength Anacin.

After denying McNeil's motion for a preliminary injunction, Judge Stewart held an expedited trial on the merits. Principally on the basis of consumer reaction surveys, he concluded that the advertisements made the following representations: (1) the television commercial represented that "Anacin is a superior analgesic generally, and not only with reference to particular conditions such as those enumerated in the ad * * * or to Anacin's alleged ability to reduce inflammation," Id. at 796, (Claim One); (2) the print advertisement claimed that "Anacin is a superior analgesic for certain kinds of pain because Anacin can reduce inflammation," Id. (Claim Two); and (3) both advertisements represented that Anacin reduces inflammation associated with the conditions specified in the advertisements. Id. (Claim Three).[9] The district court then concluded that the preponderance of the evidence indicated that Claims One and Two—that Anacin is a superior analgesic in general to Tylenol and a superior analgesic for conditions which have an inflammatory component—were false. Id. at 801–03. The court further held that it could not be determined on the basis of the evidence presented whether OTC dosages of Anacin reduce inflammation to a clinically significant extent in the conditions specified by the advertisements. Thus, Judge Stewart could not reach a definitive conclusion on the truth or falsity of the third claim. Id. at 801, 803. Nevertheless, he determined that because the three claims are "integral and inseparable," Id. at 803, "the advertisements as a whole make false representations for Anacin and falsely disparages [sic] Tylenol in violation of the Lanham Act." Id. at 803. Accordingly, he held that McNeil was entitled to an injunction against AHP, given the "substantial evidence that consumers have been and will continue to be deceived as to the relative efficacy of the two products and that this deception is injuring, and will continue to injure, Tylenol's reputation among consumers." Id. The injunction prohibits AHP from publishing or inducing television, radio or print media to publish any advertisement or promotional material which contains, in the context of a representation as to any anti-inflammatory property of Anacin or aspirin sold by AHP, any representation that at over-the-counter levels Anacin or aspirin provides superior analgesia to acetaminophen including Tylenol either (1) generally, or (2) for conditions which are associated with inflammation or have inflammatory components, or (3) because Anacin or aspirin reduces inflammation * * *.

II. THE PRINCIPAL APPEAL

A. *Whether Relief May be Afforded under Section 43(a) on the Basis of the District Court's Findings*

AHP's first contention is based on the following premises. The advertisements contain no express claim for greater analgesia; they

---

9. The judge also held that the advertising does not represent that Anacin provides faster analgesic action or that Anacin is harmless to the stomach, again on the basis of consumer reaction. American Home Prods. Corp. v. Johnson & Johnson, 436 F.Supp. 785, 796 (S.D.N.Y.1977). See Part III infra. Accordingly, no findings on the truth or falsity of these alleged representations were made.

merely assert Anacin's superiority to Tylenol in reducing inflammation, a claim which the district court found not to be false. AHP further assumes that the anti-inflammatory claim was held to be true and is in fact unambiguous. The argument is that a truthful and unambiguous product claim cannot be barred under Section 43(a) even though consumers mistakenly perceive a different and incorrect meaning. Thus, appellants urge, the court erred in finding a violation of Section 43(a) by not relying on express claims of superior pain relief, but by interpreting consumer reaction tests—one of which, incidentally, was introduced by AHP and the other of which was not objected to by AHP—as indicating that consumers derive a message of greater pain relief from the explicit "truthful" claim.

Whatever abstract validity AHP's argument may have, an issue we need not decide, it is clear that in this case the language of the advertisements is not unambiguous. The "truthfulness" of the claims, therefore, cannot be established until the ambiguity is resolved. Moreover, Judge Stewart expressly refused to characterize the anti-inflammatory claims as truthful.[10] But even assuming the literal truthfulness of the anti-inflammatory claims, appellant's position is no stronger because of the ambiguity of the total message which, as the district court found, conveys additional claims (Claims One and Two).

That Section 43(a) of the Lanham Act encompasses more than literal falsehoods cannot be questioned. * * * Were it otherwise, clever use of innuendo, indirect intimations, and ambiguous suggestions could shield the advertisement from scrutiny precisely when protection against such sophisticated deception is most needed. It is equally well established that the truth or falsity of the advertisement usually should be tested by the reactions of the public. * * *

Applying these principles to the facts of this case, we are convinced that the district court's use of consumer response data was proper. We believe that the claims of both the television commercial and the print advertisement are ambiguous. This obscurity is produced by several references to "pain" and body sensation accompanying the assertions that Anacin reduces inflammation.[12] A reader of or listener to these

---

10. The flaw in appellant's logic is its conclusion of truthfulness from the district court's candid recognition that it could not determine whether the anti-inflammatory claim was true or false.

12. The television commercial initially states that "[y]our body knows the difference between these pain relievers * * * and Adult Strength Anacin," thereby suggesting that the individual is going to *feel* the difference in pain reduction from use of Anacin. The reference to superior analgesic properties without mention of inflammation is quite apparent. The commercial then goes on to say that "[f]or pain other than headache, Anacin reduces the inflammation that often comes with pain," while

the competition does not. This statement is ambiguous because it does not state that "for *conditions* other than headache, Anacin reduces inflammation." It says "for *pain* other than headache," implying that by reducing the inflammation that often comes with pain, the pain is itself reduced. Again, after listing specific ostensibly inflammatory conditions, the television commercial states that "Anacin reduces that inflammation as Anacin relieves pain * * * fast," while the competition does not. Meanwhile, pulsating spots of inflammation of a male body are eliminated as Anacin works by "reliev[ing] pain." Quite clearly the television commercial is purposely ambiguous. Quite

advertisements could reasonably infer that Anacin is superior to Tylenol in reducing pain generally (Claim One) and in reducing certain kinds of pain (Claim Two). Given this rather obvious ambiguity, Judge Stewart was warranted in examining, and may have been compelled to examine consumer data to determine first the messages conveyed in order to determine ultimately the truth or falsity of the messages.

* * *

* * * Contrary to appellant's contentions, Judge Stewart did not use Section 43(a) to prohibit truthful representations mistakenly construed by consumers. * * * We have here deliberate ambiguity and unsubstantiated anti-inflammatory claims determined by the district court to be understood by the public as proclaiming superior analgesic results. Given the audience reaction to the advertisements, as found by the district court, the statute's proscription of "words or other symbols tending falsely to describe or represent [the goods]" was violated.

B. *Whether the Findings Are Supported by the Evidence*

1. *The findings that the advertising makes claims of greater pain relief generally and for specific conditions.*

AHP argues that even if Judge Stewart was correct in evaluating consumer perceptions, he arrived at the conclusion that the advertisements claim greater pain relief (Claims One and Two) by misinterpreting the consumer reaction data and erroneously affording no weight to the testimony of market research experts concerning the messages conveyed by the advertising. Initially, we note that the district court did take into account the expert testimony offered by both sides on the meaning of the advertisements. Recognizing that in some circumstances such testimony should be given substantial weight, Judge Stewart refrained from doing so here largely because it was neither reliable nor helpful to an understanding of the test data which it purported to interpret. The testimony, however, was used to corroborate the surveys.

The test data itself has some inherent weaknesses.[15] However, it was in the district court's province as trier of fact to weigh the evidence, and in particular the opinion research. * * *

clearly a claim for superior analgesic effect is intended.

15. Questions of reliability are raised because the two television commercial tests upon which the district court relief focused, to a considerable extent, on audience recall rather than on immediate impressions. Delayed recall measures consumer interest and advertising persuasiveness as well as message content. The Gallup and Robinson, Inc. (G & R) test was conducted approximately 24 hours after the commercial was aired by the use of telephone interviews with persons who claimed to have watched the program accompanying the commercial. The ASI Market Research, Inc. (ASI) testing was performed at special screenings for a specially selected audience. The viewers were questioned about their reactions both during and one hour after the screening. Some of the people tested by both surveys either had bad memories or paid little attention to the television commercial, resulting in inaccurate descriptions, not only of the claims made but even of the products discussed. But such inaccuracies, we suppose, are to be expected in advertising research.

The analysis of its test data by ASI Market Research, Inc. (ASI) which was made for and at the request of AHP and was heavily relied on by Judge Stewart, completely supports his finding that the television commercial made a superiority claim which was not limited to pain associated with inflammation. * * * Translated from survey jargon, the ASI survey concludes that the "Your Body Knows" television commercial produced a recollection in the selected audience of 250 members that Anacin is a superior pain reliever generally, even though the advertisement may have been phrased in terms of comparing inflammation relief.

AHP's advertising executives may, indeed, have intended to communicate that Anacin is better for relieving pain. They noted that 74% of the specifically selected audience thought of the commercial in terms of pain relief, while none thought of inflammation as such unless attention was directed specifically to inflammation. Nevertheless, they pointed out that because the references to inflammation triggered pain association, it was not necessary that inflammation relief be recalled.

What the ASI test shows, then, is the powerful "subliminal" influence of modern advertisements. See generally M. McLuhan & Q. Fiore, The Medium Is the Massage (1967). The survey reveals that the word "inflammation" triggers pain association, and pain association is what both advertisements are all about. The district court properly relied on these conclusions in finding that the commercial claimed general analgesic superiority.

Judge Stewart placed less reliance on the Gallup & Robinson, Inc. (G&R) statistical analysis of the television commercial, largely because the breakdown of responses did not differentiate anti-inflammation messages from general pain relief messages. * * *

We conclude, therefore, that the judge correctly held, principally on the basis of consumer reaction tests, that both advertisements claim greater pain relief. * * *

2. *The findings of falsity and inconclusiveness.*

* * *

We conclude that Judge Stewart's determination that ASA and APAP are equipotent as pain relievers for inflammatory conditions is not clearly erroneous. It was based on his careful consideration of medical studies, medical literature and expert testimony. The studies, which we have also examined, reveal that with one exception—in the case of rheumatoid arthritis [19]—there is little to indicate that in OTC

---

19. Two of many studies on rheumatoid arthritis found ASA superior to APAP in pain reduction. With regard to the 1974 test, which found ASA slightly more effective than APAP in reducing pain from rheumatoid arthritis, it repeatedly points out the lack of statistical significance of the subjects' responses. * * *

Judge Stewart found the second study, nearly 20 years old, to be methodologically unsound in comparison to the numerous other scientific reports introduced. Additionally, the study does not seem very helpful in resolving the issues below because it measured pain relief by noting differences in grip strength and joint stiffness. We have difficulty, therefore, understanding

dosages ASA is more effective in reducing pain from inflammatory conditions than APAP.[21]

The district court recognized that the medical experts' testimony as well as the scientifically unsupported opinions of certain members of the medical community were more conflicting. Judge Stewart was unwilling to give much weight to AHP's experts, who hypothesized that Anacin reduces pain associated with inflammation better than Tylenol, because much of this evidence admittedly consisted of mere speculation. In sum, Judge Stewart found most of the studies on the comparative analgesic effectiveness of ASA and APAP more reliable and convincing. Given the conflicting testimony of each party's experts and the sound scientific basis underlying the studies, we cannot say that Judge Stewart erred in his evaluation and weighing of the evidence.

We also conclude that on the basis of the evidence introduced at trial, the judge was justified in holding that he could not determine whether Anacin, at OTC dosages, reduces inflammation in the conditions listed in the advertisements. We think it unnecessary to detail the conflicting evidence presented on each of the conditions. For determining the validity of the district court's holding of lack of substantiation, it is sufficient to note that for each condition mentioned in the advertisements there was credible evidence suggesting that Anacin does not reduce inflammation.

There was testimony that aspirin is not used to control *inflammation* following tooth extraction because of its well-documented propensity to increase post-operative hemorrhaging. With respect to neuritis, perhaps an out-moded term, there was evidence that all but two neuropathies are noninflammatory in nature, and that the only two which are inherently inflammatory—leprosy and shingles—are not treated by aspirin. The evidence regarding sinusitis revealed that while aspirin can make the patient more comfortable by reducing fever and relieving headache and muscle ache, it has no effect whatsoever on the underlying sinus infection. There was evidence that aspirin is not used for reduction of inflammation from sprains and strains; indeed it can be counterproductive by prolonging and increasing hemorrhaging at the site of the injury. There was basic disagreement on whether tendonitis, to be distinguished from tenosynovitis, is a degenerative or an inherently inflammatory disease. Thus, it could not be determined

whether and when its conclusions are directed to pain relief (relevant to Claim Two) or to inflammation relief (relevant to Claim Three).

21. AHP heavily relies on one statement from a report of the Advisory Review Panel on OTC Internal Analgesic and Antirheumatic Products [hereinafter IAP Report], appointed by the Food and Drug Administration, which states:

The Panel concludes that acetaminophen is effective in relieving the pain of headache, and that it is a general analgesic of proven efficacy as shown by clinical testing. Thus, acetaminophen is considered to be equivalent to aspirin in its analgesic effects, although the lack of anti-inflammatory action *might* make it less useful in conditions having an inflammatory component.

42 Fed.Reg. No. 131, Book 2, at 35413 (1977) (emphasis added). We do not disagree with Judge Stewart's characterization of the inference to be drawn from the last clause in this statement as "reputable * * * speculations." 436 F.Supp. at 803.

whether aspirin at OTC dosages provides any therapeutic effect on tendonitis other than pain relief. Backaches have so many different causes, so many of which are not inherently inflammatory in origin, that the advertising simply cannot be accepted as true.

Moreover, Judge Stewart painstakingly considered the evidence most favorable to appellant's position—studies on aspirin's effectiveness in reducing inflammation from rheumatoid arthritis. However, he concluded that these studies did not sufficiently resolve the question whether at OTC levels Anacin reduces inflammation in the specified conditions, particularly in light of the conflicting medical literature and expert testimony on the subject.

Our discussion of the evidence relied on by the district court is an overall review of the thousands of pages of transcripts and documentary evidence. Nevertheless, we are confident that Judge Stewart's findings, based on his thorough review of the evidence, are not "clearly erroneous."

G. *Whether the Injunction is Sufficiently Specific.*

AHP argues that the injunctive order does not comply with Fed.R. Civ.P. 65(d) which requires specificity in terms and description in reasonable detail of the acts sought to be restrained. In particular, appellant asserts that the injunction as framed effectively bars AHP from discussing Anacin's anti-inflammatory benefits in a comparative advertisement because such claims may also contain an implicit representation of superior analgesia. Apparently, AHP objects to the fact that the injunction is not limited to express claims for superior analgesia.

We think the district court did a commendable job of drafting an order which specifies, as clearly as possible under the circumstances, the acts to be enjoined. Representations as to any anti-inflammatory properties of Anacin are enjoined only to the extent that they contain or imply three clearly described claims of analgesic superiority at OTC levels. In our view, Rule 65(d) is satisfied. More explicit language, if this is possible, will not diminish AHP's asserted difficulty in determining whether proposed advertising conveys a message of superior pain relief. We note, moreover, that the district court has retained jurisdiction to enable the parties "to apply to this court at any time for such other orders and directions as may be necessary or appropriate for the modification, construction or carrying out of [the] judgment." American Home Products Corp. v. Johnson & Johnson, supra, No. 77 Civ. 1363, at 2. If AHP encounters difficulties under the decree, it can apply to the court for guidance at such time.

NOTES ON DISPARAGEMENT UNDER § 43(a)

1. The original version of § 43(a) was interpreted not to permit a cause of action for disparagement. Bernard Food Industries v. Dietene Co., 415 F.2d 1279 (7th Cir.1969). At the same time false comparative advertisements which *both* disparaged the plaintiff's goods and made explicit claims about the

defendant's goods were actionable. Skil Corp. v. Rockwell International Corp., 375 F.Supp. 777 (N.D.Ill.1974). Is not any claim made by a producer about a competitor's goods an implicit claim about the producer's goods?

2. The 1988 amendment to § 43(a) clearly provides a cause of action for disparagement. Subparagraph (a)(2) applies to misrepresentations by a person relating to "his or her or *another person's* goods. . . ." However, the provision applies only where the statement is made "in commercial advertising or promotion". Is a salesclerk's disparagement of a competitor's product included? Could the section be applied to *Systems Operations?* Does the section apply to disparaging statements made by consumers? Does it apply to an unflattering review of a product in a magazine like Consumers Reports?

3. How much of a common law disparagement action is carried over into § 43(a)? Must the plaintiff show special damages? Is injunctive relief available? Who is "likely to be damaged" by a disparagement? Would a statement about the personal integrity of a competitor be actionable under the amended § 43(a)?

4. Are the remedial provisions in §§ 34–36 of the Lanham Act appropriate for a disparagement claim? Should an accounting for profits be awarded for disparagement?

NOTES ON DECEPTION UNDER § 43(a)

1. Can you formulate the test for deception under § 43(a) from *Coca Cola* and *American Home?* How does "puffing" fit into the formula? Do you see any danger in testing whether an advertisement is deceptive by the listener's reaction rather than the speaker's intent? Is it constitutional? Who had the burden of proof in the cases? See Cook, Perkiss and Liehe, Inc. v. Northern California Collection Service Inc., 911 F.2d 242 (9th Cir.1990) where a law firm specializing in collections brought suit under § 43(a) against a commercial debt collection service's advertisement that it could do any collection work an attorney could do at less cost. The court affirmed the magistrate's grant of a motion to dismiss. "The common theme that seems to run through cases considering puffery in a variety of contexts is that consumer reliance will be induced by specific rather that general assertions. * * * Here, the alleged misrepresentations in NCC's advertisement are merely general in nature. * * * The advertisement does not contain the kind of detailed or specific factual assertions that are necessary to state a false advertising cause of action under the Act."

2. If the advertised claim is literally true or there is an asserted interpretation that is true, do you see problems with measuring the deception by what the consumer perceives the claim is? Does this require surveys of consumers to determine the message communicated by the advertisement? What result if 51% of those surveyed interpret the claim to say what is in fact true but the other 49% interpret the claim to make a statement that is in fact false?

3. What about claims in advertisements that "consumers prefer brand "X" over brand "Y"?

The application of § 43(a) to claims of misrepresentations arising from consumer preference tests raises difficult questions for the courts. In Vidal Sassoon, Inc. v. Bristol–Myers Co., 661 F.2d 272 (2d Cir.1981) the challenge was to the reports and methodology of the tests that purported to show that consumers preferred defendant's shampoo. The court found § 43(a) applicable in that the advertisements were "used in connection with" goods and that the misrepresentations went to an "inherent quality or characteristic" of the shampoo:

> In a case like this, where many of the qualities of a product (such as "body") are not susceptible to objective measurement, it is difficult to see how the manufacturer can advertise its product's "quality" more effectively than through the dissemination of the results of consumer preference studies. In such instances, the medium of the consumer test truly becomes the message of inherent superiority. We do not hold that every misrepresentation concerning consumer test results or methodoloy can result in liability pursuant to § 43(a). But where depictions of consumer test results or methodoloy are so significantly misleading that the reasonably intelligent consumer would be deceived about the product's inherent quality or characteristics, an action under § 43(a) may lie.

On the other hand in The Proctor & Gamble Co. v. Chesebrough–Pond's Inc., 588 F.Supp. 1082 (S.D.N.Y.1984), affirmed 747 F.2d 114 (2d Cir.1984), Judge Goettel refused to establish standards for the validity of consumer testing under § 43(a). The parties used different testing methodologies in arriving at their inconsistent conclusions that their respective hand lotion was the most effective. After finding seven days of expert testimony "incomprehensible", the court refused to enjoin either advertisement:

> Here, we are confronted with somewhat inconsistent product claims based on tests that were conducted in apparent good faith but with somewhat differing results. The difference in the results, in turn, was partially caused by the different test protocols that the parties chose. As a consequence, neither of the parties has successfully proven that the other has chosen tests and conducted them in such a manner as to mislead the public. Courts are not always able to determine whether an advertising claim is true or false . . . and where this occurs, the only possible conclusion is that the moving party has failed to prove by a preponderance of the evidence that the advertising claim is false.

4. Are you comfortable with the role accepted by the court in *American Home* in relation to advertising? In footnote 27 of its opinion (omitted above) the court noted that "we do not have the same expertise as the Federal Trade Commission when it interprets the language of an advertisement to determine whether an advertisement is an unfair or deceptive practice * * *. Accordingly, we, as judges, must rely more heavily on the reactions of consumers, as found by the finder of fact."

5. For an expansive consideration of the cases and literature attempting to define "deception" see Craswell, Interpreting Deceptive Advertising, 65 B.U. Law.Rev. 657 (1985) (advocating a cost-benefit injury-minimizing approach).

NOTES ON COMPARATIVE ADVERTISING

1. The *Johnson & Johnson* case was an early forerunner to a series of cases brought under § 43(a) challenging comparative advertising in the over-the-counter (OTC) analgesic industry. These cases seem to have tested the patience of several judges: American Home Products Corp. v. Johnson & Johnson, 654 F.Supp. 568 (S.D.N.Y.1987) (Advil I) ("Small nations have fought for their very survival with less resources and resourcefulness than these

antagonists have brought to their epic struggle for commercial primacy in the OTC analgesic field."); American Home Products Corp. v. Johnson & Johnson, 671 F.Supp. 316 (S.D.N.Y.1987) (Advil II); American Home Products Corp. v. Johnson & Johnson, 672 F.Supp. 135 (S.D.N.Y.1987); McNeilab, Inc. v. American Home Products Corp., 848 F.2d 34 (2d Cir.1988) ("[this controversy] has brought anything but relief to the federal courts. Instead, repeated and protracted litigation has created a substantial headache. The competitive battlefield has shifted from the shelves of supermarkets and drugstores to the courtroom."). The fascinating history of the competition and litigation in this industry and the customary use of what Mark Twain called "stretchers"— "stories which, while not being untrue, do not tell the whole truth" is described in Mann & Plummer "The Big Headache", Atlantic Monthly, October 1988, pg. 39.

In "Advil I" the competition between aspirin and acetaminophen was complicated by the advent of ibuprofen, a new pain killer that works like aspirin but is said to cause less gastrointestinal irritation. At issue were multiple claims in advertisements by Johnson & Johnson attempting to link ibuprofen ("Advil") to aspirin in its side effects and to claim a superiority for Tylenol. The claims, for the most part, were literally true but capable of creating false impressions. The court described its fact finding process as follows:

> The trial lasted four weeks, and involved the in-court testimony of 22 witnesses, many of them world-renowned physicians and medical researchers specializing in pharmacology, nephrology, hepatology, gastroenterology, hematology, epidemiology, and more particularly in the systemic effects of analgesics. The testimony of 37 additional witnesses was presented by deposition.

> Many hundreds of exhibits, filling eight file drawers, were received in evidence, most of them copies of technical articles, couched in the arcane language of medical science, packed with numerical data and embellished with graphs and tables. * * *

> Almost a thousand pages of post-trial briefs and proposed findings were filed. But before the reply briefs had even been received by the Court, the attorneys for one of the parties sent a letter to the Court urging a prompt decision because the opposing party had recently resumed the broadcasting of certain challenged television commercials which it had voluntarily suspended in order to obtain a continuance of the trial.

In the end, the court issued an injunction prohibiting continuation or resumption of advertising practices by both parties based on its evaluation of the scientific evidence and its relation to its interpretation of the advertisements.

Are these issues the kind that judges should resolve? Can consumers police this type of deception? Is a governmental agency in a better position to develop the complex factual background necessary to measure the relative safety and effectiveness of non-prescription drugs?

2. Must a comparative advertisement fully disclose all relevant comparisons between the two products even if some are not as favorable as others or may the advertiser pick the comparison that sets off his product best? In "Advil I", *supra* note 1, the defendant advertised a checklist of side effects comparing those associated with the plaintiff's product and those associated only with its own product. It omitted some side effects associated only with its

own product. Is this a violation of § 43(a)? The court held it was. See also American Home Products Corp. v. Johnson & Johnson, 672 F.Supp. 135 (S.D. N.Y.1987) where Johnson & Johnson counterclaimed for damages under § 43(a) on the basis that AHP failed to warn consumers of the risk of Reyes Syndrome associated with its aspirin based "Anacin" even though AHP fully complied with labeling requirements imposed by the Food and Drug Administration. The court found compliance with FDA requirements a defense to any § 43(a) action.

3. It has been suggested that truthful disparagement in comparative advertisements should also be prohibited. Wolff, Unfair Competition by Truthful Disparagement, 47 Yale L.J. 1304 (1938) (reporting that French and German law prohibit the use of the competitor's name in advertising). Would an analysis based on *INS* reach that result? Could you argue that use of your competitor's name constitutes a trademark infringement? These questions will be considered in Chapter III.

4. If you were looking for the best value in laundry detergent, which of the following advertisements would be most helpful? (1) SAFE detergent is the cheapest detergent on the market. (2) SAFE detergent gives more washings per box than any other detergent. (3) SAFE detergent gives 5 more washings per box than SANE detergent. (4) Sarah Anne, otherwise unidentified, prefers SAFE detergent. (5) Independent tests by a consumer organization confirm SAFE detergent is the best value in laundry detergent. If all of the above advertisements were in advertising paid for by the manufacturer of SAFE detergent, on which would you most readily rely?

5. Is there an economic disincentive to engage in comparative advertising? Assume the case of two competing producers of disposable razors. If Producer *A* extolls the benefits of his disposable razor demonstrating its ease of operation and low cost he stands the chance of attracting new sales from customers of Producer *B* and from those persons using electric or nondisposable razors. If Producer *B* retaliates with an affirmative campaign showing only the good qualities of the razor he produces he may retain his customers, get new customers formerly buying *A* 's razor, and he may also convince some electric or nondisposable razor users to try his razor. The result may be that *A* and *B* will be sharing a larger market for disposable razors than before and may both be better off. On the other hand, if *A* initiates a campaign attacking the safety characteristics and shaving ability of *B* 's razor in comparison to his own, he may succeed in causing some of *B* 's customers to switch to nondisposable razors, and if *B* retaliates with an attack on *A* 's product, both *A* and *B* may end up with the same relative shares of a smaller market. If we now assume a five producer market in which *A* is the leading producer, *B* may decide not to expend funds to attack *A* 's razor for he may not capture all of the customers convinced by his attack. Those who cease buying from *A* may now begin buying from *C, D,* or *E.* *B* is, however, more likely to capture a higher percentage of the returns from advertising if he exclusively extolls the benefits of his own product.

Of course comparative advertising may have a mixture of self-adulation and competitor disparagement in various intensities, and this may enhance or reduce the force of the analysis.

Does the analysis lead you to any particular policy position regarding the legal rules that ought to govern comparative advertising? Does the analysis support the French and German rule against comparative advertising? In answering the last question consider for a moment what the situation would look like from Producer *A* 's perspective if in contemplating an attack on a rival's goods he knew for certain that the rival would not retaliate. Then consider in what circumstances the likelihood of retaliation would be reduced.

See Robin & Barnaby, Comparative Advertising: A Skeptical View, 67 Trademark Rptr. 358 (1977) describing the campaign of Bristol–Myers for its new nonaspirin pain reliever "Datril" against the industry leader "Tylenol." After stages in which "Datril" was advertised as cheaper than Tylenol, faster acting, and easier on the stomach, it is reported that "Datril" had acquired a share of the market but Tylenol had increased its share as well, apparently at the expense of the brands not involved in the advertising. See also Levine, Commercials that Name Competing Brands, 16 J.Adv.Research 7 (Dec. 1976) reporting the results of a study conducted by an advertising agency suggesting that comparative advertisements were more confusing, less informative, and less persuasive than noncomparative advertisements.

For the view that the economic analysis supports a legal rule that some firms should be required to engage in comparative advertising see Schabel, Conscious Parallelism and Advertising Themes: The Case for "Comparative" Advertising, 7 Antitrust L. & Econ. 11 (1975).

6. Policies of advertising media and self-regulation by business groups inhibit comparative advertisements. Until 1972 CBS and ABC television and radio networks limited comparison advertising to the "Brand X" type. A change in network policy resulted from informal negotiations with the Federal Trade Commission which felt that the old policies encouraged meaningless generalized comparisons and prevented relevant information from reaching consumers. Wall Street Journal, March 21, 1972, at 9, col. 2. In 1976 the Commission authorized a staff study to determine if industry self-regulating codes limit comparative advertising and if so, to what effect. 3 CCH Trade Reg. Rep. 10,173.

7. For a thorough analysis of the law regulating comparative advertising see Note, The Law of Comparative Advertising: How Much Worse is "Better" than "Great," 76 Colum.L.Rev. 80 (1976). See also Thomson, Problems of Proof in False Comparative Product Advertising: How Gullible is the Consumer?, 72 Trademark Rep. 385 (1982); a symposium on comparative advertising beginning at 67 Trademark Rep. 351 (1977).

U.S. HEALTHCARE, INC., v. BLUE CROSS OF GREATER PHILADELPHIA

United States Court of Appeals, Third Circuit, 1990.
898 F.2d 914.

SCIRICA, CIRCUIT JUDGE.

[U.S. Healthcare operates a Health Maintenance Organization and Blue Cross/Blue Shield, in order to compete, began offering a preferred provider organization program entitled "Personal Choice". The respective programs differ as to their operation but are designed to deliver health care while permitting some control by the insurer over costs. Both parties engaged in aggressive comparative advertising campaigns attacking features of the other's program. Among the more provocative claims, Blue Cross asserted that HMO doctors have a financial incentive not to refer patients to needed specialists while U.S. Healthcare claimed that many Personal Choice doctors did not have admitting privileges at area hospitals. Suit initially was brought by U.S. Healthcare claiming defamation, commercial disparagement, and unfair competition under § 43(a) of the Lanham Act. Blue Cross filed similar counterclaims. After initially deadlocking on all claims, the jury finally returned a verdict against Blue Cross on its counterclaims. The trial court scheduled a new trial on U.S. Healthcare's claims.]

The case was never retried. Instead, Blue Cross/Blue Shield filed a motion under Fed.R.Civ.P. 50(b) requesting the court to direct entry of judgment in its favor, on the grounds that the advertisements were entitled to heightened constitutional protection under the First Amendment, and that U.S. Healthcare had not met the applicable standard of proof, set forth in New York Times Co. v. Sullivan, 376 U.S. 254 (1964), et seq. The district court granted the motion. The court held that because the objects of the advertisements are "public figures," and because the matters in the advertisements are "community health issues of public concern," heightened constitutional protections attach to this speech. The court reasoned that the First Amendment limited the power of the state and of Congress to award damages resulting from the allegedly false and misleading advertisements. Accordingly, the district court held that in order to prevail on their respective claims of Lanham Act violation, commercial disparagement, defamation and tortious interference with contract, both parties were required to prove each claim by clear and convincing evidence: (1) that the other side published the advertisements with knowledge or with reckless disregard of their falsity, and (2) that the advertisements were false. Applying this standard of proof, the court concluded that "[a]lthough the jury could reasonably have concluded that both sides had proven falsity and actual malice by a preponderance of the evidence, neither side has presented clear and convincing evidence [of this]."

This appeal followed.

[The court reviewed the substantive elements of the various legal claims and concluded that aspects of the advertisements appeared actionable under § 43(a), defamation, and commercial disparagement. It then examined applicability of the First Amendment holding first that the advertisements fit clearly within the category of "commercial speech" because they were disseminated as part of a promotional campaign, they tout one specific product over another, they were motivated by the desire for revenue, and they are not the type of speech that is likely to be chilled by the threat of legal liability.]

At the outset, we note that it is of no consequence that the defendants (and counterclaim defendants) here are not members of the broadcast and print media. * * * In addition, we do not limit our consideration of the applicability of the *New York Times* standard to the parties' claims for defamation alone. The Supreme Court has already applied a similar analysis to other torts[.]

* * *

Therefore, while the speech here is protected by the First Amendment, we hold that the First Amendment requires no higher standard of liability than that mandated by the substantive law for each claim. The heightened protection of the actual malice standard is not "necessary to give adequate 'breathing space' to the freedoms protected by the First Amendment." Hustler Magazine, Inc. v. Falwell, 485 U.S. 46, 56, (1988).

Having concluded that the speech here is commercial speech that does not warrant heightened constitutional protection, we nonetheless proceed to consideration of the nature and weight of the state's interest in compensating individuals for injuries resulting from each of the distinct torts alleged. We have previously discussed the state and federal interests implicated. As we shall see in this case, however, traditional defamation analysis is not well suited to strike the proper balance between the state and federal interests and First Amendment values in the context of commercial speech.

In weighing the state interest, we must look to the status of the claimants. See [Gertz v. Robert Welch, Inc., 418 U.S. 323, at 342–45 (1974).] As we have noted, the Court has determined that the state has only a "limited" interest in compensating public persons for injury to reputation but has a "strong and legitimate" interest in compensating private persons for the same injury. See *Gertz*, 418 U.S. at 343 & 348–49. Contending that the actual malice standard applies because a public figure is implicated, Blue Cross/Blue Shield argues that the following factors render U.S. Healthcare a "public figure": it has voluntarily exposed itself to public comment on the issues involved in this dispute; it is a contributor to the ongoing debate concerning health care insurance; it is among the nation's largest providers of HMO-type insurance coverage; it markets its products extensively and aggressively, and has a substantial annual advertising budget; and it frequently and consistently asserts the advantages of its method of health care financing and delivery, and has done so in advertisements, press releases, professional journals, newspapers, magazines and speeches before public assemblies. These activites, Blue Cross/Blue Shield submits, "constitute a voluntary effort to influence the consuming public." Similar statements can be made regarding Blue Cross/Blue Shield.

* * *

Under traditional defamation analysis, the parties' considerable access to the media and their voluntary entry into a controversy are strong indicia that they are limited purpose public figures. Indeed, inflexible application of these factors would warrant a finding of public figure status and facilitate a finding of heightened constitutional protection. Nonetheless, we hold that these corporations are not public figures for the limited purpose of commenting on health care in this case.

As noted, *Gertz* defines the limited purpose public figure as one who has "thrust [himself] to the forefront of particular public controversies in order to influence the resolution of the issues involved." 418 U.S. at 345. Although some of the advertisements touch on matters of public concern, their central thrust is commercial. Thus, the parties have acted primarily to generate revenue by influencing customers, not to resolve "the issues involved."

While discerning motivations of the speaker is often difficult, we have a more fundamental reason for declining to find limited purpose public figure status in this case. The express analysis in *Gertz* is not helpful in the context of a comparative advertising war. Most products can be linked to a public issue. See *Central Hudson* [Gas & Elec. Corp. v. Public Serv. Comm'n, 447 U.S. 557 (1980)] at 563 n. 5. And most advertisers—including both claimants here—seek out the media. Thus, it will always be true that such advertisers have voluntarily placed themselves in the public eye. It will be equally true that such advertisers have access to the media. Therefore, under the *Gertz* rationale, speech of public concern that implicates corporate advertisers—i.e., typical comparative advertising—will always be insulated behind the actual malice standard. We believe a corporation must do more than the claimants have done here to become a limited purpose public figure under *Gertz*.

In summary, we conclude that the speech at issue does not receive heightened protection under the First Amendment. Because this speech is chill-resistant, the *New York Times* standard is not, as we have noted, "necessary to give adequate 'breathing space' to the freedoms protected by the First Amendment." Hustler Magazine, Inc. v. Falwell, 485 U.S. 46, 56 (1988). Therefore, the standard of proof needed to establish the substantive claims is that applicable under federal and state law.

For these reasons, we hold that the district court erred in applying the *New York Times* standard to the claims in this case and in directing entry of judgment under Fed.R.Civ.P. 50(b). Accordingly, we will reverse the judgment of the district court and remand for proceedings consistent with this opinion.

SECTION 44 OF THE LANHAM ACT

Section 44 of the Lanham Act is primarily designed to implement international conventions relating to trademarks and unfair competition. However, at least in the Ninth Circuit it was thought, for a time, to be applicable to suits between two American citizens as well. The language on its face seems to support this view. Subsection (b) provides foreign nationals the protection of the Lanham Act to the extent necessary to give effect to any international convention or treaty to which the United States and their home country are signatories. If a person qualifies under (b), subsection (h) gives them protection against unfair competition by making the remedies of the Lanham Act applicable on their behalf. Subsection (i) then gives United States citizens the same benefits granted to persons under (b). Subsection (i) does not appear to require that a foreign national be involved. Thus if an American citizen sued another American citizen for unfair competition, subsections (b), (h), and (i) together seem to suggest that the section would apply.

The Circuits split on the question. Stauffer v. Exley, 184 F.2d 962 (9th Cir.1950) was the first decision to apply § 44 to a suit between two American citizens. The controversy involved use in interstate commerce of the unregistered trade name "Stauffer System" by a California resident and use of the name "Stauffer" by another California resident in its business. The cause of action was for unfair competition; diversity of citizenship was not present nor was their a specific claim under federal statutory law because the tradename was unregistered.

The court in *Stauffer* held § 44 was applicable as long as the infringing use was "in commerce" reading subsections (b), (h), and (i) as making the section available to suits between American citizens.

The leading case rejecting this interpretation was L'Aiglon Apparel v. Lana Lobell, Inc., 214 F.2d 649 (3d Cir.1954). The Third Circuit relied heavily on the legislative history of the Lanham Act to conclude that the section was applicable only when a foreign national was involved. In this view, § 44 was designed solely to "implement international agreements that were not self-executing" and thus provided no rights other than those arising out of these agreements.

The Second, Fifth, and Seventh Circuits have rejected the *Stauffer* interpretation of § 44. American Auto Ass'n v. Spiegel, 205 F.2d 771 (2d Cir.1953); Royal Lace Paper Works, Inc. v. Pest-Guard Products, Inc., 240 F.2d 814 (5th Cir.1957); City Messenger of Hollywood v. City Bonded Messenger Serv., 254 F.2d 531 (7th Cir.1958). The Sixth Circuit recognized the difference in the circuits but did not decide the issue in Lyon v. Quality Courts United, Inc., 249 F.2d 790 (6th Cir.1957). The Court of Customs and Patent Appeals (a predecessor of the Federal Circuit) recognized a federal cause of action under § 44 in dictum in In re Lyndale Farm, 186 F.2d 723 (C.C.P.A.1951).

The Eighth Circuit first adopted *Stauffer* and then on rehearing rejected the decision in Iowa Farmers Union v. Farmers' Educational & Co-op Union, 247 F.2d 809 (8th Cir.1957). The Ninth Circuit limited *Stauffer* in International Order of Job's Daughters v. Lindeburg & Co., 633 F.2d 912, 915 n. 5 (9th Cir.1980) to apply to only two causes of actions: false designations of origin and infringement of registered marks. Since section 43(a) also applies to these claims, the court recognized that *Stauffer* has been "rendered * * * nugatory in suits between United States citizens." Toho Co. Ltd. v. Sears, Roebuck & Co., 645 F.2d 788 (9th Cir.1981).

NOTES

1. Resolution of the split in authority over the interpretation of § 44 of the Lanham Act does not exhaust the issue of the potential applicability of the

provisions of international conventions to purely domestic lawsuits involving unfair competitive practices. The international conventions may apply even in lawsuits between two American citizens, in an American court, involving questions unrelated to foreign commerce. The major multilateral treaty protecting industrial property and also prohibiting unfair competition including false and deceptive practices is the Convention of Paris for the Protection of Industrial Property. The United States ratified the original document in 1883, 25 Stat. 1372 (1883), and has ratified each subsequent amendment. Of particular importance here is Article 10 *bis*. The article contains in addition to a specific provision against most forms of false advertising a general prohibition against acts "contrary to honest practices".

Article VI of the United States Constitution reads in part as follows: "This Constitution, and the Laws of the United States which shall be made in Pursuance thereof; and all Treaties made, or which shall be made, under the Authority of the United States, shall be the Supreme Law of the Land; and the Judges in every State shall be bound thereby, any Thing in the Constitution or Laws of any State to the Contrary notwithstanding * * * "

Whether a private party may assert the provisions of the Convention depends on whether the Convention is "self-executing". If the provisions are self-executing, they do not depend on implementing legislation by Congress in order to be effective between private parties. The provisions become part of the domestic law of the United States through operation of the Supremacy Clause. According to American Law, a treaty is self-executing if its language indicates that the drafters intended it to be self-executing. Restatement of Foreign Relations Law, Second, § 141 (1965). The final determination rests with the courts, Id. § 154. If the convention is part of the domestic law, the federal district courts would have subject matter jurisdiction over actions thereunder. 28 U.S.C.A. § 1331. Diversity of citizenship would be unnecessary. It should be noted that a federal statute enacted after ratification of an international convention and inconsistent with the convention's provisions supersedes the convention as domestic law if Congress intended such a result. Restatement of Foreign Relations Law, Second, § 145 (1965).

The Supreme Court has suggested without a direct holding that the Convention of Paris is not self-executing. Cameron Septic Tank Co. v. City of Knoxville, 227 U.S. 39 (1913). On the other hand more recently the Court assumed that the General Inter-American Convention for Trade Mark and Commercial Protection, an agreement similar in content and scope to the Paris Convention, was self-executing. Bacardi Corp. v. Domenech, 311 U.S. 150 (1940). In early cases the First Circuit and Third Circuit split on the nature of the Paris Convention. United Shoe Mach. Co. v. Duplessis Shoe Mach. Co., 155 Fed. 842 (1st Cir.1907) (not self-executing); Hennebique Const. Co. v. Myers, 172 Fed. 869 (3d Cir.1909) (self-executing although not necessary for decision). More contemporary courts likewise disagree. Master, Wardens, etc. v. Cribben & Sexton Co., 202 F.2d 779 (C.C.P.A.1953) ("That treaty [Paris Convention] is part of our law and no special legislation in the United States was necessary to make it effective here. [citing Bacardi Corp. v. Domenech]. However, terms of the treaty applicable to the situation in the case at bar were embodied in [§ 44 of the Lanham Act.]"); Vanity Fair Mills v. The T. Eaton Co., 234 F.2d 633 (2d Cir.1956), cert. denied 352 U.S. 871 (1957) (holding that the plaintiff "would appear to be correct" in arguing the convention is self-executing); Ortman v. Stanray Corp., 371 F.2d 154 (7th Cir.1967) (not self-executing). None of the cases cited herein dealt with the problem of unfair competition but concerned rather foreign patent and trademark problems. Likewise none of the cases involved a purely domestic controversy between two American citizens.

2. In Toho Co. Ltd. v. Sears, Roebuck & Co., 645 F.2d 788 (9th Cir.1981) the court held that in a suit involving a foreign national, § 44 applies to the extent necessary to give effect to any treaty between the United States and the country of the foreign national. In *Toho* the relevant treaty provided that Japanese nationals would be given "most favored nation" treatment. The court held this required that Japanese nationals be given the same rights as domestic corporations and thus applied state unfair competition law to the § 44 claim.

3. If § 44 applies only where a foreign national is a party to the action, whether as plaintiff or defendant, consider the result where an American citizen engages in business conduct which is prohibited by a convention but not by American domestic law. The conduct results in damage to two competitors, one of whom is an American citizen and one of whom is a foreign national. Could Congress have intended to grant the foreign competitor greater rights than the American competitor? How would you apply § 44 to a class action where one member of the class is a foreign national?

(5) TESTING AGENCIES

In contrast to the preceding cases on misleading practices which generally involved statements made by the plaintiff's competitors, we consider here the liability for product evaluations or comparisons made by persons or agencies outside the competitive relationship. The basic question posed is whether the latter should be governed by different rules. If so, should testing agencies be granted wider latitude in comparing or evaluating various competing products? Or should we hold such comparisons to a stricter standard of truthfulness? The answers to these questions should force further analysis of the underpinnings to the rules governing remarks made in a competitive situation.

In determining what rules should apply to a testing agency one of the problems will be the extent to which the testing agency is independent. What problems are posed by disparaging statements made by: (1) Consumers Union which has no connection with any product; (2) a magazine publisher which certifies as "good quality" consumer products which are advertised in its magazine; (3) a celebrity who is paid to endorse a product; (4) a product testing company which is hired by a producer to test the producer's product and competing products; (5) a governmental agency which inspects and tests products to assure minimum levels of purity and quality prior to distribution to the public-at-large; and (6) a government agency which tests various products in order to assure that the agency itself is obtaining the highest quality product.

(A) PRIVATE TESTING AGENCIES

BOSE CORPORATION v. CONSUMERS UNION OF UNITED STATES, INC.

United States Court of Appeals, First Circuit, 1982.
692 F.2d 189.

[The Bose Corporation sued the publisher of Consumer Reports, a monthly consumer magazine, for product disparagement arising out of an article evaluating various stereo speakers including those of the plaintiff and containing the following paragraph:

But after listening to a number of recordings, it became clear that the panelists could pinpoint the location of various instruments much more easily with a standard speaker than with the Bose system. Worse, individual instruments heard through the Bose system seemed to grow to gigantic proportions and tended to wander about the room. For instance, a violin appeared to be 10 feet wide and a piano stretched from wall to wall. With orchestral music, such effects seemed inconsequential. But we think they might become annoying when listening to soloists. On an impulse, we also played some monophonic records through the Bose. To our surprise, they too acquired the same spacial openness and size distortions as the stereo records.

The district court found one statement false and disparaging and published with reckless disregard of its falsity and in a subsequent trial assessed damages of $115,296 plus interests and costs of $95,609.64. CU appeals both on liability and damages.]

The court determined that under the applicable law of product disparagement, it was the plaintiff's burden to prove that the statements made by CU were of a disparaging or defamatory nature and that the statements were false. After concluding that "the Article, when read as a whole is disparaging," the court proceeded to analyze in detail each alleged factual error in the article to determine if it was false and if it was disparaging.   *   *   *

The district court's finding of liability was based on part of one sentence in the article which reads: "Worse, individual instruments heard through the Bose system seemed to grow to gigantic proportions and tended to wander about the room." The court, in its analysis, divided the sentence into two parts. It found that the description "seemed to grow to gigantic proportions" had not been proven false but found the statement that the instruments "tended to wander about the room" was both false and disparaging. The evidence on which this finding was based is summarized as follows. CU's two employees who conducted the listening test "testified that the wandering sounds they heard were confined to an area within a few feet of the wall near which the Bose 901 loudspeakers were placed." CU conceded that the words "about the room" might not have described the wandering with precise accuracy, but argued that the *wandering* of sound was important to consumers, not *where* it wandered. CU maintained that the statement was substantially true because it accurately described the important observation. The district court referred to testimony that an amount of movement is expected with all stereo speakers and concluded that the location of the sounds' movement was as important to a consumer as the fact of movement. Thus, the court found the statement not to be substantially true. After rejecting CU's argument that the statements in the article about "a violin appear[ing] to be 10 feet wide and a piano stretch[ing] from wall to wall" modified the statements about wandering sounds to imply that the wandering occurred along the wall between the speakers, the court stated that the ordinary meaning of "about" the room was "around" the room. The court found the statement to be disparaging: "A statement that attributes such grotesque qualities as instruments wandering about the room to the plaintiff's product could have no effect other than to harm the reputation of the product." The use of the word "worse" to introduce the statement in the article showed that CU intended it to have a harmful effect.

Having determined that Bose had proved by a preponderance of the evidence that the statement about individual instruments tending to wander about the room was false and disparaging, the district court proceeded to analyze the impact of the first amendment on the standard of care required of CU. It cited several lower court decisions and discussed the first amendment balance between the need for an uninhibited press and the legitimate state interest in compensating victims of defamation in concluding that the actual malice standard of New York Times v. Sullivan, 376 U.S. 254, (1964), applies to product disparagement cases. It then applied the analysis of Bruno & Stillman, Inc. v. Globe Newspaper Co., 633 F.2d 583 (1st Cir.1980), to conclude that "Bose is a public figure, at least with respect to the limited issues of the characteristics and quality of the Bose," and was required to show by clear and convincing proof that CU's false statement was published with knowledge that it was false or with reckless disregard of its truth of falsity. CU's project engineer, Arnold Seligson, conducted the listening test and wrote the words upon which the statements in the article were based. Due in part to his demeanor at trial, the court found that Seligson's testimony as to what the words "about the room" meant was not credible. Seligson maintained that he perceived that the wandering sounds were confined to an area near the wall behind the loudspeakers. The court found that Seligson was too intelligent to not be aware of the ordinary meaning of "about" and thus concluded that Seligson knew at the time of publication that the article did not accurately describe the effects he had perceived during the test. In the court's view, this was clear and convincing proof that CU "published a false statement of material fact with the knowledge that it was false or with reckless disregard of its truth or falsity."

Our Review

As the parties acknowledge, the first amendment permeates our review. The question of the truth or falsity of the statement that individual instruments tended to wander about the room is intertwined with the question of whether that statement is one of opinion or fact; both questions are difficult to answer. CU argues that if the statement is considered in its full context it becomes clear that the statement is merely the opinion of the panelists who conducted the listening test. This full context includes the tentative language that "instruments * * * *seemed* to grow" and "*tended* to wander," that "[w]ith orchestral music, such effects *seemed* inconsequential [although] we *think they might* become annoying when listening to soloists," and finally that "the Bose system is so unusual that a prospective buyer must listen to it and judge for himself." CU cites numerous cases to support the proposition that a reviewer's published description of what he or she observed in a public performance, book, or restaurant is protected by the first amendment. Also, the Supreme Court has stated that "[u]nder the First Amendment there is no such thing as a false idea. However pernicious an opinion may seem, we depend for its correction not on the conscience of judges and juries but on the competition of other ideas." Gertz v. Robert Welch, Inc., 418 U.S. 323, 339–40 (1974) (dictum) (footnote omitted). This statement of the Court implies that an opinion can be neither true nor false as a matter of constitutional law. The proposition that an opinion can be neither true nor false also is reasonable as a matter of common sense. The determination of whether a statement is one of opinion or fact, however, is difficult to make and perhaps unreliable as a basis for decision. Although CU's argument that the statement is an opinion is plausible, the seeming scientific nature of the article—indicated by quantitative ratings, a description in the beginning of the article of the laboratory testing performed, and the use of such terms as "panelists" and "engineers" to describe the CU employees who performed the tests—would support the position that the statements are factual. See Hotchner v. Castillo-Puche, 551 F.2d 910, 913 (2nd Cir.), cert. denied sub nom. Hotchner v. Doubleday, 434 U.S. 834, (1977) (An expression of an opinion may become as damaging as an assertion of fact, and liability for libel thus attach, if the writer indicates that "he has private, firsthand knowledge which substantiates the opinions he expresses * * *."). Similarly, and stemming at least in part from the uncertain nature of the statement as one of fact or opinion, it is difficult to determine with confidence whether it is true or false. As the district court noted, at trial the CU panelists, Seligson and Lefkow, "testified that the wandering sounds that they heard were confined to an area within a few feet of the wall near which the Bose 901 loudspeakers were placed." Given the subjective nature of a listener's perceptions and the imprecise language employed in the CU article, we are not sure that the statement that instruments tended to wander about the room is false.

Due to our ultimate conclusion that Bose has failed to meet its burden of proof with respect to actual malice, however, we will assume that the statement was both factual and false and not explore further the intricacies of these concepts. Before analyzing actual malice, we should first briefly note our agreement with the district court that the statement in question disparaged Bose 901 speakers. CU concedes that the statement told readers that the "movement of individual instruments is more pronounced and localization therefore more difficult with the Bose than with conventional speakers." The tenor of the paragraph that contained the statement was clearly that of criticism; this is highlighted by the use of the word "worse" to introduce the statement. There can be little question that the statement was disparaging.

At oral argument Bose acknowledged that it does not dispute the finding of the district court that the corporation is a public figure with respect to the subject matter of the CU article. Bose also conceded that the rule of *New York Times v. Sullivan* applies in this case, and thus accepted the district court's conclusion that the actual malice standard applies to product disparagement cases. As we have indicated earlier, the district court analyzed both of these issues at length and we accept its conclusions for the purposes of this case.

We focus, therefore, on the district court's holding that Bose proved by clear and convincing evidence that CU published the words "individual instruments * * * tended to wander about the room" with knowledge that they were false or with reckless disregard of their truth or falsity. In performing this review we are not limited to the clearly erroneous standard of Fed.R.Civ.P. 52(a); instead, we must perform a de novo review, independently examining the record to ensure that the district court has applied properly the governing constitutional law and that the plaintiff has indeed satisfied its burden of proof.

* * *

[The court reviewed the proof of actual malice required of a plaintiff under *New York Times v. Sullivan* and its progeny noting that actual malice requires a showing that the defendant had serious doubts as to the truth of the publication which must be shown by "clear and convincing proof".]

* * *

It is helpful to compare the research and editing procedures followed by CU in publishing its article on loudspeakers with publishers' procedures that have been examined in other cases. One court, in finding that the plaintiff—a public figure—had failed to show actual malice, reviewed CU's work in publishing a series of articles in 1978 attacking the claims of certain organizations and individuals that fluoridization causes, among other things, cancer and birth defects. Yiamouyiannis v. Consumers Union of the United States, Inc., 619 F.2d 932. It stated:

It is clear that appellee, through its agents, made a thorough investigation of the facts. Scientific writings and authorities in the field were consulted; authoritative scientific bodies speaking for substantial segments of the medical and scientific community were investigated. The unquestioned methodology of the preparation of the article exemplifies the very highest order of responsible journalism: the entire article was checked and rechecked across a spectrum of knowledge and, where necessary, changes were made in the interests of accuracy.

Id. at 940. Although we would refrain from describing CU's loudspeaker article as exemplifying the very highest order of responsible journalism, CU does not have to meet such high standards to prevail. In addition, these two CU projects are distinguishable. In the fluoridization article there existed an abundance of scientific research and writing which CU merely cited in drawing its conclusions. In the instant case, CU had the much more difficult task of performing the original research.

It is important to point out that in conducting the listening test CU used experts, Seligson and Lefkow, who brought their expertise and experience to bear in evaluating the Bose speakers. In Reliance Insurance Co. v. Barron's, 442 F.Supp. 1341 (S.D.N.Y.1977), the court noted the expertise of the author and granted a motion for summary judgment because there was no triable issue of fact that the article was published with actual malice. Id. at 1350–51. The Second Circuit found lack of expertise to be evidence of malice in Goldwater v. Ginzburg, 414 F.2d 324 (2d Cir.1969). The court affirmed a jury finding of actual malice in an article stating that Senator Goldwater suffered from the mental disease of paranoia. The court noted that this conclusion "was reached only upon his [the author's] own non-expert evaluation of Senator Goldwater's life and political career." Id. at 331.

Some evidence of actual malice may be found "if there is a complete departure from the standards of investigation and reporting ordinarily adhered to by responsible publishers." Reliance Insurance, 442 F.Supp. at 1341. CU's editorial procedures reveal no evidence of actual malice. As in *Reliance Insurance,* the testimony in this case indicated that normal editorial procedures were followed; there was no evidence of CU knowingly departing from these procedures in order to publish the article regardless of its truth or falsity. After testing the loudspeakers, Seligson prepared a rough draft of the manuscript, commonly referred to as a "report to editorial," which was reviewed by an associate technical director. The Editorial Department then reviewed this report and drafted the manuscript for publication. Among other editorial alterations, the Department changed Seligson's words that instruments "suffered [from] a tendency to wander around the room" to the statement ultimately published that instruments "tended to wander about the room." This manuscript was sent back to Seligson for "line by line checking" and then forwarded to the associate technical director for his review. It was then returned to the Editorial Department. These same procedures were applied to galley proofs, second galley proofs, page proofs, and second page proofs. The associate technical director testified that when he performed his reviews the words "tended to wander about the room" conjured up "the mental image * * * of the sound moving about in front of the listener." He also testified that when he approved the article for publication he never really pondered the meaning of the word "about" in the statement. The most we can conclude from this is that in reviewing the manuscript CU employees could have inquired more painstakingly into the precise language being used.

Even though we accord relatively little weight to CU's claims of good faith and lack of any motivation to disparage the Bose 901, we are unable to find clear and convincing evidence that CU published the statement that individual instruments tended to wander about the room with knowledge that it was false or with reckless disregard of whether it was false or not. The evidence presented merely shows that the words in the article may not have described precisely what the two panelists heard during the listening test. CU was guilty of using imprecise language in the article—perhaps resulting from an attempt to produce a readable article for its mass audience. Certainly this does not support an inference of actual malice. * * * To find actual malice in this case would be to interpret that concept to require little more than proof of falsity, an interpretation that Justice Goldberg expressed fears about in his concurrence in New York Times v. Sullivan, 376 U.S. at 298 n. 2 (Goldberg, J., concurring).

Due to our holding on the issue of liability, there is no need for us to review the district court's findings on damages.

Reversed.

Levin H. Campbell, Circuit Judge (concurring).

In joining as I do in the court's opinion, I wish merely to emphasize my understanding that this court is in no way passing upon the actual merits of the district court's finding that Bose Corporation was a public figure.

BOSE CORPORATION v. CONSUMERS UNION OF UNITED STATES, INC.

Supreme Court of the United States, 1984.
466 U.S. 485, 104 S.Ct. 1949, 80 L.Ed.2d 502.

[The United States Supreme Court granted certiorari to consider solely the question whether the Court of Appeals properly rejected the "clearly erroneous" standard of review of Rule 52(a) for the lower court's finding of actual malice. The Court held that Rule 52(a) did not apply. The concluding paragraphs of the opinion read:]

The Court of Appeals entertained some doubt concerning the ruling that the *New York Times* rule should be applied to a claim of product disparagement based on a critical review of a loudspeaker system. We express no view on that ruling, but having accepted it for purposes of deciding this case, we agree with the Court of Appeals that the difference between hearing violin sounds move around the room and hearing them wander back and forth fits easily within the breathing space that gives life to the First Amendment. We may accept all of the purely factual findings of the District Court and nevertheless hold as a matter of law that the record does not contain clear and convincing evidence that Seligson or his employer prepared the loudspeaker article with knowledge that it contained a false statement, or with reckless disregard of the truth.

It may well be that in this case, the "finding" of the District Court on the actual malice question could have been set aside under the clearly erroneous standard of review, and we share the concern of the Court of Appeals that the statements at issue tread the line between fact and opinion. Moreover, the analysis of the central legal question before us may seem out of place in a case involving a dispute about the sound quality of a loudspeaker. But though the question presented reaches us on a somewhat peculiar wavelength, we reaffirm the principle of independent appellate review that we have applied uncounted times before. We hold that the clearly erroneous standard of Rule 52(a) of the Federal Rules of Civil Procedure does not prescribe the standard of review to be applied in reviewing a determination of actual malice in a case governed by New York Times v. Sullivan. Appellate judges in such a case must exercise independent judgment and determine whether the record establishes actual malice with convincing clarity.

The judgment of the Court of Appeals is affirmed.

It is so ordered.

DAIRY STORES, INC. v. SENTINEL PUB. CO.

Supreme Court of New Jersey, 1986.
104 N.J. 125, 516 A.2d 220.

[During a drought in 1981 sales of bottled spring water increased dramatically. The defendant Sentinel Publishing Co. published in its newspaper an article by defendant Kathleen Dzielak casting doubt on whether "Covered Bridge Crystal Clear Spring Water" sold by the plaintiff (Krauszer's Food Stores) was in fact pure spring water. The presence of chlorine in water is strong evidence that it is not spring water. Dzielak took a container of the water to an independent state-certified laboratory for testing. The laboratory supervisor recognized the label and told her Krauszer was a client of the lab. The supervisor nonetheless reported to Dzielak that the water contained no chlorine. Skeptical, Dzielak took the sample to two additional laboratories. One (Patterson Clinic Lab) reported the presence of chlorine. The other's report could not be understood. With this information, a story was published under a banner headline reading "Spring water/Independent lab analysis casts doubt on content" reporting the results of the Patterson lab and its director's comments that "I can't see how it could possibly be spring water unless the spring source was contaminated and chlorine was added at the source."

Both the trial court and the appellate division held the media defendant was protected by the First Amendment in the absence of proof of actual malice and that Paterson Lab, as an outside consultant to a media defendant, was also protected.]

POLLOCK, J.

At the outset, we must consider the distinction between causes of action for defamation and for product disparagement. The focus of our decision, however, is on the dispute whether the articles were privileged because they treated matters of public interest and, if so, whether the defendants were so careless that they lost the protection of any such privilege. In ruling for defendants, the lower courts looked to federal constitutional law and found that Krauszer's had not established that the defendants published the articles with "actual malice," a test that the United States Supreme Court has developed to measure statements about public officials and public figures. We find, however, that the characterization of Krauszer's as a public figure is problematic, and that the more appropriate principle is the common-law privilege of fair comment. Before embarking on a more detailed analysis of the principles of defamation law, including fair comment, we must first determine the nature of the cause of action.

–II–

Plaintiff has pursued the cause as one for defamation, but the cause could also be viewed as one for product disparagement. Indeed, the concurring opinion treats the case as if it were exclusively an action for product disparagement. We are sensitive, as was the Law Division, 191 N.J.Super. at 210 n. 2, 465 A.2d 953, to the potential implication of product disparagement principles, but we are constrained to decide the case as the parties and the lower courts have viewed it, as an action for defamation.

Although the two causes sometimes overlap, actions for defamation and product disparagement stem from different branches of tort law. A defamation action, which encompasses libel and slander, affords a remedy for damage to one's reputation. By comparison, an action for product disparagement is an offshoot of the cause of action for interference with contractual relations, such as sales to a prospective buyer. The two causes may merge when a disparaging statement about a product reflects on the reputation of the business that made, distributed, or sold it.

* * *

On the premise that the reputation of a business is more valuable than any particular product it sells, courts have responded more readily to a claim of damage to one's reputation than to a claim for product disparagement. * * *

Recent decisions of the United States Supreme Court have further blurred the dividing line between the two causes. Traditionally, a plaintiff in a product disparagement action has borne the burden of establishing that the disparaging statement was both false and injurious. By comparison, in a defamation action, the plaintiff was entitled to a presumption that the defamatory statement was both false and harmful. Just this year, however, the United States Supreme Court held that when a statement treats a matter of public concern, the plaintiff in a defamation action has the burden of proving that the statement is false. Philadelphia Newspapers, Inc. v. Hepps, 106 S.Ct. 1558, 1559 (1986). Earlier the Court had ruled that a plaintiff was not entitled to presume damages from the publication of a statement about a matter of public concern, unless the statement was published with actual malice. Gertz v. Robert Welch, Inc., 418 U.S. 323, 349–50 (1974); see also Dun & Bradstreet, Inc. v. Greenmoss Builders, Inc., 472 U.S. 749 (1985). As a result, the difference between product disparagement and defamation has narrowed further when a statement treats a matter of public concern.

* * *

* * * Thus, for the purposes of this appeal, we assume that the articles were not only disparaging, but also false and defamatory. As a result, the distinction between defamation and product disparagement disappears, and our attention shifts to whether the publications were privileged and whether the defendants abused any such privilege.

–III–

The evolution of the law of defamation reflects the tension between society's competing interests in encouraging the free flow of information about matters of public concern and in protecting an individual's reputation. At one time, the common law placed so high a premium on the protection of a person's reputation that it imposed strict liability for the publication of a defamatory statement. Prosser & Keeton, supra, § 113 at 804. More recently, the United States Supreme Court has declared that publishers may not be held liable for certain defamatory statements without showing that they were at least negligent. Gertz v. Robert Welch, Inc., supra, 418 U.S. at 346–47. That declaration is consistent with the increasing awareness of the need for public information on a wide variety of issues.

Traditionally, the common law has accommodated that need by recognizing that some otherwise defamatory statements should be "privileged," i.e., that their publication does not impose liability on the publisher. Privileges may be "absolute," which means that the statements are completely immune, or "qualified." A qualified privilege may be overcome, with the result that the publisher will be liable, if publication of a defamatory statement was made with "malice." Common-law malice, or malice-in-fact, has meant variously that the statement was published with an improper purpose or ill will, or without belief or reasonable grounds to believe in its truth.

Certain statements, such as those made in judicial, legislative, or administrative proceedings, are absolutely privileged because the need for unfettered expression is crucial to the public weal. See Rainier's Dairies v. Raritan Valley Farms, Inc., 19 N.J. 552, 558, 117 A.2d 889 (1955). Other statements, such as those made outside those forums but for the public welfare, enjoy a qualified privilege. * * *

Insofar as defenses to product disparagement are concerned, a qualified privilege should exist wherever it would exist in a defamation action. Because the common law historically has held the interest in one's reputation as more worthy of protection than the interest of a business in the products that it makes, it follows that the right to make a statement about a product should exist whenever it is permissible to make such a statement about the reputation of another.

One illustration of a qualified privilege is fair comment, which is sometimes described as rendering a statement non-libelous. No matter how described, the defense is lost upon a showing that the statement was made with malice. The roots of fair comment are imbedded in the common law, but in recent years, those roots have intertwined with others arising from constitutional law. Explanation of fair comment in its present form requires not only an exploration of its relationship to constitutional law, but also an analysis of the scope of the privilege, the extent to which it protects statements of fact and opinion, and the kind of malice that will overcome it.

The constitutional considerations begin with New York Times Co. v. Sullivan, 376 U.S. 254 (1964), in which the United States Supreme Court first declared that the first amendment protected certain otherwise defamatory statements. * * *

Three years after declaring that the actual malice test applied to public officials, the Court extended the test to public figures. Curtis Publishing Co. v. Butts; Associated Press v. Walker, 388 U.S. 130 (1967). Then, in what has come to be regarded as the high-water mark of constitutionally-protected speech, a plurality of the Court declared the actual malice standard applicable to statements about private individuals who became involved in matters of public or general interest. Rosenbloom v. Metromedia, Inc., 403 U.S. 29, 43 (1971). Since then, however, the Court has retrenched and declared that the actual malice test applies only to public figures or those private figures who become so involved in a particular public controversy that they become public figures for a limited range of issues. Gertz v. Robert Welch, Inc., supra, 418 U.S. at 351–52.

Notwithstanding withdrawal of constitutional protection from matters of general or public interest, the Court recognized that states might want to grant broader speech protection in setting the appropriate standard of care in defamation actions concerning private individuals. Gertz v. Robert Welch, Inc., supra, 418 U.S. at 348–49. Even before the United States Supreme Court accorded constitutional protection to statements about "public officials" and "public figures," the common law recognized that statements about matters of public concern should be protected. Through the principle of fair comment, courts have allowed commentary on public officials, private institutions that spend public funds, creative and scientific works presented to the public, and economic and social welfare events such as strikes and demonstrations. Although constitutional considerations have dominated defamation law in recent years, the common law provides an alternative, and potentially more stable, framework for analyzing statements about matters of public interest.

Another reason for turning to the common law is that the constitutional concepts do not comfortably fit the activities or products of a corporation. * * * The term "public figure" includes individuals who engage in a public controversy and ill fits a corporation, which ordinarily is interested not in thrusting itself into such a controversy, but in selling its products.

Lower federal courts, although differing on the nature and amount of activity needed to support the characterization of a corporation as a public figure, have concluded that corporations and their products can be viewed as public figures. * * * Other courts have noted, however, that the sale of a product "cannot easily be deemed a public controversy." * * * Nonetheless, the Supreme Court has yet to address whether corporations or their products can be classified as public figures.

*   *   *

A

Generally speaking, the doctrine of fair comment extends to virtually all matters of legitimate public interest. Through the principle of fair comment, New Jersey courts have long accorded protection to wide-ranging statements about public officials. The courts have likewise applied the principle to controversial public issues, such as internal security during the McCarthy era, and to criticism of a proposed trailer park that was perceived as posing a threat to drainage, property values, and taxes. Drinking water, the subject of the present litigation, has also been held to be a topic of vital public concern and subject to fair comment. * * *

In like fashion, federal and state courts proceeding on constitutional analysis have recognized that information concerning products intended for human consumption, such as drinking water, or other matters of public health, require the plaintiff to prove actual malice to sustain a claim for defamation.

*   *   *

We recognize that not everything that is newsworthy is a matter of legitimate public concern, and that sorting such matters from those of a more private nature may be difficult. In this regard, the assessment of public interest includes a determination whether the person "voluntarily and knowingly engaged in conduct that one in his position should reasonably know would implicate a legitimate public interest, engendering the real possibility of public attention and scrutiny." Sisler v. Gannett Co., Inc., 104 N.J. 256, 274, 516 A.2d 1083, 1092 (1986).

Some courts have developed criteria for determining whether the activities and products of corporations constitute matters of public interest. As previously indicated, matters of public interest include such essentials of life as food and water. Widespread effects of a product are yet another indicator that statements about the product are in the public interest. Still another criterion is substantial government regulation of business activities and products. * * *

It would be anomalous to consider food and drink to be a subject of public interest when purchased in a restaurant, but not when purchased in a store. This conclusion applies with particular force to bottled drinking water, which is the subject of state regulation. * * *

Because the present case involves a product that is unquestionably a matter of legitimate public concern, we believe it is more prudent to extend that standard for the time being only to such products, leaving to another day the determination whether the standard should apply to statements about all products no matter how prosaic or innocuous. To this extent, we disagree with our concurring colleague, who would extend the actual malice standard to a disparaging statement about any product.

B

Throughout the country, courts have divided on the issue whether fair comment should be restricted to statements of opinion or should extend to factual statements. Underlying the distinction is the premise that the widest possible latitude should extend to expressions of opinion on matters of public concern, but that factual misstatements should be more narrowly confined.

The majority view is that fair comment extends to opinion only, Restatement, supra, § 606; Harper & James, supra, § 5.28 at 456; Prosser & Keeton, supra, § 115 at 831; Note, Fair Comment, 62 Harv. L.Rev. 1207, 1211–12 (1949); Annot., 110 A.L.R. 412 (1937), but a respected minority view holds that statements of fact should also be protected. * * *

With respect to matters of legitimate public concern, therefore, we have edged toward the proposition that fair comment should apply not just to statements of opinion, but also to statements of fact. * * *

The need for the free flow of information and commentary on matters of legitimate public concern leads us to conclude that fair comment should extend beyond opinion to statements of fact. When confronting such a matter, a publisher should not be unduly inhibited in analyzing whether a statement is an immune opinion or a potentially culpable statement of fact. We believe we come close to fulfilling the policy considerations that underlie fair comment if we evaluate factual statements as the subject of a qualified privilege. This conclusion leads to further consideration of the facts that will constitute an abuse of the privilege.

C

* * *

The fair comment defense, the purpose of which is to foster the discussion of matters of legitimate public concern, is closely related to the constitutional protection accorded to statements about public officials and public figures. Although the adoption of the actual malice test is not constitutionally compelled, Restatement (Second), supra, § 580B comment c; 2 Harper, James & Gray, supra, § 5.27 at 233–34, we conclude that the defense of fair comment, like the constitutional protection, should be overcome only by proof of actual malice.

The term "malice" caused enough confusion when it was confined to the common law, but now that it has assumed a constitutional dimension, the confusion is compounded. * * * It is more direct to recognize the legal consequences of the publication of certain statements without recourse to so ambiguous a word with such a checkered past. For example, we need not resort to the term "malice" to state that no one has a license to lie. Although we discard the label, we adhere to the principle that to overcome a qualified or conditional privilege, a plaintiff must establish that the publisher knew the statement to be false or acted in reckless disregard of its truth or falsity. Restatement (Second), supra, § 600. With or without the term, the critical determination is whether, on balance, the public interest in obtaining information outweighs the individual's right to protect his or her reputation.

As society in general, and the sale of goods in particular, becomes more complex, the general welfare requires the dissemination of more and more information to the consuming public. Consumers, who are often separated from those in the early stages of a chain of distribution, have a legitimate need to learn about the reputation of the business entities in that chain and of the goods that are being distributed. From that need emanates the right to publish information concerning the nature and quality of goods intended for human consumption, and the reputations of those who make, distribute, and sell those goods.

D

We now turn to considering whether the actual malice test should apply to non-media, as well as media, defendants. The United States Supreme Court has never accorded preferential treatment to the media, notwithstanding that they are the common source of information on matters of public concern. * * * Hence, we conclude that the actual malice standard should apply to non-media as well as to media defendants.

Even if we did not reach that conclusion, it would be inappropriate to distinguish between the independent expert, Patterson, and the media defendants. In an era when science and technology frequently touch our lives, the media have an increasing need for scientific and technical advice. The preparation of articles on a variety of topics that are the daily fare of newspapers, particularly those describing the quality of products intended for human consumption, may require expert assistance. If an outside expert is held liable on a standard of care lower than that applicable to a media defendant, that expert may decline to conduct tests for reporters investigating important public issues. The effect would be to prevent the media from preparing publications with crucial information, or to preclude publication. This would have a chilling, or even freezing, effect on the dissemination of information that is in the public interest. We would be loathe to foreclose the media from vital sources that they need to speak intelligently on these matters. As a result, we conclude that outside experts that conduct tests and submit reports to the media are so closely related to news gathering that they should be treated like media defendants.

–IV–

Turning to Sentinel's articles, three statements are critical. The lead sentence in the article published under Dzielak's by-line states: "A sample bottle of 'Covered Bridge Crystal Clear Spring Water,' sold at Krauszer's convenient food stores, does not contain pure spring water, according to a laboratory analysis obtained by the Sentinel Newspapers." The next sentence states that the director of Paterson's laboratory said that "pure spring water should not contain any chlorine." The director continued by stating: " 'I can't see how it could possibly be spring water unless the spring source was contaminated and chlorine was added at the source.' "

We conclude that the statement that the Covered Bridge bottle "does not contain spring water" and that "pure spring water should not contain any chlorine" may fairly be viewed as statements of fact. Although testing for the presence of chlorine is a scientific procedure that results in the formulation of an opinion, the statement is more a factual assertion than an expression of an opinion.

We find, however, that the statement of the director that he "can't see how it could possibly be spring water unless the spring source was contaminated and chlorine was added at the source" is an expression of pure opinion. It states the director's opinion, and the factual basis for it. For instance, the article recites that chlorine dissipates at a "high rate" on exposure to "air or other substances," and that tests were repeated several times to rule out testing error. It also states countervailing facts, such as that the seal had already been broken on the bottle containing the tested water. We conclude that the director's opinion was made on the basis of stated facts, and is a statement of "pure opinion," entitled to absolute immunity.

*   *   *

The dispositive question, then, is whether there is a genuine issue that any of the defendants displayed reckless disregard in publishing the two factual statements. Because this issue implicates the defendants' state of mind, we approach it with due respect for the difficulty of granting summary judgment dismissing the complaint. * * *

As to the two defamatory statements, nothing in the record before us creates a genuine issue of material fact that any defendant knew the statements to be false or entertained serious doubts about their truth. Paterson, knowing that the water was supposed to be spring water, confirmed the positive test results through subsequent tests, all of which were reviewed by two other chemists. This procedure does not bespeak a reckless disregard for the truth.

Insofar as Sentinel and its reporter are concerned, Dzielak started out carefully enough by seeking the services of an independent testing laboratory. The first laboratory found that the water did not contain chlorine, but upon learning that Krauszer's was a customer of that laboratory, Dzielak understandably sought confirmation elsewhere. Upon obtaining Paterson's positive test results for chlorine, she consulted still another laboratory, but she did not understand its report. A more careful reporter might have deferred publication until all doubts were finally resolved, but we cannot conclude that Dzielak entertained serious doubts about the truth of her stories.

The judgment of the Appellate Division is affirmed.

GARIBALDI, J., concurring.

The plaintiff in this case has pursued a cause of action for defamation. The majority recognizes, however, that the cause of action could also be for product disparagement. I find that plaintiff's cause of action is solely one for product disparagement. I join in the Court's judgment because I am satisfied that the requirement of actual malice should be applied in a product disparagement case.

NOTES

1. An important early case involving an independent testing agency is Advance Music Corp. v. American Tobacco Co., 296 N.Y. 79, 70 N.E.2d 401 (1946). The plaintiff, a music publisher, claimed that the radio program "Hit Parade" which purported to play the top ten songs of the week based on extensive and accurate national surveys, intentionally excluded plaintiff's songs. The first complaint filed by plaintiff based on slander of property was dismissed because it did not allege special damages. The amended complaint alleged and the Court of Appeals approved a "prima facie tort" cause of action which makes actionable any "intentional infliction of temporal damages" unless justified by the defendant. Advance Music is often cited as the leading case adopting a generalized intentional tort to fill in the gaps between the specialized intentional torts, i.e. libel, assault, etc.

2. In Ellsworth v. Martindale-Hubbell Law Directory, Inc., 68 N.D. 425, 280 N.W. 879 (1938) plaintiff, a practicing lawyer, contended that the rating appearing after his name in defendant's legal directory regarding legal ability, recommendations, estimated worth, and promptness in paying bills, were erroneous and published with "the willful, wrongful, malicious and libelous purpose and intent * * * of defaming, derogating, and vitally injuring Plaintiff in his practice * * *." The defendant demurred on the grounds that there was not an adequate specification of special damages. Held: For plaintiff.

> He [plaintiff] alleges that he had a fairly lucrative law business that came to him from foreign territory through forwarders with whom he was not and from the nature of things could not be personally acquainted; that such business came because of the personal and professional reputation and standing which he enjoyed; that because of the defamatory publication of which he complains, this reputation and standing was disparaged in the minds of those who sent business to him, and consequently, his business fell off. From the nature of the circumstances as disclosed by the pleading the plaintiff cannot describe the particular items of business which he has lost or give the names of particular individuals who would have become his clients had it not been for the publication. But he does show a diminution of his business and of the income therefrom by pleading what that business amounted to prior to the publication and what it was after the publication, and as a result thereof.

Subsequently, the plaintiff was unable to prove that the diminution of his business was the result of the publication. Ellsworth v. Martindale-Hubbell Law Directory, Inc., 69 N.D. 610, 289 N.W. 101 (1939).

3. Both *Bose* and *Dairy Stores* involve statements by third party media defendants rather than by competitors of the plaintiff. Should that make a difference? Do you agree with the analysis in *Bose, Dairy Stores,* or *U.S. Healthcare?*

4. Do you agree with the New Jersey court that the common law privilege of fair comment is a more "stable" basis for balancing the interests in a product disparagement case than the First Amendment? Is the "public interest" test a better approach in product cases than the "public figure" test? Or should the cases be simplified by adopting the concurring judge's view that the privilege and requirement of actual malice be applied in all product disparagement cases? Or should such a broad rule apply only against media or third party statements and not against statements by competitors? Or should cases against competitors be viewed as "commercial speech" cases and subjected to less careful First Amendment *and* common law scrutiny? See, U.S. Healthcare v. Blue Cross, supra.

5. Other dimensions of the independent testing company problem should be considered. In Consumers Union of United States, Inc. v. Hobart Mfg. Co., 189 F.Supp. 275 (S.D.N.Y.1960) the plaintiff, an independent consumer testing agency, sought to preclude the defendant from copying and distributing ratings from the plaintiff's magazine involving defendant's product. Defendant's automatic dishwasher was rated second by plaintiff. Defendant thereupon published a sales bulletin critical of plaintiff's report and contending that its product was the best. In the process, defendant copied three types of information from plaintiff's copyrighted magazine: (1) facts used in criticism of the report; (2) facts favorable to defendant's dishwasher; and (3) facts critical of

defendant's competitors' products. Plaintiff sued for copyright infringement and unfair competition. The court denied plaintiff's motion for a preliminary injunction, noting that a person cannot criticize a person's product and then by copyrighting the criticism prevent that person from copying the critical remarks in the process of refuting the criticism. The court also rejected plaintiff's contentions that distribution of the sales bulletin deprived plaintiff of magazine sales and that the distribution would damage plaintiff's reputation by implying that plaintiff was in some way associated with defendant's product and was not totally independent.

In Consumers Union of United States, Inc. v. Theodore Hamm Brewing Co., Inc., 314 F.Supp. 697 (D.Conn.1970) a preliminary injunction to restrain the defendant from truthfully publicizing that its beer was highly ranked by the plaintiff was denied. The court noted that even where the defendant exaggerated the extent to which plaintiff's report praised defendant's beer "it may well be that some 'puffing' of a top rating may be found a proper license in advertising for illustrative purposes * * *."

And in Consumers Union of the United States v. General Signal Corp., 724 F.2d 1044 (2d Cir.1983), rehearing denied 730 F.2d 47 (2d Cir.1984), the court found that the first amendment may permit a manufacturer to truthfully report that its product received a high rating in "Consumers Reports" as long as the report makes clear that the magazine is not sponsoring the product.

6. Celebrities are facing potential liability for deceptive advertising endorsements. It has been reported that singer Pat Boone agreed to a settlement in a case brought by the Federal Trade Commission pursuant to which he will pay up to 25¢ per bottle to compensate consumers who purchased "Acne-Statin" on the basis of Boone's endorsement. The director of the FTC's Consumer Protection Bureau was quoted as stating:

> The negotiated order, while not a binding legal precedent, stands for the principle that an endorser must verify the claims made about the advertised product before the first commercial goes on the air or appears in print, or else risk FTC action. Unless the endorser is an expert on the subject, the endorser must look to independent reliable sources to validate claims, tests, or studies supplied by the advertisers. Failure to make a reasonable effort at independent evaluation could result in personal liability for the endorser.

The account of the settlement appears in [1978] Antitrust & Trade Reg. (BNA) No. 864 at A–12.

The Federal Trade Commission enacted "Guides Concerning Use of Endorsements and Testimonials In Advertising" in 1980. 16 C.F.R. § 255. One provision of the "Guides" requires that an endorser who claims to use the endorsed product "must have been a bona fide user of it at the time the endorsement was given * * *." Id. at § 255.1(c). See Jones, Celebrity Endorsements: A Case for Alarm and Concern for the Future, 15 New Eng.L. Rev. 521 (1980).

Certifying agencies have been held liable in product liability suits for injuries caused by rated products. In Hanberry v. Hearst Corp., 276 Cal.App.2d 680, 81 Cal.Rptr. 519 (1969) a plaintiff, injured when she slipped on a vinyl floor while wearing shoes advertised as meeting the "Good Housekeeping Consumers' Guaranty Seal," was allowed to pursue a claim for negligent misrepresentation against Good Housekeeping magazine based on the representation that products carrying the seal were "good ones." See also, Gizzi v. Texaco, 437 F.2d

308 (3d Cir.1971), cert. denied 404 U.S. 829 (1971) where the court concluded it was a jury question whether the slogan "Trust your car to the man who wears the star" was sufficient to create an agency relationship making Texaco liable for personal injuries resulting from the failure of one of its franchisees to properly repair the plaintiff's brakes.

(B) PUBLIC TESTING AGENCIES

E. GELLHORN, ADVERSE PUBLICITY BY ADMINISTRATIVE AGENCIES
86 Harv.L.Rev. 1380, 1408 (1973).

The controversy can be traced to the 1959 cranberry episode, a public announcement which was in effect an involuntary recall. In the cranberry episode, the FDA issued a national public warning for the first time, with consequences so devastating to the industry that henceforth the mere threat of a public announcement functioned to help enforce a voluntary recall procedure. On November 9, 1959, a day still known as "Black Monday" in the industry, Secretary of Health, Education, and Welfare Arthur Flemming held a news conference at which he urged the public not to buy cranberries grown in Washington and Oregon, saying they might be contaminated with a chemical weed killer, aminotriazole, that had been found to cause cancer in laboratory rats. Although the Secretary admitted he had no information suggesting that cranberries from other states were dangerous, he would not say they were safe. Answering a reporter's question, the Secretary stated he would not be eating cranberries that Thanksgiving. Not surprisingly, most of the nation followed suit. Since cranberries are purchased primarily for the holiday season, virtually the entire crop remained unsold, even though 99 percent of it was subsequently "cleared" and marketed as government "approved." *

CONSUMER PRODUCT SAFETY ACT
15 U.S.C.A. § 2055(b)(1).

[The following section governs the actions of the Consumer Product Safety Commission, an agency with broad authority to protect consumers against safety hazards in consumer goods.]

(b)(1) Except as provided by paragraph (2) of this subsection, not less than 30 days prior to its public disclosure of any information obtained under this chapter, or to be disclosed to the public in connection therewith (unless the Commission finds out that the public health and safety requires a lesser period of notice), the Commission shall, to the extent practicable, notify, and provide a summary of the information to, each manufacturer or private labeler of any consumer product to which such information pertains, if the manner in which such consumer product is to be designated or described in such information

---

* A complete description of the "cranberry crisis" can be found in Feingold, The Great Cranberry Crisis in Government   Regulation of Business (Bock ed. 1965).— Ed.

will permit the public to ascertain readily the identity of such manufac-turer or private labeler, and shall provide such manufacturer or private labeler with a reasonable opportunity to submit comments to the Commission in regard to such information. The Commission shall take reasonable steps to assure, prior to its public disclosure thereof, that information from which the identity of such manufacturer or private labeler may be readily ascertained is accurate, and that such disclosure is fair in the circumstances and reasonably related to effectuating the purposes of this chapter. If the Commission finds that, in the adminis-tration of this chapter, it has made public disclosure of inaccurate or misleading information which reflects adversely upon the safety of any consumer product, or the practices of any manufacturer, private label-er, distributor, or retailer of consumer products, it shall, in a manner similar to that in which such disclosure was made, publish a retraction of such inaccurate or misleading information.

NOTES

1. Does the statutory solution to unfavorable governmental publicity reproduced above adequately resolve the problem posed by the cranberry episode? The provision governing the Consumer Product Safety Commission is not applied to most federal agencies.

The effectiveness of § 2055 was called into question in Relco, Inc. v. Consumer Product Safety Comm., 391 F.Supp. 841 (S.D.Tex.1975) where the plaintiff's arc-welder was the subject of a press release warning welders of the possibility of fatal electric shock. The court noted that when "a product is once shrouded with suspicion, especially suspicion cast upon it by the government, the harm is irretractable, and no subsequent agency determination at a full hearing can fully lift the taint. Compounding this problem is the fact that the Congressional cure is as lethal as the disease. * * * In the American market where product alternatives abound, it is short-sighted to view a public retrac-tion as doing anything more than emphasizing the damage of the initial warning." Id. at 846. The court, although commiserating with the position of the plaintiff, refused to intervene until the plaintiff had exhausted his adminis-trative remedies. On the other hand, see GTE Sylvania Inc. v. Consumer Product Safety Comm., 404 F.Supp. 352 (D.Del.1975) where the court found the Commission's collection and verification of information relating to the safety of television sets so unreliable that threatened public disclosure would not be "fair in the circumstances" nor "reasonably related to effectuating the purposes of this chapter" and enjoined the agency from releasing the information. In GTE Sylvania Inc. v. Consumers Union of the United States, 445 U.S. 375 (1980) the Supreme Court held that the information enjoined from disclosure by the district Court in GTE Sylvania, supra, could not be obtained by interested parties under the Freedom of Information Act. And see also the unreported decision described in Morey, FDA Publicity Against Consumer Products—Time for Statutory Revitalization?, 30 Bus.Law. 165 (1974) in which a court exercised its general equity powers to require the FDA to retract a disparaging letter based on unproven information regarding the manufacturing practices of the plaintiff.

2. Plaintiffs have generally been unsuccessful in obtaining injunctions to prohibit governmental agencies from issuing press releases based on agency

complaints prior to hearings. In FTC v. Cinderella Career & Finishing Schools, Inc., 404 F.2d 1308 (D.C.Cir.1968) the court reversed a lower court injunction which would have prohibited the Federal Trade Commission from issuing a press release notifying the public of the commission's complaint charging respondent with deceptive practices. The court recognized that the respondent would likely suffer injury to his business because of the release but noted the commission's "broad delegation of power * * * to eliminate unfair or deceptive business practices in the public interest" and the specific statutory authority to "alert the public to suspected violations of the law by factual press releases * * *." The court did not decide whether a false release would be subject to injunctive relief. In B. C. Morton International Corp. v. FDIC, 305 F.2d 692 (1st Cir.1962) the court found that plaintiff had stated a cause of action for injunctive relief against a press release where the plaintiff alleged the agency deliberately misrepresented the application of federal law for the specific purpose of destroying plaintiff's business. See generally, Note, Disparaging Publicity by Federal Agencies, 67 Colum.L.Rev. 1512 (1967).

3. A producer injured by disparaging governmental publicity is unable generally to recover damages. In Hall v. United States, 274 F.2d 69 (10th Cir. 1959) inspectors for the U.S. Department of Agriculture as a result of a negligently conducted inspection declared plaintiff's cattle diseased, forcing plaintiff to sell his cattle at a substantial reduction in price. In fact the cattle were not diseased. Plaintiff brought this suit under the Federal Tort Claims Act, 28 U.S.C. § 2674 [hereafter "FTCA"], for damages resulting from the inspectors' negligence. Although the federal government has waived sovereign immunity for negligence actions, 28 U.S.C. § 2680(h) exempts the government from liability for claims arising out of "libel, slander, misrepresentation, deceit, or interference with contract rights." The court denied plaintiff recovery holding that § 2680(h) applied because loss resulted from the "misrepresentation" that the cattle were diseased and not from the "negligence" in conducting the tests. For a similar result under a state tort claims act patterned after the federal law see Hubbard v. State, 163 N.W.2d 904 (Iowa 1969). The United States Supreme Court relied heavily on the *Hall* case in United States v. Neustadt, 366 U.S. 696 (1961) when it held that "misrepresentation" in § 2680(h) included negligent as well as willful misrepresentation.

On the other hand, consumers suffering personal injury due to the government's mistaken approval of a product seem to fare better under the FTCA. Compare Berkovitz v. United States, 108 S.Ct. 1954 (1988) and United States v. Varig Airlines, 467 U.S. 797 (1984). Both cases focused on whether the governmental activity in question fell within the "discretionary function or duty" exception to the FTCA. Neither dealt with the "misrepresentation" exception.

Actions against the government officers themselves may be similarly unsuccessful. Government officials acting within the scope of their duties have an "absolute privilege" which precludes civil suits for damages for "defamation and kindred torts". Barr v. Matteo, 360 U.S. 564 (1959).

It should be noted that Congress eventually provided $9 million dollars in relief to cranberry growers injured by the adverse publicity described above.

4. The collision of interests is intense when the agency must balance its doubts about the accuracy of the information it seeks to disclose and the potential risk to public health or safety if it delays publicity. Separate issues arise when the government becomes involved in comparative product testing

comparable to that conducted by Consumers Union in "Consumer Reports." The federal government does extensive product testing to assist its own purchasing decisions. And in 1970 President Nixon established the Consumer Product Information Coordinating Center to "[p]romote the development, production, and public dissemination of government documents containing product information of possible use to consumers, including other government agencies, and the release of which may be accomplished in a manner that is both fair to producers and vendors and protective of government procurement processes." Executive Order No. 11566, 3 C.F.R. § 179 (1970). Public access to this information may also be obtained through the Freedom of Information Act. See Consumers Union of U.S., Inc. v. Veterans Administration, 301 F.Supp. 796 (S.D.N.Y.1969) one of the first skirmishes in a long battle by CU to obtain information regarding government tests of hearing aids. The information was eventually provided, in part pursuant to a court order and in part by agreement of the parties. Consumer Reports, January, 1970, at 8.

What protection is necessary for producers in this situation? Should the government be required to test all available models of a given product rather than a selected sample? Should the government be required to purchase its test samples on the open market? Should the producers of highly rated models be entitled to advertise their high ratings? Should a producer have redress for an unfair disparagement of his product or for an unduly favorable rating of his competitor's product? Should the consumer have standing to challenge errone-ous product information?

5. Professor Gellhorn in the article from which the description of the cranberry episode is taken provides a thorough review of the experience with adverse administrative agency publicity and a list of suggestions for reform. In addition to the publication of precise agency rules governing disclosure of adverse publicity, he recommends a more extensive judicial review of agency action and amendment of the Federal Torts Claims Act to provide monetary relief to persons injured by false statements. See also Administrative Confer-ence of the United States, Recommendation No. 73–1, 1 C.F.R. § 305.73–1 (1977) recommending that provisions similar to those governing the Consumer Prod-ucts Safety Commission be made applicable to all agencies.

B. PURCHASERS' REMEDIES

Consumers play an important role in policing the marketplace for deceptive practices. Through their purchasing decisions they can pe-nalize sellers who have deceived them in the past or who have devel-oped a general reputation for dishonesty. By taking precautions con-sumers can reduce the risk of being victimized by deceptive practices. In addition, the law provides an array of substantive legal remedies for consumers who are injured when products or services do not meet their expectations—expectations often formulated on the basis of what is said by the seller about his goods or services.

The potential role of the consumer in reducing the incidents of or injuries from deception is another factor that must be weighed when evaluating remedies available to competitors for deceptive practices. The notes and material that follow are designed to highlight the traditional consumer remedies available.

NOTES: CONSUMER REMEDIES

1. *Uniform Commercial Code: Express Warranties.* Most incidents of false advertising involving goods creates a potential cause of action for express warranty by an injured consumer. Section 2–313 of the Uniform Commercial Code defines an express warranty as any statement of fact or promise relating to the goods or description of the goods that "becomes part of the basis of the bargain. . . ." A warranty is not created by "an affirmation merely of the value of the goods or a statement purporting to be merely the seller's opinion or commendation of the goods. . . ."

2. *Uniform Commercial Code: Implied Warranties.* The Code recognizes warranties that are implied in each sale of goods unless properly disclaimed. Section 2–314 provides for a warranty of merchantability—goods that pass without objection in the trade and are fit for ordinary purposes—and section 2–315 creates an implied warranty of fitness for a particular purpose when the buyer relies upon the seller's skill and judgment and the seller has reason to know the particular purpose for which the goods are required.

3. *Action in Tort for Misrepresentation.* A purchaser injured by a seller's misrepresentation may have a cause of action based in tort for misrepresentation. This cause of action was originally the tort of "deceit" which required the following elements: (1) a false representation (usually of a material fact); (2) "scienter" (knowledge or belief that the statement is false or knowledge that the speaker does not have sufficient facts upon which to make the statement); (3) intent to deceive plaintiff to his detriment; (4) justifiable reliance on the part of the plaintiff, and (5) damages. In more recent years courts have expanded the cause of action for misrepresentation to include negligent and honest misstatements as well as intentional deception. See, e.g., Irwin v. Carlton, 369 Mich. 92, 119 N.W.2d 617 (1963).

Tort law distinguishes between actionable statements and "puffing", the distinction usually stated as the difference between statements of fact (actionable) and statements of opinion (puffing and not actionable). Early cases also refused to impose liability for non-disclosure or concealment but more recent cases have been willing to impose a duty to reveal information in certain contexts.

4. *Strict Liability in Tort.* Where a misrepresentation of a product's characteristics causes physical injury or property damage, the injured consumer may have a cause of action in tort based on strict liability for the sale of a defective product. In most jurisdictions, strict liability is not extended when a product causes only economic harm or the frustration of consumer expectations. The line between economic harm and property damage is not an easy one to draw and there are a few cases which suggest extension of strict liability to economic harm in some contexts. See Santor v. A & M Karagheusian, Inc., 44 N.J. 52, 207 A.2d 305 (1965).

5. *Remedies.* The Uniform Commercial Code provides various remedies for breach of warranty including the right to reject nonconforming goods, to rescind the contract, or to sue for breach. The measure of damages for breach, provided in section 2–714, is "the difference at the time and place of acceptance between the value of the goods accepted and the value they would have had if they had been as warranted, unless special circumstances show proximate damages of a different amount." Recovery is also allowed for incidental and consequential damages. The tort measure of damages in most jurisdictions

reflects this "benefit-of-the-bargain" rule but a few jurisdictions apply the "out-of-pocket" rule which authorizes recovery of the difference between the item received and the purchase price.

COLLIGAN v. ACTIVITIES CLUB OF NEW YORK, LTD.
United States Court of Appeals, Second Circuit, 1971.
442 F.2d 686.

MOORE, CIRCUIT JUDGE. This is an appeal from an order dismissing appellants' class action for money damages, an accounting for profits and an injunction brought under § 43(a) of the Lanham Act, on the ground that their claim failed to state a cause of action. The district court ruled on its own motion that the suit could not be maintained, because, as consumers, as opposed to commercial plaintiffs, appellants lacked standing to sue under § 43(a). Without the benefit of any opposition on appeal to appellants' counsel's able brief, which sets forth the issues with beguiling simplicity, for the reasons stated below we nevertheless affirm.

The two appellants, parochial school children, by their parents and next friends, brought this suit on behalf of themselves and as members of two classes: (1) 153 students of the Sacred Heart Academy of Hempstead, New York, who allegedly were deceived and damaged by "defendants' use of false descriptions and representations of the nature, sponsorship, and licensing of their interstate ski tour service", and (2) all high school students within the New York metropolitan area who are likely to be deceived and thereby injured by defendants' similarly deceptive practices in the future. The factual substance of the complaint is summarized below.

Appellants and their 151 classmates prepaid defendant Activities Club of New York, Inc. (the Club), $44.75 per person as the full price for a ski tour to Great Barrington, Massachusetts to be conducted during the weekend of January 24, 1970, in reliance upon the Club's representations that: each child would be provided with adequate ski equipment and qualified instruction; safe, reliable and properly certified transportation would be provided between New York and Great Barrington; and all meal costs would be included in the prepaid tour price. These representations were conveyed by means of flyers, allegedly deceptively similar to those of National Ski Tours, a well known and reputable ski service, and by means of other written and oral communications.

The ski weekend began as represented but was cut short and proved otherwise unsatisfactory by the following developments, which for purposes of reviewing the dismissal of a complaint we assume to be true: only 88 pairs of skis and boots were provided for the 153 children; only one "qualified" ski instructor was provided, who because of the equipment shortage spent all of Saturday morning fitting the children with such skis and boots as were available; the other "instructors" were high school and college students whose agreements with defendants provided for only a few hours of instruction per day; one of the buses broke down on a country road en route to Great Barrington, stranding 40 children and two chaperones in the middle of the night; another bus had faulty brakes and only one headlight and was ticketed by the Massachusetts police; another bus enroute back to New York poured exhaust fumes into its interior; one of the bus drivers was intoxicated and therefore unable to drive his bus on the return trip to New York; neither the buses nor the Club were licensed or certified by the Interstate Commerce Commission; and one busload of children was required to pay an unrefunded total of $71.75 for an extra meal in Great Barrington due to unsafe bus transportation.

In seeking redress of this apparently misfortune-strewn ski weekend brought about by the Club's misrepresentations, appellants have sought to invoke the jurisdiction of a federal court, rather than turning to traditionally available state court forums and remedies and have appended their state common law claims by way of invoking the doctrine of pendent jurisdiction. Seemingly unable to bring themselves within other federal statutes specially conferring federal court jurisdiction, and additionally unable to meet the minimum monetary requirements of 28 U.S.C. § 1331 or 28 U.S.C. § 1332, appellants imaginatively have brought this action pursuant to §§ 39 and 43(a) of the Lanham Act.

The issue of consumer standing to sue under § 43(a) is one of first impression for this and apparently any federal court. ∗ ∗ ∗

Appellants' principal contention is that the language of § 43(a), specifically the term "any person," is so unambiguous as to admit of no other construction than that of permitting consumers the right to sue under its aegis. On the face of the complaint all the prerequisites of § 43(a) seem to be met: (1) defendants are persons (2) who used false descriptions and misrepresentations (3) in connection with goods and services, (4) which defendants caused to enter commerce; (5) appellants are also persons (6) who believe themselves to have been in fact damaged by defendants' misdescriptions and misrepresentations.

Viewing the terms of § 43(a) in isolation there do not appear to be any vague words or inconsistent phrases which might permit any other inference than that which appellants would have us draw—i.e., that "any person" means exactly what it says.[8] It is further suggested that if Congress had desired, it could and would have limited or narrowed the class of protected plaintiffs to commercial parties merely by saying so. We reject this line of maxims of statutory construction in favor of Judge Learned Hand's more practical instruction that "[w]ords are not pebbles in alien juxtaposition," and therefore turn first to § 43(a)'s legislative history.

We agree with appellants that "[t]he Lanham Act of 1946 has a very long and convoluted legislative history," which with respect to

8. We note that the key language in § 43(a) is not "any person" but "any person who believes that he is or is likely to be damaged by the use of any such false description or representation." The prop- er focus therefore is whether appellants' claims partake of the *nature of the injury* sought to be prevented and/or remedied by Congress through § 43(a).

§ 43(a) we find to be inconclusive and therefore of little or no help in resolving the issue decided today.　*　*　*

The congressional statement of purpose of the Act is contained in § 45, which in pertinent part states: "The intent of this chapter * * * is to protect persons engaged in such commerce against unfair competition." In this, the only phrase referring to the class of persons to be protected by the Act, as defined by their conduct and the source of the injuries sought to be protected against, no mention at all is made of the "public" or of "consumers." The legislative history of the Act, such as it is, adds nothing. We do know to a reasonable certainty, however, that the consumer protection explosion and the wholesale displacement (though not preemption) of traditional state statutory and common law remedies—matters pregnant with manifold consequences of great importance—were never considered or foreseen by Congress prior to the enactment of § 43(a). We conclude, therefore, that Congress' purpose in enacting § 43(a) was to create a special and limited unfair competition remedy, virtually without regard for the interests of consumers generally and almost certainly without any consideration of consumer rights of action in particular. The Act's purpose, as defined in § 45, is exclusively to protect the interests of a purely commercial class against unscrupulous commercial conduct.

*　*　* Since Congress deliberately excluded from coverage virtually all categories of unfair competition but for false advertising, it could not have intended to create a whole new body of substantive law completely outside the substantive scope of unfair competition. Yet this is what appellants would have us find, under the guise of granting them standing, for the question of consumer standing and that of the creation of wholly new federal common law of consumer protection under § 43(a) cannot be disentwined.

Moreover, consumers' use of § 39 of the Act, which requires the allegation of neither a minimum monetary amount in controversy nor diverse citizenship, in combination with the expansive jurisdictional delineation given the phrase "in commerce," and the procedural advantages of bringing suit in federal court, would lead to a veritable flood of claims brought in already overtaxed federal district courts, while adequate private remedies for consumer protection, which to date have been left almost exclusively to the States, are readily at hand. Great strides are now being made in this area to expand the already numerous remedies available in state courts,[35] and this court has no desire to

---

35. State authorities have been far from lethargic in responding to the current consumer protection explosion. See, e.g., the Revised Uniform Deceptive Practices Act in Handbook of the National Conference of Commissioners on Uniform State Laws 306–315 (1966), which was initially approved by the Commissioners on Uniform State Laws and by the A.B.A. House of Delegates in 1964, and which has been adopted by eight states (Connecticut, Dela-ware, Florida, Georgia, Idaho, Illinois, New Mexico and Oklahoma). Section 3(a) of the Uniform Act has been construed unofficially to confer standing on defrauded consumers seeking injunctive relief (no money damages are provided) although the Uniform Act "originated as an effort to reform the law of business torts, not consumer torts." See Dole, Consumer Class Actions Under the Uniform Deceptive Practices Act, 1968 Duke L.J. 1101, 1107, 1109. Mr.

interfere with that process by an unprecedented interpretation of longstanding federal law.

One of appellants' arguments favoring a literal interpretation of "any person" is that "[h]ad Congress desired to limit actions under section 43(a) to those brought by competitors or by commercial concerns generally, it could and would have so provided." Our analysis requires that the manner in which this issue be posted is precisely the reverse: had Congress contemplated so revolutionary a departure implicit in appellants' claims, its intention could and would have been clearly expressed.[37]

Affirmed.

KIPPERMAN v. ACADEMY LIFE INSURANCE CO.

United States Court of Appeals, Ninth Circuit, 1977.
554 F.2d 377.

SNEED, CIRCUIT JUDGE:

Plaintiff-appellant Kipperman, through her father, seeks to establish a private right of action under 39 U.S.C. § 3009. Section 3009 makes the mailing of unsolicited "merchandise" a per se unfair trade practice actionable by the Federal Trade Commission. Under section 3009(b), the recipient of unsolicited "merchandise" may treat the item received as a gift. The district court found there was no implied private right of action and dismissed. While we agree that the action should be dismissed, we believe the district court erred in holding that no implied private right of action exists. Thus, we affirm the dismissal of the action on grounds developed hereafter.

Dole was a consultant to the Special Committee on Unfair Competition of the National Conference of Commissioners on Uniform States Laws from 1962 to 1965. See also the recently amended Massachusetts "Regulations of Business and Consumer Protection Act," Mass.Acts, ch. 690, ch. 814 (1969), amending Mass.Ann.L. ch. 93A, §§ 1–8 (Supp.1968); Goodman, An Act to Prohibit Unfair and Deceptive Trade Practices, 7 Harv.J.Legis. 122, 146–153 (1969).

37. Cf. Herpich v. Wallace, 430 F.2d 792, 809 (5th Cir.1970) (scope of § 10(b) of the Securities Exchange Act of 1934); 2 L. Loss, Securities Regulation 902–903 (2d ed. 1961) (scope of SEC power under § 14 of the Securities Exchange Act of 1934).

Although we hold that consumers have no right of action under § 43(a), we note that the federal government through the Federal Trade Commission has intervened in the marketplace and in the courts to vindicate the rights of the consuming public. Chief Judge Clark in his concurring opinion in the California Apparel case stated: "So far as the consumer is concerned, he is not dependent upon the private remedial actions brought by competitors for the remedies under the Federal Trade Commission Act * * * are now extensive * * *."

162 F.2d 896, 74 USPQ at 223; accord, 1 R. Callman, Unfair Competition, Trademarks and Monopolies § 18.2(b), at 626 (3d ed. 1967). That Chief Judge Clark's faith in the FTC perhaps has proved excessive, see e.g., A.B.A. Committee to Study the Federal Trade Commission Report (1969); E. Cox, R. Fellmeth & J. Schulz, The Nader Report on the Federal Trade Commission (1969); Baum, The Consumer and the Federal Trade Commission, 44 J.Urb.L. 71 (1966), does not derogate from our conclusion that commercial and consuming classes intentionally have been provided separate remedies.

I.

Facts.

Academy Life mailed Kipperman and others unsolicited promotional materials concerning their "Student Protection Policy." These materials included what appears to be a fully executed term insurance policy stating a face value of $2,000. The recipient's name and address were printed by a computer on the face of this "policy." At the bottom of this "policy" was a tear-off application form indicating a PREMIUM AMOUNT NOW DUE of $9.00. The application form and an accompanying brochure indicated coverage could be effected only upon return of the completed application and payment of the first premium. Kipperman brought a class action seeking to have the policy declared "merchandise" within the meaning of section 3009, and therefore fully in effect without payment of the premium. Kipperman also sought damages in the form of restitution for those who had sent premiums to Academy Life pursuant to the mailing, and for an injunction forbidding future mailings.

II.

Jurisdiction.

Kipperman sought to obtain jurisdiction under 28 U.S.C. § 1339. This section waives the amount in controversy requirement for civil actions "arising under any Act of Congress relating to the postal service." * * *

* * *

* * * The claims before us concerned "merely collateral aspects" of the operation of the postal service. True, enforcement of the statute may reduce postal service revenues; but the purpose of enforcement is to protect recipients of unwanted merchandise from being badgered into paying therefor, not to improve, or to impair, the operation of the postal service. Under these circumstances section 1339 jurisdiction is absent.

We may, nevertheless, make an independent examination of the question of jurisdiction. Mantin v. Broadcast Music, Inc., 244 F.2d 204 (9th Cir.1957). Because section 3009 regulates interstate commerce, we hold that our jurisdiction is derived from 28 U.S.C. § 1337, which waives the amount in controversy requirement for actions under federal statutes that regulate commerce or protect trade and commerce against restraints and monopolies. Our holding is not unique. Section 1337 has been used to provide jurisdiction for actions arising under many federal statutes. See, e.g., Sosa v. Fite, 465 F.2d 1227 (5th Cir. 1972) (Federal Consumer Protection Act, 15 U.S.C. § 1601 et seq.); Kaiser Aluminum & Chemical Corp. v. United States Consumer Product Safety Commission, 414 F.Supp. 1047 (D.C.Del.1976) (Consumer Product Safety Act, 15 U.S.C. § 2051 et seq.).

III.

Private Right of Action.

Our inquiry into whether section 3009 contains a private right of action begins with the Supreme Court's recent decision in Cort v. Ash, 422 U.S. 66 (1975). The Court states:

> In determining whether a private remedy is implicit in a statute not expressly providing one, several factors are relevant. First, is the plaintiff "one of the class for whose *especial* benefit the statute was enacted," * * * that is, does the statute create a federal right in favor of the plaintiff? Second, is there any indication of legislative intent, explicit or implicit, either to create such a remedy or to deny one? * * * Third, is it consistent with the underlying purposes of the legislative scheme to imply such a remedy for the plaintiff? * * * And finally, is the cause of action one traditionally relegated to state law * * *? 422 U.S. at 78.
>
> * * *

Inasmuch as section 3009 is specifically designed to protect the recipients of unordered merchandise, *Cort's* first factor is clearly satisfied. As to the second factor of *Cort, viz.* Congress' intent to establish or deny a private right of action, we believe Congress did not consider the question of a private right of action under section 3009. The explanation may be simple. In the usual situation the remedy provided the recipient is immediate and self-executing. If a book is received, it may be kept by the recipient. There may be occasions, however, when the recipient's rights require vindication at law or where the application of the section, as in the case before us, requires interpretation before the recipient's rights can be determined. Nonetheless, the automaticity of the remedy provided by Congress in the usual situation goes far to explain why it neither explicitly permitted nor barred private suits under section 3009.

Turning to the third *Cort* factor, we find a *limited* private right of action would be entirely consistent with the purpose of the statute. In order to protect fully the recipient's rights he must be able to bring suit to obtain a judicial declaration of those rights and, when necessary, to secure restitutionary relief. Injunctive relief, however, possibly would interfere with the Federal Trade Commission's power to enforce section 3009. In the absence of an expression on the part of Congress indicating a willingness to incur the risk of this interference, we hold that the private right of action does not embrace an injunction which enjoins the sender's activities. Cf. Holloway v. Bristol-Myers Corp., 158 U.S. App.D.C. 207, 485 F.2d 986 (1973) (holding private enforcement of the Federal Trade Commission Act would seriously interfere with the FTC's enforcement of that act).

In addressing the fourth *Cort* factor, Academy Life argues a private right of action should not be implied because this area has traditionally been the subject of state law. It is true that the practice with which section 3009 is concerned traditionally has been governed by state law. However, subjecting it to national law is within the power of Congress and the limited private right we recognize will further the purposes Congress sought to serve by enacting the section.

IV.

The Merits.

Our conclusions to this point require that we confront the merits of the appellant's case. At its heart is the appellant's contention that the insurance policy forwarded by the appellee is "merchandise" within the meaning of the statute. We reject this contention. It is no more "merchandise" than is an unsolicited offer to sell kitchen appliances. The receipt of such an offer does not permit the recipient under section 3009 to obtain a judicial determination that he is the owner of such appliances without the payment of the purchase price. Even if we assume arguendo that an intangible can constitute "merchandise," the insurance policy forwarded by the appellee is no more than an offer to sell insurance. No insurance coverage could arise until the recipient completed the application and forwarded it with the premium amount. Ransom v. Penn Mutual Life Insurance Co., 43 Cal.2d 420, 274 P.2d 633 (1954). Thus, we hold that such an unaccepted offer to insure is not merchandise in the meaning of 39 U.S.C. § 3009 and therefore does not result in free insurance coverage for the recipients of Academy Life's solicitation.

The dismissal of the appellant's complaint by the district court was a proper disposition of the case although the reason relied upon by the district court for this action was erroneous.

Affirmed.

NOTES

1. In Arnesen v. The Raymond Lee Organization, Inc., 333 F.Supp. 116 (C.D.Cal.1971) the court held that consumers had standing to sue under § 43(a) of the Lanham Act. And courts have eroded *Colligan's* limitation of § 43(a) to "purely commercial" interests. See, Dallas Cowboys Cheerleaders, Inc. v. Pussycat Cinema, LTD, 467 F.Supp. 366 (S.D.N.Y.1979), affirmed 604 F.2d 200 (2d Cir.1979) where the real Dallas Cowboys cheerleaders were given standing to challenge the distribution and advertisement for a film, "Debbie Does Dallas" as falsely suggesting an association with the real cheerleaders. In Smith v. Montoro, 648 F.2d 602 (9th Cir.1981) an actor used § 43(a) against a film distributor who was not giving the actor proper credit for his appearance in a film. And in Thorn v. Reliance Van Co., 736 F.2d 929 (3d Cir.1984) an investor who was a 45% shareholder in a corporation was granted standing under § 43(a) to sue a competitor of the corporation for false advertising to recover for harm suffered due to his individual investment. The court in *Thorn* and *Smith* held that standing was available to anyone who demonstrated a reasonable interest to be protected by the statute.

In Monkelis v. Scientific Systems Services, 653 F.Supp. 680 (W.D.Pa.1987) the court held that a former employee did not have standing to sue his former employer under § 43(a) for false advertising engaged in by the employer. See also, Halicki v. United Artists Communications Inc., 812 F.2d 1213 (9th Cir. 1987) where a movie producer whose movie was given a "PG" rating by the Motion Picture Association sued a distributor and movie theaters who advertised the movie with an "R" rating. The "R" meant that only those over 18 years of age could attend thus destroying the commercial success of the movie. The court held § 43(a) inapplicable because the injury did not arise out of competition.

2.   Does the 1988 change in § 43(a) affect the analysis in *Colligan*? Are you convinced it is proper to limit § 43(a) in light of other remedies for consumer deception available under state law or through action of the FTC? The Trademark Review Commission of the United States Trademark Association which initiated the 1988 amendments to the Lanham Act believed the standing issues of § 43(a) were beyond their scope and should be addressed "only after comprehensive study." USTA Trademark Review Commission Report, 77 Trademark Rep. 427–28 (1987).

3.   Section 43(a) remains a useful tool in the arsenal of business interests who seek protection against the activities of their competitors. A wide variety of claims can be framed to meet the requirements of the section and thus permit access to the federal courts without the need to show diversity of citizenship. The expanded remedies available also make the section attractive to plaintiffs.

4.   Does the interest in compensating injured parties and deterring prohibited conduct always merge to give a strong push in favor of private remedies? What possible motivation would Congress have to deny private relief? Is the answer dependent on whether all deceptive practices involve social costs? Or whether deception can be adequately defined? Or on the nature of the remedy—damages, injunction, penalty—that is available? Or on the size of the budget given the public agency for enforcement purposes? For an analysis of these questions see Becker & Stigler, Law Enforcement, Malfeasance and Compensation of Enforcers, 3 J.Leg.Studies 1 (1974) and Landes & Posner, The Private Enforcement of Law, 4 J.Leg.Studies 1 (1975).

THE CONSUMER CLASS ACTION

The consumer damaged by a deceptive practice is not short of substantive doctrines which, if applied, would provide relief. The major obstacle preventing purchasers from policing market deception through legal action is the difference in relative gains between the purchaser and the seller in winning a lawsuit. In many instances, the costs of litigation to the consumer will far exceed the amount of the harm suffered from the deception and accordingly the amount of recovery in the event of success. The defendant, on the other hand, faced with the widespread affects on his method of operation of an adverse decision has greater incentive to expend resources in defense of his conduct. Even in those cases where the amount of loss suffered by a single consumer justifies litigation, it is more than likely that the defendant's potential loss from an adverse decision will be greater, and therefore it will make more sense for the defendant to exert greater effort (and incur greater costs) in his defense.

When, however, the claims of multiple purchasers are combined in a single law suit, the economic equation is shifted to a more even balance between plaintiffs and defendants. The class action is the device to accomplish this result, and its acceptance in a consumer setting has been advocated with zeal by proponents, fought with fury by businessmen, and pursued only reluctantly by courts and legislators.

Our purpose here is not to pursue the mechanics of the class action device but rather to explore briefly the more fundamental question of whether class actions are a useful method of policing market deception. This exploration provides a point of reference from which we can contrast and compare the remedies provided to competitors of the deceiver and a background against which to evaluate the utility of public enforcement of market practices.

VASQUEZ v. SUPERIOR COURT OF SAN JOAQUIN COUNTY

Supreme Court of California, 1971.
4 Cal.3d 800, 94 Cal.Rptr. 796, 484 P.2d 964.

[Thirty-seven named plaintiffs brought a class action on behalf of consumers who purchased freezers and supplies of food under install-ment sales contracts against the seller and the finance company to which the contracts were assigned. It was alleged that the seller induced the purchases by falsely overstating the quality and value of the freezer. It was also alleged the seller claimed its food packages would provide a "seven month" supply when in fact the food would not last that long. The Supreme Court of California authorized the class action. It found that the allegation that salesmen memorized and used a standard sales pitch and that the food quantity provided, although different for each purchaser, was contained on a standard order form which implied the use of a standard formula for determining a purchas-er's food needs, were sufficient to create a presumption that common issues of fact existed for the class. The court also held that, if material misrepresentations were made, an inference is created that each pur-chaser relied on those misrepresentations thus eliminating the need for each purchaser to individually prove reliance. The court did note the requirement that each purchaser must prove his individual damage. In the following excerpts the court focuses on the value of the class action device:]

MOSK, JUSTICE.

* * *

II

Thirty years ago commentators, in urging the utility of the class suit to vindicate the rights of stockholders, made this incisive observa-tion: "Modern society seems increasingly to expose men to * * * group injuries for which individually they are in a poor position to seek legal redress, either because they do not know enough or because such redress is disproportionately expensive. If each is left to assert his rights alone if and when he can, there will at best be a random and fragmentary enforcement, if there is any at all. This result is not only unfortunate in the particular case, but it will operate seriously to impair the deterrent effect of the sanctions which underline much contemporary law. The problem of fashioning an effective and inclusive group remedy is thus a major one." (Kalven and Rosenfield, Function of Class Suit (1941) 8 U.Chi.L.Rev. 684, 686.)

What was noteworthy in the milieu three decades ago for stockholders is of far greater significance today for consumers. Not only have the means of communication improved and the sophistication of promotional and selling techniques sharpened in the intervening years, but consumers as a category are generally in a less favorable position than stockholders to secure legal redress for wrongs committed against them.

* * *

Protection of unwary consumers from being duped by unscrupulous sellers is an exigency of the utmost priority in contemporary society. According to the report of the Kerner Commission, many persons who reside in low income neighborhoods experience grievous exploitation by vendors using such devices as high pressure salesmanship, bait advertising, misrepresentation of prices, exorbitant prices and credit charges, and sale of shoddy merchandise. State laws governing relations between consumers and merchants are generally utilized only by informed, sophisticated parties, affording little practical protection to low income families. (Report of National Advisory Commission on Civil Disorders (Bantam ed. 1968) pp. 275–276; Hester, Deceptive Sales Practices and Form Contracts—Does the Consumer Have a Private Remedy? 1968 Duke L.J. 831.) The alternatives of multiple litigation (joinder, intervention, consolidation, the test case) do not sufficiently protect the consumer's rights because these devices "presuppose 'a group of economically powerful parties who are obviously able and willing to take care of their own interests individually through individual suits or individual decisions about joinder or intervention.'" (Dolgow v. Anderson (E.D.N.Y.1968) 43 F.R.D. 472, 484.)

Frequently numerous consumers are exposed to the same dubious practice by the same seller so that proof of the prevalence of the practice as to one consumer would provide proof for all. Individual actions by each of the defrauded consumers is often impracticable because the amount of individual recovery would be insufficient to justify bringing a separate action; thus an unscrupulous seller retains the benefits of its wrongful conduct. A class action by consumers produces several salutary by-products, including a therapeutic effect upon those sellers who indulge in fraudulent practices, aid to legitimate business enterprises by curtailing illegitimate competition, and avoidance to the judicial process of the burden of multiple litigation involving identical claims. The benefit to the parties and the courts would, in many circumstances, be substantial.

HALL v. COBURN CORP. OF AMERICA
Court of Appeals of New York, 1970.
26 N.Y.2d 396, 311 N.Y.S.2d 281, 259 N.E.2d 720.

[Two named plaintiffs brought a class action on behalf of persons who entered into retail installment sales contracts with various sellers by signing a particular form contract provided by and subsequently purchased by the defendant. Some contract provisions were in type less than 8 point in size in violation of a New York statute. The statutory penalty for the violation was recovery of the amount of credit service charge. The court refused to permit the class action.]

BERGAN, JUDGE.

* * *

Since the weight of authority seems to interdict these actions, the question is whether the court should now revise the rule it has laid down to permit class suits in this situation. It is submitted that the poor are victimized by this type of credit practice; that public authority is impotent to help them; and only by permitting self-help class actions initiated by private individuals and their lawyers can the imbalance be redressed.

The real injustice of course, is the fact the poor have to pay more for carpets and for everything else they buy on credit than people who are able to pay outright. Mr. and Mrs. Russell, for example, paid $736.92 for a $549.02 carpet for their living room and bedroom. Mrs. Hall paid $826.56 for a $580 carpet. But this was not due to the small type of which plaintiffs complain. It was due to the addition of charges which are expressly permitted by statute law.

* * *

If this is unfair, as it seems to be, the statute should be changed either to prohibit sales of this type or to reduce the legally permissible charges. On this essentially economic problem it is doubtful if any public good can be accomplished by making a finance company pay back legally permissible credit charges in an indefinite number of contracts because the type is too small on printed parts of the contract.

The small type of which plaintiffs complain was not concerned with the terms of the contract of sale itself. In large part it dealt with the remedies by repossession and recovery if the purchaser did not pay for the goods.

That a seller can get his goods back if they are not paid for is a common understanding and expectation of those who buy on credit. The terms of credit and protective insurance were also in small type, but the cost of the insurance items was boldly stated in writing next to printed references of sufficient size.

If the type were as large as the printer's font affords it would not make the slightest difference in the execution of these costly contracts by people who need goods but are unable to pay for them. The essential thing for a purchaser to be able to see in this contract is the exact amounts which make up the price and what has to be paid. These things are certainly stated in bold writing.

The public value of judicial sanction to this kind of class action which would harass a finance company underwriting credit sales without addressing itself to the real evil of retail credit buying is open to substantial doubt. The basic public problem is the heavy cost of credit to consumers.

* * *

Both congressional committees and the American Bar Association acting for the legal profession have been concerned with means of protecting consumers against fraudulent, deceptive or unfair trade practices.

Limitations on, or alternatives to, class actions have been considered as, for example, requiring a predetermination of unfair practice by a public agency or a court at suit of a public agency, before a class action might be instituted. Another alternative is a requirement that actions for recovery be maintained by the public agency itself.

These limitations would tend to answer the main objection to the privately maintained consumer class action; that without adequate public control they may become instruments of harassment benefiting largely persons who activate the litigation.

No significant public benefit is discernible from the acceptance of these present class actions which do not, on the merits asserted, justify present departure from the existing New York rule. The Legislature in the spring of 1970 created the State Consumer Protection Board, the public function of which will be to protect consumers from unfair practices. (L.1970, ch. 294.)

Besides this there has previously been adequate public authority in New York to see to it that the requirement of law as to the size of type on contracts be followed and enforcement need not rest on privately instituted actions for the public benefit.

The Banking Department may control the form of defendant's contracts and make appropriate directions as to the size of type. Besides this, the violation of the statute is a misdemeanor (Personal Property Law, § 414) and the Attorney-General may institute a prosecution based on small type.

The orders should be affirmed, without costs.

FULD, C.J., and BURKE, SCILEPPI, BREITEL, JASEN and GIBSON, JJ., concur.

Orders affirmed.

NOTES

1. For an engaging autobiographical account of the difficulties of consumer law suits see Schrag, Bleak House 1968: A Report on Consumer Test

Litigation, 44 N.Y.U.L.Rev. 115 (1969). The author participated in the *Coburn* case which originally was dismissed by the Supreme Court of New York and affirmed by the Appellate Division. His comments on the *Coburn* decision, prior to appeal to the Court of Appeals, indicates the importance attributed to the consumer class action by consumer advocates:

> In the *Hall* case, the Legal Defense Fund, Consumers' Union, the Attorney General of the State of New York, and the law firm of Paul, Weiss, Goldberg, Rifkind, Wharton & Garrison had all joined to urge the Court that it was unjust and unwise to prevent consumers from having a day in court solely because their claims were too small to justify individual litigation—we urged that class actions were essential to the vindication of consumers' rights. Each side put literally hundreds of man-hours into the case. Here then, in its entirety, is the response of the Appellate Division to what is probably the most important consumer law issue of the decade: "Order entered Aug. 28, 1968, and judgment, unanimously affirmed, without costs and without disbursements. No opinion. Order filed."

2. What are the perceptions of the California and New York courts as to the underlying goals of a consumer class action? What is the benefit to the courts asserted in *Vasquez?* Would the class action inevitably be a more efficient mechanism for resolving multiple claims? Assume that a national manufacturer misrepresented the amount of vegetables in a can of its soup and as a result consumers who paid 30 cents a can received only a 25 cent value. Can it realistically be argued that allowing a class action will utilize less judicial resources than requiring each individual claimant to sue separately? Assume a different case in which the individual loss to each purchaser is $2000. From a social perspective is it inevitably more efficient to resolve the common issues of fact in one lawsuit?

In the case of the vegetable soup assume the total loss to the consuming public resulting from the deception (or if you will the total gain derived by the manufacturer) is $1,000,000. Is there a social interest in allowing the class action to proceed? What if the proportionate cost of the litigation to each claimant including legal fees will be 3 cents? Is a similar problem confronting the court in *Hall?* Does the court suggest that the deception resulted in no injury and thus giving the statutory penalty to all members of the class would not in fact be compensatory? Is compensation to injured purchasers a necessary ingredient of a consumer class action? The court subtly suggests, as others have done more openly, that the major beneficiary of the class action is the plaintiff's attorney. Assuming this to be true, does it affect your view of the class action?

The role of the plaintiff's attorney in the class action has made some courts and commentators uneasy. There is a substantial conflict of interest between the attorney and the plaintiffs (in addition to a conflict between the named representative and the unnamed class members). The conflict was illustrated in A. Rosenfield, An Empirical Test of Class-Action Settlement, 5 J.Leg.Studies 113 (1976) by postulating a situation in which 10,000 class members are injured to the extent of $1,000 each and that by causing the harm the defendant's benefits are $8,000,000:

> In our example, the attorney for the class may propose a settlement of $9,000,000—$8,000,000 to be awarded to the class members and a $1,000,000 attorney's fee. The firm may then propose a counter-

offer of a $7,500,000 settlement but to be distributed as a $6,000,000 award to class members and a $1,500,000 attorney's fee. Under the first settlement each of the 10,000 individuals receives $800, under the second settlement each receives $750 or a marginal change of $50. However, each of the principals (the defendant and the class attorney) is much better off in the second case.

With regard to many of these problems is not the answer that the class action would have a deterrent effect on the defendant's conduct regardless of whether the plaintiffs are actually compensated and thus the class action ought to be authorized? As long as the defendant pays, does it really matter who gets the recovery? Indeed, to the extent the plaintiffs or their attorney recover, the class action device has encouraged private enforcement of legal restrictions. It has been suggested that private enforcement of penalties may result in inefficient overenforcement. Landis & Posner, The Private Enforcement of Law, 4 J.Leg.Studies 1 (1975). If this is the case, would you still authorize class actions or would you prefer to have public enforcement with the recovery (whether a fine or a sum based on the injury inflicted) being allocated to a public purpose? Some jurisdictions have adopted provisions authorizing a public official to sue as parens patriae on behalf of injured consumers to recover damages. Uniform Consumer Sales Practice Act § 9 (1972).

The above questions are posed and analyzed in Dam, Class Actions: Efficiency, Compensation, Deterrence, and Conflict of Interest, 4 J.Leg. Studies 47 (1975).

3. For what purpose would the government wish to require governmental action prior to authorizing class actions? Is it sufficient for consumer advocates to argue that without the class action the consumers will have a "right without a remedy"? Is the equation altered by the development of legal assistance programs for the poor? Does "test litigation" provide an adequate substitute for the class action? If procedural and standing rules were relaxed for competitor suits for deceptive advertising, would the pressure for consumer class actions be lessened?

4. For secondary literature on class actions see: Kalven & Rosenfield, The Contemporary Function of the Class Suit, 8 U.Chi.L.Rev. 684 (1941); Comment, Recovery of Damages in Class Actions, 32 U.Chi.L.Rev. 768 (1965); Dole, Consumer Class Actions Under Recent Consumer Credit Legislation, 44 N.Y. U.L.Rev. 80 (1969); Dole, Consumer Class Actions Under the Uniform Deceptive Trade Practices Act, [1968] Duke L.J. 1101. Dole, The Settlement of Class Actions for Damages, 71 Colo.L.Rev. 971 (1971). Weinstein, Some Reflections on the "Abusiveness" of Class Actions, 58 F.R.D. 299 (1973); Note, Developments in the Law—Class Actions, 89 Harv.L.Rev. 1319 (1976). See also, Annot., Attorneys' Fees in Class Actions, 38 A.L.R.3d 1384 (1971); Annot., Consumer Class Actions Based on Fraud and Misrepresentation, 53 A.L.R.3d 534 (1973).

5. Consider the following proposal: In cases where a large number of persons are injured in small amounts (under $500) a public penalty procedure would be authorized whereby the United States, or any private person injured, could initiate an action on behalf of the United States against the defendant for the aggregate amount of the harm done. If successful, the defendant would pay the judgment to an administrative agency that would administer the payment of claims. The litigating plaintiff would receive an "incentive fee" of attorneys fees plus a percentage of the recovery not to exceed $10,000. In an action initiated by a private plaintiff, the United States could take control of the

litigation or recommend its dismissal. Class actions for this type of case would be abolished and a judgment would bar further individual claims.

Where the injury to large numbers of persons exceed $500 per person, a traditional class action would be available but a preliminary hearing would be held after very limited discovery to determine whether there is a "reasonable possibility" that the plaintiff will prevail. Litigation costs to date would be assessed after the hearing in favor of the prevailing party. If the plaintiff prevails a subsequent certification hearing would be held to determine whether the case meets other requirements of a class action.

See U.S. Dept. of Justice Office for Improvements in the Administration of Justice, Effective Procedural Remedies for Unlawful Conduct Causing Mass Economic Injury, (Draft, Dec. 1, 1977). For reactions to the proposal see Antitrust & Trade Reg.Rep. (BNA), No. 891 at A–25 (1978) and No. 956 at A–3 (1980).

C. STATE UNFAIR COMPETITION STATUTES

During the 1960's and 1970's when national attention was focused on consumer protection, most states adopted unfair competition or consumer protection legislation. These enactments were modeled after the Uniform Deceptive Trade Practices Act (UDTPA), proposed by the National Conference of Commissioners on Uniform State Laws, or the Unfair Trade Practices and Consumer Protection Law (UTPCPL), proposed by the Federal Trade Commission for enactment by the states. These model laws are reproduced in the statutory supplement with a chart indicating those jurisdictions that have adopted versions of one or both of these proposals.

The major thrust of the UDTPA appears to codify the law of false advertising as applied between competitors. Section 2 provides a laundry list of "deceptive trade practices" all of which contain some element of misrepresentation. The remedial provision (§ 3) permits a "person likely to be damaged" to obtain injunctive relief, the costs of the action, and attorneys fees where the defendant "willfully" engaged in the deceptive practice. Although it has been argued that the act permits consumers to sue as well,[4] it is unlikely that the individual consumer's interest is satisfied with injunctive relief alone.

The UTPCPL, on the other hand, is a much broader assault on unwanted trade practices and currently dominates the field in the state courts. Most versions of the act prohibit acts that are "unfair" as well as acts that are "deceptive". The state attorney general is given broad powers to adopt rules and regulations and to seek civil penalties for violations. But private actions are authorized and, in some versions, substantial private remedies are available.

The states did not adopt and have not maintained a uniform approach to this consumer protection legislation. The model proposed by the FTC itself contained alternative provisions and some state

---

4. Dole, Merchant and Consumer Protection: The Uniform Deceptive Trade Practices Act, 76 Yale L.J. 485 (1967).

legislatures adopted their own alternatives which generally broadened the statute's applicability. More recently litigants have begun to explore the full potential of these enactments. The process of judicial interpretation followed by legislative clarification or adjustment has further eroded the uniformity of the original proposal. The notes below outline the major areas of diversity.

NOTES: VARIATIONS IN THE UTPCPL

1. *Substantive prohibitions.* The FTC's original proposal contained three alternative formulations of the substantive prohibitions. These alternatives are reproduced in the statutory supplement. Alternative 3 incorporates the list of deceptive practices in the UDTPA with the addition of the catchall provision in subparagraph (13) to include "unfair" as well as "deceptive" acts. Some states made alterations in the formulation of the specific prohibitions by, for example, adding a "knowingly" requirement to some of the prohibited acts.

One of the most significant features of the Consumer Protection Act was adopted by most states. It directs state courts when construing the substantive prohibitions of the act to give "great weight" to opinions by the federal courts and Federal Trade Commission defining unfair and deceptive acts under the Federal Trade Commission Act. Combined with the private remedial provisions of the state statutes, the effect of this provision is to incorporate FTC jurisprudence into the substantive law of each state.

Most state formulations also permit the state attorney general to adopt rules and regulations defining unfair or deceptive acts or practices which in turn can be enforced through the private remedies afforded by the act. Some state attorneys general have actively promulgated consumer protection regulations.

2. *Standing for private remedies.* The original FTC proposal contained a very limited standing provision defining who could seek private remedies under the act. Section 8 provided private actions to

> "[a]ny person who *purchases or leases goods or services primarily for personal, family or household purposes and thereby* suffers any ascertainable loss of money or property, real or personal, as a result of the use or employment by another of a method, act or practice declared unlawful by Section 2 of this Act . . . ."

This provision limits private relief to consumers purchasing for personal use. However, many jurisdictions adopted a modified form omitting the emphasized language. The revised form permits any injured person to bring suit. Massachusetts adopted a separate section providing a private remedy to "any person who engages in the conduct of any trade or commerce and who suffers any loss" from a prescribed act. Mass.Gen.Laws.Ann. 93A § 11.

3. *Private remedies.* The FTC proposal permits recovery of actual damages or $200 whichever is greater. States adopted different statutory damage amounts.

The act also authorizes punitive damages and equitable relief as well as "reasonable attorney's fees and costs". Many states have expanded on these remedies. In Massachusetts a "wilful or knowing" violation requires the court to provide "up to three but not less than two times [the actual damages]." Mass.Gen.Laws.Ann. 93A § 9. In North Carolina if damages are awarded for any violation of the act the court is *required* to treble them. N.Car.G.S. § 75–

16. In Texas the provision reads: "the court shall award two times that portion of actual damages that does not exceed $1,000. If the trier of fact finds that the conduct of the defendant was committed knowingly, the trier of fact may award not more than three times the amount of damages in excess of $1,000." Tex.Bus & Comm.Code § 17.50(b)(2). See also, Fargo Women's Health Organization, Inc. v. FM Women's Help and Caring Connection, 444 N.W.2d 683 (N.D.1989) where the court implied an action for damages including punitive damages for false advertising from a state variation that provided only for criminal penalties and injunctive relief.

4. In some jurisdictions the statutory causes of action have begun to take on increasing importance in regulating business practices. In others, the potential of these statutes has not yet been fully perceived. In part this can be explained by the differences in standing and remedial provisions. Massachusetts, North Carolina, Washington, and Texas particularly have experienced a burgeoning number of cases explained in part by the availability of multiple damages and attorneys fees and the courts' willingness to give a broad interpretation to what acts are encompassed within the statute.

5. *Bibliography.* A leading article on the state consumer protection statutes is Leafter & Lipson, Consumer Actions Against Unfair or Deceptive Acts or Practices: The Private Uses of Federal Trade Commission Jurisprudence, 48 Geo.Wash.L.Rev. 521 (1980). A treatise-like treatment of the cases can be found in National Consumer Law Center, Unfair and Deceptive Acts and Practices (1982) (Supp.1987). See United States Trademark Association, State Trademark and Unfair Competition Law (1988) for an outline by state of the statutory provisions and significant judicial interpretations.

POULIN v. FORD MOTOR COMPANY

Supreme Court of Vermont, 1986.
147 Vt. 120, 513 A.2d 1168.

PECK, JUSTICE.

The plaintiff brought an action against defendants Hayes Ford and Ford Motor Company, alleging that they illegally induced him to buy a 1979 Ford Mustang "Pace Car" by indicating that the car was a limited-production model which would increase in value. The complaint alleged violations of express and implied warranties, intentional misrepresentation and violation of the Consumer Fraud Act, 9 V.S.A. § 2453. After trial, the jury awarded the plaintiff $40,000. Defendants appeal the judgment on the verdict, the denial of a motion for a new trial, and the denial of a motion to set aside the verdict. We affirm.

In May, 1979, plaintiff, an owner of a lumber business, approached John Hayes, owner of defendant Hayes Ford, Inc., and expressed some interest in purchasing a 1979 Ford Mustang "Pace Car." The car was an exact replica of the one used to pace the field at the 1979 Indianapolis 500 motor car race. The plaintiff's interest stemmed from his knowledge that the 1978 Corvette Pace Car had increased in value, according to the evidence, from $14,000 to approximately $28,000.

After a test drive, the plaintiff met with Hayes and a representative of defendant Ford Motor Company. He expressed a continuing interest in the vehicle but also indicated that personal financial difficulties might preclude the purchase. According to the plaintiff, the representative of defendant Ford Motor Company told plaintiff that the pace car is "going to be a very lucrative type of car . . . as a collector's item . . . [W]e are stopping production as of the Indianapolis 500." Further, testimony indicated that the defendants told plaintiff the 1979 pace car was a limited edition with only about 2,800 issued, or less than one car per dealer. Defendants told plaintiff the car would increase in value similarly to the Corvette version of the pace car. Based on these representations, plaintiff purchased the car.

About one month later, plaintiff contacted Hayes and expressed his concerns about seeing "quite a few" pace cars on the road. Defendant Hayes Ford indicated to plaintiff that Ford had "flooded the market" with the cars, that Ford was still producing them and that Hayes Ford had, in fact, acquired another pace car. Plaintiff also learned that a Ford dealer in Swanton, Vermont, was offering rebates on two of the cars, asking only $7,400 for each.

After failing in his attempts to get Hayes Ford to buy back the pace car, plaintiff brought an action against the named defendants. The counts specified that: (1) defendants breached an express warranty that the vehicle was a "limited production car;" (2) defendants breached an implied warranty of fitness for a particular purpose in that defendants knew plaintiff, in purchasing the car, relied upon statements regarding its expected increase in value and that the warranted increase never occurred; (3) defendants defrauded plaintiff; and (4) defendants' actions constituted unfair and deceptive acts and practices in violation of 9 V.S.A. § 2453.

After both sides presented their cases, the trial judge, over defendants' objection, charged the jury on plaintiff's consumer fraud claim as well as the other claims. The jury found defendants liable, and awarded him $40,000. The amount of this award indicates the jury's verdict was rendered pursuant to the exemplary damage provision in the Consumer Fraud Act. 9 V.S.A. § 2461(b). Defendants moved the court to grant a new trial and to set aside the verdict. The court denied defendants' motions and issued judgment for plaintiff. Defendants appealed the order denying their motions and appealed the judgment.

The Consumer Fraud Act prohibits "unfair or deceptive acts or practices in commerce." 9 V.S.A. § 2453(a). For the Act to apply, the plaintiff must be a consumer as defined by the Act: "any person who purchases . . . merchandise or services not for resale in the ordinary course of his trade or business but for his use or benefit. . . ." 9 V.S.A. § 2451a. Defendants argue that plaintiff was not a consumer because he purchased the pace car as an investment, and because he stated he bought and sold cars. Plaintiff's expectation that the car would appreciate in value does not prohibit him from being a consumer. The issue is whether the plaintiff bought the car to resell in the ordinary course of his business. The plaintiff testified that he bought the car for his personal benefit and that although he had sold cars bought as investments, he was not a used car dealer. Based on this testimony, the jury could conclude that the plaintiff was a consumer under the Act.

The defendants' next argument is that there was insufficient evidence presented at trial to allow the claim of unfair or deceptive acts or practices to go to the jury.

In this case, the trial court charged the jury on common law fraud, apparently concluding that it was synonymous with consumer fraud. However, state statutes similar to our Consumer Fraud Act are recognized as providing a much broader right than common law fraud.

Our Consumer Fraud Act requires courts construing Vermont's consumer fraud law to "be guided by the construction of similar terms contained in section 5(a)(1) of the Federal Trade Commission Act as from time to time amended by the Federal Trade Commission and the courts of the United States." 9 V.S.A. § 2453(b).

Many federal courts have held that a misrepresentation which has the tendency and capacity to mislead consumers is a deceptive act or practice under federal law. See, e.g., American Home Products Corp. v. FTC, 695 F.2d 681, 686 (3d Cir.1982); Trans World Accounts, Inc. v. FTC, 594 F.2d 212, 214 (9th Cir.1979); FTC v. Sterling Drug, Inc., 317 F.2d 669, 674 (2d Cir.1963); see also the discussion in FTC v. Colgate–Palmolive Co., 380 U.S. 374, 384–90, (1965). Similarly, a number of courts in states with statutes similar to Vermont's Consumer Fraud Act have also adopted this definition of deception.

Recently, the Federal Trade Commission (FTC) stated that "a deception case requires a showing of three elements: (1) there must be a representation, practice, or omission likely to mislead consumers; (2) the consumers must be interpreting the message reasonably under the circumstances; and (3) the misleading effects must be 'material,' that is, likely to affect consumers' conduct or decision with regard to a product." International Harvester Co., 3 Trade Reg.Rep. (CCH) ¶ 22,217 p. 23,174, 23,178 (Dec. 21, 1984).

It is unnecessary to determine which standard should be adopted for purposes of this case under our Act, because in light of the facts presented here, both standards are satisfied. The evidence indicated that the defendants told the plaintiff the pace car was a limited edition; that production was stopping immediately; that only 2,800 cars would be produced; and that the car would increase in value by $4,000 or $5,000 in several months. Furthermore, there was evidence that one defendant later told the plaintiff that Ford had flooded the market with the cars and that Ford was still producing them. Other evidence revealed that at least one dealer was offering $1,600 rebates on the cars and that the price of the car had dropped from $9,000 to between $5,000 and $7,500. Given this evidence, we conclude that there was sufficient evidence of deceptive acts or practices to go to the jury. Because we find sufficient support for a finding of deception, we do not consider whether the acts were unfair.

The defendants further attack the trial court's charge on consumer fraud as erroneous because (1) it failed to describe what constitutes unfair or deceptive acts or practices, and (2) it directed the jury to apply the preponderance-of-the-evidence standard of proof rather than that of clear and convincing evidence. The record reveals no objection by the defendants as to the burden of proof or the text of the instructions themselves. Issues not objected to below will not be considered upon appellate review. As defendants admit, however, the jury based its decision on consumer fraud. Consumer fraud does not require the higher standard of proof. "The mere fact that the word 'fraud' appears in the title of our consumer protection statute does not give rise to an inference that the legislature intended to require a higher degree of proof than that ordinarily required in civil cases." *Dunlap,* supra, 136 Ariz. at 343, 666 P.2d at 89. The purpose of our Consumer Fraud Act is to protect consumers by adding "a claim for relief that is easier to establish than is common law fraud. To require the higher degree of proof would frustrate the legislative intent." Id. Until the legislature states otherwise, we will not presume that it intended to impose the greater burden of proof in consumer fraud cases.

Next, the defendants attack the verdict as unsupported by the evidence. They contend that deception requires an intentional misrepresentation, and that plaintiff failed to introduce any evidence that the defendants intentionally misrepresented material facts. Neither the prevailing judicial definition nor the recent FTC definition (both mentioned above) require intent.

The plaintiff claims this appeal should be dismissed for lack of jurisdiction because the lower court's decision was not final due to its failure to rule on attorney's fees. Although the plaintiff requested attorney's fees in his complaint and in his proposed jury instructions, he did not introduce any evidence on reasonable attorney's fees at trial. After plaintiff rested, he moved to reopen to introduce evidence on this issue but the court denied his motion. He did not object to the court's jury instructions which did not mention attorney's fees. After trial, he did not cross-appeal or move to amend the judgment. Under these circumstances, we think the judgment was final and the issue of attorney's fees has been waived.

Affirmed.

V.S.H. REALTY, INC. v. TEXACO, INC.

United States Court of Appeals, First Circuit, 1985.
757 F.2d 411.

Coffin, Circuit Judge.

I. Factual Background

On August 11, 1983, V.S.H. offered to purchase from Texaco a used bulk storage petroleum facility for $2.8 million. Texaco accepted the offer on September 7, and V.S.H. made a deposit of $280,000 to be applied against the purchase price. The offer to purchase required Texaco to convey the property "free and clear of all liens, encumbrances, tenancies and restrictions", except for those set forth in the offer. Attached to the offer to purchase was an acknowledgement signed by Texaco stating that, to the best of the company's knowledge and belief, it had not received "any notice, demand, or communication from any local county, state or federal department or agency regarding modifications or improvements to the facility or any part thereof." The offer also included a disclosure by Texaco that fuel oils had "migrated under [Texaco's] garage building across Marginal Street from the terminal [and that] the fuel oil underground as a result of heavy rains or high tides, seeps into the boiler room of the garage building." V.S.H., for its part, expressly stated in the offer that it had inspected the property, and accepted it "as is" without any representation on the part of Texaco as to its condition.

Problems arose when V.S.H. representatives visited the property in mid-October 1983, approximately a month after Texaco accepted the offer to purchase, and observed oil seeping from the ground at the western end of the property. During a subsequent visit, V.S.H. representatives discovered another oil seepage at the eastern end of the property. V.S.H. then notified Texaco that it would not go through with the purchase unless Texaco corrected the oil problem, provided V.S.H. with full indemnification, or reduced the purchase price. When Texaco refused, V.S.H. demanded return of its down payment. Texaco again refused, and V.S.H. filed this lawsuit on January 10, 1984.

In its three-count complaint, V.S.H. alleges first that Texaco violated Mass.Gen.Laws Ann. ch. 93A, § 2, which prohibits unfair and deceptive acts and practices, basing that assertion largely on Texaco's failure to disclose the seeping oil, and its failure to disclose an investigation of the property by the U.S. Coast Guard. V.S.H.'s second count claims relief for breach of contract, based on Texaco's alleged inability to convey the property at the specified time free of all liens, encumbrances and restrictions. V.S.H.'s contract theory is that the penalties associated with the oil seepage problem constitute an encumbrance on the property. Finally, V.S.H. charges Texaco with common law misrepresentation and deceit for failing to disclose the oil seepage problems and Coast Guard investigation "in the face of repeated inquiries by V.S.H. about the subject."

At the conclusion of a hearing on Texaco's motion to dismiss all three counts, the district court announced without explanation that the contract claims should be dismissed. It also dismissed the common law fraud count at that time, stating that V.S.H. had failed to allege the required affirmative misrepresentation or implicit misrepresentation by partial and ambiguous statements. It deferred decision on the chapter 93A count, and in a latter written decision dismissed that count on two grounds: an Attorney General's regulation upon which V.S.H. relied was not intended to apply in a transaction between two sophisticated business entities, when one party agrees to take the property "as is";

and Texaco had no duty to disclose the oil seepages to V.S.H., and so its failure to do so could not have violated chapter 93A.

* * *

II. Sufficiency of the Complaint

A. Common Law Misrepresentation

[V.S.H. alleged it had made "repeated inquiries" about oil leaks and had not received a full response from Texaco. This, the court found, was a sufficient allegation of partial and ambiguous statements to state a cause of action for common law misrepresentation.]

B. Breach of Mass.Gen.Laws Ann. ch. 93A

Mass.Gen.Laws Ann. ch. 93A generally prohibits unfair or deceptive acts or practices in business. When it was first enacted in 1967, its primary goal was protection of consumers, Manning v. Zuckerman, 388 Mass. 8, 12, 444 N.E.2d 1262 (1983), but the addition of section 11 in 1972 extended chapter 93A's coverage to business persons involved in transactions with other business persons. * * *

Chapter 93A § 2 provides no definition of an unfair or deceptive act or practice, and instead directs our attention to interpretations of unfair acts and practices under the Federal Trade Commission Act as construed by the Commission and the federal courts. The section also empowers the Attorney General to make rules and regulations interpreting § 2(a). See § 2(c). V.S.H. relies heavily on one such regulation to support its allegation that Texaco violated chapter 93A.

The Attorney General's regulation in Mass.Admin.Code tit. 20, § 3.16(2) states that an act or practice violates chapter 93A if:

"Any person or other legal entity subject to this act fails to disclose to a buyer or prospective buyer any fact, the disclosure of which may have influenced the buyer or prospective buyer not to enter into the transaction."

V.S.H.'s complaint appears to state a claim under this regulation and, in fact, mirrors its language. V.S.H. alleged in paragraph 19 of its complaint that Texaco's failure to disclose the oil leaks that V.S.H. representatives discovered in October 1983 "are facts the disclosure of which may have influenced V.S.H. not to enter into the transaction and agree to pay the sum of $2,800,000 for the premises or to pay a deposit in connection therewith of $280,000."

The district court found an inadequacy in the complaint by concluding that the disclosure language of regulation § 3.16 is incomplete. The court decided that "unless a defendant has a duty to speak, his nondisclosure of a defect does not constitute a violation of chapter 93A even if the information may have influenced the buyer not to enter into the contract." The court then went on to hold that Texaco did not have a duty to disclose the oil leaks to V.S.H. We disagree for two reasons. First, even if we were to accept the court's premise that nondisclosure is a violation of chapter 93A only when there is a duty to disclose, we would find that V.S.H. has met its burden of establishing a duty by alleging that Texaco made partial or incomplete statements regarding the oil leaks on the property. See Restatement of Torts (Second) §§ 551, 529.

We are not convinced, however, that V.S.H. needs to allege more than a failure to disclose a material fact to state a cause of action under chapter 93A. In Slaney v. Westwood Auto, Inc., 366 Mass. 688, 322 N.E.2d 768 (1975), the Massachusetts Supreme Judicial Court examined chapter 93A at length, and emphasized the distinction between that statutory cause of action and the common law action for fraud and deceit, which would require a duty to disclose. It pointed out that "the definition of an actionable 'unfair or deceptive act or practice' goes far beyond the scope of the common law action for fraud and deceit. . . . [A] § 9 [or § 11] claim for relief . . . is not subject to the traditional limitations of preexisting causes of action such as tort for fraud and deceit." Id., at 703–04, 322 N.E.2d 768. Massachusetts case law suggests that one difference between a fraud claim and the more liberal 93A is allowance of a cause of action even in the absence of a duty to disclose. See Nei v. Boston Survey Consultants, Inc., 388 Mass. 320, 323–24, 446 N.E.2d 681 (1983), where the court appeared ready to find chapter 93A liability even though it found no duty to speak.

The district court, however, had another reason for dismissing the claim. It concluded that chapter 93A liability was precluded because V.S.H. is a sophisticated buyer who had the opportunity to inspect the property and who agreed to purchase the property "as is". The court noted that "this type of contractual arrangement is expressly permitted under the Uniform Commercial Code, M.G.L. c. 106, § 2–316, in non-consumer sales of goods", and it thus "would be anomalous to hold that 'as is' contracts are permissible in sales of goods cases but not in commercial sales of land cases." It concluded:

> "Absent allegations of the non-detectability of defects on inspection or their fraudulent concealment by a defendant, a plaintiff who has inspected the premises to be purchased and has agreed to purchase the land 'as is' cannot rely on § 3.16(2) to establish a defendant's violation of chapter 93A."

We believe the district court's view of the law regarding "as is" clauses is incorrect. Although the Uniform Commercial Code does expressly permit disclaimers in the sale of goods between merchants, § 2–316 refers specifically to disclaimers of implied warranties, suggesting to us that it was intended only to permit a seller to limit or modify the contractual bases of liability which the Code would otherwise impose on the transaction. The section does not appear to preclude claims based on fraud or other deceptive conduct. * * *

We find further support for our view implicit in Marcil v. John Deere Industrial Equipment Co., 9 Mass.App. 625, 403 N.E.2d 430, app. denied, 380 Mass. 940 (1980). The court in that case upheld a disclaimer of all express and implied warranties other than the warranty specified on the purchase order, finding that there was no indication that the disclaimer was unconscionable. The court went on to note that the vaguely worded allegations of the plaintiff's complaint may have stated claims for deceit or violation of chapter 93A, but the plaintiff failed to characterize them as such to the trial judge, and so he was not allowed to do so for the first time on appeal. Our reading of *Marcil* is that even if a disclaimer on its face is not unconscionable, it is subject to challenge if a plaintiff, as in this case, properly raises allegations of deceit and violation of chapter 93A.

Our conclusion here does not mean that an "as is" clause would never be given effect in real estate transactions where the buyer alleged the seller's failure to disclose a material defect in the property. The Supreme Judicial Court has held that § 3.16(2) imposes liability only when the defendant had knowledge, or should have known of the defect, and where a direct relationship existed between the parties. It is possible that § 3.16(2) will be found inapplicable in other situations involving "as is" clauses.

Even more persuasive than this inferential reasoning based on the Uniform Commercial Code is the fact that Massachusetts case law unequivocally rejects assertion of an "as is" clause as an automatic defense against allegations of fraud:

"The same public policy that in general sanctions the avoidance of a promise obtained by deceit strikes down all attempts to circumvent the policy by means of contractual devices. In the realm of fact it is entirely possible for a party knowingly to agree that no representations have been made to him, while at the same time believing and relying upon representations which in fact have been made and in fact are false but for which he would not have made the agreement." Bates v. Southgate, 308 Mass. 170, 182, 31 N.E.2d 551 (1941).

* * *

Texaco acknowledges that a party may not contract out of liability for fraud. It argues instead that the specific language of the disclaimer in this case precludes recovery by V.S.H., (i.e., that V.S.H. did not rely on any representations); Texaco relies heavily, however, on a case from another jurisdiction to support this proposition, Landale Enterprises, Inc. v. Berry, 676 F.2d 506 (11th Cir.1982). Bates v. Southgate, 308 Mass. 170, 31 N.E.2d 551 (1941), is the controlling precedent on this issue in Massachusetts, not *Landale*. Texaco also implies that the disclaimer must be given full effect because V.S.H. is a "sophisticated" purchaser, experienced in real estate transactions.

Although we agree that V.S.H.'s experience in the real estate business, along with the presence of an "as is" clause, is relevant to the ultimate disposition of the chapter 93A claim, we do not find that either factor makes V.S.H.'s claim insufficient as a matter of law. Sophistication of the parties is not mentioned in chapter 93A and the amendment of chapter 93A to cover business entities did not limit the statute's protection to small, unsophisticated businesses. It may be that the Massachusetts Supreme Judicial Court ultimately should decide the question of whether an "as is" clause ever should be ignored in a transaction between two sophisticated businesses and, thus, whether the existence of one should preclude a chapter 93A cause of action. We do not believe, however, that it would, or could, do so without development of a factual record. For that reason, and the absence of any contrary precedent in Massachusetts law, we conclude that the district court erred in dismissing the chapter 93A claim.

C. Breach of Contract

[The court affirmed the lower court's dismissal of the breach of contract claim.]

BREYER, CIRCUIT JUDGE (concurring in part and dissenting in part).

The common law misrepresentation issue is a close one given the Supreme Judicial Court's refusal to find liability in Nei v. Burley, 388 Mass. 307, 446 N.E.2d 674 (1983) (no misleading partial disclosure where seller gave buyer percolation test showing too much water on land while failing to disclose seasonal stream). But I agree with the panel that enough is alleged to avoid dismissal of the complaint.

I do not agree, however, with the panel's suggestion that Mass.Gen. Laws ch. 93A would allow a finding of liability for pure *nondisclosure* in a case like this one, involving sophisticated business parties and an "as is" contract.

First, the panel's interpretation of chapter 93A virtually reads the "as is" contract out of Massachusetts law. If a seller knows he is liable for failing to disclose any material fact about which he "should have known," he will have to check the merchandise or property, and list every defect that he finds. Failure to do so certainly risks (if it does not assure) liability. Yet, it is the very purpose of an "as is" contract to shift the burden of inspection and the costs of hidden defects to the buyer. The Massachusetts Commercial Code, Mass.Gen.Laws ch. 106, § 2–316(3)(a) specifically authorizes "as is" contracts. As the district court pointed out, it is anomalous to read a different statute (chapter 93A) in a way that makes § 2–316(3)(a) of the UCC virtually meaningless. The panel majority says that perhaps the UCC's "as is" rule will still have meaningful life in other situations. Which situations? Where? How?

Second, there is a theoretical argument suggesting that applying chapter 93A here may not help—indeed it may hurt—the consumer. The basic object of chapter 93A, insofar as it requires disclosure, is to allow the consumer to make an informed choice, and thus to protect him from entering into a contract that he would not 'really' want were he more knowledgeable or sophisticated. See generally E. Kintner, A Primer on the Law of Deceptive Practices ix–xi (1978). That purpose is not directly served when the bargaining parties are knowledgeable, sophisticated businessmen. Moreover, where the contract explicitly states that the knowledgeable buyer runs the risk of, say, hidden defects (e.g., where the contract says "as is"), the knowledgeable business buyer quite clearly knows what kind of situation he is getting into, and, in all likelihood, it is one (given the price) that he wants.

Under such circumstances, to allow an action under chapter 93A not only fails to serve the Act's main purpose but indeed may harm those whom the Act seeks to protect. To insist that the knowledgeable business seller disclose all material facts that the seller "should have" known (to forbid, in effect, the "as is" contract), is to prevent the buyer and seller from allocating costs and risks as they choose in both the presumably rare situation involving deceptive conduct by the seller and the more typical *non*deceptive situation. And, such a prohibition, as a general matter, may raise the price of the underlying good or service by preventing the allocation of risks (e.g., of hidden defects) to the party willing to bear them most cheaply. Of course, one may think of this general price-increasing tendency as too theoretical, as ephemeral, or not worth much consideration when consumer protection is on the other side of the balance scale; but, it is, at the least, worth consideration when weighed against the need to protect those who typically need no protection (such as knowledgeable business buyers).

* * *

NOTES

1. A leading case in Massachusetts is Slaney v. Westwood Auto, Inc., 366 Mass. 688, 322 N.E.2d 768 (1975), cited in *V.S.H. Realty,* where a consumer sued a used car dealer for breach of his promise made as part of a sales transaction to repair defects in the used car purchased by the consumer. The consumer alleged breach of express and implied warranty under the Uniform Commercial Code as well as a violation of the Consumer Protection Act. The plaintiff also sought rescission and reimbursement for expenses. The trial court sustained the defendant's demurrer to the CPA claim holding (1) the statute provided no cause of action for a "classic breach of express or implied warranty under the Commercial Code" and (2) a purchaser's right of rescission is governed exclusively by the Commercial Code. The Supreme Judicial Court reversed holding the CPA created a new separate cause of action for any act or practice defined as unfair or deceptive under the statute. In an important passage the court held:

> The [CPA] claim for relief is the creation of that statute. It is, therefore, sui generis. It is neither wholly tortious nor wholly contractual in nature, and is not subject to the traditional limitations of preexisting causes of action such as tort for fraud and deceit. 322 N.E.2d at 779.

The court observed that while the common law of deceit requires reliance by the buyer and knowledge of the falsity by the seller, neither are required under the act. Similarly, a breach of warranty is actionable under the act even though it may duplicate or conflict with provisions of the Uniform Commercial Code.

2. The consumer protection acts suddenly make Federal Trade Commission rules and decisions applicable to consumer (and in many jurisdictions to

competitor) lawsuits in state courts. The general practitioner can no longer ignore Commission activity on the assumption that it is the domain of specialists or that its actions are likely to affect only large interstate sellers. The court in *Poulin* recognizes the importance of the Commission's views on what constitutes deception. The Commission cases on deception are considered in detail later in this Chapter. The *Poulin* court observed that the Commission has recently attempted to narrow the range of deception cases. Do you understand the difference between the old and the new Commission standard described in *Poulin*? Do you see what the implications are for private litigation? Can state courts under the CPA continue to utilize the older and broader Commission cases defining deception?

3.   How does the consumer protection act affect the warranty provisions of the Uniform Commercial Code? Can you think of a breach of warranty that would not, in all likelihood, be deceptive under the CPA? If not, do you think a lawyer in Massachusetts should ever rely on the Uniform Commercial Code? If the UCC permits contractual terms, such as disclaimers of warranty, can it still be unfair or deceptive under the CPA to include the terms in a contract? The court in *V.S.H. Realty* at least suggests that the "as is" disclaimer may no longer be available to Massachusetts sellers. Could it be unfair or deceptive to use such a disclaimer?

4.   Do the consumer protection acts pose a threat to the law of contracts generally? Consider Martin v. Lou Poliquin Enterprises, Inc., 696 S.W.2d 180 (Tex.App.1985). The defendant agreed to place an advertisement in the telephone directory for the plaintiff's business and subsequently assured plaintiff the advertisement would appear. When the advertisement failed to appear the plaintiff brought an action under the state's CPA. The court affirmed an award of damages and attorney's fees to the plaintiff. The court held that a consumer need not prove the passing of consideration but only that he initiated the purchasing process in good faith.

> An individual initiates the purchasing process when he (1) presents himself to the seller as a willing buyer with the subjective intent or specific 'objective' of purchasing, and (2) possesses at least some credible indicia of the capacity to consummate the transaction. 696 S.W.2d at 184–85.

The court also held that a provision in the "contract" which limited the defendant's liability to refunding the cost of the advertisement did not prevent the plaintiff from recovering under the act. Although the waiver would probably have been effective in a suit for breach of contract, "[the CPA] states . . . that a consumer's waiver of any . . . provision [thereunder] is contrary to public policy and is unenforceable and void." 696 S.W.2d at 186.

See also Smith v. Baldwin, 611 S.W.2d 611 (Tex.1980) where the court held the doctrine of substantial performance applies only to contract claims and not to claims under the consumer protection act.

Compare Helms v. Southwestern Bell Telephone Co., 794 F.2d 188 (5th Cir. 1986) where the telephone company put the wrong phone number in the plaintiff's advertisement: "An allegation of breach of contract—without more—does not constitute a false, misleading, or deceptive action such as would violate the [CPA]."

5.   Do any of the limitations on a tort action for misrepresentation of fraud survive the consumer protection act? Does the court in *V.S.H. Realty* suggest that there is general liability for non-disclosure under the CPA even if there is

no underlying duty at common law to disclose? Could there be liability for nondisclosure in the absence of reliance by the buyer or knowledge by the seller? Might the CPA be interpreted to impose on the seller an obligation to inspect the products he sells and disclose uncovered defects?

6. The scope of the transactions covered by the consumer protection acts varies from state to state. Some statutes provide specific exemptions for some industries such as banking or insurance. Where free of express statutory exemptions, courts continue to explore the reach of the statutes with some expanding the scope to include industries already regulated by other enactments. Thus some courts have provided private remedies for unfair insurance practices even though insurance companies are closely regulated by state insurance departments. Credit transactions including debt collections are subject to both state and federal regulation but it has been held that a violation of the Federal Fair Debt Collections Practices Act is automatically a violation of the Federal Trade Commission Act and thus becomes also a violation of the consumer protection act providing the consumer with private remedies. See In re Scrimpsher, 17 B.R. 999 (Bkrtcy.N.Y.1982). Courts have applied the state statutes to the franchise industry, another industry heavily regulated by other enactments. The range of application of the state acts is catalogued in National Consumer Law Center, Unfair and Deceptive Acts and Practices (1982) (1987 Cum.Supp.).

JAYS FOODS, INC. v. FRITO–LAY, INC.

United States Dist. Ct., N.D. Illinois, 1987.
664 F.Supp. 364.

MORAN, DISTRICT JUDGE.

* * *

Jays intended to show at trial that Frito–Lay attempted to influence the allocation of retail shelf space by engaging in several unfair and deceptive practices. First, Jays would show that Frito–Lay urged retailers to allocate shelf space based on total snack food sales but it failed to use the shelf space it gained that way in a profit maximizing manner. For example, Frito–Lay devoted all newly gained space to its comparatively slow-selling regular potato chips. Second, Jays would show that Frito–Lay gained additional shelf space by presenting retailers with misleading and incomplete shelf space studies. For example, one such study, Frito–Lays' "mini-analysis," examined only total sales of snack foods, ignoring other variables such as profits, inventory turnover, location and service. Jays also would show that Frito–Lay stacked its products at the front of retail shelves, leaving unused space behind ("dummying up"), and left more of its products in certain stores than sales justified, moving them to stores with higher inventory turnover only just in time to prevent them from going stale ("rolling stock"). Jays contends that these practices enabled Frito–Lay to occupy excessive shelf space at the expense of Frito–Lay's competitors, such as Jays.

Third, Jays would show that Frito–Lay engaged in promotional programs directly tied to the allocation of additional shelf space, a practice that Jays characterizes as "buying space." Finally, Jays would show that Frito–Lay took steps to skew sales when retailers were conducting shelf space tests to protect its shelf space allocations.

DISCUSSION

After the summary judgments on the antitrust claims [in favor of defendant] this court determined that the two state law claims remained, a very small tail on what had been a large and now dead dog.
*   *   *

[Jays' first state law claim, under the Illinois version of the Uniform Deceptive Trade Practices Act, was dismissed because Jays sought damages and the act provides only injunctive relief.]

If Jays is to recover damages it must proceed under the Consumer Fraud Act, which provides:

> Unfair methods of competition and unfair or deceptive acts or practices, including but not limited to the use or employment of any deception, fraud, false pretense, false promise, misrepresentation or the concealment, suppression or omission of any material fact, with the intent that others rely upon the concealment, suppression or omission of such material fact, or the use or employment of any practice described in Section 2 of the "Uniform Deceptive Trade Practices Act" . . . are hereby declared unlawful whether any person has in fact been misled, deceived or damaged thereby. In construing this section consideration shall be given to the interpretations of the Federal Trade Commission and the federal courts relating to Section 5(a) of the Federal Trade Commission Act.

Ill.Rev.Stat. ch. 121½, ¶ 262; see Ill.Rev.Stat. ch. 121½, ¶ 270a (providing for a private damage action).

The Consumer Fraud Act incorporates Section 2 of the Deceptive Trade Practices Act by reference, but it is considerably broader. Like the Federal Trade Commission Act, 15 U.S.C. § 41 et seq., the Consumer Fraud Act applies to "unfair methods of competition." Unfair methods of competition include violations of the federal antitrust laws. See, e.g., E.I. Du Pont de Nemours & Co. v. FTC, 729 F.2d 128, 136–37 (2d Cir.1984). However, Jays cannot proceed on an antitrust theory because of Frito–Lay's earlier successful summary judgment motions. Except for the possible violations of the Deceptive Trade Practices Act, Jays must show that Frito–Lay's shelf space practices were unfair even though they did not violate the antitrust laws. The Consumer Fraud Act is, by its terms, wide-ranging. In interpreting it, consideration shall be given to interpretations of the Federal Trade Commission Act, but the decision as to what is "unfair" is left to juries and the courts rather than to an administrative agency having experience and expertise. Perhaps for this reason the Illinois courts have moved cautiously in fleshing out the contours of the Act. *   *   *

In this action Jays has failed to develop any evidence showing that consumers are injured by Frito–Lay's conduct. The Illinois courts have limited liability under the Consumer Fraud Act to conduct that implicates consumer protection concerns. * * *

Several federal courts in this district, including this court, have followed that limitation. The Illinois Supreme Court has not squarely faced the issue, but its decisions also support limiting liability under the Consumer Fraud Act to conduct that deceives or exploits consumers. * * *

The Illinois courts have not uniformly formulated this consumer injury limitation and some courts have stated that it does not apply. See e.g., M & W Gear, 97 Ill.App.3d at 913–14, 53 Ill.Dec. at 730, 424 N.E.2d at 365. However, those cases have either involved consumer plaintiffs or conduct from which injury to consumers could be readily inferred. In *M & W Gear* the plaintiff successfully sued a competitor for false advertising. On appeal, the defendant argued that the plaintiff had failed to plead or prove any adverse effect on the public. The court rejected any public injury requirement and affirmed judgment for the plaintiff. However, as the court in *Newman–Green* observed, the *M & W Gear* court could easily have held that false advertising gives rise to a conclusive presumption of public injury to consumers. In Tague v. Molitor Motor Co., 139 Ill.App.3d 313, 316, 93 Ill.Dec. 769, 770–71, 487 N.E.2d 436, 437–38 (5th Dist.1985), the court rejected a public injury requirement, but there the plaintiff was a consumer complaining of odometer tampering and other misconduct in connection with the sale of a used car. In Duncavage v. Allen, 147 Ill.App.3d 88, 102, 100 Ill. Dec. 455, 463, 497 N.E.2d 433, 441 (1st Dist.1986), the court concluded that a tenant was a consumer under the Consumer Fraud Act, and relied on *Tague* in allowing a suit on behalf of a deceased tenant against a landlord.

This court concludes * * * that some consumer injury is an essential element of any claim under the Consumer Fraud Act. Perhaps where the plaintiff is a consumer, no further public injury need be shown. But where a suit is between competitors, as it is here, a plaintiff must show that the defendant's misconduct injured consumers generally.

Although the consumer injury requirement is an independent element of any Consumer Fraud Act claim, including claims based on the incorporated Deceptive Trade Practices Act violations, it is similar in some respects to the issue of unfairness. The consumer injury requirement developed in part from concepts applied in determining whether a trade practice is unfair under section 5 of the Federal Trade Commission Act, 15 U.S.C. § 45. A practice that is neither a violation of the antitrust laws nor deceptive may still be unfair under section 5 if it offends some established public policy, if it is immoral, unethical, oppressive or unscrupulous, or if it is substantially injurious to consumers. Spiegel, Inc. v. FTC, 540 F.2d 287, 293 (7th Cir.1978) (citing FTC v.

Sperry Hutchinson & Co., 405 U.S. 233, 244–45 & n. 5 (1972)) * * * The Federal Trade Commission has further refined the concept of unfairness under the FTC Act, clarifying that its primary focus is consumer injury; the public policy theory is used mainly to cross-check and confirm a finding of consumer injury, and the theory of immoral or unscrupulous conduct was abandoned altogether as an independent basis of liability. See, e.g., International Harvester Co., 104 F.T.C. 949, 1060–61, 1070–76 (1984). As the *Evanston Motor* court recognized, consumer injury under the Consumer Fraud Act can take two forms. Violations may affect consumers directly or indirectly by affecting competition. The plaintiff here has not attempted to set forth any evidence of a direct injury to consumers. Frito–Lay's alleged misconduct was directed to retailers, not to consumers. Further, although plaintiff contends that consumer's purchasing decisions were affected by changes in shelf space allocation, this court does not believe that such an effect can be characterized as an injury.

Rather, Jays' case depends on showing that consumers are injured because Frito–Lay's conduct was anti-competitive. [The court reviewed the evidence and prior precedent and concluded that while Frito–Lay was arguably an "over-zealous competitor" its activities were not anticompetitive or exclusionary.] * * *

Without evidence that Frito–Lay's shelf space activities were anti-competitive, Jays cannot establish the consumer injury element of its claim under the Consumer Fraud Act. For the same reason Jays cannot establish that Frito–Lay's non-deceptive shelf space practices were unfair. If Jays were seeking injunctive relief, perhaps plaintiff nevertheless could proceed to trial under the Illinois Deceptive Trade Practices Act, Ill.Rev.Stat. ch. 121½, ¶ 311 et seq., on its claim that Frito–Lay deceived retailers by using incomplete data in its shelf allocation "mini-analysis" or by sabotaging retailers' own shelf-space studies. However, it cannot recover damages under the Deceptive Trade Practices Act. Under the circumstances, Frito–Lay is entitled to summary judgment.

DOLINER v. BROWN

Appeals Court of Massachusetts, Norfolk, 1986.
21 Mass.App.Ct. 692, 489 N.E.2d 1036.

KAPLAN, JUSTICE.

[Doliner began negotiations to acquire an apartment house suitable for conversion to condominiums. He met with Green and Bendetsen to secure financing. These discussions were not confidential. Green and Bendetsen in turn met with Brown and described the potential transaction in order to get Brown to participate in the financing. Doliner reached an agreement on the purchase price for the property with the owners but the sales contract was not completed because Doliner's financing was uncertain. At this point Brown intervened and purchased the property from the owners.]

1. As one of the actors in this story put it, Brown "scooped" Doliner. That, however, was far from encompassing the tort of interference with prospective contractual relations. A competitor may "interfere" with another's contractual expectancy by picking the deal off for himself, if, in advancing his own interest, he refrains from employing wrongful means. See, Restatement (Second) of Torts § 768 (1979) * * *.

[The court found Brown and Doliner to be "competitors" and held that Brown committed no independent tort such as fraud in obtaining the contract for himself.]

2. The remedy of businessman against businessman of G.L. c. 93A, § 11, may be invoked against an "unfair method of competition" or an "unfair or deceptive act or practice declared unlawful by [§ 2] or by any rule or regulation issued under [§ 2(c)]" by the Attorney General. These references point to Federal Trade Commission lore as a source of interpretation. As to the first-quoted phrase, Brown was not engaged in any practice considered abusive of, or injurious to competition such as may be discerned in the theft of trade secrets, or in passing off, or in adjacent business torts. Embraced in the other quoted phrase have been examples of extortion or similar oppression, breach of warranty, misrepresentation, betrayal of fiduciary duty, violation of specific regulations of the Attorney General. It is recognized that the language is broad enough to take in some reprehensible acts committed in business contexts that elude conventional definitions and categories. The courts are not invited by the statute to punish every departure from "the punctilio of an honor the most sensitive" (Meinhard v. Salmon, 249 N.Y. 458, 464, 164 N.E. 545 [1928]), but they may enforce standards of behavior measurably higher than perfidy. They need not necessarily endorse a pattern of behavior because it happens to be current in the market place. We tried to suggest a mood, although we could not prescribe a rule, when we said in Levings v. Forbes & Wallace, Inc., 8 Mass.App.Ct. 498, 504, 396 N.E.2d 149 (1979), that a new tort may be recognized under § 11 when the questioned conduct "attain[s] a level of rascality that would raise an eyebrow of someone inured to the rough and tumble of the world of commerce." See also Spence v. Boston Edison Co., 390 Mass. 604, 616, 459 N.E.2d 80 (1983). The situations have to be sized up one by one. In our view the present case is outside § 11 unless we are prepared to say that the statute enacts a rule of noblesse oblige by which a party is to be barred from competing for a business advantage because he is made aware that another has been exerting himself to the same end. That would be an extravagant rule of law.

Judgment affirmed.

BROWN, JUSTICE (concurring in part and dissenting in part).

It is with utmost reluctance that I concur, even in part. I only wish that the law would aid the needy as assiduously as it does the greedy. Brown did more than sabotage Doliner's contractual expectancy; he "pick[ed] the deal off for himself." The judge found that were it not for Brown's closing with the owners, they would have signed a purchase and sale agreement with Doliner, assuming the latter had been able to achieve satisfactory financing.

In the real estate game, one never commits fully until the "numbers" have been canvassed fully. Here, the numbers were very clearly set out by Green and Bendetson during their visit to Brown. Brown told them that he would consider seriously taking a fifty percent position in the *secondary financing* of the deal. No sooner had the two messengers departed than the defendant rushed to the phone, putting in motion his plan to "scoop" the entire deal. If that is not wrong—and the majority opinion concludes that it is not wrong under principles of common and statutory law—then perhaps there is something amiss in the common law and in our statutory scheme.

It is not enough for me that the common law be viewed as simply a mirror of the manner and mores of the marketplace. Fundamental principles of decency and fairness, resplendent in other areas of common law, ought to be recognized here. I disapprove of a view which condones conduct as reprehensible as that exhibited by the defendant in this case. Ethics and morality do have a place in our economic system, the greatest example of capitalism in the history of the world. In this regard, see the instructive discussion in Meinhard v. Salmon, 249 N.Y. 458, 464, 164 N.E. 545 (1928). Nevertheless, having reviewed the authorities cited in the majority opinion, and mindful of the role of an intermediate appellate court not "to alter established rules of law governing principles of substantive liability" (Burke v. Toothaker, 1 Mass.App.Ct. 234, 239, 295 N.E.2d 184 [1973]), I am constrained to join in part 1 of the majority opinion.

Turning from the common law to our own statutory law, I respectfully dissent from the majority's view that the defendant's conduct was not actionable under G.L. c. 93A, § 11. In formulating applicable standards of conduct under chapter 93A, we are advised "to discover and make explicit those unexpressed standards of fair dealing which the conscience of the community may progressively develop." Commonwealth v. DeCotis, 366 Mass. 234, 242, 316 N.E.2d 748 (1974), quoting Judge Learned Hand in Federal Trade Commn. v. Standard Educ. Soc., 86 F.2d 692, 696 (2d Cir.1936), rev'd in part, 302 U.S. 112, 58 S.Ct. 113, 82 L.Ed. 141 (1937). In this case, I would characterize the totality of the defendant's conduct as having been infused with a high enough "level of rascality" (Levings v. Forbes & Wallace, Inc., 8 Mass. App.Ct. 498, 504, 396 N.E.2d 149 [1979]) not only to have raised the plaintiff's eyebrow, but also to have permitted him to recover under § 11.

Chapter 93A has established in general, for businesses as well as for consumers, a path of conduct higher than that trod by the crowd in the past. Cf. Meinhard v. Salmon, 249 N.Y. at 464, 164 N.E. 545. It troubles me to see such a substantial deviation from that path.

NOTES

1. Consider again the *American Financial Services* case reproduced in Chapter 1 of this casebook. The formulation of a standard for "unfairness" under the Federal Trade Commission Act takes on new significance for state courts under the consumer protection acts. Are you comfortable with the first FTC formulation that focused on whether the act was immoral or unscrupulous? Do you agree with Justice Kaplan or Justice Brown in *Doliner?* When the FTC "unfairness" standard was first formulated the only sanction available to the Commission was to seek a cease and desist order against the prohibited conduct. Can that standard be comfortably transported to a regime of treble and punitive damages and attorneys fees?

2. Do you agree with Judge Moran's analysis of the "consumer injury" requirement in *Jays?* If the UTPCPA is modified to permit competitors standing to bring a private action for damages, is there additional language in the UTPCPA that supports such a requirement? If there is injury to competition is there not ipso facto injury to consumers?

3. In McLaughlin Ford, Inc. v. Ford Motor Co., 192 Conn. 558, 473 A.2d 1185 (1984) an existing Ford dealer sued Ford under the CPA for creating a new dealership in his trade area. The court applied the new "unfairness" standard announced by the FTC, and considered in *American Financial Services* which requires "substantial consumer injury" that is not "outweighed by any countervailing benefits to consumers or competition". Although the court held for Ford on the ground that any injury to the plaintiff was outweighed by the benefit to the consumers from enhanced competition, the court found the test "equally applicable when a business person or competitor claims substantial injury."

4. There appears to be a growing number of competitor suits under the state statutes. Passing off and trademark infringement cases are quite common under the UDTPA and claims under the state act are often added to federal trademark actions. See, e.g., Brunswick Corp. v. Spinit Reel Co., 832 F.2d 513 (10th Cir.1987) (standards of proof under Oklahoma Act similar to that required under the Lanham Act). These claims can also be brought under the consumer protection acts with some advantages. In Polo Fashions, Inc. v. Craftex, Inc., 816 F.2d 145 (4th Cir.1987) the owner of the "Polo" and "Ralph Lauren" trademarks brought suit under the Lanham Act and the North Carolina Unfair Trade Practices Act. The court held that while damages could not be awarded under the Lanham Act because 15 U.S.C. § 1111 requires the statutory notice of registration before damages are permitted, damages were available (and trebled) under the state statute. But see, Sideshow, Inc. v. Mammoth Records, Inc., 751 F.Supp. 78 (E.D.N.C.1990) limiting *Polo Fashions* to intentional infringement and holding the North Carolina automatic trebling statute does not apply to innocent and unintentional infringement of unregistered trademarks because the plaintiff is "not an injured consumer and has several other adequate remedies."

In Unique Concepts, Inc. v. Manuel, 669 F.Supp. 185 (N.D.Ill.1987) the defendant filed counterclaims under common law disparagement and the Illinois Consumer Fraud and Deceptive Practices Act. The common law claim was rejected for failure to assert and prove special damages. "The statutory actions offer far more flexibility than do claims for common law commercial disparagement. Any conduct in a business which creates a likelihood of consumer confusion or misunderstanding is potentially actionable. . . . The apparatus of defamation does not apply; indeed, the statements made need not actually have been false, but only misleading. . . . Most importantly for the case at bar, in an action for disparagement brought under the Deceptive Practices statutes there is no need to plead or prove special damages . . . In *M & W Gear* [97 Ill.App.3d at 909–911, 424 N.E.2d at 362–363], damages were proven through expert testimony, extrapolating lost profits from sales figures before and after the disparaging communication."

5. Would you not expect to see a cause of action under the state statutes appended to most private anti-trust actions?

6. If the state statute or a rule of the Commission or of a state attorney general prohibits specific conduct, the plaintiff ordinarily can recover under the statute without further proof that the conduct is unfair or deceptive.

7. In a few jurisdictions courts have engrafted additional limitations on the applicability of the consumer protection acts in private lawsuits. In Washington the plaintiff must prove the defendant's acts affect the "public interest". Hangman Ridge Training Stables, Inc. v. Safeco Title Ins. Co., 105 Wn.2d 778, 719 P.2d 531 (1986). "[I]t is the likelihood that additional plaintiffs have been or will be injured in exactly the same fashion that changes a factual pattern from a private dispute to one that affects the public interest." It is reported that of the 42 states that allow a private cause of action under similar statutes, only six have imposed a showing of a "public interest" by a private plaintiff. Leaffer & Lipson, Consumer Actions Against Unfair or Deceptive Acts or Practices: The Private Uses of Federal Trade Commission Jurisprudence, 48 Geo.Wash.L.Rev. 521 (1980).

BROWN v. LeCLAIR

Appeals Court of Massachusetts, Suffolk, 1985.
20 Mass.App.Ct. 976, 482 N.E.2d 870.

[The statute, "G.L. c. 93A", referred to in this opinion is the Massachusetts version of the Unfair Trade Practices and Consumer Protection Law which prohibits "unfair methods of competition and unfair and deceptive acts or practices."]

RESCRIPT.

In September, 1981, Harold Brown, landlord of premises occupied by David LeClair, filed a summary process action in the Boston Housing Court against LeClair for non-payment of rent. On June 3, 1982, LeClair filed an amended answer in the summary process action in which he raised defenses and made counterclaims alleging: (1) breach of the implied warranty of habitability; (2) breach of the covenant of quiet enjoyment; [1] (3) intentional infliction of emotional distress; (4) negligence; and (5) violation of G.L. c. 93A. [2]

---

1. G.L. c. 186, § 14.

2. The primary conditions complained of were leaking ceilings, cockroach infestation, banging of pipes, and a door which provided no security. Other defective conditions reported by LeClair (some of which

were also found by the housing inspection department of the city of Boston to be violations of the Sanitary Code) included the poor condition of kitchen cabinets and countertops and stained, broken and sagging ceiling tiles.

In March of 1983, a hearing on LeClair's counterclaims was held. After receiving documentary evidence as well as hearing testimony from Brown's property manager, from a previous tenant of LeClair's apartment, from LeClair, and from a witness who photographed the premises, the judge found in favor of LeClair on four of his counterclaims and found for Brown on the claim for intentional infliction of emotional distress. Damages were awarded under G.L. c. 93A, the judge concluding that his findings of negligence and of breach of the implied warranty of habitability, and of G.L. c. 186, § 14, "also constitute a violation of G.L. c. 93A." The judge trebled the damages on the ground that Brown's violations were "wilful and knowing." He also found that "the landlord did not make a good faith offer of settlement."

Brown claims error in the judge's award of actual and treble damages under G.L. c. 93A, § 9(3), arguing that the evidence was insufficient to support the judge's findings and that the award did not disclose the basis on which damages were computed.

1. *Abatement of rent.* In calculating damages under G.L. c. 93A, the judge followed the method prescribed by Wolfberg v. Hunter, 385 Mass. 390, 399–400, 432 N.E.2d 467 (1982).[4] He abated the rent for a period from the inception of the lease until April, 1982. The judge found that LeClair made no complaints after that date.

The judge found that at the inception of LeClair's tenancy there were a number of violations of the State Sanitary Code and that these problems had caused the prior tenant to vacate the premises after living there a few months. He also found that the landlord was repeatedly notified of the ongoing leaks and other problems on several occasions, and that, despite these complaints, the leakage and the roach problem remained uncorrected through April, 1982. LeClair testified that he complained about leaks "throughout the tenancy" or "through . . . fall '81." There is no set rule as to the number of times a tenant must complain of a matter which remains unrepaired in order to preserve his right to an abatement. The judge's findings are not clearly erroneous.

2. *Property Damage.* Brown challenges the judge's award of $790 for property loss occasioned by a January 31, 1980, flood. LeClair testified that the value of various items of damaged property amounted to more than that figure.

The judge, in his discretion, could allow LeClair to testify as to the property's value.

---

4. The fair rental value of the apartment from November, 1979, to March, 1983, was $9,055, a sum equivalent to the contract rate for that time period. LeClair paid Brown $8,255 in rent for the same time period, the $800 difference reflecting rent withheld by LeClair between October 1, 1981, and December, 1982. The judge found that the value of the apartment "was reduced by $1,175 as a result of the conditions." The judge also awarded LeClair $790 in damages for property loss and $1,000 for the assault and battery discussed in part 3, infra. The three items total $2,965, which sum was tripled, for a total of $8,895. From that amount, the $800 of withheld rent was deducted, leaving a total award, apart from counsel fees, of $8,095.

3. *Assault and Battery.* Brown attacks the judge's award of $1,000 for the injuries received from an assault and battery. These damages were based on a September, 1980, incident in which LeClair was assaulted with a knife by a neighbor after the neighbor punched a hole through LeClair's hollow core front door and entered his apartment. The judge found that the construction of the door to LeClair's apartment did not provide adequate security and was in violation of the State Sanitary Code. See c. II of the State Sanitary Code, 105 Code Mass.Reg. 410.000 et seq. (1980); Regulations of the Attorney General, 940 Code Mass.Regs. § 3.16(3) (1978). There was evidence that the door was of flimsy construction. The question whether the requisite causal connection has been shown is one of fact. DiMarzo v. American Mutual Ins. Co., 389 Mass. 85, 101, 449 N.E.2d 1189 (1983). We are unable to say that the findings of the judge on this issue were clearly erroneous.

Brown also argues that there was no evidence of actual loss which he equates with out of pocket expenses by LeClair. Since the judge dismissed LeClair's counterclaim for emotional distress, Brown argues that LeClair is only entitled to damages for his physical injuries.

"Actual damages" for injuries under G.L. c. 93A comprehend all foreseeable and consequential damages arising out of conduct which violates the statute, and, we think, include, after St. 1979, c. 406, § 1, "emotional distress, occurring contemporaneously with . . . personal injuries." See Payton v. Abbott Labs, 386 Mass. 540, 548, 437 N.E.2d 171 (1982).

4. *Treble Damages.* Under G.L. c. 93A, § 9(3), inserted by St. 1969, c. 690, a successful plaintiff may be awarded "up to three but not less than two times [the actual damages] if the court finds that the use or employment of the act or practice was a "wilful or knowing" violation . . . or that the refusal to grant relief upon demand was made in bad faith." The trial judge found both a "wilful and [sic] knowing" violation and a bad faith refusal.

On October 23, 1981, LeClair sent Brown a "demand letter" seeking damages and requesting relief (repairs) under c. 93A for problems relating to leaks, the January 31, 1980, flood, cockroaches, the assault, and breach of the covenant of quiet enjoyment. Brown's agent responded by denying any unfair practice, claiming that the problems had been corrected and refusing to make repairs as they had been "made long ago." An offer of $150 to settle the matter was made.

In finding that Brown did not make a good faith offer of settlement, the judge laid stress on the refusal to repair. The record shows that Brown neither made any repairs in response to the demand letter nor investigated the merits of LeClair's complaints. Indeed, the judge found that "no further repairs were made until the landlord received notice of violations of law from the Housing Inspection Department of the City of Boston." We see no error in the judge's conclusion that Brown's response to LeClair's c. 93A demand letter was in bad faith.

The judge's award based on a wilful or knowing violation is supported by evidence that the previous tenant, who moved out in 1979, was unsuccessful in obtaining repairs and that some of the problems (leaks) had persisted for three and a half years and continued to the time of the trial in 1983. While each violation may not in itself have been wilful, e.g., the inadequate door, we think that where, as here, there were many continuing violations, some major and some minor, their cumulative effect on habitability can be considered by the trial judge in determining whether Brown's behavior was wilful. Cf. McKenna v. Begin, 5 Mass.App. at 308, 362 N.E.2d 548. Even if each violation must, for purposes of c. 93A, be considered separately, we think the judge's additional finding of bad faith in responding to LeClair's demand letter—the alternate prong permitting an assessment of punitive damages—leaves no doubt of the judge's finding sufficient ground to award treble damages.

Brown challenges the award of multiple damages on the ground that the findings do not sufficiently explain why treble rather than double damages were awarded. Although "neither c. 93A nor our cases construing that statute provide a trial judge with clear guidance in deciding how damages should be multiplied," Rita v. Carella, 394 Mass. 822, 829, 477 N.E.2d 1016 (1985), the decision is to be "[b]ased on the egregiousness of [the] defendant's conduct." International Fid. Ins. Co. v. Wilson, 387 Mass. 841, 853, 443 N.E.2d 1308 (1983). On the evidence before us, we cannot say that the determination to award treble damages was error.

Judgment affirmed.

NOTES

1. Those courts that have freed claims under the consumer protection acts from the limitations of analogous common law claims have also displayed a willingness to abandon some of the common law strictures on damages. See, e.g., Bernard v. Central Carolina Truck Sales, 68 N.C.App. 228, 314 S.E.2d 582 (1984) where the seller misrepresented the character and quality of a used tractor. The court refused to apply the common law rule of damages for fraudulent inducement which requires a plaintiff to choose between rescission with recovery of the purchase price or affirmation of the contract with recovery of the difference in market value between the goods as sold and the goods as represented. The court awarded the plaintiff full restitution including the monthly payments plus interest he had paid on the loan with no subtraction for the use by plaintiff of the tractor. The amount thus calculated was trebled under the North Carolina mandatory trebling statute.

2. The consumer protection acts may be a useful alternative or addition in tort cases. The plaintiff in *LeClair* was able to treble the normal tort damages by using the CPA. In Pope v. Rollins Protective Services Co., 703 F.2d 197 (5th Cir.1983) the plaintiff purchased a burglar alarm system from defendant. The system was represented to be far more effective than it was and burglars were able to enter plaintiff's house by disabling the system. Plaintiff was assaulted in the process. She sued defendant for the misrepresentations under the Texas Deceptive Trade Practices Act claiming physical injuries and mental anguish.

The Fifth Circuit held that Texas tort law would permit recovery for mental anguish in this circumstance and affirmed an award of $150,000 which was trebled under the Texas DTPA. See also Ellis v. Northern Star Company, 326 N.C. 219, 388 S.E.2d 127 (1990) where the court held a libel per se in a business setting is a violation of the CPA but the plaintiff must elect between punitive damages under common law libel or treble damages under the act.

3. Almost all of the state acts authorize successful plaintiffs to recover attorneys fees. To the extent that the acts now encompass a good share of what otherwise would be common law tort and contract actions, the statutes have reversed the long standing American rule against the award of attorneys fees.

4. In New York Public Interest Research Group, Inc. v. Insurance Information Institute, ___ A.D.2d ___, 554 N.Y.S.2d 590 (1st Dept.1990) personal injury plaintiffs brought suit under the deceptive practices act against the Insurance Information Institute for publishing articles critical of the explosion of civil law suits and escalating jury awards. The court held the act did not apply to advertisements intended to influence public opinion and that the Institute's advertisements were not commercial speech and thus fully protected by the First Amendment.

D. THE FEDERAL TRADE COMMISSION

HISTORICAL NOTE

In 1914 the Congress of the United States enacted the Federal Trade Commission Act which established the Federal Trade Commission and declared "that unfair methods of competition in commerce are hereby declared unlawful. The commission is hereby empowered and directed to prevent persons, partnerships, or corporations, except banks, and common carriers subject to the Acts to regulate commerce, from using unfair methods of competition in commerce." 38 Stat. 719 (1914).

The Supreme Court interpretation of the antitrust laws in Standard Oil v. United States, 221 U.S. 1 (1911) which promulgated the "rule of reason" for determining whether business conduct was in restraint of trade was a major incentive for passage of the FTC Act. Both big business and antitrust supporters were concerned with the potential impact of interstitial law-making by the federal judiciary. Business interests were concerned that normal business operations would be disrupted or challenged and antitrust advocates saw the "reasonable" standard as insulating from legal sanction activity which was clearly in restraint of trade. The proposal of a commission to administer the antitrust laws which would be more subject to control by Congress than the life-tenured federal judiciary obtained support from Democratic, Republican, and Progressive parties. The journey of the commission bill through Congress coincided and was related to the passage of the Clayton Act further supplementing the Sherman Act of 1890. Thus, the Commission was designed as an enforcer and administrator of the antitrust laws. Little, if any, thought was given in Congress to whether the Commission should or could regulate purely deceptive or fraudulent practices which had no anti-competitive impact.

The Commission felt no such reluctance in reading into its authority the power to issue cease and desist orders for deceptive practices. The first two cases reported in the Federal Trade Commission Reports resulted in cease and desist orders against deceptively advertising goods as silk which were in fact not made of silk. FTC v. Yagle, 1 F.T.C. 13 (1916); FTC v. A. Theo. Abbott & Co., 1 F.T.C. 16 (1916). In the first case the Commission found that the activity in question resulted in deception of consumers which caused damage to manufacturers of genuine silk goods. In the latter case, the Commission found that such deception "may have resulted in damage to the trade * * *."

The courts on the other hand were not as unanimous in conceding jurisdiction to the Commission over deceptive practices. In FTC v. Gratz, 253 U.S. 421 (1920) the Court held that the words "unfair methods of competition" were merely a codification of the pre-existing common law. The *Gratz* decision did not deal with deceptive practices but if so applied could have made the *American Washboard* doctrine applicable to Commission proceedings.

Two years after the *Gratz* decision, the Supreme Court in an opinion by Justice Brandeis, a friend and long-time supporter of the Commission concept, found authority for Commission activity against deceptive practices. FTC v. Winsted Hosiery Co., 258 U.S. 483 (1922). In this case, the petitioner marketed underwear made partly of cotton under labels which the Commission found indicated the underwear was all wool. The Second Circuit set aside the order on the basis of petitioner's arguments that its method of competition was not "unfair" within the meaning of the act because (1) the labels used had attained secondary meaning in the trade indicating goods partly of cotton; (2) a competitor could not maintain an action at common law against petitioner for the activity at issue; and (3) even if consumers are misled, the "result is in no way legally connected with unfair competition." Justice Brandeis rejected these arguments and found for the Commission.

The ability of the Commission to enforce honesty in the marketplace suffered a small setback when the Court, again through Justice Brandeis, narrowly interpreted the provision in § 5 of the act that the Commission could only issue a complaint "if it shall appear to the Commission that a proceeding by it in respect thereof would be to the interest of the public * * *" FTC v. Klesner, 280 U.S. 19 (1929). Justice Brandeis required that before a cease and desist order against a deceptive practice could be enforced a "specific and substantial" public interest as opposed to a private right must be shown. In *Klesner,* Sammons leased space in petitioner's building for his business of making and selling window shades under the name "The Shade Shop". Sammons, in violation of his lease, vacated the premises and set up his shop four doors away. "Out of spite to Sammons, and with the purpose and intent of injuring him and getting his trade * * *" petitioners opened their own business of making and selling window shades at Sammons' former location and used the trade name "Shade Shop".

Justice Brandeis offered the following guidelines for determining when a complaint would be in the public interest: "To justify filing a complaint the public interest must be specific and substantial. Often it is so, because the unfair method employed threatens the existence of present or potential competition. Sometimes, because the unfair method is being employed under circumstances which involve flagrant oppression of the weak by the strong. Sometimes, because, although the aggregate of the loss entailed may be so serious and widespread as to make the matter one of public consequence, no private suit would be brought to stop the unfair conduct, since the loss to each of the individuals affected is too small to warrant it. The alleged unfair competition here complained of arose out of a controversy essentially private in its nature * * *. It is not claimed that the article supplied by [petitioners] was inferior to that of Sammons, or that the public suffered otherwise financially * * *."

After *Klesner,* it appeared that proof of passing off or consumer deception alone would not justify Commission intervention. In 1931 the Court created another hurdle, of potentially greater impact on Commission action against deceptive practices. In FTC v. Raladam Co., 283 U.S. 643 (1931) the petitioner offered for sale an "obesity cure" which was advertised as safe and effective and usable without discomfort, inconvenience or danger of harmful results to health. The complaint charged that the compound contained an ingredient which would not act with reasonable uniformity on the bodies of all users or without impairing the health of a substantial portion of them. The Commission found deception but there was no finding of prejudice or injury to any competitor.

Mr. Justice Sutherland, for the majority, noting that "unfair trade methods are not per se unfair methods of competition," upheld a court of appeals reversal of the Commission's order.

> By the plain words of the act, the power of the Commission to take steps looking to the issue of an order to desist depends upon the existence of three distinct prerequisites: (1) That the methods complained of are *unfair;* (2) that they are methods of *competition* in commerce; and (3) that a proceeding by the Commission to prevent the use of the methods appears to be in the *interest of the public.*

> In a case arising under the Trade Commission Act, the fundamental questions are whether the methods complained of are "unfair," and whether, as in cases under the Sherman Act, they tend to the substantial injury of the public by restricting competition in interstate trade and "the common liberty to engage therein." The paramount aim of the act is the protection of the public from the evils likely to result from the destruction of competition or the restriction of it in a substantial degree, and this presupposes the existence of some substantial competition to

be affected, since the public is not concerned in the maintenance of competition which itself is without real substance.

It is obvious that the word "competition" imports the existence of present or potential competitors, and the unfair methods must be such as injuriously affect or tend thus to affect the business of these competitors—that is to say, the trader whose methods are assailed as unfair must have present or potential rivals in trade whose business will be, or is likely to be, lessened or otherwise injured. It is that condition of affairs which the Commission is given power to correct, and it is against that condition of affairs, and not some other, that the Commission is authorized to protect the public.

Findings of the Commission justify the conclusion that the advertisements naturally would tend to increase the business of respondent; but there is neither finding nor evidence from which the conclusion legitimately can be drawn that these advertisements substantially injured, or tended thus to injure, the business of any competitor or of competitors generally, whether legitimate or not.

The *Raladam* case had little practical effect on the Commission's pursuit of deceptive practices; thereafter, it perfunctorily found an anti-competitive effect in all deception cases. Finally Congress in 1938 enacted the Wheeler-Lea Amendments which clarified the Commission's authority over deceptive practices by adding a prohibition against "unfair or deceptive acts or practices in commerce". 52 Stat. 111 (1938). This amendment was subsequently interpreted to remove the requirement of finding an anti-competitive effect. See e.g., Pep Boys—Manny, Moe & Jack, Inc. v. FTC, 122 F.2d 158 (3d Cir.1941). Since 1938 the Commission has had clear authority to directly protect consumers from deceptive practices.

The original jurisdiction of the Commission extended to prohibited acts "in commerce." This was interpreted to exclude jurisdiction over acts local in character which "affected commerce." FTC v. Bunte Bros., Inc., 312 U.S. 349 (1941). The statute was changed in 1975 to read "in or affecting commerce." 15 U.S.C. § 45 (1975).

The substantive mission of the Commission has been somewhat enhanced. For instance, the Commission has been given responsibility to enforce a variety of product labelling acts and the terms of consumer warranties. Other changes were directed at providing the Commission with additional enforcement powers. The Magnuson-Moss Warranty-Federal Trade Commission Improvement Act of 1975, Pub.L. No. 93–637, 88 Stat. 2183 (1974) substantially broadened the type of remedies available to the Commission as well as codifying Commission regulation of product warranties and the Trans-Alaska Oil Pipeline Act, Pub.L. No. 93–153, 87 Stat. 591 (1973) expanded the Commission's ability to obtain preliminary injunctive relief.

The Commission has been periodically evaluated and found wanting, both in its procedures, its allocation of resources, and in its impact on marketplace deception. Compare, Henderson, The Federal Trade Commission: A Study in Administrative Law and Procedure (1924) and Commission on Organization of the Executive Branch of the Government, Task Force Report on Regulatory Commissions (1949) (popularly known as the Hoover Commission Report) with Report of the American Bar Association Commission to Study the Federal Trade Commission (Sept. 15, 1969). The consumer revolution of the late 1960's and early 1970's had its impact on the Commission's activities. For a current review and recommendations for improvement see Report of the American Bar Association Section of Antitrust Law Special Committee to Study the Role of the Federal Trade Commission, April 7, 1989.

For an extensive review of the history and effectiveness of the Commission, see Stone, Economic Regulation and the Public Interest: The Federal Trade Commission in Theory and Practice (1977).

Private remedies remain the principle theme of this Chapter. However, the Federal Trade Commission cases help formulate some fundamental concepts relating to deception and raise important issues regarding the interplay of private and public policing of deceptive practices. More importantly for purposes here, the consumer protection acts that are rapidly expanding in importance for private plaintiffs incorporate by reference rules and decisions of the FTC. Although plaintiffs historically have been unsuccessful in convincing courts to permit private remedies directly under the Federal Trade Commission Act, the states by adopting the consumer protection acts have indirectly made Commission activity applicable to private actions.

No attempt is made here to survey the landscape of Commission activity. Rather, we concentrate on basic themes. The Commission historically has reflected the political mood; in the 1970's during the era of consumer protection the Commission acted in a creative and expansive way. During the 1980's in more conservative times and with new appointees, the Commission has been considerably more restrained. However, there continues to be a rich body of decisions, rules, policies, and guidelines relating to marketplace deception that now suddenly become accessible to the private plaintiff, consumer or competitor, seeking relief under state law.

(1) THE POLICY QUESTION—WHEN TO REGULATE

PITOFSKY, BEYOND NADER: CONSUMER PROTECTION AND THE REGULATION OF ADVERTISING
90 Harv.L.Rev. 661, 663–71 (1977).

In typical buyer-seller transactions, it will be rare that buyers will be able efficiently to collect relevant information about the large number of products they seek or to take effective precautions against injuries sustained as a result of misplaced reliance on erroneous information. Sellers can accumulate and substantiate descriptive data about each product line once and make it available to all consumers; each consumer, if society left the task to consumers, would have to do it separately for every purchase of each individual item. As a result, it is socially useful to permit advertisers to assume expenses that substitute for search costs of consumers, and even to require advertisers to assume those expenses where market incentives are not adequate to stimulate them to do it themselves.

Beyond the objective of ensuring that consumers are provided with truthful data, advertising also should be regulated with the objective of increasing effective competition in the market. Accurate advertising can facilitate price comparisons and stimulate product improvement, while false advertising can result in misallocation of economic resources either through useless product expenditures, such as cold remedies that do not reduce lost work time due to colds, or by diverting trade to high priced premium products that differ from cheaper substitutes only in the quality and volume of advertising. Deceptive advertising if not controlled can eventually undermine the whole competitive system by reducing the extent to which consumers will rely on product claims and descriptions. In markets where product claims are viewed with utter suspicion, high price is adopted as an indication of quality, and price competition and product improvement become economically irrational.

Viewed in light of these principles, protection of consumers against advertising fraud should not be a broad, theoretical effort to achieve Truth, but rather a practical enterprise to ensure the existence of reliable data which in turn will facilitate an efficient and reliable competitive market process. A corollary of this approach would be that where consumers are fully capable, through common sense or simple observation, of protecting their interests against advertising exaggerations or distortions, there would be no reason for the law to intervene. Similarly, where cheap, safe products subject to repeat purchase are sold as a result of false advertising, there still would be little reason for government intervention if use of the product would clearly disclose that the advertising inducements had been deceptive.

POSNER, REGULATION OF ADVERTISING BY THE FTC
Amer.Ent.Inst.1973.

Deterrents to the Provision of Misleading Information by Sellers

Reliance on sellers for information about products does not provide complete assurance that the information disseminated will be truthful. The seller's general purpose is to provide information that, if believed, will induce consumers to buy his product in preference to other sellers' products. He may therefore be expected to be interested in the truth of the claims only insofar as it bears on their believability. It must be considered whether there are adequate market or legal mechanisms (apart from the type of legal regulation carried on by the Federal Trade Commission) that will deter sellers from making false claims.

There are at least four mechanisms available. The first is the knowledge and intelligence of the consumer. Many false claims would not be worth making simply because the consumer knows better than to believe them. * * *

The second factor that operates to discourage the making of false claims about products is the cost to a seller of developing a reputation for dishonesty. A seller cannot expect a false claim to go undetected indefinitely. If the profitability of his business depends on repeated sales to the same customers, as is true of most established sellers, a policy of false advertising is likely to be short-sighted and therefore bad business: customers will take their business elsewhere after they discover the fraud. Even if the seller does not depend on repeat customers, prospective customers may hear about his fraud from his former customers and be deterred from patronizing him. False advertising in these situations will be extremely costly to the seller in the long run.

Conversely, fraud may be attractive to two kinds of sellers. The first is one who sells a product (or service) whose effectiveness is so uncertain that consumers may not detect false claims about its performance even in the long run—as with providers of medical care. The second type of seller is one whose dependence on repeat customers, or on a good reputation generally, is so slight that he is immune to effective retaliation by former customers. A seller having no fixed business locale, no resources specialized to his current business, no visibility, no stable customer group, would be in this position. An example would be an itinerant peddler.

A third constraint on false advertising is competition. If A's competitor, B, makes a false claim designed to increase B's sales, and the claim is believed by consumers, A will lose sales to B. This will give A an incentive either to rebut B's false claims in an advertising campaign or to sue him. Three qualifications are necessary here, however.

First, A's incentive to rebut the falsity will be limited by the costs of doing so in relation to the gain from recapturing the sales lost to B. That gain may be slight if B's falsehood results in diverting to him a small number of sales from each of many competing firms (C, D, E, F, et cetera, as well as A). In these circumstances, no individual competitor will have an incentive to expend substantial sums in exposing B's fraud although the aggregate diversion of business to B, and hence the harm to consumers, may be great. * * *

Second, A may do just as well by matching B's falsehood as by attempting to refute it. This is not always possible—B may be falsely representing that he is A! And matching may be costly to A's reputation for honest dealing. Conversely, refuting B's false claim might, by increasing A's reputation for fair dealing, enable A not only to recapture the sales lost to B but to capture additional sales from B.

Third, if an industry is highly competitive, the costs of entry into and exit from the industry tend to be low. This suggests that the penalty for a firm that develops a reputation for dishonest dealing may be smaller in highly competitive industries.

* * *

The fourth deterrent to fraud that we will mention consists of private law remedies. * * *

NOTES

1. An important insight into market incentives that discourage deception is contained in Schwartz & Wilde, Intervening in Markets on the Basis of Imperfect Information: A Legal and Economic Analysis, 127 U.Pa.L.Rev. 630, 638 (1979). The authors describe the "conventional" analysis which justifies legal regulation of advertising where substantial numbers of consumers are found to have insufficient information to make informed purchasing decisions. The authors' alternative analysis is captured in simplified form in the following quotation:

> The presence of at least some consumer search in a market creates the possibility of a "pecuniary externality": persons who search sometimes protect nonsearchers from overreaching firms. This result can obtain because in mass transactions it is usually too expensive for firms to distinguish among extensive, moderate, and nonsearchers. Also, it would often be too expensive to draft different contracts for each of these groups even if they could conveniently be identified. Thus, if enough searchers exist, firms have incentives both to compete for their business and to offer the same terms to nonsearchers. When the preferences of searchers are positively correlated with the preferences of nonsearchers, competition among firms for searchers should tend to protect all consumers. Therefore, the conventional analysis asks the wrong question. Rather than asking whether an idealized individual is sufficiently informed to maximize his own utility, the appropriate normative inquiry is whether competition among firms for particular groups of searchers is, in any given market, sufficient to generate optimal prices and terms for all consumers.

2. Posner concludes from his analysis excerpted above that two factors should be present before the Commission intervenes: low probability that a consumer will discover he has been defrauded and an absence of effective private remedies. He also concludes that blatant and malicious fraudulent schemes should be subjected to criminal penalties. Given the Commission's modest enforcement powers at the time his piece was written, Posner concludes that these serious cases are not appropriate for Commission enforcement. Applying these factors to a sample of Commission cases in 1963, 1968, and 1973, Posner concludes that 11%, 3% and 8% respectively of the cases in those years were appropriate for Commission intervention.

3. Are any of the authors far apart in their analysis or in their empirical assumptions about the usefulness of private remedies? Are there factors other than the ones they mention that you would argue justify governmental regulation?

(2) "UNFAIR AND DECEPTIVE" PRACTICES

CHARLES OF THE RITZ DISTRIB. CORP. v. FTC

United States Circuit Court of Appeals, Second Circuit, 1944.
143 F.2d 676.

CLARK, CIRCUIT JUDGE. This is a petition to review and set aside a cease and desist order issued by the Federal Trade Commission, pursuant to a complaint charging petitioner with having violated the Federal Trade Commission Act, 15 U.S.C. § 41 et seq., by falsely advertising its cosmetic preparation "Charles of the Ritz Rejuvenescence Cream." Petitioner is a New York corporation engaged in the sale and distribution in interstate commerce of various cosmetics, one of which is the cream in issue. This is a preparation of the type commonly known to the trade as a powder base or foundation cream for make-up. During the years from 1934 until December, 1939, when sales were "temporarily discontinued" because of the issuance of the present complaint, petitioner's Rejuvenescence Cream enjoyed a vast popularity, with total sales amounting to approximately $1,000,000. The extensive advertising campaign which accompanied this business placed emphasis upon the rejuvenating proclivities of the product. The advertisements typically referred to "a vital organic ingredient" and certain "essences and compounds" which Rejuvenescence Cream allegedly contained, and stated that the preparation brings to the user's "skin quickly the clear radiance * * * the petal-like quality and texture of youth," that it "*restores natural moisture* necessary for a live, healthy skin," with the result that "Your face need know no *drought years*," and that it gives to the skin "a bloom which is wonderfully rejuvenating," and is "constantly active in keeping your skin clear, radiant, and young looking." (Emphasis as in the original.)

After a hearing, the Commission found that such advertising falsely represented that Rejuvenescence Cream will rejuvenate and restore youth or the appearance of youth to the skin, regardless of the condition of the skin or the age of the user, since external applications of cosmetics cannot overcome skin conditions which result from systemic causes or from physiological changes occurring with the passage of time and since there is no treatment known to medical science by which changes in the condition of the skin of an individual can be prevented or by which an aged skin can be rejuvenated or restored to a youthful condition. It, therefore, ordered petitioner to cease and desist disseminating in commerce any advertisement of Charles of the Ritz Rejuvenescence Cream: "(a) In which the word 'Rejuvenescence,' or any other word or term of similar import or meaning, is used to designate, describe, or refer to respondent's [petitioner's] said cosmetic preparation; or (b) which represents, directly or by inference, that respondent's said cosmetic preparation will rejuvenate the skin of the user thereof or restore youth or the appearance of youth to the skin of the user."

* * *

On the merits, petitioner first attacks the finding of fact that its preparation does not act as a rejuvenating agent and preserve or restore the youthful appearance of the skin. Two medical experts, one a leading dermatologist, testified for the Commission; and both affirmatively stated that there was nothing known to medical science which could bring about such results. There was no testimony to the contrary; but petitioner asserts that, since neither expert had ever used Rejuvenescence Cream or knew what it contained—petitioner being unwilling to reveal its secret formula—their testimony was not the substantial evidence necessary to support the final findings and order below. Despite their lack of familiarity with petitioner's product, however, the general medical and pharmacological knowledge of the doctors qualified them to testify as to the lack of therapeutic value of the cream. * * * Further, petitioner was not privileged, under the circumstances, to stand upon its refusal to disclose the true formula of its preparation as a trade secret, Coca-Cola Co. v. Joseph C. Wirthman Drug Co., 8 Cir., 48 F.2d 743, 747; 8 Wigmore on Evidence, 3d Ed. 1940, § 2212; and its failure to introduce evidence thus within its immediate knowledge and control, if existing anywhere, of the rejuvenating constituents and therapeutic effect of its preparation is strong confirmation of the Commission's charges. * * *

Next, and as the crux of its appeal, petitioner attacks the propriety of the finding that by use of the trade-mark "Rejuvenescence" it has represented that its preparation will rejuvenate and restore the appearance of youth to the skin. In view of the finding which we have just held supported on the evidence, that in fact there are no rejuvenating qualities in petitioner's cream, the question is then simply whether or not the trade-mark is deceptive and misleading within the meaning of the Federal Trade Commission Act. But the dictionaries treat "rejuvenescence" as a common word with a plain meaning of "a renewing of youth" or the perhaps more usual "rejuvenation"; cf. Webster's New International Dictionary, 2d Ed., Unabridged, 1939. Nor does the record show any other special meaning to have developed in the trade. On the contrary, the Commission's expert and practicing dermatologist testified directly that rejuvenescence still meant not only to him, but also, so far as he knew, to his female patients, the restoration of youth. In the light of this plain meaning, petitioner's contention can hardly be sustained that "rejuvenescence" is a nondeceptive "boastful and fanciful word," utilized solely for its attractiveness as a trade-mark. That the Patent Office has registered "Rejuvenescence" as a trade-mark is not controlling. Even conceding its nondescriptive quality and hence its validity as a trademark—a concession sufficiently doubtful in itself to be made only arguendo—the fact of registration does not prevent its use from falling within the prohibition of the Federal Trade Commission Act.

There is no merit to petitioner's argument that, since no straight-thinking person could believe that its cream would actually rejuvenate, there could be no deception. Such a view results from a grave misconception of the purpose of the Federal Trade Commission Act. That law was not "made for the protection of experts, but for the public—that vast multitude which includes the ignorant, the unthinking and the credulous," * * * and the "fact that a false statement may be obviously false to those who are trained and experienced does not change its character, nor take away its power to deceive others less experienced." Federal Trade Commission v. Standard Education Soc., 302 U.S. 112, 116. * * * The important criterion is the net impression which the advertisement is likely to make upon the general populace. * * * And, while the wise and the wordly may well realize the falsity of any representations that the present product can roll back the years, there remains "that vast multitude" of others who, like Ponce de Leon, still seek a perpetual fountain of youth. As the Commission's expert further testified, the average woman, conditioned by talk in magazines and over the radio of "vitamins, hormones, and God knows what," might take "rejuvenescence" to mean that this "is one of the modern miracles" and is "something which would actually cause her youth to be restored." It is for this reason that the Commission may "insist upon the most literal truthfulness" in advertisements, Moretrench Corp. v. Federal Trade Commission, 2 Cir., 127 F.2d 792, 795, and should have the discretion, undisturbed by the courts, to insist if it chooses "upon a form of advertising clear enough so that, in the words of the prophet Isaiah, 'wayfaring men, though fools, shall not err therein.'" General Motors Corp. v. Federal Trade Commission, 2 Cir., 114 F.2d 33, 36, certiorari denied 312 U.S. 682.

That the Commission did not produce consumers to testify to their deception does not make the order improper, since actual deception of the public need not be shown in Federal Trade Commission proceedings. * * * Representations merely having a "capacity to deceive" are unlawful, Federal Trade Commission v. Algoma Lumber Co., 291 U.S. 67, 81; Herzfeld v. Federal Trade Commission, supra; General Motors Corp. v. Federal Trade Commission, supra; and, as we have seen, the facts here more than warrant a conclusion of such capacity. Likewise it is not material that there was no consumer testimony as to the meaning of petitioner's representations. The testimony of the dermatologist, a person whose occupation took him among the buyers of Rejuvenescence Cream, is a qualified source of information "as to the buyers' understanding of the words they hear and use." * * *

* * *

The order is affirmed and an enforcement decree will be entered.

FEDERAL TRADE COMMISSION POLICY STATEMENT ON DECEPTION

Issued, October 14, 1983
Reprinted in, 45 Antitrust & Trade Reg.Rep. (BNA) 689
October 27, 1983

[The policy statement on deception was issued in a letter sent to the chairmen of the Senate Commerce, Science and Transportation

Committee and House Energy and Commerce Committee by the Chairman of the Commission. The Commission applied its new policy for the first time in In re Cliffdale Associates, Inc., 103 F.T.C. 110 (1984) a case that hardly tested the limits of the policy. Cliffdale had marketed the "Ball–Matic Gas Save Valve" promoted as a gas saving device. The claims were found to be untrue. The following is an excerpt from the Commission letter summarizing the new policy and an excerpt from the dissent of Commissioner Pertschuk in *Cliffdale.*]

October 14, 1983

Dear Mr. Chairman:

This letter responds to the inquiry of the Committee on Energy and Commerce of the House of Representatives regarding the Commission's enforcement policy against deceptive acts or practices. We also hope this letter will provide guidance to the public.

Section 5 of the FTC Act declares unfair or deceptive acts or practices unlawful. Section 12 specifically prohibits false ads likely to induce the purchase of food, drugs, devices or cosmetics. Section 15 defines a false ad for purposes of Section 12 as one which is "misleading in a material respect." Numerous Commission and judicial decisions have defined and elaborated on the phrase "deceptive acts or practices" under both Sections 5 and 12. Nowhere, however, is there a single definitive statement of the Commission's view of its authority. The Commission believes that such a statement would be useful to the public, as well as your Committee in its continuing review of our jurisdiction.

We have therefore reviewed the decided cases to synthesize the most important principles of general applicability. We have attempted to provide a concrete indication of the manner in which the Commission will enforce its deceptive mandate. In so doing, we intend to address the concerns that have been raised about the meaning of deception, and thereby attempt to provide a greater sense of certainty as to how the concept will be applied.

I. SUMMARY

Certain elements undergird all deception cases. First, there must be a representation, omission or practice that is likely to mislead the consumer. Practices that have been found misleading or deceptive in specific cases include false oral or written representations, misleading price claims, sales of hazardous or systematically defective products or services without adequate disclosures, failure to disclose information regarding pyramid sales, use of bait and switch techniques, failure to perform promised services and failure to meet warranty obligations.

Second, we examine the practice from the perspective of a consumer acting reasonably in the circumstances. If the representation or practice affects or is directed primarily to a particular group, the

Commission examines reasonableness from the perspective of that group.

Third, the representation, omission, or practice must be a "material" one. The basic question is whether the act or practice is likely to affect the consumer's conduct or decision with regard to a product or service. If so, the practice is material, and consumer injury is likely, because consumers are likely to have chosen differently but for the deception. In many instances, materiality, and hence injury, can be presumed from the nature of the practice. In other instances, evidence of materiality may be necessary.

Thus, the Commission will find deception if there is a representation, omission or practice that is likely to mislead the consumer acting reasonably in the circumstances, to the consumer's detriment. We discuss each of these elements below.

* * *

IN RE CLIFFDALE
103 F.T.C. 110 (1984).

COMMISSIONER PERTSCHUK, CONCURRING IN PART AND DISSENTING IN PART

I concur in the majority's findings that respondents violated Section 5. However, I disagree entirely with the legal analysis in the majority opinion.

* * *

Respondents' misrepresentations in this case were unambiguous and undoubtedly material. To put it simply, respondents grossly exaggerated the sole performance feature of their product, the Ball-Matic Gas Save Valve. Normally, there would be little more to say. However, this is the first deception case the Commission has decided since the announcement of the dubious Policy Statement on Deception of October 14, 1983. Since the validity of the bare majority vote on the Statement is open to question, apparently the new majority feels compelled to establish the Statement's legitimacy now by jumping this case through the hoops of its analytical framework for deception cases, regardless of how unhelpful that exercise may be.

Under the guise of making the law more "clear and understandable," the majority has actually raised the evidentiary threshold for deception cases. In this unusually simple case, the majority's approach does not affect the outcome. One has little difficulty in concluding that consumers reasonably relied on respondents' claims and suffered significant monetary loss as a direct result. However, in other cases the harm from the majority's legal analysis will be palpable and painful.

* * *

The new deception analysis has a more serious effect that is clearly not unintentional. That is to withdraw the protection of Section 5 from consumers who do not act "reasonably."

* * *

How will the Commission judge the conduct of consumers who succumb to sales pitches for worthless or grossly over-valued investments? Do "reasonable consumers" buy diamonds or real estate, sight unseen, from total strangers? Is a consumer "acting reasonably" when he or she falls for a hard-sell telephone solicitation to buy "valuable" oil or gas leases from an unknown corporation? Can a consumer "reasonably" rely on oral promises that are expressly repudiated in a written sales contract?

The sad fact is that a small segment of our society makes its livelihood preying upon consumers who are very trusting and unsophisticated. Others specialize in weakening the defenses of especially vulnerable, but normally cautious, consumers. Through skillful exploitation of such common desires as the wish to get rich quick or to provide some measure of security for one's old age, professional con men can prompt conduct that many of their victims will readily admit—in hindsight—is patently unreasonable.

Of course, what strikes me as "unreasonable" consumer behavior may not seem so to other commissioners. The very subjective nature of the "reasonable consumer" standard is cause for concern. How can consumer conduct be measured for reasonableness? I know of no test for it, and I am fearful of the *ad hoc* determinations that will be made in the future.

*   *   *

NOTES

1. The "fools test" was the articulated standard of the Commission until its membership changed in the 1980's and new appointees advocated the definition in the October 14th policy statement. The issue is central to any definition of deception. Should the test for deception be the same regardless of the legal context? How would you resolve the issue for purposes of a suit for damages by a purchaser of the Ball–Matic? Or a suit for injunctive relief brought by the manufacturer of "Super Gas–Saver" who claims his product actually performs as Ball–Matic was advertised to perform? The two Commissioners that dissented from the adoption of the new standard critically attack it in Bailey & Pertschuk, The Law of Deception: The Past as Prologue, 33 Amer. U.L.Rev. 849 (1984).

2. Do you agree with Commissioner's Pertschuk's separate view that the "reasonable consumer" standard is so subjective as to be meaningless? Is it more or less objective than a "fools test"? Cases applying the "fools test" can be quite amusing. See, Gelb v. FTC, 144 F.2d 580 (2d Cir.1944) (upholding Commission order that claim that Clairol colored hair "permanently" was deceptive because it had no effect on new hair even though the court thought it unlikely that "any user . . . could be so credulous."); Allen B. Wrisley Co. v. FTC, 113 F.2d 437 (7th Cir.1940) (rejecting a Commission finding that some consumers might believe "Palm and Olive Soap" was made of 100% olive oil and observing "we suppose that by the same process of mental reaction, such witness would believe that the words 'goose grease and lard' meant 100% lard and no goose grease, or that if shown a picture of a cow and a horse, would be led to believe he had seen a picture of two horses."

What are the consequences of a standard for deception that is ambiguous? Does an ambiguous standard trouble you more in a regulatory context or in the context of private litigation by consumers or competitors?

3. *Puffing.* There is a general recognition that sellers make some statements in the course of advertising their goods or services that are not to be taken seriously. These statements, regarded as "puffing", are not actionable at common law. Notwithstanding the "fools test", courts have recognized a "puffing" defense to actions brought by the FTC. See Kidder Oil Co. v. FTC, 117 F.2d 892 (7th Cir.1941).

In most contexts, a statement is categorized as puffing or actionable misrepresentation depending on whether it is a statement of opinion (puffing) or a statement of fact. Although the distinction may explain the general theme of the cases it is not without its limitations.

Judge Learned Hand recognized the problem in Vulcan Metals Co. v. Simmons Mfg. Co., 248 Fed. 853 (2d Cir.1918). Vulcan purchased from Simmons tools, equipment, inventions, applications, and letters patent relating to a vacuum cleaner. Simmons had made two classes of representations: (1) "commendations of the cleanliness, economy, and efficiency of the machine * * *." and (2) that Simmons had not sold the machine or ever made any attempt to sell it. The machines subsequently proved to be ineffective and of little or no value. It was also shown that Simmons had tried to market the cleaners prior to the sale to Vulcan with little success. Hand found the first category of misrepresentations "puffing" and the latter subject to an action for deceit.

> They [the misrepresentations of quality] raise * * * the question of law how far general "puffing" or "dealer's talk" can be the basis of an action for deceit.
>
> The conceded exception in such cases has generally rested upon the distinction between "opinion" and "fact"; but that distinction has not escaped the criticism it deserves. An opinion is a fact, and it may be a very relevant fact; the expression of an opinion is the assertion of a belief, and any rule which condones the expression of a consciously false opinion condones a consciously false statement of fact. When the parties are so situated that the buyer may reasonably rely upon the expression of the seller's opinion, it is no excuse to give a false one * * *. And so it makes much difference whether the parties stand "on an equality." * * * There are some kinds of talk which no sensible man takes seriously, and if he does he suffers from his credulity. If we were all scrupulously honest it would not be so; but, as it is, neither party usually believes what the seller says about his own opinions, and each knows it. Such statements, like the claims of campaign managers before election, are rather designed to allay the suspicion which would attend their absence than to be understood as having any relation to objective truth. * * * So far as concerns statements of value, the rule is pretty well fixed against the buyer.
>
> In the case at bar, since the buyer was allowed full opportunity to examine the cleaner and to test it out, we put the parties upon an equality. It seems to us that general statements as to what the cleaner would do, even though consciously false were not of a kind to be taken literally by the buyer. As between manufacturer and customer, it may not be so; but this was the case of taking over a business, after ample chance to investigate * * *. The standard of honesty permitted by

the rule may not be the best; but, as Holmes, J., says in Deming v. Darling, 148 Mass. 504, 20 N.E. 107 * * * the chance that the higgling preparatory to a bargain may be afterwards translated into assurances of quality may perhaps be a set-off to the actual wrong allowed by the rule as it stands.

4. *Proof of Deception.* In a deceptive advertising case, the Commission must determine the meaning of the advertisement to the consumers to which it is addressed and whether that meaning is true or false. It is probable that the process in most cases is one of defining the addressees and determining their likely perception of the advertisement. Reliance on the "fool's test" is reserved as an argument to defend the Commission if its judgment is challenged. See Gellhorn, Proof of Consumer Deception Before the Federal Trade Commission, 17 U.Kan.L.Rev. 559, 562–63 (1969). In making the judgments essential for determining whether a given advertisement is "deceptive" the Commission is given a relatively free hand. As *Charles of the Ritz* holds, the advertisement need only have a *tendency* to mislead and proof of actual deception or injury to consumers is not required. Furthermore the Commission need not consult any evidence outside its own expertise. As the Commission stated the law:

> * * * the Commission may rely on its own accumulated knowledge and experience for the determination of whether an advertisement is deceptive or misleading, without resorting to extrinsic evidence of deception. * * * The Commission "may draw its own inferences from the advertisement and need not depend on testimony or exhibits" in the record, aside from the advertisements themselves. * * * Indeed, the Commission is not bound to conduct surveys to determine the meaning and impact of the advertisements. If the law were otherwise, every deceptive advertisement litigation would be turned into a war of experts and surveys. However, in cases where, as here, extrinsic evidence exists in the record, the Commission should take it into consideration. ITT Continental Baking Co., 83 F.T.C. 865, 953–54 (1973).

See Gellhorn, supra, for a proposal that the Commission should use "nonpartisan" surveys in many cases. See also, Barnes, The Significance of Quantitative Evidence in Federal Trade Commission Deceptive Advertising Cases, 46 Law & Contemp.Prob. 25 (1983); Comment, FTC Deceptive Advertising Regulation: A Proposal for the Use of Consumer Behavior Research, 76 Nw.U.L.Rev. 946 (1982).

What "accumulated expertise" does the Commission possess to assist it in determining the effect on a consumer of a claim made in advertising? Could it make such a determination for a claim made in advertisements directed at a teenage audience? At advertisements for products used primarily by a particular racial or ethnic group?

5. Are there constitutional objections to prohibiting advertisements which do not mislead an ordinary consumer but are deceptive to a consumer of low intelligence? Are these objections intensified by a system that authorizes an administrative agency to make decisions involving the deceptiveness of advertisements without extrinsic evidence? Would it be constitutional to impose a similar system to police deceptive statements in political campaigns? See I. Millstein, The Federal Trade Commission and False Advertising, 64 Colum.L. Rev. 439, 462–65 (1964). Would your constitutional analysis depend on the nature of the injury that might result from the potential deception? Would

your analysis depend on the type of sanction the Commission could impose if it finds a statement deceptive?

6. "The law does not attempt the realization of every expectation that has been induced by a promise; the expectation must be a reasonable one. Under no system of law that has ever existed are all promises enforceable. The expectation must be one that most people would have; and the promise must be one that most people would perform." 1 Corbin, Contracts § 1 at 2 (1963). "If fools did not go to market, cracked pots could not be sold." Graffito in Men's Room, Mousetrap Restaurant, Charlottesville, Va. (circa 1975). Are either of the above quotations true?

PFIZER, INC.
81 F.T.C. 23 (1972).

BY KIRKPATRICK, COMMISSIONER:

* * *

II. THE COMPLAINT

The Commission's staff counsel, who have the burden of proving the allegations of the complaint, challenge certain advertising by Pfizer for the product "UN–BURN," a nonprescription product recommended for use on minor burns and sunburn. The complaint cited the following radio and television advertising for Un-Burn as typical and representative:

New Un-Burn actually anesthetizes *nerves* in sensitive sunburned skin.

Un-Burn relieves pain *fast.* Actually *anesthetizes nerves* in sensitive sunburned skin.

Sensitive skin * * * Sunburned skin is sensitive skin * * * Sensitive sunburned skin needs * * * UN–BURN. New UN–BURN contains the same local anesthetic doctors often use * * * Actually anesthetizes nerves in sensitive sunburned skin. I'll tell you what I like about UN–BURN. It's the best friend a blonde ever had! * * * I'm a blonde * * * and I know what it means to have sensitive skin. Why I'm half afraid of moon burn! That's why I'm mad about UN–BURN. It stops sunburn pain in * * * less time than it takes me to slip out of my bikini. That's awfully nice to know when you're the sensitive type * * *

The complaint alleges that the foregoing advertising claims were not substantiated by Pfizer by "adequate and well-controlled scientific studies or tests prior to the making of such statements."

Based on these facts, complaint counsel set forth charges alleging two separate and distinct violations of Section 5 of the Federal Trade Commission Act—first, a charge of unlawful deception, and second, a charge of unlawful unfairness. The deception charge alleged that Pfizer's advertising constituted a *deceptive practice* in representing to consumers that "each of the statements respecting the pain-relieving properties of the said product has been substantiated by respondent by adequate and well-controlled scientific studies or tests prior to the making of such statements." The unfairness charge rests upon the proposition that it is an *unfair practice* to make advertising claims of this nature lacking adequate and well-controlled studies or tests.

III. DECEPTION

* * *

[The deception charge of the complaint did not attack the veracity of the claims but rather asserted that making such claims implied that the maker had substantiated the claims. The Commission did not believe that such a representation could reasonably be implied from the advertisements]

* * *

IV. UNFAIRNESS

The Commission's jurisdiction to proscribe "unfair" commercial practices has been utilized frequently as an independent basis for Commission action. * * *

[The Commission here reviews some earlier decisions in which it finds "succinct confirmation" of its jurisdiction over unfair practices.]

An unfairness analysis will take into account many basic economic facts and considerations, and will permit a broad focus in the examination of marketing practices. Unfairness is potentially a dynamic analytical tool capable of a progressive, evolving application which can keep pace with a rapidly changing economy. Thus as consumers products and marketing practices change in number, complexity, variety, and function, standards of fairness to the consumer may also change.

Generally, the individual consumer is at a distinct disadvantage compared to the producer or distributor of goods in reaching conclusions concerning the reliability of product claims. Very often the price of a consumer product is sufficiently low that the cost to the consumer of obtaining relevant product information exceeds the benefits resulting from the increased satisfaction achieved thereby. In other cases, the complexity of a consumer product, and accordingly the large amount of detailed product information necessary to an informed decision, makes the costs of obtaining product information prohibitive. This problem is further magnified by the large number of competing products on the market. Thus, with the development and proliferation of highly complex and technical products, there is often no practical way for consumers to ascertain the truthfulness of affirmative product claims prior to buying and using the product. When faced with a vast selection of products to choose from, the typical family unit is not sufficiently large enough, and its requirements are too varied, to allow detailed investigation of the goods to be purchased. The consumer simply cannot make the necessary tests or investigations to determine whether the direct and affirmative claims made for a product are true.

Given the imbalance of knowledge and resources between a business enterprise and each of its customers, economically it is more rational, and imposes far less cost on society, to require a manufacturer to confirm his affirmative product claims rather than impose a burden upon each individual consumer to test, investigate, or experiment for himself. The manufacturer has the ability, the knowhow, the equipment, the time and the resources to undertake such information by testing or otherwise—the consumer usually does not.

Turning to that part of the complaint which challenges respondent's marketing practices as unfair, the Commission is of the view that it is an unfair practice in violation of the Federal Trade Commission Act to make an affirmative product claim without a reasonable basis for making that claim. Fairness to the consumer, as well as fairness to competitors, dictates this conclusion. Absent a reasonable basis for a vendor's affirmative product claims, a consumer's ability to make an economically rational product choice, and a competitor's ability to compete on the basis of price, quality, service or convenience, are materially impaired and impeded. * * *

The question of what constitutes a reasonable basis is essentially a factual issue which will be affected by the interplay of overlapping considerations such as (1) the type and specificity of the claim made— e.g., safety, efficacy, dietary, health, medical; (2) the type of product— e.g., food, drug, potentially hazardous consumer product, other consumer product; (3) the possible consequences of a false claim—e.g., personal injury, property damage; (4) the degree of reliance by consumers on the claims; (5) the type, and accessibility, of evidence adequate to form a reasonable basis for making the particular claims. More specifically, there may be some types of claims for some types of products for which the only reasonable basis, in fairness and in the expectations of consumers, would be a valid scientific or medical basis. The precise formulation of the "reasonable basis" standard, however, is an issue to be determined at this time on a case-by-case basis. This standard is determined by the circumstances at the time the claim was made and further depends on both those facts known to the advertiser, and those which a reasonably prudent advertiser should have discovered. Such facts should be possessed *before* the claim is made.

In like manner, the criteria listed above will serve as a touchstone for evaluating those instances in which the Commission is unlikely to proceed against advertisers for failure to have support for an advertisement. In the past, the Commission has recognized that there is a category of advertising themes, in the nature of puffing or other hyperbole, which do not amount to the type of affirmative product claims for which either the Commission or the consumer would expect documentation. * * *

In this case, complaint counsel is apparently challenging the reasonableness of the basis for two specific affirmative product claims made for Un-Burn: (1) Un-Burn actually anesthetizes nerves in sunburned skin, and (2) Un-Burn stops pain fast.

[Complaint counsel argued that the only reasonable basis for the claims could be "adequate and well-controlled scientific studies or tests." The Commission held that as a "question of fact" complaint counsel failed to support his contention. The Commission proceeded to examine possible evidentiary issues in proving a "reasonable basis." This examination is omitted here but explored more fully in the notes.]

Respondent's Efforts to Provide A Reasonable Basis for Affirmative [Product Claims]

Pfizer's director of Marketing testified that he took three measures to satisfy himself as to the efficacy of the product Un-Burn. First, he received "complete assurance" from Pfizer's medical people that the claims he planned to use for Un-Burn could be supported by the two active ingredients in the quantities in which they were to be used in the product. He was assured that the way a topical anesthetic works is to anesthetize nerves and thereby stop pain. He was also assured by the "medical people" that the product was patterned very closely after the market leader, Solarcaine. Secondly, he was assured that all available literature or information on these two active ingredients had been thoroughly reviewed and favorable conclusions derived from this review as to the efficacy of the ingredients as topical anesthetics. Finally, he personally reviewed all competitive advertising to satisfy himself that Pfizer would not be claiming anything more than other products with the same active ingredients. The director of marketing testified that Pfizer did not conduct tests on humans to determine whether the efficacy claims could be supported, but consciously "accepted another method of satisfying" themselves by going over the history of the ingredients. No specific tests were conducted on human beings to prove that Un-Burn anesthetizes nerve ends * * *.

The Pfizer medical official responsible for testing all new Pfizer products, testified that two efficacy tests were run on Un-Burn:

1.   Testing with regard to the antibacterial properties of the product, and

2.   The guinea pig wheal tests.

These latter tests involved the injection of Un-Burn into guinea pigs. His conclusions as to the results of Pfizer's testing on Un-Burn were as follows:

> [T]he products passed the safety and efficacy tests. The tests demonstrated that there were no safety hazards pertaining to the products, and that the antibacterial activity of the product would support the antiseptic claim, and finally, the guinea wheal test demonstrated to us that the active ingredi-

ent, one of the active ingredients, benzocaine, was not inactivated by anything in the formulations.

Inasmuch as complaint counsel's argument did not go directly to the reasonableness of these actions, we lack a sufficient basis for a finding in this regard. In future cases, we would be interested in both the qualifications of the medical and scientific advisors, and some showing that their judgments were rendered on an informed and unbiased basis. Also properly considered here would be the issue of whether reliance upon medical literature and clinical evidence as to the separate ingredients in Un-Burn is appropriate, or whether additional consideration must be given to (1) the combination of ingredients as they appear in the final product, and (2) the various conditions of use to which the product can reasonably be expected to be subjected, including variations as to skin types and degrees of sunburn. The Commission is not, moreover, convinced of the reasonableness of respondent's attempts to rely upon clinical experience as to the efficacy of benzocaine and menthol in general, to support the specific degree of efficacy ("anesthetizes" nerves, "stops" sunburn) claimed for Un-Burn.

Evidently respondent made no written report setting forth the actions which were taken to support the existence of a reasonable basis for its advertising claims. Such a report, if made in good faith prior to marketing, if reasonable in scope and approach, and if reasonably clear as to the evidentiary basis for the specific claims in question (be they scientific tests, specified medical references, or specific clinical evidence), would certainly have, in itself, gone a considerable distance in demonstrating the existence of a reasonable basis for their affirmative product claims.

* * *

VI. CONCLUSION

Having reviewed the record, initial decision, briefs and argument in this proceeding, the Commission has determined that the hearing examiner's dismissal of the complaint should be affirmed. The divergent approaches of complaint counsel and counsel for respondent, both to the appropriate legal standard and to the facts of this case, resulted in the issue simply not being satisfactorily joined.

While the Commission finds that respondent failed in its attempt to demonstrate affirmatively the existence of a reasonable basis for its Un-Burn advertising, the evidence is not sufficient to prove that respondent in fact *lacked* a reasonable basis for its advertising claims. The record evidence is simply inconclusive with regard to the adequacy of the medical literature and clinical experience relied upon by respondent, and with regard to the reasonableness of such reliance.

While this failure of proof might be cured by a remand, the Commission does not believe further proceedings are warranted in the public interest. The reformulation of the legal standard from "adequate and well-controlled scientific studies or tests" to "reasonable basis" might warrant an extensive trial *de novo,* and the advertising in question has already long been discontinued. The significance of this particular case lies, therefore, not so much in the entry of a cease and desist order against this individual respondent, but in the resolution of the general issue of whether the failure to possess a reasonable basis for affirmative product claims constitutes an unfair practice in violation of the Federal Trade Commission Act. As to that issue, the foregoing opinion expresses the views of the Commission. In view of these circumstances, the Commission has determined to affirm the order and initial decision of the hearing examiner except to the extent inconsistent with this opinion.

* * *

AMERICAN HOME PRODUCTS CORP. v. FEDERAL TRADE COMMISSION

United States Court of Appeals, Third Circuit, 1982.
695 F.2d 681.

ADAMS, CIRCUIT JUDGE.

[The case arises out of a complaint filed against American Home Products (AHP), the maker of Anacin a non-prescription analgesic, for deceptive advertising. On the same day complaints were filed against Bristol-Myers the maker of Bufferin and Excedrin, and Sterling Drug, the maker of Bayer Aspirin. The complaint against AHP alleged that advertisments for Anacin claimed superiority in effectiveness to all other non-prescription analgesics and superiority in producing less frequent side effects. The only pain-killing component of Anacin is aspirin. The Administrative Law Judge found AHP's practices "unfair and deceptive"; the Commission spoke only in terms of deception.

Part I of the order issued against AHP had two provisions. Part I(A) ordered AHP to cease falsely representing that Anacin had been medically proven to be superior in effectiveness and freedom from side effects. Part I(B) requires AHP, if it continues to make unequivocal claims of superiority of effectiveness or freedom from side effects, to verify the claims with two well-controlled clinical studies or to include in their advertisements that a substantial question about the truth of the claims exists.]

* * *

C. *Part I(A) of the Order*

We have no hesitation in affirming the Commission's determination that AHP represented that the superiority of Anacin had been proven or established, and that such representation was deceptive.

* * *

D. *Due Process and Part I(B) of the Order*
* * *

The "reasonable basis" doctrine of Pfizer, Inc., 81 F.T.C. 23 (1972), is that advertisers must possess and rely on an adequate "reasonable basis" for their claims. The Commission has supported this standard on the grounds that "[d]eception derives from the failure to disclose to consumers the material fact that an affirmative products claim lacks the support that would be presumed absent some qualification of it." *Pfizer* treated the question of "what constitutes a reasonable basis [as] essentially a factual issue." It listed a number of considerations in resolving the issue in particular cases but remarked that "there may be some types of claims for some types of products for which the only reasonable basis * * * would be a valid scientific or medical basis." 81 F.T.C. at 64. AHP seems to concede the validity of the reasonable basis theory.

In the Commission's complaint against AHP, it alleged that there was a "substantial question" whether the claimed superiority for Anacin and APF had been proven or established, and that failure to set forth this substantial question in advertisements claiming superiority was misleading. Complaint counsel did not deny that there was a "reasonable basis" for AHP's superiority claim but urged that the existence of a "substantial question" nevertheless rendered the advertisements misleading. The ALJ allowed both sides to present whatever they considered relevant under the "substantial question" doctrine, but excluded "reasonable basis" evidence. He ultimately found, and the Commission agreed, that a substantial question about the superiority of Anacin and APF existed in the absence of two well-controlled clinical studies supporting their superiority, and that, in the context of this case, failure to disclose this substantial question was misleading. AHP was not denied an opportunity to introduce evidence either as to when a substantial question exists in the medical-scientific community, or as to whether, in this case, failure on the part of the manufacturer to reveal a substantial question was misleading.

*   *   *

In affirming the ALJ, the Commission took a slightly different position regarding the provenance of the "substantial question" doctrine. Though complaint counsel had characterized "substantial question" as a new idea, and the ALJ appears to have agreed, the Commission reasoned that the theory was a logical application of well-established principles:

> The conclusions set forth herein are merely an elaboration, in the specific context of drug products, upon well-established principles of advertising law requiring that advertisers possess and rely upon a reasonable basis for affirmative product claims. Pfizer, Inc., 81 F.T.C. 23, 60–65 (1972). It has repeatedly been held that failure to possess a reasonable basis for advertising claims is a deceptive practice. [citations omitted] Deception derives from the failure to disclose to consumers the material fact that an affirmative product claim lacks the support that would be presumed absent some qualification of it. The appropriate measure for such support is, of course, to be determined in light of the particular claims made and the products for which they are made. For reasons noted in the

text, we believe that such support in the case of drugs consists of the two or more well-controlled clinical studies deemed necessary by a broad spectrum of relevant experts to justify assertions as to drug performance.

That is, the Commission determined that in some circumstances an advertiser lacks a "reasonable basis" for its claim where there is a substantial question about the truth of the claim. Given this determination, no evidence purporting to establish a "reasonable basis," and not purporting to eliminate the existence of a "substantial question," could have been relevant.

* * *

E. *The Merits of Part I(B) of the Order*

Because we do not vacate Part I(B) on due process grounds, it is necessary to address AHP's substantive challenge to this provision. Part I(B) deals with advertisements which claim that the products are superior, but which do not make overt claims that superiority has been proven. It directs AHP, when making unequivocal claims of superior effectiveness or freedom from side-effects for non-prescription analgesics, to verify such claims with two well-controlled clinical studies, or to reveal that there exists a substantial question about their truth. Another alternative available to AHP is to cease claiming superiority.

* * *

1. *Were the superiority claims made?*

The advertisements lend themselves to the Commission's interpretation, and there is expert testimony in favor of this reading. * * *

2. *Were the superiority claims deceptive?*

More difficult than the question whether superiority claims were made is whether the superiority claims were deceptive. In this regard, the Commission's central passage is the following:

When an analgesic advertiser claims its product to be superior in performance, even without the additional explicit claim that it has been so proven, it is reasonable for consumers to construe that claim to be the assertion of a fact that is generally accepted, within the scientific community, as established. By their nature, therapeutic drug products raise special public health concerns, in light of the risks associated with their use.

We do not decide whether such reasoning would justify a "substantial question" provision whenever advertisements make *any* affirmative product claims for *any* drugs. In the present case, the Commission declined to apply this reasoning so broadly, and limited Part I(B) to AHP's *non-prescription analgesics* and to claims of *superior effectiveness or freedom from sides effects*. The Commission expressly recognized the possibility that comparative claims for some non-prescription drugs might require less substantiation than is demanded here.

* * *

We are required to give deference to Commission findings that advertisements are deceptive. There are strong reasons why the Commission's demand for an especially high level of proof for advertising claims is justifiable under the facts of this proceeding. These reasons can be grouped into two categories: first, those based upon the special nature of the product category; and second, those relating to the particular facts of AHP's conduct.

Pervasive government regulation of drugs, and consumer expectations about such regulation, create a climate in which questionable claims about drugs have all the more power to mislead.

* * *

Non-prescription as well as prescription drugs are subject to the FDA's requirements that absolute safety and efficacy be demonstrated by well-controlled clinical tests. And the Commission concluded that many consumers could reasonably believe that the federal government demanded similarly high standards for claims of *comparative* effectiveness and safety as are imposed on *absolute* claims.

Of course the Commission is not committed to the unrealistic notion that consumers understand the clinical details of comparative drug testing or the exact mechanisms of government regulation. It merely asserts that consumers reasonably assume that the proper governmental authorities will take steps to ensure that unqualified claims of a drug's superiority are supported by whatever proof the appropriate medical or scientific experts consider sufficient.

Another consideration in favor of holding comparative effectiveness and safety claims for analgesics to high standards of substantiation is the difficulty for the average consumer to evaluate such claims through personal experience, and the consequent tenacity of advertising-induced beliefs about superiority. Several factors account for the lack of capability by consumers in this area. First, mild to moderate pain, especially headache pain, is "self-limiting"; that is, it will eventually disappear whether or not the consumer attempts a remedy. Consequently, the consumer cannot tell if relief was obtained spontaneously or as a result of the analgesic. Second, problems of memory may prevent reliable comparisons by a consumer between different preparations taken on different occasions. Third, pain varies in intensity, again undermining the reliability of any individual's judgments of comparative effectiveness. Fourth, the "placebo effect" of taking drugs ensures that many consumers will perceive relief even from totally ineffective products. As the ALJ noted, in "clinical studies of mild to moderate pain, the placebo response rate, i.e., the rate of positive responses (perceived relief) in the presence of a pharmacologically inactive drug, is commonly between 30% and 60% [citing expert witnesses]." One expert witness "demonstrated that, even on a blinded basis, individual consumers are unable to distinguish the comparative therapeutic effect of five OTC analgesics." App. 163. Because consumers cannot accurately rate the products for themselves, advertising, and the expectations which it engenders, becomes a significantly more influential source of consumer beliefs than it would otherwise be.

The health risks associated with aspirin are another special feature of the product category. The larger dosages of aspirin which AHP exhorts consumers to ingest increase the dangers of adverse side effects, with little evidence that there exist any countervailing benefits.

* * *

NOTES

1. Prior to the final decision in *Pfizer,* the Commission had adopted a resolution notifying advertisers that they would be required, on demand, to submit "with respect to any advertisement such tests, studies or other data (including testimonials or endorsements) as they had in their possession prior to the time claims were made and which purport to substantiate any claims, statements or representations made in the advertisement regarding the safety, performance, efficacy, quality, or comparative price of the product advertised." FTC Resolution, 36 Fed.Reg. 12058 (1971), as amended, 36 Fed.Reg. 14680 (1971). For a history of the ad substantiation program see, Note, 1973 Duke L.J. 563; Note, 61 Geo.L.J. 427 (1973). For an analysis of *Pfizer* see Note, Unfairness in Advertising: Pfizer, Inc., 59 Va.L.Rev. 324 (1973).

2. Commission orders similar to that in *American Home* requiring two scientifically controlled studies for comparative effectiveness and freedom from side effects claims were upheld against Bristol-Myers and Sterling Drug. Bristol-Myers Co. v. Federal Trade Commission, 738 F.2d 554 (2d Cir.1984); Sterling Drug, Inc. v. Federal Trade Commission, 741 F.2d 1146 (9th Cir.1984). In all three cases, the Commission imposed the "two controlled studies" standard only for advertising that claimed superiority over other similar products. Statements in the advertisements that merely claimed an abstract not a comparative level of effectiveness or safety were subjected to the "reasonable basis" standard. "A reasonable basis for such a claim shall consist of competent and reliable scientific evidence supporting that claim."

However, in Thompson Medical Co., Inc. v. Federal Trade Commission, 791 F.2d 189 (D.C.Cir.1986) a Commission order required two "well-controlled, double-blinded clinical studies" prior to any advertisement claiming effectiveness for Aspercreme, a topical over the counter analgesic. The court upheld the Commission noting that although the requirement had not formerly been imposed on a non-comparative efficacy claim, the Commission reserved in *Pfizer* the option of selecting the appropriate level of substantiation for all claims. The court found the Commission "employed the multi-factorial analysis first expounded in Pfizer * * *, exercised its remedial discretion, and determined that the particular facts here warranted the imposition of a clinical testing requirement."

3. Should any of these tests for deception or unfairness be applicable in a private suit by a consumer or competitor? How do either of these tests relate to implementation of the October 14th policy statement on deception?

4. The substantiation and reasonable basis rules have survived first amendment challenges. See Jay Norris, Inc. v. FTC, 598 F.2d 1244 (2d Cir. 1979).

5. Would you accept as a "reasonable basis" for an advertising claim a survey showing that other producers of products with similar ingredients make similar claims? What policy implications emerge from your decision? Does it matter whether you are an administrative agency or a court deciding a private law suit?

6. Are you clear as to the difference between advertising that is (1) unfair because not substantiated; (2) deceptive because not substantiated; (3) deceptive because a substantial question as to the advertising's accuracy is not disclosed? What incentives do each of these doctrines create for advertisers? For consumers? Do you expect the more onerous standard for comparative advertising claims to increase or decrease the amount of comparative advertising? Do you accept the proposition that there may be claims, either abstract or comparative, that are true but are too expensive to substantiate?

FEDERAL TRADE COMMISSION v. ALGOMA LUMBER CO.

Supreme Court of the United States, 1934.
291 U.S. 67, 54 S.Ct. 315, 78 L.Ed. 655.

MR. JUSTICE CARDOZO delivered the opinion of the Court.

In May, 1929, the Federal Trade Commission filed and served complaints against a group of fifty manufacturers on the Pacific Coast charging "unfair competition in interstate commerce" in violation of section 5 of the Federal Trade Commission Act. * * *

The practice complained of as unfair and enjoined by the Commission is the use by the respondents of the words "California white pine" to describe lumber, logs, or other forest products made from the pine species known as "pinus ponderosa." * * *

The respondents are engaged in the manufacture and sale of lumber and timber products which they ship from California and Oregon to customers in other states and foreign lands. Much of what they sell comes from the species of tree that is known among botanists as "pinus ponderosa." The respondents sell it under the name of "California white pine," and under that name, or at times "white pine" simply, it goes to the consumer. In truth it is not a white pine, whether the tests to be applied are those of botanical science or of commercial practice and understanding.

Pine trees, the genus "pinus," have for a long time been divided by botanists, foresters, and the public generally into two groups, the white pine and the yellow. The white pine group includes, by common consent, the northern white pine (pinus strobus), the sugar pine, and the Idaho white pine. It is much sought after by reason of its durability under exposure to weather and moisture, the proportion of its heartwood as contrasted with its sapwood content as well as other qualities. For these reasons it commands a high price as compared with pines of other species. The yellow pine group is less durable, harder, heavier, more subject to shrinkage and warping, darker in color, more resinous, and more difficult to work. It includes the long leaf yellow pine (pinus palustris), grown in the southern states, and the pinus ponderosa, a far softer wood, which is grown in the Pacific Coast states, and in Arizona and New Mexico as well as in the "inland empire" (Eastern Washington, Oregon, Idaho, and Western Montana).

Of the varieties of white pine, the northern or pinus strobus has been known better and longer than the others. It is described sometimes as northern white pine, sometimes as white pine simply, sometimes with the addition of its local origin, as Maine white pine, Michigan, Wisconsin, Minnesota, Canadian, New Brunswick. It is native to the northeastern states and to the Great Lakes region, as far west as Minnesota. It is found also in Canada and along the Appalachian highlands. It was almost the only building material for the settlers of New England, and so great is its durability that many ancient buildings made from it in the seventeenth and eighteenth centuries survive in good condition. The sugar pine is native to the upland regions of California, Southern Oregon and parts of Nevada. The Idaho white pine grows in the mountainous sections of Idaho, Washington, and Oregon and in parts of British Columbia. The white pine species "still holds an exalted reputation among the consuming public" and "in general esteem is the highest type of lumber as respects the excellences desired in soft wood material." "It is coming more and more to be a specialty wood, largely devoted to special purposes, as it becomes scarcer and higher in price. It is in great demand."

About 1880 the pinus ponderosa, though botanically a yellow pine, began to be described as a white pine when sold in the local markets of California, New Mexico, and Arizona, the description being generally accompanied by a reference to the state of origin, as "California white pine," etc. By 1886, sales under this description had spread to Nevada and Utah with occasional shipments farther east. About 1900, they entered the middle western states, and about 1915 had made their way into New England, though only to a small extent. The pines from the inland empire traveled east more slowly, and when they did were described as western white pine, a term now generally abandoned. The progress of the newcomers both from the coast and from the inland empire was not wholly a march of triumph. In their movement to the central and eastern markets they came into competition more and more with the genuine white pine with which those markets had been long familiar. Mutterings of discontent were heard. In 1924, partly as a result of complaints and official investigations, many of the producers, notably those of the "inland empire," as well as some producers in California and Arizona, voluntarily gave up the use of the adjective "white" in connection with their product, and adopted the description "pondosa pines," pondosa being a corruption or abbreviation of the ponderosa of the botanists. "Pondosa pine is the term employed for ponderosa by the representatives of producers of slightly more than half of the ponderosa marketed." The respondents and others, however, declined to make a change. During the next five years California white pine and its equivalent became an even more important factor in the lumber markets of the country. Accumulating complaints led to an inquiry by the Commission, which had its fruit in this proceeding.

The confusion and abuses growing out of these interlocking names have been developed in the findings. Many retail dealers receiving orders for white pine deliver California white pine, not knowing that it differs from the lumber ordered. Many knowing the difference deliver the inferior product because they can buy it cheaper. Still others, well informed and honest, deliver the genuine article, thus placing themselves at a disadvantage in the race of competition with the unscrupulous and the ignorant. Trade has thus been diverted from dealers in white pine to dealers in pinus ponderosa masquerading as white pine. Trade has also been diverted from dealers in pinus ponderosa under the name pinus pondosa to dealers in pinus ponderosa under the more attractive label. The diversion of trade from dealers of one class to dealers of another is not the only mischief. Consumers, architects, and retailers have also been misled. They have given orders for the respondents' product, supposing it to be white pine and to have the qualities associated with lumber of that species. They have accepted deliveries under the empire of that belief. True indeed it is that the woods sold by the respondents, though not a genuine white pine, are nearer to that species in mechanical properties than they are to the kinds of yellow pine indigenous to the south. The fact that for many purposes they are halfway between the white species and the yellow makes the practice of substitution easier than it would be if the difference were plain. Misrepresentation and confusion flourish in such a soil. From these findings and others the Commission was brought to the conclusion that the respondents compete unfairly in transacting business as they do, and that in the interest of the public their methods should be changed.

* * *

(a) * * * [The court first rejected the contention that the use of "California White Pine" was permissible because it was utilized by the United States Bureau of Standards in its "simplified practice recommendations" for the lumber industry. The standards resulted from a conference of industry representatives to simplify methods of business in the lumber industry by standardizing the commercial names for lumber of various types. The court found the function of the Bureau of Standards and of the Federal Trade Commission "essentially diverse. The aim of the one is to simplify business by substituting uniformity of methods for wasteful diversity, and in the achievement of these ends to rely upon cooperative action. The aim of the other is to make the process of competition fair. There are times when a description is deceptive from the very fact of its simplicity."]

(b) [The Court of Appeals had found no deception because the substituted wood was "so nearly equal in utility that buyers are not injured, even though misled."] The wood dealt in by the respondents is not substantially as good as the genuine white pine, nor would sales under the wrong name be fitting if it were.

The ruling of the court below as to this is infected by a twofold error. The first is one of fact. The supposed equivalence is unreal.

The second is one of law. If the equivalence existed, the practice would still be wrong.

* * *

What has been written has been aimed at the position that pinus ponderosa is as good or almost as good as the white pines of the east. We have yet to make it plain that the substitution would be unfair though equivalence were shown. This can best be done in considering another argument which challenges the finding of the Commission that there has been misunderstanding on the part of buyers. To this we now turn.

Second. The argument is made that retailers and consumers are not shown to have been confused as to the character of the lumber supplied by the respondents, and that even if there was confusion there is no evidence of prejudice.

Both as to the fact of confusion and its consequences the evidence is ample. Retailers order "white pine" from manufacturers and take what is sent to them, passing it on to their customers. At times they do this knowing or suspecting that they are supplying California white pine instead of the genuine article, and supplying a wood that is inferior, at least for the outer parts of buildings. Its comparative cheapness creates the motive for the preference. At times they act in good faith without knowledge of the difference between the California pines and others. Architects are thus misled, and so are builders and consumers. There is a suggestion by the court that for all that appears the retailers, buying the wood cheaper, may have lowered their own price, and thus passed on to the consumer the benefit of the saving. The inference is a fair one that this is not always done, and perhaps not even generally. If they lower the price at all, there is no reason to believe that they do so to an amount equivalent to the saving to themselves.

But saving to the consumer, though it be made out, does not obliterate the prejudice. Fair competition is not attained by balancing a gain in money against a misrepresentation of the thing supplied. The courts must set their faces against a conception of business standards so corrupting in its tendency. The consumer is prejudiced if upon giving an order for one thing, he is supplied with something else. Federal Trade Commission v. Royal Milling Co., 288 U.S. 212, 216; City of Carlsbad v. W.T. Thackeray & Co. (C.C.) 57 F. 18. In such matters, the public is entitled to get what it chooses, though the choice may be dictated by caprice or by fashion or perhaps by ignorance. Nor is the prejudice only to the consumer. Dealers and manufacturers are prejudiced when orders that would have come to them if the lumber had been rightly named, are diverted to others whose methods are less scrupulous. * * * The careless and the unscrupulous must rise to the standards of the scrupulous and diligent. The Commission was not organized to drag the standards down.

Third. The argument is made that the name for the respondents' lumber was adopted more than thirty years ago without fraudulent design, and that a continuation of the use is not unfair competition, though confusion may have developed when the business, spreading eastward, attained national dimensions.

The Commission made no finding as to the motives animating the respondents in the choice of the contested name. The respondents say it was chosen to distinguish their variety of yellow pine from the harder yellow pines native to the southern states. We may assume that this is so. The fact remains, however, that the pines were not white either botanically or commercially, though the opportunity for confusion may have been comparatively slight when the sales were restricted to customers in local markets, buying for home consumption. Complaints, if there were any, must have been few and inarticulate at a time when there was no supervisory body to hold business to its duty. According to the law as then adjudged, many competitive practices that today may be suppressed (Federal Trade Commission v. Winsted Hosiery Co., supra), were not actionable wrongs, the damage to the complainants being classified often as collateral and remote. American Washboard Co. v. Saginaw Mfg. Co. (C.C.A.) 103 F. 281, 286. The Federal Trade Commission was not organized till 1914, its jurisdiction then as now confined to interstate and foreign commerce. Silence up to that time is not even a faint token that the misapplied name had the approval of the industry. It may well have meant no more than this, that the evil was not great, or that there was no champion at hand to put an end to the abuse. Even silence thereafter will not operate as an estoppel against the community at large, whatever its effect upon individuals asserting the infringement of proprietary interests. French Republic v. Saratoga Vichy Spring Co., 191 U.S. 427. There is no bar through lapse of time to a proceeding in the public interest to set an industry in order by removing the occasion for deception or mistake, unless submission has gone so far that the occasion for misunderstanding, or for any so widespread as to be worthy of correction, is already at an end. Competition may then be fair irrespective of its origin. This will happen, for illustration, when by common acceptation the description, once misused, has acquired a secondary meaning as firmly anchored as the first one. Till then, with every new transaction, there is a repetition of the wrong.

The evidence here falls short of establishing two meanings with equal titles to legitimacy by force of common acceptation. On the contrary, revolt against the pretender, far from diminishing, has become increasingly acute. With the spread of business eastward, the lumber dealers who sold pines from the states of the Pacific Coast were involved in keen competition with dealers in lumber from the pines of the east and middle west. In the wake of competition came confusion and deception, the volume mounting to its peak in the four or five years before the Commission resolved to act. Then, if not before, misbranding of the pines was something more than a venial wrong. The respondents, though at fault from the beginning, had been allowed to go their way without obstruction while the mischief was not a crying one. They were not at liberty to enlarge the area of their business without adjusting their methods to the needs of new conditions. An analogy may be found in the decisions on the law of trade marks where the principle is applied that a name legitimate in one territory may generate confusion when carried into another, and must then be given up. Hanover Milling Co. v. Metcalf, 240 U.S. 403, 416; United Drug Co. v. Rectanus Co., 248 U.S. 90, 100. More than half the members of the industry have disowned the misleading name by voluntary action and are trading under a new one. The respondents who hold out are not relieved by innocence of motive from a duty to conform. Competition may be unfair within the meaning of this statute and within the scope of the discretionary powers conferred on the Commission, though the practice condemned does not amount to fraud as understood in courts of law. Indeed there is a kind of fraud, as courts of equity have long perceived, in clinging to a benefit which is the product of misrepresentation, however innocently made. Redgrave v. Hurd, L.R. 20 Ch.D. 1, 12, 13; Rawlins v. Wickham, 3 De G. & I. 304, 317; Hammond v. Pennock, 61 N.Y. 145, 152. That is the respondents' plight today, no matter what their motives may have been when they began. They must extricate themselves from it by purging their business methods of a capacity to deceive.

Fourth. Finally, the argument is made that the restraining orders are not necessary to protect the public interest (see Federal Trade Commission v. Royal Milling Co., supra), but to the contrary that the public interest will be promoted by increasing the demand for pinus ponderosa, though it be sold with a misleading label, and thus abating the destruction of the pine forests of the east.

The conservation of our forests is a good of large importance, but the end will have to be attained by methods other than a license to do business unfairly.

The finding of unfair competition being supported by the testimony, the Commission did not abuse its discretion in reaching the conclusion that no change of the name short of the excision of the word "white" would give adequate protection.

The judgment is reversed.

NOTES

1. One of the "classic" FTC cases to come before the Supreme Court was Federal Trade Commission v. Colgate-Palmolive Co., 380 U.S. 374 (1965). At issue was a Commission order attacking a television commercial purporting to show that "Rapid Shave", a shaving cream, could shave sandpaper. The viewer saw Rapid Shave applied to what appeared to be sandpaper and then "shaved" by a razor. In fact, the Rapid Shave was applied to a piece of plexiglas to which sand had been applied. The examiner found (1) Rapid Shave could in fact shave real sandpaper although not in the short time represented by the commercial, and (2) if real sandpaper had been used for the commercials, the

inadequacies of television transmission would have made it appear to viewers to be nothing more than plain colored paper.

The Court formulated the issue to be whether it was deceptive to represent the "truth" through undisclosed use of mock-ups on television. The Court upheld the Commission's order arguing that the misrepresentation was that viewers had "objective proof of a seller's product claim over and above the seller's word" and that they had seen the proof with their own eyes:

> In commercials where the emphasis is on the seller's word, and not on the viewer's own perception, the respondents need not fear that an undisclosed use of props is prohibited by the present order. On the other hand, when the commercial not only makes a claim, but also invites the viewer to rely on his own perception, for demonstrative proof of the claim, the respondents will be aware that the use of undisclosed props in strategic places might be a material deception.

Justices Harlan and Stewart dissented believing that "the proper legal test in cases of this kind concerns not what goes on in the broadcasting studio, but whether what is shown on the television screen is an accurate representation of the advertised product and of the claims made for it."

2. The Court in *Algoma* holds that the Commission is justified preventing a deception even if it produces no harm. Do you agree? If in fact all of the species of pine were functionally similar, why should the law intervene if the designation "white pine" is not entirely accurate? What if consumers were deceived to their benefit? Suppose a famous brand of shirt sells for $30. Assume a competing manufacturer makes a shirt identical in all respects and is able to sell it for $25. He uses the brand name of the original manufacturer thus deceiving consumers into saving themselves $5. Should this be prohibited? Should the same analysis apply to *Algoma* where there is no private brand involved? Could a consumer in either situation win a claim for deception?

3. Is anyone damaged in *Colgate?* What is the justification for the Commission's action in that case? Could a consumer bring a cause of action against Colgate for misrepresentation? How would the majority in *Cliffdale* react?

4. Should the intent of the advertiser play any role in these cases? Can the law prohibit unintentional deception consistent with the first amendment? Is your answer different for private remedies than for administration actions?

5. Professor Pitofsky observed that the Commission has deemphasized its campaign against mock-ups. He argues, however, that the *Colgate-Palmolive* case is correctly decided for two reasons: First, a mock-up defense could be asserted in a traditional deceptive demonstration case, and, thus on practical grounds, the rule against mock-ups tends to simplify and shorten such cases. Second, the rule is not detrimental to advertisers because a demonstration requiring a mock-up can still be performed as long as the fact that it is a simulation is disclosed. Pitofsky, Beyond Nader: Consumer Protection and the Regulation of Advertising, 90 Harv.L.Rev. 661, 689–92 (1977).

On the other hand consider the senselessness of the advertisement itself. People buy shaving cream to shave faces, not sandpaper, and the connection between shaving sandpaper and faces is less than obvious. Will not the success of Colgate shaving cream be determined in the market by its success in shaving faces? Why would Colgate bother to run such a commercial? As between that decision and the decision of the Commission to contest it, which makes the most sense?

6. Can a picture alone convey a false impression? Is a photograph of a young happy couple frolicking in the surf as part of a cigarette commercial deceptive? What message is conveyed by the picture? Should a panel of consumers be polled to see if they agree on the message? It is reported that the staff of the Commission considered these questions. Wall St.J., Aug. 11, 1978, at 6, col. 1.

7. Is there an inevitable conflict between "wasteful diversity" and fair competition? In *Algoma* the Bureau of Standards (or more realistically the lumber industry) believed that too many different designations for wood would be confusing (deceptive?). That is similar, is it not, to the complaint of some "consumer advocates" that the package sizes for some products are so diverse that price comparisons are not possible? In language, is there ever an optimum balance between specification and generalization that avoids confusion?

Labeling requirements can pose the tradeoffs between specialization and generalization in a particularly dramatic fashion. There are a variety of labeling laws promulgated both at the state and federal levels which require the listing of ingredients, quantities, or other characteristics of the product. For labeling laws to be meaningful, a common set of definitions of the characteristics must be imposed. For a fascinating account of the battle over the definition of "peanut butter" (a battle within the Food and Drug Administration that resulted in a rule that prevented "Skippy" and "Peter Pan", the two leading brands, from being marketed as "peanut butter") see Merrill & Collier, Jr., "Like Mother Used to Make": Analysis of FDA Food Standards of Identity, 74 Colum.L.Rev. 561 (1974).

FEDERAL TRADE COMMISSION v. MARY CARTER PAINT CO.

Supreme Court of the United States, 1965.
382 U.S. 46, 86 S.Ct. 219, 15 L.Ed.2d 128.

[Mary Carter Paint distributed paint under the "Mary Carter" label in more than 27 states through over 500 retail outlets. Its share of the national paint market was under one percent although the company did increase its sales from one million dollars in 1955 to 12 million in 1960. The basic business policy of Mary Carter consistently followed for ten years was to sell one gallon of "Mary Carter" paint at a price comparable to the leading national brands and to give the purchaser a second can "free". The policy arose when leading paint manufacturers succeeded in creating a public psychology equating quality paint with price. Paint priced below the "quality price" was not deemed by the consuming public to be quality paint. The Commission counsel conceded that the quality of Mary Carter paint was not at issue, and that Mary Carter paint was as good as or superior to paints marketed at the "quality price". The advertised price was the only price at which the purchaser could buy Mary Carter paint. Generally the purchaser accepted the second can but it was optional with him. He could not buy one can for half the price if he rejected the "free" can. There was no evidence at the hearing of consumer complaints or of any deception of Mary Carter customers.

The Commission entered a cease and desist order against Mary Carter to prohibit them from representing that the second can of paint was "free". The facts are taken from the Court of Appeals decision reversing the Commission's order. Mary Carter Paint Co. v. FTC, 333 F.2d 654 (5th Cir.1964).]

MR. JUSTICE BRENNAN delivered the opinion of the Court.

Although there is some ambiguity in the Commission's opinion, we cannot say that its holding constituted a departure from Commission policy regarding the use of the commercially exploitable word "free". Initial efforts to define the term in decisions [2] were followed by "Guides Against Deceptive Pricing." [3] These informed businessmen that they might advertise an article as "free," even though purchase of another article was required, so long as the terms of the offer were clearly stated, the price of the article required to be purchased was not increased, and its quality and quantity were not diminished. With specific reference to two-for-the-price-of-one offers, the Guides required that either the sales price for the two be "the advertiser's usual and customary retail price for the single article in the recent, regular course of his business," or where the advertiser has not previously sold the article, the price for two be the "usual and customary" price for one in the relevant trade areas. These, of course, were guides, not fixed rules as such, and were designed to inform businessmen of the factors which would guide Commission decision. Although Mary Carter seems to have attempted to tailor its offer to come within their terms, the Commission found that it failed; the offer complied in appearance only.

The gist of the Commission's reasoning is in the hearing examiner's finding, which it adopted, that

> "the usual and customary retail price of each can of Mary Carter paint was not, and is not now, the price designated in the advertisement [$6.98] but was, and is now, substantially less than such price. The second can of paint was not, and is not now, 'free,' that is, was not, and is not now, given as a gift or gratuity. The offer is, on the contrary, an offer of two cans of paint for the price advertised as or purporting to be the list price or customary and usual price of one can." 60 F.T.C., at 1844.

In sum, the Commission found that Mary Carter had no history of selling single cans of paint; it was marketing twins, and in allocating what is in fact the price of two cans to one can, yet calling one "free," Mary Carter misrepresented. It is true that respondent was not permitted to show that the quality of its paint matched those paints

2. Book-of-the-Month Club, Inc., 48 F.T.C. 1297 (1952); Walter J. Black, Inc., 50 F.T.C. 225 (1953); Puro Co., 50 F.T.C. 454 (1953); Book-of-the-Month Club, Inc., 50 F.T.C. 778 (1954); Ray S. Kalwajtys, 52 K.T.C. 721, enforced Kalwajtys v. FTC, 237 F.2d 654 (1956).

3. Guides Against Deceptive Pricing, Guide V, adopted October 2, 1958, 23 Fed. Reg. 7965; see also policy statement, December 3, 1953, 4 CCH Trade Reg.Rep. ¶ 40,210. For the current guide, Guide IV, effective January 8, 1964, see 29 Fed.Reg. 180.

which usually and customarily sell in the $6.98 range, or that purchasers of paint estimate quality by the price they are charged. If both claims were established, it is arguable that any deception was limited to a representation that Mary Carter has a usual and customary price for single cans of paint, when it has no such price. However, it is not for courts to say whether this violates the Act. "[T]he Commission is often in a better position than are courts to determine when a practice is 'deceptive' within the meaning of the Act." Federal Trade Comm'n v. Colgate-Palmolive Co., 380 U.S. 374, 385. There was substantial evidence in the record to support the Commission's finding; its determination that the practice here was deceptive was neither arbitrary nor clearly wrong. The Court of Appeals should have sustained it. * * *

The Commission advises us in its brief that it believes it would be appropriate here "to remand the case to it for clarification of its order." The judgment of the Court of Appeals is therefore reversed and the case is remanded to that court with directions to remand to the Commission for clarification of its order.

It is so ordered.

Judgment of Court of Appeals reversed and case remanded to the Commission.

MR. JUSTICE STEWART took no part in the decision of this case.

MR. JUSTICE HARLAN, dissenting.

In my opinion the basis for the Commission's action is too opaque to justify an upholding of its order in this case. * * *

                      * * *

At the very least the Commission should be required to demonstrate real deception and public injury in a decision that allows the courts to evaluate its reasoning and businessmen to comply with assurance with its latest views; these standards are not met by the FTC's opinion in this case. The Department of Justice suggests that the FTC regards the advertisements as implying that Mary Carter regularly sells its paint for the present per-can price without giving an extra can free; from this premise, it might be argued, the buyer may then conclude that each can of Mary Carter is the equal of similarly priced rivals with whom it has regularly competed on equal terms in the past, making the present "free" can offer appear an excellent bargain. But the advertising in the present case does not really suggest that the "free" can is a departure from Mary Carter's usual pricing policy. Certainly nothing in any of the publicity states that the extra can is a "new" bargain or asserts that the opportunity may lapse in the near future. To the contrary, a number of Mary Carter advertisements, not separately treated by the Commission, affirmatively suggest that the extra-can offer has been and will continue to be the sales policy. Far from trying to imply that its extra-can offer represents a temporary saving for the customer, Mary Carter has striven over a number of years to associate itself irrevocably in the public mind with the notion that every second can is free; the catchphrase appears in one form or another in nearly all the ads before us and is even imprinted on the top of Mary Carter paint cans. Finally, it is not without irony that the Commission, presumably seeking to protect the consumer from any unfounded ultimate conclusions that a can of Mary Carter is as good as its high-priced rivals, rejected an offer of proof from the company that a single can of Mary Carter is scientifically equal or superior to the leading paints that sell at the same per-can price level without giving bonus cans. Actually, there is no suggestion that any volume of consumer complaints has been received, which further deepens the mystery why this frail proceeding was ever initiated.

The temptation to gloss over the analytical failings of the rationale now asserted for the FTC by relying on agency expertise must be short-lived in this case. Any findings by the FTC as to what the public may conclude from particular phrasings are most inexplicit, no distinction is taken between the various ads in question, and the conduct proscribed is never sharply identified. Surely there can be no resort to uninvoked expertise to buttress an unarticulated theory.

The opaqueness of the Commission's opinion and order makes their approval difficult for yet other reasons. The bite of the FTC decision is in its order, which even the Commission recognizes to be unclear; how the Commission order can be upheld before this Court is told what exactly it means is indeed a puzzling question. Additionally, by failing to spell out its rationale the FTC decision breeds the suspicion that it is not merely *ad hoc* but quite possibly irreconcilable with the Black case seemingly reaffirmed by the Commission in this very proceeding. If the Commission is able to write an opinion and order that can cure these defects and draw the plain distinctions necessary to assure fair warning and equal treatment for other advertisers, it has not done so yet.

In administering § 5 in the context of the many elusive questions raised by modern advertising, it is the duty of the Commission to speak and rule clearly so that law-abiding businessmen may know where they stand. In proscribing a practice uncomplained of by the public, effectively harmless to the consumer, allowed by the Commission's long-established policy statement, and only a hair-breadth away from advertising practices that the Commission will continue to permit, I think that the Commission in this instance has fallen far short of what is necessary to entitle its order to enforcement.

For these reasons I would not disturb the judgment of the Court of Appeals setting aside the Commission's order.

NOTES

1. Consider the following from the concurring opinion of Judge Brown of the Court of Appeals: "At the outset I am not troubled about the so-called undemonstrated deception. One thing clear is that Mary Carter's paint is not really sold at any of the advertised prices. Thus, the price of $6.98 for the first gallon, the second one 'free' is not the price at all for one gallon. Nor is $3.49

(one-half of $6.98 for two gallons.) Rather, it is $4.50, represented by the cost of two-one quarts ($2.25), getting for each, another 'free' quart. For those who read and buy paint while running, I would suppose that Government might deem it appropriate to demand that at least one of the advertised prices be the correct one." Mary Carter Paint Co. v. FTC, 333 F.2d 654, 660 (5th Cir.1964). Judge Brown concurred because of his inability to distinguish the Mary Carter practice from others previously declared to be acceptable by the Commission.

Is there a private party with sufficient interest to police the marketplace for deception of the nature here? Is there sufficient "public interest" for the Commission to act? Is there any way Mary Carter could now advertise its paint without falling victim to the consumer belief that quality paint is always quality priced?

2. The Commission proposed in 1969 and adopted in 1970 a Guide Concerning Use of the Word "Free" and Similar Representations, 16 C.F.R. § 251.1 (1977). The Guide requires in any promotion claiming to give one product "free" upon purchase of another that the purchased product must be priced at its "regular price" which is that at which it has been "openly and actively sold * * * on a regular basis for a reasonably substantial period of time in the recent and regular course of business." The Guide also notes that continuous "free" offers "should be avoided." The Commission has also adopted Guides Against Deceptive Pricing, 16 C.F.R. Part 233 (1984), to regulate generally the use of "reduced" or "sale" prices.

3. Can disparate treatment by the Commission of firms regarding their advertising policies result in anticompetitive results? See, Schechter, Letting the Right Hand Know What the Left Hand's Doing: The Clash of the FTC's False Advertising and Antitrust Policies, 64 B.U.L.Rev. 265 (1984).

(3) PRIVATE OR PUBLIC ENFORCEMENT

Did the forms of deception practiced in these cases require the intervention of a public regulatory agency? Would reliance on private litigation have brought about acceptable results? Are there advantages to administrative enforcement over private remedies that permit or even require a limit on private causes of action?

An administrative agency may normally enforce its mandate either by case adjudication or by rulemaking. In the context of market deception, there may be advantages to rules that apply equally to all competitors and announce in advance proscribed behavior. Any evaluation of private remedies for market deception must consider this alternative form of regulation.

The Federal Trade Commission, surprisingly enough, did not have explicit authority to adopt rules until 1975 although it had previously adopted rules. For example in 1964 the Commission promulgated a rule requiring health warnings on cigarettes but was preempted by Congress which established a statutory scheme for the regulation of cigarette advertising. In 1969 the Commission adopted a rule requiring octane ratings to be posted on gas pumps. The Commission successfully defended its authority to adopt the rule after losing initially in the district court. National Petroleum Refiners Ass'n v. FTC, 482 F.2d 672 (D.C.Cir.1973), cert. denied 415 U.S. 951 (1974).

In 1975 Congress gave the Commission specific authority to promulgate "rules which define with specificity acts or practices which are unfair or deceptive acts or practices in or affecting commerce. . . ." 15 U.S.C.A. § 57(a) This new authority resulted from or coincided with strong consumer protection sentiments and the Commission used its power to take some bold and innovative steps. Some of these efforts are still in force, such as a rule that abolished the common law "holder in due course" rule for purchasers of consumer credit contracts and permitted a debtor to assert against the purchaser of the credit contract, all claims and defenses which the debtor could assert against the seller of the goods. Preservation of Consumers' Claims and Defenses, 16 C.F.R. § 433.1 et seq. (1977). Among the other controversial rules proposed were a rule requiring sellers of used cars to inspect them and report the inspection to prospective buyers and a rule that would have severely limited advertising on television directed at children.

The rapid expansion of Commission rulemaking activity and a shift in public sentiment toward deregulation collided in 1980 with enactment of the Federal Trade Commission Improvements Act of 1980, Pub. Law 96–252 (1980). Some of its significant provisions are: (1) a prohibition on promulgation of a rule relating to standards and certification except pursuant to the Commission's power to enforce the antitrust laws (§ 7); (2) a limitation on Commission rulemaking relating to television advertising directed at children (§ 11); (3) a restriction on the Commission's power to regulate the funeral industry (§ 19); and (4) most significantly, a provision subjecting any Commission rule to a review and potential veto by Congress prior to its enforcement (§ 21). The legislative veto was subsequently declared unconstitutional. United States House of Representatives v. FTC, 463 U.S. 1216 (1983).

NOTES

1. Could private remedies work to restrain the advertising of cigarettes or to insure the octane ratings on gasoline pumps? Do you predict market forces will eventually work in that direction? What about limitations on children's advertising or more disclosure within the funeral industry?

2. Public agencies often have a more diverse arsenal of remedial tools once a deception is discovered. Private litigation relies on the recovery of damages or injunctive relief. Administrative agencies in addition may have monetary penalties and may order broad-scale relief such as restitution to all purchasers or corrective advertising to cure any lingering deception. Of course, judges can fashion creative injunctions in some privately litigated cases as well.

3. The remedial authority of the FTC was limited to seeking a cease and desist order until the Federal Trade Commission Improvement Act of 1975, 15 U.S.C.A. § 57(b). That section permits the Commission to seek court approval for wider relief including "rescission or reformation of contracts, the refund of money or return of property, the payment of damages, and public notification respecting the rule violation. . . ."

4. Even without the act the Commission had experimented with more creative remedies. In Warner–Lambert Co. v. FTC, 562 F.2d 749 (D.C.Cir.1977)

a creative cease and desist order that amounted to requiring corrective advertising was upheld in order to reduce the lingering effect of the deception. Listerine advertised for several years its use could cure colds and sore throats. The Commission, finding the claim untrue, required Listerine to cease and desist from advertising unless the advertisement contained the phrase "Contrary to prior advertising, Listerine will not help prevent colds or sore throats or lessen their severity." The court upheld the order except for the words "Contrary to prior advertising", finding these to be too punitive. On the other hand a cease and desist order requiring restitution was held to be outside the Commission's authority. Heater v. FTC, 503 F.2d 321 (9th Cir.1974).

5. For a comparison of the attributes of various methods of policing deception see A. Best, Controlling False Advertising: A Comparative Study of Public Regulation, Industry Self-Policing, and Private Litigation, 20 Ga.L.Rev. 1 (1985). For a critique of FTC deceptive advertising activities see Sullivan & Marks, The FTC's Deceptive Advertising Policy: A Legal and Economic Analysis, 64 Ore.L.Rev. 593 (1986). R. Craswell, The Identification of Unfair Acts and Practices by the Federal Trade Commission, 1981 Wisc.L.Rev. 107 (1981), offers a systematic overview of Commission rulings in this area. On a more theoretical level is H. Beales, R. Craswell, & S. Salop, The Efficient Regulation of Consumer Information, 24 J. Law & Econ. 491 (1981). The economic view of false advertising is pursued in E. Jordan & P. Rubin, An Economic Analysis of the Law of False Advertising, 8 J. of Leg.Stud. 527 (1979).

Chapter III

PRODUCT AND PRODUCER IDENTITY

A. THE FUNDAMENTALS

KELLOGG CO. v. NATIONAL BISCUIT CO.
Supreme Court of the United States, 1938.
305 U.S. 111, 59 S.Ct. 109, 83 L.Ed. 73, rehearing denied 305 U.S. 674, 59 S.Ct. 246, 83 L.Ed. 437.

MR. JUSTICE BRANDEIS delivered the opinion of the Court.

This suit was brought in the federal court for Delaware [1] by National Biscuit Company against Kellogg Company to enjoin alleged unfair competition by the manufacture and sale of the breakfast food commonly known as shredded wheat. The competition was alleged to be unfair mainly because Kellogg Company uses, like the plaintiff, the name shredded wheat and, like the plaintiff, produces its biscuit in pillow-shaped form.

Shredded wheat is a product composed of whole wheat which has been boiled, partially dried, then drawn or pressed out into thin shreds and baked. The shredded wheat biscuit generally known is pillow-shaped in form. It was introduced in 1893 by Henry D. Perky, of Colorado; and he was connected until his death in 1908 with companies formed to make and market the article. Commercial success was not attained until the Natural Food Company built, in 1901, a large factory at Niagara Falls, New York. In 1908, its corporate name was changed to "The Shredded Wheat Company"; and in 1930 its business and goodwill were acquired by National Biscuit Company. *first large scale produce*

[Kellogg Company began making breakfast cereals in 1905, experimented with a product somewhat like Shredded wheat from 1912 to 1919, and in 1928 began manufacturing Kellogg's Shredded Wheat.

The district court first held against Nabisco finding that on the expiration of a patent the name of the article passes into the public domain. The Circuit Court of Appeals first affirmed and then on rehearing granted Nabisco relief, describing the trademark as "consisting of a dish, containing two biscuits submerged in milk." Nabisco sought clarification when Kellogg argued it was only prohibited from using the term "Shredded Wheat" when displayed in combination with

1. The federal jurisdiction rests on diversity of citizenship—National Biscuit Company being a New Jersey corporation and Kellogg Company a Delaware corporation. Most of the issues in the case involve questions of common law and hence are within the scope of Erie R. Co. v. Tompkins, 1938, 304 U.S. 64. But no claim has been made that the local law is any different from the general law on the subject, and both parties have relied almost entirely on federal precedents.

241

the biscuits submerged in milk. The court clarified its decree and enjoined Kellogg:

> "(1) from the use of the name 'Shredded Wheat' as its trade name, (2) from advertising or offering for sale its product in the form and shape of plaintiff's biscuit, and (3) from doing either."

The Supreme Court granted certiorari.]

The plaintiff concedes that it does not possess the exclusive right to make shredded wheat. But it claims the exclusive right to the trade name "Shredded Wheat" and the exclusive right to make shredded wheat biscuits pillow-shaped. It charges that the defendant, by using the name and shape, and otherwise, is passing off, or enabling others to pass off, Kellogg goods for those of the plaintiff. Kellogg Company denies that the plaintiff is entitled to the exclusive use of the name or of the pillow-shape; denies any passing off; asserts that it has used every reasonable effort to distinguish its product from that of the plaintiff; and contends that in honestly competing for a part of the market for shredded wheat it is exercising the common right freely to manufacture and sell an article of commerce unprotected by patent.

First. The plaintiff has no exclusive right to the use of the term "Shredded Wheat" as a trade name. For that is the generic term of the article, which describes it with a fair degree of accuracy; and is the term by which the biscuit in pillow-shaped form is generally known by the public. Since the term is generic, the original maker of the product acquired no exclusive right to use it. As Kellogg Company had the right to make the article, it had, also the right to use the term by which the public knows it. Compare Saxlehner v. Wagner, 216 U.S. 375; Holzapfel's Compositions Co. v. Rahtjen's American Composition Co., 183 U.S. 1. Ever since 1894 the article has been known to the public as shredded wheat. For many years, there was no attempt to use the term "Shredded Wheat" as a trade-mark. When in 1905 plaintiff's predecessor, Natural Food Company, applied for registration of the words "Shredded Whole Wheat" as a trade-mark under the so-called "ten year clause" of the Act of February 20, 1905, c. 592, sec. 5, 33 Stat. 725, 15 U.S.C. § 85, William E. Williams gave notice of opposition. Upon the hearing it appeared that Williams had, as early as 1894, built a machine for making shredded wheat, and that he made and sold its product as "Shredded Whole Wheat". The Commissioner of Patents refused registration. The Court of Appeals of the District of Columbia affirmed his decision, holding that "these words accurately and aptly describe an article of food which * * * has been produced for more than ten years * * *." Natural Food Co. v. Williams, 30 App.D.C. 348.[3]

---

3. The trade-marks are registered under the Act of 1920. 41 Stat. 533, 15 U.S.C. §§ 121–128 (1934), 15 U.S.C. §§ 121–128. But it is well settled that registration under it has no effect on the domestic common-law rights of the person whose trade-mark is registered. Charles Broadway Rouss, Inc., v. Winchester Co., 2 Cir., 300 F. 706, 713, 714; Kellogg Co. v. National Biscuit Co., 2 Cir., 71 F.2d 662, 666.

Moreover, the name "Shredded Wheat", as well as the product, the process and the machinery employed in making it, has been dedicated to the public. The basic patent for the product and for the process of making it, and many other patents for special machinery to be used in making the article, issued to Perky. In those patents the term "shredded" is repeatedly used as descriptive of the product. The basic patent expired October 15, 1912; the others soon after. Since during the life of the patents "Shredded Wheat" was the general designation of the patented product, there passed to the public upon the expiration of the patent, not only the right to make the article as it was made during the patent period, but also the right to apply thereto the name by which it had become known. As was said in Singer Mfg. Co. v. June Mfg. Co., 163 U.S. 169, 185:

"It equally follows from the cessation of the monopoly and the falling of the patented device into the domain of things public that along with the public ownership of the device there must also necessarily pass to the public the generic designation of the thing which has arisen during the monopoly. * * *

"To say otherwise would be to hold that, although the public had acquired the device covered by the patent, yet the owner of the patent or the manufacturer of the patented thing had retained the designated name which was essentially necessary to vest the public with the full enjoyment of that which had become theirs by the disappearance of the monopoly."

It is contended that the plaintiff has the exclusive right to the name "Shredded Wheat", because those words acquired the "secondary meaning" of shredded wheat made at Niagara Falls by the plaintiff's predecessor. There is no basis here for applying the doctrine of secondary meaning. The evidence shows only that due to the long period in which the plaintiff or its predecessor was the only manufacturer of the product, many people have come to associate the product, and as a consequence the name by which the product is generally known, with the plaintiff's factory at Niagara Falls. But to establish a trade name in the term "shredded wheat" the plaintiff must show more than a subordinate meaning which applies to it. It must show that the primary significance of the term in the minds of the consuming public is not the product but the producer. This it has not done. The showing which it has made does not entitle it to the exclusive use of the term shredded wheat but merely entitles it to require that the defendant use reasonable care to inform the public of the source of its product.

The plaintiff seems to contend that even if Kellogg Company acquired upon the expiration of the patents the right to use the name shredded wheat, the right was lost by delay. The argument is that Kellogg Company, although the largest producer of breakfast cereals in the country, did not seriously attempt to make shredded wheat, or to challenge plaintiff's right to that name until 1927, and that meanwhile plaintiff's predecessor had expended more than $17,000,000 in making the name a household word and identifying the product with its manufacture. Those facts are without legal significance. Kellogg Company's right was not one dependent upon diligent exercise. Like every other member of the public, it was, and remained, free to make shredded wheat when it chose to do so; and to call the product by its generic name. The only obligation resting upon Kellogg Company was to identify its own product lest it be mistaken for that of the plaintiff.

Second. The plaintiff has not the exclusive right to sell shredded wheat in the form of a pillow-shaped biscuit—the form in which the article became known to the public. That is the form in which shredded wheat was made under the basic patent. The patented machines used were designed to produce only the pillow-shaped biscuits. And a design patent was taken out to cover the pillow-shaped form.[4] Hence, upon expiration of the patents the form, as well as the name, was dedicated to the public. As was said in Singer Mfg. Co. v. June Mfg. Co., supra, page 185: "It is self-evident that on the expiration of a patent the monopoly granted by it ceases to exist, and the right to make the thing formerly covered by the patent becomes public property. It is upon this condition that the patent is granted. It follows, as a matter of course, that on the termination of the patent there passes to the public the right to make the machine in the form in which it was constructed during the patent. We may therefore dismiss without further comment the complaint as to the form in which the defendant made his machines."

Where an article may be manufactured by all, a particular manufacturer can no more assert exclusive rights in a form in which the public has become accustomed to see the article and which, in the minds of the public, is primarily associated with the article rather than a particular producer, than it can in the case of a name with similar connections in the public mind. Kellogg Company was free to use the pillow-shaped form, subject only to the obligation to identify its product lest it be mistaken for that of the plaintiff.

Third. The question remains whether Kellogg Company in exercising its right to use the name "Shredded Wheat" and the pillow-shaped biscuit, is doing so fairly. Fairness requires that it be done in a manner which reasonably distinguishes its product from that of plaintiff.

Each company sells its biscuits only in cartons. The standard Kellogg carton contains fifteen biscuits; the plaintiff's twelve. The Kellogg cartons are distinctive. They do not resemble those used by the plaintiff either in size, form, or color. And the difference in the labels is striking. The Kellogg cartons bear in bold script the names "Kellogg's Whole Wheat Biscuit" or "Kellogg's Shredded Whole Wheat

---

4. The design patent would have expired by limitations in 1909. In 1908 it was declared invalid by a district judge on the ground that the design had been in public use for more than two years prior to the application for the patent and theretofore had already been dedicated to the public. Natural Foods Co. v. Bulkley, No. 28,530, U.S.Dist.Ct., N.Dist.Ill., East.Div. (1908).

Biscuit" so sized and spaced as to strike the eye as being a Kellogg product. It is true that on some of its cartons it had a picture of two shredded wheat biscuits in a bowl of milk which was quite similar to one of the plaintiff's registered trade-marks. But the name Kellogg was so prominent on all of the defendant's cartons as to minimize the possibility of confusion.

Some hotels, restaurants, and lunchrooms serve biscuits not in cartons, and guests so served may conceivably suppose that a Kellogg biscuit served is one of the plaintiff's make. But no person familiar with plaintiff's product would be misled. The Kellogg biscuit is about two-thirds the size of plaintiff's; and differs from it in appearance. Moreover, the field in which deception could be practiced is negligibly small. Only 2½ per cent of the Kellogg biscuits are sold to hotels, restaurants and lunchrooms. Of those so sold 98 per cent are sold in individual cartons containing two biscuits. These cartons are distinctive and bear prominently the Kellogg name. To put upon the individual biscuit some mark which would identify it as the Kellogg product is not commercially possible. Relatively few biscuits will be removed from the individual cartons before they reach the consumer. The obligation resting upon Kellogg Company is not to insure that every purchaser will know it to be the maker but to use every reasonable means to prevent confusion.

It is urged that all possibility of deception or confusion would be removed if Kellogg Company should refrain from using the name "Shredded Wheat" and adopt some form other than the pillow-shape. But the name and form are integral parts of the goodwill of the article. To share fully in the goodwill, it must use the name and the pillow-shape. And in the goodwill Kellogg Company is as free to share as the plaintiff. Compare William R. Warner & Co. v. Eli Lilly & Co., 265 U.S. 526, 528, 530. Moreover, the pillow-shape must be used for another reason. The evidence is persuasive that this form is functional—that the cost of the biscuit would be increased and its high quality lessened if some other form were substituted for the pillow-shape.

Kellogg Company is undoubtedly sharing in the goodwill of the article known as "Shredded Wheat"; and thus is sharing in a market which was created by the skill and judgment of plaintiff's predecessor and has been widely extended by vast expenditures in advertising persistently made. But that is not unfair. Sharing in the goodwill of an article unprotected by patent or trade-mark is the exercise of a right possessed by all—and in the free exercise of which the consuming public is deeply interested. There is no evidence of passing off or deception on the part of the Kellogg Company; and it has taken every reasonable precaution to prevent confusion or the practice of deception in the sale of its product.

Fourth. By its "clarifying" decree, the Circuit Court of Appeals enjoined Kellogg Company from using the picture of the two shredded wheat biscuits in the bowl only in connection with an injunction against manufacturing the pillow-shaped biscuits and the use of the term shredded wheat, on the grounds of unfair competition. The use of this picture was not enjoined on the independent ground of trade-mark infringement. Since the National Biscuit Company did not petition for certiorari, the question whether use of the picture is a violation of that trade-mark although Kellogg Company is free to use the name and the pillow-shaped biscuit is not here for review.

Decrees reversed with direction to dismiss the bill.

MR. JUSTICE McREYNOLDS and MR. JUSTICE BUTLER are of opinion that the decree of the Circuit Court of Appeals is correct and should be affirmed. To them it seems sufficiently clear that the Kellogg Company is fraudulently seeking to appropriate to itself the benefits of a goodwill built up at great cost by the respondent and its predecessors.

NOTES

1. This chapter considers how and to what extent a manufacturer may establish and protect his identity and the identity of his product in the marketplace. Although the trademark is perhaps the most obvious device utilized for identification, it is not the only one. The *Kellogg* case, for example, involves three different allegedly identifying devices, the trademark "Shredded-Wheat", the product dress including the picture of two biscuits in a bowl of milk, and the pillow-shaped form of the product itself.

It is standard learning that trademarks serve three separate functions: (1) The mark can indicate the origin and ownership of the goods. This is an identifying function. A plaintiff injured through negligent design of a product may determine through the trademark which manufacturer bears the responsibility. (2) The mark is said to provide a guarantee of quality. The "guarantee" does not assure the acceptability or safety of the product but purports to guarantee a constancy of quality on repeated purchases. (3) The mark may also serve as an advertising device by attracting consumers and creating demand for the product. It also enables a manufacturer to reach the ultimate consumer directly rather than relying on individual retailers to promote the product. See Schechter, The Rational Basis of Trademark Protection, 40 Harv. L.Rev. 813 (1927).

Trademarks are intimately involved in the debate over the relative merits and purposes of advertising generally. For an advertiser to capture the returns from his advertising, he must be able to distinguish his goods from others. In most markets for goods or services a trademark will be used for this purpose.

Proponents of limited trademark protection utilize the economic analysis advanced by Chamberlin, The Theory of Monopolistic Competition (5th ed. 1946). See Brown, Advertising and the Public Interest: Legal Protection of Trade Symbols, 57 Yale L.J. 1165 (1948); Alexander, Honesty and Competition (1965); Galbraith, The New Industrial State (1967); Mueller, Sources of Monopoly Power: A Phenomenon Called "Product Differentiation" 18 Amer.U.L.Rev. 1 (1968).

In Chamberlain's view the ability of a producer to protect the differentiation of his product from others gave him a degree of monopoly power over price. For example, to the extent consumers prefer "Crown" brand toothpaste to other brands, the producer of "Crown" can charge a higher price being the only source of "Crown" toothpaste. At some point this higher monopoly price is thought to be disadvantageous to the consumer.

Advocates of stronger and more extensive trademark protection believe consumers are advantaged by both advertising and the identification of the source of products. This view builds upon the theories advanced in Stigler, The Economics of Information, 69 J. Political Econ. 213 (1961). In Stigler's view the consumer faces two separate costs in purchasing a product: the nominal cost of the product and the information costs associated with searching for the right product to purchase. Sellers can generally reduce consumer search costs through advertising but will do so only if they can identify their products. Similarly, if trademarks signal a constant quality, consumers, once they find their preferred product, can forego repeated costs of research and experimentation by relying on a favored brand name. In this view, trademarks (and advertising) benefit consumers by reducing the search cost component of the price they pay for their purchases. See W. Landes & R. Posner, Trademark Law: An Economic Perspective, 30 J. Law & Econ. 265 (1987). For earlier classic defenses of stronger trademark protection see Pattishall, Trade–Marks and The Monopoly Phobia, 50 Mich.L.Rev. 967 (1952); Rogers, The Lanham Act and The Social Functions of Trade–Marks, 14 Law & Contemp.Prob. 173 (1949).

2. Trademark cases involve three distinct interests. The innovator, or original trademark owner, has an interest in protecting the investment in its product's identity or good-will and reputation based on that identity. This strongly suggests property notions for legal protection. Should the owner have a "property interest" in his trademark which reflects the investment of time, creativity and promotional outlays? Does Justice Brandeis in the *Kellogg* case protect the investment of the National Biscuit Co.?

The second interest involved in imitation cases is that of the imitator or competitor of the innovator. What interest does Kellogg have in the use of the term "Shredded-Wheat"? Or in selling the produce in pillow-shape? Or in having a picture of two biscuits in a bowl of milk on their package?

The third interest, generally not directly represented in the litigation, is that of the consumer. Does the consumer care whether Kellogg uses the designation "Shredded-Wheat" if both are of the same quality? If Kellogg's is of higher quality? Lesser quality? Would a price differential in the products alter any of your answers?

In Standard Brands, Inc. v. Smidler, 151 F.2d 34 (2d Cir.1945) Judge Frank, in his concurring opinion, pondered this problem:

> If Alert & Co. sells a laundry soap, under the name "Quick Clean," at 75¢ a cake, and a competitor, Wiseacre, Inc., then begins to sell the identical soap under the same name at 50¢ a cake, Alert & Co. loses customers, and therefore money, if it maintains its price; but the purchasers are misled to their financial benefit. If the sole purpose were to protect consumers from direct financial loss, the second name-user in such a case would have a complete defense if he showed that he sold, at a lower price, precisely the same article (compounded of exactly the same ingredients) as the first user.

Do you agree? What are the transaction costs of adopting a position requiring proof of consumer injury?

3. Compare *Kellogg, American Washboard,* and *Ely Norris,* supra. Why should a competitor be allowed to sue for false indications of origin and not false indications of quality, particularly if the suit is designed to protect the

"consumer interest"? Where does the consumer have the greatest interest—in the quality or origin of the product?

4. *Bibliography.* The following is a sampling of works that may be helpful in understanding the law of trademarks:

    a. McCarthy, Trademarks and Unfair Competition (2d ed. 1984 with pocket supplements) (2 volumes).

    b. Callmann, The Law of Unfair Competition, Trademarks and Monopolies (4th ed. 1981 with supplements).

    c. The Trademark Reporter, a periodical published by the United States Trademark Association, and particularly the annual review of trademark law under the title, e.g., The Thirty-Seventh Year of Administration of the Lanham Act of 1946, 74 Trademark Rep. 469 (1984).

    d. Gilson, Trademark Protection and Practice (1976 with supplements).

    e. W.R. Cornish, Intellectual Property: Patents, Copyright, Trademarks and Allied Rights (London, Sweet & Maxwell, 1981), discusses the English unfair competition and trademark law with attention to the practices of other members of the European Common Market.

The first edition of the Restatement of Torts contained sections on the law of trademarks but these provisions were omitted from the Restatement (Second) of Torts. The American Law Institute is currently preparing a Restatement (Third) of Unfair Competition which will include the law of trademarks. Tentative Draft No. 2 (1990) and Tentative Draft No. 3 (1991) covering trademarks are available.

SHAW v. TIME–LIFE RECORDS
Court of Appeals of New York, 1975.
38 N.Y.2d 201, 379 N.Y.S.2d 390, 341 N.E.2d 817.

[Artie Shaw, a famous band leader and musician in the 1920's, 30's, and 40's, brought causes of action against Time-Life Records for invasion of his privacy, unauthorized use of his name, damage to his reputation, and unfair competition. Shaw had originally recorded several songs for RCA. RCA arranged with Reader's Digest Record Album Service to issue a four record set entitled "Swing with Artie Shaw" which were the original performances electronically enhanced for stereo. Time-Life, in competition with the RCA release and without Shaw's permission, produced a series of recordings of music of the "Swing Era" containing 25 of Shaw's arrangements. The songs were played by modern musicians and promoted as "Artie Shaw versions". Shaw received royalties from RCA but not from Time-Life. Shaw did not have copyrights to the musical compositions and the copyright law did not protect arrangements or performances.]

JASEN, JUDGE.

The plaintiff's claim for damages based on unfair competition, the fourth cause of action in the amended complaint, stands on a different footing. While Time-Life was entitled to copy Shaw's arrangements and to compete with Shaw's own records, Time-Life was under an obligation to "use reasonable care to inform the public of the source of its product" and to identify its own merchandise "lest it be mistaken for that of the plaintiff." (Kellogg Co. v. National Biscuit Co., 305 U.S. 111, 119, hearing den., 305 U.S. 674.) While the use of Shaw's name is permissible, dishonesty in the use of the name is condemned. * * * Time-Life could not "palm off" its records as being the personal work of Shaw * * *.

The essence of an unfair competition claim is that the defendant assembled a product which bears so striking a resemblance to the plaintiff's product that the public will be confused as to the identity of the products. * * * The test is whether persons exercising "reasonable intelligence and discrimination" would be taken in by the similarity. * * * The defendant's promotional materials offered consumers an opportunity to purchase "Artie Shaw versions" of Swing Era classics. It is impossible to say as a matter of law, that reasonably discriminating consumers would discern that these "versions" were not authentic Shaw performances, but were instead attempted re-creations by modern day musicians. We believe that the plaintiff has made a sufficient factual showing to entitle him to present his case to the jury. A triable issue of fact exists as to whether reasonably discriminating members of the public would be confused or misled by defendant's advertising. Thus, in this limited respect, the defendant's motion for summary judgment was properly denied. * * *

NOTES

1. At common law trademark law is a specialized part of the more general tort of unfair competition. Both involve the same species of deception, passing off one's goods as those of another. The *Shaw* case illustrates the rule outside the trademark context. Does this also explain why Justice Brandeis in *Kellogg* could conclude that even though there was no protectible interest in the term "Shredded Wheat", Kellogg was still obliged to use the mark "fairly"?

2. There is much confusion in the cases on what constitutes "palming off" or "passing off," and the extent to which it is an essential element of a claim for unfair competition. Some cases have emphasized the intent of the defendant to "palm off" his goods as those of someone else. Venetianaire Corp. of America v. A & P Import Co., 302 F.Supp. 156 (S.D.N.Y.1969), affirmed 429 F.2d 1079 (2d Cir.1970). Others, like *Shaw,* have emphasized likelihood of confusion. And it has been suggested that for the broader tort of unfair competition *either* a likelihood of confusion *or* an unsuccessful attempt to fool the public might be sufficient. Whose interest is being protected in *Shaw?* In those cases requiring intent? Is there a first amendment objection if intent or at least negligence is not required? Can you distinguish the facts in *Shaw* from a case in which a defendant publishes a report that Shaw's music is inferior? What remedy would you authorize in a case where the defendant intended to pass off his goods as another's but was unsuccessful?

3. "Passing off" cases have been classified into four categories. Borchard, Reverse Passing-Off-Commercial Robbery or Permissible Competition, 67 Trademark Rep. 1 (1977): Express passing off (X sells his own goods with Y's mark); implied passing off (X sells his own goods using a sample of Y's goods); express reverse passing off (X buys Y's goods and resells them with X's mark); and

implied reverse passing off (*X* buys *Y*'s goods and resells them unbranded). Would you impose liability in all of these cases? What interests are jeopardized in each situation? In which category does INS v. AP fall?

LEGAL SOURCES OF TRADEMARK PROTECTION

Unlike patents and copyrights, trademark protection derived from the common law rather than from legislation or constitutional provision. In England, and subsequently in the United States, a merchant obtained rights in his mark through adoption and use. No prior registration was required; the merchant merely designed his mark and applied it to his goods. The common law responded to protect his interests. In contrast, on the European Continent trademarks were protected only if registered with a governmental agency. The first merchant to register a given mark was entitled to its exclusive use.

The common law remains today as a basic source of protection for trademarks and other producer-identifying devices. Adoption and use remain acceptable first steps in obtaining protection. In 1988 Congress adopted a limited intent-to-use system of registration which moderates the adoption and use requirements of the common law. Even where registration statutes have been enacted, common law principles determine to a large extent when an individual has built up sufficient interest in his trademark to be worthy of registration and whatever protection is provided for registered marks. Thus, where trademark problems arise there is often a complex interplay between common law rules and statutory provisions. The federal registration statute is popularly known as the Lanham Act. Most states have state trademark registration laws, the language of many being patterned after the Lanham Act.

We have tried in the following materials to provide the student with a basic foundation in the issues arising out of trademark protection, including some special problems associated with the Lanham Act. This has necessitated featuring common law cases where the common law doctrine predominates and Lanham Act cases and text where the act deviates substantially from the common law. The state statutes are considered here only when they add a particular dimension to trademark law.

NOTE: A BRIEF HISTORY OF FEDERAL TRADEMARK LEGISLATION

Apparently trademarks were not of great importance during colonial times or early in the history of the United States. Although the founding fathers enshrined the patent and copyright systems into the constitution, trademarks were not mentioned. There was little public interest in trademark protection, although as early as 1791 Thomas Jefferson, as Secretary of State received a petition from one Samuel Breck and other "proprietors of a sailcloth manufactory in Boston, praying that they may have the exclusive privilege of using particular marks for designating the sailcloth of their manufactory." Jefferson transmitted the petition to the Second Congress along with his report which recognized that manufacturers should have an exclusive right to some mark on their goods and that "this should be done by general laws, extending equal right to every case to which the authority of the Legislature should be competent." 14 Amer. State Papers 48 reprinted in Report of The Commissioners Appointed to Revise the Statutes Relating to Patents, Trade and Other Marks, and Trade and Commercial Names, S.Doc. No. 20, 56th Cong., 2d Sess. 92 (1902). Congress did not act on the federal level. The first trademark statute enacted in the United States was in New York in 1845 and was designed to prevent fraud in the use of common law marks. In fact, the first reported case involving a trademark was in 1837 in Massachusetts. Thompson v. Winchester, 19 Pick. 214 (Mass.1837).

International demands rather than American public opinion led to the first federal attempt at trademark legislation. In 1868 treaties were concluded with Russia and Belgium granting reciprocal rights in trademarks for the citizens of each country trading in the other. However, for a Russian citizen to obtain rights under the treaty he had to register his mark in the United States Patent Office. The Patent Office had no authority to receive such registrations.

In 1870 Congress enacted the first federal trademark registration act, primarily to implement the treaties agreed upon two years earlier, and secondarily, to provide American citizens with the same rights that foreign merchants had in the United States. Act of July 8, 1870, ch. 230, 16 Stat. 198. This enactment was part of a substantial revision of the patent and copyright laws. Perhaps since the attention of Congress regarding trademark legislation was directed to continental Europe because of the treaties, the first statute created substantive trademark rights as well as recognizing those rights created by common law. It allowed registration by persons "who are entitled to the exclusive use of any lawful trade-mark or *who intend to adopt and use* any trademark for exclusive use within the United States." (Emphasis added). Only citizens of countries not granting reciprocal rights to citizens of the United States were precluded from registering under the act. The act provided remedies for infringement, jurisdiction in federal courts, and a thirty-year period of protection with the option to renew the registration for an additional thirty years.

Six years later finding that "The public generally, the honest manufacturers and honest dealers throughout the country are being constantly swindled by counterfeit trade-marks" and that "worthless parties engaged in such dishonest practices are not prevented by civil actions" Congress passed the Act of August 14, 1876, ch. 274, 19 Stat. 141 providing criminal penalties of up to two years imprisonment and one thousand dollars fine for infringing, counterfeiting, making, or using a registered mark with "intent to defraud."

Shortly thereafter, the United States Supreme Court held both statutes unconstitutional. In re Trade-Mark Cases, 100 U.S. 82 (1879). The Court, in an opinion by Justice Miller, noted that trademarks had always been protected by state law, and thus for Congress to act required specific authority in the Constitution. With regard to the patent and copyright clause, the Court held that a trademark could not be considered a discovery of an inventor or a writing of an author because unlike patents and copyrights, protection under the trademark acts did not "depend upon novelty, upon invention, upon discovery, or upon any work of the brain. It requires no fancy or imagination, no genius, no laborious thought. It is simply founded on priority of appropriation." The Court also refused to uphold the legislation under the commerce clause because the scope of neither statute was limited to interstate commerce.

The Court left open two important questions: (1) whether "the trademark bears such a relation to commerce in general terms as to bring it within congressional control, when used or applied to the classes of commerce which fall within that control" and (2) whether Congress has authority to enact trademark legislation from its treaty-making power and its authority to pass laws necessary to carry such treaties into effect.

Apparently the country was pleased with its short sampling of federal trademark registration for it is reported that many petitions were sent to Congress and "great publicity was given to the subject by the press of the country." See Report, supra, at 103. The New York Times on November 19, 1879, noted that the "value put upon the statute by the mercantile community is shown by the fact that, notwithstanding the large fee for registration, about 8,000 trade-marks have been registered since the law was passed in 1879. * * * State laws for this purpose cannot prove otherwise than unsatisfactory and objectionable." And a constitutional amendment to authorize Congress to regulate the "exclusive right to adopt and use trademarks" was introduced in the House.

In 1881, the act of 1870 was substantially reenacted but applied only to "owners of trade-marks used in commerce with foreign nations, or with the Indian tribes." This implemented the treaties with Russia and Belgium but did not extend federal registration to marks used in interstate commerce. Act of March 3, 1881, ch. 138, 21 Stat. 502.

Concern over the precise interpretation of the Supreme Court's view of Congressional power to enact trademark legislation explains to a large extent the omission of interstate commerce from the act of 1881. Likewise, it took Congress almost another twenty-five years before it passed another registration act for interstate commerce—the Act of February 20, 1905, ch. 592, 33 Stat. 724, which has been described as "a slovenly piece of legislation, characterized by awkward phraseology, bad grammar and involved sentences. Its draftsmen had a talent for obscurity amounting to genius." Rogers, The Expensive Futility of the United States Trade-Mark Statute, 12 Mich.L.Rev. 660 (1914).

The act allowed registration of marks used in interstate commerce for a period of twenty years with an unlimited right of renewal. Registration constituted prima facie evidence of ownership of the mark, entitled the federal courts to jurisdiction, and provided remedies for infringement. In addition, the act allowed anyone injured by the registration of a mark at any time to petition the Commissioner of Patents for cancellation of the registration.

Interpretations of the Act of 1905 were influenced by the impact of the Trade-Mark Cases. In American Steel Foundries v. Robertson, 269 U.S. 372 (1926) the Supreme Court gratuitously noted that Congress "has been given no power to legislate upon the substantive law of trade-marks" and therefore the 1905 act entitled only the registration of "such marks as that law [common law of trade-marks] and the general law of unfair competition of which it is a part, recognized as legitimate." And in American Trading Co. v. H.E. Heacock Co., 285 U.S. 247 (1932) the Court, in deciding a conflict between a mark registered under a local act in the Philippine Islands authorized by an act of Congress and a mark registered under the act of 1905, both being applied to commerce solely within the Philippine Islands, held the Philippine mark had superior rights because although Congress had the right to authorize the Philippine Commission to enact a substantive trademark statute for the Philippines, the Act of 1905 did not create substantive rights because "Congress, by virtue of the commerce clause, has no power to legislate upon the substantive law of trademarks. * * * " For a time, lower federal courts assumed no Congressional power over substantive trademark rights.

In 1943, the Seventh Circuit in a widely cited opinion directly held that not only did congress have authority to create substantive trademark rights but it had done so in the Act of 1905. Philco Corp. v. Phillips Mfg. Co., 133 F.2d 663, 668 (7th Cir.1943).

The Act of 1905 did not satisfy those who wanted a national law of trademarks. Various successful attempts at "tinkering" with the Act of 1905 were paralleled by attempts at total revision beginning as early as 1924. Finally Representative Fritz G. Lanham introduced a trademark bill in 1938 which eventually after modification was enacted in 1946 and became effective in 1947. The Lanham Act embodied the labors of several interest groups including the National Association of Manufacturers, the United States Trade-Mark Association and the American Bar Association. See Hearings on H.R. 102 Before the Subcomm. on Trade-Marks of the House Comm. on Patents, 77th Cong., 1st Sess., at 134 (1941). A fuller treatment of the background to eventual passage of the Lanham Act can be found in McCarthy, Trademarks and Unfair Competition § 5.4 (2d ed. 1984). For an extensive contemporaneous interpretation of the act see Robert, The New Trade-Mark Manual (1947) which also provides a valuable comparison between the Lanham Act and the Act of 1905. For further commentaries on the Lanham Act see Andrus & Sceales, The New Trade-Mark Act, 1947 Wis.L.Rev. 618 (1947); Diggs, The Lanham Trade-Mark Act, 35 Geo.L.J. 147 (1947).

The Trademark Revision Act of 1988, with an effective date of November 16, 1989, is the first major revision of the Lanham Act since its enactment.

AN OVERVIEW OF NATIONAL AND INTERNATIONAL REGISTRATION UNDER THE LANHAM ACT

The Lanham Act, 15 U.S.C. § 1051 et seq., enacts the federal regime of trademark registration. Administered by the Patent and Trademark Office (PTO) the Act creates two separate registers, the "principal register" (§ 1) and the "supplemental register" (§ 23).

The principal register affects trademark rights and controversies within the United States. Since 1947 the Act has provided that a "trademark owner" who has adopted and used a mark can apply for federal registration on the principal register. The PTO examines the application to determine if it is entitled to registration (§ 12) and, if so, publishes the mark in the Official Gazette of the Patent and Trademark Office. Interested persons have 30 days after publication to file an opposition to registration (§ 13). If no opposition is filed, a registration certificate is issued which remains in force for 10 years provided the owner files an affidavit in the fifth year showing the mark is still in use (§ 8). The registration can be renewed for an unlimited number of additional 10 year terms by filing an affidavit within 6 months of expiration indicating the mark is still in use. (§ 9).

Effective in 1989 trademark owners who have not yet used a mark can apply to register a mark on the principal register if they can demonstrate a bona fide intention to use a mark in the future (§ 1(b)).

The applicant must then file within six months a statement that the mark has been actually used. The PTO can give an applicant additional time to demonstrate use not to exceed 24 months after filing (§ 1(d)). No registration issues until the mark is actually used.

Controversies involving the validity of the application or registration of a mark may arise in a number of different contexts. An applicant may contest the denial of his application by the examiner (§ 20). Persons who might be injured by the registration may seek to oppose the registration prior to its issuance (§ 13) or may seek to cancel the registration after it is issued (§ 14). If the Commissioner believes the mark in an application resembles a registered mark or a mark in another pending application he can declare an interference proceeding which allows the owners of the two marks to litigate their respective rights (§ 16).

Controversies in all of these contexts are heard by the PTO's Trademark Trial and Appeal Board (§ 17). Appeal was to the Court of Customs and Patent Appeals until 1982 when Congress created the United States Court of Appeals for the Federal Circuit (§ 21(a)). Instead of a direct appeal to the Federal Circuit, a person dissatisfied with the PTO's decision may file a civil action in an appropriate federal district court (§ 21(b)).

The provisions governing registration on the principal register will be considered more fully throughout this chapter.

The primary purpose of the supplemental register is to allow American trademark owners to secure the benefit of international trademark protection. In order to facilitate the protection of trademarks in international trade, multinational trademark agreements have been negotiated and enacted by most nations. The earliest international agreement aimed at multinational registration and protection of trademarks was the International Convention for the Protection of Industrial Property, signed at Paris in 1883. The principle underlying the Convention of Paris is that member states agree to confer on nationals of other member states the same entitlements relating to the protection of marks as are extended to their own citizens.

The Paris Convention provides that once a citizen has filed for registration in his home country, he may seek registration under the laws of other member states. Registration on the supplemental register is designed to allow an American company to satisfy this requirement; it has little impact on domestic rights and, accordingly, has few restrictions as to the marks that can be registered. Section 44 of the Lanham Act is designed to implement formal international agreements relating to trademarks as well as to extend the benefits of American registration to citizens of countries that provide reciprocal rights to American citizens.

A major feature of the Convention of Paris, reflected in § 44, is that upon compliance with certain conditions the date of filing an application for registration in the applicant's home country becomes his date of filing in a foreign country for purposes of determining priority between competing marks in the foreign country. This constructive priority date applies as long as the foreign application is filed within 6 months of the domestic application. This feature causes some difficulty in the United States because the Lanham Act, unlike the law in most countries, required until the 1988 revisions adoption and use of a mark prior to registration. Thus it is possible for a foreign national to register in his home country prior to using the mark and claim priority in the United States over an American company who is the prior user of the mark in the United States.

See generally McCarthy, Trademarks and Unfair Competition § 19:23 (2d ed. 1984); Ladas, The Lanham Act and International Trade, 14 Law & Contemp.Prob. 269 (1949).

The Convention of Paris merely allows foreign nationals to obtain the benefits of the domestic law of trademarks. A trademark owner is still required to pursue a separate registration in each country in which his goods are sold. In Vienna in 1973 fourteen nations, including the United States, signed the Trademark Registration Treaty (TRT). This agreement provides for an international registration through a single application which would be given the same effect in the member states as if the applicant had obtained separate national registrations. The treaty also provides that no member state could refuse trademark registration on grounds of non-use within three years of filing of the application for international registration. The treaty allows a company to reserve a trademark for a period of time before making actual use of it. The treaty has not been ratified by the United States Senate; ratification would require substantial changes in the Lanham Act.

"TRADEMARK," "TRADENAME," AND "SECONDARY MEANING"

Trademark and tradename. The common law historically distinguished between "trademarks" and "tradenames." The former came to signify those marks or devices which were arbitrary and were distinctive enough to identify the user's goods; "tradenames" referred to those marks or devices which had a primary meaning other than identifying the user's goods, such as a surname or a descriptive word. To be protected, the "tradename" owner had to show that his mark had come to distinguish his goods in the minds of the consuming public, i.e. that it had attained a secondary meaning or significance. The Restatement of Torts § 715 (1938) outlined the requirements for a trademark: (a) it was adopted and used to denominate goods, (b) it was affixed to the goods, and (c) it was not a "common or generic name for the goods or a picture of them, or a geographical, personal, or corporate or other associate name, or a designation descriptive of the goods or of their quality, ingredients, properties or functions * * *" Section 716 defined tradename as any designation which is adopted and used to denominate goods or services or a business and has "acquired a special significance as the name thereof * * *"

There were distinctions likewise in the extent of protection accorded the designation depending on whether it was a "trademark" or "tradename." The leading article on the subject stated the difference as follows:

> A trade-mark must be affixed to the merchandise it is intended to identify; a trade name is not required to be physically attached either to the goods or packages. A trademark need not be so associated by the purchasing public with the article for which it is claimed as to acquire the "secondary meaning" or "secondary significance" demanded of trade names. A trade-mark will be protected even against innocent infringement; a trade name, only against fraudulent simulation. If a trade-mark is substantially copied, its use will be enjoined notwithstanding that it is accompanied by such distinguishing features as render it unlikely that the public will mistake the goods bearing the simulated mark for those stamped with the original. If a trade name is imitated, relief will be granted only if such confusion of the public is probable. The injunction against the imitation of a trademark is absolute, all use of the mark being prohibited; the injunction restraining simulation of a trade name is qualified or limited in the scope, preventing only those uses of the mark which render it likely that the public will confuse the products bearing the marks. Handler & Pickett, Trade-Marks and Trade Names—An Analysis and Synthesis, 30 Colum.L.Rev. 168, 759 (1930).

The passage of the Lanham Act in 1946 redefined the terms. Section 45 of the Lanham Act, 15 U.S.C. § 1127, defines "mark" "trademark" and "tradename." The definition of "trademark" does not refer to the quality of the mark, i.e. whether it is descriptive, geographical or a surname, but rather to the nature of the mark—word, name, symbol, or device.

"Tradename", on the other hand, identifies a person's "business or vocation". Under the Lanham Act, the distinction between trademark and tradename becomes whether the mark identifies the goods or services of the producer or the producer's business. Of course, in some situations a mark may function *both* as a trademark and a tradename. "Coca–Cola" may identify both the soft drink and the company that produces it.

Section 2 of the Act, 15 U.S.C. § 1052, is the heart of the registration provisions. Section 2 sets out the requirements through which a trademark owner obtains the protection of the act. The beginning clause of this section uses the term "trademark" and prohibits the Patent Office from refusing to register any "trademark" unless it fits the specifically listed prohibitions. Thus a "trademark" exists prior to registration.

Subsection 2(e) contains the Lanham Act's codification of the descriptive, geographical, or surname distinctions of the common law. By reading the introductory clause of § 2 with subsection (e) it can be seen that a trademark which is descriptive is still a trademark and yet it cannot be registered under 2(e). On the other hand, if the mark is "merely descriptive," how could it distinguish the goods of the applicant as required by the introductory clause of § 2?

Subsection (f) further complicates the question. First, grammatically it is not parallel to the other subsections. Second, it is an exception to the exception of subsection (e). Subsection (f) allows marks which are "merely descriptive," "primarily geographically descriptive," or "primarily merely a surname" to be registered notwithstanding (e) if the mark is "distinctive of the applicant's goods in commerce." What is the difference between "distinctive" in 2(f) and "distinguish" as used in the introductory clause? If a "mark" is "*merely* descriptive" how could it be "distinctive" of the applicant's goods?

The only reference to "tradename" in section 2 is in subsection (d) which precludes registration of a "mark" which so resembles a "mark or trade name previously used in the United States."

"Tradenames" as defined in § 45 are not registrable on the Principal Register. On the other hand, § 44(g) provides protection to foreign nationals for tradenames or commercial names "without the obligation of filing or registration whether or not they form parts of marks."

The Lanham Act specifically recognizes three other types of marks: service marks (§ 3), certification marks (§ 4), and collective marks (§ 4). They are each defined in § 45. You should at this point examine those sections; a more detailed consideration will be required subsequently.

The Lanham Act definitions increasingly have been adopted by courts even in common law trademark and unfair competition cases. In reading cases, some care must be taken to determine which set of definitions are being used.

Secondary meaning. Under the traditional common law, a trade name included any designation adopted which acquired "special significance." Under the Lanham Act, descriptive, geographical and surname marks can be registered if they become "distinctive of the applicant's goods." The common law referred to this "special significance" as "secondary meaning" and many of the Lanham Act cases use the term also. The classical definition of secondary meaning is by Judge Denison in G. & C. Merriam Co. v. Saalfield, 198 F. 369, 373 (6th Cir.1912):

> [Secondary meaning] contemplates that a word or phrase originally, and in that sense primarily, incapable of exclusive appropriation with reference to an article on the market, because geographically or otherwise descriptive, might nevertheless have been used so long and so exclusively by one

producer with reference to his article that, in that trade and to that branch of the purchasing public, the word or phrase had come to mean that the article was his product; in other words, had come to be, to them, his trademark. So it was said that the word had come to have a secondary meaning, although this phrase, "secondary meaning," seems not happily chosen, because, in the limited field, this new meaning is primary rather than secondary: that is to say, it is, in that field, the natural meaning.

How does Justice Brandeis define "secondary meaning" in *Kellogg*. When he requires the plaintiff to show "that the primary significance of the term in the minds of the consuming public is not the product but the producer," does he mean that the consumer must know the name of the producer?

Proof of secondary meaning is the critical issue in many trademark cases. The consumer association of the mark with the producer may be proved by direct or circumstantial evidence. Direct evidence may consist of the testimony of actual consumers or scientific surveys of actual consumers. A number of courts have noted that the direct testimony of consumers is not terribly persuasive, particularly where their selection was not in accord with recognized techniques to assure randomness and reliability. Scientific surveys have been increasingly utilized, and their probative value obviously depends on the objectivity of the sampling technique. However, as the direct evidence becomes more scientific, the Court must confront the difficult question of what percentage of the appropriate class of consumers must have formed the association in order to support a finding of secondary meaning. Would 100% be required? A majority? Would 25% be sufficient? What if 55% of the consumers associated the mark with producer *X* but 25% associated the mark with producer *Y* in a case where both claim secondary meaning?

Proof of "distinctiveness" for purposes of Lanham Act registrations is similar to proof of secondary meaning at common law. Both direct and circumstantial evidence are used. See 37 CFR 2.41 (1984). In addition two presumptions are created, one by statute and the other by regulation. Section 2(f) of the Act provides that exclusive and continuous use of a mark for 5 years "before the date on which the claim of distinctiveness is made" may be considered to be prima facie evidence of distinctiveness. The Commissioner is not required to accept the presumption in all cases.

For an in depth analysis of the secondary meaning doctrine see, Stern & Hoffman, Public Injury and the Public Interest: Secondary Meaning in the Law of Unfair Competition, 110 U.Pa.L.Rev. 935 (1962): "Courts rarely articulate precisely, if they recognize at all, the choice they make in unfair competitive cases between the two competing rationales and their underlying policies. Instead, the decisions are often shrouded in unhelpful conclusions phrased in the legal mysticism of 'secondary meaning' on the one hand or of 'property rights' on the other." The problems of proof of secondary meaning are considered in more detail in McCarthy, Trademarks and Unfair Competition §§ 15:10, 15:26 (2d ed. 1984).

B. PROBLEMS OF VALIDITY

(1) DISTINCTIVENESS

(A) DESCRIPTIVE MARKS

ZATARAINS, INC. v. OAK GROVE SMOKEHOUSE, INC.

United States Court of Appeals, Fifth Circuit, 1983.
698 F.2d 786.

GOLDBERG, CIRCUIT JUDGE:

* * *

I. FACTS AND PROCEEDINGS BELOW

A. THE TALE OF THE TOWN FRIER

Zatarain's is the manufacturer and distributor of a line of over one hundred food products. Two of these products, "Fish-Fri" and "Chick-Fri," are coatings or batter mixes used to fry foods. These marks serve as the entreè in the present litigation.

Zatarain's "Fish-Fri" consists of 100% corn flour and is used to fry fish and other seafood. "Fish-Fri" is packaged in rectangular cardboard boxes containing twelve or twenty-four ounces of coating mix. The legend "Wonderful FISH–FRI ®" is displayed prominently on the front panel, along with the block Z used to identify all Zatarain's products. The term "Fish-Fri" has been used by Zatarain's or its predecessor since 1950 and has been registered as a trademark since 1962.

Zatarain's "Chick-Fri" is a seasoned corn flour batter mix used for frying chicken and other foods. The "Chick-Fri" package, which is very similar to that used for "Fish-Fri," is a rectangular cardboard container labelled "Wonderful CHICK–FRI." Zatarain's began to use the term "Chick-Fri" in 1968 and registered the term as a trademark in 1976.

Zatarain's products are not alone in the marketplace. At least four other companies market coatings for fried foods that are denominated "fish fry" or "chicken fry." Two of these competing companies are the appellees here, and therein hangs this fish tale.

Appellee Oak Grove Smokehouse, Inc. ("Oak Grove") began marketing a "fish fry" and a "chicken fry" in March 1979. Both products are packaged in clear glassine packets that contain a quantity of coating mix sufficient to fry enough food for one meal. The packets are labelled with Oak Grove's name and emblem, along with the words "FISH FRY" OR "CHICKEN FRY." Oak Grove's "FISH FRY" has a corn flour base seasoned with various spices; Oak Grove's "CHICKEN FRY" is a seasoned coating with a wheat flour base.

Appellee Visko's Fish Fry, Inc. ("Visko's") entered the batter mix market in March 1980 with its "fish fry." Visko's product is packed in a cylindrical eighteen-ounce container with a resealable plastic lid. The words "Visko's FISH FRY" appear on the label along with a photograph of a platter of fried fish. Visko's coating mix contains corn flour and added spices.

Other food manufacturing concerns also market coating mixes.

* * *

III. THE TRADEMARK CLAIMS

A. *BASIC PRINCIPLES*

1. *Classifications of Marks*

The threshold issue in any action for trademark infringement is whether the word or phrase is initially registerable or protectable.

* * *

Courts and commentators have traditionally divided potential trademarks into four categories. A potential trademark may be classified as (1) generic, (2) descriptive, (3) suggestive, or (4) arbitrary or fanciful. These categories, like the tones in a spectrum, tend to blur at the edges and merge together. The labels are more advisory than definitional, more like guidelines than pigeonholes. Not surprisingly, they are somewhat difficult to articulate and to apply.

A *generic* term is "the name of a particular genus or class of which an individual article or service is but a member." [Vision Center v. Opticks, Inc., 596 F.2d 111, 115 (5th Cir.1980)] A generic term connotes the "basic nature of articles or services" rather than the more individualized characteristics of a particular product.

* * *

A *descriptive* term "identifies a characteristic or quality of an article or service," Vision Center, 596 F.2d at 115, such as its color, odor, function, dimensions, or ingredients. Descriptive terms ordinarily are not protectable as trademarks, Lanham Act § 2(e)(1), 15 U.S.C. § 1052(e)(1) (1976); they may become valid marks, however, by acquiring a secondary meaning in the minds of the consuming public. See id. § 2(f), 15 U.S.C. § 1052(f). Examples of descriptive marks would include "Alo" with reference to products containing gel of the aloe vera plant, Aloe Creme Laboratories, Inc. v. Milsan, Inc., 423 F.2d 845 (5th Cir.1970), and "Vision Center" in reference to a business offering optical goods and services, Vision Center, 596 F.2d at 117. As this court has often noted, the distinction between descriptive and generic terms is one of degree. The distinction has important practical consequences, however; while a descriptive term may be elevated to trademark status with proof of secondary meaning, a generic term may never achieve trademark protection.

A *suggestive* term suggests, rather than describes, some particular characteristic of the goods or services to which it applies and requires the consumer to exercise the imagination in order to draw a conclusion as to the nature of the goods and services. A suggestive mark is protected without the necessity for proof of secondary meaning. The term "Coppertone" has been held suggestive in regard to sun tanning products. *See* Douglas Laboratories, Inc. v. Copper Tan, Inc., 210 F.2d 453 (2d Cir.1954).

Arbitrary or *fanciful* terms bear no relationship to the products or services to which they are applied. Like suggestive terms, arbitrary and fanciful marks are protectable without proof of secondary meaning. The term "Kodak" is properly classified as a fanciful term for photographic supplies, *see* Eastman Kodak Co. v. Weil, 137 Misc. 506, 243 N.Y.S. 319 (1930) ("Kodak"); "Ivory" is an arbitrary term as applied to soap. Abercrombie & Fitch, 537 F.2d at 9 n. 6.

2. Secondary Meaning

As noted earlier, descriptive terms are ordinarily not protectable as trademarks. They may be protected, however, if they have acquired a secondary meaning for the consuming public.

* * * Proof of secondary meaning is an issue only with respect to descriptive marks; suggestive and arbitrary or fanciful marks are automatically protected upon registration, and generic terms are unprotectible even if they have acquired secondary meaning.

3. The "Fair Use" Defense

Even when a descriptive term has acquired a secondary meaning sufficient to warrant trademark protection, others may be entitled to use the mark without incurring liability for trademark infringement. When the allegedly infringing term is "used fairly and in good faith only to describe to users the goods or services of [a] party, or their geographic origin," Lanham Act § 33(b)(4), 15 U.S.C. § 1115(b)(4) (1976), a defendant in a trademark infringement action may assert the "fair use" defense. The defense is available only in actions involving descriptive terms and only when the term is used in its descriptive sense rather than its trademark sense. In essence, the fair use defense prevents a trademark registrant from appropriating a descriptive term for its own use to the exclusion of others, who may be prevented thereby from accurately describing their own goods. The holder of a protectable descriptive mark has no legal claim to an exclusive right in the primary, descriptive meaning of the term; consequently, anyone is free to use the term in its primary, descriptive sense so long as such use does not lead to customer confusion as to the source of the goods or services.

* * *

B. "FISH–FRI"

1. Classification

* * * The district court found that "Fish-Fri" was a descriptive term identifying a function of the product being sold. Having reviewed this finding under the appropriate "clearly erroneous" standard, we affirm.

* * * Courts and commentators have formulated a number of tests to be used in classifying a mark as descriptive.

(1) A suitable starting place is the dictionary, for "[t]he dictionary definition of the word is an appropriate and relevant indication 'of the ordinary significance and meaning of words' to the public." American Heritage, 494 F.2d at 11 n. 5; see also Vision Center, 596 F.2d at 116. Webster's Third New International Dictionary 858 (1966) lists the following definitions for the term "fish fry": "1. a picnic at which fish are caught, fried, and eaten; * * *. 2. fried fish." Thus, the basic dictionary definitions of the term refer to the preparation and consumption of fried fish. This is at least preliminary evidence that the term "Fish-Fri" is descriptive of Zatarain's product in the sense that the words naturally direct attention to the purpose or function of the product.

(2) The "imagination test" is a second standard used by the courts to identify descriptive terms. This test seeks to measure the relationship between the actual words of the mark and the product to which they are applied. If a term "requires imagination, thought and perception to reach a conclusion as to the nature of goods," Stix Products, 295 F.Supp. at 488, it is considered a suggestive term. Alternatively, a term is descriptive if standing alone it conveys information as to the characteristics of the product. In this case, mere observation compels the conclusion that a product branded "Fish-Fri" is a prepackaged coating or batter mix applied to fish prior to cooking. The connection between this merchandise and its identifying terminology is so close and direct that even a consumer unfamiliar with the product would doubtless have an idea of its purpose or function. It simply does not require an exercise of the imagination to deduce that "Fish-Fri" is used to fry fish. Accordingly, the term "Fish-Fri" must be considered descriptive when examined under the "imagination test."

(3) A third test used by courts and commentators to classify descriptive marks is "whether competitors would be likely to need the terms used in the trademark in describing their products." Union Carbide Corp. v. Ever-Ready, Inc., 531 F.2d 366, 379 (7th Cir.1976). A descriptive term generally relates so closely and directly to a product or service that other merchants marketing similar goods would find the term useful in identifying their own goods. Common sense indicates that in this case merchants other than Zatarain's might find the term "fish fry" useful in describing their own particular batter mixes. While Zatarain's has argued strenuously that Visko's and Oak Grove could have chosen from dozens of other possible terms in naming their

coating mix, we find this position to be without merit. As this court has held, the fact that a term is not the only or even the most common name for a product is not determinative, for there is no legal foundation that a product can be described in only one fashion. There are many edible fish in the sea, and as many ways to prepare them as there are varieties to be prepared. Even piscatorial gastronomes would agree, however, that frying is a form of preparation accepted virtually around the world, at restaurants starred and unstarred. The paucity of synonyms for the words "fish" and "fry" suggests that a merchant whose batter mix is specially spiced for frying fish is likely to find "fish fry" a useful term for describing his product.

A final barometer of the descriptiveness of a particular term examines the extent to which a term actually has been used by others marketing a similar service or product. This final test is closely related to the question whether competitors are likely to find a mark useful in describing their products. As noted above, a number of companies other than Zatarain's have chosen the word combination "fish fry" to identify their batter mixes. Arnaud's product, "Oyster Shrimp and Fish Fry," has been in competition with Zatarain's "Fish-Fri" for some ten to twenty years. When companies from A to Z, from Arnaud to Zatarain's, select the same term to describe their similar products, the term in question is most likely a descriptive one.

* * * The district court in this case found that Zatarain's trademark "Fish-Fri" was descriptive of the function of the product being sold. Having applied the four prevailing tests of descriptiveness to the term "Fish-Fri," we are convinced that the district court's judgment in this matter is not only not clearly erroneous, but clearly correct.

2. *Secondary Meaning*

Descriptive terms are not protectable by trademark absent a showing of secondary meaning in the minds of the consuming public. To prevail in its trademark infringement action, therefore, Zatarain's must prove that its mark "Fish-Fri" has acquired a secondary meaning and thus warrants trademark protection. The district court found that Zatarain's evidence established a secondary meaning for the term "Fish-Fri" in the New Orleans area. We affirm.

* * *

In assessing a claim of secondary meaning, the major inquiry is the consumer's attitude toward the mark. The mark must denote to the consumer "a single thing coming from a single source," Coca-Cola Co. v. Koke Co., 254 U.S. 143 (1920); Aloe Creme Laboratories, 423 F.2d at 849, to support a finding of secondary meaning. Both direct and circumstantial evidence may be relevant and persuasive on the issue.

Factors such as amount and manner of advertising, volume of sales, and length and manner of use may serve as circumstantial evidence relevant to the issue of secondary meaning. While none of these factors alone will prove secondary meaning, in combination they may establish the necessary link in the minds of consumers between a product and its source. It must be remembered, however, that "the question is not the *extent* of the promotional efforts, but their *effectiveness* in altering the meaning of [the term] to the consuming public." Aloe Creme Laboratories, 423 F.2d at 850.

Since 1950, Zatarain's and its predecessor have continuously used the term "Fish-Fri" to identify this particular batter mix. Through the expenditure of over $400,000 for advertising during the period from 1976 through 1981, Zatarain's has promoted its name and its product to the buying public. Sales of twelve-ounce boxes of "Fish-Fri" increased from 37,265 cases in 1969 to 59,439 cases in 1979. From 1964 through 1979, Zatarain's sold a total of 916,385 cases of "Fish-Fri." The district court considered this circumstantial evidence of secondary meaning to weigh heavily in Zatarain's favor.

In addition to these circumstantial factors, Zatarain's introduced at trial two surveys conducted by its expert witness, Allen Rosenzweig. In one survey, telephone interviewers questioned 100 women in the New Orleans area who fry fish or other seafood three or more times per month. Of the women surveyed, twenty-three percent specified *Zatarain's* "Fish-Fri" as a product they "would buy at the grocery to use as a coating" or a "product on the market that is especially made for frying fish." In a similar survey conducted in person at a New Orleans area mall, twenty-eight of the 100 respondents answered "*Zatarain's* 'Fish-Fri' " to the same questions.

The authorities are in agreement that survey evidence is the most direct and persuasive way of establishing secondary meaning. The district court believed that the survey evidence produced by Zatarain's, when coupled with the circumstantial evidence of advertising and usage, tipped the scales in favor of a finding of secondary meaning. Were we considering the question of secondary meaning *de novo*, we might reach a different conclusion than did the district court, for the issue is close. Mindful, however, that there is evidence in the record to support the finding below, we cannot say that the district court's conclusion was clearly erroneous. Accordingly, the finding of secondary meaning in the New Orleans area for Zatarain's descriptive term "Fish-Fri" must be affirmed.

3. The "Fair Use" Defense

* * * The district court determined that Oak Grove and Visko's were entitled to fair use of the term "fish fry" to describe a characteristic of their goods; we affirm that conclusion.

Zatarain's term "Fish-Fri" is a descriptive term that has acquired a secondary meaning in the New Orleans area. Although the trademark is valid by virtue of having acquired a secondary meaning, only that penumbra or fringe of secondary meaning is given legal protection. Zatarain's has no legal claim to an exclusive right in the original, descriptive sense of the term; therefore, Oak Grove and Visko's are still free to use the words "fish fry" in their ordinary, descriptive sense, so long as such use will not tend to confuse customers as to the source of the goods.

The record contains ample evidence to support the district court's determination that Oak Grove's and Visko's use of the words "fish fry" was fair and in good faith. Testimony at trial indicated that the appellees did not intend to use the term in a trademark sense and had never attempted to register the words as a trademark. * * * In addition, Oak Grove and Visko's consciously packaged and labelled their products in such a way as to minimize any potential confusion in the minds of consumers.

NOTES

1. Courts have had great difficulty drawing the line between suggestive and descriptive marks. In Q-Tips, Inc. v. Johnson & Johnson, 206 F.2d 144, 146 (3d Cir.1953), cert. denied 346 U.S. 867 (1953) the mark "Q-Tips" was held to be a valid mark.

> It is pretty clear that the two terms (suggestive and descriptive) are not mutually exclusive. There must be some description in almost any suggestion or the suggesting process will not take place. So what we have in any trademark case is a matter of judgment as to what side of the line the question mark falls upon. It is desirable to protect a trader who has built up public association with a product under his trademark from having his business taken by somebody else. It is also desirable to keep the channels of expression open by not giving protection to people who go out and take ordinary, descriptive words and then claim something like a property right in them.

Compare Judge Learned Hand's opinion holding the mark "Fashionknit" to be descriptive for knitted sweaters in Franklin Knitting Mills, Inc. v. Fashionit Sweater Mills, Inc., 297 Fed. 247, 248 (S.D.N.Y.1923): "It is quite impossible to get any rule out of the cases beyond this: That the validity of the mark ends where suggestion ends and description begins." See also, Union Carbide Corporation v. Ever-Ready Inc., 531 F.2d 366, 379 (7th Cir.1976) upholding the "Eveready" mark as applied to batteries: "[This distinction between descriptiveness and suggestiveness] is, undoubtedly, often made on an intuitive basis rather than as the result of a logical analysis susceptible of articulation."

In Union National Bank of Texas, Laredo v. Union National Bank of Texas, 909 F.2d 839 (5th Cir.1990) the Fifth Circuit, following *Zatarains,* reversed the lower court's decision that "Union National Bank" was descriptive as a matter of law. The court suggested the richness of the proper analysis:

> The English language, more than most, is in a constant state of flux. A word which is today fanciful may tomorrow become descriptive or generic. * * * Thus, the trier of fact must be aware of, or informed of, common, up-to-date usage of the word or phrase. Furthermore, even were usage not constantly changing, the context in which a word or phrase appears is relevant to determining the proper category for purposes of trademark protection eligibility. The word or phrase must be compared to the product or service to which it is applied. For example, the word "fish," previously discussed, was said to be generic as it describes a category of aquatic life. Yet "fish" as used in "fish market" turns "fish" into a descriptive term if it describes a type of

"market." Used in the phrase "FishWear" for dive clothing, "fish" may be suggestive if the intent is to suggest that divers who wear this clothing will be able to "swim like a fish." On the other hand, with respect to clothing worn while fishing, "FishWear" might be descriptive. Finally, "fish," used in the name of a product totally unrelated to anything having to do with fish, or suggestive thereof, such as "Fish National Bank," would appear to be arbitrary.

For a list of marks which have been held "descriptive" or "suggestive" see 3 Callmann, Unfair Competition, Trademarks and Monopolies § 71 et seq. (4th ed. 1981); McCarthy, Trademarks and Unfair Competition §§ 11.8, 11.23 (2d ed. 1984). See, e.g., Louis Rich, Inc. v. Horace W. Longacre, Inc., 423 F.Supp. 1327 (E.D.Pa.1976) ("Gobble-gobble" suggestive as applied to turkey meat products.)

2. Is the distinction between descriptive and suggestive marks a workable tool in deciding which marks will be granted legal protection? Are you satisfied that the court reached the correct decision in *Zatarains?* Can you see an analysis that concentrates on the interests of the parties rather than on the abstract consideration of the characteristics of the marks? Why do we care if a person appropriates a "descriptive" mark? Or, why shouldn't all trademark owners be forced to prove secondary meaning?

3. The courts may hesitate to protect some marks that, although not descriptive, may be of such a nature that, like descriptive marks they ought not to be withdrawn from common usage. See The Different Drummer, Ltd. v. Textron, Inc., 306 F.Supp. 672 (S.D.N.Y.1969) refusing to protect Thoreau's phrase: "The man who hears a different drummer drumming" for cologne. Although the words may even be fanciful, "their true source, Thoreau's Walden, is the property of all English-speaking peoples." But see, Roux Laboratories, Inc. v. Clairol, Inc., 427 F.2d 823 (CCPA 1970) where the slogan "Hair Color So Natural Only Her Hairdresser Knows For Sure" was permitted to be registered for hair coloring products on proof of secondary meaning.

4. *Deceptive and Misdescriptive Marks.* Section 2(e)(1) of the Lanham Act, 15 U.S.C. § 1052(2)(e)(1), precludes registration of "deceptively misdescriptive" marks as well as "merely descriptive" marks. In addition section 2(a), 15 U.S.C. § 1052(2)(a), denies registration to "deceptive" trademarks and does not permit their validity to be resurrected by showing they have become "distinctive" under section 2(f), 15 U.S.C. § 1052(2)(f). Should "Old Crow Whiskey" be denied registration under either or both provisions unless it is made from old crows?

The difference between "deceptive" and "deceptively misdescriptive" was examined in In re Quady Winery Inc., 221 U.S.P.Q. 1213 (TTAB 1984) where the word "Essensia" which originally referred to a very rare type of Hungarian Tokay wine was applied to a mass-marketed California muscat. The Board provided the following test:

> The test for deceptive misdescriptiveness has two parts. First we must determine if the matter sought to be registered misdescribes the goods. If so, then we must ask if it is also deceptive, that is, if anyone is likely to believe the misrepresentation. * * * A third question, used to distinguish between marks that are deceptive under Section 2(a) and marks that are deceptively misdescriptive under Section 2(e) (1), is whether the misrepresentation would materially affect the decision to purchase the goods.

See also, Germain, Trademark Registration Under Sections 2(a) and 2(e) of the Lanham Act: the Deception Decision, 44 Fordham L.Rev. 249 (1975).

It should also be remembered that section 43(a) of the Lanham Act, 15 U.S.C. § 1125(a), prohibits any "false description or representation" used with goods or services.

5. There seems to be growing interest in the § 2(a) provision that prohibits registration of "scandalous matter". See In re McGinley, 660 F.2d 481 (CCPA 1981) where a mark comprising an embracing nude couple "appearing to show the male genitalia" was denied registration against claims that "scandalous" was vague and in violation of the First Amendment. The court suggested that the term applied to material that is offensive to a sense of propriety or morality from the standpoint of a "substantial composite of the general public." See also In re Tinseltown, Inc., 212 U.S.P.Q. 863 (TTAB 1981) (the mark "Bullshit" denied registration as scandalous).

(B) GENERIC MARKS

KELLOGG CO. v. NATIONAL BISCUIT CO.
Supra page 235.

A.J. CANFIELD CO. v. HONICKMAN
United States Court of Appeals, Third Circuit, 1986.
808 F.2d 291.

BECKER, CIRCUIT JUDGE.

* * *

We must decide whether the designation "chocolate fudge" as applied to diet soda deserves protection as a trademark under the federal law of unfair competition. 15 U.S.C. § 1125(a) (Section 43(a) of the Lanham Act). The term is protectable if it is suggestive or if it is descriptive and is buttressed by proof of secondary meaning. The designation is unprotectable if it is generic or if it is descriptive but lacks sufficient secondary meaning. If the mark is protectable, we must also decide its geographic reach.

At the present stage of the case, we hold the designation "chocolate fudge" for diet soda generic, hence unprotectable, on the basis of two essential considerations. First, as the district court justifiably found, the term "chocolate fudge" denotes a particular full and rich chocolate flavor, that distinguishes Canfield's product from plain chocolate sodas. Second, on the basis of the present record, it appears difficult if not impossible for a competing producer to convey to the public that its product shares this functional flavor characteristic without using the words "chocolate fudge."

Unlike Athena, however, this conclusion does not emerge full grown from the existing jurisprudence. Indicative of this legal lacuna is the fact that three distinguished district judges have considered the level of inherent distinctiveness of chocolate fudge soda and have arrived at disparate conclusions. See A.J. Canfield Co. v. Vess Beverages, Inc., 612 F.Supp. 1081 (N.D.Ill.1985) (Shadur, J.), aff'd, 796 F.2d

903 (7th Cir.1986) (finding "a reasonable basis for considering term suggestive although even greater basis for holding it merely descriptive"); Canfield v. Concord Beverages Co. (Scirica, J.) (holding term descriptive); Yoo–Hoo Chocolate Beverages Corp. v. A.J. Canfield Co., 229 U.S.P.Q. 653 (D.N.J.1986) (Sarokin, J.) (finding term generic), appeal stayed per stipulation, App. No. 86–5584 (3d Cir. Oct. 17, 1986).

* * *

Because, on the present record, Chocolate Fudge Soda appears to fit our test for a generic term, and because generic designations are not protectable under trademark law, we will affirm the order of the district court denying the preliminary injunction.

* * *

Because chocolate fudge denotes a flavor, no imagination is required for a potential consumer to reach a conclusion about the nature of Canfield's soda. In accordance with the accepted definitions, "chocolate fudge" as applied to diet soda cannot be suggestive.

IV. IS CHOCOLATE FUDGE AS APPLIED TO DIET SODA DESCRIPTIVE OR GENERIC?

The question remains whether the term "chocolate fudge" as applied to diet soda is descriptive because it only describes characteristics or functions of the product or whether it is so commonly descriptive of the name of the product that we should consider it generic. That in turn depends on how we define the relevant product category, or "genus." The district court found that chocolate fudge as applied to diet soda is not generic because "(t)here is no proof that the term has come to be understood as referring to the genus of all chocolate-flavored diet sodas." 629 F.Supp. at 208 (citation omitted). This statement assumes, without any analysis, that the relevant genus is chocolate diet sodas, so that the term chocolate fudge provides a description of this particular chocolate soda. We do not consider this assumption obvious, for the relevant genus could be chocolate fudge soda, just as the relevant genus of similarly flavored ice creams could be chocolate fudge ice creams rather than chocolate ice creams (with chocolate fudge a species). If that is the case, then Canfield has chosen the generic name of the product as the name of its brand and cannot gain trademark protection.

* * *

We cannot, however, determine the relevant genus on the basis of abstract analysis, intuition or common sense alone. Rather, we first examine the principles and tests that Congress and the courts have developed for judging genericness to determine if any established method is available for distinguishing product brand from product class. We conclude, however, that neither of the two dominant principles of genericness, the primary significance test and its related test of consumer understanding, directly provide an answer to our question, for both tests become applicable only after we have determined the relevant genus. We therefore must develop our own rule out of basic principles of trademark law that is consistent with these tests.

A. The Primary Significance Test

The dominant principle for determining whether a term is generic is the primary significance test. This test has its origins in the Supreme Court case of Kellogg Co. v. National Biscuit Co. * * * Congress codified this holding in the Trademark Clarification Act of 1984, Pub.L. No. 98–620, Title I, § 102, 98 Stat. 3335 (1984) (codified at 15 U.S.C. § 1064), mandating that "the primary significance" test "shall be the test for determining whether the registered mark" has become generic. 15 U.S.C. § 1064.[9]

Although the primary significance test instructs us to inquire whether a term primarily signifies the product or the producer, a trademark need not identify source directly or explicitly. The Clarification Act endorsed the long-recognized anonymous source rule, Pub.L. 98–620, Title I, § 103(1) (codified at 15 U.S.C. § 1127), which recognizes that a term may function as an indicator of source and therefore as a valid trademark, even though consumers may not know the name of the manufacturer or producer of the product. The rule recognizes that "the primary significance" test is met even if the primary significance of a mark is not directly the producer but rather if "the primary significance of the mark to consumers . . . is to identify a product or service which emanates from a particular source, known or unknown," for it still provides the assurance to the public "that the product is of uniform quality and performance." S.Rep. No. 98–627, 98th Cong., 2d Sess., 5 (1984) * * *.

In codifying the primary significance test, Congress has also recognized that trademarks need not indicate source exclusively, but may have a "dual function—that of identifying a product while at the same time indicating its source." *Senate Report* at 5, U.S.Code Cong. & Admin.News 1984 at 5722. Because "most firms, in fact, attempt to market and promote their products as unique in some way," id. at 8, the public may understand that all goods with a certain term originate from the same producer and at the same time understand the term to indicate particular product characteristics (or a combination of characteristics) that distinguish the product from others. The Clarification Act therefore specifies, "A registered mark shall not be deemed to be the common descriptive name of goods or services solely because such mark is also used as a name of or to identify a unique product or service." Pub.L. 98–620, Title I, §§ 102, 103 (codified at 15 U.S.C. §§ 1064, 1127).

9. Although the Clarification Act changed sections of the Lanham Act that deal with registered marks, and thus did not explicitly change § 43(a) of the Lanham Act, 15 U.S.C. § 1125, which concerns us here, we consider these changes applicable to our analysis of unfair competition. The law governing unregistered marks is largely judge-made, but federal law under § 43(a) of the Lanham Act generally follows the principles established by statute and the courts for registered marks. * * *

Notwithstanding the centrality of the primary significance test to the genericness doctrine, it does not enable us to determine the relevant product genus in this case because it only becomes applicable after we have distinguished product genus from product brand. Although a term may primarily signify source if it primarily signifies a product emanating from a single, albeit anonymous, source, it does not primarily signify source if the product that emanates from a single source, e.g., shredded wheat, constitutes its own product genus. * * *

In other words, the primary significance test is generally satisfied if a term signifies a product that emanates from a single source, i.e., a product brand, but it is not satisfied if the product that emanates from a single source is not only a product brand but is also a product genus. The primary significance test does not, in and of itself, tell us how to differentiate a mere product brand from a product genus. That, however, is the crucial question in this case. Once that question is decided, the resulting question often decides itself.[12]

B. The Test of Consumer Understanding

Although the primary significance test does not itself tell us how to distinguish a product brand from a product genus, some commentators have suggested that such a distinction can be made by direct examination of consumer understanding. See, e.g., Greenbaum, Ginsburg & Weinberg, *A Proposal for Evaluating Genericism After "Anti–Monopoly"*, 73 Trademark Rep. 101, 117–22 (1984); Note, The Legislative Response to Anti–Monopoly: A Missed Opportunity to Clarify the Genericness Doctrine, 1985 U.Ill.L.Rev. 197. Congress has attributed "the classic test" of consumer understanding, see *Senate Report* at 3, U.S.Code Cong. & Admin.News 1984, at 5719, to Bayer Co. v. United Drug Co., 272 F. 505, 509 (S.D.N.Y.1921), in which Judge Learned Hand stated: "The single question, as I view it, in all these (genericness) cases, is merely one of fact: What do the buyers understand by the word for whose use the parties are contending?" Some commentators suggest that we may determine this understanding and thereby determine whether the term signifies a product brand or a product genus, by directly asking members of the relevant public whether, in their view, a term is a brand name or a "common name," i.e., the name of a product genus. See Greenbaum, Ginsburg & Weinberg, supra, at 118–22.

* * *

In contrast to the advocates of this survey technique, we do not believe that a direct survey of public views can truly measure consumer understanding if a term identifies a product that arguably constitutes its own genus. As we have discussed above, generic marks signifying goods produced by only one manufacturer may function both as generic terms, signifying the product genus, and as brand names, indicating

---

12. For example, in Kellogg, if wheat cereals were the relevant product class, then Shredded Wheat would be merely a brand. But once it was decided that cere- als containing pillow-shaped forms of wheat shreds was the relevant product class, the term "shredded wheat" was obviously generic.

continuity of source.[14]　Faced with a mark like shredded wheat, the consumer has no reason to define it either as the name of a brand or as the name of a genus because the term functions most efficiently as both.　Accordingly, a survey inquiring whether a designation like shredded wheat is a brand name or a product name forces respondents to make a false dichotomy.　Because consumers will never have had a reason to consider the question before, such a survey might not elicit real attitudes but merely answers developed on the spot that would be highly susceptible to the influences of survey phraseology.

Perhaps more significantly, directly surveying the public without first differentiating the product brand from the product genus—or at least without first offering a definition for the distinction—would not, in the context of this case, test the meaning of words to the public but would rather request a legal conclusion.　A conscientious survey respondent, when asked whether a term is a brand name or product name, might ask, "Exactly what do you mean by product name and what do you mean by brand name?"　Using the primary significance test and taking account of the anonymous source rule, we would be compelled to answer: "A brand name primarily signifies a product brand while a product name primarily signifies a product genus."　The respondent then asks: "How do I distinguish a product brand from a product genus?"　If we seek to answer this question with the results of this survey, we can only answer in a circular fashion: "That question depends on the answers we obtain from you and other respondents."　We simply cannot circumvent the requirement of defining the distinction between product brand and product genus by asking the public to tell us if a name is a brand name or the name of a product genus; we can only ignore it.

Some commentators have suggested that, instead of providing a definition of product brand and product genus, a survey may simply provide examples of brand names and product names.　See Greenbaum, Ginsburg & Weinberg, *supra,* at 118.[16]　We do not agree.　Such a technique would presumably rest on the assumption that even though we, as courts, cannot define the distinction between brand and genus names without first distinguishing between brand and genus categories, the public can.　We can think of no reason to support this assumption.

---

14. A trademark can serve a dual function in that some consumers use it to associate source while others use it to designate a product, functioning in a way some have called "discontinuously hybrid." See Folsom & Teply, [Trademarked Generic Words, 89 Yale L.J. 1323] at 1339. The problem in our case, however, is that a mark may be "simultaneously hybrid" in that it functions "for some consumers both as a generic term designating a product class and at the same time as a source-significant, commercial symbol." *Id.*

16. Such was the methodology of the well-known *Teflon* survey in E.I. DuPont de Nemours & Co. v. Yoshida International, Inc., 393 F.Supp. 502 (E.D.N.Y.1975), on which the court relied in refusing to find the word "Teflon" generic. The survey offered the example of "Chevrolet-automobile" to illustrate what it meant by brand name and product name and then asked respondents to classify many names, only one of which was Teflon, the term at issue. Such a survey would supposedly be self-authenticating in that we can examine whether the public provides answers we know are correct and thereby assure ourselves that the survey's methodology is sound.

Such a technique might also rest on the assumption that a list of examples might convey the distinction between brand and genus categories. But examples would only do so where the distinction is obvious, a situation we do not face. Finally, such a technique would not eliminate the fact that members of the public have no reason to distinguish between brand and genus name when they contemplate a genus with only one brand.

Although we agree that consumer understanding lies at the heart of any trademark evaluation, how it may aid courts in cases involving unique products is problematic. * * * In this case, however, determining the relevant product genus is our principal problem, for at least until recently no producers other than Canfield have manufactured a diet soda tasting like chocolate fudge. We therefore know that the public understands "diet chocolate fudge soda" to refer only to Canfield's product. That fact alone, however, does not mean that the brand is not also its own genus and the brand name not also a generic term.

Thus, we have come full circle. Although we recognize the importance of consumer understanding, and although we must develop a rule that uses it, the foregoing discussion demonstrates that a direct survey of the public alone furnishes us no more of a method for determining the relevant product genus, or of circumventing the need to make that determination, than that furnished by the primary significance test.[18]

C. A Rule Developed from Basic Principles

Our analysis and research have revealed no established test for differentiating between product brand and product genus. In order to resolve the issue we must therefore develop an analytical framework that is consistent with Congress's demand that genericness reflect the "primary significance" principle and at the same time that accommo-

---

18. Another method some commentators have suggested for distinguishing product brand from product genus would borrow anti-trust concepts of the relevant product market by focusing on cross-elasticities of demand, i.e., the public's willingness to substitute different goods for each other as they vary in price. See 1 McCarthy, supra, at 12:17; Note, Trademarks and Generic Words: An Effect-on-Competition Test, 51 U.Chi.L.Rev. 868, 882–85 (1984). If cross-elasticities are large, so that the consumers consider products relatively interchangeable, this argument suggests that courts should view them as belonging to the same product genus. If cross-elasticities are small, each product belongs to a different product genus. Although one court has assumed a genus on the basis of assumptions about cross-elasticity, Trak Inc. v. Benner Ski KG, 475 F.Supp. 1076, 1079 (D.Mass.1979), no court that we know of has truly attempted to apply this test.

Because of our doubts about this test, we will not be the first. In some situations, this test may be unfair to a manufacturer with strong brand loyalty. Consumers of a particular brand may consider it so superior to others that they are unwilling to shift to other brands despite a significant change in price. Under the cross-elasticity test, that brand would become its own product class, and other manufacturers could use its name. In other circumstances, we imagine that goods with clearly recognized independent product names might prove to be highly cross-elastic; we suspect, for example, that the demand for all sodas varies considerably with the price of others. Again, cross-elasticity would not supply a proper test. Accordingly, we are unwilling to endorse a cross-elasticity analysis unless and until we are shown a method of applying it suited to the subtleties of the trademark context.

dates Congress's insistence that a term is not generic merely because it also identifies a unique product or service. We are not prepared to announce a test for all cases. We do believe, however, that a direct analysis of interests underlying trademark law and the doctrine of genericness leads to a result in this case.

* * *

Underlying the genericness doctrine is the principle that some terms so directly signify the nature of the product that interests of competition demand that other producers be able to use them even if terms have or might become identified with a source and so acquire "de facto" secondary meaning. * * * Courts refuse to protect a generic term because competitors need it more to describe their goods than the claimed markholder needs it to distinguish its goods from others.

In essence, this kind of genericness requires courts to balance different kinds of confusion. If only one manufacturer can use a designation for which there is no common alternative, buyers may be confused by their ignorance that other goods possess the characteristics they seek. If a particular designation is available to all, however, customers who believe that only one manufacturer makes a product with that name may be misled into buying the goods of others, at least in the short run, and may face disappointment because these alternatives differ in subtle characteristics from the brand they wished to buy. * * * The doctrine of genericness reflects the Congressional determination that the interest in preventing the second kind of confusion does not normally justify creating the first, in large part because producers may identify their goods through the use of terms that are not necessary to competitors.

* * *

This quick summary of the genericness doctrine, we think, illuminates the primary significance test and provides a framework for analyzing the distinction between product brand and product genus. Notwithstanding its acknowledgment of the legitimate role a trademark may have in identifying a product brand, the primary significance test provides that "to function as a trademark, a term must be . . . an indicator of source, sponsorship, approval or affiliation." *Senate Report,* at 2, U.S.Code Cong. & Admin.News 1984, at 5719. To the extent that a trademark also communicates functional characteristics, it does not function as a trademark. Thus, to be consistent with the primary significance test, whether a product brand with a name used by one producer constitutes its own genus must turn on the extent to which the brand name communicates functional characteristics that differentiate the brand from the products of other producers. In making these calculations, consumer understanding will determine the extent to which a term communicates functional characteristics and the significance of a term's role in doing so because of a dearth or abundance of alternative terms that effectively communicate the same functional information.

Although we do not believe we have derived a formula that will differentiate the product brand from the product genus in all cases, we believe that application of these general principles of trademark law to this case, which involves at best a descriptive word not a coined term, is straightforward. We hold as follows: If a producer introduces a product that differs from an established product class in a particular characteristic, and uses a common descriptive term of that characteristic as the name of the product, then the product should be considered its own genus. Whether the term that identifies the product is generic then depends on the competitors' need to use it. See CES Publishing Corp. v. St. Regis Publications, Inc., 531 F.2d 11, 15 (1975). At the least, if no commonly used alternative effectively communicates the same functional information, the term that denotes the product is generic. If we held otherwise, a grant of trademark status could effectively prevent a competitor from marketing a product with the same characteristic despite its right to do so under the patent laws.

* * *

V. APPLYING THE TEST TO CHOCOLATE FUDGE SODA

Because the district court did not apply the test we have just established, we are not bound by its finding that chocolate fudge as applied to diet soda is descriptive. * * * At the present stage of this case, we believe that application of our holding to the present record plainly demonstrates that Canfield has not sustained its burden of proving that chocolate fudge, as applied to diet soda, is not generic. Canfield must make such a showing to demonstrate a likelihood of success on the merits that would justify a preliminary injunction in its favor.

Application of our rule to this case is straightforward. Canfield had the good fortune of originating a soda idea, a diet soda tasting like chocolate fudge, that proved eventually to have extraordinary appeal. Largely through the Bob Greene article, and through the press reports that followed it, abetted by Canfield's own advertising, Canfield sparked a nationwide demand for its soda. All these forms of publicity have highlighted the functional difference between a soda tasting like chocolate fudge and a mere chocolate soda, an established product class, suggesting that much of the demand for this soda arises because of its flavor. The term "chocolate fudge" is a common descriptive explanation of that functional difference. Accordingly, the relevant product class is not diet chocolate sodas but diet sodas that taste like chocolate fudge.

Having determined the relevant product genus, we must examine the need of Canfield's competitors to use the term "chocolate fudge." Often, this examination will require a factual analysis of alternative terms. Flavors, however, have unique characteristics, and we can imagine no term other than "chocolate fudge" that communicates the same functional information, namely, that this soda has the taste of chocolate fudge, a particular, full, rich chocolate taste. (The preliminary injunctive record reveals no alternative terms either.) Notwithstanding Canfield's role in creating the demand for this kind of product, the trademark laws do not give it the right to be the sole producer of a diet soda tasting like chocolate fudge. Such a right could only come from the patent laws. Accordingly, we conclude on this record that the term "chocolate fudge" as applied to diet soda is generic and is available to all potential competitors.

*   *   *

Because Canfield has not thus far made out a case that the designation chocolate fudge for diet soda is protectable, it has little likelihood of success on the merits. Accordingly, the judgment of the district court denying Canfield's request for a preliminary injunction will be affirmed.

NOTES

1. *The Lanham Act.* The original language of the Lanham Act did not expressly prohibit the registration of "generic" marks nor did it use the term "generic" mark. Section 2(e) precludes registration of "merely descriptive" marks which arguably could include generic descriptiveness. However § 2(e) marks can be registered under § 2(f) if distinctive and by definition generic marks cannot be distinctive. Section 14(c) of the original Lanham Act authorized cancellation of a registration at any time if it "becomes the common descriptive name of an article or substance" and section 15(4) prohibited a "common descriptive name" from becoming incontestible. Even with these ambiguities courts denied registration to generic marks. See, e.g., Application of G.D. Searle & Co., 360 F.2d 650 (CCPA 1966) ("the pill" for an oral contraceptive denied registration).

In the Trademark Revision Act of 1988 these provisions were amended so that the words "common descriptive name of an article or substance" became "the generic name for the goods or services".

2. A significant episode in the development of the generic mark doctrine involved the famous "Monopoly" board game. The game was invented and sold by Parker Brothers beginning in 1935 under the registered mark "Monopoly". General Mills purchased Parker Brothers. In 1973 Anti–Monopoly Inc. began selling a board game called "Anti–Monopoly". General Mills claimed trademark infringement. Twice the trial judge upheld the "Monopoly" mark and found an infringement. Twice the trial court was reversed. Anti–Monopoly, Inc. v. General Mills Fun Group, 684 F.2d 1316 (9th Cir.1982), cert. denied 459 U.S. 1227 (1983) (citing earlier decisions). The Ninth Circuit struggled with whether "Monopoly" was a source indicator or whether it was the generic name of the product. As in *Kellogg,* the product, here the board game, was unique in that it differed from other similar products. The question was whether "Monopoly" was its own genus or whether it was part of the genus "board games" or "real estate trading games". Finding the game its own genus and purporting to apply the "primary significance test" announced in *Kellogg,* the court held that the issue was whether purchasers were motivated to purchase the product because of the product or the producer—did consumers want a board game named "Monopoly" or did they want a Parker Brothers board game? Relying on a survey that disclosed 65% of those surveyed wanted the game regardless of who made it, the court held the mark generic.

The reaction to the *Anti–Monopoly* decision was largely negative. See Greenbaum, Ginsburg, and Weinberg, A Proposal for Evaluating Genericism After "Anti–Monopoly", 73 Trademark Rep. 101 (1983): "[T]he relegation of MONOPOLY to a 'unique' product category presents an extreme exercise in 'sophistry', and a substantial misconception of the way goods are promoted and marketed. . . . Furthermore, if the product is its own 'genus', its trademark is virtually, by definition, generic." *Id.* at 109. See also, Zeisel, The Surveys That Broke Monopoly, 50 U.Chi.L.Rev. 896 (1983) which suggests that the surveys relied upon by the majority were flawed and also argues that Monopoly should not be a 'genus': "It would seem that before anyone can demand that a trade name be cancelled because it had become generic, a genus must have come into existence, that is a real genus of at least two members." *Id.* at 908–909.

Congress reversed the *Anti–Monopoly* decision for Lanham Act purposes by adding the last two sentences in section 14(c) and the last sentence in the definition of "abandonment" in section 45. The legislative history describes the purposes of these amendments as follows:

> (a) Clarify that a mark may have a "dual purpose" of identifying goods and services and indicating the source of the goods and services; (b) Clarify that a mark may serve to identify a unique product or service so long as the mark serves also to identify a single source of the product or service; (c) Clarify that identification of a mark with a source does not require that the identity of a producer or producers be known by the consumer; and (d) Prohibit the use of the "motivation test" in determining genericism, and reaffirm the use of the "primary significance" test. U.S.Cong. & Admin.News, 98th Cong., Second Sess. 5718, 5725 (1984).

3. Does the *Canfield* decision successfully resolve the problem of trademarks used on unique products? For Judge Becker's test to apply the product must first differ from the established product class and second, the product name must be descriptive of the differentiating characteristic. Should the test for whether a product is its own genus depend on what the producer calls it? If Canfield had called the product "Glop X" would the product have then been a species of the genus diet soft drinks?

4. Do you agree with Judge Becker's attack on the consumer understanding test and the surveys that support it. If consumers attach *both* a generic and a source meaning to a term what result should follow as to protection of the mark? If 30% of consumers think the mark is generic and 60% think it is a brand name? The *Teflon* type survey discussed in footnote 16 is probably the most widely used survey technique currently employed in generic mark cases. Does it get close enough?

5. If you were counsel to a company about to market a game or a soft drink that had the potential for becoming as popular as "Monopoly" or "Chocolate Fudge Soda", what advice would you give regarding the naming and promotion of the product?

6. *Generic Marks and the Constitution.* Is there a constitutional dimension to the protection of generic marks? In the Amateur Sports Act, 36 U.S. C.A. § 380, Congress granted the United States Olympic Committee exclusive rights to use "for purposes of trade" or to promote "any theatrical exhibition, athletic performance, or competition" the Olympic symbols or the word "Olympic". In San Francisco Arts & Athletics Inc. v. United States Olympic

Committee, 483 U.S. 522 (1987), the Committee sought to prohibit the petitioner from promoting the "Gay Olympic Games". The petitioner argued the word "Olympic" was generic and not protectible, that the petitioner's use did not result in consumer confusion, and that protection in this context violated the first amendment. The United States Supreme Court interpreted the act as not requiring the Committee to show confusion but found no constitutional objection to the protection accorded:

> Because Congress reasonably could conclude that the USOC has distinguished the word "Olympic" through its own efforts, Congress' decision to grant the USOC a limited property right in the word "Olympic" falls within the scope of trademark law protections, and thus certainly within constitutional bounds.

The majority of the Court also found the absence of a requirement of confusion was not constitutionally objectionable in this case because the speech regulated was commercial speech and Congress had a legitimate interest in protecting not only the commercial interests of the Committee but also the "broader public interest" in promoting the Olympic Games. In dissent, Justice Brennan argued the absence of traditional elements of trademark law gave the Committee control over the word in a broad range of noncommercial contexts which infringed upon first amendment values.

IN RE SEATS

United States Court of Appeals for the Federal Circuit, 1985.
757 F.2d 274.

[The applicant sought to register the mark "Seats" as a service mark for a ticket reservation service arguing that the mark had become distinctive under 2(f). The Trademark Trial and Appeal Board made two findings. It first found the mark so inherently descriptive as to be incapable of functioning as a trademark and denied registration without regard to the evidence of distinctiveness. However the Board also found that if it had considered the evidence it would have found the mark "distinctive". Registration was denied.]

MARKEY, CHIEF JUDGE.

* * *

In discussing "incapability" however, the Board stated first the view that SEATS was so highly descriptive that "it should remain in the public domain available for all to use in describing service activities of this kind." The Board then gave as its reasons: (1) that "a common term or descriptor for some central or distinctive characteristic" may be "incapable"; (2) that "tickets" or "reservations" are such apt names for the "central commodity handled via" the services that *those terms* (for which registration was *not* being sought) would be "incapable"; (3) that the dictionary defines "seat" as a right evidenced by a "ticket"; (4) that in common parlance "seats" is used as a synonym for "tickets" or "reservations"; (5) that Seats thus deals in "seats" as much as in "tickets" or "reservations"; and (6) that *"all three terms"* are so descriptive that they "must remain freely available for competitive use". (Emphasis added.) Though, as above indicated, the Board recognized that if the registration here sought were issued others could still use "seats" descriptively in presenting the same services, it said that fact does not "remove the basic infirmities of source identification we have found". Continuing its focus on synonyms, the Board added: "Nor would it be desirable to rescue *all such terms* from the bars of 'registrability' by a rationalization that descriptive usage of *such words* remains available to others." (Emphasis added.)

Tendering a broad attack on the concept of "incapability", Seats argues strenuously that this court should overrule any predecessor court holdings that registration may be refused on a finding of "incapability" *without* considering evidence of acquired distinctiveness. In the alternative, Seats suggests that if courts may do that when the mark is "the common descriptive name" or "generic name" of the product or service, it should not be extended to situations where, as here, the Board found the mark descriptive of only "some central or distinctive characteristic" of the product or service. In any event, says Seats, the decision should rest on the facts of each case and the facts of record here establish its right to the registration it seeks under the provisions of § 2(f) of the statute.

In arguing for the demise of the notion that a term may be so generic or descriptive as to preclude forever its acquisition of trademark or service mark significance, Seats cites 3 Callmann, Unfair Competition, Trademarks & Monopolies, § 18.03 (4th Ed.1983); Folsom and Teply, *Trademarked Generic Words*, 89 Yale L.J. 1323 (1980), Gilson, Trademark Protection and Practice, pp. 17–19 (Supp.1984); 3 Callmann, Unfair Competition, Trademarks and Monopolies, p. 74 (Cumm.Supp.1982). Those writers suggest the need for courts to view all the evidence, however strong be the improbability that the mark under consideration may acquire trademark or service mark significance, and for courts to abandon *a priori* theories of what may or may not be possible. In essence, the cited commentators suggest that courts which have found marks "incapable" should have based their holdings on failure of the evidence to establish distinctiveness in the face of the genericness or descriptiveness of the mark.

* * *

Strong as are the attacks of writers on judicial creation of the concept of "incapability", and attractive as is the proposition that judicial decisions should rest on the facts of record and not on some broad notion or proposition contrary to those facts * * * we need not and accordingly do not decide in this case the general question of whether the Board may ever in future cases refuse to consider evidence of acquired distinctiveness.

* * *

The Board did not find that SEATS was generic. Nor could it have so found. The term "seats" may be generic in relation to chairs or couches or bleachers. It is clearly not generic to reservation services. Contrary to the Board's statement, Seats is not selling seats, as would for example a furniture merchant, but is selling a reservation service, and consideration of whether generic terms are *per se* unregistrable, * * * is not here involved.

It is equally clear that SEATS is not "the common descriptive name" of reservation services (assuming the quoted phrase has a meaning different from "generic"). That is true when purchasers of the services will be seated and when "standing room" is involved. Nor did the Board find that SEATS was the common descriptive name of the services involved (as stated above, it did find the mark merely descriptive of the product and function under § 2(e)(1)). On the contrary, the Board recognized that issuance of the registration here sought would not deprive others of the use of "seats" in connection with such services. Competitors would remain free to advertise "seats are available", "balcony seats—$12.00", "reserve your seats through us", etc, and theatres may employ "SEATS" in advertisements and on box offices and ticket windows.

In this application, Seats seeks registration under § 2(f) and has filed what the Board described as extensive evidence of acquired distinctiveness. The Board has found that evidence sufficient to establish "acquired distinctiveness." We cannot say on the record before us that that finding is clearly erroneous. The Board was at liberty to have found that evidence insufficient to have established an acquired distinctiveness, in light of what it considered an over-balancing descriptiveness content in the mark sought to be registered. It appeared to reach its ultimate conclusion, however, on the ground that other terms, which it considered synonymous, could not by any evidence have been shown to have acquired distinctiveness. Whether terms not sought to be registered could or could not acquire distinctiveness is irrelevant where, as here, the claim is that the mark sought to be registered has acquired distinctiveness and the Board has found that the evidence establishes the truth of that claim.

⇒ Seats was protectable

NOTES

1. *Generic Marks and Secondary Meaning.* In re Seats is illustrative of the difficulty courts have had as to whether the user of a mark believed to be generic can show that the mark has acquired secondary meaning. On the one hand there is something circular in refusing evidence on the point since if the baseline question is how consumers use the mark, evidence that they attribute source characteristics to the mark cuts against a finding it is generic. On the other hand the courts are reluctant to give ownership rights to a mark that appears to be essential to those who wish to compete in the underlying product market.

2. In American Aloe Corp. v. Aloe Creme Laboratories, Inc., 420 F.2d 1248 (7th Cir.), cert. denied 400 U.S. 820 (1970), the issue was whether the mark "Aloe Essence" infringed the mark "Alo–Hands" when both were used on cosmetics and the main ingredient of each was aloe, a gel of the aloe vera plant. The Seventh Circuit in denying protection became categorical:

The case is unlike Coca–Cola Co. v. Koke Co. of America, 254 U.S. 143 (1920) where the term Coke or Coca was originally descriptive of the extract of Coca leaves, or cocaine contained in the plant, but which lost this generic sense when the plaintiff was compelled to remove any effective cocaine from the product, after which Coca or Coke acquired a purely secondary meaning. Neither is this case controlled by those decisions which have found that exact copies or phonetic equivalents infringe purely suggestive names which have acquired trade name significance, such as Douglas Laboratories Corp. v. Copper Tan, Inc., 210 F.2d 453 (2nd Cir.1954) which said "copper tone" for sun tan lotion was suggestive rather than descriptive, and Orange Crush Co. v. California Crushed Fruit Co., 297 F. 892 (D.C.Cir.1924) which said "Crush" was not descriptive of a soft drink and was not used in its generic sense; nor is it in the same class with those which hold that terms having a general descriptive but not denominative sense acquired secondary meaning. Keller Products, Inc. v. Rubber Linings Corp., 213 F.2d 382, 47 A.L.R.2d 1108 (7th Cir.1954) (Tub Cove v. Tub Kove); Speaker v. Shaler Co., 87 F.2d 985 (7th Cir.1937) (Hot Patches v. Hot Patches—for vulcanizing products); Barton v. Rex–Oil Co., Inc., 29 F.2d 474 (3rd Cir.1928) (Dynashine v. Dye & Shine—for shoe polish). It must also be distinguished from the Supreme Court's decision in Armstrong Paint & Varnish Works v. Nu–Enamel Corp., 305 U.S. 315 (1939) where the essentially descriptive and denominative term "nu-enamel" had acquired a secondary meaning at least partially through its widespread application to products other than enamel—such as paint brushes.

This case is properly classified with those where the term in question was the common name for the article sold and hence denominative of that article regardless of source. Kellogg Co. v. National Biscuit Co., 305 U.S. 111 (1938) (shredded wheat); Henry Heide, Inc. v. George Ziegler Co., 354 F.2d 574 (7th Cir.1965) (ju-jubes); Donald F. Duncan, Inc. v. Royal Tops Manufacturing Co., 343 F.2d 655 (7th Cir. 1965) (yo-yos) and particularly with those cases where the term was denominative of the prime or distinguishing ingredient in the product. Compare LeBlume Import Co. v. Coty, 293 F. 344 (2nd Cir.1923) (Lorigan v. L'Origan de Coty—for perfume); Pinaud, Inc. v. Huebschman, 27 F.2d 531 (E.D.N.Y.1928) (Lilas De France v. Lilas De France—for perfume); Wells & Richardson Co. v. Siegel, Cooper & Co., 106 F. 77 (N.D.Ill.1900) (Celery Compound v. Celery Compound) with Dixi–Cola Laboratories, Inc. v. Coca–Cola Co., 117 F.2d 352 (4th Cir. 1941) (cola v. cola—for soft drink containing extract of cola nut). It is clear from an examination of the cases that while the test may be stated in the same language in both types of cases, it is much more difficult to establish secondary meaning in a denominative term (as used herein) than in a purely descriptive one.

In Aloe Creme Laboratories, Inc. v. Milsan, Inc., 423 F.2d 845 (5th Cir. 1970), cert. denied 398 U.S. 928 (1970), the Fifth Circuit also refused to protect the "Alo" mark but rejected the Seventh Circuit's enhanced burden of proof for secondary meaning: "By placing 'Alo' in [the denominative] category, the [Seventh Circuit] denied secondary meaning without the necessity of discussing any evidence relevant to the claim. * * * A claim of secondary meaning presents a question of fact. * * * We agree with [the Seventh Circuit] insofar as it holds that the evidentiary burden, necessary to establish secondary meaning, is substantial where the mark applied to an article designates a principal ingredient desired by the public." See also, W.E. Bassett Co. v. Revlon, Inc., 435 F.2d 656 (2d Cir.1970) holding that for generic marks the user must show he actually succeeded in making the mark source identifying whereas where a term is merely descriptive an inference of secondary meaning is enough.

3. Opinions relied upon by the Board in *Seats* have used the term "de facto secondary meaning" to describe a circumstance in which a mark may have developed some source identifying power among consumers but nonetheless the mark cannot be protected because it is generic—it cannot acquire "de jure secondary meaning". See Miller Brewing Co. v. Falstaff Brewing Corp., 655 F.2d 5 (1st Cir.1981) ("Lite" for beer); Weiss Noodle Co. v. Golden Cracknel & Speciality Co., 290 F.2d 845 (CCPA 1961) (affirmed cancellation of "Ha-Lush-Ka" for egg noodle product because it was the common Hungarian name for the product). The "de facto secondary meaning" doctrine is explored in Treece & Stephenson, A Look at American Trademark Law, 29 Sw.L.J. 547 (1975).

4. Some cases seemed to suggest that there is an automatic loss of trademark rights for any name applied to a patented article once the patent expires. An important case was Singer Mfg. Co. v. June Mfg. Co., 163 U.S. 169 (1896), relied on in *Kellogg*. The Court in *Singer* held the mark "Singer" as applied to sewing machines was generic because the patents expired.

Judge Learned Hand, however, disagreed: "The single question, as I view it, in all these cases, is merely one of fact: What do the buyers understand by the word for whose use the parties are contending. * * * The fact that it was patented until 1917 is indeed a material circumstance, but it is not necessarily controlling." Bayer Co. v. United Drug Co., 272 Fed. 505 (2d Cir.1921) (holding that the coined word "Aspirin" had become generic to the consuming public but not to manufacturing chemists, retail druggist and physicians to whom "Aspirin" indicated the plaintiff as source of the product.).

GENERIC MARK CONTROVERSIES

EASTERN AIR LINES, INC. v. NEW YORK AIR LINES, INC.

559 F.Supp. 1270 (S.D.N.Y.1983).

[Beginning in 1961 Eastern Air Lines began offering a "shuttle" service between Boston, New York, and Washington, D.C. As aggressively marketed by EAL, the "shuttle" provided hourly flights between the cities, on-board ticketing, no reservation requirement, and a separate shuttle terminal. Prior to the air controllers' strike in 1981, EAL also guaranteed seat availability on the shuttle by maintaining back-up aircraft for unexpected demand. EAL obtained a Lanham Act registration for the service mark "Air-Shuttle" in 1966. (Eastern subsequently sold this service to Trump Air.)

In 1980 in response to deregulation of the airline industry, New York Air began competing with the EAL shuttle. In 1982 NYA launched a comparative advertising campaign designed to attract EAL customers. NYA's Chief Executive Officer Mike Levine instructed his advertising agency to "Put it to the shuttle". The campaign described the NYA service as a "shuttle". The advertisements stressed NYA's on board amenities of free food, drinks and more comfort and suggested that NYA's service had everything EAL's service had and more. (The NYA service was subsequently sold to Pan American World Airways).

EAL brought suit alleging trademark infringement for the use of the word "shuttle" to describe NYA's service and for false advertising in that NYA suggested its service had all of the features of EAL's "Air-Shuttle" when in fact it did not, i.e., back-up aircraft. NYA claimed the "Air-Shuttle" mark was generic and denied the false advertising claims. After tracing the use of the word "shuttle" from the Bible, through Shakespeare and Whitman to modern transportation advertising the court concluded:]

While it is clear that the word "shuttle" does have some of the connotations of EAL's service, neither these features nor EAL itself has become the "principal significance" of the word * * *. A shuttle is still viewed as "a train, bus or plane making short, frequent trips between two points." The American Heritage Dictionary of the English Language 1969, at 1201.

The fact that the word has certain connotations does not make it any the less generic as these connotations have not altered the primary meaning of the word. As NYA's word expert testified, the development of a specialized meaning does not necessarily encroach upon the general meaning or change it.

Even if the word "shuttle" were found to be descriptive instead of generic, the mark would not be entitled to trademark protection as the survey made by EAL failed to show that it has acquired a secondary meaning. Only 10 per cent of the individuals surveyed identified the word "Air-Shuttle" with EAL. Not only is this percentage too insignificant to establish that the primary significance of the term is the producer and not the product, but the mere fact that a respondent mentioned "Eastern" when he heard the word "shuttle" does not suggest that "shuttles" are identified with Eastern. All that it demonstrates is that a likely response to any generic word is the name of the best known producer or manufacturer of that product. This evidence further demonstrates that the term "shuttle" is generic. * * *

Yet, the principle that all uses of the word "shuttle" by NYA are not prohibited does not mean that NYA can indiscriminately use the word in its advertising. Even though the word "shuttle" is generic, it has come to have certain connotations embedded in the mind of the public through twenty-two years of advertising by EAL, as established by surveys, regarding guaranteed seating, back-up plane service, lack of a reservation requirement, frequent hourly service, on-board ticketing, and a separate shuttle terminal. NYA's use of the word may not be used in any way to mislead the public into believing that NYA also provides these features if it does not. Misleading effects from its advertising could result from either the format of the advertisements or from the absence of disclaimers.

* * *

Although a party cannot block others from using a generic term by investing in that term, neither a court nor a competitor can ignore the effects of such investment on the public's understanding of the term when deciding whether advertising is misleading.

*   *   *

EAL introduced survey evidence of the reactions to one set of NYA's advertisements. Five hundred one individuals who had flown between LaGuardia and Washington and/or LaGuardia and Boston at least once during the past three years were interrogated in the survey. The advertisement evaluated in the survey listed, side-by-side, certain features of EAL's and NYA's services from LaGuardia to Washington, D.C. The side describing EAL was headed "What $65 buys on Eastern's shuttle" and lists only "A trip to Washington" followed by a substantial blank space opposite the promotional features of NYA's service. The side describing NYA's service is headed "What $45 buys on New York Air's shuttle" and lists a trip to Washington, flight attendants who attend, extra legroom, an assigned seat, free New York-style food, and free drinks, including a featured red and white wine of the month. In addition, this half of the advertisement lists NYA's flight schedule, details the fares, and informs the reader how to make a reservation.

The surveys have established that this type of advertisement misleads the public by suggesting that NYA furnishes the features of EAL's service as well as additions thereto—clearly an overrepresentation of NYA's service. *   *   *

Thus, it is well established by the canvas of the public that the type of advertising used by NYA that was the subject of the survey is misleading and thus liable to an injunction.

NOTE

New York Air changed its program and its advertising after the case. It implemented a "shuttle-shuttle"—a bus that provided bus service between New York Air and Eastern so that a passenger could get from one to the other in the event the New York Air flight was full or the passenger was late for the Eastern flight. It also scheduled its flights on the half-hour whereas Eastern's was on the hour. Eastern challenged the advertisements as in contempt of the prior order because they suggested that a person missing an Eastern flight was guaranteed a seat on New York Air even though that was not true. The court found the subsequent advertisement deceptive but failed to find a purposeful deception. Eastern Air Lines, Inc. v. New York Air Lines, Inc., 565 F.Supp. 800 (S.D.N.Y.1983).

MILLER BREWING CO. v. G. HEILEMAN BREWING CO., INC.

561 F.2d 75 (7th Cir.1977).

[In 1972 Miller Brewing acquired the registered mark "Lite" as applied to a low calorie beer which subsequently received consumer acceptance because it (is less filling) (tastes great)? In 1975 other breweries began selling "light" beer with reduced calories and Miller brought suit. The court reviewed the use of "light" in the beer industry to describe various characteristics including a beer's color, flavor, body, or alcoholic content and concluded the term was "generic or a common descriptive term when used with 'beer'."]

Miller argues that it uses the word as the name for "less filling, low calorie" beer, and that "light" has not heretofore been used in that sense. This argument fails for two reasons. First, "less filling" means essentially light in body and taste and not oppressive to the stomach, which is a common descriptive meaning of "light"; and, as Miller conceded in its brief, the caloric content of beer depends primarily on alcoholic content. Second, even if Miller had given its light beer a characteristic not found in other light beers, it could not acquire the exclusive right to use the common descriptive word "light" as a trademark for that beer. Other brewers whose beers have qualities that make them "light" as that word has commonly been used remain free to call their beer "light." Otherwise a manufacturer could remove a common descriptive word from the public domain by investing his goods with an additional quality, thus gaining the exclusive right to call his wine "rosé," his whiskey "blended," or his bread "white."

The word "light," including its phonetic equivalent "lite," being a generic or common descriptive term as applied to beer, could not be exclusively appropriated by Miller as a trademark, "despite whatever promotional effort [Miller] may have expended to exploit it."

ANHEUSER–BUSCH, INC. v. THE STROH BREWERY CO.
750 F.2d 631 (8th Cir.1984).

[In 1983 Anheuser-Busch began marketing a low alcohol beer using the mark "LA". Shortly thereafter Stroh announced plans to market a low alcohol beer under the mark "Schaefer LA". Anheuser-Busch sued for trademark infringement; Stroh claimed the mark "LA" was generic and would become the "bar call" for this type of beer. Internal documents from Anheuser-Busch revealed that the company hoped to emulate the experience of Miller in use of the term "Lite" for low calorie beer. Even though the term "Lite" was declared generic, the extensive advertising by Miller had made "light" the bar call for low-calorie beer and Miller had obtained 57% of the market for low-calorie beer. Anheuser-Busch officers in selecting "LA" observed that "Anheuser-Busch has an opportunity to 'write the book' on the reduced alcohol segment in exactly the same way Miller did in the light beer segment * * *." The district court found the mark "LA" to be suggestive rather than generic and the Eighth Circuit affirmed.]

The court first examined National Conference of Bar Examiners v. Multistate Legal Studies, 692 F.2d 478 (7th Cir.1982) where the Seventh Circuit refused to protect the marks "Multistate Bar Examination" and "MBE" used by the National Conference of Bar Examiners against the use of the marks "Preliminary Multistate Bar Examination" and "PMBE" as used by a private corporation providing review courses and practice examinations in preparation for the multistate bar examination. The court there held: "Under settled trademark law if the components of a trade name are common descriptive terms, a combination of such terms retains that quality. We note further that plaintiffs also use the initials "MBE" to designate their test is of no consequence. Abbreviations for generic or common descriptive phrases must be treated similarly." The Eighth Circuit agreed with the district court that it was significant that Anheuser-Busch had not used the accompanying phrase "low alcohol" and thus did not fit the *National Conference* analysis:]

Rather, the question in the instant case is whether, when a party seeks to protect initials alone which are also the initials of a generic or descriptive phrase, the initials are to be equated with that phrase. The key issue, as the cases demonstrate, is the nature of the relationship or tie between the initials and the generic or descriptive phrase and the relationship or tie between the initials and the product. As the district court properly held, if some operation of the imagination is required to connect the initials with the product, the initials cannot be equated with the generic phrase but are suggestive in nature, thereby rendering them protectable."

[The court dismissed the evidence that Anheuser-Busch hoped to acquire the "bar call" designation. Given that marks are judged by the reaction of the consumer public, "such matters are not relevant to the trademark status of LA . . .."]

BRIGHT, CIRCUIT JUDGE, dissenting.

The record reveals that consumers may not now associate LA with low alcohol only because this category of beer has only recently come on the market and much of the general public does not even know of its existence. Although Anheuser-Busch does not display the term "low alcohol" on the LA label, and primarily promotes LA as the brand name, the accompanying advertising does note the low alcoholic content of the beer. Little doubt exists, in my view, that LA will come to be synonymous with low alcohol in the average consumer's mind after a few months of heavy advertising. This belief is reinforced by the appearance of numerous articles in newspapers and magazines since the beginning of 1984 explaining that the term "LA" stands for low alcohol. This kind of association tends to confirm that the informed consumer exposed to the new product will more likely than not equate LA primarily with low alcohol, rather than associate the letters as an Anheuser-Busch trademark.

NOTES

1. Other marks that have recently suffered at the hands of the generic doctrine include "Toll House" for chocolate chip cookies, Nestle Co., Inc. v. Chester's Market, Inc., 571 F.Supp. 763 (D.Conn.1983), and "Cream of Wheat", Nabisco Brands, Inc. v. The Quaker Oats Co., 547 F.Supp. 692 (D.N.J.1982).

2. The *Miller Brewing* decision has been criticized for expanding the generic category to include adjectives used in connection with nouns. 1 J. Gilson, Trademark Protection and Practice § 2.02 (Supp. June 1986). By categorizing adjectives as "generic" they cannot be protected even by showing secondary meaning. If they are regarded only as "merely descriptive" then protection remains theoretically possible. The Seventh Circuit recognized the problem in Henri's Food Products Inc. v. Tasty Snacks Inc., 817 F.2d 1303 (7th Cir.1987) where it was argued that "Tas–Tee Salad Dressing" was generic. The court distinguished *Miller Brewing* arguing that "light" used with beer describes a genus of beer whereas "tastee" used with salad dressing describes the *quality* of salad dressings generally. "There really can be no suggestion that 'tasty dressings' is a kind or type or subcategory of dressing such as, for example, French dressing."

3. The *Miller Brewing* ("Lite Beer") and *Anheuser-Busch* ("LA Beer") cases suggest that there may be some advantage to the owner of having its mark become generic. In G. Heileman Brewing Co. v. Anheuser–Busch Inc., 676 F.Supp. 1436 (E.D.Wis.1987) two competing brewers claimed that Anheuser–Busch was engaging in unfair competition and attempts to monopolize under the Sherman Act by claiming rights in the "LA" mark. The court rejected the claim finding that Anheuser–Busch in prosecuting these trademark claims "was primarily motivated by a desire to obtain . . . . relief rather than by a desire to achieve anticompetitive goals. . . . ."

4. The *Eastern Airlines Case* suggests that the first user of a generic term can through advertising set the standard for the generic product. Thus, "shuttle" has now become the generic term for the type of service Eastern Airlines provides and doctrines of false advertising are available to protect against the term being used to refer, at least deceptively, to flights that do not offer similar services. If the generic mark doctrine is designed in part to protect competition, should the definition of "shuttle" be so limited?

5. Consumer surveys are playing an increasingly important role in the generic mark cases as well as in other aspects of trademark litigation. Since trademark law is built on premises involving consumer reactions to identifying devices, it seems wholly appropriate that these reactions should be sampled. Although many early courts refused to permit introduction of survey evidence under the hearsay rule, most modern courts, as the *Anti-Monopoly* opinion demonstrates, permit their introduction either holding they are not hearsay or that they fit the exception for present state of mind, attitude, or belief. Prior to admission, the surveys must be shown to be trustworthy. As stated in Toys "R" US, Inc. v. Canarsie Kiddie Shop, Inc., 559 F.Supp. 1189, 1205 (E.D.N.Y. 1983):

> The trustworthiness of surveys depends upon foundation evidence that (1) the "universe" was properly defined, (2) a representative sample of that universe was selected, (3) the questions to be asked of interviewees were framed in a clear, precise and non-leading manner, (4) sound interview procedures were followed by competent interviewers who had no knowledge of the litigation or the purpose for which the survey was conducted, (5) the data gathered was accurately reported, (6) the data was analyzed in accordance with accepted statistical principles and (7) objectivity of the entire process was assured. Failure to satisfy one or more of these criteria may lead to exclusion of the survey
> * * *.

6. What must a company do to protect itself from a claim that its mark has become generic? It has been reported that the Coca-Cola Company maintains a "Trade Research Department" consisting of 25 investigators who order "Coke" in restaurants and send the drink served back to headquarters for chemical analysis. The company also has an aggressive litigation policy against restaurants serving Coke substitutes. Coca-Cola has sued 800 retailers since 1945. The company asserts the policy is necessary to prevent its mark from becoming generic. Some retailers assert that the policy actually is designed to force restaurant owners into serving Coke since liability for infringement arises even in the absence of intent to infringe and as one owner was quoted: "There's just no way we can guarantee on a busy night—when as many as 2,000 people cram into our bar—that one of our waitresses or waiters won't forget to warn a customer who asks for a rum and Coke that we serve rum and Pepsi." Wall St.J., March 9, 1978, at 1, col. 4. The Coca-Cola Company survived an antitrust attack against its trademark enforcement policies in Coca-Cola Co. v. Overland, Inc., 692 F.2d 1250 (9th Cir.1982). Summary judgment was awarded to Coca-Cola because Overland failed to provide evidence of attempted monopolization or of specific retailers who were influenced by the enforcement policy to switch to "Coke".

7. For literature on the economic foundation of the generic doctrine see Folsom & Teply, Trademarked Generic Words, 89 Yale Law J. 1323 (1980); Swann, The Economic Approach to Genericism: A Reply to Folsom and Teply, 70 Trademark Reporter 243 (1980); Folsom and Tepley, A Comparative View of the Law of Trademarked Generic Words, 6 Hastings Int'l and Comparative L.Rev. 1 (1982).

(C) GEOGRAPHIC MARKS

IN RE NANTUCKET, INC.

United States Court of Customs and Patent Appeals, 1982.
677 F.2d 95.

MARKEY, CHIEF JUDGE.

Nantucket, Inc. (Nantucket) appeals from a decision of the Trademark Trial and Appeal Board (board) affirming a refusal to register the mark NANTUCKET for men's shirts on the ground that it is "primarily geographically deceptively misdescriptive." In re Nantucket, Inc., 209 USPQ 868 (TTAB 1981). We reverse.

BACKGROUND

On March 13, 1978, Nantucket, based in North Carolina, filed application serial number 162,716 for registration of NANTUCKET for men's shirts on the principal register in the Patent and Trademark Office (PTO), alleging a date of first use of February 2, 1978.

Refusal to register was based on § 2(e)(2) of the Lanham Act, 15 U.S.C. § 1052(e)(2) * * *.

[Trademark Manual of Examining Procedure] § 1208.02 indicates that a mark is *primarily geographical,* inter alia, if it "is the name of a place which has general renown to the public at large and which is a place from which goods and services are known to emanate as a result of commercial activity."

The examiner, citing a dictionary definition of "Nantucket" as an island in the Atlantic Ocean south of Massachusetts, concluded that the mark NANTUCKET was either primarily geographically descriptive or primarily geographically deceptively misdescriptive, depending upon whether Nantucket's shirts did or did not come from Nantucket Island.

* * *

The board correctly notes that its test for registrability of geographic terms is "easy to administer" and "*minimizes* subjective determinations by eliminating any need to make unnecessary inquiry into the nebulous question of whether the public associates particular goods with a particular geographical area in applying Section 2(e)(2)." [Emphasis in original.] Ease-of-administration considerations aside, the board's approach does raise the question of whether public association of goods with an area must be considered in applying § 2(e)(2). That question is one of first impression in this court. We answer in the affirmative.

The board's test rests mechanistically on the one question of whether the mark is recognizable, at least to some large segment of the public, as the name of a geographical area. NANTUCKET is such. That ends the board's test. Once it is found that the mark is the name of a known place, i.e., that it has "a readily recognizable geographic meaning," the next question, whether applicant's goods do or do not come from that place, becomes irrelevant under the board's test, for if they do, the mark is "primarily geographically descriptive"; if they don't, the mark is "primarily geographically deceptively misdescriptive." Either way, the result is the same, for the mark must be denied registration on the principal register unless resort can be had to § 2(f).

The Statute

One flaw in the board's test resides in its factoring out the nature of applicant's goods, in contravention of § 2(e)(2)'s requirement that the mark be evaluated "when applied to the goods of the applicant," and that registration be denied only when the mark is geographically descriptive or deceptively misdescriptive "of them" (the goods).

Another flaw in the board's test lies in its failure to give appropriate weight to the presence of "deceptively" in § 2(e)(2). If the goods do not originate in the geographic area denoted by the mark, the mark might in a vacuum be characterized as geographically misdescriptive, but the statutory characterization required for denial of registration is "geographically *deceptively* misdescriptive." [Emphasis supplied.] Before that statutory characterization may be properly applied, there must be a reasonable basis for believing that purchasers are likely to be deceived.

* * *

Section 2(e)(2) provides that registration shall not be refused *unless* the mark is primarily geographically deceptively misdescriptive of the goods. The only indication of record that NANTUCKET is primarily a geographical term resides in dictionary listings referring to Nantucket Island as a summer resort and former whaling center. There is no evidence of record to support a holding that the mark NANTUCKET as applied to men's shirts is "deceptively misdescriptive." There is no indication that the purchasing public would expect men's shirts to have their origin in Nantucket when seen in the market place with NANTUCKET on them. Hence buyers are not likely to be deceived, and registration cannot be refused on the ground that the mark is "primarily geographically deceptively misdescriptive."

Accordingly, the decision of the board is reversed.

Reversed.

NIES, JUDGE, concurring.

I join the court's holding that there must be an indication that "the purchasing public would expect men's shirts to have their origin in Nantucket when seen in the marketplace with NANTUCKET on them." Moreover, I agree that on the present record the board's decision holding that NANTUCKET for men's shirts is "primarily geographically deceptively misdescriptive" must be reversed. I choose to concur, however, because I reach the same conclusion from a different direction, and because the court leaves open what the PTO must show to make a prima facie case under § 2(e)(2) with respect to this application.

Appellant had urged that the court adopt the rule that a goods/place association can be established under § 2(e)(2) only if the place identified by the geographic name claimed as a mark was "noted for" the goods, like IDAHO for potatoes or PARIS for perfume. The standard of registrability enunciated by the court has not been restricted to such a stringent test. To have done so would have created as rigid a rule in favor of registration as the board had used to deny registration. If a geographic name were arbitrary in the absence of a reputation for the goods, any trader who is the *first* to use any geographic name for particular goods would, thereby, appropriate it to his exclusive use. Moreover, the rationale advanced by appellant is not limited to geographic names of places where the likelihood of future commercial exploitation by others is small but would be equally applicable if the claimed mark for shirts were CHICAGO. The answer to the basic question of public association of goods with a place, i.e., geographic descriptiveness, cannot be decided on this simplistic basis.

* * *

A geographic term may be used in a manner which is (1) inherently distinctive, which includes arbitrary and suggestive usage, (2) generic, (3) descriptive, (4) deceptively misdescriptive, or, (5) deceptive. Different consequences flow from the finding of what is the appropriate category or categories for the mark, which to some extent overlap. In any event, such a determination can only be made by consideration of the specific goods on which the name or term is used. In every case the issue which must be resolved is: What meaning, if any, does the term convey to the public with respect to the goods on which the name is used?

In resolving the question of registrability of geographic names, the development of the law with respect to protection of such terms provides guidance. * * * Thus, we must start with the concept that a geographic name of a place of business is a descriptive term when used on the goods of that business. There is a public goods/place association, in effect, presumed.

However, as with other terms which are descriptive when first used, it came to be recognized that through substantially exclusive and extensive use, a merchant might develop a protectible goodwill in such a geographically descriptive name upon proof that the name ceased being informational to the public and came to indicate a source of goods. Thus, if a manufacturer located in Chicago were to display the name CHICAGO on his shirts, for example, it has been the law for over a century that he could prevent another's subsequent use only if he could establish "secondary meaning" in the term. Until secondary meaning has been developed in a descriptive term, the public cannot be confused that the term indicates source in a particular user and others are free to make comparable use of the term. While a merchant in Chicago will not be deprived of his right to use the name in a non-trademark display if another acquires trademark rights in CHICAGO, he does become limited in the choice of marks for related goods or services and must operate, thereafter, under the constraints of avoiding likelihood of confusion with CHICAGO per se for shirts. * * *

Since the mark CHICAGO is, thus, unregistrable even to a Chicago manufacturer who is the first to use that name for shirts without a showing of distinctiveness, one cannot accept, as urged by appellant, that the law recognizes better rights, ipso facto, in a company not located there which happens to be the first to use that name for shirts. It is simply illogical to say that CHICAGO is descriptive of shirts if the manufacturer is located in Chicago, but arbitrary, if he is not located there. The public is not aware of the actual locations of most businesses. The public is aware of trade practice and makes, or is presumed likely to make, a goods/place association in either instance. Nor is it any less objectionable to a Chicago merchant if the term is used by a non-local rather than another local merchant. * * * Arguably any nondescriptive use, even if arbitrary, is, in a sense, misdescriptive. Accordingly, the word "deceptively" was inserted before "misdescriptive" in both § 2(e)(1) and § 2(e)(2), again, to avoid technical rejections of applications to register marks such as IVORY for soap, or ALASKA for bananas.

Thus, where usage would be understood by the public as arbitrary, i.e., misdescriptive but not "deceptively" so, the term or name claimed as a mark is registrable without a showing of distinctiveness. On the other hand, if the public would perceive a misdescriptive use of a geographic name as a descriptive use, the claimed mark is deceptively misdescriptive and unregistrable without secondary meaning. That a place is "noted for" goods is only one circumstance under which a geographic name would be barred by § 2(e)(2). "Noted for" and "public association" thus, are not equivalent tests for determining public goods/place association.

* * *

Concerning the authority cited by the appellant, it is apparent that the issue of whether the public is likely to believe a particular geographic name is informational when it appears on a product has been lost sight of in some decisions, which have applied mechanical rules wholly inappropriate to trademark cases. A geographic name is not unprotectible or unregistrable because it can be labelled a geographic name, but because it tells the public something about the product or the producer about which his competitor also has a right to inform the public. Thus, the names of places devoid of commercial activity are arbitrary usage.

* * *

It is also apparent that some opinions fail to grasp that the defense of geographic descriptiveness, put forth by an alleged infringer, should be available only to one with a legitimate personal interest in use of the name. * * *

* * *

NOTES

1. The common law also denied protection to geographic marks unless they acquired secondary meaning. In American Waltham Watch Co. v. United States Watch Co., 173 Mass. 85, 53 N.E. 141 (1899) the plaintiff, the first producer of "Waltham Watches" in Waltham, Massachusetts, proved secondary meaning in a suit against another Waltham manufacturer and obtained an injunction prohibiting the defendant from any use of the terms "Waltham Watches" in its advertising or from any indication that it was located in Waltham without an accompanying statement clearly distinguishing its watches from those of the plaintiff. The Supreme Judicial Court of Massachusetts affirmed. In 1963 the Seventh Circuit upheld a Federal Trade Commission order against the successor to the plaintiff who had purchased the good-will of the plaintiff but now sold imported watches under the name "Waltham". The Commission order required that consumers be given notice that watches were no longer made by the original company in Waltham. Waltham Watch Co. v. FTC, 318 F.2d 28 (7th Cir.1963).

2. *Lanham Act Provisions.* Which opinion in *Nantucket* provides the best analytical framework for application of the Lanham Act to geographic marks? Is it easier to focus on the mark in the context of the market or is it better to examine whether other users have any interest in preventing registration of the mark?

The *Nantucket* case was applied in In re Loew's Theatres, Inc., 769 F.2d 764 (Fed.Cir.1985) to deny registration to the mark "Durango" for chewing tobacco because it was "primarily geographically deceptively misdescriptive". To deny registration the PTO "must show only a reasonable basis for concluding that the public is likely to believe the mark identifies the place from which the goods originate and that the goods do not come from there."

In addition to § 2(e), the "deceptive" mark provision of § 2(a) has been applied to geographically misdescriptive marks. For application of a "materiality" test to distinguish between marks that are "geographically deceptively misdescriptive" under § 2(e) and those that are "deceptive" under § 2(a) see In re House of Windsor, 221 U.S.P.Q. 53 (TTAB 1983) (denying registration to the mark "Bahia" for cigars under § 2(a) because the registrant had no connection with the Bahia province of Brazil which is known for its tobacco.):

> If the evidence shows that the geographical area named in the mark is an area sufficiently renowned to lead purchasers to make a goods-place association but the record does not show that goods like applicant's or goods related to applicant's are a principal product of that geographical area, then the deception will most likely be found not to be material and the mark, therefore, not deceptive. On the other hand, if there is evidence that goods like applicant's or goods related to applicant's are a principal product of the geographical area named by the mark, then the deception will most likely be found material and the mark, therefore, deceptive.

3. *Certification Marks.* Section 45, 15 U.S.C. § 1127, defines, and section 4, 15 U.S.C. § 1054, permits to be registered certification marks "including indications of regional origins." Section 14(e), 15 U.S.C. § 1064(e), provides specific grounds for cancellation of certification marks. A certification mark, as its name suggests, is used to certify that goods produced by someone other than the mark's owner meets certain standards or comes from some particular geographic region. And § 2(e) of the Act which prevents registration of geographic marks specifically exempts from its provisions marks of regional origin registered as certification marks.

In Community of Roquefort v. William Faehndrich, Inc., 303 F.2d 494 (2d Cir.1962) the plaintiff, a municipality, owned the registered certification mark "Roquefort" for a sheep's milk blue-mold cheese cured in caves in Roquefort, France. The defendant sold cheese not made in Roquefort as "Imported Roquefort Cheese". The decision analyzes the interplay between § 2(e) and the certification mark provisions. The mark "Roquefort" could have at least three separate connotations: (1) it could refer to the city of Roquefort in which it has geographic significance; (2) it could refer to cheese made in Roquefort, France by a variety of producers in which it could be used to certify such fact; or (3) it could refer to any sheep's milk blue mold cheese wherever produced. As the court observes, a geographic term "does not require a secondary meaning in order to qualify for registration as a certification mark. * * * On the other hand, a geographical name registered as a certification mark must continue to indicate the regional origin, mode of manufacture, etc. of the goods upon which it is used, just as a trade-mark must continue to identify a producer. * * * Therefore, if a geographical name which has been registered as a certification mark, identifying certain goods, acquires principal significance as a description of those goods, the rights cease to be incontestable * * * and the mark is subject to cancellation * * *." The court found no evidence that the "Roquefort" had become descriptive of all sheep milk blue-mold cheese wherever produced and found for the plaintiff.

See also Black Hills Jewelry Mfg. Co. v. Gold Rush, Inc., 633 F.2d 746 (8th Cir.1980) where three independent producers of "Black Hills Gold Jewelry" each located in the Black Hills area of South Dakota sued to enjoin the defendant from selling his jewelry as "Black Hills Gold Jewelry" when it was made outside the region. The court affirmed the district court's holding that the plaintiffs were not entitled to exclusive use of the mark because there was no showing of secondary meaning, i.e., that the term referred to these three producers. Similarly the court refused to consider a common law certification mark because certification marks are owned by someone *other than the producers of the goods*. However, the court did affirm an injunction against the defendant finding (1) that the mark was not generic as to the particular design of the jewelry but did retain geographical significance, and (2) the defendant's use of the term for jewelry not made in the region violated section 43(a) of the Lanham Act.

4. *Collective Marks.* Certification marks should be distinguished from collective marks, the latter being marks that are adopted by organizations to identify their members or the goods and services of their members. See 15 U.S.C. § 1127. Collective marks, like certification marks, are owned by the organization but used by others. Collective marks may signify that the particular seller of goods is a member of a cooperative or other organization. In noncommercial settings, fraternal names or symbols indicating membership in an organization would be a collective mark. In theory certification marks specify that the goods or services meet particular standards or have particular characteristics while collective marks identify only membership. However, to the extent membership in an organization requires certain attributes, the line between the two becomes uncertain. Does it make a difference whether something is classified as a certification or collective mark? See, Opticians Association of America v. Independent Opticians of America, Inc., 734 F.Supp. 1171 (D.N.J.1990). See also, Restatement (Third) of Unfair Competition § 10, § 11, Comment *b* (Tent. Draft No. 2, 1990).

(D) PERSONAL NAMES

TAYLOR WINE CO., INC. v. BULLY HILL VINEYARDS, INC.

United States Court of Appeals, Second Circuit, 1978.
569 F.2d 731.

GURFEIN, CIRCUIT JUDGE:

[The grandfather of defendant Walter S. Taylor began a winery on an estate called Bully Hill in 1878 and with others formed a partnership engaging in the wine business. The assets, other than Bully Hill, were sold during the grandfather's lifetime to the plaintiff, the Taylor Wine Company, which has marketed wine under the Taylor label since 1880 and has registered 13 Taylor trademarks. The Taylor trademarks came to identify the plaintiff company.

Walter S. Taylor purchased the Bully Hill estate in 1958 from strangers and in 1970 established the defendant company which produced wine under the name of Bully Hill. In 1977 defendant began marketing a new line of "Walter S. Taylor" wine. The name was prominently displayed on the labels with the statement "Owner of the

Estate" or "Owner of the Taylor Family Estate." Plaintiff sued for trademark infringement; the lower court enjoined Bully Hill from use of the word "Taylor" on any of its labeling, packaging, advertising or promotional materials.]

Appellant contends that its use of "Taylor" as a trademark does not infringe the appellee's trademarks because the appellant's wines are better and are not in actual competition with appellee's wines. It also urges us to say that the injunction is too broad, in any case, and that it would be enough if we made Bully Hill add some distinguishing words if it chooses to use Walter S. Taylor's own surname as a trademark.

This is not a case where a first comer seeks to save himself a place in a new market he has not yet entered by denying to a man the use of his own name in exploiting that market. Cf. S.C. Johnson & Son, Inc. v. Johnson, 116 F.2d 427 (2d Cir.1940). The wines of defendant and plaintiff compete in the same general market. It is a truism that every product has its own separate threshold for confusion of origin. Wine is a product whose quality is accepted by many simply on faith in the maker. They can perhaps identify the vintner better than the wine.

It is doubtless true that some wartime soldiers did bring back from Europe an inchoate taste for wine and for some of its nuances, and that other Americans have acquired a similar taste. Yet, the average American who drinks wine on occasion can hardly pass for a connoisseur of wines. He remains an easy mark for an infringer. Whether appellant's or appellee's wines are better is not the issue. Trespass upon the secondary meaning of the Taylor brand name, developed at great cost over the years, cannot be forgiven on the ground that subtlety of taste will avoid the confusion inherent in the overlapping labels and representations of origin.

We do not doubt that Walter S. Taylor, a former employee of the plaintiff, knew well the customer appeal of the Taylor name, nor that he chose to capitalize on the name as if his grandfather had left it to him as an inheritance. The only serious question we must meet is whether the injunction is too broad.

The conflict between a first comer who has given a secondary meaning (as well as trademark registration) to a family name, and a later comer who wishes to use his own true family name as a trademark in the same industry has been one of the more interesting issues in the law of trademark infringement. The problem is made more difficult when the second comer has his own background of experience in the particular industry, and is not simply a newcomer. See John T. Lloyd Laboratories, Inc. v. Lloyd Brothers Pharmacists, Inc., 131 F.2d 703 (6th Cir.1942).

In the nineteenth and earlier twentieth centuries, both the state and federal courts tended to be highly solicitous of an individual's personal right to use his name in trade.

With the passage of the Federal Trade-Mark Act of 1905, 33 Stat. 724, and an increasing commercial reliance on marketing techniques to create name recognition and goodwill, the courts adopted a more flexible approach to the conflicting property interests involved in surname trademark infringement cases. By 1908, the Supreme Court was willing to enjoin the use of a surname unless accompanied by a disclaimer. Herring-Hall-Marvin Safe Co. v. Hall's Safe Co., 208 U.S. 554, 559–60 (1908). Shortly thereafter, in Thaddeus Davids Co. v. Davids, 233 U.S. 461 (1914) and L.E. Waterman Co. v. Modern Pen Co., 235 U.S. 88 (1914), the Supreme Court established what has since become a guiding principle in trademark surname cases. Once an individual's name has acquired a secondary meaning in the marketplace, a later competitor who seeks to use the same or similar name must take "reasonable precautions to prevent the mistake." L.E. Waterman Co., supra, at 94.

It is, however, difficult to distill general principles as to what are "reasonable precautions" from the Supreme Court's decisions in *Thaddeus Davids* and *Waterman*. In *Davids*, supra, the Court affirmed without modification a lower court decree enjoining entirely the use of the words "Davids" or "Davids Mfg. Co." in connection with the manufacturing and sale of inks. 233 U.S. at 472. In Waterman, supra, on the other hand, the Supreme Court affirmed without modification a lower court's injunction which simply prescribed the use of a full first name instead of an initial, and required a notice of disclaimer.

Since the field is one that does not lend itself to strict application of the rule of *stare decisis* because the fact patterns are so varied, we must try to identify the elements that have influenced decisions on the adequacy of the remedy.

For example, the fact that an alleged infringer has previously sold his business with its goodwill to the plaintiff makes a sweeping injunction more tolerable. So, too, if an individual enters a particular line of trade for no apparent reason other than to use a conveniently confusing surname to his advantage, the injunction is likely to be unlimited.

If, however, the second comer owns the company himself and evinces a genuine interest in establishing an enterprise in which his own skill or knowledge can be made known to the public, that argues in favor of allowing him to use his own name in some restricted fashion.
* * *

When confusion is likely, however, there must obviously be some limitation on an individual's unrestricted use of his own name. * * * Yet, he may retain a limited use of the family name even though goodwill has been conveyed to the plaintiff.

* * *

We do not doubt the necessity for an injunction in this case, but we think that its provisions were too broad. Walter S. Taylor is apparently a scholar of enology and a commentator on wines. He runs a wine museum in the Finger Lakes District, and seems to be a person sincerely concerned with the art of wine-growing. Yet, in granting him the right to let people know that he is personally a grower and distributor of regional wines, the public must be assured that he does not by his "estate bottled" nomenclature and his claims to being the "original" Taylor, confuse the public into believing that his product originates from the Taylor Wine Company which is so well-known.

We have concluded that neither Bully Hill nor Walter S. Taylor should use the "Taylor" name as a trademark, but that the defendant may show Walter's personal connection with Bully Hill. He may use his signature on a Bully Hill label or advertisement if he chooses, but only with appropriate disclaimer that he is not connected with, or a successor to, the Taylor Wine Company. He must also be restrained from using such words as "Original" or "Owner of the Taylor Family Estate." He must, in short, not pretend that his grandfather or his father passed anything on to him as a vintner. To the extent that Walter S. Taylor can exploit his *own* knowledge and techniques as a person, he may do so with the limitations noted, if he refrains from trading on the goodwill of the plaintiff company by competing unfairly.

The order is affirmed in part, modified in part, and remanded for further proceedings in accordance with this opinion.

PROBLEM

Mark Levinson is a famous designer of "high-end" audio equipment. Consumers began to attach great value to a Levinson designed system. He was employed by Madrigal, a manufacturer of audio components. During his employment he assigned the "permanent and exclusive right, title and interest to the trade name 'Mark Levinson' " for use with audio equipment. Madrigal marketed the "Mark Levinson Line" of audio components. Levinson subsequently formed Cello, his own audio manufacturing company, and through advertising and other means let consumers know that he was designing systems for this new company. In Madrigal Audio Laboratories, Inc. v. Cello, Ltd., 799 F.2d 814 (2d Cir.1986), Madrigal seeks an injunction prohibiting Levinson from generating any publicity, written or oral, that he is in any way associated with Cello. What result? The plaintiff cites the *Taylor Wine* case. Does the *Levitt* case, immediately below, make the plaintiff's case even stronger? Does Levinson have a claim against Madrigal?

LEVITT CORP. v. LEVITT

United States Court of Appeals, Second Circuit, 1979.
593 F.2d 463.

[William J. Levitt founded Levitt and Sons in 1929 and rose to national prominence in the housing industry. He constructed several "Levittowns" in the Northeast. In 1968 he sold the company and its good will including the "Levitt" marks. In 1975 he entered a covenant with the new Levitt Corporation (successor to the purchaser) agreeing not to enter the residential housing industry until 1977 and after that date not to use the name "Levitt" as a corporate title, trademark, or trade name in the construction business, although he reserved the right to use his own name publicly as a corporate officer as long as it was not likely to create confusion. Levitt Corporation began seven residential developments in Florida, seeking to capitalize on the value of the Levitt name among residents of the Northeast who were approaching retirement age. In 1978, William Levitt publicly announced that he and the International Construction Corporation would build a "new Levittown" in Orlando, Florida. He purchased advertisements in Northeast newspapers bearing the names "Levittown, Florida," and referring to "Levitt and Sons" to "Levitt's Engineering and Planning Department." The advertisements also identified William Levitt as the founder of the company responsible for the successful Levittowns in the Northeast. Levitt Corporation sued William Levitt for trademark infringement.

In addition to enjoining William Levitt's use of the "Levitt" mark and requiring him to issue corrective advertisements, the district court enjoined any publicity concerning William Levitt's connection in any way with the Orlando project for two years and in addition permanently forbid William Levitt from publicizing his former connection with Levitt and Sons in any future residential development. William Levitt argued these latter two restrictions were too broad.]

IRVING R. KAUFMAN, CHIEF JUDGE.

We believe that several persistent themes may be distilled from the judicial attempts to resolve conflicting interests in the use of trade names by imposing appropriate injunctive relief. If the infringing party has had some experience of his own in an industry, and wishes to establish a business under his own name, it is considered unfair to preclude him from using his name under all circumstances and for all times, although the first-comer has established a reputation and goodwill under the same appellation. See, e.g., Taylor Wine Co., supra, 569 F.2d at 735–36; John B. Stetson Co. v. Stephen L. Stetson Co., 85 F.2d 586 (2d Cir.), cert. denied, 299 U.S. 605 (1936).

Where, as here, however, the infringing party has previously sold his business, including use of his name and its goodwill, to the plaintiff, sweeping injunctive relief is more tolerable. * * * Goodwill is a valuable property right derived from a business's reputation for quality and service. * * * To protect the property interest of the purchaser, then, the courts will be especially alert to foreclose attempts by the seller to "keep for himself the essential thing he sold, and also keep the price he got for it," Guth v. Guth Chocolate Co., supra, 224 F. at 934. And if the district court finds that the seller has attempted to arrogate to himself the trade reputation for which he received valuable consideration, broad remedies may be effected to restore to the plaintiff the value of his purchase.

*　*　*

The record makes it plain that the promotion of William J. Levitt's name and the manner in which it has been repeatedly linked to Levitt Corporation's marks has created substantial confusion with the plaintiff's venture. We think that the remedy fashioned by Judge Pratt is a reasonable means of dispelling some of the confusion caused by the defendants' advertising campaign. It will also allow Levitt Corporation to make up some of the ground it lost in Florida due to the dissipation of its goodwill.

* * *

Based on the evidence before him, Judge Pratt concluded that any attempt to call public attention to Mr. Levitt's achievements as President of Levitt and Sons would inevitably connect his name to the "spectacular success" of that firm. Moreover, publicity associating Mr. Levitt with the corporate history would create confusion with the marks of Levitt Corporation, resulting in the dilution of the goodwill purchased by the plaintiffs. Accordingly, the district judge permanently enjoined the defendants, in connection with future residential developments, from issuing press releases, brochures, advertising, or publicity concerning Mr. Levitt's prior association with the projects of Levitt and Sons.

The findings on which Judge Pratt predicated this portion of the decree are not clearly erroneous, and justify the relief granted. Mr. Levitt's 1975 contract explicitly forbade confusing uses of his name, and Levitt Corporation's trade reputation is symbolized by the marks "Levittown," "Levitt and Sons," and "Strathmore." To permit Mr. Levitt to proclaim his "track record" by recounting his stewardship of Levitt and Sons would, perforce, free him to link his name to those marks and profit from the ensuing confusion.[12] Accordingly, since we believe that Judge Pratt reasonably determined that an injunction of this scope was necessary to prevent confusion and to protect the value of plaintiff's goodwill, we affirm.

NOTES

1. The terms of the preliminary injunction were approved with some modifications in Taylor Wine Co. Inc. v. Bully Hill Vineyards Inc., 590 F.2d 701 (2d Cir.1978). Subsequent developments are described in The Taylor Wine Co., Inc. v. Bully Hill Vineyards, Inc., 208 U.S.P.Q. 80 (W.D.N.Y.1979) in which Bully Hill was held in contempt for repeated and intentional violations of both the preliminary and permanent injunctions. From the record it appeared Walter Taylor did not think kindly of the court's decision. One example was an advertising brochure showing a portrait of Walter Taylor with the caption "Unknown But Not Unloved" and a textual paragraph which read: "Due to complex factors beyond human control, history regarding Walter S. _____ will have to be kept secret until the Federal Courts decide how much the public should know about him * * *. Where he came from and how he suddenly arrived on this planet involved with grape growing and wine making without ancestors, heritage or a father. Usually Walter S. _____ will without notice appear at his winery next to you, and as you meet him personally, he will request that you agree with the Federal Court's position on his unique status.

12. Under these circumstances, a disclaimer of any *current* relationship between Mr. Levitt and the corporation will not protect the plaintiff's rights, for the effect of such a statement would be to inform the public that the achievements to which Levitt Corporation justly lays claim really are attributable to the efforts of someone else, now in business for himself.

You will be requested to concentrate only on the unobvious, in order to satisfy his insecure competition 'down in the valley' because of his stand against 'the proliferation of Evil.'"   Id. at 85.

2. See David B. Findlay, Inc. v. Findlay, 18 N.Y.2d 12, 271 N.Y.S.2d 652, 218 N.E.2d 531 (1966), cert. denied 385 U.S. 930 (1967), where the Court of Appeals split 4–3 in affirming an injunction prohibiting Wally Findlay from using the name "Findlay" in connection with his new art gallery at 17 East 57th St. in competition with his brother's art gallery located at 13–15 East 57th St. and known in the trade as "Findlay's on 57th St."   The dissenting opinion declared that "proof of confusion—understandably inevitable when there is a similarity of name—is irrelevant since confusion resulting from the honest use of one's own name is not actionable."   See also, Brody's, Inc. v. Brody Bros., Inc., 308 Pa.Super. 417, 454 A.2d 605 (1982) applying the rule that the right to use one's own surname in business is protected even if consumer confusion results as long as there is no intent to deceive.

3. *Lanham Act Provisions.* Section 2(e) of the Lanham Act precludes registration of a mark which "is primarily merely a surname" unless it has become "distinctive" under subsection 2(f).   The most thorough analysis of the language is contained in Ex Parte Rivera Watch Corp., 106 U.S.P.Q. 145 (Com. of Pat.1955):

> A trademark is a trademark only if it is used in trade.   When it is used in trade it must have some impact upon the purchasing public, and it is that impact or impression which should be evaluated in determining whether or not the primary significance of a word when applied to a product is a surname significance.   If it is, and it is only that, then it is primarily merely a surname.   Reeves, Higgins, and Wayne are thus primarily merely surnames.   If the mark has well known meanings as a word in the language and the purchasing public, upon seeing it on the goods, may not attribute surname significance to it, it is not primarily merely a surname.   "King," "Cotton," and "Boatman" fall in this category.

> There are some names which by their very nature have only a surname significance even though they are rare surnames.   Seidenberg, if rare, would be in this class.   And there are others which have no meaning—well known or otherwise—and are in fact surnames which do not, when applied to goods as trademarks, create the impression of being surnames.

> It seems to me that the test to be applied in the administration of this provision in the Act is not the rarity of the name, nor whether it is the applicant's name, nor whether it appears in one or more telephone directories, nor whether it is coupled with a baptismal name or initials. The test should be: What is its primary significance to the purchasing public?

The *Rivera* analysis was adopted in Application of Kahan & Weisz Jewelry Mfg. Corp., 508 F.2d 831 (CCPA 1975).

Section 2(c) prohibits registration of a mark which consists of a "name * * * identifying a particular living individual except by his written consent" and § 2(a) prohibits registration of a mark which may "falsely suggest a connection with persons, living or dead * * *."   In Lucien Piccard Watch Corp. v. 1868 Crescent Corp., 314 F.Supp. 329 (S.D.N.Y.1970) the registered mark "Da Vinci" was upheld as not violating § 2(a) because it was "scarcely

likely to mislead any substantial number of purchasers into believing that
Leonardo DaVinci was in any way responsible for the design or production of
the goods" and was held not to be "primarily merely a surname" because it
"comes very near having as its exclusive connotation" the historical figure and
thus is not regarded as a current surname.

4. *Corporate Names and Service Marks.* The Lanham Act does not provide registration for "tradenames". Section 3 authorizes registration of "service marks" and provides them with the same protection as trademarks. In
theory the distinction between trademarks and tradenames is clear. "The
Coca-Cola Company" is the tradename, i.e., the name under which the company
does business, and "Coca-Cola" is the trademark, i.e., the identifier of the goods.
However, particularly with businesses that provide services rather than goods
the same mark may function as both. Thus "AAA Auto Repair" may be both
the name of the company (tradename) and may also be the mark that identifies
the services the company provides (service mark). See In re Amex Holding
Corp., 163 U.S.P.Q. 558 (TTAB 1969) (Whether or not a term used as a trade
name also performs the function of a service mark is one of fact to be
determined from the manner in which it is used and the possible impact thereof
upon purchasers.) See also Communications Satellite Corp. v. Comcet, Inc., 429
F.2d 1245 (4th Cir.1970), cert. denied 400 U.S. 942 (1971) where the mark
"Comsat" was held to be both a tradename and a service mark.

If a mark is held to be a "tradename" identifying the business itself rather
than its goods or services, there is no protection under the Lanham Act (except
under § 44 for international trade purposes). However, a business or corporate
name is protected by the common law against confusion created by uses of
similar names. One of the leading cases is Lawyers Title Ins. Co. v. Lawyers
Title Ins. Corp., 109 F.2d 35 (D.C.Cir.1939), cert. denied 309 U.S. 684 (1940):

> Some of the opinions speak in terms of "property" as the basis for
> [enjoining second users of a tradename], others in the language of
> unfair competition with a conclusive presumption of public confusion
> and of injury to the prior appropriator's business in cases of nominal
> identity. The larger number frankly assimilate corporate names to
> trade-marks or to trade names, with results varying somewhat accord-
> ing to the classification adopted but in respects not material here.

> Whether one or another approach is taken * * * relief is grant-
> ed under circumstances, upon considerations and subject to limitations
> equally applicable either to trade-marks or to trade names. Either
> confusion of the public or injury to the plaintiff's business, actual or
> probable, generally both, will be found implicit in the facts.

5. The selection of a corporate name is often dictated by a regulatory
environment. See, e.g., Massachusetts Mutual Life Insurance Co. v. Massachusetts Life Insurance Co., 356 Mass. 287, 249 N.E.2d 586 (1969) where the state
corporation and insurance laws required the plaintiff to have the words
"mutual", "life", and "insurance" in its name.

6. The corporation laws of most states prohibit incorporation under a
name which is similar to that of a corporation already registered. See, e.g.
Revised Model Business Corp. Act, §§ 4.01–4.03 (prohibits registration of name
that cannot be distinguished from the name of another domestic or registered
foreign corporation.) In addition, many states have statutes derived from the
Model State Trademark Act promulgated by the United States Trademark
Association which provides for the protection of "tradenames" which are

defined as "a word, or a name, or any combination of the foregoing in any form or arrangement used by a person to identify his business, vocation, or occupation and distinguish it from the business, vocation, or occupation of others."

(2) SUBJECT MATTER

The standard trademark case involves a conflict over the right to use a word or symbol in connection with goods and services. However, trademark or unfair competition doctrines may protect other forms of identification such as the shape of the product or the product's image as created by its packaging. Whether there are generic limits to the type of items that can be protected is not generally of concern. There are, however, some cases that press the borders of trademark law and in doing so raise interesting questions at the interface between trademark law and the copyright and patent systems.

IN RE MORTON–NORWICH PRODUCTS, INC.
United States Court of Customs and Patent Appeals, 1982.
671 F.2d 1332.

RICH, JUDGE.

* * *

Background

Appellant's application seeks to register the following container configuration as a trademark for spray starch, soil and stain removers, spray cleaners for household use, liquid household cleaners and general grease removers, and insecticides:

Appellant owns U.S. Design Patent 238,655, issued Feb. 3, 1976, on the above configuration, and U.S. Patent 3,749,290, issued July 31, 1973, directed to the mechanism in the spray top.

The above-named goods constitute a family of products which appellant sells under the word-marks FANTASTIK, GLASS PLUS, SPRAY 'N WASH, GREASE RELIEF, WOOD PLUS, and MIRAKILL. Each of these items is marketed in a container of the same configuration but appellant varies the color of the body of the container according to the product.

[The trademark examiner refused to register the design in the face of the appellant's evidence that consumers spontaneously associate the design with appellant's products, that by 1978 over 132 million containers had been sold, that competing products use differently designed sprayers, and a consumer survey. The examiner held that the design "is no more than a non-distinctive purely functional container for the goods plus a purely functional spray trigger controlled closure * * * essentially utilitarian and non-arbitrary * * *." The appeal board within the patent office affirmed holding: " * * * the configuration of which it seeks to register, is dictated primarily by functional (utilitarian) considerations, and is therefore unregistrable despite any de facto secondary meaning * * *."]

In our view, it would be useful to review the development of the principles which we must apply in order to better understand them. In doing so, it should be borne in mind that this is not a "configuration of *goods*" case but a "configuration of the *container for* the goods" case. One question is whether the law permits, on the facts before us, exclusive appropriation of the precise configuration described in the application to register. Another facet of the case is whether that configuration in fact functions as a trademark so as to be entitled to registration. We turn first to a consideration of the development of the law on "functionality."

Functional A trademark is defined as "any word, name, symbol, or device or any combination thereof adopted and used by a manufacturer or merchant *to identify his goods* and distinguish them from those manufactured or sold by others" (emphasis ours). 15 U.S.C. § 1127 (1976). Thus, it was long the rule that a trademark must be something other than, and separate from, the merchandise to which it is applied.

Aside from the trademark/product "separateness" rationale for not recognizing the bare design of an article or its container as a trademark, it was theorized that all such designs would soon be appropriated, leaving nothing for use by would-be competitors.

* * *

This limitation of permissible trademark subject matter later gave way to assertions that one or more *features* of a product or package design could legally function as a trademark. It was eventually held that the *entire* design of an article (or its container) could, without other means of identification, function to identify the source of the article and be protected as a trademark. E.g., In re Minnesota Mining and Manufacturing Co., 335 F.2d 836, 837 (CCPA 1964).

That protection was limited, however, to those designs of articles and containers, or features thereof, which were "nonfunctional." This requirement of "nonfunctionality" is not mandated by statute, but "is deduced entirely from court decisions." In re Mogen David Wine Corp., 328 F.2d 925, 932 (CCPA 1964) (Rich, J., concurring). It has as its genesis the judicial theory that there exists a fundamental right to compete through imitation of a competitor's product, which right can only be *temporarily* denied by the patent or copyright laws:

> If one manufacturer should make an advance in effectiveness of operation, or in simplicity of form, or in utility of color; and if that advance did not entitle him to a monopoly by means of a machine or process or a product or a design patent; and if by means of unfair trade suits he could shut out other manufacturers who plainly intended to share in the benefits of unpatented utilities * * * he would be given gratuitously a monopoly more effective than that of the unobtainable patent in the ratio of eternity to seventeen years. [Pope Automatic Merchandising Co. v. McCrum-Howell Co., 191 F. 979, 981–82 (7th Cir.1911).]

An exception to the right to copy exists, however, where the product or package design under consideration is "nonfunctional" and serves to identify its manufacturer or seller, and the exception exists even though the design is *not* temporarily protectible through acquisition of patent or copyright. Thus, when a design is "nonfunctional," the right to compete through imitation gives way, presumably upon balance of that right with the originator's right to prevent others from infringing upon an established symbol of trade identification.

This preliminary discussion leads to the heart of the matter—how do we define the concept of "functionality," and what role does the above balancing of interests play in that definitional process?

I. Functionality Defined

* * *

[I]t has been noted that one of the "distinct questions" involved in "functionality" reasoning is, "In what *way* is [the] subject matter functional or utilitarian, factually or legally?" In re Honeywell, Inc., 497 F.2d 1344, 1350, (CCPA 1974) (Rich, J., concurring). This definitional division, noted in "truism" (4) in *Deister,* [Application of Deister Concentrator Co., Inc., 289 F.2d 496 (CCPA 1961)], leads to the resolution that if the designation "functional" is to be utilized to denote the *legal* consequence, we must speak in terms of de facto functionality and de jure functionality, the former being the use of "functional" in the lay sense, indicating that although the design of a product, a container, or a feature of either is directed to performance of a function, it *may* be legally recognized as an indication of source. De jure functionality, of course, would be used to indicate the opposite—such a design may not be protected as a trademark.

This is only the beginning, however, for further definition is required to explain *how* a determination of whether a design is de jure functional is to be approached. We start with an inquiry into "utility."

A. "Functional" means "utilitarian"

From the earliest cases, "functionality" has been expressed in terms of "utility." * * * This broad statement of the "law", that the design of an article "having utility" cannot be a trademark, is incorrect and inconsistent with later pronouncements.

We wish to make it clear—in fact, we wish to characterize it as the *first* addition to the *Deister* "truisms"—that a discussion of "functionality" is *always* in reference to the *design* of the thing under consideration (in the sense of its *appearance*) and *not* the thing itself. No doubt, by definition, a dish always functions as a dish and has its utility, but it is the appearance of the dish which is important in a case such as this, as will become clear.

*   *   *

Thus, it is the "utilitarian" *design* of a "utilitarian" *object* with which we are concerned, and the manner of use of the term "utilitarian" must be examined at each occurrence. The latter occurrence is, of course, consistent with the lay meaning of the term. But the former is being used to denote a *legal consequence* (it being synonymous with "functional"), and it therefore requires further explication.

B.   *"Utilitarian" means "superior in function (de facto) or economy of manufacture," which "superiority" is determined in light of competitive necessity to copy*

*   *   *

Thus, it is clear that courts in the past have considered the public policy involved in this area of the law as, not the *right* to slavishly copy articles which are not protected by patent or copyright, but the *need* to copy those articles, which is more properly termed the right to compete *effectively.*   *   *   *

More recent cases also discuss "functionality" in light of competition. One court noted that the "question in each case is whether protection against imitation will hinder the competitor in competition." Truck Equipment Service Co. v. Fruehauf Corp., 536 F.2d 1210, 1218, (8th Cir.1976). Another court, upon suit for trademark infringement (the alleged trademark being plaintiff's building design), stated that "enjoining others from using the building design [would not] inhibit competition in any way." Fotomat Corp. v. Cochran, 437 F.Supp. 1231, 1235, (D.Kan.1977). This court has also referenced "hinderance of competition" in a number of the "functionality" cases which have been argued before it.   *   *   *

Given, then, that we must strike a balance between the "right to copy" and the right to protect one's method of trade identification, *   *   * what weights do we set upon each side of the scale? That is, given that "functionality" is a question of fact, *   *   * what facts do we look to in determining whether the "consuming public has an interest in making use of [one's design], superior to [one's] interest in being [its] sole vendor"? Vaughan Novelty Mfg. Co. v. G.G. Greene Mfg. Corp., 202 F.2d 172, 176, (3d Cir.), cert. denied 346 U.S. 820 (1953).

II. Determining "Functionality"

A. In general

Keeping in mind, as shown by the foregoing review, that "function-ality" is determined in light of "utility," which is determined in light of "superiority of design," and rests upon the foundation "essential to effective competition," there exist a number of factors, both positive and negative, which aid in that determination.

Previous opinions of this court have discussed what evidence is useful to demonstrate that a particular design is "superior." In In re Shenango Ceramics, Inc., 362 F.2d 287, 291 (1966), the court noted that the existence of an expired utility patent which disclosed the *utilitarian advantage of the design* sought to be registered as a trademark was *evidence* that it was "functional." It may also be significant that the originator of the design touts its utilitarian advantages through adver-tising.

Since the effect upon competition "is really the crux of the matter," it is, of course, significant that there are other alternatives available.

* * *

It is also significant that a particular design results from a compar-atively simple or cheap method of manufacturing the article. * * *

B. The case at bar

1. *The evidence of functionality*

We come now to the task of applying to the facts of this case the distilled essence of the body of law on "functionality" above discussed. The question is whether appellant's plastic spray bottle is de jure functional; is it the best or one of a few superior designs available? We hold on the basis of the evidence before the board, that it is not. * * * Of course, the spray bottle is highly useful and performs its intended functions in an admirable way, but that is not enough to render the *design* of the spray bottle—which is all that matters here—functional.

[The court examined both the spray bottle and the spray top and held that their shapes were not dictated by de facto functional con-cerns. Evidence of other spray bottles and tops with different designs suggested the design here was not a design that competitors required in order to compete.]

What is sought to be registered, however, is no single design feature or component but the overall composite design comprising both bottle and spray top. While that design must be *accommodated* to the functions performed, we see no evidence that it was *dictated* by them and resulted in a functionally or economically superior design of such a container.

Applying the legal principles discussed above, we do not see that allowing appellant to exclude others (upon proof of distinctiveness) from using this trade dress will hinder competition or impinge upon the rights of others to compete effectively in the sale of the goods named in the application, even to the extent of marketing them in *functionally* identical spray containers. The fact is that many others are doing so. Competitors have apparently had no need to simulate appellant's trade dress, in whole or in part, in order to enjoy all of the *functional* aspects of a spray top container. Upon expiration of any patent protection appellant may now be enjoying on its spray and pump mechanism, competitors may even copy and enjoy all of its functions without copying the external appearance of appellant's spray top.

* * *

2. *The relationship between "functionality" and distinctiveness*

One who seeks to register (or protect) a product or container configuration as a trademark must demonstrate that its design is "nonfunctional," as discussed above, and that the design functions as an indication of source, whether inherently so, because of its distinctive nature, or through acquisition of secondary meaning. These two requirements must, however, be kept separate from one another.

* * *

While it is certainly arguable that lack of distinctiveness may, where appropriate, permit an inference that a design was created primarily with an eye toward the utility of the *article,* that fact is by no means conclusive as to the "functionality" of the *design* of that article. Whether in fact the design is "functional" requires closer and more careful scrutiny. We cannot say that there exists an inverse proportional relationship in all cases between distinctiveness of design and functionality (de facto or de jure).

* * *

[The court remanded to the patent office for consideration of the issue of distinctiveness of the mark.]

NOTES

1. Several cases have applied or expanded on the "de jure functionality doctrine" of *Morton-Norwich.* See In re Teledyne Industries, Inc., 696 F.2d 968 (Fed.Cir.1982) (holding a shower head de jure functional in the face of no evidence that commercially feasible alternative shower head configurations were available); In re R.M. Smith, Inc., 734 F.2d 1482 (Fed.Cir.1984) (holding the design of a pistol grip water nozzle de jure functional and thus evidence of distinctiveness irrelevant). Where the overall design is functional, trademark protection might still apply to non-functional elements of the overall design if they attain secondary meaning. Petersen Manufacturing Co., Inc. v. Central Purchasing, Inc., 740 F.2d 1541 (Fed.Cir.1984). However protection for an overall design that is functional will not be saved by having one or two non-functional elements. Textron, Inc. v. United States International Trade Commission, 753 F.2d 1019 (Fed.Cir.1985). See also In re Bose Corp., 772 F.2d 866 (Fed.Cir.1985) where the pentagonal shape of the Bose speaker was held to be functional: "If the feature asserted to give a product distinctiveness is the best, or at least one, of a few superior designs for its *de facto* purpose, it follows that competition is hindered. *Morton-Norwich* does not rest on total elimination of competition in the goods."

de jure functional: There is no evidence that there is an alternate commercially available manner to make the product.

De facto: designed with function in mind

2. Can a building be protected as a trademark? See Fotomat Corp. v. Photo Drive-Thru, Inc., 425 F.Supp. 693 (D.N.J.1977) (kiosks well-suited for drive-in sales not protectible but unique or arbitrary elements of design protected if secondary meaning established). Could famous buildings be trademarks? The Sears Tower in Chicago? The Transamerica building in San Francisco? Could the companies that own these buildings prevent others from using a picture of the buildings in advertisements? Could they prevent others from building similar buildings?

3. There are many "sayings" in trademark law that you cannot trademark a color, or a number, or a variety of other symbols. None of these turn out to be universally true. See Ideal Industries, Inc. v. Gardner Bender, Inc., 612 F.2d 1018 (7th Cir.1979) granting protection to numbers that originally designated the relative size of screw-on electrical connectors but subsequently attained secondary meaning. And see In re General Electric Broadcasting Co., Inc., 199 U.S.P.Q. 560 (TTAB 1978) suggesting a sound if unique and distinctive or possessing secondary meaning could be registered.

4. Can a manufacturer appropriate a color alone as his trademark? If goods are sold in a distinctively shaped bottle with a distinctively colored label, the total image is protectible if there is secondary meaning. It is standard trademark doctrine that the color alone can not be protected because there are a limited number of colors and one producer should not be able to deplete the supply available to others. However, in In re Owens–Corning Fiberglas Corp., 774 F.2d 1116 (Fed.Cir.1985) the color pink as applied to the entire surface of fiberglass insulation was protected in the face of an extensive advertising campaign linking the color with insulation coming from Owens–Corning and the absence of evidence that the color pink added to the functional properties of the insulation. But see, First Brands Corp. v. Fred Meyer Inc., 809 F.2d 1378 (9th Cir.1987) where the lower court's refusal to award preliminary relief to protect the color yellow as applied to a functionally shaped jug containing antifreeze was affirmed on the basis of the color depletion theory. If you could show the court that there are 26 separate colors matching the number of letters in the alphabet and therefore the same theoretical number of color combinations as words available, could you put an end to the color depletion theory?

5. Titles of literary or other works are not in and of themselves protected by copyright. However, trademark and related doctrines may provide the originator with some relief. The leading title case is Warner Bros. Pictures, Inc. v. Majestic Pictures Corp., 70 F.2d 310 (2d Cir.1934) holding the title "The Gold Diggers" suggested origin and could be protected. And see Brandon v. Regents of the University of California, 441 F.Supp. 1086 (D.Mass.1977) (providing owner of title of movie a cause of action under § 43(a) of the Lanham Act.) Initially the patent office tribunals refused registration of a title to a single book because it was descriptive. Application of Cooper, 254 F.2d 611 (CCPA 1958) ("[H]owever arbitrary, novel or nondescriptive of *contents* the name of a book—its title—may be, it nevertheless *describes* the book. ＊ ＊ ＊ If the name or title of a book were not available as a description of it, an effort to denote the book would sound like the playing of the game 'Twenty Questions'.") But see, In re Frederick Warne & Co., Inc., 218 U.S.P.Q. 345 (TTAB 1983), where the court distinguished the cover illustration from the title and permitted the illustration to be registered if it were shown to have been accepted by consumers as a trademark. And see also In re DC Comics, Inc., 689 F.2d 1042 (CCPA 1982) where the court suggested that a drawing of a comic book character, i.e., "Superman", could be a legitimate trademark for a toy doll of the character

even though it had some descriptive function. Similarly, Warner Bros., Inc. v. Gay Toys, Inc., 724 F.2d 327 (2d Cir.1983) protected the design of the toy car "General Lee" from the TV series "The Dukes of Hazard" as a trademark symbol.

See generally, Nimmer, Copyright and Quasi-Copyright Protection for Characters, Titles and Phonograph Records, 59 Trademark Rptr. 63 (1969). See also, Kurtz, Protection for Titles of Literary Works in the Public Domain, 37 Rutgers L.Rev. 53 (1984).

WALLACE INTERNATIONAL SILVERSMITHS, INC. v. GODINGER SILVER ART CO., INC.

United States Court of Appeals, Second Circuit, 1990.
916 F.2d 76.

WINTER, CIRCUIT JUDGE:

Wallace International Silversmiths ("Wallace") appeals from Judge Haight's denial of its motion for a preliminary injunction under Section 43(a) of the Lanham Act, 15 U.S.C. § 1125(a) (1988), prohibiting Godinger Silver Art Co., Inc. ("Godinger") from marketing a line of silverware with ornamentation that is substantially similar to Wallace's GRANDE BAROQUE line. Judge Haight held that the GRANDE BAROQUE design is "a functional feature of 'Baroque' style silverwear" and thus not subject to protection as a trademark. We affirm.

[Wallace's GRANDE BAROQUE pattern, made of fine sterling silver, was a popular silverware line selling for several thousand dollars per place setting. The pattern is described as "ornate, massive and flowery [with] indented, flowery roots and scrolls and curls along the side of the shaft, and flower arrangements along the front of the shaft." Godinger's silverware, selling for $20 per place setting, contained "typical baroque elements including an indented root, scrolls, curls, and flowers" in a similar arrangement but with different dimensions. In denying preliminary relief, the district judge stated:]

> In the case at bar, the "Baroque" curls and flowers are not "arbitrary embellishments" adopted to identify plaintiff's product. Instead, all the "Baroque" style silverware use essentially the same scrolls and flowers as a way to compete in the free market. The "Baroque" style is a line of silverware which many manufacturers produce. Just like the patterns on the chinaware in Pagliero [v. Wallace China Co., 198 F.2d 339 (9th Cir.1952)], the "Grande Baroque" design is a functional feature of "Baroque" style silverware. Wallace may well have developed secondary meaning in the market of "Baroque"-styled silverware. In fact, I assume for purposes of this motion that anyone that sees, for instance, five lines of Baroque silverware will single out the Wallace line as being the "classiest" or the most handsome looking and will immediately exclaim "Oh! That's the Wallace line. They make the finest looking 'Baroque' forks!" That is secondary meaning. However, that

does not mean that plaintiff's design is subject to protection. The "Baroque" curls, roots and flowers are not "mere indicia of source." Instead, they are requirements to compete in the silverware market. This is a classic example of the proposition that "to imitate is to compete." Pagliero, supra, at 344. The designs are aesthetically functional. Accordingly, I conclude that plaintiff does not have a trade dress subject to the protection of the Lanham Act. . . .

*   *   *

In order to maintain an action for trade dress infringement under Section 43(a) of the Lanham Act, the plaintiff must show that its trade dress has acquired secondary meaning—that is, the trade dress identifies the source of the product—and that there is a likelihood of confusion between the original trade dress and the trade dress of the allegedly infringing product. Even if the plaintiff establishes these elements, the defendant may still avoid liability on a variety of grounds, including the so-called functionality doctrine. Our present view of that doctrine is derived from the Supreme Court's dictum in *Inwood Laboratories*, stating that "[i]n general terms, a product feature is functional if it is essential to the use or purpose of the article or if it affects the cost or quality of the article." 456 U.S. at 850 n. 10, 102 S.Ct. at 2187 n. 10. Our most recent elaboration of the doctrine was in *Stormy Clime* [Stormy Clime Ltd. v. Progroup, Inc., 809 F.2d 971, 974 (2d Cir.1987)], where Judge Newman stated:

> the functionality inquiry . . . should [focus] on whether bestowing trade dress protection upon [a particular] arrangement of features " 'will hinder competition or impinge upon the rights of others to compete effectively in the sale of goods.' " Sicilia di R. Biebow & Co. v. Cox, 732 F.2d 417, 429 (5th Cir.1984) (quoting In re Morton-Norwich Products, Inc., 671 F.2d 1332, 1342 (Cust. & Pat.App.1982)).

Id. at 976–77. *Stormy Clime* outlined the factors to be considered in determining functionality as follows:

> the degree of functionality of the similar features, the degree of similarity between non-functional (ornamental) features of the competing products, and the feasibility of alternative arrangements of functional features that would not impair the utility of the product. These factors should be considered along a continuum. On one end, unique arrangements of purely functional features constitute a functional design. On the other end, distinctive and arbitrary arrangements of predominantly ornamental features that do not hinder potential competitors from entering the same market with differently dressed versions of the product are non-functional and hence eligible for trade dress protection. In between, the case for protection weakens the more clearly the arrangement of allegedly distinc-

tive features serves the purpose of the product . . . Id. at 977 (citations omitted).

Turning to the instant case, Judge Haight found that the similarities between the Godinger and Wallace designs involved elements common to all baroque-style designs used in the silverware market. He noted that many manufacturers compete in that market with such designs and found that "[t]he 'Baroque' curls, roots and flowers are not 'mere indicia of source.' Instead, they are requirements to compete in the silverware market." Judge Haight concluded that "the 'Grande Baroque' design is a functional feature of 'Baroque' style silverware," relying on Pagliero v. Wallace China Co., 198 F.2d 339 (9th Cir.1952).

Although we agree with Judge Haight's decision, we do not endorse his reliance upon *Pagliero*. That decision allowed a competitor to sell exact copies of china bearing a particular pattern without finding that comparably attractive patterns were not available to the competitor. It based its holding solely on the ground that the particular pattern was an important ingredient in the commercial success of the china. We rejected *Pagliero* in *LeSportsac* [LeSportsac, Inc. v. K Mart Corp., 754 F.2d 71 (2nd Cir.1985)], and reiterate that rejection here. Under *Pagliero*, the commercial success of an aesthetic feature automatically destroys all of the originator's trademark interest in it, notwithstanding the feature's secondary meaning and the lack of any evidence that competitors cannot develop non-infringing, attractive patterns. By allowing the copying of an exact design without any evidence of market foreclosure, the *Pagliero* test discourages both originators and later competitors from developing pleasing designs.

Our rejection of *Pagliero*, however, does not call for reversal. Quite unlike *Pagliero*, Judge Haight found in the instant matter that there is a substantial market for baroque silverware and that effective competition in that market requires "use [of] essentially the same scrolls and flowers" as is found on Wallace's silverware. Based on the record at the hearing, that finding is not clearly erroneous and satisfies the requirement of *Stormy Clime* that a design feature not be given trade dress protection where use of that feature is necessary for effective competition. 809 F.2d at 976–77.

Stormy Clime is arguably distinguishable, however, because it involved a design that had both aesthetic and utilitarian features. If read narrowly, *Stormy Clime* might be limited to cases in which trademark protection of a design would foreclose competitors from incorporating utilitarian features necessary to compete in the market for the particular product. In the instant case, the features at issue are strictly ornamental because they neither affect the use of the silverware nor contribute to its efficient manufacture. The question, therefore, is whether the doctrine of functionality applies to features of a product that are purely ornamental but that are essential to effective competition.

Our only hesitation in holding that the functionality doctrine applies is based on nomenclature. "Functionality" seems to us to imply only utilitarian considerations and, as a legal doctrine, to be intended only to prevent competitors from obtaining trademark protection for design features that are necessary to the use or efficient production of the product. Even when the doctrine is referred to as "aesthetic" functionality, it still seems an apt description only of pleasing designs of utilitarian features. Nevertheless, there is no lack of language in caselaw endorsing use of the defense of aesthetic functionality where trademark potection for purely ornamental features would exclude competitors from a market. * * *

We put aside our quibble over doctrinal nomenclature, however, because we are confident that whatever secondary meaning Wallace's baroque silverware pattern may have acquired, Wallace may not exclude competitors from using those baroque design elements necessary to compete in the market for baroque silverware. It is a first principle of trademark law that an owner may not use the mark as a means of excluding competitors from a substantial market. Where a mark becomes the generic term to describe an article, for example, trademark protection ceases. Where granting trademark protection to the use of certain colors would tend to exclude competitors, such protection is also limited. Finally, as discussed supra, design features of products that are necessary to the product's utility may be copied by competitors under the functionality doctrine.

In the instant matter, Wallace seeks trademark protection, not for a precise expression of a decorative style, but for basic elements of a style that is part of the public domain. As found by the district court, these elements are important to competition in the silverware market. We perceive no distinction between a claim to exclude all others from use on silverware of basic elements of a decorative style and claims to generic names, basic colors or designs important to a product's utility. In each case, trademark protection is sought, not just to protect an owner of a mark in informing the public of the source of its products, but also to exclude competitors from producing similar products. We therefore abandon our quibble with the aesthetic functionality doctrine's nomenclature and adopt the Restatement's view that, where an ornamental feature is claimed as a trademark and trademark protection would significantly hinder competition by limiting the range of adequate alternative designs, the aesthetic functionality doctrine denies such protection. See Third Restatement of the Law, Unfair Competition, Ch. 3, § 17(c) at 213–14. This rule avoids the overbreadth of *Pagliero* by requiring a finding of foreclosure of alternatives [2] while still

---

2. The Restatement's Illustrations expressly reject *Pagliero*. Illustration 6 reads as follows:

A manufactures china. Among the products marketed by A is a set of china bearing a particular "overall" pattern covering the entire upper surface of each

dish. Evidence indicates that aesthetic factors play an important role in the purchase of china, that A's design is attractive to a significant number of consumers, and that the number of alternative patterns is virtually unlimited. In the absence of evidence indicating that

ensuring that trademark protection does not exclude competitors from substantial markets.[3]

Of course, if Wallace were able to show secondary meaning in a precise expression of baroque style, competitors might be excluded from using an identical or virtually identical design. In such a case, numerous alternative baroque designs would still be available to competitors. Although the Godinger design at issue here was found by Judge Haight to be "substantially similar," it is not identical or virtually identical, and the similarity involves design elements necessary to compete in the market for baroque silverware. Because according trademark protection to those elements would significantly hinder competitors by limiting the range of adequate alternative designs, we agree with Judge Haight's denial of a preliminary injunction.

Affirmed.

HARTFORD HOUSE, LTD. v. HALLMARK CARDS, INC., 846 F.2d 1268 (10th Cir.1988), cert. denied 488 U.S. 908 (1988). [Blue Mountain Arts marketed non-occasion emotional greeting cards. The district court found the cards had an inherently distinctive and highly uniform overall appearance, although individual features that comprised the overall appearance were functional. Individual features included: a two-fold card with poetry on first and third pages, deckle edge on the first page, lengthy poetry written in free verse, soft color backgrounds done with air brush or light watercolor strokes, etc. Hallmark Cards began marketing a similarly appearing set of cards. The court held that a combination of features may be nonfunctional even though elements of the combination are functional. As applied to a combination of features "the issue of functionality turns on whether protection of the combination would hinder competition or impinge upon the rights of others to compete effectively."]

NOTES

1. What exactly was the trade dress in *Wallace* and *Hartford House?* Can you now advise Godinger and Hallmark what they may or may not appropriate? How was Godinger or Hallmark originally put on notice that the plaintiffs claimed a protectible interest? Or does that matter?

similarly attractive "overall" patterns are unavailable to competing manufacturers, A's pattern design is not functional under the rule stated in this Section.

3. Restatement Illustrations 7 and 8 reflect this aspect of the rule. They read as follows:

7. The facts being otherwise as stated in Illustration 6, A's design consists solely of a thin gold band placed around the rim of each dish. Evidence indicates that a significant number of consumers prefer china decorated with only a gold rim band. Because the number of alternative designs available to satisfy the

aesthetic desires of these prospective purchasers is extremely limited, the rim design is functional under the rule stated in this Section.

8. A is the first seller to market candy intended for Valentine's Day in heart-shaped boxes. Evidence indicates that the shape of the box is an important factor in the appeal of the product to a significant number of consumers. Because there are no alternative designs capable of satisfying the aesthetic desires of these prospective purchasers, the design of the box is functional under the rule stated in this Section.

2. Trade dress is an expansive concept that can apply far beyond the packaging of a product. See Prufrock, Ltd. v. Lasater, 781 F.2d 129 (8th Cir. 1986) where the plaintiff asserted trade dress rights to the decor of a restaurant. The court provided no protection because the decor items related to the "core concept" of an informal country dining restaurant and could not be appropriated. But see, Fuddruckers Inc. v. Doc's B.R. Others Inc., 826 F.2d 837 (9th Cir.1987) where trade dress rights were recognized in the decor and layout of a restaurant.

3. Should the plaintiff in a trade dress case be required to show secondary meaning or is the packaging and image of a product inherently arbitrary? The Second Circuit in a case involving the packaging of a mattress pad under New York law found that the "possible varieties of advertising display and packaging are virtually endless" and thus secondary meaning is not required if a likelihood of confusion is shown. Perfect Fit Industries, Inc. v. Acme Quilting Co., Inc., 618 F.2d 950 (2d Cir.1980). However, it now appears that trade dress cases will be examined in the same way as trademark cases with an initial inquiry as to whether the trade dress is arbitrary or descriptive and proof of secondary meaning will be required if the latter. Blau Plumbing, Inc. v. S.O.S. Fix–It, Inc., 781 F.2d 604 (7th Cir.1986); Chevron Chemical Co. v. Voluntary Purchasing Groups, Inc., 659 F.2d 695 (5th Cir.1981); Brooks Shoe Mfg. Co., Inc. v. Suave Shoe Corp., 716 F.2d 854 (11th Cir.1983). And the Second Circuit has now recognized that a trade dress must be "distinctive" to be protected. 20th Century Wear Inc. v. Sanmark–Stardust Inc., 815 F.2d 8 (2d Cir.1987).

4. *Problem.* Automobile manufacturers do not provide interior floor mats as standard equipment but they do offer optional floor mats with the manufacturer's logo in colors and shapes designed for their automobiles. There is a consumer demand for accessories that display the logo of the automobile manufacturer. Is there any way that independent companies can compete with the automobile manufacturers in providing floor mats with logos without infringing the trademark rights in the logo? Does it matter what consumers think when they see the logo on the floor mats? See Plasticolor Molded Products v. Ford Motor Co., 713 F.Supp. 1329 (C.D.Cal.1989): "Where a copied product feature is partially functional but partially source-identifying, we are presented with three alternatives. First, we could find that the source-identifying aspects of the feature trump the functional aspects, and simply apply the standard law of trademark infringement. Second, we could find the opposite, and hold that the feature is unprotected from copying. Third, we could attempt to find an appropriate middle ground." Is there an appropriate middle ground? Compare with *Job's Daughters,* infra page 360.

5. Does the preemption doctrines of *Sears* and *Compco* affect the trade dress cases? Does the functionality doctrine permit trade dress to coexist with the copyright and patent laws? In *Bonito Boats,* supra Chapter I, the Supreme Court observed: "Congress has thus [by enactment of § 43(a) of the Lanham Act] given federal recognition to many of the concerns which underlie the state tort of unfair competition and the application of *Sears* and *Compco* to nonfunctional aspects of a product which have been shown to identify source must take account of competing federal polices in this regard." Consider how *Bonito Boats* and cases like *Wallace* or *Hallmark Cards* might interact in the following circumstances. Ferrari sells two distinctively shaped automobiles. Roberts manufactures kits of fiberglass panels that can be attached to other cars to make them imitate the Ferrari models. Are the designs of the Ferrari automobiles functional or are they protectable trade dress? Can they be

protected after *Bonito*? See Ferrari S.P.A. Esercizio Fabriche Automobili E Corse v. Roberts, 739 F.Supp. 1138 (E.D.Tenn.1990).

C. PROBLEMS OF PRIORITY AND INFRINGEMENT

(1) ADOPTION, AFFIXATION AND USE

BLUE BELL, INC. v. FARAH MFG. CO., INC.

United States Court of Appeals, Fifth Circuit, 1975.
508 F.2d 1260.

GEWIN, CIRCUIT JUDGE:

In the spring and summer of 1973 two prominent manufacturers of men's clothing created identical trademarks for goods substantially identical in appearance. Though the record offers no indication of bad faith in the design and adoption of the labels, both Farah Manufacturing Company (Farah) and Blue Bell, Inc. (Blue Bell) devised the mark "Time Out" for new lines of men's slacks and shirts. Both parties market their goods on a national scale, so they agree that joint utilization of the same trademark would confuse the buying public. Thus, the only question presented for our review is which party established prior use of the mark in trade. A response to that seemingly innocuous inquiry, however, requires us to define the chameleonic term "use" as it has developed in trademark law.[1]

* * *

Farah conceived of the Time Out mark on May 16, after screening several possible titles for its new stretch menswear. Two days later the firm adopted an hourglass logo and authorized an extensive advertising campaign bearing the new insignia. Farah presented its fall line of clothing, including Time Out slacks, to sales personnel on June 5. In the meantime, patent counsel had given clearance for use of the mark after scrutiny of current federal registrations then on file. One of Farah's top executives demonstrated samples of the Time Out garments to large customers in Washington, D.C. and New York, though labels were not attached to the slacks at that time. Tags containing the new design were completed June 27. With favorable evaluations of marketing potential from all sides, Farah sent one pair of slacks bearing the Time Out mark to each of its twelve regional sales managers on July 3. Sales personnel paid for the pants, and the garments became their property in case of loss.

[handwritten margin note: Farah 12 pants on July 3 to managers]

1. Compare Western Stove Co. v. George D. Roper Corp., 82 F.Supp. 206 (S.D.Cal.1949) (first commercial sale controls, despite opposing party's prior conception and advertisement of the mark) with Charles Pfizer & Co. v. R.J. Moran Co., 125 U.S.P.Q. 201 (1960) (prior commercial sale is not determinative; drug manufacturer who first conceived of the mark and appended it to drugs for experimental purposes has rights superior to drug producer who initially placed goods on the market).

Following the July 3 shipment, regional managers showed the goods to customers the following week. Farah received several orders and production began. Further shipments of sample garments were mailed to the rest of the sales force on July 11 and 14. Merchandising efforts were fully operative by the end of the month. The first shipments to customers, however, occurred in September.

Blue Bell, on the other hand, was concerned with creating an entire new division of men's clothing, as an avenue to reaching the "upstairs" market. Though initially to be housed at the Hicks-Ponder plant in El Paso, the new division would eventually enjoy separate headquarters. On June 18 Blue Bell management arrived at the name Time Out to identify both its new division and its new line of men's sportswear. Like Farah, it received clearance for use of the mark from counsel. Like Farah, it inaugurated an advertising campaign. Unlike Farah, however, Blue Bell did not ship a dozen marked articles of the new line to its sales personnel. Instead, Blue Bell authorized the manufacture of several hundred labels bearing the words Time Out and its logo shaped like a referee's hands forming a T. When the labels were completed on June 29, the head of the embryonic division flew them to El Paso. He instructed shipping personnel to affix the new Time Out labels to slacks that already bore the "Mr. Hicks" trademark. The new tags, of varying sizes and colors, were randomly attached to the left hip pocket button of slacks and the left hip pocket of jeans. Thus, although no change occurred in the design or manufacture of the pants, on July 5 several hundred pair left El Paso with two tags.

Blue Bell made intermittent shipments of the doubly-labeled slacks thereafter, though the out-of-state customers who received the goods had ordered clothing of the Mr. Hicks variety. Production of the new Time Out merchandise began in the latter part of August, and Blue Bell held a sales meeting to present its fall designs from September 4–6. Sales personnel solicited numerous orders, though shipments of the garments were not scheduled until October.

By the end of October Farah had received orders for 204,403 items of Time Out sportswear, representing a retail sales value of over $2,750,000. Blue Bell had received orders for 154,200 garments valued at over $900,000. Both parties had commenced extensive advertising campaigns for their respective Time Out sportswear.

Soon after discovering the similarity of their marks, Blue Bell sued Farah for common law trademark infringement and unfair competition, seeking to enjoin use of the Time Out trademark on men's clothing. Farah counter-claimed for similar injunctive relief. The district court found that Farah's July 3 shipment and sale constituted a valid use in trade, while Blue Bell's July 5 shipment was a mere "token" use insufficient at law to create trademark rights. While we affirm the result reached by the trial court as to Farah's priority of use, the legal grounds upon which we base our decision are somewhat different from those undergirding the district court's judgment.

Federal jurisdiction is predicated upon diversity of citizenship, since neither party has registered the mark pursuant to the Lanham Act. Given the operative facts surrounding manufacture and shipment from El Paso, the parties agree the Texas law of trademarks controls. In 1967 the state legislature enacted a Trademark Statute. Section 16.02 of the Act explains that a mark is "used" when it is affixed to the goods and "the goods are sold, displayed for sale, or otherwise publicly distributed." Thus the question whether Blue Bell or Farah established priority of trademark use depends upon interpretation of the cited provision. Unfortunately, there are no Texas cases construing § 16.02. This court must therefore determine what principles the highest state court would utilize in deciding such a question. In view of the statute's stated purpose to preserve common law rights, we conclude the Texas Supreme Court would apply the statutory provision in light of general principles of trademark law.

A trademark is a symbol (word, name, device or combination thereof) adopted and used by a merchant to identify his goods and distinguish them from articles produced by others. * * * Ownership of a mark requires a combination of both appropriation and use in trade. * * * Thus, neither conception of the mark * * * nor advertising alone establishes trademark rights at common law.[7] * * * Rather, ownership of a trademark accrues when goods bearing the mark are placed on the market. * * *

The exclusive right to a trademark belongs to one who first uses it in connection with specified goods. * * * Such use need not have gained wide public recognition, * * * and even a single use in trade may sustain trademark rights if followed by continuous commercial utilization. * * *

The initial question presented for review is whether Farah's sale and shipment of slacks to twelve regional managers constitutes a valid first use of the Time Out mark. Blue Bell claims the July 3 sale was merely an internal transaction insufficiently public to secure trademark ownership. After consideration of pertinent authorities, we agree.

Secret, undisclosed internal shipments are generally inadequate to support the denomination "use." Trademark claims based upon shipments from a producer's plant to its sales office, and vice versa, have often been disallowed. * * * Though none of the cited cases dealt with *sales* to intra-corporate personnel, we perceive that fact to be a distinction without a difference. The sales were not made to customers, but served as an accounting device to charge the salesmen with their cost in case of loss. The fact that some sales managers actively solicited accounts bolsters the good faith of Farah's intended use, but

---

7. We intimate no view as to whether the Texas statute's definition of use embracing "display for sale" would change the common law rule. Vernon's Tex.Code Ann., Bus. & Comm. § 16.02 (1968).

does not meet our essential objection: that the "sales" were not made to the public.

The primary, perhaps singular purpose of a trademark is to provide a means for the consumer to separate or distinguish one manufacturer's goods from those of another. Personnel within a corporation can identify an item by style number or other unique code. A trademark aids the public in selecting particular goods. As stated by the First Circuit:

> It seems to us that although evidence of sales is highly persuasive, the question of use adequate to establish appropriation remains one to be decided on the facts of each case, and that evidence showing, first, adoption, and second, *use in a way sufficiently public to identify or distinguish the marked goods in an appropriate segment of the public mind as those of the adopter of the mark,* is competent to establish ownership.

New England Duplicating Co. v. Mendes, 190 F.2d 415, 418 (1st Cir. 1951) (Emphasis added). Similarly, the Trademark Trial and Appeal Board has reasoned:

> To acquire trademark rights there has to be an "open" use, that is to say, a use has to be made to the relevant class of purchasers or prospective purchasers since a trademark is intended to identify goods and distinguish those goods from those manufactured or sold by others. There was no such "open" use rather the use can be said to be an "internal" use, which cannot give rise to trademark rights.

Sterling Drug, Inc. v. Knoll A.G. Chemische Fabriken [159 U.S.P.Q. 628 (TTAB 1968)].

Farah nonetheless contends that a recent decision of the Board so undermines all prior cases relating to internal use that they should be ignored. In Standard Pressed Steel Co. v. Midwest Chrome Process Co., 183 U.S.P.Q. 758 (TTAB 1974) the agency held that internal shipment of marked goods from a producer's manufacturing plant to its sales office constitutes a valid "use in commerce" for registration purposes.

An axiom of trademark law has been that the right to register a mark is conditioned upon its actual use in trade. * * * Theoretically, then, common law use in trade should precede the use in commerce upon which Lanham Act registration is predicated. Arguably, since only a trademark owner can apply for registration, any activity adequate to create registrable rights must perforce also create trademark rights. A close examination of the Board's decision, however, dispels so mechanical a view. The tribunal took meticulous care to point out that its conclusion related solely to registration use rather than ownership use.

Priority of use and ownership of the Time Out mark are the only issues before this court. The language fashioned by the Board clearly indicates a desire to leave the common law of trademark ownership intact. The decision may demonstrate a reversal of the presumption that ownership rights precede registration rights, but it does not affect our analysis of common law use in trade. Farah had undertaken substantial preliminary steps toward marketing the Time Out garments, but it did not establish ownership of the mark by means of the July 3 shipment to its sales managers. The gist of trademark rights is actual use in trade. Though technically a "sale", the July 3 shipment was not "publicly distributed" within the purview of the Texas statute.

Blue Bell's July 5 shipment similarly failed to satisfy the prerequisites of a bona fide use in trade. Elementary tenets of trademark law require that labels or designs be affixed to the merchandise actually intended to bear the mark in commercial transactions. Furthermore, courts have recognized that the usefulness of a mark derives not only from its capacity to identify a certain manufacturer, but also from its ability to differentiate between different classes of goods produced by a single manufacturer. * * * Here customers had ordered slacks of the Mr. Hicks species, and Mr. Hicks was the fanciful mark distinguishing these slacks from all others. Blue Bell intended to use the Time Out mark on an entirely new line of men's sportswear, unique in style and cut, though none of the garments had yet been produced.

While goods may be identified by more than one trademark, the use of each mark must be bona fide. See, e.g., Old Dutch Foods, Inc. v. Dan Dee Pretzel & Potato Chip Co., 477 F.2d 150 (6th Cir.1973) (continuous utilization of the second mark for over thirty years). Mere adoption of a mark without bona fide use, in an attempt to reserve it for the future, will not create trademark rights. * * * In the instant case Blue Bell's attachment of a secondary label to an older line of goods manifests a bad faith attempt to reserve a mark. We cannot countenance such activities as a valid use in trade. Blue Bell therefore did not acquire trademark rights by virtue of its July 5 shipment.

We thus hold that neither Farah's July 3 shipment nor Blue Bell's July 5 shipment sufficed to create rights in the Time Out mark. Based on a desire to secure ownership of the mark and superiority over a competitor, both claims of alleged use were chronologically premature. Essentially, they took a time out to litigate their differences too early in the game. The question thus becomes whether we should continue to stop the clock for a remand or make a final call from the appellate bench. * * *

Careful examination of the record discloses that Farah shipped its first order of Time Out clothing to customers in September of 1973. Blue Bell, approximately one month behind its competitor at other relevant stages of development, did not mail its Time Out garments until at least October. Though sales to customers are not the *sine qua non* of trademark use, * * * they are determinative in the instant case. These sales constituted the first point at which the public had a chance to associate Time Out with a particular line of sportswear. Therefore, Farah established priority of trademark use; it is entitled to a decree permanently enjoining Blue Bell from utilization of the Time Out trademark on men's garments.

The judgment of the trial court is affirmed.

MANHATTAN INDUSTRIES, INC. v. SWEATER BEE BY BANFF, LTD.
627 F.2d 628 (2d Cir.1980).

[General Mills abandoned the mark "Kimberly" for high quality women's clothes on May 7, 1979. In anticipation of the abandonment Don Sophisticates displayed to customers its own merchandise with labels bearing the mark "Kimberly" prior to May 9, and actually shipped merchandise with the labels on May 9. From May to October, Don Sophisticates shipped over $10,000 worth of merchandise with the mark. Sweater Bee shipped competing merchandise with the "Kimberly" mark on May 10, the day the mark's abandonment was reported in the trade press, and has since that date shipped over $130,000 worth of marked goods. A third entrant, Bayard Shirt, shipped its first merchandise on May 11 and has since sold $45,000 worth bearing the "Kimberly" mark. Bayard Shirt subsequently obtained an assignment of the mark from Don Sophisticates. This is an action under § 43(a) of the Lanham Act to sort out the priority user of the mark. The District Court held Don Sophisticates, and by way of assignment Bayard Shirt, had priority because they were the first to ship goods bearing the mark. The court enjoined Sweater Bee from using the mark.]

* * *

When General Mills abandoned its mark, Don Sophisticates and Sweater Bee "were equally free to attempt to capture the mark to their own use." Don Sophisticates won the race, for it was the first to ship merchandise with labels bearing a "Kimberly" mark after the abandonment, and it did so with the intent of acquiring the mark. Accordingly, Don Sophisticates would ordinarily have "the right to use the mark unadorned," id., and Bayard Shirt and Manhattan Industries, as its assignees, would receive that right. However, in light of the significant shipments and investment by Sweater Bee, we do not believe that Don Sophisticates' slight priority in time justifies awarding to the appellees the exclusive, nationwide right to the "Kimberly" mark. * * * Given the evenly balanced equities in this case, it would be inequitable to allow only the appellees to use the "Kimberly" mark. Sweater Bee has proved "that it entered the market sufficiently early to be equally entitled with [appellees] to the use of the ['Kimberly'] mark. In such case, to protect the public, each company [will] have to differentiate its product from that of the other company and perhaps also from the original ['Kimberly'] mark." P. Daussa Corp. v. Sutton Cosmetics (P.R.) Inc., 462 F.2d 134, 136 (2d Cir.1972).

One of the purposes of the Lanham Act is to prevent confusion among the public as to the source of goods. We have recognized, however, that the likelihood of confusion may decrease as the sophistication of the relevant purchasers increases. * * * No doubt the parties can create and present to the district court sufficiently distinct labels bearing the "Kimberly" mark so that the purchasers of high quality women's clothing can distinguish appellees' "Kimberly" goods from appellant's. We therefore remand to the district court for the fashioning of an appropriate order not inconsistent with this opinion.

NOTES

1. The acquisition of trademark rights at common law requires adoption and use of the mark. The common law, as did the Trademark Act of 1905, also requires the mark be "affixed" (physically attached) to the goods or their container. Although the common law of unfair competition protects an unaffixed mark with secondary meaning, the date of affixation is important in establishing priority of use of the mark where there are competing claims. The *Blue Bell* case illustrates part of the problem associated with the "affixation" requirement given that Blue Bell's use of Time Out was not affixed to the actual goods to be marketed with the mark.

Passage of the Lanham Act relaxed but did not abandon the affixation requirement. Prior to 1989 § 45 of the Act defined "use in commerce" as use "on the goods or their containers or the displays associated therewith or on the tags or labels affixed thereto". This was broadened in the 1988 revisions to provide that "if the nature of the goods makes such placement impracticable, then on documents associated with the goods or their sale". The amendment was directed toward trademarking goods sold in bulk. Section 45 also defines "use" of service marks.

The affixation requirement and the Lanham Act prevent the establishment of trademark priority by advertising use alone. The use must be in connection with goods. Thus a manufacturer cannot preserve his rights to a mark prior to the availability and sale of the goods. See, In re Sanger Telecasters Inc., 1 U.S.P.Q.2d 1589 (TTAB 1986) (for service marks extensive advertising does not support registration prior to the actual rendition of services.)

2. *Token use.* The requirement of use in connection with actual goods to establish trademark priority creates difficulties for firms who have substantial expenses associated with trademark development. The race for priority of the "Time Out" mark in *Blue Bell* is but one example. An alternative system might accord priority to the first to register the mark without requiring substantial use. Does the *Standard Pressed Steel* case, analyzed in *Blue Bell* move in that direction? The Patent and Trademark Office developed a "token use" doctrine which permitted registration of a mark where there was at least one bona fide sale of the goods in commerce "accompanied by activities or circumstances evidencing an intent to continue use of the mark on the product on a commercial scale." CPC International, Inc. v. The Seven–Up Co., 218 U.S. P.Q. 379, 381 (TTAB 1983). Token use was sufficient for registration even though it might not be sufficient to establish rights to the mark. At the same time registration resulted in constructive notice to others of the registrants interest in the mark.

3. *Secondary meaning "in the making".* First use of a mark is not always sufficient to establish priority, particularly where the mark is not distinctive and thus must acquire secondary meaning in the marketplace. The user of a non-distinctive mark thus remains in jeopardy of losing protection until there is

consumer recognition of his mark. This interim period of use has caused a few courts to adopt a rule of "secondary meaning in the making" which purports to protect a first user against intentional infringement during this period. Metro Kane Imports, Ltd. v. Federated Department Stores Inc., 625 F.Supp. 313 (S.D. N.Y.1985). But see Black & Decker Mfg. Co. v. Ever-Ready Appliance Mfg. Co., 684 F.2d 546 (8th Cir.1982) rejecting the doctrine. See also, Restatement (Third) of Unfair Competition, § 13, Reporters' Notes at 53 (Tent.Draft No. 2, 1990): "The [secondary meaning in the making] doctrine, if taken literally, is inimical to the purpose of the secondary meaning requirement."

4. *Intent-to-Use.* The Trademark Revision Act of 1988 added provisions to the Lanham Act that provide for a system of trademark priority based on an intention to use a mark even though the mark is not in actual use. The key provisions are § 2(b)–(d), § 7(c), and § 45 ("use in commerce"). The provisions of § 2 authorize an application for registration based on a bona fide intention to use the mark and give the applicant not more than 2 years to put the mark to actual use. Although an application based on intent to use is not entitled to actual registration, it does establish, under § 7(c), nationwide constructive use of the mark if a registration is ultimately granted. The revision of the definition of "use in commerce" in § 45 which requires use "in the ordinary course of trade" eliminates the "token use" doctrine for registration purposes.

How do these provisions relate to the common law? What result in *Blue Bell* if Blue Bell had filed an intent-to-use application on July 5? If Farah's September shipment to customers had been limited to stores in the Eastern United States, what effect would be given to an intent-to-use application by Blue Bell on October 1? Can a manufacturer who intends to use a descriptive term or a surname mark acquire some breathing room in order to obtain secondary meaning by filing an intent-to-use application?

5. Section 44 of the Lanham Act provides that a foreign national who has registered its mark in its home country is entitled to register the mark under the Lanham Act and that its priority is determined on the basis of the date of its foreign registration. Thus a foreign national who had not used a mark in commerce could nonetheless obtain priority in the United States against a domestic company who had actually used the mark. The 1988 revisions amended § 44(e) to require the foreign company as part of its application for registration in this country to show a bona fide intention to use the mark in the United States.

6. For a description of a systematic program designed to attempt to preserve marks for future use see The Proctor & Gamble Co. v. Johnson & Johnson Inc., 485 F.Supp. 1185 (S.D.N.Y.1979).

7. After *Blue Bell* does a manufacturer's priority date of first use change every time he makes some change in the underlying goods? Does your answer depend on whether the first use is for registration purposes only or for determining the priority between two users? The Trademark Trial and Appeal Board began requiring that the use, required for registration purposes, must be on goods "identical" with those for which the mark was registered. However the Board was reversed in Ralston Purina Co. v. On-Cor Frozen Foods, Inc., 746 F.2d 801 (Fed.Cir.1984).

(2) **TEST FOR INFRINGEMENT**

NOTES

1. Proof of a likelihood of confusion between competing trademarks is at the heart of trademark infringement, both under the common law and the Lanham Act. See § 32 of the Lanham Act which requires a showing that the defendant's use is "likely to cause confusion, or to cause mistake, or to deceive." But this deceptively simple idea becomes considerably more complex in practice. The Restatement (Third) of Unfair Competition §§ 21–23 (Tent.Draft No. 2, 1990) adopts a process for proof of a likelihood of confusion that requires consideration of multiple factors in each case including the resemblance between the marks, the marketing methods of the two parties, the nature of the prospective purchasers, the degree of distinctiveness of the mark, and the product and geographic markets in which the competing marks are used.

2. Purchasers may be confused in several ways. They may believe because of the similarity of the mark or trade dress that they are obtaining the same goods they received the last time they purchased the product in question. This is confusion of goods. They might, likewise, know they are not receiving the same goods but believe that the goods they are purchasing come from the same manufacturer as other goods. This is confusion of source or origin. In other situations, they may believe that the goods they are purchasing were sponsored or approved by an agency when in fact they were not. This is confusion of sponsorship.

In the ordinary case the senior (first) user of the mark complains that the junior (second) user is passing his goods off as those of the senior user. However, if the junior user is a larger company the problem may be reversed and consumers may think the junior user is the originator and the senior user is an infringer. A cause of action for this "reverse confusion" seems to be recognized when raised. In Big O Tire Dealers, Inc. v. Goodyear Tire & Rubber Co., 408 F.Supp. 1219 (D.Colo.1976), vacated on other grounds, 561 F.2d 1365 (10th Cir.1977), cert. denied 434 U.S. 1052 (1978) the "Big O Big Foot" tire, although first in the market, was overwhelmed by a massive advertising campaign by Goodyear of its "Bigfoot" tire. See also Banff Ltd. v. Federated Department Stores, 841 F.2d 486 (2d Cir.1988) where Bloomingdale's subsequent use of "B Wear" for women's clothing overwhelmed the senior use of "Bee Wear" for similar clothing. The court held there was a likelihood of both direct and reverse confusion, both of which were prohibited by § 43(a) of the Lanham Act. As to reverse confusion: ". . . consumers may consider Banff an unauthorized infringer, and Bloomingdale's use of the mark may in that way injure Banff's reputation and impair its good will."

3. In a trademark infringement case, the plaintiff is generally not required to show actual confusion in order to obtain an injunction. However, some cases require actual confusion before an accounting of profits or damages will be allowed. Evidence of actual confusion is admissible and will generally strengthen plaintiff's case. The test, however, remains likelihood of confusion by a substantial portion of the purchasing public and proof of isolated examples of actual confusion is not sufficient.

4. The defendant's intent plays an important and yet an ambiguous role in trademark cases. The plaintiff does not have to prove intent to deceive on the part of the defendant. Pattishall, The Impact of Intent in Trade Identity

No intent Finding

Cases, 65 N.W.U.L.Rev. 421, 422 (1970): "Courts today frequently and correctly comment that the intent element is not legally requisite in either trademark infringement or unfair competition law. The body of decided cases reveals, nonetheless, that in an astonishingly high percentage of trade identity decisions in which relief was granted, the defendant was found guilty, either directly or circumstantially, of intended poaching if not outright fraud. Indeed, empirical observation indicates that something in the nature of this form of animus furandi remains virtually an essential ingredient for a winning plaintiff's suit in the area of trade identity law."

If the plaintiff is able to prove intent, many courts hold that an inference arises that (a) the plaintiff's mark has secondary meaning and (b) the defendant's use created a likelihood of confusion. The assumption behind the inference is that if defendant intentionally tried to create confusion he probably succeeded (or at least should not be able to defend on the basis that he tried but failed). Courts must be careful in permitting the inference in those cases where there may be an intent to copy but not an intent to confuse. For example, competitors have the right to copy generic or functional devices. See Blau Plumbing, Inc. v. S.O.S. Fix–It, Inc., 781 F.2d 604 (7th Cir.1986) ("The problem is that evidence of intent is often ambigiuous. Maybe therefore a court should insist on other evidence of distinctiveness and not allow a trademark infringement case to get to a jury merely on proof that the defendant may have been trying to confuse consumers about whose brand they were buying. . . ."). See, Restatement (Third) of Unfair Competition § 22 (Tent.Draft No. 2, 1990).

5. The ordinary and reasonably prudent purchaser is the standard by which most courts measure confusion. See Judge Hand's astute observation in G.H. Mumm Champagne v. Eastern Wine Corp., 142 F.2d 499 (2d Cir.1944), where a domestic wine carried a label similar to the more expensive imported brand:

> Those who covet a name for taste and elegance, do indeed affect discrimination in the recognition of various brands; but, especially as an evening wears on, the label, and only a very casual glance at the label, is quite enough to assure the host and his table that he remains as free handed and careless of cost as when he began. At such stages of an entertainment nothing will be easier than for an unscrupulous restaurant keeper to substitute the domestic champagne.

Although the likelihood of confusion in most trademark cases is among prospective purchasers of the infringer, some cases have held that post-sale confusion is also prohibited. A seller of phony "Rolex" watches can not claim that his purchaser should have known the watch was not genuine when he paid only $12 for it in contrast to the very expensive genuine "Rolex" watches. There is a likelihood of confusion when the original purchaser sells it in the second-hand market. See, e.g., Rolex Watch U.S.A. Inc. v. Forrester, 2 USPQ 2d 1292 (S.D. Fla.1986) (unpublished case). And see Lois Sportswear, U.S.A. v. Levi Strauss & Co., 799 F.2d 867 (2d Cir.1986) where Lois Sportswear used the back pocket stitching on jeans registered as a trademark by Levi Strauss and argued that the labels used by both parties would prevent confusion. Finding post-sale confusion actionable the court held: "[T]his post-sale confusion would involve consumers seeing appellant's jeans outside of the retail store, perhaps being worn by a passer-by. The confusion the Act seeks to prevent in this context is that a consumer seeing the familiar stitching pattern will associate the jeans with appellee and that association will influence his buying decisions."

6. Plaintiffs attempting to prove a likelihood of confusion, where actual confusion is not available, have increasingly relied on consumer opinion polls. The attempt to introduce the surveys into evidence has not always been successful. See Note, Public Opinion Surveys as Evidence: The Pollsters Go To Court, 66 Harv.L.Rev. 498 (1953); Sorensen & Sorensen, The Admissibility and Use of Opinion Research Evidence, 28 N.Y.U.L.Rev. 1213 (1953). For an example of judicial reluctance to allow the surveys to be introduced see Sears, Roebuck & Co. v. Allstate Driving School, 301 F.Supp. 4 (E.D.N.Y.1969). The actual questionnaire used is reproduced as an appendix to the decision. A consumer survey showing 15% of a random sample of persons confused the defendant's mark with that of the plaintiff was sufficient to prove likelihood of confusion in James Burrough Ltd. v. Sign of the Beefeater, Inc., 540 F.2d 266 (7th Cir.1976).

(3) INCONTESTABILITY: SECTIONS 14, 15, & 33 OF THE LANHAM ACT

The Lanham Act introduced the concept of "incontestability" to trademark law as a device to provide more stability to trademark owners. To understand the concept the student must be familiar with the interaction of §§ 14, 15, and 33 of the Act.

Section 14 provides the grounds upon which the registration of a mark on the Principal Register can be cancelled. The section does not use the term "incontestable". It authorizes any person "who believes that he is or will be damaged" by the registration to seek its cancellation within five years after the mark is registered. However, subsections (c) through (e) provide grounds for which cancellation can be obtained without a five year limitation. Thus, for purposes of cancellation, a mark is not completely incontestable but remains subject to cancellation throughout its existence if one of the grounds in (c) through (e) exists.

Section 15, which does contain the term "incontestable," is not structured in terms of registration or cancellation. Once the mark is used for five consecutive years subsequent to the date of registration, the operative language of the section provides that "the right of the registrant *to use* such registered mark in commerce shall be incontestable." (emphasis added). Thus it would appear that unless one of the exceptions within the section were applicable, no one could prohibit the owner of an incontestable mark from using his mark in commerce. Section 15 speaks to use; § 14 speaks to registration.

Subsection (a) of section 33 describes the effect of any registration under the Act. The registration is "prima facie evidence" of the "validity of the registered mark and of the registration of the mark, of the registrant's ownership of the mark, and of the registrant's exclusive right to use the registered mark in commerce. . . ." The registration is also subject to "any legal or equitable defense or defect". In contrast, subsection (b) governs if the registration of the mark has become incontestable. The registration becomes "conclusive" evidence rather than "prima facie evidence" and the registration is subject only to listed defenses.

PARK 'N FLY, INC. v. DOLLAR PARK AND FLY, INC.
Supreme Court of the United States, 1985.
469 U.S. 189, 105 S.Ct. 658, 83 L.Ed.2d 582.

[The petitioner operates long-term parking lots near airports in a variety of cities including San Francisco and in 1971 secured a Lanham Act registration for its mark "Park'N Fly". In 1977 it filed an affidavit required by § 15, 15 U.S.C. § 1065, stating the mark had been registered and in continuous use for five consecutive years. Respondent also provides long-term airport parking services under its trademark "Dollar Park and Fly" in Portland, Oregon. Petitioner filed an infringement action against the respondent and respondent counterclaimed seeking cancellation of the registration. Respondent argued the petitioner's mark was unenforceable because it was merely descriptive. The District Court found for petitioner holding that an incontestable mark cannot be challenged on the grounds that it is merely descriptive. The Ninth Circuit reversed holding that incontestability provides a defense against cancellation but may not be used offensively to enjoin another's use. The United States Supreme Court granted certiorari to resolve a dispute between the circuits on the scope of the incontestability provisions.]

JUSTICE O'CONNOR delivered the opinion of the Court.

* * *

This case requires us to consider the effect of the incontestability provisions of the Lanham Act in the context of an infringement action defended on the grounds that the mark is merely descriptive. Statutory construction must begin with the language employed by Congress and the assumption that the ordinary meaning of that language accurately expresses the legislative purpose.

* * *

One searches the language of the Lanham Act in vain to find any support for the offensive/defensive distinction applied by the Court of Appeals. The statute nowhere distinguishes between a registrant's offensive and defensive use of an incontestable mark. On the contrary, § 33(b)'s declaration that the registrant has an "exclusive right" to use the mark indicates that incontestable status may be used to enjoin infringement by others. A conclusion that such infringement cannot be enjoined renders meaningless the "exclusive right" recognized by the statute. Moreover, the language in three of the defenses enumerated in § 33(b) clearly contemplates the use of incontestability in infringement actions by plaintiffs. See §§ 33(b)(4)–(6), 15 U.S.C. §§ 1115(b)(4)–(6).

The language of the Lanham Act also refutes any conclusion that an incontestable mark may be challenged as merely descriptive. A mark that is merely descriptive of an applicant's goods or services is not registrable unless the mark has secondary meaning. Before a mark achieves incontestable status, registration provides prima facie evidence of the registrant's exclusive right to use the mark in commerce. § 33(a), 15 U.S.C. § 1115(a). The Lanham Act expressly provides that before a mark becomes incontestable an opposing party may prove any legal or equitable defense which might have been asserted if the mark had not been registered. Ibid. Thus, § 33(a) would have allowed respondent to challenge petitioner's mark as merely descriptive if the mark had not become incontestable. With respect to incontestable marks, however, § 33(b) provides that registration is *conclusive* evidence of the registrant's exclusive right to use the mark, subject to the conditions of § 15 and the seven defenses enumerated in § 33(b) itself. Mere descriptiveness is not recognized by either § 15 or § 33(b) as a basis for challenging an incontestable mark.

* * *

III

Nothing in the legislative history of the Lanham Act supports a departure from the plain language of the statutory provisions concerning incontestability. * * * The incontestability provisions, as the proponents of the Lanham Act emphasized, provide a means for the registrant to quiet title in the ownership of his mark. The opportunity to obtain incontestable status by satisfying the requirements of § 15 thus encourages producers to cultivate the good will associated with a particular mark. This function of the incontestability provisions would be utterly frustrated if the holder of an incontestable mark could not enjoin infringement by others so long as they established that the mark would not be registrable but for its incontestable status.

Respondent argues, however, that enforcing petitioner's mark would conflict with the goals of the Lanham Act because the mark is merely descriptive and should never have been registered in the first place.

* * *

Respondent's argument that enforcing petitioner's mark will not promote the goals of the Lanham Act is misdirected. Arguments similar to those now urged by respondent were in fact considered by Congress in hearings on the Lanham Act. * * * These concerns were answered by proponents of the Lanham Act, who noted that a merely descriptive mark cannot be registered unless the Commissioner finds that it has secondary meaning. Id., at 108, 113 (testimony of Karl Pohl, U.S. Trade Mark Assn.). Moreover, a mark can be challenged for five years prior to its attaining incontestable status. Id., at 114 (remarks of Rep. Lanham).

* * *

VI

We conclude that the holder of a registered mark may rely on incontestability to enjoin infringement and that such an action may not be defended on the grounds that the mark is merely descriptive. The judgment of the Court of Appeals is reversed and the case is remanded for further proceedings consistent with this opinion.

It is so ordered.

JUSTICE STEVENS, dissenting.

*   *   *

The mark "Park'N Fly" is at best merely descriptive in the context of airport parking. *   *   * Petitioner never submitted any such proof to the Commissioner, or indeed to the District Court in this case. Thus, the registration plainly violated the Act. *no secondary meaning established.*

*   *   *

If the registrant of a merely descriptive mark complies with the statutory requirement that prima-facie evidence of secondary meaning must be submitted to the Patent and Trademark Office, it is entirely consistent with the policy of the Act to accord the mark incontestable status after an additional five years of continued use. For if no rival contests the registration in that period, it is reasonable to presume that the initial prima-facie showing of distinctiveness could not be rebutted. But if no proof of secondary meaning is ever presented, either to the Patent and Trademark Office or to a court, there is simply no rational basis for leaping to the conclusion that the passage of time has transformed an inherently defective mark into an incontestable mark.

*   *   *

Congress enacted the Lanham Act "to secure trade-mark owners in the goodwill which they have built up." But without a showing of secondary meaning, there is no basis upon which to conclude that petitioner has built up any good will that is secured by the mark "Park 'N-Fly." In fact, without a showing of secondary meaning, we should presume that petitioner's business appears to the consuming public to be just another anonymous, indistinguishable parking lot. When enacting the Lanham Act, Congress also wanted to "protect the public from imposition by the use of counterfeit and imitated marks and false trade descriptions." Upon this record there appears no danger of this occurrence, and as a practical matter, without any showing that the public can specifically identify petitioner's service, it seems difficult to believe that anyone would imitate petitioner's marks, or that such imitation, even if it occurred, would be likely to confuse anybody.

On the basis of the record in this case, it is reasonable to infer that the operators of parking lots in the vicinity of airports may make use of the words "park and fly" simply because those words provide a ready description of their businesses, rather than because of any desire to exploit petitioner's good will. There is a well-recognized public interest in prohibiting the commercial monopolization of phrases such as "park and fly." * * *

* * *

In exercising its broad power to do equity, the federal courts certainly can take into account the tension between the apparent meaning of § 33(b) and the plain command in § 2(e), (f) of the Act prohibiting the registration of a merely descriptive mark without any proof of secondary meaning. Because it would be "demonstrably at odds with the intent of Congress" to grant incontestable status to a mark that was not eligible for registration in the first place, the Court is surely authorized to require compliance with § 2(f) before granting relief on the basis of § 33(b).

The Legislative History

The language of § 2(e), (f) expressly demonstrates Congress' concern over granting monopoly privileges in merely descriptive marks. However, its failure to include mere descriptiveness in its laundry list of grounds on which incontestability could be challenged is interpreted by the Court today as evidence of congressional approval of incontestable status for all merely descriptive marks.

This history is unpersuasive because it is perfectly clear that the failure to include mere descriptiveness among the grounds for challenging incontestability was based on the understanding that such a mark would not be registered without a showing of secondary meaning. To read Congress' failure as equivalent to an endorsement of incontestable status for merely descriptive marks without secondary meaning can only be described as perverse.

The Practical Argument

The Court suggests that my reading of the Act "effectively emasculates § 33(b) under the circumstances of this case." But my reading would simply require the owner of a merely descriptive mark to prove secondary meaning before obtaining any benefit from incontestability. If a mark is in fact "distinctive of the applicant's goods in commerce" as § 2(f) requires, that burden should not be onerous. If the mark does not have any such secondary meaning, the burden of course could not be met. But if that be the case, the purposes of the Act are served, not frustrated, by requiring adherence to the statutory procedure mandated by Congress.

* * *

NOTES

1. The scope of incontestability is far from clear. Does the conclusive nature of the registration extend beyond the exact mark registered or beyond the goods or services included in the registration. If a producer has an incontestable registration for the mark "Saucer" for frisbees, may a second producer use the mark "Saw–Ser" on frisbees or the mark "Saucer" on other recreational toys? In infringement cases, the owner of the incontestable mark

must still show likelihood of confusion. But could the second producer assert the mark is descriptive?

May a company with an incontestable registration be required to prove distinctiveness when it seeks registration of the mark on closely related goods? Should an opposer be entitled to claim the mark is descriptive? Is there any good reason why the incontestability of a mark should be narrowly confined to the precise goods and services listed in the incontestable registration? See In re Loew's Theatres, Inc., 769 F.2d 764 (Fed.Cir.1985) (incontestable registration on cigars did not protect applicant for same mark on chewing tobacco); In re BankAmerica Corp., 231 U.S.P.Q. 873 (TTAB 1986) (proof of distinctiveness required on new application for "Bank of America" for financial data processing notwithstanding incontestable registrations on a wide variety of banking services.

2. Consider the facts in Wrist-Rocket Mfg. Co., Inc. v. Saunders Archery Co., 516 F.2d 846 (8th Cir.1975), cert. denied 423 U.S. 870 (1975), appeal from remand 578 F.2d 727 (8th Cir.1978):

> Howard Ellenburg is the inventor of a wrist-braced slingshot [unpatented] that he initially marketed, through an Iowa sporting goods distributor, as "Howard's Wrist Locker Slingshot." This initial marketing arrangement was soon terminated by agreement of the parties, and Ellenburg thereafter entered into a distributorship agreement with Saunders, an established distributor of archery related sporting goods. This agreement, reduced to writing in July, 1954, gave Saunders the exclusive right to sell the slingshots manufactured by Ellenburg, with the latter retaining the right to make direct sales to customers, but not to dealers. The agreement was not strictly followed by either party, and it terminated by its own force in 1964. The agreement, nevertheless, did form the basis of the parties' business relationship which continued until November, 1971, when it was terminated by Saunders. After the termination, Ellenburg revived his distributorship agreement with the Iowa company and continued to manufacture "Wrist Rocket" slingshots. Saunders also continued to market similar slingshots under the "Wrist Rocket" label after establishing his own manufacturing facility. This suit followed.

> Before the commencement of this suit, Ellenburg's right to use the trademark "Wrist Rocket" in interstate commerce had become incontestable pursuant to 15 U.S.C. § 1065.

Would you permit Ellenburg to prohibit Saunders from using the "Wrist-Rocket" mark? Would it make a difference if the public identified Saunders as the manufacturer or if the name "Saunders" had appeared on the package with the mark "Wrist Rocket"? Prior to 1989 § 33(b) provided only conclusive evidence of the registrant's right to use the mark. In 1989 the act was broadened to make conclusive the validity of the registered mark, the registration of the mark, and the ownership of the mark. Does this amendment help a claim like Ellenburg's?

3. Consider that § 33(b) (as well as § 14(c)) makes "abandonment by the registrant" a defense. Can you construct an argument that a mark that is "merely descriptive" has in fact lost "its significance as a mark" under the definition of abandonment in § 45 and accordingly has been "abandoned"? For an argument that the economic function of trademarks would best be enhanced by permitting persons to challenge an incontestable mark on the basis of lack of

current distinctiveness, see Naresh, Incontestability and Rights in Descriptive Marks, 53 U.Chi.L.Rev. 953 (1986).

4. A mark may be refused registration under § 2(d) if it is likely to cause confusion with a preexisting mark. However, after five years a registration may not be cancelled for this reason under § 14. However § 14(c) permits cancellation "at any time" if the registration was obtained contrary to § 2(a). This section provides a mark may not be registered if it falsely suggests "a connection with persons, living or dead * * *". Aren't § 2(a) and § 2(d) really the same in that a mark that creates a likelihood of confusion at the same time suggests a connection between the goods and another "person" (§ 45 defines "person" to include corporations). The courts have been troubled by this apparent method of escaping the 5 year limit for cancellation and accordingly destroying the incontestable nature of a mark. See University of Notre Dame Du Lac v. J.C. Gourmet Food Imports Co., Inc., 703 F.2d 1372 (Fed.Cir. 1983) where the University objected to the defendant's sale of "Notre Dame" cheese. The court approved of earlier rulings by the Trademark Trial and Appeal Board that in a trademark action under § 2(a) intent to deceive as well as likelihood of confusion must be shown. Even though the University had not sold cheese or related products it could also rely on § 2(a) if it could show an injury similar to violation of its right of privacy. However, that required that the use of the term "Notre Dame" "point uniquely" to the University. Noting that the term is used for churches as well as the University, the court denied relief. See also American Speech-Language-Hearing Association v. National Hearing Aid Society, 224 U.S.P.Q. 798 (TTAB 1985).

PROBLEMS

The student may find it helpful to work through the following problems relating to assessing priority between two individuals who use essentially the same mark on substantially the same goods in substantially the same geographic areas.

Problem 1. ABC Co. begins using the mark "Wham" in 1956 on its widgets. XYZ begins using the mark "Wham-O" in 1958. Neither registers. What are the rights of the parties?

Problem 2. Same facts as Problem 1 except that ABC registers its mark on the principal register in 1957. What are XYZ's rights in 1958? In 1963 if ABC's registration has become incontestable?

Problem 3. Same facts as Problem 1 except that XYZ registers its mark on the principal register in 1958. ABC does not register its mark. What are ABC's rights in 1959? In 1964 if XYZ's mark has become incontestable?

Problem 4. Would it make any difference in any of the problems above if a third company, MNP Corp. had manufactured widgets beginning in 1950 under the unregistered mark "Wham-E"? If MNP had registered the mark on the principal register in 1955? If MNP's registration had become incontestable in 1960?

(4) GEOGRAPHIC LIMITATIONS

HANOVER STAR MILLING CO. v. METCALF
Supreme Court of the United States, 1916.
240 U.S. 403, 36 S.Ct. 357, 60 L.Ed. 713.

[This case involved two separate actions involving the use of "Tea Rose" as a trademark for flour in Butler County, Alabama. In 1872 the Allen & Wheeler Company, an Ohio firm, adopted and used the mark on flour and there is evidence that they sold flour under that mark between 1872 and 1904 in Ohio, Pennsylvania, and Massachusetts. In 1904 the company was incorporated. There was no evidence to show that Allen & Wheeler or its successor corporation at any time sold flour under the contested mark in Alabama. In 1885 Hanover Star Milling Co., an Illinois company, adopted the contested mark for flour in good faith and without notice of A. & W.'s prior use. In 1904 Hanover began an extensive campaign to sell its "Tea Rose" flour in Alabama and other south-eastern states. As the Supreme Court found: " * * * the Hanover Star Milling Company has come to be known as the Tea Rose mill, the reputation of the mill is bound up with the reputation of Tea Rose flour, and 'Tea Rose' in the flour trade in the territory referred to means flour of the Hanover Company's manufacture." In the first case Allen & Wheeler sued Hanover for trademark infringement seeking to prohibit Hanover's use of the mark anywhere in the United States.

The second action was by Hanover against Metcalf as selling agent for Steeleville Milling Company, an Illinois company. Steeleville had adopted the mark in question in 1895 and used it for its flour in Illinois, Tennessee, Mississippi, Louisiana, and Arkansas. Metcalf, a flour distributor in Greenville, was unable to sell Hanover's "Tea Rose" flour because of Hanover's exclusive selling arrangement with Metcalf's competitor. Metcalf, instead, purchased Steeleville's "Tea Rose" flour and sold it in Alabama. In this second action, the Supreme Court upheld Hanover's complaint alleging unfair competition and precluded Metcalf from selling "Tea Rose" flour in Alabama. The portions of the opinion reproduced below relate to the first case between Allen & Wheeler and Hanover Star.]

MR. JUSTICE PITNEY delivered the opinion of the court.

* * *

Expressions are found in many of the cases to the effect that the exclusive right to the use of a trade-mark is founded on priority of appropriation. * * * In the ordinary case of parties competing under the same mark in the same market, it is correct to say that prior appropriation settles the question. But where two parties independently are employing the same mark upon goods of the same class, but in separate markets wholly remote the one from the other, the question of prior appropriation is legally insignificant, unless at least it appear that the second adopter has selected the mark with some design inimical to the interests of the first user, such as to take the benefit of the reputation of his goods, to forestall the extension of his trade, or the like.

Of course, if the symbol or device is already in general use, employed in such a manner that its adoption as an index of source or origin would only produce confusion and mislead the public, it is not susceptible of adoption as a trade-mark. Such a case was Columbia Mill Co. v. Alcorn, 150 U.S. 460, 464, affirming 40 Fed.Rep. 676, where it appeared that before complainant's adoption of the disputed word as a brand for its flour the same word was used for the like purpose by numerous mills in different parts of the country.

That property in a trade-mark is not limited in its enjoyment by territorial bounds, but may be asserted and protected wherever the law affords a remedy for wrongs, is true in a limited sense. Into whatever markets the use of a trade-mark has extended, or its meaning has become known, there will the manufacturer or trader whose trade is pirated by an infringing use be entitled to protection and redress. But this is not to say that the proprietor of a trade-mark, good in the markets where it has been employed, can monopolize markets that his trade has never reached and where the mark signifies not his goods but those of another. We agree with the court below (208 Fed.Rep. 519) that "since it is the trade and not the mark, that is to be protected, a trade-mark acknowledges no territorial boundaries of municipalities or states or nations, but extends to every market where the trader's goods have become known and identified by his use of the mark. But the mark, of itself, cannot travel to markets where there is no article to wear the badge and no trader to offer the article."

* * *

* * * Allowing to the Allen & Wheeler firm and corporation the utmost that the proofs disclose in their favor, they have continued their use of the "Tea Rose" trade-mark to a limited territory, leaving the south-eastern States untouched. Even if they did not know—and it does not appear that they did know—that the Hanover Company was doing so, they must be held to have taken the risk that some innocent party might, during their forty years of inactivity, hit upon the same mark and expend money and effort in building up a trade in flour under it. If, during the long period that has elapsed since the last specified sale of Allen & Wheeler "Tea Rose"—this was "in the later 70's"—that flour has been sold in other parts of the United States excluding the south-eastern States, no clearer evidence of abandonment by non-user of trademark rights in the latter field could reasonably be asked for. And when it appears, as it does, that the Hanover Company in good faith and without notice of the Allen & Wheeler mark has expended much money and effort in building up its trade in the south-eastern market, so that "Tea Rose" there means Hanover Company's flour and nothing else, the Allen & Wheeler Company is estopped to assert trade-mark infringement as to that territory.

* * *

Mr. Justice Holmes concurring.

* * *

I think state lines, speaking always of matters outside the authority of Congress, are important in another way. I do not believe that a trade-mark established in Chicago could be used by a competitor in some other part of Illinois on the ground that it was not known there. I think that if it is good in one part of the State it is good in all. But when it seeks to pass state lines it may find itself limited by what has been done under the sanction of a power coordinate with that of Illinois and paramount over the territory concerned. If this view be adopted we get rid of all questions of penumbra, of shadowy marches where it is difficult to decide whether the business extends to them. We have sharp lines drawn upon the fundamental consideration of the jurisdiction originating the right. In most cases the change of jurisdiction will not be important because the new law will take up and apply the same principles as the old, but when, as here, justice to its own people requires a State to set a limit, it may do so, and this court cannot pronounce its action wrong.

BURGER KING OF FLORIDA, INC. v. HOOTS

United States Court of Appeals, Seventh Circuit, 1968.
403 F.2d 904.

Kiley, Circuit Judge. Defendants' appeal presents a conflict between plaintiffs' right to use the trade mark "Burger King," which plaintiffs have registered under the Federal Trade Mark Act, and defendants' right to use the same trade mark which defendants have registered under the Illinois Trade Mark Act.[2] The district court resolved the conflict in favor of plaintiffs in this case of first impression in this Circuit. We affirm the judgment restraining the defendants from using the name "Burger King" in any part of Illinois except in their Mattoon, Illinois, market, and restraining plaintiffs from using their trade mark in the market area of Mattoon, Illinois.[3]

* * *

Plaintiff Burger King of Florida, Inc. opened the first "Burger King" restaurant in Jacksonville, Florida, in 1953. By 1955, fifteen of these restaurants were in operation in Florida, Georgia and Tennessee; in 1956 the number operating in Alabama, Kentucky and Virginia was twenty-nine; by 1957, in these states, thirty-eight restaurants were in operation.

In July, 1961, plaintiffs opened their first Illinois "Burger King" restaurant in Skokie, and at that time had notice of the defendants' prior registration of the same mark under the Illinois Trade Mark Act. Thereafter, on October 3, 1961, plaintiffs' certificate of federal registration of the mark was issued. Subsequently, plaintiffs opened a restau-

2. Ill.Rev.Stat., Ch. 140 §§ 8 et seq. (1967).

3. The district court defined the Mattoon market area as a circle having a radi-

us of twenty miles, and a center located at the defendants' place of business in Mattoon, Illinois.

rant in Champaign, Illinois, and at the time of the trial in November, 1967, were operating more than fifty "Burger King" restaurants in the state of Illinois.

In 1957 the defendants, who had been operating an ice cream business in Mattoon, Illinois, opened a "Burger King" restaurant there. In July, 1959, they registered that name under Illinois law as their trade mark, without notice of plaintiffs' prior use of the same mark. On September 26, 1962, the defendants, with constructive knowledge of plaintiffs' federal trade mark, opened a second similar restaurant, in Charleston, Illinois.

Both parties have used the trade mark prominently, and in 1962 they exchanged charges of infringement in Illinois. After plaintiffs opened a restaurant in Champaign, Illinois, defendants sued in the state court to restrain plaintiffs' use of the mark in Illinois. Plaintiffs then brought the federal suit, now before us, and the defendants counter-claimed for an injunction, charging plaintiffs with infringement of their Illinois trade mark.

The district court concluded, from the unchallenged findings, that plaintiffs' federal registration is prima facie evidence of the validity of the registration and ownership of the mark; that plaintiffs have both a common-law and a federal right in the mark superior to defendants' in the area of natural expansion of plaintiffs' enterprise which "logically included" all of Illinois, except where defendants had actually adopted and used the mark, innocently, i.e., without notice and in good faith; and that the defendants had adopted and continuously used the mark in the Mattoon area innocently and were entitled to protection in that market.

We hold that the district court properly decided that plaintiffs' federal registration of the trade mark "Burger King" gave them the exclusive right to use the mark in Illinois except in the Mattoon market area in Illinois where the defendants, without knowledge of plaintiffs' prior use, actually used the mark before plaintiffs' federal registration. The defendants did not acquire the exclusive right they would have acquired by their Illinois registration had they actually used the mark throughout Illinois prior to the plaintiffs' federal registration.

We think our holding is clear from the terms of the Federal Trade Mark Act. Under 15 U.S.C. § 1065 of the Act, plaintiffs, owners of the federally registered trade mark "Burger King," have the "incontestable" right to use the mark in commerce, except to the extent that such use infringes what valid right the defendants have acquired by their continuous use of the same mark prior to plaintiffs' federal registration.

Under 15 U.S.C. § 1115(b), the federal certificate of registration is "conclusive evidence" of plaintiffs' "exclusive right" to use the mark. This Section, however, also provides a defense to an exclusive right to use a trade mark: If a trade mark was adopted without knowledge of the federal registrant's prior use, and has been continuously used, then such use "shall" constitute a defense to infringement, provided that this defense applies only for the area in which such continuous prior use is proved.   Since the defendants have established that they had adopted the mark "Burger King" without knowledge of plaintiffs' prior use and that they had continuously used the mark from a date prior to plaintiffs' federal registration of the mark, they are entitled to protection in the area which that use appropriated to them.

Plaintiffs agree that the defendants as prior good faith users are to be protected in the area that they had appropriated.   Thus, the question narrows to what area in Illinois the defendants have appropriated by virtue of their Illinois registration.

At common law, defendants were entitled to protection in the Mattoon market area because of the innocent use of the mark prior to plaintiffs' federal registration.   They argue that the Illinois Trade Mark Act was designed to give more protection than they already had at common law, and that various provisions[4] of the Illinois Act indicate an intention to afford Illinois registrants exclusive rights to use trade marks throughout the state, regardless of whether they actually used the marks throughout the state or not.   However, the Act itself does not express any such intention.   And no case has been cited to us, nor has our research disclosed any case in the Illinois courts deciding whether a registrant is entitled to statewide protection even if he has used the mark only in a small geographical area.

* * *

* * * Under 15 U.S.C. § 1115(b) of the Lanham Act, the federal certificate can be "conclusive evidence" of registrant's "exclusive right."   And 15 U.S.C. § 1127 of the Act provides that "The intent of this chapter is * * * to protect registered marks used in such commerce from interference by State * * * legislation."   The Illinois Act, however, provides only that a certificate of registration "shall be admissible * * * evidence as competent and sufficient proof of the registration * * *."   Ill.Rev.Stat. Ch. 140, § 11 (1967).

Moreover, we think that whether or not Illinois intended to enlarge the common law with respect to a right of exclusivity in that state, the Illinois Act does not enlarge its right in the area where the federal mark has priority.   * * * Congress expanded the common law, however, by granting an exclusive right in commerce to federal registrants in areas where there has been no offsetting use of the mark.   Congress intended the Lanham Act to afford nationwide protection to federally-registered marks, and that once the certificate has issued, no person can acquire any additional rights superior to those obtained by the federal registrant.   See John R. Thompson Co. v. Holloway, 366 F.2d 108 (5th Cir.1966); Dawn Donut Co. v. Hart's Food Stores, Inc., 267 F.2d 358 (2d Cir.1959).

---

4. Ill.Rev.Stat., Ch. 140 §§ 9(f), 16(A)(4) (c) (1967).   These sections prohibit dual registration of a trade mark in Illinois.

* * *

We conclude that if we were to accept the defendants' argument we would be fostering, in clear opposition to the express terms of the Lanham Act, an interference with plaintiffs' exclusive right in interstate commerce to use its federal mark.

The undisputed continuous market for the defendants' "Burger King" products was confined to a twenty mile radius of Mattoon. There is no evidence before us of any intention or hope for their use of their Illinois mark beyond that market. Yet they seek to exclude plaintiffs from expanding the scope of their national exclusive right, and from operating fifty enterprises already begun in Illinois. This result would clearly burden interstate commerce.

The defendants argue also that unless they are given the right to exclusive use throughout Illinois, many persons from all parts of Illinois in our current mobile society will come in contact with the defendants' business and will become confused as to whether they are getting the defendants' product, as they intended.

We are not persuaded by this argument. Defendants have not shown that the Illinois public is likely to confuse the products furnished by plaintiffs and by defendants. John R. Thompson Co. v. Holloway, 366 F.2d 108 (5th Cir.1966), and cases cited therein. We are asked to infer that confusion will exist from the mere fact that both trade marks co-exist in the state of Illinois. However, the district court found that the defendants' market area was limited to within twenty miles of their place of business. The court's decision restricted the use of the mark by plaintiffs and defendants to sufficiently distinct and geographically separate markets so that public confusion would be reduced to a minimum. The mere fact that some people will travel from one market area to the other does not, of itself, establish that confusion will result. Since the defendants have failed to establish on the record any likelihood of confusion or any actual confusion, they are not entitled to an inference that confusion will result.

For the reasons given, the judgment of the district court is affirmed.

DAWN DONUT CO. v. HART'S FOOD STORES, INC.
United States Court of Appeals, Second Circuit, 1959.
267 F.2d 358.

[Plaintiff, Dawn Donut Co., has since 1922 continuously used the trademark "Dawn" upon various bulk packages of dough mixes for doughnuts, cakes, and other baked goods. It distributes the mixes and licenses the use of the marks "Dawn" and "Dawn Donut" principally to individuals who agree to establish retail bakeries under the name "Dawn Donut Shops." Defendant, Hart Food Stores, owns and operates a retail grocery chain within several New York counties. The products of defendant's baker are distributed through its grocery stores and since August 30, 1951 have carried the mark "Dawn". The distribution of defendant's products is limited to an area within a 45 mile radius of Rochester, New York. Plaintiff has not licensed the use of its mark at the retail level within 60 miles of defendant's trading area except for one "Dawn Donut Shop" operated in Rochester during 1926–27.

[Plaintiff's mark was registered federally in 1927 and the registration was renewed in 1947 under the Lanham Act. Defendant's mark is unregistered. The district court found that defendant's use of the mark "Dawn" was without any actual notice of plaintiff's use or registration and was adopted in good faith from the slogan "Baked at midnight, delivered at Dawn" which had been used by the defendant from 1929 to 1935.]

LUMBARD, CIRCUIT JUDGE. The principal question is whether the plaintiff, a wholesale distributor of doughnuts and other baked goods under its federally registered trademarks "Dawn" and "Dawn Donut," is entitled under the provisions of the Lanham Trade-Mark Act to enjoin the defendant from using the mark "Dawn" in connection with the retail sale of doughnuts and baked goods entirely within a six county area of New York State surrounding the city of Rochester. The primary difficulty arises from the fact that although plaintiff licenses purchasers of its mixes to use its trademarks in connection with the retail sales of food products made from the mixes, it has not licensed or otherwise exploited the mark at the retail level in defendant's market area for some thirty years.

* * *

Defendant's principal contention is that because plaintiff has failed to exploit the mark "Dawn" for some thirty years at the retail level in the Rochester trading area, plaintiff should not be accorded the exclusive right to use the mark in this area.

We reject this contention as inconsistent with the scope of protection afforded a federal registrant by the Lanham Act.

Prior to the passage of the Lanham Act courts generally held that the owner of a registered trademark could not sustain an action for infringement against another who, without knowledge of the registration, used the mark in a different trading area from that exploited by the registrant so that public confusion was unlikely. Hanover Star Milling Co. v. Metcalf, 1916, 240 U.S. 403; * * *

But the Lanham Act, 15 U.S.C. § 1072, provides that registration of a trademark on the principal register is constructive notice of the registrant's claim of ownership. Thus, by eliminating the defense of good faith and lack of knowledge, § 1072 affords nationwide protection to registered marks, regardless of the areas in which the registrant actually uses the mark.

That such is the purpose of Congress is further evidenced by 15 U.S.C. § 1115(a) and (b) which make the certificate of registration evidence of the registrant's "exclusive right to use the * * * mark in commerce." "Commerce" is defined in 15 U.S.C. § 1127 to include all the commerce which may lawfully be regulated by Congress. These two provisions of the Lanham Act make it plain that the fact that the defendant employed the mark "Dawn," without actual knowledge of plaintiff's registration, at the retail level in a limited geographical area of New York state before the plaintiff used the mark in that market, does not entitle it either to exclude the plaintiff from using the mark in that area or to use the mark concurrently once the plaintiff licenses the mark or otherwise exploits it in connection with retail sales in the area.

Plaintiff's failure to license its trademarks in defendant's trading area during the thirty odd years that have elapsed since it licensed them to a Rochester baker does not work an abandonment of the rights in that area. We hold that 15 U.S.C. § 1127, which provides for abandonment in certain cases of non-use, applies only when the registrant fails to use his mark, within the meaning of § 1127, anywhere in the nation. Since the Lanham Act affords a registrant nationwide protection, a contrary holding would create an insoluble problem of measuring the geographical extent of the abandonment. * * *

[The court rejected defendant's claim that plaintiff was prevented by laches from enjoining defendant's use of the mark "Dawn". Defendant argued that a sales representative of plaintiff and other companies called on defendant and saw the defendant's use of the mark. The court found that knowledge of the sales representative could not be imputed to the plaintiff and therefore plaintiff was "not estopped by reason of laches from enforcing its exclusive right" to use the mark.]

Accordingly, we turn to the question of whether on this record plaintiff has made a sufficient showing to warrant the issuance of an injunction against defendant's use of the mark "Dawn" in a trading area in which the plaintiff has for thirty years failed to employ its registered mark.

The Lanham Act, 15 U.S.C. § 1114, sets out the standard for awarding a registrant relief against the unauthorized use of his mark by another. It provides that the registrant may enjoin only that concurrent use which creates a likelihood of public confusion as to the origin of the products in connection with which the marks are used. Therefore if the use of the marks by the registrant and the unauthorized user are confined to two sufficiently distinct and geographically separate markets, with no likelihood that the registrant will expand his use into defendant's market, so that no public confusion is possible, then the registrant is not entitled to enjoin the junior user's use of the mark. * * *

As long as plaintiff and defendant confine their use of the mark "Dawn" in connection with the retail sale of baked goods to their present separate trading areas it is clear that no public confusion is likely.

* * *

The decisive question then is whether plaintiff's use of the mark "Dawn" at the retail level is likely to be confined to its current area of use or whether in the normal course of its business, it is likely to expand the retail use of the mark into defendant's trading area. If such expansion were probable, then the concurrent use of the marks would give rise to the conclusion that there was a likelihood of confusion.

* * *

Accordingly, because plaintiff and defendant use the mark in connection with retail sales in distinct and separate markets and because there is no present prospect that plaintiff will expand its use of the mark at the retail level into defendant's trading area, we conclude that there is no likelihood of public confusion arising from the concurrent use of the marks and therefore the issuance of an injunction is not warranted. *A fortiori* plaintiff is not entitled to any accounting or damages. However, because of the effect we have attributed to the constructive notice provision of the Lanham Act, the plaintiff may later, upon a proper showing of an intent to use the mark at the retail level in defendant's market area, be entitled to enjoin defendant's use of the mark.

* * *

APPLICATION OF BEATRICE FOODS CO.
United States Court of Customs and Patent Appeals, 1970.
429 F.2d 466.

[Beatrice Foods Co., a manufacturer and processor of food products with a home office in Chicago, Illinois, began in 1953 to market a one-pound package of oleomargarine under the brand "Homestead". Fairway Foods, Inc., having its home office in St. Paul, Minnesota, began in 1956 to market dairy products including butter, milk, ice cream and eggs using the trademark "Homestead". On June 18, 1962, Fairway (referred to by the court as "prior applicant") filed an application to register the mark "Homestead" for dairy products on the Principal Register. Beatrice Foods Co. (referred to by the court as "prior user") filed an opposition alleging prior use of the identical mark for oleomargarine. Fairway subsequently amended its application to restrict it to specified geographic areas. On March 9, 1965, Beatrice filed an application for registration on the Principal Register setting forth, as an exception to its right to exclusive use of its mark, the right of Fairway to use the mark in the specified geographical areas. The concurrent use proceedings were thereafter instituted.

The parties filed a stipulation which set out an agreement reached between the parties as to their rights to the concurrent registrations as they had geographically restricted them. Prior applicant restricted its application to Wisconsin, Minnesota, Iowa, South Dakota, North Dakota, certain counties in eastern Montana, and the Upper Peninsula of Michigan. Prior user claimed the remainder of the United States.

The Trademark Trial and Appeal Board refused to accept the stipulated agreement. The parties were then permitted to introduce evidence by way of verified showings which indicated: (1) Prior applicant, although expressing an intention to expand into the Upper Peninsula of Michigan and eastern Montana, had not in fact used the mark in those areas; and (2) Prior user established actual use of the mark in 20 states. The Board ruled first, that in concurrent use proceedings the parties are only entitled to registrations which are restricted geographically to those areas in which the marks involved have actually been used, and second, that rights claimed by a party in a mark must be in existence at the time of the filing of its application for registration. Both parties appealed.]

BALDWIN, JUDGE. This represents the first occasion on which this Court has been asked to review a decision of the Trademark Trial and Appeal Board in a Concurrent Use Proceeding instituted under § 2(d) of the Lanham Trademark Act, 15 U.S.C. § 1052(d). * * *

No. 8294

Beatrice Foods Co., the prior user, has appealed from the decisions of the board refusing to permit its registration to cover that portion of the United States lying outside both the territory of Fairway and the area where Beatrice had made actual use of the mark prior to filing its application. The issue here, simply stated, is the correctness of the board's holding that "parties involved in a concurrent use proceeding in the United States Patent Office are entitled to registrations which are limited to those areas only in which the marks involved have actually been used." * * *

The position taken by the board in this case is obviously inconsistent with the practice of granting unrestricted registrations in cases where there is only a single applicant, and must therefore find support and justification, if at all, in the language of the proviso to § 2(d) or in some policy surrounding the proviso which differs from that behind the rest of the Lanham Act upon which the practice of granting unrestricted registrations in all other cases is based.

Looking first at the language of the proviso, we find that it sets out two requirements for the issuance of concurrent registrations for the same or similar marks to more than one person: first, such persons must "have become *entitled to use* such marks as a result of their concurrent lawful *use* in commerce *prior to* (i) the earliest of the filing dates of the applications pending," (emphasis added); and, second, it must be determined "that confusion, mistake, or deception is not likely to result from the continued use" of the marks by such persons. When it is determined that the likelihood of confusion, mistake or deception will be avoided only "under conditions and limitations as to the mode or place of use of the marks or the goods in connection with which such marks are used", the Commissioner is empowered to prescribe such conditions and limitations "with which such mark is registered to the respective persons." We find nothing in the language of the proviso, which, per se, *requires* the result reached by the board in this case.

Considering now the policy behind this provision of the act, it is our view that the proviso reflects a recognition, by the framers of that statute, that occasions do and will arise where two or more persons will independently adopt the same or a similar trademark and use it under the same or similar circumstances, and indicates their concern that a mechanism be provided for an equitable resolution of the problems which such concurrent use creates. As we see it, this is nothing more than an application of the basic policies underlying the Lanham Act as a whole.

It should be emphasized that what the parties here are seeking, and what the statute, in the proviso to § 2(d), authorizes, are concurrent federal *registrations*. Much confusion can be avoided by recognizing that such registrations would not, in and of themselves, create any new right to *use* the trademark or to assert rights based on ownership of the trademark itself. Rights of trademark ownership, for example, the right to enjoin another from use of the mark, must be based upon actual use and can be enforced only in areas of existing business influence (i.e., current use or probability of expansion). United Drug Co. v. Theodore Rectanus Co., 248 U.S. 90 (1918); Hanover Star Milling Co. v. Metcalf, 240 U.S. 403 (1916). It is now well settled that the Lanham Act did not alter this aspect of the prior law. See American Foods, Inc. v. Golden Flake, Inc., 312 F.2d 619 (5th Cir.1963); Dawn Donut Co. v. Hart's Food Stores, Inc., 267 F.2d 358 (2d Cir.1959).

Rights appurtenant to the ownership of a federal trademark registration, on the other hand, may be considered supplemental to those recognized at common law, stemming from ownership of a trademark. A federal registration gives certain procedural rights, such as the right to invoke jurisdiction of the federal courts (15 U.S.C. § 1121), and the right to rely on certain evidentiary presumptions (15 U.S.C. § 1115), but more importantly, the constructive notice provision of § 22 of the Lanham Act (15 U.S.C. § 1072), takes away from future users of the mark registered the defense of innocent appropriation. The owner of a federal registration now has the security of knowing that no one else may, henceforth legitimately adopt his trademark and create rights in another area of the country superior to his own. In this respect, this provision of § 22 is, perhaps, the best example of the intent of Congress to provide for a thriving business environment by granting nationwide protection to expanding businesses. It is the right to have this protection which the party Beatrice is, in effect, seeking through this appeal. As urged by Beatrice, it would be illogical and inconsistent with the objectives of the Lanham Act, not to provide for nationwide coverage where there is more than one registration—provided there will be no public confusion created thereby. The constructive notice provision of § 22 of the act was promulgated with the hope of cutting down on the number of instances of concurrent use and the uncertainty and confusion attached thereto. See Halliday, Constructive Notice and Concurrent Registration, 38 Trademark Rep. 111 (1948). Leaving territory open, as does the requirement by the board in this case, would frustrate this policy and increase rather than reduce the possibility of confusion and litigation.

The foregoing is not intended to imply that the Patent Office is required to issue registrations covering the whole of the United States in all circumstances. Certainly the applicant or applicants may always request territorially restricted registrations. In addition, in carrying out the Commissioner's duty under the proviso of § 2(d) of determining whether confusion, mistake or deception is likely to result from the continued concurrent use of a mark by two or more parties, it may be held that such likelihood will be prevented only when each party is granted a very limited territory with parts of the United States granted to no one.

We earlier pointed out the two requirements which the proviso sets out as conditions precedent to the issuance of concurrent registrations. The first, that the parties be presently entitled to concurrently use the mark in commerce, we view as being primarily jurisdictional in nature. As with a single applicant, we consider the extent of such actual use to be irrelevant so long as it amounts to more than a mere token attempt to conform with the requirement of the statute. Cf. Fort Howard Paper Co. v. Kimberly-Clark Corp., 390 F.2d 1015 (1968). The touchstone, however, is the requirement that there be no likelihood of confusion, mistake or deception in the market place as to the source of the goods resulting from the continued concurrent use of the trademark. Only in satisfying this standard, can the Patent Office be sure that both the rights of the individual parties and those of the public are being protected. Once there has been a determination that both parties are entitled to a federal registration, the extent to which those registrations are to be restricted territorially must also be governed by the statutory standard of likelihood of confusion.

We have concluded that in concurrent use proceedings in which neither party owns a registration for the mark, the starting point for any determination as to the extent to which the registrations are to be territorially restricted should be the conclusion that the prior user is prima facie entitled to a registration covering the entire United States. Such a prior user, who applies for a registration before registration is granted to another party, is entitled to a registration having nationwide effect no less than if there were no concurrent user having registrable rights.[13] His rights and, therefore, his registration, should be limited only to the extent that any other subsequent user, who can establish

---

13. On the other hand, where the prior user does not apply for a registration before registration is granted to another, there may be valid grounds, based on a policy of rewarding those who first seek federal registration, and a consideration of the rights created by the existing registration, for limiting his registration to the area of actual use and permitting the prior registrant to retain the nationwide protec-

tion of the act restricted only by the territory of the prior user. See the opinion of Asst. Commissioner Fay in Coastal Chemical Co. v. Dust-A-Way, Inc., 139 USPQ 208 (1963). See also, Schwartz, Concurrent Registration Under the Lanham Trademark Act of 1946: What is the Impact on Section 2(d) of Section 22?, 55 Trademark Rep. 413 (1965).

the existence of rights earlier than the prior user's application for registration, can also prove a likelihood of confusion, mistake or deception.

Having decided that, once jurisdiction is settled by way of the parties' establishing prior concurrent use, the primary concern of the Patent Office, in determining whether and to what extent registrations are to be granted, is to be the avoidance of any likelihood of confusion, we see no reason why agreements such as that worked out by the parties here should not be considered. Unquestionably, such stipulations are never binding on the board. Nevertheless, if it can be determined that they are in good faith, there can be no better assurance of the absence of any likelihood of confusion, mistake or deception than the parties' promises to avoid any activity which might lead to such likelihood.

It is not to be inferred that the Patent Office should blindly adhere to any agreement or territorial stipulation made by the parties. Such arrangements should always be critically appraised. But the practical value of accepting agreements such as this, when made in good faith, should be apparent. We see no reason why they should not be given effect when it is plain that the statutory requirement of assuring the avoidance of confusion, mistake or deception is satisfied thereby. Compare In re National Distillers and Chemical Corp., 297 F.2d 941 (CCPA 1962); In re Fleet-Wing Corp., 188 F.2d 476 (CCPA 1951).[14] Surely, the action taken by the board in this case, i.e., merely restricting the parties to areas of actual use, provides little, if any, more assurance.

In summary then, we hold that the Trademark Trial and Appeal Board was in error in deciding that appellant Beatrice is entitled only to a registration restricted to the territory in which actual use prior to the earliest filing date was established. Its decision to that effect must, accordingly, be reversed. However, since it appears from the record before us that the board made no determination as to the question of likelihood of confusion, mistake or deception as required under the statute, this case is remanded for proceedings not inconsistent with the foregoing opinion.

No. 8295

Appellant, Fairway Foods, Inc., the prior applicant, appeals from the board's refusal to permit its registration to cover the Upper Peninsula of Michigan and the eastern counties of Montana. For the reasons fully set forth in our opinion in No. 8294, the board's decision with regard to Fairway must also be reversed and the case remanded.

---

14. Of course, we are not here dealing with agreements wherein one party a prior registrant, merely gives *consent* to the other party to *register* his mark. Compare In re Continental Baking Co., 390 F.2d 747 (CCPA 1968); In re Wilson Jones Co., 337 F.2d 670 (CCPA 1964). In this regard, see Derenberg, The Twenty-First Year of Administration of the Lanham Trademark Act of 1946, 58 Trademark Rep. 609, 633 (1968).

Because of the importance of the issues, however, and the fact that this case is one of first impression in this court, we will comment on the questions as to what circumstances, if any, short of actual use of the trademark, may create rights in a territory sufficient to warrant inclusion of that territory in a geographically restricted registration, and up to what time prior to registration any proof regarding the territorial extent of trademark rights be submitted. It will be remembered that Fairway asserted, on behalf of its rights to the contested areas, previous business activity, dominance of contiguous areas, a history of expansion, presently planned expansion into the two areas, and possible present penetration into Montana by way of goods bought in the Dakotas. It should also be noted that some of the activity relied on by Fairway occurred subsequent to its filing date. The board, in its decision, stated the requirements to be no less than *actual* use *prior* to the earliest filing date. We think both requirements are wrong.

The Commissioner of Patents has the statutory responsibility to make sure that concurrent registrations are limited so as to prevent the likelihood of confusion, mistake or deception from occurring. Where a party has submitted evidence sufficient to prove a strong probability of future expansion of his trade into an area, that area would then become an area of likelihood of confusion if a registration covering it was granted to the other party. For example, many forms of evidence which would ordinarily be proffered to show a likelihood of *expansion* would be the same kind submitted to argue a likelihood of *confusion* if another party began use of the mark in that area. Thus, based on the premise that territorially restricted registrations must issue and, further, that said registrations combined will encompass the entire United States, if a likelihood of confusion is to be avoided, the territories of the parties must be limited in such a way as to exclude from each the area of probable expansion of the other party. Considering the Commissioner's indicated responsibility, which, of course, is based on a desire to protect the public, submission of evidence such as that submitted by Fairway in this case should be encouraged. And reiterating what was said earlier, any attempt, by the parties themselves, to solve the problem of public confusion, should be given serious consideration by the Patent Office.

With regard to the question as to the time prior to which evidence of trademark usage must be established, we have already indicated that the board was in error. Nothing in the statute is apparent which requires that the filing date of an application for registration is the cut-off day for establishing rights by a showing of trademark use. The *fact* of trademark use in commerce, is, as we pointed out earlier, merely necessary to invoke the jurisdiction required to adjudicate the controversy. The *extent* of such use is important only in that it is necessary to consider in determining the rights to be granted each party.

* * * The extent to which concurrent registrations must be territorially restricted has an effect on the rights of both parties. In addition, there is the paramount interest of the public to be considered.

We feel, therefore, that it is both necessary and proper for the Patent Office to determine the "conditions and limitations" with which the marks are to be registered "on the basis of facts as they exist at the time when the issue of registrability is under consideration." * * * In the present type of proceeding this would apparently mean up to the close of the testimony period. We have considered the possible problems which might result from such practice, but find they are outweighed by the interests involved.

Summary

The decisions appealed from in both appeals are reversed and the cases remanded for proceedings not inconsistent with this opinion.

Reversed and remanded.

NOTES

1. Justice Holmes' concurring opinion in *Hanover Star* extending protection of trademarks state-wide did not win substantial favor. However, courts continue to use state boundaries for analytical purposes and for drawing lines when probable expansion is shown. Some state registration statutes purport to give state-wide protection.

As *Burger King* demonstrates, state power is also subject to the preemptive force of the Lanham Act. See however, Golden Door, Inc. v. Odisho, 646 F.2d 347 (9th Cir.1980) which involved a conflict between a limited prior use in conflict with a national registrant and the court held that although the prior user could not be enjoined under federal law because of the innocent prior use exemption in § 33(b) of the Lanham Act, California law could still enjoin the prior use where there was a likelihood of confusion. "By extending to federal registrants greater protection than is available under the Lanham Act, California law, like the Act, protects both the public from confusion about the services and products it is receiving and the public relations investment of plaintiff [federal registrant]."

2. What should the rule be after *Beatrice* if the junior user is the first to register the mark and is an expanding business? See Weiner King, Inc. v. Wiener King Corp., 615 F.2d 512 (CCPA 1980). The prior user (Weiner King) began using the mark in 1962 in New Jersey and remained small with a maximum of 3 restaurants all in New Jersey. The junior user (WKNC) adopted the mark in good faith in North Carolina in 1970, registered the mark in 1972, and expanded to 100 restaurants in 20 states. However much of the expansion took place *after* WKNC learned of Weiner King's prior use. In 1975 Weiner King applied for a registration and a concurrent use proceeding was instituted. Held: WKNC, the junior user, is entitled to a national registration subject to Weiner King's prior use. To Weiner King's argument that most of WKNC's expansion was in bad faith with notice of prior uses, the court responded:

> We hold that [knowledge of the prior use in this case] is insufficient to support a finding of bad faith. In so holding, we caution that such a determination must always be the product of the particular fact pattern involved in each case. While an attempt to "palm off," or a motive to "box in" a prior user by cutting into its probable area of expansion, each necessarily flowing from knowledge of the existence of

the prior user, might be sufficient to support a finding of bad faith, *mere knowledge of the existence of the prior user* should not, by itself, constitute bad faith.

3. In Noah's Inc. v. Nark, Inc., 560 F.Supp 1253 (E.D.Mo.1983), affirmed 728 F.2d 410 (8th Cir.1984), the senior user was the first to file for registration but was opposed by the junior user and a concurrent use proceeding was initiated. The senior user could show little or no expansion activity; the junior user had made plans to expand but was prevented from doing so by lawsuits threatened by senior user. The court awarded the national registration to the junior user subject to the senior user's prior use.

Does this mean the first user of a mark must seek to expand before national registrations can be secured? Or does it suggest that registration should follow quickly after first use?

4. Defining the trade area of the innocent prior user can be a difficult factual inquiry. A trade area may consist of an area of actual use, a zone of potential expansion, the area in which the firm advertises, and the area in which the firm has some reputation. A leading common law case defining the prior user's rights is Sweetarts v. Sunline, Inc., 380 F.2d 923 (8th Cir.1967) (prior user protected in area of significant market penetration and not where transactions have been "so small, sporadic, and inconsequential that present or anticipated market penetration is *di minimus*.")

See Natural Footwear Ltd. v. Hart, Schaffner & Marx, 760 F.2d 1383 (3d Cir.1985) where the court summarized *Sweetarts* as providing the following list of factors to be used to determine whether there was sufficient market penetration to establish prior use: "(1) the volume of sales of the trademarked products, (2) the growth trends (both postive and negative in the area), (3) the number of persons actually purchasing the product in relation to the potential number of customers; and (4) the amount of product advertising in the area." Id. at 1398–1399.

5. The "zone of natural expansion doctrine" was severely restricted in Raxton Corp. v. Anania Associates, Inc., 635 F.2d 924 (1st Cir.1980). The plaintiff (Rax) opened women's clothing stores in Illinois and New Jersey in 1978 using the mark "Off the Rax" and opened its first Massachusetts store in August, 1979. The defendant (Rack) began advertising its men's clothing store using the mark "Off the Rack" in Massachusetts in January, 1979, and in February located a large sign over its future store. It was notified of Rax's intent to open a store in Massachusetts in late February, 1979. In March, Rack made its first sale and in April opened its only store. The district court held that the plaintiff's first trademark use in Massachusetts was in August of 1979 but that because it maintained its executive warehouse in the state, was incorporated in the state, and had plans to open outlets in the state, Massachusetts was an area of its natural expansion. The defendant was enjoined from using its mark. The First Circuit reversed:

> A "natural expansion" doctrine that penalized innocent users of a trademark simply because they occupied what for them would be a largely undiscoverable path of some remote prior user's expansion strikes us as at once unworkable, unfair, and, in the light of statutory protection available today, unnecessary. Such a doctrine would have to weigh the remote prior user's intangible and unregistered interest in future expansion as more important than the subsequent user's actual and good faith use of its name. Besides involving the obvious practical

difficulties of defining the "natural expansion path" of a business, this doctrine would also allow trademark owners to "monopolize markets that [their] trade ha[d] never reached."   Hanover, supra, 240 U.S. at 416.

The unfairness of this doctrine vanishes if the hypothesis of an *innocent* subsequent user is dropped, or if it is shown that the disputed trademark is known to consumers in the area of subsequent use prior to the subsequent user's adoption.   In these cases it can be presumed unless demonstrated to the contrary that the subsequent user knowingly copied a mark.   At the least, this suggests that the subsequent user should have been more careful to select a name free of prior rights and should be held to assume the risk of its negligence.   At worst, this indicates a design to appropriate the good will of another.

6.   Is the expanded geographic protection afforded by the Lanham Act limited to the goods or services listed in the registration or does it extend beyond to similar goods?   Natural Footwear Ltd. v. Hart, Schaffner & Marx, 760 F.2d 1383 (3d Cir.1985) (limited to listed goods); Key Chemicals, Inc. v. Kelite Chemicals Corp., 464 F.2d 1040 (CCPA 1972) (may extend to related goods where there is a likelihood of confusion).

7.   The new intent-to-use provisions offer an additional means of securing national protection.   Section 7(c) provides such an application constitutes constructive use "nationwide in effect".

8.   What are the tradeoffs in these cases?   By providing rights that extend beyond actual use, doesn't the Lanham Act insure some consumer confusion?   Is the scope of protection of trademark rights more or less clearly defined after adoption of the Lanham Act?

PROBLEMS—PARALLEL IMPORTS (THE GRAY MARKET)

1.   A French manufacturer produces "Java" brand face powder in France. A United States company purchases an assignment of exclusive rights in the "Java" mark for the United States market.   A third party purchases authentic "Java" powder in France and imports it into the United States in competition with the domestic assignee.   Should the United States company be entitled to prevent the importation of these authentic goods?

2.   What if in problem 1 the domestic company is a subsidiary of the French manufacturer and the domestic company registers the mark "Java" in its own name for the United States market.   Should the domestic company be entitled to prevent the importation of authentic goods purchased abroad?

3.   What if in problem 1 the domestic company is the original owner of the "Java" mark and has licensed the French manufacturer to use the mark in France.   Can the domestic company prevent importation of authentic goods by a third party?

These problems reflect some of the variants of what is known as parallel importation or the gray market.   The cases raise interesting trademark problems because the mark is used on authentic goods but in violation of privately arranged market allocations.   Any confusion of source by consumers does not relate to the product purchased, and consumers may pay less for the product because discounters often rely on parallel imports as a major source of branded merchandise.

The leading trademark case is A. Bourjois & Co. v. Katzel, 260 U.S. 689 (1923) from which problem 1 is taken. Justice Holmes upheld an injunction in favor of the domestic company: "Ownership of the goods does not carry the right to sell them with a specific mark. . . . ['Java'] is the trademark of the plaintiff only in the United States and indicates in law, and, it is found, by public understanding, that the goods come from the plaintiff although not made by it." In all of the cases above, if the domestic company can demonstrate the use of the mark in the United States reflects good will attributable to the domestic company and not to the foreign company, the parallel importation of gray market goods is a trademark infringement. See Osawa & Co. v. B & H Photo, 589 F.Supp. 1163 (S.D.N.Y.1984); Weil Ceramics & Glass, Inc. v. Dash, 618 F.Supp. 700 (D.N.J.1985). However, proof of a separate good will running to the domestic company may be very difficult.

After the Court of Appeals in *Bourjois* had ruled against the domestic company but before the Supreme Court reversed, Congress responded by adopting § 526 of the Tariff Act (now 15 U.S.C. § 1526) which provides: "It shall be unlawful to import into the United States any merchandise of foreign manufacture if such merchandise * * * bears a trademark owned by a citizen of * * * the United States * * *." See also, § 42 of the Lanham Act. This apparently all-inclusive prohibition has been narrowed by United States Customs Service regulations which permit importation where the foreign manufacturer and the domestic trademark owner are "subject to common ownership or control" (problem 2 above) or where the domestic trademark owner authorizes the foreign manufacturer to use the mark (problem 3 above). 19 C.F.R. § 133.21 (1987).

This regulatory interpretation of the Tariff Act stood for over 50 years but recently the concern about imported goods led to numerous attempts to challenge the interpretation. In K Mart Corp. v. Cartier, Inc., 486 U.S. 281 (1988) a badly split Supreme Court upheld the regulations permitting importation where there is common ownership or control (problem 2) but invalidated the authorized use exception (problem 3).

How would you resolve these cases?

(5) NON–COMPETING GOODS

INTRODUCTION

One of the most recurring controversies in trademark litigation is the extent to which a trademark owner may prevent another from using the same or a confusingly similar mark on a product that does not directly compete with the goods of the original trademark owner. This issue tests the underlying principles of trademark protection. For example, should the owner of the mark "V–8" for vegetable juice be able to prevent another from using the same mark on vitamin pills? The owner cannot complain that he will lose the trade of a potentially deceived consumer since he himself does not make vitamin pills. And if we assume that "V–8" vitamin pills are a top quality product, the reputation of the original owner of the "V–8" mark is secure. By protecting the trademark owner in other product markets the law will increase the potential market power of the mark and permit the originator to preserve for future use markets in which he does not currently use the mark. And suppose the vegetable juice manufacturer intends to expand to the vitamin pill market. Should he be allowed to exploit the good will from his vegetable juice in other markets or should he be forced to "earn" new good will for vitamins on the merits of his product? On the other hand, if "V–8" is a popular mark, why should we permit someone to get a "free ride" on another's past efforts in developing the mark?

The level of confusion created by using the same mark on different goods is influenced by consumer perceptions relating to the organization of product markets. A consumer may or may not believe the producers of the two products are associated if producers generally do not produce more than one type of good. On the other hand, in an era where producers have a diversified mix of products, assumptions of association are more likely to occur.

The courts have had some difficulty sorting these various interests and policies into a coherent test for describing the product market limits to trademark protection.

NOTE

As in so many instances of business regulation the views of the Second Circuit and Judge Learned Hand in particular have been influential. Tracing the development of that Circuit's approach to the problem of non-competing goods illustrates the inherent difficulty of the issue. In Aunt Jemima Mills Co. v. Rigney & Co., 247 Fed. 407 (2d Cir.1917) the complainant used the mark "Aunt Jemima" on self-rising flour; the defendant subsequently adopted the mark for pancake syrup. The court granted relief because the goods "though different, may be so related as to fall within the mischief which equity should prevent."

Beginning in 1928 in Yale Electric Corp. v. Robertson, 26 F.2d 972 (2d Cir. 1928) ("Yale" used on electric flashlights and batteries infringes prior use on locks and keys and other hardware) Judge Hand began to explore in a rigorous way the nature of the competing interests—an exploration culminating in S.C. Johnson & Son, Inc. v. Johnson, 116 F.2d 427 (2d Cir.1940) ("Johnson's" used on a fabric cleaner attacked by a prior user who used the mark on floor cleaners, waxes and polishes but never on fabric cleaners.)

> Obviously the plaintiff cannot stand upon the usual grievance in such cases; i.e. that the defendant is diverting its customers. * * * Since in such a situation the injured party has not lost any sales, the courts have based his right upon two other interests: first, his reputation with his customers; second, his possible wish to expand his business into the disputed market. The first of these is real enough, even when the newcomer has as yet done nothing to tarnish the reputation of the first user. Nobody willingly allows another to masquerade as himself; it is always troublesome, and generally impossible, to follow the business practices of such a competitor closely enough to be sure that they are not damaging, and the harm is frequently done before it can be prevented. Yet even as to this interest we should not forget that, so long as the newcomer has not in fact misconducted himself, the injury is prospective and contingent,

and very different from taking away the first user's customers. The second interest is frequently less palpable. It is true that a merchant who has sold one kind of goods, sometimes finds himself driven to add other "lines" in order to hold or develop his existing market; in such cases he has a legitimate present interest in preserving his identity in the ancillary market, which he cannot do, if others make his name equivocal there. But if the new goods have no such relation to the old, and if the first user's interest in maintaining the significance of his name when applied to the new goods is nothing more than the desire to post the new market as a possible preserve which he may later choose to exploit, it is hard to see any basis for its protection. The public may be deceived, but he has no claim to be its vicarious champion; his remedy must be limited to his injury and by hypothesis he has none.

In 1946, the Lanham Act became effective and enacted a standard for infringement that required a use "likely to cause confusion or mistake or to deceive purchasers as to the source of origin of such goods or services." § 32(1). Proponents of the new act had high hopes that the change in language would broaden the protection for registered marks. See Robert, The New Trade-Mark Manual 159 et seq. (1947). Judge Hand refused to modify his earlier decision; instead, he argued that the Lanham Act had codified his earlier analysis in the first *Johnson* case. S.C. Johnson & Son, Inc. v. Johnson, 175 F.2d 176, 180 (2d Cir.1949).

The Circuit eventually loosened the rigid analysis imposed by Judge Hand and adopted a more flexible test that seeks to examine and weigh a number of variables in each case. See Polaroid Corp. v. Polarad Electronics Corp., 287 F.2d 492, 495 (1961). And in Triumph Hosiery Mills, Inc. v. Triumph International Corp., 308 F.2d 196 (2d Cir.1962) the court explicitly held that the absence of injury to the two interests relied upon by Judge Hand "would not necessarily be fatal to the grant of an injunction. * * *"

McGREGOR–DONIGER INC. v. DRIZZLE INC.

United States Court of Appeals, Second Circuit, 1979.
599 F.2d 1126.

[Since 1947 McGregor sold golf jackets under the trademark "Drizzler" and federally registered the mark in 1965. The jackets sell for between $25 to $50 and are the only item McGregor sells under the mark, although they sell other apparel under other marks. In 1969 the defendant, Drizzle Inc., began selling under the unregistered mark "Drizzle," women's coats priced from $100 to $900. In 1975 McGregor, after requesting Drizzle to cease using the mark, filed suit for trademark infringement, violation of § 43(a) of the Lanham Act, and unfair competition. Judge Lasker, the district judge, dismissed the complaint.]

MESKILL, CIRCUIT JUDGE.

* * *

DISCUSSION

We are once again called upon to decide when a trademark owner will be protected against the use of its mark, or one very similar, on products other than those to which the owner has applied it. As we have observed before, the question "does not become easier of solution with the years." Polaroid Corp. v. Polarad Electronics Corp., 287 F.2d 492, 495 (2d Cir.), cert. denied, 368 U.S. 820 (1961).

The crucial issue in these cases is "whether there is any likelihood that an appreciable number of ordinarily prudent purchasers are likely to be misled, or indeed simply confused, as to the source of the goods in question." Mushroom Makers, Inc. v. R.G. Barry Corp., 580 F.2d 44, 47 (2d Cir.1978), cert. denied, 439 U.S. 1116 (1979); 3 R. Callman, The Law of Unfair Competition, Trademarks and Monopolies § 84, at 929 (3d ed. 1969) (hereinafter Callman); Restatement of Torts § 717 and Comment b at 567 (1938). In assessing the likelihood of such confusion we consider the factors laid out in the now classic *Polaroid* formula:

> Where the products are different, the prior owner's chance of success is a function of many variables: the strength of his mark, the degree of similarity between the two marks, the proximity of the products, the likelihood that the prior owner will bridge the gap, actual confusion, and the reciprocal of defendant's good faith in adopting its own mark, the quality of defendant's product, and the sophistication of the buyers. Even this extensive catalogue does not exhaust the possibilities—the court may have to take still other variables into account.

Polaroid Corp. v. Polarad Electronics Corp., supra, 287 F.2d at 495, citing Restatement of Torts §§ 729, 730, 731. * * *

(1) *Strength of the Mark*

The most complex issue raised by McGregor concerns the trial court's attempt to gauge the strength of the DRIZZLER mark. Our prior opinions and those of the district courts of this Circuit have left litigants and judges uncertain as to the appropriate way to demonstrate and determine the strength of a mark. In the hope of providing some guidance to bench and bar, we set out in some detail our view of this issue.

The term "strength" as applied to trademarks refers to the distinctiveness of the mark, or more precisely, its tendency to identify the goods sold under the mark as emanating from a particular, although possibly anonymous, source. * * * The strength or distinctiveness of a mark determines both the ease with which it may be established as a valid trademark and the degree of protection it will be accorded.

In an effort to liberate this aspect of trademark law from the "welter of adjectives" which had tended to obscure its contours, we recently reviewed the four categories into which terms are classified for trademark purposes. Abercrombie & Fitch Co. v. Hunting World, Inc., 537 F.2d 4, 9 (2d Cir.1976). Arranged in ascending order of strength, these categories are: (1) generic, (2) descriptive, (3) suggestive, and (4) arbitrary or fanciful. * * *

The many cases announcing that a mark found to be suggestive, arbitrary or fanciful (i.e., more than merely descriptive) is entitled to protection without proof of secondary meaning are correct as far as they go, for any term that is more than descriptive can be established as a valid mark which others may not infringe. Where the products involved are competitive and the marks quite similar, for example, the senior user of a more-than-descriptive mark need not prove secondary meaning. * * *

And where the marks involved are virtually identical, even if the products are non-competitive, a senior user of a more-than-descriptive mark can carry its burden on the "strength of the mark" component of the *Polaroid* formula without proving secondary meaning. See, e.g., Mushroom Makers, Inc. v. R.G. Barry Corp., supra, 580 F.2d at 48 (arbitrary mark). But these cases do not require us to hold that Judge Lasker erred in considering evidence of secondary meaning in determining whether McGregor is entitled to protection against the use, on non-competitive goods, of a mark similar to its own. The cases agree that it is appropriate to consider all factors bearing on the likelihood of confusion. We view evidence concerning the origin-indicating significance of a mark in the marketplace as relevant to and probative of the strength of a mark and hence useful in assessing the likelihood of confusion.

Consideration of evidence of secondary meaning will almost always work in favor of the senior user. Its mark, if registered, is presumptively distinctive. See Abercrombie & Fitch Co. v. Hunting World, Inc., supra, 537 F.2d at 11. Proof of secondary meaning, acquired perhaps through successful advertising, can only enhance the strength of its mark and thus enlarge the scope of the protection to which it is entitled. On the other hand, the owner of a distinctive mark need not introduce evidence of secondary meaning in order to gain protection for its mark against the confusing similarity of others. Thus, for example, the relatively small size of a senior user's advertising budget or sales volume will not diminish the strength of its valid mark, and the scope of protection accorded to that mark will not be narrowed because of such evidence. Mushroom Makers, Inc. v. R.G. Barry Corp., supra, 580 F.2d at 48. Only if the junior user carries the burden of affirmatively demonstrating that a term is generic is the senior user stripped of protection. Abercrombie & Fitch Co. v. Hunting World, Inc., supra, 537 F.2d at 9–10; 15 U.S.C. § 1064(c).

McGregor claims that the district court erred in requiring proof of secondary meaning. We agree with McGregor's contention that the decision of the Patent and Trademark Office to register a mark without requiring proof of secondary meaning affords a rebuttable presumption that the mark is more than merely descriptive. Abercrombie & Fitch Co. v. Hunting World, Inc., supra, 537 F.2d at 11; West & Co. v. Arica Institute, Inc., 557 F.2d 338, 342 (2d Cir.1977). The trial court did in fact find the term DRIZZLER more than merely descriptive, although apparently only barely over the "suggestive" line. As a suggestive term, the DRIZZLER mark would be entitled to protection, regardless of proof of secondary meaning, *if* McGregor could prove that confusion of origin was likely to result from the use of a similar mark on non-competing goods. To the extent the district court held proof of secondary meaning *necessary,* it was in error. However, it was *not* error for the court to consider evidence bearing on the strength of the mark in determining the likelihood of consumer confusion and thus the scope of protection to which the DRIZZLER mark was entitled. Trademark strength is "an amorphous concept with little shape or substance when divorced from the mark's commercial context," E.I. DuPont de Nemours & Co. v. Yoshida Internat'l, Inc., supra, 393 F.Supp. at 512. We see no advantage to be derived from barring judicial consideration of the realities that give content to the concept of trademark strength.

(2) *Similarity of the Marks*

"To the degree that the determination of 'likelihood of confusion' rests upon a comparison of the marks themselves, the appellate court is in as good a position as the trial judge to decide the issue." Miss Universe, Inc. v. Patricelli, 408 F.2d 506, 509 (2d Cir.1969). * * * There are two principles especially important to performing this task.

First, even close similarity between two marks is not dispositive of the issue of likelihood of confusion. "Similarity in and of itself is not the acid test. Whether the similarity is likely to provoke confusion is the crucial question." Callman § 82.1(a), at 601–02 (footnote omitted). For this reason cases involving the alteration, addition or elimination of only a single letter from the old mark to the new reach divergent results. E.I. DuPont de Nemours & Co. v. Yoshida Internat'l, Inc., supra, 393 F.Supp. at 511–12. Second, in assessing the similarity of two marks, it is the effect upon prospective purchasers that is important. Restatement of Torts § 728, Comment b at 591.

The district court quite correctly took into consideration all the factors that could reasonably be expected to be perceived by and remembered by potential purchasers. * * * Thus while observing that the typewritten and aural similarity of the two marks "approaches identity," the district judge noted that the context in which the respective marks are generally presented reduces the impact of this similarity. The court observed that the label in each DRIZZLER jacket prominently features the McGregor name, which is printed in striking plaid letters. In addition, although there was testimony that retail stores on occasion in independent advertisements omit the McGregor logo, the evidence showed that McGregor always emphasizes the company name in its own advertising of DRIZZLER jackets. The fact that a trademark is always used in conjunction with a company name may be considered by the trial court as bearing on the likelihood of confusion. * * * The court below properly focused on the general impression conveyed by the two marks. If Drizzle had chosen consistently to present its mark in red plaid lettering or to advertise its coats as the McGregor DRIZZLE line, we would be compelled to conclude that the similarity between the DRIZZLER mark and the DRIZZLE mark, *as generally presented to the public,* had been heightened and that the likelihood of confusion had been enhanced. Conversely, the fact that only one mark generally appears in close conjunction with the red plaid McGregor name increases the likelihood that the public, even when viewing the marks individually, will not confuse the two. The likelihood of confusion is further reduced by Drizzle's use of its mark to identify itself as the producer of the products advertised by it rather than as the name of a particular jacket or line of jackets, in contrast to McGregor's practice.

The district court's reasoning is sound. The differing methods of presentation of the two marks were properly examined. We agree with Judge Lasker's appraisal that they reduce to some degree the potential for confusion inherent in the close similarity between the two marks.

(3) and (4) *Product Proximity and Quality of Defendant's Product*

The district court concluded on the basis of differences in appearance, style, function, fashion appeal, advertising orientation, and price [5] that the competitive distance between DRIZZLER jackets and DRIZZLE coats is "significant." This conclusion is too amply supported by the evidence to be characterized as clearly erroneous.

McGregor does not claim that DRIZZLER jackets and DRIZZLE coats are directly competitive. Customers shopping for an inexpensive golf jacket are not likely to become confused by the similarity of the marks and mistakenly purchase a fashionable and expensive woman's coat. Thus the degree of proximity between the two products is relevant here primarily insofar as it bears on the likelihood that customers may be confused as to the *source* of the products, rather than as to the products themselves, and the concern is not direct diversion of purchasers but indirect harm through loss of goodwill or tarnishment of reputation. Restatement of Torts § 730, Comment b at 599. It is evident that customers would be more likely to assume that DRIZZLER golf jackets and DRIZZLE golf jackets come from the same source than they would be likely to assume that DRIZZLER golf jackets and DRIZZLE steam shovels come from the same source. DRIZZLE coats for women fall between the two extremes. In locating the appropriate place for DRIZZLE coats on this continuum, the district court considered many of the factors that are generally viewed as relevant.

> The impression that noncompeting goods are from the same origin may be conveyed by such differing considerations as the physical attributes or essential characteristics of the goods, with specific reference to their form, composition, tex-

---

5. While difference in price may, when standing alone, be insufficient to establish competitive distance, it is clearly a factor to be considered along with others in measuring product proximity. Cf. Chester Barrie, Ltd. v. The Chester Laurie, Ltd., 189 F.Supp. 98, 101 (S.D.N.Y.1960). At the time of trial most DRIZZLER jackets sold for approximately $25, although a lined model was available for about $50. Retail prices of DRIZZLE coats ranged from about $100 to $900 during that same period of time.

ture or quality, the service or function for which they are intended, the manner in which they are advertised, displayed or sold, the place where they are sold, or the class of customers for whom they are designed and to whom they are sold.

Callman § 82.2(c), at 807.

Looking at these very factors, the district judge found:

Beyond the fact that they might both be crudely classified as outerwear, the "DRIZZLER" and defendant's products have nothing in common. McGregor's garment is a relatively inexpensive, light-weight, waist-length jacket—a windbreaker * * *. As is apparent from advertisements for the jacket, it is intended for casual wear, particularly in connection with sports activities. Moreover, although the DRIZZLER can be worn by either men or women, sales are pitched primarily to the former * * *. Furthermore, a DRIZZLER is ordinarily sold in the men's department of stores which carry both men's and women's garments * * *.

Unlike McGregor's products, the coats manufactured by Drizzle are distinctly and exclusively tailored for women. They are generally full-length raincoats and capes. Although it is true that Drizzle manufactures a style that might be called a jacket * * * it is longer than the DRIZZLER and entirely different in appearance. Drizzle's garments are within the medium to high fashion range * * *. The price range of Drizzle's line, running from approximately $100 to $900 * * * reflects the coats' position in the fashion hierarchy.

446 F.Supp. at 164 (footnotes and citations to record omitted).

* * *

(5) *Bridging the Gap*

In assessing the likelihood of confusion, the district court was required to consider the likelihood that DRIZZLER would "bridge the gap," that is, the likelihood that McGregor would enter the women's coat market under the DRIZZLER banner. Polaroid Corp. v. Polarad Electronics Corp., supra, 287 F.2d at 495. McGregor presented no evidence that such a step was being considered. Clearly the absence of any present intention or plan indicates that such expansion is less, rather than more, probable. Also of probative value is the fact that McGregor has for many years marketed its women's apparel under names bearing no similarity to DRIZZLER—such as BROLLY DOLLY.

* * *

The district court's finding that it is unlikely that DRIZZLER will bridge the gap is not clearly erroneous. Nor does the evidence presented below regarding McGregor's own history of trademark use, as well as industry custom, compel the conclusion that, despite the improbability that McGregor will move into the women's coat market under the DRIZZLER trademark, consumers will assume otherwise.

(6) *Actual Confusion*

McGregor's claim that the district court erred in considering the absence of proof of *actual* consumer confusion in assessing the *likelihood* of confusion is without merit. Actual confusion is one of several factors to be considered in making such a determination. * * *

(7) *Good Faith*

* * *

We recently held that adoption of the mark MUSHROOM for women's sportswear despite actual and constructive notice of another company's prior registration of the mark MUSHROOMS for women's shoes was not necessarily indicative of bad faith, because the presumption of an exclusive right to use a registered mark extends only so far as the goods or services noted in the registration certificate. Mushroom Makers, Inc. v. R.G. Barry Corp., supra, 580 F.2d at 48, citing Avon Shoe Co. v. David Crystal, Inc., 279 F.2d 607, 613 n. 7 (2d Cir.), cert. denied, 364 U.S. 909 (1960). * * *

Here, as in *Mushroom Makers,* the district court was entitled to consider and to credit the uncontradicted testimony of Drizzle's witnesses that the DRIZZLE mark was selected without knowledge of McGregor's prior use of the DRIZZLER mark. * * *

(8) *Sophistication of Buyers*

McGregor asserts that the trial court erroneously considered only the typical "sophisticated" purchaser of Drizzle's coats, to the exclusion of the casual or unsophisticated purchaser. We do not read the decision below in this manner.

McGregor offered no evidence establishing that any significant number of DRIZZLE purchasers are casual or unsophisticated. The district court was entitled to rely on the evidence indicating that the relevant purchasing group in fact tends to be sophisticated and knowledgeable about women's apparel. We cannot classify his findings in this regard as clearly erroneous.

CONCLUSION

In trademark infringement cases involving non-competing goods, it is rare that we are "overwhelmed by the sudden blinding light of the justness of one party's cause." King Research, Inc. v. Shulton, Inc., supra, 454 F.2d at 69. Most often our affirmances in such cases rest on the more modest conclusion that the trial judge was not wrong in reaching the result appealed from. See, e.g., Mushroom Makers, Inc. v. R.G. Barry Corp., supra, 580 F.2d at 47; King Research, Inc. v. Shulton, Inc., supra, 454 F.2d at 69. It is on this basis that we affirm the district judge's decision. Judge Lasker applied the correct legal standard (likelihood of confusion) and the correct criteria (those enumerated in *Polaroid*) in reaching his result. Moreover, he quite properly regarded no single factor as determinative. Triumph Hosiery Mills v. Triumph Internat'l Corp., supra, 308 F.2d at 198, 200. Although the two marks at issue are concededly quite similar, the court below found that the DRIZZLER mark is only moderately strong, that the competitive distance between the products is significant, that there was no intention to bridge the gap, that no actual confusion has occurred, and that Drizzle adopted its mark in good faith. Thus the court's conclusion that likelihood of confusion had not been proved by McGregor is amply supported by its findings, none of which is clearly erroneous. * * * Because McGregor has failed to establish a likelihood of confusion, the balance of interests of necessity tips in Drizzle's favor. Because the goods are concededly not competitive, McGregor's sales of DRIZZLER jackets cannot be expected to suffer. Where non-competitive goods are involved the trademark laws protect the senior user's interest in an untarnished reputation and his interest in being able to enter a related field at some future time. Scarves by Vera, Inc. v. Todo Imports Ltd., supra, 544 F.2d at 1172. Because consumer confusion as to source is unlikely, McGregor's reputation cannot be expected to be harmed. Because of the improbability that McGregor will enter the women's coat field under the DRIZZLER name, its right to expand into other fields has not been unduly restricted. Thus we see no injury to McGregor resulting from denial of the relief requested. On the other hand, if forced to give up its mark Drizzle could be expected to be harmed by loss of the goodwill that has been associated with the DRIZZLE name since 1969.

As we noted in Chandon Champagne Corp. v. San Marino Wine Corp., 335 F.2d 531, 536 (2d Cir.1964):

> Although this court was the leader in granting relief to a trade-mark owner when there had been and was no likelihood of actual diversion [i.e., in cases involving non-competitive products], we have likewise emphasized that, in such cases, "against these legitimate interests of the senior user are to be weighed the legitimate interests of the innocent second user" and that we must balance "the *conflicting interests* both parties have in the unimpaired continuation of their trade mark use." Avon Shoe Co. v. David Crystal, Inc. [supra, 279 F.2d at 613].

Following this approach, this Court has frequently supplemented its consideration of the *Polaroid* factors by balancing the conflicting interests of the parties involved. See, e.g., Mushroom Makers, Inc. v. R.G. Barry Corp., supra, 580 F.2d at 49; King Research, Inc. v. Shulton, Inc., supra, 454 F.2d at 69; Kiki Undies Corp. v. Promenade Hosiery Mills, Inc., supra, 411 F.2d at 1099–1100. Particularly when viewed in light of a balancing of the interests involved, the decision below warrants affirmance.

NOTES

1. After the court has so carefully considered the factors relating to likelihood of confusion, what "interests" remain to be balanced as the court

seems to require in the last few paragraphs of the opinion? Assume the court found a likelihood of confusion. Are there further interests that must be considered? In the *Mushroom Makers* case, cited in the principal case, the court did find a likelihood of confusion and still refused injunctive relief because the interests of the junior user in retaining the good will of his mark "far outweighs any conceivable injury to [the senior user]". The senior user (Barry) used the mark "Mushrooms" for footwear; the same mark was used by Mushroom Makers for women's sportswear. Although Mushroom Makers marketed its goods one year after Barry, it was far more successful in acquiring a nation-wide market and substantial sales figures. The court noted that Barry has only two legitimate interests in seeking injunctive relief—the desire to expand and the right to be free of injury to its reputation. The court found neither interest threatened because Barry did not intend to make footwear and the quality of Mushroom Makers merchandise was not likely to deteriorate or cause any harm to the reputation of the mark.

In Lambda Electronics Corp. v. Lambda Technology, Inc., 515 F.Supp. 915 (S.D.N.Y.1981) Lambda Electronics (Veeco) sold electronic components for computers under the "Lambda" trademark; the defendant used the same mark for computer software. Applying the six factors applied in the Second Circuit, the court first found a likelihood of confusion. It then proceeded to "balance the equities":

> * * * In short, where, as here, the trial court has found a likelihood of confusion, the balance of equities tilts in the first instance toward a finding of infringement. Given this fact, there still remain a number of factors that the Court must consider in striking the balance of equities. Some of these factors potentially tip the balance still further toward a finding of infringement; others potentially implicate the interests of the junior user, and hence argue against a finding of infringement. The Court considers them in turn below.
>
> 1. *Bridging the Gap.* In a case of non-competitive products, the likelihood that the senior user will "bridge the gap" between the two products is probative not only of the likelihood of confusion, but also of the balance of equities. It is well settled that the trademark laws protect the senior user's interest in being able to enter a related field at some future time. Scarves by Vera, Inc. v. Todo Imports Ltd., supra, 544 F.2d at 1172. Thus, if Veeco had any present intention of entering the software field, it could make a powerful equitable argument in favor of a finding of infringement. Unfortunately for Veeco, it has no such present intention, meaning that this factor plays no role in striking the balance of equities in this case.
>
> 2. *Quality of Junior User's Product.* Where the junior user's product is of poor quality, the interest of the senior user in enjoining the junior user's conduct, and thus avoiding any confusion between itself and the junior user, is obviously heightened. Here, however, there is no suggestion that Lambda Technology's services are of anything but high quality. This factor thus also fails to play any role in striking the balance of equities in this case.
>
> 3. *Good Faith of Junior User.* It is fundamental that the state of mind of the junior user is an important factor in striking the balance of equities. If the junior user has acted entirely in good faith, it will have a powerful equitable argument against a finding of infringement.

On the other hand, if the junior user adopted the plaintiff's mark in bad faith, the equitable balance is tipped significantly in favor of a finding of infringement. Here, Lambda Technology acted in good faith in its selection of its corporate name and its decision to adopt the tradenames "Lambda" and "Lambda Technology." However, the Court is not persuaded that Lambda Technology acted entirely in good faith throughout the events leading to this litigation. Particularly, the Court is disturbed by Lambda Technology's decision in 1978, after having received actual notice of the LAMBDA marks, to adopt a logo far more similar to Veeco's logo than Lambda Technology's original logo. * * * Moreover, when the incidents of actual confusion detailed earlier began to occur, Lambda Technology took no significant steps toward remedying the problem. In sum, while the Court is not prepared to conclude that Lambda Technology acted in bad faith, it can weigh this factor only slightly in Lambda Technology's favor in striking the balance of equities.

4. *Junior User's Good Will.* The Court of Appeals for this Circuit has held that a powerful equitable argument against finding infringement is created when the junior user, through concurrent use of an identical trademark, develops goodwill in the mark. Mushroom Makers, Inc. v. R.G. Barry Corp., supra, 580 F.2d at 49.

2. The Second Circuit has become so attached to the analysis represented in *McGregor-Doniger* that it has recently announced it to be applicable to all trademark cases, even when the products of the competing users compete directly.

Thompson Medical Co. Inc. v. Pfizer, Inc., 753 F.2d 208 (2d Cir.1985) was a contest between the senior use of "Sportscreme" for a topical analgesic and the subsequent use of "Sportsgel" for a similar product. Neither mark was registered and the claim was brought under § 43(a) of the Lanham Act. The court observed three modes of analysis for trademark infringement: (1) the classification of the trademark analysis as to whether it is generic, descriptive, suggestive, or arbitrary; (2) the likelihood of confusion analysis ("the Polaroid factors"); and (3) the "second-comer" doctrine which in directly competing goods provided protection to the senior user. Viewing the first as "merely a threshold determination" and the third as "merely emphasizing two of the Polaroid factors", the court concluded that the Polaroid analysis should be applied in *all* cases:

> The wisdom of the likelihood of confusion test lies in its recognition that each trademark infringement case presents its own unique set of facts. Indeed, the complexities attendant to an accurate assessment of likelihood of confusion require that the entire panoply of elements constituting the relevant factual landscape be comprehensively examined. No single Polaroid factor is pre-eminent, nor can the presence or absence of one without analysis of the others, determine the outcome of an infringement suit. 753 F.2d at 214.

The court left open a more straightforward grant of priority to the senior user only where there is a claim of "passing off"—a false representation by the junior user that his goods are those of the trademark owner.

Are you convinced that a comprehensive factual analysis on likelihood of confusion followed by a balancing of interests is required in all cases? Does this ruling undermine the security of trademark owners and thus create less incentives for trademarks (or more incentive for imitation)?

3. *Lanham Act.* The issue of likelihood of confusion arises in the Patent and Trademark Office. Section 2(d) prohibits registration of a mark that is likely to cause confusion with another registered mark. A multiple-factor analysis, similar to the "Polaroid analysis", has been adopted for this determination. See Application of E.I. DuPont DeNemours & Co, 476 F.2d 1357 (CCPA 1973). Prior to 1962 the critical phrase relative to the confusion issue in the Lanham Act read: "to cause confusion or mistake or to deceive purchasers". The 1962 amendments removed the word "purchasers". Did the change affect the problem of non-competing goods?

4. Should an agreement between the parties as to their respective rights in using the same mark in different product markets be given much weight in the analysis of likelihood of confusion? Should it matter whether the agreement is couched in terms of consent or in terms of a license? See Application of In re Mastic Inc., 829 F.2d 1114 (Fed.Cir.1987) (denying registration under § 2(d) of the mark "Shurlock" for vinyl siding because of the likelihood of confusion with the same mark registered for roofing shingles even though the senior user consented to registration.)

5. Concurrent use proceedings are only authorized when both parties' use began before the earliest of the filing dates or registrations. The 1988 revisions to the Lanham Act eliminated this requirement if there is consent by the owner of the application or registration.

6. Can you explain why the Lanham Act would expand the geographic scope of protection for registered marks but not also expand the scope of protection on noncompeting goods? Can you imagine a doctrine that prevented use of a registered trademark on any goods?

INTERNATIONAL ORDER OF JOB'S DAUGHTERS v. LINDEBURG & CO.

United States Court of Appeals, Ninth Circuit, 1980.
633 F.2d 912.

FLETCHER, CIRCUIT JUDGE.

[Job's Daughters, a young woman's fraternal organization, sued Lindeburg for making jewelry displaying the fraternal emblem of the organization without their permission. Job's Daughters licenses the use of its emblem by several "official jewelers" and it sells some jewelry directly to its members. Lindeburg requested a license and was refused.]

Resolution of this issue turns on a close analysis of the way in which Lindeburg is using the Job's Daughters insignia. In general, trademark law is concerned only with identification of the maker, sponsor, or endorser of the product so as to avoid confusing consumers. Trademark law does not prevent a person from copying so-called "functional" features of a product which constitute the actual benefit that the consumer wishes to purchase, as distinguished from an assurance that a particular entity made, sponsored, or endorsed a product.

* * *

Right of publicity protects individuals/persons against unauthorized use.

Application of the [functionality doctrine] to this case has a special twist because the name "Job's Daughters" and the Job's Daughters insignia are indisputably used to identify the organization, and members of Job's Daughters wear the jewelry to identify themselves as members. In that context, the insignia are trademarks of Job's Daughters. But in the context of this case, the name and emblem are functional aesthetic components of the jewelry, in that they are being merchandised on the basis of their intrinsic value, not as a designation of origin or sponsorship.

It is not uncommon for a name or emblem that serves in one context as a collective mark or trademark also to be merchandised for its own intrinsic utility to consumers. We commonly identify ourselves by displaying emblems expressing allegiances. Our jewelry, clothing, and cars are emblazoned with inscriptions showing the organizations we belong to, the schools we attend, the landmarks we have visited, the sports teams we support, the beverages we imbibe. Although these inscriptions frequently include names and emblems that are also used as collective marks or trademarks, it would be naive to conclude that the name or emblem is desired because consumers believe that the product somehow originated with or was sponsored by the organization the name or emblem signifies.

Job's Daughters relies on Boston Professional Hockey Ass'n, Inc. v. Dallas Cap & Emblem Mfg., Inc., 510 F.2d 1004 (5th Cir.), cert. denied, 423 U.S. 868 (1975), in which the Boston Bruins and other National Hockey League clubs brought a trademark infringement suit against a company that sold replicas of the NHL team emblems. The Fifth Circuit, applying the Lanham Act infringement test and focusing on the "likelihood of confusion," found infringement:

> The confusion or deceit requirement is met by the fact that the defendant duplicated the protected trademarks and sold them to the public knowing that the public would identify them as being the teams' trademarks. The certain knowledge of the buyer that the source and origin of the trademark symbols were the plaintiffs satisfies the requirement of the act. The argument that confusion must be as to the source of the manufacture of the emblem itself is unpersuasive, where the trademark, originated by the team, is the triggering mechanism for the sale of the emblem.

510 F.2d at 1012. Job's Daughters asserts that *Boston Hockey* supports its contention that even purely functional use of a trademark violates the Lanham Act. We reject the reasoning of *Boston Hockey*. Interpreted expansively, *Boston Hockey* holds that a trademark's owner has a complete monopoly over its use, including its functional use, in commercial merchandising.[10] But our reading of the Lanham Act and

---

10. The Fifth Circuit itself has apparently retreated from a broad interpretation of *Boston Hockey*. In Kentucky Fried Chicken Corp. v. Diversified Packaging Corp., 549 F.2d 368 (5th Cir.1977), the court began its analysis of Kentucky Fried Chicken's infringement claim by noting that it "reject[ed] any notion that a trade-

its legislative history reveals no congressional design to bestow such broad property rights on trademark owners. Its scope is much narrower: to protect consumers against deceptive designations of the origin of goods and, conversely, to enable producers to differentiate their products from those of others. * * * The *Boston Hockey* decision transmogrifies this narrow protection into a broad monopoly. It does so by injecting its evaluation of the equities between the parties and of the desirability of bestowing broad property rights on trademark owners. A trademark is, of course, a form of business property. See J. McCarthy, Trademarks and Unfair Competition §§ 2:6–2:7 (1973). But the "property right" or protection accorded a trademark owner can only be understood in the context of trademark law and its purposes. A trademark owner has a property right only insofar as is necessary to prevent consumer confusion as to who produced the goods and to facilitate differentiation of the trademark owner's goods. See id. The *Boston Hockey* court decided that broader protection was desirable. In our view, this extends the protection beyond that intended by Congress and beyond that accorded by any other court.

* * *

Our holding does not mean that a name or emblem could not serve simultaneously as a functional component of a product and a trademark. See Dallas Cowboys Cheerleaders, Inc. v. Pussycat Cinema, Ltd., 604 F.2d 200, 204 (2d Cir.1979). That is, even if the Job's Daughters' name and emblem, when inscribed on Lindeburg's jewelry, served primarily a functional purpose, it is possible that they could serve secondarily as trademarks if the typical customer not only purchased the jewelry for its intrinsic functional use and aesthetic appeal but also inferred from the insignia that the jewelry was produced, sponsored, or endorsed by Job's Daughters. See generally, Grimes & Battersby, The Protection of Merchandising Properties, 69 TMR 431, 441–45 (1980). We recognize that there is some danger that the consumer may be more likely to infer endorsement or sponsorship when the consumer is a member of the group whose collective mark or trademark is being marketed. Accordingly, a court must closely examine the articles themselves, the defendant's merchandising practices, and any evidence that consumers have actually inferred a connection between the defendant's product and the trademark owner.

We conclude from our examination of the trial judge's findings and of the underlying evidence that Lindeburg was not using the Job's Daughters name and emblem as trademarks. The insignia were a prominent feature of each item so as to be visible to others when worn, allowing the wearer to publicly express her allegiance to the organization. Lindeburg never designated the merchandise as "official" Job's Daughters' merchandise or otherwise affirmatively indicated sponsor-

mark is an owner's 'property' to be protected irrespective of its role in the protection of our markets," and described the *Boston Hockey* holding as premised on a finding that consumers were likely to believe that the emblems somehow originated from the hockey clubs. 549 F.2d at 389.

ship. Job's Daughters did not show a single instance in which a customer was misled about the origin, sponsorship, or endorsement of Lindeburg's jewelry, nor that it received any complaints about Lindeburg's wares. Finally, there was evidence that many other jewelers sold unlicensed Job's Daughters jewelry, implying that consumers did not ordinarily purchase their fraternal jewelry from only "official" sources. We conclude that Job's Daughters did not meet its burden of proving that a typical buyer of Lindeburg's merchandise would think that the jewelry was produced, sponsored, or endorsed by the organization. The name and emblem were functional aesthetic components of the product, not trademarks. There could be, therefore, no infringement.

The judgment of the district court is reversed and the case is remanded for the entry of judgment in favor of appellant Lindeburg.

NOTES

1. A classic confusion of sponsorship case is Triangle Publications, Inc. v. Rohrlich, 167 F.2d 969 (2d Cir.1948) where the defendant sold girdles under the mark "Miss Seventeen" and was held to have infringed the plaintiffs registered mark "Seventeen" as a title for a teenage girl's fashion magazine. The confusion was not that the magazine publisher was now making clothes but that the clothes were somehow sponsored or approved by the magazine.

A similar case is HMH Publishing Co., Inc. v. Brincat, 504 F.2d 713 (9th Cir.1974) where the owners of "Playboy" magazine sought to prohibit defendant's use of the mark "Playboy" for dune buggies and accessories. After holding that the mark must have secondary meaning in the automotive field to be protected, the court discounted the evidence that automobile manufacturers advertised heavily in Playboy magazine or that the mark had been used by some automobile manufacturers in conjunction with promotional activities. However, the court did hold that a finding that the defendant intended to trade on the good will of plaintiff shifted the burden to the defendant to show a absence of likelihood of confusion and the defendant had not met that burden.

2. The emblem cases, represented by *Job's Daughters* and *Boston Hockey,* are an extension of the confusion of sponsorship doctrine. At the heart of the issue is the assumption one makes about the market for licensed trademarks and the extent to which trademark owners license and control their marks. The Eleventh Circuit had the occasion to reaffirm *Boston Hockey* in University of Georgia Athletic Association v. Laite, 756 F.2d 1535 (11th Cir.1985) where the defendant began marketing "Battlin Bulldog Beer" in cans featuring the University's colors and a picture of the "Georgia Bulldog"—the emblem of the University's athletic program. A disclaimer—"not associated with the University of Georgia"—appeared in small lettering on the cans. The Court of Appeals affirmed the lower court's holding of likelihood of confusion and took issue with *Job's Daughters:*

> The record in the instant case reveals that, in one week, at least ten to fifteen members of the public contacted UGAA to inquire about the connection between [the beer and the University]. * * * This evidence indicates that, contrary to the unsupported assertion of the Ninth Circuit in Job's Daughters, at least some members of the public do assume that products bearing the mark of a school or a sports team

are sponsored or licensed by the school or team [citing survey showing almost half of all persons shown football jerseys of the NFL believed manufacturers were required to obtain license from the team]. 756 F.2d at 1546, n. 28.

At the same time the Fifth Circuit found *Boston Hockey* inapplicable to a fraternal jewelry case similar to *Job's Daughters.* Supreme Assembly, Order of Rainbow for Girls, et al. v. J.H. Ray Jewelry Co., 676 F.2d 1079 (5th Cir.1982). There the court found no likelihood of confusion because (1) most fraternal organizations exercise little control over the manufacture of jewelry, and (2) the existence of an "official" jeweler created the "inescapable inference for purchasers that all other Rainbow jewelry is not endorsed, sponsored, approved or otherwise associated with Rainbow."

Has the Fifth Circuit backed away from at least the broad language of its *Boston Hockey* decision? Is there, in the *Boston Hockey* and *University of Georgia* cases a heavy element of misappropriation theory? Aren't sports teams and fraternal organizations faced with a dilemma if designating an "official" producer tends to make it easier for unofficial producers to survive legal attacks?

3. In Boston Athletic Ass'n v. Sullivan, 867 F.2d 22 (1st Cir.1989) the court extended the emblem cases to their logical (?) conclusion. The BAA held registered marks for "Boston Marathon" and a unicorn logo used in association with the annual Boston Marathon. The defendants imprinted T-shirts as follows: "1987 Marathon [picture of runners] Hopkinton–Boston" and "Boston [picture of runners] 1988". The court awarded summary judgment to the plaintiff finding both confusion of goods ("public are likely to confuse defendant's shirts with those of plaintiff") and confusion of sponsorship (if "(1) defendants intentionally referred to the Boston Marathon on its shirts, and (2) purchasers were likely to buy the shirts precisely because of that reference, we think it fair to presume that purchasers are likely to be confused about the shirt's source or sponsorship."). Does this give the sponsor a monopoly on the event itself? Note the defendants did not use the plaintiff's trademark; they only referred to the event. Can the National Football League prevent others from producing any souvenirs that refer to the Super Bowl?

4. In Tuxedo Monopoly, Inc. v. General Mills Fun Group, Inc., 648 F.2d 1335 (CCPA 1981) the owner of the mark "Monopoly" for the board game opposed registration of the same mark for clothing. The court, with two dissents, affirmed the Trademark Trial and Appeal Board's decision sustaining the opposition. "[L]ikelihood of confusion must be found if the public, being familiar with appellee's use of MONOPOLY for board games and seeing the mark on *any item* that comes within the description of goods set forth by appellant in its application, is likely to believe that appellee has expanded its use of the mark, directly or under a license, for such item."

5. What is the precise injury in confusion of sponsorship cases? If it is adopted as a test for trademark infringement, are there any principles that can be developed to limit its application or does the test presage protection of marks without regard to the goods or services upon which they are used?

MEAD DATA CENTRAL, INC. v. TOYOTA MOTOR SALES, U.S.A., INC.

United States Court of Appeals, Second Circuit, 1989.
875 F.2d 1026.

VAN GRAAFEILAN, D., Circuit Judge: *DILUTION*

Toyota Motor Sales, U.S.A., Inc. and its parent, Toyota Motor Corporation, appeal from a judgment of the United States District Court for the Southern District of New York (Edelstein, J.), enjoining them from using LEXUS as the name of their new luxury automobile and the division that manufactures it. The district court held that, under New York's antidilution statute, N.Y.Gen.Bus.Law § 368–d, Toyota's use of LEXUS is likely to dilute the distinctive quality of LEXIS, the mark used by Mead Data Central, Inc. for its computerized legal research service. On March 8, 1989, we entered an order of reversal, stating that an opinion would follow. This is the opinion.

THE STATUTE

Section 368–d of New York's General Business Law, which has counterparts in at least twenty other states, reads as follows:

> Likelihood of injury to business reputation or of dilution of the distinctive quality of a mark or trade name shall be a ground for injunctive relief in cases of infringement of a mark registered or not registered or in cases of unfair competition, notwithstanding the absence of competition between the parties or the absence or confusion as to the source of goods or services.

[The court reviewed the evidence of the respective uses of the marks involved. The district court found that 76% of attorneys and accountants associated LEXIS with Mead's service but only 1% of the general adult population did so (and half of this one percent were attorneys). Toyota had plans for an $18 million advertising campaign during the first nine months for its new LEXUS cars. Toyota knew of Mead's mark prior to adopting LEXUS but its lawyers advised them there was no conflict.]

THE LAW

The brief legislative history accompanying section 368–d describes the purpose of the statute as preventing "the whittling away of an established trade-mark's selling power and value through its unauthorized use by others upon dissimilar products." 1954 N.Y. Legis.Ann. 49 (emphasis supplied). If we were to interpret literally the italicized word "its", we would limit statutory violations to the unauthorized use of the identical established mark. This is what Frank Schechter, the father of the dilution theory, intended when he wrote The Rational Basis of Trademark Protection, 40 Harv.L.Rev. 813 (1927). See id. at 830–33; see also Shire, Dilution Versus Deception Are State Antidilution Laws an Appropriate Alternative to the Law of Infringement?, 77 Trademark Rep. 273–76 (1987).　However, since the use of obvious simulations or markedly similar marks might have the same diluting effect as would an appropriation of the original mark, the concept of exact identity has been broadened to that of substantial similarity. Nevertheless, in keeping with the original intent of the statute, the similarity must be substantial before the doctrine of dilution may be applied.

Indeed, some courts have gone so far as to hold that, although violation of an antidilution statute does not require confusion of product or source, the marks in question must be sufficiently similar that confusion may be created as between the marks themselves.　We need not go that far.　We hold only that the marks must be "very" or "substantially" similar and that, absent such similarity, there can be no viable claim of dilution.

[The court disputed the district court's observation that the two marks were pronounced the same in "everyday spoken English"—"we liken LEXUS to such words as 'census', 'focus' and 'locus' and differentiate it from such words as 'axis', 'aegis' and 'iris' "—and concluded that "everyday spoken English" was not the proper test:

> We take it as a given that television and radio announcers usually are more careful and precise in their diction than is the man on the street.　Moreover, it is the rare television commercial that does not contain a visual reference to the mark and product, which in the instant case would be the LEXUS automobile.　We conclude that in the field of commercial advertising, which is the field subject to regulation, there is no substantial similarity between Mead's mark and Toyota's.]

There are additional factors that militate against a finding of dilution in the instant case.　Such a finding must be based on two elements.　First, plaintiff's mark must possess a distinctive quality capable of dilution.　Second, plaintiff must show a likelihood of dilution[.]　As section 368–d expressly states, a plaintiff need not show either competition between its product or service and that of the defendant or a likelihood of confusion as to the source of the goods or services.

Distinctiveness for dilution purposes often has been equated with the strength of a mark for infringement purposes.　It also has been defined as uniqueness or as having acquired a secondary meaning. *　*　* In sum, the statute protects a trademark's "selling power." However, the fact that a mark has selling power in a limited geographical or commercial area does not endow it with a secondary meaning for the public generally.

The strength and distinctiveness of LEXIS is limited to the market for its services—attorneys and accountants.　Outside that market, LEXIS has very little selling power.　Because only one percent of the general population associates LEXIS with the attributes of Mead's service, it cannot be said that LEXIS identifies that service to the general public and distinguishes it from others. Moreover, the bulk of Mead's advertising budget is devoted to reaching attorneys through professional journals.

This Court has defined dilution as either the blurring of a mark's product identification or the tarnishment of the affirmative associations a mark has come to convey. Mead does not claim that Toyota's use of LEXUS would tarnish affirmative associations engendered by LEXIS. The question that remains, therefore, is whether LEXIS is likely to be blurred by LEXUS.

Very little attention has been given to date to the distinction between the confusion necessary for a claim of infringement and the blurring necessary for a claim of dilution. * * * Although the antidilution statute dispenses with the requirements of competition and confusion, it does not follow that every junior use of a similar mark will dilute the senior mark in the manner contemplated by the New York Legislature.

As already stated, the brief legislative history accompanying section 368–d described the purpose of the statute as preventing "the whittling away of an established trademark's selling power and value through its unauthorized use by others upon dissimilar products." The history disclosed a need for legislation to prevent such "hypothetical anomalies" as "Dupont shoes, Buick aspirin tablets, Schlitz varnish, Kodak pianos, Bulova gowns, and so forth", and cited cases involving similarly famous marks, e.g., Tiffany & Co. v. Tiffany Productions, Inc., 147 Misc. 679 (1932), aff'd, 237 A.D. 801, aff'd, 262 N.Y. 482 (1933); Philadelphia Storage Battery Co. v. Mindlin, 163 Misc. 52 (1937). 1954 N.Y.Legis.Ann. 49–50.

It is apparent from these references that there must be some mental association between plaintiff's and defendant's marks.

> [I]f a reasonable buyer is not at all likely to link the two uses of the trademark in his or her own mind, even subtly or subliminally, then there can be no dilution. . . . [D]ilution theory presumes some kind of mental association in the reasonable buyer's mind between the two party's [sic] uses of the mark.

2 J. McCarthy [Trademarks and Unfair Competition] § 24.13 at 213–14.

This mental association may be created where the plaintiff's mark is very famous and therefore has a distinctive quality for a significant percentage of the defendant's market. However, if a mark circulates only in a limited market, it is unlikely to be associated generally with the mark for a dissimilar product circulating elsewhere. As discussed above, such distinctiveness as LEXIS possesses is limited to the narrow market of attorneys and accountants. Moreover, the process which LEXIS represents is widely disparate from the product represented by

LEXUS. For the general public, LEXIS has no distinctive quality that LEXUS will dilute.

The possibility that someday LEXUS may become a famous mark in the mind of the general public has little relevance in the instant dilution analysis since it is quite apparent that the general public associates nothing with LEXIS. On the other hand, the recognized sophistication of attorneys, the principal users of the service, has substantial relevance. Because of this knowledgeable sophistication, it is unlikely that, even in the market where Mead principally operates, there will be any significant amount of blurring between the LEXIS and LEXUS marks.

For all the foregoing reasons, we hold that Toyota did not violate section 368–d. We see no need therefore to discuss Toyota's remaining arguments for reversal.

SWEET, District Judge, concurring:

I concur, but write separately because I disagree with the majority's conclusion that LEXIS is not a strong mark capable of dilution and that LEXIS and LEXUS differ significantly in pronunciation, and I have a different view of the factors that are necessary to a finding of dilution.

* * *

By treating similarity of the marks as a separate element of a dilution cause of action and by evaluating the dilution claim without developing an analytical framework, the majority threatens to muddy the already murky waters of antidilution analysis. * * *

Defining likelihood of dilution as "tarnishing" is helpful because that principle can be applied in practice. See, e.g., Dallas Cowboys Cheerleaders, Inc. v. Pussycat Cinema, Ltd., 604 F.2d 200 (2d Cir.1979) (plaintiff's distinctive uniform diluted by defendant's use of a similar uniform in an X-rated movie); Coca-Cola Co. v. Gemini Rising, Inc., 346 F.Supp. 1183 (E.D.N.Y.1972) (plaintiff's "Coca-Cola" mark diluted by defendant's use of similar lettering in printing "Cocaine" on poster). "Blurring," however, offers practitioners and courts only marginally more guidance than "likelihood of dilution."

There is much to be gained by defining a general concept like "blurring" more specifically. As in this instance, confusion in the doctrine has created problems for trademark attorneys advising their clients about adopting trademarks, for potential litigants assessing their chances of pursuing or defending against dilution claims, and for courts attempting to apply the statute. See Shire, 77 Trademark Rep. at 288. In the trademark infringement context, Judge Friendly defined a similarly broad standard—likelihood of confusion—by articulating a multi-factor balancing test * * *. Polaroid Corp. v. Polaroid Elecs. Corp., 287 F.2d 492, 495 (2d Cir.), cert. denied, 368 U.S. 820 (1961). This test has provided practitioners and district courts a helpful framework for assessing likelihood of confusion.

Like likelihood of confusion, blurring sufficient to constitute dilution requires a case-by-case factual inquiry. A review of the anti-dilution cases in this Circuit indicates that courts have articulated the following factors in considering the likelihood of dilution caused by blurring:

(1) similarity of the marks

(2) similarity of the products covered by the marks

(3) sophistication of consumers

(4) predatory intent

(5) renown of the senior mark

(6) renown of the junior mark

The application of these factors here requires reversal of the decision below, although on a basis that I believe differs from that stated by the majority.

[Judge Sweet reviewed each factor. He thought the district court's findings were for the most part correct: that the marks were similar, the products were dissimilar, the consumers of Mead's service were sophisticated, Toyota did not have predatory intent, and the LEXIS mark was strong within its narrow market only.]

The district court found a likelihood of dilution, reasoning that Toyota's promotional campaign for its LEXUS automobile "will dwarf the LEXIS mark," and that Toyota acted in bad faith—although without predatory intent—by launching its LEXUS line "without any regard for its effect on the LEXIS mark." The district court's dilution analysis did not refer to the other factors discussed above, nor did it conduct a balancing test.

* * *

The only finding that supports a likelihood of dilution is the district court's conclusion that LEXUS eventually may become so famous that members of the general public who now associate LEXIS or LEXUS with nothing at all may associate the terms with Toyota's automobiles and that Mead's customers may think first of Toyota's car when they hear LEXIS. This analysis is problematic. First, section 368-d protects a mark's selling power among the consuming public. Because the LEXIS mark possesses selling power only among lawyers and accountants, it is irrelevant for dilution analysis that the general public may come to associate LEXIS or LEXUS with Toyota's automobile rather than nothing at all. Second, the district court offered no evidence for its speculation that LEXUS's fame may cause Mead customers to associate "LEXIS" with Toyota's cars. It seems equally plausible that no blurring will occur—because many lawyers and accountants use Mead's services regularly, their frequent association of LEXIS with those services will enable LEXIS's mark to withstand Toyota's advertising campaign.

Therefore, even if we accept the district court's finding regarding the renown of the LEXUS mark, however, reversal still is required.

The differences in the marks and in the products covered by the marks, the sophistication of Mead's consumers, the absence of predatory intent, and the limited renown of the LEXIS mark all indicate that blurring is unlikely.

NOTES

1. In Allied Maintenance Corp. v. Allied Mechanical Trades, Inc., 42 N.Y.2d 538, 399 N.Y.S.2d 628, 369 N.E.2d 1162 (1977) the plaintiff at a well-established building maintenance firm, sought to prevent an installer of ventilating equipment from using its trade name "Allied Maintenance". The New York Court of Appeals, observing that "courts which have had the opportunity to interpret an anti-dilution statute have refused to apply its provisions literally" nonetheless thought the statute extended infringement doctrines beyond a likelihood of confusion to a likelihood of dilution. The court held the statute applied only to "trade names which are truly of distinctive quality" and "Allied Maintenance" had not "attained this stature." Judge Cooke dissented: "Dilution does not occur only in the case of a name that is widely known. * * * That plaintiff's name is not distinctive enough to allow it to prevent its use by others in noncompeting industries should not be a ground for allowing one in a closely related business to dilute the distinctive quality of its name in its field."

2. At the preliminary injunction stage the Seventh Circuit found a likely dilution claim under Illinois law in Hyatt Corp. v. Hyatt Legal Services, 736 F.2d 1153 (7th Cir.1984) where the hotel chain claimed dilution of its mark by the use of "Hyatt Legal Services" for a chain of low-cost legal service offices named after its founder Joel Hyatt. Subsequently, a settlement agreement provided that the defendant could continue to use the mark as long as at the bottom of its advertisements it places the statement: "Hyatt Legal Services is named after its founder, Joel Z. Hyatt." Hyatt Corp. v. Hyatt Legal Services, 610 F.Supp. 381 (N.D.Ill.1985).

3. Dilution is exclusively a creature of state law. A 1987 study recognized twenty-three states that had dilution statutes. Trademark Review Commission, Report and Recommendations on the United States Trademark System and the Lanham Act, 77 Trademark Rep. 375, 454 (1987). The Commission proposed as one of many amendments to the Lanham Act adoption of a new § 43(c) which would create a federal dilution cause of action. The proposal authorized injunctive relief (and monetary relief against willful dilution) for owners of "famous" marks who suffered a dilution of the distinctive quality of their marks. The proposal further provided:

> In determining whether a mark is distinctive and famous, a court may consider factors such as, but not limited to: (a) the degree of inherent or acquired distinctiveness of the mark; (b) the duration and extent of use of the mark * * *; (c) the duration and extent of advertising and publicity of the mark; (d) the geographical extent of the trading area in which the mark is used; (e) the channels of trade for the goods or services * * *; (f) the degree of recognition of the registrant's mark; (g) the nature and extent of use of the same or similar mark by third parties.

Although Congress enacted most of the recommendations of the Commission, it rejected the federal dilution cause of action. Further attempts at enactment are likely.

The Commission considered and rejected proposing a "strong mark register" for distinctive marks that could not be used by others even on noncompeting goods. Marks might be eligible for the register if 75% of the consuming public associated it with the registrant's goods or services. 77 Trademark Rep. at 412.

4. Two leading articles relating to dilution are Pattishall, The Dilution Rationale for Trademark–Trade Identity Protection, Its Progress and Prospects, 71 Nw.U.L.Rev. 618 (1976); Derenberg, The Problem of Trademark Dilution and the Antidilution Statutes, 44 Calif.L.Rev. 439 (1956). See also, Restatement (Third) of Unfair Competition § 25 (Tent.Draft No. 2, 1990).

5. Do the dilution statutes raise concerns of federal preemption? Does the abandonment of the consumer confusion rationale implicate the preemption doctrine of *Sears* and *Compco?* At least one court has held that state dilution statutes as applied to interstate commerce are preempted because they interfere with the uniform scheme adopted by Congress in the Lanham Act. U.S. Jaycees v. Commodities Magazine Inc., 661 F.Supp. 1360 (N.D.Iowa 1987). And the Supreme Court's most recent explication of preemption, *Bonito Boats,* supra Chapter I, contains language that suggests the existence of consumer confusion distinguishes unfair competition cases from misappropriation cases.

6. What relief should be accorded in a dilution case. Should profits ever be awarded? Damages? If damages are awarded, how should they be measured?

L.L. BEAN, INC. v. DRAKE PUBLISHERS, INC.

United States Court of Appeals, First Circuit, 1987.
811 F.2d 26.   *dilution case*

BOWNES, CIRCUIT JUDGE.

Imitation may be the highest form of flattery, but plaintiff-appellee L.L. Bean, Inc., was neither flattered nor amused when *High Society* magazine published a prurient parody of Bean's famous catalog. Defendant-appellant Drake Publishers, Inc., owns *High Society,* a monthly periodical featuring adult erotic entertainment. Its October 1984 issue contained a two-page article entitled "L.L. Beam's Back–To–School–Sex–Catalog." (Emphasis added.) The article was labelled on the magazine's contents page as "humor" and "parody." The article displayed a facsimile of Bean's trademark and featured pictures of nude models in sexually explicit positions using "products" that were described in a crudely humorous fashion.

L.L. Bean sought a temporary restraining order to remove the October 1984 issue from circulation. The complaint alleged trademark *complaint* infringement, unfair competition, trademark dilution, deceptive trade practices, interference with prospective business advantage and trade libel. The United States District Court for the District of Maine denied Bean's request for a temporary restraining order. Thereafter, both parties sought summary judgment. The district court granted summary judgment in favor of Drake on the claims for trade libel and interference with prospective business advantage. It denied summary judgment to both parties on Bean's claims for trademark infringement, unfair competition and deceptive trade practices, leaving the factual question of "likelihood of confusion" for resolution at trial. L.L. Bean, Inc. v. Drake Publishers, Inc., 625 F.Supp. 1531 (D.Me.1986).

The district court did, however, grant Bean summary judgment with respect to the trademark dilution claim raised under Maine law. Me.Rev.Stat.Ann. tit. 10, § 1530 (1981). It ruled that the article had tarnished Bean's trademark by undermining the goodwill and reputation associated with the mark. Relying on two affidavits presented by appellee, the district court found that Bean had suffered harm from the publication of the article. The court rejected Drake's claim that the Maine statute did not encompass allegations of tarnishment caused by parody. The court also held that enjoining the publication of a parody to prevent trademark dilution did not offend the first amendment. An injunction issued prohibiting further publication or distribution of the "L.L. Beam Sex Catalog." L.L. Bean v. Drake Publishers, 625 F.Supp. at 1530. After its motion for reconsideration was denied, Drake appealed the order enjoining further publication of the Sex Catalog.

* * *

I.

* * * The Oxford English Dictionary defines parody as "(a) composition in which the characteristic turns of thought and phrase of an author are mimicked to appear ridiculous, especially by applying them to ludicrously inappropriate subjects." Chaucer, Shakespeare, Pope, Voltaire, Fielding, Hemingway and Faulkner are among the myriad of authors who have written parodies. Since parody seeks to ridicule sacred verities and prevailing mores, it inevitably offends others, as evinced by the shock which Chaucer's Canterbury Tales and Voltaire's Candide provoked among their contemporaries.

A trademark is a word, name or symbol adopted and used by a manufacturer or merchant to identify goods and distinguish them from those manufactured by others. 15 U.S.C. § 1127 (1985 Supp.). One need only open a magazine or turn on television to witness the pervasive influence of trademarks in advertising and commerce. Designer labels appear on goods ranging from handbags to chocolates to every possible form of clothing. Commercial advertising slogans, which can be registered as trademarks, have become part of national political campaigns. "Thus, trademarks have become a natural target of satirists who seek to comment on this integral part of the national culture." Dorsen, Satiric Appropriation and the Law of Libel, Trademark and Copyright: Remedies Without Wrongs, 65 B.U.L.Rev. 923, 939 (1986); Note, Trademark Parody: A Fair Use and First Amendment Analysis, 72 Va.L.Rev. 1079 (1986). The ridicule conveyed by parody inevitably conflicts with one of the underlying purposes of the Maine anti-dilution statute, which is to protect against the tarnishment of the goodwill and reputation associated with a particular trademark. Pignons, S.A. de Mecanique de Precision v. Polaroid Corp., 657 F.2d 482, 494–95 (1st Cir.1981). The court below invoked this purpose as the basis for its decision to issue an injunction. The issue before us is

whether enjoining the publication of appellant's parody violates the
first amendment guarantees of freedom of expression.

* * *

III.

* * *

A trademark owner may obtain relief under an anti-dilution statute if his mark is distinctive and there is a likelihood of dilution due to
(1) injury to the value of the mark caused by actual or potential
confusion, (2) diminution in the uniqueness and individuality of the
mark, or (3) injury resulting from use of the mark in a manner that
tarnishes or appropriates the goodwill and reputation associated with
plaintiff's mark. There is no dispute that Bean's mark is distinctive.
The basis for the district court's injunction was that Bean's trademark
had been tarnished by the parody in defendant's magazine. We think
this was a constitutionally impermissible application of the anti-dilution statute.

The district court believed that if a noncommercial parody "would
result in images of impurity in the minds of (consumers) . . . [s]uch
connotations would obviously tarnish the affirmative associations the
mark had come to convey." L.L. Bean v. Drake Publishers, 625 F.Supp.
at 1536. It thus read the anti-dilution statute as granting a trademark
owner the unfettered right to suppress the use of its name in any
context, commercial or noncommercial, found to be offensive, negative
or unwholesome. As one commentator has pointed out, there are
serious first amendment implications involved in applying anti-dilution
statutes to cover noncommercial uses of a trademark:

> Famous trademarks offer a particularly powerful means of
> conjuring up the image of their owners, and thus become an
> important, perhaps at times indispensable, part of the public
> vocabulary. Rules restricting the use of well-known trade-
> marks may therefore restrict the communication of
> ideas. . . . If the defendant's speech is particularly unflat-
> tering, it is also possible to argue that the trademark has been
> tarnished by the defendant's use. The constitutional implica-
> tions of extending the misappropriation or tarnishment ratio-
> nales to such cases, however, may often be intolerable. Since a
> trademark may frequently be the most effective means of
> focusing attention on the trademark owner or its product, the
> recognition of exclusive rights encompassing such use would
> permit the stifling of unwelcome discussion.

Denicola, Trademarks as Speech, 1982 Wis.L.Rev. at 195–96.

The district court's opinion suggests that tarnishment may be
found when a trademark is used without authorization in a context
which diminishes the positive associations with the mark. Neither the
strictures of the first amendment nor the history and theory of anti-
dilution law permit a finding of tarnishment based solely on the

presence of an unwholesome or negative context in which a trademark is used without authorization. Such a reading of the anti-dilution statute unhinges it from its origins in the marketplace. A trademark is tarnished when consumer capacity to associate it with the appropriate products or services has been diminished. The threat of tarnishment arises when the goodwill and reputation of a plaintiff's trademark is linked to products which are of shoddy quality or which conjure associations that clash with the associations generated by the owner's lawful use of the mark * * *.

* * * The Constitution is not offended when the anti-dilution statute is applied to prevent a defendant from using a trademark without permission in order to merchandise dissimilar products or services. Any residual effect on first amendment freedoms should be balanced against the need to fulfill the legitimate purpose of the anti-dilution statute. See Friedman v. Rogers, 440 U.S. 1, 15–16 (1979). The law of trademark dilution has developed to combat an unauthorized and harmful appropriation of a trademark by another for the purpose of identifying, manufacturing, merchandising or promoting dissimilar products or services. The harm occurs when a trademark's identity and integrity—its capacity to command respect in the market—is undermined due to its inappropriate and unauthorized use by other market actors. When presented with such circumstances, courts have found that trademark owners have suffered harm despite the fact that redressing such harm entailed some residual impact on the rights of expression of commercial actors. See, e.g., Dallas Cowboys Cheerleaders v. Pussycat Cinema, Ltd., 604 F.2d 200 (plaintiff's mark damaged by unauthorized use in content and promotion of a pornographic film); Chemical Corp. of America v. Anheuser–Busch, Inc., 306 F.2d 433 (5th Cir.1962), cert. denied, 372 U.S. 965 (1963) (floor wax and insecticide maker's slogan, "Where there's life, there's bugs," harmed strength of defendant's slogan, "Where there's life, there's Bud."); Original Appalachian Artworks, Inc. v. Topps Chewing Gum, 642 F.Supp. 1031 (N.D.Ga.1986) (merchandiser of "Garbage Pail Kids" stickers and products injured owner of Cabbage Patch Kids mark); D.C. Comics, Inc. v. Unlimited Monkey Business, 598 F.Supp. 110 (N.D.Ga.1984) (holder of Superman and Wonder Woman trademarks damaged by unauthorized use of marks by singing telegram franchisor); General Electric Co. v. Alumpa Coal Co., 205 U.S.P.Q. (BNA) 1036 (D.Mass.1979) ("Genital Electric" monogram on underpants and T-shirts harmful to plaintiff's trademark); Gucci Shops, Inc. v. R.H. Macy & Co., 446 F.Supp. 838 (S.D. N.Y.1977) (defendant's diaper bag labelled "Gucchi Goo" held to injure Gucci's mark); Coca-Cola Co. v. Gemini Rising, Inc., 346 F.Supp. 1183 (E.D.N.Y.1972) (enjoining the merchandise of "Enjoy Cocaine" posters bearing logo similar to plaintiff's mark).

While the cases cited above might appear at first glance to be factually analogous to the instant one, they are distinguishable for two reasons. First, they all involved unauthorized commercial uses of another's trademark. Second, none of those cases involved a defendant using a plaintiff's trademark as a vehicle for an editorial or artistic parody. In contrast to the cases cited, the instant defendant used plaintiff's mark solely for noncommercial purposes. Appellant's parody constitutes an editorial or artistic, rather than a commercial, use of plaintiff's mark. The article was labelled as "humor" and "parody" in the magazine's table of contents section; it took up two pages in a one-hundred-page issue; neither the article nor appellant's trademark was featured on the front or back cover of the magazine. Drake did not use Bean's mark to identify or promote goods or services to consumers; it never intended to market the "products" displayed in the parody.[3]

We think the Constitution tolerates an incidental impact on rights of expression of commercial actors in order to prevent a defendant from unauthorizedly merchandising his products with another's trademark.[4] In such circumstances, application of the anti-dilution statute constitutes a legitimate regulation of commercial speech, which the Supreme Court has defined as "expression related solely to the economic interests of the speaker and its audience." Central Hudson Gas & Elec. v. Public Serv. Comm'n, 447 U.S. 557, 561 (1980). * * *

If the anti-dilution statute were construed as permitting a trademark owner to enjoin the use of his mark in a noncommercial context found to be negative or offensive, then a corporation could shield itself from criticism by forbidding the use of its name in commentaries critical of its conduct. The legitimate aim of the anti-dilution statute is to prohibit the unauthorized use of another's trademark in order to market incompatible products or services. The Constitution does not, however, permit the range of the anti-dilution statute to encompass the unauthorized use of a trademark in a noncommercial setting such as an editorial or artistic context.

The district court's application of the Maine anti-dilution statute to appellant's noncommercial parody cannot withstand constitutional scrutiny. Drake has not used Bean's mark to identify or market goods or services; it has used the mark solely to identify Bean as the object of its parody. * * *

3. The issue of whether consumers were likely to believe that the "products" would be marketed is a factual issue that is not relevant to this appeal. The trial court denied summary judgment on all claims that depend upon the resolution of the issue of "likelihood of confusion" and our holding does not encompass that issue. We note that a parody which engenders consumer confusion would be entitled to less protection than is granted by our decision today. See, Note Trademark Parody, 72 Va.L.Rev. at 1112. A parody which causes confusion in the marketplace implicates the legitimate commercial and consumer protection objectives of trademark law.

4. We have no occasion to consider the constitutional limits which might be imposed on the application of anti-dilution statutes to unauthorized uses of trademarks on products whose principal purpose is to convey a message. Mutual of Omaha Ins. Co. v. Novak, 775 F.2d 247 (8th Cir. 1985) (plaintiff entitled to preliminary injunction against peace activist protesting nuclear weapons proliferation by marketing "Mutant of Omaha" T-shirts). Such a situation undoubtedly would require a balancing of the harm suffered by the trademark owner against the benefit derived by the parodist and the public from the unauthorized use of a trademark on a product designed to convey a message. * * *

Dilution only in the commercial setting

Our reluctance to apply the anti-dilution statute to the instant case also stems from a recognition of the vital importance of parody. Although, as we have noted, parody is often offensive, it is nevertheless "deserving of substantial freedom—both as entertainment and as a form of social and literary criticism." Berlin v. E.C. Publications, Inc., 329 F.2d 541 (2d Cir.), cert. denied, 379 U.S. 822 (1964). * * *

* * *

Finally, we reject Bean's argument that enjoining the publication of appellant's parody does not violate the first amendment because "there are innumerable alternative ways that Drake could have made a satiric statement concerning 'sex in the outdoors' or 'sex and camping gear' without using plaintiff's name and mark." This argument fails to recognize that appellant is parodying L.L. Bean's catalog, not "sex in the outdoors." The central role which trademarks occupy in public discourse (a role eagerly encouraged by trademark owners), makes them a natural target of parodists. Trademark parodies, even when offensive, do convey a message. The message may be simply that business and product images need not always be taken too seriously; a trademark parody reminds us that we are free to laugh at the images and associations linked with the mark. The message also may be a simple form of entertainment conveyed by juxtaposing the irreverent representation of the trademark with the idealized image created by the mark's owner. While such a message lacks explicit political content, that is no reason to afford it less protection under the first amendment. Denying parodists the opportunity to poke fun at symbols and names which have become woven into the fabric of our daily life, would constitute a serious curtailment of a protected form of expression.

Reversed and remanded.

NOTES

1. Are you comfortable with the distinction between commercial and noncommercial parody? In the Mutual of Omaha case, cited in footnote 4 of the principal case, the court, without the benefit of a dilution statute found a likelihood of confusion when the defendant marketed "Mutant of Omaha" T–Shirts, coffee mugs, and other products as part of an anti-nuclear war campaign. Mutual of Omaha sold similar items with its own logo to its agents to be used for incentives. The court relied on a consumer survey that showed that 42% of those who were shown the defendant's T–shirts said Mutual of Omaha came to mind and 25% thought Mutual "went along" with the shirts to make people aware of nuclear war. Is this sufficient for confusion?

The analysis in *Mutual of Omaha* was rejected in Rogers v. Grimaldi, 875 F.2d 994 (2d Cir.1989). The defendant distributed a movie entitled "Ginger and Fred", a story about two fictional Italian performers who imitated the style of Ginger Rogers and Fred Astaire, two famous American dancers. Ginger Rogers brought suit arguing the title of the movie violated the Lanham Act and produced market surveys suggesting that the title misled consumers into believing Rogers was connected with the film. The court held for the defendant, rejecting Roger's contention that a title is protected under the First

Amendment only if it is so related to the subject matter that there is "no alternative avenues of communication", citing Lloyd Corp., Ltd. v. Tanner, 407 U.S. 551 (1972) (a case relied upon in *Mutual*):

> We believe that in general the [Lanham] Act should be construed to apply to artistic works only where the public interest in avoiding consumer confusion outweighs the public interest in free expression. In the context of allegedly misleading titles using a celebrity's name, that balance will normally not support application of the Act unless the title has no artistic relevance to the underlying work whatsoever, or, if it has some artistic relevance, unless the title explicitly misleads as to the source or the content of the work.

The Court then held that even if the surveys were sufficient to prove likelihood of confusion, the risk of some confusion must be accepted to protect the interests in artistic expression.

2. For a parody to be successful does it not require that the target be conjured up by the audience? If the defendant in *Mutual* had given away the products rather than sold them would the case be different? Compare *Mutual* with Jordache Enterprises, Inc. v. Hogg Wyld Ltd., 828 F.2d 1482 (10th Cir. 1987) where the defendant used a large pig head and hooves with the word "Lardashe" on the backpocket of its jeans as a parody of the small patch of a horse's head and "Jordache" on the plaintiff's jeans. The court found no likelihood of confusion emphasizing that the defendant's intent was to parody not confuse and that although parody relies on an association of the two goods it also relies upon a difference from the original mark. The court also rejected a dilution claim for tarnishment of the "Jordache" mark: "If the public associates the two marks for parody purposes only and does not associate the two sources of the products, appellant suffers no actionable injury."

3. Trademark disparagement has been applied in circumstances not involving parody and without reference to a dilution statute. In Big O Tire Dealers, Inc. v. Goodyear Tire & Rubber Co., 408 F.Supp. 1219 (D.Colo.1976), *vacated on other grounds*, 561 F.2d 1365 (10th Cir.1977) Goodyear through a saturation advertising campaign of its own "Bigfoot" tire was able to consume the preexisting "Bigfoot" mark of plaintiff for tires. Consumers came to believe that plaintiff's use of the mark was an attempt to trade on the good will of Goodyear. The Tenth Circuit approved a cause of action for "trademark disparagement" which required proof of three elements: a false statement, malice, and special damages. The court awarded plaintiff substantial damages based on what plaintiff would need to counteract the defendant's advertising.

4. Trademark disparagement is implicated during the registration process. Section 2(a) prohibits registration of a mark that "may disparage . . . persons, living or dead, institutions, beliefs, or national symbols. . . ." See Greyhound Corp. v. Both Worlds, Inc., 6 U.S.P.Q. 2d 1635 (TTAB 1988) where the running dog trademark of the Greyhound Corporation was disparaged by the applicant's defecating dog mark as applied to polo shirts. Registration was denied under § 2(a).

(6) COLLATERAL USE

CHAMPION SPARK PLUG CO. v. SANDERS

Supreme Court of the United States, 1947.
331 U.S. 125, 67 S.Ct. 1136, 91 L.Ed. 1386.

MR. JUSTICE DOUGLAS delivered the opinion of the Court.

[Petitioner manufactures "Champion" spark plugs. Respondent reconditions and resells used spark plugs in boxes which retain the word "Champion" and the original letter and figure denoting style or type. Respondent also placed its legend on the box ("Perfect Process Renewed Spark Plugs") and placed the word "renewed" on each plug. Finding trademark infringement and unfair competition the Court of Appeals denied an accounting but approved an injunction permitting continued use of the "Champion" mark but requiring the plugs to be repainted with the word "repaired" or "used" stamped on the plug and requiring the Respondent to clearly indicate on boxes that it was the source of these reconditioned plugs.]

We are dealing here with second-hand goods. The spark plugs, though used, are nevertheless Champion plugs and not those of another make. There is evidence to support what one would suspect, that a used spark plug which has been repaired or reconditioned does not measure up to the specifications of a new one. But the same would be true of a second-hand Ford or Chevrolet car. And we would not suppose that one could be enjoined from selling a car whose valves had been reground and whose piston rings had been replaced unless he removed the name Ford or Chevrolet. Prestonettes, Inc. v. Coty, 264 U.S. 359, was a case where toilet powders had as one of their ingredients a powder covered by a trade mark and where perfumes which were trade marked were rebottled and sold in smaller bottles. The Court sustained a decree denying an injunction where the prescribed labels told the truth. Mr. Justice Holmes stated, "A trade mark only gives the right to prohibit the use of it so far as to protect the owner's good will against the sale of another's product as his. * * * When the mark is used in a way that does not deceive the public we see no such sanctity in the word as to prevent its being used to sell the truth. It is not taboo." P. 368.

Cases may be imagined where the reconditioning or repair would be so extensive or so basic that it would be a misnomer to call the article by its original name, even though the words "used" or "repaired" were added. Cf. Ingersoll v. Doyle, D.C., 247 F. 620. But no such practice is involved here. The repair or reconditioning of the plugs does not give them a new design. It is no more than a restoration, so far as possible, of their original condition. The type marks attached by the manufacturer are determined by the use to which the plug is to be put. But the thread size and size of the cylinder hole into which the plug is fitted are not affected by the reconditioning. The heat range also has relevance to the type marks. And there is evidence that the reconditioned plugs are inferior so far as heat range and other qualities are concerned. But inferiority is expected in most second-hand articles. Indeed, they generally cost the customer less. That is the case here. Inferiority is immaterial so long as the article is clearly and distinctively sold as repaired or reconditioned rather than as new. The result is, of course, that the second-hand dealer gets some advantage from the trade mark. But under the rule of Prestonettes, Inc. v. Coty, supra, that is wholly permissible so long as the manufacturer is not identified with the inferior qualities of the product resulting from wear and tear or the reconditioning by the dealer. Full disclosure gives the manufacturer all the protection to which he is entitled.

* * *

Affirmed.

NOTES

1. In Bulova Watch Co. v. Allerton Co., 328 F.2d 20 (7th Cir.1964) the defendant Allerton purchased Bulova watches from a third party, removed the Bulova movements, and transferred the movements into diamond decorated cases purchased from a watch case manufacturer. The movements contained the trademark "Bulova" on the dial after recasing.

The Seventh Circuit agreed with the lower court that the recasing operation resulted in a "new construction" and was no longer a "Bulova" watch. Citing *Champion Spark Plug,* the court held that the defendant could make a proper collateral reference to the source of the watch movement if done in a way that did not deceive the public. Since it was impossible to make a full disclosure on the small dial of the watch, the court enjoined any use of the word "Bulova" on the recased watches. The court also required that any use of the word "Bulova" in advertising or on the catalogue pages indicate (1) that defendant takes plaintiff's movements and recases them, and (2) this is done independently of plaintiff.

2. In Williams v. Curtiss-Wright Corp., 691 F.2d 168 (3d Cir.1982) Curtiss-Wright (CW) made a J-65 jet engine and replacement parts for military aircraft sold to several countries. In the industry replacement parts were identified by number which were keyed to the page of the design plans. Industry practice also permitted officially designated alternative suppliers of replacement parts to use the same number preceded by a letter. Williams sold three types of replacement parts for the J-65: (1) new parts manufactured by Williams after reverse engineering CW's parts; (2) unused surplus parts made by CW and purchased by Williams from other sources; and (3) used parts originally made by CW and reconditioned by Williams. The case involved a preliminary injunction to prevent Williams from using on all three types of parts CW's numbering system preceded by the letter "G". The injunction was upheld for reversed engineered parts in as much as the numbering system might misrepresent that Williams was an approved supplier. However, the injunction was reversed as to the other two categories; for surplus CW parts for procedural reasons and for reconditioned parts on the basis of *Champion Spark Plugs.*

3. See Bandag, Inc. v. Al Bolser's Tire Stores, Inc., 750 F.2d 903 (Fed.Cir. 1984) for application of the traditional rule that an independent dealer may use another's trademark to advertise that he sells or services merchandise of that

particular brand as long as he does not misrepresent that he is an "authorized service agent" or otherwise connected with the trademark owner.

4.   Monte Carlo Shirt, Inc. contracted with Daewoo, a Korean shirt manufacturer, to produce 2400 dozen shirts to its specifications and with the Monte Carlo label.   Monte Carlo rejected the shirts after they arrived in the United States because they were too late for Christmas sales.   The American subsidiary of Daewoo purchased the rejected shirts and sold them with the Monte Carlo label to discount retailers.   Monte Carlo's rejection of the goods is upheld.   Can it also sue for trademark infringement?   Monte Carlo Shirt, Inc. v. Daewoo International (America) Corp., 707 F.2d 1054 (9th Cir.1983) (no).   Would the answer be the same if the shirts had been rejected on the grounds they were defective?

5.   What are the competing interests in these cases?   Aren't the subsequent users profiting from the investment and good will of the trademark owner?

PROBLEM

Plaintiff manufactures and sells catsup under the trademark "Red River".   Most "Red River Catsup" is sold to the retail consumer but plaintiff also sells bulk quantities of the catsup bearing the plaintiff's brand and the notation "for institutional use only".   Defendant purchases the bulk quantities, repackages the catsup in smaller bottles and sells them to retail consumers.   Can plaintiff enjoin the defendant from doing this if defendant sells the catsup under the "Red River" brand?   If he sells it under his own brand with the notation "repackaged Red River catsup"?   See Clairol Inc. v. Budget Discount, 168 U.S. P.Q. 315 (Ill.Cir.Ct.1970);   Nadell & Co. v. Grasso, 175 Cal.App.2d 420, 346 P.2d 505 (1959);   Independent News Co. v. Williams, 293 F.2d 510 (3d Cir.1961).

See Clairol, Inc. v. Boston Discount Center of Berkley, Inc., 608 F.2d 1114 (6th Cir.1979) where defendant sold plaintiff's hair care products marked "Professional Use Only" to retail customers.   These "salon" products did not have the detailed instruction and warning books describing anti-allergy tests included in the packages produced for retail sale.   The court held the defendant guilty of unfair competition constituting a fraud on the public.   Does the increased risk of personal injury distinguish this case from the catsup hypothetical?

SMITH v. CHANEL, INC.
United States Court of Appeals, Ninth Circuit, 1968.
402 F.2d 562.

Browning, Circuit Judge.   Appellant R.G. Smith, doing business as Ta'Ron, Inc., advertised a fragrance called "Second Chance" as a duplicate of appellees' "Chanel No. 5," at a fraction of the latter's price. Appellees were granted a preliminary injunction prohibiting any reference to Chanel No. 5 in the promotion or sale of appellants' product. This appeal followed.

The action rests upon a single advertisement published in "Specialty Salesmen," a trade journal directed to wholesale purchasers.   The advertisement offered "The Ta'Ron Line of Perfumes" for sale.   It gave the seller's address as "Ta'Ron Inc., 26 Harbor Cove, Mill Valley, Calif."

It stated that the Ta'Ron perfumes "duplicate 100% perfect the exact scent of the world's finest and most expensive perfumes and colognes at prices that will zoom sales to volumes you have never before experienced!" It repeated the claim of exact duplication in a variety of forms.

The advertisement suggested that a "Blindfold Test" be used "on skeptical prospects," challenging them to detect any difference between a well known fragrance and the Ta'Ron "duplicate." One suggested challenge was, "We dare you to try to detect any difference between Chanel # 5 (25.00) and Ta'Ron's 2nd Chance. $7.00."

In an order blank printed as part of the advertisement each Ta'Ron fragrance was listed with the name of the well known fragrance which it purportedly duplicated immediately beneath. Below "Second Chance" appeared " *(Chanel # 5)." The asterisk referred to a statement at the bottom of the form reading "Registered Trade Name of Original Fragrance House."

Appellees conceded below and concede here that appellants "have the right to copy, if they can, the unpatented formula of appellees' products" [citing *Sears* and *Compco*]. Moreover, for the purposes of these proceedings, appellees assume that "the products manufactured and advertised by [appellants] are *in fact* equivalents of those products manufactured by appellees." (Emphasis in original.) Finally, appellees disclaim any contention that the packaging or labeling of appellants' "Second Chance" is misleading or confusing.

I

The principal question presented on this record is whether one who has copied an unpatented product sold under a trademark may use the trademark in his advertising to identify the product he has copied. We hold that he may, and that such advertising may not be enjoined under either the Lanham Act, 15 U.S.C. § 1125(a) or the common law of unfair competition, so long as it does not contain misrepresentations or create a reasonable likelihood that purchasers will be confused as to the source, identity, or sponsorship of the advertiser's product.

* * *

We have found no holdings by federal or California appellate courts contrary to the rule of these three cases. Moreover, the principle for which they stand—that use of another's trademark to identify the trademark owner's product in comparative advertising is not prohibited by either statutory or common law, absent misrepresentation regarding the products or confusion as to their source or sponsorship—is also generally approved by secondary authorities.

The rule rests upon the traditionally accepted premise that the only legally relevant function of a trademark is to impart information as to the source or sponsorship of the product. Appellees argue that protection should also be extended to the trademark's commercially more important function of embodying consumer good will created through extensive, skillful, and costly advertising. The courts, however, have generally confined legal protection to the trademark's source identification function for reasons grounded in the public policy favoring a free, competitive economy.

* * *

A related consideration is also pertinent to the present case. Since appellees' perfume was unpatented, appellants had a right to copy it, as appellees concede. There was a strong public interest in their doing so, "[f]or imitation is the life blood of competition. It is the unimpeded availability of substantially equivalent units that permits the normal operation of supply and demand to yield the fair price society must pay for a given commodity." American Safety Table Co. v. Schreiber, 269 F.2d 255, 272 (2d Cir.1959). But this public benefit might be lost if appellants could not tell potential purchasers that appellants' product was the equivalent of appellees' product. "A competitor's chief weapon is his ability to represent his product as being equivalent and cheaper * * *." Alexander, Honesty and Competition, 39 So.Cal.L.Rev. 1, 4 (1966). The most effective way (and, where complex chemical compositions sold under trade names are involved, often the only practical way) in which this can be done is to identify the copied article by its trademark or trade name. To prohibit use of a competitor's trademark for the sole purpose of identifying the competitor's product would bar effective communication of claims of equivalence. Assuming the equivalence of "Second Chance" and "Chanel No. 5," the public interest would not be served by a rule of law which would preclude sellers of "Second Chance" from advising consumers of the equivalence and thus effectively deprive consumers of knowledge that an identical product was being offered at one third the price.

Against these considerations, two principal arguments are made for protection of trademark values other than source identification.

The first of these, as stated in the findings of the district court, is that the creation of the other values inherent in the trademark require "the expenditure of great effort, skill and ability," and that the competitor should not be permitted "to take a free ride" on the trademark owner's "widespread goodwill and reputation."

A large expenditure of money does not in itself create legally protectable rights. Appellees are not entitled to monopolize the public's desire for the unpatented product, even though they themselves created that desire at great effort and expense. As we have noted, the most effective way (and in some cases the only practical way) in which others may compete in satisfying the demand for the product is to produce it and tell the public they have done so, and if they could be barred from this effort appellees would have found a way to acquire a practical monopoly in the unpatented product to which they are not legally entitled.

Disapproval of the copyist's opportunism may be an understandable first reaction, "[b]ut this initial response to the problem has been curbed in deference to the greater public good." American Safety Table Co. v. Schreiber, 269 F.2d at 272. By taking his "free ride," the copyist, albeit, unintentionally, serves an important public interest by offering comparable goods at lower prices. On the other hand, the trademark owner, perhaps equally without design, sacrifices public to personal interest by seeking immunity from the rigors of competition.

* * *

NOTES

1. On remand, the trial court in the *Smith* case found that "Second Chance" did not duplicate "Chanel # 5" 100% and thus the advertising was in violation of § 43(a) of the Lanham Act even though no passing off was shown. Chanel, Inc. v. Smith, 178 U.S.P.Q. 630 (N.D.Cal.1973), affirmed 528 F.2d 284 (9th Cir.1976). And in Saxony Products v. Guerlain, Inc., 513 F.2d 716 (9th Cir.1975) where the defendant advertised its perfumes as "like" or "similar" to the plaintiff's, the court held that expert testimony and a smell test performed for the trial judge were sufficient to create a material fact on plaintiff's § 43(a) claim.

These cases may open a new role for the trial bench in evaluating advertising claims. See G.D. Searle & Co. v. Hudson Pharmaceutical Corp., 715 F.2d 837 (3d Cir.1983) (refusal to enjoin use of "equivalent to Metamucil" for laxative because "whether one is entitled to refer to a competitor's trademark depends not on where the reference appears but on whether the reference is truthful.")

2. The clever copier can avoid proof of equivalency by not claiming it. In several perfume cases a "like/love" comparison is made, as in "If you like OBSESSION, you will love CONFESS" where "Obsession" is the well-known perfume and "Confess" is the cheaper substitute. Calvin Klein v. Parfums de Coeur, 824 F.2d 665 (8th Cir.1987). Is a "like/love" slogan a permissible use of a competitor's trademark? If you are troubled by it standing alone would you permit it with a disclaimer as in "If You Like OPIUM, a fragrance by Yves Saint Laurent, You'll Love OMNI, a fragrance by Deborah Int'l Beauty. Yves Saint Laurent and Opium are not related in any manner to Deborah Int'l Beauty and Omni"? Charles of the Ritz Group Ltd. v. Quality King Dist. Inc., 832 F.2d 1317 (2d Cir.1987) (disclaimer not sufficient to cure confusion where type size of disclaimer and position on packaging reduced its impact).

Do you suspect the courts will look more favorably on a disclaimer where the use of the mark is in good faith, the junior user has a legitimate interest in use of the mark, the junior user has taken other steps to prevent confusion, and the resulting confusion without the disclaimer is minimal? See Soltex Polymer Corp. v. Fortex Industries Inc., 832 F.2d 1325 (2d Cir.1987).

3. How are these cases best explained? Could you argue that *Sears* and *Compco* require this result because if you can copy an unpatented product you should also be able to tell the market you did so? Or could you argue more simply that there is no consumer confusion of source in these advertisements? Or could you argue that, by analogy to *Kellogg,* these trademarks are generic or descriptive in that they represent the standard in the industry to which others have the right to compare their goods?

4. Would a dilution statute alter the result of these cases?

PROBLEMS

a. A large shipment of "Dunhill" tobacco was exposed to water during shipment. The tobacco had been shipped in small airtight tins used for retail sales. It is possible, however, for water to seep underneath the lid and destroy the seal causing the tobacco to deteriorate. It is impossible to determine whether a particular tin has been damaged without opening it, an event that causes the tobacco to deteriorate. Dunhill made a claim on its insurance carrier; the insurance policy authorized the carrier on payment of loss to sell the damaged goods as salvage. Interstate purchased the tobacco from the carrier under a bill of sale that read: "Dunhill Tobacco—As Is—Salvage." No conditions were imposed on resale. Interstate sold the tobacco to retailers and the tins were marketed by them without disclosure of the potential damage. Should Dunhill be entitled to an injunction requiring Interstate to remove the "Dunhill" label or at least indicate on the tins that they were subject to possible water damage? Is it relevant that Dunhill refused to pay an extra insurance premium for "label and brand protection coverage" which would have authorized it to remove its brand prior to the salvage sale? See Alfred Dunhill Ltd. v. Interstate Cigar Co., Inc., 499 F.2d 232 (2d Cir.1974).

b. The owner of the trademark "Candie's" for shoes contracted with a Brazilian shoe manufacturer to produce several lots of "Candie's" shoes. The manufacturer complied with the trademark owner's specifications and affixed the trademark with the owner's permission. The owner subsequently rejected two shipments because of late delivery. The manufacturer then sold the rejected shoes to the defendant. Plaintiff sues defendant for trademark infringement. Who wins? See El Greco Leather Products Co. v. Shoe World Inc., 806 F.2d 392 (2d Cir.1986).

c. Marriott Corporation registers the mark "Marriott's Great America" as a service mark for an amusement park. Five labor organizations join to organize workers at the park and adopt the name "Great America Service Trade Council, AFL–CIO". Marriott sues for trademark infringement. Is it a good claim? See Marriott Corp. v. Great America Service Trades Council, AFL–CIO, 552 F.2d 176 (7th Cir.1977) (Norris-LaGuardia Act precludes injunction because controversy part of labor dispute).

d. Adolph Coors Co. produces "Coors" beer, a perishable product since it is not heat pasteurized. In order to assure high quality beer, Coors requires authorized retailers to dispose of any beer not sold within 60 days of packaging and encourages refrigerated shipment and storage. Coors cannot produce enough beer to satisfy a national market and sells only in the Western states. Genderson purchases large quantities of Coors beer from retailers in Colorado and ships it for retail sale in Maryland. The beer for sale in Maryland often loses its quality because of the manner of shipping and storage. Genderson does not represent to its customers that it is an authorized distributor of "Coors." Should Coors be able to enjoin this unauthorized sale of its beer? See Adolph Coors Co. v. A. Genderson & Sons, Inc., 486 F.Supp. 131 (D.Colo.1980).

(7) REMEDIES

MAIER BREWING CO. v. FLEISCHMANN DISTILLING CORP.

United States Court of Appeals, Ninth Circuit, 1968.
390 F.2d 117, certiorari denied 391 U.S. 966, 88 S.Ct. 2037, 20 L.Ed.2d 879.

BYRNE, DISTRICT JUDGE.   This is a trade-mark infringement case arising under the Lanham Trade-mark Act, 60 Stat. 427, 15 U.S.C.A. §§ 1051–1127 (1946).   * * *

The present appeal is from the awarding by the District Court of an accounting by the defendants of their profits ($34,912 from Maier Brewing and $29,849 from Ralph's Grocery Company) accrued from the sale of beer under the name Black & White, the trade name registered to the plaintiffs [and used by the plaintiff on a Scotch whiskey].
* * *

Although the Lanham Act would appear to provide three distinct elements of compensation or recovery to the registrant of the infringed mark, i.e., the defendant's profits accrued from the use of the mark, plaintiff's damages, and the costs of the action, the case law which has developed under this section of the Act has been far from clear in defining the scope of the relief granted by the Act.   This is particularly true as to the right of the plaintiff to an accounting of the defendant's profits.   See, Note, 34 So.Calif.L.Rev. 283, 288 (1961).

There appear to be two distinct views as to the basis for awarding an accounting of profits.   The majority of cases seem to view an accounting of profits by the defendant as a method of shifting the burden of proof as to damages for lost or potentially lost sales from the plaintiff to the defendant.   See, Note, Wash.U.L.Q. 243 (1963).   The minority view, which is apparently the more recent trend, bases the accounting of profits on the equitable concepts of restitution and unjust enrichment.   The rationale behind this view, as expressed in Monsanto Chemical Co. v. Perfect Fit Products Mfg. Co., 349 F.2d 389 (2d Cir. 1965), the leading case in this trend, is that the infringer has taken the plaintiff's property as represented by his trade-mark and has utilized this property in making a profit, and that if permitted to retain the profit, the infringer would be unjustly enriched.

Those courts which utilize an accounting of profits as a means of compensating the plaintiff for sales which he has lost as a result of his customers being diverted to the infringer, have, as a result of this premise, required that there be competition between the parties before this recovery can be granted.   Clearly, if there is no competition, there can be no diversion of customers.   See, e.g., McCormick & Co. v. B. Manischewitz Co., 206 F.2d 744 (6th Cir.1953); Admiral Corp. v. Penco, Inc., 203 F.2d 517 (2d Cir.1953); Triangle Publications, Inc. v. Rohrlich, 167 F.2d 969 (2d Cir.1948).   It does not necessarily follow, however, that just because there is no direct competition an accounting of profits can serve no reasonable end.   * * *

Earlier in our country's history it may have been necessary to copy both the trade-mark and the product of another in order to obtain a free ride on the good reputation of that product and its maker. In such an instance requiring direct competition between the parties as a prerequisite to the granting of an accounting of profits would have been both just and logical. This, however, is the age of television and mass communications. Fortunes are spent in publicizing a name, often with only slight reference to the real utility of the product. The theory behind this modern advertising is that once the name or trade-mark of a product is firmly associated in the mind of the buying public with some desired characteristic—quality, social status, etc.—the public will buy that product.

* * * Although courts will protect this psychological value of the trade-mark by means of an injunction against infringement, even where the products are of different descriptive qualities and are, therefore, not in competition (Fleischmann Distilling Corp. v. Maier Brewing Co., 314 F.2d 149 (9th Cir.1963)), those courts which treat an accounting solely as a method of compensating for the diversion of customers fail to fully effectuate the policies of the Act. Such courts are neither "securing to the owner the good will of his business [nor] protecting the public against spurious and falsely marked goods." See Monsanto Chemical Co. v. Perfect Fit Products Mfg. Co., supra, 349 F.2d at pages 395–396.

These courts are protecting the trade-mark owner from only the most obvious form of damages—the diversion of sales, and are not in fact providing protection to the value of the good will built up in the trade-mark itself. No recognition is given to the possibility that customers who believe that they are buying a product manufactured by the plaintiff—whether such product is competitive or non-competitive—may be so unhappy with that product that they will never again want to buy that product or any other product produced by the same manufacturer, who they believe to be the plaintiff. Nor do these opinions recognize that, even if the infringing product is of higher quality than that bearing the registered trade-mark, the trade-mark registrant has been deprived of his right to the exclusive use and control of the reputation of his product.

* * *

Initially it should be noted that there is nothing in the Lanham Act which would seem to preclude the use of the unjust enrichment rationale for an accounting of profits. Indeed the language of § 1117 would seem to provide that "a plaintiff is specifically entitled 'to recover (1) defendant's profits' and * * * that he need 'prove defendant's sales only,' leaving to the defendant to 'prove all elements of cost or deduction claimed.' In addition, a plaintiff may recover '(2) any damages sustained by the plaintiff.'" Monsanto, supra at page 397.

Thus, it must be determined if the concept of unjust enrichment, utilized "subject to the principles of equity", will properly serve to effectuate the policies of the Lanham Act. It would seem that it would. The utilization of this concept will not of course make an accounting of profits automatic. Situations will exist where it would be unduly harsh to grant such recovery. Cases exist where the infringement is entirely innocent; where rather than attempting to gain the value of an established name of another, the infringer has developed what he imagined to be a proper trade name only to find out later that his name caused confusion as to the source of, and therefore infringed, a product with a registered trade-mark. See e.g., Highway Cruisers of Cal., Inc. v. Security Industries, Inc., 374 F.2d 875 (9th Cir.1967). In such a case an injunction fully satisfies both the policy of the Act and the equities of the case. Champion Spark Plug Co. v. Sanders, 331 U.S. 125.

Where, however, the infringement is deliberate and wilful, and the products are non-competitive, both the trade-mark owner and the buying public are slighted, if the court provides no greater remedy than an injunction.

* * *

It would seem fairly evident that the purposes of the Lanham Act can be accomplished by making acts of deliberate trade-mark infringement unprofitable. In the case where there is direct competition between the parties, this can be accomplished by an accounting of profits based on the rationale of a returning of diverted profits. In those cases where there is infringement, but no direct competition, this can be accomplished by the use of an accounting of profits based on unjust enrichment rationale. Such an approach to the granting of accountings of profits would, by removing the motive for infringements, have the effect of deterring future infringements. The courts would therefore be able to protect the intangible value associated with trade-marks and at the same time be protecting the buying public from some of the more unscrupulous members of our economic community.

* * *

We conclude that the District Court reached the correct and proper conclusion when, upon finding that the appellants "knowingly, wilfully and deliberately infringed the said trade-mark 'Black & White'", it granted the appellees an accounting of the appellants' profits.

The appellants make two further arguments to the effect that, even if an accounting was proper in this case, the trial court committed reversible error in that (1) the amount awarded as profits failed to properly reflect certain deductions claimed by the appellants and (2) the award was of the profits of both Maier Brewing and Ralph's Grocery Company and hence constitutes more than a single full satisfaction of the appellees.

As to the first of these arguments, both the language of Section 1117 and the case law (see e.g., Mishawaka, supra) indicate that the defendant has the burden of proof as to any deductions from his gross sales. We agree with the District Court that the appellants have not sustained their burden of proof as to the claimed deductions.

As to the second of these arguments, it is apparent that this contention is based upon the assumption that the accounting of profits in this action was utilized as a method of compensating the appellees for diversion of sales. As our resolution of the question as to the appellees' right to an accounting indicates, this was not the basis for the accounting in this action. The dollar amount of the recovery in an accounting for profits under the unjust enrichment rationale has no relation to the damages, if any, sustained by the plaintiff in the action.

The decision of the District Court is affirmed.

NOTES

1. In Playboy Enterprises, Inc. v. Baccarat Clothing Co., Inc., 692 F.2d 1272 (9th Cir.1982) the Ninth Circuit confirmed its theme in *Maier* that remedies should be fashioned to "take all the economic incentives out of trademark infringement." The defendant sold jeans with "Playboy" labels and the famous rabbit head mark of the plaintiff. The district court awarded damages based on what the standard licensing royalty would have been. The Ninth Circuit reversed holding that an award of profits was the only way to remove the incentive for infringement. The Ninth Circuit went further in Polo Fashions, Inc. v. Bruhn, 793 F.2d 1132 (9th Cir.1986) where it held that a seller of counterfeit "Polo" shirts who, after realizing the shirts were not genuine sold his remaining stock to retailers at cost, must pay the full proceeds of the sale to the trademark owner. "[A]ny lesser remedy would not remove the incentive for Bruhn to ship the shirts after discovering that they were counterfeit."

See also, Cuisinarts, Inc. v. Robot-Coupe International Corp., 580 F.Supp. 634 (S.D.N.Y.1984) applying the rule that profits are recoverable only if the plaintiff shows either (1) defendant is unjustly enriched, (2) plaintiff sustained damages, or (3) willful infringement. See also Foxtrap, Inc. v. Foxtrap, Inc., 671 F.2d 636 (D.C.Cir.1982) for a good analysis of monetary remedies under § 35 of the Lanham Act.

2. Recoverable profits must in some way be derived from use of the infringing mark. The burden of disproving the connection is placed on the defendant. See Mishawaka Rubber & Woolen Mfg. Co. v. S.S. Kresge Co., 316 U.S. 203, 206–207 (1942): "There may well be a windfall to the trade-mark owner where it is impossible to isolate the profits which are attributable to the use of the infringing mark. But to hold otherwise would give the windfall to the wrongdoer."

3. Is it ever proper to deny an accounting? Can the plaintiff recover both damages and profits? In a case where the parties are in direct competition, what damages might a plaintiff incur over and above what would be represented by the profits of the defendant? In the non-competitive cases where the court uses unjust enrichment theory, is there any overlap between damages and profits? In Friend v. H.A. Friend & Co., 416 F.2d 526 (9th Cir.1969), the court affirmed a denial of an accounting where the plaintiff and defendant were in direct competition and the plaintiff had been awarded a substantial amount of damages for his lost profits. And the Supreme Court in Mishawaka Rubber, supra, concluded its opinion with the sentence: "If the petitioner suffered damages beyond the loss of profits the decree should provide for the assessment of such damages." But examine § 35 of the Lanham Act. Does it explicitly

authorize cumulative recovery of both profits and damages or does the clause "subject to the principles of equity" prevent a plaintiff's windfall?

4. In Champion Spark Plug Co. v. Sanders, 331 U.S. 125 (1947) the Court held that where the likelihood of damage to the defendant is "slight" and there is no fraud or palming off shown, injunctive relief satisfies the "equities" of the case. This has become standard doctrine both as to profits and damages. See Electronics Corp. of America v. Honeywell, Inc., 358 F.Supp. 1230 (D.Mass. 1973), affirmed per curiam 487 F.2d 513 (1st Cir.1973). However, see Big O Tire Dealers, Inc. v. Goodyear Tire & Rubber Co., 408 F.Supp. 1219 (D.Col.1976) which rejected the doctrine. That issue was not reviewed on appeal. 561 F.2d 1365 (10th Cir.1977).

In West Des Moines State Bank v. Hawkeye Bancorporation, 722 F.2d 411 (8th Cir.1983) the Eighth Circuit applied a "corrective advertising" measure of damages based on Big O Tire Dealers, Inc. v. Goodyear Tire and Rubber Co., 561 F.2d 1365 (10th Cir.1977) which measures as damages 75% of the amount of money spent by the infringer to bring the infringing mark to the public's attention. The theory is to provide the plaintiff with a sum to correct the misperception of the public caused by the infringement. The Eighth Circuit did not speculate on whether the Lanham Act would permit such a measure of damages relying instead on Iowa law. In *Cuisinarts*, supra, the court also permitted recovery of reparative advertising costs.

5. Does the language of the Lanham Act contemplate damages or profits in cases of unintentional infringement? See the last sentence of § 32(1) and § 29. The Restatement (Third) of Unfair Competition § 36 (Tent.Draft No. 3, 1991) permits recovery of pecuniary loss suffered by the plaintiff in any trademark infringement case in which loss is specifically proved, but § 37 permits recovery of profits only upon a showing that the defendant intended to cause confusion. Is there any justification for this distinction?

6. In 1975 Congress amended the Lanham Act to specifically authorize the court to award attorneys fees to the prevailing party "in exceptional circumstances." Previously the Supreme Court had held the Act did not authorize such awards. Fleischmann Distilling Corp. v. Maier Brewing Co., 386 U.S. 714 (1967).

7. *Intentional Infringement: the Trademark Counterfeiting Act of 1984.* The penalties and damage provisions for some cases of intentional infringement were substantially enhanced by the Trademark Counterfeiting Act of 1984, P.L. 98–473 § 1501 et seq. The Act establishes substantial criminal penalties for anyone who "intentionally traffics * * * in goods or services and knowingly uses a counterfeit mark * * *." A "counterfeit mark" is defined as a "spurious mark" that is "identical or substantially indistinguishable" from a registered mark and which is used with goods and services in a way that is "likely to cause confusion, to cause mistake, or to deceive." The defendant need not know that the mark is registered but is entitled to any defenses applicable under the Lanham Act. 18 U.S.C. § 2320.

Perhaps more significantly, § 35 of the Lanham Act was amended by adding what is now subsection (b) which strengthens the provisions for triple damages, triple profits, attorneys fees, and prejudgment interest in counterfeiting cases.

8. *Destruction of labels and goods.* Section 34(d) of the Lanham Act provides authority for the seizure of "goods and counterfeit marks" in a civil action for trademark infringement. Section 36 authorizes the destruction of

"labels, signs, prints, packages, wrappers, receptacles, and advertisements . . . bearing the registered mark. . . ." However, the second paragraph of § 36 uses the language "destruction of *articles*" seized under § 34(d). Can a civil plaintiff obtain destruction of the actual goods on which the offending marks are used or only the offending labels and advertising? The Trademark Counterfeiting Act (18 U.S.C. § 2320) clearly contemplates destruction of the goods themselves in a criminal prosecution. And one court has held the sections together permit destruction of the goods by a civil plaintiff where the infringement is intentional. Fendi S.a.s. Di Paola Fendi E Sorelle v. Cosmetic World Ltd., 642 F.Supp. 1143 (S.D.N.Y.1986).

9. *RICO.* Trademark owners may also find themselves able to take advantage of the Racketeer Influenced and Corrupt Organizations Act, 18 U.S.C. § 1961 et seq. (1982) which was originally enacted to attack organized crime but which has been interpreted to apply to a wide-range of business practices. The act requires a pattern of criminal activity but intentional trademark infringement may well involve mail fraud or other criminal charges that form the predicate offenses for a RICO violation. RICO provides triple damages and attorneys fees. See Cooley, RICO: Treble Damages and Attorneys Fees in Trademark Counterfeiting Actions, 73 Trademark Rep. 476 (1983).

(8) CONTRIBUTORY INFRINGEMENT

COCA–COLA CO. v. SNOW CREST BEVERAGES, INC.

United States District Court, D.Massachusetts, 1946.
64 F.Supp. 980, affirmed 162 F.2d 280, certiorari denied 332 U.S. 809, 68 S.Ct. 110, 92 L.Ed. 386.

WYZANSKI, DISTRICT JUDGE.

[Plaintiff is the owner of the trade-mark "Coca-Cola" and for many years spent millions of dollars advertising its soft drink. Defendant manufactures and sells "Polar Cola," a dark brown cola beverage similar to "Coca-Cola." Defendant convinced a distributor of liquor to run a promotion for bars whereby for every case of rum purchased the bar would receive 5 free cases of Polar Cola. A popular mixed drink at the time was a "Cuba Libre" made of rum and cola. The promotion was designed to get bartenders to use Polar Cola when customers ordered a "Cuba Libre." Polar Cola was cheaper than Coca-Cola. Thereafter plaintiff's investigators found several bars substituting Polar Cola when Coca-Cola was specifically requested. In addition to the findings discussed in the opinion below, the court found that defendants sales talk and advertising were designed to and did induce bars to use Polar Cola for orders not specifying a particular brand of cola but were not designed to encourage or suggest the substitution when Coca-Cola was requested.]

Upon these facts, the legal questions with respect to defendant's sales to bars reduce themselves to these:

(a) Was defendant under a duty not to sell its product to a bar for use by that bar in filling a customer's general order for a Cuba Libre or a rum (or whiskey) and cola?

(b) Before it had notice that some bars in filling a customer's specific order for a rum (or whiskey) and Coca-Cola used a substitute cola, was defendant under a duty to investigate possible passing off, or to take steps to safeguard against such passing off, or to eliminate or curtail sales of its product?

(c) After it had notice that some unnamed bars in filling a customer's order for a rum (or whiskey) and Coca-Cola used a substitute cola, was defendant under a duty to investigate such passing off, or to take steps to safeguard against such passing off, or to eliminate or curtail sales of its product?

The answer to the first question is simple. On the evidence in this case there is no basis for finding that plaintiff has any trademark upon or any special right to the names of "Cuba Libre" or "cola". So far as appears any one has a right to make or sell products under those names. Customers who ask for them are not asking for plaintiff's product. For them there cannot be confusion as to the source of the goods. In short, defendant was free to sell its own cola to a bar for use by the bar in filling a customer's general order for "Cuba Libre" or "rum (or whiskey) and cola."

In answering the second question these are the dominant facts. There is on this record a failure to prove that many bar customers ordinarily place specific orders for Coca-Cola, that a reasonable person in the bottling business would have known or that this defendant did know that a very large number of customers did make such specific orders or that a reasonable person in the bottling business would have known or that this defendant did know that upon receiving specific orders for Coca-Cola barkeepers would be more likely than the average man to substitute for Coca-Cola a cheaper product. So far as appears, the great majority of customers in a bar who order a drink mixed of rum or whiskey and cola do not specify the brand of the rum or the whiskey or the cola. The percentage who specify the type cola is much lower than the small percentage of drinkers who specify the type rum or whiskey they desire.

Even upon the view of the evidence most favorable to plaintiff, the testimony only shows that some customers do place specific orders for "rum (or whiskey) and Coca-Cola," that the defendant knew it, and that any man of common sense knows that in any line of business, including but not emphasizing the business of running bars and taverns, there are some unscrupulous persons who, when it is to their financial advantage to do so, will palm off on customers a different product from that ordered by the customer.

Upon these facts defendant was not under a duty to investigate possible passing off by bartenders, or to take steps to safeguard against such passing off, or to eliminate or curtail sales of its product.

It is, of course, defendant's duty to avoid intentionally inducing bars to market defendant's products as products of plaintiff. Summerfield Co. v. Prime Furniture Co., 242 Mass. 149, 155, 136 N.E. 396; Am.

L.Inst., Restatement, Torts § 713. It is also defendant's duty to avoid knowingly aiding bars which purchase defendant's products from marketing those products in such a manner as to infringe plaintiff's trademark. New England Awl & Needle Co. v. Marlborough Awl & Needle Co., 168 Mass. 154, 155, 46 N.E. 386; Reid, Murdoch & Co. v. H.P. Coffee Co., 8 Cir., 48 F.2d 815, 817, 819, 820; Am.L.Inst., Restatement, Torts § 738, comment a, illustration 2.

Under the principles just stated, it would have been a breach of duty if defendant's salesmen had induced bars to buy defendant's product for the stated or implied purpose of serving it when Coca-Cola was called for. It would also have been a breach of duty for defendant to have continued sales to bars without taking some precautionary measures if it had known or a normal bottler would have known that most bar customers specifically ordered Coca-Cola and that consequently a normal bottler would infer from defendant's large volume of sales that many bars which bought defendant's product were using defendant's product as a substitute in the case of specific orders of Coca-Cola and were not merely using it as an ordinary cola when a customer placed a general order for a "Cuba Libre" or a "rum (or whiskey) and cola." Likewise, it would have been a breach of duty if defendant had known that many bar customers specifically ordered Coca-Cola and had also known that some particular bars were in fact using defendant's product as a substitute in the case of specific orders for Coca-Cola.

But in the case at bar plaintiff seems to urge that defendant's obligation goes further. Plaintiff appears to contend that once a defendant has knowledge that some customers of bars specifically order "rum (or whiskey) and Coca-Cola," and that there are in all probability some rogues in the bar business as in other businesses, the defendant has a duty either (a) not to sell to any bar a cola until defendant first creates for that cola a special consumer demand, or (b) at least not to sell a cola to a bar before defendant has particularly cautioned the bar to be scrupulous against substitution. The law does not go that far. Before he can himself be held as a wrongdoer or contributory infringer one who supplies another with the instruments by which that other commits a tort, must be shown to have knowledge that the other will or can reasonably be expected to commit a tort with the supplied instrument. Nugrape Co. of America v. Glazier, 5 Cir., 22 F.2d 596, 597. The test is whether wrongdoing by the purchaser "might well have been anticipated by the defendant." Reid, Murdoch & Co. v. H.P. Coffee Co., 8 Cir., 48 F.2d 817, 819, last two lines.

There is no broader legal principle that always makes the defendant his brother's or his customer's keeper. Where the defendant markets a product, defendant's accountability for his customer's wrongful use of that product turns on the issue whether a reasonable person in the defendant's position would realize either that he himself had created a situation which afforded a temptation to or an opportunity for wrong by l'homme moyen sensuel or was dealing with a customer whom he should know would be peculiarly likely to use the defendant's product wrongfully. Compare Am.L.Inst., Restatement, Torts § 302, comment m.

* * *

There remains the problem raised by the third question, that is, the duty of defendant after September 1944. In solving that problem the general principles applicable are not different from those reviewed in answering the second question. That is, plaintiff would have established a case against defendant if in the fall of 1944 or at any other time prior to November 14, 1944 when this suit was brought plaintiff had given defendant either (a) credible information that would have led a normal bottler in defendant's position to believe that so many bar customers specifically ordered "rum (or whiskey) and Coca-Cola" that in view of the volume of defendant's sales many bars must necessarily be passing off defendant's product as Coca-Cola, or (b) notice that particular named bars which defendant was continuing to supply were serving defendant's product when plaintiff's product was specifically ordered. New England Awl & Needle Co. v. Marlborough Awl & Needle Co., 168 Mass. 154, 155, 46 N.E. 386. But the evidence shows no such proffer of information that would persuade a reasonable man and no such notice by plaintiff. Plaintiff did not go beyond stating in a conversation of general scope that unnamed bars in unnamed quantities were serving defendant's product when plaintiff's was called for.

* * *

Nothing herein intimates any opinion on the question whether defendant after having its attention drawn in the course of the trial of this case to testimony that particular bars have served defendant's product in response to customer's orders for plaintiff's product, is now under a duty to minimize or eliminate the risk that those or other bars will engage in a further confusion of defendant's goods with plaintiff's goods.

Decree dismissing complaint with costs.

NIKE, INC. v. RUBBER MANUFACTURERS ASS'N, INC.

United States District Court, Southern District of New York, 1981.
509 F.Supp. 919.

[The case involves a counterclaim by Brooks, an athletic shoe manufacturer, against Nike, another manufacturer. Brooks' claim under 43(a) of the Lanham Act alleges that Nike paid several professional athletes to wear Nike shoes which all carry a "swoosh-stripe" emblem on the side and the word "NIKE" on the back. Some of these athletes, including Mike Schmidt, a star for the Philadelphia Phillies and voted the most valuable player in the major leagues, and Mark Moseley, place kicker for the Washington Redskins, wore shoes other than Nikes but doctored them to look like Nike shoes by adding a "swoosh-stripe" and the word "Nike." The athletes had contracted to wear only Nike shoes, but in some instances Nike shoes were not comfortable.]

Nike contends that it has not violated the provisions of the Lanham Act because the doctoring was done without its participation, knowledge or approval. The record indicates, however, that Nike knew of Schmidt's doctoring activity, since three of its employees observed Schmidt's doctored shoes. None of them informed Schmidt that this was a breach of his agreement. Indeed, their apparent acquiescence would indicate tacit approval.

Moreover, Nike's restrictive reading of Section 43(a) is not persuasive. In Stix Products, Inc. v. United Merchants & Manufacturers, Inc., 295 F.Supp. 479 (S.D.N.Y.1969), the court granted injunctive relief against those who knowingly played a significant role in the deception involved. * * *

* * *

At the hearing, vice-president Robert Woodell testified that Nike's corporate policy has been to oppose doctoring, and that this policy is reflected in language prohibiting such acts in the agreements signed by the players. However, it appears from the evidence that Nike has on occasion been less than vigilant in enforcing this policy. The existence of lucrative contracts between Nike and prominent players leads the players, as it did in the case of Schmidt, Boone and Unser, to doctor their shoes to look like Nike shoes if they find the Nike shoes uncomfortable and do not wish to wear them. Nike certainly knew of the likelihood of doctoring, just as it knew that by paying large sums of money to players it encouraged them to wear the Nike trademark on whatever shoes they wore. Therefore, Nike's contractual prohibition against doctoring does not shield it from liability.

NOTES

1. Is there a particularly difficult balancing of interests required in the principal case that does not fully surface in the opinion? Assume that the defendant is presented credible evidence that a particular bar shows a pattern of substitution when Coca-Cola is requested. What does Judge Wyzanski expect the defendant to do?

2. Section 32(1)(b) of the Lanham Act, 15 U.S.C. § 1114(1)(b), states the controlling principles as applied to packagers, manufacturers, and reproducers. The important limitation is the requirement that no profits and damages can be recovered from such an infringer "unless the acts have been committed with knowledge that such imitation is intended to be used to cause confusion, or to cause mistake, or to deceive." The cases are not so positive. In Corning Glass Works v. Jeannette Glass Co., 308 F.Supp. 1321 (S.D.N.Y.1970), the court said that the defendant manufacturer would be liable for contributory unfair competition and trademark infringement if the jury concluded "that Jeannette should have realized that manufacture of Lady Cornelia ovenware created an opportunity for misuse." Id. at 439.

3. Section 32 of the Lanham Act is the section most directly applicable to the issue of contributory infringement. Does the express limitation of remedy against innocent printers and publishers imply that all others who aid in a trademark infringement are subject to the full range of remedies under the Act? Is an advertising agency that prepares and a television station that

broadcasts advertising for a product with an infringing label liable for damages caused the trademark owner?

PROBLEM—CAPSULE COLORS AND GENERIC DRUGS

Plaintiff manufactures a prescription drug cyclandate under the brand name "Cyclospasmol" in distinctive red and blue capsules. Can the plaintiff prevent the defendant from selling the generic drug cyclandate in similar red and blue capsules? Are the following facts of any significance?

a. Plaintiff had enjoyed a 5 year monopoly on the production of cyclandate because it was the only manufacturer able to secure FDA approval for marketing.

b. Plaintiff had enjoyed an extended monopoly on the production of cyclandate because of a now expired patent.

c. Defendant advertises to pharmacists that its cyclandate is "comparable to Cyclospasmol."

d. Patients recognize the red and blue capsules as indicative of the drug prescribed by their physician.

The case against the defendant can be seen as a direct infringement case because pharmacists may be confused as to the source of particular capsules or as a contributory infringement case because the capsules facilitate pharmacists substituting generic equivalents for branded drugs. Some consumer advocates have argued in favor of liberal substitution by pharmacists of cheaper generic drugs that are equivalent to branded drugs, even when the physician's prescription specifies the brand name drug. In some states legislation has been enacted regulating generic switching. For example a New York statute requires the physician to indicate on each prescription whether his intent is "Dispense as Written" or "Substitution Permissible." N.Y.Education Law § 6810(6). It is thought that similar capsule colors will aid in generic switching because it reduces consumer concern about whether they have received the correct medicine. In addition there is some argument for standardized color codes for prescription drugs to reduce the risk of pharmacist and consumer error. Along this line, a short note in the Wall Street Journal reported concern by Mayo Clinic doctors that similarity of names of different drugs leads to errors in drug therapy. Wall St.J., Jan. 15, 1981, p. 1, col. 5.

On the other hand, traditional trademark analysis is urged to prevent similarly colored capsules for generic drugs and it is argued that providing a generic product when the brand "Cyclospasmol" is prescribed is no different than serving "Pepsi" when someone orders "Coke."

How should trademark law be applied to prescription drugs where (1) the person who specifies the product (physician) does not pay for it; (2) the person who selects the product (pharmacist) does not pay for it; and (3) the ultimate consumer is presumed to have insufficient knowledge of the desirability or qualities of the product (it can only be purchased with a prescription) to make his own purchasing decision.

See Ives Laboratories, Inc. v. Darby Drug Co., Inc., 455 F.Supp. 939 (E.D. N.Y.1978) (temporary relief denied to owner of branded drug), affirmed 601 F.2d 631 (2d Cir.1979). The district court eventually dismissed plaintiff's complaint. Ives Laboratories, Inc. v. Darby Drug Co., Inc., 488 F.Supp. 394 (E.D.N.Y.1980), reversed 638 F.2d 538 (2d Cir.1981) (finding contributory infringement):

By using capsules of identical color, size and shape, together with a catalog describing their appearance and listing comparative prices of Cyclospasmol and generic cyclandelate, appellees could reasonably anticipate that their generic drug product would by a substantial number of druggists be substituted illegally for Ives' trademarked CYCLOSPASMOL or that bottles of their lower-priced product might be mislabeled as CYCLOSPASMOL, all to the druggists' economic advantage. This amounted to a suggestion, at least by implication, that the druggists take advantage of the opportunity to engage in such misconduct. Id. at 453.

The United States Supreme Court reversed the Court of Appeals, holding that it did not properly apply the clearly erroneous rule in reversing the District Court. Inwood Laboratories, Inc. v. Ives Laboratories, Inc., 456 U.S. 844 (1982). The Court, applying *Snow Crest,* indicated that the petitioners could be held for contributory infringement depending on:

> [W]hether, in fact, the petitioners intentionally induced the pharmacists to mislabel generic drugs or, in fact, continued to supply cyclandelate to pharmacists whom the petitioners knew were mislabeling generic drugs.

On remand the Second Circuit in *Ives* held that sale of generic substitutes did not violate § 43(a) of the Lanham Act because the color and shape of the capsule were functional and that Ives' capsules did not have secondary meaning. Ives Laboratories Inc. v. Darby Drug Co., Inc., 697 F.2d 291 (2d Cir.1982). See, however, Ciba-Geigy Corp. v. Bolar Pharmaceutical Co., Inc., 747 F.2d 844 (3d Cir.1984), cert. denied 471 U.S. 1137 (1985), in which the Third Circuit held that as to passing off under § 43(a) of the Lanham Act *Ives* permitted liability for contributory infringement where the defendant had a "reasonable apprehension" that the capsule colors would assist infringements by others. Judge Giles dissented arguing that *Ives* clearly held that as to § 32 of the Lanham Act contributory infringement required intentional inducement or continued sale of a product with knowledge that the pharmacist would engage in illegal substitution and that the standard for § 43(a) should be the same.

Which standard do you believe best resolves the issues in these cases? What should the outcome of the Lanham Act claims be if a state statute permitted pharmacists to substitute generic equivalents? Does the Lanham Act preempt the issue?

See Germain, The Supreme Court's Opinion in the *Inwood* Case: Declination of Duty, 70 Ky.L.Rev. 731 (1982); Cooper, Trademark Aspects of Pharmaceutical Product Design, 70 Trademark Rep. 1 (1980).

(9) ABANDONMENT

EXXON CORP. v. HUMBLE EXPLORATION CO., INC.
United States Court of Appeals, Fifth Circuit, 1983.
695 F.2d 96.

[The Humble Oil & Refining Company began using the mark "Humble" on gasoline stations and automotive products in the early 1960's. In 1972 the company adopted the mark "Exxon" as a substitute, changed its corporate name to Exxon Company, U.S.A., and spent 12 million dollars advertising the mark and name change. However, the Board of Directors in 1972 passed a resolution calling for continued use of the "Humble" mark after the changeover and Exxon instituted a trademark maintenance program which involved limited sales using the "Humble" mark.

The appellant, the Humble Exploration Company was formed in 1974 and selected "Humble" as a mark because it was abandoned by Exxon. The company is actively involved in oil exploration. Exxon filed this suit to enjoin use of "Humble" by the appellant. Appellant raised the issue of abandonment.]

PATRICK E. HIGGINBOTHAM, CIRCUIT JUDGE.

* * *

The district court framed the abandonment issue thus: "Is the limited use of a famous trademark solely for protective purposes a use sufficient to preclude abandonment under the common law and the Lanham Act?" It answered the question in the affirmative. Plaintiff-Appellee withdrew its Texas and common law claims in the district court, so the resolution of the abandonment issue must focus on the federal standards for abandonment set forth in the Lanham Act.

Under the Act,

A mark shall be deemed to be abandoned—

(a) When its use has been discontinued with intent not to resume use. Intent not to resume may be inferred from circumstances. Nonuse for two consecutive years shall be prima facie abandonment.

15 U.S.C. § 1127 (1982). The burden of proof is on the party claiming abandonment, but when a prima facie case of trademark abandonment exists because of nonuse of the mark for over two consecutive years, the owner of the mark has the burden to demonstrate that circumstances do not justify the inference of intent not to resume use. See Sterling Brewers, Inc. v. Schenley Industries, Inc., 441 F.2d 675, 679 (Cust. & Pat.App.1971).

Appellant argues that Exxon has not used the HUMBLE mark since its changeover program. Since that time, Exxon has (1) sold existing inventory of packaged products bearing the name "Humble Oil and Refining Company"; (2) made periodic sales of nominal amounts of Exxon gasoline, motor oil and grease in pails bearing the names HUMBLE and EXXON; (3) sold Exxon bulk gasoline and diesel fuel to selected customers, who received HUMBLE invoices, through three corporations organized for that purpose; and (4) sold 55-gallon drum products from the Baytown, Texas refinery, all bearing a stencil with the names HUMBLE and EXXON.

The existing inventory was depleted by mid-1974; the sale of 55 gallon drums began in 1977. Whether or not these sales are "uses" for the purposes of 15 U.S.C. § 1127, the period between those sales was longer than two years, and under the Lanham Act, "nonuse for two consecutive years is prima facie abandonment." 15 U.S.C. § 1127.

During that period between sales of inventory and sales of 55-gallon drum products, Exxon can point to only two types of sales as possible uses. As earlier described, Exxon made limited sales of packaged products with both EXXON and HUMBLE on the labels to targeted customers in these amounts: $9.28 in 1973, $.0 in 1974, $140.12 in 1975 and $42.05 in 1976. Second, products in bulk form and not bearing a trade name or mark were sold to selected customers who received the explanation that they were receiving Exxon products. The only use of HUMBLE in connection with these sales was on the invoices sent to the customers. The issue, thus, is whether these two categories of arranged sales through the trademark protection program during that period constitute "use" sufficient to avoid prima facie abandonment.

* * *

In this case, the mark HUMBLE was used only on isolated products or selected invoices sent to selected customers. No sales were made that depended upon the HUMBLE mark for identification of source. To the contrary, purchasers were informed that the selected shipments would bear the HUMBLE name or be accompanied by an HUMBLE invoice but were the desired Exxon products. That is, the HUMBLE mark did not with these sales play the role of a mark. That casting, however, is central to the plot that the Lanham Act rests on the idea of registration of marks otherwise born of use rather than the creation of marks by the act of registration. That precept finds expression in the Lanham Act requirement that to maintain a mark in the absence of use there must be an intent to resume use. That expression is plain. The Act does not allow the preservation of a mark solely to prevent its use by others. Yet the trial court's reasoning allows precisely that warehousing so long as there is residual good will associated with the mark. Exxon makes the same argument here. While that may be good policy, we cannot square it with the language of the statute. In sum, these arranged sales in which the mark was not allowed to play its basic role of identifying source were not "use" in the sense of section 1127 of the Lanham Act.

* * *

[The district court had cited language in Lyon Metal Products, Inc. v. Lyon Inc., 134 U.S.P.Q. 31 (TTAB 1962) that there is a residual good will that remains after a mark is abandoned and that it might prevent another party from adopting the abandoned mark particularly given the likelihood of consumer confusion. The Court of Appeals viewed the statement as dicta and the case as not factually similar.]

* * *

This court recognizes that the good-will associated with the mark HUMBLE has immense value to Exxon. That fact, coupled with the efforts under the trademark maintenance program, could suggest Exxon's intent to resume use of the mark,[4] but the trial court did not make

---

4. In Sterling Brewers, Inc. v. Schenley Industries, Inc., 441 F.2d 675 (Cust. & Pat. App.1971), the court decided that the good- will of a trademark for beer had not dissipated through eight years of nonuse. Significantly, the court found that "the

that finding. The court found that the trademark protection program evidenced "an intent not to relinquish HUMBLE" and "an intent not to abandon HUMBLE," but it did not specifically address Exxon's intent to resume use as required by section 1127 the Lanham Act. * * * There is a difference between intent not to abandon or relinquish and intent to resume use in that an owner may not wish to abandon its mark but may have no intent to resume its use. In factual contexts where there is no issue of a hoarding of a mark, the language "an intent to abandon or relinquish" may be used to express the Lanham Act requirement of an "intent not to resume use." For that reason, it is important that cases using the language of "intent to abandon" be carefully laid into their factual molds. * * * In the context of a challenge strictly under the Lanham Act to an alleged warehousing program, as the facts of this case present, the application of the statutory language is critical. That is, this court having found that the two types of uses under the trademark maintenance program were not sufficient uses to avoid prima facie proof of abandonment, the district court must specifically address Exxon's intent to resume use of the HUMBLE trademark. An "intent to resume" requires the trademark owner to have plans to resume commercial use of the mark. Stopping at an "intent not to abandon" tolerates an owner's protecting a mark with neither commercial use nor plans to resume commercial use. Such a license is not permitted by the Lanham Act.

III.   EXXON'S CLAIM UNDER § 1125

Exxon argues here that even if the HUMBLE mark were abandoned, Exxon has the right to prevent a competitor from gaining an unfair advantage by using a "false designation of origin" or "a false representation" in interstate commerce in violation of section 43(a) of the Lanham Act, 15 U.S.C. § 1125(a). The district court found that appellant Humble Exploration's use of the trade name Humble constituted a misrepresentation of goods and services in commerce in violation of § 1125(a). That conclusion flows from its finding that Exxon had not abandoned the HUMBLE mark. This court having found that Exxon has discontinued use of the mark, abandonment of the mark is yet to be decided by the inquiry into intent to resume use. Whether the mark has been abandoned is in turn precedent to Exxon's claim under § 1125. That is, to the extent that Exxon travels on a trademark infringement claim, § 1125(a) is to be read in a parallel fashion with §§ 1114 and 1115. While § 1125 has a broader reach than § 1114, and claims under it can be maintained by plaintiffs who are not owners of a trademark, see Norman M. Morris Corp. v. Weinstein, 466 F.2d 137 (5th Cir.1972), when a claim is based on alleged ownership of a mark, the two sections must be applied in a parallel manner. Otherwise

continuous activity * * * directed to maintenance of the brewery during the period of non-use, coupled with the refusal to consider periodic efforts of appellant to negotiate purchase of the rights to the mark separately, demonstrates an intent to maintain conditions conducive to resumption of production under the mark on relatively short notice." Id. at 680.

stated, the § 1125 claim rises or falls on the issue of abandonment for the reason that the only basis for the trial court's holding that § 1125 was violated was the use by appellant of the mark, a use not faulted if the mark has been abandoned. It would be incongruous to hold that Exxon had abandoned the mark, discontinued the mark with no intent to resume use, and thus that appellant had a right to use that mark because of Exxon's abandonment, and then to hold that appellant had engaged in false designation or representation of origin * * *.

The judgment is reversed and the case is remanded for further proceedings consistent with this opinion. In doing so, we emphasize that we do not decide here whether the present record would support a finding that Exxon had sufficient intent to resume use of the Humble mark so as to avoid its loss, nor do we here address Exxon's rights under the common law to block any present use of the mark in a confusing manner. Finally, we leave to the trial court the decision whether additional evidence on the issue of intent to resume use ought to be heard.

Affirmed in part, reversed and remanded in part.

[On remand, the court held there was no abandonment. Exxon Corp. v. Humble Exploration Co., Inc., 592 F.Supp. 1226 (N.D.Tex. 1984)].

NOTES

1. The Eighth Circuit adopted the *Exxon* distinction between intent not to abandon and intent to resume in Hiland Potato Chip Co. v. Culbro Snack Foods, Inc., 720 F.2d 981 (8th Cir.1983). The *Sterling Brewers* case described in footnote 4 of the *Exxon* opinion is a leading case where delayed non-use was not considered abandonment.

2. The doctrine of abandonment may arise in a number of situations. It serves as a defense to an infringement action. Abandonment may also play a significant feature in determining priority of competing marks where the current owner of a mark seeks to use the date of adoption of a prior user from whom he has purchased the mark in establishing an earlier priority. It may be argued in such cases that the prior user abandoned the mark and therefore the date of first use is the first use by the current owner. In cases where the Lanham Act preserves preexisting rights of common law trademarks against the exclusive claims of a federal registrant, the registrant often asserts that the prior user has abandoned the mark. But see Casual Corner Assoc., Inc. v. Casual Stores of Nevada, Inc., 493 F.2d 709 (9th Cir.1974) where the court held that the standards of proof relating to abandonment do not apply in determining whether a prior use has been "continuous" and thus preserved against a claim of incontestability by section 15 of the Lanham Act. The court found a one year period of non-use sufficient to defeat an assertion of "continuous" use in the absence of intent to abandon.

3. The definition of "abandonment" in § 45 provides two separate tests. The first, non-use with intent not to resume, is a traditional common law formulation. The second declares a mark abandoned if "any course of conduct of the owner, including acts of omission as well as commission, causes the mark to become the generic name for the goods or services * * * or otherwise to lose its significance as an indication of origin." For a detailed examination of

the second definition see Wallpaper Manufacturers, Ltd. v. Crown Wallcovering Corp., 680 F.2d 755 (CCPA 1982). There the court recognizes that an expansive definition of abandonment would upset the attempt in §§ 14, 15 and 33 to provide for some security for trademark owners. In *Wallpaper* the junior user argued that since there was evidence that some consumers attributed the mark to him as well as the senior user, the mark was "abandoned" because it has lost its origin significance. The court, however, held that even where there was de facto evidence of consumer attribution to more than one source, to be abandoned the mark had to lose *all* significance for the prior user.

4. The defense of "abandonment" should be carefully distinguished from the defenses of "acquiescence" or "laches". "Acquiescence" arises where the plaintiff gives some measure of assurance, either express or implied, that he will not assert his trademark rights against a particular defendant. The defense of "laches" contemplates unreasonable delay by the plaintiff in asserting his rights with resultant prejudice to the defendant. Both defenses may only be asserted by those defendants directly affected by the plaintiff's acts or omissions; abandonment is a loss of trademark rights against the world. The three defenses are analyzed in McCarthy, Trademarks and Unfair Competition ch. 17 (abandonment) & ch. 31 (laches and acquiescence) (1973), and applied in Conagra, Inc. v. Singleton, 743 F.2d 1508 (11th Cir.1984). See also, National Association for the Advancement of Colored People v. N.A.A.C.P. Legal Defense & Educational Fund, Inc., 753 F.2d 131 (D.C.Cir.1985) where the Association formed the Legal Defense Fund in 1957 as a separate entity and permitted it to use the initials N.A.A.C.P. but after acrimony developed between the two organizations a demand was made in 1965 for LDF to discontinue its use of the initials. However, no action was taken by either party for the next 12 years until this suit was filed. The court held the Association barred by laches and dismissed the suit.

5. In abandonment cases it may be important to define the scope of the abandonment in geographic or product market terms. In *Dawn Donut Co.,* supra pg. 336, the court held that a federal registrant is not considered to have abandoned his mark unless he has abandoned it on a nation-wide basis. See also, Sheila's Shine Products, Inc. v. Sheila Shine, Inc., 486 F.2d 114 (5th Cir. 1973) where with regard to a common law mark, the issue of abandonment was evaluated on a state by state basis. "Since a state is an appropriate territory by which to define trade areas when two parties are competing over the right to use the same mark [citing United Drug Co. v. Theodore Rectanus Co., 248 U.S. 90 (1918)] we deem it consistent with general principles of trademark law to hold that a user may abandon a trademark in certain states without abandoning it in others." Id. at 124. Laches and acquiescence defenses are normally limited to the geographic market where the factual basis applies. Conan Properties, Inc. v. Conans Pizza, Inc., 752 F.2d 145 (5th Cir.1985).

6. Are there general principles to guide the application of the doctrine of abandonment? Consider whether the trademark owner should be deemed to have abandoned his mark in the following cases:

a. CBS suspends use of the "Amos 'N' Andy" trademark for radio and television programs portraying black persons because of strong pressure from civil rights groups. The mark and tapes of past programs were occasionally licensed from 1934 through the 1980's for purposes of documentaries and copyrights on the programs were asserted and renewed. CBS claims an intention to hold on to the marks for a time when public attitudes change. Can a third person use the mark to represent a new musical comedy he wants to create? See Silverman v. CBS Inc., 870 F.2d 40 (2d Cir.1989).

b. A trademark originally used on fishing lures in 1910 is now used exclusively on fishing poles. Does the owner's priority relate back to 1910? Would your answer change if instead of fishing poles the mark was switched to broom handles?

c. The trademark owner substantially changes the quality of the product to which the mark is attached by altering a major ingredient?

d. The trademark owner alters the form of the mark. The word "Beechnut" is retained but the label of the tobacco is altered by changing color and other identifying aspects. In all of the cases posed above, consider the nature of the rights of a third party to use the mark if a court decides the original owner has abandoned the mark.

(10) ASSIGNMENT AND LICENSING

PEPSICO, INC. v. GRAPETTE CO.
United States Court of Appeals, Eighth Circuit, 1969.
416 F.2d 285.

LAY, CIRCUIT JUDGE. PepsiCo, Inc., a holding company of several subsidiaries including Pepsi Cola Co., a national soft drink bottler, sought an injunction against Grapette-Aristocrat, Inc. and its holding company Grapette Co. (hereinafter referred collectively as Grapette) on the alleged infringement of its trademark "Pepsi." In 1965 Grapette purchased the mark "Peppy" and intended to bottle a soft "pepper" drink with that name. The district court found that the mark "Peppy" was confusingly similar to "Pepsi" and as such would constitute infringement under 15 U.S.C. § 1114. However, notwithstanding this finding of infringement, the court denied the plaintiff injunctive relief on the ground that it was guilty of laches. 288 F.Supp. at 937. PepsiCo., Inc., appeals. We reverse.

The evidence shows that Pepsi Cola Co. has bottled beverages duly registered under trademarks "Pepsi Cola," "Pepsi" and "Pep-Kola" for many years. See 15 U.S.C. § 1065. Grapette is a national bottler and distributor of soft drinks, concentrates and syrups. In 1965 it developed a formula for a new syrup to be used in a pepper type bottled beverage as opposed to a cola beverage. In searching for a name to market the new product, defendant discovered the 1926 registration of the mark "Peppy" by H. Fox and Co., a partnership. The mark had been renewed by Fox in 1946 and 1966. Sometime between 1932 and 1937 Fox began to use the mark "Peppy" in conjunction with a cola flavored syrup which was distributed on a local basis, confined mostly to the Eastern states of New York, New Jersey and Connecticut. The cola distribution was sold exclusively as syrup. Since 1958, Fox's syrup has been sold only to jobbers in 28 ounce consumer size bottles. Some ten to twelve years prior to this time it was sold also to the fountain trade as a syrup in gallon containers.

In 1965, Grapette Co. entered into an agreement with Fox Corp. in which the trademark "Peppy" was assigned to defendant for a consideration of $7,500. At this time Fox Corp. was in a Chapter 11 bankruptcy proceeding. Although Fox Corp. made a formal assignment of "goodwill", it is conceded by defendant that none of Fox Corp.'s physical assets or plant were transferred with the trademark; no inventory, customer lists, formulas, etc. Upon acquisition of the "Peppy" mark, Grapette began arrangements to have this mark placed upon its new pepper flavored soft drink. Fox Corp. continued to sell its cola syrup under the mark "Fox Brand" as well as agreeing to act as a distributor of defendant's "Peppy." In 1965, plaintiff warned the defendant of possible litigation if it did not stop the use of its mark. On April 21, 1966, this action was begun.

Plaintiff contends (1) that the transfer of the trade-mark "Peppy" by Fox Corp. was invalid because it was an assignment in "gross" and that therefore, Grapette cannot stand in the shoes of its predecessor in order to assert the defense of laches; and (2) that the defense of laches is not supported by sufficient evidence.

It is not disputed that Grapette must stand in the place of Fox Corp. Without a valid assignment, Grapette's rights to the use of "Peppy" accrue only as of November 1965 and it could not assert the defense of laches. PepsiCo, Inc. asserts that the 1965 assignment of the trademark by Fox Corp. to Grapette was a legal nullity in that the trade-mark was transferred totally disconnected from any business or goodwill of the assignor. We must agree.

* * * [The court here set out Section 10 of the Lanham Act, 15 U.S.C. § 1060.]

The early common law rule that a trademark could not be assigned "in gross" was recognized in this circuit in Macmahan Pharmacal Co. v. Denver Chem. Mfg. Co., 113 F. 468 (8 Cir.1901) and in Carroll v. Duluth Superior Milling Co., 232 F. 675 (8 Cir.1916). This court in *Carroll* observed that a trademark could only be transferred "in connection with the assignment of the particular business in which it has been used, with its good will, and for continued use upon the same articles or class of articles." Id. at 680. We later explained "that there is no property in a trade-mark except as a right appurtenant to an established business or trade, when it becomes an element of good will." Atlas Beverage Co. v. Minneapolis Brewing Co., 113 F.2d 672, 674–675 (8 Cir.1940). The rule found derivation in Kidd v. Johnson, 100 U.S. 617 (1879). The necessity to assign more than the naked mark was premised upon the primary object of the trade-mark "to indicate by its meaning or association the *origin* of the article to which it is affixed." (Emphasis ours.) 100 U.S. at 620. * * *

Strict adherence to this rule has been vigorously criticized as impractical and legalistic. Schecter, The Rational Bases of Trademark Protection, 40 Harv.L.Rev. 813 (1926); Grismore, The Assignment of Trademarks and Tradenames, 30 Mich.L.Rev. 489 (1932); Callman,

Unfair Competition, Trademarks and Monopolies, § 78 (3d ed. 1969); Note, Trademark Protection Following Ineffective Assignment, 88 Pa.L. Rev. 863 (1940). According to these commentators, the continuum of the rule fails to comprehend the modern image of the trademark to the consuming public. Strict application of the rule undoubtedly fails to recognize the function of the trademark as representing as well (1) a guaranty of the product and (2) the inherent advertising value of the mark itself. Id.

Some recent cases have given recognition that in certain situations a naked assignment might be approved. Grapette emphasizes the case of Hy-Cross Hatchery, Inc. v. Osborne, 303 F.2d 947 (1962), as being controlling.

There the plaintiff sought cancellation of the trademark "Hy-Cross" solely on the basis that the assignee of the original registrant took nothing but the naked mark. The evidence showed that all the assignee received was the mark itself. Osborne, the assignor, did not continue in the same business of raising chickens. The court in discussing the issue of naked assignment stated the following:

> "Unlike the cases relied on, Osborne, so far as the record shows, was using the mark at the time he executed the assignment of it. He had a valid registration which he also assigned. With these two legal properties he also assigned, in the very words of the statute, 'that part of the goodwill of the business connected with the use of and symbolized by the mark * * *.' He was selling chicks which his advertising of record shows were designated as 'No. 111 HY–CROSS (Trade Mark) AMERICAN WHITES.' As part of his assignment, by assigning the goodwill, he gave up the right to sell 'HY–CROSS' chicks. This had been a part of his 'business.' By the assignment Welp, the assignee, acquired that right. The record shows that he began selling 'HY–CROSS Hatching Eggs' and chicks designated as 'HY–CROSS 501,' 'HY–CROSS 610,' and 'HY–CROSS 656.' Thus, what had once been Osborne's business in 'HY–CROSS' chicks became Welp's business. We do not see what legal difference it would have made if a crate of eggs had been included in the assignment, or a flock of chickens destined to be eaten.

> "As for the argument that the transfer should have been held illegal because Osborne sold one kind of chick and Welp sold another another [sic] under the mark, whereby the public would be deceived, we think the record does not support this. The *type* of chick appears to have been otherwise indicated than by the trademark, as by the numbers above quoted as well as by name. Osborne, moreover, was not under any obligation to the public not to change the breed of chicks he sold under the mark from time to time."

In the instant case we need not decide whether the strict common law rule must apply or whether the approach, as suggested by *Hy-Cross,* should prevail. Inherent in the rules involving the assignment of a trademark is the recognition of protection against consumer deception. Basic to this concept is the proposition that any assignment of a trademark and its goodwill (with or without tangibles or intangibles assigned) requires the mark itself be used by the assignee on a product having substantially the same characteristics. See e.g., Independent Baking Powder Co. v. Boorman, 175 F. 448 (C.C.D.N.J.1910) (alum baking powder is distinctive from phosphate baking powder); Atlas Beverage Co. v. Minneapolis Brewing Co., 113 F.2d 672 (8 Cir.1940) (whiskey is a different product than beer); H.H. Scott, Inc. v. Annapolis Electroacoustic Corp., 195 F.Supp. 208 (D.Md.1961) (audio reproduction equipment is distinctive from hi-fidelity consoles). Cf. W.T. Wagner's Sons Co. v. Orange Snap Co., 18 F.2d 554 (5 Cir.1927) (No infringement: gingerale is in a different class than fruit flavored soft drinks).

Historically, this requirement is founded in the early case of Filkins v. Blackman, 9 Fed.Cas. 50 (No. 4786) (C.C.D.Conn.1876), wherein the court observed:

> "If the assignee should make a different article, he would not derive, by purchase from Jonas Blackman, a right which a court of equity would enforce, to use the name which the inventor had given to his own article, because such a use of the name would deceive the public. The right to the use of a trade-mark cannot be so enjoyed by an assignee that he shall have the right to affix the mark to goods differing in character or species from the article to which it was originally attached." Id. at 52.

The philosophy of the rule is sound even though the pragmatic utility of it is sometimes difficult and confusing. Grapette urges that it intends to use the trademark "Peppy" on a product of the same general "classification" as Fox, its assignor. * * *

* * *

The ultimate concern in all cases is the welfare of the public. A case by case treatment of the problem as specific facts present themselves is desirable. * * *

Where a transferred trademark is to be used on a new and different product, any goodwill which the mark itself might represent cannot legally be assigned. "The trademark owner does not have the right to a particular word but to the use of the word as the symbol of particular goods." Callman, § 78.1(a) at 426. To hold otherwise would be to condone public deceit. The consumer might buy a product thinking it to be of one quality or having certain characteristics and could find it only too late to be another. To say that this would be remedied by the public soon losing faith in the product fails to give the consumer the protection it initially deserves.

It is here that Grapette's use of the mark "Peppy" meets terminal difficulty. Grapette's intended use of the mark is one to simply describe its new pepper beverage.[4] The evidence is clear that Grapette did not intend to adopt or exploit any "goodwill" from the name "Peppy" and Fox's long association and use of it *with a cola syrup.* When one considers that Grapette did not require any of the assets of Fox, did not acquire any formula or process by which the Fox syrup was made, cf. Mulhens & Kropff, Inc. v. Ferd Muelhens, Inc., 38 F.2d 287 (D.C.1929), rev'd 43 F.2d 937 (2 Cir.1930), mandate clarified 48 F.2d 206 (2 Cir.1931), and then changed the type of beverage altogether, the assignment on its face must be considered void. It seems fundamental that either the defendant did not acquire any "goodwill" as required by law or if it did, assuming as defendant argues the mark itself possesses "goodwill," by use of the mark on a totally different product, Grapette intended to deceive the public. Either ground is untenable to the validity of the assignment.

We hold that the assignment to Grapette of the trademark "Peppy" is void and that Grapette possesses no standing to raise the equitable defense of laches.

Judgment reversed and remanded for further relief to be determined by the district court.

BLACKMUN, CIRCUIT JUDGE (concurring).

I concur, but on the ground that Hy-Cross Hatchery, Inc. v. Osborne, 303 F.2d 947 (1962), the case relied upon by the district court here, is not, or should not be helpful authority for Grapette. *Hy-Cross* is a peculiar case factually in that, among other aspects, live baby chicks were the product of both assignor and assignee. The court did place some reliance on what it seemed to regard as a genuine transfer of goodwill, 303 F.2d at 950, and, accordingly, saw little legal significance in the absence of an assignment of tangible chicks themselves. See J.C. Hall Co. v. Hallmark Cards, Inc., 340 F.2d 960, 963, (1965), where the same court apparently relates the significance of *Hy-Cross* to the absence of a transfer of tangible assets.

But if, as Grapette urges, the Hy-Cross holding has greater import than its peculiar facts suggest for me, then I would regard it as aberrational to settled authority. I prefer to stay with the usual rule, long established I thought, that a trademark may not validly be assigned in gross. And product difference is only an aspect of this traditional rule. A naked assignment is all that Fox and Grapette attempted and effected. It is not enough.

---

4. Mr. Fooks, Chairman of the Board of Grapette, testified:

"We went into his [Mr. Fox's] office and I told him just frankly my situation, that I had this product ready for the market with no name and I thought his name was a very suitable name, and if it wasn't too valuable I would like to purchase it." Record at 176a–177a.

J. ATKINS HOLDINGS LTD. v. ENGLISH DISCOUNTS, INC.
United States District Court, Southern District of New York, 1990.
729 F.Supp. 945.

LEVAL, J.

[An English manufacturer, B & W–UK, owned the mark "B & W" for loudspeakers. Until 1987, Misobanke was the exclusive distributor of B & W trademarked goods in the United States pursuant to an agreement with B & W–UK. In April, 1987, Equity Investments, a Canadian company, purchased the exclusive distribution rights in the United States. This transaction was effected through an assignment by Misobanke of the distribution agreement with B & W–UK to Equity Investments and an assignment by Misobanke of its U.S. division, B & W–America, to Equity International, a company under common control with Equity Investments. Joseph Atkins, the President of Equity International, formed J. Atkins Holding, Ltd. ("Atkins"), a Massachusetts corporation and which in July, 1987, received an assignment of the United States registered trademark "B & W" from B & W–UK. This assignment agreement which purported to transfer the good-will of the business within the United States also required Atkins to license the mark to B & W–America and further provided that if the distributorship agreement were ever terminated so that B & W–America were no longer the exclusive distributor, ownership of the marks would revert to B & W–UK.

Atkins claims Sixth Avenue imported speakers bearing the B & W mark and sold them in the United States under the mark without authorization. Sixth Avenue contends that the assignment of the mark to Atkins was a transfer in gross because the business symbolized by the mark was in fact conducted by B & W–America.]

Defendant argues first that the assignment of the marks to Atkins pursuant to the Assignment Agreement was an invalid transfer in gross. It is well settled law that the transfer of a trademark or trade name without the attendant good-will of the business which it represents is an invalid "naked" or "in gross" transfer of rights. * * *

The rationale supporting this common-law rule is consumer protection. A trademark identifies the source and quality of the goods and services offered. For a company to purchase the rights to a well-known trademark to use it in a manner which is wholly unrelated to the business or products which made the trademark famous would confuse or deceive the consumer. * * *

Consonant with this purpose, courts have recognized exceptions to the general rule that trademarks cannot be assigned without the good-will of the accompanying business. For example, where there is "continuity of management," so that the assignee will continue to provide the same quality of service, a transfer without good-will is not subject to invalidation. [Marshak v. Green, 746 F.2d 927, 930 (2d Cir.1984)].

The facts in this case do not support the defendant's position. Sixth Avenue's argument seeks to substitute labels for commercial reality. To apply the rule forbidding "naked assignment" of a trademark in these circumstances would ignore the realities of the transaction. It is true that the assignment by B & W–UK to Atkins was technically "naked," if one looks only at that facet of the overall transaction. If, on the other hand, one looks at the overall facts, this is not an assignment that separates the trademark from the goods or services upon which its reputation is based. To the contrary, this was an assignment to a U.S. corporation for business convenience (and perhaps to qualify for a customs exclusion) which is designed to continue the employment of the trademarks in connection with the same goods on which their reputation is based—being the loudspeakers manufactured by B & W–UK.[4] Furthermore, B & W–America, the former distributor under B & W–UK's license to Misobanke, with its personnel essentially unchanged, but now related to Atkins, continues to exercise the license to distribute the trademarked goods.

Thus, the Atkins assignment is not a "naked assignment." It continues the association of the trademark with the very goods which created its reputation.[5] And under the "continuity of management" exception recognized in Marshak, a viable business continues to operate as licensee of the marks. The public continues to receive the same quality of goods and services which have always accompanied the B & W marks. The assignment to Atkins did not sever the relationship between the mark and the good-will which it had developed in the United States.

NOTES

1.   What is the consequence in *Pepsico* of the court's decision invalidating the transfer? Who owns the mark? Can Grapette market a cola beverage under the mark "Peppy" pursuant to the assignment from Fox? Assuming Pepsi did not object to Grapette's use of "Peppy", what rights would Grapette have against a new entrant in the market who wanted to use the mark on a spicy tomato juice? If the assignment was invalid as an assignment in gross, does Fox or its successor still have rights in the mark? Could you argue that an ineffective assignment of a mark is an act of abandonment? If the mark is separated from the good will it represents, has it lost its significance as an indication of origin?

4. * * * As both B & W–UK and Joseph Atkins agreed to register the ownership of the B & W marks in Atkins' name, this court finds no reason why such a decision should be disturbed. Although it is not for the court to inquire into the matter, it appears that the decision not to conduct business actively through Atkins was made to avoid subjecting revenues to United States taxation. Atkins Dep. pp. 71–72.

5. The assignment of trademarks among related corporate entities is not uncommon. * * * Whether the reason is to avoid nationalization, or for tax or trademark purposes, the court does not "believe that an assignment motivated at least in part by sound business judgment should be set aside as a sham transaction." Money Store v. Harriscorp Finance, Inc., 689 F.2d 666, 678 (7th Cir.1982).

2. After *Pepsico* and *Atkins*, what seems to be the crucial factor in validating an assignment, the terms of the assignment or how the assignee uses the mark subsequent to the assignment? Consider the following:

> a. *A* produces a soft drink under the mark SNAPPY for several years. Subsequently *A* sells the mark, the good will, the formula for the soft drink, and the manufacturing plant to *B*. *B* continues the business as before.

> b. *X* produces a soft drink under the mark SNAPPY for several years. Subsequently *X* assigns the mark but not the good will, the formula, or the manufacturing plant. *Y,* however, is able to duplicate the exact formulation of the original SNAPPY soft drink and continues the business as before.

Would the result change in the first situation if *B* changed the formulation of SNAPPY? If you think this would make a difference, what would you do with an original trademark owner who changed the formulation of its trademarked product? Did the change to "New Coke" destroy the validity of the "Coke" mark?

3. A trademark can be a major asset of a firm. Does the assignment in gross rule permit the pledging of a trademark as security for a loan? Is the priority of the mark affected when the debtor agrees to assign the mark to the creditor in the event of a default? After default when the creditor enforces the agreement? If you were a creditor under what conditions would you accept a mark as collateral for a loan?

4. Section 10 of the Lanham Act codifies the prohibition against assignments in gross and also provides a recording system for assignments of registered marks. Applications to register based on an intent to use are not assignable "except to the successor to the business ∗ ∗ ∗ to which the mark pertains if the business is ongoing and existing".

5. An *assignment* of a trademark should be distinguished from the *licensing* of a mark. An assignment transfers all the rights of the owner to the assignee who then becomes the owner of the mark. A license is merely an authorization to the licensee to use the mark. The restrictions on licensing marks are considered in the following case.

DAWN DONUT CO. v. HART'S FOOD STORES, INC.
United States Court of Appeals, Second Circuit, 1959.
267 F.2d 358.

[The facts of this case are reproduced supra page 336]

LUMBARD, CIRCUIT JUDGE.

* * *

The final issue presented is raised by defendant's appeal from the dismissal of its counterclaim for cancellation of plaintiff's registration on the ground that the plaintiff failed to exercise the control required by the Lanham Act over the nature and quality of the goods sold by its licensees.

We are all agreed that the Lanham Act places an affirmative duty upon a licensor of a registered trademark to take reasonable measures to detect and prevent misleading uses of his mark by his licensees or suffer cancellation of his federal registration. The Act, 15 U.S.C.

§ 1064, provides that a trademark registration may be cancelled because the trademark has been "abandoned." And "abandoned" is defined in 15 U.S.C. § 1127 to include any act or omission by the registrant which causes the trademark to lose its significance as an indication of origin.

Prior to the passage of the Lanham Act many courts took the position that the licensing of a trademark separately from the business in connection with which it had been used worked an abandonment. The theory of these cases was that:

> "A trade-mark is intended to identify the goods of the owner and to safeguard his good will. The designation if employed by a person other than the one whose business it serves to identify would be misleading. Consequently, 'a right to the use of a trade-mark or a trade-name cannot be transferred in gross.'" American Broadcasting Co. v. Wahl Co., supra, 121 F.2d at page 413.

Other courts were somewhat more liberal and held that a trademark could be licensed separately from the business in connection with which it had been used provided that the licensor retained control over the quality of the goods produced by the licensee. E.I. DuPont de Nemours & Co. v. Celanese Corporation of America, 1948, 167 F.2d 484; see also 3 A.L.R.2d 1226, 1277–1282 (1949) and cases there cited. But even in the DuPont case the court was careful to point out that naked licensing, viz. the grant of licenses without the retention of control, was invalid.

The Lanham Act clearly carries forward the view of these latter cases that controlled licensing does not work an abandonment of the licensor's registration, while a system of naked licensing does. 15 U.S.C. § 1055 provides:

> "Where a registered mark or a mark sought to be registered is or may be used legitimately by related companies, such use shall inure to the benefit of the registrant or applicant for registration, and such use shall not affect the validity of such mark or of its registration, provided such mark is not used in such manner as to deceive the public."

And 15 U.S.C. § 1127 defines "related company" to mean "any person who legitimately controls or is controlled by the registrant or applicant for registration in respect to the nature and quality of the goods or services in connection with which the mark is used."

Without the requirement of control, the right of a trademark owner to license his mark separately from the business in connection with which it has been used would create the danger that products bearing the same trademark might be of diverse qualities. If the licensor is not compelled to take some reasonable steps to prevent misuses of his trademark in the hands of others the public will be deprived of its most effective protection against misleading uses of a trademark. The public is hardly in a position to uncover deceptive uses of a trademark before they occur and will be at best slow to detect them after they happen. Thus, unless the licensor exercises supervision and control over the operations of its licensees the risk that the public will be unwittingly deceived will be increased and this is precisely what the Act is in part designed to prevent. Clearly the only effective way to protect the public where a trademark is used by licensees is to place on the licensor the affirmative duty of policing in a reasonable manner the activities of his licensees.

The critical question on these facts therefore is whether the plaintiff sufficiently policed and inspected its licensees' operations to guarantee the quality of the products they sold under its trademarks to the public. The trial court found that: "By reason of its contacts with its licensees, plaintiff exercised legitimate control over the nature and quality of the food products on which plaintiff's licensees used the trademark 'Dawn.' Plaintiff and its licensees are related companies within the meaning of Section 45 of the Trademark Act of 1946." It is the position of the majority of this court that the trial judge has the same leeway in determining what constitutes a reasonable degree of supervision and control over licensees under the facts and circumstances of the particular case as he has on other questions of fact; and particularly because it is the defendant who has the burden of proof on this issue they hold the lower court's finding not clearly erroneous.

I dissent from the conclusion of the majority that the district court's findings are not clearly erroneous because while it is true that the trial judge must be given some discretion in determining what constitutes reasonable supervision of licensees under the Lanham Act, it is also true that an appellate court ought not to accept the conclusions of the district court unless they are supported by findings of sufficient facts. It seems to me that the only findings of the district judge regarding supervision are in such general and conclusory terms as to be meaningless. In the absence of supporting findings or of undisputed evidence in the record indicating the kind of supervision and inspection the plaintiff actually made of its licensees, it is impossible for us to pass upon whether there was such supervision as to satisfy the statute. There was evidence before the district court in the matter of supervision, and more detailed findings thereon should have been made.

Plaintiff's licensees fall into two classes: (1) those bakers with whom it made written contracts providing that the baker purchase exclusively plaintiff's mixes and requiring him to adhere to plaintiff's directions in using the mixes; and (2) those bakers whom plaintiff permitted to sell at retail under the "Dawn" label doughnuts and other baked goods made from its mixes although there was no written agreement governing the quality of the food sold under the Dawn mark.

The contracts that plaintiff did conclude, although they provided that the purchaser use the mix as directed and without adulteration, failed to provide for any system of inspection and control. Without such a system plaintiff could not know whether these bakers were adhering to its standards in using the mix or indeed whether they were selling only products made from Dawn mixes under the trademark "Dawn."

The absence, however, of an express contract right to inspect and supervise a licensee's operations does not mean that the plaintiff's method of licensing failed to comply with the requirements of the Lanham Act. Plaintiff may in fact have exercised control in spite of the absence of any express grant by licensees of the right to inspect and supervise.

The question then, with respect to both plaintiff's contract and non-contract licensees, is whether the plaintiff in fact exercised sufficient control.

Here the only evidence in the record relating to the actual supervision of licensees by plaintiff consists of the testimony of two of plaintiff's local sales representatives that they regularly visited their particular customers and the further testimony of one of them, Jesse Cohn, the plaintiff's New York representative, that "in many cases" he did have an opportunity to inspect and observe the operations of his customers. The record does not indicate whether plaintiff's other sales representatives made any similar efforts to observe the operations of licensees.

Moreover, Cohn's testimony fails to make clear the nature of the inspection he made or how often he made one. His testimony indicates that his opportunity to observe a licensee's operations was limited to "those cases where I am able to get into the shop" and even casts some doubt on whether he actually had sufficient technical knowledge in the use of plaintiff's mix to make an adequate inspection of a licensee's operations.

* * *

Thus I do not believe that we can fairly determine on this record whether plaintiff subjected its licensees to periodic and thorough inspections by trained personnel or whether its policing consisted only of chance, cursory examinations of licensees' operations by technically untrained salesmen. The latter system of inspection hardly constitutes a sufficient program of supervision to satisfy the requirements of the Act.

* * *

NOTES

1. Prior to 1984 the United States Jaycees (USJ) prohibited women members and required their local "licensees" to do likewise. When some local chapters rebelled USJ sought to enjoin chapters admitting women from continuing to use the trademark "Jaycee". USJ argued it was exercising its responsibility to police the licensed mark. In United States Jaycees v. Philadelphia Jaycees, 639 F.2d 134 (3d Cir.1981) the court ruled in favor of USJ even after the Philadelphia chapter argued USJ had abandoned the mark because it did not enforce the provision against all licensees. "We conclude that, although

the United States Jaycees did display a degree of tolerance toward some of its disobedient chapters in the use of its marks, such conduct did not constitute non-use and did not demonstrate an intent to abandon, nor did it cause its marks to lose their significance." However, in United States Jaycees v. Cedar Rapids Jaycees, 794 F.2d 379 (8th Cir.1986), USJ sought to enjoin a local chapter for its past admission of women even after USJ had subsequently changed its own policy in that regard. The court refused the injunction under the "principles of equity".

2. The ability to license trademarks opened the way to the expansion of franchising as a method of product and service distribution. At the heart of a franchise agreement is the license of the trademark and method of doing business. It should be clear from the cases that trademark law, as well as the economic interest of the franchisor, dictates that there be substantial and effective policing of the franchisee to maintain quality control. However, pushing from the other direction are the anti-trust laws that may place some restraint on the licensor's method of exercising quality controls. The initial case was Siegel v. Chicken Delight, Inc., 448 F.2d 43 (9th Cir.1971) where the franchise contract required that franchisees purchase essential cooking equipment, dry-mix food items, and packages bearing the Chicken Delight trademark from the franchisor. The court held this provision to be a "tying arrangement" prohibited by the anti-trust laws. A "tying arrangement" is one in which purchasers in order to purchase one product (the tying product) must agree to purchase another product as well (the tied product). It is a violation if it is shown that the tying product has sufficient economic power to restrain trade in the tied product market. In *Siegel,* the court held the Chicken Delight trademark was the tying product and the equipment and ingredients were the tied product. Given the economic power of a trademark, an antitrust violation was found, even in the face of Chicken Delight's argument that the restraint was justified in order to police the trademark. The court held that the licensor could establish standards for equipment and ingredients rather than requiring they be purchased exclusively from the licensor.

Compare with *Siegel,* Kentucky Fried Chicken Corp. v. Diversified Packaging Corp., 549 F.2d 368 (5th Cir.1977) in which Kentucky Fried Chicken, the franchisor, included in its franchise agreement a clause requiring franchisees to purchase supplies from a franchisor approved source. Defendant placed Kentucky Fried's trademarks on boxes and other supplies and sold them to franchisees although the defendant was not one of the six approved sources. One of the approved sources was a subsidiary of the franchisor; the other five suppliers were independent. Kentucky Fried sued defendant for infringement; the defendant counterclaimed, asserting the clause in the agreement was an illegal tying arrangement. The court characterized the assertion as the "facially implausible—some might say unappetizing-contention that the man whose chicken is 'finger-lickin' good' has unclean hands." The court held the approved list policy was acceptable as long as there was no coercion on franchisees to purchase from the franchisor's subsidiary. The court also expressed a reluctance to follow *Siegel:*

> As an original matter it is less than self-evident that such arrangements [franchises] should be treated as garden-variety tie-ins, to be analyzed in accordance with the same tying principles developed in other contexts. Unlike that of the tying party in a prototypal tying case, a franchisor's own success may depend in large measure on the success of the tie's "victim," the franchisee. The franchisor will

succeed only by establishing a favorable reputation among the consuming public, and in building that reputation the franchisor must depend largely on the quality of the franchisee's performance. A franchisor will rarely have an opportunity to explain to a dissatisfied customer that the fault was only that of the particular franchisee. The franchisor may therefore have legitimate as well as illegitimate reasons for restraining the franchisee's choices in the tied product market. The tie may have a benevolent or malevolent loop. Although in the archetypal case "[t]ying arrangements serve hardly any purpose beyond the suppression of competition," Standard Oil Co. v. United States, 337 U.S. 293 (1949), in the franchising context ties may well serve acceptable purposes. Id. at 375–376.

Some courts have refused to apply to trademark tie-ins the presumption, derived from the copyright and patent cases, that sufficient economic power exists to show an antitrust violation. Capital Temporaries, Inc. v. Olsten Corp., 506 F.2d 658 (2d Cir.1974).

More recently a few courts have drawn a distinction between marks which represent the source of a product and trademarks that warrant a method of doing business. The Chicken Delight mark is in the latter category. In Hamro v. Shell Oil Co., 674 F.2d 784 (9th Cir.1982) the court refused to declare as an illegal tying arrangement a contract provision which required as a condition of licensing the Shell trademark that only Shell gasoline be sold under the mark. "[T]he nexus between the trademark and the tied product, Shell gasoline, is sufficiently close to warrant treating them as one product." Id. at 788. See also Krehl v. Baskin-Robbins Ice Cream Co., 664 F.2d 1348, 1352–53 (9th Cir. 1982), (discussing and limiting the *Chicken Delight* precedent) and Jack Walters & Sons Corp. v. Morton Building, Inc., 737 F.2d 698 (7th Cir.1984) (no illegal tie-in to require use of Morton trademark on Morton prefabricated buildings).

3. Does the consumer expect that a university that licenses the use of a likeness of its mascot can maintain effective control over the quality of the products marketed with the likeness. Does a university have the expertise to so control the quality of the underlying products? Consider here the emblem cases considered earlier in this Chapter. Does the manufacturer of the soft drink "Coca–Cola" maintain quality control over "Coca–Cola" wearing apparel? It has been suggested that for these "merchandising marks" the quality control standards for valid licensing should be relaxed. See W. Borchard & R. Osman, Trademark Sublicensing and Quality Control, 70 Trademark Rep. 99 (1980); W. Keating, Promotional Trademark Licensing: A Concept Whose Time Has Come, 89 Dick.L.Rev. 363 (1985). The United States Trademark Association Trademark Review Commission decided "the public interest in avoiding deception in the licensing context was a very sensitive issue and that statutory relaxation of the quality control requirements was not appropriate." 77 Trademark Rep. at 448.

4. The limitations on patent, copyright and trademark licensing occupies no small place in antitrust law. The complexities will not be assayed here. In summary, the following types of arrangements should be reviewed with the antitrust laws in mind. (1) Any provision which "ties" the right to use the protected rights to a requirement that something unprotected be used. (2) Any provision which measures payments due the licensor on the basis of actions which do not infringe. (3) Any provision which controls the output, resale, price, or operating policies of the licensee or his customers. (4) Any arrangement which brings formerly competitive rights under common control. (5)

Licenses which are offered only on a "block" basis—that is the licensee must take all or none of a group of separate rights. (6) Any provision which protects the licensee from additional competition. (7) Any provision which protects the licensor from competition by the licensee.

Chapter IV

PREDATORY PRACTICES

A. INTERFERENCE WITH BUSINESS RELATIONS

(1) REFUSALS TO DEAL

In a competitive marketplace, actors are expected to make buying and selling decisions in their own best interest. This means that they must decide to deal with some and refuse to deal with other actors. Competition also assumes that a trader will urge persons to deal with him and thereby induce them not to deal with other persons. As we have observed before, competition assumes some intentional attempts to injure others, at least by depriving them of sales.

At the same time, the power to withhold patronage may be used for purposes or objectives that are not permissible even in a competitive market. As *Tuttle v. Buck* makes clear, there can be actions taken that look competitive but actually take on an anticompetitive cast. It should not be surprising that the common law had a difficult time working out the rules that segregated permissible from impermissible refusals to deal.

Initially the common law divided refusals to deal into mere individual refusals to deal, concerted refusals to deal, and inducing another to refuse to deal. These categories are carried forward in the antitrust laws because of the structure of the Sherman Act which in section 1 prohibits a "contract, combination, * * * or conspiracy" in restraint of trade. Section 1 contemplates concerted activity between two or more traders. Section 2, which deals with individual activity, prohibits monopolization or attempted monopolization and thus requires a substantial market affect.

Both at common law and under the antitrust laws, individual refusals to deal were protected in most instances but concerted refusals to deal (group boycotts) were more closely scrutinized. Inducing another to refuse to deal (secondary boycotts) evoked a more complex set of regulations.

The common law doctrines were reflected in Restatement of Torts §§ 762–774 (1939). Section 762 permitted most individual refusals to deal as long as they are "not a breach of the actor's duty arising from the nature of his business or from a statute" or "not a means of illegally affecting competition." Section 765 prohibited concerted re-

416

fusals to deal unless justified. Comment d to § 765 included the following: "When the purpose of a concerted refusal to deal is solely to satisfy spite or ill will, the refusal is not justified. But self-interest, particularly a purpose to advance the business interest of the actors, may be a justification even though the harm caused by the refusal is intended to be the means of advancing that interest." Sections 766–771 dealt with inducing a refusal to deal which served as forerunners to those provisions in the Restatement (Second) applicable to intentional interference with prospective advantage. These doctrines are considered later in this chapter.

Most refusal to deal cases in the marketplace are now governed by the Sherman Act. In an early opinion, Great Atlantic & Pacific Tea Co. v. Cream of Wheat Co., 227 Fed. 46 (2d Cir.1915), the court held that the Sherman Act did not alter the common law "right" of a trader to refuse business relations with any person. Four years later in United States v. Colgate & Co., 250 U.S. 300 (1919), Colgate announced suggested retail prices and refused to sell to any wholesaler or retailer who cut the price. The United States Supreme Court emphasized the unilateral nature of the refusal to deal and held the Sherman Act "does not restrict the long recognized right of trader or manufacturer engaged in an entirely private business, freely to exercise his own independent discretion as to parties with whom he will deal. And, of course, he may announce in advance the circumstances under which he will refuse to sell * * *."

Given the structure of the Sherman Act, the search in antitrust cases is for a "contract" or "conspiracy" in refusal to deal cases. *Colgate* continues to be cited as applicable to *individual* refusals to deal. The threshold of concerted action is reflected in United States v. Parke, Davis & Co., 362 U.S. 29 (1960) where Parke, Davis announced suggested minimum retail prices and a policy of refusing to deal with wholesalers and retailers who did not abide by the price structure. However, Parke, Davis also engaged in extensive activities to police and to persuade wholesalers to refuse to deal with price cutting retailers and this, the Court thought, went too far.

NOTES

1. Two cases illustrate how sacred the right to refuse to deal has been viewed. In House of Materials, Inc. v. Simplicity Pattern Co., 298 F.2d 867 (2d Cir.1962), Simplicity Pattern terminated its business relations with plaintiffs solely out of "its desire to retaliate for the treble damage action brought against it by plaintiffs." The court found the refusal to deal justified. See also, Dart Drug Corp. v. Parke, Davis & Co., 221 F.Supp. 948 (D.D.C.1963), affirmed 344 F.2d 173 (D.C.Cir.1965) where Parke, Davis refused to deal with a retailer who had testified against Parke, Davis in an antitrust case. Judge Holtzoff, in the district court, held that the common law allowed an individual refusal to deal and the Court of Appeals affirmed, Judge Wright concurring with the statement that although the refusal to deal may not be a violation of the Sherman

Act, it was a "most reprehensible act" and is subject to prosecution under criminal statutes for obstruction of justice.

2. The common law disdain for prohibiting individual refusals to deal encouraged specific legislation to solve some specific problems. The termination of dealer franchise agreements in the automobile industry sparked passage of the Automobile Dealer Franchise Act, 15 U.S.C. §§ 1221–22, otherwise known as the Dealer's Day in Court Act. The act provides federal jurisdiction for a suit by a dealer against an automobile manufacturer for damages sustained "by reason of the failure of said automobile manufacturer * * * to act in good faith in performing or complying with any of the terms or provisions of the franchise, or in terminating, cancelling, or not renewing the franchise with said dealer." "Good faith" means the duty to act in "a fair and equitable manner * * * so as to guarantee the one party freedom from coercion, intimidation, or threats of coercion or intimidation from the other party: *Provided,* That recommendation, endorsement, exposition, persuasion, urging or argument shall not be deemed to constitute a lack of good faith." The automobile manufacturers have not fared badly under the act. See Comment, The Judicial Treatment of the Automobile Dealer Franchise Act, 62 Mich.L.Rev. 310 (1963). See Mt. Lebanon Motors, Inc. v. Chrysler Corp., 283 F.Supp. 453 (W.D.Pa.1968) (jury question whether "Chrysler's action was motivated by honest business judgment or by personal animosity * * *."); Woodard v. General Motors Corp., 298 F.2d 121 (5th Cir.1962) (requiring showing that manufacturer acted unfairly, unequitably, *and* coercively.). On the other hand, see Autowest, Inc. v. Peugeot, Inc., 434 F.2d 556 (2d Cir.1970) where the plaintiff stated a cause of action under the act by alleging coercion and subsequent termination for failure to adhere to a manufacturer's suggested resale price.

See generally, Brown & Conwill, Automobile Manufacturer-Dealer Legislation, 57 Colum.L.Rev. 219 (1957); Kessler, Automobile Dealer Franchises: Vertical Integration by Contract, 66 Yale L.J. 1135, 1173 (1957).

In several states the principle underlying the Automobile Dealer Franchise Act has been adopted for all franchise agreements. See, e.g., Conn.Gen.Stat. Ann. § 42–133 e–g (Supp.1975). And there are many other areas in which a person's common law right to refuse to engage in business with another person for any reason has been abrogated. See, e.g., Civil Rights Act of 1964, 42 U.S.C. § 2000a (1974) (preventing discrimination on the basis of race in public accommodations).

(2) UNFAIR COMPETITION

KATZ v. KAPPER

7 Cal.App.2d 1, 44 P.2d 1060 (1935).

SHINN, JUSTICE PRO TEM.

* * *

Plaintiff and defendants were rival wholesale fish dealers in the city of Los Angeles. The defendants Kapper, Isenberg, Baker, and Simon comprised a single firm doing business under the name of "Central Market." The action is for damages alleged to have been sustained to plaintiff's business by reason of the acts of defendants, and for exemplary damages. The complaint alleges that plaintiff had a well-established wholesale fish business, the good will of which was valuable; that with the sole intention "to put the plaintiff out of business, ruin him, deprive him of his customers and custom, and to take away from him all of his business and trade, together with the good will, without any benefit to themselves," the defendants maliciously called meetings of the customers of plaintiff, threatened them that they would be driven out of business and ruined if they continued to purchase fish from plaintiff, but promised that if they purchased fish from defendants, they would be given substantial reductions in price, so that they could successfully compete with plaintiff and drive him out of business; that if said customers continued to buy from plaintiff, the defendants would open a retail store and would sell fish to the customers of plaintiff's customers at such low prices that plaintiff's customers would be driven out of business. It was further alleged that the defendants did open such a store, did widely advertise and sell fish at lower prices than either plaintiff or defendants could purchase the same, and at a loss to the defendants; that all of said acts were done for the purpose of driving plaintiff out of business; and that as a result thereof "a considerable number of said retailers and peddlers and customers ceased from doing business with plaintiff and made their purchases from these defendants to plaintiff's damage," etc.

To this complaint, defendants interposed a general and special demurrer, which was sustained by the court, and plaintiff declining to amend, judgment of dismissal was entered. The general demurrer presents the questions whether the purposes of the defendants were unlawful, and, if lawful, whether they were sought to be accomplished by unlawful means.

* * *

It very clearly appears from the allegations of the complaint that the primary purpose of the defendants was to acquire for themselves the business of plaintiff's customers, and that the detriment which would result to plaintiff's business from the accomplishment of defendants' purpose was incidental thereto. This view must be taken of the complaint, notwithstanding the allegation that the sole purpose was to drive plaintiff out of business. The defendants are not charged with making any effort to deprive plaintiff of his trade except by transferring the same to themselves. This is essentially business competition. The defendants did or threatened to do nothing other than to gain a business advantage proportionate to the losses sustained by plaintiff, and by the accomplishment of that end their purposes would have been satisfied. It cannot be said that the methods used by the defendants were unlawful. They threatened plaintiff's customers with the ruination of their businesses if they continued to trade with plaintiff, but a threat is not unlawful if it is to do a lawful thing.

* * *

The threats alleged in general terms are identified and particularized by the allegations that the defendants threatened to and did undersell the plaintiff and his customers at retail prices less than the wholesale prices at which the commodities could be purchased. These must be taken as the only acts of coercion either threatened or done, since no others are alleged. They were not unlawful nor were they committed in an unlawful manner. They related solely to the aims of the defendants to engage in business competition with plaintiff for the resulting business advantage to themselves. The fact that the methods used were ruthless, or unfair, in a moral sense, does not stamp them as illegal. It has never been regarded as the duty or province of the courts to regulate practices in the business world beyond the point of applying legal or equitable remedies in cases involving acts of oppression or deceit which are unlawful. Any extension of this jurisdiction must come through legislative action. In this case no questions of statutory law are involved. The alleged acts of defendants do not fall within the category of business methods recognized as unlawful, and hence they are not actionable. The demurrer to the complaint was properly sustained.

The judgment is affirmed.

NOTES

1. What restrictions, if any, would you place on the defendant in *Katz*? Would you be prepared to watch him drive the plaintiff out of business? Could you frame a rule that distinguishes a legitimate competitive price from a pricing policy that is sufficiently predatory to require legal intervention?

2. Is it unfair competition for a business to bribe the officers of a customer in order to retain or secure their patronage? If the customer is a foreign country and such bribes are, if not legal, at least commonplace? See Coffee, Beyond the Shut-Eyed Sentry: Toward a Theoretical View of Corporate Misconduct and an Effective Legal Response, 63 Va.L.Rev. 1099 (1977).

3. *Sales Below Costs.* The desire to counteract loss leader selling, protect small independent merchants from the competition of large chain stores, and eliminate some of the agonies of intensely competitive markets led to promulgation of statutes directly prohibiting sales below cost or unreasonably low prices. These statutes, both on the state and federal levels, provided criminal penalties as well as injunctive relief. Some state statutes also authorize treble damage recoveries. Although the first state statute was passed early in the 1900's, the major push for legislation on the state level arose in the late 1930's. And Congress responded at the federal level with the passage of the Robinson-Patman Act in 1936. Section 3 of the Act reads in part as follows:

> It shall be lawful for any person engaged in commerce, in the course of such commerce * * * to sell, or contract to sell, goods at unreasonably low prices for the purpose of destroying competition or eliminating a competitor. Any person violating any of the provisions of this section shall, upon conviction thereof, be fined not more than $5,000 or imprisoned not more than one year, or both. 49 Stat. 1528, 15 U.S.C. § 13a.

At one time or another over thirty states enacted laws of general application prohibiting sales below cost and other states have passed such statutes for specific industries. The tobacco and dairy industries have been particularly subjected to such regulations. For a brief history of this type of legislation see 2 Marketing Laws Survey, Price Control Legislation XLVIII (1940).

There is little uniformity in language among the state sales below cost legislation. Most contain (1) a prohibition against sales below cost where made with the intent to injure competitors or destroy competition; (2) a definition of cost; (3) exemptions for certain types of sales such as perishable commodities or sales to governmental agencies; (4) an exemption if the sale is made in good faith to meet the price of a competitor, and (5) provisions for both criminal penalties and injunctive relief.

The heart of such provisions is the definition of "cost". Consider the California and Pennsylvania definitions produced in part below:

CALIFORNIA UNFAIR PRACTICES ACT
Cal.Bus. & Prof.Code § 17026 (1964).

"Cost" as applied to production includes the cost of raw materials, labor and all overhead expenses of the producer.

"Cost" as applied to distribution means the invoice or replacement cost, whichever is lower, of the article or product to the distributor and vendor, plus the cost of doing business by the distributor and vendor and in the absence of proof of cost of doing business a markup of 6 percent on such invoice or replacement cost shall be prima facie proof of such cost of doing business.

Discounts granted for cash payments shall not be used to reduce cost.

PENNSYLVANIA UNFAIR SALES ACT
Pa.Stat.Ann. Tit. 73 § 212 (1960).

(1) When used in this act the term "cost to the retailer" shall mean the invoice cost of the merchandise to the retailer or the replacement cost of the merchandise to the retailer, whichever is lower, less all trade discounts, except customary discounts for cash, advertising allowances, promotional allowances, display allowances and any other allowances for services rendered and any other commission or remuneration received for services performed on behalf of any governmental agencies, to which shall be added (a) freight charges not otherwise included in the invoice or the replacement cost of the merchandise, (b) a mark-up to cover in part the cost of doing business, which mark-up in the absence of proof of a lesser cost, shall be not less than four per cent of the total cost at retail outlet.

(2) When used in this act the term "cost to the wholesaler" shall mean the invoice cost of the merchandise to the wholesaler or the replacement cost of the merchandise to the wholesaler, whichever is lower, less all trade discounts, except customary discounts for cash, advertising allowances, promotional allowances, display allowances and any other allowances for services rendered and any other commission or remuneration received for services performed on behalf of any governmental agencies, to which shall be added (a) freight charges not otherwise included in the invoice or the replacement cost of the merchandise and (b) a mark-up to cover in part the cost of doing business, which mark-up in the absence of proof of a lesser cost shall be

not less than two per cent of the total cost at the wholesale establishment.

(3) Where two or more items are advertised, offered for sale or sold at a combined price, the price of each item named shall be governed by the provisions of subsection (1) or (2) of section two respectively.

There has been substantial litigation challenging the constitutionality of prohibitions against sales below cost. Because criminal penalties are imposed, many of the constitutional attacks center on the concept of vagueness. A number of cases have upheld the statutory definitions of cost against such attacks by taking a broad view of how "cost" is to be determined. See State v. Langley, 53 Wyo. 332, 84 P.2d 767 (1938): "we must presume that the legislature did not intend to prescribe that the cost must be absolutely exact, and that it must be based upon the precise method of accounting which any one merchant might adopt, but mean, by "cost", what business men generally mean, namely, the approximate cost arrived at by a reasonable rule. * * * In other words, all that a man is required to do under the statute is to act in good faith * * *."

In United States v. National Dairy Prod. Corp., 372 U.S. 29 (1963), the United States Supreme Court upheld the constitutionality of section 3 of the Robinson-Patman Act. The issue as phrased by the Court was whether "making it a crime to sell goods at 'unreasonably low prices for the purpose of destroying competition or eliminating a competitor', is unconstitutionally vague and indefinite as applied to sales made *below cost* with such purpose":

> In proscribing sales at "unreasonably low prices for the purpose of destroying competition or eliminating a competitor" we believe that Congress condemned sales made below cost for such purpose. And we believe that National Dairy and Wise could reasonably understand from the statutory language that the conduct described in the indictment was proscribed by the Act. They say, however, that this is but the same horse with a different bridle because the phrase "below cost" is itself a vague and indefinite expression in business.

> Whether "below cost" refers to "direct" or "fully distributed" cost or some other level of cost computation cannot be decided in the abstract. There is nothing in the record on this point, and it may well be that the issue will be rendered academic by a showing that National Dairy sold below any of these cost levels. Therefore, we do not reach this issue here. * * *

> Finally, we think the additional element of predatory intent alleged in the indictment and required by the Act provides further definition of the prohibited conduct. * * * The Act here, however, in prohibiting sales at unreasonably low prices for the purpose of destroying competition, listed as elements of the illegal conduct not only the intent to achieve a *result*—destruction of competition but also the *act*—selling at unreasonably low prices—done in furtherance of that design or purpose. It seems clear that the necessary specificity of warning is afforded when, as here, separate, though related, statutory elements of prohibited activity come to focus on one course of conduct.

> * * *

> This opinion is not to be construed, however, as holding that every sale below cost constitutes a violation of § 3. Such sales are not condemned when made in furtherance of a legitimate commercial

objective, such as the liquidation of excess, obsolete or perishable merchandise, or the need to meet a lawful, equally low price of a competitor. 80 Cong.Rec. 6332, 6334; see Ben Hur Coal Co. v. Wells, 242 F.2d 481 (C.A.10th Cir., 1957). Sales below cost in these instances would neither be "unreasonably low" nor made with predatory intent. But sales made below cost without legitimate commercial objective and with specific intent to destroy competition would clearly fall within the prohibitions of § 3.

* * *

4. *Intent to Injure or Destroy Competition.* Early litigation made it clear that at least where criminal penalties were involved statutes prohibiting sales below cost would be unconstitutional unless they required some form of predatory intent. See e.g., Fairmont Creamery Co. v. State, 274 U.S. 1 (1927); State v. Fleming Co., 184 Kan. 674, 339 P.2d 12 (1959).

5. Sales below cost are part of what is recognized as "predatory pricing", a pricing strategy that lowers prices in an area to drive out competition with the expectation that losses sustained can be made up by higher prices once a monopoly position is established. The success of such a strategy depends on not only the ability to obtain some market power but also to sustain it long enough to recoup past losses with interest and to secure higher profits than would have resulted in the absence of the strategy. Some commentators are skeptical that such a strategy can be successful or is often attempted. R. Bork, The Antitrust Paradox 145 (1978); Easterbrook, Predatory Strategies and Counterstrategies, 48 U.Chi.L.Rev. 263 (1981). The Supreme Court apparently adopted this view in Matsushita Elec. Indus. Co. v. Zenith Radio, 475 U.S. 574 (1986). See also Areeda & Turner, Predatory Pricing and Related Practices Under Section 2 of the Sherman Act, 88 Harv.L.Rev. 697 (1975).

6. *Fair trade laws.* For many years several states authorized resale price maintenance agreements. These "fair trade" laws provided that a producer of branded goods could announce and enforce through a civil action a pricing policy which prevented any retailer from selling branded goods at a price less than that established by the producer. Those in favor of fair trade laws argued that the use by large chain stores of famous brand name merchandise as loss leaders was an appropriation of the goodwill attached to those brands for the benefit of the chainstore and, further, that the producers of branded merchandise suffered injury because small retailers would stop carrying merchandise used as loss leaders by larger stores. Opponents of "fair trade" laws argued that price manipulation by producers prevented price competition and injured consumers. Initially price maintenance agreements were in violation of the Sherman Act if they involved interstate commerce; in 1937, the Miller-Tydings amendment was adopted exempting such agreements from antitrust scrutiny if the agreement was authorized by state statute and the exemption was refined and broadened in 1952 by the McGuire Amendment to section 5 of the Federal Trade Commission Act. The validity of resale price maintenance agreements thus depended on state law. At one time or another, 45 states enacted fair trade legislation. However, in 1975 Congress repealed both Miller-Tydings and McGuire amendments and ended fair trade pricing. Consumer Goods Pricing Act of 1975, Pub.L. 94–145, 89 Stat. 801 (1975).

For discussions of fair trade generally see Bork, The Rule of Reason: Ancillary Restraints and the Per Se Rule, 75 Yale L.J. 373, 429 (1966). Bowman, The Prerequisites and Effects of Resale Price Maintenance, 22 U.Chi. L.Rev. 825 (1955); Note, The Operation of Fair Trade Programs, 69 Harv.L.Rev.

316 (1955); Comment, Enforcement of Resale Price Maintenance, 69 Yale L.J. 168 (1959). For a lively but inconclusive debate between two economists see Adams, Resale Price Maintenance; Fact and Fancy, 64 Yale L.J. 967 (1955) refuted by Herman, A Note on Fair Trade, 65 Yale L.J. 23 (1955) with a rebuttal, Adams, Fair Trade and the Art of Prestidigitation, 65 Yale L.J. 196 (1955).

7. Provisions directed at unreasonably low prices are designed to protect competitors' short-run interests and consumers' long run interests. A consumer may have a more immediate interest in the regulation of prices that are alleged to be unreasonably high. The major legal yardstick available to measure whether a price is too high is the contractual doctrine of unconscionability. See Uniform Commercial Code § 2–302. A few cases have applied unconscionability directly to the price term. American Home Improvement Co. v. MacIver, 105 N.H. 435, 201 A.2d 886 (1964). See also, Note, Unconscionable Sales Prices, 20 Me.L.Rev. 159 (1968).

THE ROBINSON–PATMAN ACT

Regulation of differences in price is dominated by the federal Robinson-Patman Act, 15 U.S.C. § 13, enacted in 1936 to strengthen the anti-discrimination provisions of § 2 of the Clayton Act, enacted in 1914. More than half the states have statutes prohibiting discrimination in price between different sections, communities, or purchasers. But almost all require that an illegal discrimination, to paraphrase the Massachusetts statute, be malicious or for the purpose of destroying the business of a competitor and of creating a monopoly. Mass.Laws ch. 93 § 8. The Robinson-Patman Act requires no such intent.

When the Robinson-Patman Act was enacted it was aimed at the retail grocery store chains whose "abusive," "coercive," and "secretive" tactics were thought to enable them to extract special concessions from their suppliers and thus give them an unfair advantage over the independent and presumably more upright wholesale and retail grocers that they were steadily displacing. The statute was a "bill of equal rights" for the independents, designed to preserve them from the chains. Although the abuse was specific, the statute was not; it applies to all sales of commodities in interstate commerce.

The heart of the statute is § 2(a). It is violated if there is (1) a difference in price between different purchasers of (2) commodities of (3) like grade and quality where (4) either of the purchases involved is in interstate commerce and (5) where the effect of such discrimination may be to substantially lessen competition.

There are two important defenses to a violation of § 2(a). (1) That the differences in price were justified by differences in cost. (2) That the favorable price was given in good faith to meet an equally low price of a competitor.

There are five different enforcement mechanisms. (1) A Federal Trade Commission or other administrative agency proceeding. Clayton Act § 11, 15 U.S.C. § 21. If the Commission finds that the statute has been violated it can enter a cease and desist order. Each violation of the order is subject to a civil penalty of $5,000.00 and each day of a continuing violation is defined as a separate violation. Clayton Act § 11(*l*), 15 U.S.C. § 21(*l*). (2) A private civil action for treble damages, as in the case of other antitrust law violations. Clayton Act § 4, 15 U.S.C. § 15. (3) A civil action by the Department of Justice for an injunction against further violations. Clayton Act § 15, 15 U.S.C. § 25 (seldom used). (4) A private civil action for an injunction. Clayton Act § 16, 15 U.S.C. § 26. (5) A criminal prosecution of a knowing discrimination for the purpose of destroying competition with a maximum fine of $5,000.00 and a prison term of not more than one year. Clayton Act § 3, 15 U.S.C. § 13a.

1. *A Difference in Price.* The statute prohibits a "discrimination" in price, but the Supreme Court has made it clear that this is the same as a difference in price. "[A] price discrimination within the meaning of that provision [§ 2(a)] is merely a price difference." Federal Trade Commission v. Anheuser-Busch, Inc., 363 U.S. 536, 549 (1960). See also Federal Trade Commission v. Morton Salt Co., 334 U.S. 37 (1948) holding that quantity discounts offered to all but on quantities too large for many purchasers to buy constituted price discrimination under the statute.

2. *Commodities.* The act does not apply to the sale of services.

3. *Like Grade and Quality.* If the difference in price is between goods that are not of "like grade and quality," the act has no application even if the difference in price between the two commodities is unrelated to cost differences. In FTC v. Borden Co., 383 U.S. 637 (1966) the Court held that "like grade and quality" referred to physical and chemical identity and not to consumer preference. Thus milk sold under the Borden brand and the same milk sold under private labels were of like grade and quality for purposes of evaluating a discrimination in price. However, on remand, the Fifth Circuit upheld Borden's policy because of an absence of injury to competition:

> We are of the firm view that where a price differential between a premium and nonpremium brand reflects no more than a consumer preference for the premium brand, the price difference creates no competitive advantage to the recipient of the cheaper private brand product on which injury could be predicated. "[R]ather it represents merely a rough equivalent of the benefit by way of the seller's national advertising and promotion which the purchaser of the more expensive branded product enjoys." The record discloses no evidence tending to show that Borden's price differential exceeds the recognized consumer appeal of the Borden label. Nor has it been suggested that the prices are unreasonably high for Borden brand milk on the one hand, or unrealistically low for the private label milk on the other.

The Borden Co. v. FTC, 381 F.2d 175 (5th Cir.1967). See generally, Note, The Role of Consumer Preference in the "Like Grade and Quality" Concept of the Robinson-Patman Act, 23 Buff.L.Rev. 709 (1974).

4. *A Purchase in Interstate Commerce.* One of the two or more purchases involved must have been made across a state line. It does not matter whether the high or low priced sale is the one in commerce. Moore v. Mead's Fine Bread Co., 348 U.S. 115 (1954); Gulf Oil Corp. v. Copp Paving Co., 419 U.S. 186 (1974) (Robinson-Patman Act applies only to activities "in commerce" and cannot be extended to intrastate sales that "affect" commerce.)

5. *Injury to Competition.* Injury to competition is of two types. The first, and as a practical matter the only important type is down stream injury, injury to the competition between the purchasers of the discriminating seller (called secondary-line injury) or injury to the competition between one purchaser and the customers of another purchaser, or between the customers of both (called third-line injury). Second, is horizontal injury, that is injury to the competition between the discriminating seller and his competitors (called primary-line injury).

Secondary-line injury exists if there is a price difference between two purchasers who compete in the resale of the commodity. The leading case is Federal Trade Commission v. Morton Salt Co., 334 U.S. 37 (1948). The Court said:

> * * * the Commission is authorized by the Act to bar discriminatory prices upon the "reasonable possibility" that different prices for like goods to competing purchasers may have the defined effect on competition. That respondent's quantity discounts did result in price differentials between competing purchasers sufficient in amount to influence their resale prices of salt was shown by evidence. This showing in itself is adequate to support the Commission's appropriate findings that the effect of such price discriminations "may be substantially to lessen competition * * * and to injure, destroy, and prevent competition."
>
> * * * It is suggested that in considering the adequacy of the evidence to show injury to competition respondent's carload discounts and its other quantity discounts should not be treated alike. The argument is that there is an obvious saving to a seller who delivers goods in carload lots. Assuming this to be true, that fact would not tend to disprove injury to the merchant compelled to pay the less-than-carload price. For a ten-cent carload price differential against a merchant would injure him competitively just as much as a ten-cent differential under any other name. However relevant the separate carload argument might be to the question of justifying a differential by cost savings, it has no relevancy in determining whether the differential works an injury to a competitor. * * *

Since, in order for injury to competition to exist, the purchasers must be in competition, differences in price based upon the purchaser's distribution function are legal. Thus a lower price to a wholesaler than to a retailer does not injure competition. However, for purposes of applying this doctrine a purchaser is treated as performing the most "forward" function which he in fact performs. Thus a wholesaler who also directly retails ten percent of his purchases will be treated as a retailer, and a supplier who accords him a wholesale price not accorded to direct buying retailers will violate the act. This is one reason that many concerns advertise "wholesale only" although they might be perfectly able, from an economic point of view, to service retail trade as well. For if they in fact do retail, they are no longer legally entitled to wholesale discounts essential for their wholesale business. This doctrine can be avoided if separate records are kept and different prices charged for goods resold in different capacities, but the cost of the record keeping often exceeds the advantages gained.

Functional differences do not justify a higher price to an intermediate distributor than to a forward one. For instance a higher price to a wholesaler than a retailer violates the act because of the disadvantage imposed on the wholesaler's customers who compete with the direct buying retailer. The act does not require that the injury be to the competition between the immediate purchasers. See Perkins v. Standard Oil Co., 395 U.S. 642 (1969).

Since ultimate consumers do not compete in the resale of the goods they purchase, different prices to ultimate consumers do not violate the act.

Primary-line injury has been found infrequently. The theory is that a discriminating seller can lower his price in a particular part of his market in order to eliminate his competition in that market. The Supreme Court managed to find evidence of primary-line injury in Utah Pie Co. v. Continental Baking Co., 387 U.S. 949 (1967), without defining it. The evidence included an increase in the market share of the price cutting defendants, antagonistic internal memoranda, and the use of an industrial spy. The decision was criticized on economic grounds in Ward Bowman, Restraint of Trade by the Supreme Court: The Utah Pie Case, 77 Yale L.J. 70 (1967).

6. *The Defenses.* The important defenses to a violation of § 2(a) are two: cost justification and a good faith meeting of competition. The burden is on the defendant to establish the defense.

A difference in price can be justified by showing the price differential reflects a difference in the costs associated with the transactions. The cost justification defense raises many of the same problems as the sales below cost statutes. The problem of defining and allocating to particular sales the appropriate costs is complex and not infrequently insurmountable. The Report of the Attorney General's Committee to Study the Anti-Trust Laws observed that with the ambiguity of the legal criteria combined with no officially sanctioned accounting standards "only the most prosperous and patient business firm could afford pursuit of an often illusory defense." Report at 173. For an illustration, see United States v. Borden Co., 370 U.S. 460 (1962), where a cost study undertaken to justify price differentials between chain and independent grocers was rejected by the Court. The study showed that the costs of serving independents was higher than the cost of serving chains because they required services such as shelving and arrangement of the dairy cases and lower volume delivered per store. The Court rejected the study because it lumped all independents as a class without regard to whether or not any particular independent desired the services or had a low volume store or stores. See also Automatic Canteen Co. v. Federal Trade Commission, 346 U.S. 61 (1953), where a case brought under § 2(f), 15 U.S.C. § 13(f), against a buyer for "knowingly" inducing a discrimination in price the Court held that the Commission had the burden of establishing no cost justification, noting that "cost justification being what it is, too often no one can ascertain whether a price is cost justified."

The meeting competition defense, unlike cost justification, is not stated within § 2(a) but is separately stated in § 2(b). The competition "met" (not beaten) must be competition from a competitor of the seller, not his customer, Federal Trade Commission v. Sun Oil Co., 371 U.S. 505 (1963), but once established is an absolute defense, Standard Oil Co. v. Federal Trade Commission, 340 U.S. 231 (1951).

The "meeting but not beating" competition defense creates some real difficulties for buyers and sellers as illustrated by two United States Supreme Court cases. In United States v. United States Gypsum Co., 438 U.S. 422 (1978) several gypsum board manufacturers were charged with price fixing under § 1 of the Sherman Act for telephoning each other to verify prices currently being offered to a specific customer. The manufacturers argued they were forced to verify price information in order to comply with the "meeting competition" defense under Robinson-Patman. If they did not verify competitive prices, they asserted, they could not know "in good faith" whether their prices were meeting or beating competition. The government argued that price verification activities permitted the companies to fix prices. The Court held that a Sherman Act violation could not be justified by attempts to comply with Robinson-Patman. The Court noted there are other ways to verify a buyer's assertion that it has a lower bid, but the Court also recognized that "inadequate information will, in a limited number of cases, deny the [meeting competition] defense to some who, if all the facts had been known, would have been entitled to invoke it." 438 U.S. at 459, n. 32.

The buyer is not immune from difficulty either because § 2(f) makes knowingly accepting a discrimination a violation of the Act. In Great Atlantic & Pacific Tea Co. v. FTC, 440 U.S. 69 (1979), A & P received a bid from Borden for Borden's producing private label milk for A & P stores in the Chicago area. Dissatisfied with the bid, A & P contacted Bowman dairy which subsequently made a lower bid. A & P told Borden it had a substantially better bid but did not disclose the details. Borden responded with a bid lower than Bowman's which was accepted. Since A & P knew that Borden's second bid was (a) lower than that Borden offered other buyers and (b) had not only met but had beaten the competitive bid, the FTC argued A & P had violated the Robinson-Patman Act by inducing a discriminatory price. The Commission believed that buyers in A & P's position must affirmatively disclose to sellers that their subsequent bid has "beaten" the competition. The Court, recognizing that affirmative disclosure "would almost inevitably frustrate competitive bidding and, by reducing uncertainty, lead to price matching and anticompetitive cooperation among sellers" (440 U.S. at 80), held that as long as the seller made the bid in good faith to meet competition it was permissible for the buyer to accept it.

Indirect Discrimination: Sections 2(d) and (e)

Sections 2(d) and (e) of the Robinson-Patman Act, 15 U.S.C. § 13(d) and (e), were aimed at devices which had been used to evade the predecessor prohibitions of the Clayton Act. In order to avoid a discrimination in price the supplier would pay the customer for promotional services not in fact performed [§ 2(d)] or the supplier would perform special additional services for the customer without charge [§ 2(e)]. This problem could have been dealt with by means of a sham transaction doctrine. But it is always difficult to prove what the services provided or paid for are worth. Thus the act prohibits all such arrangements not available to all customers on "proportionately equal terms."

In FTC v. Simplicity Pattern Co., 360 U.S. 55 (1959) the Court held that "given competition between the two classes of customers, neither the absence of competitive injury nor the presence of 'cost justification' defeats enforcement of the provisions of § 2(e) of the Act." Presumably the same approach is applicable to § 2(d). The meeting competition defense is the only defense to an indirect discrimination. And see FTC v. Fred Meyer, Inc., 390 U.S. 341 (1968) prohibiting promotional services or payments to a direct-buying retailer that are not provided to competing retailers who purchase the supplier's products through wholesalers.

An illustrative case of the force of the indirect discrimination provisions is State Wholesale Grocers v. Great Atlantic & Pacific Tea Co., 258 F.2d 831 (7th Cir.1958), cert. denied 358 U.S. 947 (1959). Woman's Day magazine, produced by a subsidiary of A&P, was distributed exclusively through A&P grocery stores. The magazine was sold for 7¢ a copy although it cost 17¢ a copy to produce. The deficit was recovered by sales of advertising; the predominant source of advertisers were suppliers whose products were sold in A&P stores. The rates charged by Woman's Day were comparable to those charged by other national magazines. The plaintiffs, wholesale and retail grocers who compete with A&P, did not publish a similar magazine. They argued that advertisers in Woman's Day in effect furnished the magazine to A&P by buying advertising and thus violated § 2(e). The court found, however, that the transaction was "simply buying an advertisement" and not "furnishing" the magazine. The court held, on the other hand, that the transaction violated § 2(d) as a payment of value to A&P because of its ownership of Woman's Day. Even though the plaintiffs published no comparable magazine, the court noted that the language "proportionately equal terms" requires sellers to offer benefits in alternative ways so that all qualified customers can effectively participate in some form.

It is widely suspected that by placing all cooperative promotional schemes under a pall of possible illegality, sections 2(d) and (e) force sellers to promote their products by means of brand advertising aimed directly at the consumer. Where does this leave small suppliers of retailers not in a position to mount broad and unfocused promotional campaigns?

NOTES

1. The key to compliance with §§ 2(d) and (e) is services and payments "available on proportionately equal terms." Does "available" require any affirmative offer by the supplier? Does "proportionately equal terms" mean anything other than equal dollar cost per unit of customer's sales? Little law is available on these points. The Federal Trade Commission has promulgated "guidelines for advertising allowances and other merchandising payments and services," 16 C.F.R. §§ 240.7–240.17, covering this and other problems under §§ 2(d) and (e).

2. For the sake of completeness, mention should be made here of § 2(c). That section bars discounts in lieu of brokerage payments. Thus if a seller employs brokers on a five percent commission who are authorized to quote a price of $1.00 and the seller then sells directly to a customer for $.95 the act is violated! See generally Federal Trade Commission v. Henry Broch & Co., 363 U.S. 166 (1960). The seventh circuit pulled the act from the brink of total absurdity when in Central Retailer-Owned Grocers, Inc. v. Federal Trade Commission, 319 F.2d 410 (1963), it reversed a finding of the Commission that a cooperative buying agency for independent retailers violated the act by receiving prices from direct sellers net of brokerage. But then turnaround should be fair play. But the surprising sweep of § 2(c) should be suggested by Rangen, Inc. v. Sterling Nelson & Sons, 351 F.2d 851 (9th Cir.1965), holding that a bribe paid by a seller to a state purchasing agent may give rise to a private treble damage action by a competitor who would have made the sale absent the bribe.

3. The effect of the Robinson-Patman Act remains the subject of debate. A Department of Justice study concluded:

> The simple truth is that Robinson-Patman is a false promise: it provides little, long-run protection to small businessmen * * *. In return for this illusory "protection" the small businessman, and American business in general, is placed under a series of legal restrictions and administrative agency rules and guidelines that can genuinely be described as "regulatory." Moreover, the evidence also indicates that for several reasons, it is the small businessman, not the large businessman who runs afoul of Robinson-Patman and must bear the expense of litigation with the Federal Government.

The Study also concludes that the Act fosters concentration in some markets with little actual increase in competition in others. U.S. Dept. of Justice, Report on the Robinson-Patman Act 254–56 (1977).

However, a Congressional study came to opposite conclusions:

> The Robinson-Patman Act has implemented the clearly expressed national public policy " * * * that the Government should aid, counsel, assist, and protect, insofar as is possible, the interests of small business concerns in order to preserve free competitive enterprise * * *."

Ad Hoc Subcomm. on Antitrust, the Robinson-Patman Act, and Related Matters, House Comm. on Small Business, H.R.Rep. No. 94–1738, 94th Cong., 2d Sess. (1976).

(3) INTERFERENCE WITH CONTRACTUAL RELATIONSHIPS

IMPERIAL ICE CO. v. ROSSIER
Supreme Court of California, 1941.
18 Cal.2d 33, 112 P.2d 631.

TRAYNOR, JUSTICE. The California Consumers Company purchased from S.L. Coker an ice distributing business, inclusive of good will, located in territory comprising the city of Santa Monica and the former city of Sawtelle. In the purchase agreement Coker contracted as follows: "I do further agree in consideration of said purchase and in connection therewith, that I will not engage in the business of selling and or distributing ice, either directly or indirectly, in the above described territory so long as the purchasers, or anyone deriving title to the good will of said business from said purchasers, shall be engaged in a like business therein." Plaintiff, the Imperial Ice Company, acquired from the successor in interest of the California Consumers Company full title to this ice distributing business, including the right to enforce the covenant not to compete. Coker subsequently began selling in the same territory in violation of the contract ice supplied to him by a company owned by W. Rossier, J.A. Matheson, and Fred Matheson. Plaintiff thereupon brought this action in the superior court for an injunction to restrain Coker from violating the contract and to restrain Rossier and the Mathesons from inducing Coker to violate the contract. The complaint alleges that Rossier and the Mathesons induced Coker to violate his contract so that they might sell ice to him at a profit. The trial court sustained without leave to amend a demurrer to the complaint of the defendants Rossier and Matheson and gave judgment for those defendants. Plaintiff has appealed from the judgment on the sole ground that the complaint stated a cause of action against the defendants Rossier and the Mathesons for inducing the breach of contract.

The question thus presented to this court is under what circumstances may an action be maintained against a defendant who has induced a third party to violate a contract with the plaintiff.

It is universally recognized that an action will lie for inducing breach of contract by a resort to means in themselves unlawful such as libel, slander, fraud, physical violence, or threats of such action. See cases cited in 24 Cal.L.Rev. 208; 84 A.L.R. 67. Most jurisdictions also hold that an action will lie for inducing a breach of contract by the use of moral, social, or economic pressures, in themselves lawful, unless there is sufficient justification for such inducement. See cases cited in 84 A.L.R. 55; * * *

Such justification exists when a person induces a breach of contract to protect an interest which has greater social value than insuring the stability of the contract. Restat. Torts, sec. 767. Thus, a person is justified in inducing the breach of a contract the enforcement of which would be injurious to health, safety, or good morals. * * * The interest of labor in improving working conditions is of sufficient social importance to justify peaceful labor tactics otherwise lawful, though they have the effect of inducing breaches of contracts between employer and employee or employer and customer. * * * In numerous other situations, justification exists (see Restat. Torts, secs. 766 to 774) depending upon the importance of the interest protected. The presence or absence of ill-will, sometimes referred to as "malice", is immaterial, except as it indicates whether or not an interest is actually being protected. * * *

It is well established, however, that a person is not justified in inducing a breach of contract simply because he is in competition with one of the parties to the contract and seeks to further his own economic advantage at the expense of the other. See cases cited in 84 A.L.R. 83; 24 Cal.L.Rev. 208, 211; see Restat. Torts, sec. 768[2]. Whatever interest society has in encouraging free and open competition by means not in themselves unlawful, contractual stability is generally accepted as of greater importance than competitive freedom. Competitive freedom, however, is of sufficient importance to justify one competitor in inducing a third party to forsake another competitor if no contractual relationship exists between the latter two. Katz v. Kapper, 7 Cal.App. 2d 1, 44 P.2d 1060; * * * A person is likewise free to carry on his business, including reduction of prices, advertising, and solicitation in the usual lawful manner although some third party may be induced thereby to breach his contract with a competitor in favor of dealing with the advertiser. * * * Again, if two parties have separate contracts with a third, each may resort to any legitimate means at his disposal to secure performance of his contract even though the necessary result will be to cause a breach of the other contract. * * * A party may not, however, under the guise of competition actively and affirmatively induce the breach of a competitor's contract in order to secure an economic advantage over that competitor. The act of inducing the breach must be an intentional one. If the actor had no knowledge of the existence of the contractor his actions were not intended to induce a breach, he cannot be held liable though an actual breach results from his lawful and proper acts.

* * * The case of Katz v. Kapper, 7 Cal.App.2d 1, 44 P.2d 1060, 1061, relied upon by defendants, held only that a person by the use of lawful means could interfere with advantageous business relationships of a competitor by inducing customers to trade with him instead. The case did not involve a breach of contract, and the court specifically stated: "In deciding whether the conduct of defendants alleged in the complaint is actionable, it is necessary to apply certain well-settled rules relating to competition in business. These may be generally stated as follows: 'Competition in business, though carried to the extent of ruining a rival, is not ordinarily actionable, but every trader is left to conduct his business in his own way, so long as the methods he employs do not involve wrongful conduct such as fraud, misrepresentation, intimidation, coercion, obstruction, or molestation of the rival or his servants or workmen, *or the procurement of the violation of contractual relations. * * *'"* (Italics added.) In California, therefore, an action will lie for unjustifiably inducing a breach of contract.

The complaint in the present case alleges that defendants actively induced Coker to violate his contract with plaintiffs so that they might sell ice to him.

The contract gave to plaintiff the right to sell ice in the stated territory free from the competition of Coker. The defendants, by virtue of their interest in the sale of ice in that territory, were in effect competing with plaintiff. By inducing Coker to violate his contract, as alleged in the complaint, they sought to further their own economic advantage at plaintiff's expense. Such conduct is not justified. Had defendants merely sold ice to Coker without actively inducing him to violate his contract, his distribution of the ice in the forbidden territory in violation of his contract would not then have rendered defendants liable. They may carry on their business of selling ice as usual without incurring liability for breaches of contract by their customers. It is necessary to prove that they intentionally and actively induced the breach. Since the complaint alleges that they did so and asks for an injunction on the grounds that damages would be inadequate, it states a cause of action, and the demurrer should therefore have been overruled.

The judgment is reversed.

LEIGH FURNITURE & CARPET CO. v. ISOM
Supreme Court of Utah, 1982.
657 P.2d 293.

[W.S. Leigh, owner of Leigh Furniture, entered into a contract to sell his furniture business to Richard Isom. Isom agreed to maintain inventory, cash, and accounts receivable at a level of at least $60,000 as security for the balance of the purchase price. The contract provided Isom with a ten year lease of the first floor of the building in which the store was located and an option to buy the entire building once the

$60,000 was paid. The price for exercising the option was to be determined by three appraisers appointed by the parties.

This controversy arose because Leigh became dissatisfied with the contract and expressed openly that he wanted to sell the building outright and could not because of Isom's lease. Leigh, his wife, and his bookkeeper, pursued a course of making life difficult for Isom. They visited him in his store, questioned him about his operations, made various demands and were abusive. At one point Leigh suggested Isom needed a partner and he should contact one Talbot. In fact Isom entered negotiations with one Hunter until Leigh told him he would never accept Hunter in the store.

The parties eventually entered into a supplemental agreement which provided that Isom would pay an additional $20,000 in cash toward the purchase price of the business and that Leigh would have the right to approve any person to whom Isom intended to convey any interest in the business. The agreement was also intended to resolve all disputes between the parties. It did not, however, and shortly thereafter Leigh filed two frivolous suits against Isom and the campaign of visits, demands, and disruption continued. Isom finally attempted to pay off the entire purchase price of the business, add Talbot as a partner, and exercise his option to purchase the building but Leigh refused to accept the money, approve Talbot, or appoint an appraiser.

Ultimately Leigh filed a suit against Isom seeking the balance of the purchase price and a repossession of the premises. Isom counterclaimed alleging intentional interference with contract and prospective advantage. Shortly after the suit was filed, Isom declared bankruptcy. Although he had been able to make a profit at some points during this affair, he claims the disruption and actions of Leigh made it impossible to continue. Leigh, being the secured creditor, reacquired the inventory and building through the bankruptcy proceedings. The jury found for Isom on the counterclaim and awarded him compensatory and punitive damages. Leigh appealed.]

OAKS, JUSTICE:

II. INTERFERENCE WITH CONTRACT

Leigh Furniture first contends that Isom's recovery cannot be sustained as an interference with contract because the evidence showed no conduct which "intentionally and improperly interferes with the performance of a contract * * * between another and a third person by inducing or otherwise causing the third person not to perform the contract." *Restatement (Second) of Torts* § 766 (1979). In this case, the only contract in evidence was the contract between Isom and the Leigh Corporation. It is settled that one party to a contract cannot be liable for the tort of interference with contract for inducing a breach by himself or the other contracting party. Isom having failed to prove a cause of action for intentional interference with contract, we cannot sustain the verdict on that theory.

However, the right of action for interference with a specific contract is but one instance, rather than the total class, of protections against wrongful interference with advantageous economic relations. We therefore proceed to consider whether the jury's verdict for Isom can be sustained on the basis of the related tort of interference with prospective economic relations.

* * *

III. INTERFERENCE WITH PROSPECTIVE ECONOMIC RELATIONS

A. History and Elements of the Tort

The tort of intentional interference with prospective economic relations reaches beyond protection of an interest in an existing contract and protects a party's interest in prospective relationships of economic advantage not yet reduced to a formal contract (and perhaps not expected to be).

* * *

The plethora of decided cases and abundant literature on the tort of intentional interference with prospective economic relations has been helpful in our consideration.[3] In summarizing the history of this tort, the Restatement (Second) of Torts, ch. 37, "Interference with Contract or Prospective Contractual Relation" (1979), observes that its elements are a curious blend of the principles of liability for intentional torts (in which the plaintiff proves a prima facie case of liability, subject to the defendant's proof of justification) and for negligent torts (in which the plaintiff must prove liability based on the interplay of various factors). The disagreement and confusion incident to this blend of intentional and negligent tort principles has produced two different approaches to the definition of this tort.

Influenced by the model of the intentional tort, many jurisdictions and the first *Restatement of Torts* define the tort of intentional interference with prospective economic relations as a prima facie tort, subject to proof of privilege as an affirmative defense. To recover, the plaintiff need only prove a prima facie case of liability, i.e., that the defendant intentionally interfered with his prospective economic relations and caused him injury. As with other intentional torts, the burden of going forward then shifts to the defendant to demonstrate as an affirmative defense that under the circumstances his conduct, otherwise culpable, was justified and therefore privileged. This is the approach assumed in

3. See, e.g., Estes, "Expanding Horizons in the Law of Torts—Tortious Interference," 23 Drake L.Rev. 341 (1974); Harper, "Interference with Contractual Relations," 47 Nw.U.L.Rev. 873 (1953); Perlman, "Interference with Contract and Other Economic Expectancies: A Clash of Tort and Contract Doctrine," 49 U.Chi.L.Rev. 61 (1982); Sayre, "Inducing Breach of Contract," 36 Harv.L.Rev. 663 (1922–23); "Developments in the Law—Competitive Torts," 77 Harv.L.Rev. 888 (1964); Note, "Tortious Interference with Contract: A Reassertion of Society's Interest in Commercial Stability and Contractual Integrity," 81 Colum.L.Rev. 1491 (1981); "Interference with Contract Relations." 41 Harv.L.Rev. 728 (1927–28); Annot., 9 A.L.R.2d 228 (1950); Annot., 5 A.L.R.4th 9 (1981); Annot., 6 A.L.R.4th 195 (1981).

several Utah decisions describing the related tort of interference with contract.

*   *   *

The problem with the prima facie-tort approach is that basing liability on a mere showing that defendant intentionally interfered with plaintiff's prospective economic relations makes actionable all sorts of contemporary examples of otherwise legitimate persuasion, such as efforts to persuade others not to eat certain foods, use certain substances, engage in certain activities, or deal with certain entities. The major issue in the controversy—justification for the defendant's conduct—is left to be resolved on the affirmative defense of privilege. In short, the prima facie approach to the tort of interference with prospective economic relations requires too little of the plaintiff.

Under the second approach, which is modeled after other negligent torts, the plaintiff must prove liability based on the interplay of various factors. The *Restatement (Second) of Torts* now defines an actionable interference with prospective economic relations as an interference that is both "intentional" and "improper." Id. at § 766B. Under this approach, the trier of fact must determine whether the defendant's interference was "improper" by balancing and counterbalancing seven factors, including the interferor's motive, the nature of his conduct and interests, and the nature of the interests with which he has interfered. Id. at § 767. In those jurisdictions which have followed the negligence model, the plaintiff bears the burden of proving that in view of all of these factors the defendant's interference was improper. This obviously imposes a very significant burden on the plaintiff and magnifies the difficulty of resolving some contested issues on the pleadings. So far as we have been able to discover, only four states have specifically adopted the *Restatement (Second)* definition of the elements of this tort, though others have apparently applied some portion of the Restatement formulation in their own definitions.

In short, there is no generally acknowledged or satisfactory majority position on the definition of the elements of the tort of intentional interference with prospective economic relations. In its historical review, the *Restatement (Second) of Torts* states that "the law in this area has not fully congealed but is still in a formative stage" so that the "several forms of the tort * * * are often not distinguished by the courts, and cases have been cited among them somewhat indiscriminately." Id., Introductory Note to ch. 37 at 5. We concur in the *Restatement (Second)'s* rejection of the prima facie tort approach because it leaves too much uncertainty about the requirements for a recognized privilege and the defendant's burden of pleading and proving these and other matters. Id. But we also reject the *Restatement (Second)'s* definition of the tort because of its complexity. We seek a better alternative.

Oregon has outlined a middle ground by defining the tort of interference with prospective economic relations so as to require the plaintiff to allege and prove more than the prima facie tort, but not to negate all defenses of privilege.   Privileges remain as affirmative defenses.   This approach originated with Justice Linde's opinion in Top Service Body Shop, Inc. v. Allstate Insurance Co., 283 Or. 201, 582 P.2d 1365 (1978).   After summarizing the history of this tort and specifically refusing to require a plaintiff to prove that the interference was "improper" under the balancing-of-factors approach specified in the *Restatement (Second),* the court defined the cause of action for "wrongful interference with economic relationships" as follows:

> Either the pursuit of an improper objective of harming plaintiff or the use of wrongful means that in fact cause injury to plaintiff's contractual or business relationships may give rise to a tort claim for those injuries * * *.   In summary, such a claim is made out when interference resulting in injury to another is wrongful by some measure beyond the fact of the interference itself.   Defendant's liability may arise from improper motives or from the use of improper means.

Top Service Body Shop, Inc., 283 Or. at 205, 209, 582 P.2d at 1368, 1371. A subsequent decision of that court restated and elaborated what the plaintiff must prove, as follows:

> In *Top Service* we decided that the defendant's improper intent, motive or purpose to interfere was a necessary element of the plaintiff's case, rather than a lack thereof being a matter of justification or privilege to be asserted as a defense by defendant. Thus, to be entitled to go to a jury, plaintiff must not only prove that defendant intentionally interfered with his business relationship but also that defendant had a duty of non-interference; i.e., that he interfered for an improper purpose rather than for a legitimate one, or that defendant used improper means which resulted in injury to plaintiff.

Straube v. Larson, 287 Or. 357, 361, 600 P.2d 371, 374 (1979).

We recognize a common-law cause of action for intentional interference with prospective economic relations, and adopt the Oregon definition of this tort.   Under this definition, in order to recover damages, the plaintiff must prove (1) that the defendant intentionally interfered with the plaintiff's existing or potential economic relations, (2) for an improper purpose or by improper means, (3) causing injury to the plaintiff.   Privilege is an affirmative defense, Searle v. Johnson, Utah, 646 P.2d 682 (1982), which does not become an issue unless "the acts charged would be tortious on the part of an unprivileged defendant." Top Service Body Shop, Inc., 283 Or. at 210, 582 P.2d at 1371.

* * *

C.   Evidence of Intentional Interference and Causation

Reviewing the record, we conclude that there was sufficient evidence to sustain the jury's verdict against the Leigh Corporation for intentional interference with prospective economic relations that caused injury to Isom.

There was ample evidence that Isom had business relationships with various customers, suppliers, and potential business associates, and that Leigh, the former owner of the business, understood the value of those relationships. There was also substantial competent evidence that the Corporation, through Leigh, his wife, and his bookkeeper, intentionally interfered with and caused a termination of some of those relationships (actual or potential). Their frequent visits to Isom's store during business hours to confront him, question him, and make demands and inquiries regarding the manner in which he was conducting his business repeatedly interrupted sales activities, caused his customers to comment and complain, and more than once caused a customer to leave the store. Driving away an individual's existing or potential customers is the archetypical injury this cause of action was devised to remedy.

Other actions by which the Leigh Corporation imposed heavy demands on Isom's time and financial resources to the detriment of his ability to attract and retain customers and conduct the other activities of his business included: numerous letters of complaint, Leigh's demand for an audit of Isom's books and inventory during the busy holiday season, his continued threats to cancel the contract and sell the building and business to another buyer, his refusal to pay the contracted share of the heating bills or the cost of repairing the furnace and the store's broken window, his refusal of the tendered payment of the balance due under the contract, and his suit for repossession, termination, and injunction. Leigh's refusals also prevented Isom from consummating potentially advantageous business associations with Hunter, with Talbot, and finally with Applegate, all experienced retailers able to contribute expertise and additional capital to Isom's business.

Taken in isolation, each of the foregoing interferences with Isom's business might be justified as an overly zealous attempt to protect the Corporation's interests under its contract of sale. As such, none would establish the intentional interference element of this tort, though some might give rise to a cause of action for breach of specific provisions in the contract or of the duty of good faith performance which inheres in every contractual relation. Even in small groups, these acts might be explained as merely instances of aggressive or abrasive—though not illegal or tortious—tactics, excesses that occur in contractual and commercial relationships. But in total and in cumulative effect, as a course of action extending over a period of three and one-half years and culminating in the failure of Isom's business, the Leigh Corporation's acts cross the threshold beyond what is incidental and justifiable to what is tortious. The Corporation's acts provide sufficient evidence to establish two of the elements in the definition of this tort: an intentional interference with present or prospective economic relations that caused injury to the plaintiff.

D. Improper Purpose

The alternative of improper purpose (or motive, intent, or objective) will support a cause of action for intentional interference with prospective economic relations even where the defendant's means were proper. In the context of the related tort of interference with contract, Prosser had this to say about improper purpose:

> Since *Lumley v. Gye* there has been general agreement that a purely "malicious" motive, in the sense of spite and a desire to do harm to the plaintiff for its own sake, will make the defendant liable for interference with a contract. The same is true of a mere officious intermeddling for no other reason than a desire to interfere. On the other hand, in the few cases in which the question has arisen, it has been held that where the defendant has a proper purpose in view, the addition of ill will toward the plaintiff will not defeat his privilege. It may be suggested that here, as in the case of mixed motives in the exercise of a privilege in defamation and malicious prosecution, the court may well *look to the predominant purpose underlying the defendant's conduct.* [Citations omitted; emphasis added.]

W. Prosser, *Handbook of the Law of Torts* § 129 at 943 (4th ed. 1971).

Because it requires that the improper purpose predominate, this alternative takes the long view of the defendant's conduct, allowing objectionable short-run purposes to be eclipsed by legitimate long-range economic motivation. Otherwise, much competitive commercial activity, such as a businessman's efforts to forestall a competitor in order to further his own long-range economic interests, could become tortious. In the rough and tumble of the marketplace, competitors inevitably damage one another in the struggle for personal advantage. The law offers no remedy for those damages—even if intentional—because they are an inevitable byproduct of competition. Problems inherent in proving motivation or purpose make it prudent for commercial conduct to be regulated for the most part by the improper means alternative, which typically requires only a showing of particular conduct.

The alternative of improper purpose will be satisfied where it can be shown that the actor's predominant purpose was to injure the plaintiff.

* * *

As noted earlier, there is substantial evidence that the Leigh Corporation deliberately injured Isom's economic relations. But that injury was not an end in itself. It was an intermediate step toward achieving the long-range financial goal of profitably reselling the building free of Isom's interest. Because that economic interest seems to have been controlling, we must conclude that the evidence in this case would not support a jury finding that the Corporation's predominant purpose was to injure or ruin Isom's business merely for the sake of injury alone.

* * *

E. Improper Means

The alternative requirement of improper means is satisfied where the means used to interfere with a party's economic relations are contrary to law, such as violations of statutes, regulations, or recognized common-law rules. Such acts are illegal or tortious in themselves and hence are clearly "improper" means of interference, unless those means consist of constitutionally protected activity, like the exercise of First Amendment rights. NAACP v. Claiborne Hardware Co., 458 U.S. 886 (1982). "Commonly included among improper means are violence, threats or other intimidation, deceit or misrepresentation, bribery, unfounded litigation, defamation, or disparaging falsehood." Top Service Body Shop, Inc., 582 P.2d at 1371 & n. 11. Means may also be improper or wrongful because they violate "an established standard of a trade or profession." Id. at 1371.

By forcing Isom to defend what appear to have been two groundless lawsuits, the Leigh Corporation was clearly employing an improper means of interference with Isom's business. Such use of civil litigation as a weapon to damage another's business, besides being an intolerable waste of judicial resources, may give rise to independent causes of action in tort for abuse of process and malicious prosecution.

The jury's verdict can therefore be sustained on the ground that the Leigh Corporation intentionally interfered with Isom's economic relations by improper means.

There is also another basis for affirming that verdict on the basis of improper means.

A deliberate breach of contract, even where employed to secure economic advantage, is not, by itself, an "improper means." Because the law remedies breaches of contract with damages calculated to give the aggrieved party the benefit of the bargain, there is no need for an additional remedy in tort (unless the defendant's conduct would constitute a tort independent of the contract).

Neither a deliberate breach of contract nor an immediate purpose to inflict injury which does not predominate over a legitimate economic end will, by itself, satisfy this element of the tort. However, they may do so in combination. This is so because contract damages provide an insufficient remedy for a breach prompted by an immediate purpose to injure, and that purpose does not enjoy the same legal immunity in the context of contract relations as it does in the competitive marketplace. As a result, a breach of contract committed for the immediate purpose of injuring the other contracting party is an improper means that will satisfy this element of the cause of action for intentional interference with economic relations.

Two cases illustrate how breach of contract (or lease), when done with a purpose to injure, satisfy this element of the tort. In both cases, the defendant committed a breach not just to obtain relief from its obligation under the contract or lease (for which contract damages would have made the plaintiff whole), but to achieve a larger advantage by injuring the plaintiff in a manner not compensable merely by contract damages. In both cases, the defendant ruined the plaintiff's business by its breach, and in both cases the plaintiff was given substantial damages for the tort of interference with prospective economic relations.

In Buxbom v. Smith, 23 Cal.2d 535, 145 P.2d 305 (1944), a retail grocery chain contracted with the plaintiff to publish and distribute a "shopping news." In order to do so, the plaintiff abandoned his printing customers and expanded his distribution organization. After becoming the plaintiff's sole customer and acquiring complete knowledge of his business, the retailer deliberately breached its contract in order to ruin the plaintiff's business by cutting off the work required to sustain it and then hired his employees. The California Supreme Court affirmed a verdict for the plaintiff, awarding damages for breach of contract and additional damages for "tortious interference with his business" in order to give him "complete recompense for his combined injuries ＊ ＊ ＊." Id. at 546, 145 P.2d at 310. The gravamen of the tort, the court explained, was the defendant's breaching its contract with plaintiff as a means of acquiring plaintiff's employees:

＊ ＊ ＊

In Cherberg v. Peoples National Bank of Washington, 88 Wash.2d 595, 564 P.2d 1137 (1977), a lessor deliberately breached its duty to repair a structurally unsound wall on the leased premises in order to destroy the restaurant business of a lessee who had leased a portion of the premises. The lessor's purpose was to retake the entire building as soon as possible, demolish the structure, and erect a more profitable building. The jury gave a verdict of $42,000 against the lessor. Apart from the $3,100 damages for breach of the lease (economic losses from temporary closure of the restaurant business), this verdict represented a recovery of damages for inconvenience, discomfort, and mental anguish for "the tort of intentional interference with business expectancies." The Washington Supreme Court sustained the verdict in an opinion that squarely relies on the combination of improper means and improper purpose in defendant's deliberate breach for the purpose of injuring the plaintiff.

＊ ＊ ＊

＊ ＊ ＊ In *Cherberg,* the court found that the defendant had breached its lease and interfered with the plaintiff's business not for the "privileged" reason of escaping from an unsatisfactory return on its investment in the leased premises (upon payment of contract damages), but for the impermissible purpose of injuring the tenant in order to secure an advantage beyond the scope of the lease:

＊ ＊ ＊

In the case at bar, the Leigh Corporation breached its contract in various ways.

It breached its implied duty to exercise all of its rights under the contract reasonably and in good faith.

* * * Leigh's unexplained refusal to approve Isom's prospective business partners without consideration of their merits indicates an absence of good faith and provides evidence that the Corporation's breach was intended to deprive Isom's business of additional capital and valuable expertise which (at least with regard to Talbot) Leigh himself had repeatedly urged Isom to acquire. Similar refusals to approve prospective subtenants under a contract clause in order to injure the tenant's business have been held to constitute tortious interference with economic relations. In addition, Leigh, his wife, and his bookkeeper continually interrupted sales activities with their visits, letters, threats, and demands, causing customers to comment and complain and sometimes to leave. Although the contract entitled the Corporation, as lessor and secured party, to reasonable supervision of Isom's business, the jury had sufficient evidence to conclude that this conduct constituted an unreasonable exercise of contract rights and/or was done in bad faith for the purpose of injuring Isom's business relations.

The Corporation also breached its contractual duty by refusing Isom's tender of the balance of the purchase price and by refusing to appoint an appraiser to establish a price for the sale of the entire building, thereby preventing Isom from exercising his purchase option. There is evidence of Leigh's purpose in the fact that he openly regretted his contract with Isom and frequently expressed his desire to "get Richard out" of the business and building. Furthermore, he continually contacted prospective buyers for the building, even approaching two of Isom's employees for this purpose.

All of the above provide substantial evidence from which the jury could have concluded that the Corporation breached its express and implied contractual duties for the purpose of ruining Isom's business and obtaining possession of the building in order to sell it more profitably elsewhere. By themselves, the Corporation's breaches would not satisfy the requirement of "improper means," but they could do so when coupled with the improper purpose of injuring Isom. In combination, a breach of contract and an intent to injure satisfy the improper means requirement for the cause of action for intentional interference with prospective economic relations.

* * *

NOTES

1. The tort of interference with contractual relations was first formulated out of the intense controversy between Benjamin Lumley and Frederick Gye over the operatic talents extraordinary of Johanna Wagner. Miss Wagner being under contract with Mr. Lumley to sing at the Queen's Theatre, was offered more money by Mr. Gye to sing at the Covent Garden Theatre. Miss Wagner as part of her contract with Lumley engaged "herself not to use her talents at any other theatre, nor in any concert or reunion, public or private, without the written authorization of Mr. Lumley." Lumley first obtained an injunction to enforce the above quoted provision of the contract restraining Miss Wagner from singing for Gye. Lumley v. Wagner, 1 DeG., M. & G. 604

(1852). He then brought suit for damages against Gye for interfering with his contractual relations with Miss Wagner. Lumley v. Gye, 2 El. & Bl. 213, 95 Rev.Rep. 501 (Q.B.1852). In awarding judgment for the plaintiff, Crompton, J. held: "I think that we are justified in applying the principle of the action for enticing away servants to a case where the defendant maliciously procures a party, who is under a valid contract to give her exclusive personal services to the plaintiff for a specified period, to refuse to give such services during the period for which she had so contracted, whereby the plaintiff was injured."

Coleridge, J., dissenting, expressed the concern that "to draw a line between advice, persuasion, enticement and procurement is practically impossible in a court of justice; who shall say how much of a free agent's resolution flows from the interference of other minds, or the independent resolution of his own?"

The stability of the Lumley v. Gye doctrine in English jurisprudence was not fully established until Bowen v. Hall, 6 Q.B. 333 (1881) where under similar facts it was held that the broader ground of "malicious injury" was applicable to enticing away an employee of the plaintiff and Temperton v. Russell, [1893] 1 Q.B. 715 where the doctrine was applied to a labor dispute and extended to protect prospective or potential relationships as well as existing contracts.

2. Many of the interference with contract cases, like Lumley v. Gye, involve attempts by an actor to secure the employees of a competitor. These cases often illustrate the conflicting interests in stark contrast. The initial employer may expend substantial resources educating and training the employee and providing the employee with competitively advantageous information. By permitting a potential second employer to lure the employee away permits this second employer to profit from the investment of the first employer. If this is permitted it ultimately detracts from the incentives for employers to train their employees. At the same time, however, the employee has a substantial interest in marketing his services to the highest bidder. If he is unable to do so, it reduces the employee's incentives to become better trained. Society's interest in competition for goods and services is also involved.

Which approach, that in *Rossier* or in *Leigh Furniture* best accommodates these conflicting interests? And how would you advise a businessman anxious to secure a key employee of his competitor to proceed under either rule? Judge Learned Hand in Triangle Film Corp. v. Artcraft Pictures Corp., 250 Fed. 981 (2d Cir.1918) recognized the "right to offer better terms to another's employee, so long as the latter is free to leave." In a few cases courts have attached liability to attempts to systematically induce a substantial number of employees to leave one employer with the result that the first employer's business would be substantially disrupted. Morgan's Home Equipment Corp. v. Martucci, 390 Pa. 618, 136 A.2d 838 (1957); Wear-Ever Aluminum v. Townecraft Industries, 75 N.J.Super. 135, 182 A.2d 387 (Super.Ct.1962) (violation for soliciting substantial part of sales team even though most were at-will employees).

3. Consider Hannigan v. Sears, Roebuck & Co., 410 F.2d 285 (7th Cir. 1969). Fabricated had signed a contract agreeing to produce outdoor metal lockers exclusively for Hannigan so when Fabricated began selling lockers to Sears, Hannigan was paid a royalty. Subsequently to reduce its costs in purchasing lockers, Sears put pressure on Fabricated to get out of its royalty agreement. Fabricated was economically dependent on Sears for sale of its lockers; Hannigan was dependent on Fabricated as its sole supply of lockers. Thus Sears successfully forced the two parties to alter their royalty agreement

giving Hannigan substantially less royalty on lockers sold to Sears. The Seventh Circuit upheld a jury verdict against Sears for actual and punitive damages on the basis of intentional interference with the contract.

Do you agree with the result? Does the case illustrate the problems Justice Oaks foresaw in *Leigh Furniture* if the tort were interpreted broadly?

4. *Privileged interferences.* Not all activity that results in an interference with another's contract is actionable. Consider Los Angeles Airways, Inc. v. Davis, 687 F.2d 321 (9th Cir.1982) where LAA claimed interests owned by Howard Hughes orally agreed to purchase LAA but Davis, an attorney and business advisor to the Hughes interests, induced the companies to breach the agreement. LAA alleged that Davis's motives were twofold: (1) to force LAA into bankruptcy and thus permit its acquisition by Hughes at a "distress" price, and (2) to enhance Davis' position within the Hughes Organization. Observing that California law provided a privilege for inducing breach of contract by lawful means "in order to protect an interest that has greater social value than the mere stability of the particular contract in question" the court held Davis' actions privileged.

> We conclude that where, as here, an advisor is motivated in part by a desire to benefit his principal, his conduct in inducing a breach of contract should be privileged. The privilege is designed to further certain societal interests by fostering uninhibited advise by agents to their principals. The goal of the privilege is promoted by protecting advice that is motivated, even in part, by a good faith intent to benefit the principal's interest.

> We believe that advice by an agent to a principal is rarely, if ever, motivated purely by a desire to benefit only the principal. An agent naturally hopes that by providing beneficial advice to his principal, the agent will benefit indirectly by gaining the further trust and confidence of his principal. If the protection of the privilege were denied every time that an advisor acted with such mixed motive, the privilege would be greatly diminished and the societal interests it was designed to promote would be frustrated. 687 F.2d at 328.

The Restatement (Second) of Torts §§ 768–773 provides a number of privileges for inducing contractual breach. Most permit individuals with a legitimate personal interest to act to protect their interest or to give others honest advice.

5. *Competition as Privilege.* If a privilege is established when societal interests exceed the interest in contract compliance, shouldn't an act of contract interference be justified if a result of normal business competition? The Restatement (Second) of Torts § 768 provides that competition is *not* a justification for inducing breach of a contract but does justify interference with prospective relationships.

At least where there is a formal contract, is there any justification for inducing one of the parties to the contract to breach its provisions? An economic analysis of the purpose of contracts suggests that in many instances society gains from breached agreements because it permits resources to move to higher valued uses. Assume that *A* agrees to sell a widget to *B* one week hence for $5000. Two days later *C* offers *A* $7500 if it will use its factory to make a gidget instead. *A* changes production breaching his agreement with *B*. However the factory is now producing more valuable goods and *B* will be made whole by the law of contracts that will give him the difference between the contract price ($5000) and whatever he must pay to buy a widget on the open market. Assume *B* can purchase a substitute widget for $5000, he is in the same position had the contract been performed and *A* and *C* have an additional $2500 gain to split between them. Shouldn't these types of breaches be encouraged? Should we make *C* liable under the doctrines of intentional interference with a contract if he knew about the initial agreement?

6. Interference with contract or prospective advantage cases involve determining what behavior on the part of the defendant constitutes an improper inducement and the extent to which the behavior of the defendant is privileged. These issues become intertwined in many cases. It may be useful to divide the cases into at least two classes. In the first class the defendant's behavior is independently tortious. Many of the cases decided under other rubrics such as misrepresentation, disparagement, predatory pricing, and use of force can be cast as "interference" cases. In the second class are those cases that involve no independent tortious behavior and involve conduct on the part of the defendant that at least can be arguably characterized as part of the competitive process. In this class of case, the intensity of the conflict of interests is more clearly seen. Consider whether and on what basis you would impose liability on the inducer in any of the following cases:

a. *A* supplies fishing reels to both *B* and *C* under annually renewable contractual arrangements. When *A* becomes financially troubled, *B* purchases one-sixth of the stock in *A* and makes *A* an interest free loan. As part of the transaction *A* agrees not to renew the contract with *C*. *C* sues *B*. See Fury Imports, Inc. v. Shakespeare Co., 554 F.2d 1376 (5th Cir.1977).

b. *A*, *B* and *C* are associates in a major New York law firm. They decide to form their own partnership and notify the firm's clients of their actions. The firm sues *A*, *B* and *C* for interfering with its relationships with its clients. See Adler, Barish, Daniels, Levin & Creskoff v. Epstein, 252 Pa.Super. 553, 382 A.2d 1226 (1977), reversed 482 Pa. 416, 393 A.2d 1175 (1978).

c. An automobile liability insurance company offers to settle with a plaintiff in a tort case contingent on the plaintiff breaching a contingent fee contract with his lawyer. See Herron v. State Farm Mutual Ins. Co., 56 Cal.2d 202, 14 Cal.Rptr. 294, 363 P.2d 310 (1961). And, a husband in a divorce action threatens "to refuse any and all reconciliation efforts" unless the wife discharges the plaintiff as her attorney. Abrams & Fox, Inc. v. Briney, 39 Cal. App.3d 604, 114 Cal.Rptr. 328 (1974).

d. A major bank owns an apartment house. *A*, a real estate broker, initiates conversations with the bank on behalf of *B*, a potential buyer, to determine if the bank is willing to sell. Finding the bank receptive, *A* submits a contract of sale to the bank containing a requirement that the bank pay *A* a real estate commission. The bank rejects the contract. Thereafter, *B* approaches the bank directly and they enter a contract for sale, a term of the contract requires *B* to indemnify the bank against any claim to commissions by *A*. *A* sues *B* for inducing a breach of a prospective relationship. Leonard Duckworth, Inc. v. Michael L. Field & Co., 516 F.2d 952 (5th Cir.1975).

e. *A* has a contract terminable at will with *B*. *B* has a contract terminable at will with *C*. *A* threatens to terminate his contract with *B* unless *B* terminates his contract with *C*. See Smith v. Ford Motor Co., 289 N.C. 71, 221 S.E.2d 282 (1976).

7. Would you allow the party to the contract to recover a tort measure of damages against the inducer even though he would only be able to recover

contractual damages against the breaching party? The courts are divided. Punitive damages have been awarded in some cases.

8. There has been much contemporary interest in the interference tort because, viewed broadly, it is basic to the law governing competitive practices. Compare Perlman, Interference with Contract and Other Economic Expectancies: A Clash of Tort and Contract Theory, 49 U.Chi.L.Rev. 61 (1982), Epstein, Inducement of Breach of Contract as a Problem of Ostensible Ownership, 16 J.Leg.Stud. 1 (1987), and BeVier, Reconsidering Inducement, 76 Va.L.Rev. 877 (1990). See also, Rizzo, A Theory of Economic Loss in the Law of Torts, 11 J. Legal Stud. 281 (1982); Dobbs, Tortious Interference with Contractual Relationships, 34 Ark.L.Rev. 335 (1980); Note, Tortious Interference with Contractual Relations in the Nineteenth Century: The Transformation of Property, Contract, and Tort, 93 Harv.L.Rev. 1510 (1980); Note, An Analysis of the Formation of Property Rights Underlying Tortious Interference with Contracts and Other Economic Relations, 50 U.Chi.L.Rev. 1116 (1983).

9. Actions that interfere with another's contract or business opportunity may be actionable under state deceptive practices acts even though not all of the elements of the tort cause of action are present. See Sportsmen's Boating Corp. v. Hensley, 192 Conn. 747, 474 A.2d 780 (1984) (tort cause of action requires intention or malice; claim under state deceptive practice act requires only unfairness: "Conduct that might be actionable under [state statute] may not rise to a level sufficient to invoke tort liability. The reverse of that proposition, however, is seldom true.")

B. APPROPRIATION

(1) THE PROTECTION OF IDEAS

The courts have frequently considered cases where the plaintiff has disclosed his idea, plan or composition to the defendant in situations where he might reasonably expect compensation if the idea is used. In these cases the courts have frequently afforded relief on theories variously denominated implied contract, quasi-contract or unjust enrichment. Although the cases occasionally speak of property rights in ideas, it is clear that this is a misnomer. See Comment Note, 170 A.L.R. 449 (1947) at 450–52:

> Clearly, if an invention, discovery, process or trade secret were in itself, unaided by patent laws or statutory provisions, to be regarded as in truth property, the courts would not hesitate to protect its possessor therein, and this wholly aside from special cases based on allegations of fraud, theft, breach of contract, or violation of trust and confidence. The cases do contain a variety of expressions to the effect that an invention, discovery, or trade secret is 'property,' or that the inventor, discoverer or possessor has 'a property,' or 'a right of property,' or a 'kind of property' therein, but in their rulings stop short of what might be conjectured from such language.

It is true the inventor or discoverer may assign rights in the thing invented or discovered, and it may be treated as property for some special purpose; but it is not property in the full sense—as demonstrated by the fact that anyone who comes by it without a burden of wrongdoing or contract obligation, express or implied, may use it without consent.

The use of a contract theory to provide compensation for the use of ideas faces substantial difficulties. In the usual case the writer, creator or inventor will not disclose unless he is assured of compensation if the idea is used. On the other hand, the person (or more frequently, corporation) to whom the disclosure is made will understandably refuse to promise to pay anything for an unknown idea. In the usual case the plaintiff has disclosed his idea in exchange for some ambiguous promise—often made by someone without authority to make it—that "satisfactory arrangements" will be made if the idea is used. The contractual problems are:

a. Is there consideration for such a promise? If the discloser has no property rights in the idea, what does he give in exchange for the user's promise to pay?

b. Does the "contract" fail for want of definiteness? What is the measure of compensation under the contract?

c. If the promise to pay compensation is made by someone who has neither real or apparent authority to make major business decisions such as a foreman or secretary is his promise binding on the user?

The leading case denying recovery is Bristol v. Equitable Life Assurance Soc., 132 N.Y. 264, 30 N.E. 506 (1892). In *Bristol* the plaintiff sent the defendant an unsolicited letter seeking employment and communicating to the defendant a new system for soliciting life insurance. The letter concluded: "In the meantime I need hardly to say that this letter must be considered of the most confidential nature." See opinion below, 52 Hun 161, 5 N.Y.S. 131 (1st Dept. 1889). The court said:

> Without denying that there may be property in an idea, or trade secret or system, it is obvious that its originator or proprietor must himself protect it from escape or disclosure. If it cannot be sold or negotiated or used without a disclosure, it would seem proper that some contract should guard or regulate the disclosure, otherwise it must follow the law of ideas and become the acquisition of whoever receives it. * * *

> The allegation of the complaint that the defendant disclosed the system in confidence to the defendant is vague. It does not necessarily mean that the defendant agreed not to use it; it may mean something else. Defendant is at liberty to conduct its business in its own way; it obtained a valuable hint from the plaintiff and assumed no legal obligation to pay the plaintiff if it should conclude to act upon it.

The leading case allowing recovery is Liggett & Myer Tobacco Co., Inc. v. Meyer, 101 Ind.App. 420, 194 N.E. 206 (1935). The plaintiff had sent the defendant a letter stating: "I am submitting for your approval an original advertising scheme to be used in the way of billboard advertising. The idea consists of this: Two gentlemen, well groomed, in working clothes or in hunting togs apparently engaged in conversation, one extending to the other a package of cigarettes saying, 'have one of these,' the other replying, 'no thanks; I smoke Chesterfields.' I trust that this idea will be of sufficient value as to merit a reasonable charge therefor." The defendant did not answer the letter but used the idea in its newspaper and magazine advertising. The court affirmed a jury verdict for $9,000.00 on the theory that the defendant's act of using the idea constituted acceptance of the offer and the express condition to pay reasonable compensation.

If *A* gives something to *B*, is *B* obligated to pay for it unless he returns it? Is it possible to "return" an idea? If use of the idea is equivalent to acceptance, does receipt of such an offer bar the recipient from using the idea without paying the offeror in perpetuity? Can the recipient advise the offeror that he rejects the offer and then proceed to use the idea?

MURRAY v. NATIONAL BROADCASTING CO.
United States Court of Appeals, Second Circuit, 1988.
844 F.2d 988.

ALTIMARI, CIRCUIT JUDGE:

[In the 1960's Bill Cosby became the first black entertainer to star in a dramatic network series, "I Spy". In a 1965 interview Cosby disclosed that his ambition was to produce a situation comedy featuring black actors. "My series would take place in a middle-income Negro neighborhood. People who really don't know negroes would find on this show that they're just like everyone else."

In 1980 Hwesu S. Murray, an employee of NBC Television approached NBC with an idea for a future television series. He was invited to submit his proposal in writing. He submitted five proposals, one of which was entitled "Father's Day". On submission he notified NBC that if they used any of the proposals he expected to be named executive producer and to receive compensation. He was asked to flesh out "Father's Day" which he did. The proposal was for a half-hour situation comedy to star Bill Cosby and to focus on the family life of a Black American family. NBC rejected the idea on November 21, 1980. Four years later *The Cosby Show* premiered on NBC staring Bill Cosby about everyday life in an upper middle-class black family.

Murray immediately wrote NBC claiming *The Cosby Show* was derived from "Father's Day". NBC responded that the show was an outgrowth of Bill Cosby's humor and was produced by Carsey–Werner Co., an independent production company. The district court applied New York law as announced in Downey v. General Foods Corp., 31

N.Y.2d 56, 334 N.Y.S.2d 874, 286 N.E.2d 257 (1972) "[l]ack of novelty in an idea is fatal to *any* cause of action for its unlawful use." For purposes of summary judgment it assumed the defendants had used plaintiff's idea in the development of *The Cosby Show*. The trial court found the idea not novel because it "merely combined two ideas which had been circulating in the industry for a number of years—namely, the family situation comedy, which was a standard formula, and the casting of black actors in nonstereotypical roles." Defendant's motion for summary judgment was granted.]

I.

* * *

As the district court recognized, the dispositive issue in this case is whether plaintiff's idea is entitled to legal protection. Plaintiff points to "unique"—"even revolutionary"—aspects of his "Father's Day" proposal that he claims demonstrate "genuine novelty and invention," see *Educational Sales Programs, Inc. v. Dreyfus Corp.*, 65 Misc.2d 412, 317 N.Y.S.2d 840, 844 (Sup.Ct.N.Y.Cty.1970), which preclude the entry of summary judgment against him. Specifically, plaintiff contends that his idea suggesting the nonstereotypical portrayal of black Americans on television is legally protectible because it represents a real breakthrough. As he stated in his affidavit in opposition to defendants' motion,

> [w]hen I created "Father's Day", I had in mind . . . a show that . . . would portray a Black family as it had never been shown before on television. . . . I also . . . desire[d] to produce a show with strong and positive role models for the Black community, and to make a statement regarding the love and integrity of the Black family to the world. I think every Black person in this country knows there has been a need for this, and that never before on television had there been a portrayal of a Black family as I created it for "Father's Day."

Murray claims that the novelty of his idea subsequently was confirmed by the media and the viewing public which instantly recognized the "unique" and "revolutionary" portrayal of a black family on The Cosby Show.

We certainly do not dispute the fact that the portrayal of a nonstereotypical black family on television was indeed a breakthrough. Nevertheless, that breakthrough represents the achievement of what many black Americans, including Bill Cosby and plaintiff himself, have recognized for many years—namely the need for a more positive, fair and realistic portrayal of blacks on television. While NBC's decision to broadcast The Cosby Show unquestionably was innovative in the sense that an intact, nonstereotypical black family had never been portrayed on television before, the mere fact that such a decision had not been made before does not necessarily mean that the idea for the program is itself novel.

Consequently, we do not agree with appellant's contention that the nonstereotypical portrayal of a black middle-class family in a situation comedy is novel because

> [t]o argue otherwise would be the equivalent of arguing that since there had always been baseball, and blacks in baseball, there was nothing new about Jackie Robinson playing in the major leagues—or that since there had always been schools in Little Rock, Arkansas, and blacks in schools, there was nothing new about integrating schools in Little Rock.

As appellees persuasively point out in response to this analogy, Murray has "confuse[d] the 'idea' with its execution. . . . Indeed, the idea of integration . . . had been discussed for decades prior to the actual events taking place." Similarly, we believe, as a matter of law, that plaintiff's idea embodied in his "Father's Day" proposal was not novel because it merely represented an "adaption of existing knowledge" and of "known ingredients" and therefore lacked "genuine novelty and invention." *Educational Sales Programs,* 317 N.Y.S.2d at 844.

We recognize of course that even novel and original ideas to a greater or lesser extent combine elements that are themselves not novel. Originality does not exist in a vacuum. Nevertheless, where, as here, an idea consists in essence of nothing more than a variation on a basic theme—in this case, the family situation comedy—novelty cannot be found to exist. The addition to this basic theme of the portrayal of blacks in nonstereotypical roles does not alter our conclusion, especially in view of the fact that Bill Cosby previously had expressed a desire to do a situation comedy about a black family and that, as the district court found, Cosby's entire career has been a reflection of the positive portrayal of blacks and the black family on television.

Appellant would have us believe that by interpreting New York law as we do, we are in effect condoning the theft of ideas. On the contrary, ideas that reflect "genuine novelty and invention" are fully protected against unauthorized use. *Educational Sales Programs,* 317 N.Y.S.2d at 844. But those ideas that are not novel "are in the public domain and may freely be used by anyone with impunity." *Ed Graham Productions,* [Inc. v. National Broadcasting Co., 75 Misc.2d 334, 347 N.Y.S.2d 766 (Sup.Ct.N.Y.Cty.1973)] at 769. Since such non-novel ideas are not protectible as property, they cannot be stolen. In assessing whether an idea is in the public domain, the central issue is the uniqueness of the creation. Murray insists that there is at least a question of fact as to the novelty of "Father's Day" because The Cosby Show is indisputably unique. In support of this contention, plaintiff points to the fact that NBC contracted with Carsey–Werner for the right of NBC to broadcast The Cosby Show. The contract apparently was executed by the parties before there had been any written development of the proposed series. The "program idea" for The Cosby Show, however, was described in the contract as "unique, intellectual property." According to plaintiff, the inescapable conclusion is that the idea—whether it be "Father's Day" or The Cosby Show—could not possibly have been in the public domain if NBC expressly contracted to purchase it from Carsey–Werner.

We disagree. The Carsey–Werner contract contemplates a fully-produced television series. The contract refers to, inter alia, the program format, titles, set designs, theme music, stories, scripts, and art work as well as to the "program idea." Taken together, these elements no doubt would be considered original and therefore protectible as property. On the other hand, we think it equally apparent that the mere idea for a situation comedy about a nonstereotypical black family—whether that idea is in the hands of Murray, Carsey–Werner, NBC, or anyone else—is not novel and thus may be used with impunity.

Finally, as an alternative attack on the propriety of the district court's order granting summary judgment, plaintiff posits that even if his idea was not novel as a matter of law, summary judgment still was inappropriate because his proposal was solicited by defendants and submitted to them in confidence. In this regard, Murray relies on Cole v. Phillips H. Lord, Inc., 262 A.D. 116, 28 N.Y.S.2d 404 (1st Dep't 1941). Murray contends that Cole stands for the proposition that when an idea is protected by an agreement or a confidential relationship, a cause of action arises for unauthorized use of that idea irrespective of the novelty of the subject matter of the contract. Plaintiff's reliance on Cole is misplaced in light of subsequent cases, particularly the New York Court of Appeals decision in Downey v. General Foods Corp., 31 N.Y.2d 56, 334 N.Y.S.2d 874, 286 N.E.2d 257 (1972). * * *

Consequently, we find that New York law requires that an idea be original or novel in order for it to be protected as property. Since, as has already been shown, plaintiff's proposal for "Father's Day" was lacking in novelty and originality, we conclude that the district court correctly granted defendants' motion for summary judgment.

II.

Having determined that plaintiff's idea is not property under New York law, we turn now to a consideration of the district court's dismissal of the various claims in the complaint.

A. State law claims

"[W]hen one submits an idea to another, no promise to pay for its use may be implied, and no asserted agreement enforced, if the elements of novelty and originality are absent. . . ." Downey, 334 N.Y.S.2d at 877, 286 N.E.2d at 259. As the district court recognized, non-novel ideas do not constitute property. As a result, there can be no cause of action for unauthorized use of Murray's proposal since it was not unlawful for defendants to use a non-novel idea. We conclude therefore that the district court properly dismissed plaintiff's state law claims for breach of implied contract, misappropriation, conversion, and unjust enrichment. * * *

Lastly, we find that Judge Cederbaum correctly determined that plaintiff's claim for false designation of origin, see Lanham Act § 43(a), 15 U.S.C. § 1125(a), regarding the credits to The Cosby Show, cannot survive in light of the court's granting of summary judgment against plaintiff on the issue of novelty. Even assuming defendants used plaintiff's idea, NBC's failure to designate Murray as the creator of The Cosby Show does not mean that the credits to the program are false since ideas in the public domain may be used with impunity and thus do not require attribution.

* * *

Affirmed.

George C. Pratt, Circuit Judge, dissenting:

Today this court holds that the idea underlying what may well be the most successful situation comedy in television history was, in 1980, so unoriginal and so entrenched in the public domain that, as a matter of law, it did not constitute intellectual property protected under New York law. Because I am convinced that the novelty issue in this case presents a factual question subject to further discovery and ultimate scrutiny by a trier of fact, I respectfully dissent.

* * *

Novelty, by its very definition, is highly subjective. As fashion, advertising, and television and radio production can attest, what is novel today may not have been novel 15 years ago, and what is commonplace today may well be novel 15 years hence. In this instance, where Cosby expressed the concept almost a decade and a half before Murray submitted his proposal, where it was Murray's idea that NBC actually used, where there is no evidence indicating NBC knew anything of the program idea until Murray submitted it, * * * and where substantial conflicting evidence exists as to the "novelty" of the idea under New York law, there seems to be at least a triable issue.

The majority's decision prematurely denies Murray a fair opportunity to establish his right to participate in the enormous wealth generated by The Cosby Show. Accordingly, I would reverse the district court judgment and remand the case for further consideration.

LANDSBERG v. SCRABBLE CROSSWORD GAME PLAYERS, INC.

United States Court of Appeals, Ninth Circuit, 1986.
802 F.2d 1193.

Goodwin, Circuit Judge.

* * *

Plaintiff Mark Landsberg wrote a book on strategy for winning at the Scrabble board game. He contacted defendant Selchow & Righter Co. (S & R), the owner of the Scrabble trademark, to request permission to use the mark. In response, S & R requested a copy of the manuscript, which Landsberg provided. After prolonged negotiations between them regarding the possible publication by S & R of the manuscript were broken off, S & R brought out its own Scrabble strategy book. Landsberg sued S & R, its subsidiary Scrabble Crossword Game Players, Inc., Crown Publishers, Inc., the publishers of S & R's book, and several individual defendants in state court for copyright infringement and breach of contract. Defendants successfully removed under 28 U.S.C. § 1441(a) (1982). After a bench trial, the district court found that: S & R's book was based upon Landsberg's manuscript; the two works were substantially similar; defendant S & R had copied both the ideas and the form of expression of Landsberg's work; and that defendants had infringed Landsberg's rights. *Landsberg I* reversed the judgment for Landsberg on his copyright infringement claim because the S & R book lacked the degree of similarity required for infringement of a nonfiction work. *Landsberg I,* 736 F.2d at 489. We remanded for further proceedings on whether "circumstances and conduct manifesting the terms and existence of a contract precede[d] or attend[ed] disclosure of the idea." *Id.* Upon remand, the district court held a status conference and the parties submitted additional briefs. The court then made supplemental findings of fact and conclusions of law and entered judgment for plaintiff on his contract claim. Defendants now appeal from this judgment. We affirm.

* * *

Defendants' principal argument on appeal is that the idea which is the subject of the alleged implied-in-fact contract is that of a book about Scrabble strategy, and that the idea was disclosed in Landsberg's first letter to S & R. This argument treats the trial testimony regarding the distinction between ideas and their expression, which was central to the copyright claim, as determinative of the subject of the implied contract. The contract claim turns not upon the existence of a protectible property interest, however, but upon the implied promise to pay the reasonable value of the material disclosed. See Donahue v. Ziv Television Programs, Inc., 245 Cal.App.2d 593, 601, 54 Cal.Rptr. 130, 140 (1966). At issue is thus whether an implied contact was made, and whether defendants' use of the manuscript violated its terms. Landsberg's proprietary interest in the form of expression is irrelevant.

California law allows for recovery for the breach of an implied-in-fact contract when the recipient of a valuable idea accepts the information knowing that compensation is expected, and subsequently uses the idea without paying for it. Densy v. Wilder, 46 Cal.2d 715, 733, 299 P.2d 257, 267 (1956). If disclosure occurs before it is known that compensation is a condition of its use, however, no contract will be implied. *Id.* at 739, 299 P.2d 270. Thus, if Landsberg unconditionally disclosed his manuscript before informing S & R that he expected compensation for its use, his contract claim fails under California law.

* * *

In its supplemental findings, the district court found that Landsberg's initial disclosure of his manuscript was confidential and for the limited purpose of obtaining approval for the use of the Scrabble mark, and that given his expressed intention to exploit his manuscript commercially, defendants' use of any portion of it was conditioned on payment. It found, further, that the negotiations for the use of the manuscript by defendants show that Landsberg's belief that they would not use his manuscript without paying him for it was reasonable.

Defendants cite nothing in the record to suggest that these findings are incorrect. Instead, they rely upon their theory that the idea was simply that of a Scrabble strategy book, and that plaintiff blurted out that idea. This argument does not establish that the trial court was wrong. Landsberg disclosed the contents of his manuscript for a limited purpose that was made known to defendants. Defendants negotiated with him only long enough to produce a book based on his work without compensating him for his efforts. The district court's supplemental findings were not clearly erroneous.

NOTES

1. Compare the Court's approach in *Murray* and *Landsberg*. Was Landsberg's idea novel? If *Murray*'s idea had been novel, are there sufficient facts to imply an agreement by NBC to compensate? Even if *Murray*'s idea was not novel, did he contribute anything to NBC for which compensation should be paid? What of an individual who convinces a producer that the time is right to try an old idea?

2. Why can't one agree to pay compensation for the use of an idea which is not novel and new? If the cases are really based on a theory of contract rather than property, what is the role of a novelty requirement? Havighurst, The Right to Compensation for an Idea, 49 Nw.U.L.Rev. 295 (1954), offers this explanation:

> In a number of cases decided in favor of defendants in the earlier period, the lack of novelty of the idea was stressed as supporting the contention of the defendant that the idea was not used as the result of the plaintiff's submission. *Id.* at 306–07.

Would a simpler explanation be that it is reasonable to infer that the defendant would not agree to pay for the use of an idea which was already known?

3. Do you think the Cosby interview in 1965 was the determining factor in finding the Murray idea not novel?

4. What are the competing interests in cases involving the submission of an idea? If *Murray* had been decided differently, what advice would you give NBC for future dealing with persons with ideas? What advice would you give Murray if he comes up with another brainstorm?

5. What effect should *Landsberg I* have on *Landsberg II*? If the copyright claim is defeated, doesn't *Sears* and *Compco* prohibit common law relief? If you were told that copyright protects only the manner of expression of an idea and not the idea itself does that help clarify the distinction between the two cases?

PROBLEM

If a corporation requires anyone submitting an idea for consideration to accept in writing the following eight conditions is it adequately protected against additional liability? Are all the conditions necessary?

1. An idea must be submitted by its originator or his or her duly appointed attorney or agent.

2. An idea will be considered only on the understanding that its submission and the submission of any related material is not in confidence. No confidential or other unusual relationship may be established by or implied from the submission or our consideration of the idea or related material.

3. The corporation cannot and does not agree that the idea or any related material submitted will be kept a secret.

4. The corporation will give an idea only such consideration as it believes the idea merits, and no obligation is assumed other than to notify the submitter as to whether or not the company is interested in negotiating further for rights to the idea.

5. Receipt, or consideration of, or subsequent negotiation or offer with respect to any idea will be without prejudice to us. This includes, without limitation, our rights to contest the validity of any existing or future patent on the idea. Furthermore, and also without limitation, receipt or consideration of, or negotiation or offer on an idea, shall not be deemed an admission of the novelty or patentability of the idea, or of priority or originality on the part of the submitter or any other person.

6. We cannot consider any idea on condition that we shall return any material submitted.

7. If your idea is patented, and of interest to us, negotiations may be entered into. In the event that no agreement is concluded the submitter shall rely solely upon such rights as he may have under United States Patent Laws.

8. Where your idea is not patented, in the event the idea proves new, and the corporation uses it, the company agrees to pay and you agree to accept the sum of One Thousand Dollars ($1,000.00) for all rights to such idea. However, if any such unpatented idea shall later be covered by a patent, the foregoing provisions of this paragraph shall not apply to any rights under the patent, and the submitter shall thereafter rely solely upon such rights as he may have under United States Patent Laws.

See Sylvania Electric Prods., Inc. v. Brainerd, 166 U.S.P.Q. 387 (D.C.Mass. 1970).

(2) PUBLISHED AND UNPUBLISHED WORKS

(A) COMMON LAW COPYRIGHT

Prior to the revision of the Copyright Act in 1976, the doctrines of "common-law copyright" protected "unpublished" works. As a general proposition the author of a work had the right of first publication, and until he exercised that right the common law protected him from tortious misappropriations. Once the work was published, common law rights were divested and the author was forced to look to federal statutory copyright law for protection. And conveniently enough, federal copyright protection commenced when a work was published with a proper notice of copyright attached. Justice Black in *Sears* and *Compco* suggested that the existence of federal copyright protection for published works preempted any comparable protection of such works by state law. Section 2 of the 1909 Copyright Act specifically preserved state protection of unpublished works.

This deceptively simple allocation of power between state and federal law was considerably more complex in practice. First, section 12 of the 1909 Act gave authors of most types of works other than books, an option to obtain statutory protection prior to publication by depositing a complete copy of the work with the copyright office. Second, there was no requirement that publication sufficient to *divest* common law rights be construed to mean the same thing as publication to *invest* statutory copyright. Indeed, it was unclear whether publication was to be defined by state or federal law. Third, the dividing line between a published and an unpublished work was a murky one indeed. Some kinds of works can be exploited without reproduction in copies— generally by display or performance. Should the display of a painting or the performance of a play be sufficient publication to divest common law rights?

The difficulties were considerably complicated by the invention, in White v. Kimmell, 94 F.Supp. 502 (S.D.Calif.1950), reversed on other grounds 193 F.2d 744 (9th Cir.1952), of the self-contradictory doctrine of limited publication—a doctrine that a publication, if sufficiently limited, is not a publication. The courts applied themselves with energy to the task of separating general from limited publications.

King v. Mister Maestro, Inc., 224 F.Supp. 101 (S.D.N.Y.1963) is illustrative. Martin Luther King distributed an advanced text of his "I Have A Dream" speech to the press. As part of the news coverage some newspapers printed all or excerpts from the speech. The New York Post offered for sale reprints to the public. The speech was also recorded on a newsreel from which records of the speech were made and sold to the public. Dr. King did not consent to either the sale of reprints or records, and sought an injunction prohibiting the sale of unauthorized reprints or records. The issue as framed by the court was whether there had been a general publication of the speech so as to place it in the public domain.

> The word "general" with respect to publication in this sense is of greatest significance. There can be a limited publication, which is a communication of the work to others under circumstances showing no dedication of the work to the public. A general publication is one which shows a dedication to the public so as to lose copyright. The public exhibition of a painting without notice of copyright in a gallery the rules of which forbade copying is not a general publication. * * *

> The public performance of a play is not a general publication. * * *

> The public delivery of lectures on [the subject of] a memory system is not a general publication. * * *

The playing of a song in public is not a general publication of the work. * * *

The broadcast by radio of a script is not a general publication thereof. * * *

* * *

Defendants stress the delivery without copyright notice of an advance text of his speech and the distribution of it to the press. But within the concept of publication just examined, it is clear that this was a limited, as opposed to a general, publication. There is nothing to suggest that copies of the speech were ever offered to the public; the fact is clear that the "advance text" was given to the press only.

(B) THE COPYRIGHT REVISION OF 1976

The general revision of the copyright law of 1976 became effective on January 1, 1978. The Act abandoned the concept of publication as the demarcation between state and federal law. Section 102 announces that federal copyright law "subsists" in original works "fixed in any tangible means of expression." Thus, for example, a manuscript or other written work is protected by federal copyright law from the instant it is fixed on paper. The filing of an application for registration or other acts by the author are not required as a precondition to protection. Thus, at least for those works that are within the subject matter capable of being copyrighted (§ 102), common law copyright is no longer relevant. Furthermore, § 301 preempts all "legal or equitable rights that are equivalent to any of the exclusive rights within the general scope of copyright * * *" derived from the common law or statutes of any state. The section applies to works created before or after January 1, 1978. The implications and ambiguities of § 301 will be considered *infra*.

(3) A CASE STUDY OF FEDERAL–STATE CONFLICTS: MUSICAL PERFORMANCES

There are three separate interests embodied in a recording of a musical composition: the composer's, the performer's, and the recording company's. Prior to October, 1971, the Copyright Act provided protection only to the composer's interest by authorizing him to copyright the sheet music. The Act provided no protection for the sound of a performance embodied in a record or other device from which it could be reproduced. This was partly the result of White-Smith Music Pub. Co. v. Apollo Co., 209 U.S. 1 (1908). That case held that a player piano roll was not a "copy" in the technical copyright sense, and hence not an infringement of copyrighted sheet music. The 1909 Act in § 101(e), 17 U.S.C.A. § 101(e), reversed the narrow holding of *Apollo*, providing that a recording infringes copyrighted sheet music.

However, the Act also provided that once a composer authorized the recording of his composition by one person, he was obliged to allow others to record the composition on payment of 2 cents a record. The Act did not provide protection for the performer or the recording company who were forced to look to common law for a remedy against appropriation. This set the stage for a creative duel between the state courts, sensitive to the apparent unjust enrichment by those who appropriated another's work, and the federal courts, led by Judge Learned Hand, who sought to preserve the supremacy of the federal copyright and patent systems and to limit economic monopolies over creative works. The major skirmishes are outlined below:

NOTES

1. In a famous trilogy, the Second Circuit and the state courts struggled with the protection of performances. In Waring v. WDAS Broadcasting Station, Inc., 327 Pa. 433, 194 A. 631 (1937), the Pennsylvania Supreme Court held that Fred Waring was entitled to an injunction preventing the broadcast by a radio station of a recording made by Waring's orchestra and sold with a label which read: "not licensed for radio broadcast." The court enforced the limitation on the label and cited *INS* as an independent ground for the decision. Three years later in RCA Mfg. Co. v. Whiteman, 114 F.2d 86 (2d Cir.1940), cert. denied 311 U.S. 712 (1940) Judge Hand, on facts similar to *Waring,* found for the defendant on the theory that sale of the records was a general publication of the performance and to allow state law protection would be "contrary to the whole policy of the Copyright Act and of the Constitution." Although *Whiteman* was decided after *Erie* there was little New York law in conflict with Hand's view. However in Metropolitan Opera Ass'n v. Wagner-Nichols Recorder Corp., 199 Misc. 786, 101 N.Y.S.2d 483 (1950), a case again involving facts similar to *Waring* and *Whiteman,* the state courts held as a matter of *state* law that the performances were not "general publications" divesting common-law rights. *INS* was also asserted as the law of New York. In Capitol Records, Inc. v. Mercury Records, 221 F.2d 657 (2d Cir.1955), another performance appropriation case, a majority, pursuant to its *Erie* obligations, applied the New York law of misappropriation modeled after *INS* to grant recovery to the plaintiff.

Judge Hand, however, was not to be so easily converted. In dissent, he argued that whether a work was "published" must be a question of federal not state law and once a work is published it can be freely copied unless protected by copyright. In language unquestionably the forerunner of *Sears* and *Compco,* Hand argued:

> [If the states are free to determine what constitutes publication] they could grant to an author a perpetual monopoly, although he exploited the "work" with all the freedom he would have enjoyed, had it been copyrighted. I cannot believe that the failure of Congress to include within the Act all that the Clause covers should give the states so wide a power. To do so would pro tanto defeat the overriding purpose of the Clause, which was to grant only for "limited Times" the untrammelled exploitation of an author's "Writings." Either he must be content with such circumscribed exploitation as does not constitute "publication," or he must eventually dedicate his "work" to the public. The situation is no different from that of patents, where such bilateral character of the grant is a commonplace. I would hold that the clause has that much effect ex proprio vigore; and that the states are not free to follow their own notions as to when an author's right shall be

unlimited both in user and in duration. Such power of course they have as to "works" that are not "Writings"; but I submit that, once it is settled that a "work" is in that class, the Clause enforces upon the author the choice I have just mentioned; and, if so, it must follow that it is a federal question whether he has published the "work."

2. Federal supremacy was reasserted in *Sears* and *Compco*. Do these cases mandate that "publication" be defined by federal law? Could a state protect performances after *Sears* and *Compco*? In Capitol Records, Inc. v. Greatest Records, Inc., 43 Misc.2d 878, 252 N.Y.S.2d 553 (1964), decided after *Sears* and *Compco*, a temporary injunction was granted against a defendant who made "counterfeit" records of performances of "The Beatles" from Capitol's albums and marketed them at a retail price significantly lower than the Capitol album. *Sears* and *Compco* were distinguished on the basis that they dealt with acts of "imitation" and did not prevent state law protection against "unauthorized appropriation, reproduction or duplication of the actual performances. * * * Actually, what was here done was not the copying of some article or goods made and sold by another but rather *the appropriation* of the very product itself. * * *"

3. Tape and record piracy became a national issue and many states enacted penal statutes prohibiting the activity. These statutes were generally upheld by lower courts. Tape Industries Assoc. v. Younger, 316 F.Supp. 340 (C.D.Cal.1970). In spite of their successes in the lower courts, the record manufacturers continued to seek statutory copyright protection largely because the common law provided recovery only against the "pirate"—who is usually impossible to find and insolvent when found—while the copyright act provided potent remedies against distributors and retailers. When in 1971 the Copyright Revision Bill appeared hopelessly stalled in Congress, copyright protection was extended to sound recordings by Public Law 92–140, an amendment to the 1909 Act. The amendment applied only to sound recordings made after the effective date of the act and before January 1, 1975.

GOLDSTEIN v. CALIFORNIA
412 U.S. 546, 93 S.Ct. 2303, 37 L.Ed.2d 163 (1973).

MR. CHIEF JUSTICE BURGER delivered the opinion of the Court.

We granted certiorari to review petitioners' conviction under a California statute making it a criminal offense to "pirate" recordings produced by others.

In 1971, an information was filed by the State of California, charging petitioners in 140 counts with violating § 653h of the California Penal Code. The information charged that, between April 1970 and March 1971, petitioners had copied several musical performances from commercially sold recordings without the permission of the owner of the master record or tape.[1] Petitioners moved to dismiss the complaint

---

1. In pertinent part, the California statute provides:

"(a) Every person is guilty of a misdemeanor who:

"(1) Knowingly and willfully transfers or causes to be transferred any sounds recorded on a phonograph record,

* * * tape, * * * or other article on which sounds are recorded, with intent to sell or cause to be sold, * * * such article on which such sounds are so transferred, without the consent of the owner.

"(2) * * *

on the grounds that § 653h was in conflict with Art. I, § 8, cl. 8, of the Constitution, the "Copyright Clause," and the federal statutes enacted thereunder. Upon denial of their motion, petitioners entered pleas of *nolo contendere* to 10 of the 140 counts; the remaining counts were dismissed. On appeal, the Appellate Department of the California Superior Court sustained the validity of the statute. After exhausting other state appellate remedies, petitioners sought review in this Court.

I

Petitioners were engaged in what has commonly been called "record piracy" or "tape piracy"—the unauthorized duplication of recordings of performances by major musical artists. Petitioners would purchase from a retail distributor a single tape or phonograph recording of the popular performances they wished to duplicate. The original recordings were produced and marketed by recording companies with which petitioners had no contractual relationship. At petitioners' plant, the recording was reproduced on blank tapes, which could in turn be used to replay the music on a tape player. The tape was then wound on a cartridge. A label was attached, stating the title of the recorded performance—the same title as had appeared on the original recording, and the name of the performing artists. After final packaging, the tapes were distributed to retail outlets for sale to the public, in competition with those petitioners had copied.

Petitioners made no payments to the artists whose performances they reproduced and sold, or to the various trust funds established for their benefit; no payments were made to the producer, technicians, or other staff personnel responsible for producing the original recording and paying the large expenses incurred in production. No payments were made for the use of the artists' names or the album title.

The challenged California statute forbids petitioners to transfer any performance fixed on a tape or record onto other records or tapes with the intention of selling the duplicates, unless they have first received permission from those who, under state law, are the owners of the master recording. Although the protection afforded to each master recording is substantial, lasting for an unlimited time, the scope of the proscribed activities is narrow. No limitation is placed on the use of the music, lyrics, or arrangement employed in making the master

* * *

"(b) As used in this section, 'person' means any individual, partnership, corporation or association; and 'owner' means the person who owns the master phonograph record, * * * master tape, * * * or other device used for reproducing recorded sounds on phonograph records, * * * tapes, * * * or other articles on which sound is recorded, and from which the transferred recorded sounds are directly or indirectly derived."

Specifically, each count of the information alleged that, in regard to a particular recording, petitioners had, "at and in the City of Los Angeles, in the County of Los Angeles, State of California * * * wilfully, unlawfully and knowingly transferred and caused to be transferred sounds recorded on a tape with the intent to sell and cause to be sold, such tape on which such sounds [were] so transferred * * *."

recording. Petitioners are not precluded from hiring their own musicians and artists and recording an exact imitation of the performance embodied on the master recording. Petitioners are even free to hire the same artists who made the initial recording in order to duplicate the performance. In essence, the statute thus provides copyright protection solely for the specific expressions which compose the master record or tape.

Petitioners' attack on the constitutionality of § 653h has many facets. First, they contend that the statute establishes a state copyright of unlimited duration, and thus conflicts with Art. I, § 8, cl. 8, of the Constitution. Second, petitioners claim that the state statute interferes with the implementation of federal policies inherent in the federal copyright statutes. 17 U.S.C. §§ 1 et seq. According to petitioners, it was the intention of Congress, as interpreted by this Court in Sears, Roebuck & Co. v. Stiffel Co., 376 U.S. 225 (1964), and Compco Corp. v. Day-Brite Lighting, 376 U.S. 234 (1964), to establish a uniform law throughout the United States to protect original writings. As part of the federal scheme, it is urged that Congress intended to allow individuals to copy any work which was not protected by a federal copyright. Since § 653h effectively prohibits the copying of works which are not entitled to federal protection, petitioners contend that it conflicts directly with congressional policy and must fall under the Supremacy Clause of the Constitution. Finally, petitioners argue that 17 U.S.C. § 2, which allows States to protect unpublished writings, does not authorize the challenged state provision; since the records which petitioners copied had previously been released to the public, petitioners contend that they had, under federal law, been published.

[The Court held the 1971 amendments to the Copyright Act conferring copyright protection to sound recordings did not apply to this case.]

II

Petitioners' first argument rests on the premise that the state statute under which they were convicted lies beyond the powers which the States reserved in our federal system. If this is correct, petitioners must prevail, since the States cannot exercise a sovereign power which, under the Constitution, they have relinquished to the Federal Government for its exclusive exercise.

* * *

[The Court sets out to determine whether concurrent exercise of power by the states "will necessarily" lead to conflict with federal law sufficient to infer an intent on the part of the drafters to grant exclusive jurisdiction to Congress.]

Article I, § 8, cl. 8, of the Constitution gives to Congress the power—

"To promote the Progress of Science and useful Arts, by securing for limited Times to Authors and Inventors the exclusive Right to their respective Writings and Discoveries * * *."

The clause thus describes both the objective which Congress may seek and the means to achieve it. The objective is to promote the progress of science and the arts. As employed, the terms "to promote" are synonymous with the words "to stimulate," "to encourage," or "to induce." To accomplish its purpose, Congress may grant to authors the exclusive right to the fruits of their respective works. An author who possesses an unlimited copyright may preclude others from copying this creation for commercial purposes without permission. In other words, to encourage people to devote themselves to intellectual and artistic creation, Congress may guarantee to authors and inventors a reward in the form of control over the sale or commercial use of copies of their works.

The objective of the Copyright Clause was clearly to facilitate the granting of rights national in scope. While the debates on the clause at the Constitutional Convention were extremely limited, its purpose was described by James Madison in the Federalist:

> "The utility of this power will scarcely be questioned. The copyright of authors has been solemnly adjudged, in Great Britain, to be a right of common law. The right to useful inventions seems with equal reason to belong to the inventors. The public good fully coincides in both cases with the claims of individuals. The States cannot separately make effectual provision for either of the cases, and most of them have anticipated the decision of this point, by laws passed at the instance of Congress." [11]

The difficulty noted by Madison relates to the burden placed on an author or inventor who wishes to achieve protection in all States when no federal system of protection is available. To do so, a separate application is required to each state government; the right which in turn may be granted has effect only within the granting State's borders. The national system which Madison supported eliminates the need for multiple applications and the expense and difficulty involved. In effect, it allows Congress to provide a reward greater in scope than any particular State may grant to promote progress in those fields which Congress determines are worthy of national action.

Although the Copyright Clause thus recognizes the potential benefits of a national system, it does not indicate that all writings are of national interest or that state legislation is, in all cases, unnecessary or precluded. The patents granted by the States in the 18th century show, to the contrary, a willingness on the part of the States to promote those portions of science and the arts which were of local importance. Whatever the diversity of people's backgrounds, origins, and interests, and whatever the variety of business and industry in the 13 Colonies,

11. The Federalist No. 43, p. 309 (B. Wright ed. 1961).

the range of diversity is obviously far greater today in a country of 210 million people in 50 States. In view of that enormous diversity, it is unlikely that all citizens in all parts of the country place the same importance on works relating to all subjects. Since the subject matter to which the Copyright Clause is addressed may thus be of purely local importance and not worthy of national attention or protection, we cannot discern such an unyielding national interest as to require an inference that state power to grant copyrights has been relinquished to *exclusive* federal control.

The question to which we next turn is whether, in actual operation, the exercise of the power to grant copyrights by some States will prejudice the interests of other States. As we have noted, a copyright granted by a particular State has effect only within its boundaries. If one State grants such protection, the interests of States which do not are not prejudiced since their citizens remain free to copy within their borders those works which may be protected elsewhere. The interests of a State which grants copyright protection may, however, be adversely affected by other States that do not; individuals who wish to purchase a copy of a work protected in their own State will be able to buy unauthorized copies in other States where no protection exists. However, this conflict is neither so inevitable nor so severe as to compel the conclusion, that state power has been relinquished to the exclusive jurisdiction of the Congress. Obviously when some States do not grant copyright protection—and most do not—that circumstance reduces the economic value of a state copyright, but it will hardly render the copyright worthless. The situation is no different from that which may arise in regard to other state monopolies, such as a state lottery, or a food concession in a limited enclosure like a state park; in each case, citizens may escape the effect of one State's monopoly by making purchases in another area or another State. Similarly, in the case of state copyrights, except as to individuals willing to travel across state lines in order to purchase records or other writings protected in their own State, each State's copyrights will still serve to induce new artistic creations within that State—the very objective of the grant of protection. We do not see here the type of prejudicial conflicts which would arise, for example, if each State exercised a sovereign power to impose imposts and tariffs; nor can we discern a need for uniformity such as that which may apply to the regulation of interstate shipments.

Similarly, it is difficult to see how the concurrent exercise of the power to grant copyrights by Congress and the States will necessarily and inevitably lead to difficulty. At any time Congress determines that a particular category of "writing" is worthy of national protection and the incidental expenses of federal administration, federal copyright protection may be authorized. Where the need for free and unrestricted distribution of a writing is thought to be required by the national interest, the Copyright Clause and the Commerce Clause would allow Congress to eschew all protection. In such cases, a conflict would develop if a State attempted to protect that which Congress intended to be free from restraint or to free that which Congress had protected. However, where Congress determines that neither federal protection nor freedom from restraint is required by the national interest, it is at liberty to stay its hand entirely. Since state protection would not then conflict with federal action, total relinquishment of the States' power to grant copyright protection cannot be inferred.

As we have seen, the language of the Constitution neither explicitly precludes the States from granting copyrights nor grants such authority exclusively to the Federal Government. The subject matter to which the Copyright Clause is addressed may at times be of purely local concern. No conflict will necessarily arise from a lack of uniform state regulation, nor will the interest of one State be significantly prejudiced by the actions of another. No reason exists why Congress must take affirmative action either to authorize protection of all categories of writings or to free them from all restraint. We therefor conclude that, under the Constitution, the States have not relinquished all power to grant to authors "the exclusive Right to their respective Writings."

B

Petitioners base an additional argument on the language of the Constitution. The California statute forbids individuals to appropriate recordings at any time after release. From this, petitioners argue that the State has created a copyright of *unlimited* duration, in violation of that portion of Art. I, § 8, cl. 8, which provides that copyrights may only be granted "for limited Times." Read literally, the text of Art. I does not support petitioners' position. Section 8 enumerates those powers which have been granted *to Congress*. Whatever limitations have been appended to such powers can only be understood as a limit on congressional, and not state, action. Moreover, it is not clear that the dangers to which this limitation was addressed apply with equal force to both the Federal Government and the States. When Congress grants an exclusive right or monopoly, its effects are pervasive; no citizen or State may escape its reach. As we have noted, however, the exclusive right granted by a State is confined to its borders. Consequently, even when the right is unlimited in duration, any tendency to inhibit further progress in science or the arts is narrowly circumscribed. The challenged statute cannot be voided for lack of a durational limitation.

III

Our conclusion that California did not surrender its power to issue copyrights does not end the inquiry. We must proceed to determine whether the challenged state statute is void under the Supremacy Clause. * * *

By Art. I, § 8, cl. 8, of the Constitution, the States granted to Congress the power to protect the "Writings" of "Authors." These terms have not been construed in their narrow literal sense but, rather, with the reach necessary to reflect the broad scope of constitutional principles. While an "author" may be viewed as an individual who writes an original composition, the term, in its constitutional sense, has been construed to mean an "originator," "he to whom anything owes its origin." Burrow-Giles Lithographic Co. v. Sarony, 111 U.S. 53, 58 (1884). Similarly, although the word "writings" might be limited to script or printed material, it may be interpreted to include any physical rendering of the fruits of creative intellectual or aesthetic labor. Ibid.; Trade-Mark Cases, 100 U.S. 82, 94 (1879). Thus, recordings of artistic performances may be within the reach of Clause 8.

While the area in which Congress *may* act is broad, the enabling provision of Clause 8 does not require that Congress act in regard to all categories of materials which meet the constitutional definitions. Rather, whether any specific category of "Writings" is to be brought within the purview of the federal statutory scheme is left to the discretion of the Congress. The history of federal copyright statutes indicates that the congressional determination to consider specific classes of writings is dependent, not only on the character of the writing, but also on the commercial importance of the product to the national economy. As our technology has expanded the means available for creative activity and has provided economical means for reproducing manifestations of such activity, new areas of federal protection have been initiated.

* * *

Sears and *Compco,* on which petitioners rely, do not support their position. In those cases, the question was whether a State could, under principles of a state unfair competition law, preclude the copying of mechanical configurations which did not possess the qualities required for the granting of a federal design or mechanical patent. * * *

In regard to mechanical configurations, Congress had balanced the need to encourage innovation and originality of invention against the need to insure competition in the sale of identical or substantially identical products. The standards established for granting federal patent protection to machines thus indicated not only which articles in this particular category Congress wished to protect, but which configurations it wished to remain free. The application of state law in these cases to prevent the copying of articles which did not meet the requirements for federal protection disturbed the careful balance which Congress had drawn and thereby necessarily gave way under the Supremacy Clause of the Constitution. No comparable conflict between state law and federal law arises in the case of recordings of musical performances. In regard to this category of "Writings," Congress has drawn no balance; rather, it has left the area unattended, and no reason exists why the State should not be free to act.[28]

28. Petitioners place great stress on their belief that the records or tapes which they copied had been "published." We have no need to determine whether, *under state law,* these recordings had been published or what legal consequences such

IV

More than 50 years ago, Mr. Justice Brandeis observed in dissent in International News Service v. Associated Press:

"The general rule of law is, that the noblest of human productions—knowledge, truths ascertained, conceptions, and ideas—become, after voluntary communication to others, free as the air to common use." 248 U.S. 215, 250 (1918).

But there is no fixed, immutable line to tell us which "human productions" are private property and which are so general as to become "free as the air." In earlier times, a performing artist's work was largely restricted to the stage; once performed, it remained "recorded" only in the memory of those who had seen or heard it. Today, we can record that performance in precise detail and reproduce it again and again with utmost fidelity. The California statutory scheme evidences a legislative policy to prohibit "tape piracy" and "record piracy," conduct that may adversely affect the continued production of new recordings, a large industry in California. Accordingly, the State has, by statute, given to recordings the attributes of property. No restraint has been placed on the use of an idea or concept; rather, petitioners and other individuals remain free to record the same compositions in precisely the same manner and with the same personnel as appeared on the original recording.

* * *

We conclude that the State of California has exercised a power which it retained under the Constitution, and that the challenged statute, as applied in this case, does not intrude into an area which Congress has, up to now, preempted. Until and unless Congress takes further action with respect to recordings fixed prior to February 15, 1972, the California statute may be enforced against acts of piracy such as those which occurred in the present case.

Affirmed.

MR. JUSTICE DOUGLAS, with whom MR. JUSTICE BRENNAN and MR. JUSTICE BLACKMUN concur, dissenting.

* * *

California's law promotes monopoly; the federal policy promotes monopoly only when a copyright is issued, and it fosters competition in all other instances. Moreover, federal law limits its monopoly to 28 years plus a like renewal period, while California extends her monopoly into perpetuity.

Cases like *Sears* were surcharged with "unfair competition" and the present one with "pirated recordings." But free access to products

publication might have. *For purposes of federal law,* "publication" serves only as a term of the art which defines the legal relationships which Congress has adopted under the federal copyright statutes. As to categories of writings which Congress has not brought within the scope of the federal statute, the term has no application.

on the market is the consumer interest protected by the failure of Congress to extend patents or copyrights into various areas. * * *

I would reverse the judgment below.

MR. JUSTICE MARSHALL, with whom MR. JUSTICE BRENNAN and MR. JUSTICE BLACKMUN join, dissenting.

NOTES

1. Can you construct an outline of the permissible areas of state concern which is consistent with *Sears, Compco* and *Goldstein*? Are sound recordings subject matter which Congress has left completely unattended? Or is the compulsory license provision for musical compositions evidence that Congress considered the full range of problems associated with recorded music? Has Congress attended more carefully to lamp designs or sound recordings?

2. Does Chief Justice Burger adequately evaluate the various economic interests to determine the impact of state protection on a national copyright policy? He suggests that the owner of the sound recording does not receive much of a monopoly because it is limited by state boundaries. Should the interference with the economic interests of the "pirate" caused by a diverse state law system be considered? Are consumer's interests considered?

3. Is the pejorative term "pirate" as applied in *Goldstein* equally applicable in the following situations:

(a) a law student tapes a professor's lecture, reduces it to written form and sells it to other students.

(b) a student borrows his friend's copy of a popular sound recording and tapes it for his personal use.

(c) a Justice of the United States Supreme Court borrows his colleague's copy of the Virginia Law Review and photocopies an article for use in writing an opinion.

(d) a cable television company carries a televised broadcast of a live sporting event.

4. Is there a "national policy" emanating from the "limited times" provision, that works be dedicated to the public? Is this policy compromised by *Goldstein*?

5. Are you as certain as Chief Justice Burger that there is more diversity in intellectual and aesthetic tastes now than there was 200 years ago?

6. Early cable television cases were based on assertions of state misappropriation law. In Intermountain Broadcasting & Television Corp. v. Idaho Microwave, Inc., 196 F.Supp. 315 (D.Idaho 1961) the court refused to apply *INS* in a suit by a Salt Lake City plaintiff whose television broadcasts were transmitted by a cable company to Twin Falls, Idaho, an area outside the plaintiff's broadcast area, on the theory that *INS* required competition between the parties. The same court, however, found in favor of a Twin Falls station who competed with the cable company and who had an exclusive contract with the networks on the theory that the cable's transmission of broadcasts originating in Salt Lake was a tortious interference with the contract rights of the plaintiff. Cable Vision, Inc. v. KUTV, Inc., 211 F.Supp. 47 (D.Idaho 1962). On appeal, the Ninth Circuit reversed based on the intervening decisions of *Sears* and *Compco*. Cable Vision, Inc. v. KUTV, Inc., 335 F.2d 348 (9th Cir.1964), cert. denied 379 U.S. 989 (1964). Thereafter, the United States Supreme Court held

that the Federal Communications Commission had authority to regulate CATV at least where the regulations were "reasonably ancillary to the effective performance of the Commission's various responsibilities for the regulation of television broadcasting." United States v. Southwestern Cable Co., 392 U.S. 157 (1968).

7. In contrast to the CATV cases, there is precedent distinguishing between a "reproduction" and a "recreation". In Loeb v. Turner, 257 S.W.2d 800 (Tex.Civ.App.1953) a Dallas radio station assigned an agent to listen to the plaintiff's broadcast of a stock car race in Phoenix and to transmit the bare facts by long distance telephone to Dallas. In Dallas, the information was given to A.L. Turner "a talented and experienced announcer" who recreated a description of the race over the Dallas radio station as though he were present at the race. The court held that once the news was published by broadcast in Phoenix plaintiff was free to use it to recreate the description of the race. But see, National Exhibition Co. v. Fass, 143 N.Y.S.2d 767 (1955) where the defendant was enjoined and held to account for profits for listening to authorized broadcasts of the New York Giants games from the Polo Grounds and distributing the facts to radio stations for simultaneous "recreated radio broadcasts of the games." To what extent do these cases survive *Sears, Compco,* and *Goldstein?*

8. For an article critical of the craftsmanship of the *Goldstein* opinion see Abrams & Abrams, Goldstein v. California: Sound, Fury, and Significance, 1975 Sup.Ct.Rev. 147 which evaluates the case as it relates to preemption cases generally as well as to copyright and patent issues. See also, Brown, Publication and Preemption in Copyright Law: Elegiac Reflections on Goldstein v. California, 22 U.C.L.A.L.Rev. 1022 (1975).

COPYRIGHT ACT OF 1976, 17 U.S.C. § 301 *

§ 301. Preemption with respect to other laws

(a) On and after January 1, 1978, all legal or equitable rights that are equivalent to any of the exclusive rights within the general scope of copyright as specified by section 106 in works of authorship that are fixed in a tangible medium of expression and come within the subject matter of copyright as specified by sections 102 and 103, whether created before or after that date and whether published or unpublished, are governed exclusively by this title. Thereafter, no person is entitled to any such right or equivalent right in any such work under the common law or statutes of any State.

(b) Nothing in this title annuls or limits any rights or remedies under the common law or statutes of any State with respect to—

> (1) subject matter that does not come within the subject matter of copyright as specified by sections 102 and 103, including works of authorship not fixed in any tangible medium of expression; or

* In 1988 Congress amended § 301 by adding a new subsection (e) which reads: "(e) The scope of Federal preemption under this section is not affected by the adherence of the United States to the Berne Convention or the satisfaction of obligations of the United States thereunder." Pub.L. 100–568 (Oct. 31, 1988). See p. 569 for a discussion of U.S. adherence to Berne.

(2) any cause of action arising from undertakings commenced before January 1, 1978; or

(3) activities violating legal or equitable rights that are not equivalent to any of the exclusive rights within the general scope of copyright as specified by section 106.

(c) With respect to sound recordings fixed before February 15, 1972, any rights or remedies under the common law or statutes of any State shall not be annulled or limited by this title until February 15, 2047. The preemptive provisions of subsection (a) shall apply to any such rights and remedies pertaining to any cause of action arising from undertakings commenced on and after February 15, 2047. Notwithstanding the provisions of section 303, no sound recording fixed before February 15, 1972, shall be subject to copyright under this title before, on, or after February 15, 2047.

(d) Nothing in this title annuls or limits any rights or remedies under any other Federal statute.

S. 22, 94TH CONG., 2D SESS. § 301 (1976)

§ 301. Preemption with respect to other laws †

* * *

(b) Nothing in this title annuls or limits any rights or remedies under the common law or statutes of any State with respect to—

* * *

(3) activities violating legal or equitable rights that are not equivalent to any of the exclusive rights within the general scope of copyright as specified by section 106, including rights against misappropriation not equivalent to any of such exclusive rights, breaches of contract, breaches of trust, trespass, conversion, invasion of privacy, defamation, and deceptive trade practices such as passing off and false representation.

* * *

HOUSE COMM. ON THE JUDICIARY, COPYRIGHT LAW REVISION, H.R.REP. NO. 94–1476, 94TH CONG., 2D SESS. AT 132 (1976)

[The following excerpt from the report relates to the version of § 301 contained in S. 22 above.]

The examples in clause (3), while not exhaustive, are intended to illustrate rights and remedies that are different in nature from the rights comprised in a copyright and that may continue to be protected under State common law or statute. The evolving common law rights of "privacy," "publicity," and trade secrets, and the general laws of defamation and fraud, would remain unaffected as long as the causes of action contain elements, such as an invasion of personal rights or a

† The omitted subsections are identical
to the section as finally enacted—ed.

breach of trust or confidentiality, that are different in kind from copyright infringement. Nothing in the bill derogates from the rights of parties to contract with each other and to sue for breaches of contract; however, to the extent that the unfair competition concept known as "interference with contract relations" is merely the equivalent of copyright protection, it would be preempted.

The last example listed in clause (3)—"deceptive trade practices such as passing off and false representation"—represents an effort to distinguish between those causes of action known as "unfair competition" that the copyright statute is not intended to preempt and those that it is. Section 301 is not intended to preempt common law protection in cases involving activities such as false labeling, fraudulent representation, and passing off even where the subject matter involved comes within the scope of the copyright statute.

"Misappropriation" is not necessarily synonymous with copyright infringement, and thus a cause of action labeled as "misappropriation" is not preempted if it is in fact based neither on a right within the general scope of copyright as specified by section 106 nor on a right equivalent thereto. For example, state law should have the flexibility to afford a remedy (under traditional principles of equity) against a consistent pattern of unauthorized appropriation by a competitor of the facts (i.e., not the literary expression) constituting "hot" news, whether in the traditional mold of International News Service v. Associated Press, 248 U.S. 215 (1918), or in the newer form of data updates from scientific, business, or financial data bases. Likewise, a person having no trust or other relationship with the proprietor of a computerized data base should not be immunized from sanctions against electronically or cryptographically breaching the proprietor's security arrangements and accessing the proprietor's data. The unauthorized data access which should be remediable might also be achieved by the intentional interception of data transmissions by wire, microwave or laser transmissions, or by the common unintentional means of "crossed" telephone lines occasioned by errors in switching.

122 CONGRESSIONAL RECORD H. 10910
(Daily Ed. Sept. 22, 1976).

[The following debate was on Mr. Seiberling's amendment, ultimately adopted, which removed the examples from § 301(b)(3). The views of the Department of Justice, referred to in the debate, were contained in a letter to Senator Hugh Scott from Assistant Attorney General Thomas Kauper and printed at 122 Cong.Rec. S. 2042 (daily ed. Feb. 19, 1976). The Department argued against including "misappropriation" in the list of examples because the doctrine was "highly anticompetitive" and its inclusion would "defeat the underlying purpose of the preemption section."]

MR. SEIBERLING. Mr. Chairman, my amendment is intended to save the "Federal preemption" of State law section, which is section 301 of the bill, from being inadvertently nullified because of the inclusion of certain examples in the exemptions from preemption.

This amendment would simply strike the examples listed in section 301(b)(3).

The amendment is strongly supported by the Justice Department, which believes that it would be a serious mistake to cite as an exemption from preemption the doctrine of "misappropriation." The doctrine was created by the Supreme Court in 1922, and it has generally been ignored by the Supreme Court itself and by the lower courts ever since.

Inclusion of a reference to the misappropriation doctrine in this bill, however, could easily be construed by the courts as authorizing the States to pass misappropriation laws. We should not approve such enabling legislation, because a misappropriation law could be so broad as to render the preemption section meaningless.

* * *

MR. RAILSBACK. Mr. Chairman, may I ask the gentleman from Ohio, for the purpose of clarifying the amendment that by striking the word "misappropriation," the gentleman in no way is attempting to change the existing state of the law, that is as it may exist in certain States that have recognized the right of recovery relating to "misappropriation"; is that correct?

MR. SEIBERLING. That is correct. All I am trying to do is prevent the citing of them as examples in a statute. We are, in effect, adopting a rather amorphous body of State law and codifying it, in effect. Rather I am trying to have this bill leave the State law alone and make it clear we are merely dealing with copyright laws, laws applicable to copyrights.

MR. RAILSBACK. Mr. Chairman, I personally have no objection to the gentleman's amendment in view of that clarification and I know of no objections from this side.

* * *

MR. KASTENMEIER. Mr. Chairman, I too have examined the gentleman's amendment and was familiar with the position of the Department of Justice. Unfortunately, the Justice Department did not make its position known to the committee until the last day of markup.

MR. SEIBERLING. I understand.

MR. KASTENMEIER. However, Mr. Chairman, I think that the amendment the gentleman is offering is consistent with the position of the Justice Department and accept it on this side as well.

MR. SEIBERLING. I thank the gentleman.

THE CHAIRMAN. The question is on the amendment offered by the gentleman from Ohio (Mr. SEIBERLING).

The amendment was agreed to.

NOTES

1. Does § 301 announce a preemption doctrine different from that in *Goldstein?* The standard formulation for § 301 preemption requires satisfaction of two conditions: (1) the subject matter for which state protection is sought must be within the subject matter of the copyright laws and (2) the state law rights must be equivalent to the exclusive rights provided by the copyright law. Because most original works of authorship are within the copyright statute (at least once they are fixed in a tangible medium of expression) the preemption cases focus on the second condition, whether the state right is infringed by mere acts of copying (preemption) or whether the state law requires an "extra qualitative element". See Harper & Row, Publishers Inc. v. Nation Enterprises, 723 F.2d 195 (2d Cir.1983), *reversed on other grounds,* 471 U.S. 539 (1985). In *Harper* excerpts of President Ford's memoirs were published without permission. The court held that claims for conversion and tortious interference with contract were preempted because they were based on the sole act of publishing a copyrighted work. See also Ehat v. Tanner, 780 F.2d 876 (10th Cir.1985) (conversion action preempted; damages based on profits of defendant rather than fair market value is evidence that relief was granted for act of publication and not act of physical deprivation).

2. The key question under § 301 is to what extent the doctrine of "misappropriation" survives. The Second Circuit has consistently held that the New York tort of misappropriation is preempted. Warner Bros. v. American Broadcasting Co., 720 F.2d 231 (2d Cir.1983). The most significant case may be Financial Information v. Moody's Investors Service, 808 F.2d 204 (2d Cir.1986). The plaintiff sold "Daily Bond Cards" reporting information on municipal bonds called by the issuer. Defendant offered a financial "News Report" service which reported called bonds as well as other information. Evidence suggested defendant copied information from plaintiff's publications. After holding that "[f]acts may not be copyrighted" and citing the language from the House Report suggesting that "misappropriation" was not necessarily preempted the court held the plaintiff's claim was preempted:

> [The plaintiff] attempts to characterize its claim here as one of "misappropriation" of "hot" news under International News Service v. Associated Press * * *, a branch of the unfair competition doctrine not preempted by the Copyright Act according to the House Report. * * * [The plaintiff] proved neither the quantity of copying nor the immediacy of distribution necessary to sustain a "hot" news claim. * * * The "hot" news doctrine is concerned with the copying and publication of information gathered by another before he has been able to utilize his competitive edge.

Does this ruling limit the unpreempted part of misappropriation to the facts of the *INS* case?

3. In Schuchart & Associates, Professional Engineers, Inc. v. Solo Serve Corp., 540 F.Supp. 928, 944–45 (W.D.Tex.1982) the plaintiff architects and engineers prepared plans for a retail store to be built by defendants. The plans were copyrighted by plaintiffs. Subsequently, the defendant used the plans to construct additional stores without plaintiff's permission. Plaintiff sued for copyright infringement, misappropriation, and unjust enrichment. On a motion by the defendant for summary judgment on the state law claims the court

held the misappropriation claim was preempted but the unjust enrichment claim was permissible:

> By their action for unjust enrichment, Plaintiffs seek to recover the value of the architectural and mechanical services rendered to Defendants by Defendants' acceptance and use of Plaintiffs' drawings and specifications. * * * Plaintiffs seek not to enforce their rights to copy and distribute their plans and drawings. Nor do Plaintiffs seek to recover damages analogous to the actual damages provided by § 504(b). Rather, Plaintiffs seek to recover under quantum meruit theory the value of the services rendered by Defendants' use of the plans and specifications prepared by Plaintiffs. Thus, both the rights Plaintiffs seek to enforce and the measure of damages under the unjust enrichment theory differ from those under copyright law. Section 301 has not preempted Plaintiffs' cause of action for unjust enrichment.

4. When the Supreme Court reaffirmed *Sears* and *Compco* in *Bonito Boats* (see Chapter I), it also reaffirmed *Goldstein.* Notwithstanding the concern in *Bonito* of state interference with the uniformity of federal protection, the Court recognized that state law could "promote originality and creativity in their own domains" where Congress has made no decision whether protection is warranted. The Court appears to accept the idea underlying § 301 that some expressions are not within the subject matter protected by copyright and thus states may continue to provide protection. With respect to "ideas," however, the Court seems to suggest the federal patent laws preempt the field. If designs were not specifically accorded patent protection, could the states grant protection?

5. Does § 301 preempt trade dress or other causes of action built on consumer confusion? Does it affect state trademark dilution statutes? Consider *Bonito* where the court goes to some length to reaffirm that state unfair competition law protecting nonfunctional features from use resulting in consumer confusion is preserved.

6. For contrasting views of the impact of § 301 see Brown, Unification: A Cheerful Requiem for Common Law Copyright, 24 U.C.L.A. L.Rev. 1070 (1977) and Goldstein, Preempted State Doctrines, Involuntary Transfers and Compulsory Licenses: Testing the Limits of Copyright, id. at 1107; H. Abrams, Copyright, Misappropriation, and Preemption: Constitutional and Statutory Limits of State Law Protection, 1973 Sup.Ct.Rev. 509.

(4) TRADE SECRETS

(A) COMMON LAW PROTECTION

SMITH v. SNAP–ON TOOLS CORP.
United States Court of Appeals, Fifth Circuit, 1987.
833 F.2d 578.

ALVIN B. RUBIN, CIRCUIT JUDGE:

Basil Smith, a resident of Mississippi, made a ratchet by combining parts of two existing tools. Hoping to see his ratchet made available for sale, he brought it to the attention of Snap–On Tools, Inc., a corporation with its principal place of business in Wisconsin, by showing the ratchet to an independent dealer, then submitting a tool suggestion form to corporate headquarters. Snap–On began manufacturing and selling the ratchet without paying any part of the proceeds to Smith. Smith brought a diversity action against Snap–On, claiming that the ratchet was a trade secret, that he submitted the ratchet in confidence to Snap–On, that Snap–On misappropriated the trade secret, and that Snap–On was liable in damages to him for the misappropriation. The district court, applying Wisconsin law, held that Snap–On had misappropriated Smith's trade secret and awarded Smith damages in the amount of two and one-half percent of Snap–On's gross sales from the ratchet plus pre-judgment interest. Smith appealed the damage award, seeking to recover Snap–On's profits rather than a reasonable royalty. Snap–On cross-appealed * * *. Because the record does not support the finding that there was a confidential relationship between Smith and Snap–On, we reverse.

Wisconsin law prescribes two essential elements in a cause of action for misappropriation of trade secrets: an actual trade secret and a breach of confidence. The essence of the tort of trade secret misappropriation is the inequitable use of the secret. Even when a trade secret exists, a person who learns the secret legitimately, without any duty of confidentiality, is free to use it.

Wisconsin therefore follows trade secrets law as set out in § 757 of the Restatement of Torts. Under the Restatement, "[o]ne who discloses or uses another's trade secret, without a privilege to do so, is liable to the other if . . . his disclosure or use constitutes a breach of confidence reposed in him by the other in disclosing the secret to him."[5] As the comment to this provision states, the proprietor of a trade secret may not unilaterally create a confidential relationship without the knowledge or consent of the party to whom he discloses the secret.[6] No particular form of notice is necessary, however; the question is whether the recipient of the information knew or should have known that the disclosure was made in confidence.[7]

* * *

Under certain circumstances, courts have found liability for misappropriation of trade secrets in cases involving implied confidentiality between an inventor and a manufacturer. When a manufacturer has actively solicited disclosure from an inventor, then made use of the disclosed material, the manufacturer may be liable for use or disclosure of the secret in the absence of any expressed understanding as to confidentiality. In this case, however, Smith disclosed the invention on his own initiative, without any prompting from Snap–On. Alternatively, courts have imposed liability when the disclosing inventor did not specifically request confidentiality from the manufacturer, but did make clear that the disclosure was intended as part of a course of

---

5. Restatement of Torts § 757(b) (1939).

6. Id. comment j.

7. RTE, 84 Wis.2d 105, 267 N.W.2d at 232; Restatement of Torts § 757(b) comment j (1939).

negotiations aimed at creating a licensing agreement or entering into a similar business transaction. These cases are also distinguishable because Smith did not indicate that he wanted any pecuniary recompense for his suggestion. * * *

In February, 1978, more than two years after Smith showed the ratchet to Clark, Smith's lawyer sent a letter to the supervisor of Snap–On's Product Management Division in which he asked that Smith receive compensation. Reliance on confidentiality, however, must exist at the time the disclosure is made. An attempt to establish a special relationship long after an initial disclosure comes too late.

Because there was no confidential relationship between Smith and Snap–On, Snap–On violated no obligation to Smith by manufacturing the ratchet. We therefore REVERSE.

METALLURGICAL INDUSTRIES, INC. v. FOURTEK, INC.

United States Court of Appeals, Fifth Circuit, 1986.
790 F.2d 1195.

[The alleged trade secrets relate to the reclamation of carbide from scrap metals. Metallurgical Industries (MI) began to consider a newly discovered "zinc recovery process" using a furnace. MI purchased such a furnace from Therm–O–Vac but it proved unsuccessful until MI added a number of modifications. Subsequently MI sought a second furnace and disclosed its own modifications to Consarc, another furnace manufacturer. Consarc was unwilling to manufacture the furnace so MI turned once again to Therm–O–Vac which produced a second furnace incorporating the modifications. Therm–O–Vac went bankrupt and its former employees formed the defendant, Fourtek, which produced for Smith International a recovery furnace incorporating MI's modifications. MI filed suit for misappropriation of trade secrets against Smith and the former Therm–O–Vac employees (Bielefeldt, Montesino, Boehm and Sarvadi) even though Smith had never put the furnace to commercial operation. The trial court granted the defendants' motions for directed verdict finding there were no trade secrets involved.]

Gee, Circuit Judge.

* * *

III. DEFINING A "TRADE SECRET"

We begin by reviewing the legal definition of a trade secret. Of course, to qualify as one, the subject matter involved must, in fact, be a secret; "[m]atters of general knowledge in an industry cannot be appropriated by one as his secret." Wissman v. Boucher, 150 Tex. 326, 240 S.W.2d 278, 280 (1951); * * *. Smith emphasizes the absence of any secret because the basic zinc recovery process has been publicized in the trade. Acknowledging the publicity of the zinc recovery process, however, we nevertheless conclude that Metallurgical's particular modification efforts can be as yet unknown to the industry. A general description of the zinc recovery process reveals nothing about the benefits unitary heating elements and vacuum pump filters can provide to that procedure. That the scientific principles involved are generally known does not necessarily refute Metallurgical's claim of trade secrets.

Metallurgical, furthermore, presented evidence to back up its claim. One of its main witnesses was Arnold Blum, a consultant very influential in the decisions to modify the furnaces. Blum testified as to his belief that Metallurgical's changes were unknown in the carbide reclamation industry. The evidence also shows Metallurgical's efforts to keep secret its modifications. Blum testified that he noted security measures taken to conceal the furnaces from all but authorized person-nel. The furnaces were in areas hidden from public view, while signs warned all about restricted access. Company policy, moreover, re-quired everyone authorized to see the furnace to sign a non-disclosure agreement. These measures constitute evidence probative of the exis-tence of secrets. One's subjective belief of a secret's existence suggests that the secret exists. Security measures, after all, cost money; a manufacturer therefore presumably would not incur these costs if it believed its competitors already knew about the information involved.

*　　*　　*

Smith argues, however, that Metallurgical's disclosure to other parties vitiated the secrecy required to obtain legal protection. As mentioned before, Metallurgical revealed its information to Consarc Corporation in 1978; it also disclosed information in 1980 to La Floridienne, its European licensee of carbide reclamation technology. Because both these disclosures occurred before Bielefeldt allegedly misappropriated the knowledge of modifications, others knew of the information when the Smith furnace was built. This being so, Smith argues, no trade secret in fact existed.

Although the law requires secrecy, it need not be absolute. Public revelation would, of course, dispel all secrecy, but the holder of a secret need not remain totally silent:

> He may, without losing his protection, communicate it to employees involved in its use. He may likewise communicate it to others pledged to secrecy. . . . Nevertheless, a substan-tial element of secrecy must exist, so that except by the use of improper means, there would be difficulty in acquiring the information.

Restatement of Torts, § 757 Comment b (1939). We conclude that a holder may divulge his information to a limited extent without destroying its status as a trade secret. To hold otherwise would greatly limit the holder's ability to profit from his secret. If disclosure to others is made to further the holder's economic interests, it should, in appropriate circumstances, be considered a limited disclosure that does not destroy the requisite secrecy. The only question is whether we are dealing with a limited disclosure here.

Prior caselaw provides no guidance on what constitutes limited disclosure. Metallurgical cites Hyde Corp. v. Huffines, 158 Tex. 566, 314 S.W.2d 763, cert. denied, 358 U.S. 898 (1958), and Sikes v. McGraw Edison Co., 665 F.2d 731 (5th Cir.), cert. denied 458 U.S. 1108 (1982), in contending that subsequent disclosure of a trade secret does not free one from the constraint of a prior confidential disclosure. In both of these cases, however, publication of the trade secret by its holder followed an improper use by one in whom the holder had confided. This factual difference renders these cases inapposite.

Looking instead to the policy considerations involved, we glean two reasons why Metallurgical's disclosures to others are limited and therefore insufficient to extinguish the secrecy Metallurgical's other evidence has suggested. First, the disclosures were not public announcements; rather, Metallurgical divulged its information to only two businesses with whom it was dealing. This case thus differs from Luccous v. J.C. Kinley Co., 376 S.W.2d 336 (Tex.1964), in which the court concluded that the design of a device could not be a trade secret because it had been patented—and thus revealed to all the world—before any dealing between the parties. Second, the disclosures were made to further Metallurgical's economic interests. Disclosure to Consarc was made with the hope that Consarc could build the second furnace. A longstanding agreement gave La Floridienne the right, as a licensee, to the information in exchange for royalty payments. Metallurgical therefore revealed its discoveries as part of business transactions by which it expected to profit.

Metallurgical's case would have been stronger had it also presented evidence of confidential relationships with these two companies, but we are unwilling to regard this failure as conclusively disproving the limited nature of the disclosures. Smith correctly points out that Metallurgical bears the burden of showing the existence of confidential relationships. Contrary to Smith's assertion, however, confidentiality is not a requisite; it is only a factor to consider. Whether a disclosure is limited is an issue the resolution of which depends on weighing many facts. The inferences from those facts, construed favorably to Metallurgical, is that it wished only to profit from its secrets in its business dealings, not to reveal its secrets to the public. We therefore are unpersuaded by Smith's argument.

Existing law, however, emphasizes other requisites for legal recognition of a trade secret. In Huffines, 314 S.W.2d 763, a seminal case of trade secret law, Texas adopted the widely-recognized pronouncements of the American Law Institute's Restatement of the Law. The Texas Supreme Court quoted the Restatement's definition of a trade secret:

> A trade secret may consist of any formula, pattern, device or compilation information which is used in one's business, and which gives him an opportunity to obtain an advantage over competitors who do not know it. It may be a chemical compound, a process of manufacturing, treating or preserving

materials, a pattern for a machine or other device or a list of customers.

Id. at 776, *quoting* Restatement of Torts, § 757 Comment b (1939). From this the criterion of value to the holder of the alleged secret arises, a criterion we have noted before.   *   *   *

Metallurgical met the burden of showing the value of its modifications. Lawrence Lorman, the company's vice president, testified that the zinc recovery process gave Metallurgical an advantage over its two competitors by aiding in the production of the highest quality reclaimed carbide powder. The quality of the powder, in fact, makes it an alternative to the more costly virgin carbide. Lorman testified that customers regarded Metallurgical's zinc reclaimed powder as a better product than that reclaimed by the coldstream process used by others. This evidence clearly indicates that the modifications that led to the commercial operation of the zinc recovery furnace provided a clear advantage over the competition.

Another requisite is the cost of developing the secret device or process.   *   *   *   No question exists that Metallurgical expended much time, effort, and money to make the necessary changes. It clearly has met the burden of demonstrating the effort involved in making a complex manufacturing process work.

That the cost of devising the secret and the value the secret provides are criteria in the legal formulation of a trade secret shows the equitable underpinnings of this area of the law. It seems only fair that one should be able to keep and enjoy the fruits of his labor. If a businessman has worked hard, has used his imagination, and has taken bold steps to gain an advantage over his competitors, he should be able to profit from his efforts. Because a commercial advantage can vanish once the competition learns of it, the law should protect the businessman's efforts to keep his achievements secret. As is discussed below, this is an area of law in which simple fairness still plays a large role.

We do not say, however, that all these factors need exist in every case. Because each case must turn on its own facts, no standard formula for weighing the factors can be devised. Secrecy is always required, of course, but beyond that there are no universal requirements. In a future case, for example, should the defendant's breach of confidence be particularly egregious, the injured party might still seek redress in court despite the possibility that the subject matter was discovered at little or no cost or that the object of secrecy is not of great value to him. The definition of "trade secret" will therefore be determined by weighing all equitable considerations. It is easy to recognize the possibility of a trade secret here, however, because Metallurgical presented evidence of all three factors discussed above.

*   *   *

IV. EXISTENCE OF A CONFIDENTIAL RELATIONSHIP

Deciding whether a confidential relationship existed between Metallurgical and Bielefeldt must naturally precede an inquiry into his possible breach of Metallurgical's confidence. Once again, we look to the Restatement of Torts as our starting point:

> One who discloses or uses another's trade secrets, without a privilege to do so, is liable to the other if . . . (b) his disclosure or use constitutes a breach of confidence reposed in him by the other in disclosing the secret to him.
>
>   *   *   *
>
> A breach of confidence under the rule stated in this Clause may also be a breach of contract which subjects the actor to liability. . . . But whether or not there is a breach of contract, the rule stated in this Section subjects the actor to liability if his disclosure or use of another's trade secret is a breach of the confidence reposed in him by the other in disclosing the secret to him.

Huffines, 314 S.W.2d at 769, *quoting* Restatement, § 757 and comment j. In *Huffines,* the Texas Court cited several cases to emphasize this message. Quoted at great length was Adolph Gottscho v. American Marking Corp., 18 N.J. 467, 114 A.2d 438 (1955). The *Gottscho* court stressed the blameworthy conduct of the defendant as the basis of this tort:

> [Defendants] now seek to appropriate these trade secrets to their own use and profit by a violation of their contractual agreements and a betrayal of the confidence reposed in them by plaintiff. This they may not do; such conduct is abhorrent to our conception of ordinary honesty. . . . Jackson learned the plaintiff's trade secrets in confidence and, in violation of his fiduciary obligations, he disclosed and used them for purposes other than his employer's benefit. . . . His conduct was grossly improper and gave rise to the plaintiff's cause of action, based on long-settled equitable principles and supported by the marked changes in the attitude of the law towards the need for commercial morality.

114 A.2d at 441–42, quoting Julius Hyman & Co. v. Velsicol Corp., 123 Colo. 563, 604–06, 233 P.2d 977, 999 (1952), cert. denied 342 U.S. 870 (1951). Our review of the evidence on the existence of a confidential relationship is hampered to some degree by the district court's exclusion of several items of evidence. As we discuss below, the exclusions were improper; but regardless of the evidence excluded, the record contains testimony of Metallurgical's president, Ira Friedman, that he informed Bielefeldt of the confidentiality Metallurgical expected. Although these references are few, they would have sufficed to allow a reasonable jury to have believed that a confidential relationship existed between Metallurgical and Bielefeldt.

V. OBTAINING SECRETS FROM ANOTHER

At this point we must devote separate attention to Smith, which stands in a different light from Bielefeldt. It had no significant dealings with Metallurgical and apparently was not heavily involved in the design of the furnace it purchased. The question therefore becomes whether Smith as purchaser, and thus as beneficiary of Bielefeldt's alleged misappropriation, can also be held liable for it.

The law imposes liability not only on those who wrongfully misappropriate trade secrets by breach of confidence but also, in certain situations, on others who might benefit from the breach:

> One who discloses or uses another's trade secret, without a privilege to do so, is liable to the other if . . . (c) he learned the secret from a third person with notice of the facts that it was a secret and that the third person's disclosure of it was otherwise a breach of his duty to the other. . . .

> * * *

> One has notice of facts under the rule stated in this Section when he knows of them or when he should know of them. . . . He should know of them if, from the information which he has, a reasonable man would infer the facts in question, or if, under the circumstances, a reasonable man would be put on inquiry and an inquiry pursued with reasonable intelligence and diligence would disclose the facts.

Restatement, § 757 & comment 1. Under this standard, we believe a reasonable jury could find that Smith should have inquired into the relationship between Bielefeldt and Metallurgical. Testimony shows that, during negotiations for the purchase of a furnace, Bielefeldt told Smith of his current involvement in then-pending litigation with Metallurgical regarding trade secrets in New Jersey. Smith learned that Metallurgical claimed ownership of the design and manufacturing processes of the zinc recovery furnace, a furnace which Smith wished Bielefeldt to build. Apparently satisfied by Bielefeldt's assertion of the meritlessness of Metallurgical's claims, Smith eventually gave him the go-ahead for construction of the furnace. There is no indication that it ever investigated the danger that Bielefeldt was wrongfully misappropriating the ideas of others. The evidence as it stood at the end of Metallurgical's presentation thus suggests that Smith knew of possible problems and did nothing but rely on Bielefeldt's dismissals. We think that this inattention to possible wrongdoing, unless refuted, amounts to a failure to reasonably inquire into the facts involved. Under § 757(c), Smith might therefore be held accountable, provided it used any trade secrets conveyed. This brings us to the next issue.

VI. DISCLOSURE OR USE OF A TRADE SECRET

Wrongful misappropriation occurs if one "discloses or uses another's trade secret without a privilege to do so. . . ." Restatement,

§ 757. The district court directed verdict for appellees in part because it saw no evidence of Bielefeldt's actual use or disclosure of Metallurgical's secrets. In reviewing this conclusion, we keep in mind the rule of *Boeing Co. v. Shipman* by scouring the record for reasonable inferences favorable to Metallurgical. One fact jumps out from this review: in their original form, the furnaces delivered to Metallurgical differed from those that Smith purchased. The former furnaces lacked the key features needed to achieve commercial operation, while the latter possessed those features—features that Metallurgical had devised by extensive and expensive trial and error. Bielefeldt himself testified that he did not look to public sources of information in designing the Smith furnace; he instead claimed that he relied on his memory. That his earlier efforts lacked the features at issue suggests that his "memories" may well have been of working with Metallurgical. This issue is therefore an inappropriate ground for a directed verdict.

Smith's liability can arise, however, only if it in turn used the secrets gained from Bielefeldt. "Use," as it turns out, is not so easily defined. Smith claims that it never used any secrets gained because its inability to procure substantial quantities of scrap carbide prevented commercial operation of the furnace Fourtek provided. Lykes–Youngstown, 504 F.2d 518, guides us in determining commercial use. We must first recognize the unfortunate blurring of analyses in that case. The *Lykes–Youngstown* court's discussion of commercial use was in the context of inquiring whether damages might be available. It is preferable, of course, to divorce these concepts. Commercial use is an element of the tort as enounced in § 757 of the Restatement; while the nature of the use may be relevant in determining the proper extent of damages, its existence must also be shown to establish wrongdoing in the first place. Despite this confusion, *Lykes–Youngstown* provides useful analysis.

Metallurgical looked to that case in arguing that the law provides a liberal definition of "commercial use." *Lykes–Youngstown* does indeed state a broad definition; "any misappropriation, followed by an exercise of control and dominion . . . must constitute a commercial use. . . ." 504 F.2d at 542. *Lykes–Youngstown* differs from our case, however, in one very important respect. It was a case in which "the trade secret itself was what was to be sold. . . ." Id. at 540. The court there explicitly contrasted a case like ours, "where the trade secret is used to improve manufacturing, and subsequently manufactured items were sold at a profit. . . ." Id. Although the court made this distinction in determining the proper method of computing damages, we think it also applies logically to developing a definition of "use." The discussion in *Lykes–Youngstown* following this distinction is therefore inapposite to our case, for which we instead employ the everyday meaning of the term. If Smith has not put the furnace into commercial operation to produce carbide powder it can then use, then no commercial use has occurred. Because Metallurgical failed to provide any evidence that Smith has so far benefitted from any misappropriation, directed verdict in Smith's favor was proper. Should it in future seek to profit from use or sale of the furnace, a new fact situation will be presented.

* * *

VIII. REMEDIES AND OTHER MATTERS

We now come to the issue of remedies available to Metallurgical. The district court apparently found crucial Smith's inability to operate its furnace profitably. Because there was no commercial use, it concluded that damages were unavailable. We have already concluded that Smith did not "use" the alleged secrets Bielefeldt provided; to say that this circumstance precludes all remedies goes too far, however. The court failed to distinguish consideration of the individual appellees; Smith is out of the picture, but Bielefeldt remains. Should he be found liable on retrial, the appropriate damages should be based on the tenets of *Lykes–Youngstown.* We there adopted the concept of the "reasonable royalty." This does not mean a simple percentage of actual profits; instead, the trier of fact, should it find Bielefeldt liable, must determine "the actual value of what has been appropriated." 504 F.2d at 537, quoting Vitro Corp. v. Hall Chemical Co., 292 F.2d 678, 683 (6th Cir. 1961). We later expounded this concept:

> [T]he proper measure is to calculate what the parties would have agreed to as a fair price for licensing the defendant to put the trade secret to the use the defendants intended at the time the misappropriation took place. In calculating what a fair licensing price would have been had the parties agreed, the trier of fact should consider such factors as the resulting and foreseeable changes in the parties' competitive posture; the prices past purchasers or licensees may have paid; the total value of the secret to the plaintiff, including the plaintiff's development cost and the importance of the secret to the plaintiff's business; the nature and extent of the use the defendant intended for the secret, and finally whatever other unique factors in the particular case might have been affected by the parties' agreement, such as the ready availability of alternative process.

Id. at 540. Estimation of damages, however, should not be based on sheer speculation. If too few facts exist to permit the trier of fact to calculate proper damages, then a reasonable remedy in law is unavailable. In that instance, a permanent injunction is a proper remedy for the breach of a confidential relationship. * * *

The district court's order is AFFIRMED in part, REVERSED in part, and the cause is REMANDED.

NOTES

1. Trade secret law can be applied in different contexts such as where an unsolicited idea is disclosed (*Snap–On Tools*), an employee competes with his

former employer (*Metallurgical*), information is disclosed during negotiations for the sale of a business, or where persons without any relationship to or contact with the owner of the information misappropriate its value (*Christopher, infra*). Should the context make a difference in fashioning the doctrinal content of trade secret law? Are the policies at stake in each of these contexts the same?

2. *Subject matter protected.* Compare the language of § 776 of the Restatement, cited in *Metallurgical*, with the definition provided by the Uniform Trade Secrets Act: " 'Trade secret' means information, including a formula, pattern, compilation, program, device, method, technique or process, that: (1) derives independent economic value, actual or potential from not being generally known to, and not being readily ascertainable by proper means by, other persons who can obtain economic value from its disclosure or use, and (ii) is the subject of efforts that are reasonable under the circumstances to maintain its secrecy." Are there types of valuable and secret information that cannot be protected?

3. *Customer Lists.* One of the troubling issues in an employment context is the extent of protection afforded to lists of customers. Should an employee who learns the names and requirements of customers of his employer be entitled to use that information if he takes new employment with a competitor of his former employer. The paradigm cases involve delivery services. A number of jurisdictions follow the test proposed in the Restatement of Agency which prohibits a former employee from using or disclosing in competition with his principal "written lists of names" although the agent "is entitled to use * * * names of the customers retained in his memory, if not acquired in violation of his duty as agent." Restatement, Second Agency § 396 (1958). See, e.g., Progress Laundry Co. v. Hamilton, 208 Ky. 348, 270 S.W. 834 (1925)

Compare, Developments—Competitive Torts, 77 Harv.L.Rev. 888, 956 (1964) ("[E]conomic arguments for protecting customer lists are at best marginal and the case for protection rests almost entirely on the need to deter employee disloyalty. * * * This 'memory rule' in most cases seems to have little merit other than as an arbitrary rule of thumb.") and 2 Callmann, Unfair Competition, Trademarks and Monopolies, § 54.2(c)(2) at 446 ("The distinction places a premium upon good memory and a penalty upon forgetfulness, and it cannot be justified either from a logical or pragmatic point of view") with Blake, Employee Agreements Not to Compete, 73 Harv.L.Rev. 625, 656 (1960) (" * * * the distinction has survived, indeed remained vigorous, over a long period. This is some evidence that it is helpful to courts and probably approximates good sense in most cases. The explanation seems to be that the 'memory' rule of thumb, in application, allows the former employee to solicit those customers whom he has played some personal role in obtaining or retaining for the former employer, giving him the benefit of a rather wide margin of doubt."). Even the Restatement would make an exception where the employee memorized the list of customers specifically for the purpose of competing with his principal. Restatement, *supra* comment b.

The California courts have developed a balancing of factors test. See, California Intelligence Bureau v. Cunningham, 83 Cal.App.2d 197, 188 P.2d 303 (1948):

> In the first group of cases it is held that equity, at the instance of a former employer, will enjoin a former employee from using knowledge or information gained while in the employ of the former employer, and

by reason of such employment, to the former employer's detriment, if: (1) the former employee is in possession of trade or business secrets or confidential information, or the like, not readily accessible to others; (2) the former employee solicits the customers of his former employer in a competing business with intent to injure his former employer's business; (3) the former employee solicits the customers of his former employer, who comprise a list of preferred customers whose trade is profitable to a supplier of a service, knowledge of whom is a trade secret and confidential; (4) one concern is usually patronized by a customer and the lists and names and addresses of the customers are considered secret and have the character of property; (5) there is an established business relationship between the customer and the former employer which, unless interfered with, normally continues.

In the second group of cases it is held that equity will not enjoin a former employee from using knowledge or information gained while in the employ of a former employer, and by reason of such employment, even to the detriment of the former employer, if: (1) the customers solicited (a) do not constitute a trade secret, or confidential information, or a confidential list in which a proprietary interest might be claimed, or (b) are commonly known to the trade and are called upon by salesmen for various companies, or are wholesale buyers whose names appear in directories and are so few in number that anyone might readily discover them, and the list of them is not secret or confidential; (2) the former employer is in open competition with others engaged in similar business, selling in an open, competitive market; (3) the former employee was a salesman of his former employer in a commercial field where there was no assurance of an order unless he could satisfy his customer that his product was better, cheaper, or more salable than that of his competitor, where the customer usually desired to examine, inspect and compare the product and prices offered to him and each sale was a distinct transaction, not necessarily implying that another will follow; (4) no secret or trust reposed in the former employee in the course of his employment is violated and no trade or business secret or confidential information is used by the former employee.

See also Aetna Bldg. Maintenance Co. v. West, 39 Cal.2d 198, 246 P.2d 11 (1952); Hollingsworth Solderless Terminal Co. v. Turley, 622 F.2d 1324 (9th Cir. 1980).

For an encyclopedic presentation of the various approaches to the customer list problem, see Annot., Former Employee's Duty, In Absence of Express Contract, Not to Solicit Former Employer's Customers or Otherwise Use His Knowledge of Customer Lists Acquired in Earlier Employment, 28 A.L.R.3d 7 (1969).

Does it make sense to talk in terms of "trade secrets" when the issue is solicitation of a former's employer's customers? Is there an interference with contractual relationships implicit in these cases? Or, is the issue one of employee loyalty? Or, is there an element of "misappropriation" involved?

4. *Secrecy.* The secrecy required for trade secret protection is a relative secrecy which does not prevent commercial exploitation of the information. Courts often consider what active steps the trade secret owner has taken to limit access to the information and to contractually restrain disclosure by those

who do have access. And some commercially exploited secrets are more easily kept than others because the law permits reverse engineering. See Tabor v. Hoffman, 118 N.Y. 30, 23 N.E. 12 (1889):

> If a valuable medicine, not protected by patent, is put upon the market, any one may, if he can by chemical analysis and a series of experiments, or by any other use of the medicine itself, aided by his own resources only, discover the ingredients and their proportions. If he thus finds out the secret of the proprietor, he may use it to any extent that he desires without danger of interference by the courts.

In *Tabor* the defendant was held liable because rather than reverse engineer the plaintiff's pumps, he surreptitiously acquired a copy of the patterns from which the pumps were made.

5. *Confidential relationship.* In most trade secret cases, the plaintiff voluntarily has disclosed the information to the defendant, either as part of an arms-length transaction or in the context of an employment relationship. As in *Snap–On* the issue is whether the relationship between the parties was sufficient to imply an obligation not to disclose or use the information. As Justice Holmes said in E.I. DuPont De Nemours Powder Co. v. Masland, 244 U.S. 100 (1917): "The word 'property' as applied to * * * trade secrets in an unanalyzed expression of certain secondary consequences of the primary fact that the law makes some rudimentary requirements of good faith. * * * Therefore, the starting point for the present matter is not property or due process of law, but that the defendant stood in confidential relations with the plaintiffs, or one of them."

In *Metallurgical*, do you have to assume that the plaintiff could not have prevented Consarc from disclosing its trade secrets because there was no confidential relationship? Is this consistent with *Snap–On?*

6. If a claimed trade secret could be discovered in a fair way but the defendant acquires the secret in confidence, should the defendant be prohibited from using the information? In Smith v. Dravo Corp., 203 F.2d 369 (7th Cir. 1953) the defendant manufactured shipping containers based on plans acquired from plaintiff during unsuccessful negotiations over the sale of plaintiff's business to defendant. The shipping containers themselves were available on the open market and could have been reverse engineered. The court gave plaintiff relief:

> * * * Pennsylvania will not deny recovery merely because the design *could have* been obtained through inspection. Rather, the inquiry in that jurisdiction appears to be: How *did* defendant learn of plaintiffs' design? And this we regard as the proper test. It recognizes the very nature of the type of wrong with which we are here concerned. Confidential business information is not given protection merely as a reward to its accumulator. If the creator is entitled to reward it is available to him in the patent and copyright statutes. * * * Instead our function is that of condemning "the employment of improper means to procure the trade secret."

Most courts, however, disagree with *Smith!* Even in Pennsylvania, the state courts have held that no trade secret exists if the information could have been ascertained by permissible means. Van Products Co. v. General Welding & Fabricating Co., 419 Pa. 248, 213 A.2d 769 (1965).

7. *Novelty.* Should the information protected by trade secret law have to meet some standard of novelty or inventiveness? Early courts quickly rejected

any idea that the strenuous standard of inventiveness of the patent laws should apply to trade secrets. See A.O. Smith Corp. v. Petroleum Iron Works Co., 73 F.2d 531 (6th Cir.1934). At the same time courts suggest that some modest novelty standard may be imposed. Ferroline Corp. v. General Aniline & Film Corp., 207 F.2d 912 (7th Cir.1953) (secret must involve valuable contribution arising from plaintiff's independent efforts) and Nickelson v. General Motors Corp., 361 F.2d 196 (7th Cir.1966) (secret must be valuable contribution; trivial advances or differences are not protectible.)

Can you see why some authors claim that novelty and secrecy really involve the same issue? See Turner, The Law of Trade Secrets 24 (1962). Can information that is not "new" be "secret"?

8. The law in this area is synthesized in Kitch, The Law and Economics of Rights in Valuable Information, 9 J. Legal Stud. 683, 683–708 (1980). The business side of the issue is discussed in Stanley H. Lieberstein, Who Owns What Is In Your Head? (1979).

NOTES: TRADE SECRETS AND EMPLOYEES

PROBLEM

AMP, Incorporated is the world's leading producer of electrical and electronic connection devices. Molex is a principle competitor of AMP's Components and Assemblies Division. James Fleishhacker, a graduate of the University of Minnesota and MIT began working for AMP in 1973. By 1982, he had worked his way up to manager of the Components and Assemblies Division. His duties included approving business programs, implementing strategic policies and plans, and developing personnel. His evaluations were exceptional and he was told he had the potential to continue to rise within the company. In 1982 Molex created a Director of Marketing position and an executive search firm directed them to Fleischhacker. In 1984 Fleischhacker accepted Molex's offer of employment. Fleischhacker brings to Molex his general skill and experience in the business as well as his particular knowledge relating to the customers, methods of operation and plans of AMP. AMP seeks your advice on what they can do to prohibit Fleischhacker from exploiting on Molex's behalf his training and knowledge all acquired at AMP's expense.

1. The problem illustrates a common situation. Many employers make a substantial and costly investment in their employees. They provide training and experience and inevitably disclose valuable business information. The more valuable the employee becomes the more vulnerable he is to outside inducements but his increased value comes, at least in part, from the expenditures of his employer. What are the competing public policy issues that must be balanced in these circumstances?

2. The balance between an employer's interest in secrecy and an employee's interest in mobility is often drawn by the definition of what qualifies for trade secret protection. In AMP Inc. v. Fleischhacker, 823 F.2d 1199 (7th Cir. 1987) the court affirmed a judgment for the employee:

> . . . While an enforceable restrictive covenant may protect material, such as confidential information revealed to an employee during the course of his employment, which does not constitute a trade secret, an employer's protection absent a restrictive covenant is narrower and extends only to trade secrets or near-permanent customer relationships. * * *

Because Mr. Fleischhacker is not subject to any enforceable contractual restrictions, AMP was first required to establish the existence of genuine trade secrets in order for injunctive relief to be warranted. * * * It is generally recognized in Illinois that at the termination of employment, an employee may not take with him confidential, particularized plans or processes developed by his employer and disclosed to him while the employer-employee relationship existed, which are unknown to others in the industry and which give the employer an advantage over his competitors. On the other hand, an employee is free to take with him general skills and knowledge acquired during his tenure with his former employer. * * * Furthermore, while recognizing that a business must be afforded protection against the wrongful appropriation of confidential information by a prior employee who held a position of confidence and trust, the Illinois Supreme Court has emphasized that:

the right of an individual to follow and pursue the particular occupation for which he is best trained is a most fundamental right. Our society is extremely mobile and our free economy is based upon competition. One who has worked in a particular field cannot be compelled to erase from his mind all of the general skills, knowledge and expertise acquired through his experience. These skills are valuable to such employee in the market place for his services. Restraints cannot be lightly placed upon his right to compete in the area of his greatest worth.

In other cases the balance is accomplished by examining the extent to which the employment relationship imposes an implied obligation of confidentiality.

3. It is clear that the employer-employee relationship is a confidential one although not all information about the employer's business learned by the employee is protected. One factor that may be important is whether the employer gave the employee the information or whether the employee developed it himself. A leading case is Wexler v. Greenberg, 399 Pa. 569, 160 A.2d 430 (1960) where Greenberg was originally hired by Buckingham Wax Company as a chemist whose duty was to reverse engineer and reproduce competing products for sale by Buckingham. Greenberg subsequently was hired by Brite and Brite began competing with Buckingham. The court held that Greenberg had an unqualified privilege to use his technical knowledge and skill acquired during his prior employment:

The usual situation involving misappropriation of trade secrets in violation of a confidential relationship is one in which an employer *discloses to his employee* a pre-existing trade secret (one already developed or formulated) so that the employee may duly perform his work. In such a case, the trust and confidence upon which legal relief is predicated stems from the instance of the employer's *turning over to the employee* the pre-existing trade secret. It is then that a pledge of secrecy is impliedly extracted from the employee, a pledge which he carries with him even beyond the ties of his employment relationship. Since it is conceptually impossible, however, to elicit an implied pledge of secrecy from the sole act of an employee turning over to his employer a trade secret which he, the employee, has developed, as occurred in the present case, the appellees must show a different manner in which the present circumstances support the permanent cloak of confidence cast upon Greenberg by the Chancellor. The only avenue open to the appellees is to show that the nature of the employment relationship itself gave rise to a duty of nondisclosure.

The burden the appellees must thus meet brings to the fore a problem of accommodating competing policies in our law: the right of a businessman to be protected against unfair competition stemming from the usurpation of his trade secrets and the right of an individual to the unhampered pursuit of the occupations and livelihoods for which he is best suited. There are cogent socio-economic arguments in favor of either position. Society as a whole greatly benefits from technological improvements. Without some means of post-employment protection to assure that valuable developments or improvements are exclusively those of the employer, the businessman could not afford to subsidize research or improve current methods. In addition, it must be recognized that modern economic growth and development has pushed the business venture beyond the size of the one-man firm, forcing the businessman to a much greater degree to entrust confidential business information relating to technological development to appropriate employees. While recognizing the utility in the dispersion of responsibilities in larger firms, the optimum amount of "entrusting" will not occur unless the risk of loss to the businessman through a breach of trust can be held to a minimum.

On the other hand, any form of post-employment restraint reduces the economic mobility of employees and limits their personal freedom to pursue a preferred course of livelihood. The employee's bargaining position is weakened because he is potentially shackled by the acquisition of alleged trade secrets; and thus, paradoxically, he is restrained, because of his increased expertise, from advancing further in the industry in which he is most productive. Moreover, as previously mentioned, society suffers because competition is diminished by slackening the dissemination of ideas, processes and methods.

See also, Winston Research Corp. v. Minnesota Min. & Mfg. Co., 350 F.2d 134 (9th Cir.1965) where former employees of MMM produced a precision tape recorder that competed with the one they had helped develop while working for MMM:

Winston argues that information is protected from disclosure only if communicated to the employee by the employer who is seeking protection, and that the information involved in this case was not disclosed by Mincom to the employees subsequently hired by Winston, but rather was developed by these employees themselves, albeit while employed by Mincom.

We need not examine the soundness of the rule for which Winston contends, or its applicability to a case such as this in which a group of specialists engaged in related facets of a single development project change their employer. The rule is apparently based upon the notion that unless the first employer conveys the information to the employee, subsequent disclosure by the employee cannot be a breach of a duty of confidence owed that employer. Futurecraft Corp. v. Clary Corp., * * * 23 Cal.Rptr. 198. As the court in *Futurecraft* recognized, an obligation not to disclose may arise from circumstances other than communication in confidence by the employer. It may also rest upon an express or implied agreement. In the present case, an agreement not to disclose might be implied from Mincom's elaborate efforts to maintain the secrecy of its development program, and the employees' knowledge of these efforts and participation in them. In any event, Mincom and its employees entered into express written agreements binding the latter not to disclose confidential information, and these agreements did not exclude information which the employee himself contributed.

4. If an employee is hired specifically to invent or develop new ideas for his employer, the employer is entitled to any discoveries and may assert trade secret rights as well as requiring an assignment of any subsequent patents. If the employee is not hired specifically to invent, he is entitled to his discoveries even if resulting from the performance of his duties for the employer. However, if the employee uses his employer's time and facilities in developing the invention, the employer is entitled to a nonexclusive license to use the invention even if the employee subsequently obtains a patent. And the Fifth Circuit has recently held this "shop right" applies even where the employer does not provide assistance to the employee in reducing the idea to practice if the employee initially consents to the employer putting the idea into commercial use. Wommack v. Durham Pecan Co., Inc., 715 F.2d 962 (5th Cir.1983). It has been held that the employer and employee can alter the above rules by contract. Restatement, Second Agency § 397 (1958).

Section 201 of the Copyright Act, 17 U.S.C. § 201, provides that copyright vests initially in the author of a work but that in the case of a "work made for hire" the employer is considered the author, and owns the copyright unless there is a written, signed agreement to the contrary. A "work made for hire" is defined in § 101 to include a work "prepared by an employee within the scope of his or her employment. * * *" The legislative history reflects rejection of a "shop right" provision that would have given the copyright to the employee subject to the employer's royalty free right to use the work. House Comm. on Judiciary, Copyright Law Revision, H.R.Rep. No. 94–1476, 94th Cong., 2d Sess. (1976). For further discussion of the work made for hire doctrine in copyright see p. 773, infra.

Section 111 of the patent laws specifically requires that the application for a patent be made by the "inventor". If the employee is the "inventor" the application must be made in his name although he may be forced to assign the patent to his employer. On the other hand where a supervisor conceives of the invention and the employee is merely a means through which the supervisor puts his conception into practice, the supervisor would be the "inventor". In these situations there may likewise be a presumption running in favor of the employer.

5. With the doctrines considered above, how does an employer recoup the costs of training skilled employees? If employees are entitled to receive training and then establish rival business establishments will this discourage "on the job training" programs by private enterprise? Can you recommend alternatives to the present law? Consider in passing the Statute of Apprentices, 5 Eliz. 1, Ch. 4 which provided for a seven-year apprenticeship at no wages with assurance at the end of the seventh year that the apprentice could freely ply his trade. Could contractual agreements solve many of these problems?

In a similar vein, do the common law doctrines outlined above which regulate employer-employee rights to inventions serve to stimulate technological advance? See Stedman, The Employed Inventor, The Public Interest, and Horse and Buggy Law in the Space Act, 45 N.Y.U.L.Rev. 1, 6 (1970):

> From policy standpoints, trade secret law leaves much to be desired. It tends to become an arbitrary, inflexible, all-or-nothing kind of law. It is attended by considerable uncertainty as to what one can and cannot do. It is more likely to discourage than to stimulate employee inventive activity, since it does not lend itself to refined allocation procedures and tends to favor the employer rather than the employee. Trade secret law may even prevent the employee from receiving any credit for what he has done and may hinder any public benefit which could accrue from such a contribution.

Professor Stedman's article provides a useful catalogue of the possible alternatives to trade secret protection as a means of encouraging employee inventiveness. Particular note is made of 5 U.S.C. § 4501 et seq. which provides an incentive awards program for government employees.

6. Should the legal rules be tailored to pursue the primary goal of encouraging employee inventiveness or employer investment? Should parties be permitted to contract out of trade secret law and the rules allocating rights to an employee's creative activity?

7. The use by employees of an employer's confidential information may have taken on new dimensions after Carpenter v. United States, 484 U.S. 19 (1987). A reporter for the Wall Street Journal used his confidential knowledge of future "Heard on the Street" columns to profit in the stock market. The United States Supreme Court upheld the reporter's conviction under the federal mail fraud statute. The Court held the newspaper had a property interest in keeping its information secret prior to publication, citing *INS v. AP*, and the unauthorized use of that information was a scheme to defraud the newspaper even though the newspaper itself did not directly suffer financial loss. Does this implicate the mail fraud statute in every trade secret case in which the mails are utilized?

E.I. duPONT deNEMOURS & CO., INC. v. CHRISTOPHER

United States Court of Appeals, Fifth Circuit, 1970.
431 F.2d 1012, certiorari denied 400 U.S. 1024, 91 S.Ct. 581, 27 L.Ed.2d 637,
rehearing denied 401 U.S. 967, 91 S.Ct. 968, 28 L.Ed.2d 250.

GOLDBERG, CIRCUIT JUDGE. This is a case of industrial espionage in which an airplane is the cloak and a camera the dagger. The defendants-appellants, Rolfe and Gary Christopher, are photographers in Beaumont, Texas. The Christophers were hired by an unknown third party to take aerial photographs of new construction at the Beaumont plant of E.I. duPont deNemours & Company, Inc. Sixteen photographs of the DuPont facility were taken from the air on March 19, 1969, and these photographs were later developed and delivered to the third party.

DuPont employees apparently noticed the airplane on March 19 and immediately began an investigation to determine why the craft was circling over the plant. By that afternoon the investigation had disclosed that the craft was involved in a photographic expedition and that the Christophers were the photographers. DuPont contacted the Christophers that same afternoon and asked them to reveal the name of the person or corporation requesting the photographs. The Christophers refused to disclose this information, giving as their reason the client's desire to remain anonymous.

Having reached a dead end in the investigation, DuPont subsequently filed suit against the Christophers, alleging that the Christophers had wrongfully obtained photographs revealing DuPont's trade secrets which they then sold to the undisclosed third party. DuPont contended that it had developed a highly secret but unpatented process of producing methanol, a process which gave DuPont a competitive advantage over other producers. This process, DuPont alleged, was a trade secret developed after much expensive and time-consuming research, and a secret which the company had taken special precautions to safeguard. The area photographed by the Christophers was the plant designed to produce methanol by this secret process, and because the plant was still under construction parts of the process were exposed to view from directly above the construction area. Photographs of that area, DuPont alleged, would enable a skilled person to deduce the secret process for making methanol. DuPont thus contended that the Christophers had wrongfully appropriated DuPont trade secrets by taking the photographs and delivering them to the undisclosed third party. In its suit DuPont asked for damages to cover the loss it had already sustained as a result of the wrongful disclosure of the trade secret and sought temporary and permanent injunctions prohibiting any further circulation of the photographs already taken and prohibiting any additional photographing of the methanol plant.

[The trial court granted the Christophers' motion for an interlocutory appeal from the court's ruling that DuPont had stated a claim upon which relief could be granted.]

This is a case of first impression, for the Texas courts have not faced this precise factual issue, and sitting as a diversity court we must sensitize our *Erie antennae* to divine what the Texas courts would do if such a situation were presented to them. The only question involved in this interlocutory appeal is whether DuPont has asserted a claim upon which relief can be granted. The Christophers argued both at trial and before this court that they committed no "actionable wrong" in photographing the DuPont facility and passing these photographs on to their client because they conducted all of their activities in public airspace, violated no government aviation standard, did not breach any confidential relation, and did not engage in any fraudulent or illegal conduct. In short, the Christophers argue that for an appropriation of trade secrets to be wrongful there must be a trespass, other illegal conduct, or breach of a confidential relationship. We disagree.

It is true, as the Christophers assert, that the previous trade secret cases have contained one or more of these elements. However, we do not think that the Texas courts would limit the trade secret protection exclusively to these elements. On the contrary, in Hyde Corporation v. Huffines, 1958, 158 Tex. 566, 314 S.W.2d 763, the Texas Supreme Court specifically adopted the rule found in the Restatement of Torts which provides:

> "One who discloses or uses another's trade secret, without a privilege to do so, is liable to the other if
>
> (a) he discovered the secret by improper means, or
>
> (b) his disclosure or use constitutes a breach of confidence reposed in him by the other in disclosing the secret to him
> * * *." Restatement of Torts § 757 (1939).

Thus, although the previous cases have dealt with a breach of confidential relationship, a trespass, or other illegal conduct, the rule is much broader than the cases heretofore encountered. Not limiting itself to specific wrongs, Texas adopted subsection (a) of the Restatement which recognizes a cause of action for the discovery of a trade secret by any "improper" means.

The defendants, however, read Furr's Inc. v. United Specialty Advertising Co., Tex.Civ.App.1960, 338 S.W.2d 762, writ ref'd n.r.e., as limiting the Texas rule to breach of a confidential relationship. * * * We do not read *Furr's* as limiting the trade secret protection to a breach of confidential relationship when the facts of the case do raise the issue of some other wrongful conduct on the part of one discovering the trade secrets of another. If breach of confidence were meant to encompass the entire panoply of commercial improprieties, subsection (a) of the Restatement would be either surplusage or persiflage, an interpretation abhorrent to the traditional precision of the Restatement. We therefore find meaning in subsection (a) and think that the Texas Supreme Court clearly indicated by its adoption that there is a cause of action for the discovery of a trade secret by any "improper means."

The question remaining, therefore, is whether aerial photography of plant construction is an improper means of obtaining another's trade secret. We conclude that it is and that the Texas courts would so hold. The Supreme Court of that state has declared that "the undoubted tendency of the law has been to recognize and enforce higher standards of commercial morality in the business world." Hyde Corporation v. Huffines, supra, 314 S.W.2d at 773. That court has quoted with approval articles indicating that the *proper* means of gaining possession of a competitor's secret process is "through inspection and analysis" of the product in order to create a duplicate. K & G Tool & Service Co. v. G & G Fishing Tool Service, 1958, 158 Tex. 594, 314 S.W.2d 782, 783, 788. Later another Texas court explained:

> "The means by which the discovery is made may be obvious, and the experimentation leading from known factors to presently unknown results may be simple and lying in the public domain. But these facts do not destroy the value of the discovery and will not advantage a competitor who by unfair means obtains the knowledge *without paying the price expend-*

ed by the discoverer." Brown v. Fowler, Tex.Civ.App.1958, 316 S.W.2d 111, 114, writ ref'd n.r.e. (emphasis added).

We think, therefore, that the Texas rule is clear. One may use his competitor's secret process if he discovers the process by reverse engineering applied to the finished product; one may use a competitor's process if he discovers it by his own independent research; but one may not avoid these labors by taking the process from the discoverer without his permission at a time when he is taking reasonable precautions to maintain its secrecy. To obtain knowledge of a process without spending the time and money to discover it independently is *improper* unless the holder voluntarily discloses it or fails to take reasonable precautions to ensure its secrecy.

In the instant case the Christophers deliberately flew over the DuPont plant to get pictures of a process which DuPont had attempted to keep secret. The Christophers delivered their pictures to a third party who was certainly aware of the means by which they had been acquired and who may be planning to use the information contained therein to manufacture methanol by the DuPont process. The third party has a right to use this process only if he obtains this knowledge through his own research efforts, but thus far all information indicates that the third party has gained this knowledge solely by taking it from DuPont at a time when DuPont was making reasonable efforts to preserve its secrecy. In such a situation DuPont has a valid cause of action to prohibit the Christophers from improperly discovering its trade secret and to prohibit the undisclosed third party from using the improperly obtained information.

We note that that this view is in perfect accord with the position taken by the authors of the Restatement. * * *

In taking this position we realize that industrial espionage of the sort here perpetrated has become a popular sport in some segments of our industrial community. However, our devotion to free wheeling industrial competition must not force us into accepting the law of the jungle as the standard of morality expected in our commercial relations. Our tolerance of the espionage game must cease when the protections required to prevent another's spying cost so much that the spirit of inventiveness is dampened. Commercial privacy must be protected from espionage which could not have been reasonably anticipated or prevented. We do not mean to imply, however, that everything not in plain view is within the protected vale, nor that all information obtained through every extra optical extension is forbidden. Indeed, for our industrial competition to remain healthy there must be breathing room for observing a competing industrialist. A competitor can and must shop his competition for pricing and examine his products for quality, components, and methods of manufacture. Perhaps ordinary fences and roofs must be built to shut out incursive eyes, but we need not require the discoverer of a trade secret to guard against the unanticipated, the undetectable, or the unpreventable methods of espionage now available.

In the instant case DuPont was in the midst of constructing a plant. Although after construction the finished plant would have protected much of the process from view, during the period of construction the trade secret was exposed to view from the air. To require DuPont to put a roof over the unfinished plant to guard its secret would impose an enormous expense to prevent nothing more than a school boy's trick. We introduce here no new or radical ethic since our ethos has never given moral sanction to piracy. The market place must not deviate far from our mores. We should not require a person or corporation to take unreasonable precautions to prevent another from doing that which he ought not do in the first place. Reasonable precautions against predatory eyes we may require, but an impenetrable fortress is an unreasonable requirement, and we are not disposed to burden industrial inventors with such a duty in order to protect the fruits of their efforts. "Improper" will always be a word of many nuances, determined by time, place, and circumstances. We therefore need not proclaim a catalogue of commercial improprieties. Clearly, however, one of its commandments does say "thou shall not appropriate a trade secret through deviousness under circumstances in which countervailing defenses are not reasonably available."

* * *

The decision of the trial court is affirmed and the case remanded to that court for proceedings on the merits.

NOTES

1. In Chicago Lock Co. v. Fanberg, 676 F.2d 400 (9th Cir.1982) the Chicago Lock Company made a tubular lock which was particularly secure because its keys were difficult to duplicate. The Company maintained a file on all locks so that a customer could obtain a replacement key directly from the company. Owners of locks could also have a locksmith "pick" the lock and duplicate the key. When a locksmith "picks" a lock he will usually record the serial number and the tumbler combination so that if called again he does not have to repick the lock. Fanberg decided to publish to other locksmiths a compilation of the serial numbers and tumbler combinations for these tubular locks and solicited from other locksmiths their records as well as using his own. Chicago Lock, regarding this information as its tradesecret sought to prevent publication of the compilation. Held: Defendant did not use unfair means or violate a confidential relationship. Improper means under the Restatement assumes a duty not to disclose and since the tumbler combinations were in all instances secured by reverse engineering no duty not to disclose can be implied. The court also rejected the argument that since the locksmith owed a duty of confidentiality to his customers (the lock owners) that violation of this duty was also a breach of a duty to the company.

2. Compare with *Christopher,* Dow Chemical Co. v. United States, 476 U.S. 227 (1986), where it was held that the Environmental Protection Agency's aerial inspection of a chemical plant to detect violations of the Clean Air Act did not violate the Fourth Amendment.

3. How is the aerial photography in *duPont* different from reverse engineering to discover secrets? Professor Posner argues that authorizing aerial photography would not generate information but rather encourage the expenditure of resources to conceal the plant. Reverse engineering will generate information, presumably because the only self-help available is to forego exploiting the product. Posner, The Right of Privacy, 12 Ga.L.Rev. 393, 410 (1978). But can a product be designed to make it more difficult to copy, like, for instance, a dollar bill?

BRUNSWICK CORP. v. OUTBOARD MARINE CORP.

Supreme Court of Illinois, 1980.
79 Ill.2d 475, 38 Ill.Dec. 781, 404 N.E.2d 205.

*   *   * [Mercury and Outboard (OMC) compete in manufacturing and sale of outboard motors and in outboard motorboat racing. Mercury adapted a Bendix fuel-injection system for its outboard motors and had great success. Anderson, while an employee of Mercury, worked on the development and refinement of the system which was protected by Mercury as a trade secret. In January, 1975, a Mercury race driver named Van der Velden described the Mercury adaptation to officers of OMC. In December, 1976, Anderson left Mercury and began working for OMC. In May, 1977, Mercury learned that Anderson had ordered a Bendix-injection system and brought suit.]

RYAN, JUSTICE.

*   *   *

The trial court found the time required to successfully install a Bendix mechanical-fuel-injection system on an outboard engine for use in competitive boat racing would be, from conception to project completion, anywhere from 8 to 12 months. It also found that if OMC had tried to install a Bendix fuel-injection system on its racing engines, using the Van der Velden disclosures, it could have successfully completed the project by not later than November 30, 1976. In granting defendant's motion for summary judgment the trial court relied upon Northern Petrochemical Co. v. Tomlinson (7th Cir.1973), 484 F.2d 1057. In *Northern,* a diversity case governed by Illinois law, the Federal court interpreted ILG Industries, Inc. v. Scott (1971), 49 Ill.2d 88, 273 N.E.2d 393, and Schulenburg v. Signatrol, Inc. (1965), 33 Ill.2d 379, 212 N.E.2d 865, as holding that an abstention by a thief from the use of a trade secret, for a period in which it could have been developed lawfully, prevented the victim from enjoining the use at a later time. Thus, the trial court determined this action was barred.

The appellate court examined the *Northern* opinion and concluded that the Federal court of appeals misconstrued Illinois law. We do not find the holding in *Northern* to be helpful in this case. Also *ILG Industries* and *Schulenberg,* while helpful, are also not in point.

*   *   *

The judicial application of trade secret law has advanced two doctrinal bases for trade secret protection: (1) encouragement of invention and (2) maintenance of commercial morality. *   *   * Actually, a third element enters into the shaping of the remedy, that is, a public interest in having free competition in the sale and manufacture of goods not protected by a valid patent. * * *

In applying the three doctrinal bases to the facts of a case, one must consider that a permanent injunction, while punishing the wrong-doer, thereby promoting commercial morality, would, if the secret were lawfully discoverable, give to the plaintiff a windfall protection and would subvert the public interest in fostering competition and in allowing employees to make full use of their knowledge and ability. If no injunctive relief is granted, the faithless employee and wrongdoing competitor would be unpunished and would retain the benefit of a head start advantage over legitimate competitors. The innovator of the trade secret would also be afforded no protection. By enjoining the use of wrongfully acquired trade secrets for the approximate length of time it would require a legitimate competitor to develop a competitive product following a lawful disclosure of the information, the wrongdoer is deprived of any advantage from his wrongdoing, the developer of the trade secret is placed in the same position it would have occupied if the breach of confidence had not occurred, and the minimum restraint consistent with the other objectives would be placed upon competitors and the utilization of the competitors' and the employees' skills. See Winston Research Corp. v. Minnesota Mining & Manufacturing Co. (9th Cir. 1965), 350 F.2d 134, 142.

In our case there was no finding by the court that there was ever a lawful disclosure of the trade secret. The court found that it would take one year to reproduce this engine through the process of reverse engineering. This it considered to be the length of time that the defendant could be required to abstain from production. The court measured this period of time from the disclosure of the trade secret by Van der Velden and concluded that since the defendant had abstained from producing the engine longer than the time it would take to develop it, the plaintiff was not entitled to an injunction. However, the disclosure by Van der Velden is conceded to have been tortious. The plaintiff's racing engine is not sold to the general public, and the record does not indicate that there has been any lawful disclosure of the trade secret from which this information could be discovered through reverse engineering or otherwise. Furthermore, the 1-year period the trial court found as the time it would take to reproduce the trade secret comes from an affidavit of a vice-president of the company stating that it would take from 8 to 12 months at a minimum from conception to completion for a competitor to develop an engine using the Bendix fuel-injection system. This statement, however, appears to have been made in connection with the previous paragraph in the affidavit which referred to developing the system from photographs or sketches of the Mercury engine and through reverse engineering from such sketches or photographs. There appears to be no evidence in the record as to how long it would take to reproduce plaintiff's trade secret absent the tortious disclosure of the information. The facts actually involved in this case can be fully developed when the case is heard on its merits on retrial and the appropriate relief, if any, fashioned from the principles of trade secret law reviewed in this opinion.

We hold that the trial court erred in granting summary judgment in favor of the defendants. The judgment of the appellate court is therefore affirmed, and the cause is remanded to the circuit court of Lake County for further proceedings in accordance with this opinion.

Affirmed and remanded.

NOTES

1. *Northern Petrochemical,* cited in *Brunswick,* held that an injunction for trade secret appropriation could not extend beyond the date that the secret could have been acquired by lawful means. See also, Syntex Ophthalmics, Inc. v. Novicky, 745 F.2d 1423 (Fed.Cir.1984). Doesn't that make trade secret theft a winning proposition? If the theft is not detected, the thief clearly benefits, and there are many reasons to think that most trade secret thefts are not detected. See Kitch, The Law and Economics of Rights in Valuable Information, 9 J.Legal Stud. 683, 690–91 (1980). If the theft is detected, then the thief is no worse off and the monetary award is limited to his profits or the plaintiff's damages. Where the secret involved a more efficient process and the thief did not increase his market share, the plaintiff will have no damages. So the thief can turn over his profits and go right back to using the secret. Why isn't the permanent injunction, with its punitive element, appropriate in this situation? See id. at 693.

2. Some courts have suggested that *Sears* and *Compco* may require limiting injunctive relief in trade secret cases to the period of time necessary to put the plaintiff in the position he would have been in had the secret not been taken. See Hampton v. Blair Mfg. Co., 374 F.2d 969 (8th Cir.1967) reversing a perpetual injunction. Do you agree?

3. See Curtiss-Wright Corp. v. Edel-Brown Tool & Die Co., Inc., 407 N.E.2d 319 (Mass.1980) where the court approved a permanent injunction but noted that the defendant could in the future seek to have the injunction dissolved if there was a "substantial change of circumstances." The Uniform Trade Secrets Act § 2 (1979) also contemplates permanent injunctive relief subject to application for dissolution. And see Valco Cincinnati, Inc. v. N & D Machining Service, Inc., 24 Ohio St.3d 41, 492 N.E.2d 814 (1986) where a permanent injunction against an employee was affirmed because the particular actions of the employee were "so egregious and violative of the relationship of the parties involved * * * that the ultimate sanction of a permanent injunction * * *" was appropriate.

4. What is the appropriate measure for monetary relief in a trade secret case? Should the focus be on what the plaintiff has lost or what the defendant has gained? Courts have adopted both a damage and a restitution perspective, although it is generally held the plaintiff may not recover damages *and* the defendant's profits arising out of the use of the secret. The appropriate damage measure may depend on the particular facts of each case. Relevant factors will include whether the plaintiff or defendant commercially exploited the secret and whether the secrecy of the information was destroyed by defendant's use. Consider the following possibilities:

a. The secret involves a process which is not disclosed by sale of the product it produces. Plaintiff markets the product and defendant, by unlawful appropriation of the secret, is able to compete with plaintiff. Has plaintiff suffered any damage other than the loss of profits from sales plaintiff would have made but for defendant's competition? Is the measure of plaintiff's *damages* the profits of the defendant?

Or should the damages be measured by the royalty rate the plaintiff and defendant would have agreed to had they been willing to negotiate at the time of the appropriation? Or are these figures the same?

b. Assume the facts in "a" except that, in addition, the defendant's appropriation results in disclosure of the secret so that subsequently there are several innocent third party exploiters of the process.

c. Assume the facts in "a" except that the plaintiff does not exploit the process.

d. Assume the facts in "a" except that the defendant is unable to exploit the process.

Situation "d" is the *Northern Petrochemical* case supra note 1. In similar circumstances, the Fifth Circuit imposed a "reasonable royalty" rate directing the court to consider such factors as "the resulting and foreseeable changes in the parties' competitive posture; the prices past purchasers or licensees may have paid; the total value of the secret to the plaintiff, including the plaintiff's development costs and the importance of the secret to the plaintiff's business; the nature and extent of the use the defendant intended for the secret; and finally whatever other unique factors in the particular case which might have affected the parties' agreement, such as the ready availability of alternative processes." University Computing Co. v. Lykes-Youngstown Corp., 504 F.2d 518, 539 (5th Cir.1974).

In all of these cases, in establishing a reasonable royalty can you establish the maximum figure the defendant would be willing to pay for the secret? The minimum figure the plaintiff would accept? If there is a bargaining range, who should be assumed to have had the best of the bargain?

5. Over what time period should damages in trade secret cases be measured?

6. Other remedies available in trade secret infringement cases include punitive damages, attorneys fees, surrender or destruction of plans or other fruits from the appropriation, and assignment of patents acquired by the defendant as a result of the appropriation. See Milgrim, 2 Trade Secrets § 7.08 (1978). See also Johnston, Remedies in Trade Secret Litigation, 72 Nw.U.L. Rev. 1004 (1978). In recent years some American companies have become more aggressive about protecting technological information, and have been cooperating with prosecutors in the investigation and prosecution of criminal cases where employees or others have stolen trade secrets. Use of the mails as part of a scheme to appropriate trade secrets may result in a RICO violation. Formax, Inc. v. Hostert, 841 F.2d 388 (Fed.Cir.1988). Mail advertising of products that embody misappropriated trade secrets has been held to be a violation of the mail fraud statute sufficient to show a pattern of racketeering activity under RICO. Rockwell Graphic Systems, Inc. v. DEV Industries, 3 U.S. P.Q.2d 1545 (N.D.Ill.1987) (Unpublished case).

(B) INTERLUDE: GOVERNMENT DISCLOSURE OF
TRADE SECRETS

Courts have long held that the interest of a manufacturer to protect his trade secrets yields to a valid governmental interest in disclosure. Corn Products Refining Co. v. Eddy, 249 U.S. 427 (1919) (sustaining state labeling statute requiring a listing on the label of the percentage of each ingredient in a product against the argument that it deprived the manufacturer of property without due process). The owner may confront the potential for disclosure or use of its trade secrets by government in a number of different contexts. We only mention a few in passing here.

Discovery. Trade secrets are subject to discovery during litigation although Fed.R.Civil Proc. 26 authorizes federal courts to limit discovery of "trade secrets or confidential research, development, or commercial information" or to require disclosure in a specific way. It is common to have the court issue a protective order prohibiting individuals who see the material from disclosing it further.

Freedom of Information Act. The regulation of products by governmental agencies often requires the disclosure of trade secrets as part of the regulatory process. Regulation of safety, quality, or performance may require the disclosure of secret ingredients, formulas, or cost and pricing information. Agencies traditionally kept this information secret. However with passage of the Freedom of Information Act, 5 U.S. C. § 552, most information in the possession of federal agencies can be obtained by private citizens or disclosed voluntarily by the government. However, § 552(b)(4) exempts from mandatory disclosure "trade secrets and commercial or financial information obtained from a person and privileged or confidential." The definitions of "trade secret" and "commercial or financial information" in the exemption have created substantial litigation. See Public Citizen Health Research Group v. FDA, 704 F.2d 1280 (D.C.Cir.1983) (adopting narrower definition of trade secret than Restatement of Torts formulation; must be a secret that is used for making a commodity and is the end product of innovation or substantial effort); National Parks & Conservation Ass'n v. Morton, 498 F.2d 765 (D.C.Cir.1974) (defining confidential financial information as information the disclosure of which would impair the Government's ability to obtain information voluntarily from firms or that would cause substantial competitive harm to the owner of the information).

Safety and Effectiveness Testing. To market a new drug the company must secure clearance from the Food and Drug Administration as to the safety and effectiveness of the drug. To market a new pesticide the company must obtain a registration from the Environmental Protection Agency relative to the safety of the product. In both cases (and others) the firm must conduct extensive and expensive testing to convince the agency of the safety and effectiveness of the product.　Should the results of these tests be public information or regarded as trade secrets?

If Company *A* receives marketing clearance for its new drug ABC, should Company *X* be allowed to market drug XYZ if it proves that the two drugs are identical without conducting similar tests for safety and effectiveness?　To protect the testing information as a trade secret is to require other companies to engage in duplicative and wasteful testing. To disclose the test results or to permit their use by subsequent firms is to provide a competitive advantage to those firms that "appropriate" the investment in testing of other firms.

There appears to be no single solution to this problem.　The Federal Insecticide, Fungicide, and Rodenticide Act, 7 U.S.C. § 136 et seq. permits use of test results by subsequent parties but requires compensation to the original tester and provides for binding arbitration if the amount of compensation cannot be agreed upon.　The act was upheld against various claims in Thomas v. Union Carbide Agricultural Products Co., 473 U.S. 568 (1985);　Ruckelshaus v. Monsanto Co., 467 U.S. 986 (1984).　See also the Drug Price Competition and Patent Term Restoration Act of 1984, 21 U.S.C. § 301, which permits the extension of the patent term for new drugs for up to five years to account for the delays in premarket clearance by the FDA but also permits, upon expiration of the patent, subsequent parties to obtain clearance for copies of the patented drug without the need for duplicate testing.　See generally, McGarity & Shapiro, The Trade Secret Status of Health and Safety Testing Information: Reforming Agency Disclosure Policies, 93 Harv.L.Rev. 837 (1980); Kitch, The Patent System and the New Drug Application: An Evaluation of the Incentives for Private Investment in New Drug Research and Marketing, in Univ. of Chicago Center for Policy Study, Regulating New Drugs 81 (Landau ed. 1973).

(C)　THE STATUTORY ALTERNATIVE:　PATENT

The patent system often offers an alternative to the common law of trade secrets for protection of certain types of business information. This alternative protection is limited to a large degree by the requirements of subject matter and standard of invention found in the patent laws.　The purpose of this section is to suggest some of the issues in a trade secret context which the owner of valuable information must face because of the existence of the patent laws.

CONMAR PROD. CORP. v. UNIVERSAL SLIDE FASTENER CO.

United States Court of Appeals, Second Circuit, 1949.
172 F.2d 150.

[Plaintiff, Conmar Products, sued on three causes of action, the first two involving patent infringement and the third for inducing plaintiff's employees to divulge trade secrets.　The plaintiff's patents involve improvements on the manufacturing of zippers.　Zippers were originally protected under patents which at the time of this action had expired. The court held all of the claims in the plaintiff's patents invalid. The facts involving the third cause of action were these: One Voity worked for the plaintiff in a position that made him familiar with all the details of plaintiff's secrets. Voity as did other of plaintiff's employees signed a contract promising not to divulge anything which he might learn of plaintiff's methods. During the summer of 1939, Voity and others quit plaintiff and began working for defendant. While employed by defendant, Voity devised a machine embodying seven of the plaintiff's secrets. The lower court found and the court here affirmed that the defendant did not know that Voity had signed the secrecy agreement with plaintiff until November, 1940, after they had committed $40,000 for the machines. The court noted that plaintiff's active exploitation of patents for protection and a lack of custom in the art to require employee secrecy agreements would negate the inference that defendant should have known of the secrecy agreement.

Of the seven secrets alleged by plaintiff to be utilized in defendant's machine, six and part of the seventh were found in the disclosures of the two patents which the court here found, invalid. The other part of the seventh was disclosed in two patents issued in 1944–45.]

L. HAND, CHIEF JUDGE.

* * *

Courts have been accustomed to speak of trade secrets as "property," and at times to deal with them as if they were. That may be permissible and to some extent desirable, when the question is whether the wrongdoer has got access to them by some wrongful means, like breaking into a factory, or copying formulae or blue prints. When, however, the dispute turns, as it does here, upon whether the wrongdoer has acquired a secret from the employee who has himself acquired it lawfully, the wrong consists in inducing him to break his contract, or to be disloyal to a confidence reposed in him; and in either case it is a species of the tort—recognized now for over a century—of inducing an obligor to default upon an obligation. Since the specifications of the patents in suit disclosed the first six secrets and part of the seventh, that much of the secrets upon issue of the patents fell into the public demesne; and, prima facie, the defendants were free to use them. The Seventh Circuit, and apparently the Sixth as well, have, however, held that if before issue one has unlawfully obtained and used information which the specifications later disclose, he will not be free to continue to do so after issue; his wrong deprives him of the right which he would otherwise have had as a member of the public. We have twice refused to follow this doctrine; and we adhere to our decisions. Conceivably an employer might exact from his employees a contract not to disclose the information even after the patent issued. Of what possible value such a contract could be, we find it hard to conceive; but, if an employer did exact it, others would perhaps be obliged to turn to the specifications, if they would use the information. Be that as it may, we should not so construe any secrecy contract unless the intent were put in the most inescapable terms; and the plaintiff's contract had none such. In their absence we do not see why a wrongful inducement to divulge the disclosure before issue should deprive the wrongdoer of his right to avail himself of the patentee's dedication; for, as we have just said, the contract is to be construed as imposing secrecy only until issue. The doctrine must rest upon the theory that it is a proper penalty for the original wrong to deny the wrongdoer resort to the patent; and for that we can find no support in principle. Thus, any possible liability for exploiting whatever the patents in suit disclosed, ended with their issue. Since the earliest notice was on November 16, 1940, it is not necessary to resort to this reasoning as to the first six secrets and as to part of the seventh, because the two patents in suit issued before November 16, 1940; but the doctrine does become important as to the remaining part of the seventh secret.

It is almost, if not quite, impossible to learn what was that part of the seventh secret which did remain undisclosed after the issue of the Ulrich patent in suit; but for argument we will assume that the plaintiff proved that some parts did so remain. Whatever these were, they were all disclosed in two later patents to Ulrich: No. 2,338,884, issued January 11, 1944, and No. 2,370,380, issued February 27, 1945; and in any event the right to an injunction against exploiting any secrets whatever had therefore expired before the judgment was entered in November, 1947. All that could remain was the right to an accounting for profits or to a claim for damages between November 16, 1940, and the date of issue of these patents. We think, however, that the defendants had an excuse for exploiting that secret over that period, if they did so. As we have said, by November 16, 1940, they had invested $40,000 in the offending machine; that is, they had either paid or committed themselves to pay that much. The Restatement of Torts makes it an excuse for continued exploitation of a secret that at the time when one, who has theretofore been innocently exploiting it, first learns that he has induced the breach of an obligation, he has substantially changed his position. The opinions which support this are not very satisfactory; so far as we have found, in all but one or two it is doubtful whether what the judges say is more than dictum. However, they do all point the same way, for they assume that the situation is proper for the application of the doctrine that a bona fide purchaser takes free from a trust. The act of inducing the breach is the wrong, and the inducer's ignorance is an excuse only because one is not ordinarily held liable for consequences which one could not have anticipated. Although it is proper to prevent any continued use of the secret after the inducer has learned of the breach, the remedies must not invade the inducer's immunity over the period while he was ignorant. They may invade it, if the inducer has changed his position on the faith of his ignorance. We agree with the Comment of the Restatement that each case must stand on its facts; the answer depends upon weighing the loss to the inducer against the benefit to the obligee. In the case at bar we have no hesitation in deciding that issue in favor of the defendants. On November 16, 1940, when the defendants were first charged with any duty to desist, they had become free to exploit the major part of the secrets—the first six and an undetermined part of the seventh. Their duty at most extended no further than to change their machines and their methods, so as not to continue to exploit the still protected vestiges of the seventh; and even these would become free when the two other patents issued. Certainly, to compel them to make that change was seriously to invade the immunity they had enjoyed to that time; it would have compelled a disruption of their business and a redesigning of their machines. Opposed to this was a benefit to the plaintiff, the importance of which no one could even guess; for it must be measured by the advantage of suppressing only the use of the yet undisclosed part of the seventh secret, while the defendants remained free to use all the rest. The plaintiff had the burden of showing that the balance was in its favor, and we should be wholly unwarranted in deducing that conclusion from the maze of verbiage which wraps the issue.

The plaintiff finally argues that the defendants were liable because Voity was their agent, authorized to make the machines, and that while doing so, he knew of the contract and so supplied the missing factor in the liability and charged them as his principals. This reasoning would confine the excuse of ignorance to cases in which the inducer did not take the obligor into his own employ, and those are by far the greater number of cases in which he is aware of the obligation. For it will be seldom that one will innocently induce another's employees to disclose secrets of their employer's business, and yet not engage the employees in his own employ. That alone should be enough to condemn the reasoning practically. However, it is also wrong in theory. The fact that Voity knew of his own contract is immaterial; that knowledge might well have charged the defendants that he induced the breach of some other employee's obligation; but that he did not do. He did not induce himself to default in his own obligation. The transaction in which they ignorantly induced his breach was one in which Voity was the opposite party and did not represent them in any way. Having acquired the secrets innocently, they were entitled to exploit them till they learned that they had induced the breach of the contract.

Judgment affirmed.

NOTES

1. Does *Conmar* suggest the operation of the federal patent laws may have some preemptive effect on state trade secret law? What if a defendant acquires secret information by unfair means but could have acquired the same information from an issued patent subsequently held invalid. Can an injunction on the trade secret claim extend beyond the point the patent is declared invalid? Can an accounting be ordered for a time subsequent to the declaration of invalidity? See Schreyer v. Casco Prod. Corp. 190 F.2d 921 (2d Cir.1951) (accounting limited to period prior to declaration of invalidity, citing *Conmar*) and Franke v.

Wiltschek, 209 F.2d 493 (2d Cir.1953) (permanent injunction upheld under New York law with no reference to *Conmar*).

2. What does the *Conmar* decision suggest is the philosophy of the patent laws regarding the disclosure of inventions?

3. The mere filing of the application for a patent is not regarded as a disclosure of the claims to the public. A.O. Smith Corp. v. Petroleum Iron Works Co., 73 F.2d 531 (6th Cir.1934). The Patent Office is required to keep applications confidential. 35 U.S.C. § 122.

4. Should an inventor be allowed to retain his trade secret rights in an invention which the Patent Office rejects as unpatentable? Compare Brown v. Fowler, 316 S.W.2d 111 (Civ.App.1958) (protection granted where mechanical patent rejected but design patent granted after defendant breached royalty agreement) with American Gage & Mfg. Co. v. Maasdam, 245 F.2d 62 (6th Cir. 1957) (protection denied where patent rejected as fully disclosed by the prior art and examination of device disclosed elements of construction). Consider 37 C.F.R. § 1.14(b) (1985) which provides that abandoned applications are not open to public inspection and will not be returned to applicant. An application is deemed abandoned if the applicant fails to prosecute his application within six months of receiving a rejection. 37 C.F.R. § 1.135 (1988). An applicant, on the other hand, may waive his rights to an enforceable patent by giving written consent to the Patent Office. 37 C.F.R. § 1.138 (1988). It has been held that the Freedom of Information Act does not require disclosure of abandoned applications. Sears v. Gottschalk, 502 F.2d 122 (4th Cir.1974), cert. denied 422 U.S. 1056 (1975). However the Patent Office was required to disclose 175 volumes of memorandum decisions involving abandoned and rejected patents after excising exempt material—quotations from the patent applications. Irons v. Gottschalk, 548 F.2d 992 (D.C.Cir.1976).

What are the arguments in favor of disclosure of abandoned patents? Is it not wasteful to have other inventors seeking patents for innovations already rejected? Should the patent office be able to rely on an abandoned patent to prove that another applicant is not the first inventor?

5. If the applicant fails to obtain a patent from the Patent Office and prosecutes an appeal into the courts, it has been held that the court has inherent authority to seal the record and order ex camera proceedings. In re Mosher, 199 U.S.P.Q. 82 (CCPA 1978).

6. The student should examine § 102 of the patent law. This section is designed to encourage timely applications for patents, and it has a direct bearing on the interrelationship of trade secret law and patent law. The various clauses of § 102 will be examined in Chapter VI.

In general, the patent law gives priority to the first to invent. However, the date of invention is presumed to be the date of application unless the applicant can show an earlier date. Both the date of invention and the date of application are significant to the implementation of § 102. Under § 102(b) an invention which has been "in public use or on sale" for more than one year prior to application for a patent may not be patented. And § 102(g) destroys the priority of a first inventor who suppresses or conceals his invention. Exploitation of an invention in reliance on trade secret doctrine has been held to constitute, in some circumstances, both a "public use" and a suppression or concealment of the invention. The student should work through the provisions of § 102 as they relate to trade secret doctrines.

PROBLEM

A invents on January 1, 1970, and exploits his invention, relying on trade secret protection. *B* independently discovers the same innovation on January 1, 1975 and immediately applies for a patent. On July 1, 1975, *A* applies for a patent. Consider who is entitled to the patent. What are the rights of the respective parties after the patent issues?

(D) THE PRIVATE ALTERNATIVE: CONTRACT

REED, ROBERTS ASSOCIATES, INC. v. STRAUMAN

40 N.Y.2d 303, 386 N.Y.S.2d 677, 353 N.E.2d 590 (1976).

[John Strauman was hired by Reed, Roberts, a firm supplying advice to employers on compliance with State unemployment laws. Strauman signed a restrictive covenant with his employer by which he agreed not to "directly or indirectly solicit any of your clients" or for a three year period engage in competition with Reed, Roberts within the geographical area of New York. Over a 10 year period, Strauman became a valuable employee with increased responsibility for the internal affairs of the company. He was not responsible for sales or obtaining new customers. After 11 years with Reed, Roberts, Strauman formed his own company in direct competition with his former employer. This action was brought by Reed, Roberts to enforce the restrictive covenant.]

WACHTLER, JUDGE.

*   *   *

Generally negative covenants restricting competition are enforceable only to the extent that they satisfy the overriding requirement of reasonableness. Yet the formulation of reasonableness may vary with the context and type of restriction imposed. For example, where a business is sold, anticompetition covenants will be enforceable, if reasonable in time, scope and extent. These covenants are designed to protect the goodwill integral to the business from usurpation by the former owner while at the same time allowing an owner to profit from the goodwill which he may have spent years creating. *   *   * However, where an anticompetition covenant given by an employee to his employer is involved a stricter standard of reasonableness will be applied.

In this context a restrictive covenant will only be subject to specific enforcement to the extent that it is reasonable in time and area, necessary to protect the employer's legitimate interests, not harmful to the general public and not unreasonably burdensome to the employee *   *   *. Indeed, our economy is premised on the competition engendered by the uninhibited flow of services, talent and ideas. Therefore, no restrictions should fetter an employee's right to apply to his own best advantage the skills and knowledge acquired by the overall experience of his previous employment. This includes those techniques which are but "skillful variations of general processes known to the particular trade" (Restatement, Agency 2d, § 396, Comment *b*; see, also, Customer List—As Trade Secret-Factors, Ann., 28 A.L.R.3d 7).

Of course, the courts must also recognize the legitimate interest an employer has in safeguarding that which has made his business successful and to protect himself against deliberate surreptitious commercial piracy. Thus restrictive covenants will be enforceable to the extent necessary to prevent the disclosure or use of trade secrets or confidential customer information * * *.

In addition injunctive relief may be available where an employee's services are unique or extraordinary and the covenant is reasonable * * *. This latter principle has been interpreted to reach agreements between members of the learned professions (e.g., Karpinski v. Ingrasci, 28 N.Y.2d 45, 320 N.Y.S.2d 1, 268 N.E.2d 751).

With these principles in mind we consider first the issue of solicitation of customers in the case at bar. The courts below found, and Reed, Roberts does not dispute, that there were no trade secrets involved here. The thrust of Reed, Roberts' argument is that by virtue of Strauman's position in charge of internal administration he was privy to sensitive and confidential customer information which he should not be permitted to convert to his own use. The law enunciated in Leo Silfen, Inc. v. Cream, 29 N.Y.2d 387, 328 N.Y.S.2d 423, 278 N.E.2d 636 is dispositive. There, as here, the plaintiff failed to sustain its allegation that the defendant had pirated the actual customer list. Rather Silfen argued that in light of the funds expended to compile the list it would be unfair to allow the defendant to solicit the clients of his former employer. We held that where the employee engaged in no wrongful conduct and the names and addresses of potential customers were readily discoverable through public sources, an injunction would not lie. Similarly here there was no finding that Strauman acted wrongfully by either pilfering or memorizing the customer list * * *.

More important, by Reed, Roberts' own admission every company with employees is a prospective customer and the solicitation of customers was usually done through the use of nationally known publications such as Dun and Bradstreet's *Million Dollar Directory* where even the name of the person to contact regarding these services is readily available (Leo Silfen, Inc. v. Cream, supra, 29 N.Y.2d pp. 392–393, 328 N.Y.S.2d pp. 427–28, 278 N.E.2d pp. 639–40). It strains credulity to characterize this type of information as confidential. * * *

Apparently, the employer is more concerned about Strauman's knowledge of the intricacies of their business operation. However, absent any wrongdoing, we cannot agree that Strauman should be prohibited from utilizing his knowledge and talents in this area (see Restatement, Agency 2d, § 396, Comment *b*). A contrary holding would make those in charge of operations or specialists in certain aspects of an enterprise virtual hostages of their employers. Where the knowledge does not qualify for protection as a trade secret and there has been no conspiracy or breach of trust resulting in commercial piracy we see no reason to inhibit the employee's ability to realize his potential both professionally and financially by availing himself of opportunity.   Therefore, despite Strauman's excellence or value to Reed, Roberts the trial court's finding that his services were not extraordinary or unique is controlling and properly resulted in a denial of the injunction against operating a competing business.

EDEN HANNON & CO. v. SUMITOMO TRUST & BANKING CO., 914 F.2d 556 (4th Cir.1990).   [The Hannon Co. advised institutional investors on how to fashion bids for purchase of Xerox lease portfolios.   To provide this advice Hannon had to disclose to the investors its confidential methods and economic models.   To protect itself, Hannon required investors to sign a "Nondisclosure and Noncircumvention" agreement that obligated the investor not to disclose any of Hannon's methods or to independently bid on Xerox portfolios for a three year period. Sumitomo signed the agreement, received Hannon's advice, but independently and successfully bid on a portfolio.   The Fourth Circuit held the agreement valid and imposed a constructive trust on the profits from the portfolio on Hannon's behalf.]

The Noncircumvention and Nondisclosure Agreement (in the forthcoming discussion, we will call this a "noncircumvention agreement") is nearly identical in purpose to an employment agreement.   Most importantly, an employment agreement enables an employer to expose his employees to the firm's trade secrets.   Similarly, a noncircumvention agreement enables potential joint venturers to share confidential information regarding a possible deal.   In both instances, the idea is to share trade secrets so that business can be conducted without losing control over the secrets.   Often, the value of a firm is its special knowledge, and this knowledge may not be an idea protectible by patent or copyright.   If that firm cannot protect that knowledge from immediate dissemination to competitors, it may not be able to reap the benefits from the time and money invested in building that knowledge. If firms are not permitted to construct a reasonable legal mechanism to protect that knowledge, then the incentive to engage in the building of such knowledge will be greatly reduced.   Free riders will capture this information at little or no cost and produce a product cheaper than the firm which created the knowledge, because it will not have to carry the costs of creating that knowledge in its pricing.   Faced with this free rider problem, this information may not be created, and thus everybody loses.   To counteract that problem, an employer can demand that employees sign an employment agreement as a condition of their contract, and thus protect the confidential information.   This means that if an employer takes in an employee and exposes that employee to trade secrets, the employer does not have to allow the employee to go across the street and set up shop once that employee has mastered the information.   Although it was not explained in this detail, Virginia has recognized this interest in protecting confidential information.

These employment agreements (or in the present case, a noncircumvention agreement) are often necessary because it can be very difficult to prove the theft of a trade secret by a former employee. Often, the purpose of an employment agreement can be to prevent the dissemination of trade secrets, yet a mere ban on using trade secrets after the termination of employment would be difficult to enforce. Judge Lord explained the problem well in Greenberg v. Croydon Plastics Co., Inc., 378 F.Supp. 806, 814 (E.D.Pa.1974):

> Plaintiffs in trade secret cases, who must prove by a fair preponderance of the evidence disclosure to third parties and use of the trade secret by the third parties, are confronted with an extraordinarily difficult task. Misappropriation and misuse can rarely be proved by convincing direct evidence. In most cases plaintiffs must construct a web of perhaps ambiguous circumstantial evidence from which the trier of fact may draw inferences which convince him that it is more probable than not that what the plaintiffs allege happened did in fact take place. Against this often delicate construct of circumstantial evidence there frequently must be balanced defendants' witnesses who directly deny everything.

Actually, Judge Lord's description of the problem covers just the tip of the iceberg. There are several problems with trying to prevent former employees from illegally using the former employer's trade secrets, and these problems are caused by the status of the law regarding the misappropriation of trade secrets. First, as Judge Lord depicted so well, it is difficult to prove that the trade secret was actually used. Second, the former employee tends to get "one free bite" at the trade secret. Most courts will refuse to enjoin the disclosure or use of a trade secret until its illegal use is imminent or until it has already occurred. By that time, much of the damage may be done. Third, even if a clearly illegal use of the trade secret by a former employee can be shown, most courts will not enjoin that person from working for the competition on that basis. Instead, they will merely enjoin future disclosure of the trade secret. Yet, policing the former employee's compliance with that injunction will be difficult. Finally, even if the employee does not maliciously attempt to use his former employer's trade secrets in the new employer's workplace, avoiding this use can be difficult. It would be difficult for the employee to guard the trade secret of the former employer and be effective for the new employer.

In order to avoid these problems, many employers ask their employees to sign non-competition agreements. These agreements prevent an employee from working with the competition within a limited geographical range of the former employer and for a limited time. As seen above, Virginia courts will only enforce these agreements if they are reasonable. Yet, when they are valid, they make the guarding of a trade secret easier since they remove the opportunity for the former employee to pass on the trade secret to the competition, either malevolently or benevolently. This does not supplant the need for law protecting trade secrets. Non-competition agreements cannot prevent disclosure anywhere in the world and until the end of time, for they would be held unreasonable. Instead, a non-competition agreement will merely prevent the illegal use of a trade secret next door in the near future, where the use might do the most damage.

WARNER–LAMBERT PHARM. CO. v. JOHN J. REYNOLDS, INC.

United States District Court, S.D. New York, 1959.
178 F.Supp. 655, aff'd on opinion below, 280 F.2d 197.

[Plaintiff manufactured and sold an antiseptic liquid compound called "Listerine" under an exclusive license from the defendant, which is the successor in interest of the developer of the compound. The license agreement dates back to 1881 and contains a royalty payment by plaintiff to defendant based on the amount of Listerine manufactured and sold. Royalty payments at the time of the action amounted to about one and one-half million dollars per year. At the time of the original agreement, Listerine was a secret formula. Between the years 1881 and 1949, the formula became a matter of public knowledge and had been published in the United States Pharmacopia, the National Formulary and the Journal of the American Medical Association "and also as a result of proceedings brought against plaintiff's predecessor by the Federal Trade Commission." The plaintiff was not responsible for any of the publications. The plaintiff brings this action for a judgment declaring that it is no longer obligated to pay royalties because the formula is no longer secret. The court found that the unambiguous language of the agreement contemplated royalty payments as long as the plaintiff manufactured and sold "Listerine". The court rejected plaintiff's contention that this was a contract in "perpetuity" which the common law abhorred and should be interpreted as requiring royalties for a reasonable time—while the formula remained secret.]

There is nothing unreasonable or irrational about imposing such an obligation. It is entirely rational and sensible that the obligation to make payments should be based upon the business which flows from the formula conveyed. Whether or not the obligation continues is in the control of the plaintiff itself. For the plaintiff has the right to terminate its obligation to pay whenever in good faith it desires to cease the manufacture or sale of Listerine. * * * This would seem to end the matter.

However, plaintiff urges with vigor that the agreement must be differently construed because it involved the conveyance of a secret formula. The main thrust of its argument is that despite the language which the parties used the court must imply a limitation upon Lambert's obligation to pay measured by the length of time that the Listerine formula remained secret.

To sustain this theory plaintiff relies upon a number of cases involving the obligations of licensees of copyrights or patents to make continuing payments to the owner or licensor, and argues that these cases are controlling here.

It is quite plain that were it not for the patent and copyright features of such license agreements the term would be measured by use. * * *

There are other cases on which the plaintiff relies which hold that when a patent or copyright is held to be invalid before the expiration of the statutory term of the grant the obligation to pay royalties under a license terminates. This is but another aspect of the same principle. * * *

Paralleling the concept that the licensing of a patent or copyright contracts only for the statutory monopoly granted in such cases is the concept not so frequently expressed that public policy may require a termination of the obligation to pay when the patent or copyright term is ended. * * *

In the patent and copyright cases the parties are dealing with a fixed statutory term and the monopoly granted by that term. This monopoly, created by Congress, is designed to preserve exclusivity in the grantee during the statutory term and to release the patented or copyrighted material to the general public for general use thereafter. This is the public policy of the statutes in reference to which such contracts are made and it is against this background that the parties to patent and copyright license agreements contract.

Here, however, there is no such public policy. The parties are free to contract with respect to a secret formula or trade secret in any manner which they determine for their own best interests. A secret formula or trade secret may remain secret indefinitely. It may be discovered by someone else almost immediately after the agreement is entered into. Whoever discovers it for himself by legitimate means is entitled to its use. See, e.g., Tabor v. Hoffman, 118 N.Y. 30, 23 N.E. 12.

But that does not mean that one who acquires a secret formula or a trade secret through a valid and binding contract is then enabled to escape from an obligation to which he bound himself simply because the secret is discovered by a third party or by the general public. I see no reason why the court should imply such a term or condition in a contract providing on its face that payment shall be co-extensive with use. To do so here would be to rewrite the contract for the parties without any indication that they intended such a result.

* * *

One who acquires a trade secret or secret formula takes it subject to the risk that there be a disclosure. The inventor makes no representation that the secret is non-discoverable. All the inventor does is to convey the knowledge of the formula or process which is unknown to the purchaser and which in so far as both parties then know is unknown to any one else. The terms upon which they contract with reference to this subject matter are purely up to them and are governed by what the contract they enter into provides.

If they desire the payments or royalties should continue only until the secret is disclosed to the public it is easy enough for them to say so. But there is no justification for implying such a provision if the parties do not include it in their contract, particularly where the language which they use by fair intendment provides otherwise.

* * *

If plaintiff wishes to avoid its obligations under the contract it is free to do so, and, indeed, the contract itself indicates how this may be done. The fact that neither the plaintiff nor its predecessors have done so, and that the plaintiff continues to manufacture and sell Listerine under the Lawrence formula with great success, indicates how valuable the rights under the contract are and how unjust it would be to permit it to have its cake and eat it too.

Thus, I hold that under the agreements in suit plaintiff is obligated to make the periodic payments called for by them as long as it continues to manufacture and sell the preparation described in them as Listerine.

* * *

Defendants' motions for summary judgment are in all respects granted. Judgment for defendants dismissing the second amended complaint will be entered accordingly.

It is so ordered.

NOTES

1. *Reed, Roberts* involved the activities of a former employee. Should the same requirement of reasonableness be applied to the seller of the good will of a business who after the sale solicits former customers for a competing firm? In Mohawk Maintenance Co., Inc. v. Kessler, 52 N.Y.2d 276, 419 N.E.2d 324 (1981) the New York Court of Appeals held that although an anticompetition agreement must be limited in duration and geographic scope, there is an independent tort duty implied from the circumstances not to solicit former customers after selling the "good will" of a business. This duty is not limited in duration! This unlimited duty applies only to sellers of good will and not to employees or contractors, Chevron U.S.A. Inc. v. Roxen Service, Inc., 813 F.2d 26 (2d Cir. 1987). And the duty requires only a restraint on solicitation of former customers and not on subsequent transactions initiated by the customer. Hyde Park Products Corp. v. Maximilian Lerner Corp., 65 N.Y.2d 316, 491 N.Y.S.2d 302, 480 N.E.2d 1084 (1985).

2. In Ingersoll–Rand Co. v. Ciavatta, 216 N.J.Super. 667, 524 A.2d 866 (1987) the employee assigned to his employer all right, title, and interest in any invention or design that he conceived, developed, or perfected "within one year after termination of such employment if conceived as a result of and is attributable to work done during such employment and relates to [the employer's business]." Within one year of being terminated the employee invented a machine that competed with a machine of the employer. The trial judge found the employee's machine did not incorporate any trade secret or confidential information of the employer but did fit within the agreement. The trial judge ordered the employee to assign the patent to the employer. Held: Reversed. In the context of this case, as long as there are no trade secrets or confidential

information used, the post-employment restraint fails to permit the employee to use his skill and training in subsequent employment and is thus unreasonable and unenforceable.

3. The plaintiff's predecessor in *Warner-Lambert* had first manufactured and sold the formula under the trademark "Listerine," thus acquiring the common law rights to the mark. If the defendant's successor in interest had first sold the formula under the name "Listerine" and then licensed the right to use the name, there would be no doubt about the outcome. Trademark rights are, given continued use, and, under the Lanham Act § 8(a), 15 U.S.C.A. § 1058(a), given reregistration every twenty years, perpetual. If only the trademark were licensed, would the plaintiff remain free to manufacture and sell the formula under a different name? Would that be an important difference?

4. Is the effect of *Reed, Roberts* that restrictive covenants between employers and employees are useless? Does the case hold that an agreement is only enforceable if it reaches the same result that tort law would reach in the absence of the agreement? Does *Eden Hannon* cast further doubt on the efficacy of trade secret law? Is this inconsistent with *Warner-Lambert?* Judge Hand in *Conmar,* supra, suggested he would not interpret a contract for royalties on a secret to extend beyond the period of secrecy unless the terms of the contract were clear. Assume the parties clearly intended that result. Would you enforce it? Does *Eden Hannon* support enforcement of such agreements? Does the doctrine of *Sears* and *Compco* help answer these questions? Does the analysis in *Reed, Roberts* apply to a situation like *Warner-Lambert?*

5. For an excellent analysis of historical and current approaches to the problem of post-employment agreements see Blake, Employee Agreements Not to Compete, 73 Harv.L.Rev. 625 (1960).

The question of why courts are reluctant to enforce post-employment contractual restraints is discussed in Kitch, The Law and Economics of Rights in Valuable Information, 9 J.Leg.Stud. 683 (1980). The Blake article summarizes the two reasons traditionally given. First, that employees lack the sophistication and foresight necessary to bargain intelligently on their rights after the unexpected (at the time of bargaining) contingency of employment termination. Second, it is argued that post-employment contractual restraints are anti-competitive. Kitch argues that neither reason is very satisfactory.

The lack of capacity argument is unsatisfactory because the courts have permitted employees to freely bargain on far more difficult questions relating to post-employment pension rights and because the class of contracts approved and disapproved by the courts has no correspondence to the presence or absence of bargaining sophistication. Young baseball players, aspiring actors, and dairy routemen have been held to their contracts while sophisticated executives like John Strauman in *Reed, Roberts* are allowed to avoid their contracts.

Second, there is nothing more anti-competitive about a post-employment contract than there is about any long term supply contract for an input to production. The contract does not keep an employee from moving to his highest valued use. It only means that some payment must be made to the employer to compensate him for the loss of his contract rights. Consider the frequency with which professional baseball players change teams in spite of the substantial restraints on post-employment choices which the law permits.

6. It is likely, is it not, that one important piece of information that John Strauman took from his employer in *Reed, Roberts* was the knowledge that the activity was profitable? Why is he entitled to exploit that information when he did not discover or develop the profitable opportunity?

(E) PREEMPTION

BRULOTTE v. THYS CO.

Supreme Court of the United States, 1964.
379 U.S. 29, 85 S.Ct. 176, 13 L.Ed.2d 99, rehearing denied 379 U.S. 985, 85 S.Ct. 638, 13 L.Ed.2d 579.

MR. JUSTICE DOUGLAS delivered the opinion of the Court.

Respondent, owner of various patents for hop-picking, sold a machine to each of the petitioners for a flat sum [1] and issued a license for its use. Under that license there is payable a minimum royalty of $500 for each hop-picking season or $3.33⅓ per 200 pounds of dried hops harvested by the machine, whichever is greater. The licenses by their terms may not be assigned nor may the machines be removed from Yakima County. The licenses issued to petitioners listed 12 patents relating to hop-picking machines; but only seven were incorporated into the machines sold to and licensed for use by petitioners. Of those seven all expired on or before 1957. But the licenses issued by respondent to them continued for terms beyond that date.

Petitioners refused to make royalty payments accruing both before and after the expiration of the patents. This suit followed. One defense was misuse of the patents through extension of the license agreements beyond the expiration date of the patents. The trial court rendered judgment for respondent and the Supreme Court of Washington affirmed. 62 Wash.2d 284, 382 P.2d 271. The case is here on a writ of certiorari. 376 U.S. 905.

We conclude that the judgment below must be reversed insofar as it allows royalties to be collected which accrued after the last of the patents incorporated into the machines had expired.

The Constitution by Art. I, § 8 authorizes Congress to secure "for limited times" to inventors "the exclusive right" to their discoveries. Congress exercised that power by 35 U.S.C.A. § 154 which * * * [specifies a grant of seventeen years].

* * *

The Supreme Court of Washington held that in the present case the period during which royalties were required was only "a reasonable amount of time over which to spread the payments for the use of the patent." 62 Wash.2d, at 291, 382 P.2d, at 275. But there is intrinsic evidence that the agreements were not designed with that limited view. As we have seen, the purchase price in each case was a flat sum, the annual payments not being part of the purchase price but royalties for use of the machine during that year. The royalty payments due for the

---

1. One petitioner paid $3,125 for "title" to a machine, the other petitioner, $3,300.

post-expiration period are by their terms for use during that period, and are not deferred payments for use during the pre-expiration period. Nor is the case like the hypothetical ones put to us where non-patented articles are marketed at prices based on use. The machines in issue here were patented articles and the royalties exacted were the same for the post expiration period as they were for the period of the patent. That is peculiarly significant in this case in view of other provisions of the license agreements. The license agreements prevent assignment of the machines or their removal from Yakima County *after,* as well as before, the expiration of the patents.

Those restrictions are apt and pertinent to protection of the patent monopoly; and their applicability to the post-expiration period is a telltale sign that the licensor was using the licenses to project its monopoly beyond the patent period. They forcefully negate the suggestion that we have here a bare arrangement for a sale or a lease at an undetermined price, based on use. The sale or lease of *unpatented* machines on long-term payments based on a deferred purchase price or on use would present wholly different considerations. Those arrangements seldom rise to the level of a federal question. But patents are in the federal domain; and "whatever the legal device employed" * * * a projection of the patent monopoly after the patent expires is not enforceable. The present licenses draw no line between the term of the patent and the post-expiration period. The same provisions as respects both use and royalties are applicable to each. The contracts are, therefore, on their face a bald attempt to exact the same terms and conditions for the period after the patents have expired as they do for the monopoly period. We are, therefore, unable to conjecture what the bargaining position of the parties might have been and what resultant arrangement might have emerged had the provision for post-expiration royalties been divorced from the patent and nowise subject it to its leverage.

In light of those considerations, we conclude that a patentee's use of a royalty agreement that projects beyond the expiration date of the patent is unlawful *per se.* If that device were available to patentees, the free market visualized for the post-expiration period would be subject to monopoly influences that have no proper place there.

* * *

* * * We share the views of the Court of Appeals in Ar-Tik Systems, Inc. v. Dairy Queen, Inc., 302 F.2d 496, 510, that after expiration of the last of the patents incorporated in the machines "the grant of patent monopoly was spent" and that an attempt to project it into another term by continuation of the licensing agreement is unenforceable.

Reversed.

MR. JUSTICE HARLAN, dissenting.

The Court holds that the Thys Company unlawfully misused its patent monopoly by contracting with purchasers of its patented machines for royalty payments based on use beyond the patent term. I think that more discriminating analysis than the Court has seen fit to give this case produces a different result.

The patent laws prohibit post-expiration restrictions on the use of patented ideas; they have no bearing on use restrictions upon non-patented, tangible machines. We have before us a mixed case involving the sale of a tangible machine which incorporates an intangible, patented idea. My effort in what follows is to separate out these two notions, to show that there is no substantial restriction on the use of the Thys *idea,* and to demonstrate that what slight restriction there may be is less objectionable than other post-expiration use restrictions which are clearly acceptable.

I.

It surely cannot be questioned that Thys could have lawfully set a fixed price for its machine and extended credit terms beyond the patent period. It is equally unquestionable, I take it, that if Thys had had no patent or if its patent had expired, it could have sold its machines at a flexible, undetermined price based on use; for example, a phonograph record manufacturer could sell a recording of a song in the public domain to a juke-box owner for an undetermined consideration based on the number of times the record was played.

Conversely it should be equally clear that if Thys licensed another manufacturer to produce hop-picking machines incorporating any of the Thys patents, royalties could not be exacted beyond the patent term. Such royalties would restrict the manufacturer's exploitation of the *idea* after it falls into the public domain, and no such restriction should be valid. To give another example unconnected with a tangible machine, a song writer could charge a royalty every time his song—his idea—was sung for profit during the period of copyright. But once the song falls into the public domain each and every member of the public should be free to sing it.

In fact Thys sells both a machine and the use of an idea. The company should be free to restrict the use of its machine, as in the first two examples given above. It may not restrict the use of its patented idea once it has fallen into the public domain. Whether it has done so must be the point of inquiry.

Consider the situation as of the day the patent monopoly ends. Any manufacturer is completely free to produce Thys-type hop-pickers. The farmer who has previously purchased a Thys machine is free to buy and use any other kind of machine whether or not it incorporates the Thys idea, or make one himself if he is able. Of course, he is not entitled as against Thys to the *free* use of any Thys machine. The Court's opinion must therefore ultimately rest on the proposition that the purchasing farmer is restricted in using his particular machine, embodying as it does an application of the patented idea, by the fact that royalties are tied directly to use.

To test this proposition I again put a hypothetical. Assume that a Thys contract called for neither an initial flat-sum payment nor any annual minimum royalties; Thys' sole recompense for giving up ownership of its machine was a royalty payment extending beyond the patent term based on use, without any requirement either to use the machine or not to use a competitor's. A moment's thought reveals that, despite the clear restriction on use both before and after the expiration of the patent term, the arrangement would involve no misuse of patent leverage.[1] Unless the Court's opinion rests on technicalities of contract draftsmanship and not on the economic substance of the transaction, the distinction between the hypothetical and the actual case lies only in the cumulative investment consisting of the initial and minimum payments independent of use, which the purchaser obligated himself to make to Thys. I fail to see why this distinguishing feature should be critical. If anything the investment will encourage the purchaser to use his machine in order to amortize the machine's fixed cost over as large a production base as possible. Yet the gravamen of the majority opinion is restriction, not encouragement, of use.

II.

The essence of the majority opinion may lie in some notion that "patent leverage" being used by Thys to exact use payments extending beyond the patent term somehow allows Thys to extract more onerous payments from the farmers than would otherwise be obtainable. If this be the case, the Court must in some way distinguish long-term use payments from long-term installment payments of a flat-sum purchase price. For the danger which it seems to fear would appear to inhere equally in both, and as I read the Court's opinion, the latter type of arrangement is lawful despite the fact that failure to pay an installment under a conditional sales contract would permit the seller to recapture the machine, thus terminating—not merely restricting—the farmer's use of it. Furthermore, since the judgments against petitioners were based almost entirely on defaults in paying the $500 minimums and not on failures to pay for above-minimum use,[2] any such distinction of extended use payments and extended installments, even if accepted, would not justify eradicating all petitioners' obligations beyond the patent term, but only those based on use above the stated minimums; for the minimums by themselves, being payable whether or not a machine has been used, are precisely identical in substantive economic effect to flat installments.

In fact a distinction should not be accepted based on the assumption that Thys, which exploits its patents by selling its patented

1. Installment of a patented, coin-operated washing machine in the basement of an apartment building without charge except that the landlord and his tenants must deposit 25 cents for every use, should not constitute patent misuse.

2. Petitioner Charvet was indebted to Thys only to the extent of the minimums; petitioner Brulotte was in default approximately $4,500 of which $3,120 was attributable to minimums.

machines rather than licensing others to manufacture them, can use its patent leverage to exact more onerous payments from farmers by gearing price to use instead of charging a flat sum. Four possible situations must be considered. The purchasing farmer could overestimate, exactly estimate, underestimate, or have no firm estimate of his use requirements for a Thys machine. If he overestimates or exactly estimates, the farmer will be fully aware of what the machine will cost him in the long run, and it is unrealistic to suppose that in such circumstances he would be willing to pay more to have the machine on use than on straight terms. If the farmer underestimates, the thought may be that Thys will take advantage of him; but surely the farmer is in a better position than Thys or anyone else to estimate his own requirements and is hardly in need of the Court's protection in this respect. If the farmer has no fixed estimate of his use requirements he may have good business reasons entirely unconnected with "patent leverage" for wanting payments tied to use, and may indeed be willing to pay more in the long run to obtain such an arrangement. One final example should illustrate my point:

At the time when the Thys patent term still has a few years to run, a farmer who has been picking his hops by hand comes into the Thys retail outlet to inquire about the mechanical pickers. The salesman concludes his description of the advantages of the Thys machine with the price tag—$20,000. Value to the farmer depends completely on the use he will derive from the machine; he is willing to obligate himself on long credit terms to pay $10,000, but unless the machine can substantially outpick his old hand-picking methods, it is worth no more to him. He therefore offers to pay $2,000 down, $400 annually for 20 years, and an additional payment during the contract term for any production he can derive from the machine over and above the minimum amount he could pick by hand. Thys accepts, and by doing so, according to the majority, commits a *per se* misuse of its patent. I cannot believe that this is good law.[3]

III.

The possibility remains that the Court is basing its decision on the technical framing of the contract and would have treated the case differently if title had been declared to pass at the termination instead of the outset of the contract term, or if the use payments had been verbally disassociated from the patent licenses and described as a convenient means of spreading out payments for the machine. If indeed the impact of the opinion is that Thys must redraft its contracts

---

3. The Court also adverts to the provisions in the license agreements prohibiting "assignment of the machines or their removal from Yakima County" (ante, p. 32) during the terms of the agreements. Such provisions, however, are surely appropriate to secure performance of what are in effect conditional sales agreements and they do not advance the argument for patent misuse.

Furthermore, it should not be overlooked that we are dealing here with a patent, not an antitrust, case, there being no basis in the record for concluding that Thys' arrangements with its licensees were such as to run afoul of the antitrust laws.

to achieve the same economic results, the decision is not only wrong, but conspicuously ineffectual.

I would affirm.

NOTES

1. *Brulotte* was decided in the same year as *Sears* and *Compco*. Are they all based on the same basic philosophy? Could you reformulate the *Brulotte* opinion into one asserting federal preemption rather than patent misuse?

2. If Thys Co. can not extend royalty payments based on use beyond the expiration of the patents, can it exact royalty payments based on use *prior to* issuance of a patent? Would this unreasonably extend the patent monopoly? Would it make a difference if a patent application were pending? See Congoleum Industries, Inc. v. Armstrong Cork Co., 366 F.Supp. 220 (E.D.Pa.1973).

LEAR, INC. v. ADKINS
Supreme Court of the United States, 1969.
395 U.S. 653, 89 S.Ct. 1902, 23 L.Ed.2d 610.

Mr. Justice Harlan delivered the opinion of the Court.

[In 1952 Lear hired John Adkins to develop improvements in the gyroscope utilized in Lear's aircraft. The parties signed a "rudimentary one-page agreement" giving Adkins the property interest in all ideas or inventions in consideration for Adkins' agreement to license their use by Lear on a "mutually satisfactory royalty basis." Adkins' efforts bore fruit and in 1954 he applied for a patent on his gyroscope improvements. On September 15, 1955, after lengthy negotiations, Lear and Adkins signed a licensing agreement governing Lear's use of the improved gyroscope upon payment of specified royalties. The license agreement contained a clause giving Lear the right to terminate the agreement if the Patent Office refused to issue a patent or an issued patent was subsequently held invalid.

Lear began paying royalties. Adkins, however, had difficulty convincing the Patent Office of the novelty of his ideas. In 1957, Lear finally announced it would discontinue royalty payments on the belief that no patent would issue. In 1960, the Patent Office issued a patent to Adkins who immediately filed suit against Lear for royalties. Lear maintained that the patent was invalid because Adkins' inventions were anticipated by prior art. The California Supreme Court held that a licensee like Lear is estopped from asserting the invalidity of the licensed patent and accordingly approved an award for royalties owed pursuant to the agreement. In the part of the opinion omitted below, the United States Supreme Court reviews the history of the licensee estoppel doctrine, recognizes that several exceptions had been adopted, and concludes that the doctrine should be discarded in its entirety.

Recognizing that, on the one hand, "the law of contracts forbids a purchaser to repudiate his promises simply because he later becomes dissatisfied" and, on the other, that "federal law requires that all ideas in general circulation be dedicated to the common good unless they are protected by a valid patent [citing *Sears* and *Compco*]" the Court continues:]

III.

* * *

Surely the equities of the licensor do not weigh very heavily when they are balanced against the important public interest in permitting full and free competition in the use of ideas which are in reality a part of the public domain. Licensees may often be the only individuals with enough economic incentive to challenge the patentability of an inventor's discovery. If they are muzzled, the public may continually be required to pay tribute to would-be monopolists without need or justification. We think it plain that the technical requirements of contract doctrine must give way before the demands of the public interest in the typical situation involving the negotiation of a license after a patent has issued.

B.

The case before us, however, presents a far more complicated estoppel problem than the one which arises in the most common licensing context. The problem arises out of the fact that Lear obtained its license in 1955, more than four years before Adkins received his 1960 patent. Indeed, from the very outset of the relationship, Lear obtained special access to Adkins' ideas in return for its promise to pay satisfactory compensation.

Thus, during the lengthy period in which Adkins was attempting to obtain a patent, Lear gained an important benefit not generally obtained by the typical licensee. For until a patent issues, a potential licensee may not learn his licensor's ideas simply by requesting the information from the Patent Office. During the time the inventor is seeking patent protection, the governing federal statute requires the Patent Office to hold an inventor's patent application in confidence. If a potential licensee hopes to use the ideas contained in a secret patent application, he must deal with the inventor himself, unless the inventor chooses to publicize his ideas to the world at large. By promising to pay Adkins royalties from the very outset of their relationship, Lear gained immediate access to ideas which it may well not have learned until the Patent Office published the details of Adkins' invention in 1960. At the core of this case, then, is the difficult question whether federal patent policy bars a State from enforcing a contract regulating access to an unpatented secret idea.

Adkins takes an extreme position on this question. The inventor does not merely argue that since Lear obtained privileged access to his ideas *before 1960*, the company should be required to pay royalties accruing *before 1960* regardless of the validity of the patent which ultimately issued. He also argues that since Lear obtained special benefits before 1960, it should also pay royalties during the entire patent period (1960–1977), without regard to the validity of the Patent Office's grant. We cannot accept so broad an argument.

Adkins' position would permit inventors to negotiate all important licenses during the lengthy period while their applications were still pending at the Patent Office, thereby disabling entirely all those who have the strongest incentive to show that a patent is worthless. While the equities supporting Adkins' position are somewhat more appealing than those supporting the typical licensor, we cannot say that there is enough of a difference to justify such a substantial impairment of overriding federal policy.

Nor can we accept a second argument which may be advanced to support Adkins' claim to at least a portion of his post-patent royalties, regardless of the validity of the Patent Office grant. The terms of the 1955 agreement provide that royalties are to be paid until such time as the "patent * * * is held invalid," § 6, and the fact remains that the question of patent validity has not been finally determined in this case. Thus, it may be suggested that although Lear must be allowed to raise the question of patent validity in the present lawsuit, it must also be required to comply with its contract and continue to pay royalties until its claim is finally vindicated in the courts.

The parties' contract, however, is no more controlling on this issue than is the State's doctrine of estoppel, which is also rooted in contract principles. The decisive question is whether overriding federal policies would be significantly frustrated if licensees could be required to continue to pay royalties during the time they are challenging patent validity in the courts.

It seems to us that such a requirement would be inconsistent with the aims of federal patent policy. Enforcing this contractual provision would give the licensor an additional economic incentive to devise every conceivable dilatory tactic in an effort to postpone the day of final judicial reckoning. We can perceive no reason to encourage dilatory court tactics in this way. Moreover, the cost of prosecuting slow-moving trial proceedings and defending an inevitable appeal might well deter many licensees from attempting to prove patent invalidity in the courts. The deterrent effect would be particularly severe in the many scientific fields in which invention is proceeding at a rapid rate. In these areas, a patent may well become obsolete long before its 17-year term has expired. If a licensee has reason to believe that he will replace a patented idea with a new one in the near future, he will have little incentive to initiate lengthy court proceedings, unless he is freed from liability at least from the time he refuses to pay the contractual royalties. Lastly, enforcing this contractual provision would under-mine the strong federal policy favoring the full and free use of ideas in the public domain. For all these reasons, we hold that Lear must be permitted to avoid the payment of all royalties accruing after Adkins' 1960 patent issued if Lear can prove patent invalidity.

C.

Adkins' claim to contractual royalties accruing before the 1960 patent issued is, however, a much more difficult one, since it squarely raises the question whether, and to what extent, the States may protect the owners of *unpatented* inventions who are willing to disclose their ideas to manufacturers only upon payment of royalties. The California Supreme Court did not address itself to this issue with precision, for it believed that the venerable doctrine of estoppel provided a sufficient answer to all of Lear's claims based upon federal patent law. Thus, we do not know whether the Supreme Court would have awarded Adkins recovery even on his pre-patent royalties if it had recognized that previously established estoppel doctrine could no longer be properly invoked with regard to royalties accruing during the 17-year patent period. Our decision today will, of course, require the state courts to reconsider the theoretical basis of their decisions enforcing the contractual rights of inventors and it is impossible to predict the extent to which this re-evaluation may revolutionize the law of any particular State in this regard. Consequently, we have concluded, after much consideration, that even though an important question of federal law underlies this phase of the controversy, we should not now attempt to define in even a limited way the extent, if any, to which the States may properly act to enforce the contractual rights of inventors of unpatented secret ideas. Given the difficulty and importance of this task, it should be undertaken only after the state courts have, after fully focused inquiry, determined the extent to which they will respect the contractual rights of such inventors in the future. Indeed, on remand, the California courts may well reconcile the competing demands of patent and contract law in a way which would not warrant further review in this Court.

IV.

We also find it inappropriate to pass at this time upon Lear's contention that Adkins' patent is invalid.

The judgment of the Supreme Court of California is vacated and the case is remanded to that court for further proceedings not inconsistent with this opinion.

It is so ordered.

MR. JUSTICE BLACK, with whom THE CHIEF JUSTICE and MR. JUSTICE DOUGLAS join, concurring in part and dissenting in part.

I concur in the judgment and opinion of the Court, except for what is said in Part III, C, of the Court's opinion. What the Court does in this part of its opinion is to reserve for future decision the question whether the States have power to enforce contracts under which someone claiming to have a new discovery can obtain payment for disclosing it while his patent application is pending, even though the discovery is later held to be unpatentable. This reservation is, as I see it, directly in conflict with what this Court held to be the law in Sears, Roebuck v. Stiffel Co., 376 U.S. 225 (1964), and Compco Corp. v. Day-Brite Lighting, Inc., 376 U.S. 234 (1964). BROTHER HARLAN concurred in the result in those cases, saying—contrary to what the Court held—"I see no reason why the State may not impose reasonable restrictions on the future 'copying' itself." *Compco,* supra, at 239. Consequently the Court is today joining in the kind of qualification that only MR. JUSTICE HARLAN was willing to make at the time of our *Stiffel* and *Compco* decisions.

I still entertain the belief I expressed for the Court in *Stiffel* and *Compco* that no State has a right to authorize any kind of monopoly on what is claimed to be a new invention, except when a patent has been obtained from the Patent Office under the exacting standards of the patent laws. One who makes a discovery may, of course, keep it secret if he wishes, but private arrangements under which self-styled "inventors" do not keep their discoveries secret, but rather disclose them, in return for contractual payments, run counter to the plan of our patent laws, which tightly regulate the kind of inventions that may be protected and the manner in which they may be protected. The national policy expressed in the patent laws, favoring free competition and narrowly limiting monopoly, cannot be frustrated by private agreements among individuals, with or without the approval of the State.

MR. JUSTICE WHITE, concurring in part.

* * *

Although we have jurisdiction to review this state court judgment and to determine the licensee estoppel issue, it does not necessarily follow that we may or should deal with two other federal questions which come into focus once the licensee is free to challenge the patent. The first is whether the patent is valid. The second, which arises only if the patent is invalidated, is whether federal law forbids the collection of royalties which might otherwise be collectible under a contract rooted in state law. * * *

In the first place, we have no decision of the California Supreme Court affirming or denying, as a matter of federal law, that Adkins may not enforce his contract if his patent is held invalid. The California court held that the license agreement had not been terminated in accordance with its terms, that the doctrine of licensee estoppel prevented Lear from challenging the patent and that Lear was utilizing the teaching of Adkins' patent. There was thus no necessity or reason to consider whether the patent was invalid, or, if it was, whether either state or federal law prevented collection of the royalties reserved by the contract. * * *

There is no indication, however, that Lear, directly or by inference, urged in the California courts that if Adkins' patent were invalid, federal law overrode state contract law and precluded collection of the royalties which Lear had promised to pay. One of the defenses presented by Lear in its answer to Adkins' claim for royalties was that there had been a failure of consideration because of the absence of bargained-for patentability in Adkins' ideas. But failure of consideration is a state law question, and I find nothing in the record and nothing in this Court's opinion indicating that Lear at any time contended in the state courts that once Adkins' patent was invalidated, the royalty agreement was unenforceable as a matter of federal law.

Given Lear's failure below to "specially set up or claim" the federal bar to collection of royalties in the event Adkins' patent was invalidated, and without the California Supreme Court's "final judgment" on this issue, I doubt our jurisdiction to decide the issue. * * *

NOTES

1. Footnote 9 of the Court's opinion in *Lear* reads as follows:

9. Adkins also filed a second cause of action which contended that Lear had wrongfully appropriated a valuable trade secret and so was liable regardless of the validity of the inventor's contractual and quasi-contractual theories. The trial court, however, required Adkins' to choose between his contract and tort claims. Since the California Supreme Court completely vindicated the inventor's right to contractual royalties, it was not obliged to consider the propriety of this aspect of the trial judge's decision. Consequently, the tort claim is not before us at this time.

How do you evaluate Adkins' contention?

2. If, in the contract, Lear had expressly promised to pay royalties whether or not the patent was valid, would that have made any difference? Did § 6 of the agreement, providing that Lear could terminate if the patent was held invalid, have any role in the decision?

3. Suppose Adkins had entered into an agreement entitled "Agreement for compensation for services rendered to Lear, Inc. in connection with the successful development of improved vertical gyros" which provided that Adkins should be compensated for his services by royalties on the production of the devices described in the patent. Separately, Adkins executed an irrevocable, royalty free license of the patent to Lear, Inc. Would the compensation agreement be enforceable? Can Lear bring an action in the California courts to have his agreement reformed along these lines? Would section 6 be fatal to such an action?

4. *Lear* alone did not have much of an impact on patent licensing. The licensee often has a substantial interest in preserving the patent validity since the licensee shares in the patent's market power. However, the resolution of some of the questions left open in *Lear* were of great concern to patent owners. If the patent is found invalid, could a licensee recover royalties already paid? If so, the licensee could exploit the license against third parties until near the end of the patent period and then contest the patent's validity recovering, if successful, his royalty payments. The situation became more interesting after the Court decided Blonder-Tongue Laboratories, Inc. v. University of Illinois Foundation, 402 U.S. 313 (1971). The Court there held that once a patent owner has a full and fair chance to litigate the validity of his patent in one case and the patent is held invalid, the owner is estopped to assert the validity of the patent in subsequent litigation. However, a declaration of patent *validity*

would not be binding on parties not involved in the earlier litigation. See Stevenson v. Sears, Roebuck & Co., 713 F.2d 705 (Fed.Cir.1983). *Blonder-Tongue* provided additional incentive for a licensee to await the outcome of other litigation.

The leading case facing up to these difficulties is Troxel Mfg. Co. v. Schwinn Bicycle Co., 465 F.2d 1253 (6th Cir.1972) (Troxel I), and Troxel Mfg. Co. v. Schwinn Bicycle Co., 489 F.2d 968 (6th Cir.), cert. denied 416 U.S. 939 (1974) (Troxel II). Troxel was a licensee of a Schwinn patent. In unrelated litigation a California federal district court declared the patent invalid in January, 1969, and the Ninth Circuit affirmed on December 22, 1970. Troxel had stopped paying royalties in October, 1970. Troxel sued to recover all royalties paid under the invalid patent. Schwinn counterclaimed for royalties during the last quarter of 1970. In *Troxel I* the court held that *Lear* did not require or authorize the recovery of voluntarily paid royalties. In *Troxel II,* the court ordered Troxel to pay royalties through December 22, 1970. The *Troxel* cases were amplified in PPG Industries, Inc. v. Westwood Chemical, Inc., 530 F.2d 700 (6th Cir.1976). There the court held the obligation to pay royalties ceases on the earliest of the following dates: (1) on the date some other party is successful in having the patent declared invalid; (2) the licensee stops paying royalties for the purpose of prompting an adjudication of validity (the mere refusal to pay without a further indication that the licensee contests the validity of the patent is insufficient); or (3) the licensee files a suit or counterclaim attacking the validity of the patent. See also Transitron Electronic Corp. v. Hughes Aircraft, 649 F.2d 871 (1st Cir.1981) (licensee may recover back royalty payments if induced into the license by fraud).

5. The objective of the Court in *Lear* is to create an opportunity for licensees to challenge the validity of patents because, as the Court reasons, "Licensees may often be the only individuals with enough economic incentive to challenge the patentability of an inventor's discovery. If they are muzzled, the public may continually be required to pay tribute to would-be monopolists without need or justification." Is this true? The licensor and licensee are already in a close bargaining relationship. Once the *Lear* doctrine is clearly established, isn't it in both of their interests to simply renegotiate the license arrangement in light of the probabilities that the licensee could show the patent to be invalid? The licensee has no more interest than the licensor in creating a public, on-the-record determination that the patent is invalid. Thus isn't the only effect of the *Lear* decision to marginally reduce the value of all patents?

6. Does *Lear* suggest that an assignor of a patent may turn around and challenge its validity? Diamond Scientific Co. v. Ambico Inc., 848 F.2d 1220 (Fed.Cir.1988) (No). What about a party to an agreement reached to settle litigation? See Hemstreet v. Spiegel Inc., 851 F.2d 348 (Fed.Cir.1988) (No); Warner–Jenkinson Co. v. Allied Chemical Corp., 567 F.2d 184 (2d Cir.1977) (Yes). A party to a consent decree? Wallace Clark & Co. Inc. v. Acheson Industries, Inc., 532 F.2d 846 (2d Cir.1976) (No).

7. See generally, McCarthy. "Unmuzzling" The Patent Licensee: Chaos in the Wake of Lear v. Adkins, 45 Geo.Wash.L.Rev. 429 (1977), R. Dreyfuss, Dethroning *Lear*: Licensee Estoppel and the Incentive to Innovate, 72 Va.L. Rev. 677 (1986).

8. The mystery of Mr. Justice Harlan's dissent in *Brulotte* and the authorship of *Lear* becomes clear when one learns that he followed the practice

of accepting as precedent binding on him decisions from which he dissented after the end of the term in which they were handed down. See Bourguignon, The Second Mr. Justice Harlan: His Principles of Judicial Decision Making, 1979 Sup.Ct.Rev. 251, 279–81. Indeed, his authorship of the *Lear* opinion enabled him to adopt a limited if somewhat illogical reading of *Brulotte*. Doesn't the logic of *Brulotte* require that once a court determines that a patent is invalid—and hence that it always has been invalid—that all royalties ever paid be returned?

9. Does § 294 of the Patent Act, providing for arbitration by agreement of patent disputes, partially overrule the *Lear* decision? Could parties agree in arbitration to pay royalties for an invalid patent? Consider Saturday Evening Post Co. v. Rumbleseat Press, Inc., 816 F.2d 1191 (7th Cir.1987) holding arbitration and no contest clauses in a copyright licensing agreement valid.

KEWANEE OIL COMPANY v. BICRON CORPORATION
Supreme Court of the United States, 1974.
416 U.S. 470, 94 S.Ct. 1879, 40 L.Ed.2d 315.

MR. CHIEF JUSTICE BURGER delivered the opinion of the Court.

We granted certiorari to resolve a question on which there is a conflict in Courts of Appeals: whether state trade secret protection is pre-empted by operation of the federal patent law. * * *

I

Harshaw Chemical Company, an unincorporated division of Petitioner, is a leading manufacturer of a type of synthetic crystal which is useful in the detection of ionizing radiation. In 1949 Harshaw commenced research into the growth of this type crystal and was able to produce one less than two inches in diameter. By 1966, as the result of expenditures in excess of $1 million, Harshaw was able to grow a 17-inch crystal, something no one else had done previously. Harshaw had developed many processes, procedures and manufacturing techniques in the purification of raw materials and the growth and encapsulation of the crystals which enabled it to accomplish this feat. Some of these processes Harshaw considers to be trade secrets.

The individual Respondents are former employees of Harshaw who formed or later joined respondent Bicron. While at Harshaw the individual Respondents executed, as a condition of employment, at least one agreement each requiring them not to disclose confidential information or trade secrets obtained as employees of Harshaw. Bicron was formed in August 1969 to compete with Harshaw in the production of the crystals, and by April 1970, had grown a 17-inch crystal.

Petitioner brought this diversity action in United States District Court for the Northern District of Ohio seeking injunctive relief and damages for the misappropriation of trade secrets. The District Court, applying Ohio trade secret law, granted a permanent injunction against the disclosure or use by Respondents of 20 of the 40 claimed trade secrets until such time as the trade secrets had been released to the public, had otherwise generally become available to the public or had been obtained by Respondents from sources having the legal right to convey the information.

The Court of Appeals for the Sixth Circuit held that the findings of fact by the District Court were not clearly erroneous, and that it was evident from the record that the individual Respondents appropriated to the benefit of Bicron secret information on processes obtained while they were employees at Harshaw. Further, the Court of Appeals held that the District Court properly applied Ohio law relating to trade secrets. Nevertheless, the Court of Appeals reversed the District Court, finding Ohio's trade secret laws to be in conflict with the patent laws of the United States. The Court of Appeals reasoned that Ohio could not grant monopoly protection to processes and manufacturing techniques that were appropriate subjects for consideration under 35 U.S.C. § 101 for a federal patent but which had been in commercial use for over one year and so were no longer eligible for patent protection under 35 U.S. C. § 102(b).

We hold that Ohio's law of trade secrets is not preempted by the patent laws of the United States, and, accordingly, we reverse.

II

Ohio has adopted the widely relied upon definition of a trade secret found at 4 Restatement of Torts § 757, comment b (1939). * * *

The subject of a trade secret must be secret, and must not be of public knowledge or of a general knowledge in the trade or business. * * * This necessary element of secrecy is not lost, however, if the holder of the trade secret reveals the trade secret to another "in confidence, and under an implied obligation not to use or disclose it." * * * These others may include those of the holder's "employes [sic] to whom it is necessary to confide it, in order to apply it to the uses for which it is intended." * * * Often the recipient of confidential knowledge of the subject of a trade secret is a licensee of its holder. * * *

The protection accorded the trade secret holder is against the disclosure or unauthorized use of the trade secret by those to whom the secret has been confided under the express or implied restriction of nondisclosure or nonuse. The law also protects the holder of a trade secret against disclosure or use when the knowledge is gained, not by the owner's volition, but by some "improper means," 4 Restatement of Torts, § 757(a), which may include theft, wiretapping, or even aerial reconnaissance. A trade secret, however, does not offer protection against discovery by fair and honest means, such as by independent invention, accidental disclosure, or by so-called reverse engineering, that is by starting with the known product and working backward to divine the process which aided in its development or manufacture.

Novelty, in the patent law sense, is not required for a trade secret. * * * However, some novelty will be required if merely because that which does not possess novelty is usually known; secrecy, in the context of trade secrets, thus implies at least minimal novelty.

III

The first issue we deal with is whether the States are forbidden to act at all in the area of protection of the kinds of intellectual property which may make up the subject matter of trade secrets.

[Citing Goldstein v. California, the Court concludes Congress does not have exclusive power over "discoveries."]

IV

The question of whether the trade secret law of Ohio is void under the Supremacy Clause involves a consideration of whether that law "stands as an obstacle to the accomplishment and execution of the full purposes and objectives of Congress." Hines v. Davidowitz, 312 U.S. 52, 67 (1941). * * * The stated objective of the Constitution in granting the power to Congress to legislate in the area of intellectual property is to "promote the Progress of Science and useful Arts." The patent laws promote this progress by offering a right of exclusion for a limited period as an incentive for inventors to risk the often enormous costs in terms of time, research, and development. The productive effort thereby fostered will have a positive effect on society through the introduction of new products and processes of manufacture into the economy, and the emanations by way of increased employment and better lives for our citizens. In return for the right of exclusion—this "reward for inventions." Universal Oil Co. v. Globe Co., 322 U.S. 471, 484 (1944)—the patent laws impose upon the inventor a requirement of disclosure. To insure adequate and full disclosure so that upon the expiration of the 17-year period "the knowledge of the invention enures to the people, who are thus enabled without restriction to practice it and profit by its use." United States v. Dubilier Condenser Corp., 289 U.S. 178, 187 (1933), the patent laws require that the patent application shall include a full and clear description of the invention and "of the manner and process of making and using it" so that any person skilled in the art may make and use the invention. 35 U.S.C. § 112. When a patent is granted and the information contained in it is circulated to the general public and those especially skilled in the trade, such additions to the general store of knowledge are of such importance to the public weal that the Federal Government is willing to pay the high price of 17 years of exclusive use for its disclosure, which disclosure, it is assumed, will stimulate ideas and the eventual development of further significant advances on the art. The Court has also articulated another policy of the patent law: that which is in the public domain cannot be removed therefrom by action of the States.

> "[F]ederal laws requires that all ideas in general circulation be dedicated to the common good unless they are protected by a valid patent." Lear, Inc. v. Adkins, supra, 395 U.S., at 668.

See also Goldstein v. California, supra, 412 U.S., at 570–571; Sears, Roebuck & Co. v. Stiffel Co., supra; Compco Corp. v. Day-Brite Lighting, Inc., 376 U.S. 234, 237–238 (1964); International News Service v. Associated Press, 248 U.S. 215, 250 (1918) (Brandeis, J., dissenting).

The maintenance of standards of commercial ethics and the encouragement of invention are the broadly stated policies behind trade secret law. "The necessity of good faith and honest, fair dealing, is the very life and spirit of the commercial world." National Tube Co. v. Eastern Tube Co., supra, 3 Ohio Cir.Ct.R., N.S. at 462. In A.O. Smith Corp. v. Petroleum Iron Works Co., supra, 73 F.2d, at 539, the Court emphasized that even though a discovery may not be patentable, that does not

> "destroy the value of the discovery to one who makes it, or advantage the competitor who by unfair means, or as the beneficiary of a broken faith, obtains the desired knowledge without himself paying the price in labor, money, or machines expended by the discoverer."

In Wexler v. Greenberg, 399 Pa. 569, 578–579, 160 A.2d 430 (1960), the Pennsylvania Supreme Court noted the importance of trade secret protection to the subsidization of research and development and to increased economic efficiency within large companies through the dispersion of responsibilities for creative developments.

Having now in mind the objectives of both the patent and trade secret law, we turn to an examination of the interaction of these systems of protection of intellectual property—one established by the Congress and the other by a State—to determine whether and under what circumstances the latter might constitute "too great an encroachment on the federal patent system to be tolerated." Sears, Roebuck & Co. v. Stiffel Co., supra, 376 U.S., at 232.

As we noted earlier, trade secret law protects items which would not be proper subjects for consideration for patent protection under 35 U.S.C. § 101. As in the case of the recordings in Goldstein v. California, Congress, with respect to nonpatentable subject matter, "has drawn no balance; rather, it has left the area unattended, and no reason exists why the State should not be free to act." Goldstein v. California, supra, 412 U.S., at 570 (footnote omitted).

Since no patent is available for a discovery, however useful, novel, and nonobvious, unless it falls within one of the express categories of patentable subject matter of 35 U.S.C. § 101, the holder of such a discovery would have no reason to apply for a patent whether trade secret protection existed or not. Abolition of trade secret protection would, therefore, not result in increased disclosure to the public of discoveries in the area of nonpatentable subject matter. Also, it is hard to see how the public would be benefited by disclosure of customer lists or advertising campaigns; in fact, keeping such items secret encourages businesses to initiate new and individualized plans of operation, and constructive competition results. This, in turn, leads to a greater variety of business methods than would otherwise be the case if privately developed marketing and other data were passed illicitly among firms involved in the same enterprise.

Congress has spoken in the area of those discoveries which fall within one of the categories of patentable subject matter of 35 U.S.C. § 101 and which are, therefore, of a nature that would be subject to consideration for a patent. Processes, machines, manufactures, compositions of matter and improvements thereof, which meet the tests of utility, novelty, and nonobviousness are entitled to be patented, but those which do not, are not. The question remains whether those items which are proper subjects for consideration for a patent may also have available the alternative protection accorded by trade secret law.

Certainly the patent policy of encouraging invention is not disturbed by the existence of another form of incentive to invention. In this respect the two systems are not and never would be in conflict. Similarly, the policy that matter once in the public domain must remain in the public domain is not incompatible with the existence of trade secret protection. By definition a trade secret has not been placed in the public domain.

The more difficult objective of the patent law to reconcile with trade secret law is that of disclosure, the *quid pro quo* of the right to exclude. Universal Oil Co. v. Globe Co., supra, 322 U.S., at 484. We are helped in this stage of the analysis by Judge Henry Friendly's opinion in Painton & Company v. Bourns, Inc., 442 F.2d 216 (CA2 1971). There the Court of Appeals thought it useful, in determining whether inventors will refrain because of the existence of trade secret law from applying for patents thereby depriving the public from learning of the invention, to distinguish between three categories of trade secrets:

"(1) the trade secret believed by its owner to constitute a validly patentable invention; (2) the trade secret known to its owner not to be so patentable; and (3) the trade secret whose valid patentability is considered dubious." Painton & Co. v. Bourns, Inc., 442 F.2d, at 224.

Trade secret protection in each of these categories would run against breaches of confidence—the employee and licensee situations—and theft and other forms of industrial espionage.

As to the trade secret known not to meet the standards of patentability, very little in the way of disclosure would be accomplished by abolishing trade secret protection. As with trade secrets of nonpatentable subject matter, the patent alternative would not reasonably be available to the inventor. "There can be no public interest in stimulating developers of such [unpatentable] knowhow to flood an overburdened Patent Office with applications for what they do not consider patentable." Ibid. The mere filing of applications doomed to be turned down by the Patent Office will bring forth no new public knowledge or enlightenment, since under federal statute and regulation patent applications and abandoned patent applications are held by the Patent

Office in confidence and are not open to public inspection. 35 U.S.C. § 122; 37 CFR § 1.14(b).

Even as the extension of trade secret protection to patentable subject matter that the owner knows will not meet the standards of patentability will not conflict with the patent policy of disclosure, it will have a decidedly beneficial effect on society. Trade secret law will encourage invention in areas where patent law does not reach, and will prompt the independent innovator to proceed with the discovery and exploitation of his invention. Competition is fostered and the public is not deprived of the use of valuable, if not quite patentable, invention.

Even if trade secret protection against the faithless employee were abolished, inventive and exploitive effort in the area of patentable subject matter which did not meet the standards of patentability would continue, although at a reduced level. Alternatively with the effort that remained, however, would come an increase in the amount of self-help that innovative companies would employ. Knowledge would be widely dispersed among the employees of those still active in research. Security precautions necessarily would be increased, and salaries and fringe benefits of those few officers or employees who had to know the whole of the secret invention would be fixed in an amount thought sufficient to assure their loyalty. Smaller companies would be placed at a distinct economic disadvantage, since the costs of this kind of self-help could be great, and the cost to the public of the use of this invention would be increased. The innovative entrepreneur with limited resources would tend to confine his research efforts to himself and those few he felt he could trust without the ultimate assurance of legal protection against breaches of confidence. As a result, organized scientific and technological research could become fragmented, and society, as a whole would suffer.

Another problem that would arise if state trade secret protection were precluded is in the area of licensing others to exploit secret processes. The holder of a trade secret would not likely share his secret with a manufacturer who cannot be placed under binding legal obligation to pay a license fee or to protect the secret. The result would be to hoard rather than disseminate knowledge. Painton & Co. v. Bourns, Inc., 442 F.2d, at 223. Instead, then, of licensing others to use his invention and making the most efficient use of existing manufacturing and marketing structures within the industry, the trade secret holder would tend either to limit his utilization of the invention, thereby depriving the public of the maximum benefit of its use, or engage in the time-consuming and economically wasteful enterprise of constructing duplicative manufacturing and marketing mechanisms for the exploitation of the invention. The detrimental misallocation of resources and economic waste that would thus take place if trade secret protection were abolished with respect to employees or licensees cannot be justified by reference to any policy that the federal patent law seeks to advance.

Nothing in the patent law requires that States refrain from action to prevent industrial espionage. In addition to the increased costs for protection from burglary, wire-tapping, bribery and the other means used to misappropriate trade secrets, there is the inevitable cost to the basic decency of society when one firm steals from another. A most fundamental human right, that of privacy, is threatened when industrial espionage is condoned or is made profitable; the state interest in denying profit to such illegal ventures is unchallengeable.

The next category of patentable subject matter to deal with is the invention whose holder has a legitimate doubt as to its patentability. The risk of eventual patent invalidity by the courts and the costs associated with that risk may well impel some with a good-faith doubt as to patentability not to take the trouble to seek to obtain and defend patent protection for their discoveries, regardless of the existence of trade secret protection. Trade secret protection would assist those inventors in the more efficient exploitation of their discoveries and not conflict with the patent law. In most cases of genuine doubt as to patent validity the potential rewards of patent protection are so far superior to those accruing to holders of trade secrets, that the holders of such inventions will seek patent protection, ignoring the trade secret route. For those inventors "on the line" as to whether to seek patent protection, the abolition of trade secret protection might encourage some to apply for a patent who otherwise would not have done so. For some of those so encouraged, no patent will be granted and the result

> "will have been an unnecessary postponement in the divulging of the trade secret to persons willing to pay for it. If [the patent does issue], it may well be invalid, yet many will prefer to pay a modest royalty than to contest it, even though *Lear* allows them to accept a license and pursue the contest without paying royalties while the fight goes on. The result in such a case would be unjustified royalty payments from many who would prefer not to pay them rather than agreed fees from one or a few who are entirely willing to do so." Painton & Co. v. Bourns, Inc., supra, 442 F.2d, at 225.

The point is that those who might be encouraged to file for patents by the absence of trade secret law will include inventors possessing the chaff as well as the wheat. Some of the chaff—the nonpatentable discoveries—will be thrown out by the Patent Office, but in the meantime the society will have been deprived of use of those discoveries through trade secret-protected licensing. Some of the chaff may not be thrown out. This Court has noted the difference between the standards used by the Patent Office and the courts to determine patentability. Graham v. John Deere Co., 383 U.S. 1, 18 (1966). In Lear, Inc. v. Adkins, supra, the Court thought that an invalid patent was so serious a threat to the free use of ideas already in the public domain that the Court permitted licensees of the patent holder to challenge the validity of the patent. Better had the invalid patent never issued. More of those patents would likely issue if trade secret law were abolished.

Eliminating trade secret law for the doubtfully patentable invention is thus likely to have deleterious effects on society and patent policy which we cannot say are balanced out by the speculative gain which might result from the encouragement of some inventors with doubtfully patentable inventions which deserve patent protection to come forward and apply for patents. There is no conflict, then, between trade secret law and the patent law policy of disclosure, at least insofar as the first two categories of patentable subject matter are concerned.

The final category of patentable subject matter to deal with is the clearly patentable invention, i.e., that invention which the owner believes to meet the standards of patentability. It is here that the federal interest in disclosure is at its peak; these inventions, novel, useful and nonobvious, are "the things which are worth to the public the embarrassment of an exclusive patent." Graham v. John Deere Co., supra, 383 U.S., at 9 (quoting Thomas Jefferson). The interest of the public is that the bargain of 17 years of exclusive use in return for disclosure be accepted. If a State, through a system of protection, were to cause a substantial risk that holders of patentable inventions would not seek patents, but rather would rely on the state protection, we would be compelled to hold that such a system could not constitutionally continue to exist. In the case of trade secret law no reasonable risk of deterrence from patent application by those who can reasonably expect to be granted patents exists.

Trade secret law provides far weaker protection in many respects than the patent law. While trade secret law does not forbid the discovery of the trade secret by fair and honest means, e.g., independent creation and reverse engineering, patent law operates "against the world," forbidding any use of the invention for whatever purpose for a significant length of time. The holder of a trade secret also takes a substantial risk that the secret will be passed on to his competitors, by theft or by breach of a confidential relationship, in a manner not easily susceptible to discovery or proof. Painton & Co. v. Bourns, Inc., supra, 442 F.2d, at 224. Where patent law acts as a barrier, trade secret law functions relatively as a sieve. The possibility that an inventor who believes his invention meets the standards of patentability will sit back, rely on trade secret law, and after one year of use forfeit any right to patent protection, 35 U.S.C. § 102(b), is remote indeed.

Nor does society face much risk that scientific or technological progress will be impeded from the rare inventor with a patentable invention who chooses trade secret protection over patent protection. The ripeness of time concept of invention, developed from the study of the many independent multiple discoveries in history, predicts that if a particular individual had not made a particular discovery others would have, and in probably a relatively short period of time. If something is to be discovered at all very likely it will be discovered by more than one person. R. Merton, Singletons and Multiples in Science (1961), The Sociology of Science (1973); J. Cole and S. Cole, Social Stratification in Science, 12–13, 229–230 (1973); Ogburn and Thomas, Are Inventions

Inevitable?, 37 Political Science Quarterly, 83 (1922).[19] Even were an inventor to keep his discovery completely to himself, something that neither the patent nor trade secret laws forbid, there is a high probability that it will be soon independently developed. If the invention, though still a trade secret, is put into public use, the competition is alerted to the existence of the inventor's solution to the problem and may be encouraged to make an extra effort to independently find the solution thus known to be possible. The inventor faces pressures not only from private industry, but from the skilled scientists who work in our universities and our other great publicly supported centers of learning and research.

We conclude that the extension of trade secret protection to clearly patentable inventions does not conflict with the patent policy of disclosure. Perhaps because trade secret law does not produce any positive effects in the area of clearly patentable inventions, as opposed to the beneficial effects resulting from trade secret protection in the areas of the doubtfully patentable and the clearly unpatentable inventions, it has been suggested that partial pre-emption may be appropriate, and that courts should refuse to apply trade secret protection to inventions which the holder should have patented, and which would have been, thereby, disclosed.[20] However, since there is no real possibility that trade secret law will conflict with the federal policy favoring disclosure of clearly patentable inventions partial pre-emption is inappropriate. Partial preemption, furthermore, could well create serious problems for state courts in the administration of trade secret law. As a preliminary matter in trade secret actions, state courts would be obliged to distinguish between what a reasonable inventor would and would not correctly consider to be clearly patentable, with the holder of the trade secret arguing that the invention was not patentable and the misappropriator of the trade secret arguing its undoubted novelty, utility and nonobviousness. Federal courts have a difficult enough time trying to determine whether an invention, narrowed by the patent application procedure and fixed in the specifications which describe the invention for which the patent has been granted, is patentable. Although state courts in some circumstances must join federal courts in judging whether an issued patent is valid, Lear, Inc. v. Adkins, supra, it would be undesirable to impose the almost impossible burden on state courts to determine the patentability—in fact and in the mind of a reasonable inventor—of a discovery which has not been patented and remains entirely uncircumscribed by expert analysis in the administrative pro-

---

19. See J. Watson, The Double Helix (1968). If Watson and Crick had not discovered the structure of DNA it is likely that Linus Pauling would have made the discovery soon. Other examples of multiple discovery are listed at length in the Ogburn and Thomas article.

20. See Note, Patent Preemption of Trade Secret Protection Meeting Judicial Standards of Patentability, 87 Harv.L.Rev. 807 (1974); Brief for the United States as *Amicus Curiae,* presenting the view within the Government favoring limited pre-emption (which view is not that of the United States which believes that patent law does not pre-empt state trade secret law).

cess. Neither complete nor partial pre-emption of state trade secret law is justified.

*   *   *

Trade secret law and patent law have coexisted in this country for over one hundred years. Each has its particular role to play, and the operation of one does not take away from the need for the other. Trade secret law encourages the development and exploitation of those items of lesser or different invention than might be accorded protection under the patent laws, but which items still have an important part to play in the technological and scientific advancement of the Nation. Trade secret law promotes the sharing of knowledge, and the efficient operation of industry; it permits the individual inventor to reap the rewards of his labor by contracting with a company large enough to develop and exploit it. Congress, by its silence over these many years, has seen the wisdom of allowing the States to enforce trade secret protection. Until Congress takes affirmative action to the contrary, States should be free to grant protection to trade secrets.

Since we hold that Ohio trade secret law is not preempted by the federal patent law, the judgment of the Court of Appeals for the Sixth Circuit is reversed and the case is remanded to the Court of Appeals with directions to reinstate the judgment of the District Court.

It is so ordered.

Reversed and remanded for reinstatement of District Court judgment.

MR. JUSTICE POWELL took no part in the decision of this case.

MR. JUSTICE MARSHALL, concurring in the result.

Unlike the Court, I do not believe that the possibility that an inventor with a patentable invention will rely on state trade secret law rather than apply for a patent is "remote indeed." State trade secret law provides substantial protection to the inventor who intends to use or sell the invention himself rather than license it to others, protection which in its unlimited duration is clearly superior to the 17-year monopoly afforded by the patent laws. I have no doubt that the existence of trade secret protection provides in some instances a substantial disincentive to entrance into the patent system, and thus deprives society of the benefits of public disclosure of the invention which it is the policy of the patent laws to encourage. This case may well be such an instance.

But my view of sound policy in this area does not dispose of this case. Rather, the question presented in this case is whether Congress, in enacting the patent laws, intended merely to offer inventors a limited monopoly in exchange for disclosure of their invention, or instead to exert pressure on inventors to enter into this exchange by withdrawing any alternative possibility of legal protection for their inventions. I am persuaded that the former is the case. *   *   *

MR. JUSTICE DOUGLAS, with whom MR. JUSTICE BRENNAN concurs, dissenting.

NOTES

1. What is to be made of Chief Justice Burger's description of the Ohio law of trade secrets? After *Kewanee,* may a state extend "trade secret" protection beyond the law of Ohio as described? Consider the line in the opinion that reads: "If a state, through a system of protection, were to cause a substantial risk that holders of patentable inventions would not seek patents, but rather would rely on the state protection, we would be compelled to hold that such a system could not constitutionally continue to exist." For example, are states free to place their own interpretation on what is "improper means" as distinguished from "fair and honest means" or is that now a matter of federal law?

2. Are you convinced the answer to *Kewanee* is empirical?

3. Do you accept the proposition that "the patent policy of encouraging invention is not disturbed by the existence of another form of incentive to invention." Could Congress reasonably conclude that there is too much incentive for innovative activity generally or in specific areas?

4. Does *Kewanee* affect the nature of the relief that can be granted by state courts for trade secret infringement? Are permanent injunctions prohibiting the use of infringing material permissible? Is an accounting for profits? See, Stern, A Reexamination of Preemption of State Trade Secret Law After Kewanee, 42 Geo.Wash.L.Rev. 927 (1974).

5. Should the fixation of a notice of copyright on a document preclude the assertion of trade secret rights? In Technicon Medical Information Systems Corp. v. Green Bay Packaging, Inc., 687 F.2d 1032 (7th Cir.1982), cert. denied 459 U.S. 1106 (1982) the Seventh Circuit held that under the 1909 Copyright Act the owner of copyrighted documents was not estopped from asserting that the publication of the documents was not a general publication but preserved trade secret rights. Does section 301 of the 1976 Act preempt trade secret protection? See Avco Corp. v. Precision Air Parts, Inc., 210 U.S.P.Q. 894 (M.D. Ala.1980), affirmed on other grounds 676 F.2d 494 (11th Cir.1982), cert. denied 459 U.S. 1037 (1982) and Warrington Associates, Inc. v. Real-Time Engineering Systems, Inc., 522 F.Supp. 367 (N.D.Ill.1981).

PROBLEM

To test your understanding of the preemption landscape, complete the following matrix, placing in each square the extent to which state law may operate. In doing so, you should consider the applicability of *Sears, Compco, Goldstein, Lear, Kewanee,* and § 301 of the Copyright Act.

	Unpublished	Published
Outside subject matter of (C) or (P)		
Subject matter of (C) or (P)		

ARONSON v. QUICK POINT PENCIL CO.
Supreme Court of the United States, 1979.
440 U.S. 257, 99 S.Ct. 1096, 59 L.Ed.2d 296.

MR. CHIEF JUSTICE BURGER delivered the opinion of the Court.

We granted certiorari to consider whether federal patent law preempts state contract law so as to preclude enforcement of a contract to pay royalties to a patent applicant, on sales of articles embodying the putative invention, for so long as the contracting party sells them, if a patent is not granted.

(1)

In October 1955 the petitioner Mrs. Jane Aronson filed an application, Serial No. 542677, for a patent on a new form of keyholder. Although ingenious, the design was so simple that it readily could be copied unless it was protected by patent. In June 1956, while the patent application was pending Mrs. Aronson negotiated a contract with the respondent, Quick Point Pencil Company, for the manufacture and sale of the keyholder.

The contract was embodied in two documents. In the first, a letter from Quick Point to Mrs. Aronson, Quick Point agreed to pay Mrs. Aronson a royalty of 5% of the selling price in return for "the exclusive right to make and sell keyholders of the type shown in your application, Serial No. 542677." The letter further provided that the parties would consult one another concerning the steps to be taken "[i]n the event of any infringement."

The contract did not require Quick Point to manufacture the keyholder. Mrs. Aronson received a $750 advance on royalties and was entitled to rescind the exclusive license if Quick Point did not sell a million keyholders by the end of 1957. Quick Point retained the right to cancel the agreement whenever "the volume of sales does not meet our expectation." The duration of the agreement was not otherwise prescribed.

A contemporaneous document provided that if Mrs. Aronson's patent application was "not allowed within five (5) years, Quick Point Pencil Co. [would] pay two and one half percent (2½%) of sales * * * so long as you [Quick Point] continue to sell same."

In June 1961, when Mrs. Aronson had failed to obtain a patent on the keyholder within the five years specified in the agreement, Quick Point asserted its contractual right to reduce royalty payments to 2½% of sales. In September of that year the Board of Patent Appeals issued a final rejection of the application on the ground that the keyholder was not patentable, and Mrs. Aronson did not appeal. Quick Point continued to pay reduced royalties to her for 14 years thereafter.

The market was more receptive to the keyholder's novelty and utility than the Patent Office. By September 1975 Quick Point had made sales in excess of seven million dollars and paid Mrs. Aronson royalties totalling $203,963.84; sales were continuing to rise. However, while Quick Point was able to pre-empt the market in the earlier years and was long the only manufacturer of the Aronson keyholder, copies began to appear in the late 1960's. Quick Point's competitors, of course, were not required to pay royalties for their use of the design. Quick Point's share of the Aronson keyholder market has declined during the past decade.

(2)

In November 1975 Quick Point commenced an action in the United States District Court for a declaratory judgment, pursuant to 28 U.S.C. § 2201, that the royalty agreement was unenforceable. Quick Point asserted that state law which might otherwise make the contract enforceable was pre-empted by federal patent law. This is the only issue presented to us for decision.

Both parties moved for summary judgment on affidavits, exhibits, and stipulations of fact. The District Court concluded that the "language of the agreement is plain, clear and unequivocal and has no relation as to whether or not a patent is ever granted." Accordingly, it held that the agreement was valid, and that Quick Point was obliged to pay the agreed royalties pursuant to the contract for so long as it manufactured the keyholder.

The Court of Appeals reversed, one judge dissenting. It held that since the parties contracted with reference to a pending patent application, Mrs. Aronson was estopped from denying that patent law principles governed her contract with Quick Point. Although acknowledging that this Court has never decided the precise issue, the Court of Appeals held that our prior decisions regarding patent licenses compelled the conclusion that Quick Point's contract with Mrs. Aronson became unenforceable once she failed to obtain a patent. The court held that a continuing obligation to pay royalties would be contrary to "the strong federal policy favoring the full and free use of ideas in the public domain," Lear, Inc. v. Adkins, 395 U.S. 653, 674 (1969). The court also observed that if Mrs. Aronson actually had obtained a patent, Quick Point would have escaped its royalty obligations either if the patent were held to be invalid, see id., at 674, or upon its expiration after 17 years, see Brulotte v. Thys Co., 379 U.S. 29 (1964). Accordingly, it concluded that a licensee should be relieved of royalty obligations when the licensor's efforts to obtain a contemplated patent prove unsuccessful.

(3)

On this record it is clear that the parties contracted with full awareness of both the pendency of a patent application and the possibility that a patent might not issue. The clause de-escalating the royalty by half in the event no patent issued within five years makes that crystal clear. Quick Point apparently placed a significant value on exploiting the basic novelty of the device, even if no patent issued; its success demonstrates that this judgment was well founded. Assuming, *arguendo,* that the initial letter and the commitment to pay a 5% royalty was subject to federal patent law, the provision relating to the 2½% royalty was explicitly independent of federal law. The cases and principles relied on by the Court of Appeals and Quick Point do not bear on a contract that does not rely on a patent, particularly where, as here, the contracting parties agreed expressly as to alternative obligations if no patent should issue.

Commercial agreements traditionally are the domain of state law. State law is not displaced merely because the contract relates to intellectual property which may or may not be patentable; the states are free to regulate the use of such intellectual property in any manner not inconsistent with federal law. Kewanee Oil Co. v. Bicron Corp., 416 U.S. 470, 479 (1974); see Goldstein v. California, 412 U.S. 546 (1973). In this as in other fields, the question of whether federal law pre-empts state law "involves a consideration of whether that law 'stands as an obstacle to the accomplishment and execution of the full purposes and objectives of Congress.' Hines v. Davidowitz, 312 U.S. 52, 67 (1941)." Kewanee Oil Co., supra. If it does not, state law governs.

In Kewanee Oil Co., supra, at 480–481, we reviewed the purposes of the federal patent system. First, patent law seeks to foster and reward invention; second, it promotes disclosure of inventions, to stimulate further innovation and to permit the public to practice the invention once the patent expires; third, the stringent requirements for patent protection seek to assure that ideas in the public domain remain there for the free use of the public.

Enforcement of Quick Point's agreement with Mrs. Aronson is not inconsistent with any of these aims. Permitting inventors to make enforceable agreements licensing the use of their inventions in return for royalties provides an additional incentive to invention. Similarly, encouraging Mrs. Aronson to make arrangements for the manufacture of her keyholder furthers the federal policy of disclosure of inventions; these simple devices display the novel idea which they embody wherever they are seen.

Quick Point argues that enforcement of such contracts conflicts with the federal policy against withdrawing ideas from the public domain and discourages recourse to the federal patent system by allowing states to extend "perpetual protection to articles too lacking in novelty to merit any patent at all under federal constitutional standards," Sears Roebuck & Co. v. Stiffel Co., 376 U.S. 225, 232 (1964).

We find no merit in this contention. Enforcement of the agreement does not withdraw any idea from the public domain. The design for the keyholder was not in the public domain before Quick Point obtained its license to manufacture it. See Kewanee Oil Co., supra, at 484. In negotiating the agreement, Mrs. Aronson disclosed the design in confidence. Had Quick Point tried to exploit the design in breach of that confidence, it would have risked legal liability. It is equally clear that the design entered the public domain as a result of the manufacture and sale of the keyholders under the contract.

Requiring Quick Point to bear the burden of royalties for the use of the design is no more inconsistent with federal patent law than any of the other costs involved in being the first to introduce a new product to the market, such as outlays for research and development and marketing and promotional expenses. For reasons which Quick Point's experience with the Aronson keyholder demonstrate, innovative entrepreneurs have usually found such costs to be well worth paying.

Finally, enforcement of this agreement does not discourage anyone from seeking a patent. Mrs. Aronson attempted to obtain a patent for over five years. It is quite true that had she succeeded, she would have received a 5% royalty only on keyholders sold during the 17-year life of the patent. Off-setting the limited terms of royalty payments, she would have received twice as much per dollar of Quick Point's sales, and both she and Quick Point could have licensed any others who produced the same keyholder. Which course would have produced the greater yield to the contracting parties is a matter of speculation; the parties resolved the uncertainties by their bargain.

(4)

No decision of this Court relating to patents justifies relieving Quick Point of its contract obligations. We have held that a state may not forbid the copying of an idea in the public domain which does not meet the requirements for federal patent protection. Compco Corp. v. Day-Brite Lighting, Inc., 376 U.S. 234 (1964); Sears Roebuck & Co. v. Stiffel Co., 376 U.S. 225 (1964). Enforcement of Quick Point's agreement, however, does not prevent anyone from copying the keyholder. It merely requires Quick Point to pay the consideration which it promised in return for the use of a novel device which enabled it to preempt the market.

In Lear, Inc. v. Adkins, 395 U.S. 653 (1969), we held that a person licensed to use a patent may challenge the validity of the patent, and that a licensee who establishes that the patent is invalid need not pay the royalties accrued under the licensing agreement subsequent to the issuance of the patent. Both holdings relied on the desirability of encouraging licensees to challenge the validity of patents, to further the strong federal policy that only inventions which meet the rigorous requirements of patentability shall be withdrawn from the public domain. Id., at 670–671, 673–674. Accordingly, neither the holding nor the rationale of *Lear* controls when no patent has issued, and no ideas have been withdrawn from public use.

Enforcement of the royalty agreement here is also consistent with the principles treated in Brulotte v. Thys Co., 379 U.S. 29 (1964). There, we held that the obligation to pay royalties in return for the use of a patented device may not extend beyond the life of the patent. The principle underlying that holding was simply that the monopoly granted *under a patent* cannot lawfully be used to "negotiate with the leverage of that monopoly." The Court emphasized that to "use that leverage to project those royalty payments beyond the life of the patent is analogous to an effort to enlarge the monopoly of a patent * * *." Id., at 33. Here the reduced royalty which is challenged, far from being negotiated "with the leverage" of a patent, rested on the contingency that no patent would issue within five years.

No doubt a pending patent application gives the applicant some additional bargaining power for purposes of negotiating a royalty agreement. The pending application allows the inventor to hold out the hope of an exclusive right to exploit the idea, as well as the threat that the other party will be prevented from using the idea for 17 years. However, the amount of leverage arising from a patent application depends on how likely the parties consider it to be that a valid patent will issue. Here, where no patent ever issued, the record is entirely clear that the parties assigned a substantial likelihood to that contingency, since they specifically provided for a reduced royalty in the event no patent issued within five years.

This case does not require us to draw the line between what constitutes abuse of a pending application and what does not. It is clear that whatever role the pending application played in the negotiation of the 5% royalty, it played no part in the contract to pay the 2½% royalty indefinitely.

Our holding in Kewanee Oil Co., supra, puts to rest the contention that federal law pre-empts and renders unenforceable the contract made by these parties. There we held that state law forbidding the misappropriation of trade secrets was not pre-empted by federal patent law. We observed:

> "Certainly the patent policy of encouraging invention is not disturbed by the existence of another form of incentive to invention. In this respect the two systems [patent and trade secret law] are not and never would be in conflict." Id., at 484.

Enforcement of this royalty agreement is even less offensive to federal patent policies than state law protecting trade secrets. The most commonly accepted definition of trade secrets is restricted to confidential information which is not disclosed in the normal process of exploitation. See Restatement of Torts § 757, comment b (1939). Accordingly, the exploitation of trade secrets under state law may not satisfy the federal policy in favor of disclosure, whereas disclosure is inescapable in exploiting a device like the Aronson keyholder.

Enforcement of these contractual obligations, freely undertaken in arm's length negotiation and with no fixed reliance on a patent or a probable patent grant, will:

> "encourage invention in areas where patent law does not reach, and will prompt the independent innovator to proceed with the

discovery and exploitation of his invention. Competition is fostered and the public is not deprived of the use of valuable, if not quite patentable, invention." [Footnote omitted.] Id., at 485.

The device which is the subject of this contract ceased to have any secrecy as soon as it was first marketed, yet when the contract was negotiated the inventiveness and novelty were sufficiently apparent to induce an experienced novelty manufacturer to agree to pay for the opportunity to be first in the market. Federal patent law is not a barrier to such a contract.

Reversed.

MR. JUSTICE BLACKMUN, concurring in the result.

For me, the hard question is whether this case can meaningfully be distinguished from Brulotte v. Thys Co., 379 U.S. 29 (1964). There the Court held a patent licensor could not use the leverage of its patent to obtain a royalty contract that extended beyond the patent's 17-year term. Here Mrs. Aronson has used the leverage of her patent application to negotiate a royalty contract which continues to be binding even though the patent application was long ago denied.

The Court, * * * asserts that her leverage played "no part" with respect to the contingent agreement to pay a reduced royalty if no patent issued within five years. Yet it may well be that Quick Point agreed to that contingency in order to obtain its other rights that depended on the success of the patent application. The parties did not apportion consideration in the neat fashion the Court adopts.

In my view, the holding in *Brulotte* reflects hostility toward extension of a patent monopoly whose term is fixed by statute, 35 U.S.C. § 154. Such hostility has no place here. A patent application which is later denied temporarily discourages unlicensed imitators. Its benefits and hazards are of a different magnitude from those of a granted patent that prohibits all competition for 17 years. Nothing justifies estopping a patent application licensor from entering into a contract whose term does not end if the application fails. The Court points out, * * * that enforcement of this contract does not conflict with the objectives of the patent laws. The United States, as *amicus curiae*, maintains that patent application licensing of this sort is desirable because it encourages patent applications, promotes early disclosure, and allows parties to structure their bargains efficiently.

On this basis, I concur in the Court's holding that federal patent law does not pre-empt the enforcement of Mrs. Aronson's contract with Quick Point.

NOTES

1. In the 1989 decision in *Bonito Boats,* supra Chapter I, the Supreme Court reaffirmed not only *Sears* and *Compco* but also *Lear, Kewanee,* and *Aronson.* After reiterating the analysis in *Kewanee* the Court observed:

We have since reaffirmed the pragmatic approach which *Kewanee* takes to the pre-emption of state laws dealing with the protection of intellectual property. See, *Aronson* * * *. At the same time, we have consistently reiterated the teaching of *Sears* and *Compco* that ideas once placed before the public without the protection of a valid patent are subject to appropriation without significant restraint. *Aronson* * * *.

2. The opinion of the Eighth Circuit in *Quick Point* concluded:

Aronson believed her invention was patentable and she submitted a patent application. Had a patent issued she would have had 17 years of exclusive rights to her invention before it became part of the public domain. She approached Quick Point with her idea and the parties entered into a contract anticipating that a patent would issue. If that had happened, under Brulotte v. Thys Co., supra, 379 U.S. at 32, Quick Point's liability for royalties would have ended after 17 years *in spite of the contract.* Furthermore, if a patent had issued and Quick Point had later questioned the patentability of the keyholder, under Lear, Inc. v. Adkins, supra, 395 U.S. at 674, it could have stopped making royalty payments and challenged the patent in court. If such a challenge were successful, Quick Point's liability for payments would have ended *in spite of the contract.* We do not believe the result should be different here. The principles discussed above strongly indicate that any other conclusion would violate public policy.

567 F.2d at 762 (8th Cir.1977). Do you think the Supreme Court adequately addressed this argument?

3. The combined effect of *Brulotte, Lear, Kewanee,* and *Aronson* is far from clear. *Brulotte* involved a patent license. *Lear* involved an agreement followed by the issuance of a patent. *Kewanee* did not involve patents. *Aronson* involved only the potential for a patent that subsequently failed to materialize. And *Aronson* involved a license agreement that adjusted the royalty rate depending on the validity of the patent. Several cases have attempted to determine to what extent contractual arrangements are enforceable where they contemplate a hybrid transfer of both patented or patentable ideas and tradesecrets or "know-how":

(a) Pitney Bowes v. Mestre, 701 F.2d 1365 (11th Cir.1983). The parties signed a royalty agreement on machines for which patent applications were pending. The patents issued but the royalty agreement required payment beyond the patent period. The court held *Brulotte* applied and if the patent issues, all claims to royalties end at the patent's expiration.

(b) Boggild v. Kenner Products, 776 F.2d 1315 (6th Cir.1985). The parties entered into a royalty agreement prior to filing the patent application. The patent subsequently issued but the agreement required royalty payments beyond the patent period. The court held *Brulotte* applied because the parties entered the agreement with "clear expectations that a valid patent would issue." See also Meehan v. PPG Industries, Inc., 802 F.2d 881 (7th Cir.1986) following *Boggild* and holding royalty payments unenforceable after expiration of United States patent even though a Canadian patent still valid.

(c) Universal Gym Equipment Inc. v. ERWA Exercise Equipment Ltd., 827 F.2d 1542 (Fed.Cir.1987). The parties entered a distribution contract permitting defendant to distribute the plaintiff's exercise equipment. The contract specified that upon termination the defendant would not sell any equipment containing any of the features or designs of the plaintiff's equipment. After termination defendant manufactured and sold its own equipment. Plaintiff sued for both patent infringement and breach of contract claiming defendant's equipment had features similar to plaintiff's. The court held there was no patent infringement but defendant's equipment did contain similar features. The court upheld a damage award for breach of contract even though the similar features were not trade secrets, rejecting a *Sears* and *Compco* preemption defense. The Federal Circuit does not appear sympathetic to preemption. It had upheld a plug molding statute against preemption claims, a view rejected by the Supreme Court in *Bonito Boats,* supra Chapter I. Could *Universal Gym* survive Supreme Court scrutiny?

4. Is the difference between the leverage of a patent and the leverage of a patent application a difference of kind or degree? Chief Justice Burger says that the leverage from an application depends on "how likely the parties consider it to be that a valid patent will issue." Isn't the leverage associated with a granted patent related to how likely it is that a court will enforce the patent? The Court leaves open the possibility that a patent applicant might abuse his patent application, perhaps a reference to the problem in *Brulotte.* Can you construct a situation where this might be true?

5. How would you decide a case in which a former employer seeks to enjoin a former employee from disclosing the employers trade secrets even though the secrets are already public? Would it make a difference if the employee had signed a non-disclosure agreement which extended beyond the disclosure of the secret?

6. Should there be a presumption that the license terminates on public disclosure unless there is an explicit agreement to the contrary?

7. Consider a case like *Aronson* in an industry in which the number of potential users of the secret is very small? Isn't *Brulotte* the most significant precedent?

8. Do the realities of private transactions prevent the enforcement of the licensing agreement from interfering with federal patent policies. If the licensee has agreed to pay a royalty which after disclosure of the secret makes it difficult for him to compete with others, will not the licensor have an incentive to reduce the royalty? Does the case change if, like *Brulotte,* the licensee agrees to a minimum royalty payment? Would any sensible licensee agree to such a provision?

9. Assume *A* and *B* entered into an agreement whereby *A* licenses a trade secret to *B*. *B* agrees to pay a 10¢ per unit royalty, to be increased to 20¢ per unit if and when a patent issues and to be reduced to 1¢ per unit if the patent is subsequently declared invalid. Is the agreement enforceable?

(5) A CASE STUDY: EXPLOITATION OF CHARACTERS AND PERSONALITIES

This section explores the extent to which a celebrity may prevent others from using his or her name, likeness, or personality without the celebrity's permission. The cases evolve under the tort of "invasion of the right of publicity" which is thought by some to be an aspect of the right of privacy. See Prosser, Privacy, 48 Calif.L.Rev. 383 (1960). In the first case to recognize a right of publicity by name, the plaintiff who held exclusive contracts to use certain baseball player's photographs on cards distributed with chewing gum successfully prevented a competing chewing gum manufacturer to use pictures of the same ballplayers. Haelan Laboratories, Inc. v. Topps Chewing Gum, Inc., 202 F.2d 866 (2d Cir.1953). Since then, cases applying the publicity right have protected the commercial value of the celebrity's creative efforts and provide an interesting review of concepts of misappropriation, trademark, and copyright preemption played against a background of first amendment concerns.

GROUCHO MARX PRODUCTIONS, INC. v. DAY AND NIGHT CO., INC.

United States Court of Appeals, Second Circuit, 1982.
689 F.2d 317.

NEWMAN, CIRCUIT JUDGE.

For the second time in just two years, exercise of the diversity jurisdiction requires us to determine whether state law protects a person's so-called right of publicity—the right to exploit the commercial value of his name, likeness, or attributes—after his death. See Factors Etc., Inc. v. Pro Arts, Inc., 652 F.2d 278 (2d Cir.1981), cert. denied, 456 U.S. 927 (1982), leave to file petition for rehearing granted, 652 F.2d 278 (2d Cir.1982). * * *

The subject matter of this litigation is the musical play "A Day in Hollywood/A Night in the Ukraine," which enjoyed a successful run on Broadway beginning in May, 1980. The play is described by its authors as a "satiric comment" on Hollywood in the 1930's. The second ("Ukraine") half of the play purports to be the way the Marx Brothers would have dramatized Chekhov's novel "The Bear." Though the names of the Marx Brothers are not used, the script calls for the three principal performers to reproduce the appearance and comedy style made memorable by Groucho, Chico, and Harpo. Plaintiffs-appellees are Groucho Marx Productions, Inc., ("GMP") and Susan Marx, Harpo's widow. Defendants-appellants are Day and Night Company, Inc. and Alexander Cohen, producers of the play; third-party defendants-appellants are Richard K. Vosburgh and Frank Lazarus, authors of the play.

The plaintiffs' amended complaint sought damages "in the nature of a license fee" because of the defendants' exhibition of the play allegedly in derogation of plaintiffs' "exclusive rights of publicity relating to the commercialization of the characters of Groucho, Chico and Harpo." * * * The claim based on a right of publicity, with which this appeal is concerned, appears to be grounded solely on diversity jurisdiction.

Plaintiffs moved for summary judgment on the issue of liability based on the alleged appropriation of their right of publicity in the names and likenesses of the Marx Brothers. After determining that under appropriate choice of law rules, New York law governed the substantive rights of the plaintiffs, the District Court ruled that New York recognizes a right of publicity and that such a right is assignable and descendible. Judge Conner also concluded that whatever exploitation of the right during a celebrity's life is necessary to render the right descendible is satisfied by his normal professional performing. The Marx Brothers' every performance, the Court ruled, was sufficient exploitation without the need for them to "endorse dance studios, candy bars or tee shirts." 523 F.Supp. at 492. Judge Conner then rejected the defendants' claim that the First Amendment protected their right to exhibit the play without paying damages to the plaintiffs. He reasoned that the play was neither biographical nor an attempt to convey information and that whatever literary merit it possessed was outweighed by its "wholesale appropriation of the Marx Brothers characters." Id. at 493. He therefore granted the plaintiffs' motion for partial summary judgment on the issue of liability and certified his ruling for interlocutory appeal, 28 U.S.C. § 1292(b) (1976), which this Court accepted.

We need not rule on the correctness of these interpretations of New York common law and federal constitutional law, for in our opinion, the initial decision to look to the law of New York was incorrect. * * * [W]e conclude that the law governing the existence of plaintiffs' rights is California law. * * *

Two decisions of the California Supreme Court appear to establish that under the law of that State, an individual's right of publicity terminates at his death, Guglielmi v. Spelling-Goldberg Productions, 25 Cal.3d 860, 603 P.2d 454, 160 Cal.Rptr. 352 (1979) (per curiam), and Lugosi v. Universal Pictures, 25 Cal.3d 813, 603 P.2d 425, 160 Cal.Rptr. 323 (1979). *Guglielmi* was a suit by the alleged nephew of the actor Rudolph Valentino for damages and an injunction because of the televised showing of a fictionalized version of Valentino's life. The California Supreme Court affirmed dismissal of the nephew's suit in the following paragraph:

> In Lugosi v. Universal Pictures, 160 Cal.Rptr. 323, 603 P.2d 425, we hold that the right of publicity protects against the unauthorized use of one's name, likeness or personality, but that the right is not descendible and expires upon the death of the person so protected. *Lugosi* controls the disposition of the present case and makes it unnecessary to discuss any further issues raised by the parties.

603 P.2d at 455, 160 Cal.Rptr. at 353. The unequivocal nature of that statement is surely a sufficient basis for this Court, exercising diversity jurisdiction, to be satisfied that plaintiffs in this case hold no rights that California would recognize after the deaths of the Marx Brothers. Nevertheless, we explore the issue further because the *Lugosi* decision, on which *Guglielmi* relies, is at least open to the interpretation that its holding is narrow and therefore it is arguable that the broadly stated rule of *Guglielmi* should also be understood to have a narrower meaning than first appears.

Lugosi, decided two days prior to *Guglielmi*, was a suit by the heirs of the actor Bela Lugosi against the motion picture company that had produced several films based on the character Count Dracula. The best known of these films was the 1930 version in which Lugosi starred. In contracting to play the part, Lugosi gave the film studio rights to use his name and likeness to advertise the movie. After his death, his heirs sued the studio for the profits it had made in licensing "the use of the Count Dracula character to commercial firms" for merchandising products other than the film. 603 P.2d at 427, 160 Cal.Rptr. at 325. The trial court ruled in favor of the heirs, finding that the studio had appropriated the right Lugosi had in his facial characteristics and the individual manner of his likeness and appearance *as* Count Dracula. The California Court of Appeals reversed in an opinion adopted, with minor amendment, by the California Supreme Court.

Though the case presented the novel issue of whether a celebrity had a right of publicity in his appearance in a part already well known before he portrayed it, the California Supreme Court focused much of its attention on whether Lugosi had exploited his right of publicity during his lifetime. Acknowledging that Lugosi had exploited his right to a limited extent by contracting with Universal Pictures to use his likeness to promote the film, the Court nevertheless concluded that the heirs were claiming a descendible right of publicity for "commercial situations he left unexploited." 603 P.2d at 431, 160 Cal.Rptr. at 329. The Court noted that Lugosi had not availed himself of the opportunity it was willing to assume he had to exploit his name and likeness "in association with the Dracula character," suggesting that he might have "established a business under the name Lugosi Horror Pictures and sold licenses to have 'Lugosi as Dracula' imprinted on shirts." Id. at 429, 160 Cal.Rptr. at 327 (footnote omitted). But since he did not, the Court considered it "rather novel to urge that * * * *the opportunity* to have done so is property which descends to his heirs." Id. at 430, 160 Cal.Rptr. at 328 (emphasis in original). "We hold," the Court concluded, "that the right to exploit name and likeness is personal to the artist and must be exercised, if at all, by him during his lifetime." Id. at 431, 160 Cal.Rptr. at 329.

Without question, *Lugosi* established that California law does not recognize a descendible right of publicity available to the heirs of a celebrity who did not exploit his own right during his lifetime. What is less certain, however, is whether the right is descendible when the celebrity does exploit it during his lifetime. To take the California Court's example, what rights would Lugosi's heirs have had if he had established a company to market "Lugosi as Dracula" T-shirts?

There are three possible answers. If the broad rule stated in *Guglielmi* is taken literally, the heirs would have had no right of publicity that could prevent others from marketing Lugosi's likeness, even on T-shirts. Or they might have had a right of publicity that could prevent others from marketing his likeness on T-shirts, but not on any other product. Or they might have had a right of publicity that could prevent others from profiting in any way from the use of his likeness. It may well be that the broad rule that *Guglielmi* extracts from *Lugosi* is to be taken literally, at least by a diversity court trying to discern, not refine or evolve, state law. One passage of the *Lugosi* opinion, in particular, supports such a reading. The Court dwells on Dean Prosser's formulation that the right of publicity is one of four parts of an overall right of privacy, *see* 603 P.2d at 428, 160 Cal.Rptr. at 326 (quoting at length from Prosser, Privacy, 48 Calif.L.Rev. 383, 389 (1960)). Though noting that California law does not follow Prosser in thinking that a right of publicity is not assignable, the Court quotes with explicit approval Prosser's statement that " '*there is no common law right of action for a publication concerning one who is already dead.*' " Id. at 429, 160 Cal.Rptr. at 327 (quoting Prosser, Law of Torts 815 (4th ed. 1971)) (emphasis in Court's opinion).[3]

If we did not follow the literal rule stated in *Guglielmi*, we could read *Lugosi* to permit the second, but not the third, of the three possible answers to our query as to what right of publicity Lugosi's heirs would have had if he had created the T-shirt business. At most, California would recognize a descendible right of publicity that would have enabled the heirs to prevent others from using Lugosi's name and likeness on T-shirts or any other product he had promoted during his life.[4] But we can be reasonably confident that California would not accept the third alternative, which would recognize a descendible right of publicity so broad as to enable the heirs to prevent *any* use of a celebrity's name and likeness so long as the celebrity exploited his right of publicity to promote at least one product or service during his lifetime. The California Supreme Court acknowledged that Lugosi had exploited his name and likeness to promote his Count Dracula film, but that did not entitle his heirs to assert a descendible right of publicity against use of Lugosi's name and likeness in connection with "commercial situations he left unexploited." 603 P.2d at 431, 160 Cal.Rptr. at 329. The Court's rationale on this point is revealed in an earlier

---

3. Arguably also supporting a literal reading is the passage in which the Court endeavors to illustrate what benefits the heirs might have derived if Lugosi had organized or licensed the T-shirt company. The one example offered is the right to receive installment payments or royalties due after his death arising from a sale of his interest before his death. 603 P.2d at 429, 160 Cal.Rptr. at 327. Of course, contractual rights to receive accrued benefits are descendible. What is significant is that the Court does not even intimate the possibility that the heirs would receive royalties from T-shirt sales occurring after Lugosi's death. An available inference is that, even if the business had been created during his life, any exclusive rights of its proprietors protected by a right of publicity would have ended at Lugosi's death.

4. This is a much narrower view than the one expressed by some courts that have upheld a descendible right of publicity assertable against any commercial use of a celebrity's name and likeness, so long as the celebrity made some commercial exploitation of his right during his life. *See,* e.g., Hicks v. Casablanca Records, 464 F.Supp. 426, 429 (S.D.N.Y.1978) (to create a descendible right of publicity decedent must have "acted in such a way as to evidence his or her own recognition of the extrinsic commercial value of his or her name or likeness, and manifested that recognition in some overt manner, e.g., making an *inter vivos* transfer of the rights * * *, or posing for bubble gum cards").

passage, where it notes that Lugosi had not used his likeness as Dracula "in connection with any business, product or service so as to impress a *secondary meaning* on *such* business, product or service." Id. at 428, 160 Cal.Rptr. at 326 (emphasis added). This is the language of trademark law, under which the strength or public recognition of a mark as identifying the source of a particular product is significant in determining whether the proprietor may prevent use of the mark on similar products. Perhaps *Lugosi* was relegating the heirs solely to their rights under trademark law. But even if it was recognizing a distinct descendible right of publicity, the right is limited to the particular "commercial situations"—products or services—that the celebrity promoted with his name and likeness during his lifetime.[5]

Lugosi also makes clear that playing a part is not the sort of exploitation of one's likeness or attributes that enables heirs to enjoy a descendible right of publicity. The California Supreme Court was willing to assume, for purposes of the *Lugosi* case, that Lugosi had an inchoate right of publicity to his appearance as Dracula—an opportunity to exploit the right in connection with one or more commercial products. Nevertheless, the Court rejected the heirs' suit. The Court was willing to find the requisite exploitation of this inchoate right only as to the film which Lugosi had agreed to promote with his name and likeness. Thus, applying California law, we must reject Judge Conner's view that the Marx Brothers, simply by performing as Groucho, Chico, and Harpo, exploited their rights of publicity so as to create descendible rights.

We conclude that *Lugosi* is subject to two interpretations. It may mean that California does not recognize any descendible right of publicity and that the heirs of a celebrity must rely on trademark law to protect the good will that the celebrity brought to a product during his lifetime. Alternatively, *Lugosi* might mean that, wholly apart from trademark law, California recognizes a descendible right of publicity that enables the heirs to prevent the use of a celebrity's name and likeness on any product or service the celebrity promoted by exploiting his right of publicity during his lifetime. Under either of the two possible views of California law we have discerned, the plaintiffs in this litigation cannot prevail. Obviously, if no right of publicity survives death, the plaintiffs have no rights after the deaths of the Marx Brothers. Even if there is a limited descendible right, applicable to a product or service promoted by the celebrity, the defendants are not using the names or likenesses of the Marx Brothers in connection with any product or service that the comedians promoted during their lives.

---

5. The *Lugosi* opinion comments in passing that an *inter vivos* assignment of the right would be "synonymous with its exercise." 603 P.2d at 431, 160 Cal.Rptr. at 329. However, the repeated emphasis elsewhere in the opinion of the need to create a "tie-up * * * with a business, product or service," id. at 428, 160 Cal. Rptr. at 326, indicates that such an assignment would create a survivable interest only to the extent that the assigned right was transformed from a potential interest into a realized commercial interest by exploitation in connection with a particular commercial activity.

Since California would recognize, at most, a descendible right of publicity only in connection with particular commercial situations—products and services—that a celebrity promoted during his lifetime, we conclude that California would not recognize a descendible right of publicity that protects against an original play using a celebrity's likeness and comedic style.

For these reasons, we reverse the District Court's ruling granting partial summary judgment to the plaintiffs on the issue of liability for appropriation of a right of publicity and remand for the District Court's consideration of any issues that may remain.[9]

NOTES

1. What is the interest protected by the right of publicity? What is the appropriate measure of damages in such cases? Should the plaintiff be limited to recovery of the defendant's profits attributable to the use of the plaintiff's name or likeness? Do you want to prohibit the unauthorized use of a celebrity's name or likeness in all cases or do you merely want to insure the celebrity receives the returns from his investment in attaining celebrity status? How do the celebrity cases differ from a situation in which a photograph of a non-celebrity taken in a public place is used as part of a television commercial? Is the celebrity's endorsement of a product a "free good"?

2. The Second Circuit has twice deferred to the law of other jurisdictions in ruling that the right of publicity does not survive the death of the owner. In the *Factors* decision, cited in the opinion, the court deferred to the Sixth Circuit's interpretation of Tennessee law, in denying protection to the heirs of Elvis Presley. In an earlier appeal in that case, the Second Circuit had held that New York law would indeed permit protection after death. Factors, Etc., Inc. v. Pro Arts, Inc., 579 F.2d 215 (2d Cir.1978). And, in Tennessee, ex. rel. The Elvis Presley International Memorial Foundation v. Crowell, 733 S.W.2d 89 (Tenn.App.1987) a Tennessee Court found that Tennessee law does in fact permit descendibility.

Can you justify permitting the right to descend to heirs? Is such a right necessary to encourage celebrities to develop and exploit their personas? If a celebrity secures a contract that specifically contemplates royalty payments after death, should the contract be enforceable? Does the issue depend on whether the right of publicity protects against misappropriation or confusion?

3. In Midler v. Ford Motor Co., 849 F.2d 460 (9th Cir.1988) Ford Motor, after unsuccessfully seeking the services of Bette Midler for an advertising commercial, hired another person to imitate Midler's voice singing a famous Midler song. The court upheld a cause of action for appropriating the plaintiff's identity, rejecting a copyright preemption claim because a "voice is not copyrightable" and a First Amendment argument because the use here was not informative or culture but exploitive. "We need not and do not go so far as to

---

9. In addition to the state law claim based on a descendible right of publicity, plaintiffs also alleged causes of action for false representation in violation of section 43(a) of the Lanham Act, 15 U.S.C. § 1125(a) (1976), and state law claims of misappropriation, interference with contractual relations and unfair competition, and infringement of common-law copyright. Though appellants urge us to direct dismissal of the complaint upon reversal of the certified ruling on appeal, we prefer to have the District Court consider whether any of plaintiffs' other claims, which are not before us, survive our rejection of their right of publicity claim.

hold that every imitation of a voice to advertise merchandise is actionable. We hold only that when a distinctive voice of a professional singer is widely known and is deliberately imitated in order to sell a product, the sellers have appropriated what is not theirs and have committed a tort in California." See also, Lombardo v. Doyle, Dane & Bernbach, Inc., 58 A.D.2d 620, 396 N.Y.S.2d 661 (1977) (Guy Lombardo has a proprietary interest in his public personality sufficient to prevent the use of an imitation of his New Years Eve performance in a commercial). But see, Sinatra v. Goodyear Tire & Rubber Co., 435 F.2d 711, cert. denied 402 U.S. 906 (1970), where the court relied on *Sears* and *Compco* to dismiss a complaint by Nancy Sinatra for imitation of her distinctive manner of singing "These Boots Are Made for Walking" in a commercial advertising Goodyear's "wide boots" tires. The commercial was sung by a different singer who imitated the Sinatra style. See also Booth v. Colgate-Palmolive Co., 362 F.Supp. 343 (S.D.N.Y.1973) (denying recovery for imitation in a commercial of Shirley Booth's voice).

Is there an appropriate distinction to be drawn between imitation and appropriation in these cases? Are there now additional risks for the comedian whose basic routine consists of satirically impersonating celebrities? If a manufacturer can reverse engineer a product to produce a competing copy, why should not an entertainer "reverse engineer" a successful performer and provide competition? Do *Sears* and *Compco* apply here?

4. Not all courts have required that the celebrity exploit his right of publicity during his lifetime in order to have a property right that descends to his heirs. In Martin Luther King, Jr., Center for Social Change, Inc. v. American Heritage Products, Inc., 250 Ga. 135, 296 S.E.2d 697 (1982) the heirs and successors to Martin Luther King sought to prevent the defendant from selling an unauthorized bust of King. In holding for the plaintiff, the court argued that the exploitation requirement would deny protection to heirs of public figures and grant protection only to entertainers who contracted for bubble gum cards, posters, and tee shirts:

> Without doubt, Dr. King could have exploited his name and likeness during his lifetime. That this opportunity was not appealing to him does not mean that others have the right to use his name and likeness in ways he himself chose not to do. Nor does it strip his family and estate of the right to control, preserve and extend his status and memory and to prevent unauthorized exploitation thereof by others. Here, they seek to prevent the exploitation of his likeness in a manner they consider unflattering and unfitting. We cannot deny them this right merely because Dr. King chose not to exploit or commercialize himself during his lifetime.

See generally, Felcher & Rubin, The Descendibility of the Right of Publicity: Is there Commercial Life After Death?, 89 Yale L.J. 1125 (1980).

5. Consider the following factual contexts in which the right of publicity has been raised. In which would you grant protection?

a. Playgirl magazine published in its magazine a portrait of a nude black man seated in the corner of a boxing ring. The man was allegedly recognizeable as Muhammad Ali, the former heavyweight boxing champion. The picture was captioned "Mystery Man" and was accompanied by a verse referring to the man as "the Greatest." Ali v. Playgirl, Inc., 447 F.Supp. 723 (S.D.N.Y.1978) (right of publicity infringed).

b. In 1978, Ann-Margret appeared nude from the waist up in the film "Magic." She said her decision to disrobe was based on artistic necessity. Subsequently a picture taken from the movie appeared in a magazine entitled "High Society Celebrity Skin" which specialized in printing nude photographs of celebrities. Ann-Margret did not consent to publication of the picture. See Ann-Margret v. High Soc'y Magazine, Inc., 498 F.Supp. 401 (S.D.N.Y.1980) (right of publicity not applicable).

Compare Brinkley v. Casablancas, 80 A.D.2d 428, 438 N.Y.S.2d 1004 (1981) where a famous fashion model posed for photographs for a poster series, selected the proof, but did not give written consent authorizing distribution of the poster. Held: right of publicity under New York statute infringed by distribution of the poster.

c. The defendant publishes a true but unauthorized biography of a celebrity. See Frosch v. Grossett & Dunlap, Inc., 75 A.D.2d 768, 427 N.Y.S.2d 828 (1980).

ZACCHINI v. SCRIPPS–HOWARD BROADCASTING CO.

Supreme Court of the United States, 1977.
433 U.S. 562, 97 S.Ct. 2849, 53 L.Ed.2d 965.

MR. JUSTICE WHITE delivered the opinion of the Court.

Petitioner, Hugo Zacchini, is an entertainer. He performs a "human cannonball" act in which he is shot from a cannon into a net some 200 feet away. Each performance occupies some 15 seconds. In August and September, 1972, petitioner was engaged to perform his act on a regular basis at the Geauga County Fair in Burton, Ohio. He performed in a fenced area, surrounded by grandstands, at the fair grounds. Members of the public attending the fair were not charged a separate admission fee to observe his act.

On August 30, a freelance reporter for Scripps-Howard Broadcasting Company, the operator of a television broadcasting station and respondent in this case, attended the fair. He carried a small movie camera. Petitioner noticed the reporter and asked him not to film the performance. The reporter did not do so on that day; but on the instructions of the producer of respondent's daily newscast, he returned the following day and videotaped the entire act. This film clip approximately 15 seconds in length, was shown on the 11 o'clock news program that night, together with favorable commentary.[1]

Petitioner then brought this action for damages, alleging that he is "engaged in the entertainment business," that the act he performs is one "invented by his father and * * * performed only by his family for the last fifty years," that respondent "showed and commercialized

---

1. The script of the commentary accompanying the film clip read as follows:

"This * * * now * * * is the story of a *true spectator* sport * * * the sport of human cannonballing * * * in fact, the great *Zacchini* is about the only human cannonball around, these days * * * just happens that, *where* he is, is the Great Geauga County Fair, in Burton * * * and believe me, although it's not a *long* act, it's a thriller * * * and you really need to see it *in person* * * * to appreciate it. * * *" (Emphasis in original.) App. 12.

the film of his act without his consent," and that such conduct was an "unlawful appropriation of plaintiff's professional property." * * *

[The trial court summarily granted respondent's motion for summary judgment. The Ohio Court of Appeals reversed finding the complaint stated a cause of action for conversion and for infringement of a common law copyright. The Supreme Court of Ohio reversed, holding that although the petitioner had a "right of publicity," the newscast was a matter of public interest and thus privileged.]

We granted certiorari, 429 U.S. 1037 (1977), to consider an issue unresolved by this Court: whether the First and Fourteenth Amendments immunized respondent from damages for its alleged infringement of petitioner's state law "right of publicity." Petition for Certiorari 2. Insofar as the Ohio Supreme Court held that the First and Fourteenth Amendments of the United States Constitution required judgment for respondent, we reverse the judgment of that court.

III

The Ohio Supreme Court held that respondent is constitutionally privileged to include in its newscasts matters of public interest that would otherwise be protected by the right of publicity, absent an intent to injure or to appropriate for some nonprivileged purpose. If under this standard respondent had merely reported that petitioner was performing at the fair and described or commented on his act, with or without showing his picture on television, we would have a very different case. But petitioner is not contending that his appearance at the fair and his performance could not be reported by the press as newsworthy items. His complaint is that respondent filmed his entire act and displayed that film on television for the public to see and enjoy. This, he claimed, was an appropriation of his professional property. The Ohio Supreme Court agreed that petitioner had "a right of publicity" that gave him "personal control over the commercial display and exploitation of his personality and the exercise of his talents." This right of "exclusive control over the publicity given to his performance" was said to be such a "valuable part of the benefit which may be attained by his talents and efforts" that it was entitled to legal protection. It was also observed, or at least expressly assumed, that petitioner had not abandoned his rights by performing under the circumstances present at the Geauga County Fair Grounds.

The Ohio Supreme Court nevertheless held that the challenged invasion was privileged, saying that the press "must be accorded broad latitude in its choice of how much it presents of each story or incident, and of the emphasis to be given to such presentation. No fixed standard which would bar the press from reporting or depicting either an entire occurrence or an entire discrete part of a public performance can be formulated which would not unduly restrict the 'breathing room' in reporting which freedom of the press requires." 47 Ohio St., at 235,

351 N.E.2d, at 461. Under this view, respondent was thus constitutionally free to film and display petitioner's entire act.

The Ohio Supreme Court relied heavily on Time, Inc. v. Hill, [385 U.S. 374 (1967)], but that case does not mandate a media privilege to televise a performer's entire act without his consent. Involved in Time, Inc. v. Hill was a claim under the New York "Right of Privacy" statute that Life Magazine, in the course of reviewing a new play, had connected the play with a long-past incident involving petitioner and his family and had falsely described their experience and conduct at that time. The complaint sought damages for humiliation and suffering flowing from these nondefamatory falsehoods that allegedly invaded Hill's privacy. The Court held, however, that the opening of a new play linked to an actual incident was a matter of public interest and that Hill could not recover without showing that the Life report was knowingly false or was published with reckless disregard for the truth—the same rigorous standard that had been applied in New York Times v. Sullivan, [376 U.S. 254 (1964)].

Time, Inc. v. Hill, which was hotly contested and decided by a divided court, involved an entirely different tort than the "right of publicity" recognized by the Ohio Supreme Court. As the opinion reveals in Time, Inc. v. Hill, the Court was steeped in the literature of privacy law and was aware of the developing distinctions and nuances in this branch of the law. The Court, for example, cited Prosser, Handbook of the Law of Torts (3d ed. 1964), and the same author's well-known article, Privacy, 48 Calif.L.Rev. 383 (1960), both of which divided privacy into four distinct branches. The Court was aware that it was adjudicating a "false light" privacy case involving a matter of public interest, not a case involving "intrusion," 385 U.S., at 384–385, n. 9, "appropriation" of a name or likeness for the purposes of trade, Id., at 381, or "private details" about a non-newsworthy person or event, Id., at 383 n. 7. It is also abundantly clear that Time, Inc. v. Hill did not involve a performer, a person with a name having commercial value, or any claim to a "right of publicity." This discrete kind of "appropriation" case was plainly identified in the literature cited by the Court and had been adjudicated in the reported cases.

The differences between these two torts are important. First, the State's interests in providing a cause of action in each instance are different. "The interest protected" in permitting recovery for placing the plaintiff in a false light "is clearly that of reputation, with the same overtones of mental distress as in defamation." Prosser, supra, 48 Calif.L.Rev., at 400. By contrast, the State's interest in permitting a "right of publicity" is in protecting the proprietary interest of the individual in his act in part to encourage such entertainment.[10] As we

10. The Ohio Supreme Court expressed the view "that plaintiff's claim is one for invasion of the right of privacy by appropriation, and should be considered as such." 47 Ohio St., at 226, 351 N.E.2d, at 456. It should be noted, however, that the case before us is more limited than the broad category of lawsuits that may arise under the heading of "appropriation." Petitioner does not merely assert that some

later note, the State's interest is closely analogous to the goals of patent and copyright law, focusing on the right of the individual to reap the reward of his endeavors and having little to do with protecting feelings or reputation. Second, the two torts differ in the degree to which they intrude on dissemination of information to the public. In "false light" cases the only way to protect the interests involved is to attempt to minimize publication of the damaging matter, while in "right of publicity" cases the only question is who gets to do the publishing. An entertainer such as petitioner usually has no objection to the widespread publication of his act as long as he gets the commercial benefit of such publication. Indeed, in the present case petitioner did not seek to enjoin the broadcast of his act; he simply sought compensation for the broadcast in the form of damages.

Nor does it appear that our later cases, such as Rosenbloom v. Metromedia, Inc., 403 U.S. 29 (1971); Gertz v. Robert Welch, Inc., 418 U.S. 323 (1974); and Time, Inc. v. Firestone, 424 U.S. 448, (1976), require or furnish substantial support for the Ohio court's privilege ruling. These cases, like *New York Times,* emphasize the protection extended to the press by the First Amendment in defamation cases, particularly when suit is brought by a public official or a public figure. None of them involve an alleged appropriation by the press of a right of publicity existing under state law.

Moreover, Time, Inc. v. Hill, *New York Times, Metromedia, Gertz,* and *Firestone* all involved the reporting of events; in none of them was there an attempt to broadcast or publish an entire act for which the performer ordinarily gets paid. It is evident, and there is no claim here to the contrary, that petitioner's state-law right of publicity would not serve to prevent respondent from reporting the newsworthy facts about petitioner's act. Wherever the line in particular situations is to be drawn between media reports that are protected and those that are not, we are quite sure that the First and Fourteenth Amendments do not immunize the media when they broadcast a performer's entire act without his consent. The Constitution no more prevents a State from requiring respondent to compensate petitioner for broadcasting his act on television than it would privilege respondent to film and broadcast a copyrighted dramatic work without liability to the copyright owner.

* * *

The broadcast of a film of petitioner's entire act poses a substantial threat to the economic value of that performance. As the Ohio court recognized, this act is the product of petitioner's own talents and energy, the end result of much time, effort and expense. Much of its economic value lies in the "right of exclusive control over the publicity given to his performance"; if the public can see the act for free on

general use, such as advertising, was made of his name or likeness; he relies on the much narrower claim that respondent tele-

vised an entire act that he ordinarily gets paid to perform.

television, they will be less willing to pay to see it at the fair.[12] The effect of a public broadcast of the performance is similar to preventing petitioner from charging an admission fee. "The rationale for [protecting the right of publicity] is the straightforward one of preventing unjust enrichment by the theft of good will. No social purpose is served by having the defendant get for free some aspect of the plaintiff that would have market value and for which he would normally pay." Kalven, Privacy in Tort Law—Were Warren and Brandeis Wrong?, 31 Law and Contemporary Problems 326, 331 (1966). Moreover, the broadcast of petitioner's entire performance, unlike the unauthorized use of another's name for purposes of trade or the incidental use of a name or picture by the press, goes to the heart of petitioner's ability to earn a living as an entertainer. Thus in this case, Ohio has recognized what may be the strongest case for a "right of publicity"—involving not the appropriation of an entertainer's reputation to enhance the attractiveness of a commercial product, but the appropriation of the very activity by which the entertainer acquired his reputation in the first place.

Of course, Ohio's decision to protect petitioner's right of publicity here rests on more than a desire to compensate the performer for the time and effort invested in his act; the protection provides an economic incentive for him to make the investment required to produce a performance of interest to the public. This same consideration underlies the patent and copyright laws long enforced by this Court. As the Court stated in Mazer v. Stein, 347 U.S. 201, 219 (1954),

> "The economic philosophy behind the clause empowering Congress to grant patents and copyrights is the conviction that encouragement of individual effort by personal gain is the best way to advance public welfare through the talents of authors and inventors in 'Science and useful Arts.' Sacrificial days devoted to such creative activities deserve rewards commensurate with the services rendered."

These laws perhaps regard the "reward to the owner [as] a secondary consideration," United States v. Paramount Pictures, 334 U.S. 131, 158 (1948), but they were "intended definitely to grant valuable, enforceable rights" in order to afford greater encouragement to the production of works of benefit to the public. Washingtonian Publishing Co. v. Pearson, 306 U.S. 30, 36 (1939). The Constitution does not prevent Ohio from making a similar choice here in deciding to protect the entertainer's incentive in order to encourage the production of this type of work. Cf. Goldstein v. California, 412 U.S. 546 (1973); Kewanee Oil Co. v. Bicron Corp., 416 U.S. 470 (1974).

---

12. It is possible, of course, that respondent's news broadcast increased the value of petitioner's performance by stimulating the public's interest in seeing the act live. In these circumstances, petitioner would not be able to prove damages and thus would not recover. But petitioner has alleged that the broadcast injured him to the extent of $25,000, and we think the State should be allowed to authorize compensation of this injury if proven.

There is no doubt that entertainment, as well as news, enjoys First Amendment protection. It is also true that entertainment itself can be important news. Time, Inc. v. Hill, supra. But it is important to note that neither the public nor respondent will be deprived of the benefit of petitioner's performance as long as his commercial stake in his act is appropriately recognized. Petitioner does not seek to enjoin the broadcast of his performance; he simply wants to be paid for it. Nor do we think that a state-law damages remedy against respondent would represent a species of liability without fault contrary to the letter or spirit of Gertz, supra. Respondent knew exactly that petitioner objected to televising his act, but nevertheless displayed the entire film.

We conclude that although the State of Ohio may as a matter of its own law privilege the press in the circumstances of this case, the First and Fourteenth Amendments do not require it to do so.

Reversed.

MR. JUSTICE POWELL, with whom MR. JUSTICE BRENNAN and MR. JUSTICE MARSHALL join, dissenting.

Disclaiming any attempt to do more than decide the narrow case before us, the Court reverses the decision of the Supreme Court of Ohio based on repeated incantation of a single formula: "a performer's entire act." * * *

I doubt that this formula provides a standard clear enough even for resolution of this case.[1] In any event, I am not persuaded that the Court's opinion is appropriately sensitive to the First Amendment values at stake, and I therefore dissent.

* * *

* * * When a film is used, as here, for a routine portion of a regular news program, I would hold that the First Amendment protects the station from a "right of publicity" or "appropriation" suit, absent a strong showing by the plaintiff that the news broadcast was a subterfuge or cover for private or commercial exploitation.

I emphasize that this is a "reappropriation" suit, rather than one of the other varieties of "right of privacy" tort suits identified by Dean Prosser in his classic article. Prosser, Privacy, 48 Calif.L.Rev. 383 (1960). In those other causes of action the competing interests are considerably different. The plaintiff generally seeks to avoid any sort of public exposure, and the existence of constitutional privilege is

---

1. Although the record is not explicit, it is unlikely that the "act" commenced abruptly with the explosion that launched petitioner on his way, ending with the landing in the net a few seconds later. One may assume that the actual firing was preceded by some fanfare, possibly stretching over several minutes, to heighten the audience's anticipation: introduction of the performer, description of the uniqueness and danger, last-minute checking of the apparatus, and entry into the cannon, all accompanied by suitably ominous commentary from the master of ceremonies. If this is found to be the case on remand, then respondent could not be said to have appropriated the "entire act" in its 15-second newsclip—and the Court's opinion then would afford no guidance for resolution of the case. Moreover, in future cases involving different performances, similar difficulties in determining just what constitutes the "entire act" are inevitable.

therefore less likely to turn on whether the publication occurred in a news broadcast or in some other fashion. In a suit like the one before us, however, the plaintiff does not complain about the fact of exposure to the public, but rather about its timing or manner. He welcomes some publicity, but seeks to retain control over means and manner as a way to maximize for himself the monetary benefits that flow from such publication. But having made the matter public—having chosen, in essence, to make it newsworthy—he cannot, consistently with the First Amendment, complain of routine news reportage. * * *

Since the film clip here was undeniably treated as news and since there is no claim that the use was subterfuge, respondent's actions were constitutionally privileged. I would affirm.

NOTES

1. What measure of damages would you adopt for cases like *Zacchini*? Does the majority opinion place any first amendment limits on your range of choice? Isn't *Zacchini* really like the *DuPont* case [aerial photography]? Would it make any difference if the ticket to see Zacchini's act carried the legend "No Photographs".

2. Is the Ohio law of publicity preempted by § 301 of the Copyright Act? Does it matter that Zacchini's act was not fixed in a tangible medium of expression under § 102? Does Zacchini's act fit within one of the protectible categories mentioned in § 102? Is the right of publicity "equivalent" to a right in § 106? The Seventh Circuit struggled with these problems in Baltimore Orioles v. Major League Baseball Players, 805 F.2d 663 (7th Cir.1986) where major league baseball players argued they owned the broadcast rights to their performances during baseball games. As to the games that were videotaped, the court held the right of publicity was preempted by § 301. As to other games the court left open whether the employer owns the names, likenesses, and performances of employees within the scope of their employment. What do you think? See D. Shipley, Three Strikes and They're Out at the Old Ball Game: Preemption of Performers' Rights of Publicity Under the Copyright Act of 1976, 20 Ariz.St.L.J. 369 (1988).

3. Should the constitutional fault standard of the defamation and privacy cases apply to publicity cases? If a publisher publishes nude photographs he claims are of a particular celebrity and they turn out to be of someone else, should the celebrity be required to prove "actual malice". Does it matter whether the celebrity wants (a) an injunction against publication, or (b) royalties? See Lerman v. Flynt Distributing Co., Inc., 745 F.2d 123 (2d Cir.1984). See also Tellado v. Time–Life Books, Inc., 643 F.Supp. 904 (D.N.J.1986) where the plaintiff objected to the use of his picture, taken during battle in Vietnam, as an advertisement for a series of picture books on the Vietnam war. The court held that a misappropriation claim was available for "predominantly commercial uses" of a person's likeness and such a cause of action would not violate the First Amendment.

4. Can you frame a response to the assertion that Scripps-Howard's activity in *Zacchini* is similar to broadcasting a copyrighted dramatic work as part of news coverage?

5. In New Kids on the Block v. New America Publishing, Inc., 745 F.Supp. 1540 (C.D.Cal.1990) the defendants, USA Today and Star Magazine, advertised

surveys to determine which member of the musical group "New Kids on the Block" was regarded by fans as the "favorite" or "sexiest". Readers were invited to call a 900 telephone number to cast their vote and each caller was charged a fee when doing so. The "New Kids" sued claiming trademark infringement and misappropriation of their name and likeness. The court first held on the trademark claim that any risk that some people might believe the musical group sponsored or endorsed the 900 number was "outweighed by the danger of restricting news gathering and dissemination." On the misappropriation claim the court after noting that California has "specifically allowed incidental commercial exploitation of a public figure's name and likeness in the context of a publication's advertising activities * * * [but] total commercial exploitation is not allowed," held the use of the group's name in this context was descriptive rather than exploitative and thus constitutionally protected.

> [T]his is not a case that would fall under the rule created by the United States Supreme Court in [Zacchini]. * * * The Court weighed defendant's First Amendment rights against plaintiff's right to earn a livelihood. The Court found that "[t]he broadcast of a film of petitioner's entire act poses a substantial threat to the economic value of that performance." * * * Because there is no similar substantial threat to the economic value of the New Kids' name, the Court should not adopt the *Zacchini* rule in this case. The Court finds, as a matter of law, that the defendants' use of the New Kids' name and likeness was related to news gathering and not mere commercial exploitation. Thus, the First Amendment immunizes USA Today and Star Magazine from plaintiffs' misappropriation claims.

Do you think a state lottery could operate a lottery which required players to pick the winner of professional football games if the lottery cards and associated advertising used the trademarks and logos of the professional football teams to identify the games to be played each week, i.e., Chicago Bears v. Philadelphia Eagles?

6. How would you expect the Supreme Court to handle a case in which the owner of a copyright on a medical journal sued a library for photocopying an article from the journal at the request of a medical researcher?

ESTATE OF ELVIS PRESLEY v. RUSSEN
United States District Court, District of New Jersey, 1981.
513 F.Supp. 1339.

BROTMAN, DISTRICT JUDGE.

During his lifetime, Elvis Presley established himself as one of the legends in the entertainment business. On August 16, 1977, Elvis Presley died, but his legend and worldwide popularity have survived. As Presley's popularity has subsisted and even grown, so has the capacity for generating financial rewards and legal disputes.[1] Although the present case is another in this line, it presents questions not previously addressed. As a general proposition, this case is concerned

---

1. See Memphis Development Foundation v. Factors Etc., Inc., 616 F.2d 956 (6th Cir.), cert. denied, 449 U.S. 953 (1980); Factors Etc., Inc. v. Pro Arts, Inc., 496 F.Supp. 1090 (S.D.N.Y.1980) (permanent injunc- tion); 444 F.Supp. 288 (S.D.N.Y.1977) (preliminary injunction) affirmed, 579 F.2d 215 (2nd Cir.1978), cert. denied, 440 U.S. 908, (1979); Factors Etc., Inc. v. Creative Card Co., 444 F.Supp. 279, 282 (S.D.N.Y.1977).

with the rights and limitations of one who promotes and presents a theatrical production designed to imitate or simulate a stage perform- ance of Elvis Presley.

* * *

* * * Plaintiff seeks a permanent injunction, an impounding and delivery to plaintiff of promotional and advertising materials, letter- heads, business cards and other materials, an accounting of defendant's profits, and an award of treble damages and reasonable attorneys' fees. Defendant answered the allegations contained in the complaint and also filed a counterclaim alleging that the plaintiff's actions were in violation of the anti-trust laws of the United States.

* * *

FINDINGS OF FACT

Plaintiff

1. Plaintiff is the Estate of Elvis Presley (hereafter the Estate) located in Memphis, Tennessee, created by the Will of Elvis Presley and is, under the laws of the State of Tennessee, a legal entity with the power to sue and be sued.

* * *

Defendant

31. Defendant, Rob Russen d/b/a THE BIG EL SHOW (hereafter Russen) is the producer of THE BIG EL SHOW.

32. THE BIG EL SHOW is a stage production patterned after an actual Elvis Presley stage show, albeit on a lesser scale, and featuring an individual who impersonates the late Elvis Presley by performing in the style of Presley. The performer wears the same style and design of clothing and jewelry as did Presley, hands out to the audience scarves as did Presley, sings songs made popular by Presley, wears his hair in the same style as Presley, and imitates the singing voice, distinctive poses, and body movements made famous by Presley.

33. Russen charges customers to view performances of THE BIG EL SHOW or alternatively charges fees to those in whose rooms or auditoriums THE BIG EL SHOW is performed who in turn charge customers to view THE BIG EL SHOW.

34. THE BIG EL SHOW production runs for approximately nine- ty minutes. The show opens with the theme from the movie "2001—A Space Odyssey" which Elvis Presley also used to open his stage shows. The production centers on Larry Seth, "Big El," doing his Elvis Presley impersonation and features musicians called the TCB Band. The TCB Band was also the name of Elvis Presley's band; however THE BIG EL SHOW TCB Band does not consist of musicians from Presley's band.

* * *

A. *Likelihood of Success on the Merits*

1. *Right of Publicity*

The plaintiff has asserted that the defendant's production, THE BIG EL SHOW, infringes on the right of publicity which plaintiff inherited from Elvis Presley.

* * *

In the present case, we are faced with the following issues: * * *

b. Assuming the existence and inheritability of a right of publicity, does the presentation of THE BIG EL SHOW infringe upon the plaintiff's right of publicity?

* * *

b. *Theatrical Imitations and The Right of Publicity*

Having found that New Jersey supports a common law right of publicity, we turn our attention to a resolution of whether this right of publicity provides protection against the defendant's promotion and presentation of THE BIG EL SHOW. In deciding this issue, the circumstances and nature of defendant's activity, as well as the scope of the right of publicity, are to be considered. In a recent law journal article, the authors conducted an extensive and thorough analysis of the cases and theories bearing on media portrayals, i.e., the portrayal of a real person by a news or entertainment media production. Felcher & Rubin, Privacy, Publicity, and the Portrayal of Real People by the Media, [hereinafter "Portrayal"] 88 Yale L.J. 1577, 1596 (1979). They concluded that "[t]he primary social policy that determines the legal protection afforded to media portrayals is based on the First Amendment guarantee of free speech and press." Id. at 1596. Thus, the purpose of the portrayal in question must be examined to determine if it predominantly serves a social function valued by the protection of free speech. If the portrayal mainly serves the purpose of contributing information, which is not false or defamatory, to the public debate of political or social issues or of providing the free expression of creative talent which contributes to society's cultural enrichment, then the portrayal generally will be immune from liability. If, however, the portrayal functions primarily as a means of commercial exploitation, then such immunity will not be granted. See generally Portrayal, supra, at 1596–99.[13]

---

13. The authors also discuss other, albeit less important, policies bearing on media portrayals. These policies focus on the harm to the plaintiff and include: the protection of the freedom of the individual against the disclosure of certain types of information; the prevention of fraudulent business practices; and that of encouraging individual achievement by allowing people to profit from their own efforts. Id. at 1599–1601. These three policies emphasize that a showing of identifiable harm, either noneconomic or economic, supports recovery for unauthorized media portrayals where the portrayal is predominantly exploitative and not protected by First Amendment considerations. Id. at 1608–16.

Taking the two sets of principles (First Amendment concerns and identifiable harm) into account, the authors have proposed a two-step process whereby:

The first step is to determine whether the portrayal in question is exploitative [in that it does not serve a recognized

The idea that the scope of the right of publicity should be measured or balanced against societal interests in free expression has been recognized and discussed in the case law and by other legal commentators. In general, in determining whether a plaintiff's right of publicity can be invoked to prevent a defendant's activity, the courts have divided along the lines set out above. In cases finding the expression to be protected, the defendant's activity has consisted of the dissemination of such information as "thoughts, ideas, newsworthy events, * * * matters of public interest," Rosemont Enterprises, Inc. v. Random House, Inc., 58 Misc.2d 1, 6, 294 N.Y.S.2d 122, 129 (Sup.Ct.1968), aff'd mem., 32 App.Div.2d 892, 301 N.Y.S.2d 948 (1969) (biography of Howard Hughes) and fictionalizations. The importance of protecting fictionalizations and related efforts as against rights of publicity was explained by Chief Justice Bird of the California Supreme Court:

> Contemporary events, symbols and people are regularly used in fictional works. Fiction writers may be able to more persuasively, more accurately express themselves by weaving into the tale persons or events familiar to their readers. The choice is theirs. No author should be forced into creating mythological worlds or characters wholly divorced from reality. The right of publicity derived from public prominence does not confer a shield to ward off caricature, parody and satire. Rather, prominence invites creative comment.

Guglielmi v. Spelling—Goldberg Productions, 25 Cal.3d at 869, 160 Cal. Rptr. at 358, 603 P.2d at 460 (Bird, C.J., concurring).

On the other hand, most of those cases finding that the right of publicity, or its equivalence, prevails have involved the use of a famous name or likeness predominantly in connection with the sale of consumer merchandise or "solely 'for purposes of trade—e.g., merely to attract attention.' [without being artistic, informational or newsworthy] Grant v. Esquire, Inc., 367 F.Supp. 876, 881 (S.D.N.Y.1973) [unauthorized use of photo of Cary Grant in fashion article]." Ali v. Playgirl, Inc., 447 F.Supp. 723, 727, 728–29 (S.D.N.Y.1978) (unauthorized drawing of nude man, recognizable as Muhammed Ali, seated in corner of boxing ring). In these cases, it seems clear that the name or likeness of the public figure is being used predominantly for commercial exploitation, and thus is subject to the right of publicity. * * *

In the present case, the defendant's expressive activity, THE BIG EL SHOW production, does not fall clearly on either side. Based on the current state of the record, the production can be described as a live theatrical presentation or concert designed to imitate a performance of

social function of an informative or cultural nature]. If the portrayal is found to be exploitative, the next step is to determine whether the plaintiff has suffered any identifiable harm, of either an economic or dignitary nature.

We have not incorporated the harm element into our determination of likelihood of success on the merits. However, we have discussed the need for identifiable harm in the section, infra, on irreparable injury and the right of publicity.

Id. at 1620.

the late Elvis Presley. The show stars an individual who closely resembles Presley and who imitates the appearance, dress, and characteristic performing style of Elvis Presley. The defendant has made no showing, nor attempted to show, that the production is intended to or acts as a parody, burlesque, satire, or criticism of Elvis Presley. As a matter of fact, the show is billed as "A TRIBUTE TO ELVIS PRESLEY." In essence, we confront the question of whether the use of the likeness of a famous deceased entertainer in a performance mainly designed to imitate that famous entertainer's own past stage performances is to be considered primarily as a commercial appropriation by the imitator or show's producer of the famous entertainer's likeness or as a valuable contribution of information or culture. After careful consideration of the activity, we have decided that although THE BIG EL SHOW contains an informational and entertainment element, the show serves primarily to commercially exploit the likeness of Elvis Presley without contributing anything of substantial value to society. In making this decision, the court recognizes that certain factors distinguish this situation from the pure commercial use of a picture of Elvis Presley to advertise a product. In the first place, the defendant uses Presley's likeness in an entertainment form and, as a general proposition, "entertainment * * * enjoys First Amendment protection." Zacchini v. Scripps-Howard Broadcasting Co., 433 U.S. 562, 578 (1977). However, entertainment that is merely a copy or imitation, even if skillfully and accurately carried out, does not really have its own creative component and does not have a significant value as pure entertainment. As one authority has emphasized:

> The public interest in entertainment will support the sporadic, occasional and good-faith imitation of a famous person to achieve humor, to effect criticism or to season a particular episode, but it does not give a privilege to appropriate another's valuable attributes on a continuing basis as one's own without the consent of the other.

Netterville, "Copyright and Tort Aspects of Parody, Mimicry and Humorous Commentary," 35 S.Cal.L.Rev. 225, 254 (1962).

In the second place, the production does provide information in that it illustrates a performance of a legendary figure in the entertainment industry. Because of Presley's immense contribution to rock 'n roll, examples of him performing can be considered of public interest. However, in comparison to a biographical film or play of Elvis Presley or a production tracing the role of Elvis Presley in the development of rock 'n roll, the information about Presley which THE BIG EL SHOW provides is of limited value.

This recognition that defendant's production has some value does not diminish our conclusion that the primary purpose of defendant's activity is to appropriate the commercial value of the likeness of Elvis Presley. * * *

In Zacchini v. Scripps-Howard Broadcasting Co., 433 U.S. 562 (1977) the Supreme Court addressed a situation which implicated both a performer's right of publicity and the First Amendment. The Court held that the First Amendment did not prevent a state from deciding that a television news show's unauthorized broadcast of a film showing plaintiff's "entire act," a fifteen second human cannonball performance, infringed plaintiff's right of publicity.

In reaching its conclusion, the Court, reasoned that "[t]he broadcast of [the] film of petitioner's entire act poses a substantial threat to the economic value of that performance," id. at 576; that

> the broadcast of petitioner's entire performance, unlike the unauthorized use of another's name for purposes of trade or the incidental use of a name or picture by the press, goes to the heart of petitioner's ability to earn a living as an entertainer. Thus, in this case, Ohio has recognized what may be the strongest case for a "right of publicity"—involving, not the appropriation of an entertainer's reputation to enhance the attractiveness of a commercial product, but the appropriation of the very activity by which the entertainer acquired his reputation in the first place.

Id. at 576; and that the "protection [of the right of publicity] provides an economic incentive for the performer to produce a performance of interest to the public." Id.

In the present case, although the defendant has not shown a film of an Elvis Presley performance, he has engaged in a similar form of behavior by presenting a live performance starring an imitator of Elvis Presley. To some degree, the defendant has appropriated the "very activity [live stage show] by which [Presley initially] acquired his reputation * * *" id. at 576, and from which the value in his name and likeness developed. The death of Presley diminishes the impact of certain of the court's reasons, especially the one providing for an economic incentive to produce future performances. However, through receiving royalties, the heirs of Presley are the beneficiaries of the "right of the individual to reap the reward of his endeavors." Id. at 573. Under the state's right of publicity, they are entitled to protect the commercial value of the name or likeness of Elvis Presley from activities such as defendant's which may diminish this value.

We thus find that the plaintiff has demonstrated a likelihood of success on the merits of its right of publicity claim with respect to the defendant's live stage production. In addition, we find this likelihood of success as to the defendant's unauthorized use of Elvis Presley's likeness on the cover or label of any records or on any pendants which are sold or distributed by the defendant.

* * *

NOTES

1. For an interesting discussion of the right of publicity see Carson v. Here's Johnny Portable Toilets, Inc., 698 F.2d 831 (6th Cir.1983) where the entertainer Johnny Carson objected to the use of his famous introduction "Here's Johnny" on portable toilets. Denying protection under a theory of trademark law because there was no likelihood of confusion, the court nonetheless provided protection under the publicity right. Rejecting the dissent's contention that the right of publicity only applied to name or likeness, the court held that "a celebrity's legal right of publicity is invaded whenever his identity is intentionally appropriated for commercial purposes." Does this give celebrities greater rights to their identification than trademark owners are accorded? If what is appropriated is not the actual name or likeness, shouldn't some likelihood of confusion be required?

2. Compare with *Carson*, Allen v. National Video, Inc., 610 F.Supp. 612 (S.D.N.Y.1985) in which Woody Allen seeks to enjoin the use of a "look-alike" actor in an advertisement for a national video rental chain. The advertisement portrayed the look-alike as a satisfied customer of the chain. The court first examined the right of publicity claim under New York law. The New York courts have held that any publicity claim must be made under the New York Civil Rights Law §§ 50–51 which prohibits the use of another's "name, portrait, or picture" for commercial purposes without consent. Stephano v. News Group Publications, Inc., 64 N.Y.2d 174, 485 N.Y.S.2d 220, 474 N.E.2d 580 (1984). In *Allen* the court, recognizing that the "look-alike" had the right to exploit his own likeness, denied Allen a summary judgment on the publicity claim because the defendant had not used Allen's picture. However, the court went on to grant summary judgment under § 43(a) of the Lanham Act after a detailed examination that resulted in a finding of likelihood of confusion as a matter of law.

In Pirone v. MacMillan, Inc., 894 F.2d 579 (2d Cir.1990) the daughters of Babe Ruth, who owned the registered mark "Babe Ruth," sued the defendant for trademark infringement for including three pictures of the famous baseball player in its baseball engagement calendar. The Second Circuit held that a trademark in the name did not cover all photos of Babe Ruth, the pictures were not used as a trademark by the defendant, and there could not possibly be a likelihood of confusion. In a jurisdiction that recognized the right of publicity, could Babe Ruth's daughters prevail?

3. The first amendment was asserted as justification for denying Cher relief against the unauthorized publication of an interview with her. Cher had given the interview to one magazine without securing contractual protection against use by others and ultimately the "Star" published part of the interview. The court held the first amendment protected reports, commentaries, and interviews with public figures from claims of violation of the right of publicity. Cher v. Forum Int'l Ltd., 692 F.2d 634 (9th Cir.1982).

4. There is an expanding literature on the right of publicity. See generally, Denicola, Institutional Publicity Rights: An Analysis of the Merchandising of Famous Trade Symbols, 62 N.C.L.Rev. 603 (1984), reprinted in 75 Trademark Rep. 41 (1985); Samuelson, Reviving *Zacchini:* Analyzing First Amendment Defenses in Right of Publicity and Copyright Cases, 57 Tulane L.Rev. 836 (1983).

Chapter V

COPYRIGHT

In many respects copyright is simple. An exclusive right to exploit belongs to the author of a work of authorship for a period of the life of the author plus 50 years. For most authors and their attorneys obtaining copyright protection will present few problems beyond the simple and routine submission of a registration form and copies of the work to the copyright office, steps no longer required but often prudent.

Copyright law is codified in Title 17, a relatively coherent and comprehensive statute passed in 1976. Predecessor statutes date back to the first Congress. The text of Title 17 should be the first (and last) stopping place for the puzzled student of copyright. This statute is cited here by section number alone. The United States Code section numbers are the same.

The present statute has a long legislative history. The first proposed revision bill was H.R. 11947 of the 88th Cong., introduced July 20, 1964. Public Law 94–553 was signed by the President on October 19, 1976. The intervening 12 years generated a voluminous legislative record. The most authoritative document is House Report 94–1476 on S. 22, of September 3, 1976. That was the report of the Committee on the Judiciary to the House. The bill moved from the Committee to the House, conference and Presidential signature with only a few minor changes. This report is cited in these materials as House Report 94–1476. The legislative history is collected in A. Latman & J. Lightstone (eds.), The Kamenstein Legislative History Project: A Compendium and Analytic Index of Materials Leading to the Copyright Act of 1976 (Fred Rothman, 1981). The statute and its relationship to this extended legislative history is essayed in Jessica Litman, Copyright, Compromise, and Legislative History, 72 Cornell Law Rev. 857 (1987), and Jessica Litman, Copyright Legislation and Technological Change, 68 Oregon Law Review 275 (1989). As Litman documents, an unusual aspect of the legislative process was the openness with which the private interests of those groups involved in the lobbying process were addressed and compromised.

Copyright is a system of protection for the intellectual arts. The title to the first copyright statute, enacted in 1790, read:

"AN ACT for the encouragement of learning, by securing the copies of maps, charts, and books, to the authors and proprietors of such copies, during the times therein mentioned." 1 Stat. 124.

The protection of this statute did not extend to other artistic works such as painting, sculpture and drama.

The coverage of the copyright statute has steadily expanded, largely in response to new technologies of reproduction and communication, until it now reaches works with no similarity to books.

The expansion of statutory copyright has occurred largely through a process of statutory revision. In 1802 the statute was extended to those "who shall invent and design, engrave, etch or work * * * any historical or other print or prints." 2 Stat. 171. In 1831 the statute was extended to musical compositions and cuts. 4 Stat. 436. In 1856 the owner of the copyright in a printed drama was given the exclusive right of public performance. 11 Stat. 138. In 1865 photographs and negatives were added to the list of copyrightable works. 13 Stat. 540. In 1870 paintings, drawings, chromos, statuettes, statuary and models or designs intended as works of fine art were added to the enumerated list. 16 Stat. 212. In 1874 protection of engravings, cuts and prints was limited to "pictorial illustrations or works connected with the fine arts." 18 Stat. 79. In 1909 the owner of the copyright in sheet music was given the exclusive right to make mechanical reproductions of the music subject to a complex compulsory licensing provision, 35 Stat. 1075, compilations (previously thought to have been included as books) were explicitly mentioned, 35 Stat. 1077, and lectures, sermons and addresses prepared for oral delivery were added. 35 Stat. 1076. In 1912, motion pictures, previously thought to have been included within the category of photographs, were added. 37 Stat. 488. See generally "The Meaning of 'Writings' in the Copyright Clause of the Constitution," Copyright Office Study No. 3 (1956).

The 1976 revision again expanded the scope of copyrightable subject matter. The scope of the kinds of works protected was expanded from an enumerated list to a general principle expressed in § 102: "Copyright protection subsists * * * in original works of authorship fixed in any tangible medium of expression, now known or later developed, from which they can be perceived, reproduced, or otherwise communicated, either directly or with the aid of a machine or device."

A major expansion of copyright protection since the 1976 revision act has been in the area of computer programs or "software." Public Law 96–517, erroneously titled: "To amend the patent and trademark laws," amended 17 U.S.C.A. § 117, which had previously limited rights "with respect to the use of the work in conjunction with automatic systems capable of storing, processing, retrieving, or transferring information" to those rights in existence prior to the passage of the 1976 revision bill. Under the prior law, use of a work which did not involve making a tangible copy in a standard language and did not involve a performance did not infringe, which meant that as a practical matter there was no protection for software. The new § 117 changed all of that, and computer programs are now one of the most active areas of copyright litigation.

In 1990, copyright protection was extended to architectural works in the Architectural Works Copyright Protection Act.

NOTES

1. For an introductory guide see Arthur R. Miller and Michael H. Davis, Intellectual Property: Patents, Trademarks, and Copyright in a Nutshell (St. Paul: West Pub. Co., 2d. ed. 1990). Melville B. Nimmer, Nimmer on Copyright: A Treatise on the Law of Literature, Musical and Artistic Property, and the Protection of Ideas (New York: Matthew Bender, 1978) and Paul Goldstein, Copyright: Principles, Law and Practice (Boston: Little, Brown and Co., 1989) are the leading treatises.

Prior to the introduction of the revision bill, the Copyright Office commissioned a series of preparatory studies. They contain a wealth of information on American and foreign copyright law and are conveniently available in Copyright Society of the U.S.A., Studies on Copyright (Arthur Fisher Memorial Edition, 2 vols. 1963).

The economics of copyright protection is discussed in Arnold Plant, The Economic Aspects of Copyright in Books, 1 Economics 167 (new series 1934), reprinted in Arnold Plant, Selected Economic Essays and Addresses (1974); Hurt & Schuchman, The Economic Rationale of Copyright, 56 Am.Econ.Rev. 421 (1966); Stephen Breyer, The Uneasy Case for Copyright: A Study of Copyright in Books, Photocopies, and Computer Programs, 84 Harv.L.Rev. 281 (1970); Tyerman, The Economic Rationale for Copyright Protection for Published Books: A Reply to Professor Breyer, 18 U.C.L.A. Law Rev. 1100 (1971); Novos & Waldman, The Effects of Increased Copyright Protection: An Analytic Approach, 92 J.P.E. 236 (1984); William R. Johnson, The Economics of Copying, 93 J.P.E. 158 (1985); and William Landes & Richard Posner, An Economic Analysis of Copyright Law, 18 J. of Legal Stud. 325 (1989).

Rochelle Cooper Dreyfuss, The Creative Employee and the Copyright Act of 1976, 54 Univ. of Chicago Law Rev. 590 (1987), offers an "author-based" view of the purposes of copyright protection.

AN OVERVIEW OF THE STATUTE

The following discussion will be more helpful if you refer to the sections of the statute as you read it.

The statute begins with a comprehensive set of definitions in § 101 which apply throughout the statute. These definitions are often critical to a correct reading of the statute, and analysis of any section should always be undertaken with an eye to the question of whether it contains terms defined in § 101.

The statute has eight titles. The first, "Subject matter and Scope of Copyright" defines what works are, and what works are not, copyrightable and sets out the scope of the rights conferred by copyright. The key sections are 102, which sets out the general subject matter of copyright, and 106, which sets out the scope of the exclusive rights conferred upon the owner of works that are copyrighted. Section 106A, added by the Visual Artists Rights Act of 1990, confers rights of attribution and integrity on authors of works of visual art [a defined term]. Sections 103 to 105 are but amplifying footnotes to 102, and sections 107 through 120 (although very complex) are amplifying footnotes to 106. For the moment skip these sections, except for a brief glance at 107, which sets out the concept of "fair use," an important limit on the scope of copyright and a concept to which we devote considerable attention.

Chapter 2, "Copyright Ownership and Transfer," deals with the question of who initially owns the copyright in a work, establishes the way in which the right can be transferred, and sets up a recording system for transfers of the right.

Chapter 3, is incompletely entitled: "Duration of Copyright" because it also contains the important section 301 (which has already been addressed in this book, supra pp. 468–473 dealing with the effect of the statute upon equivalent state law rights).   The rest of the Chapter provides, in brief, that the term of a copyright is the life of the author plus fifty years, or in the case of a work made for hire [defined term], that the term of the copyright is 75 years (the employer that hires the employee who creates a work made for hire will usually be an institution, which cannot die).   Seventy-five years was thought to be roughly equivalent, on average, to the remaining life expectancy of an author plus fifty years.   (Should an old author set up a corporation and write for it in order to get the 75 year term?).

Chapter 4, "Copyright Notice, Deposit and Registration," deals with notice, registration and deposit.   Prior to the U.S. adherence to the Berne Convention in 1989 (of which more shortly), these steps were required in order to obtain full copyright protection.   Berne does not permit formalities as a condition of protection, so these steps are no longer mandatory.   However, the statute confers enforcement advantages upon those who do comply with them, so copyright claimants will continue to follow these procedural steps.

The notice has three elements.   The symbol "©", or the word "Copyright" or the abbreviation "Copr."; the year of first publication [defined term] of the work; and the name of the owner of the copyright. The notice is to be affixed to the copies in such manner and location "as to give reasonable notice of the claim of copyright."   § 401(c).

Deposit and registration are other formalities.   They are not necessary for protection, but registration for works originating in the United States is necessary in order to be able to bring a lawsuit enforcing copyright (§ 411) and deposit of works published in the United States must be made upon demand of the Registrar of Copyrights (§ 407(d)). (The deposit requirement has been an important source of the collection of the Library of Congress, but the Registrar does not exactly care to be inundated by every trivial item for which copyright is claimed, and the Registrar has power to exempt classes of works from deposit.)   Registration and deposit creates a record of the origin and content of the work for which copyright is claimed and can simplify factual issues in subsequent infringement litigation.

A copyright owner may register his work at any time under § 408. Registration requires deposit (unless the work is exempt), payment of a fee, and submission of an application for copyright registration (§ 409).

Chapter 5 sets out the remedies for infringement of copyright. They are unusually sweeping. In addition to recovery of damages and lost profits (§ 504) and injunctions (§ 502), they include special statutory damages (§ 504(c)), impoundment and destruction of infringing works and the means for making further infringements (§ 503), and the award of costs and attorney's fees (§ 505). In addition, infringement "willfully and for purposes of commercial advantage or private financial gain" is a crime (§ 506). (The penalties are set forth in 18 U.S.C. § 2319: one year and $25,000 for small scale infringement, five years and $250,000 for large scale infringement.)

Chapter 6, § 601, (now expired) relates to a requirement of U.S. manufacture of certain copyrighted works, a protectionist provision dating from the nineteenth century designed to protect the U.S. printing industry. Sec. 602 makes importation into the United States of a copy (defined term) or phonorecord (defined term) of a copyrighted work an infringement, and § 603 gives the Post Office and the Customs Service authority to enforce this provision.

Chapter 7 establishes the Copyright Office within the Library of Congress, to be headed by the Registrar of Copyrights, and contains provisions relating to the operation of the office.

Chapter 8 establishes the Copyright Royalty Tribunal to administer provisions of the act relating to compulsory licenses.

NOTES

1. In Ladd v. Law & Technology Press, 762 F.2d 809 (9th Cir.1985), the publisher of a specialized newsletter called "The Scott Report" (probably sold to subscribers at a high price) refused to comply with the Registrar's notice demanding deposit. The Ninth Circuit rejected the publisher's argument that the deposit requirement is an unconstitutional taking of property without compensation.

2. The items exempted by the Registrar (where are we going to put all of these things?) are set out in 37 C.F.R. § 202.19(c). They include: architectural or engineering blueprints; mechanical drawings; anatomical models; greeting cards; picture postcards; stationery; lectures; sermons; speeches and addresses when published individually; literary dramatic and musical works published only as embodied in phonorecords (the record must be deposited); computer programs and automated data bases, published only in the form of machine readable copies such as magnetic tape or disks or punched cards; three-dimensional sculptural works and works published only on jewelry, dolls, toys, games, plaques, floor coverings, wallpaper, and textile or other fabrics; prints labels and advertising; and tests and answers to tests.

BERNE CONVENTION ADHERENCE

On March 1, 1989, the United States joined the Berne Convention for the Protection of Literary and Artistic Works. Thus ended more than a century of American isolation from the mainstream of world copyright law. The changes in American law made in order to conform to the requirements of the Berne Convention were made by the Berne

Convention Implementation Act of 1988, Public Law 100–568, Oct. 31, 1988.

In the nineteenth century, Europe was the center of the literary world and the authors of Great Britain the most important writers in the English language. The United States was a net importer of copyrighted works.

The United States declined to join the Berne Convention in 1886. Instead, the United States developed its own system of international copyright relationships beginning with the Chace Act of 1891, which provided that we would extend protection to foreign authors under our law when the foreign author's country did the same for our authors. But even this avenue of protection was limited by the requirement that the copies required to be deposited had to be actually printed in the United States. This latter provision evolved into the so-called manufacturing clause which survives in § 601 of the present act but which has expired as of July 1, 1986. Apparently some portions of the printing industry whose business was based upon the printing of pirated foreign works feared that they would lose this business if the authors obtained copyright protection and sold in the United States works printed abroad. The manufacturing clause itself became a further obstacle to U.S. adherence to Berne. The manufacturing clause was subsequently extended to provide that all works distributed in or imported into the United States and protected by U.S. copyright had to be printed in the United States.

In the Twentieth Century the conditions that had made the case for adherence to Berne seem less than compelling to the United States changed. The United States itself became a major exporter of copyrighted works, with an interest in assuring protection for U.S. authors abroad. In the American period of hegemony after World War II, the United States took the lead in the formulation and widespread adoption of the Universal Copyright Convention [hereafter the "UCC"], based upon a system of national treatment of the nationals of all signatories—i.e., the author of any member country is entitled to the same treatment as a national of any member country gets in that country. Although this was also a basic principle of Berne, Berne went further in guaranteeing some minimum level of substantive protection free of any formalities. The UCC itself accepted the continuing preeminence of Berne by providing that where any two countries were signatories of both Berne and the UCC, the more demanding provisions of Berne should control. This meant that in reality the UCC was little more than a uniform system of bilateral relationships between the United States and the other countries of the world.

The UCC did, however, eliminate the operation of the manufacturing clause as applied to works of the authors of member countries. This meant that the only important, continuing function of the manufacturing clause was to prevent publishers of the works of American authors from making use of lower cost foreign printers. The American printing industry continued to fight for this protection.

Strong voices had advocated U.S. adherence to Berne from the beginning, and repeated efforts were made to move the U.S. in that direction. It had become clear by the 1970's that the U.S. incentives to join Berne were growing. The export of U.S. origin copyrighted works was becoming ever more important and the problem of foreign piracy was increasing. Berne and its affiliated organizations were the center of international copyright policy formulation and advancement. And it was difficult for the U.S. to deplore nonprotectionist policies of the underdeveloped countries who saw advantages to themselves in weak copyright protection (just as the U.S. had seen for itself in the nineteenth century) when the U.S. itself declined to join the dominant system of world copyright protection.

The first decisive move toward U.S. adherence to Berne came in the 1976 Copyright Revision Act. The act committed American copyright law to the concept of a broad scope of protected subject matter (§ 102), adopted the Berne Convention term of life plus 50 years, and placed an expiration date in the manufacturing clause. And for the first time the idea that an absence of notice upon publication would not destroy the underlying copyright was introduced.

After one more extension of the manufacturing clause at the behest of the printing industry and over the veto of President Reagan, the clause expired on July 1, 1986. The way was then open for U.S. adherence to Berne by eliminating mandatory formalities, and this the Berne Implementation Act accomplished.

Works published after the effective date of the act do not have to carry copyright notice in order to be protected. Works whose country of origin is not the United States do not have to be registered prior to suing for infringement. However, there are significant advantages to taking both steps, and it is expected that persons claiming copyright in the United States will continue to take these steps.

The elimination of the formality rule applies only to works published after the date of the act. Presumably most works published in the United States before the act were published with notice. However, some works were probably published abroad without notice (in conformity with Berne procedures) and those works will not regain any protection in the United States. To emphasize this point, § 12 of the implementation act provides that "Title 17, United States Code, as amended by this Act [the implementation act], does not provide copyright protection for any work that is in the public domain in the United States."

NOTES

1. *Moral Rights.* Article 6 *bis* of the Berne Convention requires that member states recognize, independently of the author's economic rights, that "the author shall have the right to claim authorship of the work and object to

any distortion, mutilation or other modification of, or other derogatory action in relation to, the said work, which would be prejudicial to his honor or reputation." This concept of "moral rights" has been generally unknown in U.S. copyright law, but is well developed in some other member states, particularly France. A major issue in U.S. adherence to Berne was whether U.S. copyright law would be amended to protect these hitherto unknown non-economic rights.

The solution of the implementation act was to take the position that existing U.S. law does protect moral rights, not under the copyright statute, but under common law principles of unfair competition. This topic is addressed further *infra* page 784.

2. *Self-executing.* There was concern that U.S. adherence to Berne would affect U.S. law in unforeseen ways because litigants would argue to the courts that U.S. law had adopted certain rules or principles in conformity with Berne simply by ratifying the treaty. The implementation act goes to great lengths to insist that this does not happen, that the treaty is not (in the parlance of treaty law) "self-executing," and that the only changes in U.S. law occur as the result of the implementation act itself. Section 3 makes this point:

"The provisions of the Berne Convention—

(1) shall be given effect under title 17, as amended by the Act, and any other relevant provision of federal or state law, including the common law; and

(2) shall not be enforceable in any action brought pursuant to the provisions of the Berne Convention itself.

(b) Certain Rights Not Affected.—The provisions of the Berne Convention, the adherence of the United States thereto, and satisfaction of United States obligations thereunder, do not expand or reduce any right of an author of a work, whether claimed under Federal, State, or the common law—

(1) to claim authorship of the work; or

(2) to object to any distortion, mutilation, or other modification of, or other derogatory action in relation to, the work, that would prejudice the author's honor or reputation."

The act also amended Title 17 to make the same point in § 104(c), and again in § 301(e).

3. The United States in 1990, itself, adopted a limited type of moral right for visual works in § 106A. See p. 776 *infra*.

A. COPYRIGHTABLE SUBJECT MATTER

---

(1) THE NATURE OF THE MATERIAL

Section 102 defines copyrightable subject matter. The first sentence, which contains no defined terms, sets out what appears to be a general principle of coverage. The second sentence offers eight categories of copyrightable works. Three are undefined: "musical works," "dramatic works," and "pantomimes and choreographic works." The other five are defined and it is important to consult the definitions.

The natural construction is that the list of eight merely illustrates by specific example the range of works included in the first sentence, a construction confirmed by House Report 94–1476 at 53.

Subsection (b) of 102 is stated in the form of a qualification of 102(a), but note that the things excluded from copyright by (b) are not explicitly included by (a). The House Report says of this section: "[It] * * * in no way enlarges or contracts the scope of copyright protection under the present law. Its purpose is to restate in the context of the new single Federal system of copyright, that the basic dichotomy between expression and idea remains unchanged." Id. at 57.

BAKER v. SELDEN
Supreme Court of the United States, 1879.
101 U.S. (11 Otto) 99, 25 L.Ed. 841.

MR. JUSTICE BRADLEY delivered the opinion of the court.

Charles Selden, the testator of the complainant in this case, in the year 1859 took the requisite steps for obtaining the copyright of a book, entitled "Selden's Condensed Ledger, or Bookkeeping Simplified," the object of which was to exhibit and explain a peculiar system of bookkeeping. In 1860 and 1861, he took the copyright of several other books, containing additions to and improvements upon the said system. The bill of complaint was filed against the defendant, Baker, for an alleged infringement of these copyrights.

* * *

The book or series of books of which the complainant claims the copyright consists of an introductory essay explaining the system of bookkeeping referred to, to which are annexed certain forms or blanks, consisting of ruled lines, and headings, illustrating the system and showing how it is to be used and carried out in practice. This system effects the same results as bookkeeping by double entry; but, by a peculiar arrangement of columns and headings, presents the entire operation, of a day, a week, or a month, on a single page, or on two pages facing each other, in an account book. The defendant uses a similar plan so far as results are concerned; but makes a different arrangement of the columns, and uses different headings. If the complainant's testator had the exclusive right to the use of the system explained in his book it would be difficult to contend that the defendant does not infringe it, notwithstanding the difference in his form of arrangement; but if it be assumed that the system is open to public use, it seems to be equally difficult to contend that the books made and sold by the defendant are a violation of the copyright of the complainant's book considered merely as a book explanatory of the system. Where the truths of a science or the methods of an art are the common property of the whole world, any author has the right to express the one, or explain and use the other, in his own way. As an author, Selden explained the system in a particular way. It may be conceded that Baker makes and uses account books arranged on substantially the same system; but the proof fails to show that he has violated the copyright of Selden's book, regarding the latter merely as an explanatory work; or that he has infringed Selden's right in any way, unless the latter became entitled to an exclusive right in the system.

The evidence of the complainant is principally directed to the object of showing that Baker uses the same system as that which is explained and illustrated in Selden's books. It becomes important, therefore, to determine whether, in obtaining the copyright of his books, he secured the exclusive right to the use of the system or method of bookkeeping which the said books are intended to illustrate and explain. It is contended that he has secured such exclusive right, because no one can use the system without using substantially the same ruled lines and headings which he has appended to his books in illustration of it. * * *

It cannot be pretended, and indeed it is not seriously urged, that the ruled lines of the complainant's account book can be claimed under any special class of objects, other than books, named in the law of copyright existing in 1859. The law then in force was that of 1831, and specified only books, maps, charts, musical compositions, prints, and engravings. An account book, consisting of ruled lines and blank columns, cannot be called by any of these names unless by that of a book.

There is no doubt that a work on the subject of bookkeeping, though only explanatory of well-known systems, may be the subject of a copyright; but, then, it is claimed only as a book. Such a book may be explanatory either of old systems, or of an entirely new system; and, considered as a book, as the work of an author, conveying information on the subject of bookkeeping, and containing detailed explanations of the art, it may be a very valuable acquisition to the practical knowledge of the community. But there is a clear distinction between the book, as such, and the art which it is intended to illustrate. * * * The same distinction may be predicted of every other art as well as that of bookkeeping. A treatise on the composition and use of medicines, be they old or new; on the construction and use of ploughs, or watches, or churns; or on the mixture and application of colors for painting or dyeing; or on the mode of drawing lines to produce the effect of perspective,—would be the subject of copyright; but no one would contend that the copyright of the treatise would give the exclusive right to the art or manufacture described therein. * * * To give to the author of the book an exclusive property in the art described therein, when no examination of its novelty has ever been officially made, would be a surprise and a fraud upon the public. That is the province of letters-patent, not of copyright. The claim to an invention or discovery of an art or manufacture must be subjected to the examination of the Patent Office before an exclusive right therein can be obtained; and it can only be secured by a patent from the government.

The difference between the two things, letters-patent and copyright, may be illustrated by reference to the subject just enumerated. Take the case of medicines. Certain mixtures are found to be of great value in the healing art. If the discoverer writes and publishes a book on the subject (as regular physicians generally do), he gains no exclusive right to the manufacture and sale of the medicine; he gives that to the public. If he desires to acquire such exclusive right he must obtain a patent for the mixture as a new art, manufacture, or composition of matter. * * *

Of course, these observations are not intended to apply to ornamental designs, or pictorial illustrations addressed to the taste. Of these it may be said, that their form is their essence, and their object, the production of pleasure in their contemplation. This is their final end. They are as much the product of genius and the result of composition, as are the lines of the poet or the historian's periods. * * *

Recurring to the case before us, we observe that Charles Selden, by his books, explained and described a peculiar system of bookkeeping, and illustrated his method by means of ruled lines and blank columns, with proper headings on a page, or on successive pages. Now, whilst no one has a right to print or publish his book, or any material part thereof, as a book intended to convey instruction in the art, any person may practice and use the art itself which he has described and illustrated therein. The use of the art is a totally different thing from a publication of the book explaining it. The copyright of a book on bookkeeping cannot secure the exclusive right to make, sell, and use account books prepared upon the plan set forth in such book. Whether the art might or might not have been patented, is a question which is not before us. It was not patented, and is open and free to the use of the public. And, of course, in using the art, the ruled lines and headings of accounts must necessarily be used as incident to it.

The plausibility of the claim put forward by the complainant in this case arises from a confusion of ideas produced by the peculiar nature of the art described in the books which have been made the subject of copyright. In describing the art, the illustrations and diagrams employed happen to correspond more closely than usual with the actual work performed by the operator who uses the art. Those illustrations and diagrams consist of ruled lines and headings of accounts; and it is similar ruled lines and headings of accounts which, in the application of the art, the bookkeeper makes with his pen, or the stationer with his press; whilst in most other cases the diagrams and illustrations can only be represented in concrete forms of wood, metal, stone, or some other physical embodiment. But the principle is the same in all. The description of the art in a book, though entitled to the benefit of copyright, lays no foundation for an exclusive claim to the art itself. The object of the one is explanation; the object of the other is use. The former may be secured by copyright. The latter can only be secured, if it can be secured at all, by letters-patent.

* * *

The conclusion to which we have come is, that blank account books are not the subject of copyright; and that the mere copyright of Selden's book did not confer upon him the exclusive right to make and use account books, ruled and arranged as designated by him and described and illustrated in said book.

The decree of the Circuit Court must be reversed, and the cause remanded with instructions to dismiss the complainant's bill; and it is

So ordered.

MORRISSEY v. PROCTOR & GAMBLE CO.
United States Court of Appeals, First Circuit, 1967.
379 F.2d 675.

ALDRICH, CHIEF JUDGE. This is an appeal from a summary judgment for the defendant. The plaintiff, Morrissey, is the copyright owner of a set of rules for a sales promotional contest of the "sweepstakes" type involving the social security numbers of the participants. Plaintiff alleges that the defendant, Proctor & Gamble Company, infringed, by copying, almost precisely, Rule 1. In its motion for summary judgment, based upon affidavits and depositions, defendant denies that plaintiff's Rule 1 is copyrightable material, and denies access. The district court held for the defendant on both grounds.

Taking the second ground first, the defendant offered affidavits or depositions of all of its allegedly pertinent employees, all of whom denied having seen plaintiff's rules. Although the plaintiff, by deposition, flatly testified that prior to the time the defendant conducted its contest he had mailed to the defendant his copyrighted rules with an offer to sell, the court ruled that the defendant had "proved" nonaccess, and stated that it was "satisfied that no material issue as to access * * * lurks * * * [in the record.]"

[The court held that in view of the "presumption arising from mailing" the facts were insufficiently clear to support summary judgment on the issue of access, relying on cases such as Arnstein v. Porter, 154 F.2d 464 (2d Cir.1946). In a footnote, the court observed that "the [district] court did not discuss, nor need we, the additional fact that the almost exact following of plaintiff's wording and format in an area in which there is at least some room for maneuverability, might be found of itself to contradict defendant's denial of access."]

The second aspect of the case raises a more difficult question. Before discussing it we recite plaintiff's Rule 1, and defendant's Rule 1, the italicizing in the latter being ours to note the defendant's variations or changes.

"1. Entrants should print name, address and social security number on a boxtop, or a plain paper. Entries must be accompanied by * * * boxtop or by plain paper on which the name * * * is copied from any source. Official rules are explained on * * * packages or leaflets obtained from dealer. If you do not have a social security number you may use the name and number of any member of your immediate family living with you. Only the person named on the entry will be deemed an entrant and may qualify for prize.

"Use the correct social security number belonging to the person named on entry * * * wrong number will be disqualified."

(Plaintiff's Rule)

"1. Entrants should print name, address and Social Security number on a Tide boxtop, or on [a] plain paper. Entries must be accompanied by Tide boxtop (*any size*) or by plain paper on which the name 'Tide' is copied from any source. Official rules are *available* on Tide Sweepstakes packages, or *on* leaflets *at* Tide dealers, or *you can send a stamped, self-addressed, envelope* to: Tide 'Shopping Fling' Sweepstakes, P.O. Box 4459, Chicago 77, Illinois.

"If you do not have a Social Security number, you may use the name and number of any member of your immediate family living with you. Only the person named on the entry will be deemed an entrant and may qualify for a prize.

"Use the correct Social Security number, belonging to the person named on *the* entry—wrong numbers will be disqualified."

(Defendant's Rule)

The district court, following an earlier decision, Gaye v. Gillis, D.Mass., 1958, 167 F.Supp. 416, took the position that since the substance of the contest was not copyrightable, which is unquestionably correct, Baker v. Selden, 1879, 101 U.S. 99; Affiliated Enterprises v. Gruber, 1 Cir., 1936, 86 F.2d 958; Chamberlin v. Uris Sales Corp., 2 Cir., 1945, 150 F.2d 512, and the substance was relatively simple, it must follow that plaintiff's rule sprung directly from the substance and "contains no original creative authorship." 262 F.Supp. at 738. This does not follow. Copyright attaches to form of expression, and defendant's own proof, introduced to deluge the court on the issue of access, itself established that there was more than one way of expressing even this simple substance. Nor, in view of the almost precise similarity of the two rules, could defendant successfully invoke the principle of a stringent standard for showing infringement which some courts apply when the subject matter involved admits of little variation in form of expression. E.g., Dorsey v. Old Surety Life Ins. Co., 10 Cir., 1938, 98 F.2d 872, 874 ("a showing of appropriation in the exact form or substantially so."); Continental Casualty Co. v. Beardsley, 2 Cir., 1958, 253 F.2d 702, 705, cert. denied 358 U.S. 816, ("a stiff standard for proof of infringement.")

Nonetheless, we must hold for the defendant. When the uncopyrightable subject matter is very narrow, so that "the topic necessarily requires," Sampson & Murdock Co. v. Seaver-Radford Co., 1 Cir.,

1905, 140 F. 539, 541; cf. Kaplan, An Unhurried View of Copyright, 64–65 (1967), if not only one form of expression, at best only a limited number, to permit copyrighting would mean that a party or parties, by copyrighting a mere handful of forms, could exhaust all possibilities of future use of the substance. In such circumstances it does not seem accurate to say that any particular form of expression comes from the subject matter. However, it is necessary to say that the subject matter would be appropriated by permitting the copyrighting of its expression. We cannot recognize copyright as a game of chess in which the public can be checkmated. Cf. Baker v. Selden, supra.

Upon examination the matters embraced in Rule 1 are so straightforward and simple that we find this limiting principle to be applicable. Furthermore, its operation need not await an attempt to copyright all possible forms. It cannot be only the last form of expression which is to be condemned, as completing defendant's exclusion from the substance. Rather, in these circumstances, we hold that copyright does not extend to the subject matter at all, and plaintiff cannot complain even if his particular expression was deliberately adopted.

Affirmed.

NOTES

1. In Consumers Union v. Hobart Mfg. Co., 189 F.Supp. 275 (S.D.N.Y. 1960), followed on summary judgment, 199 F.Supp. 860 (S.D.N.Y.1961), Consumers Union was denied a preliminary injunction against use by defendant of quotations from Consumers Reports in its sales literature directed to its distributors. The literature was designed to answer criticisms and emphasize favorable comments about defendant's KitchenAid dishwashers made in Consumers Reports. "In no instance did material which was copied into the [sales] Bulletin have any original literary form which would entitle it to copyright protection. Each item was a bald statement of fact which could hardly have been stated in any different fashion." 189 F.Supp. at 278. Plaintiff argued that it was injured because the use of its findings by manufacturers for sales purposes destroys the confidence of its subscribers in its integrity.

2. Can legal documents be copyrighted? Suppose you had worked long and hard to create a particularly clever and useful contract, bylaws or other document which might have multiple uses? Can you copyright it and then earn royalty income whenever other lawyers want to use part or all of your document? Continental Casualty Co. v. Beardsley, 253 F.2d 702 (2d Cir.1958) held a copyright in a plan for a blanket bond to cover replacement of lost securities valid but not infringed. Merritt Forbes & Co. v. Newman Investment Securities, Inc., 604 F.Supp. 943 (S.D.N.Y.1985), was an action for copyright infringement and trademark infringement for the documents implementing the "TENDER OPTION PROGRAM ™ ". The program was an offering of municipal bonds in which the seller gave the buyer the option to tender the bonds back to the seller prior to maturity. The presence of such an option would provide the buyer some protection against interest rate fluctuations. Although the concept of a repurchase option was not new, the plaintiffs claimed that the offering had a combination of unique features. Defendant's motion for summary judgment on the ground of lack of copyrightable subject matter was denied.

3. The effort to obtain protection for written systems and forms under the patent law, suggested in Baker v. Selden, has generally been unavailing due to a failure to satisfy the requirements of the patent statute. An exceptional case is Cincinnati Traction Co. v. Pope, 210 Fed. 443 (6th Cir.1913), which upheld a patent on a particular type of transfer ticket. The form of the ticket made it possible to distinguish between transfers issued in the morning from those issued in the afternoon. This was done by means of a detachable coupon. When the coupon was detached, the hour indicated on the ticket was an A.M. hour. The court said:

> "[W]hile the case is perhaps near the border line, we think the device should be classed as an article to be used in a method of doing business and thus a 'manufacture' within the statute * * *. The device of the patent clearly involves structure. The claims themselves are * * * limited to such structure." 210 Fed. at 446.

In Berardini v. Tocci, 190 Fed. 329 (S.D.N.Y.1911), the court held invalid a patent on a code system for transmitting instructions for disbursements of sums of money by cable without fear of mistakes arising out of errors in transmission. The court distinguished cases like *Cincinnati Traction Co.* on the ground that the patent was on the physical structure of the paper and the writing while the patent involved in *Beradini* was for a "system of devising code messages." The patent, said the court, "is for an art only in the sense that one speaks of the art of painting, or the art of curving the thrown baseball. Such arts, however ingenious, difficult, or amusing, are not patentable within any statute of the United States."

In Wier v. Coe, 33 F.Supp. 142 (D.D.C.1940), the court affirmed a patent office denial of an application for a patent on an improved system of musical notation. In the course of its opinion, the court said: "the claimed series of musically staffed sheets are merely printed matter for conveying intelligence. They do not involve physical structure and are not subject matter which may be protected under the patent laws." 83 F.Supp. at 143.

The Supreme Court has held that many computer programs are unpatentable. See infra pp. 823–825, 832–840.

4. The distinction between a copy and a use lies at the heart of *Baker*. The distinction is more difficult to apply where the right of performance, as opposed to the right to copy is involved. If a dramatist obtains a copyright on a script which includes detailed instructions for the scenery to be used in the play, can he prevent another from incorporating scenery constructed in accordance with the directions in a different play? Consider the case of Daly v. Palmer, 6 F.Cas. 1132 (No. 3,552) (S.D.N.Y.1868). Plaintiff's play had achieved great success, largely because of a "railroad scene" in which "one of the characters is represented as secured by another, and laid helpless upon the rails of a railroad track, in such manner, and with the presumed intent, that the railroad train, momentarily expected, shall run him down and kill him, and, just at the moment when such a fate seems inevitable, another of the characters contrives to reach the intended victim, and to drag him from the track as the train rushes in and passes over the spot." Defendant used a similar scene in his play, otherwise dissimilar. The court found infringement. Would this infringe the new right of display? § 106(5).

APPLE COMPUTER, INC. v. FORMULA INTERNATIONAL INC.

United States Court of Appeals, Ninth Circuit, 1984.
725 F.2d 521.

FERGUSON, CIRCUIT JUDGE.

Formula International, Inc. (Formula) appeals from the district court's grant of a preliminary injunction in favor of the plaintiff, Apple Computer, Inc. (Apple). The injunction prohibits Formula from copying computer programs having copyrights registered to Apple, from importing, selling, distributing, or advertising those copies.

* * * Because we find that the district court did not abuse its discretion or rely on erroneous legal premises in issuing the injunction, we affirm.

FACTS

Formula is a wholesaler and retailer of electronic parts and electronic kits. In May 1982, Formula entered the computer market, selling a computer kit under the trademark "Pineapple." The computer was designed to be compatible with application software written for the home computer manufactured by Apple, the Apple II. Included within Formula's computer kit were two computer programs embodied in semiconductor devices called ROM's (Read Only Memory). Formula concedes for purposes of appeal that the two programs are substantially similar to two programs for which Apple has registered copyrights. Apple also introduced evidence to show that Formula had sold copies of three other programs for which Apple holds the copyright. These three programs are not sold as part of a computer by either Apple or Formula, but are distributed separately.

The computer programs involved in this lawsuit are operating systems programs, that is, programs that are designed to manage the computer system. For example, one program translates instructions written in a higher-level language that is more understandable to the computer user into a lower-level object code that the computer understands. As such, the programs are distinguishable from application programs, which are programs that directly interact with the computer user.

Apple brought suit against Formula claiming copyright, trademark, and patent infringement, as well as unfair competition. Formula counterclaimed for antitrust violations and unfair competition and sought declaratory relief as to the validity of certain patents and copyrights. After a brief period of discovery, Apple moved for a preliminary injunction based on its copyright and trademark infringement claims, and on its unfair competition claims. The district court granted the motion on April 12, 1983, and the district court's opinion is reported at 562 F.Supp. 775 (C.D.Cal.1983).

Standard of Review:

To obtain a preliminary injunction, a party must show either (1) a likelihood of success on the merits and the possibility of irreparable injury, or (2) the existence of serious questions going to the merits and the balance of hardships tipping in its favor. * * * The district court held that Apple had shown a likelihood of success on the merits of its copyright and trademark infringement claims and significant irreparable harm. 562 F.Supp. at 783, 785. Our review of the district court at this stage of the proceeding is very limited. * * * The district court's grant of the preliminary injunction must be affirmed unless the court abused its discretion or based its decision on an erroneous legal standard or on clearly erroneous findings of fact.

* * *

A. *Likelihood of success on the merits*

On the basis of the evidence before the district court, we cannot conclude that the court erred in finding that Apple had demonstrated a likelihood of success on the merits of its copyright infringement claim. Under the Copyright Act, Apple's certificates of copyright registration constitute *prima facie* evidence of the validity of Apple's copyrights, 17 U.S.C. § 410(c), and Formula has the burden of overcoming the presumption of validity. Williams Electronics, Inc. v. Artic International, Inc., 685 F.2d 870, 873 (3d Cir.1982).

Formula asserts that the district court erred in granting the preliminary injunction by relying on the legal premise that the Copyright Act, 17 U.S.C. § 101 et seq., extends protection to all computer programs regardless of the function which those programs perform. Formula contends that the computer programs involved in this lawsuit, because they control the internal operation of the computer, are only "ideas" or "processes," and therefore, unlike application programs, they are not protected by copyright. See 17 U.S.C. § 102(b) ("In no case does copyright protection for an original work of authorship extend to any *idea, procedure, process, system, method of operation,* concept, principle or discovery, regardless of the form in which it is described, explained, illustrated, or embodied in such work.") (emphasis added). Formula also points to the idea/expression dichotomy recognized in case law, see, e.g., Baker v. Selden, 101 U.S. 99 (1879); Sid & Marty Krofft Television Productions, Inc. v. McDonald's Corp., 562 F.2d 1157, 1163–64 (9th Cir. 1977), and contends that a computer program is protected under the Copyright Act only if the program embodies expression *which is communicated to the user when the program is run on a computer.*

Formula's position, however, is contrary to the language of the Copyright Act, the legislative history of the Act, and the existing case law concerning the copyrightability of computer programs. An examination of the legislative history reveals that Formula's arguments were considered and rejected by Congress when copyright protection was extended to computer programs.

In 1974, the National Commission on New Technological Uses of Copyright Works (CONTU) was established by Congress to consider, *inter alia,* to what extent computer programs should be protected by copyright law. The CONTU Final Report recommended that the copyright law be amended "to make it explicit that computer programs, to the extent that they embody an author's original creation, are proper subject matter of copyright." National Commission on New Technological Uses of Copyrighted Works, Final Report 1 (1979) [hereafter CONTU Report].

Commissioner Hersey dissented from this recommendation, arguing that "[t]he Act of 1976 should be amended to make it explicit that copyright protection does not extend to a computer program in the form in which it is capable of being used to control computer operations." CONTU Report at 1. Hersey's dissent was based on his belief, similar to the argument advanced by Formula, that "[w]orks of authorship have always been intended to be circulated to human beings and to be used by them—to be read, heard, or seen, for either pleasurable or practical ends. Computer programs, in their mature phase, are addressed to machines." Id. at 28.

Commissioner Nimmer, while concurring in the Commission's opinion and recommendation, provided a possible line of demarcation for computer programs to be considered in the future if the Commission's recommendation proved to be too open-ended. Nimmer suggested that it might be desirable to limit copyright protection for software to those computer programs which produce works which themselves qualify for copyright protection. CONTU Report at 27.

The majority of the Commission, however, expressly considered and rejected both the Hersey and Nimmer positions:

> It has been suggested by Vice-Chairman Nimmer in his separate opinion that programs be copyrighted only when their use leads to copyrighted output. * * * This distinction is not consistent with the design of the Act of 1976, which was clearly to protect all works of authorship from the moment of their fixation in any tangible medium of expression. Further, it does not square with copyright practice past and present, which recognizes copyright protection for a work of authorship regardless of the uses to which it may be put. *The copyright status of the written rules for a game or a system for the operation of a machine is unaffected by the fact that those rules direct the actions of those who play the game or carry out the process.* Nor has copyright been denied to works simply because of their utilitarian aspects. It follows, therefore, that there should likewise be no distinction made between programs which are used in the production of further copyrighted works and those which are not.

* * *

> *That the words of a program are used ultimately in the*
> *implementation of a process, should in no way affect their*
> *copyrightability.*

CONTU Report at 21 (emphasis added) (footnote omitted).

In 1980, Congress accepted the CONTU majority's recommended statutory changes verbatim. See 17 U.S.C. §§ 101, 117. Among other changes not relevant here, the Copyright Act was amended to add the following definition of "computer program":

> A "computer program" is a set of statements or instructions to be used *directly or indirectly* in a computer in order to bring about a certain result.

17 U.S.C. § 101 (emphasis added). As recommended by the CONTU majority, the Act makes no distinction between the copyrightability of those programs which directly interact with the computer user and those which simply manage the computer system.

Formula's reliance on the idea/expression dichotomy to argue that computer programs are copyrightable only if they provide expression to the computer user is misplaced. The distinction between ideas and expression is intended to prohibit the monopolization of an idea when there are a limited number of ways to express that idea:

> The "idea-expression identity" exception provides that copyrighted language may be copied without infringing when there is but a limited number of ways to express a given idea. This rule is the logical extension of the fundamental principle that copyright cannot protect ideas. In the computer context this means that when specific instructions, even though previously copyrighted, are the only and essential means of accomplishing a given task, their later use by another will not amount to an infringement.

* * *

> When other language *is* available, programmers are free to read copyrighted programs and use the ideas embodied in them in preparing their own works.

CONTU Report at 20 (footnotes omitted). See also Apple Computer, Inc. v. Franklin Computer Corp., 714 F.2d 1240, 1253 (3d Cir.1983) ("We * * * thus focus on whether the idea is capable of various modes of expression. If other programs can be written or created which perform the same function as an Apple's operating system program, then that program is an expression of the idea and hence copyrightable."). As in *Franklin,* Apple "does not seek to copyright the method which instructs the computer to perform its operating functions but only the instructions themselves." Id. at 1251. Apple introduced evidence that numerous methods exist for writing the programs involved here, and Formula does not contend to the contrary. 562 F.Supp. at 787. Thus, Apple seeks to copyright only its particular set of instructions, not the underlying computer process.

Further, Formula provides absolutely no authority for its contention that the "expression" required in order for a computer program to be eligible for copyright protection is expression that must be communicated to the computer user when the program is run on a computer. The Copyright Act extends protection to "original works of authorship fixed in any tangible medium of expression, now known or later developed, from which they can be perceived, reproduced, or otherwise communicated, either directly or with the aid of a machine or device." 17 U.S.C. § 102(a). The computer program when written embodies expression; never has the Copyright Act required that the expression be communicated to a particular audience.

B. *Irreparable Harm*

Formula contends that Apple presented no evidence of harm to Apple if Formula were allowed to continue distributing copies of the programs to which Apple possesses the copyright during the pendency of the lawsuit.

A showing of a reasonable likelihood of success on the merits in a copyright infringement claim raises a presumption of irreparable harm. Apple Computer, Inc. v. Franklin Computer Corp., 714 F.2d at 1254; Atari, Inc. v. North American Philips Consumer Electronics Corp., 672 F.2d 607, 620 (7th Cir.), cert. denied, 459 U.S. 880 (1982). Further, Apple introduced evidence of the considerable time and money that it had invested in the development of the computer programs. "[T]he jeopardy to Apple's investment and competitive position caused by [the defendant's] wholesale copying of many of its key operating programs * * * satisf[ies] the requirement of irreparable harm needed to support a preliminary injunction." Apple Computer, Inc. v. Franklin Computer Corp., 714 F.2d at 1254.

Formula contends that it will be irreparably harmed by the injunction because the injunction will inhibit Formula's entry into the computer market. At the time Formula filed its response to Apple's motion for a preliminary injunction, however, it had sold only 49 "Pineapple" computer kits. Further, Formula's revenues from the sale of computer products constitute only a small percentage of its total sales. 562 F.Supp. at 777.

* * *

CONCLUSION

The district court did not abuse its discretion or rely on erroneous legal premises in issuing the preliminary injunction.

Affirmed.

NOTES

1. Prior to the amendment of § 117 in 1980, computer programs could be copyrighted as books, and many were copyrighted in this form. However, a copy of a book in machine readable form was not a copy, and hence not an

infringement of the copyrighted program. See the discussion of the analogous problem of audio and video tape recording, infra page 704.

2. Apple Computer, Inc. v. Franklin Computer Corp., 714 F.2d 1240 (3d Cir.1983), cited in the principal case, involved the manufacturer of the Franklin Computer, advertised as "Apple Compatible" and using operating programs copied from Apple (one of the Franklin programs still had the name of an Apple programmer embedded within it). After the Court of Appeals reversed the order of the District Court denying a preliminary injunction, the case was settled by the payment of substantial damages and an agreement giving Franklin some time to write new, noninfringing operating system programs.

3. Williams Electronics, Inc. v. Artic International, Inc., 685 F.2d 870 (3d Cir.1982), cited in the principal case, was an action by the manufacturer of the coin-operated electronic video game DEFENDER. The game program, embedded in ROM (read only memory), and the visual screen displays were copyrighted. The Court of Appeals affirmed the grant of a preliminary injunction.

4. Atari, Inc. v. North American Philips Consumer Electronics Corp., 672 F.2d 607 (7th Cir.1982), was an action by the owners of the copyright in the game "PAC-MAN," alleging that the game "K.C. Munchkin" was an infringement. The Court of Appeals reversed the district court's denial of a preliminary injunction.

5. The principal case is one of a number of early copyright software cases which tested the subject matter scope of copyright protection of computer programs after the amendment of § 117 in 1980. These cases established the principle that all computer programs are eligible for protection. The litigation over computer software has shifted to the issue: what forms of copying infringe? The leading case on this topic is Whelan Associates, Inc. v. Jaslow Dental Laboratory, Inc., infra page 672.

BLEISTEIN v. DONALDSON LITHOGRAPHING

Supreme Court of the United States, 1903.
188 U.S. 239, 23 S.Ct. 298, 47 L.Ed. 460.

MR. JUSTICE HOLMES delivered the opinion of the court.

This case comes here from the United States Circuit Court of Appeals for the Sixth Circuit by writ of error. * * * It is an action brought by the plaintiffs in error to recover the penalties prescribed for infringements of copyrights.

* * * The alleged infringements consisted in the copying in reduced form of three chromolithographs prepared by employés of the plaintiffs for advertisements of a circus owned by one Wallace. Each of the three contained a portrait of Wallace in the corner and lettering bearing some slight relation to the scheme of decoration, indicating the subject of the design and the fact that the reality was to be seen at the circus. One of the designs was of an ordinary ballet, one of a number of men and women, described as the Stirk family, performing on bicycles, and one of groups of men and women whitened to represent statues. The Circuit Court directed a verdict for the defendant on the ground that the chromolithographs were not within the protection of the copyright law, and this ruling was sustained by the Circuit Court of

Appeals. Courier Lithographing Co. v. Donaldson Lithographing Co., 104 Fed.Rep. 993.

* * *

We shall do no more than mention the suggestion that painting and engraving unless for a mechanical end are not among the useful arts, the progress of which Congress is empowered by the Constitution to promote. The Constitution does not limit the useful to that which satisfies immediate bodily needs. Burrow-Giles Lithographic Co. v. Sarony, 111 U.S. 53. It is obvious also that the plaintiffs' case is not affected by the fact, if it be one, that the pictures represent actual groups—visible things. They seem from the testimony to have been composed from hints or description, not from sight of a performance. But even if they had been drawn from the life, that fact would not deprive them of protection. The opposite proposition would mean that a portrait by Velasquez or Whistler was common property because others might try their hand on the same face. Others are free to copy the original. They are not free to copy the copy. The copy is the personal reaction of an individual upon nature. Personality always contains something unique. It expresses its singularity even in hand-writing, and a very modest grade of art has in it something irreducible, which is one man's alone. That something he may copyright unless there is a restriction in the words of the act.

* * *

These chromolithographs are "pictorial illustrations." The word "illustrations" does not mean that they must illustrate the text of a book, and that the etchings of Rembrandt or Steinla's engraving of the Madonna di San Sisto could not be protected to-day if any man were able to produce them. Again, the act however construed, does not mean that ordinary posters are not good enough to be considered within its scope. * * * Certainly works are not the less connected with the fine arts because their pictorial quality attracts the crowd and there-fore gives them a real use—if use means to increase trade and to help to make money. A picture is none the less a picture and none the less a subject of copyright that it is used for an advertisement. And if pictures may be used to advertise soap, or the theatre, or monthly magazines, as they are, they may be used to advertise a circus. Of course, the ballet is as legitimate a subject for illustration as any other. A rule cannot be laid down that would excommunicate the paintings of Degas.

Finally, the special adaptation of these pictures to the advertise-ment of the Wallace shows does not prevent a copyright. That may be a circumstance for the jury to consider in determining the extent of Mr. Wallace's rights, but it is not a bar. Moreover, on the evidence, such prints are used by less pretentious exhibitions when those for whom they were prepared have given them up.

It would be a dangerous undertaking for persons trained only to the law to constitute themselves final judges of the worth of pictorial illustrations, outside of the narrowest and most obvious limits. At the one extreme some works of genius would be sure to miss appreciation. Their very novelty would make them repulsive until the public had learned the new language in which their author spoke. It may be more than doubted, for instance, whether the etchings of Goya or the paintings of Manet would have been sure of protection when seen for the first time. At the other end, copyright would be denied to pictures which appealed to a public less educated than the judge. Yet if they command the interest of any public, they have a commercial value—it would be bold to say that they have not an aesthetic and educational value—and the taste of any public is not to be treated with contempt. It is an ultimate fact for the moment, whatever may be our hopes for a change. That these pictures had their worth and their success is sufficiently shown by the desire to reproduce them without regard to the plaintiffs' rights.   *   *   *

We are of opinion that there was evidence that the plaintiffs have rights entitled to the protection of the law.

[Reversed.]

Mr. Justice Harlan, with whom concurred Mr. Justice McKenna, dissenting.

*   *   *

I entirely concur in the views [of the court below] and therefore dissent from the opinion and judgment of this court. The clause of the Constitution giving Congress power to promote the progress of science and useful arts, by securing for limited terms to authors and inventors the exclusive right to their respective works and discoveries, does not, as I think, embrace a mere advertisement of a circus.   *   *   *

NOTE

1. Justice Holmes' ringing assertion that "It would be a dangerous undertaking for persons trained only to the law to constitute themselves final judges of the worth of pictorial illustrations, outside of the narrowest and most obvious limits" has exerted a strong influence on the development of copyright law. But is that really the issue? Why couldn't "artistic worth" be treated as a question of fact, and resolved through the testimony of experts, just as many other questions involving subjects beyond the scope of legal training are resolved?

The right of the author of a work of visual art to prevent the destruction of a work of "recognized stature" in new § 106A will require the courts to determine what is, and what is not, such a work.

MAZER v. STEIN

Supreme Court of the United States, 1954.
347 U.S. 201, 74 S.Ct. 460, 98 L.Ed. 630, rehearing denied 347 U.S. 949, 74 S.Ct. 637, 98 L.Ed. 1096.

Mr. Justice Reed delivered the opinion of the Court.

This case involves the validity of copyrights obtained by respondents for statuettes of male and female dancing figures made of semivitreous china. The controversy centers around the fact that although copyrighted as "works of art," the statuettes were intended for use and used as bases for table lamps, with electric wiring, sockets and lamp shades attached.

Respondents are partners in the manufacture and sale of electric lamps. One of the respondents created original works of sculpture in the form of human figures by traditional clay-model technique. From this model, a production mold for casting copies was made. The resulting statuettes, without any lamp components added, were submitted by the respondents to the Copyright Office for registration as "works of art" or reproductions thereof under § 5(g) or § 5(h) of the copyright law, and certificates of registration issued. Sales (publication in accordance with the statute) as fully equipped lamps preceded the applications for copyright registration of the statuettes. 17 U.S.C. (Supp. V, 1952) §§ 10, 11, 13, 209; Rules and Regulations, 37 CFR, 1949, §§ 202.8 and 202.9. Thereafter, the statuettes were sold in quantity throughout the country both as lamp bases and as statuettes. The sales in lamp form accounted for all but an insignificant portion of respondents' sales.

Petitioners are partners and, like respondents, make and sell lamps. Without authorization, they copied the statuettes, embodied them in lamps and sold them.

* * *

Petitioners, charged by the present complaint with infringement of respondents' copyrights of reproductions of their works of art, seek here a reversal of the Court of Appeals decree upholding the copyrights. Petitioners in their petition for certiorari present a single question:

> "Can statuettes be protected in the United States by copyright when the copyright applicant intended primarily to use the statuettes in the form of lamp bases to be made and sold in quantity and carried the intentions into effect? * * * "

It is not the right to copyright an article that could have utility under §§ 5(g) and (h), * * * that petitioners oppose. Their brief accepts the copyrightability of the great carved golden saltcellar of Cellini but adds:

> "If, however, Cellini designed and manufactured this item in quantity so that the general public could have salt cellars, then an entirely different conclusion would be reached. In such case, the salt cellar becomes an article of manufacture having utility in addition to its ornamental value and would therefore have to be protected by design patent."

It is publication as a lamp and registration as a statue to gain a monopoly in manufacture that they assert is such a misuse of copyright as to make the registration invalid.

* * *

The practice of the Copyright Office, under the 1870 and 1874 Acts and before the 1909 Act, was to allow registration "as works of the fine arts" of articles of the same character as those of respondents now under challenge. Seven examples appear in the Government's brief *amicus curiae.*[22] * * * The *amicus* brief gives sixty examples selected at five-year intervals, 1912–1952, said to be typical of registrations of works of art possessing utilitarian aspects.[25] * * * So we have a contemporaneous and long-continued construction of the statutes by the agency charged to administer them that would allow the registration of such a statuette as is in question here.

* * *

The successive acts, the legislative history of the 1909 Act and the practice of the Copyright Office unite to show that "works of art" and "reproductions of works of art" are terms that were intended by Congress to include the authority to copyright these statuettes. * * *

The conclusion that the statues here in issue may be copyrighted goes far to solve the question whether their intended reproduction as lamp stands bars or invalidates their registration. This depends solely on statutory interpretation. Congress may after publication protect by copyright any writing of an author. Its statute creates the copyright. It did not exist at common law even though he had a property right in his unpublished work.

But petitioners assert that congressional enactment of the design patent laws should be interpreted as denying protection to artistic articles embodied or reproduced in manufactured articles. They say:

> "Fundamentally and historically, the Copyright Office is the repository of what each claimant considers to be a cultural treasure, whereas the Patent Office is the repository of what each applicant considers to be evidence of the advance in industrial and technological fields."

Their argument is that design patents require the critical examination given patents to protect the public against monopoly. Attention is called to Gorham Co. v. White, 14 Wall. 511, interpreting the design patent law of 1842, 5 Stat. 544, granting a patent to anyone who by "their own industry, genius, efforts, and expense, may have invented or produced any new and original design for a manufacture. * * *" A pattern for flat silver was there upheld. The intermediate and present law differs little. "Whoever invents any new, original and ornamental design for an article of manufacture may obtain a patent therefor, * * *" subject generally to the provisions concerning patents for invention. § 171, 66 Stat. 805. As petitioner sees the effect of the design patent law:

---

22. E.g., "A female figure bearing an urn in front partly supported by drapery around the head. The figure nude from the waist up and below this the form concealed by conventionalized skirt draperies which flow down and forward forming a tray at the base. Sides and back of skirt in fluted form. The whole being designed as a candlestick with match tray. The figure standing and bent forward from hips and waist."

25. E.g., "*Lighting fixture design.* By F.E. Guitini. [Bowl-shaped bracket embellished with figure of half-nude woman standing in bunch of flowers.] Copyright December 28, 1912. Registration number G 42645. Copyright claimant: Kathodion Bronze Works, New York."

"If an industrial designer can not satisfy the novelty requirements of the design patent laws, then his design as used on articles of manufacture can be copied by anyone."

Petitioner has furnished the Court a booklet of numerous design patents for statuettes, bases for table lamps and similar articles for manufacture, quite indistinguishable in type from the copyrighted statuettes here in issue. Petitioner urges that overlapping of patent and copyright legislation so as to give an author or inventor a choice between patents and copyrights should not be permitted. * * *[36]

As we have held the statuettes here involved copyrightable, we need not decide the question of their patentability. Though other courts have passed upon the issue as to whether allowance by the election of the author or patentee of one bars a grant of the other, we do not. We do hold that the patentability of the statuettes, fitted as lamps or unfitted, does not bar copyright as works of art. Neither the Copyright Statute nor any other says that because a thing is patentable it may not be copyrighted. We should not so hold.

Unlike a patent, a copyright gives no exclusive right to the art disclosed; protection is given only to the expression of the idea—not the idea itself. Thus, in Baker v. Selden, 101 U.S. 99, the Court held that a copyrighted book on a peculiar system of bookkeeping was not infringed by a similar book using a similar plan which achieved similar results where the alleged infringer made a different arrangement of the columns and used different headings. The distinction is illustrated in Fred Fisher, Inc. v. Dillingham, 298 F. 145, 151, when the court speaks of two men, each a perfectionist, independently making maps of the same territory. Though the maps are identical, each may obtain the exclusive right to make copies of his own particular map, and yet neither will infringe the other's copyright. Likewise a copyrighted directory is not infringed by a similar directory which is the product of independent work. The copyright protects originality rather than novelty or invention—conferring only "the sole right of multiplying copies." Absent copying there can be no infringement of copyright. Thus, respondents may not exclude others from using statuettes of human figures in table lamps; they may only prevent use of copies of their statuettes as such or as incorporated in some other article. Regulation § 202.8, supra, makes clear that artistic articles are protected in "form but not their mechanical or utilitarian aspects." See Stein v. Rosenthal, 103 F.Supp. 227, 231.

* * *

36. The English Copyright Act, 1911, § 22, 4 Halsbury's Statutes of England (2d ed.), p. 800, does not protect designs registrable under the Patents and Designs Act (now the Registered Designs Act, 1949, 17 Halsbury's Statutes of England (2d ed.)) unless such designs are not used or intended to be used as models or patterns to be multiplied by any industrial process. The Board of Trade has ruled that a design shall be deemed to be used as a model or pattern to be multiplied by industrial process within the meaning of § 22 when the design is reproduced or intended to be reproduced in more than fifty single articles. The Copyright (Industrial Designs) Rules, 1949, No. 2367, 1 Statutory Instruments 1949, p. 1453.

The economic philosophy behind the clause empowering Congress to grant patents and copyrights is the conviction that encouragement of individual effort by personal gain is the best way to advance public welfare through the talents of authors and inventors in "Science and useful Arts." Sacrificial days devoted to such creative activities deserve rewards commensurate with the services rendered.

Affirmed.

*   *   *

HOUSE REPORT NO. 94–1476
pp. 54–55.

In accordance with the Supreme Court's decision in Mazer v. Stein, 347 U.S. 201 (1954), works of "applied art" encompass all original pictorial, graphic, and sculptural works that are intended to be or have been embodied in useful articles, regardless of factors such as mass production, commercial exploitation, and the potential availability of design patent protection. The scope of exclusive rights in these works is given special treatment in section 113, to be discussed *   *   * [infra page 595].

The Committee has added language to the definition of "pictorial, graphic, and sculptural works" in an effort to make clearer the distinction between works of applied art protectable under the bill and industrial designs not subject to copyright protection. The declaration that "pictorial, graphic, and sculptural works" include "works of artistic craftsmanship insofar as their form but not their mechanical or utilitarian aspects are concerned" is classic language; it is drawn from Copyright Office regulations promulgated in the 1940's and expressly endorsed by the Supreme Court in the *Mazer* case.

The second part of the amendment states that "the design of a useful article *   *   * shall be considered a pictorial, graphic, or sculptural work only if, and only to the extent that, such design incorporates pictorial, graphic, or sculptural features that can be identified separately from, and are capable of existing independently of, the utilitarian aspects of the article." A "useful article" is defined as "an article having an intrinsic utilitarian function that is not merely to portray the appearance of the article or to convey information." This part of the amendment is an adaptation of language added to the Copyright Office Regulations in the mid-1950's in an effort to implement the Supreme Court's decision in the *Mazer* case.

In adopting this amendatory language, the Committee is seeking to draw as clear a line as possible between copyrightable works of applied art and uncopyrighted works of industrial design. A two-dimensional painting, drawing, or graphic work is still capable of being identified as such when it is printed on or applied to utilitarian articles such as textile fabrics, wallpaper, containers, and the like. The same is true when a statue or carving is used to embellish an industrial product or, as in the *Mazer* case, is incorporated into a product without losing its ability to exist independently as a work of art. On the other hand, although the shape of an industrial product may be aesthetically satisfying and valuable, the Committee's intention is not to offer it copyright protection under the bill. Unless the shape of an automobile, airplane, ladies' dress, food processor, television set, or any other industrial product contains some element that, physically or conceptually, can be identified as separable from the utilitarian aspects of that article, the design would not be copyrighted under the bill. The test of separability and independence from "the utilitarian aspects of the article" does not depend upon the nature of the design—that is, even if the appearance of an article is determined by esthetic (as opposed to functional) considerations, only elements, if any, which can be identified separately from the useful article as such are copyrightable. And, even if the three-dimensional design contains some such element (for example a carving on the back of a chair or a floral relief design on silver flatware), copyright protection would extend only to that element, and would not cover the over-all configuration of the utilitarian article as such.

A special situation is presented by architectural works. An architect's plans and drawings would, of course, be protected by copyright, but the extent to which that protection would extend to the structure depicted would depend on the circumstances. Purely nonfunctional or monumental structures would be subject to full copyright protection under the bill, and the same would be true of artistic sculpture or decorative ornamentation or embellishment added to a structure. On the other hand, where the only elements of shape in an architectural design are conceptually inseparable from the utilitarian aspects of the structure, copyright protection for the design would not be available.

The Committee has considered, but chosen to defer, the possibility of protecting the design of typefaces. A "typeface" can be defined as a set of letters, numbers, or other symbolic characters, whose forms are related by repeating design elements consistently applied in a notational system and are intended to be embodied in articles whose intrinsic utilitarian function is for use in composing text or other cognizable combinations of characters. The Committee does not regard the design of typeface, as thus defined, to be a copyrightable "pictorial, graphic, or sculptural work" within the meaning of this bill and the application of the dividing line in section 101.

NOTE

1. Robert C. Denicola, Applied Art and Industrial Design: A Suggested Approach to Copyright in Useful Articles, 67 Minn.L.Rev. 707 (1983), argues that the test for separating copyrightable from uncopyrightable commercial designs should focus on the design process rather than the physical object. His argument puts considerable weight upon the use of the term "conceptually" in the following sentence from the portion of the house report just quoted: "Unless the shape of an automobile, airplane, ladies' dress, food processor, television set, or any other industrial product contains some element that,

physically or conceptually, can be identified as separable from the utilitarian aspects of that article, the design would not be copyrighted under the bill."

Denicola argues that the critical distinction between decorative art and industrial design is the role of functional considerations in the design process. If the design is dictated solely by aesthetic considerations, he argues, it should be copyrightable no matter what the style, even if it is sleek and modern. On the other hand, if the design has emerged out of the close relationship between form and function, it should not be copyrightable.

Denicola argues that a test of physical separability does not accurately reflect the case law because the courts have held many designs (such as fabric designs) copyrightable which cannot in fact be removed from the commercial product on which they exist.

2. Is an original type face or other symbol system eligible for copyright? Can a copy of a public domain work be protected against photographic reproduction by the use of an original, unusual type face or symbols? In Perris v. Hexamer, 99 U.S. 674 (1878), the court held that a map of Philadelphia did not infringe a map of New York even though it employed the same original, specialized system of symbols. The Court said: "The complainants have no more an exclusive right to use the form of the characters they employ to express their ideas upon the face of the map, than they have to use the form of type they select to print the key. Scarcely any map is published on which certain arbitrary signs, explained by a key printed at some convenient place for reference, are not used to designate objects of special interest, such as rivers, railroads, boundaries, cities, towns, etc.; and yet we think it has never been supposed that a simple copyright of the map gave the publisher an exclusive right to the use upon other maps of the particular signs and key which he saw fit to adopt for the purposes of his delineations. That, however, is what the complainants seek to accomplish in this case. The defendant has not copied their maps. All he has done at any time has been to use to some extent their system of arbitrary signs and their key." 99 U.S. 676.

In Eltra Corporation v. Ringer, 579 F.2d 294 (4th Cir.1978), the plaintiff sought a writ of mandamus to compel the Registrar of Copyrights to register a typeface design which had been prepared by a well-known typeface designer for a fee of $11,000. Both the district court and the court of appeals held that a typeface design was not a work of art under the 1909 act.

G. Ricordi & Co. v. Haendler, 194 F.2d 914 (2d Cir.1952) (Learned Hand), held the plaintiff could not maintain an action for unfair competition by photocopying the plaintiff's sheet music after the copyright on the sheet music had expired. But in Grove Press, Inc. v. Collectors Publication, Inc., 264 F.Supp. 603 (C.D.Cal.1967), the court held that such an action could be maintained for a photo offset reproduction of plaintiff's edition of "My Secret Life," a work in the public domain. The court said that *Sears* and *Compco* did not bar the action. What result under § 301?

COMMERCIAL PRINTS AND LABELS

Copyright protection has been accorded to commercial prints and labels by statute since 1874.

Copyright protection of commercial labels is attractive for two reasons. First, the plaintiff need only show copying, not consumer confusion. Where the copying is clear, this may make it easier to obtain a preliminary injunction, and in some cases it may even be possible to prevail on copyright where trademark would fail. See Kitchens of Sara Lee, Inc. v. Nifty Food Corp., 266 F.2d 541 (2d Cir. 1959), where plaintiff succeeded in copyright for the copying of pictures of cakes on its labels, but failed in unfair competition because of the absence of customer confusion. Secondly, copyright protection affords protection against use of the label in a non-trademark manner. This is particularly important where a company plans a continuing promotional campaign built around central symbols. Think, for instance, of the anguish at the Green Giant Co. if the Jolly Green Giant, a copyrighted figure to be sure, were made the subject of a cartoonist's satire, or worse, portrayed as the villain of the piece.

See generally, Pattishall, Protection of Labels Through Copyright Infringement and Unfair Competition Laws, 56 Trademark Rep. 408 (1966).

Commercial prints and labels are not specifically enumerated in § 102. The House Report states that "there is no intention whatever to narrow the scope of the subject matter now characterized in § 5(k) as 'prints or labels used for articles of merchandise.' However, since this terminology suggests the material object in which a work is embodied rather than the work itself, the bill does not mention this category separately." House Report No. 94–1476 at 54.

DESIGNS

American law provides little protection for commercial and industrial designs. Design statutes have been repeatedly proposed to the Congress but have never passed. Their proponents argue that the lack of protection for applied design contributes to low aesthetic standards in an area of great importance, and that as a result American industrial design standards are lower than those of some other countries.

For a number of years while it was under consideration by the Congress the Revision Bill contained a Title III for the protection of designs. The Title provided protection for a period of five years for an "original ornamental design of a useful article." The system was modelled on copyright, i.e. it required notice and registration but not "invention." This title was removed from the bill just before passage with a statement from the House Committee that the matter would be considered again in the next session of the Congress. It has not been.

Absent a federal design statute, protection is available under copyright following *Mazer,* under the design patent statute, under the Lanham Act and unfair competition doctrines. The protection that is available in the end amounts to very little.

Under *Mazer* protection is regularly obtained on fabric designs, toys, jewelry and household decorative items, at least to judge by the active Second Circuit infringement docket in these areas.

Mazer would provide the basis for broad protection of industrial designs if the following stratagem were successful. Say, for instance, that you desired to obtain protection on a new design for a shoe. Take the shoe, glue it to a base, and title it: "Shoe in modern life." Register it as a statue and manufacture the shoe. Would a competitor who copied your shoe design infringe the copyright?

Does *Mazer* answer this question? How would Denicola answer this question?

Section 113(a) appears to answer this question in the affirmative. But it is limited by section 113(b). Protection "in a work that portrays a useful article as such" is to be no greater than existed under the 1909 law. House Report 94–1476 states:

> Section 113 deals with the extent of copyright protection in "works of applied art." The section takes as its starting point the Supreme Court's decision in Mazer v. Stein, 347 U.S. 201 (1954), and the first sentence of subsection (a) restates the basic principle established by that decision. The rule of *Mazer*, as affirmed by the bill, is that copyright in a pictorial, graphic, or sculptural work will not be affected if the work is employed as the design of a useful article, and will afford protection to the copyright owner against the unauthorized reproduction of his work in useful as well as nonuseful articles. The terms "pictorial, graphic, and sculptural works" and "useful article" are defined in section 101, and these definitions are discussed above in connection with section 102.

> The broad language of section 106(1) and of subsection (a) of section 113 raises questions as to the extent of copyright protection for a pictorial, graphic, or sculptural work that portrays, depicts, or represents an image of a useful article in such a way that the utilitarian nature of the article can be seen. To take the example usually cited, would copyright in a drawing or model of an automobile give the artist the exclusive right to make automobiles of the same design?

> The 1961 Report of the Register of Copyrights stated, on the basis of judicial precedent, that "copyright in a pictorial, graphic, or sculptural work, portraying a useful article as such, does not extend to the manufacture of the useful article itself," and recommended specifically that "the distinctions drawn in this area by existing court decisions" not be altered by the statute. The Register's Supplementary Report, at page 48, cited a number of these decisions, and explained the insuperable difficulty of finding "any statutory formulation that would express the distinction satisfactorily." Section 113(b) reflects the Register's conclusion that "the real need is to make clear that there is no intention to change the present law with respect to the scope of protection in a work portraying a useful article as such." Id. at 105.

The design patent statute is a brief addition to the patent statute, 35 U.S.C. §§ 171–173. Protection is "subject to the conditions and requirements of this title" and there are few, designs that can meet the standard of non-obviousness required by section 103. See infra, page 883.

The *Sears* and *Compco* cases checked the development of state law as a source of design protection by analogy to unfair competition. Some designs have been registered on the principal register of the Lanham Act, but the requirement of secondary meaning restricts that protection. One successful example is the Haig and Haig Pinch Bottle. In re Haig & Haig Ltd., 118 U.S.P.Q. 229 (Comm'r of Patents, 1958). But see Haig & Haig Ltd. v. Maradel Products, Inc., 249 F.Supp. 575 (S.D.N.Y.1966) (no injunction against use of pinch-shaped bottle to market after shave lotion and bubble bath). See generally, supra page 301.

NOTES

1. In Esquire, Inc. v. Ringer, the plaintiff sought mandamus to compel the Registrar to register under the 1909 act a design for contemporary light fixtures with rounded or elliptically shaped housings. Mandamus denied because the refusal to register was within the discretion of the Registrar. 591 F.2d 796 (D.C.Cir.1978), cert. denied 440 U.S. 908 (1979).

2. Defining the line between copyright and industrial design, and finding a satisfactory approach to the protection of industrial design is a problem that has been difficult for other legal systems as well. The story of developments in numerous other systems, with careful parallels to issues faced in American law, is chronicled in an ambitious two-part study by Professor J.H. Reichman. J.H. Reichman, Design Protection in Domestic and Foreign Copyright Law: From the Berne Revision of 1948 to the Copyright Act of 1976, 1983 Duke L.J. 1143 (1983) and J.H. Reichman, Design Protection after the Copyright Act of 1976: A Comparative View of the Emerging Interim Models, 31 J. of the Copyright Soc. of the U.S.A. 267 (1984). The American legal system has been more hostile to providing any meaningful protection to industrial designs than that of almost any other industrial nation, a phenomenon that may reflect the unusual role of antitrust concerns in American law and complexities created by the mixed system of state and national protection.

ARCHITECTURAL WORKS

The U.S. adherence to the Berne Convention aided the arguments of those who favored protection for architectural works because the Berne Convention explicitly requires their protection. Protection was extended to architectural works in 1990 by the Architectural Works Copyright Protection Act.

Prior to that act, U.S. law protected an architect's plans and drawings, but did not protect the expression of the architect's work fixed in the structure itself. See the discussion in H.R. 1476, quoted supra p. 591. Under this law, one could copy from the structure itself, but not from the plans or drawings used to construct the structure.

See Imperial Homes Corp. v. Lamont, 458 F.2d 895 (5th Cir.1972). The Architectural Works Copyright Protection Act added architectural works to the list of expressly listed copyrighted works in § 102(a), and added a definition of architectural works in 101. "An 'architectural work' is the design of a building as embodied in any tangible medium of expression, including a building, architectural plans, or drawings. The work includes the overall form as well as the arrangement and composition of spaces and elements of the design, but does not include individual standard features."

The scope of the copyright in architectural works is limited by new § 120(a), which permits the making, distribution and display of pictorial representations of an architectural work "if the building in which the work is embodied is located in or ordinarily visible from a public place." Otherwise, one could not take photographs of a copyrighted architectural work without the permission of the copyright owner.

Section 120(b) permits the owner of an architectural work to alter or destroy the work without possible liability for creating a derivative work under § 106(2).

(2) PUBLIC POLICY

Do any considerations of "public policy" limit the scope of copyrightable subject matter? The court in Mitchell Bros. Film Group v. Cinema Adult Theater, 604 F.2d 852 (5th Cir.1979), thought not. The defendants argued that the plaintiff's film was not copyrightable because obscene and that the court should not enjoin infringement because the plaintiff had "unclean hands." (A technical equity doctrine which is a grounds for denying injunctive relief.) "Denying copyright protection to work adjudged obscene by the standards of one era would frequently result in lack of copyright protection (and thus lack of financial incentive to create) for works that later generations might consider to be not only non-obscene but even of great literary merit." 604 F.2d 857.

In Merritt Forbes & Co. v. Newman Investment Securities, Inc., 604 F.Supp. 943 (S.D.N.Y.1985), the defendants argued that it is against public policy to permit a copyright in legal documents. The effect of copyright, they argued, would be to force competitors who wished to offer a product under the same contractual terms (relating, for instance, to a product warranty or, as in the case itself, to the terms of a bond offering) to change the language of the legal document although the purpose would be to create the same legal relationship. This would have two effects contrary to public policy. First, it would make it more difficult for purchasers to compare the offerings of competitors because they would have to "decode" the different legal language of the documents in order to decide whether there are significant differences. Second, it would undermine the usefulness of precedent since a decision construing the language of one document might or might not apply to a variant. The court held that there was no public policy doctrine limiting copyrightability, and said that these arguments would be relevant only to an argument that the claimed infringement was fair use under § 107. "The issue of whether or not bond underwriting documents are the proper subject for copyright protection has apparently never been addressed in this or any other jurisdiction. * * * [N]o court * * * [has] concluded that there is a public policy exemption for a particular classification of literary works which would otherwise be subject to copyright protection." 604 F.Supp. 949–951.

In Hutchinson Telephone Co. v. Fronteer Directory Co., 770 F.2d 128 (8th Cir.1985), the plaintiff sought to enforce its copyright in its "white pages." The district court held the copyright invalid on the ground that the telephone company was required by law to publish a directory, and thus no copyright was needed to create the incentive. The Eighth Circuit reversed. "[N]o policy analysis is required." 770 F.2d 132.

PROBLEM

Are the arguments in *Merritt Forbes & Co.* that copyright for legal documents will result in a needless cacophony of meaningless variants persuasive? Consider the fact that the leading operating system for personal computers, MS–DOS (for Microsoft Disk Operating System) is copyrighted by the Microsoft Corporation. Yet the system is used on many different brands of personal computers, each maker of which (including IBM, the leading manufacturer) has obtained a license from Microsoft. Does this example have any relevance to the case of legal forms? If not, why not?

(3) ORIGINALITY

Section 102 requires a "work of authorship," echoing the Constitutional clause conferring upon Congress the power to enact the statute: "[t]o promote the Progress of Science and useful Arts, by securing for limited Times to Authors and Inventors the exclusive Right to their respective Writings and Discoveries." U.S. Const. art. I, § 8, cl. 8. Does the status of "authorship" require any originality, creativity or effort?

ALFRED BELL & CO. v. CATALDA FINE ARTS, INC.
United States Court of Appeals, Second Circuit, 1951.
191 F.2d 99.

[The plaintiff is a British print producer and dealer who had copyrighted in the United States mezzotint engravings of old masters. The mezzotint method lends itself to realistic reproduction of oil paintings. It is a tedious process requiring skill and patience and is therefore expensive compared to modern color photographic processes. The artists employed to produce these mezzotint engravings attempt faithfully to reproduce the original paintings. The defendants produced and sold color lithographs of the plaintiff's mezzotints.]

FRANK, CIRCUIT JUDGE. 1. Congressional power to authorize both patents and copyrights is contained in Article 1, § 8 of the Constitution. In passing on the validity of patents, the Supreme Court recurrently insists that this constitutional provision governs. On this basis, pointing to the Supreme Court's consequent requirement that to be valid, a patent must disclose a high degree of uniqueness, ingenuity and inventiveness, the defendants assert that the same requirement constitutionally governs copyrights. As several sections of the Copyright Act—e.g., those authorizing copyrights of "reproductions of works of art," maps, and compilations—plainly dispense with any such high standard, defendants are, in effect, attacking the constitutionality of those sections. But the very language of the Constitution differentiates (a) "authors" and their "writings" from (b) "inventors" and their "discoveries." Those who penned the Constitution, of course, knew the difference. The pre-revolutionary English statutes had made the distinction. In 1783, the Continental Congress had passed a resolution recommending that the several states enact legislation to "secure" to authors the "copyright" of their books. Twelve of the thirteen states (in 1783–1786) enacted such statutes. Those of Connecticut and North Carolina covered books, pamphlets, maps, and charts.

Moreover, in 1790, in the year after the adoption of the Constitution, the first Congress enacted two statutes, separately dealing with patents and copyrights. The patent statute, enacted April 10, 1790, 1 Stat. 109, provided that patents should issue only if the Secretary of State, Secretary of War and the Attorney General, or any two of them "shall deem the invention or discovery sufficiently useful and important"; the applicant for a patent was obliged to file a specification "so particular" as "to distinguish the invention or discovery from other things before known and used * * *"; the patent was to constitute *prima facie* evidence that the patentee was "the first and true inventor or * * * discoverer * * * of the thing so specified." The Copyright Act, enacted May 31, 1790, 1 Stat. 124, covered "maps, charts, and books". A printed copy of the title of any map, chart or book was to be recorded in the Clerk's office of the District Court, and a copy of the map, chart or book was to be delivered to the Secretary of State within six months after publication. Twelve years later, Congress in 1802, 2 Stat. 171, added, to matters that might be copyrighted, engravings, etchings and prints.

Thus legislators peculiarly familiar with the purpose of the Constitutional grant, by statute, imposed far less exacting standards in the case of copyrights. They authorized the copyrighting of a mere map which, patently, calls for no considerable uniqueness. They exacted far more from an inventor. And, while they demanded that an official should be satisfied as to the character of an invention before a patent issued, they made no such demand in respect of a copyright. In 1884, in Burrow-Giles Lithographic Co. v. Sarony, 111 U.S. 53, 57, 4 S.Ct. 279, 28 L.Ed. 349, the Supreme Court, adverting to these facts said: "The construction placed upon the constitution by the first act of 1790 and the act of 1802, by the men who were contemporary with its formation, many of whom were members of the convention which framed it, is of itself entitled to very great weight, and when it is remembered that the rights thus established have not been disputed during a period of nearly a century, it is almost conclusive." Accordingly, the Constitution, as so interpreted, recognizes that the standards for patents and copyrights are basically different.

The defendants' contention apparently results from the ambiguity of the word "original." It may mean startling, novel or unusual, a marked departure from the past. Obviously this is not what is meant when one speaks of "the original package," or the "original bill," or (in connection with the "best evidence" rule) an "original" document; none of those things is highly unusual in creativeness. "Original" in reference to a copyrighted work means that the particular work "owes its origin" to the "author." No large measure of novelty is necessary.

[The court then quoted passages from Baker v. Selden, supra page 573, and Bleistein v. Donaldson Lithographing Co., supra page 585, in support of this position.] * * *

On that account, we have often distinguished between the limited protection accorded a copyright owner and the extensive protection granted a patent owner. So we have held that "independent reproduction of a copyrighted * * * work is not infringement", whereas it is *vis a vis* a patent. Correlative with the greater immunity of a patentee is the doctrine of anticipation which does not apply to copyrights: The alleged inventor is chargeable with full knowledge of all the prior art, although in fact he may be utterly ignorant of it. The "author" is entitled to a copyright if he independently contrived a work completely identical with what went before; similarly, although he obtains a valid copyright, he has no right to prevent another from publishing a work identical with his, if not copied from his. A patentee, unlike a copyrightee, must not merely produce something "original"; he must also be "the first inventor or discoverer." "Hence it is possible to have a plurality of valid copyrights directed to closely identical or even identical works. Moreover, none of them if independently arrived at without copying, will constitute an infringement of the copyright of the others."

2. We consider untenable defendants' suggestion that plaintiff's mezzotints could not validly be copyrighted because they are reproductions of works in the public domain. Not only does the Act include "Reproductions of a work of art", but—while prohibiting a copyright of "the original text of any work * * * in the public domain"—it explicitly provides for the copyrighting of "translations, or other versions of works in the public domain". The mezzotints were such "versions". They "originated" with those who made them, and—on the trial judge's findings well supported by the evidence—amply met the standards imposed by the Constitution and the statute. There is evidence that they were not intended to, and did not, imitate the

paintings they reproduced. But even if their substantial departures from the paintings were inadvertent, the copyrights would be valid. A copyist's bad eyesight or defective musculature, or a shock caused by a clap of thunder, may yield sufficiently distinguishable variations. Having hit upon such a variation unintentionally, the "author" may adopt it as his and copyright it.

Accordingly, defendants' arguments about the public domain become irrelevant. They could be relevant only in their bearing on the issue of infringement, i.e., whether the defendants copied the mezzotints. But on the findings, again well grounded in the evidence, we see no possible doubt that defendants, who did deliberately copy the mezzotints, are infringers. For a copyright confers the exclusive right to copy the copyrighted work—a right not to have others copy it. Nor were the copyrights lost because of the reproduction of the mezzotints in catalogues.

* * * The judgment is affirmed.

NOTES

1. In Burrow-Giles Lithographic Co. v. Sarony, 111 U.S. 53 (1884), the Court upheld a copyright on a photograph of Oscar Wilde. The statute provided for a copyright on photographs and the Court decided that the statute, at least as applied to the photograph in issue, was constitutional. The Court relied on the finding below that the photograph was the result of the photographer's "original mental conception, to which he gave visible form by posing the said Oscar Wilde in front of the camera, selecting and arranging the costume draperies, and other various accessories in said photograph, arranging the subject so as to present graceful outlines, arranging and disposing the light and shade, suggesting and evoking the desired expression, and from such disposition, arrangement, or representation, made entirely by plaintiff, he produced the picture in suit." The Court expressed no opinion on the copyrightability of the "ordinary production of a photograph." That question was answered in Time, Inc. v. Bernard Geis Assoc., 293 F.Supp. 130 (S.D.N.Y.1968), upholding the copyrightability of a movie of the assassination of President Kennedy taken by an amateur bystander with his home movie camera.

2. Doesn't Judge Frank confuse two different issues? First, whether in order to be copyrightable the work must be distinguishable from what has gone before? And second, whether in order to be copyrightable the work must incorporate skill or effort of some degree? The only issue in *Catalda* was the first, was it not?

FINANCIAL INFORMATION, INC. v. MOODY'S INVESTORS SERVICE, INC.

United States Court of Appeals, Second Circuit, 1986.
808 F.2d 204, certiorari denied 484 U.S. 820, 108 S.Ct. 79, 98 L.Ed.2d 42 (1987).

Lumbard, Circuit Judge:

In this case, before us for the second time, Financial Information, Inc. ("FII"), which publishes a financial reporting service, charged Moody's Investors Service, Inc. ("Moody's"), another financial publisher, with copyright infringement and unfair competition. After a bench trial, the District Court for the Southern District (Carter, J.) held for the defendants. It found that the material in question was copyrightable, but that Moody's made "fair use" of it under the copyright statute. In Financial Information, Inc. v. Moody's Investors Service, Inc., 751 F.2d 501 (2d Cir.1984) (Financial Information I), we reversed and remanded for further factual findings to determine whether the material in question was copyrightable. On remand, Judge Carter found that FII's material was not copyrightable and also dismissed the plaintiff's pendent state claim. Because we agree that FII's service is not a copyrightable compilation and that the state claims were preempted by federal law, we affirm.

I.

The relevant facts are set forth at length in Judge Oakes' opinion cited above. FII is a financial publisher. One of its works is called the "Financial Daily Card Service," from which it alleges Moody's stole copyrighted information. This service (hereafter "Daily Bond Cards") consists of packets of 4″ by 6″ index cards on which are printed information regarding municipal bonds which the issuer has elected to redeem, or "call." The information typically includes the identity of the issuing authority, the series of bonds being called, the date and price of the redemption, and the name of the trustee or paying agent.

The Daily Bond Cards seek to report all municipal redemptions. When a municipality or other government body calls a bond for redemption—and, consequently, stops paying interest—it publishes a notice of the call in one or more newspapers. Because these notices are not published in a single place, the "back offices" of financial institutions, which are ill-equipped to keep track of thousands of call notices each year, subscribe to called bond services such as FII's. FII's approximately 500 subscribers pay $279 per year for the daily reports, an annual cumulative volume and a filing cabinet.

The defendant Moody's offers a service called the Municipal and Government News Reports ("News Reports"), a bi-weekly supplement to a yearly publication called the Municipal and Government Manual. The Moody's publication provides substantially more information than FII's—including Moody's own rating of the quality of the bonds. In addition, unlike FII, Moody's does not seek to report on all municipal bond redemptions; it reports on only those bonds which the company also rates. The Moody's service costs $840 per year, which includes not only the bi-weekly news reports, but also the annual Municipal and Government Manual, which is a comprehensive work containing a great deal of financial information about municipalities. The Moody's publication serves a far wider audience than the Daily Bond Cards, including libraries and government agencies as well as financial institutions.

According to FII, it noticed in 1980 a "coincidence of Moody's errata publishing after FII," and suspected that Moody's was copying FII's data. In December of that year, FII began planting some false information in its Daily Bond Cards. Moody's reproduced seven of FII's ten common errors in 1980, and eight of eight errors in 1981. FII's expert witness stated that it was more than 95% certain that Moody's had copied 40–50% of FII's information in 1980 and 1981. Moody's, in response, presented substantial evidence of what it called the "independent creation" of its News Reports. It presented evidence that its research cost $700,000 to $1,000,000 per year.

The crucial issue on remand involved FII's efforts to produce its Bond Cards—which the district court described as a "simple clerical task." The cards contain only five basic facts about the bonds: the name of the issuer and a description of the bond (e.g. water, sewage, etc.); the redemption date; the redemption agent; the identification of the specific bonds being called, and the redemption price. Indeed, FII's advertising for its bond service called attention to the simplicity and conciseness of the cards, describing them as appearing in "outline form" without any "superfluous matter." As the district court found, "all (FII) does is provide its subscribers with the requisite bond redemption data in simplified form for easy and ready reference."

FII's procedure for collecting the information for its cards was as rudimentary as the cards themselves. The FII clerks usually did nothing more than look through newspapers and write down the redemption information from the "tombstone" advertisements. When the "tombstone" contained additional or unusually complex information, the clerks would simply attach a photocopy of the "tombstone" to the FII card. Occasionally, the FII clerks would telephone the issuers or agents to verify or clarify information.

Theresa Moore, a former FII researcher, testified at the initial trial that she and her colleagues were clerks with no special skills who exercised no discretion in their jobs. According to the district court, "[s]he used no subjective analysis, but 'just took the information from what I saw in the tombstones and the articles in the paper.'" Also at the first trial, the FII managing editor, George Sheekey, described the researchers' duties much as Moore did: he said their jobs consisted essentially of doing a simple, repetitive task by rote.

Following remand, the district court afforded FII another opportunity to describe its editorial processes. FII called only one witness, Frances Zawilski, an FII assistant editor who formerly supervised Theresa Moore. The district court found that Zawilski "gave a far more inflated version of [Moore's] training process as an FII researcher." The district court questioned the credibility of Zawilski's testimony, stating that "the court is now convinced that the testimony on remand was an attempt to enlarge and embellish a straight forward, simple but time consuming operation that had been fully and adequately explicated at the initial trial." Judge Carter concluded that "FII's researchers perform a simple clerical task. They go through the various publications, cut out the tombstones or redemption notices, extract from the notices the raw data—name of issuer, description of issue, redemption price, date, agent and serial number of bonds being called. . . . The only selectivity involved is principally one of format. . . . With this data, there is no room for selection or choices or judgment." Accordingly, the court held that the Daily Bond Cards were not copyrightable.

II.

Facts may not be copyrighted. The Copyright Act of 1976 does, however, expressly provide for the protection of "compilations," which are defined as works "formed by the collection and assembling of preexisting materials or of data that are selected, coordinated or arranged in such a way that the resulting work as a whole constitutes an original work of authorship." 17 U.S.C. § 101 (1982). The remand order instructed the district court to determine whether the Daily Bond Cards qualify as a copyrightable compilation.

Our leading case on the copyrightability of compilations is Eckes v. Card Prices Update, 736 F.2d 859 (2d Cir.1984). "Card Prices Update" was a publication which comprehensively listed all baseball cards manufactured from 1909 to 1979. The Guide listed 18,000 different cards and in each case furnished the author's estimation of the going market price. The Guide also gave the price for each card according to its condition: "mint, very good/excellent and fair/good." Id. at 860. In addition, the Guide divided all cards into premium (that is, valuable) and common (or less valuable) cards.

At the outset in *Eckes*, we noted our well-established reluctance to grant copyright protection to works of non-fiction—chiefly on the ground that facts may not be copyrighted. See id. at 862; Hoehling v. Universal City Studios, Inc., 618 F.2d 972, 979 (2d Cir.), cert. denied, 449 U.S. 841 (1980); Rosemont Enterprises, Inc. v. Random House, Inc., 366 F.2d 303, 310 (2d Cir.1966), cert. denied 385 U.S. 1009 (1967). See also Harper & Row Publishers, Inc. v. Nation Enterprises, 471 U.S. 539 (1985) (copyright protects only the expression of facts, not the facts themselves). We stated in *Eckes* that "we have been particularly restrictive in the protection of non-fiction works indicating, for example, that the fruits of another's labor in lieu of independent research obtained through the sweat of a researcher's brow, does not merit copyright protection absent, perhaps, wholesale appropriation." *Eckes*, supra, 736 F.2d at 862. The statute thus requires that copyrightability not be determined by the amount of effort the author expends, but rather by the nature of the final result. To grant copyright protection based merely on the "sweat of the author's brow" would risk putting large areas of factual research material off limits and threaten the public's unrestrained access to information.[1]

---

1. FII alleges that Moody's engaged in "wholesale appropriation" under *Eckes*, su- pra, 736 F.2d at 862. Judge Carter did not directly address the question of "wholesale

Applying these principles in *Eckes*, we concluded that the Report was copyrightable, stating that "[w]e have no doubt that appellants exercised selection, creativity and judgment in choosing among the 18,000 or so different baseball cards in order to determine which were the 5,000 premium cards." Id. at 863. Here, in contrast, the district court concluded that FII's efforts fell far short of those involved in the production of the "Card Prices Update." The district court's determination of whether the work was sufficiently original to merit copyright protection was one of fact. * * *. Relying in significant measure on its evaluation of the credibility of witnesses—which we are ill-disposed to disturb on appeal—the district court found that there was insufficient proof of "independent creation" to render the Daily Bond Cards copyrightable. The researchers had five facts to fill in on each card—nothing more and nothing less. They sometimes did minor additional research in order to find these facts, but little "independent creation" was involved. This conclusion is amply supported by the record and certainly not "clearly erroneous." [3]

III.

* * *[In this section of the opinion the Court of Appeals held that the plaintiff's common law claim for misappropriation of its data by copying is preempted by 17 U.S.C. § 301.]

IV.

The judgment of the district court is affirmed.

WEST PUBLISHING CO. v. MEAD DATA CENTRAL, INC.

United States Court of Appeals, Eighth Circuit, 1986.
799 F.2d 1219, certiorari denied 479 U.S. 1070, 107 S.Ct. 962, 93 L.Ed.2d 1010 (1987).

ARNOLD, CIRCUIT JUDGE.

Mead Data Central, Inc. (MDC) appeals from a preliminary injunction issued by the District Court for the District of Minnesota in a copyright infringement action brought by West Publishing Company (West). West's claim is based upon MDC's proposed introduction of

---

appropriation," but it is fair to infer from his observation that "both FII and Moody's regularly used each other for source material" that he would have found no such action by Moody's. The record supports a finding of no "wholesale appropriation." At most Moody's used the FII information to provide one small piece of information for its News Reports. FII's expert witness testified that at the "statistical fringe," he would say that Moody's had copied 91% of the time, but that he was statistically certain that Moody's had copied only 40–50% of the time; Moody's submitted an exhibit

demonstrating that of Moody's 1,400 called bond entries in one year, 789 could not possibly have come from copying FII.

3. Judge Newman suggested hypothetically in his concurrence in Financial Information I, supra, 751 F.2d at 511, that the cards might be copyrightable as a series, but not as individual items. The district court rejected this theory, because there was no coordination or relationship between the cards. This conclusion was also fully supported by the record.

"star pagination," keyed to West's case reports, into the LEXIS system of computer-assisted legal research.

For more than a century, West has been compiling and reporting opinions of state and federal courts. West publishes these opinions in a series of books known as the "National Reporter System." Before it publishes an opinion, West checks the accuracy of case and statutory citations in the opinion and adds parallel citations, prepares headnotes and a synopsis for the opinion, and arranges the opinion in West's style and format. West then assigns its report of each opinion to one of the individual series in the National Reporter System, such as *Federal Reporter, Second Series* or *Bankruptcy Reporter;* this assignment is based on the court and/or the subject matter of the opinion. Next, West assigns the case to a volume in the series, further categorizes and arranges the cases within the volume, and prepares additional materials, such as indices and tables of cases, for each volume. Volumes and pages are numbered sequentially to facilitate precise reference to West reports; citing the proper volume number, series name, and page number communicates the exact location of a West report, or a portion thereof, within the National Reporter System. West represents that upon completion of each volume, it registers a copyright claim with the Register of Copyrights and receives a Certificate of Registration for the volume.

MDC developed, owns, and operates LEXIS, a computer-assisted, on-line legal research service first marketed in 1973. LEXIS, like West's National Reporter System, reports the decisions of state and federal courts. Since LEXIS's inception, MDC has included on the first computer screen of each LEXIS case report the citation to the first page of West's report of the opinion. West concedes that citation to the first page of its reports is a noninfringing "fair use" under 17 U.S.C. § 107, so these citations are not at issue here.

On June 24, 1985, MDC announced that it planned to add "star pagination" to the text of opinions stored in the LEXIS data-base. This new service, named the LEXIS Star Pagination Feature, was to be available to LEXIS users by September or October of 1985. This feature would insert page numbers from West's National Reporter System publications into the body of LEXIS reports, providing "jump" or "pinpoint" citations to the location in West's reporter of the material viewed on LEXIS. Thus, with the LEXIS Star Pagination Feature, LEXIS users would be able to determine the West page number corresponding to the portion of an opinion viewed on LEXIS without ever physically referring to the West publication in which the opinion appears.

In response to MDC's announcement, West brought this action, claiming, *inter alia,* that the LEXIS Star Pagination Feature is an appropriation of West's comprehensive arrangement of case reports in violation of the Copyright Act of 1976, 17 U.S.C. §§ 101–810. West sought, and was granted, a preliminary injunction. West Publishing

Co. v. Mead Data Central, Inc., 616 F.Supp. 1571 (D.Minn.1985). The District Court held that there is a substantial likelihood that West's arrangements of case reports are protected by copyright law, that MDC's copying of West's pagination constitutes copyright infringement, and that MDC's star pagination is not a fair use of West's copyrighted works. The Court further held that the balance of the harms to West and to MDC involved in granting or denying a preliminary injunction weighed in favor of granting an injunction, and that the public interest also favored preliminary injunctive relief. We affirm.

ANALYSIS

* * *

I.

MDC's principal contention here is that there is no likelihood that West will succeed on the merits of its copyright claim. MDC readily concedes that portions of West's National Reporter System publications that are not at issue here, such as headnotes prepared by West, merit copyright protection. Yet, MDC maintains that any aspects of West's reporters affected by the LEXIS Star Pagination Feature are not copyrightable. The dominant chord of MDC's argument is that West claims copyright in mere page numbers. MDC adds that in any event, whether West claims copyright in its case arrangement or simply in its pagination, West's claim must fail because neither case arrangement nor pagination can ever qualify as the original work of an author. Even were this possible, MDC goes on, West's case arrangement and pagination do not in fact meet this standard. Finally, MDC contends that even were West's arrangement of cases protected by copyright, the proposed use of West's page numbers in LEXIS reports would not constitute infringement.

We do not agree with MDC that West's claim here is simply one for copyright in its page numbers. Instead, we concur in the District Court's conclusion that West's arrangement is a copyrightable aspect of its compilation of cases, that the pagination of West's volumes reflects and expresses West's arrangement, and that MDC's intended use of West's page numbers infringes West's copyright in the arrangement.

A. Copyright Protection

The Copyright Act provides copyright protection for "original works of authorship fixed in any tangible medium of expression." 17 U.S.C. § 102(a). The standard for "originality" is minimal. It is not necessary that the work be novel or unique, but only that the work have its origin with the author—that it be independently created. * * *

To be the original work of an author, a work must be the product of some "creative intellectual or aesthetic labor." Goldstein v. California, 412 U.S. 546, 561 (1973). However, "a very slight degree of such labor[,]

. . . almost any ingenuity in selection, combination or expression, no matter how crude, humble or obvious, will be sufficient" to make the work copyrightable. M. Nimmer, 1 Nimmer on Copyright, supra, § 1.08[c][1]; *id.,* § 1.06. See Rockford Map Publishers v. Directory Service Company, 768 F.2d 145, 148–149 (7th Cir.1985) (map based on Agriculture Department photographs and legal descriptions is copyrightable, no matter how quickly or with what little effort it is produced), cert. denied, 474 U.S. 1061 (1986); Universal Athletic Sales Co. v. Salkeld, 511 F.2d 904, 908 (3d Cir.) ("even a modicum of creativity may suffice for a work to be protected"), cert. denied, 423 U.S. 863 (1975).

MDC argues that case arrangement is per se uncopyrightable because it cannot meet these standards. However, it is apparent on the face of the Copyright Act that it is possible for an arrangement of pre-existing materials to be an independently produced work of intellectual creation. Section 103 of the Act, 17 U.S.C. § 103, establishes that "the subject matter of copyright . . . includes compilations and derivative works." * * * An arrangement of opinions in a case reporter, no less than a compilation and arrangement of Shakespeare's sonnets, can qualify for copyright protection.

We find support for this view in Callaghan v. Myers, 128 U.S. 617 (1888), which indicates that an original arrangement of opinions is copyrightable whenever it is the product of labor, talent, or judgment. The plaintiff in that case, Myers, held copyrights for several volumes of reports of the Supreme Court of Illinois. He had purchased these rights from the official reporter of that Court, who had prepared the volumes. In addition to the Court's opinions, the volumes contained a substantial amount of material original to the reporter, including headnotes, statements of facts, tables of cases, indices, and so on. Myers brought an infringement action against the publishers of a competing reporter of Illinois Supreme Court opinions who had copied from Myers's reports material created by the official reporter, as well as the arrangement and pagination of some volumes. The trial court found Myers's copyrights valid and infringed. The Supreme Court affirmed, holding that the fact that Myers sought to protect material prepared by the official court reporter did not bar his claim, since no Illinois legislation forbade the reporter to obtain a copyright for matter that was the product of his intellectual labor. 128 U.S. at 646–647.

As MDC points out, the treatment of case arrangement and pagination in Callaghan was not crucial to the Court's decision, since the defendants had also made use of other portions of Myers's volumes, such as headnotes and statements of facts. Nonetheless, we find Callaghan's discussion of the copyrightability of case arrangements instructive. The Supreme Court noted that while the reporter could claim no copyright in the opinions themselves, 128 U.S. at 649 citing Wheaton v. Peters, 33 U.S. 591, 668 (1834), he could copyright other portions of his reports. Mr. Justice Blatchford wrote that, in addition to headnotes, statements of facts, arguments of counsel, case tables, and indices,

> "[s]uch work of the reporter, which may be the lawful subject of copyright, comprehends . . . the order of arrangement of the cases, the division of the reports into volumes, the numbering *and paging* of the volumes, the table of the cases cited in the opinions, (where such table is made,) and the subdivision of the index into appropriate, condensed titles, involving the distribution of the subjects of the various head-notes, and cross-references, where such exist."

Callaghan, 128 U.S. at 649 (emphasis ours).

Later in its opinion, however, when considering several volumes that Myers claimed the defendants had infringed by copying their case arrangement and pagination, the Court quoted with approval the opinion of the Circuit Court, which stated:

> "Undoubtedly, in some cases, where are involved labor, talent, judgment, the classification and disposition of subjects in a book entitle it to a copyright. But the arrangement of law cases and the paging of the book may depend simply on the will of the printer, of the reporter, or publisher, or the order in which the cases have been decided, or upon other accidental circumstances."

128 U.S. at 662 quoting Myers v. Callaghan, 20 Fed. 441, 442 (C.C. N.D.Ill.1883). Evaluating the volumes at issue, the Circuit Court concluded that their case arrangement and pagination involved little labor; it therefore found the defendants' copying of the case arrangement and pagination of Myers's volumes not an independent infringement, but a matter to be considered in connection with other similarities in the parties' reporters. Id. The teaching of *Callaghan* with respect to the issues before us does not come through with unmistakable clarity. But as we read it, *Callaghan* establishes at least that there is no *per se* rule excluding case arrangement from copyright protection, and that instead, in each case the arrangement must be evaluated in light of the originality and intellectual-creation standards.

* * *

Having determined that there is no per se rule that case arrangements are not copyrightable, we turn to examine the District Court's findings that West's arrangements in fact meet originality and intellectual-creation requirements.

West publishes opinions not from just one court, but from every state and all the federal courts in the United States. As it collects these opinions, West separates the decisions of state courts from federal-court decisions. West further divides the federal opinions and the state opinions and then assigns them to the appropriate West reporter series. State court decisions are divided by geographic region and assigned to West's corresponding regional reporter. Federal decisions are first divided by the level of the court they come from into district court decisions, court of appeals decisions, and Supreme Court decisions; Court of Claims and military court decisions are also separated out. Before being assigned to a reporter, district court decisions are subdivided according to subject matter into bankruptcy decisions, federal rules decisions, and decisions on other topics. After an opinion is assigned to a reporter, it is assigned to a volume of the reporter and then arranged within the volume. Federal court of appeals decisions, for example, are arranged according to circuit within each volume of West's *Federal Reporter, Second Series*, though there may be more than one group of each circuit's opinions in each volume.

We conclude, as did the District Court, that the arrangement West produces through this process is the result of considerable labor, talent, and judgment. As discussed above, to meet intellectual-creation requirements a work need only be the product of a modicum of intellectual labor; West's case arrangements easily meet this standard. Further, since there is no allegation that West copies its case arrangements from some other source, the requirement of originality poses no obstacle to copyrighting the arrangements. In the end, MDC's position must stand or fall on its insistence that all West seeks to protect is numbers on pages. If this is a correct characterization, MDC wins: two always comes after one, and no one can copyright the mere sequence of Arabic numbers. As MDC points out, the specific goal of this suit is to protect some of West's page numbers, those occurring within the body of individual court opinions. But protection for the numbers is not sought for their own sake. It is sought, rather, because access to these particular numbers—the "jump cites"—would give users of LEXIS a large part of what West has spent so much labor and industry in compiling, and would pro tanto reduce anyone's need to buy West's books. The key to this case, then, is not whether numbers are copyrightable, but whether the copyright on the books as a whole is infringed by the unauthorized appropriation of these particular numbers. On the record before us (and subject to reconsideration if materially new evidence comes in at the plenary trial on the merits), the District Court's findings of fact relevant to this issue are supportable. We therefore hold (again subject to reexamination after the record has closed) that West's case arrangements, an important part of which is internal page citations, are original works of authorship entitled to copyright protection.

* * *

Affirmed.

NOTES

1. Is *West* consistent with *FII?* Substantially more expertise and effort is required to compile the West reporters than the FII bond redemption cards. But the only issue in *West* is the protection of the page numbers, and surely the page numbers fall out as a purely mechanical consequence of all the other decisions made in the editing process: the number of cases, their sequence, the extent of the summaries and notes, the size of the type, the page format and so

on. Is the key distinction suggested by note 3 in *FII,* supra page 605? That is, Lexis proposed to take the entire system of page numbers? Is there a distinction between copying the citation (as Lexis had done without provoking litigation) and copying *every* page number? Does this explain the court's stress in *West,* supra page 605, on the fact that if Lexis can offer the West page numbers, it will reduce the incentive to purchase West's books because there will be no need to consult the West volumes?

In a passage deleted from the *West* opinion the court distinguished the case of Toro Co. v. R & R Products Co., 787 F.2d 1208 (8th Cir.1986). In that case Toro sued a manufacturer of replacement parts who used the Toro part numbers to identify its parts. The court held that Toro's copyright on its parts numbering system was invalid for lack of originality. The evidence showed that part numbers were assigned in a completely random manner. In *West* the court distinguished *Toro* on the ground that "the copyright we recognize here is in West's arrangement, not in its numbering system; MDC's use of West's page numbers is problematic because it infringes West's copyrighted arrangement, not because the numbers themselves are copyrighted." Suppose Toro had had a system for assigning parts numbers, i.e. wheel parts begin with 1, engine parts with 2, mower parts with 3, etc. Would that have been sufficient creativity?

2. After the principal opinion the case was settled and Lexis agreed not to introduce pagination information based on West's reporters. Lexis then introduced its own system of citation called Lexis cites. If you were a judge considering a court rule on citation practice, would you accept citations to either the West reporters or Lexis? Would your answer be affected by whether or not you and your colleagues had cost-free access to Lexis? Should the legal profession insist upon page citations to West's reporter system if West claims exclusive rights in that system of citation?

3. In Matthew Bender & Co. v. Kluwer Law Book Publishers, 672 F.Supp. 107 (S.D.N.Y.1987) the court relied upon *FII* to find that a compilation of information about personal injury awards divided by body part categories and other information about the cases was not protected by copyright.

4. In spite of the "black letter" rule that no level of creativity or originality is required for copyright protection, the courts intermittently suggest that there is some level of authorship required in cases involving compilations of various types, derivative works, and simple commercial designs. This probably reflects a poorly-articulated judgment that some items are so trivial as to not merit protection, much less the time required for the judge to address the case. Recent examples: Sherry Mfg. Co. v. Towel King of Florida, Inc., 753 F.2d 1565 (11th Cir.1985) (copyright on a beach towel imprinted with palm trees, beach and sailboat invalid for lack of originality); John Muller & Co. v. New York Arrows Soccer Team, Inc., 802 F.2d 989 (8th Cir.1986) (Registrar of Copyrights can refuse to register a logo for the New York Arrows soccer team, consisting of four angled lines which form an arrow and the word "Arrows" in cursive script below the arrow); and Magic Marketing, Inc. v. Mailing Services of Pittsburgh, Inc., 634 F.Supp. 769 (W.D.Pa.1986) (envelopes printed with solid black stripes and a few words such as "Priority Message" or "Gift Check" did not exhibit the minimal level of creativity necessary).

5. Some cases relating to catalogues, directories, maps and other compilations of information have long expressed this theme. The statutes have always been clear that they are to be protected, although the merit of a compilation

lies in its fidelity to the underlying information compiled rather than in any originality or creativity. Think, for instance, of an alphabetized directory or of an accurate map using conventional cartographic symbols. What has the author contributed? Certainly not the underlying information (at least if it is accurate). Certainly not the method of alphabetization or the methods of cartography. The only discernable contribution of this author is the labor and effort that has gone into making the work. This line of reasoning led some courts to suggest that works of this type require at least some original work or effort to be copyrightable. E.g., Amsterdam v. Triangle Publications, Inc., 189 F.2d 104 (3d Cir.1951) ("modicum of creative work" required for map), a standard echoed in O.W. Donald v. Zack Meyer's T.V. Sales and Service, 426 F.2d 1027 (5th Cir.1970), holding a copyright on a form for a conditional sales agreement invalid for lack of originality. The case law, however, keeps returning to the contrary proposition. For instance, the Ninth Circuit expressly refused to follow *Amsterdam* in United States v. Hamilton, 583 F.2d 448 (9th Cir.1978). The application of the copyright law to such "fact works" was carefully summarized and analyzed in Robert A. Gorman, Copyright Protection for the Collection and Representation of Facts, 76 Harv.L.Rev. 1569 (1963). The meaning of copyright in this context is further clarified by § 103, which makes it clear that the copyright in such works "extends only to the material contributed by the author of such work, as distinguished from preexisting material employed in the work."

6. Originality appears to survive as an operative test of copyright validity in the case of derivative works. See L. Batlin & Son, Inc. v. Synder, 536 F.2d 486 (2d Cir.1976), in which the Second Circuit, sitting en banc, held a copyright on a plastic Uncle Sam bank invalid because it was a nearly exact (but reduced scale) reproduction of an antique metal bank. Batlin was followed in Gracen v. The Bradford Exchange, 698 F.2d 300 (7th Cir.1983), holding a copyright on a painting depicting Judy Garland as Dorothy in the movie The Wizard of Oz invalid for lack of originality. Judge Posner, writing for the Court, said: "[T]he concept of originality in copyright law has as one would expect a legal rather than aesthetic function—to prevent overlapping claims. * * * Suppose Artist A produces a reproduction of the Mona Lisa, a painting in the public domain, which differs slightly from the original. B also makes a reproduction of the Mona Lisa. A, who has copyrighted his derivative work, sues B for infringement. B's defense is that he was copying the original, not A's reproduction. But if the difference between the original and A's reproduction is slight, the difference between A's and B's reproductions will also be slight, so that if B had access to A's reproductions the trier of fact will be hard-pressed to decide whether B was copying A or copying the Mona Lisa itself." 698 F.2d 304. But why couldn't this problem be handled by according the copyright owner no presumption of copying from similarity in this situation? Note the similarity of this hypothetical to the Bleistein case, supra page 585.

7. Computers and telecommunications have made it possible to offer widespread access to large and current databases to many different users without the need to distribute large, costly and quickly outdated books. Is copyright protection necessary to create sufficient incentives to offer and maintain these services? Or can providers of these services handle the problem by requiring all of their customers to sign agreements limiting their use of the information?

8. In Feist Publications, Inc. v. Rural Telephone Service Co., 111 S.Ct. 40 (1990), the Supreme Court granted certiorari to consider whether the "copy-

right in a telephone directory by a telephone company prevents access to that directory as a source of names and numbers to compile a competing directory, or does copyright protection extend only to selection, coordination, or arrangement of those names and numbers." In an unpublished opinion, the Tenth Circuit held that defendant's differently organized directory infringed plaintiff's copyright.

PROBLEM

Can computer output be copyrighted? Can a machine be an "author?" Can the machine operator "adopt" the output as his own. Consider, for instance, whether a computer generated table of random numbers is copyrightable.

B. INFRINGEMENT

As the materials in the previous section repeatedly illustrate, Congress has imposed few limits on copyrightable subject matter, and the courts have considered it unwise to imply any, sensibly recognizing the difficulty of separating good from bad works. To conclude that a work is copyrightable, however, says little about the scope of the protection actually conferred. In this section we turn to the issue of what uses of the copyrighted work infringe, i.e. what uses are in violation of the rights conferred by the statute?

Whether or not a work protected by copyright has been infringed depends on three questions.

1. Has one of the exclusive rights of the copyright owner been violated?

The copyright law does not give to the copyright owner the exclusive right to control all uses of his work. An infringer must have made some use which is within the scope of the exclusive rights conferred by § 106. To illustrate, you will be relieved to know that you are not infringing the copyright on this book by reading it. There is no exclusive right to read.

2. Is the use of the work of a type that infringes the copyright?

In brief, an infringement must have been taken from the copyrighted work and must constitute a taking of the protected elements of the work.

3. Is the use authorized by a provision of §§ 107 through 118?

The scope of the exclusive rights conferred by § 106 is limited by §§ 107 through 118. An example is the right of an owner of copy to resell the copy under § 109(a). Another example is the doctrine of fair use, now codified in § 107. For example, if you write into your notes verbatim short passages from this book, you will have violated § 106(1) because you will have made a copy. But you will not have infringed because that is a classic example of "fair use."

(1) THE EXCLUSIVE RIGHTS

HOUSE REPORT NO. 94–1476
PAGES 61–65.

SECTION 106. EXCLUSIVE RIGHTS IN COPYRIGHTED WORKS

General Scope of Copyright

The five fundamental rights that the bill gives to copyright own-ers—the exclusive rights of reproduction, adaptation, publication, per-formance, and display—are stated generally in section 106. These exclusive rights, which comprise the so-called "bundle of rights" that is a copyright, are cumulative and may overlap in some cases. * * *

The approach of the bill is to set forth the copyright owner's exclusive rights in broad terms in section 106, and then to provide various limitations, qualifications, or exemptions in the 12 sections that follow. Thus, everything in section 106 is made "subject to sections 107 through 118," and must be read in conjunction with those provisions. [Sections 119 and 120 were added in later amendments to the 1976 act.]

The exclusive rights accorded to a copyright owner under section 106 are "to do and to authorize" any of the activities specified in the five numbered clauses. Use of the phrase "to authorize" is intended to avoid any questions as to the liability of contributory infringers. For example, a person who lawfully acquires an authorized copy of a motion picture would be an infringer if he or she engages in the business of renting it to others for purposes of unauthorized public performance.

Rights of Reproduction, Adaptation, and Publication

The first three clauses of section 106, which cover all rights under a copyright except those of performance and display, extend to every kind of copyrighted work. The exclusive rights encompassed by these clauses, though closely related, are independent; they can generally be characterized as rights of copying, recording, adaptation, and publish-ing. A single act of infringement may violate all of these rights at once, as where a publisher reproduces, adapts, and sells copies of a person's copyrighted work as part of a publishing venture. Infringe-ment takes place when any one of the rights is violated: where, for example, a printer reproduces copies without selling them or a retailer sells copies without having anything to do with their reproduction. The references to "copies or phonorecords," although in the plural, are intended here and throughout the bill to include the singular (1 U.S.C. § 1).

Reproduction.—Read together with the relevant definitions in sec-tion 101, the right "to reproduce the copyrighted work in copies or phonorecords" means the right to produce a material object in which the work is duplicated, transcribed, imitated, or simulated in a fixed form from which it can be "perceived, reproduced, or otherwise commu-nicated, either directly or with the aid of a machine or device." As under the present law, a copyrighted work would be infringed by reproducing it in whole or in any substantial part, and by duplicating it exactly or by imitation or simulation. Wide departures or variations from the copyrighted works would still be an infringement as long as the author's "expression" rather than merely the author's "ideas" are taken. An exception to this general principle, applicable to the reproduction of copyrighted sound recordings, is specified in section 114.

"Reproduction" under clause (1) of section 106 is to be distinguished from "display" under clause (5). For a work to be "reproduced," its fixation in tangible form must be "sufficiently permanent or stable to permit it to be perceived, reproduced, or otherwise communicated for a period of more than transitory duration." Thus, the showing of images on a screen or tube would not be a violation of clause (1), although it might come within the scope of clause (5).

Preparation of Derivative Works.—The exclusive right to prepare derivative works, specified separately in clause (2) of section 106, overlaps the exclusive right of reproduction to some extent. It is broader than that right, however, in the sense that reproduction requires fixation in copies or phonorecords, whereas the preparation of a derivative work, such as a ballet, pantomime, or improvised performance, may be an infringement even though nothing is ever fixed in tangible form.

To be an infringement the "derivative work" must be "based upon the copyrighted work," and the definition in section 101 refers to "a translation, musical arrangement, dramatization, fictionalization, motion picture version, sound recording, art reproduction, abridgment, condensation, or any other form in which a work may be recast, transformed, or adapted." Thus, to constitute a violation of section 106(2), the infringing work must incorporate a portion of the copyrighted work in some form; for example, a detailed commentary on a work or a programmatic musical composition inspired by a novel would not normally constitute infringements under this clause.

* * *

Public Distribution.—Clause (3) of section 106 establishes the exclusive right of publications: The right "to distribute copies or phonorecords of the copyrighted work to the public by sale or other transfer of ownership, or by rental, lease, or lending." Under this provision the copyright owner would have the right to control the first public distribution of an authorized copy or phonorecord of his work, whether by sale, gift, loan, or some rental or lease arrangement. Likewise, any unauthorized public distribution of copies or phonorecords that were unlawfully made would be an infringement. As section 109 makes clear, however, the copyright owner's rights under section 106(3) cease with respect to a particular copy or phonorecord once he has parted with ownership of it.

Rights of Public Performance and Display

Performing Rights and the "For Profit" Limitation.—The right of public performance under section 106(4) extends to "literary, musical, dramatic, and choreographic works, pantomimes, and motion pictures and other audiovisual works and sound recordings" and, unlike the equivalent provisions now in effect, is not limited by any "for profit" requirement. The approach of the bill, as in many foreign laws, is first to state the public performance right in broad terms, and then to provide specific exemptions for educational and other nonprofit uses.

This approach is more reasonable than the outright exemption of the 1909 statute. The line between commercial and "nonprofit" organizations is increasingly difficult to draw. Many "non-profit" organizations are highly subsidized and capable of paying royalties, and the widespread public exploitation of copyrighted works by public broadcasters and other noncommercial organizations is likely to grow. In addition to these trends, it is worth noting that performances and displays are continuing to supplant markets for printed copies and that in the future a broad "not for profit" exemption could not only hurt authors but could dry up their incentive to write.

The exclusive right of public performance is expanded to include not only motion pictures, including works [such as] records on film, video tape, and video disks, but also audiovisual works such as filmstrips and sets of slides. This provision of section 106(4), which is consistent with the assimilation of motion pictures to audiovisual works throughout the bill, is also related to amendments of the definitions of "display" and "perform" discussed below. The important issue of performing rights in sound recordings is discussed in connection with section 114.

Right of Public Display.—Clause (5) of section 106 represents the first explicit statutory recognition in American copyright law of an exclusive right to show a copyrighted work, or an image of it, to the public. The existence or extent of this right under the present statute is uncertain and subject to challenge. The bill would give the owners of copyright in "literary, musical, dramatic, and choreographic works, pantomimes, and pictorial, graphic, or sculptural works", including the individual images of a motion picture or other audiovisual work, the exclusive right "to display the copyrighted work publicly."

Definitions

Under the definitions of "perform," "display," "publicly," and "transmit" in section 101, the concepts of public performance and public display cover not only the initial rendition or showing, but also any further act by which that rendition or showing is transmitted or communicated to the public. Thus, for example: a singer is performing when he or she sings a song; a broadcasting network is performing when it transmits his or her performance (whether simultaneously or from records); a local broadcaster is performing when it transmits the network broadcast; a cable television system is performing when it retransmits the broadcast to its subscribers; and any individual is performing whenever he or she plays a phonorecord embodying the performance or communicates the performance by turning on a receiving set. Although any act by which the initial performance or display is transmitted, repeated, or made to recur would itself be a "performance" or "display" under the bill, it would not be actionable as an infringement unless it were done "publicly," as defined in section 101. Certain other performances and displays, in addition to those that are "private," are exempted or given qualified copyright control under sections 107 through 118.

To "perform" a work, under the definition in section 101, includes reading a literary work aloud, singing or playing music, dancing a ballet or other choreographic work, and acting out a dramatic work or pantomime. A performance may be accomplished "either directly or by means of any device or process," including all kinds of equipment for reproducing or amplifying sounds or visual images, any sort of transmitting apparatus, any type of electronic retrieval system, and any other techniques and systems not yet in use or even invented.

The definition of "perform" in relation to "a motion picture or other audio visual work" is "to show its images in any sequence or to make the sounds accompanying it audible." The showing of portions of a motion picture, filmstrip, or slide set must therefore be sequential to constitute a "performance" rather than a "display", but no particular order need be maintained. The purely aural performance of a motion picture sound track, or of the sound portions of an audiovisual work, would constitute a performance of the "motion picture or other audiovisual work"; but, where some of the sounds have been reproduced separately on phonorecords, a performance from the phonorecord would not constitute performance of the motion picture or audiovisual work.

The corresponding definition of "display" covers any showing of a "copy" of the work, "either directly or by means of a film, slide, television image, or any other device or process." Since "copies" are defined as including the material object "in which the work is first fixed," the right of public display applies to original works of art as well as to reproductions of them. With respect to motion pictures and other audiovisual works, it is a "display" (rather than a "performance") to show their "individual images nonsequentially." In addition to the direct showings of a copy of a work, "display" would include the projection of an image on a screen or other surface by any method, the transmission of an image by electronic or other means, and the showing of an image on a cathode ray tube, or similar viewing apparatus connected with any sort of information storage and retrieval system.

Under clause (1) of the definition of "publicly" in section 101, a performance or display is "public" if it takes place "at a place open to the public or at any place where a substantial number of persons outside of a normal circle of a family and its social acquaintances is gathered." One of the principal purposes of the definition was to make clear that, contrary to the decision in Metro-Goldwyn-Mayer Distributing Corp. v. Wyatt, 21 C.O.Bull. 203 (D.Md.1932), performances in "semipublic" places such as clubs, lodges, factories, summer camps, and schools are "public performances" subject to copyright control. The term "a family" in this context would include an individual living alone, so that a gathering confined to the individual's social acquaintances would normally be regarded as private. Routine meetings of businesses and governmental personnel would be excluded because they do not represent the gathering of a "substantial number of persons."

Clause (2) of the definition of "publicly" in section 101 makes clear that the concepts of public performance and public display include not only performances and displays that occur initially in a public place, but also acts that transmit or otherwise communicate a performance or display of the work to the public by means of any device or process. The definition of "transmit"—to communicate a performance or display "by any device or process whereby images or sound are received beyond the place from which they are sent"—is broad enough to include all conceivable forms and combinations of wired or wireless communications media, including but by no means limited to radio and television broadcasting as we know them. Each and every method by which the images or sounds comprising a performance or display are picked up and conveyed is a "transmission," and if the transmission reaches the public in * * * [any] form, the case comes within the scope of clauses (4) or (5) of section 106.

Under the bill, as under the present law, a performance made available by transmission to the public at large is "public" even though the recipients are not gathered in a single place, and even if there is no proof that any of the potential recipients was operating his receiving apparatus at the time of the transmission. The same principles apply whenever the potential recipients of the transmission represent a limited segment of the public, such as the occupants of hotel rooms or the subscribers of a cable television service. Clause (2) of the definition of "publicly" is applicable "whether the members of the public capable of receiving the performance or display receive it in the same place or in separate places and at the same time or at different times."

HOUSE REPORT NO. 94–1476
PAGE 106.

SECTION 114. SCOPE OF EXCLUSIVE RIGHTS IN SOUND RECORDINGS

Subsection (a) of Section 114 specifies that the exclusive rights of the owner of copyright in a sound recording are limited to the rights to reproduce the sound recording in copies or phonorecords, to prepare derivative works based on the copyrighted sound recording, and to distribute copies or phonorecords of the sound recording to the public. Subsection (a) states explicitly that the owner's rights "do not include any right of performance under section 106(4)." The Committee considered at length the arguments in favor of establishing a limited performance right, in the form of a compulsory license, for copyrighted sound recordings, but concluded that the problem requires further study.

*   *   *

Subsection (b) of section 114 makes clear that statutory protection for sound recordings extends only to the particular sounds of which the recording consists, and would not prevent a separate recording of another performance in which those sounds are imitated. Thus, infringement takes place whenever all or any substantial portion of the actual sounds that go to make up a copyrighted sound recording are reproduced in phonorecords by repressing, transcribing, recapturing off the air, or any other method, or by reproducing them in the soundtrack or audio portion of a motion picture or other audiovisual work. Mere imitation of a recorded performance would not constitute a copyright infringement even where one performer deliberately sets out to simulate another's performance as exactly as possible.

Under section 114, the exclusive right of owner of copyright in a sound recording to prepare derivative works based on the copyrighted sound recording is recognized. However, in view of the expressed intention not to give exclusive rights against imitative or simulated performances and recordings, the Committee adopted an amendment to make clear the scope of rights under section 106(2) in this context. Section 114(b) provides that the "exclusive right of the owner of copyright in a sound recording under clause (2) of section 106 is limited to the right to prepare a derivative work in which the actual sounds fixed in the sound recording are rearranged, remixed, or otherwise altered in sequence or quality."

Another amendment deals with the use of copyrighted sound recordings "included in educational television and radio programs *   *   * distributed or transmitted by or through public broadcasting entities." This use of recordings is permissible without authorization from the owner of copyright in the sound recording, as long as "copies or phonorecords of said programs are not commercially distributed by or through public broadcasting entities to the general public."

MIRAGE EDITIONS, INC. v. ALBUQUERQUE A.R.T. CO.

United States Court of Appeals, Ninth Circuit, 1988.
856 F.2d 1341, certiorari denied 489 U.S. 1018, 109 S.Ct. 1135, 103 L.Ed.2d 196
(1989).

BRUNETTI, CIRCUIT JUDGE:

Albuquerque A.R.T. (appellant or A.R.T.) appeals the district court's granting of summary judgment in favor of appellees Mirage, Dumas, and Van Der Marck (Mirage). The district court, in granting summary judgment, found that appellant had infringed Mirage's copyright and issued an order enjoining appellant from further infringing Mirage's copyright.

Patrick Nagel was an artist whose works appeared in many media including lithographs, posters, serigraphs, and as graphic art in many magazines, most notably Playboy. Nagel died in 1984. * * *. Mirage is the exclusive publisher of Nagel's works and also owns the copyrights to many of those works. * * *. Appellee Alfred Van Der Marck Editions, Inc. is the licensee of Dumas [Nagel's widow] and Mirage and the publisher of the commemorative book entitled *NAGEL: The Art of Patrick Nagel* ("the book"), which is a compilation of selected copyrighted individual art works and personal commentaries.

Since 1984, the primary business of appellant has consisted of: 1) purchasing artwork prints or books including good quality artwork page prints therein; 2) gluing each individual print or page print onto a rectangular sheet of black plastic material exposing a narrow black margin around the print; 3) gluing the black sheet with print onto a major surface of a rectangular white ceramic tile; 4) applying a transparent plastic film over the print, black sheet and ceramic tile surface; and 5) offering the tile with artwork mounted thereon for sale in the retail market.

It is undisputed, in this action, that appellant did the above process with the Nagel book. The appellant removed selected pages from the book, mounted them individually onto ceramic tiles and sold the tiles at retail.

Mirage * * * brought an action alleging infringement of registered copyrights in the artwork of Nagel and in the book. Mirage also alleged trademark infringement and unfair competition under the Lanham Act * * * and the state law of unfair competition * * *.

Appellant moved for summary judgment on the Lanham Act and Copyright Act causes of action. The district court granted summary judgment as to the Lanham Act cause of action but denied summary judgment on the copyright cause of action. Mirage then moved for summary judgment on the copyright claim which was granted. The court also enjoined appellants from removing individual art images from the book, mounting each individual image onto a separate tile and advertising for sale and/or selling the tiles with the images mounted thereon.

* * *

The district court concluded appellant infringed the copyrights in the individual images through its tile-preparing process and also concluded that the resulting products comprised derivative works.

Appellant contends that there has been no copyright infringement because (1) its tiles are not derivative works, and (2) the "first sale" doctrine precludes a finding of infringement.

The Copyright Act of 1976, 17 U.S.C. § 101 defines a derivative work as:

(A) work based upon one or more preexisting works such as a translation, musical arrangement, dramatization, fictionalization, motion picture version, sound recording, art reproduction, abridgment, condensation *or any other form in which a work may be recast, transformed, or adapted.* A work consisting of editorial revisions, annotations, elaborations, or other modifications which, as a whole, represent an original work of authorship is a "derivative work."

(Emphasis added).

The protection of derivative rights extends beyond mere protection against unauthorized copying to include the right to make other versions of, perform, or exhibit the work. Lone Ranger Television v. Program Radio Corp., 740 F.2d 718, 722 (9th Cir.1984); Russell v. Price, 612 F.2d 1123, 1128 n. 16 (9th Cir.1979).

Melvin Nimmer in his treatise on copyright law wrote:

"[A] work will be considered a derivative work only if it would be considered an infringing work if the material which it has derived from a preexisting work had been taken without the consent of a copyright proprietor of such preexisting work."

1 *Nimmer on Copyright* § 3.01 (1986) * * *.

What appellant has clearly done here is to make another version of Nagel's art works, *Lone Ranger,* supra, and that amounts to preparation of a derivative work. By borrowing and mounting the preexisting, copyrighted individual art images without the consent of the copyright proprietors—Mirage and Dumas as to the art works and Van Der Marck as to the book—appellant has prepared a derivative work and infringed the subject copyrights. Nimmer, supra.

Appellant's contention that since it has not engaged in "art reproduction" and therefore its tiles are not derivative works is not fully dispositive of this issue. Appellant has ignored the disjunctive phrase "or any other form in which a work may be recast, transformed or adapted." The legislative history of the Copyright Act of 1976 indicates that Congress intended that for a violation of the right to prepare derivative works to occur "the infringing work must incorporate a portion of the copyrighted work in *some form.*" 1976 U.S. Code Cong. & Admin. News 5659, 5675. (emphasis added). The language "recast, transformed or adapted" seems to encompass other alternatives besides simple art reproduction. By removing the individual images from the book and placing them on the tiles, perhaps the appellant has not accomplished reproduction. We conclude, though, that appellant has certainly recast or transformed the individual images by incorporating them into its tile-preparing process.

The "first sale" doctrine, which appellant also relies on in its contention that no copyright infringement has occurred, appears at 17 U.S.C. § 109(a). * * *

In United States v. Wise, 550 F.2d 1180 (9th Cir.1977), which concerned a criminal prosecution under the pre–1976 Copyright Act, this court held that:

"[T]he 'first sale' doctrine provides that where a copyright owner parts with title to a particular copy of his copyrighted work, he divests himself of his exclusive right to vend that particular copy. While the proprietor's other copyright rights (reprinting, copying, etc.) remain unimpaired, the exclusive right to vend the transferred copy rests with the vendee, who is not restricted by statute from further transfers of that copy."

550 F.2d at 1187.

We recognize that, under the "first sale" doctrine as enunciated at 17 U.S.C. § 109(a) and as discussed in *Wise,* appellant can purchase a copy of the Nagel book and subsequently alienate its ownership in that book. However, the right to transfer applies only to the particular copy of the book which appellant has purchased and nothing else. The mere sale of the book to the appellant without a specific transfer by the copyright holder of its exclusive right to prepare derivative works, does not transfer that right to appellant. The derivative works right, remains unimpaired and with the copyright proprietors * * *. As we have previously concluded that appellant's tile-preparing process results in derivative works and as the exclusive right to prepare derivative works belongs to the copyright holder, the "first sale" doctrine does not bar the appellees' copyright infringement claims.

We AFFIRM.

PROBLEMS

1. The result in *Mirage* should be contrasted with the result in C.M. Paula Co. v. Logan, 355 F.Supp. 189 (N.D.Tex.1973), involving similar facts. The court held: no infringement under the 1909 Act. Under the different provisions of that act, the court held that the ceramic plaques involved in that case were not "adaptations." The scope of first sale doctrine suggested by *Mirage* will doubtless result in further litigation on these questions.

2. Can the operators of a hotel make videotapes available to their guests for viewing in the guest rooms, conveniently equipped with a video cassette player? Assume that the tapes have been purchased at a video store where they were sold for home viewing. Would it make any difference if a separate fee was charged for the tape rental? Whether or not a big sign out front said: "Stop in and See our Movies"? Compare Columbia Pictures Indus. v. Professional Real Estate Investors, 228 U.S.P.Q. 743 (C.D.Cal.1986). Can nursing homes show videotapes (purchased or rented) to their residents? See CCH Copyright Law Rep. ¶ 20,600, Agreement on Showing Videotaped Movies in Nursing Homes, Aug. 3, 1990 (major firms in the movie business agreed to license Nursing Homes without charge to view videotaped movies.)

3. Can a photographer make and sell photographs of a performance of a copyrighted work of choreography (explicitly included as a copyrightable work under § 102(4)) without the permission of the owner of the copyright? What exclusive right would be violated? Would the photograph be a "derivative work?" Compare Horgan v. Macmillan, Inc., 789 F.2d 157 (2d Cir.1986).

4. Are you now able to determine which state law doctrines are not "equivalent to any of the exclusive rights within the general scope of copyright" for purposes of § 301?

5. Many computer programs are sold with a licensing agreement in which the buyer "agrees" not to make copies of the program and with built-in copy-protection schemes designed to make it difficult to copy the program. Other companies sell programs with names like "Nibble" that are designed to defeat the protection schemes and make copies of the protected programs. Does the seller of the copy-protected program have any cause of action (under either state or federal law) against the seller or user of the program designed to defeat the copy-protection scheme? Consider that § 117(2) provides that "it is not an infringement for the owner of a copy of a computer program to make or authorize the making of another copy or adaptation of that computer program provided * * * that such new copy or adaptation is for archival purposes only and that all archival copies are destroyed in the event that continued possession of the computer program should cease to be rightful." See Vault Corp. v. Quaid Software Ltd., 847 F.2d 255 (5th Cir. 1988).

(2) THE INFRINGING WORK

In order to infringe a work must

(1) have been taken (the verb "copied" is usually used but we shall use the term "taken" in order to clearly distinguish the technical copyright noun "copy") from the copyrighted work and not from some other source or from an independent imagination; and

(2) have taken those elements of the copyrighted work which are protected by the copyright.

Because a copyright owner is seldom in a position to actually prove that the alleged infringing work was in fact taken from his work, the courts shift the burden of persuasion to the alleged infringer to show that it was not taken upon proof

(1) that the source of the alleged infringing work had access to the plaintiff's work; and

(2) that the alleged infringing work is so similar to aspects of the copyrighted work not otherwise available to the source of the alleged infringing work that it is unlikely to have been created independently.

When the alleged infringing work is not a duplicate of the copyrighted work, a determination of whether protected elements have been taken requires a close analysis of the differences and similarities between the two works.

The statute does not codify the law of infringement.

GASTE v. KAISERMAN

United States Court of Appeals, Second Circuit, 1988.
863 F.2d 1061.

JON O. NEWMAN, CIRCUIT JUDGE:

This appeal involves a copyright infringement action against the composer and publisher of the highly successful popular song "Feelings," brought by Louis Gaste, the composer of an obscure French song written nearly 17 years earlier. The appeal is from a judgment of the District Court for the Southern District of New York (William C. Conner, Judge), entered after a jury found defendants Morris Kaiserman and Fermata International Melodies, Inc. ("Fermata") liable for copyright infringement. The jury awarded damages of $268,000 against Fermata and $233,000 against Kaiserman. The District Court also issued a permanent injunction against further infringement. Judge Conner reduced the damages against Kaiserman to $135,140 after excluding profits attributable to foreign performances. Judge Conner denied defendants' motions for a judgment notwithstanding the verdict or a new trial.

Defendants appeal from Judge Conner's denial of a new trial or judgment notwithstanding the verdict on several grounds. They argue that: * * * (2) plaintiff failed to prove copying [taking] as a matter of law; (3) the District Court incorrectly instructed the jury on the issues of "access" and "striking similarity"; and (4) * * *. For the reasons stated below, we reject appellants' arguments and affirm the judgment.

Background

In 1956, plaintiff-appellee Gaste, a resident and citizen of France, composed the music to a song entitled "Pour Toi" as part of the score of a motion picture Le Feu aux Poudres, which was released in France that same year.[1] Gaste registered the sheet music for the song in the United States Copyright Office in 1957. Neither the movie nor the song, which was published and recorded separately in France, had great success. Worldwide revenues of "Pour Toi" have amounted to less than $15,000.

From France, the scene shifts to Brazil, nearly two decades later. In 1973, the then unheralded and relatively unknown Brazilian singer and composer Morris Kaiserman, known professionally as Morris Albert, composed and recorded the song "Feelings." "Feelings" became a smash hit internationally, winning "gold records" in a number of countries.

Gaste contended at trial that Kaiserman had gained access to Gaste's virtually unknown song through Enrique Lebendiger, the owner of Fermata, which was Kaiserman's publisher. Gaste's evidence, de-

---

1. Gaste did not compose the lyrics to "Pour Toi." His infringement suit involves only the music to the song.

tailed below in the discussion of access, established that Fermata had had some dealings with Gaste's publishing company, Les Editions Louis Gaste, in the 1950s.

Discussion

* * *

II. Copying [Taking]

Appellants next attack the jury's conclusion that they copied Gaste's work. Because copiers are rarely caught red-handed, copying has traditionally been proven circumstantially by proof of access and substantial similarity. * * * Appellants argue that there was insufficient evidence for the jury to find access directly or to infer it from striking similarity.

A. Access. Kaiserman and Fermata argue that Gaste's proof of access was too remote and speculative to have sustained a reasonable finding of access.

The guiding principle in deciding whether to overturn a jury verdict for insufficiency of evidence is " 'whether the evidence is such that, without weighing the credibility of the witnesses or otherwise considering the weight of the evidence, there can be but one conclusion as to the verdict that reasonable men could have reached.' " Mattivi v. South African Marine Corp., 618 F.2d 163, 167 (2d Cir.1980) (quoting Simblest v. Maynard, 427 F.2d 1, 4 (2d Cir.1970)). In the context of copyright, it is well established that there must be evidence of a reasonable possibility of access. Access must be more than a bare possibility and may not be inferred through speculation or conjecture. See Ferguson v. National Broadcasting Co., 584 F.2d 111, 113 (5th Cir. 1978); 3 M. & D. Nimmer, [*Nimmer on Copyright*] § 13.02(A), at 13–12 [(1988)].

In this case, Gaste's principal theory of access was that Fermata's owner, Lebendiger, received a copy of "Pour Toi" in the 1950s, when Gaste was trying to market the song to subpublishers, and that Kaiserman obtained it from Lebendiger in 1973. Georges Henon, a former employee of Gaste who had been responsible for distributing materials to foreign subpublishers, testified that he gave a recording of "Pour Toi" to Lebendiger in France in the 1950s and that he sent copies of the sheet music and record to Lebendiger in Brazil.

Lebendiger testified that he never heard or saw copies of "Pour Toi" prior to the litigation. Defendants also presented several witnesses, including Kaiserman, in an effort to establish that Kaiserman composed "Feelings" in September 1973 and that he had had no contact with Lebendiger's publishing company before that date. The credibility of both this testimony and these witnesses' prior affidavits was significantly undercut, however, when Gaste introduced a contract between Kaiserman and Editora Augusta Ltd., a publishing company owned in part by Lebendiger; the contract was dated July 1, 1973, and Kaiserman's signature was notarized on July 11, 1973. The initial contract for "Feelings" was not signed until May 10, 1974.

Although Gaste's theory of access relies on a somewhat attenuated chain of events extending over a long period of time and distance, we cannot say as a matter of law that the jury could not reasonably conclude that Kaiserman had access to the song through Lebendiger. Access through third parties connected to both a plaintiff and a defendant may be sufficient to prove a defendant's access to a plaintiff's work. * * *. The lapse of time between the original publication of "Pour Toi" and the alleged infringement and the distance between the locations of the two events may make copying less likely but not an unreasonable conclusion. Indeed, a copier may be more likely to plagiarize an obscure song from the distant past and a faraway land than a recent well-known hit.

Kaiserman and Gaste also challenge the District Court's instructions to the jury on the issue of access. Appellants asked for an instruction that would have told the jury it could not base its findings on mere speculation or conjecture. The District Judge declined to give such an instruction, saying he did not want the jurors to think they could not draw inferences from the evidence. Judge Conner did tell the jurors several times, however, that they could find access only if Kaiserman had a "reasonable opportunity" to see or hear "Pour Toi."

We find no error in Judge Conner's instruction. Requiring a finding of a "reasonable opportunity" for access adequately states the appropriate standard. It might have been helpful for the District Court to have added that, although the jurors could draw inferences from the evidence presented, they could not find access on the basis of mere conjecture or surmise. But we do not find that the omission of such a caution rendered the charge misleading or permitted the jury to apply an incorrect standard.

B. Striking Similarity. Appellants argue that the District Court incorrectly permitted the jury to find copying on the basis of "striking similarity." As with access, appellants again challenge both the District Court's instruction and the sufficiency of the evidence.

Judge Conner instructed the jury that if a copyrighted work and an allegedly infringing work are strikingly similar, "then access does not have to be proven." [3] Appellants, relying principally on Selle v. Gibb,

---

3. The District Court's full instruction on striking similarity was as follows: Now, there is one circumstance in which access does not have to be proven. If the two works, that is the copyrighted work and the allegedly infringing work, are what we call strikingly similar, then access does not have to be proven. By striking similarity what we mean is that the two songs are so much alike that the only reasonable explanation for such a great degree of similarity is that the later song was copied from the first. In other words, if they are so nearly alike that it is virtually inconceivable that the second was independently composed without knowledge of the first, then you may find that there was infringement without finding actual access. In other words, you are in effect presuming access from the fact of striking similarity. So what you will have to decide is whether or not the songs are so much alike that it is virtually inconceivable that Feelings was independently composed without any derivation from Pour Toi. That issue as to whether the two works are strikingly simi-

741 F.2d 896, 901 (7th Cir.1984), argue that even where there is striking similarity, there must be at least some other evidence that would establish a "reasonable possibility" that the plaintiff's work was available to the alleged infringer.

In this Circuit, the test for proof of access in cases of striking similarity is less rigorous. In Arnstein v. Porter, 154 F.2d 464 (2d Cir. 1946), Judge Frank said, "In some cases, the similarities between the plaintiff's and defendant's work are so extensive and striking as, *without more*, both to justify an inference of copying and to prove improper appropriation." Id. at 468–69 (emphasis added); see also Ferguson v. National Broadcasting Co., supra, 584 F.2d at 113 ("If the two works are so strikingly similar as to preclude the possibility of independent creation, 'copying' may be proved without a showing of access."); 3 M. & D. Nimmer, supra, § 13.02(B), at 13–17 (criticizing the Selle requirement that there be a "reasonable possibility" of access—not just a "bare possibility"—even in cases of striking similarity).

Appellants contend that undue reliance on striking similarity to show access precludes protection for the author who independently creates a similar work. However, the jury is only permitted to infer access from striking similarity; it need not do so. Though striking similarity alone can raise an inference of copying, that inference must be reasonable in light of all the evidence. A plaintiff has not proved striking similarity sufficient to sustain a finding of copying if the evidence as a whole does not preclude any reasonable possibility of independent creation. See Arnstein v. Porter, supra, 154 F.2d at 468 ("If evidence of access is absent, the similarities must be so striking as to preclude the possibility that plaintiff and defendant independently arrived at the same result."); Ferguson v. National Broadcasting Co., supra, 584 F.2d at 113.

Thus, we find Judge Conner's instruction, taken as a whole, a correct statement of the law. Judge Conner said the issue was whether the plaintiff's proof "preclude(d) any reasonable possibility of independent creation" of the allegedly infringing work, and he instructed the jury to make its determination "on the basis of all of the evidence."

We also conclude that there was sufficient evidence to permit the jury to infer access based on striking similarity. Gaste's proof of striking similarity consisted of both aural renditions of the songs and expert testimony. Gaste's expert testified not merely to common musical phrases in the songs but said that "there is not one measure of 'Feelings' which . . . cannot be traced back to something which occurs in 'Pour Toi.' " He also pointed to a unique musical "fingerprint"—an

lar in the sense that I have defined, in other words, so as to preclude any reasonable possibility of independent creation, is an issue which is to be determined by you on the basis of all of the evidence, including the expert testimony. Judge Conner also instructed the jury that independent creation of a copyrighted song was not infringement because there is no copying and that there is no infringement if the similarities between two songs are the result of the use of common musical sources or techniques.

"evaded resolution" [4]—that occurred in the same place in the two songs. The witness said that while modulation from a minor key to its relative major was very common, he had never seen this particular method of modulation in any other compositions.[5]

Appellants' expert criticized the analytical methods of Gaste's expert and disagreed with his conclusions. But these criticisms go to the weight of the evidence, which, along with the credibility of the witnesses, was for the jury to determine.

In assessing this evidence, we are mindful of the limited number of notes and chords available to composers and the resulting fact that common themes frequently reappear in various compositions, especially in popular music. See Arnstein v. Edward B. Marks Music Corp., 82 F.2d 275, 277 (2d Cir.1936). Thus, striking similarity between pieces of popular music must extend beyond themes that could have been derived from a common source or themes that are so trite as to be likely to reappear in many compositions. See Selle v. Gibb, supra, 741 F.2d at 905.

In their defense, Kaiserman and Fermata presented examples of prior art—by composers ranging from Bach and Schumann to Stan Kenton—to demonstrate that some of the similarities between "Feelings" and "Pour Toi" also appear in other works. But Gaste's expert analyzed these other works and testified that they were not substantially similar. In his opinion, similarity of themes in these works could not explain the extensive similarities between "Feelings" and "Pour Toi." He testified that he did not believe it would be possible to compose "Feelings" without copying from "Pour Toi." The dispute was properly left to the jury.

The judgment of the District Court is affirmed.

NOTE

One of the important differences between the patent and copyright systems is that the copyright system places no burden on the copyright holder to identify the elements of his work for which he claims protection. While 35 U.S.C. § 112 requires the patentee to make "one or more claims particularly pointing out and distinctly claiming the subject matter which the applicant regards as his invention," a copyright owner who has published his work with

---

4. As explained by Gaste's expert, in most compositions, a dominant seventh chord "resolves" or leads into the major or minor chord four tones up. Thus, a B seventh chord would resolve to E minor or major. But in "Pour Toi" and "Feelings," this normal resolution is "evaded." The dominant seventh chord leads to a different key. In "Pour Toi," a B seventh chord resolves to C, in the key of G major. In "Feelings," an E dominant seventh chord, which would normally resolve to an A chord, resolves to C, again in the key of G major.

5. It is axiomatic that copyright protects only an author's expression, not his ideas. Drawing the line between ideas and expression, however, is not always easy, particularly in musical works. The "evaded resolution" described by Gaste's expert is arguably more a musical idea than expression. But the evaded resolution was identically placed in the two songs, and this sequencing of the technique could properly be considered expression.

the appropriate notice is protected against infringement of any part of his work that is protected. To illustrate, a person who publishes a book containing 2 original pages and 300 pages from the public domain is protected against infringement of the 2 pages even if inspection of the book would not have revealed which 2 pages were protected. In patent cases, the issue of the scope of patent rights is often raised by the question: is the claim valid? In copyright, the scope of copyright rights is raised by the question: is the work infringed?

The copyright statute departs narrowly from this approach in § 403, applying to works consisting preponderantly of works of the United States Government.

The failure of the copyright system to require the copyright owner to define the scope of his claimed rights is related to the difference between infringement under the two statutes. A patent is infringed by anyone who makes, uses or sells the claimed invention whether or not it was taken from the patentee. This draconian sweep requires procedural devices to narrow the scope of claimed rights. Copyright infringement, on the other hand, can (at least in theory) be avoided by not "taking."

NICHOLS v. UNIVERSAL PICTURES CORP.

United States Circuit Court of Appeals, Second Circuit, 1930.
45 F.2d 119.

L. HAND, CIRCUIT JUDGE. The plaintiff is the author of a play, "Abie's Irish Rose," which it may be assumed was properly copyrighted under section five, subdivision (d), of the Copyright Act, 17 U.S.C. § 5(d). The defendant produced publicly a motion picture play, "The Cohens and The Kellys," which the plaintiff alleges was taken from it. As we think the defendant's play too unlike the plaintiff's to be an infringement, we may assume, arguendo, that in some details the defendant used the plaintiff's play, as will subsequently appear, though we do not so decide. It therefore becomes necessary to give an outline of the two plays.

"Abie's Irish Rose" presents a Jewish family living in prosperous circumstances in New York. The father, a widower, is in business as a merchant, in which his son and only child helps him. The boy has philandered with young women, who to his father's great disgust have always been Gentiles, for he is obsessed with a passion that his daughter-in-law shall be an orthodox Jewess. When the play opens the son, who has been courting a young Irish Catholic girl, has already married her secretly before a Protestant minister, and is concerned to soften the blow for his father, by securing a favorable impression of his bride, while concealing her faith and race. To accomplish this he introduces her to his father at his home as a Jewess, and lets it appear that he is interested in her, though he conceals the marriage. The girl somewhat reluctantly falls in with the plan; the father takes the bait, becomes infatuated with the girl, concludes that they must marry, and assumes that of course they will, if he so decides. He calls in a rabbi, and prepares for the wedding according to the Jewish rite.

Meanwhile the girl's father, also a widower, who lives in California, and is as intense in his own religious antagonism as the Jew, has been called to New York, supposing that his daughter is to marry an Irishman and a Catholic. Accompanied by a priest, he arrives at the house at the moment when the marriage is being celebrated, but too late to prevent it, and the two fathers, each infuriated by the proposed union of his child to a heretic, fall into unseemly and grotesque antics. The priest and the rabbi become friendly, exchange trite sentiments about religion, and agree that the match is good. Apparently out of abundant caution, the priest celebrates the marriage for a third time, while the girl's father is inveigled away. The second act closes with each father, still outraged, seeking to find some way by which the union, thus trebly insured, may be dissolved.

The last act takes place about a year later, the young couple having meanwhile been abjured by each father, and left to their own resources. They have had twins, a boy and a girl, but their fathers know no more than that a child has been born. At Christmas each, led by his craving to see his grandchild, goes separately to the young folks' home, where they encounter each other, each laden with gifts, one for a boy, the other for a girl. After some slapstick comedy, depending upon the insistence of each that he is right about the sex of the grandchild, they become reconciled when they learn the truth, and that each child is to bear the given name of a grandparent. The curtain falls as the fathers are exchanging amenities, and the Jew giving evidence of an abatement in the strictness of his orthodoxy.

"The Cohens and The Kellys" presents two families, Jewish and Irish, living side by side in the poorer quarters of New York in a state of perpetual enmity. The wives in both cases are still living, and share in the mutual animosity, as do two small sons, and even the respective dogs. The Jews have a daughter, the Irish a son; the Jewish father is in the clothing business; the Irishman is a policeman. The children are in love with each other, and secretly marry, apparently after the play opens. The Jew, being in great financial straits, learns from a lawyer that he has fallen heir to a large fortune from a great-aunt, and moves into a great house, fitted luxuriously. Here he and his family live in vulgar ostentation, and here the Irish boy seeks out his Jewish bride, and is chased away by the angry father. The Jew then abuses the Irishman over the telephone, and both become hysterically excited. The extremity of his feelings makes the Jew sick, so that he must go to Florida for a rest, just before which the daughter discloses her marriage to her mother.

On his return the Jew finds that his daughter has borne a child; at first he suspects the lawyer, but eventually learns the truth and is overcome with anger at such a low alliance. Meanwhile, the Irish family who have been forbidden to see the grandchild, go to the Jew's house, and after a violent scene between the two fathers in which the Jew disowns his daughter, who decides to go back with her husband, the Irishman takes her back with her baby to his own poor lodgings.

The lawyer, who had hoped to marry the Jew's daughter, seeing his plan foiled, tells the Jew that his fortune really belongs to the Irishman, who was also related to the dead woman, but offers to conceal his knowledge, if the Jew will share the loot. This the Jew repudiates, and, leaving the astonished lawyer, walks through the rain to his enemy's house to surrender the property. He arrives in great dejection, tells the truth, and abjectly turns to leave. A reconciliation ensues, the Irishman agreeing to share with him equally. The Jew shows some interest in his grandchild, though this is at most a minor motive in the reconciliation, and the curtain falls while the two are in their cups, the Jew insisting that in the firm name for the business, which they are to carry on jointly, his name shall stand first.

It is of course essential to any protection of literary property, whether at common-law or under the statute, that the right cannot be limited literally to the text, else a plagiarist would escape by immaterial variations. That has never been the law, but, as soon as literal appropriation ceases to be the test, the whole matter is necessarily at large, so that, as was recently well said by a distinguished judge, the decisions cannot help much in a new case. Fendler v. Morosco, 253 N.Y. 281, 292, 171 N.E. 56. When plays are concerned, the plagiarist may excise a separate scene [Daly v. Webster, 56 F. 483 (C.C.A.2); Chappell v. Fields, 210 F. 864 (C.C.A.2); Chatterton v. Cave, L.R. 3 App. Cas. 483]; or he may appropriate part of the dialogue (Warne v. Seebohm, L.R. 39 Ch.D. 73). Then the question is whether the part so taken is "substantial," and therefore not a "fair use" of the copyrighted work; it is the same question as arises in the case of any other copyrighted work. Marks v. Feist, 290 F. 959 (C.C.A.2); Emerson v. Davies, Fed.Cas.No. 4436, 3 Story, 768, 795–797. But when the plagiarist does not take out a block in situ, but an abstract of the whole, decision is more troublesome. Upon any work, and especially upon a play, a great number of patterns of increasing generality will fit equally well, as more and more of the incident is left out. The last may perhaps be no more than the most general statement of what the play is about, and at times might consist only of its title; but there is a point in this series of abstractions where they are no longer protected, since otherwise the playwright could prevent the use of his "ideas," to which, apart from their expression, his property is never extended. Holmes v. Hurst, 174 U.S. 82, 86; Guthrie v. Curlett, 36 F.(2d) 694 (C.C.A.2). Nobody has ever been able to fix that boundary, and nobody ever can. In some cases the question has been treated as though it were analogous to lifting a portion out of the copyrighted work (Rees v. Melville, MacGillivray's Copyright Cases [1911–1916], 168); but the analogy is not a good one, because, though the skeleton is a part of the body, it pervades and supports the whole. In such cases we are rather concerned with the line between expression and what is expressed. As respects plays, the controversy chiefly centers upon the characters and sequence of incident, these being the substance.

We did not in Dymow v. Bolton, 11 F.(2d) 690, hold that a plagiarist was never liable for stealing a plot; that would have been flatly against our rulings in Dam v. Kirk La Shelle Co., 175 F. 902 and Stodart v. Mutual Film Co., 249 F. 513, affirming my decision in (D.C.) 249 F. 507; neither of which we meant to overrule. We found the plot of the second play was too different to infringe, because the most detailed pattern, common to both, eliminated so much from each that its content went into the public domain; and for this reason we said, "this mere subsection of a plot was not susceptible of copyright." But we do not doubt that two plays may correspond in plot closely enough for infringement. How far that correspondence must go is another matter. Nor need we hold that the same may not be true as to the characters, quite independently of the "plot" proper, though, as far as we know, such a case has never arisen. If Twelfth Night were copyrighted, it is quite possible that a second comer might so closely imitate Sir Toby Belch or Malvolio as to infringe, but it would not be enough that for one of his characters he cast a riotous knight who kept wassail to the discomfort of the household, or a vain and foppish steward who became amorous of his mistress. These would be no more than Shakespeare's "ideas" in the play, as little capable of monopoly as Einstein's Doctrine of Relativity, or Darwin's theory of the Origin of Species. It follows that the less developed the characters, the less they can be copyrighted; that is the penalty an author must bear for marking them too indistinctly.

In the two plays at bar we think both as to incident and character, the defendant took no more—assuming that it took anything at all—than the law allowed. The stories are quite different. One is of a religious zealot who insists upon his child's marrying no one outside his faith; opposed by another who is in this respect just like him, and is his foil. Their difference in race is merely an obbligato to the main theme, religion. They sink their differences through grandparental pride and affection. In the other, zealotry is wholly absent; religion does not even appear. It is true that the parents are hostile to each other in part because they differ in race; but the marriage of their son to a Jew does not apparently offend the Irish family at all, and it exacerbates the existing animosity of the Jew, principally because he has become rich, when he learns it. They are reconciled through the honesty of the Jew and the generosity of the Irishman; the grandchild has nothing whatever to do with it. The only matter common to the two is a quarrel between a Jewish and an Irish father, the marriage of their children, the birth of grandchildren and a reconciliation.

If the defendant took so much from the plaintiff, it may well have been because her amazing success seemed to prove that this was a subject of enduring popularity. Even so, granting that the plaintiff's play was wholly original, and assuming that novelty is not essential to a copyright, there is no monopoly in such a background. Though the plaintiff discovered the vein, she could not keep it to herself; so defined, the theme was too generalized an abstraction from what she wrote. It was only a part of her "ideas."

Nor does she fare better as to her characters. It is indeed scarcely credible that she should not have been aware of those stock figures, the low comedy Jew and Irishman. The defendant has not taken from her more than their prototypes have contained for many decades. If so, obviously so to generalize her copyright, would allow her to cover what was not original with her. But we need not hold this as matter of fact, much as we might be justified. Even though we take it that she devised her figures out of her brain de novo, still the defendant was within its rights.

There are but four characters common to both plays, the lovers and the fathers. The lovers are so faintly indicated as to be no more than stage properties. They are loving and fertile; that is really all that can be said of them, and anyone else is quite within his rights if he puts loving and fertile lovers in a play of his own, wherever he gets the cue. The plaintiff's Jew is quite unlike the defendant's. His obsession is his religion, on which depends such racial animosity as he has. He is affectionate, warm and patriarchal. None of these fit the defendant's Jew, who shows affection for his daughter only once, and who has none but the most superficial interest in his grandchild. He is tricky, ostentatious and vulgar, only by misfortune redeemed into honesty. Both are grotesque, extravagant and quarrelsome; both are fond of display; but these common qualities make up only a small part of their simple pictures, no more than any one might lift if he chose. The Irish fathers are even more unlike; the plaintiff's a mere symbol for religious fanaticism and patriarchal pride, scarcely a character at all. Neither quality appears in the defendant's, for while he goes to get his grandchild, it is rather out of a truculent determination not to be forbidden, than from pride in his progeny. For the rest he is only a grotesque hobbledehoy, used for low comedy of the most conventional sort, which any one might borrow, if he chanced not to know the exemplar.

The defendant argues that the case is controlled by my decision in Fisher v. Dillingham (D.C.) 298 F. 145. Neither my brothers nor I wish to throw doubt upon the doctrine of that case, but it is not applicable here. We assume that the plaintiff's play is altogether original, even to an extent that in fact it is hard to believe. We assume further that, so far as it has been anticipated by earlier plays of which she knew nothing, that fact is immaterial. Still, as we have already said, her copyright did not cover everything that might be drawn from her play; its content went to some extent into the public domain. We have to decide how much, and while we are as aware as any one that the line, wherever it is drawn, will seem arbitrary, that is no excuse for not drawing it; it is a question such as courts must answer in nearly all cases. Whatever may be the difficulties a priori, we have no question on which side of the line this case falls. A comedy based upon conflicts between Irish and Jews, into which the marriage of their children enters, is no more susceptible of copyright than the outline of Romeo and Juliet.

The plaintiff has prepared an elaborate analysis of the two plays, showing a "quadrangle" of the common characters, in which each is represented by the emotions which he discovers. She presents the resulting parallelism as proof of infringement, but the adjectives employed are so general as to be quite useless. Take for example the attribute of "love" ascribed to both Jews. The plaintiff has depicted her father as deeply attached to his son, who is his hope and joy; not so, the defendant, whose father's conduct is throughout not actuated by any affection for his daughter, and who is merely once overcome for the moment by her distress when he has violently dismissed her lover. "Anger" covers emotions aroused by quite different occasions in each case; so do "anxiety," "despondency" and "disgust." It is unnecessary to go through the catalogue for emotions are too much colored by their causes to be a test when used so broadly. This is not the proper approach to a solution; it must be more ingenuous, more like that of a spectator, who would rely upon the complex of his impressions of each character.

We cannot approve the length of the record, which was due chiefly to the use of expert witnesses. Argument is argument whether in the box or at the bar, and its proper place is the last. The testimony of an expert upon such issues, especially his cross-examination, greatly extends the trial and contributes nothing which cannot be better heard after the evidence is all submitted. It ought not to be allowed at all; and while its admission is not a ground for reversal, it cumbers the case and tends to confusion, for the more the court is led into the intricacies of dramatic craftsmanship, the less likely it is to stand upon the firmer, if more naive, ground of its considered impressions upon its own perusal. We hope that in this class of cases such evidence may in the future be entirely excluded, and the case confined to the actual issues; that is, whether the copyrighted work was original, and whether the defendant copied it, so far as the supposed infringement is identical.

* * *

Decree affirmed.

NOTES

1. *Nichols* was closely followed in Reyher v. Children's Television Workshop, 533 F.2d 87 (2d Cir.1976). In that case the court found that the defendants did not infringe plaintiff's copyright on her children's book "My Mother Is The Most Beautiful Woman In The World" by publishing and selling the illustrated story "The Most Beautiful Woman in the World" in Sesame Street Magazine and elsewhere. Both works had a similar plot line involving a child separated from its homely mother who considers her the most beautiful woman in the world. The court found no infringement because of the differences in detail.

2. Learned Hand uses the term "fair use" to mean a taking that is not substantial enough to be infringing. The doctrine of fair use codified in § 107

and considered page 696 infra is a different doctrine, which excuses a taking substantial enough to be an infringement. It reduces confusion to reserve the term "fair use" for the latter doctrine.

SHELDON v. METRO–GOLDWYN PICTURES CORP.
United States Circuit Court of Appeals, Second Circuit, 1936.
81 F.2d 49, certiorari denied 298 U.S. 669, 56 S.Ct. 835, 80 L.Ed. 1392.

L. HAND, CIRCUIT JUDGE. The suit is to enjoin the performance of the picture play "Letty Lynton," as an infringement of the plaintiffs' copyrighted play, "Dishonored Lady." The plaintiffs' title is conceded, so too the validity of the copyright; the only issue is infringement. The defendants say that they did not use the play in any way to produce the picture; the plaintiffs discredit this denial because of the negotiations between the parties for the purchase of rights in the play, and because the similarities between the two are too specific and detailed to have resulted from chance. The judge thought that, so far as the defendants had used the play, they had taken only what the law allowed, that is, those general themes, motives, or ideas in which there could be no copyright. Therefore he dismissed the bill.

An understanding of the issue involves some description of what was in the public demesne, as well as of the play and the picture. In 1857 a Scotch girl, named Madeleine Smith, living in Glasgow, was brought to trial upon an indictment in three counts; two for attempts to poison her lover, a third for poisoning him. The jury acquitted her on the first count, and brought in a verdict of "Not Proven" on the second and third. The circumstances of the prosecution aroused much interest at the time not only in Scotland but in England; so much indeed that it became a cause célèbre, and that as late as 1927 the whole proceedings were published in book form. An outline of the story so published, which became the original of the play here in suit, is as follows: The Smiths were a respectable middle-class family, able to send their daughter to a "young ladies' boarding school"; they supposed her protected not only from any waywardness of her own, but from the wiles of seducers. In both they were mistaken, for when at the age of twenty-one she met a young Jerseyman of French blood, Emile L'Angelier, ten years older, and already the hero of many amorous adventures, she quickly succumbed and poured out her feelings in letters of the utmost ardor and indiscretion, and at times of a candor beyond the standards then, and even yet, permissible for well-nurtured young women. They wrote each other as though already married, he assuming to dictate her conduct and even her feelings; both expected to marry, she on any terms, he with the approval of her family. Nevertheless she soon tired of him and engaged herself to a man some twenty years older who was a better match, but for whom she had no more than a friendly complaisance. L'Angelier was not, however, to be fobbed off so easily; he threatened to expose her to her father by showing her letters. She at first tried to dissuade him by appeals to their tender memories, but finding this useless and thinking herself otherwise undone, she affected a return of her former passion and invited him to visit her again. Whether he did, was the turning point of the trial; the evidence, though it really left the issue in no doubt, was too indirect to satisfy the jury, perhaps in part because of her advocate's argument that to kill him only insured the discovery of her letters. It was shown that she had several times bought or tried to buy poison,—prussic acid and arsenic,—and that twice before his death L'Angelier became violently ill, the second time on the day after her purchase. He died of arsenical poison, which the prosecution charged that she had given him in a cup of chocolate. At her trial, Madeleine being incompetent as a witness, her advocate proved an alibi by the testimony of her younger sister that early on the night of the murder as laid in the indictment, she had gone to bed with Madeleine, who had slept with her throughout the night. As to one of the attempts her betrothed swore that she had been with him at the theatre.

This was the story which the plaintiffs used to build their play. As will appear they took from it but the merest skeleton, the acquittal of a wanton young woman, who to extricate herself from an amour that stood in the way of a respectable marriage, poisoned her lover. The incidents, the characters, the mis en scène, the sequence of events, were all changed; nobody disputes that the plaintiffs were entitled to their copyright. All that they took from the story they might probably have taken, had it even been copyrighted. Their heroine is named Madeleine Cary; she lives in New York, brought up in affluence, if not in luxury; she is intelligent, voluptuous, ardent and corrupt; but, though she has had a succession of amours, she is capable of genuine affection. Her lover and victim is an Argentinian, named Moreno, who makes his living as a dancer in night-clubs. Madeleine has met him once in Europe before the play opens, has danced with him, has excited his concupiscence; he presses presents upon her. The play opens in his rooms, he and his dancing partner who is also his mistress, are together; Madeleine on the telephone recalls herself to him and says she wishes to visit him, though it is already past midnight. He disposes of his mistress by a device which does not deceive her and receives Madeleine; at once he falls to wooing her, luring her among other devices by singing a Gaucho song. He finds her facile and the curtain falls in season.

The second act is in her home, and introduces her father, a bibulous dotard, who has shot his wife's lover in the long past; Laurence Brennan, a self-made man in the fifties, untutored, self-reliant and reliable, who has had with Madeleine a relation, half paternal, half-amorous since she grew up; and Denis Farnborough, a young British labor peer, a mannekin to delight the heart of well ordered young women. Madeleine loves him; he loves Madeleine; she will give him no chance to declare himself, remembering her mottled past and his supposedly immaculate standards. She confides to Brennan, who makes clear to her the imbecility of her self-denial; she accepts this enlightenment and engages herself to her high-minded paragon after confessing vaguely her evil life and being assured that to post-war generations all such lapses are peccadillo.

In the next act Moreno, who has got wind of the engagement, comes to her house. Disposing of Farnborough, who chances to be there, she admits Moreno, acknowledges that she is to marry Farnborough, and asks him to accept the situation as the normal outcome of their intrigue. He refuses to be cast off, high words pass, he threatens to expose their relations, she raves at him, until finally he knocks her down and commands her to go to his apartment that morning as before. After he leaves full of swagger, her eye lights on a bottle of strychnine which her father uses as a drug; her fingers slowly close upon it; the audience understands that she will kill Moreno. Farnborough is at the telephone; this apparently stiffens her resolve, showing her the heights she may reach by its execution.

The scene then shifts again to Moreno's apartment; his mistress must again be put out, most unwillingly for she is aware of the situation; Madeleine comes in; she pretends once more to feel warmly, she must wheedle him for he is out of sorts after the quarrel. Meanwhile she prepares to poison him by putting the strychnine in coffee, which she asks him to make ready. But in the course of these preparations during which he sings her again his Gaucho song, what with their proximity, and this and that, her animal ardors are once more aroused and drag her, unwillingly and protesting, from her purpose. The play must therefore wait for an hour or more until, relieved of her passion, she appears from his bedroom and while breakfasting puts the strychnine in his coffee. He soon discovers what has happened and tries to telephone for help. He does succeed in getting a few words through, but she tears away the wire and fills his dying ears with her hatred and disgust. She then carefully wipes away all traces of her finger prints and manages to get away while the door is being pounded in by those who have come at his call.

The next act is again at her home on the following evening. Things are going well with her and Farnborough and her father, when a district attorney comes in, a familiar of the household, now in stern mood; Moreno's mistress and a waiter have incriminated Madeleine, and a cross has been found in Moreno's pocket, which he superstitiously took off her neck the night before. The district attorney cross-questions her, during which Farnborough several times fatuously intervenes; she is driven from point to point almost to an avowal when as a desperate plunge she says she spent the night with Brennan. Brennan is brought to the house and, catching the situation after a moment's delay, bears her out. This puts off the district attorney until seeing strychnine brought to relieve the father, his suspicions spring up again and he arrests Madeleine. The rest of the play is of no consequence here, except that it appears in the last scene that at the trial where she is acquitted, her father on the witness stand accounts for the absence of the bottle of strychnine which had been used to poison Moreno.

At about the time that this play was being written an English woman named Lowndes wrote a book called Letty Lynton, also founded on the story of Madeleine Smith. Letty Lynton lives in England; she is eighteen years old, beautiful, well-reared and intelligent, but wayward. She has had a more or less equivocal love affair with a young Scot, named McLean, who worked in her father's chemical factory, but has discarded him, apparently before their love-making had gone very far. Then she chances upon a young Swede—half English—named Ekebon, and their acquaintance quickly becomes a standardized amour, kept secret from her parents, especially her mother, who is an uncompromising moralist, and somewhat estranged from Letty anyway. She and her lover use an old barn as their place of assignation; it had been fitted up as a play house for Letty when she was a child. Like Madeleine Smith she had written her lover a series of indiscreet letters which he has kept, for though he is on pleasure bent Ekebon has a frugal mind, and means to marry his sweetheart and set himself up for life. They are betrothed and he keeps pressing her to declare it to her parents, which she means never to do. While he is away in Sweden Letty meets an unmarried peer considerably older than she, poor, but intelligent and charming; he falls in love with her and she accepts him, more because it is a good match than for any other reason, though she likes him well enough, and will make him suppose that she loves him.

Thereupon Ekebon reappears, learns of Letty's new betrothal, and threatens to disclose his own to her father, backing up his story with her letters. She must at once disown her peer and resume her engagement with him. His motive, like L'Angelier's, is ambition rather than love, though conquest is a flattery and Letty a charming morsel. His threats naturally throw Letty into dismay; she has come to loathe him and at any cost must get free, but she has no one to turn to. In her plight she thinks of her old suitor, McLean, and goes to the factory only to find him gone. He has taught her how to get access to poisons in his office and has told of their effect on human beings. At first she thinks of jumping out the window, and when she winces at that, of poisoning herself; that would be easier. So she selects arsenic which is less painful and goes away with it; it is only when she gets home that she thinks of poisoning Ekebon. Her mind is soon made up, however, and she makes an appointment with him at the barn; she has told her father, she writes, and Ekebon is to see him on Monday, but meanwhile on Sunday they will meet secretly once more. She has prepared to go on a week-end party and conceals her car near the barn. He comes; she welcomes him with a pretence of her former ardors, and tries to get back her letters. Unsuccessful in this she persuades him to drink a cup of chocolate into which she puts the arsenic. After carefully washing the pans and cups, she leaves with him, dropping him from her car near his home; he being still unaffected. On her way to her party she pretends to have broken down and by asking the help of a passing cyclist establishes an alibi. Ekebon dies at his home attended by his mistress; the letters are discovered and Letty is brought before the coroner's inquest and acquitted chiefly through the alibi, for things look very bad for her until the cyclist appears.

The defendants, who are engaged in producing speaking films on a very large scale in Hollywood, California, had seen the play and wished to get the rights. They found, however, an obstacle in an association of motion picture producers presided over by Mr. Will Hays, who thought the play obscene; not being able to overcome his objections, they returned the copy of the manuscript which they had had. That was in the spring of 1930, but in the autumn they induced the plaintiffs to get up a scenario, which they hoped might pass moral muster. Although this did not suit them after the plaintiffs prepared it, they must still have thought in the spring of 1931 that they could satisfy Mr. Hays, for they then procured an offer from the plaintiffs to sell their rights for $30,000. These negotiations also proved abortive because the play continued to be objectionable, and eventually they cried off on the bargain. Mrs. Lowndes' novel was suggested to Thalberg, one of the vice-presidents of the Metro-Goldwyn Company, in July, 1931, and again in the following November, and he bought the rights to it in December. At once he assigned the preparation of a play to Stromberg, who had read the novel in January, and thought it would make a suitable play for an actress named Crawford, just then not employed. Stromberg chose Meehan, Tuchock and Brown to help him, the first two with the scenario, the third with the dramatic production. All these four were examined by deposition; all denied that they had used the play in any way whatever; all agreed that they had based the picture on the story of Madeleine Smith and on the novel, "Letty Lynton." All had seen the play, and Tuchock had read the manuscript, as had Thalberg, but Stromberg, Meehan and Brown swore that they had not; Stromberg's denial being however worthless, for he had originally sworn the contrary in an affidavit. They all say that work began late in November or early in December, 1931, and the picture was finished by the end of March. To meet these denials, the plaintiffs appeal to the substantial identity between passages in the picture and those parts of the play which are original with them.

The picture opens in Montevideo where Letty Lynton is recovering from her fondness for Emile Renaul. She is rich, luxurious and fatherless, her father having been killed by his mistress's husband; her mother is seared, hard, selfish, unmotherly; and Letty has left home to escape her, wandering about in search of excitement. Apparently for the good part of a year she has been carrying on a love affair with Renaul; twice before she has tried to shake loose, has gone once to Rio where she lit another flame, but each time she has weakened and been drawn back. Though not fully declared as an amour, there can be no real question as to the character of her attachment. She at length determines really to break loose, but once again her senses are too much for her and it is indicated, if not declared, that she spends the night with Renaul. Though he is left a vague figure only indistinctly associated with South America somewhere or other, the part was cast for an actor with a marked foreign accent, and it is plain that he was meant to be understood, in origin anyway, as South American, like Moreno in the play. He is violent, possessive and sensual; his power over Letty lies in his strong animal attractions. However, she escapes in the morning while he is asleep, whether from his bed or not is perhaps uncertain; and with a wax figure in the form of a loyal maid—Letty in the novel had one—boards a steamer for New York. On board she meets Darrow, a young American, the son of a rich rubber manufacturer, who is coming back from a trip to Africa. They fall in love upon the faintest provocation and become betrothed before the ship docks, three weeks after she left Montevideo. At the pier she finds Renaul who has flown up to reclaim her. She must in some way keep her two suitors apart, and she manages to dismiss Darrow and then to escape Renaul by asking him to pay her customs duties, which he does. Arrived home her mother gives her a cold welcome and refuses to concern herself with the girl's betrothal. Renaul is announced; he has read of the betrothal in the papers and is furious. He tries again to stir her sensuality by the familiar gambit, but this time he fails; she slaps his face and declares that she hates him. He commands her to come to his apartment that evening; she begs him to part with her and let her have her life; he insists on renewing their affair. She threatens to call the police; he rejoins that if so her letters will be published and then he leaves. Desperate, she chances on a bottle of strychnine, which we are to suppose is an accoutrement of every affluent household, and seizes it; the implication is of intended suicide, not murder. Then she calls Darrow, tells him that she will not leave with him that night for his parents' place in the Adirondacks as they had planned; she renews to him the pledge of her love, without him she cannot live, an intimation to the audience of her purpose to kill herself.

That evening she goes to Renaul's apartment in a hotel armed with her strychnine bottle, for use on the spot; she finds him cooling champagne, but in bad temper. His caresses which he bestows plentifully enough, again stir her disgust not her passions, but he does not believe it and assumes that she will spend the night with him. Finding that he will not return the letters, she believes herself lost and empties the strychnine into a wine glass. Again he embraces her; she vilifies him; he knocks her down; she vilifies him again. Ignorant of the poison he grasps her glass, and she, perceiving it, lets him drink. He woos her again, this time with more apparent success, for she is terrified; he sings a Gaucho song to her, the same one that has been heard at Montevideo. The poison begins to work and, at length supposing that she has meant to murder him, he reaches for the telephone; she forestalls him, but she does not tear out the wire. As he slowly dies, she stands over him and vituperates him. A waiter enters; she steps behind a curtain; he leaves thinking Renaul drunk; she comes out, wipes off all traces of her fingerprints and goes out, leaving however her rubbers which Renaul had taken from her when she entered.

Next she and Darrow are found at his parents' in the Adirondacks; while there a detective appears, arrests Letty and takes her to New York; she is charged with the murder of Renaul; Darrow goes back to New York with her. The finish is at the district attorney's office; Letty and Darrow, Letty's mother, the wax serving maid are all there. The letters appear incriminating to an elderly rather benevolent district attorney; also the customs slip and the rubbers. Letty begins to break down; she admits that she went to Renaul's room, not to kill him but to get him to release her. Darrow sees that that story will not pass, and volunteers that she came to his room at a hotel and spent the night with him. Letty confirms this and mother, till then silent, backs up their story; she had traced them to the hotel and saw the lights go out, having ineffectually tried to dissuade them. The maid still further confirms them and the district attorney, not sorry to be discomfited, though unbelieving, discharges Letty.

We are to remember that it makes no difference how far the play was anticipated by works in the public demesne which the plaintiffs did not use. The defendants appear not to recognize this, for they have filled the record with earlier instances of the same dramatic incidents and devices, as though, like a patent, a copyrighted work must be not only original, but new. That is not however the law as is obvious in the case of maps or compendia, where later works will necessarily be anticipated. At times, in discussing how much of the substance of a play the copyright protects, courts have indeed used language which seems to give countenance to the notion that, if a plot were old, it could not be copyrighted. London v. Biograph Co. (C.C.A.) 231 F. 696; Eichel v. Marcin (D.C.) 241 F. 404. But we understand by this no more than that in its broader outline a plot is never copyrightable, for it is plain beyond peradventure that anticipation as such cannot invalidate a copyright. Borrowed the work must indeed not be, for a plagiarist is not himself pro tanto an "author"; but if by some magic a man who had never known it were to compose anew Keats's Ode on a Grecian Urn, he would be an "author," and, if he copyrighted it, others might not copy that poem, though they might of course copy Keats's. Bleistein v. Donaldson Lithographing Co., 188 U.S. 239, 249; Gerlach-Barklow Co. v. Morris & Bendien, Inc., 23 F.(2d) 159, 161 (C.C.A.2); Weil, Copyright Law, p. 234. But though a copyright is for this reason less vulnerable than a patent, the owner's protection is more limited, for just as he is no less an "author" because others have preceded him, so another who follows him, is not a tort-feasor unless he pirates his work. Jewelers' Circular Publishing Co. v. Keystone Co., 281 F. 83, 92, 26 A.L.R. 571 (C.C.A.2); General Drafting Co. v. Andrews, 37 F.(2d) 54, 56 (C.C.A.2); Williams v. Smythe (C.C.) 110 F. 961; American, etc., Directory Co. v. Gehring Pub. Co. (D.C.) 4 F.(2d) 415; New Jersey, etc., Co. v. Barton Business Service (D.C.) 57 F.(2d) 353. If the copyrighted work is therefore original, the public demesne is important only on the issue of infringement; that is, so far as it may break the force of the inference to be drawn from likenesses between the work and the putative piracy. If the defendant has had access to other material which would have served him as well, his disclaimer becomes more plausible.

In the case at bar there are then two questions: First, whether the defendants actually used the play; second, if so, whether theirs was a "fair use." The judge did not make any finding upon the first question, as we said at the outset, because he thought the defendants were in any case justified; in this following our decision in Nichols v. Universal Pictures Corporation, 45 F.(2d) 119. The plaintiffs challenge that opinion because we said that "copying" might at times be a "fair use"; but it is convenient to define such a use by saying that others may "copy" the "theme," or "ideas," or the like, of a work, though not its "expression." At any rate so long as it is clear what is meant, no harm is done. In the case at bar the distinction is not so important as usual, because so much of the play was borrowed from the story of Madeleine Smith, and the plaintiffs' originality is necessarily limited to the variants they introduced. Nevertheless, it is still true that their whole contribution may not be protected; for the defendants were entitled to use, not only all that had gone before, but even the plaintiffs' contribution itself, if they drew from it only the more general patterns; that is, if they kept clear of its "expression." We must therefore state in detail those similarities which seem to us to pass the limits of "fair use." Finally, in concluding as we do that the defendants used the play pro tanto, we need not charge their witnesses with perjury. With so many sources before them they might quite honestly forget what they took; nobody knows the origin of his inventions; memory and fancy merge even in adults. Yet unconscious plagiarism is actionable quite as much as deliberate. Buck v. Jewell-La Salle Realty Co., 283 U.S. 191, 198; Harold Lloyd Corporation v. Witwer, 65 F.(2d) 1, 16 (C.C.A.9); Fred Fisher, Inc., v. Dillingham (D.C.) 298 F. 145.

The defendants took for their mis en scène the same city and the same social class; and they chose a South American villain. The heroines had indeed to be wanton, but Letty Lynton "tracked" Madeleine Cary more closely than that. She is overcome by passion in the first part of the picture and yields after announcing that she hates Renaul and has made up her mind to leave him. This is the same weakness as in the murder scene of the play, though transposed. Each heroine's waywardness is suggested as an inherited disposition; each has had an errant parent involved in scandal; one killed, the other becoming an outcast. Each is redeemed by a higher love. Madeleine Cary must not be misread; it is true that her lust overcomes her at the critical moment, but it does not extinguish her love for Farnborough; her body, not her soul, consents to her lapse. Moreover, her later avowal, which she knew would finally lose her her lover, is meant to show the basic rectitude of her nature. Though it does not need Darrow to cure Letty of her wanton ways, she too is redeemed by a nobler love. Neither Madeleine Smith, nor the Letty of the novel, were at all like that; they wished to shake off a clandestine intrigue to set themselves up in the world; their love as distinct from their lust, was pallid. So much for the similarity in character.

Coming to the parallelism of incident, the threat scene is carried out with almost exactly the same sequence of event and actuation; it has no prototype in either story or novel. Neither Ekebon nor L'Angelier went to his fatal interview to break up the new betrothal; he was beguiled by the pretence of a renewed affection. Moreno and Renaul each goes to his sweetheart's home to detach her from her new love; when he is there, she appeals to his better side, unsuccessfully; she abuses him, he returns the abuse and commands her to come to his rooms; she pretends to agree, expecting to finish with him one way or another. True, the assault is deferred in the picture from this scene to the next, but it is the same dramatic trick. Again, the poison in each case is found at home, and the girl talks with her betrothed just after the villain has left and again pledges him her faith. Surely the sequence of these details is pro tanto the very web of the authors' dramatic expression; and copying them is not "fair use."

The death scene follows the play even more closely; the girl goes to the villain's room as he directs; from the outset he is plainly to be poisoned while they are together. (The defendants deny that this is apparent in the picture, but we cannot agree. It would have been an impossible dénoument on the screen for the heroine, just plighted to the hero, to kill herself in desperation, because the villain has successfully enmeshed her in their mutual past; yet the poison is surely to be used on some one.) Moreno and Renaul each tries to arouse the girl by the memory of their former love, using among other aphrodisiacs the Gaucho song; each dies while she is there, incidentally of strychnine not arsenic. In extremis each makes for the telephone and is thwarted by the girl; as he dies, she pours upon him her rage and loathing. When he is dead, she follows the same ritual to eradicate all traces of her presence, but forgets telltale bits of property. Again these details in the same sequence embody more than the "ideas" of the play; they are its very raiment.

Finally in both play and picture in place of a trial, as in the story and the novel, there is substituted an examination by a district attorney; and this examination is again in parallel almost step by step. A parent is present; so is the lover; the girl yields progressively as the evidence accumulates; in the picture, the customs slip, the rubbers and the letters; in the play, the cross and the witnesses, brought in to confront her. She is at the breaking point when she is saved by substantially the same most unexpected alibi; a man declares that she has spent the night with him. That alibi there introduced is the turning point in each drama and alone prevents its ending in accordance with the classic canon of tragedy; i.e., fate as an inevitable consequence of past conduct, itself not evil enough to quench pity. It is the essence of the authors' expression, the very voice with which they speak.

We have often decided that a play may be pirated without using the dialogue. Daly v. Palmer, Fed.Cas. No. 3,552, 6 Blatch. 256; Daly v. Webster, 56 F. 483, 486, 487; Dam v. Kirke La Shelle Co., 175 F. 902, 907; Chappell & Co. v. Fields, 210 F. 864. Dymow v. Bolton, 11 F.(2d) 690; and Nichols v. Universal Pictures Corporation, supra, 45 F.(2d) 119, do not suggest otherwise. Were it not so, there could be no piracy of a pantomime, where there cannot be any dialogue; yet nobody would deny to pantomime the name of drama. Speech is only a small part of a dramatist's means of expression; he draws on all the arts and compounds his play from words and gestures and scenery and costume and from the very looks of the actors themselves. Again and again a play may lapse into pantomime at its most poignant and significant moments; a nod, a movement of the hand, a pause, may tell the audience more than words could tell. To be sure, not all this is always copyrighted, though there is no reason why it may not be, for those decisions do not forbid which hold that mere scenic tricks will not be protected. Serrana v. Jefferson (C.C.) 33 F. 347; Barnes v. Miner (C.C.) 122 F. 480; Bloom et al. v. Nixon (C.C.) 125 F. 977. The play is the sequence of the confluents of all these means, bound together in an inseparable unity; it may often be most effectively pirated by leaving out the speech, for which a substitute can be found, which keeps the whole dramatic meaning. That as it appears to us is exactly what the defendants have done here; the dramatic significance of the scenes we have recited is the same, almost to the letter. True, much of the picture owes nothing to the play; some of it is plainly drawn from the novel; but that is entirely immaterial; it is enough that substantial parts were lifted; no plagiarist can excuse the wrong by showing how much of his work he did not pirate. We cannot avoid the conviction that, if the picture was not an infringement of the play, there can be none short of taking the dialogue.

The decree will be reversed and an injunction will go against the picture together with a decree for damages and an accounting. The plaintiffs will be awarded an attorney's fee in this court and in the court below, both to be fixed by the District Court upon the final decree.

Decree reversed.

NOTES

1. The analysis of the *Sheldon* opinion suggests that in some situations a character could be protected by copyright if the copying of the character's features and behavior were sufficiently detailed. In Warner Bros. v. American Broadcasting Companies, 654 F.2d 204 (2d Cir.1981) (denial of preliminary injunction affirmed), 720 F.2d 231 (2d Cir.1983) (summary judgment of no infringement affirmed), the owners of the copyright on Superman were unable to stop the ABC series "The Greatest American Hero" featuring the exploits of one Ralph Hinkley whose abilities and activities lightly spoofed the Superman story. Superman did once prevail against a comic book competitor in Detective Comics, Inc. v. Bruns Publications, Inc., 111 F.2d 432 (2d Cir.1940), holding that the defendant's Wonderman infringed. In Selmon v. Hasbro Bradley, Inc., 669

F.Supp. 1267 (S.D.N.Y.1987), the Whats were unable to stop the Wuzzles. The pun laden opinion is illustrated by ten pages of sketches of both Whats and Wuzzles. "The questions before us are really quite simple: 'Just what's a "What," what's the similarity between a "What" and a "Wuzzle," and "Wuzzle" we do about it?' "

2. The subject of legal protection of characters is carefully examined in Leslie A. Kurtz, The Independent Legal Lives of Fictional Characters, 1986 Wisc.L.Rev. 429 (1986).

ARNSTEIN v. PORTER

United States Circuit Court of Appeals, Second Circuit, 1946.
154 F.2d 464.

Action by Ira B. Arnstein against Cole Porter for infringement of copyrights, infringement of right to uncopyrighted musical compositions and wrongful use of the titles of others. From a judgment dismissing action on defendant's motion for summary judgment, the plaintiff appeals.

Modified in part; otherwise reversed and remanded.

Plaintiff, a citizen and resident of New York, brought this suit, charging infringement by defendant, a citizen and resident of New York, of plaintiff's copyrights to several musical compositions, infringement of his rights to other uncopyrighted musical compositions, and wrongful use of the titles of others. Plaintiff, when filing his complaint, demanded a jury trial. Plaintiff took the deposition of defendant, and defendant, the deposition of plaintiff. Defendant then moved for an order striking out plaintiff's jury demand, and for summary judgment. Attached to defendant's motion papers were the depositions, phonograph records of piano renditions of the plaintiff's compositions and defendant's alleged infringing compositions, and the court records of five previous copyright infringement suits brought by plaintiff in the court below against other persons, in which judgments had been entered, after trials, against plaintiff. Defendant also moved for dismissal of the action on the ground of "vexatiousness."

Plaintiff alleged that defendant's "Begin the Beguine" is a plagiarism from plaintiff's "The Lord Is My Shepherd" and "A Mother's Prayer." Plaintiff testified, on deposition, that "The Lord Is My Shepherd" had been published and about 2,000 copies sold, that "A Mother's Prayer" had been published, over a million copies having been sold. In his depositions, he gave no direct evidence that defendant saw or heard these compositions. He also alleged that defendant's "My Heart Belongs to Daddy" had been plagiarized from plaintiff's "A Mother's Prayer."

Plaintiff also alleged that defendant's "I Love You" is a plagiarism from plaintiff's composition "La Priere," stating in his deposition that the latter composition had been sold. He gave no direct proof that plaintiff knew of this composition.

He also alleged that defendant's song "Night and Day" is a plagiarism of plaintiff's song "I Love You Madly," which he testified had not been published but had once been publicly performed over the radio, copies having been sent to divers radio stations but none to defendant; a copy of this song, plaintiff testified, had been stolen from his room. He also alleged that "I Love You Madly" was in part plagiarized from "La Priere." He further alleged that defendant's "You'd Be So Nice To Come Home To" is plagiarized from plaintiff's "Sadness Overwhelms My Soul." He testified that this song had never been published or publicly performed but that copies had been sent to a movie producer and to several publishers. He also alleged that defendant's "Don't Fence Me In" is a plagiarism of plaintiff's song "A Modern Messiah" which has not been published or publicly performed; in his deposition he said that about a hundred copies had been sent to divers radio stations and band leaders but that he sent no copy to defendant. Plaintiff said that defendant "had stooges right along to follow me, watch me, and live in the same apartment with me," and that plaintiff's room had been ransacked on several occasions. Asked how he knew that defendant had anything to do with any of these "burglaries," plaintiff said, "I don't know that he had to do with it, but I only know that he could have." He also said " * * * many of my compositions had been published. No one had to break in to steal them. They were sung publicly."

Defendant in his deposition categorically denied that he had ever seen or heard any of plaintiff's compositions or had had any acquaintance with any persons said to have stolen any of them.

The prayer of plaintiff's original complaint asked "at least one million dollars out of the millions the defendant has earned and is earning out of all the plagiarism." In his amended complaint the prayer is "for judgment against the defendant in the sum of $1,000,000 as damages sustained by the plagiarism of all the compositions named in the complaint." Plaintiff, not a lawyer, appeared pro se below and on this appeal.

FRANK, CIRCUIT JUDGE. * * * The principal question on this appeal is whether the lower court, under Rule 56, properly deprived plaintiff of a trial of his copyright infringement action. * * * It is important to avoid confusing two separate elements essential to a plaintiff's case in such a suit: (a) that defendant copied from plaintiff's copyrighted work and (b) that the copying (assuming it to be proved) went so far as to constitute improper appropriation.

As to the first—copying—the evidence may consist (a) of defendant's admission that he copied or (b) of circumstantial evidence—usually evidence of access—from which the trier of the facts may reasonably infer copying. Of course, if there are no similarities, no amount of evidence of access will suffice to prove copying. If there is evidence of access and similarities exist, then the trier of the facts must determine whether the similarities are sufficient to prove copying. On this issue, analysis ("dissection") is relevant, and the testimony of experts may be received to aid the trier of the facts. If evidence of access is absent, the similarities must be so striking as to preclude the possibility that plaintiff and defendant independently arrived at the same result.

If copying is established, then only does there arise the second issue, that of illicit copying (unlawful appropriations). On that issue (as noted more in detail below) the test is the response of the ordinary lay hearer, accordingly, on that issue, "dissection" and expert testimony are irrelevant.

In some cases, the similarities between the plaintiff's and defendant's work are so extensive and striking as, without more, both to justify an inference of copying and to prove improper appropriation. But such double-purpose evidence is not required; that is, if copying is otherwise shown, proof of improper appropriation need not consist of similarities which, standing alone, would support an inference of copying.

Each of these two issues—copying and improper appropriation—is an issue of fact. If there is a trial, the conclusions on those issues of the trier of the facts—of the judge if he sat without a jury, or of the jury if there was a jury trial—bind this court on appeal, provided the evidence supports those findings, regardless of whether we would ourselves have reached the same conclusions. But a case could occur in which the similarities were so striking that we would reverse a finding of no access, despite weak evidence of access (or no evidence thereof other than the similarities); and similarly as to a finding of no illicit appropriation.

We turn first to the issue of copying. After listening to the compositions as played in the phonograph recordings submitted by defendant, we find similarities; but we hold that unquestionably, standing alone, they do not compel the conclusion, or permit the inference that defendant copied. The similarities, however, are sufficient so that, if there is enough evidence of access to permit the case to go to the jury, the jury may properly infer that the similarities did not result from coincidence.

Summary judgment was, then, proper if indubitably defendant did not have access to plaintiff's compositions. Plainly that presents an issue of fact. On that issue, the district judge who heard no oral testimony, had before him the depositions of plaintiff and defendant. The judge characterized plaintiff's story as "fantastic"; and, in the light of the references in his opinion to defendant's deposition, the judge obviously accepted defendant's denial of access and copying. Although part of plaintiff's testimony on deposition (as to "stooges" and the like) does seem "fantastic," yet plaintiff's credibility, even as to those improbabilities, should be left to the jury. If evidence is "of a kind that greatly taxes the credulity of the judge, he can say so, or if he totally disbelieves it, he may announce that fact, leaving the jury free to believe it or not." If, said Winslow, J., "evidence is to be always disbelieved because the story told seems remarkable or impossible, then a party whose rights depend on the proof of some facts out of the usual course of events will always be denied justice simply because his story is improbable." We should not overlook the shrewd proverbial admonition that sometimes truth is stranger than fiction.

But even if we were to disregard the improbable aspects of plaintiff's story, there remain parts by no means "fantastic." On the record now before us, more than a million copies of one of his compositions were sold; copies of others were sold in smaller quantities or distributed to radio stations or band leaders or publishers, or the pieces were publicly performed. If, after hearing both parties testify, the jury disbelieves defendant's denials, it can, from such facts, reasonably infer access. It follows that, as credibility is unavoidably involved a genuine issue of material fact presents itself. With credibility a vital factor, plaintiff is entitled to a trial where the jury can observe the witnesses while testifying. Plaintiff must not be deprived of the invaluable privilege of cross-examining the defendant—the "crucial test of credibility"—in the presence of the jury. Plaintiff, or a lawyer on his behalf, on such examination may elicit damaging admissions from defendant; more important, plaintiff may persuade the jury, observing defendant's manner when testifying, that defendant is unworthy of belief.

* * *

With all that in mind, we cannot now say—as we think we must say to sustain a summary judgment—that at the close of a trial the judge could properly direct a verdict.

* * * Assuming that adequate proof is made of copying, that is not enough; for there can be "permissible copying," copying which is not illicit. Whether (if he copied) defendant unlawfully appropriated presents, too, an issue of fact. The proper criterion on that issue is not an analytic or other comparison of the respective musical compositions as they appear on paper or in the judgment of trained musicians.[19] The plaintiff's legally protected interest is not, as such, his reputation as a musician but his interest in the potential financial returns from his compositions which derive from the lay public's approbation of his efforts. The question, therefore, is whether defendant took from plaintiff's works so much of what is pleasing to the ears of lay listeners, who comprise the audience from whom such popular music is composed, that defendant wrongfully appropriated something which belongs to the plaintiff.

Surely, then, we have an issue of fact which a jury is peculiarly fitted to determine. Indeed, even if there were to be a trial before a judge, it would be desirable (although not necessary) for him to summon an advisory jury on this question.

19. Where plaintiff relies on similarities to prove copying (as distinguished from improper appropriation) paper comparisons and the opinions of experts may aid the court.

We should not be taken as saying that a plagiarism case can never arise in which absence of similarities is so patent that a summary judgment for defendant would be correct.   Thus suppose that Ravel's "Bolero" or Shostakovitch's "Fifth Symphony" were alleged to infringe "When Irish Eyes Are Smiling."   But this is not such a case.   For, after listening to the playing of the respective compositions, we are, at this time, unable to conclude that the likenesses are so trifling that, on the issue of misappropriation, a trial judge could legitimately direct a verdict for defendant.

At the trial, plaintiff may play, or cause to be played, the pieces in such manner that they may seem to a jury to be inexcusably alike, in terms of the way in which lay listeners of such music would be likely to react.   The plaintiff may call witnesses whose testimony may aid the jury in reaching its conclusion as to the responses of such audiences.   Expert testimony of musicians may also be received, but it will in no way be controlling on the issue of illicit copying, and should be utilized only to assist in determining the reactions of lay auditors.   The impression made on the refined ears of musical experts or their views as to the musical excellence of plaintiff's or defendant's works are utterly immaterial on the issue of misappropriation;   for the views of such persons are caviar to the general—and plaintiff's and defendant's compositions are not caviar.

In copyright infringement cases cited by defendant,[26] we have sustained judgments in favor of defendants based on findings of fact made by trial judges after trials, findings we held not to be "clearly erroneous."   *   *   *

[R]eversed and remanded.

CLARK, CIRCUIT JUDGE (dissenting).

While the procedure followed below seems to me generally simple and appropriate, the defendant did make one fatal tactical error.   In an endeavor to assist us, he caused to be prepared records of all the musical pieces here involved, and presented these transcriptions through the medium of the affidavit of his pianist.   Though he himself did not stress these records and properly met plaintiff's claims as to the written music with his own analysis, yet the tinny tintinnabulations of the music thus canned resounded through the United States Courthouse to the exclusion of all else, including the real issues in the case.   Of course, sound is important in a case of this kind, but it is not so important as to falsify what the eye reports that the mind teaches.   Otherwise plagiarism would be suggested by the mere drumming of repetitious sound from our usual popular music, as it issues from a piano, orchestra, or hurdy-gurdy—particularly when ears may be dulled by long usage, possibly artistic repugnance or boredom, or mere distance which causes all sounds to merge.   And the judicial eardrum may be peculiarly insensitive after long years of listening to the "beat, beat,

---

26. See, e.g., Arnstein v. Edward B. Marks Music Corporation, 2 Cir., 82 F.2d   275, 277;   Arnstein v. Broadcast Music, Inc., 2 Cir., 137 F.2d 410, 412.   *   *   *

beat" (I find myself plagiarizing from defendant and thus in danger of my brothers' doom) of sound upon it, though perhaps no more so than the ordinary citizen juror—even if tone deafness is made a disqualification for jury service, as advocated.

Pointing to the adscititious fortuity inherent in the stated standard is, it seems to me, the fact that after repeated hearings of the records, I could not find therein what my brothers found. The only thing definitely mentioned seemed to be the repetitive use of the note e in certain places by both plaintiff and defendant, surely too simple and ordinary a device of composition to be significant. In our former musical plagiarism cases we have, naturally, relied on what seemed the total sound effect; but we have also analyzed the music enough to make sure of an intelligible and intellectual decision. Thus in Arnstein v. Edward B. Marks Music Corp., 2 Cir., 82 F.2d 275, 277, Judge L. Hand made quite an extended comparison of the songs, concluding, inter alia: " * * * the seven notes available do not admit of so many agreeable permutations that we need be amazed at the re-appearance of old themes, even though the identity extend through a sequence of twelve notes." See also the discussion in Marks v. Leo Feist, Inc., 2 Cir., 290 F. 959, and Darrell v. Joe Morris Music Co., 2 Cir., 113 F.2d 80, where the use of six similar bars and of an eight-note sequence frequently repeated were respectively held not to constitute infringement, and Wilkie v. Santly Bros., 2 Cir., 91 F.2d 978, affirming D.C.S.D.N.Y., 13 F.Supp. 136, certiorari denied Santly Bros. v. Wilkie, 302 U.S. 735, where use of eight bars with other similarities amounting to over three-quarters of the significant parts was held infringement.[1]

It is true that in Arnstein v. Broadcast Music, Inc., 2 Cir., 137 F.2d 410, 412, we considered "dissection" or "technical analysis" not the proper approach to support a finding of plagiarism, and said that it must be "more ingenuous, more like that of a spectator, who would rely upon the complex of his impressions." But in its context that seems to me clearly sound and in accord with what I have in mind. Thus one may look to the total impression to repulse the charge of plagiarism where a minute "dissection" might dredge up some points of similarity.

---

1. In accord is Shafter, Musical Copyright, 2d Ed.1939, c. 6, particularly p. 205, where the author speaks of "the 'comparative method,' worked out by Judge Learned Hand with great success," and "his successful method of analysis," citing Hein v. Harris, C.C.S.D.N.Y., 175 F. 875, affirmed 2 Cir., 183 F. 107, and Haas v. Leo Feist, Inc., D.C.S.D.N.Y., 234 F. 105; and p. 194, where he approves of Judge Yankwich's course in attaching an exhibit of analysis to his opinion in Hirsch v. Paramount Pictures, Inc., D.C.S.D.Cal., 17 F.Supp. 816— "this sensible procedure," "a splendid model for future copyright decisions." I find nowhere any suggestion of two steps in adjudication of this issue, one of finding copying which may be approached with musical intelligence and assistance of experts, and another that of illicit copying which must be approached with complete ignorance; nor do I see how rationally there can be any such difference, even if a jury—the now chosen instrument of musical detection—could be expected to separate those issues and the evidence accordingly. If there is actual copying, it is actionable, and there are no degrees; what we are dealing with is the claim of similarities sufficient to justify the inference of copying. This is a single deduction to be made intelligently, not two with the dominating one to be made blindly.

Hence one cannot use a purely theoretical disquisition to supply a tonal resemblance which does not otherwise exist. Certainly, however, that does not suggest or compel the converse—that one must keep his brain in torpor for fear that otherwise it would make clear differences which do exist. Music is a matter of the intellect as well as the emotions; that is why eminent musical scholars insist upon the employment of the intellectual faculties for a just appreciation of music.

Consequently I do not think we should abolish the use of the intellect here even if we could. When, however, we start with an examination of the written and printed material supplied by the plaintiff in his complaint and exhibits, we find at once that he does not and cannot claim extensive copying, measure by measure, of his compositions. He therefore has resorted to a comparative analysis—the "dissection" found unpersuasive in the earlier cases—to support his claim of plagiarism of small detached portions here and there, the musical fillers between the better known parts of the melody. And plaintiff's compositions, as pointed out in the cases cited above, are of the simple and trite character where small repetitive sequences are not hard to discover. It is as though we found Shakespeare a plagiarist on the basis of his use of articles, pronouns, prepositions, and adjectives also used by others. The surprising thing, however, is to note the small amount of even this type of reproduction which plaintiff by dint of extreme dissection has been able to find.

Though it is most instructive, it will serve no good purpose for me to restate here this showing as to each of the pieces in issue. As an example of the rest, we may take plaintiff's first cause of action. This involves his "A Modern Messiah" with defendant's "Don't Fence Me In." The first is written in 6/8 time, the second in common or 4/4 time; and there is only one place where there is a common sequence of as many as five consecutive notes, and these without the same values. Thus it goes. The usual claim seems to be rested upon a sequence of three, or four, or of five—never more than five—identical notes, usually of different rhythmical values. Nowhere is there anything approaching the twelve-note sequence of the Marks case supra. Interesting is the fact that the closest tonal resemblance is to be found between a piece by defendant written back in 1930 and an uncopyrighted waltz by plaintiff (rejected here by my brothers because it is uncopyrighted) which was never published, but, according to his statement, was publicly performed as early as 1923, 1924, and 1925.

In the light of these utmost claims of the plaintiff, I do not see a legal basis for the claim of plagiarism. So far as I have been able to discover, no earlier case approaches the holding that a simple and trite sequence of this type, even if copying may seem indicated, constitutes proof either of access or of plagiarism. In addition to the cases already cited, see the fine statements of Bright, J., in Arnstein v. Broadcast Music, Inc., D.C.S.D.N.Y., 46 F.Supp. 379, 381, affirmed 2 Cir., 137 F.2d 410, supra, and of Yankwich, J., in Carew v. R.K.O. Radio Pictures, D.C. S.D.Cal., 43 F.Supp. 199. That being so, the procedure whereby the demonstration is made does not seem to me over-important. A court is a court whether sitting at motion or day calendar; and when an issue of law is decisively framed, it is its judicial duty to pass judgment. Hence on the precedents I should feel dismissal required on the face of the complaint and exhibits.

* * *

* * * Here I think we ought to assume the responsibility of decision now. If, however, we are going to the other extreme of having all decisions of musical plagiarism made by ear, the more unsophisticated and musically naive the better, then it seems to me we are reversing our own precedents to substitute chaos, judicial as well as musical.

NOTES

1. In Heim v. Universal Pictures Co., 154 F.2d 480 (2d Cir.1946), decided five days later, the court affirmed a judgment of non-infringement in spite of proof of access and considerable similarity. Judge Frank said:

> In effect, [the trial judge] * * * found that plaintiff's method of dealing with the common trite note sequence did not possess enough originality, raising it above the level of banal, to preclude coincidence as an adequate explanation of the identity. We cannot say that the judge erred. Whether, had he reached a contrary conclusion, we would have affirmed, we do not consider. Id. at 488.

Judge Clark, concurring in the result, observed:

> Surely, if the Arnstein case teaches us anything, it must be that banality is no bar to a claim for plagiarism. That results at once so divergent and so musically astonishing as the decisions in these two cases can occur simultaneously I can attribute only to the novel conceptions of legal plagiarism first announced in the Arnstein case and now repeated here. By these the issue is no longer one of musical similarity or identity to justify the conclusion of copying—an issue to be decided with all the intelligence, musical as well as legal, we can bring to bear upon it—but is one first, of copying, to be decided more or less intelligently, and, second, of illicit copying, to be decided blindly on a mere cacophony of sounds. Just at which stage decision here has occurred, I am not sure. Id. at 491.

2. In Fred Fisher, Inc. v. Dillingham, 298 Fed. 145 (S.D.N.Y.1924), Judge L. Hand held that Jerome Kern's "Kalua" had infringed the plaintiff's "Dardanella."

> There is no similarity between the melodies of the two pieces in any part, but the supposed infringement is in the accompaniment of the chorus or refrain of 'Kalua,' which has in part an absolute identity with the accompaniment of the verse, though not the chorus, of 'Dardanella.' This accompaniment introduces the copyrighted song, and is known in music as an 'ostinato,' or constantly repeated figures, which produces the effect of a rolling underphrase for the melody, something like the beat of a drum or tomtom, except that it has a very simple melodic character of its own. It consists of only eight notes, written in two measures and repeated again and again, with no

changes, except the variation of a musical fifth in the scale to accommodate itself harmonically to the changes in the melody. Precisely the same eight notes are in the accompaniment to the chorus or refrain of 'Kalua,' used also as an 'ostinato,' precisely as they are used in 'Dardanella,' giving the same effect, and designed, as the composer says, to indicate the booming of a surf upon the beach. 298 Fed. at 146.

Is *Fisher* consistent with the position that mere phrases, titles and slogans are not copyrightable?

3. The *Arnstein* case illustrates the fact that although in theory an infringing work must actually be taken from the copyrighted work, in practice copyright protection is somewhat greater. In the *Fisher* case, supra, Kern testified that he was not aware of any plagiarism. Although Hand was willing to believe him, he was unimpressed.

Whether he unconsciously copied the figures, he cannot say, and does not try to. Everything registers somewhere in our memories, and no one can tell what may evoke it. On the whole, my belief is that, in composing the accompaniment to the refrain of 'Kalua,' Mr. Kern must have followed, probably unconsciously, what he had certainly often heard only a short time before. I cannot really see how else to account for a similarity, which amounts to identity. 298 Fed. at 147.

4. Judge Frank says: "On that issue [unlawful appropriation] * * * the test is the response of the ordinary lay hearer. * * * The question, therefore, is whether defendant took from plaintiff's works so much of what is pleasing to the ears of lay listeners, who comprise the audience from whom such popular music is composed, that defendant wrongfully appropriated something which belongs to the plaintiff." (supra p. 648). Is that statement consistent with Judge Hand's approach in *Nichols* and *Sheldon?* Do different standards apply to drama and music? If so, is that because they have different audiences? How does Judge Frank (or the jury) know when "so much of what is pleasing" is too much?

PROBLEMS

1. Is the standard for infringement of serious music the same as for popular music?

2. Should a judge who does not regularly listen to popular music disqualify himself as a trier of fact in a case involving infringement of such music? Can a juror be excluded for cause on such a ground? Cf. note 22 of the *Arnstein* opinion: "It would * * * be proper to exclude tone-deaf persons from the jury." 154 F.2d at 473.

SAUL STEINBERG v. COLUMBIA PICTURES INDUSTRIES

United States District Court for the Southern District of New York, 1987.
663 F.Supp. 706.

STANTON, DISTRICT JUDGE.

In these actions for copyright infringement, plaintiff Saul Steinberg is suing the producers, promoters, distributors and advertisers of the movie "Moscow on the Hudson" ("Moscow"). Steinberg is an artist whose fame derives in part from cartoons and illustrations he has drawn for *The New Yorker* magazine. Defendant Columbia Pictures Industries, Inc. (Columbia) is in the business of producing, promoting and distributing motion pictures, including "Moscow." * * *

Plaintiff alleges that defendants' promotional poster for "Moscow" infringes his copyright on an illustration that he drew for The New Yorker and that appeared on the cover of the March 29, 1976 issue of the magazine, in violation of 17 U.S.C. §§ 101–810. Defendants deny this allegation and assert the affirmative defenses of fair use as a parody, estoppel and laches.

Defendants have moved, and plaintiff has cross-moved, for summary judgment. For the reasons set forth below, this court rejects defendants' asserted defenses and grants summary judgment on the issue of copying to plaintiff.

I

* * *

Summary judgment is often disfavored in copyright cases, for courts are generally reluctant to make subjective comparisons and determinations. Hoehling v. Universal City Studios, Inc., 618 F.2d 972, 977 (2d Cir.1980), citing Arnstein v. Porter, 154 F.2d 464, 474 (2d Cir. 1946). Recently, however, this circuit has "recognized that a court may determine non-infringement as a matter of law on a motion for summary judgment." Warner Brothers v. American Broadcasting Cos., 720 F.2d 231, 240 (2d Cir.1983) * * *.

The voluminous submissions that accompanied these cross-motions leave no factual issues concerning which further evidence is likely to be presented at a trial. Moreover, the factual determinations necessary to this decision do not involve conflicts in testimony that would depend for their resolution on an assessment of witness credibility. In addition, this case is different from most copyright infringement actions, in which it is preferable to leave the determination of the issue to a jury: each party has implied that its case is complete by moving for summary judgment, and as neither side has requested a jury, the court would be the trier of fact at trial. Finally, the interests of judicial economy are also served by deciding the case at its present stage. Summary judgment is therefore appropriate.

II

The essential facts are not disputed by the parties despite their disagreements on nonessential matters. On March 29, 1976, *The New Yorker* published as a cover illustration the work at issue in this suit, widely known as a parochial New Yorker's view of the world. The magazine registered this illustration with the United States Copyright Office and subsequently assigned the copyright to Steinberg. Approximately three months later, plaintiff and *The New Yorker* entered into an agreement to print and sell a certain number of posters of the cover illustration.

It is undisputed that unauthorized duplications of the poster were made and distributed by unknown persons, although the parties disagree on the extent to which plaintiff attempted to prevent the distribution of those counterfeits. Plaintiff has also conceded that numerous posters have been created and published depicting other localities in the same manner that he depicted New York in his illustration. These facts, however, are irrelevant to the merits of this case, which concerns only the relationship between plaintiff's and defendants' illustrations.

Defendants' illustration was created to advertise the movie "Moscow on the Hudson," which recounts the adventures of a Muscovite who defects in New York. In designing this illustration, Columbia's executive art director, Kevin Nolan, has admitted that he specifically referred to Steinberg's poster, and indeed, that he purchased it and hung it, among others, in his office. Furthermore, Nolan explicitly directed the outside artist whom he retained to execute his design, Craig Nelson, to use Steinberg's poster to achieve a more recognizably New York look. Indeed, Nelson acknowledged having used the facade of one particular edifice, at Nolan's suggestion that it would render his drawing more "New York-ish." While the two buildings are not identical, they are so similar that it is impossible, especially in view of the artist's testimony, not to find that defendants impermissibly copied plaintiff's copyright.[1]

To decide the issue of infringement, it is necessary to consider the posters themselves. Steinberg's illustration presents a bird's eye view across a portion of the western edge of Manhattan, past the Hudson River and a telescoped version of the rest of the United States and the Pacific Ocean, to a red strip of horizon, beneath which are three flat land masses labeled China, Japan and Russia. The name of the magazine, in *The New Yorker's* usual typeface, occupies the top fifth of the poster, beneath a thin band of blue wash representing a stylized sky.

The parts of the poster beyond New York are minimalized, to symbolize a New Yorker's myopic view of the centrality of his city to the world. The entire United States west of the Hudson River, for example, is reduced to a brown strip labeled "Jersey," together with a light green trapezoid with a few rudimentary rock outcroppings and the names of only seven cities and two states scattered across it. The few blocks of Manhattan, by contrast, are depicted and colored in detail. The four square blocks of the city, which occupy the whole lower half of the poster, include numerous buildings, pedestrians and cars, as well as parking lots and lamp posts, with water towers atop a few of the buildings. The whimsical, sketchy style and spiky lettering are recognizable as Steinberg's.

The "Moscow" illustration depicts the three main characters of the film on the lower third of their poster, superimposed on a bird's eye

---

1. Nolan claimed also to have been inspired by some of the posters that were inspired by Steinberg's; such secondary inspiration, however, is irrelevant to whether or not the "Moscow" poster infringes plaintiff's copyright by having impermissibly copied it.

view of New York City, and continues eastward across Manhattan and the Atlantic Ocean, past a rudimentary evocation of Europe, to a clump of recognizably Russian-styled buildings on the horizon, labeled "Moscow." The movie credits appear over the lower portion of the characters. The central part of the poster depicts approximately four New York city blocks, with fairly detailed buildings, pedestrians and vehicles, a parking lot, and some water towers and lamp posts. Columbia's artist added a few New York landmarks at apparently random places in his illustration, apparently to render the locale more easily recognizable. Beyond the blue strip labeled "Atlantic Ocean," Europe is represented by London, Paris and Rome, each anchored by a single landmark (although the landmark used for Rome is the Leaning Tower of Pisa).

The horizon behind Moscow is delineated by a red crayoned strip, above which are the title of the movie and a brief textual introduction to the plot. The poster is crowned by a thin strip of blue wash, apparently a stylization of the sky. This poster is executed in a blend of styles: the three characters, whose likenesses were copied from a photograph, have realistic faces and somewhat sketchy clothing, and the city blocks are drawn in a fairly detailed but sketchy style. The lettering on the drawing is spiky, in block-printed handwritten capital letters substantially identical to plaintiff's, while the printed texts at the top and bottom of the poster are in the typeface commonly associated with The New Yorker magazine.[2]

III

* * * [T]he sole issue * * * with respect to liability is whether there is such substantial similarity between the copyrighted and accused works as to establish a violation of plaintiff's copyright. The central issue of "substantial similarity," which can be considered a close question of fact, may also validly be decided as a question of law. * * *

"Substantial similarity" is an elusive concept. This circuit has recently recognized that

> [t]he 'substantial similarity' that supports an inference of copying sufficient to establish infringement of a copyright is not a concept familiar to the public at large. It is a term to be used in a courtroom to strike a delicate balance between the protection to which authors are entitled under an act of Congress and the freedom that exists for all others to create their works outside the area protected by infringement.

Warner Bros., 720 F.2d at 245.

The definition of "substantial similarity" in this circuit is "whether an average lay observer would recognize the alleged copy as having been appropriated from the copyrighted work." Ideal Toy Corp. v. Fab–

2. The typeface is not a subject of copyright, but the similarity reinforces the impression that defendants copied plaintiff's illustration.

Lu Ltd., 360 F.2d 1021, 1022 (2d Cir.1966) * * *. A plaintiff need no longer meet the severe "ordinary observer" test established by Judge Learned Hand in Peter Pan Fabrics, Inc. v. Martin Weiner Corp., 274 F.2d 487 (2d Cir.1960). Uneeda Doll Co., Inc. v. Regent Baby Products Corp., 355 F.Supp. 438, 450 (E.D.N.Y.1972). Under Judge Hand's formulation, there would be substantial similarity only where "the ordinary observer, unless he set out to detect the disparities, would be disposed to overlook them, and regard their aesthetic appeal as the same." 274 F.2d at 489.

Moreover, it is now recognized that "[t]he copying need not be of every detail so long as the copy is substantially similar to the copyrighted work." Comptone Co. v. Rayex Corp., 251 F.2d 487, 488 (2d Cir. 1958). * * *

In determining whether there is substantial similarity between two works, it is crucial to distinguish between an idea and its expression. It is an axiom of copyright law, established in the case law and since codified at 17 U.S.C. § 102(b), that only the particular expression of an idea is protectible, while the idea itself is not. * * *

There is no dispute that defendants cannot be held liable for using the idea of a map of the world from an egocentrically myopic perspective. No rigid principle has been developed, however, to ascertain when one has gone beyond the idea to the expression, and "[d]ecisions must therefore inevitably be ad hoc." Peter Pan Fabrics, Inc. v. Martin Weiner Corp., 274 F.2d 487, 489 (2d Cir.1960) (L. Hand, J.). As Judge Frankel once observed, "Good eyes and common sense may be as useful as deep study of reported and unreported cases, which themselves are tied to highly particularized facts." Couleur International Ltd. v. Opulent Fabrics, Inc., 330 F.Supp. 152, 153 (S.D.N.Y.1971).

Even at first glance, one can see the striking stylistic relationship between the posters, and since style is one ingredient of "expression," this relationship is significant. Defendants' illustration was executed in the sketchy, whimsical style that has become one of Steinberg's hallmarks. Both illustrations represent a bird's eye view across the edge of Manhattan and a river bordering New York City to the world beyond. Both depict approximately four city blocks in detail and become increasingly minimalist as the design recedes into the background. Both use the device of a narrow band of blue wash across the top of the poster to represent the sky, and both delineate the horizon with a band of primary red.[3]

---

3. Defendants claim that since this use of thin bands of primary colors is a traditional Japanese technique, their adoption of it cannot infringe Steinberg's copyright. This argument ignores the principle that while "[o]thers are free to copy the original . . . [t]hey are not free to copy the copy." Bleistein v. Donaldson Lithographing Co.,

188 U.S. 239, 250 (1903) (Holmes, J.). Cf. Dave Grossman Designs, Inc. v. Bortin, 347 F.Supp. 1150, 1156–57 (N.D.Ill.1972) (an artist may use the same subject and style as another "so long as the second artist does not substantially copy [the first artist's] specific expression of his idea.").

The strongest similarity is evident in the rendering of the New York City blocks. Both artists chose a vantage point that looks directly down a wide two-way cross street that intersects two avenues before reaching a river. Despite defendants' protestations, this is not an inevitable way of depicting blocks in a city with a grid-like street system, particularly since most New York City cross streets are one-way. Since even a photograph may be copyrighted because "no photograph, however simple, can be unaffected by the personal influence of the author," Time Inc. v. Bernard Geis Assoc., 293 F.Supp. 130, 141 (S.D.N.Y.1968) [described p. 601, n. 1 supra], quoting Bleistein [supra page 585], one can hardly gainsay the right of an artist to protect his choice of perspective and lay-out in a drawing, especially in conjunction with the overall concept and individual details. Indeed, the fact that defendants changed the names of the streets while retaining the same graphic depiction weakens their case: had they intended their illustration realistically to depict the streets labeled on the poster, their four city blocks would not so closely resemble plaintiff's four city blocks. Moreover, their argument that they intended the jumble of streets and landmarks and buildings to symbolize their Muscovite protagonist's confusion in a new city does not detract from the strong similarity between their poster and Steinberg's.

While not all of the details are identical, many of them could be mistaken for one another; for example, the depiction of the water towers, and the cars, and the red sign above a parking lot, and even many of the individual buildings. The shapes, windows, and configurations of various edifices are substantially similar. The ornaments, facades and details of Steinberg's buildings appear in defendants', although occasionally at other locations. In this context, it is significant that Steinberg did not depict any buildings actually erected in New York; rather, he was inspired by the general appearance of the structures on the West Side of Manhattan to create his own New York-ish structures. Thus, the similarity between the buildings depicted in the "Moscow" and Steinberg posters cannot be explained by an assertion that the artists happened to choose the same buildings to draw. The close similarity can be explained only by the defendants' artist having copied the plaintiff's work. Similarly, the locations and size, the errors and anomalies of Steinberg's shadows and streetlight, are meticulously imitated.

In addition, the Columbia artist's use of the childlike, spiky block print that has become one of Steinberg's hallmarks to letter the names of the streets in the "Moscow" poster can be explained only as copying. There is no inherent justification for using this style of lettering to label New York City streets as it is associated with New York only through Steinberg's poster.

While defendants' poster shows the city of Moscow on the horizon in far greater detail than anything is depicted in the background of plaintiff's illustration, this fact alone cannot alter the conclusion. "Substantial similarity" does not require identity, and "duplication or near identity is not necessary to establish infringement." *Krofft,* 562 F.2d at 1167. Neither the depiction of Moscow, nor the eastward perspective, nor the presence of randomly scattered New York City landmarks in defendants' poster suffices to eliminate the substantial similarity between the posters. As Judge Learned Hand wrote, "no plagiarist can excuse the wrong by showing how much of his work he did not pirate." Sheldon v. Metro–Goldwyn Pictures Corp. [supra page 644] * * *.

Defendants argue that their poster could not infringe plaintiff's copyright because only a small portion of its design could possibly be considered similar. This argument is both factually and legally without merit. "[A] copyright infringement may occur by reason of a substantial similarity that involves only a small portion of each work." Burroughs v. Metro–Goldwyn–Mayer, Inc., 683 F.2d 610, 624 n. 14 (2d Cir.1982). Moreover, this case involves the entire protected work and an iconographically, as well as proportionately, significant portion of the allegedly infringing work. * * *

The process by which defendants' poster was created also undermines this argument. The "map," that is, the portion about which plaintiff is complaining, was designed separately from the rest of the poster. The likenesses of the three main characters, which were copied from a photograph, and the blocks of text were superimposed on the completed map.

I also reject defendants' argument that any similarities between the works are unprotectible *scenes a faire,* or "incidents, characters or settings which, as a practical matter, are indispensable or standard in the treatment of a given topic." Walker [v. Time–Life Films, Inc.], 615 F.Supp. [430] at 436 [(S.D.N.Y.1985), aff'd, 784 F.2d 44 (2d Cir.1986), cert. denied, 106 S.Ct. 2278 (1986)]. See also Reyher [v. Children's Television Workshop], 533 F.2d [87] at 92 [(2d Cir.1976)]. It is undeniable that a drawing of New York City blocks could be expected to include buildings, pedestrians, vehicles, lampposts and water towers. Plaintiff, however, does not complain of defendants' mere use of these elements in their poster; rather, his complaint is that defendants copied his expression of those elements of a street scene.

While evidence of independent creation by the defendants would rebut plaintiff's *prima facie* case, "the absence of any countervailing evidence of creation independent of the copyrighted source may well render clearly erroneous a finding that there was not copying." Roth Greeting Cards v. United Card Co., 429 F.2d 1106, 1110 (9th Cir.1970). * * *.

Moreover, it is generally recognized that ". . . since a very high degree of similarity is required in order to dispense with proof of access, it must logically follow that where proof of access is offered, the required degree of similarity may be somewhat less than would be necessary in the absence of such proof." 2 *Nimmer* § 143.4 at 634, quoted in Krofft, 562 F.2d at 1172. As defendants have conceded access to plaintiff's copyrighted illustration, a somewhat lesser degree of similarity suffices to establish a copyright infringement than might otherwise be required. Here, however, the demonstrable similarities are such that proof of access, although in fact conceded, is almost unnecessary.

[The court also held that the copying was not fair use under 17 U.S.C. § 107.] * * *

For the reasons set out above, summary judgment is granted to plaintiffs as to copying.

HOEHLING v. UNIVERSAL CITY STUDIOS, INC.

United States Court of Appeals, Second Circuit, 1980.
618 F.2d 972.

IRVING R. KAUFMAN, CHIEF JUDGE. A grant of copyright in a published work secures for its author a limited monopoly over the expression it contains. The copyright provides a financial incentive to those who would add to the corpus of existing knowledge by creating original works. Nevertheless, the protection afforded the copyright holder has never extended to history, be it documented fact or explanatory hypothesis. The rationale for this doctrine is that the cause of knowledge is best served when history is the common property of all, and each generation remains free to draw upon the discoveries and insights of the past. Accordingly, the scope of copyright in historical accounts is narrow indeed, embracing no more than the author's original expression of particular facts and theories already in the public domain. As the case before us illustrates, absent wholesale usurpation of another's expression, claims of copyright infringement where works of history are at issue are rarely successful.

I.

This litigation arises from three separate accounts of the triumphant introduction, last voyage, and tragic destruction of the Hindenburg, the colossal dirigible constructed in Germany during Hitler's reign. The zeppelin, the last and most sophisticated in a fleet of luxury airships, which punctually floated its wealthy passengers from the Third Reich to the United States, exploded into flames and disintegrated in 35 seconds as it hovered above the Lakehurst, New Jersey Naval Air Station at 7:25 p.m. on May 6, 1937. Thirty-six passengers and crew were killed but, fortunately, 52 persons survived. Official investigations conducted by both American and German authorities could ascertain no definitive cause of the disaster, but both suggested the plausibility of static electricity or St. Elmo's Fire, which could have ignited the highly explosive hydrogen that filled the airship. Throughout, the investigators refused to rule out the possibility of sabotage.

The destruction of the Hindenburg marked the concluding chapter in the chronicle of airship passenger service, for after the tragedy at Lakehurst, the Nazi regime permanently grounded the Graf Zeppelin I and discontinued its plan to construct an even larger dirigible, the Graf Zeppelin II.

The final pages of the airship's story marked the beginning of a series of journalistic, historical, and literary accounts devoted to the Hindenburg and its fate. Indeed, weeks of testimony by a plethora of witnesses before the official investigative panels provided fertile source material for would-be authors. Moreover, both the American and German Commissions issued official reports, detailing all that was then known of the tragedy. A number of newspaper and magazine articles had been written about the Hindenburg in 1936, its first year of trans-Atlantic service, and they, of course, multiplied many fold after the crash. In addition, two passengers—Margaret Mather and Gertrud Adelt—published separate and detailed accounts of the voyage, C.E. Rosendahl, commander of the Lakehurst Naval Air Station and a pioneer in airship travel himself, wrote a book titled *What About the Airship?*, in which he endorsed the theory that the Hindenburg was the victim of sabotage. In 1957, Nelson Gidding, who would return to the subject of the Hindenburg some 20 years later, wrote an unpublished "treatment" for a motion picture based on the deliberate destruction of the airship. In that year as well, John Toland published *Ships in the Sky* which, in its seventeenth chapter, chronicled the last flight of the Hindenburg. In 1962, Dale Titler released *Wings of Mystery*, in which he too devoted a chapter to the Hindenburg.[1]

Appellant A.A. Hoehling published *Who Destroyed the Hindenburg?*, a full-length book based on his exhaustive research in 1962. Mr. Hoehling studied the investigative reports, consulted previously published articles and books, and conducted interviews with survivors of the crash as well as others who possessed information about the Hindenburg. His book is presented as a factual account, written in an objective, reportorial style.

The first half recounts the final crossing of the Hindenburg, from Sunday, May 2, when it left Frankfurt, to Thursday, May 6, when it exploded at Lakehurst. Hoehling describes the airship, its role as an instrument of propaganda in Nazi Germany, its passengers and crew, the danger of hydrogen, and the ominous threats received by German officials, warning that the Hindenburg would be destroyed. The second portion, headed *The Quest,* sets forth the progress of the official investigations, followed by an account of Hoehling's own research. In the final chapter, spanning eleven pages, Hoehling suggests that all proffered explanations of the explosion, save deliberate destruction, are unconvincing. He concludes that the most likely saboteur is one Eric Spehl, a "rigger" on the Hindenburg crew who was killed at Lakehurst.

According to Hoehling, Spehl had motive, expertise, and opportunity to plant an explosive device, constructed of dry-cell batteries and a

---

1. Titler's account was published after the release of appellant's book. In an affidavit in this litigation, Titler states that he copied Hoehling's theory of sabotage. Hoehling, however, has never instituted a copyright action against Titler.

flashbulb, in "Gas Cell 4," the location of the initial explosion. An amateur photographer with access to flashbulbs, Spehl could have destroyed the Hindenburg to please his ladyfriend, a suspected communist dedicated to exploding the myth of Nazi invincibility.

Ten years later appellee Michael MacDonald Mooney published his book, *The Hindenburg.* Mooney's endeavor might be characterized as more literary than historical in its attempt to weave a number of symbolic themes through the actual events surrounding the tragedy. His dominant theme contrasts the natural beauty of the month of May, when the disaster occurred, with the cold, deliberate progress of "technology." The May theme is expressed not simply by the season, but also by the character of Spehl, portrayed as a sensitive artisan with needle and thread. The Hindenburg, in contrast, is the symbol of technology, as are its German creators and the Reich itself. The destruction is depicted as the ultimate triumph of nature over technology, as Spehl plants the bomb that ignites the hydrogen. Developing this theme from the outset, Mooney begins with an extended review of man's efforts to defy nature through flight, focusing on the evolution of the zeppelin. This story culminates in the construction of the Hindenburg, and the Nazis' claims of its indestructibility. Mooney then traces the fateful voyage, advising the reader almost immediately of Spehl's scheme. The book concludes with the airship's explosion.

Mooney acknowledges, in this case, that he consulted Hoehling's book, and that he relied on it for some details. He asserts that he first discovered the "Spehl-as-saboteur" theory when he read Titler's *Wings of Mystery.* Indeed, Titler concludes that Spehl was the saboteur, for essentially the reasons stated by Hoehling. Mooney also claims to have studied the complete National Archives and New York Times files concerning the Hindenburg, as well as all previously published material. Moreover, he traveled to Germany, visited Spehl's birthplace, and conducted a number of interviews with survivors.

After Mooney prepared an outline of his anticipated book, his publisher succeeded in negotiations to sell the motion picture rights to appellee Universal City Studios. Universal then commissioned a screen story by writers Levinson and Link, best known for their television series, *Columbo,* in which a somewhat disheveled, but wise detective unravels artfully conceived murder mysteries. In their screen story, Levinson and Link created a Columbo-like character who endeavored to identify the saboteur on board the Hindenburg. Director Robert Wise, however, was not satisfied with this version, and called upon Nelson Gidding to write a final screenplay. Gidding, it will be recalled, had engaged in preliminary work on a film about the Hindenburg almost twenty years earlier.

The Gidding screenplay follows what is known in the motion picture industry as a "Grand Hotel" formula, developing a number of fictional characters and subplots involving them. This formula has become standard fare in so-called "disaster" movies, which have enjoyed a certain popularity in recent years. In the film, which was released in late 1975, a rigger named "Boerth," who has an anti-Nazi ladyfriend, plans to destroy the airship in an effort to embarrass the Reich. Nazi officials, vaguely aware of sabotage threats, station a Luftwaffe intelligence officer on the zeppelin, loosely resembling a Colonel Erdmann who was aboard the Hindenburg. This character is portrayed as a likeable fellow who soon discovers that Boerth is the saboteur. Boerth, however, convinces him that the Hindenburg should be destroyed and the two join forces, planning the explosion for several hours after the landing at Lakehurst, when no people would be on board. In Gidding's version, the airship is delayed by a storm, frantic efforts to defuse the bomb fail, and the Hindenburg is destroyed. The film's subplots involve other possible suspects, including a fictional countess who has had her estate expropriated by the Reich, two fictional confidence men wanted by New York City police, and an advertising executive rushing to close a business deal in America.

Upon learning of Universal's plans to release the film, Hoehling instituted this action against Universal for copyright infringement and common law unfair competition in the district court for the District of Columbia in October 1975. Judge Smith declined to issue an order restraining release of the film in December, and it was distributed throughout the nation.

In January 1976, Hoehling sought to amend his complaint to include Mooney as a defendant. The district court, however, decided that it lacked personal jurisdiction over Mooney. In June 1976, Hoehling again attempted to amend his complaint, this time to add Mooney's publishers as defendants. Judge Smith denied this motion as well, but granted Hoehling's request to transfer the litigation to the Southern District of New York, 28 U.S.C. § 1404(a), where Mooney himself was successfully included as a party. Judge Metzner, with the assistance of Magistrate Sinclair, supervised extensive discovery through most of 1978. After the completion of discovery, both Mooney and Universal moved for summary judgment, Fed.R.Civ.P. 56, which was granted on August 1, 1979.

II.

It is undisputed that Hoehling has a valid copyright in his book. To prove infringement, however, he must demonstrate that defendants "copied" his work and that they "improperly appropriated" his "expression." See Arnstein v. Porter, 154 F.2d 464, 468 (2d Cir.1946). Ordinarily, wrongful appropriation is shown by proving a "substantial similarity" of *copyrightable* expression. See Nichols v. Universal Pictures Corp., 45 F.2d 119, 121 (2d Cir.1930), cert. denied, 282 U.S. 902 (1931). Because substantial similarity is customarily an extremely close question of fact, see Arnstein, supra, 154 F.2d at 468, summary judgment has traditionally been frowned upon in copyright litigation, id. at 474. Nevertheless, while *Arnstein*'s influence in other areas of the law has been diminished, see SEC v. Research Automation Corp., 585 F.2d 31 (2d Cir.1978); 6 Moore's Federal Practice ¶ 56.17[14] (2d ed. 1976), a series of copyright cases in the Southern District of New York have granted defendants summary judgment when all alleged similarity related to *non*-copyrightable elements of the plaintiff's work, see, e.g., Alexander v. Haley, 460 F.Supp. 40 (S.D.N.Y.1978); Musto v. Meyer, 434 F.Supp. 32 (S.D.N.Y.1977); Gardner v. Nizer, 391 F.Supp. 940 (S.D. N.Y.1975); Fuld v. National Broadcasting Co., 390 F.Supp. 877 (S.D. N.Y.1975). These cases signal an important development in the law of copyright, permitting courts to put "a swift end to meritless litigation" and to avoid lengthy and costly trials. Quinn v. Syracuse Model Neighborhood Corp., 613 F.2d 438, 445 (2d Cir.1980); accord, Donnelly v. Guion, 467 F.2d 290, 293 (2d Cir.1972); American Manufacturers Mutual Insurance Co. v. American Broadcasting-Paramount Theatres, Inc., 388 F.2d 272, 278 (2d Cir.1967). Drawing on these cases, Judge Metzner assumed both copying and substantial similarity, but concluded that all similarities pertained to various categories of non-copyrightable material. Accordingly, he granted appellees' motion for summary judgment. We affirm the judgment of the district court.

A

Hoehling's principal claim is that both Mooney and Universal copied the essential plot of his book—i.e., Eric Spehl, influenced by his girlfriend, sabotaged the Hindenburg by placing a crude bomb in Gas Cell 4. In their briefs, and at oral argument, appellees have labored to convince us that their plots are not substantially similar to Hoehling's. While Hoehling's Spehl destroys the airship to please his communist girlfriend, Mooney's character is motivated by an aversion to the technological age. Universal's Boerth, on the other hand, is a fervent anti-fascist who enlists the support of a Luftwaffe colonel who, in turn, unsuccessfully attempts to defuse the bomb at the eleventh hour.

Although this argument has potential merit when presented to a fact finder adjudicating the issue of substantial similarity, it is largely irrelevant to a motion for summary judgment where the issue of substantial similarity has been eliminated by the judge's affirmative assumption. Under Rule 56(c), summary judgment is appropriate only when "there is no genuine issue as to any material fact." Accord, Heyman v. Commerce & Industry Insurance Co., 524 F.2d 1317 (2d Cir. 1975). Perhaps recognizing this, appellees further argue that Hoehling's plot is an "idea," and ideas are not copyrightable as a matter of law. See Sheldon v. Metro-Goldwyn Pictures Corp., 81 F.2d 49, 54 (2d Cir.), cert. denied, 298 U.S. 669 (1936).

Hoehling, however, correctly rejoins that while ideas themselves are not subject to copyright, his "expression" of *his* idea is copyrightable. Id. at 54. He relies on Learned Hand's opinion in *Sheldon,* supra, at 50, holding that *Letty Lynton* infringed *Dishonored Lady* by copying its story of a woman who poisons her lover, and Augustus

Hand's analysis in Detective Comics, Inc. v. Bruns Publications, Inc., 111 F.2d 432 (2d Cir.1940), concluding that the exploits of "Wonderman" infringed the copyright held by the creators of "Superman," the original indestructible man. Moreover, Hoehling asserts that, in both these cases, the line between "ideas" and "expression" is drawn, in the first instance, by the fact finder.

Sheldon and *Detective Comics*, however, dealt with works of fiction,[4] where the distinction between an idea and its expression is especially elusive. But, where, as here, the idea at issue is an interpretation of an historical event, our cases hold that such interpretations are not copyrightable as a matter of law. In Rosemont Enterprises, Inc. v. Random House, Inc., 366 F.2d 303 (2d Cir.1966), cert. denied, 385 U.S. 1009 (1967), we held that the defendant's biography of Howard Hughes did not infringe an earlier biography of the reclusive alleged billionaire. Although the plots of the two works were necessarily similar, there could be no infringement because of the "public benefit in encouraging the development of historical and biographical works and their public distribution." Id. at 307; accord, Oxford Book Co. v. College Entrance Book Co., 98 F.2d 688 (2d Cir.1938). To avoid a chilling effect on authors who contemplate tackling an historical issue or event, broad latitude must be granted to subsequent authors who make use of historical subject matter, including theories or plots. Learned Hand counseled in Myers v. Mail & Express Co., 36 C.O.Bull. 478, 479 (S.D.N.Y.1919), "[t]here cannot be any such thing as copyright in the order of presentation of the facts, nor, indeed, in their selection."[5]

In the instant case, the hypothesis that Eric Spehl destroyed the Hindenburg is based entirely on the interpretation of historical facts, including Spehl's life, his girlfriend's anti-Nazi connections, the explosion's origin in Gas Cell 4, Spehl's duty station, discovery of a dry-cell battery among the wreckage, and rumors about Spehl's involvement dating from a 1938 Gestapo investigation. Such an historical interpretation, whether or not it originated with Mr. Hoehling, is not protected by his copyright and can be freely used by subsequent authors.

4. In *Sheldon*, both works were loosely based on an actual murder committed by a young Scottish girl. Judge Hand, however, clearly dealt only with the fictional plots conceived by the respective authors. See Sheldon v. Metro-Goldwyn Pictures Corp., 81 F.2d 49, 54 (2d Cir.) cert. denied, 298 U.S. 669 (1936).

5. This circuit has permitted extensive reliance on prior works of history. See, e.g., Gardner v. Nizer, 391 F.Supp. 940 (S.D.N.Y.1975) (the story of the Rosenberg trial not copyrightable); Fuld v. National Broadcasting Co., 390 F.Supp. 877 (S.D. N.Y.1975) ("Bugsy" Siegel's life story not copyrightable); Greenbie v. Noble, 151 F.Supp. 45 (S.D.N.Y.1957) (the life of Anna Carroll, a member of Lincoln's cabinet, not copyrightable). The commentators are in accord with this view. See, e.g. 1 Nimmer on Copyright § 2.11[A] (1979); Chafee, Reflections on the Law of Copyright: I, 45 Colum.L.Rev. 503, 511 (1945).

B

The same reasoning governs Hoehling's claim that a number of specific facts, ascertained through his personal research, were copied by appellees.[6] The cases in this circuit, however, make clear that factual information is in the public domain. See, e.g., Rosemont Enterprises, Inc., supra, 366 F.2d at 309; Oxford Book Co., supra, 98 F.2d at 691. Each appellee had the right to "avail himself of the facts contained" in Hoehling's book and to "use such information, whether correct or incorrect, in his own literary work." Greenbie v. Noble, 151 F.Supp. 45, 67 (S.D.N.Y.1957). Accordingly, there is little consolation in relying on cases in other circuits holding that the fruits of original research are copyrightable. See, e.g., Toksvig v. Bruce Publications Corp., 181 F.2d 664, 667 (7th Cir.1950); Miller v. Universal City Studios, Inc., 460 F.Supp. 984 (S.D.Fla.1978). Indeed, this circuit has clearly repudiated *Toksvig* and its progeny. In Rosemont Enterprises, Inc., supra, 366 F.2d at 310, we refused to "subscribe to the view that an author is absolutely precluded from saving time and effort by referring to and relying upon prior published material. * * * It is just such wasted effort that the proscription against the copyright of ideas and facts * * * are designed to prevent." Accord, 1 Nimmer on Copyright § 2.11 (1979).

* * *

D

All of Hoehling's allegations of copying, therefore, encompass material that is non-copyrightable as a matter of law, rendering summary judgment entirely appropriate. We are aware, however, that in distinguishing between themes, facts, and *scenes a faire* on the one hand, and copyrightable expression on the other, courts may lose sight of the forest for the trees. By factoring out similarities based on non-copyrightable elements, a court runs the risk of overlooking wholesale usurpation of a prior author's expression. A verbatim reproduction of another work, of course, even in the realm of nonfiction, is actionable as copyright infringement. See Wainwright Securities, Inc. v. Wall Street Transcript Corp., 558 F.2d 91 (2d Cir.1977), cert. denied, 434 U.S. 1014 (1978). Thus, in granting or reviewing a grant of summary

---

6. In detailed comparisons of his book with Mooney's work and Universal's motion picture, Hoehling isolates 266 and 75 alleged instances of copying, respectively. Judge Metzner correctly pointed out that many of these allegations are patently frivolous. The vast majority of the remainder deals with alleged copying of historical facts. It would serve no purpose to review Hoehling's specific allegations in detail in this opinion. The following ten examples, however, are illustrative: (1) Eric Spehl's age and birthplace; (2) Crew members had smuggled monkeys on board the Graf Zeppelin; (3) Germany's abassador to the United States dismissed threats of sabotage; (4) A warning letter had been received from a Mrs. Rauch; (5) The Hindenburg's captain was constructing a new home in Zeppelinheim; (6) Eric Spehl was a photographer; (7) The airship flew over Boston; (8) The Hindenburg was "tail heavy" before landing; (9) A member of the ground crew had etched his name in the zeppelin's hull; and (10) The navigator set the Hindenburg's course by reference to various North Atlantic islands.

judgment for defendants, courts should assure themselves that the works before them are not virtually identical. In this case, it is clear that all three authors relate the story of the Hindenburg differently.

In works devoted to historical subjects, it is our view that a second author may make significant use of prior work, so long as he does not bodily appropriate the expression of another. Rosemont Enterprises, Inc., supra, 366 F.2d at 310. This principle is justified by the fundamental policy undergirding the copyright laws—the encouragement of contributions to recorded knowledge. The "financial reward guaranteed to the copyright holder is but an incident of this general objective, rather than an end in itself." Berlin v. E.C. Publications, Inc., 329 F.2d 541, 543-44 (2d Cir.), cert. denied, 379 U.S. 822 (1964). Knowledge is expanded as well by granting new authors of historical works a relatively free hand to build upon the work of their predecessors.[7]

III.

Finally, we affirm Judge Metzner's rejection of Hoehling's claims based on the common law of "unfair competition." Where, as here, historical facts, themes, and research have been deliberately exempted from the scope of copyright protection to vindicate the overriding goal of encouraging contributions to recorded knowledge, the states are preempted from removing such material from the public domain. See, e.g., Sears, Roebuck & Co. v. Stiffel Co., 376 U.S. 225 (1964); Compco Corp. v. Day-Brite Lighting, Inc., 376 U.S. 234 (1964). "To forbid copying" in this case, "would interfere with the federal policy * * * of allowing free access to copy whatever the federal patent and copyright laws leave in the public domain." Id. at 237.

The judgment of the district court is affirmed.

NOTE

The Fifth Circuit followed *Hoehling* and the other Second Circuit precedents in Miller v. Universal City Studios, 650 F.2d 1365 (5th Cir.1981). Plaintiff was a reporter for the Miami Herald who had written in collaboration with the victim a book entitled "83 Hours Till Dawn," the story of the ordeal of the college-aged daughter of a wealthy Florida land developer who was abducted from an Atlanta motel room and buried alive in a plywood and fiberglass capsule from which she was rescued after five days. A Universal City Studios producer read the book and thought it good material for a television movie. When negotiations for purchase of the screen rights to "83 Hours Till Dawn" broke down, the studio proceeded with the project, instructing the scriptwriter that no use was to be made of the book in preparing the script. The movie was completed and shown as the ABC Movie of the Week with the title "The Longest Night." Plaintiff sued for copyright infringement and won a jury verdict. The appellate court reversed because the instructions (and plaintiff's

---

7. We note that publication of Mooney's book and release of the motion picture revived long dormant interest in the Hindenburg. As a result, Hoehling's book, which had been out of print for some time, was actually re-released after the film was featured in theaters across the country.

arguments) to the jury included the statement that "if an author, in writing a book concerning factual matters, engages in research on these matters, his research is copyrightable." 650 F.2d 1368.

The infringement cases studied so far have involved works of fiction, drama, history, music and graphic art, all close to the core of traditional copyright protection. In the past half century, however, there has been an expansion in the use of copyright to protect "works" which are more like commercial than artistic products—fabric designs, computer programs and data bases, promotional campaigns and symbols. Is the standard of infringement different for each kind of protected work? Or is the concept of infringement a unitary concept that applies in the same way to works extending all the way from a novel to a movie of a jazz concert to a patterned napkin to a directory of gardening suppliers?

The statute itself makes no distinction among the types of protected works in §§ 106 and 107, which define the scope of the "exclusive right" for all classes of copyrighted works. That is not to say that the statute does not show an awareness of differences between different kinds of works and different uses of those works, for they are addressed in complex detail in § 108 (reproduction of copies or phonorecords by libraries and archives), § 110 (non-profit teaching), § 111 (secondary transmission by cable systems and others), § 114 (limits on application of § 106 to sound recordings), § 115 (use of nondramatic musical works in phonorecords), § 116 (performance of phonorecords by juke boxes), § 117 (use of computer programs), and § 118 (use of works by public broadcasting). Thus the statute can easily be read to support the position that infringement is a unitary concept that does not vary depending upon the class of work to be protected.

Nevertheless, the view of the most thoughtful commentators, see, e.g., Robert A. Gorman, Copyright Protection for the Collection and Representation of Facts, 76 Harv.L.Rev. 1569 (1963), is that the range of works protected is so great, and the differences among them so substantial, that it is necessary to adapt the test of infringement to the nature of the work involved. Even if a court uses the same verbal formula for determining what is an infringement, the process is necessarily very different as between, for instance, drama and music, not to say as between a design upon a T-shirt and a map.

1. *Fact Works.* Gorman (in 76 Harv., supra) coined the term "fact works" to apply to works as varied as maps, news stories, directories, advertisements, photographs, and legal and business forms. They all have in common that many of the works in these categories will consist of no more than a collection and organization of data supplied by the environment. Now included within this category would be computer programs and data bases. What are the protectible elements of such a work?

Consider the simple example of an alphabatized directory. What is protected? The names and addresses alphabitized are the names and addresses of the persons listed, and are not the subject of copyright, for they are not created by the "author" of the directory but simply copied from some other source. The alphabetical method of organization is not protected, for it is a long-known technique, surely in the public domain. Does this mean that a competitor who wants to make and sell a competitive directory can just copy the first one? Of course, if the second firm literally copies every detail of the first, including the art work (if any), then there will be infringement of the art work. But suppose that the second firm sets new type, using the first directory as its guide? Suppose the competitor copies the listings but reorganizes them? In Leon v. Pacific Tel. & Tel. Co., 91 F.2d 484 (9th Cir.1937), it was held that a directory organized by number infringed the alphabetized directory from which it was prepared. And in Addison-Wesley Publishing Co. v. Brown, 223 F.Supp. 219 (E.D.N.Y.1963), the court held that it infringed the copyright on a math book to publish a separate book containing the answers.

Producers of materials of this type have long anticipated this problem by inserting into their work phony, arbitrary elements. The blatant copier copies these phony elements and thereafter is hard pressed to argue that he took only the "unprotected elements." For instance, a dictionary might contain fifty or so entries for words that do not exist and do not appear in any other dictionary. Examples abound in the litigated cases. Rockford Map Publishers, Inc. v. Directory Service Company of Colorado, Inc., 768 F.2d 145 (7th Cir.1985), was a suit by a firm in the business of preparing "plat maps," maps prepared from the local land records which show the ownership of the tracts within a township, useful to people in the real estate business and others. The defendant admitted to having used the plaintiff's map as a "guide," but to have independently verified the information from the land records. However Rockford Map had inserted fake middle initials into a row of names on the plat which spelled out "ROCKFORD MAP INC." These had been faithfully copied by the defendant, and the case was lost. Or in Apple Computer, Inc. v. Franklin Computer Corp., 714 F.2d 1240 (3d Cir.1983), the defendant might have been able to argue that its programs were identical to the plaintiff's only because of the functional constraints presented by the demands of efficient program design and the vocabulary of assembly language programming had its program not included the obviously non-functional feature of the name of an Apple programmer. Inadvertent errors of fact or typographical errors perform a similar role in other cases.

The long-litigated issue in these cases has been the extent of the use that the second firm can make of the work of the first. For instance, can the second firm send a copy of the entry in the first directory to the listed firm or person and ask for verification that it is correct? Suppose the second firm does this, but the process does not catch all errors? In Jewlers' Circular Publishing Co. v. Keystone

Publishing Co., 274 Fed. 932 (S.D.N.Y.1921), affirmed 281 Fed. 83 (2d Cir.1922), Judge Hand was able to avoid these issues. The plaintiff was the publisher of a directory containing the names and addresses of jewelers along with a reproduction of their trade name and trademark. The defendant had clipped the entries out of the directory and sent them to each jeweler for verification. Judge Hand found infringement on the ground that the reproductions of the trademarks were themselves copyrighted works, and that copying them was itself infringement.

In Southern Bell Telephone & Telegraph Co. v. Associated Telephone Directory Publishers, 756 F.2d 801 (11th Cir.1985), the defendant was preparing to publish a competing "Yellow Pages." To this end, it made copies of pages of the plaintiff's classified directory, cut them up by firm, and mailed them to the firms offering to publish the ad in its own directory. The Court of Appeals held that making copies of whole pages of the plaintiff's directory for this purpose was itself infringement.

The confused state of the law is illustrated by the following two cases:

In Universal Athletic Sales Co. v. Salkeld, 511 F.2d 904 (3d Cir. 1975), the parties were competitors in the sale of structurally similar weight-lifting machines. The plaintiff had prepared a chart using stick figures to illustrate the exercises to be performed with the machine. The defendant copied the chart, illustrating the same exercises but changing the color, layout, and design. The plaintiff claimed that preparation of the chart had required obtaining medical and physiological information on the correct way to perform the illustrated exercises. The district court held the copyright infringed on a motion for summary judgment. On appeal: reversed and remanded with instructions to enter judgment for the defendant. The visual differences between the charts preclude a finding of infringement.

> "A review of copyright infringement decisions confirms the observation that most cases are decided on an *ad hoc* basis. * * * [C]opyright does not protect ideas—only expressions. * * * The ideas are similar, but the expressions are not substantially so." 511 F.2d 907–09.

In Schroeder v. William Morrow & Co., 566 F.2d 3 (7th Cir.1977), the plaintiff had prepared a directory called *The Green Thumbook* which contained names, addresses and detailed descriptive information about plant suppliers and plant societies. The plaintiff had compiled her list from other published lists, with some further verification and checking. The defendant published a larger book on gardening called *The Gardner's Catalogue,* which contained a directory section. To save time, the defendant copied, without independent verification, only the names and addresses (but none of the other information) from *The Green Thumbook* into *The Gardner's Catalogue.* The District Court held that there was no infringement because the defendant's copying was limited to information in the public domain. On appeal: reversed. "An original compilation of names and addresses is copyrightable even though the individual names and addresses are in the public domain and not copyrightable." 566 F.2d 5, citing Leon, supra, and Jewler's Circular, supra.

In Miller v. Universal City Studios, 650 F.2d 1365 (5th Cir.1981), noted supra, the plaintiff newspaper reporter argued that the directory cases were precedent for the protection of compilations of facts, which should be extended to compilations of historical fact. The Fifth Circuit suggested that "it may be better to recognize the directory cases as being in a category by themselves rather than to attempt to bring their result and rationale to bear on nondirectory cases. Under the 1909 Copyright Act [in effect at the time of the alleged infringement], directories are specifically identified as copyrightable subject matter . . . and the rule is now well settled that they can be copyrighted." 650 F.2d 1370. In a footnote the court noted without comment that § 103 of the revised act extends protection to a broader category of "compilations" (defined term). 650 F.2d 1370 n. 4. Does that change the result of the *Miller* case?

An ambitious effort to integrate this area is offered by Robert C. Denicola, Copyright in Collections of Facts: A Theory for the Protection of Nonfiction Literary Works, 81 Col.L.Rev. 516 (1981). Denicola points out that if copyright does not protect compilations there is no economic incentive to create them. He argues that the cases can largely be explained and the desirable result reached if it is recognized that there is copyright protection which inheres not in particular facts, but in a particular *collection* of facts. Others can take particular facts from the collection without infringing, but if they take a substantial part of the *collection* they are infringing (unless they can demonstrate that their use is "fair use," a doctrine to be addressed in the next section). Note that this position makes the taking in International News Service, supra page 17, copyright infringement.

Denicola's analysis has been followed in two district court decisions. In National Business Lists v. Dun & Bradstreet, 552 F.Supp. 89 (N.D.Ill.1982), the court concluded that the use of information from a copyrighted directory of businesses to compile commercial mailing lists could be copyright infringement. And in Rand McNally & Co. v. Fleet Management Systems, 600 F.Supp. 933 (N.D.Ill.1984), the court held that creating a computerized data base of mileages between points (helpful to truckers in calculating charges) taken from plaintiff's maps was copyright infringement.

2. *Commercial art and design.* The *Mazer* doctrine has operated to bring to the courts many cases of infringement involving fabrics, dolls and other toys, and various novelties. Here the "ordinary observer" test is clearly the standard, and the "ordinary observer" is the person in the market for which the product is intended. For instance, in Peter Pan Fabrics, Inc. v. Martin Weiner Corp., 274 F.2d 487 (2d Cir.

1960), Judge Hand said that "In deciding that question [of how much similarity is too much] one should consider the uses for which the design is intended, especially the scrutiny that observers will give to it as used. In the case at bar we must try to estimate how far its overall appearance will determine its aesthetic appeal when the cloth is made into a garment." 274 F.2d at 489. This is in spite of the fact that the copyright act provides no protection for dress designs, only fabric designs. In Ideal Toy Corp. v. Sayco Doll Corp., 302 F.2d 623 (2d Cir. 1962), the court affirmed a preliminary injunction against defendant's "Chubby Toddler" doll. The district judge had found that a visual comparison between the copyrighted doll and the defendant's "establishes that the head of defendant's doll incorporates so many distinctive features and characteristics of the head of plaintiff's doll as to lead to the conclusion *prima facie* that defendant's doll head was copied." Judge Clark dissented, finding that it was not at all surprising that the heads of two dolls modeled on babies should have many distinctive features in common, and arguing that under the guise of affirming a finding of fact the court was creating an important commercial monopoly never intended by Congress.

An "ordinary observer in the market" test makes sense if one views the purpose of copyright in this area as one of conferring protection on the commercial designs involved. However, if one views the copyright protection as a secondary by-product of the protection afforded to the "work of art," then it would be logical to define the scope of the protection on the perspective of the art world rather than the market in which the fabric, toys and novelties are sold.

WHELAN ASSOCIATES, INC. v. JASLOW DENTAL LABORATORY, INC.

United States Court of Appeals, Third Circuit, 1986.
797 F.2d 1222.

BECKER, CIRCUIT JUDGE.

This appeal involves a computer program for the operation of a dental laboratory, and calls upon us to apply the principles underlying our venerable copyright laws to the relatively new field of computer technology to determine the scope of copyright protection of a computer program. More particularly, in this case of first impression in the courts of appeals, we must determine whether the structure (or sequence and organization) [1] of a computer program is protectible by copyright, or whether the protection of the copyright law extends only as far as the literal computer code. The district court found that the copyright law covered these non-literal elements of the program, and we agree. This conclusion in turn requires us to consider whether there was sufficient evidence of substantial similarity between the structures of the two programs at issue in this case to uphold the

---

1. We use the terms "structure," "sequence," and "organization" interchangeably when referring to computer programs, and we intend them to be synonymous in this opinion.

district court's finding of copyright infringement. Because we find that there was enough evidence, we affirm.

I. FACTUAL BACKGROUND

Appellant Jaslow Dental Laboratory, Inc. ("Jaslow Lab") is a Pennsylvania corporation in the business of manufacturing dental prosthetics and devices. Appellant Dentcom, Inc. ("Dentcom") is a Pennsylvania corporation in the business of developing and marketing computer programs for use by dental laboratories. Dentcom was formed out of the events that gave rise to this suit, and its history will be recounted below. Individual appellants Edward Jaslow and his son Rand Jaslow are officers and shareholders in both Jaslow Lab and Dentcom. Appellants were defendants in the district court. Plaintiff-appellee Whelan Associates, Inc. ("Whelan Associates") is also a Pennsylvania corporation, engaged in the business of developing and marketing custom computer programs.

Jaslow Lab, like any other small- or medium-sized business of moderate complexity, has significant bookkeeping and administrative tasks. Each order for equipment must be registered and processed; inventory must be maintained; customer lists must be continually updated; invoicing, billing, and accounts receivable, must be dealt with. While many of these functions are common to all businesses, the nature of the dental prosthetics business apparently requires some variations on the basic theme.

Although Rand Jaslow had not had extensive experience with computers, he believed that the business operations of Jaslow Lab could be made more efficient if they were computerized. In early 1978, he therefore bought a small personal computer and tried to teach himself how to program it so that it would be of use to Jaslow Lab. Although he wrote a program for the computer, he was ultimately not successful, limited by both his lack of expertise and the relatively small capacity of his particular computer.

A few months later, stymied by his own lack of success but still confident that Jaslow Lab would profit from computerization, Rand Jaslow hired the Strohl Systems Group, Inc. ("Strohl"), a small corporation that developed custom-made software to develop a program that would run on Jaslow Lab's new IBM Series One computer and take care of the Lab's business needs. Jaslow Lab and Strohl entered into an agreement providing that Strohl would design a system for Jaslow Lab's needs and that after Strohl had installed the system Strohl could market it to other dental laboratories. Jaslow Lab would receive a 10% royalty on all such sales.[2] The person at Strohl responsible for the

---

2. A letter of August 31, 1978, explained what the program would do for Jaslow Lab and how much it would cost. A letter from Strohl to Jaslow Lab dated September 20, 1978, supplemented the August 31 proposal as follows: This communi-cation is a supplement to our proposal letter dated 8/31/78. We (Strohl) propose that all software developed by us for your dental laboratory system remain under our ownership. This basic system can then be marketed to similar laboratories by our

Jaslow Lab account was Elaine Whelan, an experienced programmer who was an officer and half-owner of Strohl.

Ms. Whelan's first step was to visit Jaslow Lab and interview Rand Jaslow and others to learn how the laboratory worked and what its needs were. She also visited other dental laboratories and interviewed people there, so that she would better understand the layout, workflow, and administration of dental laboratories generally. After this education into the ways of dental laboratories, and Jaslow Lab, in particular, Ms. Whelan wrote a program called Dentalab for Jaslow Lab. Dentalab was written in a computer language known as EDL (Event Driven Language), so that it would work with IBM Series One machines. The program was completed and was operative at Jaslow Lab around March 1979.

Presumably with an eye towards exploiting the economic potential of the Dentalab program, Ms. Whelan left Strohl in November, 1979, to form her own business, Whelan Associates, Inc., which acquired Strohl's interest in the Dentalab program. Shortly thereafter, Whelan Associates entered into negotiations with Jaslow Lab for Jaslow Lab to be Whelan Associates' sales representative for the Dentalab program. Whelan Associates and Jaslow Lab entered into an agreement on July 30, 1980, according to which Jaslow Lab agreed to use its "best efforts and to act diligently in the marketing of the Dentalab package," and Whelan Associates agreed to "use its best efforts and to act diligently to improve and augment the previously successfully designed Dentalab package." The agreement stated that Jaslow Lab would receive 35% of the gross price of any programs sold and 5% of the price of any modifications to the programs. The agreement was for one year and was then terminable by either party on thirty days' notice. The parties' business relationship worked successfully for two years.[3] During this time, as Rand Jaslow became more familiar with computer programming, he realized that because Dentalab was written in EDL it could not be used on computers that many of the smaller dental prosthetics firms were using, for which EDL had not been implemented. Sensing that there might be a market for a program that served essentially the same function as Dentalab but that could be used more widely, Rand Jaslow began in May or June of 1982 to develop in his spare time a program in the BASIC language for such computers. That

organization. A royalty of ten percent of the basic package price would be returned to Jaslow Dental Laboratory for each system sold. Whelan Associates v. Jaslow Dental Laboratory, 609 F.Supp. 1307, 1310 (E.D.Pa.1985) (the district court inadvertently identified the letter as dated September 30, 1978). Although no representative of Jaslow Lab ever signed either agreement, the district court found that

Jaslow Lab had, through its conduct, accepted the terms of the letter. Id. at 1310.

3. Rand Jaslow on behalf of Jaslow Lab sent a letter to Whelan Associates on June 22, 1982, stating its intention to terminate business relations in 30 days. However, the parties continued to do business under the agreement of July 30, 1980 until the termination letter of May 31, 1983, discussed below.

program, when completed, became the alleged copyright infringer in this suit; it was called the Dentcom PC program ("Dentcom program").[4]

It appears that Rand Jaslow was sanguine about the prospects of his program for smaller computers. After approximately a year of work, on May 31, 1983, his attorney sent a letter to Whelan Associates giving one month notice of termination of the agreement between Whelan Associates and Jaslow Lab.[5] The letter stated that Jaslow Lab considered itself to be the exclusive marketer of the Dentalab program which, the letter stated, "contains valuable trade secrets of Jaslow Dental Laboratory." The letter concluded with a thinly veiled threat to Whelan Associates: "I . . . look for your immediate response confirming that you will respect the rights of Jaslow and not use or disclose to others the trade secrets of Jaslow."

Approximately two months later, on about August 1, Edward and Rand Jaslow, Paul Mohr, and Joseph Cerra formed defendant-appellant Dentcom to sell the Dentcom program.[6] At about the same time, Rand Jaslow and Jaslow Lab employed a professional computer programmer, Jonathan Novak, to complete the Dentcom program. The program was soon finished, and Dentcom proceeded to sell it to dental prosthetics companies that had personal computers. Dentcom sold both the Dentalab and Dentcom programs, and advertised the Dentcom program as "a new version of the Dentalab computer system."

Despite Jaslow Lab's May 31 letter warning Whelan Associates not to sell the Dentalab program, Whelan Associates continued to market Dentalab. This precipitated the present litigation.

II. PROCEDURAL HISTORY

On June 30, 1983, Jaslow Lab filed suit in the Court of Common Pleas of Montgomery County (Pennsylvania), alleging that Whelan Associates had misappropriated its trade secrets. Whelan Associates responded by filing the instant suit in the United States District Court for the Eastern District of Pennsylvania on September 21, 1983. As set forth in its amended complaint, Whelan Associates alleged that

---

4. The record indicates that Whelan Associates also developed a BASIC version of the Dentalab, written specially for the IBM–Datamaster 26 computer. That program (the "Datamaster" program), did not succeed commercially. Whelan Associates has also written a second program in BASIC for dental laboratories' business operations. The second program was intended for use on IBM–PC's. Neither the Datamaster program nor Whelan Associates' program for the IBM–PC is directly at issue here. But see infra 677 (use of Datamaster program by defendants' expert witness at trial).

5. The district court inadvertently referred to this as the letter of January 31, 1983. See Whelan Associates v. Jaslow

Dental Laboratory, 609 F.Supp. 1307, 1313 (E.D.Pa.1985).

6. Joseph Cerra had, from January until June, 1983, been in the employ of Whelan Associates in charge of marketing. In this position, he had had close contact with Rand Jaslow. When he left Whelan Associates, he made a verbal promise to Elaine Whelan that he would not become associated in any business ventures with Rand Jaslow. There was, however, no written agreement. App. at 1088. Although Mr. Cerra was originally named as a defendant, he settled prior to trial. The record contains no information about Paul Mohr's employment history or of his previous associations with Whelan Associates or any of the defendants.

Dentcom's licensing of the Dentalab and Dentcom programs infringed Whelan Associates' copyright in Dentalab; that Dentcom's use of the terms "Dentlab" or "Dentalab," violated Pennsylvania common law and 15 U.S.C. § 1125(a) (Lanham Trademark Act of 1946) (false designation of origin); and that Dentcom's activities violated various other federal and state laws pertaining to unfair competition and tortious interference with contractual relations. Whelan Associates sought injunctive relief, as well as compensatory and punitive damages.

Jaslow Lab and its co-defendants answered, denying all liability. They claimed that Whelan Associates' copyright was invalid for two reasons. First, they said that although he had not been listed in the copyright registration, Rand Jaslow had been a co-author (with Elaine Whelan) of the Dentalab program. The omission of Rand Jaslow from the registration form, defendants averred, rendered the copyright defective. Second, the defendants maintained that even if Rand Jaslow had not co-authored the program, he owned the copyright because the program had been written by someone employed by him. Defendants also averred that Rand Jaslow had developed the Dentcom system independently, and therefore could not have violated Whelan Associate's copyright, even if the copyright were valid.[7] Finally, defendants claimed that their use of "Dentalab" or "Dentlab" violated neither federal nor state law, for, inter alia, those terms are merely general descriptions of goods and services, not names of particular products. Defendants counterclaimed that Whelan Associates had usurped defendants' copyright and that by continuing to sell Dentalab, Whelan Associates was engaging in unfair competition. By agreement of the parties, the trade secret action was removed from the Court of Common Pleas to the district court and became a counterclaim.

The first procedural blow was struck by the defendants, who moved almost immediately for a preliminary injunction to enjoin Whelan Associates from using Jaslow Labs' trade secrets. After a three-day hearing, the district court denied the motion in a bench opinion delivered on November 2, 1983. The court held that the defendants had not shown a likelihood of success on the merits because they had failed to prove that any of Jaslow Lab's trade secrets were in the Dentalab program. Moreover, the court held that the defendants had not proven irreparable harm and that they had approached the court with "unclean hands" on account of their use of the term "Dentlab," which could be and was confused for Dentalab.

A quick victory proving beyond the defendants' reach, the parties prepared for a protracted battle. Discovery proceeded on each side, and a three-day bench trial began on July 9, 1984. At trial, Whelan

---

7. 17 U.S.C. § 106 (1982), which prescribes copyright holders' exclusive rights, forbids the copying of copyrighted works. The independent creation of even identical works is therefore not a copyright infringement, and independent creation is a complete defense to a claim of copyright infringement. See also Fred Fisher, Inc. v. Dillingham, 298 F. 145, 147 (S.D.N.Y.1924) (L. Hand, J.) ("the law imposes no prohibition upon those who, without copying, independently arrive at the precise combination of words or notes which have been copyrighted.").

Associates continued to press all of its claims—copyright violations, unfair competition, and tortious interference with contractual relations. The defendants abandoned the trade secret claim that had failed them in the preliminary injunction battle, but maintained their position that Rand Jaslow owned the copyright to Dentalab. Defendants continued to deny Whelan Associates' allegations.

The principal witnesses were Elaine Whelan, Rand Jaslow, and two expert witnesses, Dr. Thomas Moore for Whelan Associates and Stephen Ness on behalf of the defendants. Whelan and Jaslow testified about the dealings and negotiations between the parties. Dr. Moore and Mr. Ness examined the programs and testified about the programs' similarities and differences. Dr. Moore testified that although the Dentcom program was not a translation of the Dentalab system, the programs were similar in three significant respects. He testified that most of the file structures, and the screen outputs, of the programs were virtually identical. He also testified that five particularly important "subroutines" within both programs—order entry, invoicing, accounts receivable, end of day procedure, and end of month procedure—performed almost identically in both programs.[8] Mr. Ness compared the source and object codes [9] of the Dentalab, Dentcom, and Datamaster programs, see supra n. 4, and testified at length about the many ways that the programs differed from one another. He concluded that "substantive differences in programming style, in programming structure, in algorithms and data structures, all indicate that the Dentcom system is not directly derived from either of the other systems." In his written report, however, which was entered into evidence, Mr. Ness conceded that the Dentalab and Dentcom programs had "overall structural similarities."

The district court ruled for Whelan Associates on all grounds. Whelan Associates v. Jaslow Dental Laboratory, 609 F.Supp. 1307 (E.D. Pa.1985). It found that Elaine Whelan was the sole author of the Dentalab system (and, hence, that Rand Jaslow was not a co-author) and that the contract between Strohl and Rand Jaslow, see supra n. 2, made clear that Strohl would retain full ownership over the software. The court thus concluded that Whelan Associates' copyright in the Dentalab System was valid, and that Dentcom's sales of the Dentalab program were violations of that copyright.[10]

The court also found that Rand Jaslow had not created the Dentcom system independently, and that the Dentcom system, although written in a different computer language from the Dentalab, and although not a direct transliteration of Dentalab, was substantially similar to Dentalab because its structure and overall organization were substantially similar. This substantial similarity, in conjunction with Rand Jaslow's acknowledged access to the Dentalab system, led the

---

8. Dr. Moore's testimony is discussed in greater detail infra at 689–695.

9. Source and object code are defined infra at 679–680.

10. There were two such sales by Dentcom.

district court to conclude that each sale of the Dentcom program by Dentcom [11] violated Whelan Associates' copyright on the Dentalab system. The court therefore awarded Whelan Associates damages for these copyright infringements, and enjoined Dentcom from selling any more copies of the Dentalab or Dentcom programs. The court also held that plaintiffs had exclusive use of the term "Dentalab," and enjoined defendants from using either "Dentalab" or "Dentlab" in their business.

* * * On appeal, * * * [the defendants] raise a single issue: whether the district court erred in its finding that the Dentcom program infringes the copyright of plaintiffs' Dentalab system.

III. TECHNOLOGICAL BACKGROUND

We begin with a brief description of computer programs and an explanation of how they are written. This introduction is necessary to our analysis of the issue in this case. A computer program is a set of instructions to the computer.[13] Most programs accept and process user-supplied data. The fundamental processes utilized by a program are called algorithms (mechanical computational procedures) and are at the heart of the program. See Keplinger, Computer Software—Its Nature and its Protection, 30 Emory L.J. 483, 484–85 (1984). These algorithms must be developed by the human creativity of the programmer, and the program therefore cannot contain any algorithms not already considered by humans. Although a computer cannot think or develop algorithms, it can execute them faster and more accurately than any human possibly could. See R. Saltman, Copyright in Computer–Readable Works 59 (1977).

The creation of a program often takes place in several steps, moving from the general to the specific.[14] Because programs are intended to accomplish particular tasks, the first step in creating the program is identifying the problem that the computer programmer is trying to solve. In this case, Rand Jaslow went to Strohl and stated that his problem was recordkeeping for his business. Although this was an accurate statement of the problem, it was not specific enough to guide Elaine Whelan. Before she could write the Dentalab program, she needed to know more about Jaslow Lab's business—how orders were processed, what special billing problems might arise, how inventory might be correlated to orders, and other characteristics of the dental prosthetics trade.

As the programmer learns more about the problem, she or he may begin to outline a solution. The outline can take the form of a flowchart, which will break down the solution into a series of smaller

---

11. There were 23 such sales.

13. Title 17 U.S.C. § 101 (1982), gives a more technical [definition] * * *.

14. More detailed descriptions of this process can be found in D. Bender, Computer Law—Software Protection § 2.06(3) (1985); Yohe, An Overview of Programming Tactics, 6 Computing Surveys 221 (1974).

units called "subroutines" or "modules," each of which deals with elements of the larger problem. See Note, Defining the Scope of Copyright Protection for Computer Software, 38 Stan.L.Rev. 497, 500–01 (1986). A program's efficiency depends in large part on the arrangements of its modules and subroutines; although two programs could produce the same result, one might be more efficient because of different internal arrangements of modules and subroutines. Because efficiency is a prime concern in computer programs (an efficient program being obviously more valuable than a comparatively inefficient one), the arrangement of modules and subroutines is a critical factor for any programmer. In the present case, the Dentalab program had numerous modules pertaining to inventory, accounts receivable, various dentist-patient matters, and payroll, among others. Some of the modules were simple; others were quite complex and involved elaborate logical development.

As the program structure is refined, the programmer must make decisions about what data are needed, where along the program's operations the data should be introduced, how the data should be inputted, and how it should be combined with other data. The arrangement of the data is accomplished by means of data files, and is affected by the details of the program's subroutines and modules, for different arrangements of subroutines and modules may require data in different forms. Once again, there are numerous ways the programmer can solve the data-organization problems she or he faces. Each solution may have particular characteristics—efficiencies or inefficiencies, conveniences or quirks—that differentiate it from other solutions and make the overall program more or less desirable. Because the Dentalab program was intended to handle all of the business-related aspects of a dental laboratory, it had to accommodate and interrelate many different pieces and types of data including patients' names, dentists' names, inventory, accounts receivable, accounts payable, and payroll.[16]

Once the detailed design of the program is completed, the coding begins.[17] Each of the steps identified in the design must be turned into a language that the computer can understand. This translation process in itself requires two steps. The programmer first writes in a "source code," which may be in one of several languages, such as COBOL, BASIC, FORTRAN, or EDL.[18] The choice of language depends upon which computers the programmer intends the program to be used by,

16. Elaine Whelan's material on the various elements, files and subroutines of the Dentalab system are voluminous, taking up over 200 pages of the record. See App. at 1222–1469. The material consisted of detailed outlines on how the program was to be structured.

17. The discussion in this paragraph draws heavily from Note, Copyright Protection of Computer Program Object Code, 96 Harv.L.Rev. 1723, 1724–25 (1983).

18. We ignore the distinction between "high level language" and "assembly language," see Note, 96 Harv.L.Rev. 1723, 1725 (1983), which is not relevant to the issues in this case. Both of these may be referred to as "source codes." See Apple Computer, Inc. v. Franklin Computer Corp, 714 F.2d 1240, 1243 (3d Cir.1983), cert. dismissed, 464 U.S. 1033.

for some computers can read only certain languages.[19] Once the program is written in source code, it is translated into "object code," which is a binary code, simply a concatenation of "0"s and "1"s. In every program, it is the object code, not the source code, that directs the computer to perform functions. The object code is therefore the final instruction to the computer.[20]

As this brief summary demonstrates, the coding process is a comparatively small part of programming. By far the larger portion of the expense and difficulty in creating computer programs is attributable to the development of the structure and logic of the program, and to debugging, documentation and maintenance, rather than to the coding. See Frank, *Critical Issues in Software* 22 (1983) (only 20% of the cost of program development goes into coding); Zelkowitz, *Perspective on Software Engineering,* 10 Computing Surveys 197–216 (June, 1978). See also *InfoWorld,* Nov. 11, 1985 at 13 ("the 'look and feel' of a computer software product often involves much more creativity and often is of greater commercial value than the program code which implements the product . . .."). The evidence in this case shows that Ms. Whelan spent a tremendous amount of time studying Jaslow Labs, organizing the modules and subroutines for the Dentalab program, and working out the data arrangements, and a comparatively small amount of time actually coding the Dentalab program.

IV. LEGAL BACKGROUND

A. *The elements of a copyright infringement action*—To prove that its copyright has been infringed, Whelan Associates must show two things: that it owned the copyright on Dentalab, and that Rand Jaslow copied Dentalab in making the Dentacom program. * * *; Reyher v. Children's Television Workshop, 533 F.2d 87, 90 (2d Cir.), cert. denied, 429 U.S. 980 (1976); 3 Nimmer On Copyright § 13.01 (1985) (referred to hereinafter as "Nimmer"). Although it was disputed below, the district court determined, and it is not challenged here, that Whelan Associates owned the copyright to the Dentalab program. We are thus concerned only with whether it has been shown that Rand Jaslow copied the Dentalab program.

As it is rarely possible to prove copying through direct evidence, Roth Greeting Cards v. United Card Co., 429 F.2d 1106, 1110 (9th Cir. 1970), copying may be proved inferentially by showing that the defendant had access to the allegedly infringed copyrighted work and that the allegedly infringing work is substantially similar to the copyrighted work. * * *. The district court found, and here it is uncontested, that Rand Jaslow had access to the Dentalab program, both because

---

19. The IBM Series One, for example, can read EDL but not BASIC; the IBM–PC can read BASIC, but not EDL.

20. The discussion assumes that the program is "compiled" or "assembled." If a program is "interpreted," then the source and object codes are joined in a single step. Whether a program is compiled or interpreted depends on the program and the machine on which it is run. The difference is not important in this case.

Dentalab was the program used in Jaslow Labs and because Rand Jaslow acted as a sales representative for Whelan Associates.[22] Thus, the sole question is whether there was substantial similarity between the Dentcom and Dentalab programs.[23]

B. *The appropriate test for substantial similarity in computer program cases*—The leading case of Arnstein v. Porter, 154 F.2d 464, 468–69 (2d Cir.1946), suggested a bifurcated substantial similarity test whereby a finder of fact makes two findings of substantial similarity to support a copyright violation. First, the fact-finder must decide whether there is sufficient similarity between the two works in question to conclude that the alleged infringer used the copyrighted work in making his own. On this issue, expert testimony may be received to aid the trier of fact. (This has been referred to as the "extrinsic" test of substantial similarity. Sid & Marty Krofft Television Prods., Inc. v. McDonald's Corp., 562 F.2d at 1164–65.) Second, if the answer to the first question is in the affirmative, the fact-finder must decide without the aid of expert testimony, but with the perspective of the "lay observer," whether the copying was "illicit," or "an unlawful appropriation" of the copyrighted work. (This has been termed an "intrinsic" test of substantial similarity. Id.) The Arnstein test has been adopted in this circuit. See Universal Athletic Sales Co., 511 F.2d at 907.

The district court heard expert testimony. It did not bifurcate its analysis, however, but made only a single finding of substantial similarity. It would thus appear to have contravened the law of this circuit. Nevertheless, for the reasons that follow, we believe that the district court applied an appropriate standard.

The ordinary observer test, which was developed in cases involving novels, plays, and paintings, and which does not permit expert testimony, is of doubtful value in cases involving computer programs on account of the programs' complexity and unfamiliarity to most members of the public. See Note, Copyright Infringement of Computer Programs: A Modification of the Substantial Similarity Test, 68 Minn. L.Rev. 1264, 1285–88 (1984). Cf. Note, Copyright Infringement Actions: The Proper Role for Audience Reactions in Determining Substantial Similarity, 54 S.Cal.L.Rev. 385 (1981) (criticizing lay observer standard when objects in question are intended for particular, identifiable audiences). Moreover, the distinction between the two parts of the Arnstein test may be of doubtful value when the finder of fact is the same person for each step: that person has been exposed to expert evidence

22. The district court found, inter alia, that Rand Jaslow "had surreptitiously and without consent of either Strohl Systems or Whelan Associates obtained a copy of the (Dentalab) source code," and that he had "utilized the source code in his attempt to develop the IBM–PC Dentcom program."

23. Although not an issue in this case, see infra n. 47, it is important to note that even the showing of substantial similarity is not dispositive, for it is still open to the alleged infringer to prove that his work is an original creation, see supra n. 7, or that the similarities between the works was not on account of copying but because both parties drew from common sources that were part of the public domain. The cause of the substantial similarity—legitimate or not—is a question of fact.

in the first step, yet she or he is supposed to ignore or "forget" that evidence in analyzing the problem under the second step. Especially in complex cases, we doubt that the "forgetting" can be effective when the expert testimony is essential to even the most fundamental understanding of the objects in question.

On account of these problems with the standard, we believe that the ordinary observer test is not useful and is potentially misleading when the subjects of the copyright are particularly complex, such as computer programs. We therefore join the growing number of courts which do not apply the ordinary observer test in copyright cases involving exceptionally difficult materials, like computer programs, but instead adopt a single substantial similarity inquiry according to which both lay and expert testimony would be admissible. * * *. That was the test applied by the district court in this case.

C. *The arguments on appeal* —On appeal, the defendants attack on two grounds the district court's holding that there was sufficient evidence of substantial similarity. First, the defendants argue that because the district court did not find any similarity between the "literal" elements (source and object code) of the programs, but only similarity in their overall structures, its finding of substantial similarity was incorrect, for the copyright covers only the literal elements of computer programs, not their overall structures. Defendants' second argument is that even if the protection of copyright law extends to "non-literal" elements such as the structure of computer programs, there was not sufficient evidence of substantial similarity to sustain the district court's holding in this case. We consider these arguments in turn.

V. THE SCOPE OF COPYRIGHT PROTECTION OF COMPUTER PROGRAMS

It is well, though recently, established that copyright protection extends to a program's source and object codes. * * * In this case, however, the district court did not find any copying of the source or object codes, nor did the plaintiff allege such copying. Rather, the district court held that the Dentalab copyright was infringed because the overall structure of Dentcom was substantially similar to the overall structure of Dentalab. The question therefore arises whether mere similarity in the overall structure of programs can be the basis for a copyright infringement, or, put differently, whether a program's copyright protection covers the structure of the program or only the program's literal elements, i.e., its source and object codes.

Title 17 U.S.C. § 102(a)(1) extends copyright protection to "literary works," and computer programs are classified as literary works for the purposes of copyright. * * * The copyrights of other literary works can be infringed even when there is no substantial similarity between the works' literal elements. One can violate the copyright of a play or book by copying its plot or plot devices. See, e.g., Twentieth Century-

Fox Film Corp. v. MCA, Inc., 715 F.2d 1327, 1329 (9th Cir.1983) (13 alleged distinctive plot similarities between Battlestar Galactica and Star Wars may be basis for a finding of copyright violation); Sid & Marty Krofft Television Productions, Inc., 562 F.2d at 1167 (similarities between McDonaldland characters and H.R. Pufnstuf characters can be established by " 'total concept and feel' " of the two productions (quoting Roth Greeting Cards v. United Card Co., 429 F.2d 1106, 1110 (9th Cir.1970)); Sheldon v. Metro–Goldwyn Pictures Corp., 81 F.2d 49, 54–55 (2nd Cir.1936) [page 635 supra]; Nichols v. Universal Pictures Corp., 45 F.2d 119, 121 (2d Cir.1930) [page 629 supra] (copyright "cannot be limited literally to the text, else a plagiarist would escape by immaterial variations"). By analogy to other literary works, it would thus appear that the copyrights of computer programs can be infringed even absent copying of the literal elements of the program. Defendants contend, however, that what is true of other literary works is not true of computer programs. They assert two principal reasons, which we consider in turn.

A. *Section 102(b) and the dichotomy between idea and expression* —It is axiomatic that copyright does not protect ideas, but only expressions of ideas. This rule, first enunciated in Baker v. Selden, 101 U.S. (11 Otto) 99 (1879) [page 573 supra], has been repeated in numerous cases. See, e.g., Mazer v. Stein, 347 U.S. 201, 217 (1954) [page 587 supra] ("Unlike a patent, a copyright gives no exclusive right to the art disclosed; protection is given only to the expression of the idea—not the idea itself." (citation omitted)); Universal Athletic Sales Co., 511 F.2d at 906; Dymow v. Bolton, 11 F.2d 690, 691 (2d Cir.1926); see generally A. Latman, The Copyright Law 31–35 (5th ed. 1979); 1 Nimmer § 2.03(D). The rule has also been embodied in statute. [17 U.S.C. § 102(b)] * * *.

The legislative history of this section, adopted in 1976, makes clear that § 102(b) was intended to express the idea-expression dichotomy. See H.R.Rep. No. 1476 at 57 (§ 102(b) is intended to "restate . . . that the basic dichotomy between expression and idea remains unchanged.") See also Apple Computer, supra, 714 F.2d at 1252.

Defendants argue that the structure of a computer program is, by definition, the idea and not the expression of the idea, and therefore that the structure cannot be protected by the program copyright. Under the defendants' approach, any other decision would be contrary to § 102(b). We divide our consideration of this argument into two parts. First, we examine the caselaw concerning the distinction between idea and expression, and derive from it a rule for distinguishing idea from expression in the context of computer programs. We then apply that rule to the facts of this case.

1. *A rule for distinguishing idea from expression in computer programs* —It is frequently difficult to distinguish the idea from the expression thereof. No less an authority than Learned Hand, after a career that included writing some of the leading copyright opinions,

concluded that the distinction will "inevitably be ad hoc." Peter Pan Fabrics, Inc. v. Martin Weiner Corp., 274 F.2d 487, 489 (2d Cir.1960). * * *. Although we acknowledge the wisdom of Judge Hand's remark, we feel that a review of relevant copyright precedent will enable us to formulate a rule applicable in this case. In addition, precisely because the line between idea and expression is elusive, we must pay particular attention to the pragmatic considerations that underlie the distinction and copyright law generally. In this regard, we must remember that the purpose of the copyright law is to create the most efficient and productive balance between protection (incentive) and dissemination of information, to promote learning, culture and development.

We begin our analysis with the case of *Baker v. Selden* [supra page 573], which, in addition to being a seminal case in the law of copyright generally, is particularly relevant here because, like the instant case, it involved a utilitarian work, rather than an artistic or fictional one. In *Baker v. Selden*, the plaintiff Selden obtained a copyright on his book, "Selden's Condensed Ledger, or Bookkeeping Simplified," which described a new, simplified system of accounting. * * *. The dispute centered on whether Selden's blank forms were part of the method (idea) of Selden's book, and hence non-copyrightable, or part of the copyrightable text (expression).

In deciding this point, the Court distinguished what was protectible from what was not protectible as follows:

> "[W]here the art [i.e., the method of accounting] it teaches cannot be used without employing the methods and diagrams used to illustrate the book, or such as are similar to them, such methods and diagrams are to be considered as necessary incidents to the art, and given to the public."

Applying this test, the Court held that the blank forms were necessary incidents to Selden's method of accounting, and hence were not entitled to any copyright protection.

The Court's test in Baker v. Selden suggests a way to distinguish idea from expression. Just as Baker v. Selden focused on the end sought to be achieved by Selden's book, the line between idea and expression may be drawn with reference to the end sought to be achieved by the work in question. In other words, the purpose or function of a utilitarian work would be the work's idea, and everything that is not necessary to that purpose or function would be part of the expression of the idea. * * * Where there are various means of achieving the desired purpose, then the particular means chosen is not necessary to the purpose; hence, there is expression, not idea.

Consideration of copyright doctrines related to *scenes a faire* and fact-intensive works supports our formulation, for they reflect the same underlying principle. *Scenes a faire* are "incidents, characters or settings which are as a practical matter indispensable . . . in the treatment of a given topic." Atari, Inc. v. North American Philips

Consumer Elecs. Corp., 672 F.2d 607, 616 (7th Cir.), cert. denied, 459 U.S. 880 (1982). See also See v. Durang, 711 F.2d 141, 143 (9th Cir. 1983). It is well-settled doctrine that *scenes a faire* are afforded no copyright protection.

Scenes a faire are afforded no protection because the subject matter represented can be expressed in no other way than through the particular *scene a faire*. Therefore, granting a copyright "would give the first author a monopoly on the commonplace ideas behind the *scenes a faire*." Landsberg v. Scrabble Crossword Game Players, Inc., 736 F.2d at 489. This is merely a restatement of the hypothesis advanced above, that the purpose or function of a work or literary device is part of that device's "idea" (unprotectible portion). It follows that anything necessary to effecting that function is also, necessarily, part of the idea, too.

Fact intensive works are given similarly limited copyright coverage. See, e.g., Landsberg, 736 F.2d at 488; Miller v. Universal City Studios, Inc., 650 F.2d 1365, 1372 (5th Cir.1981). Once again, the reason appears to be that there are only a limited number of ways to express factual material, and therefore the purpose of the literary work—telling a truthful story—can be accomplished only by employing one of a limited number of devices. Landsberg, 736 F.2d at 488. Those devices therefore belong to the idea, not the expression, of the historical or factual work.

Although the economic implications of this rule are necessarily somewhat speculative, we nevertheless believe that the rule would advance the basic purpose underlying the idea/expression distinction, "the preservation of the balance between competition and protection reflected in the patent and copyright laws." Herbert Rosenthal Jewelry Corp. v. Kalpakian, 446 F.2d 738, 742 (9th Cir.1971); * * *. As we [have] stated * * * among the more significant costs in computer programming are those attributable to developing the structure and logic of the program. The rule proposed here, which allows copyright protection beyond the literal computer code, would provide the proper incentive for programmers by protecting their most valuable efforts, while not giving them a stranglehold over the development of new computer devices that accomplish the same end.

The principal economic argument used against this position—used, that is, in support of the position that programs' literal elements are the only parts of the programs protected by the copyright law—is that computer programs are so intricate, each step so dependent on all of the other steps, that they are almost impossible to copy except literally, and that anyone who attempts to copy the structure of a program without copying its literal elements must expend a tremendous amount of effort and creativity. In the words of one commentator: "One cannot simply 'approximate' the entire copyrighted computer program and create a similar operative program without the expenditure of almost the same amount of time as the original programmer expended." Note, 68 Minn.L.Rev. at 1290 (footnote omitted). According to this argument, such work should not be discouraged or penalized. A further argument against our position is not economic but jurisprudential; another commentator argues that the concept of structure in computer programs is too vague to be useful in copyright cases. Radcliffe, Recent Developments in Copyright Law Related to Computer Software, 4 Computer L.Rep. 189, 194–97 (1985). He too would therefore appear to advocate limiting copyright protection to programs' literal codes.

Neither of the two arguments just described is persuasive. The first argument fails for two reasons. In the first place, it is simply not true that "approximation" of a program short of perfect reproduction is valueless. To the contrary, one can approximate a program and thereby gain a significant advantage over competitors even though additional work is needed to complete the program. Second, the fact that it will take a great deal of effort to copy a copyrighted work does not mean that the copier is not a copyright infringer. The issue in a copyright case is simply whether the copyright holder's expression has been copied, not how difficult it was to do the copying. Whether an alleged infringer spent significant time and effort to copy an original work is therefore irrelevant to whether he has pirated the expression of an original work.

As to the second argument, it is surely true that limiting copyright protection to computers' literal codes would be simpler and would yield more definite answers than does our answer here. Ease of application is not, however, a sufficient counterweight to the considerations we have adduced on behalf of our position.

Finally, one commentator argues that the process of development and progress in the field of computer programming is significantly different from that in other fields, and therefore requires a particularly restricted application of the copyright law. According to this argument, progress in the area of computer technology is achieved by means of "stepping-stones," a process that "requires plagiarizing in some manner the underlying copyrighted work." Note, 68 Minn.L.Rev. at 1292 (footnote omitted). As a consequence, this commentator argues, giving computer programs too much copyright protection will retard progress in the field.

We are not convinced that progress in computer technology or technique is qualitatively different from progress in other areas of science or the arts. In balancing protection and dissemination, * * *, the copyright law has always recognized and tried to accommodate the fact that all intellectual pioneers build on the work of their predecessors. Thus, copyright principles derived from other areas are applicable in the field of computer programs.

2. *Application of the general rule to this case* —The rule proposed here is certainly not problem-free. The rule has its greatest force in the analysis of utilitarian or "functional" works, for the purpose of such works is easily stated and identified. By contrast, in cases involving

works of literature or "non-functional" visual representations, defining the purpose of the work may be difficult. Since it may be impossible to discuss the purpose or function of a novel, poem, sculpture or painting, the rule may have little or no application to cases involving such works. The present case presents no such difficulties, for it is clear that the purpose of the utilitarian Dentalab program was to aid in the business operations of a dental laboratory.[34] * * * It is equally clear that the structure of the program was not essential to that task: there are other programs on the market, competitors of Dentalab and Dentcom, that perform the same functions but have different structures and designs.

This fact seems to have been dispositive for the district court:

> "The mere idea or concept of a computerized program for operating a dental laboratory would not in and of itself be subject to copyright. Copyright law protects the manner in which the author expresses an idea or concept, but not the idea itself. Albert E. Price v. Metzner, 574 F.Supp. 281 (E.D.Pa. 1983). Copyrights do not protect ideas—only expressions of ideas. Universal Athletic Sales Co. v. Salkeld, 511 F.2d 904, 908 (3d Cir.1975). There are many ways that the same data may be organized, assembled, held, retrieved and utilized by a computer. *Different computer systems may functionally serve similar purposes without being copies of each other. There is evidence in the record that there are other software programs for the business management of dental laboratories in competition with plaintiff's program. There is no contention that any of them infringe although they may incorporate many of the same ideas and functions.* The 'expression of the idea' in a software computer program is the manner in which the program operates, controls and regulates the computer in receiving, assembling, calculating, retaining, correlating, and producing useful information either on a screen, print-out or by audio communication."

(Emphasis added). We agree. The conclusion is thus inescapable that the detailed structure of the Dentalab program is part of the expression, not the idea, of that program.

* * *

The Copyright Act of 1976 provides further support, for it indicates that Congress intended that the structure and organization of a literary work could be part of its expression protectible by copyright. Title 17 U.S.C. § 103 (1982) specifically extends copyright protection to compila-

---

34. We do not mean to imply that the idea or purpose behind every utilitarian or functional work will be precisely what it accomplishes, and that structure and organization will therefore always be part of the expression of such works. The idea or purpose behind a utilitarian work may be to accomplish a certain function in a certain way, see, e.g., Baker v. Selden, 101 U.S. at 100 (referring to Selden's book as explaining "a peculiar system of book-keeping"), and the structure or function of a program might be essential to that task. There is no suggestion in the record, however, that the purpose of the Dentalab program was anything so refined; it was simply to run a dental laboratory in an efficient way.

tions and derivative works. * * * Although the Code does not use the terms "sequence," "order" or "structure," it is clear from the definition of compilations and derivative works, and the protection afforded them, that Congress was aware of the fact that the sequencing and ordering of materials could be copyrighted, i.e., that the sequence and order could be parts of the expression, not the idea, of a work.

Our solution may put us at odds with Judge Patrick Higginbotham's scholarly opinion in Synercom Technology, Inc. v. University Computing Co., 462 F.Supp. 1003 (N.D.Tex.1978), which dealt with the question whether the "input formats" of a computer program—the configurations and collations of the information entered into the program—were idea or expression. The court held that the input formats were ideas, not expressions, and thus not protectible. *Synercom* did not deal with precisely the materials at issue here—input formats are structurally simple as compared to full programs—and it may therefore be distinguishable. However, insofar as the input formats are devices for the organization of data into forms useful for computers, they are similar to programs; thus, *Synercom* is relevant and we must come to grips with it.

Central to Judge Higginbotham's analysis was his conviction that the organization and structure of the input formats was inseparable from the idea underlying the formats. Although the court acknowledged that in some cases structure and sequence might be part of expression, not idea * * *, it stated that in the case of input formats, structure and organization were inherently part of the idea. The court put its position in the form of a powerful rhetorical question: "if sequencing and ordering [are] expression, what separable idea is being expressed?" * * *

To the extent that *Synercom* rested on the premise that there was a difference between the copyrightability of sequence and form in the computer context and in any other context, we think that it is incorrect. As just noted, the Copyright Act of 1976 demonstrates that Congress intended sequencing and ordering to be protectible in the appropriate circumstances * * *, and the computer field is not an exception to this general rule. Although Congress was aware that computer programs posed a novel set of issues and problems for the copyright law, Congress did not then make, and has not since made, any special provision for ordering and sequencing in the context of computer programs. There is thus no statutory basis for treating computer programs differently from other literary works in this regard.

Despite the fact that copyright protection extends to sequence and form in the computer context, unless we are able to answer Judge Higginbotham's powerful rhetorical question—"if sequencing and ordering [are] expression, what separable idea is being expressed?"—in our own case, we would have to hold that the structure of the Dentalab program is part of its idea and is thus not protectible by copyright. Our answer has already been given, however: the idea is the efficient organization of a dental laboratory (presumably, this poses different problems from the efficient organization of some other kinds of laboratories or businesses). Because there are a variety of program structures through which that idea can be expressed, the structure is not a necessary incident to that idea.[36] * * *

* * *

VI. EVIDENCE OF SUBSTANTIAL SIMILARITY

Defendants' second argument is that even if copyright protection is not limited to computer programs' literal elements as a matter of law, there is insufficient evidence of substantial similarity presented in this case to support a finding of copyright infringement. The defendants claim that all three parts of Dr. Moore's expert testimony as to the similarity of the programs * * *, were flawed, and also that the district court erred in evaluating the relative weight of Dr. Moore's and Mr. Ness' testimony. We consider these arguments in turn.

A. *File structures*—Defendants claim that Dr. Moore's examination and conclusions with respect to file structures are irrelevant to the question whether there was a copyright violation. Defendants analogize files to blank forms, which contain no information but merely collect and organize information that is entered from another source. They argue, relying on *Baker v. Selden,* that, as a matter of law, blank forms cannot be copyrighted. Thus, they conclude, neither can file structures be part of the copyright of a program.

Defendants' description of the file structures is indeed correct. Dr. Moore himself described a computer's file as "a storage place for data, and it's really no different in a computer than it is in a file drawer, it's like a manila folder that contains all the data on a particular subject category in a computer." (Another analogy, particularly accessible to lawyers, is to a very complex cataloguing structure like the structure of Lexis or Westlaw without any entries yet made.) Defendants' legal conclusion is not correct, however. Although some courts have stated that the meaning of *Baker v. Selden* is that blank forms cannot be copyrighted, this circuit, like the majority of courts that have considered the issue, has rejected this position and instead have held that blank forms may be copyrighted if they are sufficiently innovative that their arrangement of information is itself informative. * * *. See * * * Manpower, Inc. v. Temporary Help of Harrisburg, Inc., 246 F.Supp. 788 (E.D.Pa.1965) (upholding copyrightability of form for vacation schedules).

---

36. It is not clear whether the end sought to be accomplished by the input formats involved in *Synercom* could be accomplished with different sequences and orders. Compare 462 F.Supp. at 1013 ("there are many . . . possible choices of computer formats, and the decision among them [is] arbitrary") with id. at 1014 ("The 'idea or principle' behind the forms in question, and the 'method or system' involved in them, [are] no more or less than the formats."). Moreover, as noted above, the input formats involved in *Synercom* are not identical to the structures of computer programs that concern us here.

This is not to say that all blank forms or computer files are copyrightable. Only those that by their arrangement and organization convey some information can be copyrighted. Cf. 1 Nimmer at 2–201: "Thus books intended to record the events of baby's first year, or a record of a European trip, or any one of a number of other subjects, may evince considerable originality in suggestions of specific items of information which are to be recorded, and in the arrangement of such items." (footnote omitted). Defendants do not contend, however, that the file structures convey no information, and it appears to us that the structures are sufficiently complex and detailed that such an argument would not succeed. As we have noted * * * there are many ways in which the same goal—the organization of the business aspects of a dental laboratory—might be accomplished, and several of these approaches might use significantly different file structures.[43] The file structures in the Dentalab and Dentcom systems require certain information and order that information in a particular fashion. Other programs might require different information or might use the same information differently. When we compare the comprehensiveness and complexity of the file structures at issue here with the "blank forms" at issue in the cases mentioned above, we have no doubt that these file structures are sufficiently informative to deserve copyright protection.

B. *Screen outputs*—Defendants' second line of argument is slightly confusing. Defendants appear to argue that to the extent that the district court relied upon the similarity of the screen outputs of Dentalab and Dentcom its finding of substantial similarity was erroneous. * * *

* * * [T]he question is whether the screen outputs have probative value concerning the nature of the programs that render them sufficient to clear the hurdles of Fed.R.Evid. 401 and 403. The defendants argue that the screen outputs have no probative value with respect to the programs because many different programs can create the same screen output. Defendants rely on Stern Electronics Inc. v. Kaufman, 669 F.2d at 855 ("many different computer programs can produce the same 'results,' whether those results are an analysis of financial records or a sequence of images and sounds."), and Midway Manufacturing Co., 564 F.Supp. at 749 ("it is quite possible to design a game that would infringe Midway's audiovisual copyright but would use an entirely different computer program."). Neither court, however, was presented with the question that faces us today, the evidentiary

---

43. Defendants' expert, Mr. Ness, testified that, given the problem to be solved, there were in fact few possible, efficient, file structures, and that the similarity in the programs' file structures was therefore neither surprising nor probative. The district court apparently did not find Mr. Ness persuasive on this point, however, and we defer to the court's assessment. Had the defendants offered more evidence to support their position, our answer might have been different. It is true that for certain tasks there are only a very limited number of file structures available, and in such cases the structures might not be copyrightable and similarity of file structures might not be strongly probative of similarity of the program as a whole. We are simply not convinced that this is such a case.

value of screen outputs in a suit for infringement of the underlying program.

Insofar as everything that a computer does, including its screen outputs, is related to the program that operates it, there is necessarily a causal relationship between the program and the screen outputs. The screen outputs must bear some relation to the underlying programs, and therefore they have some probative value. The evidence about the screen outputs therefore passes the low admissibility threshold of Fed. R.Evid. 401.

* * *

C. *The five subroutines*—With respect to the final piece of evidence, Dr. Moore's testimony about the five subroutines found in Dentalab and Dentcom, defendants state that they "fail to understand how a substantial similarity in structure can be established by a comparison of only a small fraction of the two works." The premise underlying this declaration is that one cannot prove substantial similarity of two works without comparing the entirety, or at least the greater part, of the works. We take this premise to be the defendants' argument.

The premise does not apply in other areas of copyright infringement. There is no general requirement that most of each of two works be compared before a court can conclude that they are substantially similar. In the cases of literary works—novels, movies, or plays, for example—it is often impossible to speak of "most" of the work. The substantial similarity inquiry cannot be simply quantified in such instances. Instead, the court must make a qualitative, not quantitative, judgment about the character of the work as a whole and the importance of the substantially similar portions of the work. * * *

Computer programs are no different. Because all steps of a computer program are not of equal importance, the relevant inquiry cannot therefore be the purely mechanical one of whether most of the programs' steps are similar. Rather, because we are concerned with the overall similarities between the programs, we must ask whether the most significant steps of the programs are similar. * * * This is precisely what Dr. Moore did. He testified as follows:

> What I decided to do was to look at the programs that had the primary, or let's say most important, tasks of the system, and also ones which manipulate files, because there are a lot of programs that simply print lists, or answer a question when you ask him it, but I thought that the programs which actually showed the flow of information, through the system, would be the ones that would illustrate the system back.

Dr. Moore's testimony was thus in accord with general principles of copyright law. As we hold today that these principles apply as well to computer programs, we therefore reject the defendants' argument on this point.

D. *Sufficiency of the evidence*—Defendants' final argument is that the district court erred in evaluating the testimony of Dr. Moore and Mr. Ness. They contend that, properly evaluated, Mr. Ness' testimony was sufficiently strong and Dr. Moore's sufficiently weak, that there was not sufficient evidence of substantial similarity for plaintiff to prevail.

We have described the testimony of Dr. Moore and Mr. Ness * * *, and it is recounted in the district court opinion, Whelan Associates v. Jaslow Dental Laboratory, 609 F.Supp. at 1316. The district court explained its evaluation of the evidence as follows:

> I conclude . . . that Dr. Moore, plaintiffs' expert, had greater knowledge as to the particular programs at issue. Dr. Hess [sic], the defendants' expert witness, reviewed only the source and object codes of the IBM–Series 1 (Dentalab program), the IBM Datamaster [see supra n. 4], and the IBM–PC Dentcom system. He never observed the computer in operation nor viewed the various screens or the user's manual. He stated he was not familiar with EDL coding. More basically, however, his comparison as to dissimilarities was between the IBM Datamaster and the IBM–PC Dentcom systems. Plaintiff contends that the IBM–PC Dentcom is a copy of the IBM Series 1 System—not the IBM–Datamaster system. Dr. Hess's conclusions were that although the overall structures of those systems is similar, the code in the IBM–PC Dentcom is not "directly derived" from either plaintiff's IBM Series–1 or its IBM–Datamaster system. To the extent that Dr. Moore's testimony supports plaintiff's contentions of copying, I find his testimony more credible and helpful because of his detailed and thorough analysis of the many similarities.

Determinations of credibility and the relative weight to be given expert witnesses are, of course, left primarily to the discretion of the district court. Our review of the record convinces us that the district court's analysis of the two experts' opinions was far from being erroneous. As the district court pointed out, Mr. Ness had studied the programs, but he had never observed them at work in computers. The district court also pointed out that Mr. Ness was unfamiliar with EDL coding. These factors suffice to support the court's conclusion.

In addition, we believe, on re-reading the trial transcript, that although Mr. Ness' testimony was quite competent, Dr. Moore's was more persuasive on the issues relevant to this appeal. Whereas the greater part of Mr. Ness' testimony was concerned with the dissimilarities between the two programs' source and object codes, Dr. Moore discussed the crucial issue in this case, the similarities and differences in the programs' structures. For example, when he discussed the programs' invoicing subroutine, Dr. Moore testified as follows:

> In the DentaLab system, the same kind of thing again, same information is up there, description, unit price, exten-

sion, items and program reads all those things in from te [sic] number of files actually, and displays them and then gives the operator a number of options to change the order as it appears on the screen to skip this one, to cancel it, or to accept it.

The same choices are given in Dentalab systems, change, skip, cancel.

Assuming that the order is accepted, both systems then calculate the money, calculate the amount of money that will be billed, and at this point they use the price code to find which of the four prices are to be charged for this particular customer. Both systems do that. They pick that one of the four prices and calculate the total amount, write [sic] then the record of this invoice that has been formed to show the invoice's file, sets the flag in the order's file to show that this order has now been invoiced so that it doesn't get reinvoiced.

Q. What is a flag?

A. Well, a flag would be, in this case, a certain location is marked I for invoices, just an indicator that invoicing has been done on this record.

Q. Both used it?

A. Both used a flag. I don't remember whether Dentcom uses a letter I or some other symbol, but there is a flag there that it's a field number 12, in which it's indicated that this file has been invoiced or this order has been invoiced.

* * *

Q. Do you have any comment about the invoicing?

A. *Well, I think it should be clear, it was clear to me from going through these programs that there is a very marke[d] similarity between the two, that they, item by item, are doing pretty much the same thing with the same fields in the same files, and accomplishing roughly the same results.*

So there was quite a match, line by line, between these two, flow in these two.

Q. What do you conclude from that?

A. Well, back together with the file's structure, sort of set up with the—how the programs have to proceed. I would think that the person who designed or constructed the DentaLab system must have been thoroughly familiar with the Dentcom system.

The person who constructed the Dentcom system must have been familiar with the series one system, because the same file structure and same program steps are followed, same overall flow takes place in both systems.

(Emphasis added).　Dr. Moore's testimony about Dentcom's and Dentalab's month-end subroutines also demonstrates the structural comparisons in which he engaged:

Q.　What did you find in month-end?

A.　Okay.　Month-end, the calling program in Dentcom, this obviously is done at the end of each month.

In the Dentcom system there is a program called MOEND, which claims all these other programs, that is, MOEND calls MOPRDL, and after that program runs, goes back to MEEND, calls the print sale and so on.

In the Dentalab system there is a supervisory program also called MOEND, and that system calls or runs a series of programs doing various functions.

Now *if we look at the functions done by the programs in order, we find that they are the same except for a flipping of the order in the first two things.*

The Dentcom system, it first prints product group report, and then prints the monthly customer sales analysis.

In Dentalab, just reverses, prints sales analysis first, product group report second.

After that, both systems do the same thing in the same order.

They now do accounts receivable aging, since a month has gone by they have to update all the 30 days, 60 days, et cetera, calculate service charges.　Then they print the monthly AR reports that had to do with service charges, only those that involve service charges, they both do that. Then they both print the age file balance, balance report, and following that they print the month and accounts receivable report.　That's the total accounts receivable rport [sic].

Then they both go through and look for accounts that are not active that month, and print a list of these accounts, accounts not serviced, an account that doesn't have any access.

The final thing that the Dentcom system does is to calculate the new AR total for the entire lab, which I mentioned is contained in the company file.

DentaLab doesn't keep that total, so that's the last item, that is not as far as I can tell, done by DentaLab.　I may have said—did I say Dentcom keeps that total?　DentaLab does not.　That's the only difference.

(Emphasis added).　Dr. Moore testified in similar detail and to similar effect about the other three subroutines that he felt were particularly important, order entry, accounts receivable, and day's end.

This testimony, in addition to Dr. Moore's exhaustive comparison of the two programs' file structures and his testimony about the screen outputs, demonstrates the marked similarity between the programs. Defendants' argument as to sufficiency of the evidence therefore fails.[47]

VII.　CONCLUSION

We hold that (1) copyright protection of computer programs may extend beyond the programs' literal code to their structure, sequence, and organization, and (2) the district court's finding of substantial similarity between the DentaLab and Dentcom programs was not clearly erroneous. The judgment of the district court will therefore be affirmed.

NOTES

1. The opinions of both the Court of Appeals and the District Court confuse the issue of (1) the amount of similarity sufficient to support an inference of taking in the presence of access with (2) the amount and type of similarity necessary to constitute an infringement. Nevertheless, it is clear that the Court is addressing only the second issue, isn't it?

2. Critics of the *Whelan* opinion have been concerned that it accords too broad a scope of protection to software, and that the protection will prevent programmers from copying useful programming ideas and techniques developed by others, to the detriment of advances in the programming art. The critics read the sentence in the opinion that says "it is clear that the purpose of the utilitarian Dentalab program was to aid in the business operations of a dental laboratory", supra page 687, as leading to the conclusion that every other aspect of a program is protected. Do you agree?

3. The most widely publicized litigation in the computer field involves claims by Apple against Microsoft that Microsoft's Windows program copies the "look and feel" of the Apple MacIntosh copyrighted system screens and claims by Lotus against seller's of Lotus 1–2–3 "clones" that they have infringed the "look and feel" of the Lotus 1–2–3 copyright. The 1–2–3 clone of Paperback Software was held to infringe the Lotus copyright in Lotus Development Corp. v. Paperback Software Intern., 740 F.Supp. 37 (D.Mass.1990).

4. An important and closely followed case has been NEC Corporation v. Intel Corp., 645 F.Supp. 590 (N.D.Cal.1986), in which Intel alleged that NEC had infringed the copyrights on its 8088 and 8086 microprocessors (the central processing unit or "brain" of the original IBM Personal Computer and clones) in its V20, V30, and V50 microprocessors (designed to be compatible with the 8088 and 8086). Intel is a leading designer and producer of microprocessors in the United States. NEC is the Nippon Electronics Corporation, the Japanese

---

47. Of course structural similarities between two programs can also arise in completely legitimate ways—e.g., where the authors of the two programs have included subroutines from common, unprotected subroutine libraries, or where the authors of both programs have consulted common, public domain, reference books. There can be no bright line rules as to when similarities are evidence of infringement and when they are legitimate—that is a determination to be made by the trier of fact. See supra note 23. There is no suggestion in the present case that the similarities between Dentalab and Dentcom were the result of such common ground, however, and so the court's inference of copyright infringement from its finding of substantial similarity was correct.

"A.T. & T." and a leading electronics manufacturer in Japan. On February 6, 1989, the district court held that Intel had lost its copyright due to the omission of notice from a large number of the chips and that the NEC chips did not infringe. 1989 WL 67434.

5. The use of copyright to protect computer software raises fundamental issues of copyright and patent law, as well as requiring an examination of basic policies concerning the protection of both intellectual and industrial property. In addition, computers are fascinating and fast evolving technological tools, increasingly familiar to many people, including lawyers. As a result, the subject of protection of software has generated an enormous literature in the last few years.

C. FAIR USE

Prior to 1970 there were few fair use cases, and examples of takings thought to be clear examples of fair use fell into the following three categories.

1. Notes taken from a copyrighted work for the private use of the reader.

2. Quotations from a work used as part of a critical essay or response to the work and reasonably necessary to that purpose. In Consumers Union v. Hobart Mfg. Co., 189 F.Supp. 275 (S.D.N.Y.1960), followed on summary judgment, 199 F.Supp. 860 (S.D.N.Y.1961), the defendant had quoted criticisms of its KitchenAid dishwashers from Consumers Report in order to answer them. In the course of holding for the defendant on the ground of non-copyrightable subject matter, see supra page 592, the court observed: "[I]t must be admitted that one cannot, by copyrighting his unfavorable remarks about another, prevent that other from quoting those remarks and refuting them." 189 F.Supp. at 278.

3. Copyrighted material which is included incidentally in a documentary or commentary as part of the atmosphere without any special gain accruing to the user as a result of the inclusion. Karll v. Curtis Publishing Co., 39 F.Supp. 836 (E.D.Wisc.1941), was a suit for infringement of the chorus of the official Green Bay Packer song "Go! You Packers Go!" which appeared in an article entitled "Little Town That Leads 'Em" appearing in the Saturday Evening Post. The article told of the history of the Packer organization and the strength of its community support, the song was quoted in passing. The court found fair use. And in Broadway Music Corp. v. F–R Publishing Corp., 31 F.Supp. 817 (S.D.N.Y.1940), the court found that the New Yorker's use of twelve lines from the plaintiff's humorous song "Poor Pauline" in the course of a comment on the death of the actress Pauline White was fair use.

The frequency of reported litigation whose outcome involves the fair use concept has increased greatly since 1970. This is the result of three factors. First, the increased commercial value of copyrightable materials in a knowledge-based and entertainment-focused era. Second, the expansion of the subject matter of (§ 102) and exclusive rights conferred by (§ 106) copyright in the 1976 act. And third, the development of inexpensive and widely available copying technologies.

SONY CORP. OF AMERICA v. UNIVERSAL CITY STUDIOS, INC.

Supreme Court of the United States, 1984.
464 U.S. 417, 104 S.Ct. 774, 78 L.Ed.2d 574.

JUSTICE STEVENS delivered the opinion of the Court.

Petitioners manufacture and sell home video tape recorders. Respondents own the copyrights on some of the television programs that are broadcast on the public airwaves. Some members of the general public use video tape recorders [in the opinion called "VTR's", but commonly known as "VCR's", for video cassette recorders] sold by petitioners to record some of these broadcasts, as well as a large number of other broadcasts. The question presented is whether the sale of petitioners' copying equipment to the general public violates any of the rights conferred upon respondents by the Copyright Act.

* * *

After a lengthy trial, the District Court denied respondents all the relief they sought and entered judgment for petitioners. 480 F.Supp. 429 (1979). The United States Court of Appeals for the Ninth Circuit reversed the District Court's judgment on respondent's copyright claim, holding petitioners liable for contributory infringement and ordering the District Court to fashion appropriate relief. 659 F.2d 963 (1981). We granted certiorari, 457 U.S. 1116 (1982); since we had not completed our study of the case last Term, we ordered reargument, 463 U.S. 1226 (1983).

We now reverse.

An explanation of our rejection of respondents' unprecedented attempt to impose copyright liability upon the distributors of copying equipment requires a * * * recitation of the findings of the District Court. In summary, those findings reveal that the average member of the public uses a VTR principally to record a program he cannot view as it is being televised and then to watch it once at a later time. This practice, known as "time-shifting," enlarges the television viewing audience. For that reason, a significant amount of television programming may be used in this manner without objection from the owners of the copyrights on the programs. For the same reason, even the two respondents in this case, who do assert objections to time-shifting in this litigation, were unable to prove that the practice has impaired the commercial value of their copyrights or has created any likelihood of future harm. Given these findings, there is no basis in the Copyright Act upon which respondents can hold petitioners liable for distributing VTR's to the general public. The Court of Appeals' holding that respondents are entitled to enjoin the distribution of VTR's, to collect royalties on the sale of such equipment, or to obtain other relief, if affirmed, would enlarge the scope of respondents' statutory monopolies to encompass control over an article of commerce that is not the subject of copyright protection. Such an expansion of the copyright privilege is beyond the limits of the grants authorized by Congress.

I

The two respondents in this action, Universal Studios, Inc. and Walt Disney Productions, produce and hold the copyrights on a substantial number of motion pictures and other audiovisual works. In the current marketplace, they can exploit their rights in these works in a number of ways: by authorizing theatrical exhibitions, by licensing limited showings on cable and network television, by selling syndication rights for repeated airings on local television stations, and by marketing programs on prerecorded videotapes or videodiscs. Some works are suitable for exploitation through all of these avenues, while the market for other works is more limited.

*   *   *

Several capabilities of the * * * [VTR] are noteworthy. The separate tuner in the Betamax enables it to record a broadcast off one station while the television set is tuned to another channel permitting the viewer, for example, to watch two simultaneous news broadcasts by watching one "live" and recording the other for later viewing. Tapes may be reused, and programs that have been recorded may be erased either before or after viewing. A timer in the Betamax can be used to activate and deactivate the equipment at predetermined times, enabling an intended viewer to record programs that are transmitted when he or she is not at home. Thus a person may watch a program at home in the evening even though it was broadcast while the viewer was at work during the afternoon. The Betamax is also equipped with a pause button and a fast-forward control. The pause button, when depressed, deactivates the recorder until it is released, thus enabling a viewer to omit a commercial advertisement from the recording, provided, of course, that the viewer is present when the program is recorded. The fast forward control enables the viewer of a previously recorded program to run the tape rapidly when a segment he or she does not desire to see is being played back on the television screen.

The respondents and Sony both conducted surveys of the way the Betamax machine was used by several hundred owners during a sample period in 1978. Although there were some differences in the surveys, they both showed that the primary use of the machine for most owners was "time-shifting,"—the practice of recording a program to view it once at a later time, and thereafter erasing it. Time-shifting enables viewers to see programs they otherwise would miss because they are not at home, are occupied with other tasks, or are viewing a program on another station at the time of a broadcast that they desire to watch. Both surveys also showed, however, that a substantial number of interviewees had accumulated libraries of tapes. Sony's survey indicated that over 80% of the interviewees watched at least as much regular television as they had before owning a Betamax. Respondents offered no evidence of decreased television viewing by Betamax owners.

Sony introduced considerable evidence describing television programs that could be copied without objection from any copyright holder, with special emphasis on sports, religious, and educational programming. For example, their survey indicated that 7.3% of all Betamax use is to record sports events, and representatives of professional baseball, football, basketball, and hockey testified that they had no objection to the recording of their televised events for home use.

Respondents offered opinion evidence concerning the future impact of the unrestricted sale of VTR's on the commercial value of their copyrights. The District Court found, however, that they had failed to prove any likelihood of future harm from the use of VTR's for time-shifting.

* * *

II

From its beginning, the law of copyright has developed in response to significant changes in technology.[11] Indeed, it was the invention of a new form of copying equipment—the printing press—that gave rise to the original need for copyright protection. Repeatedly, as new developments have occurred in this country, it has been the Congress that has fashioned the new rules that new technology made necessary. * * *

* * *

In a case like this, in which Congress has not plainly marked our course, we must be circumspect in construing the scope of rights created by a legislative enactment which never contemplated such a calculus of interests.

* * *

[The law] * * * has never accorded the copyright owner complete control over all possible uses of his work. Rather, the Copyright Act grants the copyright holder "exclusive" rights to use and to authorize the use of his work in five qualified ways, including reproduction of the copyrighted work in copies. § 106. * * *

* * *

The two respondents in this case do not seek relief against the Betamax users who have allegedly infringed their copyrights. Moreover, this is not a class action on behalf of all copyright owners who

---

11. Thus, for example, the development and marketing of player pianos and perforated roles of music, see White-Smith Music Publishing Co. v. Apollo Co., 209 U.S. 1 (1908), preceded the enactment of the Copyright Act of 1909; innovations in copying techniques gave rise to the statutory exemption for library copying embodied in § 108 of the 1976 revision of the Copyright law; the development of the technology that made it possible to retransmit television programs by cable or by microwave systems, see Fortnightly Corp. v. United Artists, 392 U.S. 390 (1968), and Teleprompter Corp. v. CBS, 415 U.S. 394 (1974), prompted the enactment of the complex provisions set forth in 17 U.S.C. § 111(d)(2)(B) and § 111(d)(5) after years of detailed congressional study, see Eastern Microwave, Inc. v. Doubleday Sports, Inc., 691 F.2d 125, 129 (CA2 1982).

* * *

license their works for television broadcast, and respondents have no right to invoke whatever rights other copyright holders may have to bring infringement actions based on Betamax copying of their works. As was made clear by their own evidence, the copying of the respondents' programs represents a small portion of the total use of VTR's. It is, however, the taping of respondents own copyright programs that provides them with standing to charge Sony with contributory infringement. To prevail, they have the burden of proving that users of the Betamax have infringed their copyrights and that Sony should be held responsible for that infringement.

III

[In part III of the opinion the Court considered what the plaintiffs had to prove in order to hold that the defendants' sale of VTR's made them subject to remedies for the possible infringements of the purchasers. The Court concluded:] Accordingly, the sale of copying equipment, like the sale of other articles of commerce, does not constitute contributory infringement if the product is widely used for legitimate, unobjectionable purposes. Indeed, it need merely be capable of substantial noninfringing uses.

IV

[The Court then turned to the question of whether the Betamax is capable of significant noninfringing uses. It focused on two types of time-shifting (the record, relating to the period prior to 1978 when home video rentals were not widely available, showed that time-shifting was the principal consumer use): authorized and unauthorized time-shifting. The record revealed that owners of rights in sports, religious and educational programming had no objection to time-shifting. The Court made specific mention of] the testimony of Fred Rogers, president of the corporation that produces and owns the copyright on *Mr. Rogers' Neighborhood.* The program is carried by more public television stations than any other program. Its audience numbers over 3,000,000 families a day. He testified that he had absolutely no objection to home taping for noncommercial use and expressed the opinion that it is a real service to families to be able to record children's programs and to show them at appropriate times.

If there are millions of owners of VTR's who make copies of televised sports events, religious broadcasts, and educational programs such as *Mister Rogers' Neighborhood,* and if the proprietors of those programs welcome the practice, the business of supplying the equipment that makes such copying feasible should not be stifled simply because the equipment is used by some individuals to make unauthorized reproductions of respondents' works. The respondents do not represent a class composed of all copyright holders. Yet a finding of contributory infringement would inevitably frustrate the interests of broadcasters in reaching the portion of their audience that is available only through time-shifting.

B. *Unauthorized Time-Shifting*

Even unauthorized uses of a copyrighted work are not necessarily infringing. An unlicensed use of the copyright is not an infringement unless it conflicts with one of the specific exclusive rights conferred by the copyright statute. Twentieth Century Music Corp. v. Aiken, 422 U.S. 151, 154–155. Moreover, the definition of exclusive rights in § 106 of the present Act is prefaced by the words "subject to sections 107 through 118." Those sections describe a variety of uses of copyrighted material that "are not infringements of copyright notwithstanding the provisions of § 106." The most pertinent in this case is § 107, the legislative endorsement of the doctrine of "fair use."

That section identifies various factors that enable a Court to apply an "equitable rule of reason" analysis to particular claims of infringement. Although not conclusive, the first factor requires that "the commercial or nonprofit character of an activity" be weighed in any fair use decision. If the Betamax were used to make copies for a commercial or profit-making purpose, such use would presumptively be unfair. The contrary presumption is appropriate here, however, because the District Court's findings plainly establish that time-shifting for private home use must be characterized as a noncommercial, nonprofit activity. Moreover, when one considers the nature of a televised copyrighted audiovisual work, see 17 U.S.C. § 107(2), and that time-shifting merely enables a viewer to see such a work which he had been invited to witness in its entirety free of charge, the fact that the entire work is reproduced, see § 107(3), does not have its ordinary effect of militating against a finding of fair use.

This is not, however, the end of the inquiry because Congress has also directed us to consider "the effect of the use upon the potential market for or value of the copyrighted work." § 107(4). The purpose of copyright is to create incentives for creative effort. Even copying for noncommercial purposes may impair the copyright holder's ability to obtain the rewards that Congress intended him to have. But a use that has no demonstrable effect upon the potential market for, or the value of, the copyrighted work need not be prohibited in order to protect the author's incentive to create. The prohibition of such noncommercial uses would merely inhibit access to ideas without any countervailing benefit.

Thus, although every commercial use of copyrighted material is presumptively an unfair exploitation of the monopoly privilege that belongs to the owner of the copyright, noncommercial uses are a different matter. A challenge to a noncommercial use of a copyrighted work requires proof either that the particular use is harmful, or that if it should become widespread, it would adversely affect the potential market for the copyrighted work. Actual present harm need not be shown; such a requirement would leave the copyright holder with no defense against predictable damage. Nor is it necessary to show with certainty that future harm will result. What is necessary is a showing by a preponderance of the evidence that *some* meaningful likelihood of future harm exists. If the intended use is for commercial gain, that likelihood may be presumed. But if it is for a noncommercial purpose, the likelihood must be demonstrated.

In this case, respondents failed to carry their burden with regard to home time-shifting. The District Court described respondents' evidence as follows:

> "Plaintiffs' experts admitted at several points in the trial that the time-shifting without librarying would result in 'not a great deal of harm.' Plaintiffs' greatest concern about time-shifting is with 'a point of important philosophy that transcends even commercial judgment.' They fear that with any Betamax usage, 'invisible boundaries' are passed: 'the copyright owner has lost control over his program.' " 480 F.Supp., at 467.

Later in its opinion, the District Court observed:

> "Most of plaintiffs' predictions of harm hinge on speculation about audience viewing patterns and ratings, a measurement system which Sidney Sheinberg, MCA's president, calls a 'black art' because of the significant level of imprecision involved in the calculations."

There was no need for the District Court to say much about past harm. "Plaintiffs have admitted that no actual harm to their copyrights has occurred to date."

On the question of potential future harm from time-shifting, the District Court offered a more detailed analysis of the evidence. It rejected respondents' "fear that persons 'watching' the original telecast of a program will not be measured in the live audience and the ratings and revenues will decrease," by observing that current measurement technology allows the Betamax audience to be reflected. It rejected respondents' prediction "that live television or movie audiences will decrease as more people watch Betamax tapes as an alternative," with the observation that "[t]here is no factual basis for [the underlying] assumption." It rejected respondents' "fear that time-shifting will reduce audiences for telecast reruns," and concluded instead that "given current market practices, this should aid plaintiffs rather than harm them." And it declared that respondents' suggestion "that theater or film rental exhibition of a program will suffer because of time-shift recording of that program" "lacks merit."

* * *

The District Court's conclusions are buttressed by the fact that to the extent time-shifting expands public access to freely broadcast television programs, it yields societal benefits. * * *

When these factors are all weighed in the "equitable rule of reason" balance, we must conclude that this record amply supports the District Court's conclusion that home time-shifting is fair use. In light of the findings of the District Court regarding the state of the empirical data, it is clear that the Court of Appeals erred in holding that the statute as presently written bars such conduct.

* * *

The Betamax is * * * capable of substantial noninfringing uses. Sony's sale of such equipment to the general public does not constitute contributory infringement of respondent's copyrights.

V

One may search the Copyright Act in vain for any sign that the elected representatives of the millions of people who watch television every day have made it unlawful to copy a program for later viewing at home, or have enacted a flat prohibition against the sale of machines that make such copying possible.

It may well be that Congress will take a fresh look at this new technology, just as it so often has examined other innovations in the past. But it is not our job to apply laws that have not yet been written. Applying the copyright statute, as it now reads, to the facts as they have been developed in this case, the judgment of the Court of Appeals must be reversed.

It is so ordered.

[JUSTICES BLACKMUN, MARSHALL, POWELL, and REHNQUIST dissented.]

NOTE

1. The impact of time-shifting upon the demand for copyrighted program material is not clear. It is plausible that the effect of time-shifting is to make television viewing more convenient and accessible and thus to increase the viewing audience. Persons who are unable to view television during certain hours can record the program and view it at other times. Broadcast capacity during off hours such as the early morning can be used to broadcast programs which are taped by the viewer for viewing at another time. If time-shifting does increase the demand for programming in general (by lowering the costs of transmitting the program to some viewers), wouldn't it have been odd for the court to limit or bar the sale of VCR's at the behest of only a few copyright owners?

2. The Statement in the *Sony* case that "every commercial use of copyrighted material is presumptively an unfair exploitation of the monopoly privilege that belongs to the owner of the copyright" has been frequently repeated in the cases. But is it correct? Why isn't home videotaping a "commercial" use of the copyrighted program which saves the homeowner the cost of buying or renting a copy of the program? Can't home videotaping have a large impact on the commercial market for videotapes?

The Court may simply be trying to express the thought that organized copying within the context of a business organization is enforceable illegality, while dispersed copying in the private home is unstoppable, even if illegal.

That certainly seems to be the practice in the case of computer software, musical tapes, and videotaping, where there is widespread and quite open copying in dispersed, personal settings (and the less personal setting of the colleges and universities, which are centers of massive copyright infringement), while the owners of the copyrights focus their enforcement efforts on commercial distribution and use. But in spite of this language in *Sony,* there are cases which have held commercial use a fair use. For instance consider the use by KitchenAid of the Consumers Union comments, or the use of quotes by the Saturday Evening Post or the New Yorker Magazine, supra p. 696. Or the use by fee-charging doctors of the copies of articles from the National Library of Medicine in *Williams & Wilkins,* infra p. 711. Or the use of a magazine cover in a competing advertisement in *Triangle Publications,* infra p. 741. Are these uses so distinctively "fair" that they overcame the presumption? How?

The Supreme Court said that journalistic use is commercial use in the *Nation* case, infra p. 715, offering a somewhat odd definition. "In arguing that the purpose of news reporting is not purely commercial, The Nation misses the point entirely. The crux of the profit/nonprofit distinction is not whether the sole motive of the use is monetary gain but whether the user stands to profit from exploitation of the copyrighted material without paying the customary price." Infra pp. 724–725. Does this mean that if it is customary not to pay the price, then the use is non-commercial, even though it is for the purpose of making money?

PROBLEM

Does a law firm that has copies made of copyrighted material such as case reports including headnotes and articles in academic journals to put into case files for easy retention and subsequent access infringe the copyright in those works? Is use by a law firm a commercial use? What about a judge, whose clerks do the same thing?

THE PRE–1976 LAW, ANALOGOUS AUDIO RECORDING PRACTICES AND THE SCOPE OF THE *SONY* HOLDING

The expansion of the scope of the rights conferred by copyright in § 106 (interacting with the definitions in § 101) played an important role in the *Sony* litigation. Prior to the new statute, a recording was not treated like a copy of a protected work because the concept of copy was limited to things which were visually similar to the original. White-Smith Music Publishing Co. v. Apollo Co., 209 U.S. 1 (1908) (perforated roll for player piano not an infringement of the copyright in the sheet music). Thus making a video tape was not a copying and not itself an infringement of the copyright on an underlying work. This was changed by the new definition of "Copies" in § 101: " 'Copies' are material objects * * * in which a work is fixed by any method * * * and from which the work can be perceived, reproduced, or otherwise communicated, either directly or with the aid of a machine or device." Video tapes fall within this definition.

Also important was the development of a relatively low cost and hence widely available copying technology for television programs. Similar devices had developed for audio recording (the sound tape recorder which had developed prior to the video recorder, now widely available in a standardized cassette form) and for copying the printed page (a technology now dominated by xerography), and their availability has raised similar fair use issues.

Audio Recording. The practices that had developed in relation to the audio tape recorder were relevant to the *Sony* litigation, for it is clear that the audio tape recorder is widely used to make copies of recorded music and broadcasts, and that these copies are (to use the argot of the *Sony* litigation) "libraried." No lawsuit has ever been filed to challenge this practice for personal, non-commercial use, perhaps because home recording is not a sufficiently good substitute for records to affect the market (the only people satisfied with cassette copies may be those who don't have the money to buy the record). Prior to the 1976 Act, the illegality of making personal audio recordings was less than clear. In a compromise at the time of the 1909 statute, adopted long before home recording was a possibility, much less a gleam in an engineer's eye, the statute provided that a recorded copy only entitled the owner of the copyright in the music (copyrighted in the form of transcribed sheet music) to collect a royalty fee, not to enjoin an infringement or pursue the other infringement remedies. So the personal use, home recorder could simply be viewed as someone from whom the owner of the copyright had not yet bothered to collect the few cents of compulsory royalty due. (Parenthetically, the compulsory royalty provisions live on in § 115, but restructured so that it is clear that they are not available to the casual, personal home recorder. For instance, a person claiming a compulsory license must have served notice of his intention to do so on the copyright owner.) Prior to 1976 the practice of home "librarying" of sound recordings developed in this legal setting (home video recording had just begun in 1976).

It was clear enough to any copyright lawyer that the revision bill would significantly affect this situation. Yet it was rarely addressed in the legislative history. The district court in *Sony* (which found fair use) used the audio analogy in the following excerpt.

UNIVERSAL CITY STUDIOS v. SONY CORP. OF AMERICA
United States District Court, Central District, 1979.
480 F.Supp. 429.

FERGUSON, DISTRICT JUDGE.

*   *   *

In 1955, Congress began revising the Copyright Act of 1909. From 1955 to 1976, the Office of the Register of Copyrights worked with Congress to draft the new legislation and focus issues of concern. Comprehensive revision was a complex and controversial effort. In 1971, the process was impeded by strong disagreement about the treatment of cable television in the revised statutory framework. By the same year, the problem of record piracy had become severe. Relief for this problem was blocked by the dispute over the cable television portions of the revision act. Rather than waiting for complete revision, Congress passed an amendment to the Old Act to deal with sound recording piracy. This amendment became subsection (f) of § 1 of the Old Act and established limited copyright protection for owners of sound recordings. This subsection (f) was not distinct and separate from the comprehensive revision under way in Congress. Its language was lifted from the earlier general revision bills, and it was incorporated virtually verbatim into § 106 *et seq.* of the New Act. As the Librarian of Congress wrote to the Chairman of the Senate Judiciary Committee on January 19, 1971:

> In general, we also support the amendatory language adopted in the bill which *draws heavily upon the language of the bill for general revision of the copyright law (S.543)* * * *
>
>   *   *   *
>
> The most fundamental question raised by the bill is its relationship to the program for general revision of the copyright law. The revision bill before your committee this past session and which Senator McClellan proposes to reintroduce, has parallel provisions, and if general revision were on the threshold of enactment S. 4592 would be unnecessary. However, some fundamental problems impeding the progress of general revision of the copyright law, notably the issue of cable television, have not yet been resolved. We agree that the national and international problem of record piracy is too urgent to await comprehensive action on copyright law revision, and that the amendments proposed in S. 4592 are badly needed now. *Upon enactment of the revision bill, they would, of course, be merged into the larger pattern of the revised statute as a whole.*

S.Rep. No. 72, 92d Cong., 1st Sess., 7–8 (1971) (emphasis added).

A comparison of the statutory language shows that the amendment was merged into the New Act. This incorporation is significant because Congress, in passing the legislation, clearly expressed its intent not to restrain home sound recording from broadcasts, tapes or records where the recording is for private, non-commercial use. As the House Report which accompanied the 1971 Amendment stated:

Home Recording

> In approving the creation of a limited copyright in sound recordings it is the intention of the Committee that this limited copyright not grant any broader rights than are accorded to other copyright proprietors under the existing title 17. Specifically, it is not the intention of the Committee to restrain the home recording, from broadcasts or from tapes or records, of recorded performances, where the home recording is for private use and with no purpose of reproducing or otherwise capitalizing commercially on it. This practice is common and unrestrained today, and the record producers and performers

would be in no different position from that of the owners of copyright in recorded musical compositions over the past 20 years.

H.Rep. No. 487, 92d Cong., 1st Sess. 7, reprinted in [1971] U.S.Code Cong. & Admin.News, pp. 1566, 1572.

Thus, while the language of § 106 of the New Act appears to give copyright holders exclusive rights over all recordings, the Congressional intent was that home-use sound recording was not prohibited. Holders of copyrights in sound recordings were not to have any "broader rights than are accorded to other copyright proprietors." U.S.Code Cong. & Admin.News 1971, p. 1572. Defendants contend that, as with home-use sound recording, Congress did not intend to protect copyright holders from off-the-air audiovisual recording for home-use, even though the statute does not expressly so state.

The issue of home-use recording was not addressed in any subsequent House or Senate report. The reports accompanying the 1976 general revision legislation did not restate Congressional refusal to give monopoly power over home-use recording, but the language of the 1971 Amendment was incorporated into the New Act without any suggestion that legislative intent had changed.

The 1971 House Report is not the only support for a finding that the Copyright Act does not prohibit home-use recording. Home-use recording from radio and television broadcasts was discussed in committee hearings, floor debates and reports from the Office of Copyrights. Statements from all three sources are relevant to a determination of legislative intent.

In June, 1971, Subcommittee No. 3 of the House Committee on the Judiciary met in hearings on the sound recording amendment. Representative Beister of Pennsylvania engaged in the following dialogue about off-the-air recording with Ms. Barbara Ringer, then Assistant Register of Copyrights:

MR. BEISTER. I do not know that I can add very much to the questions which you have been asked so far.

I can tell you I must have a small pirate in my own home.

My son has a cassette tape recorder, and as a particular record becomes a hit, he will retrieve it onto his little set.

Now, he may retrieve in addition something else onto his recording, but nonetheless, he does retrieve the basic sound, *and this legislation, of course, would not point to his activities, would it?*

MISS RINGER. I think the answer is clearly, *"No, it would not."*

I have spoken at a couple of seminars on *video cassettes lately, and this question is usually asked: "What about the home recorders?"*

The answer I have given and will give again is that *this is something you cannot control. You simply cannot control it.*

Hearings on S. 646 before the Subcomm. No. 3 of the House Judiciary Comm., 92d Cong., 1st Sess. 22 (June 9 and 10, 1971).

Ms. Ringer proceeded to discuss the problem of unauthorized video recordings finding their way into the market. She recognized that this was a problem which Congress might face in the future but stated that it could not be met by carrying copyright enforcement into the home or by banning devices for off-the-air recording. Her testimony continued:

But *I do not see anybody going into anyone's home and preventing this sort of thing, or forcing legislation that would engineer a piece of equipment not to allow home taping.*

MR. BEISTER: Secondly, *with respect to video cassettes,* are we approaching an additional problem, *not with respect to private use,* but with respect to public distribution after it has been retrieved over a home set?

MISS RINGER: The answer is very definitely, "yes."

For years the motion picture industry has been faced with bootlegging problems, much of it deriving from the 10 mm prints that were distributed to the Armed Forces and got out of control. The film industry has had a very active policing activity for years.

I think that this problem is going to undergo a quantum increase when video cassette recorders are freely available. But I would say that there is a big difference, and I think it is something that you might consider. In that area, they have got copyright protection, and in this area, who knows? *It is certainly not protectable under the Federal statute.*

Id. pp. 22–23.

When the 1971 Amendment reached the House floor, the question of noncommercial home recording was raised by Representative Kazen of Texas and answered by Representative Kastenmeier. Representative Kastenmeier was chairman of the House Judiciary Subcommittee responsible for the New Act, a sponsor of the general revision legislation, and a member of the Conference Committee which put the New Act in final form. The dialogue was as follows:

MR. KAZEN. Am I correct in assuming that the bill protects copyrighted material that *is duplicated for commercial purposes only?*

MR. KASTENMEIER. Yes.

MR. KAZEN. In other words, if your child were to *record off of a program which comes through the air on* the radio or *television, and then used it for her own personal pleasure, for listening pleasure, this would not be included under the penalties of this bill?*

MR. KASTENMEIER. *This is not included in the bill. I am glad the gentleman raises the point.*

On page 7 of the report, under "Home Recordings," Members will note that under the bill the same practice which prevails today is called for; namely, *this is considered both presently and under the proposed law to be fair use. The child does not do this for commercial purposes.* This is made clear in the report.

117 Cong.Rec. 34, 748 (1971).

Treatment of home-use recording is consistent outside the legislative history, as well. Indeed, since 1955, the Copyright Office of the Library of Congress and the Register of Copyright consistently avoided and even opposed efforts to protect copyright owners against home-use recording.

In 1961, the Office issued a report which urged that private performance of a copyrighted film or motion picture not be restrained. The Register contended that statutory damages for such infringement "would be grossly excessive" and that "private performances could rarely be discovered or controlled." The Register directly confronted the issue of home-use videotape recording:

New technical devices will probably make it practical in the future to reproduce televised motion pictures in the home. We do not believe the private use of such a reproduction can or should be precluded by copyright.

Copyright Law Revision, Report of the Register of Copyrights (July, 1961), p. 30.

As discussed above, the Copyright Office, through Barbara Ringer, continued to advocate this view throughout the years of legislative revision. The Office was an active participant in drafting, promoting and explaining the legislation for Congress and always maintained that home-use recording is not an infringement.

This position of the Office developed in part from a concern about invasion of the individual's privacy in his home. As Ms. Ringer testified, home recording simply cannot be controlled. Nobody is going into anyone's home to prevent it. The fears of Representatives Beister and Kazen that the legislation would reach their children's activities in their homes were not realized. Of course, not all activity is made legal by virtue of occurring in a private home. Congress can constitutionally legislate against some activity which may occur in the home, but doing so necessarily requires caution. Here, legislative history shows that, in balance, Congress did not find that protection of copyright holders' rights over reproduction of their works was worth the privacy and enforcement problems which restraint of home-use recording would create.

[The district court found fair use, broadly upholding all home, non-commercial taping.]

These arguments were made to the Supreme Court, which responded to them at the end of a footnote. "Sony argues that the legislative history of that Act [The Sound Recording Amendment of 1971, 85 Stat. 391, which extended copyright protection to sound recordings on an interim basis pending passage of the revision bill], see especially H.Rep. No. 487, 92nd Cong., 1st Sess., p. 7, [quoted at length by the district court, supra] indicates that Congress did not intend to prohibit the private home use of either audio or video tape recording equipment. In view of our disposition of the contributory infringement issue, we express no opinion on that question." 104 S.Ct. 782 n. 11. Thus the Court in *Sony* chose to avoid addressing the issue of fair use in relation to audio recordings, and in relation to both audio and video recordings when "librarying" is present. What does that suggest about how the Court might rule if those issues were clearly before it?

In 1984 Congress passed the Record Rental Amendment of 1984, which amended § 109 to prohibit commercial record rental services by adding new subsection § 109(b) and making other conforming amendments to the copyright act. The purpose of this amendment was to enable the copyright owner to refuse to consent to a commercial rental service offered by an owner of a phonorecord. The reason given was that commercial record rental establishments existed to facilitate making home recorded cassettes from the rental record. One such establishment advertised: "Never, ever buy another record."

The House Report said: "The Committee * * * declines at this time to address the issue of home taping of copyrighted works for private, noncommercial use. No precedential value, therefore, should be implied for any other legislation." House Report No. 98–987, p. 2, 1984 U.S.Code Cong. & Admin.News, vol. 4, p. 2899.

The Committee also considered, but did not recommend, legislation designed to change the law in relation to movies. Why are establishments that rent video tape copies of movies different than establishments that rent records?

In recent years the Digital Audio Tape, or DAT, format recorders have been controversial because they make it possible to produce high quality copies of digital compact disks at home. Music copyright owners have unsuccessfully asked Congress to make them illegal. The DAT tape recorders now being sold permit the user to make a copy, but not a copy of a copy.

Congress extended the prohibition of rental to computer software by amending § 109(b) in the Computer Software Rental Amendments Act of 1990.

Copying of printed materials. There has been no litigation involving personal use of copying machines to make copies of books, articles and other printed material. The problem has been partially addressed in the context of schools, infra p. 754. Up to a point, personal copying can be analogized to the long-recognized fair use privilege of taking notes. But a copy of a whole book or article can serve as a substitute for the book or article itself.

A relevant case is Williams & Wilkins Co. v. United States, 203 Ct. Cl. 74, 487 F.2d 1345 (1973), affirmed without opinion by an equally divided Court 420 U.S. 376 (1975). A private publisher of four special-ized medical journals sued the United States government for copyright infringement based upon actions of the library of the National Institute of Health [known as the "NIH"] and the National Library of Medicine [the "NLM"].

The court described the activities of the library of the NIH as follows:

> The NIH library subscribes to about 3,000 different journal titles, four of which are the journals in suit. The library subscribes to two copies of each of the journals involved. As a general rule, one copy stays in the library reading room and the other copy circulates among interested NIH personnel. Demand by NIH research workers for access to plaintiff's journals (as well as other journals to which the library sub-scribes) is usually not met by in-house subscription copies. Consequently, as an integral part of its operation, the library runs a photocopy service for the benefit of its research staff. On request, a researcher can obtain a photocopy of an article from any of the journals in the library's collection. Usually, researchers request photocopies of articles to assist them in their on-going projects; sometimes photocopies are requested simply for background reading. The library does not monitor the reason for requests or the use to which the photocopies are put. The photocopies are not returned to the library; and the record shows that, in most instances, researchers keep them in their private files for future reference.

> The library's policy is that, as a rule, only a single copy of a journal article will be made per request and each request is limited to about 40 to 50 pages, though exceptions may be, and have been, made in the case of long articles, upon approval of the Assistant Chief of the library branch. Also, as a general rule, requests for photocopying are limited to only a single article from a journal issue. Exceptions to this rule are routinely made, so long as substantially less than an entire journal is photocopied, i.e., less than about half of the journal. Coworkers can, and frequently do, request single copies of the same article and such requests are honored.

> Four regularly assigned employees operate the NIH photo-copy equipment. The equipment consists of microfilm cameras and Xerox copying machines. In 1970, the library photocopy

budget was $86,000 and the library filled 85,744 requests for photocopies of journal articles (including plaintiff's journals), constituting about 930,000 pages. On the average, a journal article is 10 pages long, so that, in 1970, the library made about 93,000 photocopies of articles. 487 F.2d 1347–48.

The court described the activities of the NLM as follows:

NLM, located on the Bethesda campus of NIH, was formerly the Armed Forces Medical Library. In 1956, Congress transferred the library from the Department of Defense to the Public Health Service (renaming it the National Library of Medicine), and declared its purpose to be " * * * to aid the dissemination and exchange of scientific and other information important to the progress of medicine and to the public health * * *." 42 U.S.C. § 275 (1970). NLM is a repository of much of the world's medical literature, in essence a "librarians' library." As part of its operation, NLM cooperates with other libraries and like research-and-education-oriented institutions (both public and private) in a so-called "interlibrary loan" program. Upon request, NLM will loan to such institutions, for a limited time, books and other materials in its collection. In the case of journals, the "loans" usually take the form of photocopies of journal articles which are supplied by NLM free of charge and on a no-return basis. NLM's "loan" policies are fashioned after the General Interlibrary Loan Code, which is a statement of self-imposed regulations to be followed by all libraries which cooperate in interlibrary loaning. The Code provides that each library, upon request for a loan of materials, shall decide whether to loan the original or provide a photoduplicate. The Code notes that photoduplication of copyrighted materials may raise copyright infringement problems, particularly with regard to "photographing *whole issues* of periodicals or books with *current copyrights,* or in making *multiple copies* of a publication." [Emphasis in original text.] NLM, therefore, will provide only one photocopy of a particular article, per request, and will not photocopy on any given request an entire journal issue. Each photocopy reproduced by NLM contains a statement in the margin, "This is a single photostatic copy made by the National Library of Medicine for purposes of study or research in lieu of lending the original."

In recent years NLM's stated policy has been not to fill requests for copies of articles from any of 104 journals which are included in a so-called "widely-available list." Rather, the requester is furnished a copy of the "widely-available list" and the names of the regional medical libraries which are presumed to have the journals listed. Exceptions are sometimes made to the policy, particularly if the requester has been unsuccessful in obtaining the journal elsewhere. The four journals involved in this suit are listed on the "widely-available list." A rejection on the basis of the "widely-available list" is made only if the article requested was published during the preceding 5 years, but requests from Government libraries are not refused on the basis of the "widely-available list."

Also, NLM's policy is not to honor an excessive number of requests from an individual or an institution. As a general rule, not more than 20 requests from an individual, or not more than 30 requests from an institution, within a month, will be honored. In 1968, NLM adopted the policy that no more than one article from a single journal issue, or three from a journal volume, would be copied. Prior to 1968, NLM had no express policy on copying limitations, but endeavored to prevent "excessive copying." Generally, requests for more than 50 pages of material will not be honored, though exceptions are sometimes made, particularly for Government institutions. Requests for more than one copy of a journal article are rejected, without exception. If NLM receives a request for more than one copy, a single copy will be furnished and the requester advised that it is NLM's policy to furnish only one copy.

In 1968, a representative year, NLM received about 127,000 requests for interlibrary loans. Requests were received, for the most part, from other libraries or Government agencies. However, about 12 percent of the requests came from private or commercial organizations, particularly drug companies. Some requests were for books, in which event the book itself was loaned. Most requests were for journals or journal articles; and about 120,000 of the requests were filled by photocopying single articles from journals, including plaintiff's journals. Usually, the library seeking an interlibrary loan from NLM did so at the request of one of its patrons. If the "loan" was made by photocopy, the photocopy was given to the patron who was free to dispose of it as he wished. NLM made no effort to find out the ultimate use to which the photocopies were put; and there is no evidence that borrowing libraries kept the "loan" photocopies in their permanent collections for use by other patrons. 487 F.2d 1348–49.

The Court of Claims held that these practices were fair use, concluding that the publisher had not shown concrete harm in the form of lost subscription income and that medicine and medical research would be injured by holding these practices infringing. How would a requirement that the libraries pay a royalty fee of some sort (or choose to buy more copies) be injurious to medicine? Is copyright in non-informational works produced to provide entertainment stronger than copyright in works that contain important and useful information?

If the large scale and organized practices of the NIH and the NLM are fair use, then it would seem *a fortiorari* that occasional, personal copying of articles or sections of books for personal consultation and reference would also. Does the *Sony* opinion suggest the possibility that a majority of the Supreme Court would reverse the Court of Claims today? Do the widespread practices and customs that have developed since the *Williams & Wilkins* decision (relying in part on the decision) make that unlikely?

The statute now addresses copying by libraries in § 108. Does § 108(d) codify the result in *Williams and Wilkins?*

NOTE

The *Williams & Wilkins* decision is discussed at length in Wendy J. Gordon, Fair Use as Market Failure: A Structural and Economic Analysis of the *Betamax* Case and its Predecessors, 82 Columbia L.Rev. 1600 (1982). In the article Professor Gordon develops a general theory of the doctrine of fair use as a doctrine designed to prevent market failures that would otherwise arise from the copyright system. For instance an author might want to quote from a copyrighted work and the author of the copyrighted work might welcome the quotation (because of the attendant publicity for instance) but the cost of identifying the copyright owner and writing to get permission could easily exceed the benefit of using the quotation for the second author. If the quotation is fair use (and it is less costly to ascertain that it is fair use than it is to write for permission) then a quotation of benefit to all parties will be used. Or to illustrate in the context of the *Betamax* case (Professor Gordon is critical of the Ninth Circuit analysis of fair use, subsequently reversed by the Supreme Court), the owner of a program copyright might welcome home recording, and users might benefit from it, yet no such recording would take place because the cost of getting permission on a program by program basis would exceed the benefits of the recording. Id. at 1655. Professor Gordon applauds the court of claims in *Williams and Wilkins* for its cost-benefit approach, but is critical of its application in the particular situation. Id. at 1647–52. But why couldn't Mr. Rogers and other program owners who welcome recording grant consent for recording in a brief written message at the outset of their program and why couldn't journal publishers place an authorizing legend in their journals?

PROBLEMS

1. Suppose there had been a finding by the trial court in *Sony* that consumers use VCR's not only for time-shifting, but that when watching the recorded program they used the remote, fast-forward controls on the VCR to skip over the commercials? Different result? Doesn't the viewer's ability to avoid the commercials destroy the value of the program? Just how would the owners of the copyright enforce their rights, if they have them? Would an injunction enjoining the manufacture and sale of machines with remote fast-forward controls be appropriate?

2. Does it violate the copyright law to operate a used record store if it can be established that a large percentage of the customers resell the used record to the store a short time after they buy it?

HARPER & ROW, PUBLISHERS, INC. v. NATION ENTERPRISES

Supreme Court of the United States, 1985.
471 U.S. 539, 105 S.Ct. 2218, 85 L.Ed.2d 588.

JUSTICE O'CONNOR delivered the opinion of the Court.

This case requires us to consider to what extent the "fair use" provision of the Copyright Revision Act of 1976 sanctions the unauthorized use of quotations from a public figure's unpublished manuscript. In March 1979, an undisclosed source provided The Nation magazine with the unpublished manuscript of "A Time to Heal: The Autobiography of Gerald R. Ford." Working directly from the purloined manuscript, an editor of The Nation produced a short piece entitled "The Ford Memoirs—Behind the Nixon Pardon." The piece was timed to "scoop" an article scheduled shortly to appear in Time magazine. Time had agreed to purchase the exclusive right to print prepublication excerpts from the copyright holders, Harper & Row Publishers, Inc. (hereinafter Harper & Row) and Reader's Digest Association, Inc. (hereinafter Reader's Digest). As a result of The Nation article, Time canceled its agreement. Petitioners brought a successful copyright action against The Nation. On appeal, the Second Circuit reversed the lower court's finding of infringement, holding that The Nation's act was sanctioned as a "fair use" of the copyrighted material. We granted certiorari, and we now reverse.

I

In February 1977, shortly after leaving the White House, former President Gerald R. Ford contracted with petitioners Harper & Row and The Reader's Digest, to publish his as yet unwritten memoirs. The memoirs were to contain "significant hitherto unpublished material" concerning the Watergate crisis, Mr. Ford's pardon of former President Nixon and "Mr. Ford's reflections on this period of history, and the morality and personalities involved." In addition to the right to publish the Ford memoirs in book form, the agreement gave petitioners the exclusive right to license prepublication excerpts, known in the trade as "first serial rights." Two years later, as the memoirs were nearing completion, petitioners negotiated a prepublication licensing agreement with Time, a weekly news magazine. Time agreed to pay $25,000, $12,500 in advance and an additional $12,500 at publication, in exchange for the right to excerpt 7,500 words from Mr. Ford's account of the Nixon pardon. The issue featuring the excerpts was timed to appear approximately one week before shipment of the full length book version to bookstores. Exclusivity was an important consideration; Harper & Row instituted procedures designed to maintain the confidentiality of the manuscript, and Time retained the right to renegotiate the second payment should the material appear in print prior to its release of the excerpts.

Two to three weeks before the Time article's scheduled release, an unidentified person secretly brought a copy of the Ford manuscript to Victor Navasky, editor of The Nation, a political commentary magazine. Mr. Navasky knew that his possession of the manuscript was not authorized and that the manuscript must be returned quickly to his "source" to avoid discovery. He hastily put together what he believed was "a real hot news story" composed of quotes, paraphrases and facts drawn exclusively from the manuscript. Mr. Navasky attempted no independent commentary, research or criticism, in part because of the need for speed if he was to "make news" by "publish[ing] in advance of publication of the Ford book." The 2,250 word article * * * appeared on April 3, 1979. As a result of The Nation's article, Time canceled its piece and refused to pay the remaining $12,500.

Petitioners brought suit in the District Court for the Southern District of New York, alleging conversion, tortious interference with contract and violations of the Copyright Act. After a 6-day bench trial, the District Judge found that "A Time to Heal" was protected by copyright at the time of The Nation publication and that respondents' use of the copyrighted material constituted an infringement under the Copyright Act * * *. The District Court rejected respondents' argument that The Nation's piece was a "fair use" sanctioned by § 107 of the Act. Though billed as "hot news," the article contained no new facts. The magazine had "published its article for profit," taking "the heart" of "a soon-to-be-published" work. This unauthorized use "caused the *Time* agreement to be aborted and thus diminished the value of the copyright." Although certain elements of the Ford memoir, such as historical facts and memoranda, were not *per se* copyrightable, the District Court held that it was "the totality of these facts and memoranda collected together with Ford's reflections that made them of value to The Nation, [and] this * * * totality * * * is protected by the copyright laws." The court awarded actual damages of $12,500.

A divided panel of the Court of Appeals for the Second Circuit reversed. The majority recognized that Mr. Ford's verbatim "reflections" were original "expression" protected by copyright. But it held that the District Court had erred in assuming the "coupling [of these reflections] with uncopyrightable fact transformed that information into a copyrighted 'totality.'" 723 F.2d 195, 205 (CA2 1983). The majority noted that copyright attaches to expression, not facts or ideas. It concluded that, to avoid granting a copyright monopoly over the facts underlying history and news, "'expression' [in such works must be confined] to its barest elements—the ordering and choice of the words themselves." Id., at 204. Thus similarities between the original and the challenged work traceable to the copying or paraphrasing of uncopyrightable material, such as historical facts, memoranda and other public documents, and quoted remarks of third parties, must be disregarded in evaluating whether the second author's use was fair or infringing.

"When the uncopyrighted material is stripped away, the article in *The Nation* contains, at most, approximately 300 words that are copyrighted. These remaining paragraphs and scattered phrases are all verbatim quotations from the memoirs which had not appeared previously in other publications. They include a short segment of Ford's conversations with Henry Kissinger and several other individuals. Ford's impressionistic depictions of Nixon, ill with phlebitis after the resignation and pardon, and of Nixon's character, constitute the major portion of this material. It is these parts of the magazine piece on which [the court] must focus in [its] examination of the question whether there was a 'fair use' of copyrighted matter."

Examining the four factors enumerated in § 107, the majority found the purpose of the article was "news reporting," the original work was essentially factual in nature, the 300 words appropriated were insubstantial in relation to the 2,250 word piece, and the impact on the market for the original was minimal as "the evidence [did] not support a finding that it was the very limited use of expression *per se* which led to Time's decision not to print the excerpt." The Nation's borrowing of verbatim quotations merely "len[t] authenticity to this politically significant material * * * complementing the reporting of the facts." The Court of Appeals was especially influenced by the "politically significant" nature of the subject matter and its conviction that it is not "the purpose of the Copyright Act to impede that harvest of knowledge so necessary to a democratic state" or "chill the activities of the press by forbidding a circumscribed use of copyrighted words."

II

We agree with the Court of Appeals that copyright is intended to increase and not to impede the harvest of knowledge. But we believe the Second Circuit gave insufficient deference to the scheme established by the Copyright Act for fostering the original works that provide the seed and substance of this harvest. The rights conferred by copyright are designed to assure contributors to the store of knowledge a fair return for their labors. * * * As we noted last Term, "[this] limited grant is a means by which an important public purpose may be achieved. It is intended to motivate the creative activity of authors and inventors by the provision of a special reward, and to allow the public access to the products of their genius after the limited period of exclusive control has expired." Sony Corp. v. Universal City Studios, Inc., 464 U.S. 417, 429 (1984). "The monopoly created by copyright thus rewards the individual author in order to benefit the public." Id., at 477 (dissenting opinion). This principle applies equally to works of fiction and nonfiction. The book at issue here, for example, was two years in the making, and began with a contract giving the author's copyright to the publishers in exchange for their services in producing and marketing the work. In preparing the book, Mr. Ford drafted essays and word portraits of public figures and participated in hundreds of taped interviews that were later distilled to chronicle his personal viewpoint. It is evident that the monopoly granted by copyright actively served its intended purpose of inducing the creation of new material of potential historical value.

*　*　*

Creation of a nonfiction work, even a compilation of pure fact, entails originality. See, e.g., Schroeder v. William Morrow & Co., 566 F.2d 3 (CA7 1977) (copyright in gardening directory); cf. Burrow-Giles Lithographic Co. v. Sarony, 111 U.S. 53, 58 (1884) (originator of a photograph may claim copyright in his work). *　*　* [T]here is no dispute that the unpublished manuscript of "A Time to Heal," as a whole, was protected by § 106 from unauthorized reproduction. Nor do respondents dispute that verbatim copying of excerpts of the manuscript's original form of expression would constitute infringement unless excused as fair use. See 1 M. Nimmer, Nimmer on Copyright § 2.11[B], p. 2–159 (1984) (hereinafter Nimmer). Yet copyright does not prevent subsequent users from copying from a prior author's work those constituent elements that are not original—for example, quotations borrowed under the rubric of fair use from other copyrighted works, facts, or materials in the public domain—as long as such use does not unfairly appropriate the author's original contributions. Ibid.; A. Latman, Fair Use of Copyrighted Works (1958), reprinted as Study No. 14 in Copyright Law Revision Studies Nos. 14–16, Prepared for the Senate Committee on the Judiciary, 86th Cong., 2d Sess., 7 (1960) (hereinafter Latman). Perhaps the controversy between the lower courts in this case over copyrightability is more aptly styled a dispute over whether The Nation's appropriation of unoriginal and uncopyrightable elements encroached on the originality embodied in the work as a whole. Especially in the realm of factual narrative, the law is currently unsettled regarding the ways in which uncopyrightable elements combine with the author's original contributions to form protected expression. Compare Wainwright Securities Inc. v. Wall Street Transcript Corp., 558 F.2d 91 (CA2 1977) (protection accorded author's analysis, structuring of material and marshaling of facts), with Hoehling v. Universal City Studios, Inc., 618 F.2d 972 (CA2 1980) (limiting protection to ordering and choice of words). See, e.g., 1 Nimmer § 2.11[D], at 2–164—2–165.

We need not reach these issues, however, as The Nation has admitted to lifting verbatim quotes of the author's original language totalling between 300 and 400 words and constituting some 13% of The Nation article. In using generous verbatim excerpts of Mr. Ford's unpublished manuscript to lend authenticity to its account of the forthcoming memoirs, The Nation effectively arrogated to itself the right of first publication, an important marketable subsidiary right. For the reasons set forth below, we find that this use of the copyrighted manuscript, even stripped to the verbatim quotes conceded by The Nation to be copyrightable expression, was not a fair use within the meaning of the Copyright Act.

III

A

Fair use was traditionally defined as "a privilege in others than the owner of the copyright to use the copyrighted material in a reasonable manner without his consent." H. Ball, Law of Copyright and Literary Property 260 (1944) (hereinafter Ball). The statutory formulation of the defense of fair use in the Copyright Act of 1976 reflects the intent of Congress to codify the common-law doctrine. 3 Nimmer § 13.05. Section 107 requires a case-by-case determination whether a particular use is fair, and the statute notes four nonexclusive factors to be considered. This approach was "intended to restate the [pre-existing] judicial doctrine of fair use, not to change, narrow, or enlarge it in any way." H.R. Rep. No. 94–1476, p. 66 (1976) (hereinafter House Report), U.S.Code Cong. & Admin.News 1976, pp. 5659, 5680.

"[T]he author's consent to a reasonable use of his copyrighted works ha[d] always been implied by the courts as a necessary incident of the constitutional policy of promoting the progress of science and the useful arts, since a prohibition of such use would inhibit subsequent writers from attempting to improve upon prior works and thus * * * frustrate the very ends sought to be attained." Ball 260. Professor Latman, in a study of the doctrine of fair use commissioned by Congress for the revision effort, see Sony Corp. v. Universal City Studios, Inc., 464 U.S., at 462–463, n. 9 (dissenting opinion), summarized prior law as turning on the "importance of the material copied or performed from the point of view of the reasonable copyright owner. In other words, would the reasonable copyright owner have consented to the use?" Latman 15.[3]

As early as 1841, Justice Story, gave judicial recognition to the doctrine in a case that concerned the letters of another former President, George Washington.

"[A] reviewer may fairly cite largely from the original work, if his design be really and truly to use the passages for the purposes of fair and reasonable criticism. On the other hand, it is as clear, that if he thus cites the most important parts of the work, with a view, not to criticise, but to supersede the use of the original work, and substitute the review for it, such a use will be deemed in law a piracy." Folsom v. Marsh, 9 F.Cas. 342, 344–345 (No. 4,901) (CC Mass.)

---

3. Professor Nimmer notes, "[perhaps] no more precise guide can be stated than Joseph McDonald's clever paraphrase of the Golden Rule: 'Take not from others to such an extent and in such a manner that you would be resentful if they so took from you.'" 3 Nimmer § 13.05[A], at 13–66, quoting McDonald, Non-infringing Uses, 9 Bull. Copyright Soc. 466, 467 (1962). This "equitable rule of reason," Sony Corp. v. Universal City Studios, Inc., 464 U.S., at 448, "permits courts to avoid rigid application of the copyright statute when, on occasion, it would stifle the very creativity which that law is designed to foster." Iowa State University Research Foundation, Inc. v. American Broadcasting Cos., 621 F.2d 57, 60 (CA2 1980). * * *

As Justice Story's hypothetical illustrates, the fair use doctrine has always precluded a use that "supersede[s] the use of the original." Ibid. Accord S.Rep. No. 94–473, p. 65 (1975) (hereinafter Senate Report).

Perhaps because the fair use doctrine was predicated on the author's implied consent to "reasonable and customary" use when he released his work for public consumption, fair use traditionally was not recognized as a defense to charges of copying from an author's as yet unpublished works. Under common-law copyright, "the property of the author * * * in his intellectual creation [was] absolute until he voluntarily part[ed] with the same." American Tobacco Co. v. Werckmeister, 207 U.S. 284, 299 (1907); 2 Nimmer § 8.23, at 8–273. This absolute rule, however, was tempered in practice by the equitable nature of the fair use doctrine. In a given case, factors such as implied consent through *de facto* publication on performance or dissemination of a work may tip the balance of equities in favor of prepublication use. * * * But it has never been seriously disputed that "the fact that the plaintiff's work is unpublished * * * is a factor tending to negate the defense of fair use." Ibid. Publication of an author's expression before he has authorized its dissemination seriously infringes the author's right to decide when and whether it will be made public, a factor not present in fair use of published works. Respondents contend, however, that Congress, in including first publication among the rights enumerated in § 106, which are expressly subject to fair use under § 107, intended that fair use would apply *in pari materia* to published and unpublished works. The Copyright Revision Act does not support this proposition.

The Copyright Revision Act of 1976 represents the culmination of a major legislative reexamination of copyright doctrine. Among its other innovations, it eliminated publication "as a dividing line between common law and statutory protection," House Report at 129, U.S.Code Cong. & Admin.News 1976, p. 5745, extending statutory protection to all works from the time of their creation. It also recognized for the first time a distinct statutory right of first publication, which had previously been an element of the common-law protections afforded unpublished works. The Report of the House Committee on the Judiciary confirms that "Clause (3) of section 106, establishes the exclusive right of publications. * * * Under this provision the copyright owner would have the right to control the first public distribution of an authorized copy * * * of his work." Id. at 62, U.S.Code Cong. & Admin.News 1976, p. 5675.

Though the right of first publication, like the other rights enumerated in § 106 is expressly made subject to the fair use provision of § 107, fair use analysis must always be tailored to the individual case. Id., at 65; 3 Nimmer § 13.05[A]. The nature of the interest at stake is highly relevant to whether a given use is fair. From the beginning, those entrusted with the task of revision recognized the "overbalancing reasons to preserve the common law protection of undisseminated works until the author or his successor chooses to disclose them."

Copyright Law Revision, Report of the Register of Copyrights on the General Revision of the U.S. Copyright Law, 87th Cong., 1st Sess., 41 (Comm. Print 1961). The right of first publication implicates a threshold decision by the author whether and in what form to release his work. First publication is inherently different from other § 106 rights in that only one person can be the first publisher; as the contract with Time illustrates, the commercial value of the right lies primarily in exclusivity. Because the potential damage to the author from judicially enforced "sharing" of the first publication right with unauthorized users of his manuscript is substantial, the balance of equities in evaluating such a claim of fair use inevitably shifts.

The Senate Report confirms that Congress intended the unpublished nature of the work to figure prominently in fair use analysis. In discussing fair use of photocopied materials in the classroom the Committee Report states:

> "A key, though not necessarily determinative, factor in fair use is whether or not the work is available to the potential user. If the work is 'out of print' and unavailable for purchase through normal channels, the user may have more justification for reproducing it. * * * The applicability of the fair use doctrine to unpublished works is narrowly limited since, although the work is unavailable, this is the result of a deliberate choice on the part of the copyright owner. Under ordinary circumstances, the copyright owner's 'right of first publication' would outweigh any needs of reproduction for classroom purposes." Senate Report, at 64.

Although the Committee selected photocopying of classroom materials to illustrate fair use, it emphasized that "the same general standards of fair use are applicable to all kinds of uses of copyrighted material." Id., at 65. We find unconvincing respondent's contention that the absence of the quoted passage from the House Report indicates an intent to abandon the traditional distinction between fair use of published and unpublished works. It appears instead that the fair use discussion of photocopying of classroom materials was omitted from the final report because educators and publishers in the interim had negotiated a set of guidelines that rendered the discussion obsolete. House Report, at 67. The House Report nevertheless incorporates the discussion by reference, citing to the Senate Report and stating that "The Committee has reviewed this discussion, and considers it still has value as an analysis of various aspects of the [fair use] problem." Ibid.

Even if the legislative history were entirely silent, we would be bound to conclude from Congress' characterization of § 107 as a "restatement" that its effect was to preserve existing law concerning fair use of unpublished works as of other types of protected works and not to "change, narrow, or enlarge it." Id., at 66. We conclude that the unpublished nature of a work is "[a] key, though not necessarily determinative, factor" tending to negate a defense of fair use. Senate

Report, at 64. See 3 Nimmer § 13.05, at 13–62, n. 2; W. Patry, The Fair Use Privilege in Copyright Law 125 (1985) (hereinafter Patry).

We also find unpersuasive respondents' argument that fair use may be made of a soon-to-be-published manuscript on the ground that the author has demonstrated he has no interest in nonpublication. This argument assumes that the unpublished nature of copyrighted material is only relevant to letters or other confidential writings not intended for dissemination. It is true that common-law copyright was often enlisted in the service of personal privacy. See Brandeis & Warren, The Right to Privacy, 4 Harv.L.Rev. 193, 198–199 (1890). In its commercial guise, however, an author's right to choose when he will publish is no less deserving of protection. The period encompassing the work's initiation, its preparation, and its grooming for public dissemination is a crucial one for any literary endeavor. The Copyright Act, which accords the copyright owner the "right to control the first public distribution" of his work, House Report, at 62, echos the common law's concern that the author or copyright owner retain control throughout this critical stage. The obvious benefit to author and public alike of assuring authors the leisure to develop their ideas free from fear of expropriation outweighs any short term "news value" to be gained from premature publication of the author's expression. See Goldstein, Copyright and the First Amendment, 70 Colum.L.Rev. 983, 1004–1006 (1970) (The absolute protection the common law accorded to soon-to-be published works "[was] justified by [its] brevity and expedience"). The author's control of first public distribution implicates not only his personal interest in creative control but his property interest in exploitation of prepublication rights, which are valuable in themselves and serve as a valuable adjunct to publicity and marketing. * * * Under ordinary circumstances, the author's right to control the first public appearance of his undisseminated expression will outweigh a claim of fair use.

B

Respondents, however, contend that First Amendment values require a different rule under the circumstances of this case. The thrust of the decision below is that "[t]he scope of [fair use] is undoubtedly wider when the information conveyed relates to matters of high public concern." Consumers Union of the United States, Inc. v. General Signal Corp., 724 F.2d 1044, 1050 (CA2 1983) (construing Harper & Row Publishers, Inc. v. Nation Enterprises, 723 F.2d 195 (CA2 1983) (case below), as allowing advertiser to quote Consumer Reports), cert. denied, 469 U.S. 823 (1984). Respondents advance the substantial public import of the subject matter of the Ford memoirs as grounds for excusing a use that would ordinarily not pass muster as a fair use—the piracy of verbatim quotations for the purpose of "scooping" the authorized first serialization. Respondents explain their copying of Mr. Ford's expression as essential to reporting the news story it claims the book itself represents. In respondents' view, not only the facts contained in Mr. Ford's memoirs, but "the precise manner in which [he] expressed himself was as newsworthy as what he had to say." Brief for Respondents 38–39. Respondents argue that the public's interest in learning this news as fast as possible outweighs the right of the author to control its first publication.

The Second Circuit noted, correctly, that copyright's idea/expression dichotomy "strike[s] a definitional balance between the First Amendment and the Copyright Act by permitting free communication of facts while still protecting an author's expression." 723 F.2d, at 203. No author may copyright his ideas or the facts he narrates. 17 U.S.C. § 102(b). See, e.g., New York Times Co. v. United States, 403 U.S. 713, 726, n.* (1971) (BRENNAN, J., concurring) (Copyright laws are not restrictions on freedom of speech as copyright protects only form of expression and not the ideas expressed); 1 Nimmer § 1.10[B][2]. As this Court long ago observed: "[T]he news element—the information respecting current events contained in the literary production—is not the creation of the writer, but is a report of matters that ordinarily are *publici juris;* it is the history of the day." International News Service v. Associated Press, 248 U.S. 215, 234 (1918). But copyright assures those who write and publish factual narratives such as "A Time to Heal" that they may at least enjoy the right to market the original expression contained therein as just compensation for their investment. Cf. Zacchini v. Scripps-Howard Broadcasting Co., 433 U.S. 562, 575 (1977).

Respondents' theory, however, would expand fair use to effectively destroy any expectation of copyright protection in the work of a public figure. Absent such protection, there would be little incentive to create or profit in financing such memoirs and the public would be denied an important source of significant historical information. The promise of copyright would be an empty one if it could be avoided merely by dubbing the infringement a fair use "news report" of the book.

*   *   *[6]

In our haste to disseminate news, it should not be forgotten that the Framers intended copyright itself to be the engine of free expression. By establishing a marketable right to the use of one's expression, copyright supplies the economic incentive to create and disseminate ideas. *   *   *

*   *   *

In view of the First Amendment protections already embodied in the Copyright Act's distinction between copyrightable expression and uncopyrightable facts and ideas, and the latitude for scholarship and comment traditionally afforded by fair use, we see no warrant for expanding the doctrine of fair use to create what amounts to a public figure exception to copyright. Whether verbatim copying from a public

---

6. It bears noting that Congress in the Copyright Act recognized a public interest warranting specific exemptions in a number of areas not within traditional fair use, see, e.g., 17 U.S.C. § 115 (compulsory license for records); § 105 (no copyright in government works). No such exemption limits copyright in personal narratives written by public servants after they leave government service.

figure's manuscript in a given case is or is not fair must be judged according to the traditional equities of fair use.

IV

Fair use is a mixed question of law and fact. * * *. Where the District Court has found facts sufficient to evaluate each of the statutory factors, an appellate court "need not remand for further factfinding * * * [but] may conclude as a matter of law that [the challenged use] do[es] not qualify as a fair use of the copyrighted work." * * *. [quoting note 8 in Pacific and Southern Co. v. Duncan, 744 F.2d 1490 (11th Cir.1984), infra page 745.] Thus whether The Nation article constitutes fair use under § 107 must be reviewed in light of the principles discussed above. The factors enumerated in the section are not meant to be exclusive: "[S]ince the doctrine is an equitable rule of reason, no generally applicable definition is possible, and each case raising the question must be decided on its own facts." House Report, at 65, U.S.Code Cong. & Admin.News 1976, p. 5678. The four factors identified by Congress as especially relevant in determining whether the use was fair are: (1) the purpose and character of the use; (2) the nature of the copyrighted work; (3) the substantiality of the portion used in relation to the copyrighted work as a whole; (4) the effect on the potential market for or value of the copyrighted work. We address each one separately.

Purpose of the Use. The Second Circuit correctly identified news reporting as the general purpose of The Nation's use. News reporting is one of the examples enumerated in § 107 to "give some idea of the sort of activities the courts might regard as fair use under the circumstances." Senate Report, at 61. This listing was not intended to be exhaustive, see *id.;* § 101 (definition of "including" and "such as"), or to single out any particular use as presumptively a "fair" use. The drafters resisted pressures from special interest groups to create presumptive categories of fair use, but structured the provision as an affirmative defense requiring a case by case analysis. See H.R.Rep. No. 83, 90th Cong., 1st Sess., 37 (1967); Patry 477, n. 4. "[W]hether a use referred to in the first sentence of section 107 is a fair use in a particular case will depend upon the application of the determinative factors, including those mentioned in the second sentence." Senate Report, at 62. The fact that an article arguably is "news" and therefore a productive use is simply one factor in a fair use analysis.

* * *

The fact that a publication was commercial as opposed to non-profit is a separate factor that tends to weigh against a finding of fair use. "[E]very commercial use of copyrighted material is presumptively an unfair exploitation of the monopoly privilege that belongs to the owner of the copyright." Sony Corp. v. Universal City Studios, Inc., 464 U.S., at 451. In arguing that the purpose of news reporting is not purely commercial, The Nation misses the point entirely. The crux of the profit/nonprofit distinction is not whether the sole motive of the use is monetary gain but whether the user stands to profit from exploitation of the copyrighted material without paying the customary price.

In evaluating character and purpose we cannot ignore The Nation's stated purpose of scooping the forthcoming hardcover and Time abstracts.[7] The Nation's use had not merely the incidental effect but the *intended purpose* of supplanting the copyright holder's commercially valuable right of first publication. See Meredith Corp. v. Harper & Row Publishers, Inc., 378 F.Supp. 686, 690 (SDNY), (purpose of text was to compete with original), aff'd, 500 F.2d 1221 (CA2 1974). Also relevant to the "character" of the use is "the propriety of the defendant's conduct." 3 Nimmer § 13.05[A], at 13–72. "Fair use presupposes 'good faith' and 'fair dealing.'" Time Inc. v. Bernard Geis Associates, 293 F.Supp. 130, 146 (SDNY 1968), quoting Schulman, Fair Use and the Revision of the Copyright Act, 53 Iowa L.Rev. 832 (1968). The trial court found that The Nation knowingly exploited a purloined manuscript. Unlike the typical claim of fair use, The Nation cannot offer up even the fiction of consent as justification. Like its competitor newsweekly, it was free to bid for the right of abstracting excerpts from "A Time to Heal." Fair use "distinguishes between 'a true scholar and a chiseler who infringes a work for personal profit.'" Wainwright Securities Inc. v. Wall Street Transcript Corp., 558 F.2d, at 94, quoting from Hearings on Bills for the General Revision of the Copyright Law before the House Committee on the Judiciary, 89th Cong., 1st Sess., ser. 8, pt. 3, p. 1706 (1966) (Statement of John Schulman).

Nature of the Copyrighted Work. Second, the Act directs attention to the nature of the copyrighted work. "A Time to Heal" may be characterized as an unpublished historical narrative or autobiography. The law generally recognizes a greater need to disseminate factual works than works of fiction or fantasy. See Gorman, Fact or Fancy? The Implications for Copyright, 29 J. Copyright Soc. 560, 561 (1982).

> "[E]ven within the field of fact works, there are gradations as to the relative proportion of fact and fancy. One may move from sparsely embellished maps and directories to elegantly written biography. The extent to which one must permit expressive language to be copied, in order to assure dissemination of the underlying facts, will thus vary from case to case." Id., at 563.

Some of the briefer quotes from the memoir are arguably necessary adequately to convey the facts; for example, Mr. Ford's characterization of the White House tapes as the "smoking gun" is perhaps so integral to the idea expressed as to be inseparable from it. Cf. 1 Nimmer § 1.10[C]. But The Nation did not stop at isolated phrases and

---

7. The dissent excuses The Nation's unconsented use of an unpublished manuscript as "standard journalistic practice," taking judicial notice of New York Times articles regarding the memoirs of John Erlichman, John Dean's "Blind Ambition," and Bernstein & Woodward's "The Final Days" as proof of such practice. * * * Amici curiae sought to bring this alleged practice to the attention of the Court of Appeals for the Second Circuit, citing these same articles. The Court of Appeals, at Harper & Row's motion, struck these exhibits for failure of proof at trial, Record Doc. No. 19, thus they are not a proper subject for this Court's judicial notice.

instead excerpted subjective descriptions and portraits of public figures whose power lies in the author's individualized expression. Such use, focusing on the most expressive elements of the work, exceeds that necessary to disseminate the facts.

The fact that a work is unpublished is a critical element of its "nature." 3 Nimmer § 13.05[A]; Comment, 58 St. John's L.Rev., at 613. Our prior discussion establishes that the scope of fair use is narrower with respect to unpublished works. While even substantial quotations might qualify as fair use in a review of a published work or a news account of a speech that had been delivered to the public or disseminated to the press, see House Report, at 65, the author's right to control the first public appearance of his expression weighs against such use of the work before its release. The right of first publication encompasses not only the choice whether to publish at all, but also the choices when, where and in what form first to publish a work.

In the case of Mr. Ford's manuscript, the copyrightholders' interest in confidentiality is irrefutable; the copyrightholders had entered into a contractual undertaking to "keep the manuscript confidential" and required that all those to whom the manuscript was shown also "sign an agreement to keep the manuscript confidential." While the copyrightholders' contract with Time required Time to submit its proposed article seven days before publication, The Nation's clandestine publication afforded no such opportunity for creative or quality control. It was hastily patched together and contained "a number of inaccuracies." (testimony of Victor Navasky). A use that so clearly infringes the copyrightholder's interests in confidentiality and creative control is difficult to characterize as "fair."

Amount and Substantiality of the Portion Used. Next, the Act directs us to examine the amount and substantiality of the portion used in relation to the copyrighted work as a whole. In absolute terms, the words actually quoted were an insubstantial portion of "A Time to Heal." The district court, however, found that "[T]he Nation took what was essentially the heart of the book." We believe the Court of Appeals erred in overruling the district judge's evaluation of the qualitative nature of the taking. See, e.g., Roy Export Co. Establishment v. Columbia Broadcasting System, Inc., [503 F.Supp. 1137 (S.D. N.Y.1980)] supra, at 1145 (taking of 55 seconds out of one hour and twenty-nine minute film deemed qualitatively substantial). A Time editor described the chapters on the pardon as "the most interesting and moving parts of the entire manuscript." The portions actually quoted were selected by Mr. Navasky as among the most powerful passages in those chapters. He testified that he used verbatim excerpts because simply reciting the information could not adequately convey the "absolute certainty with which [Ford] expressed himself," or show that "this comes from President Ford," or carry the "definitive quality" of the original. In short, he quoted these passages precisely because they qualitatively embodied Ford's distinctive expression.

As the statutory language indicates, a taking may not be excused merely because it is insubstantial with respect to the *infringing* work. As Judge Learned Hand cogently remarked, "[N]o plagiarist can excuse the wrong by showing how much of his work he did not pirate." Sheldon v. Metro-Goldwyn Pictures Corp., 81 F.2d 49, 56 (CA2), cert. denied, 298 U.S. 669 (1936). Conversely, the fact that a substantial portion of the infringing work was copied verbatim is evidence of the qualitative value of the copied material, both to the originator and to the plagiarist who seeks to profit from marketing someone else's copyrighted expression.

Stripped to the verbatim quotes, the direct takings from the unpublished manuscript constitute at least 13% of the infringing article. See Meeropol v. Nizer, 560 F.2d 1061, 1071 (CA2 1977) (copyrighted letters constituted less than 1% of infringing work but were prominently featured). The Nation article is structured around the quoted excerpts which serve as its dramatic focal points. * * * In view of the expressive value of the excerpts and their key role in the infringing work, we cannot agree with the Second Circuit that the "magazine took a meager, indeed an infinitesimal amount of Ford's original language."

Effect on the Market. Finally, the Act focuses on "the effect of the use upon the potential market for or value of the copyrighted work." This last factor is undoubtedly the single most important element of fair use.[9] See 3 Nimmer § 13.05[A], at 13–76, and cases cited therein. "Fair use, when properly applied, is limited to copying by others which does not materially impair the marketability of the work which is copied." 1 Nimmer § 1.10[D], at 1–87. The trial court found not merely a potential but an actual effect on the market. Time's cancellation of its projected serialization and its refusal to pay the $12,500 were the direct effect of the infringement. The Court of Appeals rejected this fact finding as clearly erroneous, noting that the record did not establish a causal relation between Time's nonperformance and respondents' unauthorized publication of Mr. Ford's *expression* as opposed to the facts taken from the memoirs. We disagree. Rarely will a case of copyright infringement present such clear cut evidence of actual damage. Petitioners assured Time that there would be no other authorized publication of *any* portion of the unpublished manuscript prior to April 23, 1979. *Any* publication of material from chapters 1 and 3 would permit Time to renegotiate its final payment. Time cited The Nation's article, which contained verbatim quotes from the unpublished manuscript, as a reason for its nonperformance. With respect to apportion-

---

9. Economists who have addressed the issue believe the fair use exception should come into play only in those situations in which the market fails or the price the copyright holder would ask is near zero. See, e.g., T. Brennan, Harper & Row v. The Nation, Copyrightability and Fair Use, Dept. of Justice Economic Policy Office Discussion Paper, 13–17 (1984); Gordon, Fair Use as Market Failure: A Structural and Economic Analysis of the *Betamax* Case and its Predecessors, 82 Colum.L.Rev. 1600, 1615 (1982). As the facts here demonstrate, there is a fully functioning market that encourages the creation and dissemination of memoirs of public figures. In the economists' view, permitting "fair use" to displace normal copyright channels disrupts the copyright market without a commensurate public benefit.

ment of profits flowing from a copyright infringement, this Court has held that an infringer who commingles infringing and noninfringing elements "must abide the consequences, unless he can make a separation of the profits so as to assure to the injured party all that justly belongs to him." Sheldon v. Metro-Goldwyn Pictures Corp., 309 U.S. 390, 406 (1940). Cf. 17 U.S.C. § 504(b) (the infringer is required to prove elements of profits attributable to other than the infringed work). Similarly, once a copyrightholder establishes with reasonable probability the existence of a causal connection between the infringement and a loss of revenue, the burden properly shifts to the infringer to show that this damage would have occurred had there been no taking of copyrighted expression. See 3 Nimmer § 14.02, pp. 14–7—14–8.1. Petitioners established a prima facie case of actual damage that respondent failed to rebut. The trial court properly awarded actual damages and accounting of profits. See 17 U.S.C. § 504(b).

More important, to negate fair use one need only show that if the challenged use "should become widespread, it would adversely affect the *potential* market for the copyrighted work." Sony Corp. v. Universal City Studios, Inc., 464 U.S., at 451 (emphasis added); id., at 484, and n. 36 (collecting cases) (dissenting opinion). This inquiry must take account not only of harm to the original but also of harm to the market for derivative works. "If the defendant's work adversely affects the value of any of the rights in the copyrighted work (in this case the adaptation [and serialization] right) the use is not fair." 3 Nimmer § 13.05[B], at 13–77—13–78 (footnote omitted).

It is undisputed that the factual material in the balance of The Nation's article, besides the verbatim quotes at issue here, was drawn exclusively from the chapters on the pardon. The excerpts were employed as featured episodes in a story about the Nixon pardon— precisely the use petitioners had licensed to Time. The borrowing of these verbatim quotes from the unpublished manuscript lent The Nation's piece a special air of authenticity—as Navasky expressed it, the reader would know it was Ford speaking and not The Nation. Thus it directly competed for a share of the market for prepublication excerpts. The Senate Report states:

> "With certain special exceptions * * * a use that supplants any part of the normal market for a copyrighted work would ordinarily be considered an infringement." Senate Report, at 65.

Placed in a broader perspective, a fair use doctrine that permits extensive prepublication quotations from an unreleased manuscript without the copyright owner's consent poses substantial potential for damage to the marketability of first serialization rights in general. "Isolated instances of minor infringements, when multiplied many times, become in the aggregate a major inroad on copyright that must be prevented." Ibid.

V

The Court of Appeals erred in concluding that The Nation's use of the copyrighted material was excused by the public's interest in the subject matter. It erred, as well, in overlooking the unpublished nature of the work and the resulting impact on the potential market for first serial rights of permitting unauthorized prepublication excerpts under the rubric of fair use. Finally, in finding the taking "infinitesimal," the Court of Appeals accorded too little weight to the qualitative importance of the quoted passages of original expression. In sum, the traditional doctrine of fair use, as embodied in the Copyright Act, does not sanction the use made by The Nation of these copyrighted materials. Any copyright infringer may claim to benefit the public by increasing public access to the copyrighted work. But Congress has not designed, and we see no warrant for judicially imposing, a "compulsory license" permitting unfettered access to the unpublished copyrighted expression of public figures.

The Nation conceded that its verbatim copying of some 300 words of direct quotation from the Ford manuscript would constitute an infringement unless excused as a fair use. Because we find that The Nation's use of these verbatim excerpts from the unpublished manuscript was not a fair use, the judgment of the Court of Appeals is reversed and remanded for further proceedings consistent with this opinion.

It is so ordered.

[JUSTICES BRENNAN, WHITE and MARSHALL dissented.]

NOTES

1. Rosemont Enterprises v. Random House, 366 F.2d 303 (2d Cir.1966), was an action by a shell corporation controlled by the secretive and reclusive (but always newsworthy and mysterious) millionaire Howard Hughes brought to stop the publication of a biography of Hughes. The biography, "Howard Hughes—a Biography by John Keats," was published in May 1966 and made use of some verbatim passages lifted from an article that appeared in *Look* magazine in 1954. In May, 1966 the plaintiff corporation purchased the copyright to the 1954 article and commenced an action for copyright infringement. The district court granted a preliminary injunction. The Court of Appeals reversed with an opinion that mingled the concepts of fair use and the equitable doctrine of "unclean hands," although the Court clearly stated that "The only issue presently before this court is: Was the preliminary injunction erroneously issued as a matter of law?" 366 F.2d 304. The court viewed the lawsuit as a stratagem designed to punish Random House for having undertaken to publish a book about Hughes by disrupting the production and promotion schedule while the offending passages were rewritten into paraphrase.

2. In Wainwright Securities Inc. v. Wall Street Transcript Corporation, 558 F.2d 91 (2d Cir.1977), a brokerage house sued the publisher of a weekly newspaper concerned with economic, business and financial news, for publishing abstracts of its research reports for clients in its "Wall Street Roundup"

column. The defendant argued fair use and pointed out that the *Wall Street Journal* does exactly the same thing in its "Heard on the Street" column. "The copying by the Transcript is easily distinguishable from the reporting of the Wainwright research reports by other publications. The *Wall Street Journal* articles referred to by appellants [also summarizing Wainwright reports], for example, were published a year apart. There apparently was no attempt to provide readers regularly with summaries of the Wainwright reports and there is no indication that the Wall Street Journal launched an advertising campaign portraying itself as a publisher of the same financial analyses available to large investors, but at a lower price. By contrast, the appellants' use of the Wainwright reports was blatantly self-serving, with obvious intent, if not the effect, of fulfilling the demand for the original work. * * *. This was not legitimate coverage of a news event; instead it was, and there is no other way to describe it, chiseling for personal profit." 558 F.2d 96–97. Held: not fair use.

Presumably the plaintiff objected to finding summaries of the essence of its research reports in the *Wall Street Transcript* each week, but didn't mind the publicity that came from an occasional mention in the much more widely read *Wall Street Journal*. If the plaintiff objected to the *Wall Street Journal's* summaries of its research reports, could the Wall Street Journal continue to summarize them when, in the judgment of its editorial staff, they constituted financial news?

3. In Meeropol v. Nizer, 560 F.2d 1061 (2d Cir.1977), the defendant (a lawyer who has also enjoyed a successful writing career) had written an account of the events surrounding the espionage trial of Julius and Ethel Rosenberg entitled *The Implosion Conspiracy*. In the book there were reproduced substantial quotations from 28 letters written by the Rosenbergs. The plaintiffs were the sons of the Rosenbergs who had inherited the copyright in the letters (it has long been conventional doctrine that the copyright in a letter remains the property of the author-sender). The district court decided for the defendants on grounds of fair use. Reversed and remanded for further hearings on the purpose of the use and damages. *Rosemont* was distinguished on the ground that the taking there was less substantial, involved taking from a work about the subject, not by the subject, and was a bad faith action to suppress publication of the book.

4. Consumers Union of United States, Inc. v. General Signal Corp., 724 F.2d 1044 (2d Cir.1983), rehearing denied 730 F.2d 47 (2d Cir.1984), cert. denied 469 U.S. 823 (1985), was decided after the *Nation* case had been decided in the Second Circuit. Consumers Union a non-profit corporation that publishes the widely-circulated magazine *Consumer Reports* has long had the policy of prohibiting the use in product advertising of its product ratings and reports. Consumers Union had adopted this policy so that consumers can be confident that there is no relationship between Consumers Union and the manufacturers of products it recommends. In its July 1983 issue *Consumer Reports* evaluated lightweight vacuum cleaners and gave its highest "check-rated" rating to the Regina Powerteam. The manufacturer of the product made use of the rating and a brief quotation in television advertisements, accompanied by the statement that "*Consumer Reports* is not affiliated with Regina and does not endorse Regina products or any other products." The district court granted a preliminary injunction. On appeal, reversed. The court of appeals concluded that the ad would have no negative effect on sales of the magazine issue reviewing light

weight vacuum cleaners, and that Consumers Union concern about its reputation for independence and integrity is not an interest protected by copyright.

If manufacturers are free to disseminate without payment favorable ratings from *Consumer Reports,* what is the effect on the consumer's incentive to buy the magazine?

5. In Maxtone–Graham v. Burtchaell, 803 F.2d 1253 (2d Cir.1986), the plaintiff authored a book consisting of 17 anonymous interviews of women who had undergone unwanted pregnancies, some leading to adoption, others to abortion. The book was sympathetic to abortion. The defendant, a Catholic priest and professor of theology published a book of essays entitled *Rachel Weeping.* The title essay, critical of abortion, contained 37,000 words, of which 7,000 were quotations (with full attribution) from the plaintiff's book. The defendant requested permission to quote, but the permission was denied. The defendant justified the copying on the ground that "it [was] essential for the credibility of my essay that the words of abortion veterans themselves appear." He also felt that as a Catholic priest it would be impossible for him to conduct his own credible interviews and that his book would be perceived as fairer if he relied on interviews conducted by those sympathetic to the pro-choice position. The court held the copying fair use, relying heavily on the fact that the defendant's book did not injure the market for the plaintiff's book.

6. Prior to the 1976 revision act, copyright in unpublished works was provided by the states under the doctrine of "common law copyright." The 1976 act provided unitary federal protection for both published and unpublished works, and in § 301 preempted state common law copyright. Under common law copyright there was no precedent to suggest that one could copy unpublished works under the doctrine of fair use, and indeed much to suggest that the right to prevent copying was absolute on the ground that copying invaded the author's absolute and privacy-like right to control release of his own work. The 1976 revision act, by incorporating protection of unpublished works into its structure and expressly codifying the doctrine of fair use in § 107 without an exception for unpublished works, made it difficult to maintain any such absolute position. The Supreme Court's opinion in the *Nation* case, however, makes it clear that any claim of a right to copy unpublished works on grounds of fair use will be evaluated skeptically.

7. In Salinger v. Random House, Inc., 811 F.2d 90 (2d Cir.1987), rehrg. denied 818 F.2d 252 (1987) cert. denied 108 S.Ct. 213 (1987), the author of *Catcher in the Rye* sued to stop publication of a biography. The author of the biography, working without Salinger's assistance, had located in university libraries letters donated by recipients of letters from Salinger, and used them as a source of first-hand accounts of Salinger's life experiences. The sender of a letter, of course, continues to own the copyright. Following the *Nation* opinion, the Second Circuit rejected a claim of fair use, overruling Judge Leval of the district court. "To deny a biographer like Hamilton the opportunity to copy the expressive content of unpublished letters is not, as appellees contend, to interfere in any significant way with the process of enhancing public knowledge of history or contemporary events. The facts may be reported. . . . Public awareness of the expressive content of the letters will have to await either Salinger's decision to publish or the expiration of his copyright, save such special circumstances as might fall within the 'narrower' scope of fair use available for unpublished works. . . ." Of course, the same result would follow, even if the letters had been published, wouldn't it?

8. In New Era Publications International, ApS v. Henry Holt and Co. Inc., 873 F.2d 576 (2d Cir.1989), a corporation holding copyrights from the Church of Scientology founded by one Ron Hubbard (who had bequeathed the copyrights to the church) sued to stop the publication of a highly critical biography of Hubbard called *The Bare Faced Messiah*. The biography contended that Hubbard was a fraud and religious charlatan. The suit alleged infringement of many of Hubbard's writings, including substantial copying from unpublished writings. Judge Leval, who was also the District Judge in the *Salinger* case, found that the copied passages were fair use. New Era Publications International, ApS v. Henry Holt and Co. Inc., 695 F.Supp. 1493 (S.D.N.Y.1988). He found that verbatim quotation rather than paraphrase helped the biographer to make his point that Hubbard's very own words supported the biographer's view of the subject. "I conclude . . . that the very large majority of Miller's [the biographer] takings of Hubbard material display a powerful and compelling fair use purpose. These are not . . . appropriations of the literary talent of the subject to enliven and improve the secondary work. They are, rather, instances . . . where the critic exhibits chosen words of the subject to prove a critical point or to demonstrate a flaw in the subject's character." 695 F.Supp. 1507– 08. In his analysis Judge Leval developed an interesting set of hypothetical examples to illustrate this point. See 695 F.Supp. at 1502. Judge Leval also concluded that since Hubbard was dead, he had no continuing privacy interest in the works, unlike Salinger.

The Second Circuit affirmed, but only on the grounds that laches barred an injunction. The majority opinion explicitly rejected Judge Leval's fair use analysis, placing heavy weight on the unpublished status of the copied works. Judge Leval's analysis was defended in an elaborate separate opinion by Judge Oakes, 873 F.2d at 585.

9. What are unpublished works for purposes of the restrictive scope of fair use of unpublished works suggested by the *Nation* case? Does unpublished for this purpose mean the same thing as unpublished (and hence protected by common law copyright) meant under the 1909 Act? (Note that this definition is carried forward in the definition of publication in § 101, and remains important for issues such as national origin under § 104, notice, and some aspects of the copyright term.) Or does it mean something else? The copyright definition of unpublished, particularly if we include as a gloss the concept of limited publication, includes many works that are publicly known and available. In the *Nation* case the manuscript had been stolen, and this improper method of acquisition clearly influenced the Court's attitude toward the defendant's copying. But that was not the situation in either *Salinger* or *New Era*, even though the Second Circuit thought it necessary to adopt the Supreme Court's attitude toward "unpublished" works.

In *Salinger* the letters had been obtained from university libraries, which had acquired them from recipients of the letters and made them available for research. Information contained in the letters was publicly available to researchers. It is true that the letters had not been published because sending a letter is not publication. But the sender does lose control of the substance of its content, if not of the copyright.

In *New Era* the biographer Miller learned of some documents by freedom of information requests to the federal government (for instance, Hubbard had written to the F.B.I. accusing his former wife of being a communist, and the letter was found in F.B.I. files) to which Hubbard had sent them. He apparently learned the content of others because the Church of Scientology permitted a dedicated member to undertake a biography of Hubbard. The member, one Armstrong, was given access to six filing cabinets of material, "only to become totally disillusioned with contradictory material on Hubbard's family background, naval and academic careers, fraudulent business background, tax evasion and evasion of the law." 873 F.2d at 585–86. The Church sued to get the documents back, and Miller learned of the documents from the lawsuit. Of this, Judge Leval said:

> Holt argues that many of these works were effectively published when they became part of the court record and were placed on public display during the conduct of a trial brought by the Church of Scientology in an effort to recover the documents from a member (Armstrong) who it claimed had taken them without authorization. Plaintiff disputes whether the court in fact placed the works on public display and also disputes whether such display would alter their unpublished status. Combining the fact that any public display in the course of the Armstrong litigation was over objection, with the small number of persons, at most, who saw the works, plaintiff has the better of the argument. If the bringing of a lawsuit to enforce a right necessarily resulted in its sacrifice, the right would be chimerical. 695 F.Supp. at 1500 n. 3.

This is too quick. There are procedures such as protective orders, closed proceedings, etc. that can be used to protect confidential material involved in litigation. If the biographer Miller had been subject to a protective order, he could not have used the material in violation of the order. But there is no suggestion that he was, in which case the materials were in fact part of a public record. Both *Salinger* and *New Era* involve conduct that is substantially different from that involved in *Nation*. Should the Second Circuit have considered the *Nation* case as controlling? It is easy to see why the Supreme Court found theft of the Ford manuscript "unfair." But is that true of the research methods involved in *Salinger* and *New Era?*

(1) PARODY

BENNY v. LOEW'S INCORPORATED

United States Court of Appeals, Ninth Circuit, 1956.
239 F.2d 532, affirmed 356 U.S. 43, 78 S.Ct. 667, 2 L.Ed.2d 583, rehearing
denied 356 U.S. 934, 78 S.Ct. 770, 2 L.Ed.2d 764.

MCALLISTER, CIRCUIT JUDGE. Patrick Hamilton, an English author and a British subject, some time prior to December, 1938, conceived and wrote an original play entitled, "Gas Light." It was published and protected by copyright in February, 1939. Shortly thereafter, it was publicly performed in England, first, in Richmond, and later, in London. On December 5, 1941, it was produced as a play in New York under the name, "Angel Street," and had a successful run of 1,295 consecutive performances, extending over a period of more than 37 months.

On October 7, 1942, the exclusive motion picture rights for "Gas Light" were acquired by Loew's, Inc., better known under its trade name of Metro-Goldwyn-Mayer.

Loew's spent $2,458,000 in the production and distribution of the motion picture photoplay of "Gas Light." The actual making of the film extended over a period of more than two and a half years.

In producing the motion picture, Loew's acquired the services of three great artists in the cinema field, Charles Boyer, Ingrid Bergman, and Joseph Cotten.

The photoplay, "Gas Light," was exhibited in the United States and fifty-six foreign countries. Approximately fifty-two million persons paid admission to see it. The gross receipts in rentals for the play amounted to $4,857,000.

There is no question of the right of the dramatic work to protection under the copyright laws of both Great Britain and the United States.

On October 14, 1945, Jack Benny, a successful performer in the field of comedy, after securing Loew's consent to present a parody of "Gas Light" on radio, caused to be written, produced, performed, and broadcast over a national radio network a fifteen-minute burlesque of the play. In preparing the program, the radio writers for Benny had access to the acting script of the motion picture, "Gas Light."

More than six years later, on January 27, 1952, the Columbia Broadcasting System caused to be written and produced a half-hour-long television show burlesquing "Gas Light," with Jack Benny in the leading role. It was broadcast over the Columbia Broadcasting System network and was "sponsored" by the American Tobacco Company. Neither Mr. Benny nor the Columbia Broadcasting System nor the American Tobacco Company secured consent from Loew's or Mr. Hamilton to publish and broadcast the television burlesque, or, as it is sometimes called, the parody.

Immediately after the presentation of the television show, Loew's dispatched a telegram to the Columbia Broadcasting System, notifying that company that Loew's was the owner of the exclusive rights of production and recording of the play, "Gas Light," and adaptations thereof by means of talking films, sound tracks, and television; that Columbia had used substantial portions of the play in its television program; and that Loew's intended to enforce its rights against infringement. A short time thereafter, counsel for Columbia replied to the above telegram, informing Loew's that its burlesque appropriation of the play, "Gas Light," was a "fair use" of the dramatic work, and that Columbia had the right to parody it as it did in the television show. Loew's, in turn, informed Columbia that the burlesque television show constituted an infringement of the copyright of "Gas Light"; and when Columbia prepared for a similar presentation over several television channels, Loew's filed this action, and secured a temporary restraining order.

Upon a trial of the issues, the district court found that the Benny television play was copied in substantial part from Loew's motion picture photoplay, "Gas Light"; that the portion so copied was a substantial part of the copyrighted material in such photoplay; and that the Benny television presentation was an infringement of the copyrighted photoplay, "Gas Light." The court, accordingly, granted injunctive relief, restraining the showing of the television play, all of which appears in the able and comprehensive opinion by Judge James M. Carter, reported in 131 F.Supp. 165.

On review, the chief contention advanced by appellants is that the burlesque presentation of "Gas Light" was a "fair use" of appellees' photoplay; that, although the play was copyrighted, and neither Benny, Columbia, nor the American Tobacco Company had received any consent on the part of the copyright owners to adapt the play in the way they did, nevertheless, they had the right to adapt the original copyrighted dramatic work of the author of the play and of the photoplay version as a burlesque, and to present, vend, and appropriate it thus, for their own profit.

Appellees submit that the Copyright Act insures to the copyright owners the exclusive right to any lawful use of their property, whereby they may get a profit out of it. They further submit that there is no doctrine of fair use which justifies the appropriation of substantial copyrighted material of a dramatic work without the consent of the copyright owner, whether such appropriation is made for the purpose of pirating the work openly, or under the guise of a burlesque or a parody.

In considering the law and its application to this case, the facts themselves are most important. The play is a remarkable dramatic production. As outlined by appellees and somewhat supplemented by the record, the play tells the story of a man who sets out upon a deliberate plan to drive his wife insane. He is motivated in this endeavor by the need of having access to a house which was inherited by his wife and in which they live. Some years prior, he had murdered the aunt of his wife for the sake of some valuable jewels which he had intended to steal, but in which he had been frustrated. His method of achieving his objective of finding the jewels without the wife's knowledge, and, at the same time, avoiding her suspicion, is to keep her attention diverted by inducing in her the belief that she is having hallucinations, suffering great lapses of memory, and gradually losing her mind. He does this by abstracting, without her knowledge, articles which he had entrusted to his wife, and by removing a portrait from the wall, making her believe that she had been responsible for the misplacement of the articles and the removal of the picture, of which she had lost all recollection. He fosters such a belief in her, in part, by causing the servants to bear witness that they did not remove the portrait. The suspense aroused by the picture is focused upon whether he will succeed in his scheme of finding the jewels and driving his wife insane. He fails, because of the intervention of a detective from Scotland Yard who, suspicious of the husband's conduct, has become interested in, and then obviously enamoured, of the heroine. The detective apprehends the husband at the climax of the plot, binds him to a chair in his own home to secure his arrest, and then reveals the truth, which he has learned, to the wife. At her request, she is given an opportunity to talk to the husband, who attempts once again, through his personal charm, to subdue her to his will. She, however, resists. In this scene, at her husband's request, she procures a knife, which he has kept nearby. The suspense is heightened by the question whether she will use the knife to cut her husband's bonds, as he has asked her to do, or whether she has come to a determination to kill him. She does neither, but contents herself with denouncing him, and turning him over to the police.

A comparison of appellees' "Gas Light" and the Columbia television show discloses the following: The locale of Loew's photoplay is in the early 1870's when the story begins. In the burlesque television show, the story begins in 1871. The setting is a gloomy old four-story Victorian house. The characters are a murderer, his wife, a detective from Scotland yard, and a maid. The murderer has killed a woman ten years before in this house. (In the Columbia television show, the time of the murder is fifteen years before.) Thereafter, the murderer marries the young girl who has inherited the house from the murdered woman, so that he can pursue his search for the jewels for which he had committed the crime. All of the foregoing is the same in the Columbia television show except that it does not mention that the wife had inherited the house.

In carrying out his objective, the husband follows the above mentioned plan of driving his wife insane, so that she may eventually be placed in an asylum. He leaves the house nightly and then secretly returns through another entrance to the attic to search for the jewels. In one of the incidents, the husband questions, in the presence of the wife, the maid, concerning the picture which has been removed from its place on the wall, in spite of the wife's begging the husband not to humiliate her before a servant. The maid denies having touched the picture, and the husband uses this incident also to make his wife believe that she has lost her mind. The husband is finally caught by the Scotland Yard detective, who has deduced that he is the murderer.

During the entire play, except at the climax, the wife is deeply in love with her husband and is grieved that he leaves her alone each night. Because of the husband's machinations, she fears that she is losing her mind and repeatedly begs for the sympathy and understanding of her husband, who coldly repels her. The detective from Scotland Yard, who has been noticing the husband's suspicious actions and watching the house for some time, calls on the wife when her husband is away and tells her of his past and of the murder several years previously. In talking with the wife, the detective gets her to admit that she knows it is her husband who is prowling in the attic and making the mysterious noises there at night. Upon the return of the husband, the detective conceals himself in the house, but appears as the husband commences to bully his wife. He then places the husband under arrest, allows the wife to talk with him alone for a few minutes while he waits outside the door, and then, at her call, returns and takes him into custody. The foregoing is similar in both the photoplay and the television play.

*   *   *

The district court found, as a fact, that appellants' television play was copied by them, in substantial part, from appellees' motion picture photoplay "Gas Light," and that the "part so copied was and is a substantial part of [appellants' television] play, and of the copyrightable and copyrighted material in [appellees'] motion picture photoplay." The district court found as facts "(1) that the locale and period of the works are the same; (2) the main setting is the same; (3) the characters are generally the same; (4) the story points are practically identical; (5) the development of the story, the treatment (except that defendants' treatment is burlesque), the incidents, the sequences of events, the points of suspense, the climax are almost identical and finally, (6) there has been a detailed borrowing of much of the dialogue with some variation in wording. There has been a substantial taking by defendants from the plaintiffs' copyrighted property." Accordingly, the district court found that appellants were guilty of infringement of appellees' photoplay, "Gas Light."

The photoplay is an original dramatic work. It deals with incidents familiar in life and fiction, but the grouping of those incidents presents a novel arrangement of events; and it is that originality which is protected by copyright.

A comparison of the photoplay and the television play indicates how much was copied. If the material taken by appellants from "Gas Light" is eliminated, there are left only a few gags, and some disconnected and incoherent dialogue. If the television play were presented without appellants' contribution, there would be left the plot, story, principal incidents, and same sequence of events as in the photoplay.

A review of the record, a comparison of the scripts of appellees' photoplay and appellants' television play, and a viewing of the motion picture photoplay and the television play, as projected upon the screen—all convince us that the findings of fact of the district court that appellants copied the photoplay in substantial part, and that the part so copied was a substantial part of the television play and of the material in appellees' photoplay, are clearly supported by the evidence.

Appellants' chief defense is that the use which they made of appellees' photoplay in their television play was a fair use, by reason of the fact that the material which they appropriated from the motion picture, "Gas Light," was used in the creation of a burlesque, and that by reason of such circumstance they are not guilty of infringement.

The so-called doctrine of fair use of copyrighted material appears in cases in federal courts having to do with compilations, listings, digests, and the like, and is concerned with the use made of prior compilations, listings and digests. In certain of these cases, it is held that a writer may be guided by earlier copyrighted works, may consult original authorities, and may use those which he considers applicable in support of his own original text; but even in such cases, it is generally held that if he appropriate the fruits of another's labors, without alteration, and without independent research, he violates the rights of the copyright owner. In these instances, as has been said, there are certain to be considerable resemblances, "just as there must be between the work of two persons compiling a directory, or a dictionary, or a guide for railroad trains, or for automobile trips. In such cases the question is whether the writer has availed himself of the earlier writer's work without doing any independent work himself." Chautauqua School of Nursing v. National School of Nursing, 2 Cir., 238 F. 151, 153. See also cases digested in 18 F.Dig., Copyrights, Section 55. But up to the time of the present controversy, no federal court, in any adjudication, has supposed that there was a doctrine of fair use applicable to copying the substance of a dramatic work, and presenting it, with few variations, as a burlesque. The fact that a serious dramatic work is copied practically verbatim, and then presented with actors walking on their hands or with other grotesqueries, does not avoid infringement of the copyright. "Counsel have not disclosed a single authority, nor have we been able to find one, which lends any support to the proposition that wholesale copying and publication of copyrighted material can *ever* be fair use." Leon v. Pacific Telephone & Telegraph Co., 9 Cir., 91 F.2d 484, 486. (Emphasis supplied.) Whether the audience is gripped with tense emotion in viewing the original drama, or, on the other hand, laughs at the burlesque, does not absolve the copier. Otherwise, any individual or corporation could appropriate, in its entirety, a serious and famous dramatic work, protected by copyright, merely by introducing comic devices of clownish garb, or movement, or facial distortion of the actors, and presenting it as burlesque. One person has the sole right to do this—the copyright owner, inasmuch as, under Title 17 U.S.C. § 1 [of the 1909 Act], he has the exclusive right to make any other version of the work that he desires. He can have it read or sung or danced or pantomimed or burlesqued, because, in the language of the statute, he has the sole right to "exhibit, perform, represent, produce, or reproduce it in any manner or by any method whatsoever."

The fact that it has been Mr. Benny's custom to present from time to time, his, or the Columbia Broadcasting System's "version" of various dramatic works during the past twenty-five years, is no defense to this action for infringement of copyright. Appellants cannot copy and present another's dramatic work as they have in the instance before us, unless they receive the consent of the copyright owner.

An apparently alternative contention that the presentation of the burlesque was, in effect, literary or dramatic criticism and, therefore, not subject to an action for infringement of copyright, would seem to be a parody upon the meaning of criticism.

The record in this case includes a beguiling dissertation on the history of the drama, of English literature, of parody, and of burlesque, by Dr. Frank C. Baxter, a widely recognized and eminent authority in this field of study. Briefs of appellants' counsel, too, disclose a wealth of literary appreciation. However, there is only a single decisive point in the case: One cannot copy the substance of another's work without infringing his copyright. A burlesque presentation of such a copy is no defense to an action for infringement of copyright. As was said by the district judge, a "parodized or burlesque taking is to be treated no differently from any other appropriation; that, as in all other cases of alleged taking, the issue becomes first one of fact, i.e., what was taken and how substantial was the taking; and if it is determined that there was a substantial taking, infringement exists."

The finding of the district court that appellants had copied a substantial part of appellees' photoplay is clearly supported by the evidence. The judgment is affirmed upon the findings of fact and conclusions of law of the district court and for the reasons set forth in the opinion of Judge James M. Carter.

NOTES

1. Affirmed without opinion by an equally divided Court, 356 U.S. 43 (1958).

2. In Columbia Pictures Corp. v. National Broadcasting Co., 137 F.Supp. 348 (S.D.Calif.1955), the District Court that had decided the principal case found that a burlesque of "From Here to Eternity" entitled "From Here to Obscurity" did not infringe. The court said: "Some limited taking should be permitted under the doctrine of fair use, in the case of burlesque, to bring about * * * [the] recalling or conjuring up of the original." Id. at 350.

3. Berlin v. E.C. Publications, 329 F.2d 541 (2d Cir.1964):

> "Through depression and boom, war and peace, Tin Pan Alley has light-heartedly insisted that 'the whole world laughs' with a laugher, and that 'the best things in life are free.' In an apparent departure from these delightful sentiments, the owners of the copyrights upon some twenty-five popular songs instituted this action against the publishers, employees and distributors of 'Mad Magazine,' alleging that Mad's publication of satiric parody lyrics to plaintiffs' songs infringed the copyrighted originals, despite Mad's failure to reproduce the music of plaintiffs' compositions in any form whatsoever. * * * The parodies were published as a 'special bonus' to the Fourth Annual Edition of Mad, whose cover characterized its contents as 'More Trash From Mad—A Sickening Collection of Humor and Satire From Past Issues,' and almost prophetically carried this admonition for its readers: 'For Solo or Group Participation (Followed by Arrest).' Defendants' efforts were billed as a collection of parody lyrics to 57 old standards which reflect the idiotic world we live in today. Divided into nine categories, ranging from 'Songs of Space & The Atom' to 'Songs of Sports,' they were accompanied by the notation that they were to be 'Sung to' or 'Sung to the tune of' a well-known popular song—in twenty-five cases, the plaintiffs' copyrighted compositions. So that this musical direction might feasibly be obeyed, the parodies were written in the same meter as the original lyrics.

> "The District Court observed that the theme and content of the parodies differed markedly from those of the originals. Thus, 'The

Last Time I Saw Paris,' originally written as a nostalgic ballad which tenderly recalled pre-war France, became in defendants' hands 'The First Time I Saw Maris,' a caustic commentary upon the tendency of a baseball hero to become a television pitchman, more prone to tempt injury with the razor blade which he advertises than with the hazards of the game which he plays. Similarly, defendants transformed the plaintiffs' 'A Pretty Girl Is Like a Melody', into 'Louella Schwartz Describes Her Malady'; what was originally a tribute to feminine beauty became a burlesque of a feminine hypochondriac troubled with sleeplessness and a propensity to tell the world of her plight."

The court found no infringement. Is the doctrine of fair use necessary to reach such a result?

4. In Walt Disney Productions v. Air Pirates, 345 F.Supp. 108 (N.D.Cal. 1972), the defendant had parodied Mickey Mouse and other cartoon characters of Walt Disney. Defendant argued that it was necessary to copy the characters in order to parody them. The court found infringement, following *Benny*. The court of appeals affirmed on the ground that the taking was too extensive without deciding whether *Benny* allowed sufficient room for parody. 581 F.2d 751 (9th Cir.1978).

5. The Fifth Circuit had no trouble affirming a preliminary injunction against infringement of a copyrighted poster of five members of the Dallas Cowboys cheerleaders. The infringing poster displayed five ex-members of the Dallas Cowboys cheerleaders with bare breasts. The court rejected the argument that the poster was parody and hence fair use. Dallas Cowboys Cheerleaders, Inc. v. Scoreboard Posters, Inc., 600 F.2d 1184 (5th Cir.1979).

6. In Hustler Magazine, Inc. v. Moral Majority, Inc., 796 F.2d 1148 (9th Cir.1986), *Hustler* magazine ran an ad which was a parody of Campari liquor advertisements. Campari advertisements consist of interviews with famous people about the first time they drank Campari, using double entendre to conflate the first drink of Campari and a first sexual experience. The parody ad featured the Rev. Jerry Falwell, a nationally famous fundamentalist minister, describing his "first time" as being incest with his mother in an outhouse. Falwell used copies of the ad in fund raising appeals (while also suing *Hustler* for libel) and Hustler sued Falwell for infringement. Falwell's use of the copies of the ad was held to be fair use.

7. Elsmere Music, Inc. v. National Broadcasting Co., Inc., 482 F.Supp. 741 (S.D.N.Y.1980), affirmed 623 F.2d 252 (2d Cir.1980), was an action for infringement of the promotional song "I Love New York." The song was parodied on Saturday Night Live as "I Love Sodom." Held: fair use because the parody did not affect the value of the plaintiff's copyrighted song. But didn't the parody reduce the value of the song as a successful promotional device since viewers of the Saturday Night Live skit might be reminded of it every time they heard "I Love New York"? Note that the defendants in *Elsmere*, unlike the defendants in *Berlin*, supra note 3, sang the entire (albeit quite simple) melody of "I Love New York." In Fisher v. Dees, 794 F.2d 432 (9th Cir.1986), the court found that defendant's "when Sonny Sniffs Glue" was fair use of plaintiff's "When Sunny Gets Blue."

8. Suppose the *Nation* had combined its excerpts from the Ford memoirs with more extended and critical editorial material along the lines of "This is what Ford said he said or did, and isn't that ridiculous?" Would that have changed the outcome of the litigation? Can a copyright infringer find safety by

combining infringement with controversial editorial material about the work infringed (just as magazines containing sexually explicit pictorials have found it helpful to add anti-establishment and anti-government articles)?

9. A factor to be considered but not enumerated in § 107 is the conduct of the defendant after the infringement has been detected, according to Iowa State Univ. Research Foundation, Inc. v. American Broadcasting Companies, 621 F.2d 57 (2d Cir.1980). In that case students at Iowa State University had produced a 28 minute film entitled *Champion,* a short biography of fellow student and champion wrestler Dan Gable. ABC used several minutes of the film in connection with Gable's successful competition for a gold medal at the 1972 Olympics and in connection with Gable's appearance on an ABC program "Superstars." ABC unsuccessfully argued fair use. "We cannot ignore the fact, found by the district judge, that ABC copied *Champion* while purporting to assess its value for possible purchase, or that the network repeatedly denied that it had ever used the film. * * * ABC's conduct in the instant case is not irrelevant to the fairness of its use." 621 F.2d at 62. The district court awarded $15,250 in statutory damages and $17,500 in attorney's fees. 475 F.Supp. 78 (S.D.N.Y.1979).

10. A recent study of satire and fair use is Michael C. Albin, Beyond Fair Use: Putting Satire in its Proper Place, 33 UCLA Law Rev. 518 (1985).

(2) OTHER NON–COMPETING USES

TRIANGLE PUBLICATIONS, INC. v. KNIGHT–RIDDER NEWSPAPERS, INC.

United States Court of Appeals, Fifth Circuit, 1980.
626 F.2d 1171.

JOHN R. BROWN, CIRCUIT JUDGE:

* * *

The plaintiff-appellant, Triangle Publications (Triangle), is the publisher of "TV Guide," a periodical containing television schedules and articles relating to television entertainment. The defendant-appellee, Knight-Ridder Newspapers (Knight-Ridder), publishes the Miami Herald Newspaper (the Herald). During the fall of 1977, Knight-Ridder began a campaign to promote a newly developed television booklet which was to be included as a supplement to the Sunday edition of the Herald. Like TV Guide, the booklet contains television schedules and articles related to that media. * * *

[T]he booklet was advertised in two thirty second television commercials. The first is based on the theme "Goldilocks and the Three Bears." It compares the size of the Herald's former television guide with the Herald's new supplement and with TV Guide, concluding that the former supplement is too large, that TV Guide is too small, but that the new supplement is just the right size for human beings.[3] While TV Guide is not mentioned by name, one of the actors in the commercial is

---

3. This is the script of the commercial:

[Narrator]: "This is the story of Sidney Bear, Cindy Bear and Junior Bear. They all love to watch TV, but . . ."

[Middle Aged Man]: "This TV book is too small."

[Child]: "This TV book is too big."

shown briefly with a back-dated copy of TV Guide in hand. The cover of the TV Guide issue is clearly visible. The commercial was used for several weeks and was then discontinued. The second commercial is a monologue. After identifying TV Guide as the competing product, the announcer suggests that the Herald's supplement is a better value for the money because the purchaser gets the entire newspaper, not merely a TV booklet.[4] During the course of his statement, the announcer holds up a backdated issue of TV Guide with the cover clearly visible. The announcer then puts down the TV Guide and holds up first a copy of the Herald's supplement and then a copy of the Sunday edition of the Herald. This commercial was being used at the time of the District Court's hearing and Knight-Ridder contemplated using it in the future.

The only conduct by the Herald being challenged here is the reproducing of TV Guide covers. The verbal reference to TV Guide made in the second commercial is not being attacked. Since each issue of TV Guide is individually copyrighted, and since magazine covers have in the past been afforded copyright protection, see, e.g., Conde Nast Publications, Inc. v. Vogue School of Fashion Modeling, Inc., 105 F.Supp. 325 (S.D.N.Y.1952), Triangle claims that the Herald's showing of TV Guide covers violates § 106 of the new Copyright Act, 17 U.S.C. § 106. Triangle moved in the District Court for preliminary and permanent injunctions (and also sought damages). [The district court rejected the defendant's fair use defense, but nevertheless decided for the defendant on the ground that an injunction against infringement would violate free speech.]

* * *

In analyzing the fair use question, the District Court did not get beyond the first factor [of § 107]. The Court deemed it controlling that the use of the TV Guide covers by the Miami Herald was to obtain commercial advantage. The Court established what amounts to virtually a per se rule that commercial motive destroys the defense of fair use.

Clearly, § 107 makes commercial motive relevant to fair use analysis. But it is certainly not decisive. As the legislative history makes clear:

> This amendment is not intended to be interpreted as any sort of not-for-profit limitation on educational uses of copyrighted

[Middle Aged Woman]: "This TV section is just right."

[Narrator]: "It was the Sunday Herald's new TV book at no extra cost. The three bears loved the new . . . just-right size with its up-to-date and more complete listings. 'Til one day this little blonde kid—uh, but that's another story. . . . Something for everybody. Every day of the week." (Dots indicate pauses, not omitted material.)

4. This is the script of the commercial:

"This is TV Guide. When you buy it, that's all you get. No extras. This is The Miami Herald's TV Book. When you buy it, you get a few extras. Like more up-to-date listings, charts that let you see what's on at a glance. It even has extras on top of the extras. And the best part is, even if there's nothing good on TV . . . you can always sit back and read some of the extras. The Miami Herald."

(Dots indicate pauses, not omitted material.)

works. It is an express recognition that, as under the present law, the commercial and non-profit character of an activity, while not conclusive with respect to fair use, can and should be weighed along with other factors in fair use decisions.

House Report, at 66; U.S.Code Cong. & Admin.News, at 5679. See also Senate Report, at 62; 3 Nimmer on Copyright, § 13.05[A], at 13–52 (1978) (stating that commercial use does not necessarily negate fair use defense and citing string of cases to support proposition).

* * *

We believe that in viewing commercial motive as conclusive on the question of fair use, the District Court incorrectly applied § 107. Accordingly, its finding of no fair use defense is not subject to a clearly erroneous standard. Rather, we are more free to determine the question of fair use.

As § 107 makes clear, the first factor to consider in a fair use analysis is the purpose and character of the use. Here, Knight-Ridder used TV Guide covers for advertisements, and any commercial use tends to cut against a fair use defense. On the other hand, the precise characteristics of the commercial use in this case caution against too much weight being given to the fact that the use is commercial. Specifically, there was no attempt to palm off Triangle's product as that of the Herald's. Compare Conde Nast Publications, Inc. v. Vogue School of Fashion Modeling, Inc., supra. Rather, the advertisement was a comparative advertisement done in a manner which is generally accepted in the advertising industry.[13]

The second factor specified in § 107 is the nature of the copyrighted work. One commentator has argued that because the copyrighted work—TV Guide—is itself commercial, the defense of fair use should

---

13. As stated, the fact that the commercial use occurred in the course of a truthful comparative advertisement undercuts the significance of the commercial nature of the use. Congress emphasized that the doctrine of fair use must be flexible. House Report, at 66; U.S.Code Cong. & Admin.News, at 5680; Senate Report at 62. Today, the public interest in comparative advertising is well-recognized. As the Federal Trade Commission has stated:

The Commission has supported the use of brand comparisons where the bases of comparison are clearly identified. Comparative advertising, when truthful and nondeceptive, is a source of important information to consumers and assists them in making rational purchase decisions. Comparative advertising encourages product improvement and innovation, and can lead to lower prices in the marketplace. For these reasons, the Commission will continue to scrutinize carefully restraints upon its use.

16 C.F.R. § 14.15(c) (1980). One affidavit received as a part of the record cites several examples of comparative advertising, including many magazine ads reproducing covers of competing magazines. For example, the January 9, 1978 issue of Advertising Age contains an advertisement for Americana magazine with a display of covers of competing magazines. The December 1977 issue of Media Decisions contains an ad promoting Horizon magazine featuring pictures of covers of competing magazines. An advertisement in the July 8, 1977 issue of New Times promoting that magazine shows covers of Time and Newsweek, two newsweeklys with which New Times competes. Affidavit of Ken Keoughan, Director of Marketing Services, Beber, Silverstein & Partners, Inc. Thus, while the Miami Herald is clearly out to make a profit from its advertisements, there is certainly no palming off of Triangle's work. Rather, the Herald has used various covers of TV Guide for purposes of comparative advertisements.

more readily apply. See Wisconsin Note ["Copyright and the First Amendment—Triangle Publications, Inc. v. Knight–Ridder Newspapers, Inc., 445 F.Supp. 875 (S.D.Fla.1978), 1979 Wisc.L.Rev. 242], supra, at 261. However, other commentators have argued that "courts have tended to be most receptive to unauthorized use of educational, scientific, and historical works." Note, Copyright Infringement and the First Amendment, 79 Colum.L.Rev. 320, 326 n. 42 (hereafter referred to as Columbia Note), citing Eisenschiml v. Fawcett Publications, supra. In our view, the fact that TV Guide is a commercial publication neither supports nor hurts Knight-Ridder's claim that a fair use defense is appropriate here.

The third factor to consider under § 107 is the amount and substantiality of the portion used in relation to the copyrighted work as a whole. Here, Knight-Ridder did not copy what is the essence of TV Guide—the television schedules and articles. It simply reproduced covers of old TV Guide issues. We do not mean to trivialize the covers of TV Guide, but simply emphasize that this factor would have been entitled to more weight had, for example, some of the contents been used.

The fourth factor to analyze under § 107—the factor which is widely accepted to be the most important, is the effect of the use upon the potential market for, or the value of, the copyrighted work. We are simply unable to find any effect—other than possibly de minimus—on the commercial value of the copyright. To be sure, the Herald's advertisements may have had the effect of drawing customers away from TV Guide. But this results from the nature of advertising itself and in no way stems from the fact that TV Guide covers were used. Indeed, assuming that TV Guide covers offer positive artistic enjoyment, the reproduction of these covers in the Herald's ads may have shown why TV Guide is a better product than the Herald's guide and may have decreased the effectiveness of the ads. At no point has Triangle offered a cogent explanation of the logical link between the showing of TV Guide covers and the alleged harm to the copyright. We cannot see it. * * *

Applying the four factors specified in § 107—and giving heavy emphasis to the fourth factor—we conclude that the fair use defense applies in this case and that the District Court erred in holding that it did not. We simply cannot see how Triangle was harmed by the Herald's advertisements. Moreover, the public as well as the Herald benefits from comparative advertising, thus minimizing the importance of the fact that a commercial use was involved.

* * *

We affirm the decision of the District Court denying Triangle's motions for preliminary and permanent injunctions. * * *

Affirmed.

PACIFIC AND SOUTHERN CO. v. DUNCAN
United States Court of Appeals, Eleventh Circuit, 1984.
744 F.2d 1490.

JOHNSON, CIRCUIT JUDGE:

[WXIA], a television station, charges that Carol Duncan, d/b/a TV News Clips, has infringed its copyright by videotaping its news broadcasts and selling the tapes to the subjects of the news reports. We hold that the appellant has violated the copyright laws because her activities do not constitute "fair use" of the material. We also conclude that the television station is entitled to a permanent injunction preventing the appellant from continuing to infringe its copyright. Accordingly, we affirm in part and reverse in part.

I. Facts

* * * WXIA–TV, a television station in Atlanta, Georgia * * * broadcasts four local news programs each day and places a notice of copyright at the end of each newscast. A program consists of self-contained news stories originating outside the studio and linked together by live commentary from the anchor persons, along with weather reports and shorter news reports originating from the studio itself. WXIA records the entire program on videotape and audiotape. It retains a written transcript of the program for a year and the audiotape for an indefinite period of time; it also maintains videotape copies of all the news stories taped before broadcast and stories originating live from a location outside the studio. The station erases the videotape of the entire program after seven days, a practice that destroys any record of the visual element of segments of the show broadcast live from within the studio.

WXIA does not currently market videotape copies of its news stories. Nevertheless, some people ask the station for a chance to view a tape at the station or to purchase a copy for personal use. WXIA has always honored requests to view tapes and usually allows persons to buy the tapes they want.[1] The revenue from tape sales is a small portion of WXIA's total profits.

Carol Duncan operates a business known as TV News Clips, a commercial enterprise belonging to a nationwide association of news clipping organizations.[2] TV News Clips videotapes television news programs, identifies the persons and organizations covered by the news reports, and tries to sell them copies of the relevant portion of the newscast.[3] It does not seek the permission of WXIA or any other

---

1. The tapes cost one hundred dollars. WXIA will not sell tapes to political candidates because the sale could appear to be an endorsement or other show of support for the candidate. Out of a similar concern over favoritism, the station asks for a subpoena before selling a tape that will be used in litigation.

2. TV News Clips belongs to the International Association of Broadcast Monitors, an organization of 20 to 30 members. Ms. Duncan is a past president of the association.

3. The customers pay $65 for an initial purchase and $25 for subsequent purchases.

broadcaster before selling the tapes, nor does it place a notice of copyright on the tapes. A label on each tape does say, however, that it is "for personal use only not for rebroadcast." TV News Clips erases all tapes after one month.

This case began when TV News Clips sold a copy of a news feature to Floyd Junior College, the subject of a story aired by WXIA on March 11, 1981. WXIA obtained the tape purchased by Floyd Junior College, registered its copyright,[4] and brought this action to obtain damages for the infringement of its copyright and an injunction preventing unauthorized copying and sales of its news program. The district court found that the news feature was protected by the copyright laws and that TV News Clips had not made "fair use" of the material. It rejected the fair use defense without reaching the four factors listed in 17 U.S.C. § 107 (1977), because TV News Clips had not met its threshold burden of showing that its activity served a purpose such as "criticism, comment, news reporting, teaching * * * scholarship, or research," categories listed in the preamble to Section 107. Yet despite finding that TV News Clips had clearly violated WXIA's copyright, the district court denied the request for an injunction for three reasons. First, the sales did not seriously threaten WXIA's creativity, so an injunction would not significantly further the main objective of the copyright laws, fostering creativity. Second, the court feared that an injunction would threaten First Amendment values served by the increased public availability of the news made possible by TV News Clips. Finally, the court found that WXIA had abandoned its copyright on several portions of the newscasts; it declined to formulate a decree that would distinguish between the abandoned and unabandoned portions.

II. "Fair Use" Defense to Statutory Liability

The news feature broadcast by WXIA undoubtedly falls within the protection of the copyright laws. The editorial judgment used to present effectively the events covered by the broadcast made it an "original" work of authorship, and the feature became "fixed" in a tangible medium when it was recorded at the time of transmission.[5] Thus, it met the requirements of 17 U.S.C. § 102. The fact that the infringing tape is the only exact copy of the transmission still in existence does not nullify the copyright. The statute requires only that the original work be "fixed" for a period of "more than transitory duration," not for the entire term of the copyright. 17 U.S.C. §§ 101, 102.

* * *

TV News Clips argued in the district court that its use of the news broadcast was a fair use of the material because it served an important

---

4. WXIA does not normally register the copyright for its news programs.

5. The feature in this case was prerecorded, but the final product broadcast by WXIA included a live introduction by the anchor person and graphics (stating the reporter's name and location) superimposed over the pretaped version.

societal interest in full access to the news. The court rejected the fair use defense without considering the four statutory factors because TV News Clips did not copy and distribute the material for purposes such as the ones listed in the preamble. The district court reasoned that since TV News Clips' use was not "inherently productive or creative," like each of the preamble uses, analysis of the four factors was unnecessary.

We agree with TV News Clips that the district court should have considered the four factors set out in the statute. The statute uses mandatory language to the effect that in a fair use determination, the "factors to be considered *shall* include" (emphasis added) the four listed. The preamble merely illustrates the sorts of uses likely to qualify as fair uses under the four listed factors.

* * * The district court fashioned a per se rule that a use must be inherently productive or creative before it can be a fair use, but a doctrine meant to resolve unforeseen conflicts of values should not turn on such a narrow inquiry. The Supreme Court, in its recent fair use decision in Sony Corp. v. Universal City Studios, 464 U.S. 417 (1984), did not conduct any preliminary tests before analyzing the four statutory factors. It expressly refused to look to productivity alone in determining what constituted a fair use. Id. at n. 40. * * *

Despite the district court's erroneous interpretation of the law, we need not remand this case for further factfinding. The district court resolved all the issues of fact necessary for us to conclude as a matter of law that TV News Clips' activities do not qualify as a fair use of the copyrighted work. See Triangle Publications, Inc. v. Knight-Ridder Newspapers, Inc., 626 F.2d 1171, 1175 (5th Cir.1980) (analyzing usage under the four statutory factors where district court had made findings under an erroneous view of controlling legal principles).[8]

The purpose and character of TV News Clips' use of WXIA's work heavily influences our decision in this case. TV News Clips copies and distributes the broadcast for unabashedly commercial reasons despite the fact that its customers buy the tapes for personal use. The district court characterized TV News Clips as a "full-fledged commercial operation." TV News Clips denies that its activities have a commercial purpose; instead, it says that its purpose is "private news reporting," meant to provide the public with a record of news reports. Of course, every commercial exchange of goods and services involves both the giving of the good or service and the taking of the purchase price. The fact that TV News Clips focuses on the giving rather than the taking cannot hide the fact that profit is its primary motive for making the exchange.

8. Fair use is probably best characterized as a mixed question of law and fact that can be decided by an appellate court if the trial court has found facts sufficient to evaluate each of the four statutory factors. Cf. Meeropol v. Nizer, 560 F.2d 1061, 1070 (2d Cir.1977) (trial court erroneously determined fair use as a matter of law before allowing case to go to jury because there were no factual findings regarding first or fourth statutory factors).

* * *

We also note that TV News Clips' use is neither productive nor creative in any way. It does not analyze the broadcast or improve it at all. Indeed, WXIA expressed concern over the technical inferiority of the tapes. TV News Clips only copies and sells. As the uses listed in the preamble to Section 107 indicate, fair uses are those that contribute in some way to the public welfare. * * *

The fourth fair use factor, the effect on the potential market for the work, is closely related to the first. By examining the effect of a use, a reviewing court can measure the success of the original purpose and single out those purposes that most directly threaten the incentives for creativity which the copyright tries to protect. Some commercial purposes, for example, might not threaten the incentives because the user profits from an activity that the owner could not possibly take advantage of. See Triangle Publications, Inc. v. Knight-Ridder Newspapers, Inc., supra. But in this case, TV News Clips uses the broadcasts for a purpose that WXIA might use for its own benefit. The fact that WXIA does not actively market copies of the news programs does not matter, for Section 107 looks to the "potential market" in analyzing the effects of an alleged infringement. Copyrights protect owners who immediately market a work no more stringently than owners who delay before entering the market. TV News Clips sells a significant number of copies that WXIA could itself sell if it so desired; therefore, TV News Clips competes with WXIA in a potential market and thereby injures the television station. This evidence is reinforced by a presumption established in *Sony* that a commercial use naturally produces harmful effects. 104 S.Ct. at 793. The actual harmful effect, along with the presumption, undermines any fair use defense.

The third factor directs our attention to the amount and substantiality of the portion used in relation to the copyrighted work as a whole. The Floyd Junior College story stands alone as a coherent narrative, and WXIA saves it as a distinct unit for future reference apart from the rest of the March 11 broadcast. The Register of Copyrights issued a certificate of copyright for the Floyd Junior College segment and for the entire broadcast. Moreover, the district court found that WXIA had properly registered the story and the whole broadcast.[9] We agree with the district court that the feature stands alone as a copyrighted work in this case.[10] Hence, TV News Clips copied an entire work. And even if

9. TV News Clips contends that the district court erred in its finding that WXIA had properly registered the Floyd Junior College story because WXIA had deposited, pursuant to 17 U.S.C. § 408(b) (1977), the copy made by News Clips. This invalidated the registration, it argues, because the copy was not fixed "under authority of the author." It is true that a work must be fixed under authority of the author in order for the protections of copyright to take effect. 17 U.S.C. § 101 (1977). But the tape that "fixes" a broadcast need not be the same tape that is deposited for registration.

10. This case differs from Triangle Publications, Inc. v. Knight-Ridder Newspapers, Inc., supra, where the court held that the cover of a magazine was not a copyrighted work apart from the whole magazine. There was no evidence in that case that the cover had been registered apart

the story could not stand independent of the entire newscast, we could not ignore the fact that TV News Clips tapes virtually all of the broadcast on a daily basis. By bringing a suit for injunctive relief as well as damages, WXIA is challenging the entire practice of copying and selling news stories, not just the sale of the Floyd Junior College story.[11] Because TV News Clips uses virtually all of a copyrighted work, the fair use defense drifts even further out of its reach.

Finally, the second factor calls on us to analyze the nature of the copyrighted work. This is the only factor that arguably works in favor of TV News Clips. The importance to society of the news could affect the definition of a fair use for a number of reasons.[12] But the courts should also take care not to discourage authors from addressing important topics for fear of losing their copyright protections. The necessarily limited impact of this second factor, along with the commercial and unproductive purpose of the use, the injury to the potential market, and the substantial amount of copying, leads us to conclude that TV News Clips has not made fair use of the protected work.

*   *   *

[Part III of the opinion, rejecting defendant's First Amendment defense, is omitted.]

IV. Remedy

WXIA has proven that TV News Clips infringed its copyright. The district court found that TV News Clips had regularly copied the newscast and sold the tapes, and would continue to do so. Unless it can obtain an injunction, WXIA can only enforce its copyrights against TV News Clips by finding out which stories have been copied and sold, registering those stories, and bringing many different infringement actions against TV News Clips. Each infringement action would yield a rather small damage recovery. This is a classic case, then, of a past infringement and a substantial likelihood of future infringements which would normally entitle the copyright holder to a permanent injunction against the infringer pursuant to 17 U.S.C. § 502(a). The question is whether the district court abused its discretion in refusing

from the magazine or that they were stored or used separately.

11. In addition, we mention that a small portion of a work may be especially significant. The single story involving a particular subject is by far the most significant portion of the newscast for that potential customer.

12. The Supreme Court has mentioned that use of a news program may give rise to a fair use defense more easily than use of a full-length motion picture. Sony, supra, 104 S.Ct. at 795, n. 40. The Court does not fully explain this distinction, but the context sugests that the large secondary market for motion picture copies makes fair use less appropriate in that context. As discussion of the fourth factor revealed, significant commercial harm is present in this case. Another court found that the great public interest in the contents of a book (the memoirs of Gerald Ford) called for application of the fair use doctrine. Harper & Row, Publishers, Inc. v. National Enterprises, 723 F.2d 195 (2d Cir.1983). But the *Harper & Row* court also relied on other factors, particularly the fact that the alleged infringer used material from the book that was for the most part not copyrightable at all. Furthermore, the public interest in the average news story is far less than the interest in presidential memoirs.

to issue the injunction.[17]   Because none of the three grounds relied upon by the court for denying injunctive relief are legally sufficient to support the decision, we hold that the court did abuse its discretion.

The court began its discussion by noting that an injunction would not greatly further the ends of the copyright laws, because the post-broadcast market is relatively unimportant to WXIA as a creative incentive. We agree but find that fact standing alone to be irrelevant. The disincentive to creativity caused by the infringement would be just as small if WXIA were to wait and bring infringement actions in the future. The weakness of WXIA's interest in stopping this infringement has no bearing on the choice between present injunctive relief and future damage relief unless some independent consideration weighs against the use of an injunction in this case.

The "modest" furtherance of First Amendment rights accomplished by TV News Clips, the second ground relied upon by the court, does not provide any such independent reason to disfavor an injunction. It is undoubtedly true that TV News Clips (like any copyright infringer) increases public access to the copyrighted work. But the First Amendment issue of public access was duly considered when resolving the liability issue. If the First Amendment would not prevent WXIA from recovering for individual infringements in the future, it should not bar an injunction in the present. The scope of liability affects First Amendment interests, but the choice of the form of relief in this case does not.

Finally, the district court found injunctive relief inappropriate because WXIA regularly abandons the copyright on a portion of its program when it erases the videotape of the entire broadcast. Certainly the erasure shows that WXIA did not desire to distribute post-broadcast copies of parts of the program. Failure to distribute a work does not mean, however, that an owner intends to allow others to use the work, and it is questionable whether WXIA had such an intent. Destroying the only known copy of a work would seem to be the best way to assure that it will not be used by another. Still, we do not say

---

17. TV News Clips insists that WXIA is not legally entitled to an injunction, because it seeks an injunction against the infringement of works that have not been created (future newscasts) rather than an injunction applicable only to the March 11 program. The statute itself does not impose such a requirement, for it empowers district courts to issue injunctions "on such terms as it may deem reasonable to prevent or restrain infringement of a copyright." 17 U.S.C. § 502(a) (1977). The appellant bases its argument on the requirement that an author register a work before instituting an infringement action. 17 U.S.C. § 411 (1977). An injunction against the use of unregistered works would bypass this requirement.

The district court in this case had the power to issue such an injunction because the statute provides for injunctions to prevent infringement of "*a* copyright" (emphasis added), not necessarily the registered copyright that gave rise to the infringement action. The opposite result would be especially unjust in a case such as this one in which the registered work and the future works are so closely related, part of a series of original works created with predictable regularity and similar format and function. To refuse injunctive relief under these conditions would render meaningless the fact that registration is "not a condition of copyright protection." 17 U.S.C. § 408(a).

that destruction of the only copy of a work can never establish intent to abandon. We defer to the trial court's factual finding that WXIA intended to abandon portions of its program.

Nevertheless, WXIA erased only a small portion of its broadcast. The entire audiotape still survives, along with many portions of the videotape. The district court, while recognizing this fact, declined to issue an injunction against the use of segments of the news program not erased by WXIA. It said that "the precise wording of an appropriately limited decree is unapparent." The fact that a court must make some difficult judgments should not prevent it from effectuating established legal rights. Moreover, the clear-cut test used by the district court to find an intent to abandon the copyright (destruction of the only copy) should make the formulation of the decree more manageable.

Thus, the trial court relied on irrelevant and insufficient grounds in its refusal to grant injunctive relief. It correctly found that TV News Clips had infringed the copyright of WXIA but abused its discretion by refusing to grant injunctive relief. Accordingly, the judgment is affirmed in part, reversed in part, and remanded for further proceedings consistent with this opinion.

NOTES

1. If TV News Clips had been engaged in fair use, what legal uses could the purchaser make of recordings purchased from TV News Clips?

2. Can anyone make and keep copies of copyrighted newscasts and other informational television programming? Such programs contain a wealth of information about contemporary society, and could be a valuable resource for future historians. If the television stations themselves do not go to the time and trouble to preserve them, does that mean they are lost forever? Section 108(a) appears to authorize any qualifying library or archive to make one copy of television broadcasts as long as the "reproduction or distribution is made without any purpose of direct or indirect commercial advantage." Section 108(f) permits "reproduction and distribution by lending of a limited number of copies and excerpts by a library or archives of an audiovisual news program [but no other type of program]." Does limiting this activity to the noncommercial sector assure that there will be little of it? Is that a wise policy?

The American Television and Radio Archives Act, 5 U.S.C. § 170, authorizes the Librarian of Congress to establish an American Radio and Television Archive within the Library of Congress, to record newscasts off the air, and to distribute reproductions to libraries or archives which meet the requirements of § 108(a) "for use only in research and not for further reproduction or performance." Does that solve any problem?

3. The reliance by the district judge in *Pacific and Southern Co.* on the discretion of a court to refuse to issue an injunction has been an alternative theme in some fair use decisions. It was the principal ground of decision in Rosemont Enterprises v. Random House, 366 F.2d 303 (2d Cir.1966), noted supra page 729, where the court felt the injunction was sought not to further the purpose of the copyright laws (compensation for works of authorship) but to suppress information about Howard Hughes.

In [Judith Jacklin] Belushi v. [Bob] Woodward, 598 F.Supp. 36 (D.D.C.1984), the defendant had written *Wired: The Short Life & Fast Times of John Belushi.* The book contained numerous photographs, including one entitled "John and Nena" which plaintiff claimed belonged to her and had been used without permission. One hundred and seventy-five thousand copies of the book had been printed, of which 145,000 had been distributed to bookstores. Plaintiff sought a preliminary injunction against distribution of the 30,000 copies remaining in the publisher's possession. "Defendants assert that if relief issues their carefully orchestrated and costly plans for selling and marketing the book will be disrupted, costing them a substantial amount in lost sales. Defendants emphasize that successful marketing of a book like *Wired* depends upon the coordination of advertising, serialization, author appearances, and reviews, and the release to the public of the book." Injunction denied. "The public interest clearly favors maintaining the integrity of the copyright laws. In this case, however, it appears that legal remedies would vindicate any rights that may have been impinged [through the award of damages]. Further, there is a competing public interest in this case: the promotion of free expression and robust debate. If this were a case in which relief would enjoin the distribution of an average commercial product, relief would not be so drastic." 598 F.Supp. 37.

How is the court to compute damages? What is the value of a single picture which was by itself probably not necessary for the book and which would have limited alternative commercial uses? Or will the amount of the recovery be determined in part by the success of the book, so that a remedy which undermines its effective promotion harms both parties? Suppose the plaintiff had refused to license the use of the photo at any price? Same result?

4. In New York Times Co. v. Roxbury Data Interface, Inc., 434 F.Supp. 217 (D.N.J.1977), the defendant had published a name index to the annual index published by the New York Times. The defendants were publishing a multi-volume index of all names that appeared in any annual volume of the New York Times Index which listed them alphabetically and showed the volume and page of the plaintiff's index where the name appeared. The plaintiff argued that the defendants had copied the names and page numbers from its copyrighted index. The court denied a preliminary injunction on grounds of fair use. The court was influenced by the fact that the New York Times did not itself publish such an index and that the defendant's index would require the user to also use the plaintiff's index before he would be able to locate the item in the newspaper itself.

5. If the fact that the copyright owner does not itself exploit the copyright in the market being exploited by the defendant is a factor favoring fair use, what happens if the copyright owner subsequently decides to enter the defendant's market? Does the infringement then cease to be fair use? In National Business Lists, Inc. v. Dun & Bradstreet, Inc., 552 F.Supp. 89 (N.D.Ill.1982), Dun & Bradstreet did not at first object when National Business Lists began using information from Dun & Bradstreet directories to create a computerized data base that enabled it to produce mailing lists with particular characteristics—for instance, businesses of a certain size, or in certain product markets, or located in certain places. After National Business had developed this business, Dun & Bradstreet decided to itself enter the field of providing specialized mailing lists using its own information. The court held that because of National Business List's reliance on Dun & Bradstreet's failure to object, that Dun & Bradstreet

was estopped from using its copyright to stop the practice—even as to future editions of the Dun & Bradstreet Directories.

PROBLEMS

1. Can individuals who are interested in the TV news (or what the TV news is saying about them) make copies of newscasts on their own VCR's, and save them for review or a possible defamation suit?

2. If the answer to one is yes, can individuals hire a service like that of TV Clips to do the recording for them, with an advance understanding that a copy will be made available if the newscast is of interest to the subscribing client?

3. WXIA had the policy of not providing tapes to political candidates, see note 1 of the opinion. Could TV Clips provide its service to political candidates only?

EDUCATIONAL, ARCHIVAL AND NON–PROFIT USE

Does the fact that infringement is undertaken in support of a particularly worthy or useful activity excuse the infringement? As a general matter, the answer is no. Sponsors of a charity benefit cannot make use of the popular songs of the day without paying a license fee simply because the fee will decrease the net amount raised. The owners of copyright are not singled out to provide subsidies to worthy causes through limitations on their rights. But the statute does not adhere strictly to this principle. Buried within sections 108 through 118 are sometimes economically substantial benefits for particular "good" organizations (usually nonprofit or governmental). They are briefly summarized below. No doubt a good deal of legal effort goes into construing the exact limits of these privileges as various groups maneuver to get within them.

Section 108 limits its privileges for libraries and archives to "reproduction or distribution ∗ ∗ ∗ without any purpose of direct or indirect commercial advantage." The effect of this test is to limit these privileges for libraries maintained by for-profit, commercial organizations, or at least the House Report says that it is. See H.R. 94–1476, pp. 74–75.

Section 110 limits the exclusive rights of performance or display in a number of specific situations, many of which are defined in part by the character of the organization involved. Section 110(1) permits performance or display of works "by instructors or pupils in the course of face-to-face teaching activities of a nonprofit educational institution." Section 110(2) permits transmission of works into classrooms if "the performance or display is a regular part of the systematic instructional activities of a governmental body or a nonprofit educational institution." Section 110(3) permits performance or display in the course of religious services. Section 110(4) permits performance if there is no admission charge and the net proceeds "are used exclusively for educational, religious or charitable purposes," subject to the right of the copyright owner to object in advance. (There is no mechanism for ensuring that the copyright owner learns of the planned performance.) Section 110(6) confers limited protection on nonprofit agricultural or horticultural organizations in the course of annual fairs. Subsections (8) and (9) are designed to make specialized transmissions for the blind and deaf cheaper. Subsection (10) confers a special privilege upon nonprofit veterans' organizations or nonprofit fraternal organization where the net proceeds are for charitable purposes, with a more restrictive test applicable to college fraternities or sororities (lest every fraternity dance become an exempt occasion).

Section 111(4) confers a broad privilege of secondary transmission upon "a governmental body, or other nonprofit organization."

Section 114(b) protects public broadcasting entities who distribute educational television or radio programs from the copyright in the sound recording.

Section 118 confers upon public broadcasting stations the right to infringe copyrights, subject to the payment of royalties as determined by the Copyright Royalty Tribunal.

A major area of controversy during the consideration of the revision bill was the right of teachers to use copyrighted materials in the classroom. For instance a teacher might want to make copies of a poem for discussion in class, or to have the class perform a song in a school assembly. The wrath of the nation's teachers came down on the head of Congress when the National Education Association informed them that the new statute would make these practices infringement of copyright (failing to inform them that the existing statute already did. See Wihtol v. Crow, 309 F.2d 777 (8th Cir.1962), holding a music teacher liable for duplicating copies of his arrangement of a copyrighted song.) These concerns were addressed in guidelines, described as follows in House Report No. 94–1476.

HOUSE REPORT NO. 94–1476

Pages 68–72.

Intention as to Classroom Reproduction

Although the works and uses to which the doctrine of fair use is applicable are as broad as the copyright law itself, most of the discussion of section 107 has centered around questions of classroom reproduction, particularly photocopying. The arguments on the question are summarized at pp. 30–31 of this Committee's 1967 report (H.R.Rep. No. 83, 90th Cong., 1st Sess.), and have not changed materially in the intervening years.

The Committee also adheres to its earlier conclusion, that "a specific exemption freeing certain reproductions of copyrighted works for educational and scholarly purposes from copyright control is not justified." At the same time the Committee recognizes, as it did in 1967, that there is a "need for greater certainty and protection for teachers." In an effort to meet this need the Committee has not only adopted further amendments to section 107, but has also amended section 504(c) to provide innocent teachers and other non-profit users of copyrighted material with broad insulation against unwarranted liability for infringement. * * *

In a joint letter to Chairman Kastenmeier, dated March 19, 1976, the representatives of the Ad Hoc Committee of Educational Institutions and Organizations on Copyright Law Revision, and of the Authors League of America, Inc., and the Association of American Publishers, Inc., stated:

> You may remember that in our letter of March 8, 1976 we told you that the negotiating teams representing authors and publishers and the Ad Hoc Group had reached tentative agreement on guidelines to insert in the Committee Report covering educational copying from books and periodicals under Section 107 of H.R. 2223 and S. 22, and that as part of that tentative agreement each side would accept the amendments to Sections 107 and 504 which were adopted by your Subcommittee on March 3, 1976.
>
> We are now happy to tell you that the agreement has been approved by the principals and we enclose a copy herewith. We had originally intended to translate the agreement into language suitable for inclusion in the legislative report dealing with Section 107, but we have since been advised by committee staff that this will not be necessary.
>
> As stated above, the agreement refers only to copying from books and periodicals, and it is not intended to apply to musical or audiovisual works.

The full text of the agreement is as follows:

AGREEMENT ON GUIDELINES FOR CLASSROOM COPYING IN NOT-FOR-PROFIT EDUCATIONAL INSTITUTIONS

WITH RESPECT TO BOOKS AND PERIODICALS

The purpose of the following guidelines is to state the minimum standards of educational fair use under Section 107 of H.R. 2223. The parties agree that the conditions determining the extent of permissible copying for educational purposes may change in the future; that certain types of copying permitted under these guidelines may not be permissible in the future; and conversely that in the future other types of copying not permitted under these guidelines may be permissible under revised guidelines.

Moreover, the following statement of guidelines is not intended to limit the types of copying permitted under the standards of fair use under judicial decision and which are stated in Section 107 of the Copyright Revision Bill. There may be instances in which copying which does not fall within the guidelines stated below may nonetheless be permitted under the criteria of fair use.

GUIDELINES

I. *Single Copying for Teachers*

A single copy may be made of any of the following by or for a teacher at his or her individual request for his or her scholarly research or use in teaching or preparation to teach a class:

    A. A chapter from a book;

    B. An article from a periodical or newspaper;

    C. A short story, short essay or short poem, whether or not from a collective work;

    D. A chart, graph, diagram, drawing, cartoon or picture from a book, periodical, or newspaper.

II. *Multiple Copies for Classroom Use*

Multiple copies (not to exceed in any event more than one copy per pupil in a course) may be made by or for the teacher giving the course for classroom use or discussion; *provided that:*

    A. The copying meets the tests of brevity and spontaneity as defined below; *and,*

    B. Meets the cumulative effect test as defined below; *and,*

    C. Each copy includes a notice of copyright.

Definitions

Brevity

    (*i*) Poetry: (a) A complete poem if less than 250 words and if printed on not more than two pages or, (b) from a longer poem, an excerpt of not more than 250 words.

    (*ii*) Prose: (a) Either a complete article, story or essay of less than 2,500 words, or (b) an excerpt from any prose work of not more than 1,000 words or 10% of the work, whichever is less, but in any event a minimum of 500 words.

    [Each of the numerical limits stated in "i" and "ii" above may be expanded to permit the completion of an unfinished line of a poem or of an unfinished prose paragraph.]

    (*iii*) Illustration: One chart, graph, diagram, drawing, cartoon or picture per book or per periodical issue.

    (*iv*) "Special" works: Certain works in poetry, prose or in "poetry prose" which often combine language with illustrations and which are intended sometimes for children and at other times for a more general audience fall short of 2,500 words in their entirety. Paragraph "ii" above notwithstanding such "special works" may not be reproduced in their entirety; however, an excerpt comprising not more than two of the published pages of such special work and containing not more than 10% of the words found in the text thereof, may be reproduced.

Spontaneity

(*i*) The copying is at the instance and inspiration of the individual teacher, and

(*ii*) The inspiration and decision to use the work and the moment of its use for maximum teaching effectiveness are so close in time that it would be unreasonable to expect a timely reply to a request for permission.

Cumulative Effect

(*i*) The copying of the material is for only one course in the school in which the copies are made.

(*ii*) Not more than one short poem, article, story, essay or two excerpts may be copied from the same author, nor more than three from the same collective work or periodical volume during one class term.

(*iii*) There shall not be more than nine instances of such multiple copying for one course during one class term.

[The limitations stated in "ii" and "iii" above shall not apply to current news periodicals and newspapers and current news sections of other periodicals.]

III. *Prohibitions as to I and II Above*

Notwithstanding any of the above, the following shall be prohibited:

(A) Copying shall not be used to create or to replace or substitute for anthologies, compilations or collective works. Such replacement or substitution may occur whether copies of various works or excerpts therefrom are accumulated or reproduced and used separately.

(B) There shall be no copying of or from works intended to be "consumable" in the course of study or of teaching. These include workbooks, exercises, standardized tests and test booklets and answer sheets and like consumable material.

(C) Copying shall not:

(a) substitute for the purchase of books, publishers' reprints or periodicals;

(b) be directed by higher authority;

(c) be repeated with respect to the same item by the same teacher from term to term.

(D) No charge shall be made to the student beyond the actual cost of the photocopying.

Agreed March 19, 1976.

Ad Hoc Committee on Copyright Law Revision:

By SHELDON ELLIOTT STEINBACH.

Author-Publisher Group:

Authors League of America:

By IRWIN KARP, *Counsel.*

Association of American Publishers, Inc.:

By ALEXANDER C. HOFFMAN,

Chairman, Copyright Committee.

[The House Report then set out similar guidelines negotiated by interested organizations covering fair use of musical scores in an educational setting.]

* * *

The Committee appreciates and commends the efforts and the cooperative and reasonable spirit of the parties who achieved the agreed guidelines on books and periodicals and on music. Representatives of the American Association of University Professors and of the Association of American Law Schools have written to the Committee strongly criticizing the guidelines, particularly with respect to multiple copying, as being too restrictive with respect to classroom situations at the university and graduate level. However, the Committee notes that the Ad Hoc group did include representatives of higher education, that the stated "purpose of the * * * guidelines is to state the minimum and not the maximum standards of educational fair use" and that the agreement acknowledges "there may be instances in which copying which does not fall within the guidelines * * * may nonetheless be permitted under the criteria of fair use."

The Committee believes the guidelines are a reasonable interpretation of the minimum standards of fair use. Teachers [w]ill know that copying within the guidelines is fair use. Thus, the guidelines serve the purpose of fulfilling the need for greater certainty and protection for teachers. The Committee expresses the hope that if there are areas where standards other than these guidelines may be appropriate, the parties will continue their efforts to provide additional specific guidelines in the same spirit of good will and give and take that has marked the discussion of this subject in recent months.

* * *

MARCUS v. ROWLEY

United States Court of Appeals for the Ninth Circuit, 1983.
695 F.2d 1171.

PFAELZER, DISTRICT JUDGE:

This is an appeal from a dismissal on the merits of a suit for copyright infringement brought by a public school teacher who is the owner of a registered copyright to a booklet on cake decorating. The defendant, also a public school teacher, incorporated a substantial portion of the copyrighted work into a booklet which she prepared for use in her classes. Both parties moved the district court for summary judgment. The district court denied both motions and dismissed the action on the merits on the ground that defendant's copying of plaintiff's material constituted fair use. We reverse.

From September 1972 to June 1974, plaintiff, Eloise Toby Marcus was employed by the defendant, San Diego Unified School District ("District") as a teacher of home economics. Plaintiff resigned from the District's employ in 1974 and taught adult education classes intermittently from 1975 to 1980. Shortly after leaving her teaching position with the District, she wrote a booklet entitled "Cake Decorating Made Easy".

* * *

Plaintiff sold all but six of the copies of her booklet for $2.00 each to the students in the adult education cake decorating classes which she taught. Plaintiff's profit was $1.00 on the sale of each booklet. Copies of plaintiff's booklet were never distributed to or sold by a bookstore or other outlet. Plaintiff never authorized anyone to copy or reproduce her booklet or any part of it.

Defendant, Shirley Rowley ("Rowley"), teaches food service career classes in the District. In the spring of 1975, she enrolled in one of plaintiff's cake decorating classes and purchased a copy of plaintiff's book. During the following summer, Rowley prepared a booklet entitled "Cake Decorating Learning Activity Package" ("LAP") for use in her food service career classes. The LAP consisted of twenty-four pages and was designed to be used by students who wished to study an optional section of her course devoted to cake decorating. Defendant had fifteen copies of the LAP made and put them in a file so that they would be available to her students. She used the LAP during the 1975, 1976 and 1977 school years. The trial court found that sixty of Rowley's two hundred twenty-five students elected to study cake decorating. The trial court further found that neither Rowley nor the District derived any profit from the LAP.

Rowley admits copying eleven of the twenty-four pages in her LAP from plaintiff's booklet. The eleven pages copied consisted of the supply list, icing recipes, three sheets dealing with color flow and mixing colors, four pages showing how to make and use a decorating bag, and two pages explaining how to make flowers and sugar molds.

* * *. Rowley did not give plaintiff credit for the eleven pages she copied, nor did she acknowledge plaintiff as the owner of a copyright with respect to those pages.

Plaintiff learned of Rowley's LAP in the summer of 1977 when a student in plaintiff's adult education class refused to purchase plaintiff's book. The student's son had obtained a copy of the LAP from Rowley's class. After examining Rowley's booklet, the student accused plaintiff of plagiarizing Rowley's work. Following these events, plaintiff made a claim of infringement against Rowley and the District. Both denied infringement and the plaintiff filed suit.

The parties filed cross-motions for summary judgment. The trial court denied both motions for summary judgment and dismissed the case on the merits. The ground for dismissal was that the defendant's copying of the plaintiff's material for nonprofit educational purposes constituted fair use.

* * *

The first factor to be considered in determining the applicability of the doctrine of fair use is the purpose and character of the use, and specifically whether the use is of a commercial nature or is for a nonprofit educational purpose. It is uncontroverted that Rowley's use of the LAP was for a nonprofit educational purpose and that the LAP was distributed to students at no charge. These facts necessarily weigh in Rowley's favor. Nevertheless, a finding of a nonprofit educational purpose does not automatically compel a finding of fair use.[5]

This court has often articulated the principle that a finding that the alleged infringers copied the material to use it for the same intrinsic purpose for which the copyright owner intended it to be used is strong indicia of no fair use. Jartech, Inc. v. Clancy, 666 F.2d 403 (1982); Universal City Studios, Inc. v. Sony Corp., 659 F.2d 963 at 969. See also Iowa State University v. American Broadcasting Cos., 621 F.2d

---

5. In MacMillan v. King, 223 F. 862 (D.Mass.1914), the district court was presented with the question of fair use in an educational setting. In that case, plaintiff, a teacher of economics at Harvard University, had written a textbook entitled "Principles of Economics" for use in university economics courses.

The defendant acted as a private tutor of a variety of subjects, including economics. Some of the defendant's students were using the plaintiff's textbook in their economics class and sought tutoring from the defendant in that course. In preparation for the tutoring sessions, defendant prepared a typewritten outline of the week's lessons. The outline was written to mirror the organization of plaintiff's textbook and often contained quotations from the textbook. None of the outlines were ever sold and the defendant claimed that the fee charged for the tutoring sessions was the same whether or not an outline was prepared for the session. The court found that plaintiff's copyright had been infringed due to "an appropriation [by the defendant] of the author's ideas and language more extensive than the copyright law permits." Id. at 866. With respect to the argument that the copying was permissible because it was done in furtherance of educational pursuits, the court stated:

If the above conclusions are right, I am unable to believe that the defendant's use of the outlines is any the less infringement of the copyright because he is a teacher, because he uses them in teaching the contents of the book, because he might lecture upon the contents of the book without infringing, or because his pupils might have taken their own notes of his lectures without infringing.

Id. at 867.

57 (the scope of fair use is constricted when the original and the copy serve the same function).

This same function test is addressed in the House of Representatives' 1967 Report, specifically in relation to classroom materials. The Report states that, with respect to the fair use doctrine, "[t]extbooks and other material prepared primarily for the school market would be less susceptible to reproduction for classroom use than material prepared for general public distribution." H.R.Rep. (1967) at 34.

In this case, both plaintiff's and defendant's booklets were prepared for the purpose of teaching cake decorating, a fact which weighs against a finding of fair use.[6]

Because fair use presupposes that the defendant has acted fairly and in good faith, the propriety of the defendant's conduct should also be weighed in analyzing the purpose and character of the use. See 3 Nimmer, supra, § 13.05[A][1] at 13–61.

Here, there was no attempt by defendant to secure plaintiff's permission to copy the contents of her booklet or to credit plaintiff for the use of her material even though Rowley's copying was for the most part verbatim.[8] Rowley's conduct in this respect weighs against a finding of fair use.

*   *   *

[Another] *   *   * factor to be considered is the amount and substantiality of the portion used in relation to the copyrighted work as a whole.   *   *   *

With respect to this factor, this court has long maintained the view that wholesale copying of copyrighted material precludes application of the fair use doctrine. Benny v. Loew's, Inc., 239 F.2d 532 (9th Cir.1956), aff'd by an equally divided Court sub nom. Columbia Broadcasting System v. Loew's, Inc., 356 U.S. 43 (1958). See also Walt Disney Productions v. Air Pirates, 581 F.2d 751 at 758, and Universal City Studios, Inc. v. Sony Corp., 659 F.2d 963 at 973. Other courts are in accord with this principle, and two courts have specifically addressed the issue in relation to copying for educational purposes.

Wihtol v. Crow, 309 F.2d 777 (8th Cir.1962), involved alleged infringement by the defendant, a school teacher and church choir director, of a hymn entitled "My God and I". The defendant Crow incorporated plaintiff's original piano and solo voice composition into an arrangement for his choirs. He made forty-eight copies of his arrangement and had the piece performed on two occasions: once by the high school choir at the school chapel, and once in church on Sunday. The music was identified as "arranged Nelson E. Crow", but

---

6. Of course, this finding is not decisive on the issue of fair use. The fact that both works were used for the same intrinsic purpose carries less weight in a case such as this, because plainly the doctrine of fair use permits some copying of educational materials for classroom use. The critical issues here are the nature and the extent of defendant's copying.

8. Attribution is, of course, but one factor. Moreover, acknowledgement of a source does not excuse infringement when the other factors listed in section 107 are present. *   *   *

no reference was made to plaintiff as the original composer. The Eighth Circuit affirmed the trial court's finding that Crow had infringed plaintiff's copyright and in addressing the issue of whether Crow's copying constituted fair use, the court stated that "[w]hatever may be the breadth of the doctrine of 'fair use', it is not conceivable to us that the copying of all, or substantially all, of a copyrighted song can be held to be a 'fair use' merely because the infringer had no intent to infringe." Id. at 780.

The court in Encyclopaedia Britannica Educational Corp. v. Crooks, 447 F.Supp. 243 (W.D.N.Y.1978), also considered the issue of fair use in the educational context. In that case, three corporations which produced educational motion picture films sued the Board of Cooperative Educational Services of Erie County ("BOCES") for videotaping several of plaintiffs' copyrighted films without permission. BOCES distributed the copied films to schools for delayed student viewing. Defendants' fair use defense was rejected on the ground that although defendants were involved in noncommercial copying to promote science and education, the taping of entire copyrighted films was too excessive for the fair use defense to apply. Id. at 251.[9] * * *

In this case, almost 50% of defendant's LAP was a verbatim copy of plaintiff's booklet and that 50% contained virtually all of the substance of defendant's book. Defendant copied the explanations of how to make the decorating bag, how to mix colors, and how to make various decorations as well as the icing recipes. In fact, the only substantive pages of plaintiff's booklet which defendant did not put into her booklet were hints on how to ice a cake and an explanation of how to make leaves. Defendant argues that it was fair to copy plaintiff's booklet because the booklet contained only facts which were in the public domain. Even if it were true that plaintiff's book contained only facts, this argument fails because defendant engaged in virtually verbatim copying. Defendant's LAP could have been a photocopy of plaintiff's booklet but for the fact that defendant retyped plaintiff's material. This case presents a clear example of both substantial quantitative and qualitative copying.

* * *

The final factor to be considered with respect to the fair use defense is the effect which the allegedly infringing use had on the potential market for or value of the copyrighted work. The 1967 House Report points out that this factor is often seen as the most important criterion of fair use, but also warned that it "must almost always be judged in conjunction with the other three criteria." H.R.Rep. (1967) at 35. The Report explains that "a use which supplants any part of the normal market for a copyrighted work would ordinarily be considered an infringement." Id. Here, despite the fact that at least one of

9. Contra, Williams & Wilkins Co. v. United States, 487 F.2d 1345, 1352, 1354 (Ct.Cl.1973), aff'd, 420 U.S. 376 (1975) (the existence of verbatim copying was not dispositive when the conduct encouraged scientific progress and did not cause plaintiff substantial monetary harm).

plaintiff's students refused to purchase her booklet as a result of defendant's copying, the trial court found that it was unable to conclude that the defendant's copying had any effect on the market for the plaintiff's booklet. Even assuming that the trial court's finding was not erroneous, and that that finding must be accepted and weighed in Rowley's favor, Sid & Marty Krofft Television Productions, Inc. v. McDonald's Corp., 562 F.2d 1157, 1166 (9th Cir.1977), it does not alter our conclusion. The mere absence of measurable pecuniary damage does not require a finding of fair use. Universal City Studios, Inc. v. Sony Corp., 659 F.2d 963 at 974. Fair use is to be determined by a consideration of all of the evidence in the case. Mathews Conveyor Co. v. Palmer-Bee Co., 135 F.2d 73, 85 (6th Cir.1943). Thus, despite the trial court's finding, we conclude that the factors analyzed weigh decisively in favor of the conclusion of no fair use. This conclusion is in harmony with the Congressional guidelines which, as a final point, also merit consideration with respect to the issue of fair use in an educational context.

* * *

The question of how much copying for classroom use is permissible was of such major concern to Congress that, although it did not include a section on the subject in the revised Act, it approved a set of guidelines with respect to it. The guidelines represent the Congressional Committees' view of what constitutes fair use under the traditional judicial doctrine developed in the case law. Conf.Rep. No. 1733, 94th Cong., 2d Sess. 70, reprinted in 1976 U.S.Cong. & Ad.News 5810, 5811. The guidelines were designed to give teachers direction as to the extent of permissible copying and to eliminate some of the doubt which had previously existed in this area of the copyright laws. The guidelines were intended to represent minimum standards of fair use. 3 Nimmer, supra, § 13.05[E][3] at 13–75. Thus, while they are not controlling on the court, they are instructive on the issue of fair use in the context of this case.

The guidelines relating to multiple copies for classroom use indicate that such copying is permissible if three tests are met. First, the copying must meet the test of "brevity" and "spontaniety." "Brevity" is defined, for prose, as "[e]ither a complete article, story or essay of less than 2,500 words, or an excerpt from any prose work of not more than 1,000 words or * * * 10% of the work, whichever is less * * *." H.R.Rep. (1976) at 68, U.S.Code Cong. & Admin.News 1976, p. 5682. Rowley's copying would not be permissible under either of these tests.

The guidelines also provide a separate definition of "brevity" for "special works." "Special works" are works "which often combine language with illustrations and which are intended sometimes for children and at other times for a more general audience." Id. at 69. Plaintiff's booklet arguably would fall into this category. The guidelines provide that, notwithstanding the guidelines for prose, " 'special works' may not be reproduced in their entirety; however, an excerpt comprising not more than two of the published pages of such special work and containing not more than 10% of the words found in the text thereof, may be reproduced." Id. Rowley's copying would not be permissible under this test.

Under the guidelines, "spontaneity" requires that "[t]he copying is at the instance and inspiration of the individual teacher, and * * * [t]he inspiration and decision to use the work and the moment of its use for maximum teaching effectiveness are so close in time that it would be unreasonable to expect a timely reply to a request for permission." Id. Defendant compiled her LAP during the summer of 1975 and first used it in her classes during the 1975–76 school year. She also used the LAP for the following two school years. Rowley's copying would not meet this requirement either.

The second test under the guidelines is that of "cumulative effect". Id. This test requires that the copied material be for only one course in the school. This aspect of the test would probably be met on these facts. The test also limits the number of pieces which may be copied from the same author and the number of times a teacher may make multiple copies for one course during one term. These latter two tests also appear to be met. The facts indicate that defendant copied only one piece of plaintiff's work. Defendant's conduct, therefore, would satisfy the second test under the guidelines.

The third test requires that each copy include a notice of copyright. As stated, defendant's LAP did not acknowledge plaintiff's authorship or copyright and therefore would not meet this test.

In conclusion, it appears that Rowley's copying would not qualify as fair use under the guidelines.

We conclude that the fair use doctrine does not apply to these facts as that doctrine has been articulated in the common law, in section 107 of the revised Copyright Act, or in the special guidelines approved by Congress for nonprofit educational institutions. Rowley's LAP work, which was used for the same purpose as plaintiff's booklet, was quantitatively and qualitatively a substantial copy of plaintiff's booklet with no credit given to plaintiff. Under these circumstances, neither the fact that the defendant used the plaintiff's booklet for nonprofit educational purposes nor the fact that plaintiff suffered no pecuniary damage as a result of Rowley's copying supports a finding of fair use.

The order of the district court is reversed, summary judgment is entered for the plaintiff, and the case is remanded for a determination of damages pursuant to the provisions of the Copyright Act.

Reversed and remanded.

NOTE

The opinion in Encyclopaedia Britannica Educational Corp. v. Crooks, 447 F.Supp. 243 (W.D.N.Y.1978), cited in the *Marcus* case, rejected the fair use defense in the context of a motion for a preliminary injunction, which was granted. Final judgment against the defendants was entered in 1982. 542

F.Supp. 1156 (W.D.N.Y.1982). The defendant in that case made recordings of off-the-air broadcasts of educational programs and permanently retained them for use by the area school systems. Under § 118(d)(3) the defendant (a government body) could make such recordings, but they have to be used within seven days and destroyed at the end of that period.

(3) FAIR USE AND THE BURDEN OF PERSUASION

None of the case law developed under the fair use doctrine has addressed the issue of the burden of proof, which is of central importance given the ambiguities of the doctrine. Indeed, since issues of burden are the first thing a trained lawyer thinks of when confronted by a difficult issue, the failure of the Supreme Court to address it seems purposeful. One possibility is that the issue was not briefed, and in the absence of briefing the Court was reluctant to address the subject. There are two issues: (1) Who has the burden of proof once the plaintiff has shown an invasion of the exclusive right conferred by § 106? And second, is the burden of proving fair use affected by whether or not the challenged conduct is similar to any of the conduct protected by §§ 108 to 120? In other words do §§ 108 thru 120 simply create safe harbors for conduct that may otherwise be (or not be) fair use, or are they designed to create precise limits on what is permitted?

At first glance, the answer to the first question might seem to be that all of the sections following § 106 provide defenses, and that therefore it is part of the plaintiff's burden to prove only a violation of § 106, and then it is the defendant's burden to prove the applicability of one of the defenses.

However, the text of the statute suggests that sections 106 thru 120 are to be construed as an integral whole, which together define the scope of the exclusive right conferred by copyright. Section 106 begins: "Subject to sections 107 through 120." And many of those sections begin: "Notwithstanding the provisions of section 106." H.R.Rep. 1476 says: "The approach of the bill is to set forth the copyright owner's exclusive rights *in broad terms* in section 106, and then to provide various *limitations, qualifications, or exemptions* in the 12 sections [sections 119 and 120 were added later] that follow." Id. at 61 [emphasis added]. This is not the same as saying that § 106 sets out the copyright owner's rights, and the subsequent sections set out defenses.

In the *Sony* case the court asserts, without explanation, that "A challenge to a noncommercial use of copyrighted work requires proof either that the particular use is harmful, or that if it should become widespread, it would adversely affect the potential market for the copyrighted work. . . . What is necessary is a showing by a preponderance of the evidence that *some* meaningful likelihood of future harm exists. If the intended use is for commercial gain, that likelihood may be presumed. But if it is for a noncommercial purpose, the likelihood must be demonstrated." Supra, pp. 701–702. How these burdens are determined by the Court is not explained.

The argument that conduct falling close to but not within one of the provisions of §§ 108 to 120 should be presumed not to be fair use is that Congress having explicitly drawn a line, that line should not be blurred through interpretation of § 107. For instance § 110(3) provides that "performance of a nondramatic literary or musical work or of a dramatico-musical work of a religious nature, or display of a work, in the course of services at a place of worship or other religious assembly" is not infringement. This provision does not provide that performance of a dramatic literary work in the course of a religious service is not infringement. Should a court be open to the suggestion that such a performance might be fair use? Or should a court conclude that since Congress carefully drew a line between nondramatic and dramatic literary works, it surely was the Congressional intent that a performance of a dramatic literary work in a religious service should never be fair use?

Such a construction places heavy weight on the lines drawn in §§ 108 thru 120. It would be one thing to construe these as safe harbors, which clearly permit the conduct described, and perhaps illustrate kinds of unlicensed uses Congress thought proper. It is another thing to read them as prohibiting by negative implication the conduct not permitted. This is in part because these sections reflected more pervasively than any other part of the act the implementation of arbitrary compromises between private interests described at length in Jessica Litman, Copyright, Compromise, and Legislative History, 72 Cornell Law Review 857 (1987) and Jessica Litman, Copyright Legislation and Technological Change, 68 Oregon Law Review 275 (1989). Just inspect the odd lines drawn in these sections. To go beyond treating these compromises as safe harbors, and read in a negative implication from their provisions is to give them more weight than they will bear.

Section 107 is the one section that permits the courts to apply a rule of reason that can arbitrate between the broad and abstract rights conferred by § 106 and the narrow and arbitrary exemptions conferred by §§ 108 thru 120. The broad concepts of 106 reach conduct surely unforeseen and unforeseeable by the Congress. Sections 108 thru 120 reach out to protect narrowly described situations brought to Congressional attention by those active in the lobbying process. Only section 107 provides the courts with a rule of reason that can be used by the courts to do justice in the particular case, and to construe the statute in a fair and reasonable manner as applied to the myriad of unforseen situations that will arise. Section 107 cannot play this role if its availability is virtually foreclosed by the assignment of the burden of proof.

D. OWNERSHIP OF COPYRIGHT

1. *The Author as Initial Owner.* "Copyright in a work protected under this title vests initially in the author or authors of the work." 17

U.S.C. § 201(a).　Who, then is the "author"?　The term is not further defined in the statute.　However authorship is an idea central to the subject of copyrightable subject matter, supra pp. 598–613, because a work must be the work of an author to be copyrightable.　17 U.S.C. § 102(a).　That law incorporates an expansive and undemanding test of authorship: finding almost any "work" copyrightable if it incorporates a minimal creative contribution.

It can be argued that the definition of author for purposes of assigning ownership should be more focused and demanding than the definition used for determining whether there is any element of copyrightable subject matter in a work.　For purposes of identifying the owner of the copyright, the law of copyrightable subject matter suggests that works may have impracticably many authors.　The writer of a novel is an author.　But what about the book editor, the book publisher, or the book designer, each of whom make some contribution to the final "work"?　What about the author's friends, from whom he may borrow ideas and suggestions?　Are all these persons authors of the finished work, and is it necessary to trace the chain of title to all of them?　And if a book, often the work of a single, identifiable writer, may present difficulties, what about works such as movies and television programs, which may involve the coordinated efforts of hundreds of people?　The cases, without evidencing much thought about the problem, point in the direction of equating the minimal test of authorship used under § 102(b) with the test required to determine who owns the copyright under § 201.

These problems can all be dealt with by agreements that transfer any resulting copyright to the intended person or entity, and it is an important function of a lawyer to review the contracts in connection with a project leading to the production of copyrightable material to ensure that the property rights end up where the parties to the transaction intend them to be.　The catch is that the intent of the parties alone will not control.　A transfer of copyright must be in writing.　An oral or implied term is not sufficient.　"A tranfer of copyright ownership . . . is not valid unless an instrument of conveyance, or a note or memorandum of the transfer, is in writing and signed by the owner of the rights conveyed or such owner's duly authorized agent."　17 U.S.C. § 204(a).

The ownership of the copyright is also important to buyers of copyrightable works.　It is widely understood that the person who buys a copy of a book gets only the right to read, possess and resell the single copy purchased.　But it is probably not so widely understood that a person who pays millions of dollars for an original painting or sculpture may be buying only the painting, not the right to prevent [or authorize] the reproduction and sale of copies of the painting.　Or that a person who pays millions for a computer system (or for any of the many machines which include specialized computer sub-systems) containing extensive copyrighted software may not acquire the right to use all the features of the software.　Just as a buyer may want to be assured of good title in the object, he or she may also want rights in relation to the copyright.

The complexity presented by the possibility of multiple authors of a work is ameliorated by the concept of works made for hire. "In the case of a work made for hire, the employer or other person for whom the work is prepared is considered the author . . . and, unless the parties have expressly agreed otherwise in a written instrument signed by them, owns all of the rights comprised in the copyright." 17 U.S.C. § 201(b). If all the persons who contribute to a work and thus are possible authors are employees of the same entity, then there is only one author, the employer, and there is no need for any further agreement about who owns the copyright.

As a general rule, the statute does not permit the parties to make a work into a "work made for hire" by agreement. A work made for hire is defined as "a work prepared by an employee within the scope of his or her employment," 17 U.S.C. § 101, "work made for hire" (1), and this is interpreted to mean a person who is in a common law employment relationship. Community for Creative Non-Violence v. Reid, 490 U.S. 730 (1989).

There is an exception to this rule for a curious list of works. "[A] work specially ordered or commissioned for use as a contribution to a collective work, as a part of a motion picture or other audiovisual work, as a translation, as a supplementary work, as a compilation, as an instructional text, as a test, as answer material for a test, or as an atlas." 17 U.S.C. § 101, "work made for hire" (2). In the case of these works, "if the parties expressly agree in a written instrument signed by them that the work shall be considered a work made for hire," then the work is a work made for hire. The reasons for this exception cannot be understood until we get to the subject of renewal and termination rights, infra pp. 770–774, but the exception makes it clear that unless a work falls within this list, the issue of whether or not a work is made for hire is not to be answered by what the parties in their agreements said it was.

The registration procedure under the statute can work to foreclose subsequent issues about authorship status. The application for registration must include "the name and nationality or domicile of the author or authors," 17 U.S.C. § 409. This information is contained in the certificate of registration, 17 U.S.C. § 410(a), and "[i]n any judicial proceedings the certificate of a registration . . . shall constitute prima facie evidence . . . of the facts stated in the certificate." 17 U.S.C. § 410(c). A claim of authorship status made long after a work has been published and registered by others is unlikely to fare well against this presumption.

If a work is "prepared by two or more authors with the intention that their contributions be merged into inseparable or interdependent parts of a unitary whole," 17 U.S.C. § 101, then the work is defined as a joint work, and the joint authors are coowners of the copyright in the work.   17 U.S.C. § 201(a).

One purpose of the definition of joint works in the 1976 Act was to narrow the application of the concept to situations where there was a pre-existing plan to create a single work.   For instance, if a lyricist and a composer collaborate in writing a song, they create a single joint work.   However, if the composer first writes the music, and then a lyricist, hearing the tune, writs lyrics for it, each is an author of separate copyrightable works—the composer of the music and the lyricist of the lyrics.*   This is not simply a difference of terminology. In the case of the joint work, each author as a coowner has the right to perform or reproduce the song or authorize others to do so (although he or she must account for a share of the profits to the coowner), while if there are two separate works no one—neither the authors nor any third party—can perform or reproduce the music and the lyrics without permission from both authors.   In the joint work situation there is the possibility of multiple coowners, each with the right to exploit all rights in the work in competition with the other coowners.   In the multiple copyrightable works situation, there is the possibility of overlapping rights, none of which can be exploited without the consent of all.   Both the coownership and multiple separate rights situations can present difficulties in the absence of either a willingness of the multiple authors to cooperate or some binding agreement that assigns to some person or entity the ability to manage the exploitation of the work.

The difficulties that can arise for multiple authors in the absence of careful legal planning are illustrated by the facts of Community for Creative Non-Violence v. Reid, 490 U.S. 730 (1989).   The Community for Creative Non-Violence (CCNV) is a nonprofit unincorporated association dedicated to eliminating homelessness in America, and Mitch Snyder was a member and trustee of CCNV.   In the fall of 1985 CCNV decided to participate in the annual Christmastime Pageant of Peace in Washington, D.C., by sponsoring a display to dramatize the plight of the homeless.

Snyder and fellow CCNV members conceived of a display: a sculpture of a modern Nativity scene in which, in lieu of the traditional Holy Family, the two adult figures and the infant would appear as contemporary homeless people huddled on a streetside steam grate.   The figures were to be life-sized, and the steam grate would be positioned atop a platform pedestal, or base within which special-effects equipment would be enclosed to emit simulated steam through the grate to swirl about the figures.   They also settled upon a title for the work—"Third World America"—and a legend for the pedestal: "and still there is no room at the inn."

---

* This was the situation in Shapiro, Bernstein & Co. v. Jerry Vogel Music Co., 221 F.2d 569, on reh'g 223 F.2d 252 (2d Cir. 1955) (known as the "Twelfth Street Rag case"), which held that the resulting song was a joint work.   The decision was much criticized, and the definition in the 1976 Act was intended to reverse the result of this case.   Among other things, it meant that two authors who had never worked together became coowners of a single work.

The project thus conceived, Snyder undertook to locate a local artist to produce the sculpture. He found James Earl Reid, a professional sculptor. In the course of two telephone calls, Reid agreed to sculpt the three human figures in a non-durable synthetic material. CCNV agreed to obtain the steam grate and pedestal for the statue. Reid agreed to donate his services and charge $15,000 for materials.

Reid and CCNV members collaborated on details of the sculpture—the choice of models, their position in relation to the steam grate, the use of a shopping cart. The statue was completed by Reid, delivered to Washington and there joined with the steam grate and pedestal. CCNV paid Reid the $15,000. The display was apparently a success.

The parties then fell into a dispute over the ownership of the copyright in the statue, something they had never discussed. Snyder saw further fundraising possibilities for the sculpture, and began planning for a national tour. Reid, happy enough to donate his labor for the Christmas display, did not want to donate the copyright. He urged that the statue be cast in bronze or that a master mold be created from which multiple copies could be made. Perhaps Reid now foresaw that the statue might become famous. If CCNV had the copyright, he would be unable to make any further copies.

At this point the rights of the parties might seem easy enough to figure out. Since CCNV had purchased the statue, it owned the material object and was entitled to publicly display it, 17 U.S.C. § 109(c). Reid, the sculptor, was the author of a copyrightable work, and since there had been no transfer of the ownership of the copyright, he still owned the copyright, and could stop CCNV from making any copy of the work. For instance, CCNV would have the right to conduct a national tour of the sculpture in which it would be publicly displayed, but Reid could stop CCNV from selling souvenir copies of the statue.

CCNV sued Reid for a declaration that it owned the statue and the copyright. The District Court decided for CCNV on the ground that CCNV had commissioned the statue and that the intent of the parties was that CCNV should own it and the copyright. To reach this result, the court relied on cases under the 1909 Act which had held that commissioned works were works made for hire, and which had been followed in some circuits under the 1976 Act. On this point the Court of Appeals reversed, Community for Creative Non-Violence v. Reid, 846 F.2d 1485 (D.C.Cir.1988), relying on the definition of works made for hire in § 101. The court of appeals was affirmed by the Supreme Court. Since Reid was not an employee of CCNV, but an independent contractor, the statue was not a work made for hire. Since Reid had not executed a writing transferring the copyright to CCNV, he still owned it. Reid's copyright troubles, however, were not over.

The Court of Appeals remanded the case to the District Court to consider whether the statue was a joint work, consisting of the pedestal, the steam grate, and the sculpted figures contributed by Reid. Not only did the Court of Appeals suggest that Reid and CCNV might be "joint authors," but raised the possibility that the cabinet maker who constructed the base and various persons who assisted Reid might also be joint authors, thus firmly embracing an approach to authorship under 17 U.S.C. § 201 which tracks the cases under 17 U.S.C. § 102 and opening wide the specter of multiple authorship problems in many situations. The court instructed the district court to determine if there were other parties who might be joint authors who should be joined in the action. The Supreme Court affirmed this aspect of the Court of Appeals decision in a single sentence, 490 U.S. at 753, 109 S.Ct. at 2180.

2. *Right of Termination and Renewal.* The ownership of copyright is complicated by the fact that the statute attempts to retain for the benefit of the author and his family an interest in roughly the last half of the copyright term. This objective adds considerable technical complexity to issues of ownership. The idea is implemented differently under the 1976 Act than it was under the 1909 Act. As to some works whose term extends across the effective date of the 1976 Act, the 1976 Act makes both the 1909 and the 1976 structures applicable. §§ 303, 304. These transition provisions (transition only in the sense that they will eventually fade away—they will matter until 2005) will not be further discussed here.

The basic problem which the statute attempts to address can be illustrated as follows. A young, unknown and struggling writer sells the copyright in a manuscript for a pittance. Years later, the manuscript turns out to be a famous and still popular book. The publisher gets rich, the writer (now, perhaps, old, infirm and penniless) gets nothing. There is no relief for the author, except for what under the 1909 act was a provision for a renewal term, and under the 1976 act is a provision for a termination right. Under these provisions, our penniless writer may get the copyright back, and can negotiate a new license reflecting the fame and success of the work.

The number of authors whose works retain commercial value long enough to make these provisions economically significant is very small. The appeal of the destitute but successful artist has nevertheless been thought by Congress to justify introducing substantial complexity into the statutory scheme.

Under the 1909 Act the copyright term of 56 years from publication consisted of two separate 28 year terms. (This two term structure actually goes back to the Statute of Anne, which in 1709 provided for two fourteen year terms.) The first term belonged to the author. The second term belonged to the author if he was then living, and if not to "the widow, widower, or children of the author," or if such author, widow, widower or children be not living, "then the author's executors, or in the absence of a will, his next of kin." 1909 Copyright Act § 24. The second term was obtained only if the eligible person made an application for renewal in the twenty-seventh year of the copyright. In the case of the many works for which no renewal was filed, they entered the public domain at the end of the twenty-eighth year.

The Supreme Court held that the author's contingent interest in the second term was fully assignable. Fred Fisher Music Co. v. M. Witmark & Sons, 318 U.S. 643 (1943) (involving the copyright for "When Irish Eyes are Smiling.") In the Court's view, the statute gave the author the ability not to assign the renewal term if he chose not to do so, but did not invalidate an otherwise valid assignment. So if publishers and others made it a standard provision of their contracts (which they did) that the author assigned both terms, then the publisher had both terms if the author was living in the twenty-seventh year. However, the author's assignment of his or her interest in the second term, would not include his wife's, or his children's, etc. Thus if the author had signed a contract which included the second term, but was still living in the twenty-seventh year, neither he or his family would get any benefit from the second term. If, however, he had died, and the statutory owner of the renewal term (most typically the widow or widower and children) filed for the renewal term, they could assert copyright free of any agreement signed by the author. This led to the rather odd result that the author would benefit from the renewal term only if dead.

The 1976 Act created a new scheme designed to protect the author in every case. "A provision of this sort is needed because of the unequal bargaining position of authors, resulting in part from the impossibility of determining a work's value until it has been exploited." H.R.Rep. No. 1476, p. 124. The term was made a single term, eliminating the need for a renewal application. But transfers made by the author were made subject to a termination right that can be exercised in every case by the author, or if the author is deceased, by the widow, widower, children and children of deceased children, in the five year period beginning at the end of the thirty-fifth year. If the author exercised the right to terminate, any prior "exclusive or nonexclusive grant of a transfer or license of copyright or of any right under a copyright, executed by the author on or after January 1, 1978, otherwise than by will," § 203(a), is set aside and "all rights under this title that were covered by the terminated grants revert to the author" or the persons owning the termination interest. § 203(b). Section 203 sets out the procedures for exercising the termination interest, which include an advance notice in writing which must be served not less than two or more than ten years before the date of the proposed termination. "Termination of the grant may be effected notwithstanding any agreement to the contrary, including an agreement to make a will or to make any future grant." § 203(a)(5).

One problem that had arisen under the renewal mechanism of the 1909 Act was the impact of the renewal term on derivative works. Suppose the author of a novel had granted movie rights. If the author of the novel was deceased in the twenty-seventh year, the renewal term would pass to the widow and children, who would be in a position to block any further showing of the movie. For an example of the problems that could arise, see G. Ricordi & Co. v. Paramount Pictures, 189 F.2d 469 (2d Cir.1951), involving the ownership of the movie rights to the opera *Madam Butterfly* in light of the copyrights in the separately authored novel, play, and opera.

To ameliorate these problems, the statute provides an exception from the termination right for derivative works. Section 203(b) provides that "A derivative work prepared under authority of the grant before its termination may continue to be utilized under the terms of the grant after termination, but this privilege does not extend to the preparation after the termination of other derivative works based upon the copyrighted work covered by the terminated grant."

Although the termination provisions are conceived of as protecting authors, they have the fault of all paternal legislation: they actually reduce the author's rights. The author cannot give up the right of termination even if he or she wants to do so. The practical importance of the right of termination, however, is rduced by the fact that as to all transfers other than transfers including the right of publication, the right of termination begins thirty-five years after the date of the *grant.* This means that if the licensee gets a new grant every few years (perhaps in connection with promises to further promote or exploit the work) the time period starts over again. But suppose an author's work was published thirty years ago, and the work has fallen into obscurity. The author now wants to get a publisher to put out a new edition. Maybe he is willing to negotiate a more favorable contract with the original publisher, or to accept a reassignment of the copyright and approach another publisher. How can he induce any publisher to publish the book if the contract will be subject to termination in five years?

3. *Works Made for Hire and Renewal and the Right of Termination.* Both the renewal term under the 1909 Act and the right of termination under the 1976 Act do not extend to a "work made for hire." Under the 1909 Act, works made for hire had a single 56 year term. Under the 1976 Act, there is no right of termination in works made for hire. The theory, if theory there be, is that an employer, the author of a work made for hire, would be sophisticated and not in need of the "protection" of a right of termination. Paul Goldstein, *Copyright: Principles, Law and Practice* (1989), vol. I, p. 484, § 4.9.1.3. The issue of whether a work is a work made for hire is important both for purposes of identifying who is the author for ownership purposes, but also for purposes of determining whether that author has any right to terminate.

It is the connection between works made for hire and the termination right that explains clause 2 of the definition of works made for hire in the 1976 act. "The right of termination would not apply to 'works made for hire,' which is one of the principal reasons the definition of that term assumed importance in the development of the bill." H.R. Rep. No. 1476, p. 125. The exception was not needed in order to affect the ownership of the copyright. The parties could provide for that equally well by requiring each possible "author" to assign the copyright in writing. Clause 2 permits "authors" of the enumerated types of works to contract out of the right of termination provisions by signing a written agreement that the work is a work made for hire.

The types of works covered by clause 2 have the following in common. (1) They are works of a type commonly involving creative input from a large number of people. (2) Many of the contributors will not be employees of the entity that funds the project, but rather will be specially commissioned to contribute. For instance, a textbook publisher may commission professors to contribute sections to the textbook, or to review and revise drafts, or a movie producer may hire composers, set and costume designers, and script writers to work on some aspect of the movie. (3) The works are produced by an organized industry that had the sophisticated representation necessary to participate in the long, technical process of copyright revision that unfolded in the Congress. The leading examples are the publishers of instructional materials ("an instructional text, as a test, as answer material for a test") and the movie industry ("as a part of a motion picture or other audiovisual work"). These industries feared the problems that would emerge if years after their creation of a copyrightable work all of the commissioned contributors could come forward and assert their termination rights.

NOTES

1. The concept of "work made for hire" is also important to the copyright term, because the term of a "work made for hire" is 75 years. Note that this is true even if the employer and statutory author are natural persons. Section 302(c).

2. Why are grants by will excluded from the termination right?

3. Even though the statute attempts to preserve the termination right for authors in the face of the demands of publishers and others to abandon the right, there is much that can be done to affect the right. Suppose for instance that the publisher of pulp novels who commissions writers to write for a set fee wants to make sure that there is no termination right. The publisher could, of course, hire the writers as employees, but might not want to do so because of tax withholding, labor regulation, and liability concerns. But suppose the publisher insists that it will only commission authors who first form their own wholly owned corporation and enter into an employment agreement with it providing that they are to be "President and staff novelist." The publisher then enters into an agreement not with the writer, but with the corporation. Doesn't this convert the commissioned novel into a "work made for hire?" Or will the courts examine the substance of the transaction to determine what it "really" was?

4. The position of the owner of a derivative work under the renewal rights provisions applicable to pre-1976 Act copyrights is illustrated by Stewart v. Abend, 110 S.Ct. 1750 (1990), involving the right to show the Alfred Hitchcock movie "Rear Window." In 1942 Cornell Woolrich authored the story "It Had to Be Murder," which was published in Dime Detective Magazine. Woolrich retained all rights except the magazine publication rights. In 1945 he assigned the rights to make motion picture versions of six of his stories, including "It Had to Be Murder" and including both the first and renewal terms to a third party for $9,250.00. In 1953 actor Jimmy Stewart and director Alfred Hitchcock formed a production company which obtained these movie rights. "Rear Window" was the resulting picture. Woolrich died in 1968 without a widow or children, so under the renewal provisions of the 1909 Act the renewal right passed as directed in his will to a trust for the benefit of Columbia University. In 1969, Chase Manhattan Bank as trustee filed the renewal application. The trust then assigned the renewal rights to Abend for $650 plus ten percent of all proceeds from exploitation of the story. Abend sued and won, and the Supreme

Court granted certiorari to resolve a conflict with the Second Circuit in Rohauer v. Killiam Shows, Inc., 551 F.2d 484 (2d Cir.1977), which held that the owner of the derivative work could continue to exploit it even in the face of objection from the owner of the renewal term, relying in part on the provisions of the 1976 Act relating to the post-termination exploitation of pre-existing derivative works. The Court affirmed the Ninth Circuit, rejected the interpretation of the Second, and held that Abend could enforce the renewal term against "Rear Window."*

The significance of *Abend* is reduced by the fact that the Ninth Circuit held that even though the copyright was valid, Abend could not obtain an injunction.

> The "Rear Window" film resulted from the collaborative efforts of many talented individuals other than Cornell Woolrich, the author of the underlying story. The success of the movie resulted in large part from factors completely unrelated to the underlying story, "It Had To Be Murder." It would cause a great injustice for the owners of the film if the court enjoined them from further exhibition of the movie. An injunction would also effectively foreclose defendants from enjoying legitimate profits derived from exploitation of the "new matter" comprising the derivative work. . . . We also note that an injunction could cause public injury by denying the public the opportunity to view a classic film for many years to come. 863 F.2d at 1479.

This aspect of the decision converted Abend's rights into a right only to receive damages, a kind of compulsory license, which might be quite favorable to the defendant depending on how the courts applied § 504 of the 1976 Act. The Supreme Court did not review this aspect of the Ninth Circuit decision. 110 S.Ct. at 1757–58.

5. *The Author's Right to Protect the Integrity of the Work.* The owner of a copyright is in a position to maintain (or not) the integrity of the work. Adaptations, translations, abridgments and other modifications of the work can only be undertaken with the permission of the copyright owner. If he does not like the new version, he can refuse to authorize it. See Rochelle Cooper Dreyfuss, The Creative Employee and the Copyright Act of 1976, 54 U. of Chi.L. Rev. 590 (1987) for numerous examples of how the author's continuing control over his or her own work can be an important aspect of the author's creativity.

These are important powers, but ones usually given up by the creator of the work. Authors customarily sign contacts with publishers which transfer the copyright to the publisher. Sculptors and painters sell their works, and that sale can include a transfer of the copyright.

Other legal systems, most notably the French, create a separate, non-transferable right called the "moral right" which remains with the author or creator of the work and enables him to invoke the aid of the courts in protecting the integrity of the work (which includes protection against alteration, mutilation or destruction) after the copyright has been transferred to others.

---

* Note that the enforcement of the renewal terms against the owners of the derivative work was particularly harsh in *Abend* because the author had died without a widow or children and under the 1909 Act renewal provisions the renewal right passed back to the executors, where it passed under the author's will. But the author had already agreed to give the owners of the derivative work rights in the renewal term. In *Rohauer* the renewal right had passed to a daughter. The Court considered *Abend* as if it were factually indistinguishable from *Rohauer*.

During the last two decades, a version of this concept, applicable only to fine art, made its way into the statutory law of several states. See Edward J. Damich, The New York Artists' Authorship Rights Act: A Comparative Critique, 84 Col.L.Rev. 1733 (1984), which describes and compares the French, California and New York law.

In 1990 the Copyright Statute was amended to provide such protection. The Visual Artists Rights Act of 1990 added a new § 106A to the Copyright Act which created new rights of attribution and integrity. One consequence of this extension of federal law is that the state statutes are now preempted, as is spelled out in a new § 301(f).

Section 106A gives the author of a work of visual art the right to claim authorship, to prevent false attributions of authorship, and to prevent the use of his or her name in the event of a distortion of the work. Most importantly the statute gives the author the right "to prevent any intentional distortion, mutilation, or other modification of the work which would be prejudicial to his or her honor or reputation, and any intentional distortion, mutilation or modification of that work is a violation of that right and (B) to prevent any destruction of a work of recognized stature, and any intentional or grossly negligent destruction of that work is a violation of that right." A definition of "work of visual art" is added to § 101. It is: "a painting, drawing, print, or sculpture, existing in a single copy, in a limited edition of 200 copies or fewer that are signed and consecutively numbered by the author, or, in the case of a sculpture, in multiple cast, carved or fabricated sculptures of two hundred or fewer that are consecutively numbered by the author and bear the signature or other identifying mark of the author," and a still photographic image subject to similar restrictions.

The § 106A rights to attribution and integrity are the property of the author or authors and are non-transferable. However, they can be waived. § 106A(e).

There are special provisions relating to the removal or alteration of works of visual art incorporated in buildings, contained in new § 113(d).

6. *The Significance of a Transfer of a Copy.* Under the common law it was understood that the sale of certain kinds of works implicitly included ownership in the copyright in the work. The purchaser of an original oil painting or an unpublished manuscript acquired both the object and the copyright. (Unlike the purchaser, for instance, of a published book, who everyone understood, acquired only the single copy, not the right to the copyright.) The 1976 revision changed this law. House Report No. 94–1476, p. 124 says:

> The principle restated in section 202 is a fundamental and important one: that copyright ownership and ownership of a material object in which the copyrighted work is embodied are entirely separate things. Thus, transfer of a material object does not of itself carry any rights under the copyright, and this includes transfer of the copy or phonorecord—the original manuscript, the photographic negative, the unique painting or statue, the master tape recording, etc.—in which the work was first fixed. Conversely, transfer of a copyright does not necessarily require the conveyance of any material object.

As a result of the interaction of this section and the provisions of section 204(a) and 301, the bill would change a common law doctrine exemplified by the decision in Pushman v. New York Graphic Society,

Inc., 287 N.Y. 302, 39 N.E.2d 249 (1942). Under that doctrine, authors or artists are generally presumed to transfer common law literary property rights when they sell their manuscript or work of art, unless those rights are specifically reserved. This presumption would be reversed under the bill, since a specific written conveyance of rights would be required in order for a sale of any material object to carry with it a transfer of copyright.

The statute requires a written agreement for an effective transfer. § 204(a).

The transfer of a copy does give the purchaser the right to use it free of further copyright restrictions. This doctrine of exhaustion is codified in § 109(a) which permits the purchaser of a copy to resell it, § 109(c) which permits the purchaser of a copy to display it, and § 117 which permits the purchaser of a copy of software to make copies necessary to use the software and to back it up. The purchaser of a copy is also permitted to do anything with the copy that is not infringing, for instance to read and observe it because these actions are not infringement under § 106.

Section 109(a) is a codification of Bobbs-Merrill Co. v. Straus, 210 U.S. 339 (1908), which held that a first sale exhausts the copyright, and that it cannot be enforced against a purchaser even if the seller attempts to retain copyright rights. In *Bobbs-Merrill* the publisher attempted to enforce resale price maintenance by putting a notice on the book licensing the copyright for resale only at a minimum resale price. There are similar decisions under the patent statute.

If, however, the copy is not sold then the copyright is not "exhausted." This is recognized in § 109(d). In recent years, sellers of computer software have attempted to take advantage of this provision by licensing rather than selling mass marketed software. The reasons why these "licenses" are likely to be held unenforceable by the courts are spelled out in David Rice, Licensing the Use of Computer Program Copies and the Copyright Act First Sale Doctrine, 30 Jurimetrics 157 (1990).

GILLIAM v. AMERICAN BROADCASTING COMPANIES, INC.

United States Court of Appeals, Second Circuit, 1976.
538 F.2d 14.

LUMBARD, CIRCUIT JUDGE:

Plaintiffs, a group of British writers and performers known as "Monty Python," [1] appeal from a denial by Judge Lasker in the Southern District of a preliminary injunction to restrain the American Broadcasting Company (ABC) from broadcasting edited versions of three separate programs originally written and performed by Monty Python for broadcast by the British Broadcasting Corporation (BBC). We agree with Judge Lasker that the appellants have demonstrated that the excising done for ABC impairs the integrity of the original work. We further find that the countervailing injuries that Judge Lasker found might have accrued to ABC as a result of an injunction at

---

1. Appellant Gilliam is an American citizen residing in England.

a prior date no longer exist. We therefore direct the issuance of a preliminary injunction by the district court.

Since its formation in 1969, the Monty Python group has gained popularity primarily through its thirty-minute television programs created for BBC as part of a comedy series entitled "Monty Python's Flying Circus." In accordance with an agreement between Monty Python and BBC, the group writes and delivers to BBC scripts for use in the television series. This scriptwriters' agreement recites in great detail the procedure to be followed when any alterations are to be made in the script prior to recording of the program.[2] The essence of this section of the agreement is that, while BBC retains final authority to make changes, appellants or their representatives exercise optimum control over the scripts consistent with BBC's authority and only minor changes may be made without prior consultation with the writers. Nothing in the scriptwriters' agreement entitles BBC to alter a program once it has been recorded. The agreement further provides that, subject to the terms therein, the group retains all rights in the script.

Under the agreement, BBC may license the transmission of recordings of the television programs in any overseas territory. The series has been broadcast in this country primarily on non-commercial public broadcasting television stations, although several of the programs have been broadcast on commercial stations in Texas and Nevada. In each instance, the thirty-minute programs have been broadcast as originally recorded and broadcast in England in their entirety and without commercial interruption.

In October 1973, Time-Life Films acquired the right to distribute in the United States certain BBC television programs, including the Monty Python series. Time-Life was permitted to edit the programs only

---

2. The Agreement provides:

V. When script alterations are necessary it is the intention of the BBC to make every effort to inform and to reach agreement with the Writer. Whenever practicable any necessary alterations (other than minor alterations) shall be made by the Writer. Nevertheless the BBC shall at all times have the right to make (a) minor alterations and (b) such other alterations as in its opinion are necessary in order to avoid involving the BBC in legal action or bringing the BBC into disrepute. Any decision under (b) shall be made at a level not below that of Head of Department. It is however agreed that after a script has been accepted by the BBC alterations will not be made by the BBC under (b) above unless (i) the Writer, if available when the BBC requires the alterations to be made, has been asked to agree to them but is not willing to do so and (ii) the Writer has had, if he so requests and if the BBC agrees that time permits if rehearsals and recording are to proceed as planned, an opportunity to be represented by the Writers' Guild of Great Britain (or if he is not a member of the Guild by his agent) at a meeting with the BBC to be held within at most 48 hours of the request (excluding weekends). If in such circumstances there is no agreement about the alterations then the final decision shall rest with the BBC. Apart from the right to make alterations under (a) and (b) above the BBC shall not without the consent of the Writer or his agent (which consent shall not be unreasonably withheld) make any structural alterations as opposed to minor alterations to the script, provided that such consent shall not be necessary in any case where the Writer is for any reason not immediately available for consultation at the time which in the BBC's opinion is the deadline from the production point of view for such alterations to be made if rehearsals and recording are to proceed as planned.

"for insertion of commercials, applicable censorship or governmental * * * rules and regulations, and National Association of Broadcasters and time segment requirements." No similar clause was included in the scriptwriters' agreement between appellants and BBC. Prior to this time, ABC had sought to acquire the right to broadcast excerpts from various Monty Python programs in the spring of 1975, but the group rejected the proposal for such a disjoined format. Thereafter, in July 1975, ABC agreed with Time-Life to broadcast two ninety-minute specials each comprising three thirty-minute Monty Python programs that had not previously been shown in this country.

Correspondence between representatives of BBC and Monty Python reveals that these parties assumed that ABC would broadcast each of the Monty Python programs "in its entirety." On September 5, 1975, however, the group's British representative inquired of BBC how ABC planned to show the programs in their entirety if approximately 24 minutes of each 90 minute program were to be devoted to commercials. BBC replied on September 12, "we can only reassure you that ABC have decided to run the programmes 'back to back,' and that there is a firm undertaking not to segment them."

ABC broadcast the first of the specials on October 3, 1975. Appellants did not see a tape of the program until late November and were allegedly "appalled" at the discontinuity and "mutilation" that had resulted from the editing done by Time-Life for ABC. Twenty-four minutes of the original 90 minutes of recording had been omitted. Some of the editing had been done in order to make time for commercials; other material had been edited, according to ABC, because the original programs contained offensive or obscene matter.

In early December, Monty Python learned that ABC planned to broadcast the second special on December 26, 1975. The parties began negotiations concerning editing of that program and a delay of the broadcast until Monty Python could view it. These negotiations were futile, however, and on December 15 the group filed this action to enjoin the broadcast and for damages. Following an evidentiary hearing, Judge Lasker found that "the plaintiffs have established an impairment of the integrity of their work" which "caused the film or program * * * to lose its iconoclastic verve." According to Judge Lasker, "the damage that has been caused to the plaintiffs is irreparable by its nature." Nevertheless, the judge denied the motion for the preliminary injunction on the grounds that it was unclear who owned the copyright in the programs produced by BBC from the scripts written by Monty Python; that there was a question of whether Time-Life and BBC were indispensable parties to the litigation; that ABC would suffer significant financial loss if it were enjoined a week before the scheduled broadcast; and that Monty Python had displayed a "somewhat disturbing casualness" in their pursuance of the matter.

Judge Lasker granted Monty Python's request for more limited relief by requiring ABC to broadcast a disclaimer during the December

26 special to the effect that the group dissociated itself from the program because of the editing. A panel of this court, however, granted a stay of that order until this appeal could be heard and permitted ABC to broadcast, at the beginning of the special, only the legend that the program had been edited by ABC. We heard argument on April 13 and, at that time, enjoined ABC from any further broadcast of edited Monty Python programs pending the decision of the court.

We * * * reach the question whether there is a likelihood that appellants will succeed on the merits. In concluding that there is a likelihood of infringement here, we rely especially on the fact that the editing was substantial, i.e., approximately 27 per cent of the original program was omitted, and the editing contravened contractual provisions that limited the right to edit Monty Python material. * * *

Judge Lasker denied the preliminary injunction in part because he was unsure of the ownership of the copyright in the recorded program. Appellants first contend that the question of ownership is irrelevant because the recorded program was merely a derivative work taken from the script in which they hold the uncontested copyright. Thus, even if BBC owned the copyright in the recorded program, its use of that work would be limited by the license granted to BBC by Monty Python for use of the underlying script. We agree.

* * *

Since the copyright in the underlying script survives intact despite the incorporation of that work into a derivative work, one who uses the script, even with the permission of the proprietor of the derivative work, may infringe the underlying copyright. See Davis v. E. I. DuPont deNemours & Co., 240 F.Supp. 612 (S.D.N.Y.1965) (defendants held to have infringed when they obtained permission to use a screenplay in preparing a television script but did not obtain permission of the author of the play upon which the screenplay was based).

If the proprietor of the derivative work is licensed by the proprietor of the copyright in the underlying work to vend or distribute the derivative work to third parties, those parties will, of course, suffer no liability for their use of the underlying work consistent with the license to the proprietor of the derivative work. Obviously, it was just this type of arrangement that was contemplated in this instance. The scriptwriters' agreement between Monty Python and BBC specifically permitted the latter to license the transmission of the recordings made by BBC to distributors such as Time-Life for broadcast in overseas territories.

One who obtains permission to use a copyrighted script in the production of a derivative work, however, may not exceed the specific purpose for which permission was granted. Most of the decisions that have reached this conclusion have dealt with the improper extension of the underlying work into media or time, i.e., duration of the license, not covered by the grant of permission to the derivative work proprietor.

* * *

The rationale for finding infringement when a licensee exceeds time or media restrictions on his license—the need to allow the proprietor of the underlying copyright to control the method in which his work is presented to the public—applies equally to the situation in which a licensee makes an unauthorized use of the underlying work by publishing it in a truncated version. Whether intended to allow greater economic exploitation of the work, as in the media and time cases, or to ensure that the copyright proprietor retains a veto power over versions desired for the derivative work, the ability of the copyright holder to control his work remains paramount in our copyright law. We find, therefore, that unauthorized editing of the underlying work, if proven, would constitute an infringement of the copyright in that work similar to any other use of a work that exceeded the license granted by the proprietor of the copyright.

If the broadcast of an edited version of the Monty Python program infringed the group's copyright in the script, ABC may obtain no solace from the fact that editing was permitted in the agreements between BBC and Time-Life or Time-Life and ABC. BBC was not entitled to make unilateral changes in the script and was not specifically empowered to alter the recordings once made; Monty Python, moreover, had reserved to itself any rights not granted to BBC.

* * *

Our resolution of these technical arguments serves to reinforce our initial inclination that the copyright law should be used to recognize the important role of the artist in our society and the need to encourage production and dissemination of artistic works by providing adequate legal protection for one who submits his work to the public. See Mazer v. Stein, 347 U.S. 201 (1954). We therefore conclude that there is a substantial likelihood that, after a full trial, appellants will succeed in proving infringement of their copyright by ABC's broadcast of edited versions of Monty Python programs. In reaching this conclusion, however, we need not accept appellants' assertion that any editing whatsoever would constitute infringement. Courts have recognized that licensees are entitled to some small degree of latitude in arranging the licensed work for presentation to the public in a manner consistent with the licensee's style or standards. That privilege, however, does not extend to the degree of editing that occurred here especially in light of contractual provisions that limited the right to edit Monty Python material.

II

It also seems likely that appellants will succeed on the theory that, regardless of the right ABC had to broadcast an edited program, the cuts made constituted an actionable mutilation of Monty Python's work. This cause of action, which seeks redress for deformation of an artist's work, finds its roots in the continental concept of droit moral, or moral right, which may generally be summarized as including the right of the artist to have his work attributed to him in the form in which he created it. See 1 M. Nimmer, supra, at § 110.1.

American copyright law, as presently written, does not recognize moral rights or provide a cause of action for their violation, since the law seeks to vindicate the economic, rather than the personal, rights of authors. Nevertheless, the economic incentive for artistic and intellectual creation that serves as the foundation for American copyright law, Goldstein v. California, 412 U.S. 546 (1973); Mazer v. Stein, 347 U.S. 201 (1954), cannot be reconciled with the inability of artists to obtain relief for mutilation or misrepresentation of their work to the public on which the artists are financially dependent. Thus courts have long granted relief for misrepresentation of an artist's work by relying on theories outside the statutory law of copyright, such as contract law, Granz v. Harris, 198 F.2d 585 (2d Cir.1952) (substantial cutting of original work constitutes misrepresentation), or the tort of unfair competition, Prouty v. National Broadcasting Co., 26 F.Supp. 265 (D.Mass.1939). See Strauss, The Moral Right of the Author 128–138, in Studies on Copyright (1963). Although such decisions are clothed in terms of proprietary right in one's creation, they also properly vindicate the author's personal right to prevent the presentation of his work to the public in a distorted form. ＊ ＊ ＊

Here, the appellants claim that the editing done for ABC mutilated the original work and that consequently the broadcast of those programs as the creation of Monty Python violated the Lanham Act § 43(a), 15 U.S.C. § 1125(a). This statute, the federal counterpart to state unfair competition laws, has been invoked to prevent misrepresentations that may injure plaintiff's business or personal reputation, even where no registered trademark is concerned. ＊ ＊ ＊ It is sufficient to violate the Act that a representation of a product, although technically true, creates a false impression of the product's origin. See Rich v. RCA Corp., 390 F.Supp. 530 (S.D.N.Y.1975) (recent picture of plaintiff on cover of album containing songs recorded in distant past held to be a false representation that the songs were new); ＊ ＊ ＊. [A]n allegation that a defendant has presented to the public a [garbled], ＊ ＊ ＊ distorted version of plaintiff's work seeks to redress the very rights sought to be protected by the Lanham Act, 15 U.S.C. § 1125(a), and should be recognized as stating a cause of action under that statute. ＊ ＊ ＊

During the hearing on the preliminary injunction, Judge Lasker viewed the edited version of the Monty Python program broadcast on December 26 and the original, unedited version. After hearing argument of this appeal, this panel also viewed and compared the two versions. We find that the truncated version at times omitted the climax of the skits to which appellants' rare brand of humor was leading and at other times deleted essential elements in the schematic development of a story line.[12] We therefore agree with Judge Lasker's

---

12. A single example will illustrate the extent of distortion engendered by the editing. In one skit, an upper class English family is engaged in a discussion of the tonal quality of certain words as "woody" or "tinny." The father soon begins to sug-

conclusion that the edited version broadcast by ABC impaired the integrity of appellants' work and represented to the public as the product of appellants what was actually a mere caricature of their talents. We believe that a valid cause of action for such distortion exists and that therefore a preliminary injunction may issue to prevent repetition of the broadcast prior to final determination of the issues.[13]

For these reasons we direct that the district court issue the preliminary injunction sought by the appellants.

GURFEIN, CIRCUIT JUDGE (concurring):

I believe that this is the first case in which a federal appellate court has held that there may be a violation of Section 43(a) of the Lanham Act with respect to a common-law copyright. The Lanham Act is a trademark statute, not a copyright statute. Nevertheless, we must recognize that the language of Section 43(a) is broad. It speaks of the affixation or use of false designations of origin or false descriptions or representations, but proscribes such use "in connection with any goods or services." It is easy enough to incorporate trade names as well as trademarks into Section 43(a) and the statute specifically applies to common law trademarks, as well as registered trademarks. Lanham Act § 45, 15 U.S.C. § 1127.

In the present case, we are holding that the deletion of portions of the recorded tape constitutes a breach of contract, as well as an infringement of a common-law copyright of the original work. There is literally no need to discuss whether plaintiffs also have a claim for relief under the Lanham Act or for unfair competition under New York law. I agree with Judge Lumbard, however, that it may be an exercise of judicial economy to express our view on the Lanham Act claim, and I do not dissent therefrom. I simply wish to leave it open for the District Court to fashion the remedy.

The Copyright Act provides no recognition of the so-called *droit moral,* or moral right of authors. Nor are such rights recognized in the field of copyright law in the United States. See 1 Nimmer on Copyright, § 110.2 (1975 ed.). If a distortion or truncation in connection with a use constitutes an infringement of copyright, there is no need for an additional cause of action beyond copyright infringement. Id. at

gest certain words with sexual connotations as either "woody" or "tinny," whereupon the mother fetches a bucket of water and pours it over his head. The skit continues from this point. The ABC edit eliminates this middle sequence so that the father is comfortably dressed at one moment and, in the next moment, is shown in a soaked condition without any explanation for the change in his appearance.

13. Judge Gurfein's concurring opinion suggests that since the gravamen of a complaint under the Lanham Act is that the origin of goods has been falsely described, a legend disclaiming Monty Python's approval of the edited version would preclude violation of that Act. We are doubtful

that a few words could erase the indelible impression that is made by a television broadcast, especially since the viewer has no means of comparing the truncated version with the complete work in order to determine for himself the talents of plaintiffs. Furthermore, a disclaimer such as the one originally suggested by Judge Lasker in the exigencies of an impending broadcast last December would go unnoticed by viewers who tuned into the broadcast a few minutes after it began.

We therefore conclude that Judge Gurfein's proposal that the district court could find some form of disclaimer would be sufficient might not provide appropriate relief.

§ 110.3.   An obligation to mention the name of the author carries the implied duty, however, as a matter of contract, not to make such changes in the work as would render the credit line a false attribution of authorship, Granz v. Harris, 198 F.2d 585 (2 Cir.1952).

So far as the Lanham Act is concerned, it is not a substitute for *droit moral* which authors in Europe enjoy.   If the licensee may, by contract, distort the recorded work, the Lanham Act does not come into play.   If the licensee has no such right by contract, there will be a violation in breach of contract.   The Lanham Act can hardly apply literally when the credit line correctly states the work to be that of the plaintiffs which, indeed it is, so far as it goes.   The vice complained of is that the truncated version is not what the plaintiffs wrote.   But the Lanham Act does not deal with artistic integrity.   It only goes to misdescription of origin and the like.   *   *   *

The misdescription of origin can be dealt with, as Judge Lasker did below, by devising an appropriate legend to indicate that the plaintiffs had not approved the editing of the ABC version.[1]   With such a legend, there is no conceivable violation of the Lanham Act.   If plaintiffs complain that their artistic integrity is still compromised by the distorted version, their claim does not lie under the Lanham Act, which does not protect the copyrighted work itself but protects only against the misdescription or mislabelling.

*   *   *

NOTES

1.   The *Gilliam* case is Exhibit 1 in support of the position that U.S. law met the Berne Convention requirement that moral rights be protected.

2.   Section 43(a) of the Lanham Act has also been successfully invoked by authors and artists claiming that they were not being given proper credit for their work.   Smith v. Montoro, 648 F.2d 602 (9th Cir.1981), involved an actor claiming that the film distributors had removed his name from the film credits and the advertising, and inserted another name.   The court said this was "reverse passing off" actionable under § 43(a).   In Dodd v. Fort Smith Special School Dist. No. 100, 666 F.Supp. 1278 (W.D.Ark.1987), a junior high teacher and her students obtained a preliminary injunction enjoining the school district from publishing a book they had prepared without giving them authorship credit.

3.   The case of an author who did not want credit was before the court in Follett v. Arbor House Publishing Co., 497 F.Supp. 304 (S.D.N.Y.1980).   There the author complained that the publisher was going to erroneously describe him as the author.   The work was an account of a notorious bank robbery in Nice, France.   Follett had translated the work into English from an account written by three French journalists.   The work was first published in England, where Follett had pressed his publisher for authorship credit.   But by the time the work was scheduled for publication in the United States, Follett had achieved great success here with *Eye of the Needle* and *Triple*.   The American publisher of the translation wanted to capitalize on this success and Follett

---

1.   I do not imply that the appropriate legend be shown only at the beginning of   the broadcast.   That is a matter for the District Court.

wanted to stop it, in part because of a forthcoming book with another publisher. The proposed description was: "by the author of TRIPLE and EYE OF THE NEEDLE KEN FOLLETT with Rene Louis Maurice." Rene Louis Maurice was a pseudonym used by the three French journalists. The court decreed that Follett and Maurice should be given equal credit.

4. Can the author of a letter to the editor keep control over the use made of the letter by claiming copyright? In Diamond v. Am-Law Publishing Corp., 745 F.2d 142 (2d Cir.1984), the *American Lawyer* ran a story reporting that Diamond, a New York lawyer, had had a dispute over a $1,608.50 legal fee with a client, and that as a result of his persistent efforts to collect it the client had filed a grievance against him with the New York bar association. Diamond wrote to Stephen Brill, editor of the magazine, demanding a retraction and apology. Brill wrote to Diamond inviting him to write a letter for publication in the magazine stating that no grievance had been filed. Diamond wrote such a letter, criticizing the story and the reportorial work of the magazine. The letter stated "You are authorized to publish this letter but only in its entirety." Brill published the letter in edited form. Diamond sued for copyright infringement. Held: fair use. "[Section 107] expressly protects comments and news reporting, and Diamond's own demands for a retraction with regard to whether [the client] * * * had filed a grievance are more than enough to render the portion of the letter published newsworthy. A paraphrase of Diamond's version of the facts relating to the grievance would not have been a basis for an infringement action, and we fail to see why using his own words creates such liability." 745 F.2d 147. Does this holding survive the Supreme Court's *Nation* decision?

5. In Bonner v. Westbound Records, Inc., 49 Ill.App.3d 543, 7 Ill.Dec. 409, 364 N.E.2d 570 (1977), the court held that the Uniform Deceptive Trade Practices Act provides a cause of action against unauthorized alteration of an artist's work where consumers will believe that the altered version is in fact the work of the plaintiff. The defendants were enjoined from selling rock albums assembled from unfinished tapes made while the plaintiffs were still under contract to the defendant.

6. An issue related to the continuing rights of the author vis-a-vis the owner of the work is the right of the author to continue to make use of themes, ideas, and techniques incorporated in the (now transferred) copyrighted work. Artists and writers tend to work in similar or related styles or themes over a period of time. Think of the characters like Falstaff, who appears in several of Shakespeare's plays, or the practice of an author using a detective character like Sherlock Holmes through a series of books, or of Monet's water lilies. This is not surprising since it has probably taken considerable effort to find a successful approach, and the artist may even be able to enrich his work through subtle development and interplay among the various realizations of the idea. This is, like the other issues in this section, an issue that can be addressed at the time of the original transfer. But if the copyright has simply been transferred without further elaboration, what can the author or artist continue to use? The simple answer is, of course, that he can continue to use those elements of the work not protected by copyright. But some decisions suggest that the courts may be more receptive to the claim of an author or artist to use elements of his "own" work than they would be to a similar claim from a third-party.

In Warner Bros. Pictures, Inc. v. Columbia Broadcasting System, Inc., 216 F.2d 945 (9th Cir.1954), Dashiell Hammett wrote a mystery-detective story entitled "The Maltese Falcon." The detective was named Sam Spade. Warner Brothers acquired the ownership of the copyright from Hammett and his publisher Knopf. Hammett used the characters from "The Maltese Falcon" in later works, and Warner Bros. sued for infringement. The court construed the transfer of copyright to Warner Brothers as not including the right to use the characters in subsequent stories (although there was only one copyright, which the instrument made no effort to divide). "The conclusion that these rights are not within the granting instruments is strongly buttressed by the fact that historically and presently detective fiction writers have and do carry the leading characters with their names and individualisms from one story into succeeding stories. This was the practice of Edgar Allen Poe, Sir Arthur Conan Doyle, and others. * * * If the intention of the contracting parties had been to avoid this practice which was a very valuable one to the author, it is hardly reasonable that it would be left to a general clause following specific grants." 216 F.2d 945.

In Franklin Mint Corp. v. National Wildlife Art Exchange, Inc., 575 F.2d 62 (3d Cir.1978), Gilbert, a nationally recognized wildlife artist, had painted a water color of cardinals entitled "Cardinals on Apple Blossom." Gilbert sold the painting to National Wildlife in exchange for a check bearing the notation "For Cardinal painting 20 × 24 including all rights—reproduction etc." National sold an edition of 300 prints of the painting. Gilbert later painted and sold to the Franklin Mint Corporation four water color bird life pictures, including one of cardinals with similarities to the National Wildlife painting. Franklin Mint made engravings of the four paintings, which were sold as a group. National Wildlife sued for infringement. In the course of affirming a finding of no infringement, the court observed that "There was also testimony on the tendency of some painters to return to certain basic themes time and time again. Winslow Homer's schoolboys, Monet's facade of Rouen Cathedral, and Bingham's flatboat characters were cited. Franklin Mint relied upon these examples of 'variations on a theme' as appropriate examples of the freedom which must be extended to artists to utilize basic subject matter more than once. National vigorously objects to the use of such a concept as being contrary to the theory of copyright. We do not find the phrase objectionable, however, because a 'variation' probably is not a copy and if a 'theme' is equated with an 'idea,' it may not be monopolized. We conceive of 'variations on a theme,' therefore, as another way of saying that an 'idea' may not be copyrighted and only its 'expressions may be protected'." 575 F.2d at 66.

7. French law provides the artist with the *droit de suite* or right to share in the sale price of a work after its initial sale. The right enables artists who sell their early works for low prices, but who later achieve success in the market, to share in the later appreciation in the value of the paintings. See generally, Monroe Price, Government Policy and Economic Security for Artists: The Case of the Droit de Suite, 77 Yale L.J. 1333 (1968). California has enacted a statute based upon the *droit de suite,* California Civil Code § 986. It provides that whenever a work of fine art is sold and the seller resides in California, or the sale takes place in California, the seller shall pay to the artist five percent of the amount of the sale. The statute was upheld against constitutional attack in Morseburg v. Balyon, 621 F.2d 972 (9th Cir.1980). The statute is discussed in Stephen S. Ashley, Critical Comment on California's Droit de Suite, Civil Code Section 986, 29 Hast.L.J. 249 (1977) and Comment, The Droit de Suite Has Arrived: Can it Thrive in California as it Has in Calais?, 11 Creighton L.Rev. 529 (1977).

The statute was amended in 1982 to provide that the artist could assign this right to another entity (not the purchaser). This would make it possible to have an enforcement organization like ASCAP, infra this page, to monitor and enforce these rights. John E. McInerney III, California Resale Royalties Act: Private Sector Enforcement, 19 U. of San Francisco L.Rev. 1 (1984), discusses these amendments. The article concedes that "Apparent lack of effective means to collectively enforce the Act has made it virtually irrelevant." Id. at 2.

Can the California statute be avoided by directing the sale to an out-of-state (New York?) auction house?

If art work rises in value after the first sale, isn't that rise likely to be in part due to promotional efforts of the artist subsequent to the first sale? Doesn't the owner of an artist's work have an interest in giving the artist an incentive to promote the market for his work, including pieces already sold?

The *Morseburg* case was decided under the 1909 act. Different result under § 301? Note, The California Resale Royalties Act as a Test Case for Preemption, 81 Colum.L.Rev. 1315 (1981), concludes no preemption.

8. Section 608(b) of the Visual Artists Rights Act of 1990 directed the Copyright Office to study resale royalties and report to Congress in 18 months.

E. COPYRIGHT ENFORCEMENT

1. *The performing rights organizations.* Copyright law has led to the formation of an unusual kind of organization—the performing rights organization—which plays an important role in the enforcement of the performing rights. The principal organizations are ASCAP—the American Society of Composers, Authors and Publishers—and BMI—Broadcast Music, Inc.

ASCAP arose to provide a feasible system for the owners of musical copyrights to enforce their performance rights against broadcasters, theatres, bars, nightclubs and such. Musical performances (whether live or by playing a record) on every radio (and later TV) station, and at every theatre, bar and night club in the land are infringements unless licensed, but it is hardly feasible for the copyright owner to go from bar to bar (or listen all night to the radio) until he finds an unauthorized performance of his song. Instead, the owner authorizes the society to license his work, and the society offers blanket licenses to enable the licensee to use all of the songs in the society's catalogue. If the society learns of a broadcaster or other establishment that has not obtained a license, it can listen to the station or send an investigator into the establishment. Given the size of the ASCAP catalogue, it will not be long before several unauthorized performances of ASCAP songs occur. A suit for infringement, complete with a claim for statutory damages and attorney's fees, follows shortly thereafter.

BMI is a non-profit corporation owned and operated by the broadcasters to compete with ASCAP. Both BMI and ASCAP obtain most of their revenues from the broadcasting industry.

The performing rights organizations have elaborate procedures for allocating the revenues they receive among the participating publishers and authors. These procedures depend upon sampling techniques to estimate the relative amount of time works are being played by licensees.

NOTE

1. ASCAP, as a combination of many of the music authors and publishers, has been the subject of numerous suits under the antitrust laws and operates under the terms of a consent decree entered in the Southern District of New York. The decree was first entered in 1941 and has been subject to many subsequent revisions. In Broadcast Music, Inc. v. Columbia Broadcasting System, Inc., 441 U.S. 1 (1979), the Supreme Court decided that the policy of both ASCAP and BMI of refusing to license on a work-by-work basis and offering only blanket licenses (licenses to use any song in the catalogue) was not a per se violation of the Sherman Act. CBS wanted the courts to force ASCAP and BMI to offer it licenses covering only the songs CBS wanted to use. The Court relied heavily on the right of members of ASCAP or licensors of BMI to separately and independently license their works if they wish to do so. This right is rarely if ever exercised, presumably because broadcasters find it too costly to deal with many separate authors and publishers.

---

2. *The Copyright Royalty Tribunal.* The Copyright Royalty Tribunal was an innovation of the 1976 Act. Its function is to fix compulsory royalty rates under §§ 111 (cable TV), 115 (records), 116 (juke boxes) and 118 (public broadcasting), and to distribute the funds generated by the cable T.V. royalty, § 111(d)(5), and the juke box royalty, § 116(c).

Three of the four areas of its responsibility originated in partial or no copyright protection under the 1909 Act.

a. Cable TV. While the copyright act was pending in Congress the question arose in the courts as to whether a cable system which picked up a broadcast signal and transmitted it to subscribers was infringing the copyright. The Supreme Court held that it was not. Teleprompter Corp. v. Columbia Broadcasting System, 415 U.S. 394 (1974); Fortnightly Corp. v. United Artists Television, Inc., 392 U.S. 390 (1968). The cases turned on the Court's conclusion that the cable systems were not publicly performing the retransmitted works under the 1909 Act.

Meanwhile the issue was hotly contested in Congress in connection with the statutory revision effort. The broad protective sweep of § 106 threatened the immune status of the cable operators. In addition, the economic role of cable was increasing rapidly. Congress compromised between full copyright protection and no copyright protection by setting a compulsory royalty and gave the Copyright Royalty Tribunal authority to readjust the royalty level.

b. Records. The 1909 Act, as almost an afterthought (records had just appeared) set a compulsory royalty of 2 cents per record. Sec. 1(e).

By the 1970's long playing records and inflation had made the fee hopelessly obsolete. Congress raised the fee to 2 and three-fourths cents or half a cent a minute, whichever is greater, and gave the Copyright Royalty Tribunal authority to revise it periodically.

3. Juke boxes had enjoyed a complete exemption under the 1909 Act, again practically as an afterthought. The exemption had no justification but juke box operators were nevertheless ready to defend it. Congress again compromised on a compulsory license.

4. Public broadcasting. Public broadcasting is always looking for forms of non-budget subsidy, and found one in § 118.

NOTES

1. Because the standards under which the Royalty Tribunal is to set and distribute royalties leave considerable latitude in their administration, and because large amounts of money are at stake, the proceedings of the Tribunal have been vigorously contested and challenged in the courts, particularly the Court of Appeals for the District of Columbia. It has generally affirmed the decisions of the Tribunal, but not without complaint about the lack of clarity in the Tribunal's reasons. See National Cable Television Association v. Copyright Royalty Tribunal, 689 F.2d 1077 (D.C.Cir.1982); Christian Broadcasting Network, Inc. v. Copyright Royalty Tribunal, 720 F.2d 1295 (D.C.Cir.1983).

The Tribunal was again affirmed in National Association of Broadcasters v. Copyright Royalty Tribunal, 772 F.2d 922 (D.C.Cir.1985). The court concluded: "We have thus concluded this third lengthy expedition into the arena of copyright royalty distributions. We emerge from our analysis of these inherently subjective judgment calls and rough balancing of hotly competing claims with one overriding conclusion: it is the Tribunal which Congress, for better or worse, has entrusted with an unenviable mission of dividing up the booty among copyright holders. Given the potential monetary stakes, the claimants studied tack to date of 'boundless litigiousness' * * * directed at the various nooks and crannies of the Tribunal's decisions is perhaps understandable. But with today's decision joining the ranks of our two prior exercises of review, the broad discretion necessarily conferred upon the Copyright Royalty Tribunal in making its distributions is emphatically clear. We will not hesitate henceforth, should this tack of litigation-to-the-hilt continue to characterize the aftermath of CRT distribution decisions, to refrain from elaborately responding to the myriad of claims and contentions advanced by a highly litigious copyright-owner subculture." 772 F.2d at 940.

2. Does the model of the performing rights society have application in other areas? If the *Sony* case had been decided differently, would a collective organization have arisen to license owners of VCR's? In the area of photocopying, The Copyright Clearance Center, a private, non-profit corporation, administers a centralized system of advance authorization and fee collection for works registered with it.

3. Because Article 11(1) of the Berne Convention provides that authors of musical works "shall enjoy the exclusive right authorizing the public performance of their works," the Berne Convention Implementation Act of 1988, P.L. 100–568, Oct. 31, 1988, modified the juke box provisions to provide for "voluntary negotiations" between the juke box operators and the copyright owners, subject to the ultimate control of the Copyright Royalty Tribunal.

4. *Criminal Enforcement.* Criminal enforcement of the copyright laws has become important. Infringement of copyright has long been a federal crime. (Unlike infringement of a patent and until the enactment of the Trademark Counterfeiting Act of 1984, a trademark. Can you explain why?) But it was a rarely prosecuted crime until low-cost reproduction equipment made organized, large-scale sale of infringing records, tapes and movies big business. There are now numerous reported criminal prosecutions.

Dowling v. United States, 473 U.S. 207 (1985), involved a prosecution of three young men who had established a thriving business in the manufacture, promotion and sale of records with Elvis Presley performances, all made without copyright license. The records were not copies of commercially available records, but rather recordings made from unreleased performances such as movie sound tracks, broadcasts and so on, and of particular interest to Presley cultists. Conviction was obtained not only for criminal copyright infringement, but for interstate transportation of stolen property. Held: defendant did not engage in the interstate transportation of stolen property when he engaged in the interstate distribution of infringing records. The Court said:

> The broad consequences of the Government's theory, both in the field of copyright and in kindred fields of intellectual property law, provide a final and dispositive factor against reading § 2314 in the manner suggested. For example, in Harper & Row, supra, this Court very recently held that The Nation, a weekly magazine of political commentary, had infringed former President Ford's copyright in the unpublished manuscript of his memoirs by verbatim excerpting of some 300 words from the work. It rejected The Nation's argument that the excerpting constituted fair use. Presented with the facts of that case as a hypothetical at oral argument in the present litigation, the Government conceded that its theory of § 2314 would permit prosecution of the magazine if it transported copies of sufficient value across state lines. Tr. of Oral Arg. 35. Whatever the wisdom or propriety of The Nation's decision to publish the excerpts, we would pause, in the absence of any explicit indication of congressional intention, to bring such conduct within the purview of a criminal statute making available serious penalties for the interstate transportation of goods "stolen, converted or taken by fraud."

> Likewise, the field of copyright does not cabin the Government's theory, which would as easily encompass the law of patents and other forms of intellectual property. If "the intangible idea protected by the copyright is effectively made tangible by its embodiment upon the tapes," United States v. Gottesman, 724 F.2d 1517, 1520 (11th Cir. 1984), phonorecords, or films shipped in interstate commerce as to render those items stolen goods for purposes of § 2314, so too would the intangible idea protected by a patent be made tangible by its embodiment in an article manufactured in accord with patented specifications. Thus, as the Government as much as acknowledged at argument, Tr. of Oral Arg. 29, its view of the statute would readily permit its application to interstate shipments of patent-infringing goods. Despite its undoubted power to do so, however, Congress has not provided criminal penalties for distribution of goods infringing valid patents.[19]

---

19. Congress instead had relied on provisions affording patent owners a civil cause of action. 35 U.S.C. §§ 281–294.   Among the available remedies are treble damages for willful infringement. § 284; see, e.g., American Safety Table Co. v.

Thus, the rational supporting application of the statute under the circumstances of this case would equally justify its use in wide expanses of the law which Congress has evidenced no intention to enter by way of criminal sanction.[20] This factor militates strongly against the reading proffered by the Government, Cf. Williams v. United States, 458 U.S., at 287, 102 S.Ct., at 3093.

473 U.S., at 225–227.

Schreiber, 415 F.2d 373, 378–379 (2d Cir. 1969), cert. denied 396 U.S. 1038 (1970). * * *. The only criminal provision relating to patents is 18 U.S.C. § 497, which proscribes the forgery, counterfeiting, or false alteration of letters patent, or the uttering thereof. See also 35 U.S.C. § 292 ($500 penalty, one-half to go to person suing and one-half to the United States, for false marking of patent status).

[20] The Government's rationale would also apply to goods infringing trademark rights. Yet, despite having long and extensively legislated in this area, see federal Trademark Act of 1946 (Lanham Act), 15 U.S.C. § 1051 et seq., in the modern era Congress only recently has resorted to criminal sanctions to control trademark infringement. See Trademark Counterfeiting Act of 1984, Pub.L. 98–473, ch. XV, 98 Stat. 2178. * * *.

Chapter VI

PATENTS

The patent statute (35 U.S.C. §§ 1–376, hereafter cited by Section number only) establishes nine major requirements for a valid patent. Five of the requirements are substantive, that is, they define what can be patented. Four are procedural, that is, they define the steps that must be taken to obtain a valid patent. The five substantive requirements are:

1. Patentable subject matter (§ 101);
2. Originality (§§ 101, 115);
3. Novelty (§§ 101, 102);
4. Utility (§ 101);
5. Non-obviousness (§ 103).

The four procedural requirements are:

1. An application filed with the patent office by the inventor or his representative (§§ 111, 115, 116, 117, 118);
2. within one year of the public use or publication of the invention (§ 102(b));
3. with a specification containing "a written description of the invention, and of the manner and process of making and using it, in such full, clear, concise, and exact terms as to enable any person skilled in the art to which it pertains * * * to make and use the same" (§§ 112, 113, 114), and concluding;
4. with one or more claims "pointing out and distinctly claiming the subject matter" which constitutes the invention, and no more (§ 112).

A patent is issued to an applicant only after the Patent and Trademark Office determines, based upon an examination of the application (§ 131), that it meets the statutory requirements (§ 151). If a patent owner subsequently wishes to enforce the patent, a suit for infringement is brought in a United States District Court. The District Courts have exclusive jurisdiction over infringement actions. 28 U.S.C. § 1338(a). The fact that the patent has already been reviewed and issued by the patent office does not prevent the defendant in an infringement action from proving that the patent does not meet the requirements of the statute, although an issued patent enjoys a presumption of validity (§ 282).

A valid patent confers upon its owner the exclusive right to make, use or sell the patented invention within the United States during the term of the patent, which is seventeen years (§ 154) (except for design patents, which have a term of fourteen years (§ 173)).

792

A patent is more difficult to obtain than a copyright, but confers more sweeping rights. In particular, there is no requirement that the infringer of a patent have copied from the patent (§ 271). Even if the infringer developed his own technology independently of any knowledge of the patent, he infringes if his technology falls within the claim of the patent. The burden is on the firm designing or purchasing a new product or using a new process to examine the record of issued patents in the patent office and determine whether or not any patents are infringed.

Patent law appeals are now almost exclusively within the jurisdiction of a specialized court—the United States Court of Appeals for the Federal Circuit. This court was created in 1982 through a merger of the previously existing United States Court of Claims and the United States Court of Customs and Patent Appeals. The Court of Customs and Patent Appeals had had a specialized patent jurisdiction (shared with the United States Court of Appeals for the District of Columbia) over appeals from actions of the Patent and Trademark Office. The most significant new jurisdiction conferred upon the Federal Circuit (in addition to the previous jurisdictions of the merging courts) was the review of the patent decisions of the district courts, decisions that had previously been reviewed in the geographic circuits along with all the other decisions of the district courts. The purpose was to reduce the burdens of the other circuit courts, thought to be increasingly overworked, and to increase the uniformity of patent law. Patent appeals constituted about five percent of their business, and it was widely believed that patent cases were particularly burdensome for them to hear and decide. The court was given the imposing title of "Court of Appeals for the Federal Circuit" to reflect the fact that it would now—like the other courts of appeal—review decisions of the district courts.

Because all patent cases are decided by the Federal Circuit, it is unlikely that there will be a conflict with other circuits on issues of patent law. Since conflict is one of the most important reasons that the Supreme Court decides to review a case, it is probable that in the future the Supreme Court will infrequently, if ever, review a case turning on an issue of patent law. Thus the decisions of the Federal Circuit are likely to be controlling precedents. The Federal Circuit has ruled that precedents of the Court of Claims and Court of Customs and Patent Appeals announced prior to September 30, 1982, are binding precedent for it. South Corp. v. United States, 690 F.2d 1368 (Fed.Cir. 1982) (en banc). However, in patent cases on appeal from the district courts, issues in those cases other than patent law issues are to be governed by the law of the circuit in which the district court sits. Atari, Inc. v. JS & A Group, Inc., 747 F.2d 1422 (Fed.Cir.1984).

The creation of the Federal Circuit had more than procedural significance for patent law. The jurisdiction of the Court of Customs and Patent Appeals was limited to reviewing decisions of the patent and trademark office denying patent applications. It was widely believed that the patent office was more liberal in construing the standard for a valid patent than were the District Courts and the Courts of Appeal, and the Court of Customs and Patent Appeal was part of the application process. Thus in transferring jurisdiction to review the validity of patents from the Courts of Appeal to the Federal Circuit, there was an implicit message that Congress would not particularly mind if the standard of patent validity was more generous to patents. Decisions of the Federal Circuit have been consistent with that implication.

NOTES

1. The patent office costs money to run. Since patent owners are the ones who benefit directly from patents, there is much to be said for a system of finance which imposes the costs of operating the patent system on the patent owners. One advantage of such charges is that it eliminates the incentive to obtain patents on inventions whose value is so low that it would be negative if the costs of administering the system are taken into account. A problem with charging the full cost of the patent office to patent owners is that it may make patent protection economically unavailable to pioneering inventors who are poorly funded and are the only ones to perceive the future value of their inventions.

In recent years, Congress has reorganized the finance of the PTO to take these principles into account. In addition to application ($300) and issue fees ($500), there are maintenance fees to be paid during the life of the patent ($400 after 3.5 years, $800 after 7.5 years, and $1,200 after 11.5 years). § 41. The advantages of a maintenance fee are two. First, it is payable only after the patent has issued and there has been time to determine the commercial value of the invention. Second, it operates to remove from the patent register those patents whose owners have determined have little value. This makes it easier to search the files to determine if any particular product or process infringes a patent which has not expired. The PTO is to adjust these fees every three years in proportion to the consumer price index (§ 41(f)) and to set "fees for all other processing, services, or materials related to patents not specified * * * to recover the estimated average cost to the Office of such processing, services, or materials." § 41(d).

The theory of this fee structure is that it is to recover the cost of operating the office. Congress has then instructed the Commissioner to reduce these fees by fifty percent for the benefit of three groups—independent inventors, nonprofit organizations and small business organizations—and has authorized the appropriation of funds to cover the shortfall caused by these "discount" fees. Public Law 97–247 § 1, 96 Stat. 317 (Aug. 27, 1982). An independent inventor and a nonprofit organization are defined in 37 C.F.R. § 1.9, and a small business organization is defined by the Small Business Administration. Patent and Trademark Office user fees were increased as part of the budget compromise legislation passed in the fall of 1990. H.R. 5835 § 10101.

2. Donald S. Chisum, Patents: A Treatise on the Law of Patentability, Validity and Infringement (New York: Matthew Bender, 1978, 5 vols. with supplements), is a useful resource. Peter D. Rosenberg, Patent Law Fundamentals (New York: Clark Boardman Co., Ltd., 1980) is a three-volume updated, loose leaf text. For an introduction see Arthur R. Miller and Michael H. Davis,

Intellectual Property: Patents, Trademarks, and Copyright in a Nutshell (St. Paul: West Pub. Co. 2d ed. 1990).

3. The economic effects of a patent system have been extensively analyzed. Fritz Machlup, An Economic Review of the Patent System, Study No. 15 of the Subcommittee on Patents, Trademarks and Copyrights of the Committee on the Judiciary, U.S. Senate, 85th Cong.2d Sess. (1958), is a comprehensive review of the literature up to 1958. More recent contributions are Kenneth Arrow, Economic Welfare and the Allocation of Resources for Invention, in National Bureau of Economic Research, The Rate and Direction of Inventive Activity (Princeton: Princeton Univ. Press, 1962) at 617; Harold Demsetz, Information and Efficiency: Another Viewpoint, 12 J. of Law & Econ. 12 (1969); Edmund W. Kitch, The Nature and Function of the Patent System, 20 J. of Law & Econ. 265 (1977); Robert Merges and Richard Nelson, On the Complex Economics of Patent Scope, 90 Colum.L.Rev. 839 (1990).

An intriguing episode in world patent history was the failure of the Netherlands and Switzerland to provide patents during the nineteenth century. Their experience is described and analyzed in Eric Schiff, Industrialization Without National Patents (Princeton Univ. Press, 1971).

4. The right to obtain a patent is the right of the particular person (or persons, see § 116) who makes the invention (§ 111, with exceptions in §§ 117 and 118), even if the person has done the work on the invention while a full time research employee of a business. Such an employee is probably subject to an obligation to assign the patent to the employer if it is issued, and the employer probably handles the application and pays the expense of obtaining and enforcing the patent, but the application is pursued on behalf of the individual. This is in contrast to the copyright law, where a "work made for hire" [defined term] is treated as the work of the employer. 17 U.S.C. § 201(b).

A. PATENTABLE SUBJECT MATTER

The statute provides that a patent may issue on "any new and useful process, machine, manufacture, or composition of matter, or any new and useful improvement thereof" (§ 101).

O'REILLY v. MORSE
Supreme Court of the United States, 1853.
56 U.S. (15 How.) 62, 14 L.Ed. 601.

MR. CHIEF JUSTICE TANEY delivered the opinion of the court.

In proceeding to pronounce judgment in this case, the court is sensible, not only of its importance, but of the difficulties in some of the questions which it presents for decision. * * *

The appellants take three grounds of defense. In the first place they deny that Professor Morse, was the first and original inventor of the Electro-Magnetic Telegraphs described in his two reissued patents of 1848. Secondly, they insist that if he was the original inventor, the patents under which he claims have not been issued conformably to the acts of Congress, and do not confer on him the right to the exclusive use. And thirdly, if these two propositions are decided against them, they insist that the Telegraph of O'Reilly is substantially different from that of Professor Morse, and the use of it, therefore, no infringement of his rights. * * *

In relation to the first point (the originality of the invention), many witnesses have been examined on both sides.

It is obvious that, for some years before Professor Morse made his invention, scientific men in different parts of Europe were earnestly engaged in the same pursuit. Electro-magnetism itself was a recent discovery, and opened to them a new and unexplored field for their labors, and minds of a high order were engaged in developing its power and the purposes to which it might be applied.

Professor Henry, of the Smithsonian Institute, states in his testimony that, prior to the winter of 1819–20, an electro-magnetic telegraph—that is to say a telegraph operating by the combined influence of electricity and magnetism—was not possible; that the scientific principles on which it is founded were until then unknown; and that the first fact of electro-magnetism was discovered by Oersted, of Copenhagen, in that winter, and was widely published, and the account everywhere received with interest.

He also gives an account of the various discoveries, subsequently made from time to time, by different persons in different places, developing its properties and powers, and among them his own. He commenced his researches in 1828, and pursued them with ardor and success, from that time until the telegraph of Professor Morse was established and in actual operation. And it is due to him to say that no one has contributed more to enlarge the knowledge of electro-magnetism, and to lay the foundations of the great invention of which we are speaking, than the professor himself.

It is unnecessary, however, to give in detail the discoveries enumerated by him—either his own or those of others. But it appears from his testimony that very soon after the discovery made by Oersted, it was believed by men of science that this newly-discovered power might be used to communicate intelligence to distant places. And before the year 1823, Ampere of Paris, one of the most successful cultivators of physical science, proposed to the French Academy a plan for that purpose. But his project was never reduced to practice. And the discovery made by Barlow, of the Royal Military Academy of Woolwich, England, in 1825, that the galvanic current greatly diminished in power as the distance increased, put at rest, for a time, all attempts to construct an electro-magnetic telegraph. Subsequent discoveries, however, revived the hope; and in the year 1832, when Professor Morse appears to have devoted himself to the subject, the conviction was general among men of science everywhere that the object could, and sooner or later would, be accomplished.

The great difficulty in their way was the fact that the galvanic current, however strong in the beginning, became gradually weaker as it advanced on the wire; and was not strong enough to produce a mechanical effect, after a certain distance had been traversed. But, encouraged by the discoveries which were made from time to time, and strong in the belief that an electro-magnetic telegraph was practicable, many eminent and scientific men in Europe, as well as in this country, became deeply engaged in endeavoring to surmount what appeared to be the chief obstacle to its success. And in this state of things it ought not to be a matter of surprise that four different magnetic telegraphs, purporting to have overcome the difficulty, should be invented and made public so nearly at the same time that each has claimed a priority; and that a close and careful scrutiny of the facts in each case is necessary to decide between them. The inventions were so nearly simultaneous, that neither inventor can justly be accused of having derived any aid from the discoveries of the other.

* * *

We perceive no well-founded objection to the description which is given of the whole invention and its separate parts, nor to his right to a patent for the first seven inventions set forth in the specification of his claims. The difficulty arises on the eighth.

It is in the following words:

"Eighth. I do not propose to limit myself to the specific machinery or parts of machinery described in the foregoing specification and claims; the essence of my invention being the use of the motive power of the electric or galvanic current, which I call electromagnetism, however developed for marking or printing intelligible characters, signs, or letters, at any distances, being a new application of that power of which I claim to be the first inventor or discoverer."

It is impossible to misunderstand the extent of this claim. He claims the exclusive right to every improvement where the motive power is the electric or galvanic current, and the result is the marking or printing intelligible characters, signs, or letters at a distance.

If this claim can be maintained, it matters not by what process or machinery the result is accomplished. For aught that we now know some future inventor, in the onward march of science, may discover a mode of writing or printing at a distance by means of the electric or galvanic current, without using any part of the process or combination set forth in the plaintiff's specification. His invention may be less complicated—less liable to get out of order—less expensive in construction, and in its operation. But yet if it is covered by this patent the inventor could not use it, nor the public have the benefit of it without the permission of this patentee.

* * *

No one we suppose will maintain that Fulton could have taken out a patent for his invention of propelling vessels by steam, describing the process and machinery he used, and claimed under it the exclusive right to use the motive power of steam, however developed, for the purpose of propelling vessels. It can hardly be supposed that under such a patent he could have prevented the use of the improved machinery which science has since introduced; although the motive power is steam, and the result is the propulsion of vessels. * * *

Again, the use of steam as a motive power in printing presses is comparatively a modern discovery. Was the first inventor of a machine or process of this kind entitled to a patent, giving him the exclusive right to use steam as a motive power, however developed, for the purpose of marking or printing intelligible characters? Could he have prevented the use of any other press subsequently invented where steam was used? * * *

* * *

The leading case * * * is that of Neilson and others v. Harford and others in the English Court of Exchequer. It was elaborately argued and appears to have been carefully considered by the court. The case was this:

Neilson, in his specification, described his invention as one for the improved application of air to produce heat in fires, forges, and furnaces, where a blowing apparatus is required. And it was to be applied as follows: The blast or current of air produced by the blowing apparatus was to be passed from it into an air-vessel or receptacle made sufficiently strong to endure the blast; and through or from that vessel or receptacle by means of a tube, pipe, or aperture into the fire, the receptacle be kept artificially heated to a considerable temperature by heat externally applied. He then described in rather general terms the manner in which the receptacle might be constructed and heated, and the air conducted through it to the fire: stating that the form of the receptacle was not material, nor the manner of applying heat to it. * * * [T]he defendant among other defences insisted that a patent for throwing hot air into the furnace, instead of cold, and thereby increasing the intensity of the heat, was a patent for a principle, and that a principle was not patentable.

Baron Parke, who delivered the opinion of the court, said:

"It is very difficult to distinguish it from the specification of a patent for a principle, and this at first created in the minds of the court much difficulty; but after full consideration we think that the plaintiff does not merely claim a principle, but a machine, embodying a principle and a very valuable one. We think the case must be considered as if the principle being well known, the plaintiff had first invented a mode of applying it by a mechanical apparatus to furnaces, and his invention then consists in this: by interposing a receptacle for heated air between the blowing apparatus and the furnace. In this receptacle he directs the air to be heated by the application of heat externally to the receptacle, and thus he accomplishes the object of applying the blast, which was before cold air, in a heated state to the furnace."

We see nothing in this opinion differing in any degree from the familiar principles of law applicable to patent cases. Neilson claimed no particular mode of constructing the receptacle, or of heating it. He pointed out the manner in which it might be done; but admitted that it might also be done in a variety of ways; and at a higher or lower temperature; and that all of them would produce the effect in a greater or less degree, provided the air was heated by passing through a heated receptacle. And hence it seems that the court at first doubted, whether it was a patent for anything more than the discovery that hot air would promote the ignition of fuel better than cold. And if this had been the construction, the court, it appears, would have held his patent to be void; because the discovery of a principle in natural philosophy or physical science, is not patentable.

But after much consideration, it was finally decided that this principle must be regarded as well known, and that the plaintiff had invented a mechanical mode of applying it to furnaces; and that his invention consisted in interposing a heated receptacle, between the blower and the furnace, and by this means heating the air after it left the blower, and before it was thrown into the fire. Whoever, therefore, used this method of throwing hot air into the furnace, used the process he had invented, and thereby infringed his patent, although the form of the receptacle or the mechanical arrangements for heating it, might be different from those described by the patentee. For whatever form was adopted for the receptacle, or whatever mechanical arrangements were made for heating it, the effect would be produced in a greater or less degree, if the heated receptacle was placed between the blower and the furnace, and the current of air passed through it.

Undoubtedly, the principle that hot air will promote the ignition of fuel better than cold, was embodied in this machine. But the patent was not supported because this principle was embodied in it. He would have been equally entitled to a patent, if he had invented an improvement in the mechanical arrangements of the blowing apparatus, or in the furnace, while a cold current of air was still used. But his patent was supported, because he had invented a mechanical apparatus, by which a current of hot air, instead of cold, could be thrown in. And this new method was protected by his patent. The interposition of a heated receptacle, in any form, was the novelty he invented.

* * *

This court has decided, that the specification required by this law is a part of the patent; and that the patent issues for the invention described in the specification.

Now whether the Telegraph is regarded as an art or machine, the manner and process of making or using it must be set forth in exact terms. The act of Congress makes no difference in this respect between an art and a machine. An improvement in the art of making bar iron or spinning cotton must be so described; and so must the art of printing by the motive power of steam. And in all of these cases it has always been held that the patent embraces nothing more than the improvement described and claimed as new, and that any one who afterwards discovered a method of accomplishing the same object, substantially and essentially differing from the one described, had a right to use it.

* * *

The provisions of the acts of Congress in relation to patents may be summed up in a few words.

Whoever discovers that a certain useful result will be produced, in any art, machine, manufacture, or composition of matter, by the use of certain means, is entitled to a patent for it; provided he specifies the means he uses in a manner so full and exact, that any one skilled in the science to which it appertains, can, by using the means he specifies, without any addition to, or subtraction from them, produce precisely the result he describes. And if this cannot be done by the means he describes, the patent is void. And if it can be done, then the patent confers on him the exclusive right to use the means he specifies to produce the result or effect he describes, and nothing more. And it makes no difference, in this respect, whether the effect is produced by chemical agency or combination; or by the application of discoveries or principles in natural philosophy known or unknown before his invention; or by machinery acting altogether upon mechanical principles. In either case he must describe the manner and process as above mentioned, and the end it accomplishes. And any one may lawfully accomplish the same end without infringing the patent, if he uses means substantially different from those described.

Indeed, if the eighth claim of the patentee can be maintained, there was no necessity for any specification, further than to say that he had discovered that, by using the motive power of electromagnetism, he could print intelligible characters at any distance. We presume it will be admitted on all hands, that no patent could have issued on such a specification. Yet this claim can derive no aid from the specification field. It is outside of it, and the patentee claims beyond it. And if it stands, it must stand simply on the ground that the broad terms above-mentioned were a sufficient description, and entitled him to a patent in terms equally broad. In our judgment the act of Congress cannot be so construed. * * * [The Court then held that although the eighth claim was illegal and void, the rest of the claims were good.] The only remaining question is, whether they or either of them have been infringed by the defendants.

* * *

It is a well-settled principle of law, that the mere change in the form of the machinery (unless a particular form is specified as the means by which the effect described is produced) or an alteration in some of its unessential parts; or in the use of known equivalent powers, not varying essentially the machine, or its mode of operation or organization, will not make the new machine a new invention. It may be an improvement upon the former; but that will not justify its use without the consent of the first patentee.

The Columbian (O'Reilly's) Telegraph does not profess to accomplish a new purpose, or produce a new result. Its object and effect is to communicate intelligence at a distance, at the end of the main line, and at the local circuits on its way. And this is done by means of signs or

letters impressed on paper or other material. The object and purpose of the Telegraph is the same with that of Professor Morse.

Does he use the same means? Substantially, we think he does, both upon the main line and in the local circuits. He uses upon the main line the combination of two or more galvanic or electric circuits, with independent batteries for the purpose of obviating the diminished force of the galvanic current and in a manner varying very little in form from the invention of Professor Morse.

* * *

All of the efficient elements of the combination are retained, or their places supplied by well-known equivalents. Its organization is essentially the same.

Neither is the substitution of marks and signs, differing from those invented by Professor Morse, any defense to this action. His patent is not for the invention of a new alphabet; but for a combination of powers composed of tangible and intangible elements, described in his specification, by means of which marks or signs may be impressed upon paper at a distance, which can there be read and understood. And if any marks or signs or letters are impressed in that manner by means of a process substantially the same with his invention, or with any particular part of it covered by his patent, and those marks or signs can be read, and thus communicate intelligence, it is an infringement of his patent. The variation in the character of the marks would not protect it, if the marks could be read and understood.

* * *

The invasion of the plaintiff's rights, already stated, authorized the injunction granted by the Circuit Court, and so much of its decree must be affirmed. But, for the reasons hereinbefore assigned, the complainants are not entitled to costs, and that portion of the decree must be reversed, and a decree passed by this court, directing each party to pay his own costs, in this and in the Circuit Court.

NOTE

The development of the telegraph is described in Malcolm MacLaren, The Rise of the Electrical Industry During the Nineteenth Century (Princeton: Princeton University Press, 1943) at 32–47. Henry's testimony in the litigation, which tended to minimize Morse's contribution, greatly irritated Morse. In 1855 Morse launched a bitter attack against Henry's personal integrity. Henry asked the Board of Regents of the Smithsonian Institution to investigate the charges on the ground that they related to his fitness for the office of Secretary. The Board exonerated Henry. Id. at 43.

TILGHMAN v. PROCTOR

Supreme Court of the United States, 1880.
102 U.S. (12 Otto) 707, 26 L.Ed. 279.

MR. JUSTICE BRADLEY delivered the opinion of the Court.

* * *

The patent in question relates to the treatment of fats and oils, and is for a process of separating their component parts so as to render them better adapted to the uses of the arts. It was discovered by Chevreul, an eminent French chemist, as early as 1813, that ordinary fat, tallow and oil are regular chemical compounds, consisting of a base which has been termed glycerine, and of different acids, termed generally fat acids, but specifically, stearic, margaric, and oleic acids. These acids, in combination severally with glycerine, form stearine, margarine, and oleine. They are found in different proportions in the various neutral fats and oils; stearine predominating in some, margarine in others, and oleine in others. When separated from their base (glycerine), they take up an equivalent of water, and are called free fat acids. In this state they are in a condition for being utilized in the arts. The stearic and margaric acids form a whitish, semi-transparent, hard substance, resembling spermaceti, which is manufactured into candles. They are separated from the oleic acid, which is a thin oily fluid, by hydrostatic or other powerful pressure; the oleine being used for manufacturing soap, and other purposes. The base, glycerine, when purified, has come to be quite a desirable article for many uses.

The complainant's patent is dated the third day of October, 1854, and relates back to the ninth day of January of that year, being the date of an English patent granted to the patentee for the same invention. It has but a single claim, the words of which are as follows: "Having now described the nature of my said invention, and the manner of performing the same, I hereby declare that I claim, as of my own invention, the manufacturing of fat acids and glycerine from fatty bodies by the action of water at a high temperature and pressure."

* * *

As having some bearing upon the proper construction of the patent in suit (which will presently be more particularly examined), it is proper to observe that Tilghman's actual invention, as demonstrated in his experiments made in 1853, before making any application for a patent, was not confined to the use of a coil of pipe in a heated chamber or furnace for effecting the process which he claims, but was frequently exhibited by using a simple digester, filled nearly full with a mixture of fat and water, and heated in a gas stove, or in a vertical position over a gas lamp; the mixture of fat with the water being kept up by a loose metallic rod or jumper, which thoroughly mixed the contents when the digester was shaken. * * *

An examination of the patent itself, which the preceding remarks will enable us better to understand, will show, we think, that it was intended to and does cover and secure to the patentee the general process which has been described, although only one particular method of applying and using it is pointed out.

The specification describes the invention as follows:—

"My invention consists of a process for producing free fat acids and solution of glycerine from those fatty and oily bodies of animal and vegetable origin which contain glycerine as their base. For this purpose, I subject these fatty or oily bodies to the action of water at a high temperature and pressure, so as to cause the elements of those bodies to combine with water, and thereby obtain at the same time free fat acids and solution of glycerine. I mix the fatty body to be operated upon with from a third to a half of its bulk of water, and the mixture may be placed in any convenient vessel in which it can be heated to the melting point of lead, until the operation is complete. The vessel must be closed and of great strength, so that the requisite amount of pressure may be applied to prevent the conversion of the water into steam.

"The process may be performed more rapidly and also continuously by causing the mixture of fatty matter and water to pass through a tube or continuous channel, heated to the temperature already mentioned; the requisite pressure for preventing the conversion of water into steam being applied during the process; and this I believe is the best mode of carrying my invention into effect. In the drawing hereunto annexed are shown figures of an apparatus for performing this process speedily and continuously, but which apparatus I do not intend to claim as any part of my invention."

The specification then goes on to describe, by the aid of the drawing referred to, the particular device mentioned. But it is evident, and indeed is expressly announced, that the process claimed does not have reference to this particular device, for the apparatus described was well known, being similar to that used for producing the hot-blast and for heating water for the purpose of warming houses. It consists of a coil of iron pipe, or other metallic tubing, erected in an oven or furnace, where it can be subjected to a high degree of heat; and through this pipe the mixture (of nearly equal parts of fat and water), made into an emulsion in a separate vessel by means of a rapidly vibrating piston, or dasher, is impelled by a force-pump in a nearly continuous current, with such regulated velocity as to subject it to the heat of the furnace for a proper length of time to produce the desired result; which time, when the furnace is heated to the temperature of 612 degrees Fahrenheit, is only about ten minutes. The fat and water are kept from separating by the vertical position of the tubes, as well as by the constant movement of the current; and are prevented from being converted into steam by weighting the exit valve by which the product is discharged into the receiving vessel, so that none of it can escape except as it is expelled by the pulsations produced by the working of the force-pump. Before arriving at the exit valve, the pipe is passed, in a second coil, through an exterior vessel filled with water, by which the temperature of the product is reduced. After the product is discharged into the receiving vessel, it is allowed to stand and cool until the glycerine settles to the bottom and separates itself from the fat acids. The latter are then subjected to washing and hydraulic pressure in the usual way.

After describing this apparatus it is added:—

"Although the decomposition of the neutral facts by water takes place with great quickness at the proper heat, yet I prefer that the pump should be worked at such a rate, in proportion to the length or capacity of the heating tubes, that the mixture, while flowing through them, should be maintained at the desired temperature for ten minutes before it passes into the refrigerator or cooling part of the apparatus."

It is evident that the passing of the mixture of fat and water through a heated coil of pipe standing in a furnace is only one of several ways in which the process may be applied. The patentee suggests it as what he conceived to be the best way, apparently because the result is produced with great rapidity and completeness. But other forms of apparatus, known and in public use at the time, can as well be employed without changing the process. A common digester, or boiler, can evidently be so used, provided proper means are employed to keep up the constant admixture of the water and fat, which is a *sine qua non* in the operation. Tilghman himself, as we have seen, often used such digesters in making his experiments before applying for his patent; and, in putting up machinery for his licensees after his patent was obtained, he did the same thing when the parties desired it. Yet surely the identity of the process was not changed by thus changing the form of apparatus. No great amount of invention was required to adapt different forms of well-known apparatus to the application of the process. The principal difficulty would be in providing an internal arrangement in the boiler, or digester, for successfully keeping up the intimate commixture of the fat and water. It is evident that this could be accomplished by means of revolving reels armed with buckets, or of a force-pump constantly transferring the heavy stratum of water from the bottom of the mass to the top, aided by horizontal diaphragms partially sectionizing the digester. These devices were resorted to by Tilghman and others when they used a boiler instead of a coil of pipe.

Whilst Tilghman in his patent recommends the high degree of heat named, he does not confine himself to that. It had been fully developed in his experiments, and was well known to him, that a lower degree of heat could be employed by taking longer time to perform the operation; and this would be necessary when boilers, or digesters, of considerable size were used instead of the coil of pipe, on account of the decreasing power of large vessels to resist the internal pressure. The specification, after describing the use of a metallic coil of pipe, proceeds to add:—

"The melting-point of lead has been mentioned as the proper heat to be used in this operation, because it has been found to give good results. But the change of fatty matters into fat acid and glycerine takes place with some materials (such as palm-oil) at or below the melting point of bismuth [510 degrees Fahrenheit]; yet the heat has been carried considerably above the melting-point of lead without any apparent injury, and the decomposing action of the water becomes more powerful as the heat is increased. By starting the apparatus at a low heat, and gradually increasing it, the temperature giving products most suitable to the intended application of the fatty body employed can easily be determined."

* * *

What did Tilghman discover? And what did he, in terms, claim by his patent? He discovered that fat can be dissolved into its constituent elements by the use of water alone under a high degree of heat and pressure; and he patented *the process* of "manufacturing fat acids and glycerine from fatty bodies by the action of water at a high temperature and pressure." Had the process been known and used before, and not been Tilghman's invention, he could not then have claimed anything more than the particular apparatus described in his patent; but being the inventor of the process, as we are satisfied was the fact, he was entitled to claim it in the manner he did.

That a patent can be granted for a process, there can be no doubt. The patent law is not confined to new machines and new compositions of matter, but extends to any new and useful art or manufacture. A manufacturing process is clearly an art, within the meaning of the law. Goodyear's patent was for a process, namely, the process of vulcanizing India-rubber by subjecting it to a high degree of heat when mixed with sulphur and a mineral salt. The apparatus for performing the process was not patented, and was not material. The patent pointed out how the process could be effected, and that was deemed sufficient. Neilson's patent was for the process of applying the hot-blast to furnaces by forcing the blast through a vessel or receptacle situated between the blowing apparatus and the furnace, and heated to a red heat; the form of the heated vessel being stated by the patent to be immaterial. These patents were sustained after the strictest scrutiny and against the strongest opposition.

* * *

It has been supposed that the decision in O'Reilly v. Morse was adverse to patents for mere processes. The mistake has undoubtedly arisen from confounding a patent for a process with a patent for a mere principle. We think that a careful examination of the judgment in that case will show that nothing adverse to patents for processes is contained in it. The eighth claim of Morse's patent was held to be invalid, because it was regarded by the court as being not for a process, but for a mere principle. It amounted to this, namely, a claim of the exclusive right to the use of electro-magnetism as a motive power for making intelligible marks at a distance; that is, a claim to the exclusive use of one of the powers of nature for a particular purpose. It was not a claim of any particular machinery, nor a claim of any particular process for utilizing the power; but a claim of the power itself,—a claim put forward on the ground that the patentee was the first to discover that it *could* be thus employed. This claim the court held could not be sustained.

* * *

The claim of the patent is not for a mere principle. The chemical principle or scientific fact upon which it is founded is, that the elements of neutral fat require to be severally united with an atomic equivalent of water in order to separate from each other and become free. This chemical fact was not discovered by Tilghman. He only claims to have invented a particular mode of bringing about the desired chemical union between the fatty elements and water. He does not claim every mode of accomplishing this result. He does not claim the lime-saponification process, nor the sulphuric-acid distillation process, and if, as contended, the result was accomplished by Dubrunfaut, Wilson, and Scharling, by means of steam distillation, he does not claim that process. He only claims the process of subjecting to a high degree of heat a mixture continually kept up, of nearly equal quantities of fat and water in a convenient vessel strong enough to resist the effort of the mixture to convert itself into steam. This is most certainly a process. It is clearly pointed out in the specification, and one particular mode of applying it and carrying it into effect is described in detail.

* * *

[The Court then held the patent valid and infringed.]

APPLICATION OF ZOLTAN TARCZY–HORNOCH
United States Court of Customs and Patent Appeals, 1968.
397 F.2d 856.

RICH, JUDGE. This appeal is from a decision of the Patent Office Board of Appeals affirming the examiner's rejection of claims 31–35 and 40 in appellant's application serial No. 23,739, filed April 21, 1960, entitled "Pulse Sorting Apparatus and Method." Claims 16–28, 29, 30 and 36–39 have been allowed.

The invention of the claims on appeal is a method for sorting or counting electrical pulses, effective in counting of such pulses of varying amplitudes even at extremely high repetition rates, i.e., at rates greater than 50,000,000 (50 megacycles per second). Appellant's method envisions the use of a multistage apparatus. The first stage counts every pulse within its capacity. Cancelling orders in the form of "inhibit" pulses are then sent to each of the succeeding stages to prevent another counting of those same pulses. Should the initial stage be unable to handle a pulse, no cancellation order is given the second stage. The pulse, then, is counted by the second stage. Thereupon, cancellation orders are sent to succeeding stages.

Claim 31 is illustrative:

> 31. In a method for sorting a plurality of input pulses by utilizing a plurality of serially connected stages adapted to accept pulses, causing each input pulse to be applied to each stage sequentially in time, generating an inhibit pulse in each stage which accepts an input pulse and applying the inhibit pulse to each succeeding stage in substantial coincidence with the input pulse so that the input pulse is canceled to thereby prevent registration of the same input pulse in a succeeding stage.

The examiner allowed appellant's apparatus claims. However, he rejected all the method claims on the ground that they merely defined the function of appellant's apparatus. * * *

The issue, therefore, is whether a process claim, otherwise patentable, should be rejected because the application, of which it is a part, discloses apparatus which will *inherently* carry out the recited steps. * * *

We have determined that our decisions requiring the rejection of such claims are justified neither by history nor policy. Today we overrule those decisions.

The expression "function of an apparatus" is our legacy of 19th century controversy over the patentability of processes. Early cases proscribed a kind of overweening claim in which the desirable result first effected by an invention was itself appropriated by the inventor. Two notorious examples will suffice.

Wyeth had obtained a patent for a machine for cutting ice into blocks of uniform size. His specification read: "It is claimed as new, to cut ice of a uniform size, by means of an apparatus worked by any other power than human. The invention of this art, as well as the particular method of the application of the principle, are claimed by * * * [Wyeth]." In an infringement suit, in 1840, Justice Story, sitting on circuit, held the claimed matter "unmaintainable" in point of law and a patent, granted for such, void as for an abstract principle and broader than the invention. "A claim broader than the actual invention of the patentee is, for that very reason, upon the principles of the common law, utterly void, and the patent is a nullity." Wyeth v. Stone, Fed.Cas. No.18,107, 1 Story 273, 285–286 (C.C.Mass.1840).

The first comprehensive review of process patents by the Supreme Court was occasioned some thirteen years later by Morse's attempt to enforce his telegraph patent. Chief Justice Taney wrote the opinion for the Court, which held several apparatus claims valid and infringed. O'Reilly v. Morse, 56 U.S. (15 How.) 62 (1854).

* * *

The [eighth] claim was, of course, held invalid because it did not correspond in scope to Morse's invention.

The [opinion in Morse] * * * apparently cast some doubt on the validity of claims for processes generally, whether mechanical or not. See Risdon Iron & Locomotive Works v. Medart, 158 U.S. 68, 75 (1894); Tilghman v. Proctor, 102 U.S. 707, 726 (1880); O'Reilly v. Morse, 56 U.S. (15 How.) 62 (1853) (Grier, J., dissenting). It shortly became clear, however, that the patentability of chemical processes at least had been unaffected. In Corning v. Burden, 56 U.S. (15 How.) 252 (1853), a case decided after *Morse* but during the same term, the issue was whether Burden's ambiguous claim was properly interpreted as for a process. The patent was ostensibly directed toward a machine for rolling puddle balls in the manufacture of iron. But the lower court had instructed the jury that the patent was for a new *method* of converting puddle balls to blooms "by continuous pressure and rotation * * * between converging surfaces." The Supreme Court held the claim limited to the machine, since, in the Court's mind, a contrary decision would call into question the validity of the claim. In an influential aside on the way to this conclusion, Justice Grier, for a unanimous Court, discussed the patentability of processes:

> A process, *eo nomine,* is not made the subject of a patent in our act of Congress. It is included under the general term "useful art." An art may require one or more processes or machines in order to produce a certain result or manufacture. The term machine includes every mechanical device or combination of mechanical powers and devices to perform some function and produce a certain effect or result. But where the result or effect is produced by chemical action, by the operation or application of some element or power of nature, or of one substance to another, such modes, methods, or operations, are called processes. A new process is usually the result of a discovery; a machine, of invention. The arts of tanning, dyeing, making water-proof cloth, vulcanizing India rubber, smelting ores, and numerous others are usually carried on by processes, as distinguished from machines. One may discover a new and useful improvement in the process of tanning, dyeing, & c., irrespective of any particular form of machinery or mechanical device. And another may invent a labor-saving machine by which this operation or process may be performed, and each may be entitled to his patent. As, for instance, A has discovered that by exposing India rubber to a certain degree of heat, in mixture or connection with certain metallic salts, he can produce a valuable product or manufacture; he is entitled to a patent for his discovery, as a process or improvement in the art, irrespective of any machine or mechanical device. B, on the contrary, may invent a new furnace or stove, or steam apparatus, by which this process may be carried on with much saving of labor, and expense of fuel; and he will be entitled to a patent for his machine, as an improvement in the art. Yet A could not have a patent for a machine, or B for a process; but each would have a patent for the means or method of producing a certain result, or effect, and not for the result or effect produced. It is for the discovery or invention of some practicable method or means of producing a beneficial result or effect, that a patent is granted, and not for the result or effect itself. It is when the term process is used to represent the means or method of producing a result that it is patentable, and it will include all methods or means which are not effected by mechanism or mechanical combinations.

But the term process is often used in a more vague sense, in which it cannot be the subject of a patent. Thus we say that a board is undergoing the process of being planed, grain of being ground, iron of being hammered, or rolled. Here the term is used subjectively or passively as applied to the material operated on, and not to the method or mode of producing that operation, which is by mechanical means, or the use of a machine, as distinguished from a process.

In this use of the term it represents the function of a machine, or the effect produced by it on the material subjected to the action of the machine. But it is well settled that a man cannot have a patent for the function or abstract effect of a machine, but only for the machine which produces it.

The dictum is interesting for its reflection of the context in which the "function of a machine" objection to patentability was initially applied. It is clear that some processes were thought patentable and others not. It is also clear that "function of a machine" was symbolic of the latter. It is yet unclear, at this point in the development of the law, whether the dividing line marks a difference between means and result or chemistry and mechanics. In any event, the simple notion of undue breadth has been abandoned or, at least, considerably refined.

Several subsequent cases upheld process patents. Cochrane v. Deener, 94 U.S. 780 (1876); Tilghman v. Proctor, 102 U.S. 707 (1880). In the first of these a patent for a process of sifting flour was held valid and infringed. Justice Bradley wrote for the Court:

That a process may be patentable, irrespective of the particular form of the instrumentalities used, cannot be disputed. If one of the steps of a process be that a certain substance is to be reduced to a powder, it may not be at all material what instrument or machinery is used to effect that object, whether a hammer, a pestle and mortar, or a mill. Either may be pointed out; but if the patent is not confined to that particular tool or machine, the use of the others would be an infringement, the general process being the same. A process is a mode of treatment of certain materials to produce a given result. It is an act, or a series of acts, performed upon the subject-matter to be transformed and reduced to a different state or thing. If new and useful, it is just as patentable as is a piece of machinery. In the language of the patent law, it is an art. The machinery pointed out as suitable to perform the process may or may not be new or patentable; whilst the process itself may be altogether new, and produce an entirely new result. The process requires that certain things should be done with certain substances, and in a certain order; but the tools to be used in doing this may be of secondary consequence. [94 U.S. at 787–88]

This discussion as well as the validation itself of the flour-sifting process seemed to show that the connotation of the "function of a machine" rejection was not an objection to mechanical processes but rather to mere effects masquerading as processes.

Justice Bradley's language in Tilghman v. Proctor tended to reinforce this idea. In that case although the process in question was a chemical one, he again took up the patentability of processes in general and discussed, among other cases, O'Reilly v. Morse, supra, to show that Chief Justice Taney "fully acquiesced in the legality and validity of a patent for a process." The "true ground" of that decision, the opinion points out, was that Morse's eighth claim was directed to a principle, not a process, a claim to a power of nature itself by one who had only first employed that power.

In the Telephone Cases, 126 U.S. 1 (1888), the Court reiterated this theme in upholding the validity of Bell's fifth claim which read:

> 5. The method of, and apparatus for, transmitting vocal or other sounds telegraphically, as herein described, by causing electrical undulations, similar in form to the vibrations of the air accompanying the said vocal or other sounds, substantially as set forth.

It was urged that the decision in O'Reilly v. Morse required that this claim be held invalid. Chief Justice Waite, who wrote for the Court, replied that that case, on the contrary, required validation of the claim. Bell's claim, he observed, was for a method of using electricity, not for electricity "in its natural state."

The Court made it clear that as long as the claim *delineated a means and not a result,* the inventor would not be penalized for having invented the *only* means for effecting the result.

> It may be that electricity cannot be used at all for the transmission of speech, except in the way Bell has discovered, and that therefore, practically, his patent gives him its exclusive use for that purpose, but that does not make his claim one for the use of electricity distinct from the particular process with which it is connected in his patent. It will, if true, show more clearly the great importance of his discovery, but it will not invalidate his patent.

Only a few years later, however, the Court seemed to turn away from the means-result dichotomy. In Risdon Locomotive Works v. Medart, 158 U.S. 68 (1894), the validity of a patent for a process of manufacturing belt pulleys was an issue. The process involved the following steps: centering the pulley center or spider; grinding the ends of the arms of the spider concentrically with the axis of the pulley; boring the center; securing the rim to the spider; grinding the face of the rim concentrically with the axis of the pulley; and grinding or squaring the edges of the rim. The Court rightly observed that the process was "purely a mechanical one" and proceeded to declare it unpatentable. The Court's reasoning began with an analysis of the "great case" of O'Reilly v. Morse, supra, and asked whether Chief Justice Taney's comments on "processes involving chemical effects" were not too broad to be supported by subsequent cases. After a review of several of those cases, the Court concluded that the validity of process patents had, in fact, been upheld when the process was chemical or involved the use of one of the agencies of nature for a practical purpose. 158 U.S. at 77. See e.g., Telephone Cases, supra; New Process Fermentation Co. v. Maus, 122 U.S. 413 (1887).

The Court then cited Corning v. Burden, supra; Wyeth v. Stone, supra, and several fairly contemporaneous circuit court decisions for the proposition that it was "equally clear" that no valid patent could be obtained "for a process which involves nothing more than the operation of a piece of mechanism, or, in other words, for the function of a machine." The patent in issue was, of course, invalid since "it clearly falls within this category." * * *

This decision was understandably taken as proscribing patents for mechanical processes. * * * [The court then discussed extensively the subsequent, erratic history of the "function of a machine" doctrine in the Supreme Court, the lower courts, the patent office and the text writers] * * *

Our present review of the major precedents has persuaded us that the decisions of the Supreme Court have not required the rejection of process claims merely because the process apparently could be carried out only with the disclosed apparatus. These rejections have been the product of decisions in the lower courts and especially in this court. We decide today that we will no longer follow those decisions.

In taking this step we are moved, to some extent, by the fact that the doctrine has been shown not to proceed from its purported wellsprings. Even so, we would leave it undisturbed were it not the product of an essentially illogical distinction unwarranted by, and at odds with, the basic purposes of the patent system and productive of a range of undesirable results from the harshly inequitable to the silly.

* * *

* * * We feel that the basic rationale of the patent system demands the upholding of properly drawn claims for new, useful and unobvious processes, regardless of whether the inventor has invented one, two, or more machines to carry them out. Cf. Waxham v. Smith, supra.

* * *

[P]erpetuation of this doctrine only invites inequitable consequences. The essential difficulty is in the fact that, although at the time of the application only one apparatus may be known which is capable of carrying out the process, others may become available later. In which case, of course, the inventor may be cheated of his invention. It is peculiarly our responsibility to see that the decisional law does not require this kind of inequity.

In the *Telephone Cases,* supra, it was pointed out that Bell's invention, primarily a method, would have been lost to him had his process claim been held invalid since he had failed to claim the apparatus which later became commercially important. But the Court upheld the method claim: "Surely, a patent for such a discovery is not to be confined to the mere means he improvised to prove the reality of his conception." We think it clear that justice militates against so confining any process patent.

This case illustrates one of the peculiarities of the doctrine. Several method claims, generic to those rejected, have been allowed, simply because they admit of operation by two sets of apparatus. This would suggest that any two process claims, each unpatentable under the "function of the apparatus" theory could be merged into a patentable claim. We see no interest of the Patent System well served by such a practice.

Accordingly, the decision of the board is reversed.

Reversed.

NOTES

1. Prior to the 1952 revision, the patent statute provided:

> "Any person who has invented or discovered any new and useful art, machine, manufacture, or composition of matter, or any new and useful improvements thereof, * * * may * * * obtain a patent therefor." 35 U.S.C. § 31 (1940); R.S. § 4886.

Does the explicit addition of "processes" in § 101 by Congress in 1952 have any bearing on the problem of the principal case?

2. Similar to the "function of an apparatus" doctrine is the rule that a patent cannot be obtained on a new use for an old product. Under this doctrine if A patents a chemical compound useful as an additive for a motor oil, B cannot later patent the compound as a cure for cancer. The compound, having already been disclosed to the art, is (subject to A's patent) available for any use. This doctrine was announced by Learned Hand in Old Town Ribbon & Carbon Co. v. Columbia Ribbon & Carbon Mfg. Co., 159 F.2d 379 (2d Cir.1947). The patent in that case was on a device for making masters in a "gelatin pad" process of duplication. The same device had been disclosed in an earlier patent for use in a "spirit" process. The inventor had perceived the usefulness of the device in the "gelatin pad" process. In holding the patent invalid, Hand said:

> "[T]here is no * * * reason for saying that Congress might not, if it chose, issue a patent for a new use of an old physical object, which is in fact closely akin to, if not identical with, an 'art,' like a process. There would be nothing unreasonable in so doing; substantially no 'machine, manufacture or composition of matter' is ever new throughout; usually it is a combination of elements, all of which are severally old, and the invention consists in the mental act of fabricating the combination. Nevertheless, since 1793, unless a patent disclosed a 'new and useful art,' a new 'machine,' a new 'manufacture,' or a new 'composition of matter,' it has not been a valid patent. If it be merely for a new employment of some 'machine, manufacture or composition of matter' already known, it makes not the slightest difference how beneficial to the public the new function may be, how long a search it may end, how many may have shared that search, or how high a reach of imaginative ingenuity the solution may have demanded. All the mental factors which determine invention may have been present to the highest degree, but it will not be patentable because it will not be within the terms of the statute. * * * It is scarcely necessary to

add that the claims in suit are not for an 'art' or 'process.' "   159 F.2d at 382.

The force of Hand's opinion is somewhat weakened by the fact that the actual claims in suit, not set out in his opinion, were not limited to the use of the master in the gelatin process. See the opinion below, 66 F.Supp. 929, 930 (E.D. N.Y.1946).

Does the inclusion of a "new use of a known process, machine, manufacture, composition of matter, or material" in the definition of process in § 100(b) of the 1952 Act change the result? Is the solution for the applicant to claim a new process rather than the old product?

FUNK BROS. SEED CO. v. KALO INOCULANT CO.

Supreme Court of the United States, 1948.
333 U.S. 127, 68 S.Ct. 440, 92 L.Ed. 588.

MR. JUSTICE DOUGLAS delivered the opinion of the Court.

This is a patent infringement suit brought by respondent. The charge of infringement is limited to certain product claims [1] of Patent No. 2,200,532 issued to Bond on May 14, 1940. Petitioner filed a counterclaim asking for a declaratory judgment that the entire patent be adjudged invalid.[2] The District Court held the product claims invalid for want of invention and dismissed the complaint. It also dismissed the counterclaim. Both parties appealed. The Circuit Court of Appeals reversed, holding that the product claims were valid and infringed and that the counterclaim should not have been dismissed. 161 F.2d 981. The question of validity is the only question presented by this petition for certiorari.

Through some mysterious process leguminous plants are able to take nitrogen from the air and fix it in the plant for conversion to organic nitrogenous compounds. The ability of these plants to fix nitrogen from the air depends on the presence of bacteria of the genus Rhizobium which infect the roots of the plant and form nodules on them. These root-nodule bacteria of the genus Rhizobium fall into at least six species. No one species will infect the roots of all species of leguminous plants. But each will infect well-defined groups of those plants.[3] Each species of root-nodule bacteria is made up of distinct strains which vary in efficiency. Methods of selecting the strong

1. The product claims in suit are 1, 3, 4, 5, 6, 7, 8, 13, and 14. Claim 4 is illustrative of the invention which is challenged. It reads as follows:

"An inoculant for leguminous plants comprising a plurality of selected mutually non-inhibitive strains of different species of bacteria of the genus Rhizobium, said strains being unaffected by each other in respect to their ability to fix nitrogen in the leguminous plant for which they are specific."

2. The patent also contains process claims.

3. The six well-recognized species of bacteria and the corresponding groups (cross-inoculation groups) of leguminous plants are:

Rhizobium trifolii	Red clover, crimson clover, mammoth clover, alsike clover
Rhizobium meliloti	Alfalfa, white or yellow sweet clovers
Rhizobium phaseoli	Garden beans
Rhizobium leguminosarum	Garden peas and vetch
Rhizobium lupini	Lupines
Rhizobium japonicum	Soy beans

strains and of producing a bacterial culture from them have long been known. The bacteria produced by the laboratory methods of culture are placed in a powder or liquid base and packaged for sale to and use by agriculturists in the inoculation of the seeds of leguminous plants. This also has long been well known.

It was the general practice, prior to the Bond patent, to manufacture and sell inoculants containing only one species of root-nodule bacteria. The inoculant could therefore be used successfully only in plants of the particular cross-inoculation group corresponding to this species. Thus if a farmer had crops of clover, alfalfa, and soy beans he would have to use three separate inoculants.[4] There had been a few mixed cultures for field legumes. But they had proved generally unsatisfactory because the different species of the Rhizobia bacteria produced an inhibitory effect on each other when mixed in a common base, with the result that their efficiency was reduced. Hence it had been assumed that the different species were mutually inhibitive. Bond discovered that there are strains of each species of root-nodule bacteria which do not exert a mutually inhibitive effect on each other. He also ascertained that those mutually non-inhibitive strains can, by certain methods of selection and testing, be isolated and used in mixed cultures. Thus he provided a mixed culture of Rhizobia capable of inoculating the seeds of plants belonging to several cross-inoculation groups. It is the product claims which disclose that mixed culture that the Circuit Court of Appeals has held valid.

We do not have presented the question whether the methods of selecting and testing the non-inhibitive strains are patentable. We have here only product claims. Bond does not create a state of inhibition or of non-inhibition in the bacteria. Their qualities are the work of nature. Those qualities are of course not patentable. For patents cannot issue for the discovery of the phenomena of nature. See Le Roy v. Tatham, 14 How. 156, 175. The qualities of these bacteria, like the heat of the sun, electricity, or the qualities of metals, are part of the storehouse of knowledge of all men. They are manifestations of laws of nature, free to all men and reserved exclusively to none. He who discovers a hitherto unknown phenomenon of nature has no claim to a monopoly of it which the law recognizes. If there is to be invention from such a discovery, it must come from the application of the law of nature to a new and useful end. See Telephone Cases, 126 U.S. 1, 532–533; De Forest Radio Co. v. General Electric Co., 283 U.S. 664, 684–685; Mackay Radio & Tel. Co. v. Radio Corp., 306 U.S. 86, 94; Cameron Septic Tank Co. v. Saratoga Springs, 159 F. 453, 462–463. The Circuit Court of Appeals thought that Bond did much more than discover a law of nature, since he made a new and different composition of non-inhibitive strains which contributed utility and economy to the manufacture and distribution of commercial inoculants. But we think that

---

4. See note 3, supra.

that aggregation of species fell short of invention within the meaning of the patent statutes. *There is no synergism (old doctrine)*

Discovery of the fact that certain strains of each species of these bacteria can be mixed without harmful effect to the properties of either is a discovery of their qualities of non-inhibition. It is no more than the discovery of some of the handiwork of nature and hence is not patentable. The aggregation of select strains of the several species into one product is an application of that newly-discovered natural principle. But however ingenious the discovery of that natural principle may have been, the application of it is hardly more than an advance in the packaging of the inoculants. Each of the species of root-nodule bacteria contained in the package infects the same group of leguminous plants which it always infected. No species acquires a different use. The combination of species produces no new bacteria, no change in the six species of bacteria, and no enlargement of the range of their utility. Each species has the same effect it always had. The bacteria perform in their natural way. Their use in combination does not improve in any way their natural functioning. They serve the ends nature originally provided and act quite independently of any effort of the patentee.

There is, of course, an advantage in the combination. The farmer need not buy six different packages for six different crops. He can buy one package and use it for any or all of his crops of leguminous plants. And, as respondent says, the packages of mixed inoculants also hold advantages for the dealers and manufacturers by reducing inventory problems and the like. But a product must be more than new and useful to be patented; it must also satisfy the requirements of invention or discovery. Cuno Engineering Corp. v. Automatic Devices Corp., 314 U.S. 84, 90, 91, and cases cited; 35 U.S.C. § 31, R.S. § 4886. The application of this newly-discovered natural principle to the problem of packaging of inoculants may well have been an important commercial advance. But once nature's secret of the non-inhibitive quality of certain strains of the species of Rhizobium was discovered, the state of the art made the production of a mixed inoculant a simple step. Even though it may have been the product of skill, it certainly was not the product of invention. There is no way in which we could call it such unless we borrowed invention from the discovery of the natural principle itself. That is to say, there is no invention here unless the discovery that certain strains of the several species of these bacteria are non-inhibitive and may thus be safely mixed is invention. But we cannot so hold without allowing a patent to issue on one of the ancient secrets of nature now disclosed. All that remains, therefore, are advantages of the mixed inoculants themselves. They are not enough.

Since we conclude that the product claims do not disclose an invention or discovery within the meaning of the patent statutes, we do not consider whether the other statutory requirements contained in 35 U.S.C. § 31, R.S. § 4886, are satisfied.

Reversed.

MR. JUSTICE FRANKFURTER, concurring.

My understanding of Bond's contribution is that prior to his attempts, packages of mixed cultures of inoculants presumably applicable to two or more different kinds of legumes had from time to time been prepared, but had met with indifferent success. The reasons for failure were not understood, but the authorities had concluded that in general pure culture inoculants were alone reliable because mixtures were ineffective due to the mutual inhibition of the combined strains of bacteria. Bond concluded that there might be special strains which lacked this mutual inhibition, or were at all events mutually compatible. Using techniques that had previously been developed to test efficiency in promoting nitrogen fixation of various bacterial strains, Bond tested such efficiency of various mixtures of strains. He confirmed his notion that some strains were mutually compatible by finding that mixtures of these compatible strains gave good nitrogen fixation in two or more different kinds of legumes, while other mixtures of certain other strains proved mutually incompatible.

If this is a correct analysis of Bond's endeavors, two different claims of originality are involved: (1) the idea that there are compatible strains, and (2) the experimental demonstration that there were in fact some compatible strains. Insofar as the court below concluded that the packaging of a particular mixture of compatible strains is an invention and as such patentable, I agree, provided not only that a new and useful property results from their combination, but also that the particular strains are identifiable and adequately identified. I do not find that Bond's combination of strains satisfies these requirements. The strains by which Bond secured compatibility are not identified and are identifiable only by their compatibility.

Unless I misconceive the record, Bond makes no claim that Funk Brothers used the same combination of strains that he had found mutually compatible. He appears to claim that since he was the originator of the idea that there might be mutually compatible strains and had practically demonstrated that some such strains exists, everyone else is forbidden to use a combination of strains whether they are or are not identical with the combinations that Bond selected and packaged together. It was this claim that, as I understand it, the District Court found not to be patentable, but which, if valid, had been infringed.

The Circuit Court of Appeals defined the claims to "cover a composite culture in which are included a plurality of species of bacteria belonging to the general Rhizobium genus, carried in a conventional base." 161 F.2d 981, 983. But the phrase "the claims cover a composite culture" might mean "a particular composite culture" or "any composite culture." The Circuit Court of Appeals seems to me to have proceeded on the assumption that only "a particular composite culture" was devised and patented by Bond, and then applies it to "any composite culture" arrived at by deletion of mutually inhibiting strains, but strains which may be quite different from Bond's composite culture.

The consequences of such a conclusion call for its rejection. Its acceptance would require, for instance in the field of alloys, that if one discovered a particular mixture of metals, which when alloyed had some particular desirable properties, he could patent not merely this particular mixture but the idea of alloying metals for this purpose, and thus exclude everyone else from contriving some other combination of metals which, when alloyed, had the same desirable properties. In patenting an alloy, I assume that both the qualities of the product and its specific composition would need to be specified. The strains that Bond put together in the product which he patented can be specified only by the properties of the mixture. The District Court, while praising Bond's achievement, found want of patentability. The Circuit Court of Appeals reversed the judgment of the District Court by use of an undistributed middle—that the claims cover a "composite culture"— in the syllogism whereby they found patentability.

It only confuses the issue, however, to introduce such terms as "the work of nature" and the "laws of nature." For these are vague and malleable terms infected with too much ambiguity and equivocation. Everything that happens may be deemed "the work of nature," and any patentable composite exemplifies in its properties "the laws of nature." Arguments drawn from such terms for ascertaining patentability could fairly be employed to challenge almost every patent. On the other hand, the suggestion that "if there is to be invention from such a discovery, it must come from the application of the law of nature to a new and useful end" may readily validate Bond's claim. Nor can it be contended that there was no invention because the composite has no new properties other than its ingredients in isolation. Bond's mixture does in fact have the new property of multi-service applicability. Multi-purpose tools, multivalent vaccines, vitamin complex composites, are examples of complexes whose sole new property is the conjunction of the properties of their components. Surely the Court does not mean unwittingly to pass on the patentability of such products by formulating criteria by which future issues of patentability may be prejudged. In finding Bond's patent invalid I have tried to avoid a formulation which, while it would in fact justify Bond's patent, would lay the basis for denying patentability to a large area within existing patent legislation.

NOTES

1. In Merck & Co. v. Olin Mathieson Chemical Corp., 253 F.2d 156 (4th Cir.1958), the court upheld a patent on a Vitamin B_{12}—Active Composition which was a concentrate of Vitamin B_{12} obtained by extraction and purification from fermentation materials. The district court held the patent invalid on the ground that Vitamin B_{12} was a "product of nature". The court reversed:

A product of nature which is not a 'new and useful * * * machine, manufacture, or composition of matter' is not patentable, for it is not within the statutory definition of those things which may be patented. Even though it be a new and useful composition of matter it still may be unpatentable if the subject matter as a whole was obvious within the meaning of § 103 (35 U.S.C. 103), or if other conditions of patentability are not satisfied.

In dealing with such considerations, unpatentable products have been frequently characterized as 'products of nature.' See Funk Brothers Seed Company v. Kalo Inoculant Company, 333 U.S. 127 * * *. But where the requirements of the Act are met, patents upon products of nature are granted and their validity sustained. * * *

To the extent that the product of nature defense has validity, as urged here, it is a contention that the patented compositions are not 'new and useful * * * compositions of matter' within the meaning of § 101 of the Act. This defense may be separated into two doctrines, (1) that a patent may not be granted upon an old product though it be derived from a new source by a new and patentable process, and (2) that every step in the purification of a product is not a patentable advance, except, perhaps, as to the process, if the new product differs from the old 'merely in degree, and not in kind.'

In the first aspect of this defense, reliance is placed upon American Wood Paper Company v. Fibre Disintegrating Company, 90 U.S. 566, in which a patent upon cellulose produced from wood products was held invalid because cellulose derived from other sources was old and long had been used for paper making, and upon Cochrane v. Badische Anilin & Soda Fabrik, 111 U.S. 293, in which a patent upon synthetic alizarine was held invalid because alizarine, having the same chemical properties and uses, derived from the madder root, had long been known and used in dye-stuff.

It can hardly be doubted that, as was said in 'The Wood-Paper Patent case,' '* * * if one should discover a mode or contrive a process by which prussic acid could be obtained from a subject in which it is not now known to exist, he might have a patent for his process, but not for prussic acid.' The fact that the product, itself, is not a 'new and useful * * * machine, manufacture, or composition of matter,' within the meaning of § 101, is fatal to the product claims. The facts here, however, are far from the premise of the principle. Until the patentees produced them, there were no such B_{12} active compositions. No one had produced even a comparable product. The active substance was unidentified and unknown. The new product, not just the method, had such advantageous characteristics as to replace the liver products. What was produced was, in no sense, an old product.

The second aspect of the defense is equally inapplicable to the facts. Each slight step in purification does not produce a new product. What is gained may be the old product, but with a greater degree of purity. Alpha alumina purified is still alpha alumina, In re Ridgway, 76 F.2d 602, and ultramarine from which flotable impurities have been removed is still ultramarine, In re Merz, 97 F.2d 599. The fact, however, that a new and useful product is the result of processes of extraction, concentration and purification of natural materials does not defeat its patentability. As was said in the aspirin case, Kuehmsted v. Farbenfabriken of Elberfeld Co., 7 Cir., 179 F. 701, 705:

"Hoffmann has produced a medicine indisputably beneficial to mankind—something new in a useful art, such as our patent policy was intended to promote. Kraut and his contemporaries, on the other hand, had produced only, at best, a chemical compound in an impure state. And it makes no difference, so far as patentability is concerned, that the medicine thus produced is lifted out of a mass that contained, chemically, the compound; for, though the difference between Hoffmann and Kraut be one of purification only—strictly marking the line, however where the one is therapeutically available and the others were therapeutically unavailable—patentability would follow. In the one case the mass is made to yield something to the useful arts; in the other case what is yielded is chiefly interesting as a fact in chemical learning."

* * * The patentees have given us for the first time a medicine which can be used successfully in the treatment of pernicious anemia, a medicine which avoids the dangers and disadvantages of the liver extracts, the only remedies available prior to this invention, a medicine subject to accurate standardization and which can be produced in large quantities and inexpensively, a medicine which is valuable for other purposes, as well as for the treatment of pernicious anemia. It did not exist in nature in the form in which the patentees produced it and was produced by them only after lengthy experiments. Nothing in the prior art either anticipated or suggested it.

The same patent was again upheld on a different record in Merck & Co. v. Chase Chemical Co., 273 F.Supp. 68 (D.N.J.1967).

2. "Our reading of the Supreme Court's opinion in Funk leads us to conclude that the test of patentability of a natural phenomenon is as follows: Would an artisan, knowing the newly discovered natural phenomenon require more than ordinary skill to discover the process by which to apply that phenomenon as the patentee had done?" Armour Pharmaceutical Co. v. Richardson-Merrell, Inc., 396 F.2d 70, 74 (3d Cir.1968). Is this test consistent with the holding in *Merck*? In *Armour Pharmaceutical* the court held invalid a patent on the use of an already known compound for use as an anti-inflammatory agent. The compound was to be taken orally in the form of a coated pill. The coating permitted the compound to pass through the acidic environment of the stomach and into the intestine, where it would be absorbed through the wall of the small intestine into the body. The critical discovery was the hitherto unknown fact that the compound would be absorbed by the lining of the small intestine—a fact discovered by experiments on rats. Once that fact was known, the preparation of a coated pill to deliver the compound to the small intestine required no new art. Is *Armour* distinguishable from *Merck* on the ground that extraction of Vitamin B_{12} was a difficult process requiring many years of experimentation before it was achieved, even though the fact that there was an "anti-pernicious anemia principle" later found to be Vitamin B_{12} had long been known?

3. In Scripps Clinic & Research Foundation v. Genentech Inc., 666 F.Supp. 1379 (N.D.Cal.1987), on motion for reconsideration 678 F.Supp. 1429 (1988), the Court held that a concentrated preparation of Factor VIII:C, a component of blood that facilitates clotting and which hemophiliacs lack, was patentable subject matter although Factor VIII:C naturally occurs in blood. The Scripps patent was on concentrated Factor VIII:C which Scripps obtained by purification of human blood. Since human blood is in short supply, the resulting

Factor VIII:C was very expensive. Genentech used biotechnology to place human genes in a hamster so that the genetically modified hamsters became producers of Factor VIII:C. The court held that the Genentech product infringed the Scripps patent, but denied a preliminary injunction pending a determination of patent validity.

4. Is a newly discovered plant patentable under 35 U.S.C. § 101? Is a plant a "composition of matter?" The assumption that a plant was not patentable led to a 1930 amendment to the patent act explicitly providing for plant patents. The provisions for plant patents are now contained in 35 U.S.C. §§ 161–64. Note the explicit exclusion of a "plant found in an uncultivated state" and the limitation of the patent owner's right to the right "to exclude others from asexually reproducing the plant or selling or using the plant so reproduced." What policy considerations led to these limitations on plant patents?

The House Report described the purpose of the amendment as follows:

The purpose of the bill is to afford agriculture, so far as practicable, the same opportunity to participate in the benefits of the patent system as has been given industry, and thus assist in placing agriculture on a basis of economic equality with industry. The bill will remove the existing discrimination between plant developers and industrial inventors. To these ends the bill provides that any person who invents or discovers a new and distinct variety of plant shall be given by patent an exclusive right to propagate that plant by asexual reproduction; that is, by *grafting, budding, cuttings, layering, division, and the like, but not by seeds.* The bill does not provide for patents upon varieties of plants newly found by plant explorers or others, growing in an uncultivated or wild state.

* * * To-day plant breeding and research is dependent, in large part, upon Government funds to Government experiment stations, or the limited endeavors of the amateur breeder. It is hoped that the bill will afford a sound basis for investing capital in plant breeding and consequently stimulate plant development through private funds,

In addition, the breeder to-day must make excessive charges for specimens of the new variety disposed of by him at the start in order to avail himself of his only opportunity for financial reimbursement. Under the bill the breeder may give the public immediate advantage of the new varieties at a low price with the knowledge that the success of the variety will enable him to recompense himself through wide public distribution by him during the life of the patent. The farmers and general public that buy plants will be able promptly to obtain new improved plants at a more moderate cost.

In re Arzberger, 112 F.2d 834 (C.C.P.A.1940), held that the plant patent statute did not extend to newly discovered bacteria even though a bacteria is scientifically a type of plant. "We think that Congress, in the use of the word 'plant,' was speaking 'in the common language of the people,' and did not use the word in its strict, scientific sense." 112 F.2d at 838.

5. The United States Plant Variety Protection Act, 84 Stat. 1542 (1970), 7 U.S.C. § 2321 et seq., is administered by the Agricultural Marketing Service of the U.S. Department of Agriculture. The statute is modelled in part on the patent statute, with numerous alterations to fit the plant context. It provides for protection of any novel variety of sexually reproduced plant other than

fungi, bacteria, or first generation hybrids. Non-obviousness is not required. The term is 17 years.

6. Morton v. New York Eye Infirmary, 17 F. Cases 879 (No. 9,865) (C.C. S.D.N.Y.1862), held a patent invalid on the discovery that ether when administered to an animal would make the animal insensitive to pain and enable a surgeon to operate. The discovery was an important and famous one, laying the basis for modern surgical techniques. The court said:

> [T]he specification presents nothing new except the effect produced by well-known agents, administered in well-known ways on well-known subjects. This new or additional effect [of rendering the patient insensitive to pain] is not produced by any new instrument by which the agent is administered nor by a different application of it to the body of the patient. It is simply produced by increasing the quantity of the vapor inhaled. And even this quantity is to be regulated by the discretion of the operator, and may vary with the susceptibilities of the patient to its influence. It is nothing more, in the eye of the law, than the application of a well-known agent, by well-known means, to a new or more perfect use, which is not sufficient to support a patent.

> * * * [T]he beneficient and imposing character of the discovery cannot change the legal principles upon which the law of patents is founded, nor abrogate the rules by which judicial construction must be governed. * * * No matter through what long, solitary vigils, or by what importunate efforts, the secret may have been wrung from the bosom of Nature, or to what useful purpose it may be applied. Something more is necessary. The new force or principle brought to light must be embodied and set to work, and can be patented only in connection or combination with the means by which, or the medium through which, it operates.

17 F. Cases 883–84. This decision, along with the "rule" of Cochrane v. Deener, 94 U.S. 780 (1877), that a process must work to transform or change the thing which is the subject of the process, has been repeatedly cited for the proposition that medical processes are not patentable.

In Ex parte Scherer, 103 U.S.P.Q. 107 (Pat.Off.Bd.App.1954), the Patent Office granted a patent on a method of injecting medications into the human body by means of a high pressure jet. The invention made it possible to give injections without the use of a needle. The Board appeared to distinguish the *Morton* case on the ground that the materials used there were old and well known whereas Scherer's apparatus was itself novel. A number of lower court decisions involving patents on various medical procedures and devices are discussed in Note, 23 Geo.Wash.L.Rev. 238 (1954).

7. Should the patent system exclude any technological advance from its coverage? Isn't the effect of including some technologies and excluding others to skew the incentive created by the patent system toward those fields that are covered? Is there any relationship between the scope of the patent laws and the fact that large government subsidies have been found necessary for agricultural and medical research?

8. Could Mr. Justice Frankfurter's concern about obtaining a unique description of the invention be solved by submitting a specimen of the composition to the PTO? Specimens can be provided in appropriate cases, but where the specimen is alive how is the PTO to care for it? This problem is now solved by the use of a third-party depository for microorganisms, presumably equipped

to maintain the specimen. See U.S. Patent and Trademark Office, Manual of Patent Examining Procedure § 608.01(p) part C (5th Ed. 1983, Rev. 1989).

DIAMOND v. CHAKRABARTY

Supreme Court of the United States, 1980.
447 U.S. 303, 100 S.Ct. 2204, 65 L.Ed.2d 144.

MR. CHIEF JUSTICE BURGER delivered the opinion of the Court.

We granted certiorari to determine whether a live, human-made micro-organism is patentable subject matter under 35 U.S.C. § 101.

I

In 1972, respondent Chakrabarty, a microbiologist, filed a patent application, assigned to the General Electric Company. The application asserted 36 claims related to Chakrabarty's invention of "a bacterium from the genus *Pseudomonas* containing therein at least two stable energy-generating plasmids, each of said plasmids providing a separate hydrocarbon degradative pathway." [1] This human-made, genetically engineered bacterium is capable of breaking down multiple components of crude oil. Because of this property, which is possessed by no naturally occurring bacteria, Chakrabarty's invention is believed to have significant value for the treatment of oil spills. [2]

Chakrabarty's patent claims were of three types: first, process claims for the method of producing the bacteria; second, claims for an inoculum comprised of a carrier material floating on water, such as straw, and the new bacteria; and third, claims to the bacteria themselves. The patent examiner allowed the claims falling into the first two categories, but rejected claims for the bacteria. His decision rested on two grounds: (1) that micro-organisms are "products of nature," and (2) that as living things they are not patentable subject matter under 35 U.S.C. § 101.

Chakrabarty appealed the rejection of these claims to the Patent Office Board of Appeals, and the Board affirmed the Examiner on the second ground. [3] Relying on the legislative history of the 1930 Plant

1. Plasmids are hereditary units physically separate from the chromosomes of the cell. In prior research Chakrabarty and an associate discovered that plasmids control the oil degredation abilities of certain bacteria. In particular, the two researchers discovered plasmids capable of degrading camphor and octane, two components of crude oil. In the work represented by the patent application at issue here, Chakrabarty discovered a process by which four different plasmids, capable of degrading four different oil components, could be transferred to and maintained stably in a single *Pseudomonas* bacteria, which itself has no capacity for degrading oil.

2. At present, biological control of oil spills requires the use of a mixture of natu-rally occurring bacteria, each capable of degrading one component of the oil complex. In this way, oil is decomposed into simpler substances which can serve as food for aquatic life. However, for various reasons, only a portion of any such mixed culture survives to attack the oil spill. By breaking down multiple components of oil, Chakrabarty's micro-organism promises more efficient and rapid oil-spill control.

3. The Board concluded that the new bacteria were not "products of nature," because *Pseudomonas* bacteria containing two or more different energy-generating plasmids are not naturally occurring.

Patent Act, in which Congress extended patent protection to certain asexually reproduced plants, the Board concluded that § 101 was not intended to cover living things such as these laboratory created micro-organisms.

The Court of Customs and Patent Appeals, by a divided vote, reversed on the authority of its prior decision in *In re Bergy,* 563 F.2d 1031 (1978), which held that "the fact that microorganisms * * * are alive * * * [is] without legal significance" for purposes of the patent law.[4] Subsequently, we granted the Government's petition for certiorari in *Bergy,* vacated the judgment, and remanded the case "for further consideration in light of Parker v. Flook, 437 U.S. 584, 438 U.S. 902 (1978). The Court of Customs and Patent Appeals then vacated its judgment in *Chakrabarty* and consolidated the case with *Bergy* for reconsideration. After re-examining both cases in the light of our holding in *Flook,* that court, with one dissent, reaffirmed its earlier judgments. 596 F.2d 952 (1979).

The Government again sought certiorari, and we granted the writ as to both *Bergy* and *Chakrabarty.* 444 U.S. 924 (1979). Since then, *Bergy* has been dismissed as moot, 444 U.S. 1028 (1980), leaving only *Chakrabarty* for decision.

II

* * *

The question before us in this case is a narrow one of statutory interpretation requiring us to construe 35 U.S.C. § 101 * * *.

Specifically, we must determine whether respondent's microorganism constitutes a "manufacture" or "composition of matter" within the meaning of the statute.

* * *

[This case followed two decisions in which the Supreme Court had reversed Court of Customs and Patent Appeals decisions construing § 101 broadly. They were:

Gottschalk v. Benson, 409 U.S. 63 (1972). The Patent Office had rejected an application for a patent claiming a method of programming a general-purpose digital computer to convert code from binary-coded decimal form into pure binary form. The Court of Customs and Patent Appeals had reversed, holding that the claim was for a useful process. The Supreme Court, in turn, reversed the Court of Customs and Patent Appeals and upheld the Patent Office position.

All information is stored in a computer in binary or "on-off" form. The information "on" or "off" can be treated as equivalent to 0 or 1, and 0 and 1 can be used together to represent all numbers in the form 0, 1, 10, 11, 100, 101, 111, and so on. These numbers can in turn be used in codes to represent letters or numbers. Binary-coded decimal form is a decimal number in which each position in the decimal

---

4. *Bergy* involved a patent application for a pure culture of the micro-organism *Streptomyces vellosus* found to be useful in the production of lincomycin, an antibiotic.

number is represented by the appropriate binary number for the number in that position. This is a useful way for a computer to store numbers when they are to be displayed or printed in decimal form. The binary-coded decimal form, however, requires more machine memory than the pure binary form, so for purposes of storing the numbers or performing calculations it is useful to convert the numbers from binary-coded decimal form to pure binary form.

The claim of the patent was for a series of mechanical, computational steps which, when followed, converted a number from binary coded decimal form to pure binary form. The court read the claim as covering any use of the computational steps, whether performed with or without a computer. (The claim was limited to a "data processing method," which could have been read to limit the procedure to use in data processing, i.e., use on a machine, since we do not normally speak of penciled calculations as "data processing.")

There are passages in the opinion which suggest that the Court thought it was holding that all programs for digital computers are unpatentable subject matter. For instance: "If these programs are to be patentable, considerable problems are raised which only committees of Congress can manage, for broad powers of investigations are needed, including hearings which canvass the wide variety of views which those operating in this field entertain." 409 U.S. at 73.

But there were other passages that suggested that the Court was only holding that a claim on a formula, not limited to a particular use, was invalid. "Here the 'process' claim is so abstract and sweeping as to cover both known and unknown uses of the BCD to pure binary conversion. The end use may (1) vary from the operation of a train to verification of drivers' licenses to researching the law books for precedents and (2) be performed through any existing machinery or future-devised machinery or without any apparatus. ⁎ ⁎ ⁎ What we come down to in a nutshell is the following. It is conceded that one may not patent an idea. But in practical effect that would be the result if the formula for converting BCD numerals to pure binary numerals were patented in this case. The mathematical formula involved here has no substantial practical application except in connection with a digital computer, which means that if the judgment below is affirmed, the patent would wholly pre-empt the mathematical formula and in practical effect would be a patent on the algorithm itself." 409 U.S. at 68–73.

Gottschalk was followed by Parker v. Flook, 437 U.S. 584 (1978). The patent office rejected an application for a method for updating alarm limits. The C.C.P.A. again reversed, and the Supreme Court again reversed the C.C.P.A.

As in *Gottschalk* the only novel element in the patent was a formula, in this case a formula which used a number to generate another number. But unlike *Gottschalk*, the claim was drafted to read only on the use of the formula in connection with the computation of process alarms limits in the catalytic chemical conversion of hydrocar-

bons. This claim, argued the applicant, did not "wholly preempt the mathematical formula."

The Court's opinion clearly held that a patent on a computer program was not patentable subject matter. "Difficult questions of policy concerning the kinds of programs that may be appropriate for patent protection and the form and duration of such protection can be answered by Congress on the basis of current empirical data not equally available to this tribunal." 437 U.S. at 595.]

III

* * *

Guided by * * * canons of construction, this Court has read the term "manufacture" in § 101 in accordance with its dictionary definition to mean "the production of articles for use from raw materials prepared by giving to these materials new forms, qualities, properties, or combinations, whether by hand labor or by machinery." American Fruit Growers, Inc. v. Brogdex Co., 283 U.S. 1, 11 (1931). Similarly, "composition of matter" has been construed consistent with its common usage to include "all compositions of two or more substances and * * * all composite articles, whether they be the results of chemical union, or of mechanical mixture, or whether they be gases, fluids, powders, or solids." Shell Dev. Co. v. Watson, 149 F.Supp. 279, 280 (D.C.1957) (citing 1 A. Deller, Walker on Patents § 14, p. 55 (1st ed. 1937)). In choosing such expansive terms as "manufacture" and "composition of matter," modified by the comprehensive "any," Congress plainly contemplated that the patent laws would be given wide scope.

The relevant legislative history also supports a broad construction. The Patent Act of 1793, authored by Thomas Jefferson, defined statutory subject matter as "any new and useful art, machine, manufacture, or composition of matter, or any new or useful improvement [thereof]." Act of Feb. 21, 1793, ch. 11, § 1, 1 Stat. 318. The Act embodied Jefferson's philosophy that "ingenuity should receive a liberal encouragement." V Writings of Thomas Jefferson, at 75–76. See Graham v. John Deere Co., 383 U.S. 1, 7–10 (1966). Subsequent patent statutes in 1836, 1870, and 1874 employed this same broad language. In 1952, when the patent laws were recodified, Congress replaced the word "art" with "process," but otherwise left Jefferson's language intact. The Committee Reports accompanying the 1952 act inform us that Congress intended statutory subject matter to "include anything under the sun that is made by man." S.Rep. No. 1979, 82d Cong., 2d Sess., 5 (1952); H.R.Rep. No. 1923, 82d Cong., 2d Sess., 6 (1952).

This is not to suggest that § 101 has no limits or that it embraces every discovery. The laws of nature, physical phenomena, and abstract ideas have been held not patentable. See Parker v. Flook, 437 U.S. 584 (1978); Gottschalk v. Benson, 409 U.S. 63, 67 (1973); Funk Seed Co. v. Kalo Co., 333 U.S. 127, 130 (1948); O'Reilly v. Morse, 15 How. 62, 112–

121 (1853); Le Roy v. Tatham, 14 How. 156, 175 (1852). Thus, a new mineral discovered in the earth or a new plant found in the wild is not patentable subject matter. Likewise, Einstein could not patent his celebrated law that $E=mc^2$; nor could Newton have patented the law of gravity. Such discoveries are "manifestations of * * * nature, free to all men and reserved exclusively to none." Funk, supra, 333 U.S., at 130.

Judged in this light, respondent's micro-organism plainly qualifies as patentable subject matter. His claim is not to a hitherto unknown natural phenomenon, but to a nonnaturally occurring manufacture or composition of matter—a product of human ingenuity "having a distinctive name, character [and] use." Hartranft v. Wiegmann, 121 U.S. 609, 615 (1887). The point is underscored dramatically by comparison of the invention here with that in *Funk*. There, the patentee had discovered that there existed in nature certain species of root-nodule bacteria which did not exert a mutually inhibitive effect on each other. He used that discovery to produce a mixed culture capable of inoculating the seeds of leguminous plants. Concluding that the patentee had discovered "only some of the handiwork of nature," the Court ruled the product nonpatentable:

> "Each of the species of root-nodule bacteria contained in the package infects the same group of leguminous plants which it always infected. No species acquires a different use. The combination of the six species produces no new bacteria, no change in the six bacteria, and no enlargement of the range of their utility. Each species has the same effect it always had. The bacteria perform in their natural way. Their use in combination does not improve in any way their natural functioning. They serve the same ends nature originally provided and act quite independently of any effort by the patentee." 333 U.S., at 131.

Here, by contrast, the patentee has produced a new bacterium with markedly different characteristics from any found in nature and one having the potential for significant utility. His discovery is not nature's handiwork, but his own; accordingly it is patentable subject matter under § 101.

IV

Two contrary arguments are advanced, neither of which we find persuasive.

(A)

The Government's first argument rests on the enactment of the 1930 Plant Patent Act, which afforded patent protection to certain asexually reproduced plants [35 U.S.C. § 161], and the 1970 Plant Variety Protection Act, which authorized patents for certain sexually reproduced plants but excluded bacteria from its protection [7 U.S.C.

§ 2402(a)]. In the Government's view, the passage of these Acts evidences congressional understanding that the terms "manufacture" or "composition of matter" do not include living things; if they did, the Government argues, neither Act would have been necessary.

We reject this argument. Prior to 1930, two factors were thought to remove plants from patent protection. The first was the belief that plants, even those artificially bred, were products of nature for purposes of the patent law. This position appears to have derived from the decision of the patent office in Ex parte Latimer, 1889 C.D. 123, in which a patent claim for fiber found in the needle of the *Pinus australis* was rejected. The Commissioner reasoned that a contrary result would permit "patents [to] be obtained upon the trees of the forests and the plants of the earth, which of course would be unreasonable and impossible." Id., at 126. The *Latimer* case, it seems, came to "se[t] forth the general stand taken in these matters" that plants were natural products not subject to patent protection. H. Thorne, Relation of Patent Law to Natural Products, 6 J.Pat.Off.Soc. 23, 24 (1923). The second obstacle to patent protection for plants was the fact that plants were thought not amendable to the "written description" requirement of the patent law. See 35 U.S.C. § 112. Because new plants may differ from old only in color or perfume, differentiation by written description was often impossible. See Hearings on H.R. 11372 before the House Committee on Patents, 71 Cong., 2d Sess. 4 (1930), p. 7 (memorandum of Patent Commissioner Robertson).

In enacting the Plant Patent Act, Congress addressed both of these concerns. It explained at length its belief that the work of the plant breeder "in aid of nature" was patentable invention. S.Rep. No. 315, 71st Cong., 2d Sess., 6–8 (1930); H.R.Rep. No. 1129, 71st Cong., 2d Sess., 7–9 (1930). And it relaxed the written description requirement in favor of "a description * * * as complete as is reasonably possible." 35 U.S.C. § 162. No Committee or Member of Congress, however, expressed the broader view, now urged by the Government, that the terms "manufacture" or "composition of matter" exclude living things. The sole support for that position in the legislative history of the 1930 Act is found in the conclusory statement of Secretary of Agriculture Hyde, in a letter to the Chairmen of the House and Senate Committees considering the 1930 Act, that "the patent laws * * * at the present time are understood to cover only inventions or discoveries in the field of inanimate nature." See S.Rep. No. 315, supra, at Appendix A; H.R. Rep. No. 1129, supra, at Appendix A. Secretary Hyde's opinion, however, is not entitled to controlling weight. His views were solicited on the administration of the new law and not on the scope of patentable subject matter—an area beyond his competence. Moreover, there is language in the House and Senate Committee reports suggesting that to the extent Congress considered the matter it found the Secretary's dichotomy unpersuasive. The reports observe:

"There is a clear and logical distinction *between the discovery of a new variety of plant and of certain inanimate things,* such, for example, as a new and useful natural mineral. The mineral is created wholly by nature unassisted by man. * * * On the other hand, a plant discovery resulting from cultivation is unique, isolated, and is not repeated by nature, nor can it be reproduced by nature unaided by man. * * *" S.Rep. No. 315, supra, at 6; H.R.Rep. No. 1129, supra, at 7 (emphasis added).

Congress thus recognized that the relevant distinction was not between living and inanimate things, but between products of nature, whether living or not, and human-made inventions. Here, respondent's micro-organism is the result of human ingenuity and research. Hence, the passage of the Plant Patent Act affords the Government no support.

Nor does the passage of the 1970 Plant Variety Protection Act support the Government's position. As the Government acknowledges, sexually reproduced plants were not included under the 1930 Act because new varieties could not be reproduced true-to-type through seedlings. Brief for United States 27, n. 31. By 1970, however, it was generally recognized that true-to-type reproduction was possible and that plant patent protection was therefore appropriate. The 1970 Act extended that protection. There is nothing in its language or history to suggest that it was enacted because § 101 did not include living things.

In particular, we find nothing in the exclusion of bacteria from plant variety protection to support the Government's position. * * * The legislative history gives no reason for this exclusion. As the Court of Customs and Patent Appeals suggested, it may simply reflect congressional agreement with the result reached by that court in deciding In re Arzberger, 112 F.2d 834 (1940), which held that bacteria were not plants for the purposes of the 1930 Act. Or it may reflect the fact that prior to 1970 the Patent Office had issued patents for bacteria under § 101.[9] In any event, absent some clear indication that Congress "focused on [the] issues * * * directly related to the one presently before the Court," SEC v. Sloan, 436 U.S. 103, 120–121 (1978), there is no basis for reading into its actions an intent to modify the plain meaning of the words found in § 101. See TVA v. Hill, 437 U.S. 153, 189–193 (1978); United States v. Price, 361 U.S. 304, 313 (1960).

(B)

The Government's second argument is that micro-organisms cannot qualify as patentable subject matter until Congress expressly authorizes such protection. Its position rests on the fact that genetic technology

---

9. In 1873, the Patent Office granted Louis Pasteur a patent on "yeast, free from organic germs of disease, as an article of manufacture." And in 1967 and 1968, immediately prior to the passage of the Plant Variety Protection Act, that office granted two patents which, as the Government concedes, state claims for living micro-organisms.

was unforeseen when Congress enacted § 101. From this it is argued that resolution of the patentability of inventions such as respondent's should be left to Congress. The legislative process, the Government argues, is best equipped to weigh the competing economic, social, and scientific considerations involved, and to determine whether living organisms produced by genetic engineering should receive patent protection. In support of this position, the Government relies on our recent holding in Parker v. Flook, 437 U.S. 584 (1978), and the statement that the judiciary "must proceed cautiously when * * * asked to extend patent rights into areas wholly unforeseen by Congress." Id., at 596.

It is, of course, correct that Congress, not the courts, must define the limits of patentability; but it is equally true that once Congress has spoken it is "the province and duty of the judicial department to say what the law is." Marbury v. Madison, 1 Cranch 137, 177 (1803). Congress has performed its constitutional role in defining patentable subject matter in § 101; we perform ours in construing the language Congress has employed. In so doing, our obligation is to take statutes as we find them, guided, if ambiguity appears, by the legislative history and statutory purpose. Here, we perceive no ambiguity. The subject matter provisions of the patent law have been cast in broad terms to fulfill the constitutional and statutory goal of promoting "the Progress of Science and the useful Arts" with all that means for the social and economic benefits envisioned by Jefferson. Broad general language is not necessarily ambiguous when congressional objectives require broad terms.

Nothing in *Flook* is to the contrary. That case applied our prior precedents to determine that a "claim for an improved method of calculation, even when tied to a specific end use, is unpatentable subject matter under § 101." 437 U.S., at 595, n. 18. The Court carefully scrutinized the claim at issue to determine whether it was precluded from patent protection under "the principles underlying the prohibition against patents for 'ideas' or phenomena of nature." Id., at 593. We have done that here. *Flook* did not announce a new principle that inventions in areas not contemplated by Congress when the patent laws were enacted are unpatentable *per se*.

To read that concept into *Flook* would frustrate the purposes of the patent law. This Court frequently has observed that a statute is not to be confined to the "particular application[s] * * * contemplated by the legislators." Barr v. United States, 324 U.S. 83, 90 (1945). This is especially true in the field of patent law. A rule that unanticipated inventions are without protection would conflict with the core concept of the patent law that anticipation undermines patentability. See Graham v. John Deere Co., 383 U.S., at 12–17. Mr. Justice Douglas reminded that the inventions most benefiting mankind are those that "push back the frontiers of chemistry, physics, and the like." A. & P.

Tea Co. v. Supermarket Corp., 340 U.S. 147, 154 (1950) (concurring opinion). Congress employed broad general language in drafting § 101 precisely because such inventions are often unforeseeable.[10]

To buttress its argument, the Government, with the support of *amicus,* points to grave risks that may be generated by research endeavors such as respondent's. The briefs present a gruesome parade of horribles. Scientists, among them Nobel laureates, are quoted suggesting that genetic research may pose a serious threat to the human race, or, at the very least, that the dangers are far too substantial to permit such research to proceed apace at this time. We are told that genetic research and related technological developments may spread pollution and disease, that it may result in a loss of genetic diversity, and that its practice may tend to depreciate the value of human life. These arguments are forcefully, even passionately presented; they remind us that, at times, human ingenuity seems unable to control fully the forces it creates—that with Hamlet, it is sometimes better "to bear those ills we have than fly to others that we know not of."

It is argued that this Court should weigh these potential hazards in considering whether respondent's invention is patentable subject matter under § 101. We disagree. The grant or denial of patents on micro-organisms is not likely to put an end to genetic research or to its attendant risks. The large amount of research that has already occurred when no researcher had sure knowledge that patent protection would be available suggests that legislative or judicial fiat as to patentability will not deter the scientific mind from probing into the unknown any more than Canute could command the tides. Whether respondent's claims are patentable may determine whether research efforts are accelerated by the hope of reward or slowed by want of incentives, but that is all.

What is more important is that we are without competence to entertain these arguments—either to brush them aside as fantasies generated by fear of the unknown, or to act on them. The choice we are urged to make is a matter of high policy for resolution within the legislative process after the kind of investigation, examination, and study that legislative bodies can provide and courts cannot. That process involves the balancing of competing values and interests, which in our democratic system is the business of elected representatives. Whatever their validity, the contentions now pressed on us should be addressed to the political branches of the government, the Congress and the Executive, and not to the courts.

* * *

10. Even an abbreviated list of patented inventions underscores the point: telegraph (Morse, No. 1647); telephone (Bell, No. 174,465); electric lamp (Edison, No. 223,898); airplane (the Wrights, No. 821,393); transistor (Bardeen & Brattain, No. 2,524,035); neutronic reactor (Fermi & Szilard, No. 2,708,656); laser (Schawlow & Townes, No. 2,929,922). See generally Revolutionary Ideas, Patents & Progress in America, Office of Patents (1976).

Accordingly, the judgment of the Court of Customs and Patent Appeals is affirmed.

Affirmed.

MR. JUSTICE BRENNAN, with whom MR. JUSTICE WHITE, MR. JUSTICE MARSHALL, and MR. JUSTICE POWELL join, dissenting.

* * *

* * * The sweeping language of the Patent Act of 1793, as re-enacted in 1952, is not the last pronouncement Congress had made in this area. In 1930 Congress enacted the Plant Patent Act affording patent protection to developers of certain asexually reproduced plants. In 1970 Congress enacted the Plant Variety Protection Act to extend protection to certain new plant varieties capable of sexual reproduction. Thus, we are not dealing—as the Court would have it—with the routine problem of "unanticipated inventions." * * * In these two Acts Congress has addressed the general problem of patenting animate inventions and has chosen carefully limited language granting protection to some kinds of discoveries, but specifically excluding others. These Acts strongly evidence a congressional limitation that excludes bacteria from patentability.

* * *

NOTES

1. If living micro-organisms can be patented, then why not any living thing? Pat. No. 4,736,866, granted to Harvard University, claims a living mouse, particularly suitable for cancer research because it develops cancers not naturally occurring in mice. If a rodent, why not a mammal such as a cow which gives unusually good milk. And if a cow, why not a man, perhaps improved to exhibit more satisfactory social behavior? On April 21, 1987, the Commissioner issued a notice taking the position that all nonnaturally occurring nonhuman multicellular organisms, including animals, are patentable. 1077 Pat. & Trademark Off. Gazette 24. The position provoked hearings in Congress and attention in the press. The issue is essayed in Robert P. Merges, Intellectual Property in Higher Life Forms: The Patent System and Controversial Technologies, 47 Md.L.Rev. 1051 (1988); and Note, Altering Nature's Blueprints for Profit: Patenting Multicellular Animals, 74 Va.L.Review 1327 (1988).

2. The interest in animal patents has arisen as a result of techniques of biotechnology, which enable scientists to manipulate the genetic structure of living cells in order to produce biological products including animals with predictable and non-naturally occurring properties. This new technology has generated large investments as well as much patent litigation as firms compete to establish a position in what they hope will be a very profitable technology. An example of a biotechnology patent that has been held valid is Patent No. 4,376,110 for immunometric assays using monoclonal antibodies, held valid in Hybritech Inc. v. Monoclonal Antibodies, 802 F.2d 1367 (Fed.Cir.1986), cert. denied 480 U.S. 947 (1987).

DIAMOND v. DIEHR

Supreme Court of the United States, 1981.
450 U.S. 175, 101 S.Ct. 1048, 67 L.Ed.2d 155.

MR. JUSTICE REHNQUIST delivered the opinion of the Court.

We granted certiorari to determine whether a process for curing synthetic rubber which includes in several of its steps the use of a mathematical formula and a programmed digital computer is patentable subject matter under 35 U.S.C. § 101.

I

The patent application at issue was filed by the respondents on August 6, 1975. The claimed invention is a process for molding raw, uncured synthetic rubber into cured precision products. The process uses a mold for precisely shaping the uncured material under heat and pressure and then curing the synthetic rubber in the mold so that the product will retain its shape and be functionally operative after the molding is completed.[1]

Respondents claim that their process ensures the production of molded articles which are properly cured. Achieving the perfect cure depends upon several factors including the thickness of the article to be molded, the temperature of the molding process, and the amount of time that the article is allowed to remain in the press. It is possible using well-known time, temperature, and cure relationships to calculate by means of the Arrhenius equation [2] when to open the press and remove the cured product. Nonetheless, according to the respondents, the industry has not been able to obtain uniformly accurate cures because the temperature of the molding press could not be precisely measured thus making it difficult to do the necessary computations to determine cure time.[3] Because the temperature *inside* the press has heretofore been viewed as an uncontrollable variable, the conventional industry practice has been to calculate the cure time as the shortest

---

1. A "cure" is obtained by mixing curing agents into the uncured polymer in advance of molding and then applying heat over a period of time. If the synthetic rubber is cured for the right length of time at the right temperature, it becomes a useable product.

2. The equation is named after its discoverer Svante Arrhenius and has long been used to calculate the cure time, in rubber molding presses. The equation can be expressed as follows:

$$\ln v = CZ + x$$

wherein ln v is the natural logarithm of v, the total required cure time; C is the activation constant, a unique figure for each batch of each compound being molded, determined in accordance with rheometer

measurements of each batch; Z is the temperature in the mold; and x is a constant dependent on the geometry of the particular mold in the press. A rheometer is an instrument to measure flow of viscous substances.

3. During the time a press is open for loading, it will cool. The longer it is open, the cooler it becomes and the longer it takes to re-heat the press to the desired temperature range. Thus, the time necessary to raise the mold temperature to curing temperature is an unpredictable variable. The respondents claim to have overcome this problem by continuously measuring the actual temperature in the closed press through the use of a thermocouple.

time in which all parts of the product will definitely be cured, assuming a reasonable amount of mold-opening time during loading and unloading. But the shortcoming of this practice is that operating with an uncontrollable variable inevitably led in some instances to overestimating the mold-opening time and overcuring the rubber, and in other instances to underestimating that time and undercuring the product.

Respondents characterize their contribution to the art to reside in the process of constantly measuring the actual temperature inside the mold. These temperature measurements are then automatically fed into a computer which repeatedly recalculates the cure time by use of the Arrhenius equation. When the recalculated time equals the actual time that has elapsed since the press was closed, the computer signals a device to open the press. According to the respondents, the continuous measuring of the temperature inside the mold cavity, the feeding of this information to a digital computer which constantly recalculates the cure time, and the signaling by the computer to open the press, are all new in the art.

The patent examiner rejected the respondents' claims on the sole ground that they were drawn to nonstatutory subject matter under 35 U.S.C. § 101.[5] He determined that those steps in respondents' claims that are carried out by a computer under control of a stored program

---

5. Respondents' application contained 11 different claims. Three examples are claims 1, 2, and 11 which provide:

"1. A method of operating a rubber-molding press for precision molded compounds with the aid of a digital computer, comprising:

"providing said computer with a data base for said press including at least,

"natural logarithm conversion data (1n),

"the activation energy constant (C) unique to each batch of said compound being molded, and

"a constant (x) dependent upon the geometry of the particular mold of the press,

"initiating an interval timer in said computer upon the closure of the press for monitoring the elapsed time of said closure,

"constantly determining the temperature (Z) of the mold at a location closely adjacent to the mold cavity in the press during molding,

"constantly providing the computer with the temperature (Z),

"repetitively calculating in the computer, at frequent intervals during each cure, the Arrhenius equation for reaction time during the cure, which is

"$1n \ v = CZ + x$

"where v is the total required cure time,

"repetitively comparing in the computer at said frequent intervals during the cure each said calculation of the total required cure time calculated with the Arrhenius equation and said elapsed time, and

"opening the press automatically when a said comparison indicates equivalence.

"2. The method of claim 1 including measuring the activation energy constant for the compound being molded in the press with a rheometer and automatically updating said data base within the computer in the event of changes in the compound being molded in said press as measured by said rheometer.

"11. A method of manufacturing precision molded articles from selected synthetic rubber compounds in an openable rubber molding press having at least one heated precision mold, comprising:

"(a) heating said mold to a temperature range approximating a pre-determined rubber curing temperature,

"(b) installing prepared unmolded synthetic rubber of a known compound in a molding cavity of a predetermined geometry as defined by said mold,

"(c) closing said press to mold said rubber to occupy said cavity in conformance with the contour of said mold and

constituted nonstatutory subject matter under this Court's decision in Gottschalk v. Benson, 409 U.S. 63 (1972). The remaining steps— installing rubber in the press and the subsequent closing of the press— were "conventional in nature and cannot be the basis of patentability." The examiner concluded that respondents' claims defined and sought protection of a computer program for operating a rubber molding press.

The Patent and Trademark Office Board of Appeals agreed with the examiner, but the Court of Customs and Patent Appeals reversed. The court noted that a claim drawn to subject matter otherwise statutory does not become nonstatutory because a computer is involved. The respondents' claims were not directed to a mathematical algorithm or an improved method of calculation but rather recited an improved process for molding rubber articles by solving a practical problem which had risen in the molding of rubber products.

The Government sought certiorari arguing that the decision of the Court of Customs and Patent Appeals was inconsistent with prior decisions of this Court. Because of the importance of the question presented, we granted the writ. 445 U.S. 926 (1980).

II

Last Term in Diamond v. Chakrabarty, 447 U.S. 303 (1980), this Court discussed the historical purposes of the patent laws and in particular 35 U.S. § 101. As in *Chakrabarty,* we must here construe 35 U.S.C. § 101:

* * *

The Patent Act of 1793 defined statutory subject matter as "any new and useful art, machine, manufacture or composition of matter, or any new or useful improvement [thereof]." Act of Feb. 21, 1793, ch. 11, § 1, 1 Stat. 318. Not until the patent laws were recodified in 1952 did Congress replace the word "art" with the word "process." It is that

to cure said rubber by transfer of heat thereto from said mold,

"(d) initiating an interval timer upon the closure of said press for monitoring the elapsed time of said closure,

"(e) heating said mold during said closure to maintain the temperature thereof within said range approximating said rubber curing temperature,

"(f) constantly determining the temperature of said mold at a location closely adjacent said cavity thereof throughout closure of said press,

"(g) repetitively calculating at frequent periodic invervals throughout closure of said press the Arrhenius equation for reaction time of said rubber to determine total required cure time v as follows:

"$\ln v = CZ + x$

"wherein c is an activation energy constant determined for said rubber being molded and cured in said press, z is the temperature of said mold at the time of each calculation of said Arrhenius equation, and x is a constant which is a function of said predetermined geometry of said mold,

"(h) for each repetition of calculation of said Arrhenius equation herein comparing the resultant calculated total required cure time with the monitored elapsed time measured by said interval timer,

"(i) opening said press when a said comparison of calculated total required cure time and monitored elapsed time indicates equivalence, and

"(j) removing from said mold the resultant precision molded and cured rubber article."

latter word which we confront today, and in order to determine its meaning we may not be unmindful of the Committee Reports accompanying the 1952 Act which inform us that Congress intended statutory subject matter to "include anything under the sun that is made by man." S.Rep. No. 1979, 82d Cong., 2d Sess., 5 (1952), H.R.Rep. No. 1923, 82d Cong., 2d Sess., 6 (1952), U.S.Code Cong. & Admin.News 1952, pp. 2394, 2399.

Although the term "process" was not added to 35 U.S.C. § 101 until 1952 a process has historically enjoyed patent protection because it was considered a form of "art" as that term was used in the 1793 Act. In defining the nature of a patentable process, the Court stated:

> "That a process may be patentable, irrespective of the particular form of the instrumentalities used, cannot be disputed. * * * A process is a mode of treatment of certain materials to produce a given result. It is an act, or a series of acts, performed upon the subject matter to be transformed and reduced to a different state or thing. If new and useful, it is just as patentable as is a piece of machinery. In the language of the patent law, it is an art. The machinery pointed out as suitable to perform the process may or may not be new or patentable; whilst the process itself may be altogether new, and produce an entirely new result. The process requires that certain things should be done with certain substances, and in a certain order; but the tools to be used in doing this may be of secondary consequence." Cochrane v. Deener, 94 U.S. 780, 787–788 (1876).

Analysis of the eligibility of a claim of patent protection for a "process" did not change with the addition of that term to § 101. Recently, in Gottschalk v. Benson, 409 U.S. 63 (1972), we repeated the above definition recited in Cochrane v. Deener, adding "Transformation and reduction of an article 'to a different state or thing' is the clue to the patentability of a process claim that does not include particular machines." Id., at 70.

Analyzing respondents' claims according to the above statements from our cases, we think that a physical and chemical process for molding precision synthetic rubber products falls within the § 101 categories of possibly patentable subject matter. That respondents' claims involve the transformation of an article, in this case raw uncured synthetic rubber, into a different state or thing cannot be disputed. The respondents' claims describe in detail a step-by-step method for accomplishing such beginning with the loading of a mold with raw uncured rubber and ending with the eventual opening of the press at the conclusion of the cure. Industrial processes such as this are the type which have historically been eligible to receive the protection of our patent laws.

III

Our conclusion regarding respondents' claims is not altered by the fact that in several steps of the process a mathematical equation and a programmed digital computer are used. This Court has undoubtedly recognized limits to § 101 and every discovery is not embraced within the statutory terms. Excluded from such patent protection are laws of nature, physical phenomena and abstract ideas. See Parker v. Flook, 437 U.S. 584 (1978); Gottschalk v. Benson, 409 U.S. 63 (1973); Funk Bros. Seed Co. v. Kalo Co., 333 U.S. 127, 130 (1948). "An idea of itself is not patentable," Rubber-Tip Pencil Co. v. Howard, 20 Wall. 498, 507 (1874). "A principle, in the abstract, is a fundamental truth; an original cause; a motive; these cannot be patented, as no one can claim in either of them an exclusive right." Le Roy v. Tatham, 14 How. 156, 175 (1852).

* * *

Our recent holdings in Gottschalk v. Benson, supra, and Parker v. Flook, supra, both of which are computer-related, stand for no more than these long established principles. In *Benson,* we held unpatentable claims for an algorithm used to convert binary code decimal numbers to equivalent pure binary numbers. The sole practical application of the algorithm was in connection with the programming of a general purpose digital computer. We defined "algorithm" as a "procedure for solving a given type of mathematical problem," and we concluded that such an algorithm, or mathematical formula, is like a law of nature, which cannot be the subject of a patent.[9]

Parker v. Flook, supra, presented a similar situation. The claims were drawn to a method for computing an "alarm limit." An "alarm limit" is simply a number and the Court concluded that the application sought to protect a formula for computing this number. Using this formula, the updated alarm limit could be calculated if several other variables were known. The application, however, did not purport to explain how these other variables were to be determined,[10] nor did it

---

9. The term "algorithm" is subject to a variety of definitions. The Government defines the term to mean:

"1. A fixed step-by-step procedure for accomplishing a given result; usually a simplified procedure for solving a complex problem, also a full statement of a finite number of steps. 2. A defined process or set of rules that leads [*sic*] and assures development of a desired output from a given input. A sequence of formulas and/or algebraic/logical steps to calculate or determine a given task; processing rules."

This definition is significantly broader than the definition this Court employed in *Benson* and *Flook.* Our previous decisions regarding the patentability of "algorithms" are necessarily limited to the more narrow definition employed by the Court and we do not pass judgment on whether processes falling outside the definition previously used by this Court, but within the definition offered by the Government, would be patentable subject matter.

10. As we explained in *Flook,* in order for an operator using the formula to calculate an updated alarm limit the operator would need to know the original alarm base, the appropriate margin of safety, the time interval that should elapse between each updating, the current temperature (or other process variable) and the appropriate weighing factor to be used to average the alarm base and the current temperature. 437 U.S. 584, 586. The patent application

purport "to contain any disclosure relating to the chemical processes at work, the monitoring of process variables, or the means of setting off an alarm system. All that is provided is a formula for computing an updated alarm limit." 437 U.S., at 586.

In contrast, the respondents here do not seek to patent a mathematical formula. Instead, they seek patent protection for a process of curing synthetic rubber. Their process admittedly employs a well known mathematical equation, but they do not seek to pre-empt the use of that equation. Rather, they seek only to foreclose from others the use of that equation in conjunction with all of the other steps in their claimed process. These include installing rubber in a press, closing the mold, constantly determining the temperature of the mold, constantly recalculating the appropriate cure time through the use of the formula and a digital computer, and automatically opening the press at the proper time. Obviously, one does not need a "computer" to cure natural or synthetic rubber, but if the computer use incorporated in the process patent significantly lessens the possibility of "overcuring" or "undercuring," the process as a whole does not thereby become unpatentable subject matter.

Our earlier opinions lend support to our present conclusion that a claim drawn to subject matter otherwise statutory does not become nonstatutory simply because it uses a mathematical formula, computer program or digital computer. In Gottschalk v. Benson, supra, we noted "it is said that the decision precludes a patent for any program servicing a computer. We do not so hold." 409 U.S., at 71. Similarly, in Parker v. Flook, supra, we stated, "A process is not unpatentable simply because it contains a law of nature or a mathematical algorithm." 437 U.S., at 590. It is now common-place that an *application* of a law of nature or mathematical formula to a known structure or process may well be deserving of patent protection. See, e.g., Funk Bros. Seed Co. v. Kalo Co., 333 U.S. 127 (1948); Eibel Process Co. v. Minnesota & Ontario Paper Co., 261 U.S. 45 (1923); Cochrane v. Deener, 94 U.S. 780 (1876); O'Reilly v. Morse, 15 How. 62 (1853); and Le Roy v. Tatham, 14 How. 156 (1852). As Mr. Justice Stone explained four decades ago:

> "While a scientific truth, or the mathematical expression of it, is not a patentable invention, a novel and useful structure created with the aid of knowledge of scientific truth may be." Mackay Radio & Telegraph Co. v. Radio Corp. of America, 306 U.S. 86, 94 (1939).

We think this statement in *Mackay* takes us a long way toward the correct answer in this case. Arrhenius' equation is not patentable in isolation, but when a process for curing rubber is devised which incorporates in it a more efficient solution of the equation, that process is at the very least not barred at the threshold by § 101.

did not "explain how to select the approximate margin of safety, the weighing factor or any of the other variables." Ibid.

In determining the eligibility of respondents' claimed process for patent protection under § 101, their claims must be considered as a whole. It is inappropriate to dissect the claims into old and new elements and then to ignore the presence of the old elements in the analysis. This is particularly true in a process claim because a new combination of steps in a process may be patentable even though all the constituents of the combination were well known and in common use before the combination was made. The "novelty" of any element or steps in a process, or even of the process itself, is of no relevance in determining whether the subject matter of a claim falls within the § 101 categories of possibly patentable subject matter.[12]

It has been urged that novelty is an appropriate consideration under § 101. Presumably, this argument results from the language in § 101 referring to any "new and useful" process, machine, etc. Section 101, however, is a general statement of the type of subject matter that is eligible for patent protection "subject to the conditions and requirements of this title." Specific conditions for patentability follow and § 102 covers in detail the conditions relating to novelty. The question therefore of whether a particular invention is novel is "fully apart from whether the invention falls into a category of statutory subject matter." In re Bergy, 596 F.2d 952, 961 (Cust. & Pat.App., 1979). See also Nickola v. Peterson, 580 F.2d 898 (CA6 1978). The legislative history of the 1952 Patent Act is in accord with this reasoning. The Senate Report provided:

> "Section 101 sets forth the subject matter than can be patented, 'subject to the conditions and requirement of this title.' The conditions under which a patent may be obtained follow, and *Section 102 covers the conditions relating to novelty*." S.Rep. No. 1979, 82d Cong., 2d Sess., 5 (1952), U.S.Code Cong. & Admin.News, 1952, p. 2399 (emphasis supplied).

It is later stated in the same report:

> "Section 102, in general, may be said to describe the statutory novelty required for patentability, and includes, in effect, the amplification and definition of 'new' in Section 101." Id., at 6, U.S.Code Cong. & Admin.News, 1952, p. 2399.

---

12. It is argued that the procedure of dissecting a claim into old and new elements is mandated by our decision in *Flook* which noted that a mathematical algorithm must be assumed to be within the "prior art." It is from this language that the Government premises its argument that if everything other than the algorithm is determined to be old in the art, then the claim cannot recite statutory subject matter. The fallacy in this argument is that we did not hold in *Flook* that the mathematical algorithm could not be considered at all when making the § 101 determination. To accept the analysis proffered by the Government would, if carried to its extreme, make all inventions unpatentable because all inventions can be reduced to underlying principles of nature which, once known, make their implementation obvious. The analysis suggested by the Government would also undermine our earlier decisions regarding the criteria to consider in determining the eligibility of a process for patent protection. See, e.g., Gottschalk v. Benson, 409 U.S. 63 (1973); and Cochrane v. Deener, 94 U.S. 780 (1876).

Finally, it is stated in the "Revision Notes":

> "The corresponding section of [the] existing statute is split into two sections, Section 101 relating to the subject matter for which patents may be obtained, and Section 102 defining statutory novelty and stating other conditions for patentability." Id., at 17, U.S.Code Cong. & Admin.News, 1952, p. 2409.

See also H.R.Rep. No. 1923, 82d Cong., 2d Sess. (1952), at 6, 7 and 17.

In this case, it may later be determined that the respondents' process is not deserving of patent protection because it fails to satisfy the statutory conditions of novelty under § 102 or nonobviousness under § 103. A rejection on either of these grounds does not affect the determination that respondents' claims recited subject matter which was eligible for patent protection under § 101.

IV

We have before us today only the question of whether respondents' claims fall within the § 101 categories of possibly patentable subject matter. We view respondents' claims as nothing more than a process for molding rubber products and not as an attempt to patent a mathematical formula. We recognize, of course, that when a claim recites a mathematical formula (or scientific principle or phenomenon of nature), an inquiry must be made into whether the claim is seeking patent protection for that formula in the abstract. A mathematical formula as such is not accorded the protection of our patent laws, Gottschalk v. Benson, supra, and this principle cannot be circumvented by attempting to limit the use of the formula to a particular technological environment. Parker v. Flook, supra. Similarly, insignificant post-solution activity will not transform an unpatentable principle into a patentable process. Ibid.[14] To hold otherwise would allow a competent

---

14. Arguably, the claims in *Flook* did more than present a mathematical formula. The claims also solved the calculation in order to produce a new number or "alarm limit" and then replaced the old number with the number newly produced. The claims covered all uses of the formula in processes "comprising the catalytic chemical conversion of hydrocarbons." There are numerous such processes in the petrochemical and oil refinery industries and the claims therefore covered a broad range of potential uses, 437 U.S., at 586. The claims, however, did not cover every conceivable application of the formula. We rejected in *Flook* the argument that because all possible uses of the mathematical formula were not pre-empted, the claim should be eligible for patent protection. Our reasoning in *Flook* is in no way inconsistent with our reasoning here. A mathematical formula does not suddenly become patentable subject matter simply by having the applicant acquiesce to limiting the reach of the patent for the formula to a particular technological use. A mathematical formula in the abstract is nonstatutory subject matter regardless of whether the patent is intended to cover all uses of the formula or only limited uses. Similarly, a mathematical formula does not become patentable subject matter merely by including in the claim for the formula token post-solution activity such as the type claimed in *Flook*. We were careful to note in *Flook* that the patent application did not purport to explain how the variables used in the formula were to be selected, nor did the application contain any disclosure relating to chemical processes at work or the means of setting off an alarm or adjusting the alarm unit. 437 U.S., at 586. All the application provided was a "formula for computing an up-dated alarm limit." 437 U.S., at 586.

draftsman to evade the recognized limitations on the type of subject matter eligible for patent protection. On the other hand, when a claim containing a mathematical formula implements or applies that formula in a structure or process which, when considered as a whole, is performing a function which the patent laws were designed to protect (e.g., transforming or reducing an article to a different state or thing), then the claim satisfies the requirements of § 101. Because we do not view respondents' claims as an attempt to patent a mathematical formula, but rather to be drawn to an industrial process for the molding of rubber products, we affirm the judgment of the Court of Customs and Patent Appeals.

* * *

PROBLEM

Is a "word processing program" patentable subject matter? A word processing program is a program for a digital computer which, operated through instructions entered from the keyboard by the user, enables the user to create, store, edit, format and print documents with the assistance of automatic routines executed by the computer.

DESIGNS

The patent statute provides protection for "new, original and ornamental design for an article of manufacture." 35 U.S.C. § 171. The term of a design patent is fourteen years, 35 U.S.C. § 173. A design patent must meet all the requirements of the patent statute. Most importantly, this means a design patent must be non-obvious under 35 U.S.C. § 103, discussed infra page 883.

A patent on a design which primarily serves a utilitarian or functional purpose is invalid.

A design which has been copyrighted (see the discussion supra page 575) can also be the subject of a design patent. Application of Yardley, 493 F.2d 1389 (C.C.P.A.1974) (Copyright registration of Spiro Agnew watch does not bar design patent).

MASK WORKS

The Semiconductor Chip Protection Act of 1984, Pub.L. 98–620, 17 U.S.C. §§ 901–914, extends a copyright-type protection to "mask works."

The purpose of the statute is to protect the investment necessary to design integrated circuits to be embodied in particular semiconductor designs. A firm could spend thousands or even millions of dollars on the engineering for a chip to perform a particular function—to act as a processor for a computer, or to control the functions of a microwave oven or a television set—and a competitor could simply photograph the chip and use the photograph together with available techniques and machinery to make an exact copy. Although the engineering of the chip was expensive, it employed known design methods and hence was probably unpatentable because "obvious" to one skilled in that art. Since the "form" of the circuit was dictated not by design considerations, but by the functional imperatives of the circuit components, it was not copyrightable. Congress passed the statute in order to protect the private incentive to design such chips in spite of the fact that they could be so easily copied.

Mask works are defined as a "series of related images, however fixed or encoded, having or representing the predetermined, three-dimensional pattern of metallic, insulating, or semiconductor material present or removed from the layers of a semiconductor chip product; and in which series the relation of the images to one another is that each image has the pattern of the surface of one form of the semiconductor chip product."

The protection is for a period of ten years. Protection is limited to "reproduction" of the mask work (§ 905), and there is an express defense to infringement of independent, reverse engineering which produces a different, but functionally equivalent chip (§ 906).

PROBLEM

Is the approach taken by Congress in the Semiconductor Chip Protection Act of 1984 and in the Plant Variety Protection Act of 1970—creating specialized types of protection with provisions specifically directed to the type of technology protected—a desirable approach? Would this be a good approach to use in the area of industrial designs? Would such an approach inevitably turn the process of Congressional consideration of each specialized statute into a kind of pork barrel system as each technology struggled to obtain more favorable protection from Congress?

B. UTILITY

BRENNER v. MANSON

Supreme Court of the United States, 1966.
383 U.S. 519, 86 S.Ct. 1033, 16 L.Ed.2d 69.

MR. JUSTICE FORTAS delivered the opinion of the Court.

This case presents two questions of importance to the administration of the patent laws: First, whether this Court has certiorari jurisdiction, upon petition of the Commissioner of Patents, to review decisions of the Court of Customs and Patent Appeals; and second, whether the practical utility of the compound produced by a chemical process is an essential element in establishing a prima facie case for the patentability of the process. The facts are as follows:

In December 1957, Howard Ringold and George Rosenkranz applied for a patent on an allegedly novel process for making certain known steroids.[1] They claimed priority as of December 17, 1956, the

---

1. The applicants described the products of their process as "2-methyl dihydrotestosterone derivatives and esters thereof as well as 2-methyl dihydrotestos-

date on which they had filed for a Mexican patent. United States Patent No. 2,908,693 issued late in 1959.

In January 1960, respondent Manson, a chemist engaged in steroid research, filed an application to patent precisely the same process described by Ringold and Rosenkranz. He asserted that it was he who had discovered the process, and that he had done so before December 17, 1956. Accordingly, he requested that an "interference" be declared in order to try out the issue of priority between his claim and that of Ringold and Rosenkranz.

A Patent Office examiner denied Manson's application, and the denial was affirmed by the Board of Appeals within the Patent Office. The ground for rejection was the failure "to disclose any utility for" the chemical compound produced by the process. Letter of Examiner, dated May 24, 1960. This omission was not cured, in the opinion of the Patent Office, by Manson's reference to an article in the November 1956 issue of the Journal of Organic Chemistry, 21 J.Org.Chem. 1333–1335, which revealed that steroids of a class which included the compound in question were undergoing screening for possible tumor-inhibiting effects in mice, and that a homologue [3] adjacent to Manson's steroid had proven effective in that role. Said the Board of Appeals, "It is our view that the statutory requirement of usefulness of a product cannot be presumed merely because it happens to be closely related to another compound which is known to be useful."

The Court of Customs and Patent Appeals (hereinafter CCPA) reversed, Chief Judge Worley dissenting. 52 C.C.P.A. (Pat.) 739, 745, 333 F.2d 234, 237–238. The court held that Manson was entitled to a declaration of interference since "where a claimed process produces a known product it is not necessary to show utility for the product," so long as the product "is not alleged to be detrimental to the public interest." Certiorari was granted, 380 U.S. 971, to resolve this running dispute over what constitutes "utility" in chemical process claims, as well as to answer the question concerning our certiorari jurisdiction.

* * *

[The Court held that it had certiorari jurisdiction over the Court of Customs and Patent Appeals.]

Our starting point is the proposition, neither disputed nor disputable, that one may patent only that which is "useful."

* * *

As is so often the case, however, a simple, everyday word can be pregnant with ambiguity when applied to the facts of life. That this is

---

terone derivatives having a C–17 lower alkyl group. The products of the process of the present invention have a useful high anabolic-androgenic ratio and are especially valuable for treatment of those ailments where anabolic or antiestrogenic effect together with a lesser androgenic effect is desired."

3. "A homologous series is a family of chemically related compounds, the composition of which varies from member to member by CH_2 (one atom of carbon and two atoms of hydrogen). * * * Chemists knowing the properties of one member of a series would in general know what to expect in adjacent members." * * *

so is demonstrated by the present conflict between the Patent Office and the CCPA over how the test is to be applied to a chemical process which yields an already known product whose utility—other than as a possible object of scientific inquiry—has not yet been evidenced.

* * *

It is not remarkable that differences arise as to how the test of usefulness is to be applied to chemical processes. Even if we knew precisely what Congress meant in 1790 when it devised the "new and useful" phraseology and in subsequent re-enactments of the test, we should have difficulty in applying it in the context of contemporary chemistry where research is as comprehensive as man's grasp and where little or nothing is wholly beyond the pale of "utility"—if that word is given its broadest reach.

Respondent does not—at least in the first instance—rest upon the extreme proposition, advanced by the court below, that a novel chemical process is patentable so long as it yields the intended product and so long as the product is not itself "detrimental." * * *

* * * [O]n the assumption that the process would be patentable were respondent to show that the steroid produced had a tumor-inhibiting effect in mice, we would not overrule the Patent Office finding that respondent has not made such a showing. The Patent Office held that, despite the reference to the adjacent homologue, respondent's papers did not disclose a sufficient likelihood that the steroid yielded by his process would have similar tumor-inhibiting characteristics. Indeed, respondent himself recognized that the presumption that adjacent homologues have the same utility has been challenged in the steroid field because of "a greater known unpredictability of compounds in that field." In these circumstances and in this technical area, we would not overturn the finding of the Primary Examiner, affirmed by the Board of Appeals and not challenged by the CCPA.

The second and third points of respondent's argument present issues of much importance. Is a chemical process "useful" within the meaning of § 101 either (1) because it works—i.e., produces the intended product? or (2) because the compound yielded belongs to a class of compounds now the subject of serious scientific investigation? These contentions present the basic problem for our adjudication.

* * *

In support of his plea that we attenuate the requirement of "utility," respondent relies upon Justice Story's well-known statement that a "useful" invention is one "which may be applied to a beneficial use in society, in contradistinction to an invention injurious to the morals, health, or good order of society, or frivolous and insignificant" [20]—and upon the assertion that to do so would encourage inven-

---

20. Note on the Patent Laws, 3 Wheat. App. 13, 24. See also Justice Story's decisions on circuit in Lowell v. Lewis, 15 Fed. Cas. 1018 (No. 8568) (C.C.D.Mass.), and Bedford v. Hunt, 3 Fed.Cas. 37 (No. 1217) (C.C.D.Mass).

tors of new processes to publicize the event for the benefit of the entire scientific community, thus widening the search for uses and increasing the fund of scientific knowledge. Justice Story's language sheds little light on our subject. Narrowly read, it does no more than compel us to decide whether the invention in question is "frivolous and insignificant"—a query no easier of application than the one built into the statute. Read more broadly, so as to allow the patenting of any invention not positively harmful to society, it places such a special meaning on the word "useful" that we cannot accept it in the absence of evidence that Congress so intended. There are, after all, many things in this world which may not be considered "useful" but which, nevertheless, are totally without a capacity for harm.

It is true, of course, that one of the purposes of the patent system is to encourage dissemination of information concerning discoveries and inventions. And it may be that inability to patent a process to some extent discourages disclosure and leads to greater secrecy than would otherwise be the case. The inventor of the process, or the corporate organization by which he is employed, has some incentive to keep the invention secret while uses for the product are searched out. However, in light of the highly developed art of drafting patent claims so that they disclose as little useful information as possible—while broadening the scope of the claim as widely as possible—the argument based upon the virtue of disclosure must be warily evaluated. Moreover, the pressure for secrecy is easily exaggerated, for if the inventor of a process cannot himself ascertain a "use" for that which his process yields, he has every incentive to make his invention known to those able to do so. Finally, how likely is disclosure of a patented process to spur research by others into the uses to which the product may be put? To the extent that the patentee has power to enforce his patent, there is little incentive for others to undertake a search for uses.

Whatever weight is attached to the value of encouraging disclosure and of inhibiting secrecy, we believe a more compelling consideration is that a process patent in the chemical field, which has not been developed and pointed to the degree of specific utility, creates a monopoly of knowledge which should be granted only if clearly commanded by the statute. Until the process claim has been reduced to production of a product shown to be useful, the metes and bounds of that monopoly are not capable of precise delineation. It may engross a vast, unknown, and perhaps unknowable area. Such a patent may confer power to block off whole areas of scientific development, without compensating benefit to the public. The basic *quid pro quo* contemplated by the Constitution and the Congress for granting a patent monopoly is the benefit derived by the public from an invention with substantial utility. Unless and until a process is refined and developed to this point— where specific benefit exists in currently available form—there is insufficient justification for permitting an applicant to engross what may prove to be a broad field.

These arguments for and against the patentability of a process which either has no known use or is useful only in the sense that it may be an object of scientific research would apply equally to the patenting of the product produced by the process. Respondent appears to concede that with respect to a product, as opposed to a process, Congress has struck the balance on the side of nonpatentability unless "utility" is shown. Indeed, the decisions of the CCPA are in accord with the view that a product may not be patented absent a showing of utility greater than any adduced in the present case. We find absolutely no warrant for the proposition that although Congress intended that no patent be granted on a chemical compound whose sole "utility" consists of its potential role as an object of use-testing, a different set of rules was meant to apply to the process which yielded the unpatentable product. That proposition seems to us little more than an attempt to evade the impact of the rules which concededly govern patentability of the product itself.

This is not to say that we mean to disparage the importance of contributions to the fund of scientific information short of the invention of something "useful," or that we are blind to the prospect that what now seems without "use" may tomorrow command the grateful attention of the public. But a patent is not a hunting license. It is not a reward for the search, but compensation for its successful conclusion. "[A] patent system must be related to the world of commerce rather than to the realm of philosophy. * * * "

The judgment of the CCPA is

Reversed.

MR. JUSTICE HARLAN, * * * dissenting in part.

* * *

Respondent has contended that a workable chemical process, which is both new and sufficiently nonobvious to satisfy the patent statute, is by its existence alone a contribution to chemistry and "useful" as the statute employs that term. Certainly this reading of "useful" in the statute is within the scope of the constitutional grant, which states only that "[t]o promote the Progress of Science and useful Arts," the exclusive right to "Writings and Discoveries" may be secured for limited times to those who produce them. Art. I, § 8. Yet the patent statute is somewhat differently worded and is on its face open both to respondent's construction and to the contrary reading given it by the Court. In the absence of legislative history on this issue, we are thrown back on policy and practice. Because I believe that the Court's policy arguments are not convincing and that past practice favors the respondent, I would reject the narrow definition of "useful" and uphold the judgment of the Court of Customs and Patent Appeals (hereafter CCPA).

The Court's opinion sets out about half a dozen reasons in support of its interpretation. Several of these arguments seem to me to have almost no force. For instance, it is suggested that "[u]ntil the process claim has been reduced to production of a product shown to be useful, the metes and bounds of that monopoly are not capable of precise delineation" * * * and "[i]t may engross a vast, unknown, and perhaps unknowable area" * * *. I fail to see the relevance of these assertions; process claims are not disallowed because the products they produce may be of "vast" importance nor, in any event, does advance knowledge of a specific product use provide much safeguard on this score or fix "metes and bounds" precisely since a hundred more uses may be found after a patent is granted and greatly enhance its value.

The further argument that an established product use is part of "[t]he basic *quid pro quo*" * * * for the patent or is the requisite "successful conclusion" * * * of the inventor's search appears to beg the very question whether the process is "useful" simply because it facilitates further research into possible product uses. The same infirmity seems to inhere in the Court's argument that chemical products lacking immediate utility cannot be distinguished for present purposes from the processes which create them, that respondent appears to concede and the CCPA holds that the products are nonpatentable, and that therefore the processes are nonpatentable. Assuming that the two classes cannot be distinguished, a point not adequately considered in the briefs, and assuming further that the CCPA has firmly held such products nonpatentable, this permits us to conclude only that the CCPA is wrong either as to the products or as to the processes and affords no basis for deciding whether both or neither should be patentable absent a specific product use.

More to the point, I think, are the Court's remaining, prudential arguments against patentability: namely, that disclosure induced by allowing a patent is partly undercut by patent-application drafting techniques, that disclosure may occur without granting a patent, and that a patent will discourage others from inventing uses for the product. How far opaque drafting may lessen the public benefits resulting from the issuance of a patent is not shown by any evidence in this case but, more important, the argument operates against all patents and gives no reason for singling out the class involved here. The thought that these inventions may be more likely than most to be disclosed even if patents are not allowed may have more force; but while empirical study of the industry might reveal that chemical researchers would behave in this fashion, the abstractly logical choice for them seems to me to maintain secrecy until a product use can be discovered. As to discouraging the search by others for product uses, there is no doubt this risk exists but the price paid for any patent is that research on other uses or improvements may be hampered because the original patentee will reap much of the reward. From the standpoint of the public interest the Constitution seems to have resolved that choice in favor of patentability.

What I find most troubling about the result reached by the Court is the impact it may have on chemical research. Chemistry is a highly interrelated field and a tangible benefit for society may be the outcome of a number of different discoveries, one discovery building upon the next. To encourage one chemist or research facility to invent and disseminate new processes and products may be vital to progress, although the product or process be without "utility" as the Court defines the term, because that discovery permits someone else to take a further but perhaps less difficult step leading to a commercially useful item. In my view, our awareness in this age of the importance of achieving and publicizing basic research should lead this Court to resolve uncertainties in its favor and uphold the respondent's position in this case.

This position is strengthened, I think, by what appears to have been the practice of the Patent Office during most of this century. While available proof is not conclusive, the commentators seem to be in agreement that until Application of Bremner, 37 C.C.P.A. (Pat.) 1032, 182 F.2d 216, in 1950, chemical patent applications were commonly granted although no resulting end use was stated or the statement was in extremely broad terms.[3] Taking this to be true, *Bremner* represented a deviation from established practice which the CCPA has now sought to remedy in part only to find that the Patent Office does not want to return to the beaten track. If usefulness was typically regarded as inherent during a long and prolific period of chemical research and development in this country, surely this is added reason why the Court's result should not be adopted until Congress expressly mandates it, presumably on the basis of empirical data which this Court does not possess.

Fully recognizing that there is ample room for disagreement on this problem when, as here, it is reviewed in the abstract, I believe the decision below should be affirmed.

NOTES

1. Is United States Patent No. 2,908,693, mentioned in the second paragraph of the opinion, valid?

2. Mr. Justice Story's language, which the Court quotes on page 843 was thought to have settled the question until the decision of the Supreme Court in *Manson.* He was not the only one to take the position that utility should mean only "not detrimental to the public interest." An editorial writer for the New York Times in 1871 set the argument out at length. "We see no warrant in sense or equity for these examiners sitting in judgment upon the prospective

3. See, e.g., the statement of a Patent Office Examiner-in-Chief: "Until recently it was also rather common to get patents on chemical compounds in cases where no use was indicated for the claimed compounds or in which a very broad indication or suggestion as to use was included in the application. [*Bremner* and another later ruling] * * * have put an end to this practice." Wolffe, Adequacy of Disclosure as Regards Specific Embodiment and Use of Invention, 41 J.Pat.Off.Soc. 61, 66 (1959).

The Government's brief in this case is in accord: "[I]t was apparently assumed by the Patent Office [prior to 1950] * * * that chemical compounds were necessarily useful * * * and that specific inquiry beyond the success of the process was therefore unnecessary. * * * " Brief for the Commissioner, p. 25. See also Cohen & Schwartz, Do Chemical Intermediates Have Patentable Utility? 29 Geo.Wash.L. Rev. 87, 91 (1960); Note, 53 Geo.L.J. 154, 183 (1964); 14 Am.U.L.Rev. 78 (1964).

fate of the invention or its probabilities of utility, for these are matters which lie entirely between the patentee and the public. At all events, it seems a hardship to deny a patent on grounds which are merely hypothetical, particularly in instances where a failure of success with the public might lead to improvements which would be useful in the end. There are instances innumerable where our Patent Office has summarily, and even whimsically, denied applications made in good faith by men who had spent years upon schemes whose success *they,* at least, were willing to take the risk of. Such a course appears to us calculated to discourage, rather than foster, the inventive faculty, and to chill the enthusiasm which, if not useful, certainly is harmless. Any new invention is entitled to a patent, so long as the inventor is willing to pay the regulation fees. It is for the public to say whether the invention is practicable or useful, and that verdict is pretty sure to be a correct one." New York Times, p. 4, col. 5, Oct. 15, 1871.

3. Is it true, as Mr. Justice Fortas says, that a patent creates a "monopoly of knowledge?" Is it true, that "to the extent that the patentee has power to enforce his patent, there is little incentive for others to undertake a search for uses?" What is the probable effect of the *Manson* decision on research?

4. In Application of Bergel, 292 F.2d 955 (C.C.P.A.1961) the court reversed a decision of the Board of Appeals of the United States Patent Office affirming a rejection of an application on a chemical shown to have tumor inhibiting effects in rats. The Board of Appeals reasoned that "protection of rats, or mice, from the growth of cancer * * * is not in itself a sufficient usefulness within the purview of the patent statutes * * *," and went on to observe that "the elimination of rodents themselves would seem to be a more desirable objective." "The continued disease-free existence of rodents," said the Board, "is not a desirable objective." Id. at 957. In reversing, the Court of Customs and Patent Appeals said "our conclusion is influenced by a background of common knowledge that cancer is one of the dreadest of all diseases; that for years untold measures of time, talent, and treasure have been devoted to a search for means to prevent its spread and discover a cure; and that as of now those measures have been largely unsuccessful." Was this relevant? In light of *Manson,* was the decision in *Bergel* correct?

5. The utility requirement has been a convenient ground on which to reject applications such as those for perpetual motion machines, thus avoiding an argument as to whether or not the invention in fact works. Compare Puharich v. Brenner, 415 F.2d 979 (D.C.Cir.1969), affirming the patent office's denial of an application for a cage said to expand powers of extra sensory perception. The patent office had rejected on grounds of lack of utility and inoperability. Applicant refused to replicate his experiments which showed the cage worked on the ground that "it would be onerous to the point of practical impossibility to arrange a duplication." And in Application of Ferens, 417 F.2d 1072 (C.C.P.A.1969), the court affirmed a denial of a patent on a method of curing baldness in spite of affidavits from 21 persons that the method had worked on them.

One particularly persistent inventor obtained an order from the District Court requiring that his perpetual motion machine be tested by the government. See *In re Newman* 782 F.2d 971 (Fed.Cir.1986). The tests, which the Government claimed cost $75,000, showed the device did not work.

6. Disputes over utility will seldom arise in an infringement suit since if the patent is worth infringing it must have some use. "We have no doubt that

by copying and using the patented device the defendant has estopped itself from claiming want of utility in the sense of the patent statute." Nestle-Le Mur Co. v. Eugene, Ltd., 55 F.2d 854, 856 (6th Cir.1932).

7. Mr. Justice Fortas assumed in *Manson* that an experimental use would infringe. But see Kaz Mfg. Co. v. Chesebrough-Pond's, Inc., 211 F.Supp. 815, 818 (S.D.N.Y.1962), affirmed 317 F.2d 679 (2d Cir.1963):

> " 'The use of the patented machine for experiments for the sole purpose of gratifying a philosophical taste or curiosity or for instruction and amusement does not constitute an infringing use.' Ruth v. Stearns Roger Manufacturing Co., 13 F.Supp. 697, 713 (D.C.Colo.1935), reversed on other grounds, 87 F.2d 35 (10th Cir., 1936). Nor does construction of an infringing device purely for experimental purposes constitute an actionable infringement. Chesterfield v. United States, 159 F.Supp. 371, 376, 141 Ct.Cl. 838 (1958); Dugan v. Lear Avia, 55 F.Supp. 223, 229 (S.D.N.Y.1944), aff'd. 156 F.2d 29 (2d Cir., 1946); see also, Beidler v. Photostat Corp., 10 F.Supp. 628, 630 (W.D.N.Y.1935), aff'd. 81 F.2d 1015 (2d Cir., 1936); but cf., Northill Co. v. Danforth, 51 F.Supp. 928, 929 (N.D.Cal.1942)."

In Spray Refrigeration Co. v. Sea Spray Fishing, Inc., 322 F.2d 34 (9th Cir.1963), the court agreed that a purely experimental use would not infringe, but held that use of a machine in regular commercial operations in order to determine whether or not it was satisfactory constituted infringement.

In Roche Products v. Bolar Pharmaceutical Co., 733 F.2d 858 (Fed.Cir.1984), the plaintiff, a large, research-oriented pharmaceutical company, sought to enjoin Bolar, a manufacturer of generic drugs, from taking during the final year of a patent term the steps necessary to obtain regulatory approval for marketing a generic competitor from the Food and Drug Administration. A so-called "generic" drug is a copy of a successful branded drug, usually sold and promoted under its chemical or "generic" name on the basis of price. The generic competitor who is able to first introduce the drug after the patent expires has an advantage in establishing market share. Bolar imported a large quantity of the patented drug to form into "dosage form capsules, to obtain stability data, dissolution rates, bioequivalency studies, and blood serum studies" necessary for a marketing application to the F.D.A. Roche sued for infringement. The District Court denied relief on the ground that the use was experimental. The Federal Circuit reversed. "Bolar's intended 'experimental' use is solely for business reasons and not for amusement, to satisfy idle curiosity, or for strictly philosophical inquiry. * * * Bolar may intend to perform 'experiments,' but unlicensed experiments conducted with a view to the adaption of the patented invention to the experimentor's business is a violation of the rights of the patentee to exclude others from using his patented invention." 733 F.2d at 863.

8. When a new substance with a valuable use is found there are two contributions to the art, are there not? First, the discovery of the substance. And second, the discovery of the use. Should there not be two patents, one for the substance and one for the use? Can that be done in the medical area by making process claims? Are the therapeutic effects of a known substance a patentable process? Is it feasible to enforce such a claim? If such claims are not patentable, doesn't that skew drug research toward the discovery of the therapeutic properties possessed by new and hence patentable substances?

Time, April 20, 1970, p. 46 reported:

"Last week ＊ ＊ ＊ lithium carbonate was approved by the U.S. Food and Drug Administration for the treatment of mental patients in the overexcited mania phase of manic-depressive psychosis.

"No less remarkable than the properties of the metal itself is the way its compound has won approval, primarily due to the work of Australian Psychiatrist John Frederick Joseph Cade. After $3\frac{1}{2}$ years as a prisoner of war, Cade began to work in a mental hospital at Bundoora, near Melbourne, concentrating on possible biochemical differences between the manic and depressive phases of the same patient. Nothing was farther from his mind than lithium, which had been discredited as a hypnotic and again in 1949 as a substitute for table salt. 'One can hardly imagine,' says Cade, 'a less propitious year,' especially as the work was being done 'by an unknown psychiatrist, in a small hospital, with no research training, primitive techniques and negligible equipment.' Cade was led indirectly to lithium by inconclusive experiments with other substances. What he learned from his crude equipment and his guinea pigs was that lithium carbonate had a profound effect on the manic patient. He took it himself and suffered no harm. He gave it to a male patient, 51, who was 'restless, dirty, destructive, who had been in a back ward for five years and bade fair to remain there the rest of his life.' In three weeks the patient was better, and he soon went home and back to work. Lithium carbonate, Cade found, appeared to be of little or no value in the treatment of other psychotic states, notably schizophrenia, or in the depressive phase into which most manic patients usually subside.

"Danish investigators extended Cade's findings: lithium-treated patients, after remission of their mania, did not become depressed as soon again or as often as those receiving other drugs. But lithium carbonate posed a problem for the drug industry. A common chemical, it could not be patented, so there could be little profit in its manufacture. Any schoolboy could buy it from a chemical supply house for his basement laboratory; the FDA insisted that only research psychiatrists could use it clinically, under rigid rules."

The following proposal was advanced by Paul H. Eggert, Uses, New Uses and Chemical Patents—A Proposal, 51 J.P.O.S. 768, 784–87 (1969):

"In reality, there are two, and only two, contributions in applied chemistry: discovery and disclosure of (1) how to make a compound and (2) how to put it to use. These basic contributions, for want of better terminology and to avoid confusion with established terms, will be designated a 'howtomake' and a 'howtouse.' A howtomake is defined as a contribution to the useful arts comprising the discovery, reduction to practice, and disclosure of a *method* of synthesizing a given compound. A howtouse is defined as a contribution to the useful arts comprising the discovery, reduction to practice, and disclosure of a *method* of achieving a given result with a given compound.

"A howtomake and a howtouse are independent contributions to the progress of the useful arts. A howtomake may exist without a substantial, corresponding howtouse, and vice versa. Since these contributions are distinct and nondependent, they should be rewarded independently. The public should reward each new howtomake and each new howtouse pertaining to a given compound if and when they are reduced to practice and disclosed. There should not be a reward covering any or all howtouses potentially discoverable in the future merely because one howtouse has been disclosed.

"In what form should the public grant its reward? Traditionally it is done in the form of a patent. The patent grant would confer control over use of the *contribution* for a reasonable time.

"The howtomake inventor should receive control over what he has contributed. If his contribution is truly beneficial, he will derive great economic benefit. If his contribution is valueless (although inventive), he will receive an appropriate economic reward, which may be nothing. In such a case, no harm will have been done, except perhaps a small economic waste. No unearned restriction of the field will result from patenting an unneeded howtomake.

"The howtouse inventor should acquire control over what he has contributed. If his howtouse is a method of tanning leather, he should be granted control over *that* contribution. However, if a later inventor contributes an additional howtouse, perhaps as a cervicitis treatment, he, and not the earlier howtouse discoverer, should receive credit for that contribution. Or, if another inventor discloses an additional, nonobvious method of tanning leather with the specified compound, he should receive credit for that contribution. In this way no inventor will be granted control over more than he has contributed. A chemist will not virtually foreclose experimentation or reap the financial benefits of all future howtouses by virtue of his discovery of one.

"Still unanswered is the question of what form control of the howtouse should take. Should the patentee be allowed to designate who, if anyone, will manufacture the metacresolsulfonic acid used to treat cervicitis, or should he be allowed only to designate who will treat cervicitis with compound? That is, should there be a free market in the compound which is the subject of the howtouse?

"From an economic standpoint, it would seem more beneficial to the nation to permit control only at the user level. A free market in the compound would encourage competition within the chemical industry by allowing the existence of more than one source. Competition could induce lower prices and encourage the development of superior howtomakes for that chemical.

"The following proposals would implement these policies:

"1. Any method of producing a chemical (howtomake) should be patentable.

"2. Any method of using a chemical (howtouse) should be patentable.

"3. No chemical compound should be patentable.

"('Patentable' is used here in the sense of 'allowable subject matter for a patent.' The other conditions of patentability, particularly nonobviousness, would still have to be met.)

"Enactment would restore a balance between reward and contribution. No longer could an inventor profit, at the expense of the real contributor, from a use he never contemplated or disclosed. No longer would a chemist who finds an inventive use for a compound occurring

Not the law, England [handwritten margin note]

in nature be denied a patent or restricted to one on the extraction process. No longer would an inventor of a long-sought, 'useless' molecule be denied a patent on his process. The first inventor would not be able to close the field to others by his securing a patent on the compound. Others could experiment and patent uncontemplated uses without fear of being blocked by a product patent. Vigorous competition in the sale of chemicals would be possible. One corporation could not control the availability of a chemical merely because it was the first to create it (unless it also held the sole process patent)."

See Kitch, The Nature and Function of the Patent System, 20 J. of Law 6 Econ. 265 (1977), for an explanation of how a grant of all howtouse rights to the first inventor can enhance public welfare.

9. Although patents have played an important role in creating incentives for pharmaceutical research, and the advances resulting from privately-funded, patent-induced pharmaceutical research in the past fifty years have been remarkable, the relationship between patent law and drugs has been somewhat awkward. Patents are available for a new chemical substance showing some promise of utility, but a commercial product results only after years of investigation and testing have proven the existence of a safe and efficacious drug. In recent decades rising standards of investigational rigor, more stringent product liability law, and increased FDA regulatory requirements have made the process of bringing a new pharmaceutical product to market more costly and time consuming.

The FDA responded to this situation by creating an exclusive market position for the firm that first obtained regulatory approval for a drug. It did this by requiring the second firm that wanted to market a drug to complete the same clinical testing that was required of the first firm. The second firm was not permitted to simply copy the approved drug (already shown to be safe and efficacious by the first firm) and market it, but had to replicate the tests of the first firm. (It was such testing that Bolar Pharmaceutical wanted to complete prior to the expiration of the patent in Roche Products v. Bolar Pharmaceutical Co., 733 F.2d 858 (Fed.Cir.1984), supra note 7). Since these tests were costly and the effect of the entry of the second firm would be to drive the price of the drug toward marginal cost (leaving little profit margin to contribute to recovery of the already-incurred testing costs), the effect of this requirement was to give the first firm a form of protection from competition which helped to overcome the disincentives for introducing new drugs created by the costs of complying with the FDA regulation and other factors. These practices of the FDA were not contemplated by the statute, which provided only for marketing approval of "a drug," and were successfully challenged in some courts.

Congress addressed the relationship between the Food and Drug Act, the incentives for development of new drugs, and the regulatory position of generic competitors in the Drug Price Competition and Patent Term Restoration Act of 1984, Pub.L. 98–417. Title I of the Act amended the Federal Food, Drug, and Cosmetic Act by adding a new 21 U.S.C. § 355(j) that permits the second firm to submit an "abbreviated new drug application" which asserts a right to approval based only on the fact that the same drug has already been approved, but permits such a new drug application to be granted only five years after the drug on which the application is based was approved. This gives the first firm a five year period of exclusive marketing rights under the regulation (apart from whatever exclusive rights are conferred by a patent).

Title II of the Act amended the Patent Statute by adding a new § 156 that permits extension of the patent term for the period that the marketing of the drug is delayed by the time required for regulatory approval. It also amended § 271 by adding a new § 271(e) which makes it possible for competitors to undertake FDA required testing prior to the expiration of the patent term. (Thus reversing the outcome of Roche Products v. Bolar Pharmaceutical Co., 733 F.2d 858 (Fed.Cir.1984), supra note 7). (The student who looks at § 156 may also notice § 155, an earlier provision for extension of the patent term narrowly drafted to provide an extension for the artificial sweetener aspartame, marketed as Nutrasweet®.)

In Eli Lilly and Co. v. Medtronic, Inc., 110 S.Ct. 2683 (1990), the Court held that § 271(e)(1) applies to a medical device.

10. What, under *Manson,* is a sufficient disclosure of utility? A disclosure that the substance smells? Lubricates? Can be converted to steam? Has a low boiling point? A high boiling point? Is a pretty color? Can be used to make another substance which can be used to make another substance which is known to be useful?

11. In spite of the fact that it has been generally assumed that utility need not be shown to obtain a patent, it was common in the 19th century to emphasize in advertising the fact that an article was patented. For instance the phrase "patent medicine" arises from the widespread sale of patented compounds as medical remedies of various degrees of efficacy.

Does the government by issuing a patent on an invention of little or no utility aid and abet consumer fraud? In Decker v. F.T.C., 176 F.2d 461 (D.C.Cir. 1949), the petitioners sought reversal of an F.T.C. cease and desist order enjoining them from making certain representations in relation to a device they sold under the name Vacudex. In their advertising the petitioners represented that Vacudex, when attached to the exhaust mechanism of automobiles, saved gasoline and oil; increased the power of the motor; caused it to give better performance; drew carbon, oil and moisture from the muffler; eliminated or reduced back pressure; reduced vibration of the motor; gave the motor greater acceleration, caused the motor to run more smoothly, and saved tires. The petitioners argued that their advertising representations were the same as the representations in the specifications of their patent on the Vacudex and argued that the cease and desist order was improper because it was in effect an attack on the patent, beyond the jurisdiction of the F.T.C. The Court rejected the argument, pointing out that the cease and desist order related only to the advertising, not the patent. One judge dissented, arguing that "if the utility of the invention as portrayed in the specification which is made a part of the Letters Patent cannot be advertised, then the invention, as a practical matter, cannot be sold."

C. NONOBVIOUSNESS

GRAHAM v. JOHN DEERE CO.
Supreme Court of the United States, 1966.
383 U.S. 1, 86 S.Ct. 684, 15 L.Ed.2d 545.

MR. JUSTICE CLARK delivered the opinion of the Court.

After a lapse of 15 years, the Court again focuses its attention on the patentability of inventions under the standard of Art. I, § 8, cl. 8, of the Constitution and under the conditions prescribed by the laws of the United States. Since our last expression on patent validity, A. & P. Tea Co. v. Supermarket Corp., 340 U.S. 147 (1950), the Congress has for the first time expressly added a third statutory dimension to the two requirements of novelty and utility that had been the sole statutory test since the Patent Act of 1793. This is the test of obviousness, i.e., whether "the subject matter sought to be patented and the prior art are such that the subject matter as a whole would have been obvious at the time the invention was made to a person having ordinary skill in the art to which said subject matter pertains. Patentability shall not be negatived by the manner in which the invention was made." § 103 of the Patent Act of 1952, 35 U.S.C. § 103 (1964 ed.).

The questions, involved in each of the companion cases before us, are what effect the 1952 Act had upon traditional statutory and judicial tests of patentability and what definitive tests are now required. We have concluded that the 1952 Act was intended to codify judicial precedents embracing the principle long ago announced by this Court in Hotchkiss v. Greenwood, 11 How. 248 (1851), and that, while the clear language of § 103 places emphasis on an inquiry into obviousness, the general level of innovation necessary to sustain patentability remains the same.

The Cases.

(a). No. 11, Graham v. John Deere Co., an infringement suit by petitioners, presents a conflict between two Circuits over the validity of a single patent on a "Clamp for vibrating Shank Plows." The invention, a combination of old mechanical elements, involves a device designed to absorb shock from plow shanks as they plow through rocky soil and thus to prevent damage to the plow. In 1955, the Fifth Circuit had held the patent valid under its rule that when a combination produces an "old result in a cheaper and otherwise more advantageous way," it is patentable. Jeoffroy Mfg., Inc. v. Graham, 219 F.2d 511, cert. denied 350 U.S. 826. In 1964, the Eighth Circuit held, in the case at bar, that there was no new result in the patented combination and that the patent was, therefore, not valid. 333 F.2d 529, reversing 216 F.Supp. 272. We granted certiorari, 379 U.S. 956. Although we have determined that neither Circuit applied the correct test, we conclude that the patent is invalid under § 103 and, therefore, we affirm the judgment of the Eighth Circuit.

(b). No. 37, Calmar, Inc. v. Cook Chemical Co., and No. 43, Colgate-Palmolive Co. v. Cook Chemical Co., both from the Eighth Circuit, were separate declaratory judgment actions, but were filed contemporaneously. Petitioner in *Calmar* is the manufacturer of a finger-operated sprayer with a "hold-down" cap of the type commonly seen on grocers' shelves inserted in bottles of insecticides and other liquids prior to shipment. Petitioner in *Colgate-Palmolive* is a purchaser of the sprayers and uses them in the distribution of its products. Each action sought a declaration of invalidity and noninfringement of a patent on similar sprayers issued to Cook Chemical as assignee of Baxter I. Scoggin, Jr., the inventor. By cross-action, Cook Chemical claimed infringement. The actions were consolidated for trial and the patent was sustained by the District Court. 220 F.Supp. 414. The Court of Appeals affirmed, 336 F.2d 110, and we granted certiorari, 380 U.S. 949. We reverse.

* * *

At the outset it must be remembered that the federal patent power stems from a specific constitutional provision which authorizes the Congress "To promote the Progress of * * * useful Arts, by securing for limited Times to * * * Inventors the exclusive Right to their * * * Discoveries." Art. I, § 8, cl. 8. The clause is both a grant of power and a limitation. This qualified authority, unlike the power often exercised in the sixteenth and seventeenth centuries by the English Crown, is limited to the promotion of advances in the "useful arts." It was written against the backdrop of the practices—eventually curtailed by the Statute of Monopolies—of the Crown in granting monopolies to court favorites in goods or businesses which had long before been enjoyed by the public. See Meinhardt, Inventions, Patents and Monopoly, pp. 30–35 (London, 1946). The Congress in the exercise of the patent power may not overreach the restraints imposed by the stated constitutional purpose. Nor may it enlarge the patent monopoly without regard to the innovation, advancement or social benefit gained thereby. Moreover, Congress may not authorize the issuance of patents whose effects are to remove existent knowledge from the public domain, or to restrict free access to materials already available. Innovation, advancement, and things which add to the sum of useful knowledge are inherent requisites in a patent system which by constitutional command must "promote the Progress of * * * useful Arts." This is the *standard* expressed in the Constitution and it may not be ignored. And it is in this light that patent validity "requires reference to a standard written into the Constitution." A. & P. Tea Co. v. Supermarket Corp., supra, at 154 (concurring opinion).

* * *

This Court formulated a general condition of patentability in 1851 in Hotchkiss v. Greenwood, 11 How. 248. The patent involved a mere substitution of materials—porcelain or clay for wood or metal in doorknobs—and the Court condemned it, holding:

"[U]nless more ingenuity and skill * * * were required * * * than were possessed by an ordinary mechanic acquainted with the business, there was an absence of that degree of skill and ingenuity which constitute essential elements of every invention. In other words, the improvement is the work of the skilful mechanic, not that of the inventor." At p. 267.

Hotchkiss, by positing the condition that a patentable invention evidence more ingenuity and skill than that possessed by an ordinary mechanic acquainted with the business, merely distinguished between new and useful innovations that were capable of sustaining a patent and those that were not.

* * *

The language in the case, and in those which followed, gave birth to "invention" as a word of legal art signifying patentable inventions. Yet, as this Court has observed, "[t]he truth is the word ['invention'] cannot be defined in such manner as to afford any substantial aid in determining whether a particular device involves an exercise of the inventive faculty or not." McClain v. Ortmayer, 141 U.S. 419, 427 (1891); A. & P. Tea Co. v. Supermarket Corp., supra, at 151. Its use as a label brought about a large variety of opinions as to its meaning both in the Patent Office, in the courts, and at the bar. The *Hotchkiss* formulation, however, lies not in any label, but in its functional approach to questions of patentability. In practice, *Hotchkiss* has required a comparison between the subject matter of the patent, or patent application, and the background skill of the calling. It has been from this comparison that patentability was in each case determined.

The 1952 Patent Act.

The Act sets out the conditions of patentability in three sections. An analysis of the structure of these three sections indicates that patentability is dependent upon three explicit conditions: novelty and utility as articulated and defined in § 101 and § 102, and non-obviousness, the new statutory formulation, as set out in § 103. The first two sections, which trace closely the 1874 codification, express the "new and useful" tests which have always existed in the statutory scheme and, for our purposes here, need no clarification. The pivotal section around which the present controversy centers is § 103.

* * *

The section is cast in relatively unambiguous terms. Patentability is to depend, in addition to novelty and utility, upon the "non-obvious" nature of the "subject matter sought to be patented" to a person having ordinary skill in the pertinent art.

The first sentence of this section is strongly reminiscent of the language in *Hotchkiss*. Both formulations place emphasis on the pertinent art existing at the time the invention was made and both are implicitly tied to advances in that art. The major distinction is that Congress has emphasized "nonobviousness" as the operative test of the section, rather than the less definite "invention" language of *Hotchkiss* that Congress thought had led to "a large variety" of expressions in decisions and writings. In the title itself the Congress used the phrase "Conditions for patentability; *non-obvious subject matter*" (italics added), thus focusing upon "nonobviousness" rather than "invention."

* * *

We believe that * * * [the] legislative history, as well as other sources, shows that the revision was not intended by Congress to change the general level of patentable invention. We conclude that the section was intended merely as a codification of judicial precedents

Longfelt demand — amt of research
Commercial success (advertising? → you need advertising to create demand
Commercial acquiescence
Simultaneous solution (by other means)

embracing the *Hotchkiss* condition, with congressional directions that inquiries into the obviousness of the subject matter sought to be patented are a prerequisite to patentability.

Approached in this light, the § 103 additional condition, when followed realistically, will permit a more practical test of patentability. The emphasis on nonobviousness is one of inquiry, not quality, and, as such, comports with the constitutional strictures.

While the ultimate question of patent validity is one of law, A. & P. Tea Co. v. Supermarket Corp., supra, at 155, the § 103 condition, which is but one of three conditions, each of which must be satisfied, lends itself to several basic factual inquiries. Under § 103, the scope and content of the prior art are to be determined; differences between the prior art and the claims at issue are to be ascertained; and the level of ordinary skill in the pertinent art resolved. Against this background, the obviousness or nonobviousness of the subject matter is determined. Such secondary considerations as commercial success, long felt but unsolved needs, failure of others, etc., might be utilized to give light to the circumstances surrounding the origin of the subject matter sought to be patented. As indicia of obviousness or nonobviousness, these inquiries may have relevancy. See Note, Subtests of "Nonobviousness": A Nontechnical Approach to Patent Validity, 112 U.Pa.L.Rev. 1169 (1964).

This is not to say, however, that there will not be difficulties in applying the nonobviousness test. What is obvious is not a question upon which there is likely to be uniformity of thought in every given factual context. The difficulties, however, are comparable to those encountered daily by the courts in such frames of reference as negligence and scienter, and should be amenable to a case-by-case development. We believe that strict observance of the requirements laid down here will result in that uniformity and definiteness which Congress called for in the 1952 Act.

While we have focused attention on the appropriate standard to be applied by the courts, it must be remembered that the primary responsibility for sifting out unpatentable material lies in the Patent Office. To await litigation is—for all practical purposes—to debilitate the patent system. We have observed a notorious difference between the standards applied by the Patent Office and by the courts. While many reasons can be adduced to explain the discrepancy, one may well be the free rein often exercised by Examiners in their use of the concept of "invention." In this connection we note that the Patent Office is confronted with a most difficult task. Almost 100,000 applications for patents are filed each year. Of these, about 50,000 are granted and the backlog now runs well over 200,000. 1965 Annual Report of the Commissioner of Patents 13–14. This is itself a compelling reason for the Commissioner to strictly adhere to the 1952 Act as interpreted here. This would, we believe, not only expedite disposition but bring about a closer concurrence between administrative and judicial precedent.

Professional approval
Patent officer readiness to grant approval

Although we conclude here that the inquiry which the Patent Office and the courts must make as to patentability must be beamed with greater intensity on the requirements of § 103, it bears repeating that we find no change in the general strictness with which the overall test is to be applied. We have been urged to find in § 103 a relaxed standard, supposedly a congressional reaction to the "increased standard" applied by this Court in its decisions over the last 20 or 30 years. The standard has remained invariable in this Court. Technology, however, has advanced—and with remarkable rapidity in the last 50 years. Moreover, the ambit of applicable art in given fields of science has widened by disciplines unheard of a half century ago. It is but an evenhanded application to require that those persons granted the benefit of a patent monopoly be charged with an awareness of these changed conditions. The same is true of the less technical, but still useful arts. He who seeks to build a better mousetrap today has a long path to tread before reaching the Patent Office.

We now turn to the application of the conditions found necessary for patentability to the cases involved here:

A. *The Patent in Issue in No. 11,* Graham v. John Deere Co.

This patent, No. 2,627,798 (hereinafter called the '798 patent) relates to a spring clamp which permits plow shanks to be pushed upward when they hit obstructions in the soil, and then springs the shanks back into normal position when the obstruction is passed over. The device, which we show diagrammatically in the accompanying sketches (Appendix, Fig. 1) [infra page 869], is fixed to the plow frame as a unit. The mechanism around which the controversy centers is basically a hinge. The top half of it, known as the upper plate (marked 1 in the sketches), is a heavy metal piece clamped to the plow frame (2) and is stationary relative to the plow frame. The lower half of the hinge, known as the hinge plate (3), is connected to the rear of the upper plate by a hinge pin (4) and rotates downward with respect to it. The shank (5), which is bolted to the forward end of the hinge plate (at 6), runs beneath the plate and parallel to it for about nine inches, passes through a stirrup (7), and then continues backward for several feet curving down toward the ground. The chisel (8), which does the actual plowing, is attached to the rear end of the shank. As the plow frame is pulled forward, the chisel rips through the soil, thereby plowing it. In the normal position, the hinge plate and the shank are kept tight against the upper plate by a spring (9), which is atop the upper plate. A rod (10) runs through the center of the spring, extending down through holes in both plates and the shank. Its upper end is bolted to the top of the spring while its lower end is hooked against the underside of the shank.

When the chisel hits a rock or other obstruction in the soil, the obstruction forces the chisel and the rear portion of the shank to move upward. The shank is pivoted (at 11) against the rear of the hinge plate and pries open the hinge against the closing tendency of the spring. (See sketch labeled "Open Position," Appendix, Fig. 1.) This closing tendency is caused by the fact that, as the hinge is opened, the connecting rod is pulled downward and the spring is compressed. When the obstruction is passed over, the upward force on the chisel disappears and the spring pulls the shank and hinge plate back into their original position. The lower, rear portion of the hinge plate is constructed in the form of a stirrup (7) which brackets the shank, passing around and beneath it. The shank fits loosely into the stirrup (permitting a slight up and down play). The stirrup is designed to prevent the shank from recoiling away from the hinge plate, and thus prevents excessive strain on the shank near its bolted connection. The stirrup also girds the shank, preventing it from fishtailing from side to side.

In practical use, a number of spring-hinge-shank combinations are clamped to a plow frame, forming a set of ground-working chisels capable of withstanding the shock of rocks and other obstructions in the soil without breaking the shanks.

Background of the Patent.

Chisel plows, as they are called, were developed for plowing in areas where the ground is relatively free from rocks or stones. Originally, the shanks were rigidly attached to the plow frames. When such plows were used in the rocky, glacial soils of some of the Northern States, they were found to have serious defects. As the chisels hit buried rocks, a vibratory motion was set up and tremendous forces were transmitted to the shank near its connection to the frame. The shanks would break. Graham, one of the petitioners, sought to meet that problem, and in 1950 obtained a patent, U.S. No. 2,493,811 (hereinafter '811), on a spring clamp which solved some of the difficulties. Graham and his companies manufactured and sold the '811 clamps. In 1950, Graham modified the '811 structure and filed for a patent. That patent, the one in issue, was granted in 1953. This suit against competing plow manufacturers resulted from charges by petitioners that several of respondents' devices infringed the '798 patent.

The Prior Art.

Five prior patents indicating the state of the art were cited by the Patent Office in the prosecution of the '798 application. Four of these patents, 10 other United States patents and two prior-use spring-clamp arrangements not of record in the '798 file wrapper were relied upon by respondents as revealing the prior art. The District Court and the Court of Appeals found that the prior art "as a whole in one form or another contains all of the mechanical elements of the 798 Patent." One of the prior-use clamp devices not before the Patent Examiner—Glencoe—was found to have "all of the elements."

We confine our discussion to the prior patent of Graham, '811, and to the Glencoe clamp device, both among the references asserted by respondents. The Graham '811 and '798 patent devices are similar in all elements, save two: (1) the stirrup and the bolted connection of the shank to the hinge plate do not appear in '811; and (2) the position of the shank is reversed, being placed in patent '811 above the hinge plate, sandwiched between it and the upper plate. The shank is held in place by the spring rod which is hooked against the bottom of the hinge plate passing through a slot in the shank. Other differences are of no consequence to our examination. In practice the '811 patent arrangement permitted the shank to wobble or fishtail because it was not rigidly fixed to the hinge plate; moreover, as the hinge plate was below the shank, the latter caused wear on the upper plate, a member difficult to repair or replace.

Graham's '798 patent application contained 12 claims. All were rejected as not distinguished from the Graham '811 patent. The inverted position of the shank was specifically rejected as was the bolting of the shank to the hinge plate. The Patent Office examiner found these to be "matters of design well within the expected skill of the art and devoid of invention." Graham withdrew the original claims and substituted the two new ones which are substantially those in issue here. His contention was that wear was reduced in patent '798 between the shank and the heel or rear of the upper plate.[11] He also emphasized several new features, the relevant one here being that the bolt used to connect the hinge plate and shank maintained the upper face of the shank in continuing and constant contact with the underface of the hinge plate.

Graham did not urge before the Patent Office the greater "flexing" qualities of the '798 patent arrangement which he so heavily relied on in the courts. The sole element in patent '798 which petitioners argue before us is the interchanging of the shank and hinge plate and the consequences flowing from this arrangement. The contention is that this arrangement—which petitioners claim is not disclosed in the prior art—permits the shank to flex under stress for its *entire* length. As we have sketched (see sketch, "Graham '798 Patent" in Appendix, Fig. 2 [infra page 869]), when the chisel hits an obstruction the resultant force (A) pushes the rear of the shank upward and the shank pivots against the rear of the hinge plate at (C). The natural tendency is for that portion of the shank between the pivot point and the bolted connection (i.e., between C and D) to bow downward and away from the hinge plate. The maximum distance (B) that the shank moves away from the plate is slight—for emphasis, greatly exaggerated in the sketches. This is so because of the strength of the shank and the short—nine inches or so—length of that portion of the shank between

---

11. In '811, where the shank was above the hinge plate, an upward movement of the chisel forced the shank up against the underside of the rear of the upper plate. The upper plate thus provided the fulcrum about which the hinge was pried open. Because of this, as well as the location of the hinge pin, the shank rubbed against the heel of the upper plate causing wear both to the plate and to the shank. By relocating the hinge pin and by placing the hinge plate between the shank and the upper plate, as in '798, the rubbing was eliminated and the wear point was changed to the hinge plate, a member more easily removed or replaced for repair.

(C) and (D). On the contrary, in patent '811 (see sketch, "Graham '811 Patent" in Appendix, Fig. 2), the pivot point is the upper plate at point (c); and while the tendency for the shank to bow between points (c) and (d) is the same as in '798, the shank is restricted because of the underlying hinge plate and cannot flex as freely. In practical effect, the shank flexes only between points (a) and (c), and not along the entire length of the shank, as in '798. Petitioners say that this difference in flex, though small, effectively absorbs the tremendous forces of the shock of obstructions whereas prior art arrangements failed.

The Obviousness of the Differences.

We cannot agree with petitioners. We assume that the prior art does not disclose such an arrangement as petitioners claim in patent '798. Still we do not believe that the argument on which petitioners' contention is bottomed supports the validity of the patent. The tendency of the shank to flex is the same in all cases. If free-flexing, as petitioners now argue, is the crucial difference above the prior art, then it appears evident that the desired result would be obtainable by not boxing the shank within the confines of the hinge.[12] The only other effective place available in the arrangement was to attach it below the hinge plate and run it through a stirrup or bracket that would not disturb its flexing qualities. Certainly a person having ordinary skill in the prior art, given the fact that the flex in the shank could be utilized more effectively if allowed to run the entire length of the shank, would immediately see that the thing to do was what Graham did, i.e., invert the shank and the hinge plate.

Petitioners' argument basing validity on the free-flex theory raised for the first time on appeal is reminiscent of Lincoln Engineering Co. v. Stewart-Warner Corp., 303 U.S. 545 (1938), where the Court called such an effort "an afterthought. No such function * * * is hinted at in the specifications of the patent. If this were so vital an element in the functioning of the apparatus it is strange that all mention of it was omitted." At p. 550. No "flexing" argument was raised in the Patent Office. Indeed, the trial judge specifically found that "flexing is not a claim of the patent in suit * * *" and would not permit interrogation as to flexing in the accused devices. Moreover, the clear testimony of petitioners' experts shows that the flexing advantages flowing from the '798 arrangement are not, in fact, a significant feature in the patent.[13]

---

12. Even petitioners' expert testified to that effect:

"Q. Given the same length of the forward portion of the clamp * * * you would anticipate that the magnitude of flex [in '798] would be precisely the same or substantially the same as in 811, wouldn't you?

"A. I would think so."

13. "Q. * * * Do you regard the small degree of flex in the forward end of the shank that lies between the pivot point and the point of spring attachment to be of any significance or any importance to the functioning of a device such as 798? A. Unless you are approaching the elastic limit, I think this flexing will reduce the maximum stress at the point of pivot there, where the maximum stress does occur. I

We find no nonobvious facets in the '798 arrangement. The wear and repair claims were sufficient to overcome the patent examiner's original conclusions as to the validity of the patent. However, some of the prior art, notably Glencoe, was not before him. There the hinge plate is below the shank but, as the courts below found, all of the elements in the '798 patent are present in the Glencoe structure. Furthermore, even though the position of the shank and hinge plate appears reversed in Glencoe, the mechanical operation is identical. The shank there pivots about the underside of the stirrup, which in Glencoe is *above* the shank. In other words, the stirrup in Glencoe serves exactly the same function as the heel of the hinge plate in '798. The mere shifting of the wear point to the heel of the '798 hinge plate from the stirrup of Glencoe—itself a part of the hinge plate—presents no operative mechanical distinctions, much less nonobvious differences.

B. *The Patent in Issue in No. 37,* Calmar, Inc. v. Cook Chemical Co., *and in No. 43,* Colgate-Palmolive Co. v. Cook Chemical Co.

The single patent involved in these cases relates to a plastic finger sprayer with a "hold-down" lid used as a built-in dispenser for containers or bottles packaging liquid products, principally household insecticides. Only the first two of the four claims in the patent are involved here and we, therefore, limit our discussion to them. We do not set out those claims here since they are printed in 220 F.Supp., at 417–418.

In essence the device here combines a finger-operated pump sprayer, mounted in a container or bottle by means of a container cap, with a plastic overcap which screws over the top of and depresses the sprayer (see Appendix, Fig. 3 [infra page 869]). The pump sprayer passes through the container cap and extends down into the liquid in the container; the overcap fits over the pump sprayer and screws down on the outside of a collar mounting or retainer which is molded around the body of the sprayer. When the overcap is screwed down on this collar mounting a seal is formed by the engagement of a circular ridge or rib located above the threads on the collar mounting with a mating shoulder located inside the overcap above its threads.[15] The overcap, as it is screwed down, depresses the pump plunger rendering the pump inoperable and when the seal is effected, any liquid which might seep into the overcap through or around the pump is prevented from leaking out of the overcap. The overcap serves also to protect the sprayer head and prevent damage to it during shipment or merchandising. When the overcap is in place it does not reach the cap of the container or

think it will reduce that. I don't know how much.

"Q. Do you think it is a substantial factor, a factor of importance in the functioning of the structure? A. Not a great factor, no."

The same expert previously testified similarly in Jeoffroy Mfg. Inc. v. Graham, 219 F.2d 511.

15. Our discussion here relates to the overcap seal. The container itself is sealed in the customary way through the use of a container gasket located between the container and the container cap.

bottle and in no way engages it since a slight space is left between those two pieces.

The device, called a shipper-sprayer in the industry, is sold as an integrated unit with the overcap in place enabling the insecticide manufacturer to install it on the container or bottle of liquid in a single operation in an automated bottling process. The ultimate consumer simply unscrews and discards the overcap, the pump plunger springs up and the sprayer is ready for use.

The Background of the Patent.

For many years manufacturers engaged in the insecticide business had faced a serious problem in developing sprayers that could be integrated with the containers or bottles in which the insecticides were marketed. Originally, insecticides were applied through the use of tin sprayers, not supplied by the manufacturer. In 1947, Cook Chemical, an insecticide manufacturer, began to furnish its customers with plastic pump dispensers purchased from Calmar. The dispenser was an unpatented finger-operated device mounted in a perforated cardboard holder and hung over the neck of the bottle or container. It was necessary for the ultimate consumer to remove the cap of the container and insert and attach the sprayer to the latter for use.

Hanging the sprayer on the side of the container or bottle was both expensive and troublesome. Packaging for shipment had to be a hand operation, and breakage and pilferage as well as the loss of the sprayer during shipment and retail display often occurred. Cook Chemical urged Calmar to develop an integrated sprayer that could be mounted directly in a container or bottle during the automated filling process and that would not leak during shipment or retail handling. Calmar did develop some such devices but for various reasons they were not completely successful. The situation was aggravated in 1954 by the entry of Colgate-Palmolive into the insecticide trade with its product marketed in aerosol spray cans. These containers, which used compressed gas as a propellent to dispense the liquid, did not require pump sprayers.

During the same year Calmar was acquired by the Drackett Company. Cook Chemical became apprehensive of its source of supply for pump sprayers and decided to manufacture its own through a subsidiary, Bakan Plastics, Inc. Initially, it copied its design from the unpatented Calmar sprayer, but an officer of Cook Chemical, Scoggin, was assigned to develop a more efficient device. By 1956 Scoggin had perfected the shipper-sprayer in suit and a patent was granted in 1959 to Cook Chemical as his assignee. In the interim Cook Chemical began to use Scoggin's device and also marketed it to the trade. The device was well received and soon became widely used.

In the meanwhile, Calmar employed two engineers, Corsette and Cooprider, to perfect a shipper-sprayer and by 1958 it began to market its SS–40, a device very much similar to Scoggin's. When the Scoggin patent issued, Cook Chemical charged Calmar's SS–40 with infringement and this suit followed.

The Opinions of the District Court and the Court of Appeals.

At the outset it is well to point up that the parties have always disagreed as to the scope and definition of the invention claimed in the patent in suit. Cook Chemical contends that the invention encompasses a unique combination of admittedly old elements and that patentability is found in the result produced. Its expert testified that the invention was "the first commercially successful, inexpensive integrated shipping closure pump unit which permitted automated assembly with a container of household insecticide or similar liquids to produce a practical, ready-to-use package which could be shipped without external leakage and which was so organized that the pump unit with its hold-down cap could be itself assembled and sealed and then later assembled and sealed on the container without breaking the first seal." Cook Chemical stresses the long-felt need in the industry for such a device; the inability of others to produce it; and its commercial success—all of which, contends Cook, evidences the nonobvious nature of the device at the time it was developed. On the other hand, Calmar says that the differences between Scoggin's shipper-sprayer and the prior art relate only to the design of the overcap and that the differences are so inconsequential that the device as a whole would have been obvious at the time of its invention to a person having ordinary skill in the art.

Both courts accepted Cook Chemical's contentions. While the exact basis of the District Court's holding is uncertain, the court did find the subject matter of the patent new, useful and nonobvious. It concluded that Scoggin "had produced a sealed and protected sprayer unit which the manufacturer need only screw onto the top of its container in much the same fashion as a simple metal cap." 220 F.Supp., at 418. Its decision seems to be bottomed on the finding that the Scoggin sprayer solved the long-standing problem that had confronted the industry.[16] The Court of Appeals also found validity in the "novel 'marriage' of the sprayer with the insecticide container" which took years in discovery and in "the immediate commercial success" which it enjoyed. While finding that the individual elements of the invention were "not novel per se" the court found "nothing in the prior art suggesting Scoggin's unique combination of these old features * * * as would solve the * * * problems which for years beset the insecticide industry." It concluded that "the * * * [device] meets the exacting standard required for a combination of old elements to rise to the level of patentable invention by fulfilling the long-felt need with an

---

16. "By the same reasoning, may it not also be said that if [the device] solved a long-sought need, it was likewise novel? If it meets the requirements of being new, novel and useful, it was the subject of invention, although it may have been a short step, nevertheless it was the last step that ended the journey. The last step is the one that wins and he who takes it when others could not, is entitled to patent protection." 220 F.Supp., at 421.

economical, efficient, utilitarian apparatus which achieved novel results and immediate commercial success." 336 F.2d, at 114.

The Prior Art.

Only two of the five prior art patents cited by the Patent Office Examiner in the prosecution of Scoggin's application are necessary to our discussion, i.e., Lohse U.S. Patent No. 2,119,884 (1938) and Mellon U.S. Patent No. 2,586,687 (1952). Others are cited by Calmar that were not before the Examiner, but of these our purposes require discussion of only the Livingstone U.S. Patent No. 2,715,480 (1953). Simplified drawings of each of these patents are reproduced in the Appendix, Figs. 4–6 [infra page 869] for comparison and description.

The Lohse patent (Fig. 4) is a shipper-sprayer designed to perform the same function as Scoggin's device. The differences, recognized by the District Court, are found in the overcap seal which in Lohse is formed by the skirt of the overcap engaging a washer or gasket which rests upon the upper surface of the container cap. The court emphasized that in Lohse "[t]here are no seals above the threads and below the sprayer head." 220 F.Supp., at 419.

The Mellon patent (Fig. 5), however, discloses the idea of effecting a seal above the threads of the overcap. Mellon's device, likewise a shipper-sprayer, differs from Scoggin's in that its overcap screws directly on the container, and a gasket, rather than a rib, is used to effect the seal.

Finally, Livingstone (Fig. 6) shows a seal above the threads accomplished without the use of a gasket or washer.[17] Although Livingstone's arrangement was designed to cover and protect pouring spouts, his sealing feature is strikingly similar to Scoggin's. Livingstone uses a tongue and groove technique in which the tongue located on the upper surface of the collar, fits into a groove on the inside of the overcap. Scoggin employed the rib and shoulder seal in the identical position and with less efficiency because the Livingstone technique is inherently a more stable structure, forming an interlock that withstands distortion of the overcap when subjected to rough handling. Indeed, Cook Chemical has now incorporated the Livingstone closure into its own shipper-sprayers as had Calmar in its SS–40.

The Invalidity of the Patent.

Let us first return to the fundamental disagreement between the parties. Cook Chemical, as we noted at the outset, urges that the invention must be viewed as the overall combination, or—putting it in the language of the statute—that we must consider the subject matter sought to be patented taken as a whole. With this position, taken in the abstract, there is, of course, no quibble. But the history of the

---

17. While the sealing feature was not specifically claimed in the Livingstone patent, it was disclosed in the drawings and specifications. Under long-settled law the feature became public property. Miller v. Brass Co., 104 U.S. 350, 352 (1882).

prosecution of the Scoggin application in the Patent Office reveals a substantial divergence in respondent's present position.

As originally submitted, the Scoggin application contained 15 claims which in very broad terms claimed the entire combination of spray pump and overcap. No mention of, or claim for, the sealing features was made. All 15 claims were rejected by the Examiner because (1) the applicant was vague and indefinite as to what the invention was, and (2) the claims were met by Lohse. Scoggin canceled these claims and submitted new ones. Upon a further series of rejections and new submissions, the Patent Office Examiner, after an office interview, at last relented. It is crystal clear that after the first rejection, Scoggin relied entirely upon the sealing arrangement as the exclusive patentable difference in his combination. It is likewise clear that it was on that feature that the Examiner allowed the claims. In fact, in a letter accompanying the final submission of claims, Scoggin, through his attorney, stated that "agreement was reached between the Honorable Examiner and applicant's attorney relative to *limitations* which must be in the claims in order to define novelty over the previously applied disclosure of Lohse when considered in view of the newly cited patents of Mellon and Darley, Jr." (Italics added.)

Moreover, those limitations were specifically spelled out as (1) the use of a rib seal and (2) an overcap whose lower edge did not contact the container cap. Mellon was distinguished, as was the Darley patent, infra, n. 18, on the basis that although it disclosed a hold-down cap with a seal located above the threads, it did not disclose a rib seal disposed in such position as to cause the lower peripheral edge of the overcap "to be maintained out of contacting relationship with [the container] cap * * * when * * * [the overcap] was screwed [on] tightly. * * *" Scoggin maintained that the "obvious modification" of Lohse in view of Mellon would be merely to place the Lohse gasket above the threads with the lower edge of the overcap remaining in tight contact with the container cap or neck of the container itself. In other words, the Scoggin invention was limited to the use of a rib—rather than a washer or gasket—and the existence of a slight space between the overcap and the container cap.

It is, of course, well settled that an invention is construed not only in the light of the claims, but also with reference to the file wrapper or prosecution history in the Patent Office. Hogg v. Emerson, 11 How. 587 (1850); Crawford v. Heysinger, 123 U.S. 589 (1887). Claims as allowed must be read and interpreted with reference to rejected ones and to the state of the prior art; and claims that have been narrowed in order to obtain the issuance of a patent by distinguishing the prior art cannot be sustained to cover that which was previously by limitation eliminated from the patent. Powers-Kennedy Co. v. Concrete Co., 282 U.S. 175, 185–186 (1930); Schriber Co. v. Cleveland Trust Co., 311 U.S. 211, 220–221 (1940).

Here, the patentee obtained his patent only by accepting the limitations imposed by the Examiner. The claims were carefully drafted to reflect these limitations and Cook Chemical is not now free to assert a broader view of Scoggin's invention. The subject matter as a whole reduces, then, to the distinguishing features clearly incorporated into the claims. We now turn to those features.

As to the space between the skirt of the overcap and the container cap, the District Court found:

"Certainly without a space so described, there could be no inner seal within the cap, but such a space is not new or novel, but it is necessary to the formation of the seal within the hold-down cap.

"*To me this language is descriptive of an element of the patent but not a part of the invention.* It is too simple, really, to require much discussion. In this device the hold-down cap was intended to perform two functions—to hold down the sprayer head and to form a solid tight seal between the shoulder and the collar below. In assembling the element it is necessary to provide this space in order to form the seal." 220 F.Supp., at 420. (Italics added.)

The court correctly viewed the significance of that feature. We are at a loss to explain the Examiner's allowance on the basis of such a distinction. Scoggin was able to convince the Examiner that Mellon's cap contacted the bottle neck while his did not. Although the drawings included in the Mellon application show that the cap might touch the neck of the bottle when fully screwed down, there is nothing—absolutely nothing—which indicates that the cap was designed at any time to *engage* the bottle neck. It is palpably evident that Mellon embodies a seal formed by a gasket compressed between the cap and the bottle neck. It follows that the cap in Mellon will not seal if it does not bear down on the gasket and this would be impractical, if not impossible, under the construction urged by Scoggin before the Examiner. Moreover, the space so strongly asserted by Cook Chemical appears quite plainly on the Livingstone device, a reference not cited by the Examiner.

The substitution of a rib built into a collar likewise presents no patentable difference above the prior art. It was fully disclosed and dedicated to the public in the Livingstone patent. Cook Chemical argues, however, that Livingstone is not in the *pertinent* prior art because it relates to liquid containers having pouring spouts rather than pump sprayers. Apart from the fact that respondent made no such objection to similar references cited by the Examiner,[18] so restricted a view of the applicable prior art is not justified. The problems

---

18. In addition to Livingstone and Mellon, the Examiner cited Slade, U.S. Patent No. 2,844,290 (hold-down cap for detergent cans having a pouring spout); Nilson, U.S. Patent No. 2,118,222 (combined cap and spout for liquid dispensing containers); Darley, Jr., U.S. Patent No. 1,447,712 (containers for toothpaste, cold creams and other semi-liquid substances).

confronting Scoggin and the insecticide industry were not insecticide problems; they were mechanical closure problems. Closure devices in such a closely related art as pouring spouts for liquid containers are at the very least pertinent references. See, II Walker on Patents § 260 (Deller ed. 1937).

Cook Chemical insists, however, that the development of a workable shipper-sprayer eluded Calmar, who had long and unsuccessfully sought to solve the problem. And, further, that the long-felt need in the industry for a device such as Scoggin's together with its wide commercial success supports its patentability. These legal inferences or subtests do focus attention on economic and motivational rather than technical issues and are, therefore, more susceptible of judicial treatment than are the highly technical facts often present in patent litigation. See Judge Learned Hand in Reiner v. I. Leon Co., 285 F.2d 501, 504 (1960). See also Note, Subtests of "Nonobviousness": A Nontechnical Approach to Patent Validity, 112 U.Pa.L.Rev. 1169 (1964). Such inquiries may lend a helping hand to the judiciary which, as Mr. Justice Frankfurter observed, is most ill-fitted to discharge the technological duties cast upon it by patent legislation. Marconi Wireless Co. v. United States, 320 U.S. 1, 60 (1943). They may also serve to "guard against slipping into use of hindsight," Monroe Auto Equipment Co. v. Heckethorn Mfg. & Sup. Co., 332 F.2d 406, 412 (1964), and to resist the temptation to read into the prior art the teachings of the invention in issue.

However, these factors do not, in the circumstances of this case, tip the scales of patentability. The Scoggin invention, as limited by the Patent Office and accepted by Scoggin, rests upon exceedingly small and quite nontechnical mechanical differences in a device which was old in the art. At the latest, those differences were rendered apparent in 1953 by the appearance of the Livingstone patent, and unsuccessful attempts to reach a solution to the problems confronting Scoggin made before that time became wholly irrelevant. It is also irrelevant that no one apparently chose to avail himself of knowledge stored in the Patent Office and readily available by the simple expedient of conducting a patent search—a prudent and nowadays common preliminary to well organized research. Mast, Foos & Co. v. Stover Mfg. Co., 177 U.S. 485 (1900). To us, the limited claims of the Scoggin patent are clearly evident from the prior art as it stood at the time of the invention.

We conclude that the claims in issue in the Scoggin patent must fall as not meeting the test of § 103, since the differences between them and the pertinent prior art would have been obvious to a person reasonably skilled in that art.

The judgment of the Court of Appeals in No. 11 is affirmed. The judgment of the Court of Appeals in Nos. 37 and 43 is reversed and the cases remanded to the District Court for disposition not inconsistent with this opinion.

It is so ordered.

* * *

Figure 1.—GRAHAM '798 PATENT

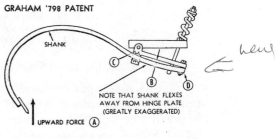

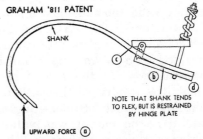

Figure 2.—FLEX COMPARISON

GRAHAM '798 PATENT

SHANK

NOTE THAT SHANK FLEXES
AWAY FROM HINGE PLATE
(GREATLY EXAGGERATED)

UPWARD FORCE (A)

NORMAL POSITION

SPRING (9)
ROD (10)
PLOW FRAME (2)
UPPER PLATE (1)
HINGE PIN (4)
HINGE PLATE (3)
SHANK (5)   STIRRUP (7)
BOLT (6)
CHISEL (8)

PLOW PULLED IN THIS DIRECTION ⟶

OPEN POSITION

UPWARD FORCE LIFTS CHISEL

[241Z]

GRAHAM '811 PATENT

SHANK

NOTE THAT SHANK TENDS
TO FLEX, BUT IS RESTRAINED
BY HINGE PLATE

UPWARD FORCE (a)

FIG. 3. SCOGGIN PATENT 2,870,943
(The Patent in Issue)

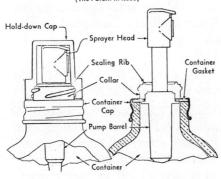

Hold-down Cap
Sprayer Head
Sealing Rib
Collar
Container Cap
Pump Barrel
Container Gasket
Container

FIG. 4. LOHSE PATENT 2,119,884
(Prior art 1938)

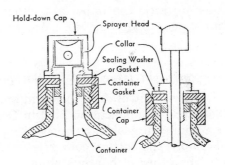

Hold-down Cap
Sprayer Head
Collar
Sealing Washer or Gasket
Container Gasket
Container Cap
Container

FIG. 5. MELLON PATENT 2,586,687
(Prior art 1952)

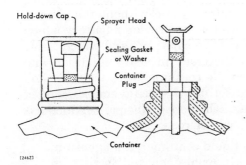

Hold-down Cap
Sprayer Head
Sealing Gasket or Washer
Container Plug
Container

[246Z]

FIG. 6. LIVINGSTONE PATENT 2,715,480
(Prior art 1953)

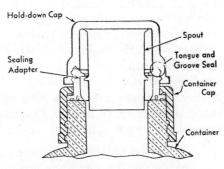

Hold-down Cap
Spout
Tongue and Groove Seal
Sealing Adapter
Container Cap
Container

UNITED STATES v. ADAMS

Supreme Court of the United States, 1966.
383 U.S. 39, 86 S.Ct. 708, 15 L.Ed. 572.

MR. JUSTICE CLARK delivered the opinion of the Court.

This is a companion case to No. 11, Graham v. John Deere Co., decided this day along with Nos. 37 and 43, Calmar, Inc. v. Cook Chemical Co. and Colgate-Palmolive Co. v. Cook Chemical Co. The United States seeks review of a judgment of the Court of Claims, holding valid and infringed a patent on a wet battery issued to Adams. This suit under 28 U.S.C.A. § 1498 (1964 ed.) was brought by Adams and others holding an interest in the patent against the Government charging both infringement and breach of an implied contract to pay compensation for the use of the invention. The Government challenged the validity of the patent, denied that it had been infringed or that any contract for its use had ever existed. The Trial Commissioner held that the patent was valid and infringed in part but that no contract, express or implied, had been established. The Court of Claims adopted these findings, initially reaching only the patent questions, 165 Ct.Cl. 576, 330 F.2d 622, but subsequently, on respondents' motion to amend the judgment, deciding the contract claims as well. 165 Ct.Cl., at 598. The United States sought certiorari on the patent validity issue only. We granted the writ, along with the others, in order to settle the important issues of patentability presented by the four cases. 380 U.S. 949. We affirm.

* * *

The Patent in Issue and Its Background.

The patent under consideration, U.S. No. 2,322,210, was issued in 1943 upon an application filed in December 1941 by Adams. It relates to a nonrechargeable, as opposed to a storage, electrical battery. Stated simply, the battery comprises two electrodes—one made of magnesium, the other of cuprous chloride—which are placed in a container. The electrolyte, or battery fluid, used may be either plain or salt water.

The specifications of the patent state that the object of the invention is to provide constant voltage and current without the use of acids, conventionally employed in storage batteries, and without the generation of dangerous fumes. Another object is "to provide a battery which is relatively light in weight with respect to capacity" and which "may be manufactured and distributed to the trade in a dry condition and rendered serviceable by merely filling the container with water." Following the specifications, which also set out a specific embodiment of the invention, there appear 11 claims. Of these, principal reliance has been placed upon Claims 1 and 10, which read:

"1. A battery comprising a liquid container, a magnesium electropositive electrode inside the container and having an exterior terminal, a fused cuprous chloride electronegative electrode, and a terminal connected with said electronegative electrode."

"10.　In a battery, the combination of a magnesium electropositive electrode, and an electronegative electrode comprising cuprous chloride fused with a carbon catalytic agent."

For several years prior to filing his application for the patent, Adams had worked in his home experimenting on the development of a wet battery.　He found that when cuprous chloride and magnesium were used as electrodes in an electrolyte of either plain water or salt water an improved battery resulted.

The Adams invention was the first practical, water-activated, constant potential battery which could be fabricated and stored indefinitely without any fluid in its cells.　It was activated within 30 minutes merely by adding water.　Once activated, the battery continued to deliver electricity at a voltage which remained essentially constant regardless of the rate at which current was withdrawn.　Furthermore, its capacity for generating current was exceptionally large in comparison to its size and weight.　The battery was also quite efficient in that substantially its full capacity could be obtained over a wide range of currents.　One disadvantage, however, was that once activated the battery could not be shut off; the chemical reactions in the battery continued even though current was not withdrawn.　Nevertheless, these chemical reactions were highly exothermic, liberating large quantities of heat during operation.　As a result, the battery performed with little effect on its voltage or current in very low temperatures.　Relatively high temperatures would not damage the battery.　Consequently, the battery was operable from 65° below zero Fahrenheit to 200° Fahrenheit.　See findings at 330 F.2d, at 632.

Less than a month after filing for his patent, Adams brought his discovery to the attention of the Army and Navy.　Arrangements were quickly made for demonstrations before the experts of the United States Army Signal Corps.　The Signal Corps scientists who observed the demonstrations and who conducted further tests themselves did not believe the battery was workable.　Almost a year later, in December 1942, Dr. George Vinal, an eminent government expert with the National Bureau of Standards, still expressed doubts.　He felt that Adams was making "unusually large claims" for "high watt hour output per unit weight," and he found "far from convincing" the graphical data submitted by the inventor showing the battery's constant voltage and capacity characteristics.　He recommended, "Until the inventor can present more convincing data about the performance of his [battery] cell, I see no reason to consider it further."

However, in November 1943, at the height of World War II, the Signal Corps concluded that the battery was feasible.　The Government thereafter entered into contracts with various battery companies for its procurement.　The battery was found adaptable to many uses.　Indeed, by 1956 it was noted that "[t]here can be no doubt that the addition of water activated batteries to the family of power sources has brought about developments which would otherwise have been technically or economically impractical." See Tenth Annual Battery Research and Development Conference, Signal Corps Engineering Laboratories, Fort Monmouth, N.J., p. 25 (1956). Also, see Finding No. 24, 330 F.2d, at 632.

Surprisingly, the Government did not notify Adams of its changed views nor of the use to which it was putting his device, despite his repeated requests. In 1955, upon examination of a battery produced for the Government by the Burgess Company, he first learned of the Government's action. His request for compensation was denied in 1960, resulting in this suit.

The Prior Art.

The basic idea of chemical generation of electricity is, of course, quite old. Batteries trace back to the epic discovery by the Italian scientist Volta in 1795, who found that when two dissimilar metals are placed in an electrically conductive fluid an electromotive force is set up and electricity generated. Essentially, the basic elements of a chemical battery are a pair of electrodes of different electrochemical properties and an electrolyte which is either a liquid (in "wet" batteries) or a moist paste of various substances (in the so-called "dry-cell" batteries). Various material which may be employed as electrodes, various electrolyte possibilities and many combinations of these elements have been the object of considerable experiment for almost 175 years. See generally, Vinal, Primary Batteries (New York 1950).

At trial, the Government introduced in evidence 24 patents and treatises as representing the art as it stood in 1938, the time of the Adams invention.[2] Here, however, the Government has relied primarily upon only six of these references [3] which we may summarize as follows.

The Niaudet treatise describes the Marie Davy cell invented in 1860 and De La Rue's variations on it. The battery comprises a zinc anode and a silver chloride cathode. Although it seems to have been capable of working in an electrolyte of pure water, Niaudet says the battery was of "little interest" until De La Rue used a solution of ammonium chloride as an electrolyte. Niaudet also states that "[t]he capital advantage of this battery, as in all where zinc with sal ammoniac [ammonium chloride solution] is used, consists in the absence of any local or internal action as long as the electric circuit is open; in other words, this battery does not work upon itself." Hayes likewise discloses the De La Rue zinc-silver chloride cell, but with certain mechanical

2. The references are listed in the opinion of the Court of Claims, 165 Ct.Cl., at 590, 330 F.2d, at 631.

3. Niaudet, Elementary Treatise on Electric Batteries (Fishback translation 1880); Hayes U.S. Patent No. 282,634 (1883); Wood U.S. Patent No. 1,696,873 (1928); Codd, Practical Primary Cells (London 1929); Wensky British Patent No. 49 of 1891; and Skrivanoff British Patent No. 4,341 (1880).

differences designed to restrict the battery from continuing to act upon itself.

The Wood patent is relied upon by the Government as teaching the substitution of magnesium, as in the Adams patent, for zinc. Wood's patent, issued in 1928, states: "It would seem that a relatively high voltage primary cell would be obtained by using * * * magnesium as the * * * [positive] electrode and I am aware that attempts have been made to develop such a cell. As far as I am aware, however, these have all been unsuccessful, and it has been generally accepted that magnesium could not be commercially utilized as a primary cell electrode." Wood recognized that the difficulty with magnesium electrodes is their susceptibility to chemical corrosion by the action of acid or ammonium chloride electrolytes. Wood's solution to this problem was to use a "neutral electrolyte containing a strong soluble oxidizing agent adapted to reduce the rate of corrosion of the magnesium electrode on open circuit." There is no indication of its use with cuprous chloride, nor was there any indication that a magnesium battery could be water-activated.

The Codd treatise is also cited as authority for the substitution of magnesium. However, Codd simply lists magnesium in an electromotive series table, a tabulation of electrochemical substances in descending order of their relative electropositivity. He also refers to magnesium in an example designed to show that various substances are more electropositive than others, but the discussion involves a cell containing an acid which would destroy magnesium within minutes. In short, Codd indicates, by inference, only that magnesium is a theoretically desirable electrode by virtue of its highly electropositive character. He does not teach that magnesium could be combined in a water-activated battery or that a battery using magnesium would have the properties of the Adams device. Nor does he suggest, as the Government indicates, that cuprous chloride could be substituted for silver chloride. He merely refers to the cuprous *ion*—a generic term which includes an infinite number of copper compounds—and in no way suggests that cuprous chloride could be employed in a battery.

The Government then cites the Wensky patent which was issued in Great Britain in 1891. The patent relates to the use of cuprous chloride as a depolarizing agent. The specifications of his patent disclose a battery comprising zinc and copper electrodes, the cuprous chloride being added as a salt in an electrolyte solution containing zinc chloride as well. While Wensky recognized that cuprous chloride could be used in a constant-current cell, there is no indication that he taught a water-activated system or that magnesium could be incorporated in his battery.

Finally, the Skrivanoff patent depended upon by the Government relates to a battery designed to give intermittent, as opposed to continuous, service. While the patent claims magnesium as an electrode, it specifies that the electrolyte to be used in conjunction with it must be a solution of "alcoline, chloro-chromate, or a permanganate strengthened with sulphuric acid." The cathode was a copper or carbon electrode faced with a paste of "phosphoric acid, amorphous phosphorous, metallic copper in spangles, and cuprous chloride." This paste is to be mixed with hot sulfuric acid before applying to the electrode. The Government's expert testified in trial that he had no information as to whether the cathode, as placed in the battery, would, after having been mixed with the other chemicals prescribed, actually contain cuprous chloride. Furthermore, respondents' expert testified, without contradiction, that he had attempted to assemble a battery made in accordance with Skrivanoff's teachings, but was met first with a fire when he sought to make the cathode, and then with an explosion when he attempted to assemble the complete battery.

The Validity of the Patent.

The Government challenges the validity of the Adams patent on grounds of lack of novelty under 35 U.S.C.A. § 102(a) as well as obviousness under 35 U.S.C.A. § 103. As we have seen in Graham v. John Deere, Co., * * * novelty and nonobviousness—as well as utility—are separate tests of patentability and all must be satisfied in a valid patent.

The Government concludes that wet batteries comprising a zinc anode and silver chloride cathode are old in the art; and that the prior art shows that magnesium may be substituted for zinc and cuprous chloride for silver chloride. Hence, it argues that the "combination of magnesium and cuprous chloride in the Adams battery was not patentable because it represented either no change or an insignificant change as compared to prior battery designs." And, despite "the fact that, wholly unexpectedly, the battery showed certain valuable operating advantages over other batteries [these advantages] would certainly not justify a patent on the essentially old formula."

There are several basic errors in the Government's position. First, the fact that the Adams battery is water-activated sets his device apart from the prior art. It is true that Claims 1 and 10, supra, do not mention a water electrolyte, but, as we have noted, a stated object of the invention was to provide a battery rendered serviceable by the mere addition of water. While the claims of a patent limit the invention, and specifications cannot be utilized to expand the patent monopoly, Burns v. Meyer, 100 U.S. 671, 672 (1880); McCarty v. Lehigh Valley R. Co., 160 U.S. 110, 116 (1895), it is fundamental that claims are to be construed in the light of the specifications and both are to be read with a view to ascertaining the invention, Seymour v. Osborne, 11 Wall. 516, 547 (1871); Schriber-Schroth Co. v. Cleveland Trust Co., 311 U.S. 211 (1940); Schering Corp. v. Gilbert, 153 F.2d 428 (1946). Taken together with the stated object of disclosing a water-activated cell, the lack of reference to any electrolyte in Claims 1 and 10 indicates that water alone could be used. Furthermore, of the 11 claims in issue, three of the narrower ones include references to specific electrolyte solutions comprising water and certain salts. The obvious implication from the absence of any mention of an electrolyte—a necessary element in any battery—in the other eight claims reinforces this conclusion. It is evident that respondents' present reliance upon this feature was not the afterthought of an astute patent trial lawyer. In his first contact with the Government less than a month after the patent application was filed, Adams pointed out that "no acids, alkalines or any other liquid other than plain water is used in this cell. Water does not have to be distilled. * * *" Letter to Charles F. Kettering (January 7, 1942), R., pp. 415, 416. Also see his letter to the Department of Commerce (March 28, 1942), R., p. 422. The findings, approved and adopted by the Court of Claims, also fully support this conclusion.

Nor is Sinclair & Carroll Co. v. Interchemical Corp., 325 U.S. 327 (1945), apposite here. There the patentee had developed a rapidly drying printing ink. All that was needed to produce such an ink was a solvent which evaporated quickly upon heating. Knowing that the boiling point of a solvent is an indication of its rate of evaporation, the patentee merely made selections from a list of solvents and their boiling points. This was no more than "selecting the last piece to put into the last opening in a jig-saw puzzle." 325 U.S., at 335. Indeed, the Government's reliance upon *Sinclair & Carroll* points up the fallacy of the underlying premise of its case. The solvent in *Sinclair & Carroll* had no functional relation to the printing ink involved. It served only as an inert carrier. The choice of solvent was dictated by known, required properties. Here, however, the Adams battery is shown to embrace elements having an interdependent functional relationship. It begs the question, and overlooks the holding of the Commissioner and the Court of Claims, to state merely that magnesium and cuprous chloride were individually known battery components. If such a combination is novel, the issue is whether bringing them together as taught by Adams was obvious in the light of the prior art.

We believe that the Court of Claims was correct in concluding that the Adams battery is novel. Skrivanoff disclosed the use of magnesium in an electrolyte completely different from that used in Adams. As we have mentioned, it is even open to doubt whether cuprous chloride was a functional element in Skrivanoff. In view of the unchallenged testimony that the Skrivanoff formulation was both dangerous and inoperable, it seems anomalous to suggest that it is an anticipation of Adams. An inoperable invention or one which fails to achieve its intended result does not negative novelty. Smith v. Snow, 294 U.S. 1, 17 (1935). That in 1880 Skrivanoff may have been able to convince a foreign patent examiner to issue a patent on his device has little significance in the light of the foregoing.

Nor is the Government's contention that the electrodes of Adams were mere substitutions of pre-existing battery designs supported by the prior art. If the use of magnesium for zinc and cuprous chloride for silver chloride were merely equivalent substitutions, it would follow that the resulting device—Adams'—would have equivalent operating

characteristics. But it does not. The court below found, and the
Government apparently admits, that the Adams battery "wholly unexpectedly" has shown "certain valuable operating advantages over other
batteries" while those from which it is claimed to have been copied
were long ago discarded. Moreover, most of the batteries relied upon
by the Government were of a completely different type designed to give
intermittent power and characterized by an absence of internal action
when not in use. Some provided current at voltages which declined
fairly proportionately with time.[4] Others were so-called standard cells
which, though producing a constant voltage, were of use principally for
calibration or measurement purposes. Such cells cannot be used as
sources of power.[5] For these reasons we find no equivalency.[6]

We conclude the Adams battery was also nonobvious. As we have
seen, the operating characteristics of the Adams battery have been
shown to have been unexpected and to have far surpassed then-existing
wet batteries. Despite the fact that each of the elements of the Adams
battery was well known in the prior art, to combine them as did Adams
required that a person reasonably skilled in the prior art must ignore
that (1) batteries which continued to operate on an open circuit and
which heated in normal use were not practical; and (2) water-activated
batteries were successful only when combined with electrolytes detrimental to the use of magnesium. These long-accepted factors, when
taken together, would, we believe, deter any investigation into such a
combination as is used by Adams. This is not to say that one who
merely finds new uses for old inventions by shutting his eyes to their
prior disadvantages thereby discovers a patentable innovation. We do
say, however, that known disadvantages in old devices which would
naturally discourage the search for new inventions may be taken into
account in determining obviousness.

Nor are these the only factors bearing on the question of obviousness. We have seen that at the time Adams perfected his invention
noted experts expressed disbelief in it. Several of the same experts
subsequently recognized the significance of the Adams invention, some
even patenting improvements on the same system. Fischbach et al.,
U.S. Patent No. 2,636,060 (1953). Furthermore, in a crowded art
replete with a century and a half of advancement, the Patent Office
found not one reference to cite against the Adams application. Against
the subsequently issued improvement patents to Fischbach, supra, and
to Chubb, U.S. Reissue Patent No. 23,883 (1954), it found but three

4. It is interesting to note in this connection that in testing the Adams cell the
Signal Corps compared it with batteries of
this type. The graphical results of the
comparison are shown in respondents'
brief, p. 51.

5. The standard text in the art states:
"The best answer to the oft-repeated question: 'How much current can I draw from
my standard cell?' is 'None.'" Vinal, Pri-

mary Batteries, p. 212 (New York 1950);
see also Ruben U.S. Patent No. 1,920,151
(1933).

6. In their motion to dismiss the writ of
certiorari as improvidently granted, respondents asserted that the Government
was estopped to claim equivalency of cuprous chloride and silver chloride. We
find no merit in this contention and, therefore, deny the motion.

references prior to Adams—none of which are relied upon by the Government.

We conclude that the Adams patent is valid. The judgment of the Court of Claims is affirmed.

It is so ordered.

NOTES

1. *The history.* The history of the development of the invention requirement is assayed in depth in Kitch, Graham v. John Deere Co.: New Standards for Patents, 1966 Sup.Ct.Rev. 293, 303–327, 49 J.P.O.S. 237 (1967). The law has been confused. An important source of the confusion has been the statute itself which prior to 1954 provided in a single sentence:

> That any person or persons, having discovered or invented any new and useful art, machine, manufacture, or composition of matter, or any new and useful improvement on any art, machine, manufacture, or composition of matter, not known or used by others before his or their discovery or invention thereof, and not, at the time of his application for a patent, in public use or on sale, with his consent or allowance, as the inventor or discoverer; and shall desire to obtain an exclusive property therein, may make application, in writing, to the Commissioner of Patents * * *.

Patent Act of 1836 § 6, 5 Stat. 119.

(The language is from the 1836 Act but the same basic wording structure was used from 1836 to 1952.) This language did not even require invention, since the applicant might merely have discovered something "new and useful." Simple novelty was, indeed, the test of patentability in the first decades of the nineteenth century. But this test was altogether unsatisfactory to the courts and they attempted to develop tests which would distinguish the really new from the simply different. These "novelty" tests were the central tests of invention during the nineteenth century. Because it is easier to say what is not new than what is, the tests tended to be put in negative form. The authoritative formulation of these tests was offered by Walker in his Text Book of the Patent Laws in 1883. He said:

> § 23. It has been shown that the word 'discovered,' in Section 4886 of the Revised Statutes, has the meaning of the word 'invented.' It follows that patents are grantable for things invented, and not for things otherwise produced. Novelty and utility must indeed characterize the subject of a patent, but they alone are not enough to make anything patentable; for the statute provides that things to be patented must be invented things, as well as new and useful things. The courts have therefore declared that not all improvement is invention, and entitled to protection as such, but that, to be thus entitled, a thing must be the produce of some exercise of the inventive faculties.

> § 24. The abstract rule stated in the last section is as certainly true as it is universally just, but its application to particular cases cannot be made without the guidance of more concrete propositions. The ideal line which separates things invented from things otherwise produced has never been completely defined nor described. There is no affirmative rule by which to determine the presence or absence of invention in every case. But there are several negative rules, each of

which applies to a large class of cases, and all of which are entirely authoritative and sufficiently clear. To formulate those rules, and to state their qualifications and exceptions, and to review and explain the adjudged cases from which those rules, qualifications, and exceptions are deducible, is the scope of several sections which immediately follow.

§ 25. It is not invention to produce a device or process which any skillful mechanic or chemist would produce whenever required.

§ 26. But if a particular result was long desired and sometimes sought, but never attained, want of invention cannot be predicated of a device or process which first reached that result, on the ground that the simplicity of the means is so marked that many believe they could readily have produced it if required. * * *

§ 27. It is not invention to produce an article which differs from some older thing only in excellence of workmanship. * * *

§ 28. It is not invention to substitute superior for inferior materials, in making one or more or all of the parts of a thing. * * *

§ 29. The rule of the last section is not without exceptions. If the substitution involved a new mode of construction, or if it developed new uses and properties of the article made, it may amount to invention. * * *

§ 30. It is not invention to so enlarge and strengthen a machine that it will operate on larger materials than before. * * *

§ 31. It is not invention to change the degree of a thing, or of one feature of a thing. * * *

§ 32. Aggregation is not invention.

§ 33. The rule of the last section does not state nor imply that all the parts of a patentable combination must act at the same time. * * *

§ 34. It is not invention to duplicate one or more of the parts of a machine. * * *

§ 35. It is not invention to omit one or more of the parts of an existing thing, unless that omission causes a new mode of operation of the parts retained. * * *

§ 36. It is not invention to improve a known structure by substituting an equivalent for either of its parts. * * *

§ 37. It is not invention to combine old devices into a new article without producing any new mode of operation. * * *

§ 38. It is not invention to use an old thing or process for a new purpose. * * *

§ 39. The rule of the last section is an easy one to apply to a case to which it is relevant, if the thing or process covered by the patent in that case, is used for the new purpose, without being changed either in construction or mode of operation. That is, however, not always the fact, and where it is not the fact the rule is of but minor practical utility as a guide to a just conclusion. It does not apply to using any new thing for a new purpose; and in order to apply it to anything which differs somewhat from the most similar thing that preceded it, it is necessary first to determine whether that difference constitutes legal novelty; to determine whether the thing covered by the patent is really old. That question must be investigated by the aid of rules other than that of the last section, and when it is determined in the negative it will follow that the rule of that section does not apply to the case.

§ 40. Want of invention, if it really exists in a particular process or thing, can nearly always be detected by one or another of the foregoing rules. When a case arises to which neither of them applies, and relevant to which the mind remains in uncertainty, that uncertainty may be removed by means of the rule in Smith v. The Dental Vulcanite Co., namely: When the other facts in a case leave the question of invention in doubt, the fact that the device has gone into general use, and has displaced other devices which had previously been employed for analogous uses, is sufficient to turn the scale in favor of the existence of invention.

§ 41. To change the form of a machine or manufacture is sometimes invention, and sometimes it is not invention. Where a change of form is within the domain of mere construction, it is not invention, but where it involves a change of mode of operation, or a change of result, it is invention, unless it is held to be otherwise in pursuance of some rule other than any which relates to form.

§ 42. A question of invention is a question of fact and not of law; though it is to be determined by means of the rules of law set forth in this chapter.

§ 43. Every inventor or constructor is presumed by the law to have borrowed from another whatever he produces that was actually first invented and used by that other. It follows that such of the foregoing rules as involve an inquiry into the state of the art to which the thing or process in controversy pertains, may involve an inquiry into the date and the character of inventions which were in fact unknown to the patentee, when he produced that thing or that process.

These tests had two important difficulties. First, almost anything can be characterized as a new mode of use, a new result or a new effect. Second, many things that clearly could qualify under the tests were also, unfortunately, trivial. These deficiencies led the courts and the writers to formulate two additional tests. One test centered on the way in which the invention was made. It was most colorfully phrased as the "flash of genius" test. This test never did anything except add to the ambiguity surrounding the problem, and it was expressly eliminated from the law by the last sentence of 103 in the 1952 Act. The second additional test was the test which, although formulated in many varying ways, and foreshadowed by Walker's § 25, became the nonobviousness test of § 103.

The courts, however, never thought of these three approaches as different but rather as all aspects of the law of invention. All too typical is the language of Mr. Justice Douglas in Cuno Eng'r Corp. v. Automatic Devices Corp., 314 U.S. 84, 91 (1941):

> [T]he new device, however useful it may be, must reveal the flash of creative genius not merely the skill of the calling. * * * Tested by that principle Mead's device was not patentable. We cannot conclude that his skill in making this contribution reached the level of inventive genius. * * * A new application of an old device may not

be patented if the "result claimed as new is the same in character as the original result. ⁕ ⁕ ⁕ "

Section 103 should interpreted to constitute a legislative choice of one of the three tests.

2. Under 35 U.S.C. § 282 a patent is presumed valid. This is an important assist to the holder of an issued patent, but some circuit courts had held that the presumption was weakened or disappeared where prior art was introduced in the infringement case that had not been considered by the patent examiner. Since this is often the case in infringement litigation, these holdings significantly weakened the effect of § 282. Perhaps the single most significant consequence of the creation of the Federal Circuit for patent law is that the circuit follows CCPA precedents that held that the presumption of § 282 is never weakened.

Judge Rich explained the Federal Circuit view of § 282 in American Hoist & Derrick Co. v. Sowa & Sons, Inc., 725 F.2d 1350 (Fed.Cir.1984), a decision that reversed a jury verdict of invalidity where the jury had been instructed (following the precedents of the circuit in which the district court sat) that "If ⁕ ⁕ ⁕ you find any of the prior art references which defendant has cited are more pertinent than the art utilized by the examiner ⁕ ⁕ ⁕ then that presumption of validity disappears." He explained:

> The two sentences of ⁕ ⁕ ⁕ § 282 ⁕ ⁕ ⁕ amount in substance to different statements of the same thing: the burden is on the attacker. And, as this court has been saying in other cases, that burden never shifts. The only question to be decided is whether the attacker is successful. When no prior art other than that which was considered by the PTO examiner is relied on by the attacker, he has the added burden of overcoming the deference that is due to a qualified government agency presumed to have properly done its job, which includes one or more examiners who are assumed to have some expertise in interpreting the references and to be familiar from their work with the level of skill in the art and whose duty it is to issue only valid patents. In some cases a PTO board of appeals may have approved the issuance of the patent.
>
> When an attacker, in sustaining the burden imposed by § 282, produced prior art or other evidence not considered in the PTO, there is, however, *no reason to defer* to the PTO so far as its effect on validity is concerned. Indeed, new prior art not before the PTO may so clearly invalidate a patent that the burden is fully sustained merely by proving its existence and applying the proper law; but that has no effect on the presumption or on who has the burden of proof. They are static and in reality different expressions of the same thing—a single hurdle to be cleared. Neither does the *standard* of proof change; it must be by clear and convincing evidence or its equivalent, by whatever form of words it may be expressed. What the production of new prior art or other invalidating evidence not before the PTO does is to eliminate, or at least reduce, the element of deference due the PTO, thereby partially, if not wholly, *discharging* the attacker's burden, but neither shifting nor lightening it or changing the standard of proof. When an attacker simply goes over the same ground travelled by the PTO, part of the burden is to show that the PTO was wrong in its decision to grant the patent. When new evidence touching validity of

the patent not considered by the PTO is relied on, the tribunal considering it is not faced with having to *disagree* with the PTO or with *deferring* to its judgment or with taking its expertise into account. The evidence may, therefore, carry more weight and go further toward sustaining the attacker's unchanging burden.

To summarize on this point, § 282 creates a presumption that a patent is valid and imposes the burden of proving invalidity on the attacker. That burden is constant and never changes and is to convince the court of invalidity by clear evidence. Deference is due the Patent and Trademark Office decision to issue the patent with respect to evidence bearing on validity which it considered but no such deference is due with respect to evidence it did not consider. All evidence bearing on the validity issue, whether considered by the PTO or not, is to be taken into account by the tribunal in which validity is attacked.

725 F.2d 1359–1360.

3. The reliability of the examination process in the Patent and Trademark Office is in part a product of the procedures used. A patent application is a secret and ex-parte procedure in the patent office in which the applicant attempts to persuade the examiner to issue the patent and the examiner (who has many applications to review at one time) has the burden of determining whether the applicant's position is consistent with the statute and the nature of the prior art. The examiner has no assistance from outside interested parties or experts, although he does have the use of the patent office files and library, consultation with fellow examiners and patent office employees, and the expertise that comes from dealing with many related applications. One advantage of this approach is that it helps to simplify the application procedure. An inventor (who may be poorly funded, particularly before he can use the issued patent to raise venture capital) might find it difficult to overcome obstacles erected by potential competitors if a more open and adversarial procedure were used.

4. A procedure for reexamination is now codified in chapter 30 of Title 35 as the result of P.L. 96–517, Patent and Trademark Laws, December 12, 1980. This procedure enables a patent owner, after the commercial value of the invention has been established, and perhaps when litigation is in the offing, to request a reexamination of the patent by the PTO. A reexamination proceeds basically just like an original application. It can be used to obtain a patent office ruling on additional prior art and to reshape the claims in light of the patent owner's present understanding of that art.

An important procedural innovation in connection with reexaminations is provision for limited third party participation in the reexamination process. Under § 301 a third party can provide prior art to be included in the patent file. Under § 302 a third party can request a reexamination of a patent. And under § 304 the person requesting the reexamination can file a statement in writing replying to any statement filed by the patent owner.

A reexamination has now become a standard aspect of patent infringement litigation. Either the patent owner, the defendant, or others who fear that the patent may be upheld, will consider it strategically advantageous to request a reexamination. In Gould v. Control Laser Corp., 705 F.2d 1340 (Fed.Cir.1983), the PTO had decided to conduct a reexamination upon the request of a person other than the patent owner. The District Court stayed the infringement action until completion of the reexamination. The court dismissed the appeal for lack of jurisdiction, but in dictum quoted portions of the legislative history which imply that such stays should be routinely granted. As a result, a fresh examination of the patent office based upon a current review of the record and conducted with the knowledge that the patent is valuable and in dispute will frequently exist in patent cases. If the PTO does a good job of conducting these reexaminations, it is likely that the courts will increasingly defer to them. The Federal Circuit upheld the constitutionality of the reexamination procedure in Patlex Corp. v. Mossinghoff, 758 F.2d 594 (Fed.Cir.1985).

5. The Court's favorable reference to the Note, Subtests of "Nonobviousness": A Nontechnical Approach to Patent Validity, 112 U.Pa.L.Rev. 1169 (1964), in *Graham* has given the note unusual importance in the lower courts, although it is impossible to determine from the opinions whether the judges rely on the tests in deciding the nonobviousness question or whether the tests are simply added to the opinions in support of decisions already made. The subtests discussed in the note are: (1) long-felt demand for the innovation which was only satisfied by the patentee's invention; (2) the commercial success of the invention in the marketplace; (3) acquiescence by competitors to the validity of the patent; (4) simultaneous solution of the problem solved by the patentee by others (tending to show no invention); (5) approval of the invention by technologists, scientific commentators, and university professors; (6) difficulty in obtaining a patent from the patent office (tending to show no invention). The note endorses all of these tests but the last one, with some cautionary qualifications.

These tests offer promise of a non-technical grounding for a non-obviousness determination, but they also lend themselves to misleading inferences. For instance, the patentee's innovation may have been made possible by some other technological advance, such as the development of a new material or testing procedure, which was not available to others who tried to satisfy the long felt demand. Commercial success may have been due to good timing, changes in consumer markets, or attractive packaging. Commercial acquiescence simply reflects the judgments of competitors that a license or non-infringement is cheaper than litigation, and constitutes a form of hearsay opinion evidence. Simultaneous solution by others may simply show that the problem solved by the invention was widely regarded as important so that many able researchers were put to work on it. Approval by experts is ambiguous because usually not addressed to the technical patent question and constitutes a form of hearsay expert testimony. Difficulties in obtaining a patent from the patent office can result from many things, including an incompetent patent attorney.

Of all these tests, commercial success is the most troubling because it seems to create a presumption of validity whenever the patented innovation is commercially successful. Of course, if the patented innovation is not commercially successful, resolution of the patent question has little economic significance. The Supreme Court treated the commercial success test as not controlling in Anderson's-Black Rock, Inc. v. Pavement Salvage Co., 396 U.S. 57 (1969). In the course of holding a patent on a machine for laying bituminous concrete employing a radiant burner heater to achieve good bonding between strips invalid, the Court observed that "Use of the radiant burner in this important field marked a successful venture. But * * * more than that is needed for invention." 396 U.S. 63. The patented invention in the *Calmar* case was very successful, but the Supreme Court found the patent invalid, as the Eighth

Circuit (which was reversed in *Calmar*) noted in General Mills, Inc. v. Pillsbury Co., 378 F.2d 666, 670 (8th Cir.1967).

Cable Electric Products, Inc. v. Genmark, Inc., 770 F.2d 1015, 1027 (Fed.Cir. 1985): "[T]his court ∗ ∗ ∗ has unequivocally stated that for commercial success of a product embodying a claimed invention to have true relevance to the issue of nonobviousness, that success must be shown to have in some way been due to the nature of the claimed invention, as opposed to other economic and commercial factors unrelated to the technical quality of the patented subject matter. Thus, a 'nexus is required between the merits of the claimed invention and the evidence offered, if the evidence is to be given substantial weight enroute to [a] conclusion on the obviousness issue.'"

6. Perhaps the most curious test, but one which appears not infrequently in the cases, is a test based upon the fact that the defendant's product is an exact copy of the plaintiff's. It is possible to reason that such exact copying shows that the patent owner has found the only way to accomplish the purpose of the patent. But if the patent is invalid, isn't the defendant entitled to copy? In Cable Electric Products, Inc. v. Genmark, Inc., 770 F.2d 1015, 1027–28 (Fed. Cir.1985), the court said: "Access to, and analysis of, other products in the market is hardly rare, even in the design stages of competing devices ∗ ∗ ∗ It is our conclusion that more than the mere fact of copying by an accused infringer is needed to make that action significant to a determination of the obviousness issue." In Vandenberg v. Dairy Equipment Co., 740 F.2d 1560, 1567 (Fed.Cir.1984), the court said that "The copying of an invention may constitute evidence that the invention is not an obvious one. ∗ ∗ ∗ This would be particularly true where the copyist had itself attempted for a substantial length of time to design a similar device, and had failed."

7. The *Adams* case contains an example of highly persuasive evidence in support of a conclusion of nonobviousness: contemporary expert opinion that the invention was impossible. Given that evidence, what was the problem in *Adams?* Is there a problem in *Adams* not present in *Graham?* See Kitch, Graham v. John Deere Co.: New Standards for Patents, 1966 Sup.Ct.Rev. 293, 327–330, 49 J.P.O.S. 237, 277–81 (1967).

8. What is a nonobvious design? In re Nalbandian, 661 F.2d 1214, 1216 (CCPA 1981): "In design cases we will consider the fictitious person identified in § 103 as 'one of ordinary skill in the art' to be the designer of ordinary capability who designs articles of the type presented in the application." Thus the CCPA overruled its own earlier precedent which had applied a standard of the "ordinary intelligent man" or "ordinary observer," a test dating back to Smith v. Whitman, 148 U.S. 674 (1893). The CCPA had been concerned that the application of the § 103 approach to designs would virtually eliminate valid design patents and that designing, unlike applied technologies, was not an organized field which made it possible to reach meaningful conclusions about what one of ordinary skill in the field could or could not do. It was persuaded to return to a § 103 standard by the weight of decisions in the circuit courts and the language of the statute itself.

D. THE RELEVANT PRIOR ART

Section 103 requires a determination of the content of the prior art. "Prior art" for purposes of § 103 is a technical term. It consists of two things. First, the body of knowledge known to a person skilled in the art. And second, certain enumerated documents and events which are constructively in the art whether or not actually known to those skilled in the art. This second category is closely related to the novelty, time bar and priority provisions of § 102. We will defer examination of it until we reach § 102. As an example of constructive prior art, any issued United States or foreign patent is in the prior art whether or not it is known to the contemporary practitioners of the art.

What types of technology are in the prior art? (This question is sometimes phrased as: what arts are "pertinent," or: what arts are "analogous".) The cases long reflected, usually unconsciously, two approaches to the question of the scope of the prior art. Sometimes they treated the prior art as the art of those who used the technology. Other times they treated the prior art as the art of those who were skilled in the art of solving the kind of technological problem to which the invention is addressed (which would include, in part, the knowledge of those who use the technology). This second approach is the approach that was followed by the CCPA, and now by the Federal Circuit. The following two cases illustrate its application.

Application of Van Wanderham, 378 F.2d 981 (CCPA 1967). The application was for a system of providing a regular flow of extremely cold fuel such as liquid hydrogen to the pumps of a rocket engine. The problem was that the fuel would boil as it left the fuel tank and came in contact with warmer tubing and valves on its way to the pumps. The boiling introduced air into the fuel, causing the pumps to produce an uneven flow to the engine, with bad effects on the performance of the rocket (burp, burp). The solution for which a patent was claimed was to coat the inside of the tubing with a layer of thermal insulating material. The reference cited against the application was a report on the use of a coating by Japanese cutlery makers prior to quenching in order to obtain a perfect hardening of the metal. The cited reference reported that this process worked because the coating prevented the formation of a vapor film on the metal when it was first immersed, speeding up the rate of cooling. The patent office argued that this reference was prior art because the patent was directed to a problem of heat transfer, and one attempting to solve a problem of heat transfer would look to practices in metallurgy. The CCPA rejected the relevance of this reference. "[I]t does not seem to us that one seeking to eliminate pump cavitation problems *and* the problem of vapor in cryogenic liquid propellant flow system would turn to the cutlery art." 378 F.2d at 988.

Stratoflex, Inc. v. Aeroquip Corp., 713 F.2d 1530 (Fed.Cir.1983). The patent was on tubing made of polytetrafluorethylene (or PTFE, trademarked by Du Pont as TEFLON) used in the aircraft and missile industry to convey pressurized fuel, lubricants, and other fluids. Tubing of PTFE had been in use since 1956, but after 1959, when hydrocarbon jet fuels were introduced, leaks developed. Engineers studied the matter and discovered that the leaks were caused by the arcing of electrostatic charges through the wall of the dielectric (nonconducting)

PTFE. The patent claimed PTFE tubing lined with an inner layer of PTFE with sufficient carbon in it so that it is conductive. Such tubing is not subject to electrostatic buildup because the static charge is dissipated by the conductive layer. The trial court held the patent invalid, relying in part on prior art relating to rubber hoses. The patentee argued "that the scope of the relevant prior art excludes rubber hose because PTFE is a unique material, possessing properties that differ significantly from rubber, and that, because the claims are limited to PTFE, the rubber hose art could at most be peripherally relevant as background information." The Federal Circuit rejected this argument and affirmed. "The scope for the prior art has been defined as that 'reasonably pertinent to the particular problem with which the inventor was involved.' * * * The problem confronting * * * [the inventor] was preventing electrostatic buildup in PTFE tubing caused by hydrocarbon fuel flow while precluding leakage of fuel. None of the unique properties of PTFE would change the nature of that problem. Nor would anything of record indicate that one skilled in the art would not include the rubber hose art in his search for a solution to that problem." 713 F.2d at 1535.

E. DOES THE NONOBVIOUSNESS OF THE PROCESS USED TO MAKE A PRODUCT MEAN THAT THE PRODUCT ITSELF IS NONOBVIOUS?

SHAW v. E.B. & A.C. WHITING CO.
United States Court of Appeals, Second Circuit, 1969.
417 F.2d 1097, certiorari denied 397 U.S. 1076, 90 S.Ct. 1518, 25 L.Ed.2d 811,
rehearing denied 398 U.S. 954, 90 S.Ct. 1866, 26 L.Ed.2d 298.

The Shaw invention consists of an artificial filament. These filaments are particularly adapted for use as brush bristles. Shaw's search for such a product began in the mid-1940's in order to provide the market with an artificial filament at a relatively low cost that could compete with the use of natural (animal and vegetable) fibers and bristles in brooms and related products. The primary advantages of a synthetic filament are its durability and the uniformity in size, shape and stiffness between one filament or bristle and another, for filaments from natural sources occur in widely divergent forms, vary in stiffness, and tend to wear more rapidly than the synthetic variety. Artificial filaments had been produced as early as the 1920's, but Shaw wished both to improve upon the qualities of such filaments and to lower the cost of synthetic filament manufacture. In 1947 Shaw found what he was looking for and, after testing his product, he applied for a patent in March, 1949.

I. The Shaw Filament

The elements of the "manufacture" or article covered by the Shaw patent may be briefly stated: (1) The filament is composed of a long chain linear stable thermoplastic polymer. (2) The filament has a uniform cross-sectional shape along its length and has a central portion with webs radiating outwardly at about right angles from the center. The cruciform or Y-shape so created not only gives the filament a high degree of stiffness, but a savings in production cost is realized due to a savings in material because the creation provides a greater surface area for a given amount of polymer. The angular shape is achieved by melt-extruding the filament through a die. (3) The filament is linearly oriented, an orientation in which the major axis of each molecule of polymer lies along the length of the filament. This type of orientation, achieved by stretching or tension-drawing the filament after it has been shaped, imparts tensile strength, resiliency, and resistance to lateral impact. If this particular orientation process is not undertaken a heterogeneous orientation results in which the molecules lie at random generally askew to the major axis of the filament length. A filament so heterogeneously oriented has spots of low lateral impact resistance which may cause breakage when the filament is subjected to brush use.

II. The Prior Art

In concluding that Shaw's patent is invalid the district court relied primarily upon five references to the prior art. It found that linear orientation of rounded or oval filaments made of a polymer used by Shaw by stretching or tension-drawing was well known in the art as disclosed in two Carothers patents [on nylon], the Rugeley patent, the Brubaker patent, and from Shaw's admissions at trial. Two prior art patents, Brubaker and Taylor, reveal that Polymer filaments could be given various shapes, such as, for example, star shapes, by passing the filament through a die having an orifice of the desired configuration. The Taylor patent, nevertheless, did not indicate that a die shaped filament could be linearly oriented. The Brubaker patent specifically stated that drawing the filament through the forming die involved compressive forces, thereby necessarily leading to some heterogeneous orientation of the molecules along the length of the filament axis.

III. Validity

A. *Novelty*

The district court's first ground for holding the Shaw patent invalid is its conclusion that the subject matter of the patent was not novel within the meaning of Section 101, and Section 102(a). This result rested upon the court's findings that all the elements found in the Shaw patent are contained in the prior art patents above discussed and that the Shaw product is not greater than the sum of its parts. However, the fact that each element of a creation sought to be patented is found in the prior art does not negate novelty if the old elements are combined in such a way that as a result of the combining an improved, useful, and more advantageous innovation is obtained. * * *

The Shaw patent meets the fairly liberal test of Section 101 and Section 102(a) because nowhere in the prior art is the Shaw filament "identically disclosed," nor is it plain from the prior art references that linear orientation of rounded filaments was functionally equivalent to linear orientation of angular shaped filaments. The fact that prior to Shaw's invention no filament of the shape described by Shaw had been linearly oriented sets Shaw's product apart from the prior art. See United States v. Adams. * * *

B. Obviousness

* * *

The crucial question here is whether in light of the prior art the bringing of linear orientation to a cruciform-shaped filament would be obvious to a person having ordinary skill in the art. In dealing with this question the district court while discussing the Brubaker patent stated:

> 32. * * * The die drawing process of the [Brubaker] patent involves compressive as well as tension forces * * * while Shaw claims that his patent involves tension forces only. However, Shaw also testified in this regard that, 'One would expect the molecules, some of them, to be aligned in the direction of the axis by the tension force * * *.' From this statement, I find that Shaw expected an alignment in the direction of the axis by the tension forces mentioned in his patent * * *. In other words, Shaw did not obtain an unexpected result.

The court then summed up its findings with respect to obviousness by stating:

> 36. I have seriously considered the scope and content of the prior art * * * and particularly the Rugeley patent * * *, [the Carothers patents] * * *, Brubaker patent * * *, and the Taylor patent * * * set forth in findings 29 to 33, respectively, and have considered the differences and similarity between the prior art and the claim in the Shaw patent, and find that there is no material difference between such prior art and the Shaw claim. I have further considered the level of ordinary skill in the pertinent art. From the foregoing, I find that the subject matter of the Shaw patent would be obvious to a person having ordinary skill in the art to which the subject matter pertains within the meaning of 35 U.S.C. § 103.

* * *

While the above is the extent of the district court's elaboration in support of the holding that the Shaw patent is obvious, it would seem that the court reached its conclusion by reasoning as follows: Given the facts that linear orientation techniques for rounded filaments were well known in the prior art, as disclosed by Carothers and Rugeley and recognized by Brubaker, and that Brubaker disclosed filaments of other than rounded, circular or oval shapes, it would be an obvious step for Shaw to stretch his filaments to achieve linear orientation *after* they were extruded through a die into the shape desired and, although Brubaker did not take this final step in the production of his filaments, it would seem but a simple and logical advance for one skilled in the art to borrow the stretching techniques disclosed in earlier patents, and therefore the new step taken by Shaw was so obvious as not to justify its patentability. * * *

As will be demonstrated, we believe that the trial court failed adequately to resolve the factual inquiries required by Graham, * * * by ignoring an abundance of unchallenged uncontroverted evidence in the record which tends to demonstrate that Shaw's patent was not obvious.

As already shown, implicit in the district court's reasoning is the assumption that no material difference was known in the art at the time of Shaw's invention between filaments of a circular nature and filaments of a precise angular shape from which an inference was drawn that orientation of one could be achieved as easily as orientation of the other and that men skilled in the art knew or should have known this. The same prior art, however, so relied upon by the court to sustain its conclusion of obviousness, contains uncontroverted evidence that clearly negates the assumption and the inference drawn therefrom.

We return to the Brubaker patent, which postdated all other prior art patents reviewed by the court and which can be viewed as embodying all the relevant teachings which would or would not point the obvious way for Shaw to innovate.

The specifications of the Brubaker patent point out two significant difficulties encountered by that patentee in reaching his discovery: (1) Brubaker found that tension drawing or stretching a circular polymer filament produced a linearly oriented filament of oval shape. In other words, the process of aligning the molecules along the filament axis distorted the original shape. The example recited disclosed a round filament having cross-sectional dimensions of 57 and 58 mils (one thousandth of an inch = 1 mil) after having been die drawn. Stretching or cold (tension) drawing this filament resulted in an oval cross-section of 43 and 62 mils. Brubaker, therefore, utilized the die drawing method to insure that the filament would not lose its shape; the patentee admitted that "[d]ie drawn filaments tend to be more uniform both in cross-sectional area and in shape than tension drawn filaments." U.S. Patent No. 2,291,873 issued to Brubaker, August 4, 1942, p. 4, col. 1, ll. 51–53; p. 2, col. 2, ll. 42–54; p. 4, col. 2, ll. 1–7. (2) Brubaker also found that there was limited distortion in the shape of the filament even when a die was used to impart shape (i.e., star) and assigned as a reason therefore the compressive forces at work as the filament was solid-extruded (drawn) through the die. Id. p. 4, col. 2, 11. 1–9. The patentee, therefore, admitted that his filament could only "*approach* being triangular, square, rectangular, oval, star, etc." Id. p. 4, col. 1, 11. 60–61 (Emphasis supplied).

Obviously, then, disclosures used by the trial court to negate validity demonstrate that, if the Brubaker patent were taken at face value, Shaw's filament could not be produced. Rather than serving to point the way to innovation, therefore, Brubaker's teachings would tend to discourage one skilled in the art from investigating the methods ultimately used by Shaw to achieve production of an improved polymer filament.

* * * [The court here quotes from Adams, supra page 870]

The district court failed to evaluate the problem posed by the prior art and appears to have relied on the proposition that, as Shaw's solution to the problem seemed a simple one, his filament was an obvious outgrowth. The simplicity of an invention or an improvement thereof is not, however, the test of its obviousness. Further, the burden is on the appellee to show *facts* that would lead to the conclusion that appellant's product was obvious. The mere recital of the known elements in the art does not, without more, invalidate the patent under Section 103. There must appear evidence that the *bringing together* of these elements would have been obvious. Doubt as to validity, no matter how strong, cannot justify resort to unfounded assumptions or supply deficiencies in the factual background. * * *

Furthermore, it appears that the court below may have used the benefit of hindsight when it stated that "I find that Shaw expected an alignment in the direction of the axis by the tension forces mentioned in his patent. * * * In other words, Shaw did not obtain an unexpected result." The issue, however, is not what the patentee expected to produce, but what a hypothetical person "having ordinary skill in the art" would expect to develop if he had thought about the problem. 35 U.S.C. § 103; Graham v. John Deere Co., supra. In resolving the question of obviousness, the judicial view must not include the knowledge contributed by the patentee, the teachings of his patent are irrelevant when determining what "would have been obvious" to one skilled in the prior art before he created his "manufacture."

It is curious that the trial court made no mention of the statements, not significantly challenged, of plaintiff's expert witnesses, Drs. Martin Kuehne and Fred Kidd, who corroborated the negative teachings of Brubaker.

Dr. Kidd, head of the British Brush Manufacturers Research Association when Shaw's filament was first brought to his attention in 1957, testified that he was quite surprised that someone could produce a linearly oriented filament of a precise X-shape because his previous experience had taught that the process of stretching or tension drawing would tend to distort the filament's shape or to round it out.

Dr. Kuehne, a professor at the University of Vermont and an expert in organic chemistry, testified that the Shaw filament posed for him an unexpected result because the stretching process would tend to induce, on the basis of chemical or molecular theory, a loss in filament shape, causing it to become more circular.

Moreover, it is significant that E.I. du Pont de Nemours & Company, which owns the Carothers and the Brubaker patents and which may be considered a leader in the plastics field, took out a license under the Shaw patent. Also, Shaw has enjoyed considerable commercial success, and licenses have issued under his patent, in addition to that issued to du Pont, to seven domestic and foreign manufacturers, one of which, Celanese Corporation of America, owns the Taylor patent. Furthermore, it does not appear that the Brubaker and Taylor patents, the only prior art references disclosing similar shapes to those produced by Shaw, have met with commercial success or acceptability.

Finally, there is considerable evidence that indicates that the defendant Whiting, having been informed that Shaw's filaments were being purchased and used by several manufacturers, obtained samples of Shaw's products and sought other relevant information in order to develop similar filaments so as to compete in the market heretofore enjoyed by Shaw. It has been said of such conduct:

> "The imitation of a thing patented by a defendant, who denies invention, has often been regarded, perhaps especially in this circuit, as conclusive evidence of what the defendant thinks of the patent, and persuasive of what the rest of the world ought to think. Kurtz v. Belle Hat Lining Co., 280 F. 277, 281 (2 Cir. 1922)."

Although these "subtests" or secondary considerations of validity cannot be given talismanic importance in our deliberations, they may be utilized to "guard against hindsight" and "to resist the temptation to read into the prior art the teachings of the invention in issue." [The court here cites *Graham* and the Note, 112 U.Pa.L.Rev. 1169 (1964).]

* * *

Reversed on the issue of validity, affirmed on the issues of infringement, and remanded to the district court to determine the extent of infringement, and to issue a permanent injunction consistent with this opinion.

Appendix

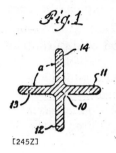

Diagram of Shaw's polymer filament

KAUFMAN, CIRCUIT JUDGE (dissenting).

While I find myself in full agreement with my brother Waterman's general discussion of the applicable patent law, I disagree with his ultimate conclusion as to the obviousness, and hence the validity, of Shaw's patent under 35 U.S.C. § 103 (1964). The Act, 35 U.S.C. § 101, authorizes patents on " * * * any new and useful process, machine, manufacture, or composition of matter * * *." Shaw's patent was for a "manufacture," or in the common parlance, was a product patent, not a process patent. Product patents cover only the article—here the shaped synthetic bristle—and not the process, or method by which it is produced. Although a product claim "may, and indeed must, be read upon the specifications," Musher Foundation v. Alba Trading Co., 150 F.2d 885 (2d Cir.1945) (L. Hand, J.),

> " * * * the invention in the case of such a product patent must lie exclusively in the conception of the product, and regardless of any method of its production, though of course the patent must disclose one way by which it can be made. While that imposes a severe standard, it is no severer than it should be, if the monopoly is to extend to the product however made. Unless conception alone is the test, and if the inventor may eke out his right by recourse to the ingenuity involved in any process or the machine, he gains an unfair advantage; for the claims cover the product produced by other machines and processes, to which by hypothesis he has contributed nothing. * * * At times indeed a process may leave traces in the product and the difficulty is avoided, but that is seldom or never true of the product of a machine; * * *." Buono v. Yankee Maid Dress Corporation, 77 F.2d 274, 279 (2d Cir.1935) (L. Hand, J.). See also General Electric Co. v. Wabash Co., 304 U.S. 364, 373–375 (1938).

Applying the test announced in Buono, for Shaw to succeed, he must show that the idea shaping linear filaments to improve stiffness must have been a new "conception," one that would not have been obvious to one skilled in the art. Prior patents seem to me to indicate precisely the contrary. Most damning of all, in my view, is the Brubaker patent, which discusses drawing linear polymers through shaping dies, and concludes:

> "The present invention through the selection of different shape openings in the die makes possible the production of filaments of various forms, for example, filaments which approach being triangular, square, rectangular, oval, star, etc. * * * *Bristles having a star shaped cross-section have better stiffness* than those having the same cross-sectional area in the form of a circle." [Emphasis added.]

I find the Brubaker patent conclusive evidence that the *product* Shaw patented—a shaped bristle—was obvious even from a cursory examination of the prior art. The point is not that creating such a product was not difficult, or that it did not involve some ingenuity in devising a process; it is that devising the product itself was obvious. The law is clearly different where a process patent is involved; but that is not this case.

I would affirm on the ground of obviousness.

APPLICATION OF PILKINGTON

United States Court of Customs and Patent Appeals, 1969.
411 F.2d 1345.

WORLEY, CHIEF JUDGE. Appellant is the inventor of the "float glass" process for making sheet glass. According to the specification, a ribbon of glass is drawn on to the horizontal surface of a bath of molten metal, considerably wider than the ribbon, and is then heated above its melting point. The glass liquefies and, under the influence of gravitational and surface tension forces, flows freely across the surface of the bath without any lateral restraint until it attains a condition of equilibrium on that surface. At this time the molten glass is in the form of a thin layer of uniform thickness with upper and lower parallel surfaces which are flat except at the very edges. The glass is cooled sufficiently to solidify it, and then withdrawn from the bath. The application on appeal is directed to the sheet glass product produced by the float process. According to appellant, that glass has qualities including a fire finish on both surfaces as well as flatness and freedom from imperfections, stresses and distortion, which render his sheet glass superior to sheet glass produced in other ways.

The application as originally filed contained conventional product claims and also product-by-process claims. In response to the first and second letters from the examiner criticizing the inclusion of product-by-process claims, appellant cancelled the initial product-by-process claims but reserved the right to reinstate those claims if the invention could not be patentably distinguished by conventional product claims. Subsequent to another letter of the examiner confirming the examiner's final rejection of the article claims, appellant submitted an amendment cancelling all the claims and substituting a single product-by-process claim, claim 17, which reads:

"17.   A sheet of glass cut from a ribbon of glass produced by delivering glass at a controlled rate to a bath of molten metal and advancing the glass along the surface of the bath under thermal conditions which assure that a layer of molten glass is established on the bath, maintaining said glass layer in molten condition until there is developed on the surface of the bath a buoyant body of molten glass of stable thickness by permitting said layer of molten glass to flow laterally unhindered to the limit of its free flow under the influence of gravity and surface tension, and thereafter continuously advancing the buoyant body in ribbon form along the bath, and sufficiently cooling this ribbon as it is advanced to permit it to be taken undamaged out of the bath by mechanical means.

In the examiner's Answer, the following rejections of claim 17 were set forth:

> (1) rejection as an improper product-by-process claim, the examiner taking the position that the product could be claimed without resort to a product-by-process claim, as exemplified by the other product claims that had been sought.

> (2) rejection as unpatentable over either of the following references, separately:

> Pedersen et al. 2,167,905 Aug. 1, 1939

> Tooley, "Handbook of Glass Manufacture," published by Ogden Publishing Co., (N.Y.), 1953, (Vol. 1, pages 391–420).

Pedersen discloses a process for making sheet glass, which is most readily described by reference to Figure 1 of that patent [infra].

In Fig. 1, a sheet of glass S is drawn upwardly from the surface of a bath of molten glass and passes in "wiping or sliding contact" over the surface of a cooled guide member 18 having a ground and polished surface. Of the guide members, the patent states:

> * * * Tendencies toward irregularities in the sheet are smoothed out by the wiping action of roll 18 in sliding contact with the sheet, and the coolers 22 and 23 then set the sheet so that above this zone the glass sheet is set to final thickness substantially non-plastic. This is highly desirable, since if stretching and thinning of the sheet occurs thereafter by the pull of the drawing rolls the sheet is liable to become warped or drawn out of line in parts thereof.

The Tooley article relates to annealing and tempering sheet glass and discusses control of the internal stress in plate glass by those methods.

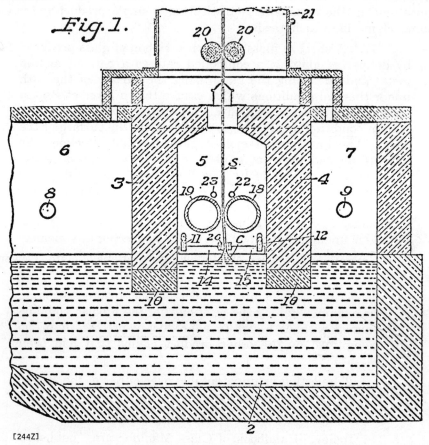

Fig.1.

[244Z]

The board, sustaining the rejection of claim 17 as an improper product-by-process claim, stated:

> We are not convinced that the product characteristics of parallelism, reflective properties, and internal stresses cannot be definitely defined, and that sufficient physical characteristics cannot be drawn to distinguish from the prior art if they are present.

The board also sustained the rejection of the claims under 35 U.S.C. 103 in view of the references cited by the examiner, stating:

> We share the examiner's view that claim 17 does not patentably distinguish over Pedersen et al. or Tooley. We are left in ignorance as to what degree that parallelism, smoothness, flatness, homogeneity and other physical characteristics of appellant's glass sheet differs from the glass of Pedersen et al. These are all characteristics that the glass of Pedersen et al. would in some degree possess. Appellant's product is not patentable [merely] because the process by which it is made is

patentable as pointed out in the Examiner's Answer. The differences in the product over the prior art must be such that they are not obvious to a person having ordinary skill in the art. The Pedersen et al. patent points out on page 7, lines 17 to 33, as noted by the examiner, that the fire-polished surfaces of their glass are substantially as optically correct as that of ground and polished plate glass.

We are not persuaded that appellant's product patentably distinguishes over the prior art cited.

We sustain the rejection of claim 17 on the references applied under 35 U.S.C.A. 103.

In resolving this appeal, we take as a starting point the position that patentability of a claim to a *product* does not rest merely on a difference in the method by which that product is made. Rather, it is the product itself which must be new and unobvious. As we said in In re Dilnot, 300 F.2d 945 (1962):

> The addition of a method step in a product claim, which product is not patentably distinguishable from the prior art, cannot impart patentability to the old product. In re Moeller, 117 F.2d 565; In re Lifton, 189 F.2d 261; In re Shortell, 173 F.2d 993.

See also Tri-Wall Containers, Inc. v. United States, 408 F.2d 748, and cases therein. Thus our inquiry here must be directed to a comparison of appellant's sheet glass with the sheet glass of the references to determine whether any differences between them are such that the subject matter as a whole would be unobvious.

Turning first to Tooley, the examiner's Answer states:

> * * * Tooley discloses that internal stresses in glass is a primary concern in the glass art and it is a matter of choice whether or not internal stresses are desired characteristics * * *. * * *

The application of that statement to the question of obviousness of appellant's claim is not readily apparent to us, and we note that the board also chose not to discuss the Tooley disclosure apart from observing that " * * * claim 17 does not patentably distinguish over Pedersen et al. or Tooley."

Tooley does, however, refer to plate glass which it is appropriate to compare with appellant's sheet glass. Conventional processes of manufacturing plate glass, we are informed by appellant, involve passing molten glass between opposed sizing and cooled casting rolls. As a result of imperfections on the roll surfaces, the glass is subject to corresponding defects on its surfaces which must be removed by subsequent grinding and polishing operations. Appellant further points out that such grinding and polishing necessarily leaves grinding and polishing marks, and that even the original glass lacks a lustrous fire finish because it was cooled and solidified in contact with a solid surface. In line with this argument, we think that appellant's float glass differs from conventional plate glass in certain important respects—it has a lustrous fire finish and lacks the surface distortion or scoring resulting from grinding and polishing of the latter glass.

Turning now to Pedersen, we observe that in all the various embodiments of the process there shown, the sheet of glass is pulled in wiping and sliding contact over at least one forming member for the stated purpose of smoothing out irregularities in the sheet. However, it seems clear that if the sheet at the time of contact with the forming member is sufficiently malleable to have irregularities smoothed out, then it must also be sufficiently malleable to reproduce in the sheet any surface imperfections of the forming member itself. As it is unlikely that Pedersen's forming members should be lacking in local surface imperfections, it seems reasonable to conclude that the sheet glass product of Pedersen possesses at least some amount of surface deviations. Thus, although Pedersen does describe his glass as having fire finished surfaces, all that is reasonably obvious from Pedersen is a sheet of glass which is as free of distortion as he can make it, but which one skilled in the art would recognize would always have an irreducible minimum degree of distortion imposed by the limitations on perfection of the forming member. Thus we think that a sheet of glass having such surface perfection and freedom from internal stress as appellant obtains by floating his liquid glass on the surface of liquid metal is both new and unobvious even in view of Pedersen.

We therefore decide that the rejection uder 35 U.S.C. 103 in view of Tooley or Pedersen cannot be sustained. There remains the review of the rejection of claim 17 as an improper product-by-process claim.

On that point the board felt the invention could be adequately claimed by the physical characteristics of appellant's sheet glass and that a product-by-process claim was therefore improper. In considering the problem presented in claiming a product by a recital in the claim of the process by which it is made, we observed in In re Steppan, 394 F.2d 1013 (1968):

> The problem, in essence, is thus one of determining who shall decide how best to state what the invention *is*. By statute, 35 U.S.C. 112, Congress has placed no limitations on *how* an applicant claims *his invention,* so long as the specification concludes with claims which particularly point out and distinctly claim that invention.

With that in mind, it appears that appellant has distinctly pointed out and claimed what he regards as his invention in accordance with 35 U.S.C. 112. While we are satisfied that the references of record do not anticipate appellant's glass or demonstrate that it would be obvious, the differences between that glass and the glass of the prior art do not appear to us to be particularly susceptible to definition by the conventional recitation of properties or structure. Under the circumstances, it seems to us that the present product-by-process claim satisfies the requirements of 35 U.S.C. 112 and is appropriate here.

For the foregoing reasons, the decision of the board is reversed.

NOTE

Because 35 U.S.C.A. § 103 requires that the subject matter of the invention be non-obvious and 35 U.S.C.A. § 112 requires that the claims particularly point out and distinctly claim the subject matter of the invention, it would seem to follow that it is the subject matter of the claim that must be non-obvious. Thus where the claim is on the thing, and the non-obviousness lies in the way of making it or in its useful properties, there seems to be a powerful statutory argument that the claim is invalid.

There is much precedent to the contrary, but none of it confronts the statute head on. The only way around the argument is to take the position that invention is not a defined term in the statute, and is used in different senses in 103 and 112. The purpose of 103 is to ensure that the inventor has made a significant contribution, and in this context invention should be construed broadly to refer to the whole contribution. This reading is supported by the phrase "subject matter as a whole" in § 103. The purpose of claims in § 112 is to provide clear boundaries to the scope of the rights so that third parties will know the limits of the patent. There are many advantages to product claims. First, their boundaries are easier to interpret. Second, the alternative process claims are difficult to enforce. The process can often be practiced in privacy and the infringement is difficult to detect.

This problem is particularly acute for patents on therapeutic drugs. There are doubts about the validity of claims on the therapeutic process in the human body, and a process claim on the therapeutic administration of the substance may be difficult to enforce. There is, however, controlling authority that a patent on a compound can be non-obvious because of the discovery of its therapeutic properties. In Application of Papesch, 315 F.2d 381 (C.C.P.A.1963), the Court of Customs and Patent Appeals took the position that a compound is a claim on the properties of the compound. This approach was followed in Commissioner of Patents v. Deutsche Gold—Und-Silber-Scheideanstalt Vormals Roessler, 397 F.2d 656 (D.C.Cir.1968) (Burger, J.), and by the Federal Circuit in In re Chupp, 816 F.2d 643 (Fed.Cir.1987). Many chemical components are "structurally obvious" in the sense that the existence of the molecule would be predicted by a chemist. The "nonobviousness" lies either in the method of synthesizing the compound or in its beneficial (and previously unknown) therapeutic properties.

F. SECTION 102

(1) INTRODUCTION

JAMESBURY CORP. v. LITTON INDUSTRIAL PRODUCTS, INC.

United States Court of Appeals, Federal Circuit, 1985.
756 F.2d 1556.

NIES, CIRCUIT JUDGE.

I.

Jamesbury Corp., the plaintiff below, charged Litton Industrial Products with infringing claims 7 and 8 of its U.S. Patent No. 2,945,666 to Freeman entitled "Ball Valve". Following a seven day jury trial, the jury returned a verdict for Litton, concluding, in answer to an interrogatory, that the asserted claims did not differ in any "significant particulars" from the prior art.[2] Under the court's instructions, this finding meant that the claims were invalid under 35 U.S.C. § 102(a) for lack of novelty. Jamesbury had timely objected to the jury charge on the issue of novelty and to the wording of the particular interrogatory under review, as well as to other instructions. No instructions were given with respect to obviousness of the claimed inventions, Litton having agreed that obviousness was not asserted as a ground for holding the claims invalid. Following entry of judgment, Jamesbury filed a motion under Fed.R.Civ.P. 50(b) for judgment notwithstanding the verdict, which was denied by the district court. In ruling on the motion, the district court stated:

> The jury returned a verdict for the defendant in this patent infringement suit. The plaintiff has moved for judgment notwithstanding the verdict. The plaintiff is seeking judgment on all disputed issues: the validity of the patent, infringement of the patent, the amount of damages, and the defenses of laches and estoppel.
>
> In its response to a special interrogatory, the jury made explicit its finding that the patent was invalid because of lack of novelty over the prior art. Thus the crucial issue to be resolved is whether the jury's finding of invalidity should be set aside. * * *

2. Jury interrogatory No. 1 reads as follows:

1. Does the ball valve construction shown and described in the Saunders British patent or any other prior art differ in any significant particulars from the ball valve defined by the express language of claims 7 and 8 of the Freeman patent?

As to claim 7   Yes___   No X

As to claim 8   Yes___   No X

* * *

If you answer "No" as to both claim 7 and claim 8, do not answer any further questions. * * *

* * * The plaintiff alleges that the defendant has produced no evidence regarding the level of ordinary skill in the ball valve art. Although such proof is essential to support a finding of invalidity because of obviousness, see *Environmental Designs v. Union Oil Co.,* 713 F.2d 693, 695 (Fed.Cir.1983), the plaintiff has cited no authority requiring such proof to support a finding of invalidity because of lack of novelty over the prior art. On the issue of novelty, there was ample evidence to support the jury's verdict; there was certainly not an overwhelming amount of evidence in the plaintiff's favor that reasonable and fair minded men could not arrive at a verdict against it.

For the foregoing reasons, the motion for judgment n.o.v. is denied.

In this appeal, Jamesbury argues that because of erroneous and prejudicial error in the instructions to the jury, it is entitled at least to a new trial. Jamesbury further asserts that because lack of novelty was not established and other grounds asserted for holding the claims invalid, namely, obviousness and inequitable conduct, were withdrawn or waived, the court erred in its ruling on Jamesbury's motion JNOV. We agree and, therefore, reverse the holding of invalidity of claims 7 and 8. The case is remanded for resolution of other issues.

II.

* * *

A.

Jamesbury first attacks the following instruction which laid the foundation for the jury's deliberations:

> [T]he public is a silent but nevertheless an important, an interested party in all patent litigation and it is entitled to protection against the monopolization of what is not lawfully patentable. In other words, it's not simply between Jamesbury and Litton. Other people are affected by it.
>
> So I charge you that it is your duty to *subject the invention* defined in claims seven and eight of the Freeman patent *to careful scrutiny before endorsing Jamesbury's right to the patent monopoly* defined by such claims. [Emphasis added.]

Jamesbury argues that the effect of this instruction was to create a presumption of invalidity requiring Jamesbury to prove, beyond careful scrutiny, that it was entitled to maintain a monopoly, which, impliedly, was against the public interest. We agree that this instruction is legally erroneous and prejudicial.

The language that the jury must give "careful scrutiny" before "endorsing" the "patent monopoly" cannot be approved. While the language does not rise to the level of a presumption of invalidity, it does incorrectly suggest that the jury must affirmatively find the patent valid, which is never appropriate. * * *

Further, this court has disapproved of a challenger's characterization of a patentee by the term "monopolist", which is commonly regarded as pejorative. Union Carbide Corp. v. American Can Co., 724 F.2d 1567, 1574 n. 4 (Fed.Cir.1984); Schenck v. Nortron Corp., 713 F.2d 782, 784 (Fed.Cir.1983). In both of the cited cases, a bench trial was involved. Here, not only was Litton's counsel not admonished for so characterizing Jamesbury before the jury, a more serious impropriety than in a bench trial, but also the characterization found its way into the instructions. As stated in Connell v. Sears, Roebuck & Co., 722 F.2d 1542, 1548 (Fed.Cir.1983), the characterization of a patent as a "monopoly" is misdirected:

> The phrase "patent monopoly" appears at various points. Under the statute, 35 U.S.C. § 261, a patent is a form of property right, and the right to exclude recognized in a patent is but the essence of the concept of property. Schenck v. Nortron Corp., 713 F.2d 782 (Fed.Cir.1983).

Instructions which supplement the statutory body of law governing patent validity by interjecting language to the effect that the public must be "protected" against a "monopoly," a term found nowhere in the statute, are likely to be prejudicial and should be avoided.

B.

* * *

[The court held that the instructions on the burden of proof were in error.]

C.

Jamesbury's objections (also made to the district court) that the instructions and interrogatory No. 1, reproduced at note 2, supra, misstate the law respecting novelty were legitimate. The instruction * * * to the effect that the claims are invalid if the prior art Saunders patent discloses "substantially the same things" as claims 7 and 8, and Interrogatory No. 1 which speaks of the claims not differing in "significant particulars", are not legally correct.

The error in this interpretation of the statutory requirement of novelty is the same as that which was addressed in Connell, 722 F.2d at 1548:

> The opinion says anticipation may be shown by less than "complete anticipation" if one of ordinary skill may in reliance on the prior art "complete the work required for the invention", and that "it is sufficient for an anticipation 'if the general aspects are the same and the differences in minor matters is only such as would suggest itself to one of ordinary skill in the art.'" Those statements relate to obviousness, not anticipation. Anticipation

requires the presence in a single prior art disclosure of all elements of a claimed invention arranged as in the claim. Soundscriber Corp. v. U.S., 360 F.2d 954, 960 (Ct.Claims 1966). A prior art disclosure that "almost" meets that standard may render the claim invalid under § 103; it does not "anticipate."

Here, as well, anticipation is not shown by a prior art disclosure which is only "substantially the same" as the claimed invention.

Litton argues that elsewhere the district court amplified its interpretation by speaking of the prior art disclosing the claimed invention "in complete terms." However, that additional paragraph of instructions also speaks of "*substantially* the same subject matter * * * *in complete terms, thus enabling* a man skilled in the art to understand and practice the invention." We see no correction of the legal standard in the above statement.

III.

Because of the above legal errors, the verdict of invalidity for lack of novelty (i.e., anticipation) cannot stand.

* * *

IV.

Because the issues of infringement, laches and estoppel were not resolved at the conclusion of the trial, the case must be remanded for their disposition. * * *

* * *

Conclusion

For the foregoing reasons, the judgment is reversed and the case is remanded for disposition of all remaining issues other than the validity of claims 7 and 8 of Freeman Patent No. 2,945,666.

Reversed and remanded.

NOTES

1. The sharp distinction made by the Federal Circuit between anticipation under § 102 and obviousness under § 103 is consistent with the first sentence of § 103, which begins: "A patent may not be obtained though the invention is not *identically disclosed or described* as set forth in section 102 of this title * * *." Nevertheless, there was authority to the contrary in the other circuits. See, for instance, the opinion of Mr. Justice Stevens, then a circuit judge, in Frantz Manufacturing Co. v. Phenix Manufacturing Co., 457 F.2d 314 (7th Cir.1972).

2. Although there is an important difference between anticipation under § 102 and obviousness under § 103, § 102 plays an important role in § 103 because § 102 has been held to inform the meaning of "prior art." The relationship between § 102 and § 103 is an issue that will recur in subsequent cases.

(2) "KNOWN OR USED"

Section 102(a) of Title 35 provides that "a person shall be entitled to a patent unless the invention was known or used by others in this country, or patented or described in a printed publication in this or a foreign country, before the invention thereof by the applicant for patent." It is less than satisfactory. If knowledge alone is sufficient to anticipate the invention, why does the statute proceed to enumerate use, a patent and a publication as things which also anticipate? Surely, knowledge encompasses and necessarily precedes use, a patent or a publication. Although the Supreme Court has not to this day resolved the matter, the answer of the best authorities—Judge Learned Hand again, as you might have guessed by now—is that "known" in § 102 means known in a manner accessible to the public. But the importation of "public" into § 102(a) is at odds with the explicit use of the term in § 102(b). But that is not only to simplify, but to jump ahead of the story. The extant Supreme Court precedent—most of it nineteenth century—does not provide a complete answer.

GAYLER v. WILDER
Supreme Court of the United States, 1850.
51 U.S. (10 How.) 477, 13 L.Ed. 504.

Mr. Chief Justice Taney delivered the opinion of the court.

* * *

The remaining question is upon the validity of the patent on which the suit was brought. [The patent was issued to one Fitzgerald for the invention of a fire-proof safe. The safe was made by constructing an inner and an outer safe of iron and then filling the space in between with plaster of paris. The circuit court (a trial court) held the patent valid.]

It appears that James Conner, who carried on the business of a stereotype founder in the city of New York, made a safe for his own use between the years 1829 and 1832, for the protection of his papers against fire; and continued to use it until 1838, when it passed into other hands. It was kept in his counting-room and known to the persons engaged in the foundry; and after it passed out of his hands, he used others of a different construction.

It does not appear what became of this safe afterwards. And there is nothing in the testimony from which it can be inferred that its mode of construction was known to the person into whose possession it fell, or that any value was attached to it as a place of security for papers against fire; or that it was ever used for that purpose.

Upon these facts the court instructed the jury, "that if Conner had not made his discovery public, but had used it simply for his own private purpose, and it had been finally forgotten or abandoned, such a discovery and use would be no obstacle to the taking out of a patent by

Fitzgerald or those claiming under him, if he be an original, though not the first, inventor or discoverer."

The instruction assumes that the jury might find from the evidence that Conner's safe was substantially the same with that of Fitzgerald, and also prior in time. And if the fact was so, the question then was whether the patentee was "the original and first inventor or discoverer," within the meaning of the act of Congress.

* * *

[Where an inventor takes out an American patent on an invention which has been known or used in a foreign country] * * * the party who invents is not strictly speaking the first and original inventor. The law assumes that the improvement may have been known and used before his discovery. Yet his patent is valid if he discovered it by the efforts of his own genius, and believed himself to be the original inventor. * * * If the foreign invention had been printed or patented, it was already given to the world and open to the people of this country, as well as of others, upon reasonable inquiry. They would therefore derive no advantage from the invention here. It would confer no benefit upon the community, and the inventor therefore is not considered to be entitled to the reward. But if the foreign discovery is not patented, nor described in any printed publication, it might be known and used in remote places for ages, and the people of this country be unable to profit by it. The means of obtaining knowledge would not be within their reach; and, as far as their interest is concerned, it would be the same thing as if the improvement had never been discovered. It is the inventor here that brings it to them, and places it in their possession. And as he does this by the effort of his own genius, the law regards him as the first and original inventor, and protects his patent, although the improvement had in fact been invented before, and used by others.

So, too, as to the lost arts. It is well known that centuries ago discoveries were made in certain arts the fruits of which have come down to us, but the means by which the work was accomplished are at this day unknown. The knowledge has been lost for ages. Yet it would hardly be doubted, if any one now discovered an art thus lost, and it was a useful improvement, that, upon a fair construction of the act of Congress, he would be entitled to a patent. Yet he would not literally be the first and original inventor. But he would be the first to confer on the public the benefit of the invention. He would discover what is unknown, and communicate knowledge which the public had not the means of obtaining without his invention.

Upon the same principle and upon the same rule of construction, we think that Fitzgerald must be regarded as the first and original inventor of the safe in question. * * *

We do not understand the Circuit Court to have said that the omission of Conner to try the value of his safe by proper tests would deprive it of its priority; nor his omission to bring it into public use.

He might have omitted both, and also abandoned its use, and been ignorant of the extent of its value; yet, if it was the same with Fitzgerald's, the latter would not upon such grounds be entitled to a patent, provided Conner's safe and its mode of construction were still in the memory of Conner before they were recalled by Fitzgerald's patent.

* * *

Upon the whole, therefore, we think there is no error in the opinion of the Circuit Court, and the judgment is therefore affirmed.

NOTES

1. In Coffin v. Ogden, 85 U.S. (18 Wall.) 120 (1874), the court held a patent invalid due to prior construction of the invention by another. In dictum, the Court cast doubt upon the statement in *Gayler* that Conner need not have tried his safe:

> "The case arose while the Patent Act of 1836 was in force, and must be decided under its provision. The sixth section of that act requires that to entitle the applicant to a patent, his invention or discovery must be one 'not known or used by others before his invention or discovery thereof.' The fifteenth section allowed a party sued for infringement to prove, among other defences, that the patentee 'was not the original and first inventor of the thing patented, or of a substantial and material part thereof claimed to be new.'"

> "The whole act is to be taken together and construed in the light of the context. The meaning of these sections must be sought in the import of their language, and in the object and policy of the legislature in enacting them. The invention or discovery relied upon as a defence, must have been complete, and capable of producing the result sought to be accomplished; and this must be shown by the defendant. The burden of proof rests upon him, and every reasonable doubt should be resolved against him. If the thing were embryotic or inchoate; if it rested in speculation or experiment; if the process pursued for its development had failed to reach the point of consummation, it cannot avail to defeat a patent founded upon a discovery or invention which was completed, while in the other case there was only progress, however near that progress may have approximated to the end in view. The law requires not conjecture, but certainty. If the question relate to a machine, the conception must have been clothed in substantial forms which demonstrate at once its practical efficacy and utility. The prior knowledge and use by a single person is sufficient. The number is immaterial. Until his work is done, the inventor has given nothing to the public. In Gayler v. Wilder the views of this court upon the subject were thus expressed: 'We do not understand the Circuit Court to have said that the omission of Conner to try his safe by the proper tests would deprive it of its priority; nor his omission to bring it into public use. He might have omitted both, and also abandoned its use and been ignorant of the extent of its value; yet if it was the same with Fitzgerald's, the latter would not, upon such grounds, be entitled to a patent; provided Conner's safe and its mode of construction were still in the memory of Conner before they were recalled by Fitzgerald's patent.' Whether the proposition expressed by the proviso in the last

sentence is a sound one, it is not necessary in this case to consider." Id. at 124–25.

The law relating to reduction to practice, infra page 947, is involved here. In summary, an invention is not reduced to practice, i.e. made, until it is proven operable. The relevance of this law arises from the argument that an invention cannot be known unless it has been made, that is reduced to practice, since something that does not exist cannot be known. *Gayler* seemed to reject this argument, *Coffin* to accept it.

2. Judge Hand's statement was this: "To be patentable, an invention cannot have been 'known or used by others' in this country before the inventor 'invented or discovered' it. ＊ ＊ ＊ Knowledge in this sense is to be distinguished from a public use or sale by the inventor himself for more than a year before he files his application, which is ipso facto an abandonment. ＊ ＊ ＊ It is also true that another's experiment, imperfect and never perfected, will not serve either as an anticipation or as part of the prior art, for it has not served to enrich it. The patented invention does not become 'known' by such a use or sale, or by anything of which the art cannot take hold and make use as it stands. But the mere fact that an earlier 'machine' or 'manufacturer', sold or used, was an experiment does not prevent its becoming an anticipation or a part of the prior art, provided it was perfected and thereafter became publicly known. Whether it does become so depends upon how far it becomes a part of the stock of knowledge of the art in question." Picard v. United Aircraft Corp., 128 F.2d 632, 635 (2d Cir.1942). As Supreme Court authority for this statement Hand cited *Coffin* and one other nineteenth century case, both holding that a prior invention had been sufficiently developed to anticipate.

3. The most useful authorities on anticipating knowledge are those cases dealing with anticipating public uses, infra pp. 910–923, because if a decision holds that a use did not anticipate, then it by implication holds that knowledge of that use did not anticipate.

APPLICATION OF BORST

United States Court of Customs and Patent Appeals, 1965.
345 F.2d 851, certiorari denied 382 U.S. 973, 86 S.Ct. 537, 15 L.Ed.2d 465.

SMITH, JUDGE. The invention for which appellant seeks a patent comprises means for safely and effectively controlling a relatively large neutron output by varying a small and easily controlled neutron input source. The application, serial No. 654,837, filed April 24, 1957, is aptly titled "Neutron Amplifier." Claim 27 is illustrative of appealed claims 27–33 and reads:

"27. A subcritical neutron amplifier having a controllable neutron source and, associated with said source in cascade, an input region of neutron moderator material in which neutrons of epithermal energy from the source are moderated to thermal energy levels, a sequent fuel region containing neutron fissionable material in mass concentration and geometric configuration adapted to augment the neutron flow by a subcritical reaction, and an output region comprising a thermal neutron barrier substantially opaque to thermal neutrons but transmissive to epithermal neutrons, whereby an amplified neutron output is subcritically produced."   *   *   *

Appellant asserts that the claimed invention affords a revolutionary approach to the safety problem in the nuclear reactor art. As the amplifier is said to be inherently safe from divergent nuclear chain reaction, the intricate systems needed to monitor and control the operation of conventional neutron amplifiers to prevent an explosion are unnecessary.

The single reference relied upon by the Patent Office in rejecting the appealed claims is an Atomic Energy Commission document entitled "KAPL–M–RWS–1, A Stable Fission Pile with High Speed Control." The document is in the form of an unpublished memorandum authored by one Samsel, and will hereinafter be referred to as "Samsel." Samsel is dated February 14, 1947 and was classified as a secret document by the Commission until March 9, 1957, when it was declassified. In essence, Samsel sets forth and discusses the problems present in the control of a nuclear reactor, the concept of use of successive fuel stages to effect such control, and a description of the arrangement, composition and relative proportions of materials required to obtain the sought-for results. Samsel is prefaced by a statement that it was made to record an idea, and it nowhere indicates that the idea had been tested in an operating reactor.

The Patent Office does not invoke Samsel as a publication (which it apparently was not, at any pertinent date). Rather, the contention is that Samsel constitutes evidence of prior knowledge within the meaning of 35 U.S.C. § 102(a).   *   *   *

In the case of In re Schlittler, 234 F.2d 882, this court was presented with the following situation: A manuscript containing an anticipatory disclosure of the appellants' claimed invention had been submitted to The Journal of the American Chemical Society and was later published. The date to which the appellants' application was entitled for purposes of constructive reduction to practice was earlier than the publication date of the Journal article, and therefore the Patent Office did not contend that the "printed publication" portion of section 102(a) was applicable. However, the manuscript bore a notation that it had been received by the publisher on a date prior to the effective filing date of the appellants' application. On the basis of this notation the Patent Office argued that the article constituted sufficient evidence of prior knowledge under section 102(a).

After an exhaustive review of the authorities, and of the legislative history of the Patent Act of 1952, this court rejected the contention of the Patent Office, and concluded that such a document was not proper evidence of prior knowledge. In reversing, the court stated (234 F.2d at 886):

> "In our opinion, one of the essential elements of the word 'known' as used in 35 U.S.C. § 102(a) is knowledge of an invention which has been completed by reduction to practice,

actual or constructive, and is not satisfied by disclosure of a conception only."

And therefore, since the Journal article, "at best, could be evidence of nothing more than conception and disclosure of the invention," the

> " * * * placing of the Nystrom article in the hands of the publishers did not constitute either prima facie or conclusive evidence of knowledge or use by others in this country of the invention disclosed by the article, within the meaning of Title 35, § 102(a) of the United States Code, since the knowledge was of a conception only and not of a reduction to practice."

Another aspect of the court's discussion in Schlittler involved the well-established principle that "prior knowledge of a patented invention would not invalidate a claim of the patent unless such knowledge was available to the public." After reaffirming that principle, the court went on to state:

> "Obviously, in view of the above authorities, the mere placing of a manuscript in the hands of a publisher does not necessarily make it available to the public within the meaning of said authorities."

However, the court did not go on to determine whether the Journal article was in fact available to the public, since such determination was deemed unnecessary for disposition of the case, under the court's theory.

We shall consider first the public availability aspect of the Schlittler case. Although that portion of the Schlittler opinion is clearly dictum, we think it just as clearly represents the settled law. The knowledge contemplated by section 102(a) must be accessible to the public. * * *

In the instant case, Samsel was clearly not publicly available during the period it was under secrecy classification by the Atomic Energy Commission. We note that the date of declassification, however, was prior to appellant's filing date, and it is perhaps arguable that Samsel became accessible to the public upon declassification. But we do not find it necessary to decide that difficult question, for there is a statutory provision which is, we think, dispositive of the question of publicity. Section 155 of the Atomic Energy Act of 1954 (42 U.S.C. § 2185) provides:

> "In connection with applications for patents covered by this subchapter, the fact that the invention or discovery was known or used before shall be a bar to the patenting of such invention or discovery even though such prior knowledge or use was under secrecy within the atomic energy program of the United States."

We think the meaning and intent of this provision is so clear as to admit of no dispute: With respect to subject matter covered by the patent provisions of the Atomic Energy Act, prior knowledge or use under section 102(a) *need not* be accessible to the public. Therefore, Samsel is available as evidence of prior knowledge insofar as the requirement for publicity is concerned.

The remaining consideration regarding the status of Samsel as evidence of prior knowledge directly calls into question the correctness of the unequivocal holding in Schlittler that the knowledge must be of a reduction to practice, either actual or constructive. After much deliberation, we have concluded that such a requirement is illogical and anomalous, and to the extent Schlittler is inconsistent with the decision in this case, it is hereby expressly overruled.

The mere fact that a disclosure is contained in a patent or application and thus "constructively" reduced to practice, or that it is found in a printed publication, does not make the disclosure itself any more meaningful to those skilled in the art (and thus, ultimately, to the public). Rather, the criterion should be whether the disclosure is *sufficient to enable one skilled in the art to reduce the disclosed invention to practice.* In other words, the disclosure must be such as will give possession of the invention to the person of ordinary skill. Even the act of publication or the fiction of constructive reduction to practice will not suffice if the disclosure does not meet this standard. See In re Sheppard and In re LeGrice, supra.

Where, as is true of Samsel, the disclosure constituting evidence of prior knowledge contains, in the words of the Board of Appeals, "a description of the invention fully commensurate with the present patent application," we hold that the disclosure need not be of an invention reduced to practice, either actually or constructively. We therefore affirm the rejection of claim 27.

* * *

NOTES

1. Your understanding of *Gayler, Borst* and subsequent cases will be facilitated if you ascertain the position of the court and answer to your own satisfaction each of the following five *separate* questions:

   a. Was the patentee an original inventor? §§ 102(f), 115, 116.

   b. Was the patentee the first inventor? §§ 102(a), 102(g).

   c. Even though the patentee was not the first inventor, did he acquire the rights of a first inventor due to acts of the true first inventor constituting abandonment? § 102(g).

   d. Was the patent blocked by a time bar? § 102(b).

   e. Was the invention obvious to one skilled in the art? § 103.

2. *Borst* is discussed in the Note, Novelty and Reduction to Practice: Patent Confusion, 75 Yale L.J. 1194 (1966). See also William C. Roch, Prior Knowledge Compared with Prior Invention as a Statutory Bar, 50 J.P.O.S. 409 (1968).

3. The "unknown" anticipation. In Tilghman v. Proctor, 102 U.S. 707 (1880), supra page 801, one of the arguments made against the patent was that

it was anticipated by the occurrence of the same process in the course of the operation of Perkins' steam cylinder, Daneill's water barometer and Walther's process for purifying fats and oils preparatory to soapmaking. The Court conceded that in the course of these processes saponification did indeed occur, but dismissed them as anticipation. "If the acids were accidentally and unwittingly produced, whilst the operators were in pursuit of other and different results, without exciting attention and without its even being known what was done or how it had been done, it would be absurd to say that this was an anticipation of Tilghman's discovery." Id. at 711–712. To the same effect, see Davey Tree Expert Co. v. Easton, 283 Fed. 840 (S.D.N.Y.1920). The limit of the principle is suggested by Vitamin Technologists, Inc. v. Wisconsin Alumni Research Foundation, 146 F.2d 941 (9th Cir.1944). Patent on a process for producing vitamin D by exposing organic substances of dietary value to ultraviolet rays. The Court held those claims which encompassed irradiation by sunlight but not those claims limited to artificial sources of ultraviolet light invalid because of anticipation by "immemorial" agricultural processes:

"It is an undisputed fact that man in all historic time has used the process of cutting hays, whereby, by oozing from the cuts, is extracted their pro-vitamin containing sap, which is exposed to sun irradiation, and copra, thus so exposing the pro-vitamin-containing coconut oil so extracted from the meat of that fruit. Thereby the sun's ultra violet rays have created vitamin D in such 'carbohydrates,' 'organic substances of dietary value,' covered by claim 1 of the first patent. Such hays fed to animals and copra, the food of both man and animals, aids or cures rachitic conditions in both classes of mammals. We refuse to entertain the absurd proposition that because the farmer and copra grower did not know the photo chemical process involved in their immemorial practice, they may be enjoined as infringers.

"Assuming that Dr. Steenbock discovered, as he claims, that the sun's rays coming from millions of miles away could irradiate foods with vitamin D and that this was the reason, unknown to them, why farmers and coconut growers regarded their sun-cured hays and sun-dried copra were good foods, such a discovery does not entitle him to a patent on their processes.

"This court has held that it is a well established principle that if a process is disclosed in a prior art, a patent whose validity is attacked is anticipated even though the prior patent failed to state and the inventor did not know that his invention brought the process into operation. In Celite Corp. v. Dicalite Co., 9 Cir., 96 F.2d 242, 248, we stated:

" ' * * * In answer to appellant's contention that the purpose of the North process was simply to remove organic matter and bleach the product, it is sufficient to state that, as the patented process in suit was disclosed by the North patent, it was anticipated by that process even though it be assumed that the North did not know, of the increased flow rate of the product produced. * * * '

" * * * Under the cases, this discovery of the reason of a prior used process is not a patentable invention." 146 F.2d 948–49.

PROBLEMS

1. Suppose that vitamin B_{12}, the patent involved in Merck & Co. v. Olin Mathieson Chemical Corp., 253 F.2d 156 (4th Cir.1958), supra page 817 had always existed in a pure form in the livers of cats. Would the patent have then been invalid? Assume (1) that the existence of a substance in the liver of cats useful for treating pernicious anemia was known, or (2) that the existence of a substance with no known utility, only later found to be vitamin B_{12}, was known, or (3) that no one knew what was in cat liver. Is Acme Flexible Clasp Co. v. Cary Mfg. Co., 96 Fed. 344 (S.D.N.Y.1899) relevant? Is it right? *Acme* held that staples used to construct a shipping box imported from China did not anticipate a patent on the same staple because they were covered by wrapping and therefore unknown to Americans.

2. The chemical maleic hydrazide (MH) was discovered in 1894. In 1947 employees of Uniroyal, Inc. discovered that when mixed with a wetting agent MH could inhibit the growth of certain plants without otherwise harming them. The discovery of this property was non-obvious. Mixing a chemical with a wetting agent is a standard procedure. Is a claim for MH mixed with a wetting agent valid? See Ansul Co. v. Uniroyal, Inc., 448 F.2d 872 (2d Cir. 1971).

EGBERT v. LIPPMANN

Supreme Court of the United States, 1881.
104 U.S. (14 Otto) 333, 26 L.Ed. 755.

MR. JUSTICE WOODS delivered the opinion of the court.

This suit was brought for an alleged infringement of the complainant's reissued letters-patent, No. 5216, dated Jan. 7, 1873, for an improvement in corset-springs. * * *

We have * * * to consider whether the defence that the patented invention had, with the consent of the inventor, been publicly used for more than two years prior to his application for the original letters, is sustained by the testimony in the record.

The sixth, seventh, and fifteenth sections of the act of July 4, 1836, c. 357 (5 Stat. 117), as qualified by the seventh section of the act of March 3, 1839, c. 88 (id. 353), were in force at the date of his application. Their effect is to render letters-patent invalid if the invention which they cover was in public use, with the consent and allowance of the inventor, for more than two years prior to his application. Since the passage of the act of 1839 it has been strenuously contended that the public use of an invention for more than two years before such application, even without his consent and allowance, renders the letters-patent therefor void.

It is unnecessary in this case to decide this question, for the alleged use of the invention covered by the letters-patent to Barnes is conceded to have been with his express consent.

The evidence on which the defendants rely to establish a prior public use of the invention consists mainly of the testimony of the complainant.

friend & wife wear corsets

She testifies that Barnes invented the improvement covered by his patent between January and May, 1855; that between the dates named the witness and her friend Miss Cugier were complaining of the breaking of their corset-steels. Barnes, who was present, and was an intimate friend of the witness, said he thought he could make her a pair that would not break. At their next interview he presented her with a pair of corset-steels which he himself had made. The witness wore these steels a long time. In 1858 Barnes made and presented to her another pair, which she also wore a long time. When the corsets in which these steels were used wore out, the witness ripped them open and took out the steels and put them in new corsets. This was done several times.

It is admitted, and, in fact, is asserted, by complainant, that these steels embodied the invention afterwards patented by Barnes and covered by the reissued letters-patent on which this suit is brought.

Joseph H. Sturgis, another witness for complainant, testifies that in 1863 Barnes spoke to him about two inventions made by himself, one of which was a corset-steel, and that he went to the house of Barnes to see them. Before this time, and after the transactions testified to by the complainant, Barnes and she had intermarried. Barnes said his wife had a pair of steels made according to his invention in the corsets which she was then wearing, and if she would take them off he would show them to witness. Mrs. Barnes went out, and returned with a pair of corsets and a pair of scissors, and ripped the corsets open and took out the steels. Barnes then explained to witness how they were made and used.

This is the evidence presented by the record, on which the defendants rely to establish the public use of the invention by the patentee's consent and allowance.

The question for our decision is, whether this testimony shows a public use within the meaning of the statute. * * *

* * * [S]ome inventions are by their very character only capable of being used where they cannot be seen or observed by the public eye. An invention may consist of a lever or spring, hidden in the running gear of a watch, or of a rachet, shaft, or cog-wheel covered from view in the recesses of a machine for spinning or weaving. Nevertheless, if its inventor sells a machine of which his invention forms a part, and allows it to be used without restriction of any kind, the use is a public one. So, on the other hand, a use necessarily open to public view, if made in good faith solely to test the qualities of the invention, and for the purpose of experiment, is not a public use within the meaning of the statute. Elizabeth v. Pavement Company, 97 U.S. 126; Shaw v. Cooper, 7 Pet. 292.

Expt is not a public use

Tested by these principles, we think the evidence of the complainant herself shows that for more than two years before the application for the original letters there was, by the consent and allowance of Barnes, a public use of the invention, covered by them. * * * He

One person using it is public use.
Even if it is private by because of the
way it is used.

imposed no obligation of secrecy, nor any condition or restriction, whatever. They were not presented for the purpose of experiment, nor to test their qualities. * * *

According to the testimony of the complainant, the invention was completed and put to use in 1855. The inventor slept on his rights for eleven years. * * * In the meantime, the invention had found its way into general, and almost universal use. * * *. It is fair to presume that having learned from this general use that there was some value in his invention, he attempted to resume, by an application for a patent, what by his acts he had clearly dedicated to the public. * * *

We are of opinion that the defence of two years' public use, by the consent and allowance of the inventor, before he made application for letters-patent, is satisfactorily established by the evidence.

Decree affirmed.

MR. JUSTICE MILLER dissenting.

* * * If the little steel spring inserted in a single pair of corsets and used by only one woman, covered by her outer-clothing, and in a position always withheld from public observation, is a public use of the piece of steel, I am at a loss to know the line between a private and a public use. * * *

NOTES

The statutory provisions relating to prior public use developed as follows.

1. Patent Act of 1793 § 1: "[W]hen any person * * * shall allege that he * * * [has] invented any new and useful art, machine, manufacture, or composition of matter, not known or used before the application * * * it shall * * * be lawful * * * [to issue letters-patent].

Patent Act of 1793 § 6: "[T]he defendant in such action [for infringement] shall be permitted to * * * prove * * * that the thing thus secured by patent was not originally discovered by the patentee, but had been in use, or had been described in some public work anterior to the supposed discovery of the patentee."

but

2. The contradiction between §§ 1 and 6 of the 1793 act came before the Court in Pennock v. Dialogue, 27 U.S. (2 Peters) 1 (1829). Patent for making pressure-tight joints in hose. The patent was applied for in 1818. Between 1811 and 1818 upward of 13,000 feet of hose were constructed and sold in the city of Philadelphia which followed the teaching of the patent, with the consent of the patentee. The court held the patent invalid, against the argument that section 6 of the act limited the defense of prior public use to uses prior to the date of invention. Mr. Justice Story said:

"We think, then, the true meaning must be, not known or used by the public, before the application. And thus construed, there is much reason for the limitation thus imposed by the act. While one great object was, by holding out a reasonable reward to inventors, and giving them an exclusive right to their inventions for a limited period, to stimulate the efforts of genius; the main object was 'to promote the progress of science and useful arts;' and this could be done best, by giving the public at large a right to make, construct, use and vend the thing invented, at as early a period as possible, having a due regard to the rights of the inventor. If an inventor should be permitted to hold back from the knowledge of the public the secrets of his invention; if he should, for a long period of years, retain the monopoly, and make and sell his invention publicly, and thus gather the whole profits of it, relying upon his superior skill and knowledge of the structure; and then, and then only, when the danger of competition should force him to secure the exclusive right, he should be allowed to take out a patent, and thus exclude the public from any further use than what should be derived under it, during his fourteen years; it would materially retard the progress of science and the useful arts, and give a premium to those who should be least prompt to communicate their discoveries." Id. at 18.

The Court brushed aside § 6 by observing: "The sixth section certainly does not enumerate all the defenses which a party may make. * * * It gives the right to the first and true inventor, and to him only; if known or used, before his supposed discovery, he is not the first, although he may be a true inventor; and that is the case to which the clause looks. But it is not inconsistent with this doctrine, that although he is the first, as well as the true inventor, yet if he shall put it into public use, or sell it for public use, before he applies for a patent, that this should furnish another bar to his claim." Id. at 21–23.

3. Patent Act of 1836 § 6: "That any person * * * having discovered or invented any new and useful art, machine, manufacture, or composition of matter, * * * not known or used by others before his * * * invention thereof, and not, at the time of his application for a patent, in public use or on sale with his consent or allowance, as the inventor or discoverer * * * [may receive a patent therefor]."

4. Patent Act of 1839 § 7: "That every person or corporation who has, or shall have, purchased or constructed any newly invented machine, manufacture, or composition of matter, prior to the application by the inventor or discoverer for a patent, shall be held to possess the right to use, and vend to others to be used, the specific machine, manufacture, or composition of matter so made or purchased, without liability therefor to the inventor, or any other person interested in such invention; and no patent shall be held to be invalid, by reason of such purchase, sale, or use prior to the application for a patent as aforesaid, except on proof of abandonment of such invention to the public; or that such purchase, sale, or prior use has been for more than two years prior to such application for a patent."

5. In *Egbert* the Court apparently construed § 7 as applying to public uses with the consent of the applicant, creating a two year grace period both for uses by the applicant and by third parties. Is this what section 7 appears to do? Was the Court's construction influenced by the following statute?

Patent Act of 1870 § 24, Rev.Stat. § 4886: "That any person who has invented or discovered any new and useful art, machine, manufacture, or composition of matter * * * not known or used by others in this country, and not patented, or described in any printed publication in this or any foreign country, before his invention or discovery thereof, and not in public use or on sale for more than two years prior to his application, unless the same is proved to have been abandoned, may * * * obtain a patent therefor."

6. The statute remained essentially the same from 1870 until the codification of 1952, except that in 1897 the two-year time bar was extended to "not

patented or described in any printed publication in this or any foreign country" and in 1939 the two year period was reduced to one year. 28 Stat. 692 (1897); 53 Stat. 1212 (1939).

GILLMAN v. STERN

United States Circuit Court of Appeals, Second Circuit, 1940.
114 F.2d 28, certiorari denied 311 U.S. 718, 61 S.Ct. 441, 85 L.Ed. 468.

L. HAND, CIRCUIT JUDGE. Both the plaintiffs and the defendant appeal from the judgment in this action. The plaintiffs filed the usual complaint, asking an injunction for the infringement of Patent No. 1,919,674, issued on July 25, 1933, to the Sterling Airbrush Co., assignee of Laszlo Wenczel, for a pneumatic "puffing machine." * * *

The patent was for a pneumatic machine for quilting; i.e., it blew thread or yarn "into pockets formed in the fabric to stuff the same to impart a raised or embossed design" (p. 1, *ll*, 3–5). It was made of a hollow needle through which the thread or yarn passed; the inner end of the needle being within a frame which contained an air-duct leading from a blower. When the blower was turned on, it blew the yarn through the needle and stuffed the pocket which the needle point had entered. Before passing into the needle the thread passed through a "tube, 40," one end of which telescoped within the inner end of the needle, but did not quite block the access of air from the blower, which passed around the end of the "tube," sucked the thread or yarn, as it emerged from the "tube," and carried it through the needle. In operation, after the yarn has once been started, the "tube" was somewhat withdrawn (being for that purpose mounted in a "threaded shank") in order to secure a stronger air-flow through the needle.

The art contained nothing of the kind before except Haas' machine, of which more later. It is true, it had been common practice in many arts to introduce an air blast around the outside of a hollow tube introduced into the entrance of a larger tube through which the air escaped, and by this means to suck material from the smaller, through the larger tube. The Venturi carbureter is an example of this; the circle of swiftly moving air entering the larger tube creates a vacuum at the end of the smaller and sucks the gasoline forward to make the mixture. The first attack upon the patent is that it was merely for a new use of an old device. However, the only objection to patenting a new use is that the statute, § 31, Title 35, U.S. Code, 35 U.S.C.A. § 31, does not include "uses" among what can be patented, except so far as they are included within "arts"—i.e., processes. If, however, an old article must be physically changed, even slightly, to fit the new use, it becomes itself a new "machine" or "manufacture," and the statute is satisfied. In that case the only question open is whether the discovery of the new use demands enough original thought to be deemed an invention. Constitutionally only "discoveries" can be patented at all, and the ingenuity needed for the new conception, not the amount of physical readjustment, is the test of a valuable "discovery." Topliff v. Topliff, 145 U.S. 156, 163, 164; C. & A. Potts & Co. v. Creager, 155 U.S.

597, 608; Rockwood v. General Fire Extinguisher Co., 2 Cir., 8 F.2d 682, 686; Gordon Form Lathe Co. v. Walcott, 6 Cir., 32 F.2d 55, 58. No machines on the Venturi principle would have served to quilt fabrics; they were sand-blasters, sand engravers, vaporizers, grain conveyors, inspirators, air brushes, sprayers, separators, carbureters and the like. Most, if not all of them, were, moreover, of the true Venturi type; that is, they always worked by suction. As we have said, Wenczel's "puffer" did so too for as long as the end of the "tube, 40" was telescoped within the inner end of the needle; but not after it was withdrawn, as it had to be for "puffing." In that phase there was no suction at the end of the "tube," but probably some back-flow, though obviously not enough to counteract the increased air-flow through the needle. However, this modification of the old devices we need not count in holding that Wenczel made an invention; it was because he selected for an old need—quilting—a theretofore unused device that we think he showed more than ordinary insight, else it would have been made before.

However, upon the issue of invalidity the defendant relies less upon prior patents than upon the prior use by Haas. Haas at some time undoubtedly did invent a "puffing machine" designed to perform the same work as plaintiff's machine. Further, his first "puffer" was substantially the same as the plaintiff's; and, if it had been properly proved, it might be hard to support the patent. However, not only was there no evidence as to the date of it except the word of Haas and his wife—who knew incidentally nothing of its construction—but again and again, Haas spoke of it as an unsatisfactory temporary device which he had discarded before he began to do any business. It must certainly be considered an abandoned experiment and is therefore immaterial. Haas also testified that in the autumn of 1929 he invented another "puffer" * * * [the plaintiff's application was filed January 21, 1931] in general structure like the first, except that there was no means—as in Wenczel's machine—to vary the air pressure by changing the position of any member like the "tube, 40." The plaintiff insists that for this reason it cannot anticipate, and literally that is true; but possibly, if it could be deemed a part of the prior art, the step between it and Wenczel's disclosure would not justify a monopoly. Besides, claim one does not incorporate the "regulating valve," i.e., the "tube, 40." We need not, however, pass upon this question, or indeed whether the evidence of its date of production satisfied the exacting standard set by the Barbed Wire Patent Case, 143 U.S. 275, for it is clear that it was never in prior "public use," and that Haas was not a "first inventor." It was always kept as strictly secret as was possible, consistently with its exploitation. In general, everybody was carefully kept out of Haas' shop where the four machines were used. He testified that "no one was allowed to enter but my employees," girls he had had "for years"; and that he "had instructed my girls that if anybody should ask to get any kind of information simply tell them you don't know. In fact I have my shop door so arranged that it could only be opened from the inside." He also enjoined secrecy on his wife who testified "no one ever got into the place and no one ever saw the machine. He made everything himself." Indeed, as a condition upon even testifying in the case at bar Haas insisted, and the judge ordered, that the lawyers should be sworn to keep secret all he said about the construction of the "puffer," and that it should not be printed in the record, but typed and sealed for the inspection of the judges alone. It does not appear that the "girls" knew how the machines which they used were made, or how they operated. The only exception to this was a disclosure, such as it was, to two members of a firm going by the name of the Bona Fide Embroidery Co.—Custer and Kadison. In the same autumn of 1929 they and Haas testified that they had seen some of his quilting and were anxious to get the whole of his output. They went to his shop to satisfy themselves; Custer said that "it was very vital at that time that I should know the workings of the machine for my production of the proper designs." (By "workings" he could only have meant how it performed for he never learned its construction.) After this visit the two agreed that Haas should give them his whole production and that they should sell it; they even talked about taking out a patent, but did not have the necessary money. Thus, Haas kept his machine absolutely secret from the outside world except to secure selling agents for its product, and then it was only its performance, not its construction that even they learned. Moreover, Custer and Kadison had the same motive to suppress whatever information they got that Haas had, for without a patent the secret was all that protected their market.

Such a use is clearly not a "public" one, and such an inventor is not a "first inventor." In Gayler v. Wilder, 10 How. 477, 481, 497, the question was whether the condition—which has always been in the statute—that the patentee must be the "first and original inventor" was defeated by anyone who had earlier conceived the same invention, or only by one who had also in some way made public his results. A majority of the court held that only the second would defeat a patent on the ground that what had not in fact enriched the art, should not count; and the doctrine is now well fixed. Alexander Milburn Co. v. Davis-Bournonville Co., 270 U.S. 390. Just as a secret use is not a "public use," so a secret inventor is not a "first inventor." Acme Flexible Clasp Co. v. Cary Mfg. Co., C.C., 96 F. 344; Diamond Patent Co. v. S. E. Carr Co., 9 Cir., 217 F. 400, 404; A. Schrader's Sons v. Wein Sales Corp., 2 Cir., 9 F.2d 306; Peerless Roll Leaf Co. v. H. Griffin & Sons Co., 2 Cir., 29 F.2d 646. Haas' user was one where "the machine, process, and product were not well known to the employes in the plant," and where "efforts were made to conceal them from anyone who had a legitimate interest in understanding them," if by "legitimate interest" one means something more than curiosity or mischief. Electric Battery Co. v. Shimadzu, 307 U.S. 5, 20. * * *

We are to distinguish between a public user which does not inform the art (Hall v. Macneale, 107 U.S. 90, 97) and a secret user; some confusion has resulted from the failure to do so. It is true that in each case the fund of common knowledge is not enriched, and that might indeed have been good reason originally for throwing out each as anticipations. But when the statute made any "public use" fatal to a patent, and when thereafter the court held that it was equally fatal, whether or not the patentee had consented to it, there was no escape from holding—contrary to the underlying theory of the law—that it was irrelevant whether the use informed the public so that they could profit by it. Nevertheless, it was still true that secret uses were not public uses, whether or not public uses might on occasion have no public value. Perhaps it was originally open to argument that the statute merely meant to confine prior "public uses" to the prospective patentee and to be evidence of abandonment, and that "first inventor" meant to include anyone who first conceived the thing in tangible enough form to be persuasive. But, rightly or wrongly, the law did not develop so, and it is now too late to change. Hence the anomaly that, by secreting a machine one may keep it from becoming an anticipation, even though its public use would really have told nobody anything about it.

* * *

The judgment is reversed and the usual judgment will be entered for the plaintiffs on all claims. The counterclaim will of course be dismissed.

METALLIZING ENGINEERING CO. v. KENYON BEARING & AUTO PARTS CO.

United States Circuit Court of Appeals, Second Circuit, 1946.
153 F.2d 516, certiorari denied 328 U.S. 840, 66 S.Ct. 1016, 90 L.Ed. 1615, rehearing denied 328 U.S. 881, 66 S.Ct. 1364, 90 L.Ed. 1648.

L. HAND, CIRCUIT JUDGE. The defendants appeal from the usual decree holding valid and infringed all but three of the claims of a reissued patent, issued to the plaintiff's assignor, Meduna; the original patent issued on May 25, 1943, upon an application filed on August 6, 1942. The patent is for the process of "so conditioning a metal surface that the same is, as a rule, capable of bonding thereto applied spray metal to a higher degree than is normally procurable with hitherto known practices". It is primarily useful for building up the worn metal parts of a machine. The art had for many years done this by what the patent calls "spray metal," which means metal sprayed in molten form upon the surface which it is desired to build up. This process is called "metalizing," and it had been known for nearly thirty years before Meduna's invention; but about fifteen or twenty years ago it was found that, to secure a satisfactory bond between the "spray metal" and the surface, the surface must be roughened so that there would be fine undercut areas in it upon which the sprayed surface could take hold; and of course the surface must itself be clean. The art had developed two ways of producing such a surface; one, by sand-blasting, and the other, by a tool, so adjusted in a lathe as to tear tiny channels: "screw-threading." Meduna's invention was to prepare the surface by first depositing upon it a preliminary layer of metal by means of a process, disclosed in Patent No.1,327,267, issued to Brewster and Weisehan, on January 6, 1920. This process was practiced by what the art knew as the "McQuay-Norris" machine, which was "more particularly adapted and intended for use in the filling of cavities which may occur in castings or other metal objects". The "McQuay-Norris" device was operated by electric power, one terminal of the circuit being connected with the work, and the other being a fusable electrode, which melted at the temperature developed in the circuit, and deposited parts of itself at the places desired upon closing of the circuit by contact with the work. The process was described as follows: "The electrode is moved from spot to spot in the cavity and the foregoing operation repeated until the surface of the blow-hole is covered by a deposit of the metal by the electrode. It will thus be seen that the surface of the blow-hole is covered by a number of small particles of metal of the electrode, all of which particles are welded to the particular portion of the surface of the blow-hole with which the elctrode contacted." After this has been done, "a peening hammer is employed to peen the metal which has been introduced into the blow-hole, thus causing the metal to be compacted, and any inequalities of the surface of the metal reduced". Meduna did not peen the metal, indeed peening would have been entirely unfitted to his purpose, as it would have pressed together the undercut deposits which later serve to catch and hold the "spray metal." Moreover, his purpose was not to fill up "blow-holes," or fissures; but, as we have said, to prepare worn surfaces for rebuilding. However, he used the McQuay-Norris machine unchanged, prescribing a voltage of preferably not more than twenty volts—ordinarily between two and nine—and an amperage of between two hundred and three or four hundred. The surface was to be "repetitiously contacted and preferably repetitiously contact stroked with the electrode on successive areas, the stroking action depositing on these areas small amounts of electrode material firmly bonded thereto. Alternatively the electrode may be applied with a stippling action to the metal surface. While these procedures essentially involve breaking and making contact between the metal surface and the electrode, it is also possible, and sometimes advisable, to move the electrode relative to the base while maintaining resistant heating contact therebetween".

The only question which we find necessary to decide is as to Meduna's public use of the patented process more than one year before August 6, 1942. The district judge made findings about this, which are supported by the testimony and which we accept. They appear as findings 8, 9, 10, 11, 12 and 13 on pages 46 and 47 of volume 62 of the Federal Supplement; and we cannot improve upon his statement. The kernel of them is the following: "the inventor's main purpose in his use of the process prior to August 6, 1941, and especially in respect to all jobs for owners not known to him, was commercial, and * * * an experimental purpose in connection with such use was subordinate only." Upon this finding he concluded as matter of law that, since the use before the critical date—August 6, 1941—was not primarily for the purposes of experiment, the use was not excused for that reason. Smith & Griggs Manufacturing Co. v. Sprague, 123 U.S. 249, 256; Aerovox Corp. v. Polymet Manufacturing Corp., 2 Cir., 67 F.2d 860, 862. Moreover, he also concluded that the use was not public but secret, and for that reason that its predominantly commercial character did prevent it from invalidating the patent. For the last he relied upon our decisions in Peerless Roll Leaf Co. v. Griffin & Sons, 29 F.2d 646, and Gillman v. Stern, 114 F.2d 28. We think that his analysis of Peerless Roll Leaf Co. v. Griffin & Sons, was altogether correct, and that he had no alternative but to follow that decision; on the other hand, we now think that we were then wrong and that the decision must be overruled for reasons we shall state. Gillman v. Stern, supra, was, however, rightly decided.

Section one of the first and second Patent Acts, 1 Stat. 109 and 318, declared that the petition for a patent must state that the subject matter had not been "before known or used." Section six of the Act of 1836, 5 Stat. 117, changed this by providing in addition that the invention must not at the time of the application for a patent have been "in public use or on sale" with the inventor's "consent or allowance"; and § 7 of the Act of 1839, 5 Stat. 353, provided that "no patent shall be held to be invalid by reason of such purchase, sale, or use prior to the application for a patent * * * except on proof of abandonment of such invention to the public; or that such purchase, sale, or prior use has been for more than two years prior to such application * * *." Section 4886 of the Revised Statutes made it a condition upon patentability that the invention shall not have been "in public use or on sale for more than two years prior to his application," and that it shall not have been "proved to have been abandoned." This is in substance the same as the Act of 1839, and is precisely the same as § 31 of Title 35, U.S.C.A. except that the prior use is now limited to the United States, and to one year before the application. § 1, Chap. 391, 29 Stat. 692; § 1, Chap. 450, 53 Stat. 1212, 35 U.S.C.A. § 31. So far as we can find, the first case which dealt with the effect of prior use by the patentee was Pennock v. Dialogue, 2 Pet. 1, 4, in which the invention had been completed in 1811, and the patent granted in 1818 for a process of making hose by which the sections were joined together in such a way that the joints resisted pressure as well as the other parts. It did not appear that the joints in any way disclosed the process; but the patentee, between the discovery of the invention and the grant of the patent, had sold 13,000 feet of hose; and as to this the judge charged: "If the public, with the knowledge and tacit consent of the inventor, be permitted to use the invention, without opposition, it is a fraud on the public afterwards to take out a patent." The Supreme Court affirmed a judgment for the defendant, on the ground that the invention had been "known or used before the application." "If an inventor should be permitted to hold back from the knowledge of the public the secrets of his invention; if he should * * * make and sell his invention publicly, and thus gather the whole profits, * * * it would materially retard the progress of science and the useful arts" to allow him fourteen years of legal monopoly "when the danger of competition should force him to secure the exclusive right" 2 Pet. at page 19. In Shaw v. Cooper, 7 Pet. 292, the public use was not by the inventor, but he had neglected to prevent it after he had learned of it, and this defeated the patent. "Whatever may be the intention of the inventor, if he suffers his invention to go into public use, through any means whatsoever, without an immediate assertion of his right, he is not entitled to a patent" 7 Pet. at page 323. In Kendall v. Winsor, 21 How. 322, the inventor had kept the machine secret, but had sold the harness which it produced, so that the facts presented the same situation as here. Since the jury brought in a verdict for the defendant on the issue of abandonment, the case adds nothing except for the dicta on page 328 of 21 How.: "the inventor who designedly, and with the view of applying it indefinitely and exclusively for his own profit, withholds his invention from the public, comes not within the policy or objects of the Constitution or acts of Congress." In Egbert v. Lippmann, 104 U.S. 333, although the patent was for the product which was sold, nothing could be learned about it without taking it apart, yet it was a public use within the statute. In Hall v. Macneale, 107 U.S. 90, the situation was the same.

In the lower courts we may begin with the often cited decision in Macbeth-Evans Glass Co. v. General Electric Co., 6 Cir., 246 F. 695, which concerned a process patent for making illuminating glass. The patentee had kept the process as secret as possible, but for ten years had sold the glass, although this did not, so far as appears, disclose the process. The court held the patent invalid for two reasons, as we understand them: the first was that the delay either indicated an intention to abandon, or was of itself a forfeiture, because of the inconsistency of a practical monopoly by means of secrecy and of a later legal monopoly by means of a patent. So far, it was not an interpretation of "prior use" in the statute; but, beginning on page 702 of 246 F. 695 Judge Warrington seems to have been construing that phrase and to hold that the sales were such a use. In Allinson Manufacturing Co. v. Ideal Filter Co., 8 Cir., 21 F.2d 22, the patent was for a machine for purifying gasoline: the machine was kept secret, but the gasoline had been sold for a period of six years before the application was filed. As in Macbeth-Evans Glass Co. v. General Electric Co., supra, 6 Cir., 246 F. 695, the court apparently invalidated the patent on two grounds: one was that the inventor had abandoned the right to a patent, or had forfeited it by his long delay. We are disposed however to read the latter part—pages 27 and 28 of 21 F.2d—as holding that the sale of gasoline was a "prior use" of the machine, notwithstanding its concealment. Certainly, the following quotation from Pitts v. Hall, Fed.Cas. No.11,192, 2 Blatchf. 229, was not otherwise apposite; a patentee "is not allowed to derive any benefit from the sale or use of his machine, without forfeiting his right, except within two years prior to the time he makes his application." On the other hand in Stresau v. Ipsen, 77 F.2d 937, 22 C.C.P.A. (Patents) 1352, the Court of Customs and Patent

Appeals did indeed decide that a process claim might be valid when the inventor had kept the process secret but had sold the product.

Coming now to our own decisions (the opinions in all of which I wrote), the first was Grasselli Chemical Co. v. National Aniline & Chemical Co., 2 Cir., 26 F.2d 305, in which the patent was for a process which had been kept secret, but the product had been sold upon the market for more than two years. We held that, although the process could not have been discovered from the product, the sales constituted a "prior use," relying upon Egbert v. Lippmann, supra, 104 U.S. 333, and Hall v. Macneale, supra, 107 U.S. 90. There was nothing in this inconsistent with what we are now holding. But in Peerles Roll Leaf Co. v. Griffin & Sons, supra, 2 Cir., 29 F.2d 646, where the patent was for a machine, which had been kept secret, but whose output had been freely sold on the market, we sustained the patent on the ground that "the sale of the product was irrelevant, since no knowledge could possibly be acquired of the machine in that way. In this respect the machine differs from a process * * * or from any other invention necessarily contained in a product" 29 F.2d at page 649. So far as we can now find, there is nothing to support this distinction in the authorities, and we shall try to show that we misapprehended the theory on which the prior use by an inventor forfeits his right to a patent. In Aerovox Corp. v. Polymet Manufacturing Corp., supra, 2 Cir., 67 F.2d 860, the patent was also for a process, the use of which we held not to have been experimental, though not secret. Thus our decision sustaining the patent was right; but apparently we were by implication reverting to the doctrine of the Peerless case when we added that it was doubtful whether the process could be detected from the product, although we cited only Hall v. Macneale, supra, 107 U.S. 90, and Grasselli Chemical Co. v. National Aniline Co., supra (2 Cir., 26 F.2d 305). In Gillman v. Stern, supra, 2 Cir., 114 F.2d 28, it was not the inventor, but a third person who used the machine secretly and sold the product openly, and there was therefore no question either of abandonment or forfeiture by the inventor. The only issue was whether a prior use which did not disclose the invention to the art was within the statute; and it is well settled that it is not. As in the case of any other anticipation, the issue of invention must then be determined by how much the inventor has contributed any new information to the art. Gayler v. Wilder, 10 How. 477, 496, 497; Tilghman v. Proctor, 102 U.S. 707, 711; Carson v. American B. & R. Co., 9 Cir., 11 F.2d 766, 770, 771; Boyd v. Cherry, C.C.Iowa, 50 F. 279, 283; Acme Flexible Clasp Co. v. Cary Manufacturing Co., C.C.N.Y., 96 F. 344, 347; Ajax Metal Co. v. Brady Brass Co., C.C.N.Y., 155 F. 409, 415, 416; Anthracite Separator Co. v. Pollock, C.C.Pa., 175 F. 108, 111.

From the foregoing it appears that in Peerless Roll Leaf Co. v. Griffin & Sons, supra, 2 Cir., 29 F.2d 646, we confused two separate doctrines: (1) The effect upon his right to a patent of the inventor's competitive exploitation of his machine or of his process; (2) the contribution which a prior use by another person makes to the art.

Both do indeed come within the phrase, "prior use"; but the first is a defence for quite different reasons from the second. It had its origin—at least in this country—in the passage we have quoted from Pennock v. Dialogue, supra, 2 Pet. 1, 7 L.Ed. 327; i.e., that it is a condition upon an inventor's right to a patent that he shall not exploit his discovery competitively after it is ready for patenting; he must content himself with either secrecy, or legal monopoly. It is true that for the limited period of two years he was allowed to do so, possibly in order to give him time to prepare an application; and even that has been recently cut down by half. But if he goes beyond that period of probation, he forfeits his right regardless of how little the public may have learned about the invention; just as he can forfeit it by too long concealment, even without exploiting the invention at all. Woodbridge v. United States, 263 U.S. 50; Macbeth-Evans Glass Co. v. General Electric Co., supra, 6 Cir., 246 F. 695. Such a forfeiture has nothing to do with abandonment, which presupposes a deliberate, though not necessarily an express, surrender of any right to a patent. Although the evidence of both may at times overlap, each comes from a quite different legal source: one, from the fact that by renouncing the right the inventor irrevocably surrenders it; the other, from the fiat of Congress that it is part of the consideration for a patent that the public shall as soon as possible begin to enjoy the disclosure.

It is indeed true that an inventor may continue for more than a year to practice his invention for his private purposes or his own enjoyment and later patent it. But that is, properly considered, not an exception to the doctrine, for he is not then making use of his secret to gain a competitive advantage over others; he does not thereby extend the period of his monopoly. Besides, as we have seen, even that privilege has its limits, for he may conceal it so long that he will lose his right to a patent even though he does not use it at all. With that question we have not however any concern here.

Judgment reversed; complaint dismissed.

NOTE

W. L. Gore & Associates, Inc. v. Garlock, Inc., 721 F.2d 1540 (Fed.Cir.1983), involves the patent on a permeable but waterproof material made from polytetrafluorethylene (PTFE, trademarked by Du Pont as TEFLON) by rapid stretching. One of the products made by this process is widely marketed under the trademark GORETEX.

The District Court had held the patent invalid under § 102(b) because of a third-party practice of the invention. The Federal Circuit reversed, following *Metallizing Engineering* with no discussion of the statutory language. The third party had used a machine whose nature and operation it had promised to keep secret from all but its employees. The defendant argued that since the machine was not hidden from employees and was shown to some Du Pont employees, § 102(b) invalidated the patent. The court rejected the defense because the employees had signed confidentiality agreements and there was no evidence that the Du Pont employees could have learned anything about the particular process used to make the claimed product.

LORENZ v. COLGATE–PALMOLIVE–PEET CO.

United States Circuit Court of Appeals, Third Circuit, 1948.

167 F.2d 423.

BIGGS, CIRCUIT JUDGE. * * * In the District Court Lorenz and Wilson (Lorenz), persons interested in Lorenz Patent No. 2,084,446, one of two interfering patents, brought suit under R.S. § 4918, 35 U.S.C. § 66, against Colgate-Palmolive-Peet Company (Colgate), the owner of the other interfering patent, Ittner, No. 1,918,603. The complaint prayed for an adjudication that Lorenz was the first and original inventor of the process disclosed in his patent, that the Lorenz patent was valid and that the Ittner patent was void. Colgate filed an answer and a counterclaim praying for a judgment that Ittner was the inventor of the process disclosed, that his patent was valid and that the Lorenz patent was invalid. Both patents cover a process for the manufacture of soap and the recovery of glycerine. The patents were in interference within the purview of R.S. § 4918 for the nineteen claims of Lorenz's patent were copied verbatim from Ittner's patent.

The interference between Lorenz and Ittner in the Patent Office arose under the following circumstances. Lorenz had filed an application for his process in the Patent Office on January 24, 1920. Shortly thereafter he communicated the substance of the disclosures of his application to Ittner, who was Colgate's chief chemist, in order that Colgate might exploit the process if it so desired. After examination Ittner expressed himself as uninterested in the process. Next, the Patent Office rejected Lorenz's application and he abandoned the prosecution of the application. On July 18, 1933, Patent No. 1,918,603 was issued to Ittner on an application filed by him on February 19, 1931. Lorenz, learning of the Ittner patent, filed a petition in the Patent Office to revive his original application. This petition was rejected. On November 8, 1934, more than a year after the issuance of the Ittner patent, Lorenz filed a new application in which he adopted as his own nineteen claims of Ittner's patent, asserting that the subject matter of Ittner's patent had been disclosed by him to Ittner in 1920. The Patent Office declared an interference. The examiner of interferences decided in Lorenz's favor and for reasons which need not be gone into here no appeal was taken.

* * *

[The court held Ittner's patent invalid because Ittner was not an original inventor.]

* * * [T]he court below held among other things that "the process of the patent, measured by the commonly accepted criteria, was an invention within the meaning of the statute" but that the patent was invalid because of prior public use. 60 F.Supp. 824, 826, 827. Lorenz appealed. * * *

We proceed immediately to an examination of the defense of prior public use. R.S. § 4886, Title 35 U.S.C. § 31, provided at the time of Lorenz's second application, viz., on November 8, 1934, as well as at the time of the issuance of the patent on that application, viz., June 22, 1937, as follows: "Any person who has invented or discovered any new and useful art, * * * or any new and useful improvement thereof, * * * *not known or used by others in this country, before his invention or discovery thereof,* and not patented or described in any printed publication in this or any foreign country, before his invention or discovery thereof, *or more than two years* prior to his application, *and not in public use* or on sale in this country for more than two years prior to his application, * * * may, * * * obtain a patent therefor."

The court below found that: "It clearly appears from the undisputed testimony and the documentary evidence offered in support thereof that the process of the patent was in public use in the factory of the defendant from November 1931 until November 1932, approximately one year, but more than two years prior to the Lorenz application of November 8, 1934. This use was preceded by several months of experimentation, but commercial production of soap and glycerine by the process of the patent was accomplished in November of 1931 and continued thereafter until 1932, when the use of the process was either discontinued or abandoned. This public use, although it did not enrich the art, was sufficient under the statute to preclude the issuance of a valid patent."

We have carefully examined the evidence in the case at bar and have perused not only the transcript but the numerous physical exhibits as well. Agreeing with Lorenz that under the peculiar circumstances of this case an unusually heavy burden rests upon Colgate in order to prove prior public use, we have made generous allowance for the difficulties which Lorenz encountered in procuring evidence to rebut Colgate's proof of prior public use. But we cannot say that the court below erred in finding that the process of Lorenz's patent was in public use in Colgate's plant for a period of a year more than two years preceding the filing of Lorenz's second patent application on November 8, 1934. We are not the trier of the facts but if we were we would feel compelled to make the same finding as did the court below.

We come then to the question whether the public use under the circumstances was such as to be within the purview of R.S. § 4886. Lorenz contends that it was not such a use; that Congress did not intend the provision of the statute to bar the grant of a valid monopoly to an inventor whose disclosures have been "pirated" by the person to whom he confided them. The court below made no finding on this point. We ruled in the earlier appeal, as has been stated, that Ittner followed the disclosures made to him by Lorenz in 1920 and that the award of priority to Lorenz by the Patent Office necessarily followed that undeniable fact. 122 F.2d at pages 879–880. The examiner of interferences had said, after referring to the circumstances under which Lorenz had communicated his invention to Ittner: "It is clear therefore since Ittner saw a copy of the earlier [Lorenz's] application that he is not the original inventor of [the claims contained in] Counts 1 to 19." Under all the circumstances and in the light of the documentary and uncontradicted evidence the conclusion is inevitable that Ittner did appropriate Lorenz's process for the benefit of Colgate and that if a finding to such effect had been made by the court below it would have found full support in the evidence. For the purposes of the appeals we will treat the case as if an express finding had been made by the court below that Ittner appropriated Lorenz's disclosures made by the latter to him in 1920.

Colgate asserts that its use was neither fraudulent nor piratical and that the disclosures made by Lorenz to Ittner in 1920 carried no pledge, express or implied, that Ittner or Colgate should not make use of Ittner's invention; that Lorenz had filed a patent application and that Ittner knew this and that otherwise Ittner would have refused to receive the disclosures; that since these were made under a then pending application Ittner and Colgate were at liberty to make use of Lorenz's process and answer to Lorenz in a patent infringement suit for profits or damages; that no confidential or trust relationship in Lorenz's favor was or could be imposed on either Ittner or Colgate under the circumstances. We are aware of the ordinary practice under which manufacturers refuse to receive an inventor's disclosures unless there is a pending patent application which covers the discovery. This proper practice is one which usually inures to the benefit of both inventor and manufacturer since it settles in written terms the nature of the disclosure and lessens the probability of future disputes. In the case at bar, however, Ittner immediately rejected Lorenz's disclosures as commercially impractical only to make substantial commercial use of them some eleven years later. The circumstances of the instant case are therefore unusual and reflect a very different pattern from that which customarily ensues when an inventor makes a disclosure to a manufacturer. Usually if the manufacturer declares himself interested in the process a contract is drawn up whereby the rights of the parties are fixed for the periods of manufacture both prior to the issuance of the patent as well as thereafter. No such opportunity was given to Lorenz in the case at bar because of Ittner's rejection of the process as soon as it had been disclosed to him.

We do not doubt that Lorenz's disclosures were made to Ittner with the implicit understanding that if Ittner was to make use of them an arrangement was to be effected whereby Lorenz was to be compensated. Certainly Lorenz was not offering his process to Ittner gratis. Under these circumstances we cannot say that an inventor may not invoke the aid of a court of equity to impose an accounting on the manufacturer, provided the inventor moves to protect his rights with reasonable promptness. Cf. Bohlman v. American Paper Goods Co., D.C.N.J., 53 F.Supp. 794. We have found no case which is on all fours with the circumstances at bar but a helpful analogy is supplied by Hoeltke v. C. M. Kemp Mfg. Co., 4 Cir., 80 F.2d 912, 922–924. In this case Hoetlke disclosed his invention to Kemp after he had filed an application but before the issuance of a patent to him Kemp made use of the device, claiming to have developed it independently. The court had no difficulty in holding Kemp liable. It stated, 80 F.2d at page 923: "It would be a reproach to any system of jurisprudence to permit one who has received a disclosure in confidence to thus appropriate the ideas of another without liability for the wrong." See also Chesapeake & O. R. Co. v. Kaltenbach, 4 Cir., 95 F.2d 801, and Booth v. Stutz Motor Car Co. of America, 7 Cir., 56 F.2d 962. We think it clear that Ittner received the disclosures cum onere and that Colgate cannot now be heard to assert that it owes no duty to Lorenz.

But Colgate's position in this regard is not really an issue in the instant case. The scope which Congress intended the public use statute to have is the important question. Here the defense of prior public use in reality is asserted on behalf of the public, albeit by Colgate. Was it the intention of Congress that public use by one who employs a process in breach of a fiduciary relationship, who tortiously appropriates it or who pirates it, should bar the inventor from the fruits of his monopoly?

* * *

* * * The prior-public-use proviso of R.S. § 4886 was enacted by Congress in the public interest. It contains no qualification or exception which limits the nature of the public use. We think that Congress intended that if an inventor does not protect his discovery by an application for a patent within the period prescribed by the Act, and an intervening public use arises from any source whatsoever, the inventor must be barred from a patent or from the fruits of his monopoly, if a patent has issued to him. There is not a single word in the statute which would tend to put an inventor, whose disclosures have been pirated, in any different position from one who has permitted the use of his process. * * * [I]t is apparent that if fraud or piracy be held to prevent the literal application of the prior-public-use provision a fruitful field for collusion will be opened and the public interest which R.S. § 4886 is designed to protect will suffer. While we cannot fail to view Lorenz's predicament with sympathy, we may not render our decision on such a basis. For these reasons we hold, as did the court below, that the Lorenz patent is void by reason of prior public use.

* * *

The judgment of the court below will be affirmed.

NOTE

In O'Brien v. Westinghouse Electric Co., 293 F.2d 1 (3d Cir.1961), the patentee had been dissuaded from filing a timely patent application by the secretary of the suggestion committee, who wrongly informed him that patent applications could not be filed during the war. The court rejected the argument that this estopped the employer from asserting the defense of its own public use.

CALI v. EASTERN AIRLINES, INC.

United States Court of Appeals, Second Circuit, 1971.
442 F.2d 65.

KAUFMAN, CIRCUIT JUDGE. Cali, plaintiff and appellant in this patent infringement action, is a mechanic employed by one of the pioneers in the airlines industry, Pan American World Airways (Pan Am). The kernel of the patented invention which is the subject of this suit was contained in an idea which Cali submitted to Pan Am on a standard form soliciting employees' suggestions in December 1962. Although of course Eastern Airlines, Inc., the appellee and alleged infringer, seeks to minimize its value, Cali's proposal apparently resulted in the correction of a persistent defect in the design of the JT–4 jet engine, then used in Pan Am's Boeing 707 and Douglas DC–8 aircraft before the introduction of the fan jet. Cali's "suggestion-box" solution had eluded the industry's professional engineers.

The sole question raised on this appeal is whether the trial court properly concluded on the basis of the pleadings, affidavits, and depositions before it, that no material fact remained to be tried, thus justifying the grant of Eastern's motion for summary judgment. Judge Dooling, whose opinion is reported at 318 F.Supp. 474, decided that Cali's "invention was * * * in public use" and not used primarily for experimental purposes "more than one year prior to the date" Cali filed his application for a patent and hence the patent was invalid, 35 U.S. C.A. § 102(b). Accordingly, the action was dismissed. While Eastern may yet ultimately prevail on the question of prior use or on other defenses raised below which are not before us on this appeal, we disagree with the district court that the relevant factual issues have been resolved with such clarity at this stage in the litigation as to justify summary judgment.

I.

Cali applied for his patent on September 1, 1964. The key date for purposes of the "public use" bar of Section 102(b) is thus September 1, 1963. As will appear in more detail, the central question before us involves the nature and purposes of the uses to which Pan Am put Cali's invention prior to that date. Before we evaluate those uses, the contours of Cali's concept must first be sketched.

Cali's patent relates to the design of the front or low pressure compression section of the "axial-flow" compressor, the type of compressor used on the JT–4, manufactured by Pratt & Whitney Aircraft Division of United Aircraft Corporation (Pratt & Whitney). This front end section includes several cylindrical stages, consisting of alternating fanlike rotor sections sandwiched between stationary "stator" sections. Successive rotors blow air back against the blades (or vanes) of the stators (or shrouds), which in turn guide the air inward through the tapering compressor chamber to an outlet section called the fairing.

The last, or seventh, stator on the JT–4 was designed by Pratt & Whitney so that it connected loosely to the fairing by means of lugs and slats. The loose interconnection permitted the "floating" fairing to vibrate against the seventh stator assembly, causing abrasive wear of the stator lugs and fairing.

As a mechanic employed by Pan Am since 1957, Cali became familiar with the usual practice of periodically repairing worn stators and fairings. This was done by first rebuilding the worn surfaces by welding them and then machining the rebuilt surfaces to their proper dimensions. Cali's suggestion, submitted to his supervisor in December 1962, proposed as an alternative to this practice "to permanently weld the fairing to the 7th stage vane and shroud" and thus by rigidly interconnecting them to eliminate the abrasive wear and hence the need for periodic repairs. Although this solution was "simplicity itself once it was conceived and expressed," as Judge Dooling characterized it, "introducing rigidity may have been powerfully counterindicated by engine building lore," 318 F.Supp. at 475, primarily because of the danger of damage from stresses that might accumulate in the two vibrating assemblies.

While precise temporal relationships are unclear in many respects from this record, at approximately the time that Cali's suggestion was being evaluated, Pan Am engineers devised a variant application of the basic rigid-connection idea suggested by Cali's proposed weld technique. By this alternative method, the vibrating parts would be connected by means of long bolts or tie-rods. The tie-rod technique is conceded by both parties to be within the teaching of Cali's patent, whose critical language describes the two vibrating parts as being "rigidly connected" or secured. The primary advantage of the tie-rod variant appears to have been to permit easier assembly and servicing of the engine.

Both parties agree that Cali's suggestion initiated a period of indefinite length during which Pan Am, in the words of Eastern's brief, evaluated the rigid-connection concept at least with the object "of finding out whether the idea was worth using." Specifically, Judge Dooling identified three foci of "problems and hesitations that preceded Pan Am's unrestricted use of the invention." Thus, Pan Am was concerned with the relative merits of the weld and tie-rod methods. Second, as indicated above, the weld method caused difficulty in assembling the compressor (the solution finally hit upon for this problem, the details of which are irrelevant here, is included in Cali's patent). Third, the court referred to certain "consequential effect," such as cracking of the welded assembly which may have caused Pan Am for a time to doubt the efficacy of Cali's approach. 318 F.Supp. at 475–76.

Certain essential details of this period prior to Pan Am's unreserved acceptance of Cali's concept, are not in dispute. Thus, by a telegram dated January 4, 1963, Pratt & Whitney authorized use of the tie rod on a "trial basis." Similarly, on February 8, 1963, Pratt & Whitney wired Pan Am that it had "no objection" to use of the weld "on token number of engines based on your assertion that no assembly difficulty will be encountered." Pursuant to this authorization,[1] Pan Am subsequently installed and used engines incorporating the tie rod technique on one engine and incorporating the weld approach on at least three other engines. In each instance, the engines were installed and used on commercial aircraft in the normal course of Pan Am's business.

II.

The district court viewed each of these commercial uses as a "public use" within the meaning of Section 102(b), and this conclusion can hardly be challenged. That an invention or process employed in the regular conduct of a business is a "public use" for this purpose is a proposition settled long ago and never disturbed. * * * This settled concept of "public use" is "extraordinarily broad," Watson v. Allen, 254 F.2d 342, 345 (D.C.Cir.1958) (Burger, Circuit Judge). It is a matter of legal indifference that the "public" use may be necessarily concealed from public awareness by the structure of the design or the manner of its use, Hall v. Macneale, 107 U.S. 90 (1882); Egbert v. Lippmann [104 U.S. 333 (1881)]; Metallizing Engineering Co. v. Kenyon Bearing & Auto Parts Co., 153 F.2d 516 (2d Cir.1946), cert. denied 328 U.S. 840 (1946). Public use by a third party, with or without the knowledge or consent of the patentee, will generally defeat the patent as readily as public use by the inventor himself. * * *

We have previously explained the purposes of this sometimes harsh standard as intended "to require the inventor to see to it that he filed his application within [the statutory period] from the completion of his invention, so as to cut off all question of the defeat of his patent by a use or sale of it by others more than [the statutory period] prior to his application" and as designed to avoid the "perplexing questions which must frequently arise when the intent of the user and the bona fides of the use are questions to be determined. * * *." Eastman v. Mayor, etc., City of New York, 134 F. 844, 854 (2d Cir.1904). See Walker on Patents 700 (2d Ed.1964). It is thus clear beyond cavil that Pan Am's use of Cali's invention in commercial aircraft prior to September 1, 1963, would defeat Cali's patent, were the uses not included within the "experimental use" exception to the prior use bar which we shall discuss below.

On the other hand, although the parties have not dwelt on the matter, it is necessary to add that the present record would not appear to support a holding that Cali's action in submitting his suggestion to Pan Am constituted a "public use" regardless of the manner of Pan

---

1. The tentative nature of the initial uses of Cali's idea at this early stage is indicated by two internal memoranda that passed between a Pan Am engineer, Frederick D. Curtin, and Pan Am's Inspection Department in February, 1963. These memoranda refer to an impending "trial installation" of the tie rod and "a service test" of the weld method. The tie rod was expressly forbidden for use "on any other engines until the results of the service testing were known."

Am's subsequent exploitation of his idea. Cali did not conceal his invention from the public while using it to his commercial advantage more than a year before his application, thus extending the period of his monopoly beyond that protected by the patent laws. To prevent such an abuse and evasion of the patent laws seems to have been accepted by courts as an important purpose of the "public use" bar, see Watson v. Allen, supra, 254 F.2d at 346; Koehring v. National Auto Tool Co., 362 F.2d 100, 103 (7th Cir.1966); Metallizing Engineering Co. v. Kenyon Bearing & Auto Parts Co., supra, 153 F.2d at 520, but one which has little importance in the circumstances of this case. Cali does not appear to stand in the position of an inventor who sells his patented device in the ordinary course of his business, for a predominantly commercial purpose, and without restriction or control over the uses to be made of the invention by the buyer. In such a case, the *buyer's* acts and purposes become irrelevant since the inventor's sale of the device is itself sufficient to defeat the patent. See Tool Research & Engineering Corp. v. Honcor Corp., 367 F.2d 449 (9th Cir.1966), cert. denied 387 U.S. 919 (1967).

Eastern does stress the absence of any indication in this record that Cali attempted to control or in any way limit Pan Am's use of his idea. Similarly, the district court observed that Cali "put no restrictions on Pan Am's use" nor did he or *could* he "control the time * * * extent and nature of [Pan Am's] use" of his conception. 318 F.Supp. at 478. But the absence of any control by Cali, or any attempt to impose control, should not be elevated to the status of a per se test under the circumstances disclosed here and in the posture in which we receive this case. Cali lacked the means to develop his idea on his own resources beyond the bare conception of it. See Ry. Register Manuf. Co. v. Broadway & 7th Ave. Ry., 22 F. 655 (2d Cir.1884); Harmon v. Struthers, 57 F. 637 (W.D.Pa.1893). Nor was Cali, as an employee of Pan Am, in any position to dictate or even propose the terms of Pan Am's entirely gratuitous application of his concept. See General Electric Co. v. Continental Fibre Co., 256 F. 660, 663 (2d Cir.1919). No purpose consonant with the scheme of the patent laws would be served were the statutory "public use" period to run in every case from the time that an employee communicated a raw idea to his superiors for evaluation and exploitation in their unfettered discretion. Indeed, such a doctrine might stifle inventiveness. See Note, The Public Use Bar to Patentability: Two New Approaches to the Experimental Use Exception, 52 Minn.L.Rev. 851, 855–56 (1968).

We do not imply that an inventor in Cali's situation might sell an idea to his employer and thereafter manifest no interest in the development, success, or failure of his invention, and yet take advantage of his employer's trial or experimental period. Such inaction and indifference would indicate that the inventor's intent was commercial—to secure the reward for the submission of the submitted concept, whatever its value—and not experimental, and would therefore constitute a "public" and nonexperimental use within the meaning of Section

102(b). Cali's acceptance of a financial reward for his idea, however, *after it was examined, tried, and ultimately adopted by Pan Am,* is consistent with a purpose to follow the idea through to its ultimate perfection and fate. Moreover, we do not see the purposes of the patent laws enhanced were the public use period to run from the date of submission, assuming Cali at that time and thereafter continued to maintain an interest in the progress of his suggestion, merely because Cali's inventiveness and thereafter his interest in the invention may have been whetted by the possibility of a financial reward should the concept prove useful to Pan Am.

Eastern does not now contend that Cali ever abandoned his idea to Pan Am in the sense suggested by the preceding paragraph. In any event, the evidence that Cali remained interested in the progress of his idea until and beyond the time it was unreservedly accepted by Pan Am is more than sufficient for purposes of our review of a grant of summary judgment. Accordingly, the determinative question becomes the nature and purpose of Pan Am's use of Cali's idea, as the parties and district court apparently seemed to agree.

III.

We turn to the issue principally briefed and argued, viz., whether Pan Am's public use of Cali's invention prior to September 1, 1963 falls within the judicially created exception to the "public use" bar for uses which are shown by "full, unequivocal, and convincing" proof, Smith & Griggs Manuf. Co., 123 U.S. 249, 264 (1888) to have been primarily intended as experimental rather than commercial. Aerovox Corp. v. Polymet Mfg. Corp., 67 F.2d 860 (2d Cir.1933). Specifically, the question is whether this factual issue was resolved by the papers before the district court with sufficient clarity to permit an award of summary judgment.

At the threshold, we differ with the district court's interpretation of the scope of the "experimental use" exception. Judge Dooling appears to have believed that even Pan Am's "first use" of the tie rod and weld was not predominantly experimental even assuming that the primary purpose of the use was to determine whether Cali's idea should be adopted or rejected. Apparently the district court assumed that a use may not be "experimental" if the purpose is to see if the idea in question has any value at all, rather than to explore ways of improving the invention or "to determine or guide the direction of *modification of an emergent* inventive concept." 318 F.Supp. at 477 (emphasis added). The district court appears to have equated "experimental" with "developmental." Id. *ie development of partial concepts*

This conception of the scope of the experimental use exception apparently underlay the whole of the district court's decision. We find it unduly restrictive. We see no good purpose in attempting to distinguish sharply between experimentation with an eye to going "back to the drawing board" for modification and rethinking in the event of *rather than test of final concept* initial failure on the one hand and experimentation directed more toward discovering whether a novel invention should be adopted and marketed or discarded in its entirety. Indeed, we have previously said as much in Aerovox Corp. v. Polymet Mfg. Corp., 67 F.2d 860, 862 (2d Cir.1933) where we "assumed" that an inventor may experiment with an idea "not only to put it into definitive form, but to see whether his ideas are worth exploiting."

The leading case defining the reach of the experimental use exception, Elizabeth v. Pavement Co., 97 U.S. 126 (1877), involved experimentation to test the *durability* of the inventor's new kind of pavement. There was no indication that the inventor put the pavement to the test of six years' public wear to determine what improvements he might make, rather than simply to discover whether the idea was worth pursuing. Indeed, the Court's decision in favor of the patentee was premised on the assumption that the aim of the test might be "to bring his invention to perfection *or* to ascertain whether it [would] answer the purpose intended." 97 U.S. at 137 (emphasis added). Either sort of experimental use—if indeed any such sorting is tenable—would bring the invention within the experimental use exception because "it is the interest of the public, as well as [of the inventor] that the invention should be perfect *and* properly tested. * * *." Id. (Emphasis added.)

IV.

The crucial date therefore becomes that when Pan Am first publicly used Cali's concept with a predominantly commercial intent, rather than with the primary purpose of determining whether or in what form the idea should be put into general use.

In sum, we find that the record discloses a genuine issue of fact as to whether Pan Am publicly used Cali's invention prior to September 1, 1963, for predominantly non-experimental purposes.

Reversed.

NOTES

1. In re Smith, 714 F.2d 1127 (Fed.Cir.1983). The court affirmed a PTO rejection of an application on a powdered carpet—treating composition, marketed as CARPET FRESH, on the basis of a § 102(b) public use. The product is sprinkled onto a carpet prior to vacuuming and is said to impart deodorizing, antistatic and antisoil characteristics to the carpet. More than a year prior to the application the applicant's company, Airwick, had conducted a consumer test of the product in St. Louis, using 76 customers. The test was conducted by first showing a video presentation introducing the product, and the consumers were then questioned about the pricing of the product, the believability of the claims made for the product, and their purchase intent. The consumers were then given samples of the product, without any express restrictions, to use in their own homes. After two weeks they were questioned further about their experience with the product. The applicant argued the use was experimental. "Contrary to appellants' contention that the St. Louis test was needed to obtain scientific data on their invention's operation and usefulness, such data could

have been easily obtained in their own facilities. The operability and other properties of the claimed invention could have been verified without the assistance of 'typical housewives' (consumers). Instead, there was a more dominant purpose behind the St. Louis test, viz. to determine whether potential consumers would buy the product and how much they would pay for it—commercial exploitation." 714 F.2d at 1135. Would this test not have invalidated the patent if the 76 consumers had first been asked to sign confidentiality agreements?

2. Preemption Devices, Inc. v. Minnesota Mining & Mfg. Co., 732 F.2d 903 (Fed.Cir.1984), affirming 559 F.Supp. 1250 (E.D.Pa.1983), was an action for infringement of a patent on a device to enable emergency vehicles to control traffic lights, marketed under the trademark OPTICOM. The device involved the installation of a pulsed, high-intensity light on the emergency vehicle and a receiver-controller device at the traffic lights. As the emergency vehicle proceeds down the street it can send the light signal to the controller, which turns the traffic signal green in the direction of the oncoming vehicle. The infringer argued that the installation and demonstration of prototypes of the invention in two California cities and an application for a trademark registration on OPTICOM more than a year prior to the patent application invalidated the patent. The installed equipment was not sold, and was monitored by the inventor for the purpose of testing the performance of the equipment under actual use conditions and design changes were made in light of the experience. 559 F.Supp. at 1255–56. The patent owner successfully argued that the prototype installations were experimental. Of the trademark application, the Federal Circuit said: "We find particularly unconvincing * * * [the] argument based on the declaration filed in connection with the application to register the trademark OPTICOM, stating the date of first use and first use in commerce [more than one year prior to the patent application]. Those statements were not made with respect to the use of the invention but the use of the mark. The description of goods in the registration is very general and defines no particular apparatus." 732 F.2d 906.

3. Almost all cases which have applied the experimental use exception have been cases of experimental use by the inventor himself or others under his control. Indeed, it has been stated that the experimental use exception does not apply to public uses by third parties. Magnetics, Inc. v. Arnold Engineering Co., 438 F.2d 72, 74 (7th Cir.1971). Should an experimental, non-secret use by a third party prior to the applicant's invention anticipate? Does it? Lyon v. Bausch & Lomb Optical Co., 224 F.2d 530, 534 (2d Cir.1955) (Hand, J.), is helpful.

4. The ambiguities of public use and the draconian nature of the one year time bar make it important for an attorney, the minute he is consulted, to ascertain what steps his client has taken and will take to develop and exploit the invention. See Robert A. Choate, "On Sale"—Review and Circumspection, 47 J.Pat.Off.Soc'y 906 (1965). Even a present contract for the future sale of a product not yet manufactured can activate the time bar. Barmag Barmer Maschinenfabrik AG v. Murata Machinery, Ltd., 731 F.2d 831 (Fed.Cir.1984). In UMC Electronics Co. v. United States, 816 F.2d 647 (Fed.Cir.1987), cert. denied 108 S.Ct. 748 (1988), the court held that an invention could be on sale at a time when it had not yet been completed or "reduced to practice."

(3) PATENTS

ALEXANDER MILBURN CO. v. DAVIS–BOURNONVILLE CO.

Supreme Court of the United States, 1926.
270 U.S. 390, 46 S.Ct. 324, 70 L.Ed. 651.

MR. JUSTICE HOLMES delivered the opinion of the Court.

This is a suit for the infringement of the plaintiff's patent for an improvement in welding and cutting apparatus alleged to have been the invention of one Whitford. The suit embraced other matters but this is the only one material here. The defense is that Whitford was not the first inventor of the thing patented, and the answer gives notice that to prove the invalidity of the patent evidence will be offered that one Clifford invented the thing, his patent being referred to and identified. The application for the plaintiff's patent was filed on March 4, 1911, and the patent was issued June 4, 1912. There was no evidence carrying Whitford's invention further back. Clifford's application was filed on January 31, 1911, before Whitford's, and his patent was issued on February 6, 1912. It is not disputed that this application gave a complete and adequate description of the thing patented to Whitford, but it did not claim it. The District Court gave the plaintiff a decree, holding that, while Clifford might have added this claim to his application, yet as he did not, he was not a prior inventor, 297 Fed.Rep. 846. The decree was affirmed by the Circuit Court of Appeals. 1 Fed. (2d) 227. There is a conflict between this decision and those of other Circuit Courts of Appeals, especially the sixth. Lemley v. Dobson-Evans Co., 243 Fed. 391. Naceskid Service Chain Co. v. Perdue, 1 Fed. (2d) 924. Therefore a writ of certiorari was granted by this Court. 266 U.S. 596.

The patent law authorizes a person who has invented an improvement like the present, "not known or used by others in this country, before his invention," &c., to obtain a patent for it. Rev.Sts. § 4886, amended, March 3, 1897, c. 391, § 1, 29 Stat. 692. Among the defences to a suit for infringement the fourth specified by the statute is that the patentee "was not the original and first inventor or discoverer of any material and substantial part of the thing patented." Rev.Sts. § 4920, amended, March 3, 1897, c. 391, § 2, 29 Stat. 692. Taking these words in their natural sense as they would be read by the common man, obviously one is not the first inventor if, as was the case here, somebody else has made a complete and adequate description of the thing claimed before the earliest moment to which the alleged inventor can carry his invention back. But the words cannot be taken quite so simply. In view of the gain to the public that the patent laws mean to secure we assume for purposes of decision that it would have been no bar to Whitford's patent if Clifford had written out his prior description and kept it in his portfolio uncommunicated to anyone. More than that, since the decision in the case of The Cornplanter Patent, 23 Wall. 181, it is said, at all events for many years, the Patent Office has made no search among abandoned patent applications, and by the words of the statute a previous foreign invention does not invalidate a patent granted here if it has not been patented or described in a printed publication. Rev.Sts. § 4923. See Westinghouse Machine Co. v. General Electric Co., 207 Fed. 75. These analogies prevailed in the minds of the Courts below.

On the other hand, publication in a periodical is a bar. This as it seems to us is more than an arbitrary enactment, and illustrates, as does the rule concerning previous public use, the principle that, subject to the exceptions mentioned, one really must be the first inventor in order to be entitled to a patent. Coffin v. Ogden, 18 Wall. 120. We understand the Circuit Court of Appeals to admit that if Whitford had not applied for his patent until after the issue to Clifford, the disclosure by the latter would have had the same effect as the publication of the same words in a periodical, although not made the basis of a claim. 1 Fed. (2d) 233. The invention is made public property as much in the one case as in the other. But if this be true, as we think that it is, it seems to us that a sound distinction cannot be taken between that case and a patent applied for before but not granted until after a second patent is sought. The delays of the patent office ought not to cut down the effect of what has been done. The description shows that Whitford was not the first inventor. Clifford had done all that he could do to make his description public. He had taken steps that would make it public as soon as the Patent Office did its work, although, of course, amendments might be required of him before the end could be reached. We see no reason in the words or policy of the law for allowing Whitford to profit by the delay and make himself out to be the first inventor when he was not so in fact, when Clifford had shown knowledge inconsistent with the allowance of Whitford's claim, [Webster] Loom Co. v. Higgins, 105 U.S. 580, and when otherwise the publication of his patent would abandon the thing described to the public unless it already was old. McClain v. Ortmayer, 141 U.S. 419, 424. Underwood v. Gerber, 149 U.S. 224, 230.

The question is not whether Clifford showed himself by the description to be the first inventor. By putting it in that form it is comparatively easy to take the next step and say that he is not an inventor in the sense of the statute unless he makes a claim. The question is whether Clifford's disclosure made it impossible for Whitford to claim the invention at a later date. The disclosure would have had the same effect as at present if Clifford had added to his description a statement that he did not claim the thing described because he abandoned it or because he believed it to be old. It is not necessary to show who did invent the thing in order to show that Whitford did not.

It is said that without a claim the thing described is not reduced to practice. But this seems to us to rest on a false theory helped out by the fiction that by a claim it is reduced to practice. A new application and a claim may be based on the original description within two years, and the original priority established notwithstanding intervening claims. Chapman v. Wintroath, 252 U.S. 126, 137. A description that would bar a patent if printed in a periodical or in an issued patent is equally effective in an application so far as reduction to practice goes.

As to the analogies relied upon below, the disregard of abandoned patent applications, however explained, cannot be taken to establish a principle beyond the rule as actually applied. As an empirical rule it no doubt is convenient if not necessary to the Patent Office, and we are not disposed to disturb it, although we infer that originally the practice of the Office was different. The policy of the statute as to foreign inventions obviously stands on its own footing and cannot be applied to domestic affairs. The fundamental rule we repeat is that the patentee must be the first inventor. The qualifications in aid of a wish to encourage improvements or to avoid laborious investigations do not prevent the rule from applying here.

Decree reversed.

HAZELTINE RESEARCH, INC. v. BRENNER

Supreme Court of the United States, 1965.
382 U.S. 252, 86 S.Ct. 335, 15 L.Ed.2d 304, rehearing denied 382 U.S. 1000, 86 S.Ct. 527, 15 L.Ed.2d 489.

MR. JUSTICE BLACK delivered the opinion of the Court.

The sole question presented here is whether an application for patent pending in the Patent Office at the time a second application is filed constitutes part of the "prior art" as that term is used in 35 U.S.C. § 103 * * *.

The question arose in this way. On December 23, 1957, petitioner Robert Regis filed an application for a patent on a new and useful improvement on a microwave switch. On June 24, 1959, the Patent Examiner denied Regis' application on the ground that the invention was not one which was new or unobvious in light of the prior art and thus did not meet the standards set forth in § 103. The Examiner said that the invention was unpatentable because of the joint effect of the disclosures made by patents previously issued, one to Carlson (No. 2,491,644) and one to Wallace (No. 2,822,526). The Carlson patent had been issued on December 20, 1949, over eight years prior to Regis' application, and that patent is admittedly a part of the prior art insofar as Regis' invention is concerned. The Wallace patent, however, was pending in the Patent Office when the Regis application was filed. The Wallace application had been pending since March 24, 1954, nearly three years and nine months before Regis filed his application and the Wallace patent was issued on February 4, 1958, 43 days after Regis filed his application.[1]

After the Patent Examiner refused to issue the patent, Regis appealed to the Patent Office Board of Appeals on the ground that the

---

1. It is not disputed that Regis' alleged invention, as well as his application, was made after Wallace's application was filed. There is, therefore, no question of priority of invention before us.

prior art = when a patent is filed
⟹ (under 103) or what 102 says is art

Wallace patent could not be properly considered a part of the prior art because it had been a "co-pending patent" and its disclosures were secret and not known to the public. The Board of Appeals rejected this argument and affirmed the decision of the Patent Examiner. Regis and Hazeltine, which had an interest as assignee, then instituted the present action in the District Court pursuant to 35 U.S.C. § 145 to compel the Commissioner to issue the patent. The District Court agreed with the Patent Office that the co-pending Wallace application was a part of the prior art and directed that the complaint be dismissed. 226 F.Supp. 459. On appeal the Court of Appeals affirmed per curiam. 340 F.2d 786. We granted certiorari to decide the question of whether a co-pending application is included in the prior art, as that term is used in 35 U.S.C. § 103. 380 U.S. 960.

Petitioners' primary contention is that the term "prior art," as used in § 103, really means only art previously publicly known. In support of this position they refer to a statement in the legislative history which indicates that prior art means "what was known before as described in section 102." [2] They contend that the use of the word "known" indicates that Congress intended prior art to include only inventions or discoveries which were already publicly known at the time an invention was made.

If petitioners are correct in their interpretation of "prior art," then the Wallace invention, which was not publicly known at the time the Regis application was filed, would not be prior art with regard to Regis' invention. This is true because at the time Regis filed his application the Wallace invention, although pending in the Patent Office, had never been made public and the Patent Office was forbidden by statute from disclosing to the public, except in special circumstances, anything contained in the application.[3]

The Commissioner, relying chiefly on Alexander Milburn Co. v. Davis-Bournonville Co., 270 U.S. 390, contends that when a patent is issued, the disclosures contained in the patent become a part of the prior art as of the time the application was filed, not, as petitioners contend, at the time the patent is issued. In that case a patent was held invalid because, at the time it was applied for, there was already pending an application which completely and adequately described the invention. In holding that the issuance of a patent based on the first application barred the valid issuance of a patent based on the second application, Mr. Justice Holmes, speaking for the Court, said, "The delays of the patent office ought not to cut down the effect of what has been done. * * * [The first applicant] had taken steps that would make it public as soon as the Patent Office did its work, although, of

2. H.R.Rep.No.1923, 82d Cong., 2d Sess., p. 7 (1952).

3. 35 U.S.C. § 122 states: "Applications for patents shall be kept in confidence by the Patent Office and no information concerning the same given without authority of the applicant or owner unless necessary to carry out the provisions of any Act of Congress or in such special circumstances as may be determined by the Commissioner."

course, amendments might be required of him before the end could be reached. We see no reason in the words or policy of the law for allowing [the second applicant] to profit by the delay. * * * " At p. 401.

In its revision of the patent laws in 1952, Congress showed its approval of the holding in *Milburn* by adopting 35 U.S.C. § 102(e) which provides that a person shall be entitled to a patent unless "(e) the invention was described in a patent granted on an application for patent by another filed in the United States before the invention thereof by the applicant for patent." Petitioners suggest, however, that the question in this case is not answered by mere reference to § 102(e), because in *Milburn*, which gave rise to that section, the co-pending applications described the same identical invention. But here the Regis invention is not precisely the same as that contained in the Wallace patent, but is only made obvious by the Wallace patent in light of the Carlson patent. We agree with the Commissioner that this distinction is without significance here. While we think petitioners' argument with regard to § 102(e) is interesting, it provides no reason to depart from the plain holding and reasoning in the *Milburn* case. The basic reasoning upon which the Court decided the *Milburn* case applies equally well here. When Wallace filed his application, he had done what he could to add his disclosures to the prior art. The rest was up to the Patent Office. Had the Patent Office acted faster, had it issued Wallace's patent two months earlier, there would have been no question here. As Justice Holmes said in *Milburn*, "The delays of the patent office ought not to cut down the effect of what has been done." P. 401.

To adopt the result contended for by petitioners would create an area where patents are awarded for unpatentable advances in the art. We see no reason to read into § 103 a restricted definition of "prior art" which would lower standards of patentability to such an extent that there might exist two patents where the Congress has plainly directed that there should be only one.

Affirmed.

G. SECTION 102 REFERENCES AS PRIOR ART

APPLICATION OF FOSTER

United States Court of Customs and Patent Appeals, 1965.
343 F.2d 980, certiorari denied 383 U.S. 966, 86 S.Ct. 1270, 16 L.Ed.2d 307, rehearing denied 384 U.S. 934, 86 S.Ct. 1441, 16 L.Ed.2d 535.

ALMOND, JUDGE. This is an appeal from the decision of the Board of Appeals affirming the rejection of the claims in appellant's patent application.

The invention relates to elastomeric synthetic polymers said to combine the desirable properties of natural Hevea rubber and the presently employed synthetic rubbers. These properties are described in the specification:

> "Hevea natural rubber is characterized by excellent tack, especially after milling; thus being ideal for tire building operations. Hevea produces vulcanizates having excellent resilience and low hysteresis properties, high tensile, strength, and good flexibility at low temperatures. Gum vulcanizates formed from Hevea also possess high tensile strength. Hevea natural rubber is characterized by a crystallinity of at least about 40% and displays a crystalline X-ray diffraction pattern when stretched.

> "Heretofore, the synthetic rubbers, in comparison with Hevea rubber, have exhibited low tack and no crystalline properties while their vulcanizates have been characterized by undesirably low tensile strengths and resilience, and undesirably high hysteresis. The synthetic rubbers, particularly the butadiene/styrene copolymer (GR–S), have been greatly superior to natural rubber in resisting crack initiation in service but have been markedly inferior to Hevea in resisting crack and cut growth. The undesirably high hysteresis of the synthetic rubber polymers has prevented their use in any substantial quantity in the production of such articles as the large tires employed on trucks, buses, and large off-the-road vehicles."

Infrared analysis of Hevea rubber has shown that the polymer consists of about 97.8% *cis*–1,4–structure. That is, the units of the rubber molecules are connected to each other in 1,4–addition to produce a linear chain with the spatial arrangement of the units in what is called the *cis*, as opposed to the *trans*, stereospecific configuration.

In contrast, the specification notes that "The butadiene portion of a typical GRS emulsion copolymer contains about 64% *trans*–1,4–structure, 18% *cis*–1.4–structure and 18% 1,2-structure."

By increasing the amount of *cis*–1,4–structure butadiene, the properties of the synthetic rubber are greatly improved.

* * *

The examiner and the Board of Appeals rejected all of the claims on the basis of the Binder reference. The record indicates that Binder, an employee of appellant's assignee, wrote an article in the magazine "Industrial and Engineering Chemistry." The article reports analyses of the microstructures of polybutadiene homopolymers and copolymers with styrene. The portions particularly relied upon by the Patent Office are:

1. Table V which lists polymer "39–1" as having 22.7% *cis*–1,4; 60.0% *trans*–1,4; and 17.3% 1,2 enstructures of butadiene. It is noted that the catalyst employed was a peroxide.

2. Conclusion: "The results of the analyses reported here show that while the amount of *cis*–1,4 addition increases with increasing

temperature of polymerization, a polybutadiene containing 100% *cis*–1,4 or *trans*–1,4 addition cannot be made at any practical temperature."

It also should be noted that the Binder report at the outset states: "During the past 2 years, a large number of polybutadienes and butadiene-styrene copolymers have been prepared in these laboratories, in which various changes were made in the recipes with the object, mainly, of increasing the amount of *cis*–1,4 addition."

* * *

It is assumed by both parties—and it is unquestionably true—that when a reference fully discloses in every detail the subject matter of a claim, the statutory basis of a rejection on that reference is 35 U.S.C.A. § 102(a) if the reference date is before the applicant's *date of invention*, thereby establishing want of novelty, and section 102(b) if the reference date is more than one year prior to the actual United States *filing date*, thereby establishing a so-called "statutory bar," more accurately, a one-year time-bar which results in loss of right to a patent, regardless of when the invention was made. In either of these situations, it is often said that the invention is "anticipated" by the reference and the reference is termed an "anticipation."

Proofs submitted in this case under Patent Office Rule 131 with respect to a reference not before us (because it was overcome thereby) have established that the applicant's invention date was prior to December 26, 1952. The Binder reference is the August 1954 issue of a periodical. It is seen, therefore, that it is subsequent to the date of invention but more than one year prior to the filing date, which was August 21, 1956. * * * Since the date of invention is earlier than the reference date, section 102(a) is necessarily inapplicable because the printed publication was not "before the invention thereof by the applicant" and there is statutory novelty. This leaves paragraph (b) of section 102 as the only paragraph of that section having possible relevancy.

* * *

Because of the importance of the question to the law of patents, we have deemed it desirable to reconsider what is the statutory basis of this "unpatentable over" or obviousness type of rejection * * * under the circumstance that *the reference or references have effective dates more than one year prior to the filing date of the applicant*. More specifically, we have reconsidered the result again urged on us here, as allegedly authorized by section 103, that a reference having a date more than a year prior to the filing date may be disposed of by showing an invention date prior to the reference date, contrary to the express provision in Patent Office Rule 131.[8]

8. *"131. Affidavit of prior invention to overcome cited patent or publication.* (a) When any claim of an application is rejected on reference to a domestic patent which substantially shows or describes but does not claim the rejected invention, or on reference to a foreign patent or to a printed publication, and the applicant shall make oath to facts showing a completion of the invention in this country before the filing date of the application on which the domestic patent issued, or before the date of the foreign patent, or before the date of the printed publication, then the

Sections 101, 102 and 103, generally speaking, deal with two different matters: (1) the factors to be considered in determining whether a patentable invention has been *made*, i.e., novelty, utility, unobviousness, and the categories of patentable subject matter; and (2) "loss of right to patent" as stated in the heading of section 102, even though an otherwise patentable invention has been made. On the subject of loss of right, appellant's brief contains a helpful review of the development of the statutory law since 1793. It says:

> "In 1897 the patent laws were amended to make the * * * two-year bar period apply to all public uses, publications and patents *regardless of the source* from which they emanated. The change was a consequence, primarily, of greatly improved communications within the country which had rendered inventors easily able to acquire knowledge of the public acts of others within their own fields. It was reasoned that any inventor who *delayed in filing* a patent application for more than two years after a public disclosure of the invention would obtain *an undeserved reward in derogation of the rights of the public* if he were granted a patent.

> "In 1939, in recognition of further improvements in communications, Congress reduced the two-year bar period to one year. * * *

> "That 1939 Act was carried over unchanged in the 1952 recodification of the patent laws as 35 U.S.C. § 102(b).

> * * *

> "Manifestly, Section 102(b) from its earliest beginnings has been and was intended to be directed toward the encouragement of *diligence* in the filing of patent applications and the protection of the public from monopolies on subject matter which had already been fully disclosed to it."

These statements are in accord with our understanding of the history and purposes of section 102(b). It presents a sort of statute of limitations, formerly two years, now one year, within which an inventor, even though he has made a patentable invention, must act on penalty of loss of his right to patent. What starts the period running is clearly the availability of the invention *to the public* through the categories of disclosure enumerated in 102(b), which include "a printed publication" anywhere describing the invention. There appears to be no dispute about the operation of this statute in "complete anticipation" situations but *the contention seems to be that 102(b) has no*

patent or publication cited shall not bar the grant of a patent to the applicant, *unless the date of such patent or printed publication be more than one year prior to the date on which the application was filed in this country.*" [Emphasis ours.]

The italicized clause at the end of the foregoing paragraph or its equivalent has been present in the rule and its predecessor Rule 75 since January 1, 1898, when the rule was amended to include:

> " * * * unless the date of such patent or printed publication is more than two years prior to the date on which application was filed in this country."

objected

applicability where the invention is not completely disclosed in a single patent or publication, that is to say where the rejection involves the addition to the disclosure of the reference of the ordinary skill of the art or the disclosure of another reference which indicates what those of ordinary skill in the art are presumed to know, *and to have known for more than a year before the application was filed.* Upon a complete reexamination of this matter, we are convinced that the contention is contrary to the policy consideration which motivated the enactment by Congress of a statutory bar. On logic and principle we think this contention is unsound, and we also believe it is contrary to the patent law as it has actually existed since at least 1898.

rejected

* * *

As to dealing with the express language of 102(b), for example, "described in a printed publication," technically, we see no reason to so read the words of the statute as to preclude the use of more than one reference; nor do we find in the context anything to show that "a printed publication" cannot include two or more printed publications.[9]

* * *

As to what the law has been, more particularly what it was prior to 1953, when the new patent act and its section 103 became effective, there is a paucity of direct precedents on the precise problem. We think there is a reason for this. Under the old law (R.S. § 4886, where 102(b) finds its origin) patents were refused or invalidated on references dated more than a year before the filing date because the invention was anticipated or, if they were not, then *because there was no "invention,"* the latter rejection being based either on (a) a single nonanticipatory reference plus the skill of the art *or (b) on a plurality of references.* There was no need to seek out the precise statutory basis because it was R.S. § 4886 in any event, read in the light of the Supreme Court's interpretation of the law that there must always be "invention." This issue was determined on the disclosures of the references relied on and if they had dates more than one year before the filing date, it was assumed they could be relied on to establish a "statutory bar." There was an express prohibition in Rule 131 and in its predecessor Rule 75 against antedating a reference having a date more than a year prior to the filing date and there was no basis on which to contest it. The accepted state of law is exemplified by the following sentences in McCrady's Patent Office Practice, 4th ed. (1959), Sec. 127, p. 176:

> "Prior art specified by 35 U.S.C. § 102, which has an effective date more than one year prior to the effective filing date of an application, constitutes a bar under the language of that statute. Until 1940 the period was two years.

* * *

9. The construction of section 102(b) is subject to the provision of 1 U.S.C. § 1 which provides in pertinent part:

"In determining the meaning of any Act of Congress, unless the context indi-

cates otherwise—words importing the singular include and apply to several persons, parties, or things; * * *.

"Procedurally, the significance of the statutory bar lies in the fact that it cannot be antedated by evidence of applicant's earlier invention, as by affidavits under Rule 131, or by evidence presented in an infringement suit."

Our decision in Palmquist [Application of Palmquist, 319 F.2d 547] appears to have been the first to hold otherwise.

* * *

It would seem that the practical operation of the prior law was that references having effective dates more than a year before applicant's filing date were always considered to be effective as references, regardless of the applicant's date of invention, and that rejections were then predicated thereon for "lack of invention" without making the distinction which we now seem to see as implicit in sections 102 and 103, "anticipation" or no novelty situations under 102 and "obviousness" situations under 103. But on further reflection, we now feel bound to point out that of equal importance is the question of *loss of right* predicated on a one-year *time-bar* which, it seems clear to us, has never been limited to "anticipation" situations, involving only a single reference, but has included as well "no invention" (now "obviousness") situations. It follows that where the time bar is involved, *the actual date of invention becomes irrelevant* and that it is not in accordance with either the letter or the principle of the law, or its past interpretation over a very long period, to permit an applicant to dispose of a reference having a date more than one year prior to his filing date by proving his actual date of invention.

Such a result was permitted by our decision in Palmquist and to the extent that it permitted a reference, having a publication date more than one year prior to the United States filing date to which the applicant was entitled, to be disposed of by proof of a date of invention earlier than the date of the reference, that decision is hereby overruled.

* * *

Since we must reject Foster's contention that he can dispose entirely of Binder by showing an earlier invention date, it becomes necessary for us to consider whether there was a loss of right to a patent, i.e., whether the invention became obvious to the public at the time of the Binder publication. Appellant has fully argued this issue in his briefs.

* * *

[The Court found that the invention became obvious at the time of the Binder publication.]

We, accordingly, reverse the decision of the Board of Appeals with regard to claims 22, 23, 25, 26, 28, 34 and 35. The rejection of claims 12, 13, 17, 18, 29, 30, 33, 36, 39 and 40 having been affirmed because the appellant has lost his right to these claims, the decision is modified.

Modified.

WORLEY, CHIEF JUDGE (concurring).

NOTES

1. The casenote on Palmquist (the decision overruled in Foster) at 32 Geo. Wash.L.Rev. 656 concludes as follows:

"An interpretation of § 103 which will encompass the one-year statutory bar clearly is possible in view of legislative and case history. The phrase 'at the time the invention was made' apparently was inserted to establish a fictional consideration of an invention before it was disclosed to the Patent Office. However, the fiction does not stop there; the artificial period 'at the time the invention was made' is coupled with a second fiction, 'the prior art.' The 'prior art' as used in § 103 was intended to encompass the type of prior art set forth in § 102. The 'prior art' has been interpreted to include copending applications which were not public knowledge 'at the time the invention was made,' but of which the inventor is fictionally apprised. Furthermore, an applicant's own public use more than a year before his filing date and references uncovered in an interference are considered prior art. Even under § 103, prior art published more than a year before applicant's filing date is entitled to greater weight than recent prior art.

"Further, events subsequent to invention may bar an applicant's opportunity to obtain a patent, as when his invention becomes obvious to those skilled in the art through his or another's disclosure. This bar arises from lack of diligence in filing a patent application, and the public reliance upon the knowledge obtained relative to the invention. The 'prior art' therefore may include all public knowledge subsequent to invention limited only by a period of grace one year prior to the filing of a patent application. This interpretation of the statutory one-year bar as applicable equally to §§ 102(b) and 103 appears preferable to the creation of a basic distinction between the two sections.

"The policy which requires a prospective patentee to contribute to the state of the art and proceed diligently does not distinguish between an invention placed in the public domain fully disclosed in a reference and one obvious to those skilled in the art. Indeed, the distinction between a complete anticipation and a difference merely obvious to those skilled in the art might approach the trivial. There appears to be no sound reason to cast the former as a statutory bar capable of cutting off an applicant's rights while allowing the latter, regardless of its date, to be removed as a reference by affidavit." Id. at 662–63.

2. Section 102(b) requires a printed publication. In In re Bayer, 568 F.2d 1357 (CCPA 1978), the question was whether the inventor's master's thesis became a printed publication as of the date it was deposited with the University library or the date on which it was catalogued and made accessible on the library shelves. The court held that it was the date the thesis became available to the public.

3. *Hazeltine* held that the items described in § 102(e) are prior art. *Foster* held that the items described in § 102(b) are prior art. That left the question whether "an invention * * * made by another * * * who has not abandoned, suppressed, or concealed it" (§ 102(g)) is prior art. In Application of Bass, 474 F.2d 1276 (CCPA 1973), the court said that it is. The *Bass* construction had the advantage of statutory symmetry—all subsections in § 102 dealing

with novelty were treated as defining a form of prior art for purposes of § 103. But the implication of that reading was that secret inventions of others unknown to the "art" and unknown to the inventor were nevertheless prior art. The court retreated from that implication of Bass by suggesting in In re Clemens, 622 F.2d 1029, 1039–40 (CCPA 1980), that Bass did not operate where the inventor did not know of the work of others. That took care of the secret inventions of others, but created a difficult problem in the management of laboratories. If co-researchers working on related problems communicated with each other about their work, then there was the danger that their work would become prior art, each to the other. Thus a large industrial laboratory with a sophisticated staff doing work at a level far above that of the "art" in general might find that none of the work of its employees was patentable because as to an invention by any one employee, the inventions of all the other employees would be prior art. See Kimberly-Clark Corp. v. Johnson & Johnson, 745 F.2d 1437 (Fed.Cir.1984), where the prior art considered in connection with a Kimberly-Clark patent on a sanitary napkin structure was work by other technicians employed by Kimberly-Clark. That problem could be solved under *Clemens* by forbidding the employees to tell each other about their work, but then the gains from sharing information within the laboratory would be lost and the employer might find itself paying separate research teams each to rediscover what other of its employees already knew. In *Kimberly-Clark* the court rejected the notion that knowledge of the invention was required under § 102(g), since the section doesn't mention it. 745 F.2d 1445. Then, in dictum, it suggested disaffection with *Bass*. "[T]he use of * * * secret art—as § 103 'prior art'—except as required by § 102(e), is not favored for reasons of public policy." 745 F.2d 1446. The Court, however, followed both *Bass* and *Kimberly-Clark* in E.I. DuPont de Nemours & Co. v. Phillips Petroleum Co., 849 F.2d 1430 (Fed.Cir.1988).

The problems created by this doctrine for research management led Congress to add the last sentence of present § 103 in the Patent Law Amendments of 1984, P.L. 98–622: "Subject matter developed by another person, which qualifies as prior art only under subsection (f) or (g) of section 102 of this title, shall not preclude patentability under this section where the subject matter and the claimed invention were, at the time the invention was made, owned by the same person or subject to an obligation of assignment to the same person." Doesn't this amendment codify *Bass* when the "subject matter and the claimed invention" are not commonly owned?

H. FIRST INVENTOR   102(g)

Title 35 § 102(g) provides that "[a] person shall be entitled to a patent unless before the applicant's invention thereof the invention was made in this country by another who had not abandoned, suppressed, or concealed it." Questions of priority most frequently arise in the context of interference proceedings under 35 U.S.C. § 135. In an interference proceeding the Patent Office determines which of two or more applicants claiming the same invention is entitled to the patent. But questions of priority are equally important in infringement cases, for proof that the patentee was not the first inventor invalidates the patent.

It is important to note that prior invention must be prior invention in the United States. Aside from the narrow exception created by the last sentence of 35 U.S.C. § 104, prior inventive acts must have taken place within the United States. For instance in O'Reilly v. Morse, 56 U.S. (15 How.) 62 (1853), the Court disregarded proof of prior inventions by several Europeans partly on the ground that they were foreign inventions. Other aspects of the *Morse* opinion appear supra page 795. Does knowledge by a person in the United States of an invention that has been made abroad anticipate? In the space era the requirement has led to some difficulties not anticipated by the statutory draftsmen. See Robert F. Kempf, Reduction to Practice of Space Inventions, 50 J.P. O.S. 105 (1968).

The "hornbook" rule of priority can be stated with relative ease:

The first inventor is (a) the person who first conceived of the invention and who from the time *of* the entry into the "field" of any other person claiming to be the first inventor was diligent in his efforts to reduce his invention to practice or, if no such person exists, (b) the person who first reduced the invention to practice.

Definition of reduction to practice: An invention can be reduced to practice either by actually making it and demonstrating its operability or by filing a patent application which adequately discloses under 35 U.S.C. § 112 how to make and practice the invention. Reduction to practice by filing is called constructive reduction to practice.

In 1990 the Inventions in Outer Space Act added a new § 105 to Title 35 that provides in essence that outer space on U.S. space vehicles is part of the United States "for purposes of this title".

(1) INTERFERENCE PRACTICE

Interferences in the Patent Office are decided by the Board of Patent Appeals and Interferences 37 C.F.R. § 1.201(a). An interference can arise in two ways. First, an Examiner who becomes aware of two applications covering the same subject matter can suggest a common claim to each of the applicants under Rule 203(b), 37 C.F.R. § 1.203(b). The applicants must both adopt the suggested claim if they desire the interference, and if they do not adopt the claim they are taken to have disclaimed the invention covered by the suggested claim. Second, an applicant who becomes aware of an issued patent (or in rare instances a pending application) covering the same subject matter as his application can copy claims from the issued patent. The Patent Office policy is that:

"If doubts exist as to whether there is an interference, an interference should not be declared." U.S. Patent and Trademark Office, Manual of Patent Examining Procedure § 2301.01(f) (5th ed. 1983, rev. 1989).

(2) REDUCTION TO PRACTICE

In Sydeman v. Thoma, 32 App.D.C. 362 (1909), the court said:

"Decisions involving this often-litigated question of actual reduction to practice may be divided into three general classes. The first class includes devices so simple and of such obvious efficacy that the complete construction of one of a size and form intended for and capable of practical use is held sufficient without test in actual use. Mason v. Hepburn, 13 App.D.C. 86, 89. * * * The second class consists of those where a machine embodying every essential element of the invention, having been tested and its practical utility for the intended purpose demonstrated to reasonable satisfaction, has been held to have been reduced to practice notwithstanding it may not be a mechanically perfect machine. In other words, it is sufficient reduction to practice, although a more desirable commercial result may be obtained by some simple and obvious mechanical improvement, or by substituting another well-known material for the one used in the original construction, as, for example, metal for wood, cast metal for sheet metal, and the like. * * * The third class includes those where the machine is of such a character that the particular use for which it is intended must be given special consideration, and requires satisfactory operation in the actual execution of the object.

"In cases falling within the second and third classes described, long delay in putting the machine in actual use for the intended purpose has always been regarded as a potent circumstance in determining whether the test was successful, or only an abandoned experiment."

LAND v. REGAN

United States Court of Customs and Patent Appeals, 1965.
342 F.2d 92.

Interference

Worley, Chief Judge. Land and Morse, junior party in Interference No. 90,976, appeal from the decision of the Board of Patent Interferences awarding priority of invention to Regan, Lincoln and Hanson, the senior party.

The invention relates to a photomechanical reproduction process for producing a master copy of an original document for use in printing further copies, as defined in the single count:

"2. A process comprising the steps of applying to a photoexposed silver halide stratum and a superposed hydrophilic, water-receptive, silver-receptive stratum which contains nuclei for precipitation of silver from a water-soluble silver complex, an aqueous alkaline solution of a silver halide developer and a silver halide solvent, reducing the exposed silver halide in the silver halide stratum to silver, forming from unreduced silver halide in the silver halide stratum a water-soluble silver complex, diffusing the complex to the silver-receptive stratum, producing from the complex in conjunction with said nuclei a visible image on the silver-receptive stratum, said image having first areas that contain silver concentrated primarily at the surface of said silver-receptive stratum in thin but substantially continuous, oleophilic dense masses and second areas that are substantially silver-free, thereafter stripping the silver halide stratum from the silver-receptive stratum coating said silver-receptive stratum, with an ink which will preferentially wet said first areas, and pressing the image onto a copy sheet in order to transfer said ink thereto."

We find the following portion of Regan's brief which describes both the photomechanical reproduction process known as lithography and the process of the count to be helpful toward understanding the issues and subject matter involved in this appeal:

"In lithographic reproduction, use is made of a lithographic master or plate having a hydrophilic,[3] water receptive, ink repellent surface that is imaged with an ink receptive, water repellent material. In the copy process, the imaged plate is first wet with an aqueous medium followed by application of a greasy ink composition. The aqueous medium only wets out the non-imaged portions of the master which are hydrophilic or water receptive. When the imaged master is subsequently treated with the greasy ink composition, the ink is repelled by the wet, non-imaged portions of the plate and received only by the unwetted ink receptive imaged portions of the plate.

"When the plate thereafter is brought into contact with an offset blanket (in offset printing) or copy sheets (in direct printing), ink composition transfers from the inked portions of the plate and not from the uninked, non-imaged portions of the plate thereby to produce inked reproductions or copy of the image that is formed on the plate. The wetting and inking operations can be repeated any number of times for multiple copy reproduction.

"The critical relationship for the production of copy by lithography is the maintenance of a high contrast between the ink receptivity and water repellency of the imaged portions as compared to the hydrophilic, water receptivity and ink repellency of the non-imaged portions of the plate whereby the aqueous medium goes only to the non-imaged portions while the ink goes only to the imaged portions of the plate.

3. Hackh's Chemical Dictionary (3rd Edition, 1944) defines "hydrophilic" as "describing a substance which absorbs or absorbs water," and "hydrophile" as "A substance, usually in the colloidal state or an emulsion, which is wetted by water, that is: attracts water or water adheres to it."

"In the practice of the invention covered by the count in interference, a negative having a silver halide in a colloid coating is exposed to an original. The exposed negative is then brought into surface contact with a master, defined as a receiving sheet having a *hydrophilic, water receptive* stratum which contains nuclei for precipitation of silver. The exposed negative is wet with a developing solution containing a silver halide developer and a silver halide solvent which operates to convert the exposed silver halide in the negative to silver while the unreacted silver halide in the unexposed portions of the negative are dissolved and formed into a complex which then transfers by diffusion from the negative to the silver receptive stratum of the master wherein the nuclei functions to reduce the complex to a silver image on the master.

"The important discovery that is represented by the count is that, when the diffusion transfer process is carried out on a receiving sheet in which the silver receptive stratum has a *hydrophilic water receptive* surface, the silver image that is formed by diffusion transfer of silver halide from the unexposed portions of the negative is highly ink receptive and water repellent, while the unsilvered non-imaged portions of the plate remain hydrophilic and water receptive thereby to provide the necessary contrast between the water repellent, ink receptive silver image and the hydrophilic, water receptive, and ink repellent non-imaged or non-silvered portions of the plate. To achieve the desired contrast, it is desirable that the silver in the imaged portions be concentrated primarily at the surface in thin but substantially continuous oleophilic dense masses while the non-imaged portions of the plate are substantially free of silver."

Regan took no testimony and is accordingly restricted to his filing date of March 31, 1955, for conception and constructive reduction to practice. Land makes no claim of diligence from a date prior to Regan's filing date until his own filing date. The principal issue before us, therefore, is whether Land has proved by a preponderance of the evidence that he reduced the invention to practice prior to Regan's filing date. Land stipulated the direct testimony of his witnesses and introduced several exhibits to show actual reduction to practice in September-October 1954. Five of those witnesses were cross-examined on Regan's behalf:

Miss Meroe Morse—coapplicant and manager of black-and-white photographic research, Polaroid Corp.

Miss Elizabeth Yankowski—laboratory technician.

Eugene Emerson—physicist.

Frederick Binda—laboratory assistant.

Frank Martin—asst. manager of black-and-white photographic research.

The board, in considering the testimony of those witnesses in its relation to each of the process steps and results which must be proved to establish Land's contention that the invention was reduced to practice in September and October 1954, regarded the last step of the count, viz. pressing the image onto a copy sheet in order to transfer ink thereto, "as important as all the remainder combined, for it is necessary for Land to prove * * * that the result was a useful one and satisfied the goals laid out by or for Land in performing the experiments." It devoted a large portion of its opinion to a summary of the testimony it considered on that aspect of the case, saying:

"* * * Miss Morse identified as Exhibit 3 * * * a notebook containing work performed by Mrs. Johnson, as Exhibit 4 a notebook containing a great deal of other work * * * and testified that

"'she was particularly pleased with the work of Mrs. Johnson and considered her experiments completely indicative of the commercial applicability of the process in photomechanical reproduction.'

"Mrs. Johnson * * * did not confirm or corroborate her satisfaction or that of Miss Morse concerning the results * * *. She * * * did not testify that reasonably good results were attained with any degree of consistency or that any knowledge of how to attain such results * * * accrued from her experiments. The failure to follow through with other work between the date of the experiments (September and October 1954) and the patent application (July 22, 1955) gives credence to Regan's theory that the opposite was the case. * * *

"Miss Elizabeth Yankowski was a laboratory technician of longer experience than Mrs. Johnson and was assigned by Miss Morse as an advisor to Mrs. Johnson in this work, which she closely observed. * * * she gave no positive testimony on direct examination that the results of Mrs. Johnson's work were those desired. She did, however, refer * * * to 'the good clear images of excellent contrast' and * * * 'the good ink reproductions affixed in the notebook.'

"On cross examination, Miss Morse referred to a problem called 'silvering', involving packing of the silver in too dense form * * *, and indicated that this phenomenon could prevent satisfactory performance of the process * * *. She did not say whether Mrs. Johnson ran into this problem or fairly solved it in relation to her work on this invention. In referring to the fact that Mrs. Johnson obtained only four copies in her work, Miss Morse testified * * *:

"'I think we were looking for a high quality, * * *.'

and that 'four seemed adequate to demonstrate the quality.' In referring to the ink in the background of Exhibit 3, * * * 'the most successful copies', she admitted that this problem existed and that it might have been caused by 'a trace of silver in the background', and stated that this was 'one of the things we were studying.'   *   *   *

"In response to a question as to whether the copy of Exhibit 3 was 'really satisfactory copy as a commercial operation' she testified *   *   *:

     " 'This is a fine point because as far as the experiment and something *potentially commercially interesting,* I thought it was very exciting. It was exciting *as an experiment* and exciting from the *possibility of being potentially commercial.* If you ask me would I recommend to our sales department that they put on the market something that looked like that—I don't think you would ask such a question.'   *   *   * [Board's emphasis]

*   *   * Miss Yankowski, in responding to a question as to why on some of the exhibits 'the non-imaged portions took ink and the imaged portions did not, ['] answered *   *   *:

     " 'I think it was done under very crude conditions.'

                 *   *   *

"When we refer to the exhibits themselves and relate them to this testimony we conclude that Land's case, viewed in its most favorable light, does not prove that he demonstrated the usefulness of the process prior to Regan's filing date and priority will accordingly be awarded to Regan."

We have quoted almost the entire portion of the board's opinion directed to Land's efforts to establish usefulness of the claimed process in order to present a clear picture of the board's reasoning. We shall now set forth our reasons for concluding the board erred in holding that Land failed to demonstrate the usefulness of the process which was practiced prior to Regan's filing date.

                 *   *   *

Land relies most heavily on experiments performed September 16, 1954, yielding the copies constituting Exhibit 3,[6] as embodying a successful reduction to practice. We have examined those copies, and agree with the characterization of them by Miss Morse:

"XQ188. It shows *   *   * [ink] in the background, does it not, Miss Morse? A. It does show ink. *Nevertheless, it also clearly shows that the experiment was effective and operative.* We

---

6. Exhibit 3 includes a memorandum dated September 16, 1954, from Mrs. Johnson to a Polaroid patent attorney describing how *"the most successful copies were made."* [Emphasis added] The record establishes that the negative silver halide emulsion utilized was a commercially available du-Pont X-ray film known as Fine Grain Industrial-type 506. The aqueous developer solution was coded "0180;" Martin identified that solution as containing hydroquinone as developing agent, sodium hydroxide as alkali, and sodium thiosulfate as silver halide solvent. The silver receptive stratum was coded "RC–2350" and, according to Martin, contained silver sulfide as a silver precipitating agent.

transferred from a silver image made by our technique—we transferred a legible *dense* ink image." [Emphasis supplied]

That testimony, coupled with her statements that she "was particularly pleased with the work of Mrs. Johnson" and that she thought the experiments were "very exciting" and "potentially commercial" convince us that Miss Morse was satisfied with the results of the work.

* * *

This court has said many times that a commercially acceptable embodiment of the invention is not necessary to proof of actual reduction to practice. Tansel v. Higonnet et al., 215 F.2d 457; Schnick v. Fenn, 277 F.2d 935; Creamer v. Kirkwood and Torre, 305 F.2d 486. While the board recognized that performance of a commercially acceptable quality is not necessarily required, its emphasis on Miss Morse's answer to the question whether Exhibit 3 "was really satisfactory as a commercial operation" we think demonstrates, in final analysis, that it did not apply the standard of those cases in analyzing the testimony and exhibits before it. We do not consider the fact that the witnesses stated the process to be "potentially commercial" or "commercially promising" to be any justification for applying the test of whether the process results were *in fact* commercially acceptable in determining the success of the process. We daresay it is the ultimate goal of every inventor to develop a process which is successful in a competitive commercial market. Simply because the ultimate goal—a process of commercial quality—has not been achieved is no reason to conclude that the practicality of the process has not otherwise been demonstrated or that it does not perform the function for which it was designed.

Other evidence which convinces us that Land and Miss Morse were satisfied with the results obtained by Mrs. Johnson is the following statement in their patent application that

"* * * Commercially available, gelatino silver halide emulsions which have been found to produce good results are sold by DuPont under the trade designations 'X-Ray Fine Grain Industrial 506 * * *.' "

That emulsion is the same as used in Exhibit 3 * * *. We do not have here the situation of the embodiments relied on for reduction to practice being different from those specifically disclosed in the application, as was the case in Walkup v. Grieg, 332 F.2d 800.

* * *

The board referred to the fact that Mrs. Johnson obtained *only* four copies in some of her work. We must assume the board regarded that fact as further indication that the results achieved by Land were not successful. If, indeed, the board would require a showing that *many* copies could be obtained from the process, it went far beyond the terms of the count and Land's specification to glean Land's intended purpose. The count requires but one transfer of ink, and Land's specification, in describing the preferred embodiment of his invention, says "In this way, four good copies * * * were produced without reinking." Cf. Conner v. Joris, 241 F.2d 944.

In referring to the ink in the background of Exhibit 3, which Mrs. Johnson termed "the most successful copies," both the board and Regan apparently regarded Miss Morse's testimony that "There may be a trace of silver in the background here which was retaining a trace of ink" and that "This is one of the things we were studying" as further evidence that the process had not been successfully reduced to practice.

We do not agree. A successful reduction to practice does not require perfection or incapability of improvement. Furthermore, the interference count calls for "second areas [background] that are *substantially* silver-free," and coating "with an ink which will *preferentially* wet said first areas [which contain silver in dense masses]." [Emphasis added] That the process of the count was not intended to exclude a trace of silver in the background is evident from the decision of the Primary Examiner who granted motions by both Land and Regan to dissolve the interference as to an earlier count reading "second areas that are silver-free." The examiner said:

> "*Both* parties are in accord that the present count embodies certain language which is inappropriate to a proper description of the invention. The language of the instant count pertaining to the second areas produced in the silver receptive layer as being silver-free is objectionable since apparently *some small amount of silver halide may transfer over from exposed areas of the silver halide stratum.* Moreover, since both parties disclose the use of colloidal silver as silver precipitating nuclei, *manifestly, the second areas are not entirely silver-free.*
> * * *

>   * * *

> "* * * there is a more acceptable term * * * [in the expression] 'substantially'." [Emphasis added]

We believe the results achieved are clearly within the purview of the count.

One further point deserves comment before leaving this aspect of the case. In his brief, Regan places great emphasis on nine of Land's 35 experiments identified as Exhibits 4D1–4D9, all of which show *negative* copies obtained when the ink adhered to the *nonimaged* portions of the master rather than to the silvered portions. Relying on Sherwood v. Drewson, 29 App.D.C. 161; E. I. duPont de Nemours & Co. v. American Cyanamid Co., 120 F.Supp. 697; and Harding v. Steingiser et al., 318 F.2d 748, Regan's position is that Land's experiments as a whole only indicated promise or future fulfillment and that they had not attained a certainty demonstrating the capacity of the invention to produce the desired result.

We think Regan and the board have placed undue emphasis on that minority of exhibits showing poor results and have neglected to accord proper weight to the good results shown in the exhibits. As we noted earlier, Land's experiments were directed to testing the process using a wide variety of materials under different conditions. The mere fact that Exhibits 4D1–4D9 illustrate that tests using some materials under some conditions were not successful does not mitigate the fact that the successful tests do establish with a reasonable certainty or probability that the process will operate in the intended manner.

Regan's argument might have merit if reproducible results with a given combination of negative, processing composition and silver-receptive stratum had not been achieved by Land. See Conner v. Joris, supra. But distributed throughout Land's Exhibit 4 are copies obtained using the same materials employed in producing the copies of Exhibit 3. We find those copies to be equal in quality to Exhibit 3, and note that they were obtained on various dates throughout September and October of 1954. Copies obtained by employing other commercial negatives, e.g. Kodak Fine Grain Positive and duPont Fine Grain Pan, are equally as good. The record does not support the board's finding that reasonably good results were not obtained with any degree of consistency, or that Mrs. Johnson was unable to learn how to repeat her better results.

In short, we regard the pattern of results as a whole to be positive in nature, not negative and erratic, and believe Land has proved by a preponderance of the evidence that the tested process operated satisfactorily.

For the purpose of that portion of its opinion evaluating the results as set forth above, the board assumed that the individual steps performed by Mrs. Johnson conformed to the details recited in the remaining steps of the count. Upon consideration of the testimony on the latter point, it found such conformity had not been proved. In reaching that conclusion, the board granted Regan's motions to strike the testimony of Miss Morse, Mrs. Johnson, Mr. Martin, and Miss Yankowski, directed to establishing certain details of the process, "to the extent that we have refused to consider the testimony of these witnesses on these points."

The record shows that 22 times during cross-examination of the above witnesses, Regan's counsel moved to strike their testimony. Those motions were occasioned by instructions to the witnesses from Land's counsel to refuse to answer certain questions on the grounds that (1) the questions were directed to subject matter not relevant and not material to the invention as defined in the count, and (2) answers to the questions would reveal trade secrets and confidential information.

We consider the following colloquy which took place during cross-examination of the witnesses to be exemplary of the proceedings:

"XQ32, 33. In your testimony as to the preparation of Exhibits 3 and 4 * * * what compositions are those? A. [Miss Yankowski] They contain the necessary ingredients, the alkali, the silver halide solvent and the developing agent.

"XQ34. Is that all that was present in those compositions? A. I don't remember. There were probably others *but those were the necessary ones.*

"XQ35. *What are the other ingredients present in those compositions?* [Emphasis added]

"Mr. Isaacs: I am going to object to this question as immaterial, beyond the scope of the direct, and as involving secret and confidential information as to the specific other ingredients, and I therefore instruct the witness not to answer.

"XQ36. Will you answer the question, Miss Yankowski? A. No.

"Mr. Hersh: In the light of the witness' refusal to answer the question, and in the light of her disclosure of only part of the compositions which were employed by her as a basis of her testimony and in the production of Exhibits 3 and 4, and through the experimentation on the subject matter of the application in interference and the count in interference, the senior party is unable to either prove or disprove the testimony of this witness and therefore, is incapable of conducting proper cross examination, and is also incapable of taking rebuttal testimony to prove or disprove the statements of this witness. In the light of our inability to cross examine fully and completely, I move to strike the testimony of this witness, and particularly her testimony with respect to the essential description of the compositions employed by her or by Mrs. Johnson or by Miss Morse in the experimentation. This is withholding critical and essential evidence.

* * *

"XQ123. In paragraph 22 of your stipulated testimony you state that the developing compositions were formulated to contain hydroquinone, sodium hydroxide, and sodium thiosulfate; do you know this of your own knowledge? A. [Miss Yankowski] Yes.

"XQ124. *What else did they contain?* [Emphasis added]

"Mr. Isaacs: * * * [Objection]

* * *

"Mr. Hersh: * * * [Motion to strike]"

Similar objections and motions to strike were made when Martin, after explaining that the silver-receptive stratum RC–2350 contained silver sulfide as silver precipitating nuclei, was questioned as to "what other materials were present" in addition to the silver sulfide.

The board stated:

" * * * the refusal to answer questions directly related to the process details, which might have enabled Regan to disprove

Land's contentions by rebuttal or further cross-examination or might have enabled Regan and this Board to judge whether the conclusions of Land's witnesses were in fact well founded, leaves us no alternative except to ignore the testimony * * * on these points (See Kelly v. Park et al., 1897 C.D. 182; Miller v. Kelley, 1901 C.D. 405; Rinehart v. Gibson, 1912 C.D. 587 [sic: 387]; Rogers v. Willoughby and Lowell [1 F.2d 824] 55 App.D.C. 65, 1924 C.D. 342; and 98 Corpus Juris Secundum [Witnesses], paragraph 381 page 141) * * *. * * * refusal to answer questions as to composition pertinent to the direct examination effectively vitiates the examination process. * * * the testimony withheld was necessary to fill out critical information, and might well have confirmed or refuted Land's contentions in support of the counts. * * * "

The testimony sought by Regan was, in the board's judgment, "both relevant and material."

We have examined all of the testimony, as the board must necessarily have done in reaching its conclusion. In relating that testimony to the count, we observe initially that the process steps set forth in the count are recited in broad terms. The negative utilized is a "silver halide stratum;" the developer solution is recited as "an aqueous alkaline solution of a silver halide developer and a silver halide solvent;" and the "silver-receptive stratum" is defined in terms of its "hydrophilic, water-receptive, silver-receptive" properties and as containing "nuclei for precipitation of silver." It is only those materials and properties which the count requires in the operation of the process.

It is apparent from the foregoing that the witnesses did not withhold information directly material and relevant to the issues defined by the count. The witnesses had already testified specifically as to all the actual ingredients and properties called for by the count when Regan, on cross-examination, collaterally asked, for example, "What else did * * * [the composition] contain?", and the witnesses refused to answer. We think those refusals insufficient grounds to warrant striking the testimony of the witnesses, recalling that a motion to strike, if granted, renders the evidence *inadmissible*. The four cases cited by the board in support of granting the motions to strike are hardly authority for the action taken. Rather, those cases appear to stand for the proposition that refusal of a witness to answer *pertinent* questions affects the *weight* to be accorded the testimony of the witness. Our further consideration of Land's testimony directed to establishing reduction to practice of the remaining steps of the count will be on the basis that all of the testimony is admissible in evidence because of its obvious material and relevant nature. The refusal of the witnesses to answer Regan's questions will be accorded appropriate significance in our determination of its probative value, credibility and weight.[8]

8. The view we take of this case renders it unnecessary to consider whether the questions propounded by Regan on cross-examination were directed to material and relevant subject matter. It should also be readily apparent that this court is not ca-

To establish a reduction to practice of the process steps of the count, Land has the burden of establishing by sufficient credible testimony that the limitations as to materials, properties, steps, and results required by the count were present in the work performed by Mrs. Johnson and Miss Yankowski in September and October of 1954. Unlike the board, we are satisfied that Land has proven by a preponderance of the evidence the hydrophilic character of the silver-receptive stratum, the presence of nuclei for precipitation of silver, the recited constituents of the developer composition, the specific mechanism of silver diffusion and precipitation, the concentration of the silver at the surface of the master, the substantial freedom from silver of the non-imaged areas, and the preferential wetting of the imaged (silvered) areas by the ink.

* * *

Our study of the entire record in light of Regan's arguments convinces us that the process practiced by Land and his associates in September and October of 1954 conformed to the limitations of the count.

The decision is reversed.

NOTES

1. The *Land* case dramatizes the role of the claim in the issue of reduction to practice. It is the *claim* that must have been practiced. By drafting a claim so that it centers on those features of the invention achieved by the applicant at an early date, the patent attorney can give his client an advantage in a priority dispute. The advantage of choosing the most favorable ground will usually accrue to a senior party in an interference because most interferences occur when the junior party copies the senior's claim and adds it to his application.

2. When is a claim for a new compound reduced to practice? When the compound is made? When a use for the compound is discovered? The CCPA has regularly held that the reduction to practice is not achieved until the use is discovered. See, e.g., Archer v. Papa, 265 F.2d 954 (CCPA 1959). This conclusion is, of course, reinforced by Brenner v. Manson, 383 U.S. 519 (1966), supra page 841.

3. The *Brenner* case itself arose out of the refusal of the Patent Office to declare an interference, a fact little noted in the opinion of the Court. The reason for the refusal was that since Manson alleged no utility he could not show prior reduction to practice. See 333 F.2d at 235. The CCPA reversed on the ground that the successful practice of a process to make a useless compound was reduction to practice of the process. Application of Manson, 333 F.2d 234 (CCPA 1964). The distinction between a patent on a useless product and a patent to make a useless product, ridiculed by the Court in Brenner v. Manson, is difficult to support under 35 U.S.C. § 101. But it might be supported by the requirements of 35 U.S.C. § 112. An application, in order to be a constructive reduction to practice, must comply with the requirements of § 112. One of these is that the application disclose "how to use" the claimed invention. One

pable, on this record, to determine the validity of Land's second ground for refusal to answer Regan's allegedly material questions, that of privilege arising from trade secrets.

can use a process to make a useless product, but not the product itself since, by assumption, no use is disclosed.

PROBLEMS

1. A claim is for stops on gates of hydraulic turbines placed so as not to interfere with the normal opening and closing of the gates but so as to prevent the movement of the gates into the turbine blades if the controls on the gates fail. A turbine embodying the invention was constructed and the stops were tested in the shop by manually swinging the gates from open to closed position very violently. The forces involved in the manual testing were substantially less than those that would be experienced under operating conditions upon failure of the controls. The controls on the turbine have never failed in operation and thus the stops have never been brought into play. The stops were engineered to withstand very large forces, but the forces that would be experienced upon failure of the controls cannot be calculated with assured accuracy. Was the claim reduced to practice (1) when the turbine was built, (2) when the gates were swung in the shop, (3) when the turbine was installed, (4) when the patent application was filed? See White v. Syvertsen, 46 F.2d 364 (CCPA 1931). See also Elmore v. Schmitt, 278 F.2d 510 (CCPA 1960) ("Bench" tests of binary counter held: not reduction to practice where it was not proven that the bench tests reproduced conditions that would be encountered in any practical use of the invention.). Was the Land patent practiced under conditions of practical use? Is it important that the *White* and *Elmore* cases involved patents on a machine rather than a process?

2. Can an applicant for a patent on a compound overcome a publication prior to his filing date which discloses the structure of the compound but no utility for the compound by showing only that he had discovered the structure of the compound prior to the publication? See Application of Moore, 444 F.2d 572 (CCPA 1971).

(3) BURDEN OF PROOF

The application of the priority rules involves factual questions of considerable difficulty which must often be decided on the basis of the testimony of an interested party. Thus the burden of proof rules are of particular importance. In an interference the party first to file is called the senior party, the other party the junior party. If the junior party filed before the issuance of the senior party's patent, then the junior party must prove priority by a preponderance of the evidence. If the junior party filed after the issuance of a patent to the senior party then the junior party must prove priority beyond a reasonable doubt. The Patent Office will not award priority to a junior party on the basis of the junior applicant's uncorroborated testimony. For a striking application of that principle see Bainbridge v. Walton, 104 F.2d 808 (CCPA 1939).

Note that any application filed more than one year after the issuance of the senior patent is blocked by the time bar, 35 U.S.C. § 102(b). Furthermore, any claim filed more than one year after the issuance of a patent claiming the same subject matter is barred by 35

U.S.C. § 135(b), even if the claim is a proper amendment to a pending application entitled to an earlier filing date.

The applicable burden of proof on the issue of anticipation in an infringement proceeding is not clear because the Supreme Court has not faced the issue. The best available statement is Cardozo's:

> "A patent regularly issued, and even more obviously a patent issued after a hearing of all the rival claimants, is presumed to be valid until the presumption has been overcome by convincing evidence of error. The force of that presumption has found varying expression in this and other courts. Sometimes it is said that in a suit for infringement, when the defense is a prior invention, "the burden of proof to make good this defense' is 'upon the party setting it up,' and 'every reasonable doubt should be resolved against him.' * * *
>
> "Again it is said that 'the presumption of the validity of the patent is such that the defense of invention by another must be established by the clearest proof—perhaps beyond reasonable doubt.' * * * The context suggests that in these and like phrases the courts were not defining a standard in terms of scientific accuracy or literal precision, but were offering counsel and suggestion to guide the course of judgment. Through all the verbal variances, however, there runs this common core of thought and truth, that one otherwise an infringer who assails the validity of a patent fair upon its face bears a heavy burden of persuasion, and fails unless his evidence has more than a dubious preponderance." Radio Corp. of America v. Radio Engineering Laboratories, Inc., 293 U.S. 1, 7–8 (1934).

PROBLEMS

1. *X* and *Y* are involved in an interference. They settle their differences and file a copy of their agreement as required by 35 U.S.C. § 135(c). Under the terms of the settlement *X* concedes that *Y's* patent is valid. In a suit for infringement by *Y* against *A*, a third party, can *A* defend on the ground that the patent is invalid because *X* was in fact the first inventor? In a suit for infringement by *Y* against *X*, can *X* defend on that ground?

2. *Y* is issued a patent by the Patent Office. There is no interference. In an action for infringement the defendant proves by "clear and convincing" evidence that he invented the invention two months before *Y's* application date. What is the burden of proof on *Y* if he wishes to rebut the defense by proving that his actual date of invention was one year prior to the application date? Compare Karr v. Botkins Grain & Feed Co., 329 F.Supp. 411, 413 (S.D.Ohio 1970), United Shoe Machinery Corp. v. Brooklyn Wood Heel Corp., 77 F.2d 263, 264 (2d Cir.1935) (Hand, L., J.), Thayer v. Hart, 20 Fed. 693 (S.D.N.Y.1884) ("beyond a reasonable doubt") with Webster Loom Co. v. Higgins, 29 Fed. Cases 563, 567 (S.D.N.Y.1879) ("The burden of proof rests upon the defendants, to show, beyond any fair doubt, the prior knowledge and use set up; but, where they have sustained that burden by showing such knowledge and use prior to

the patent, the burden of showing the still prior invention claimed, by at least a fair balance of proof, must rest upon the plaintiff."). Can Learned Hand be wrong?

(4) CONCEPTION AND DILIGENCE

GRIFFITH v. KANAMARU

United States Court of Appeals, Federal Circuit, 1987.
816 F.2d 624.

NICHOLS, SENIOR CIRCUIT JUDGE.

Owen W. Griffith (Griffith) appeals the decision of the Board of Patent Appeals and Interferences (board) * * * that Griffith failed to establish a prima facie case that he is entitled to an award of priority against the filing date of Tsuneo Kanamaru, et al. (Kanamaru) for a patent on aminocarnitine compounds. We affirm.

Background

This patent interference case involves the application of Griffith, an Associate Professor in the Department of Biochemistry at Cornell University Medical College, for a patent on an aminocarnitine compound, useful in the treatment of diabetes, and a patent issued for the same invention to Kanamaru, an employee of Takeda Chemical Industries. The inventors assigned their rights to the inventions to the Cornell Research Foundation, Inc. (Cornell) and to Takeda Chemical Industries respectively. The technology established by this invention is not at issue in this appeal and is therefore not described further.

Griffith had established conception by June 30, 1981, and reduction to practice on January 11, 1984. Kanamaru filed for a United States patent on November 17, 1982. The board found, however, that Griffith failed to establish reasonable diligence for a prima facie case of prior invention and issued an order to show cause under 37 C.F.R. § 1.617 as to why summary judgment should not be issued.

The board considered the additional evidence submitted by Griffith pursuant to the show cause order and decided that Griffith failed to establish a prima facie case for priority against Kanamaru's filing date. This result was based on the board's conclusion that Griffith's explanation for inactivity between June 15, 1983, and September 13, 1983, failed to provide a legally sufficient excuse to satisfy the "reasonable diligence" requirement of 35 U.S.C. § 102(g). Griffith appeals on the issue of reasonable diligence.

Analysis

I

This is a case of first impression and presents the novel circumstances of a university suggesting that it is reasonable for the public to wait for disclosure until the most satisfactory funding arrangements are made. The applicable law is the "reasonable diligence" standard contained in 35 U.S.C. § 102(g). * * *

Griffith must establish a prima facie case of reasonable diligence, as well as dates of conception and reduction to practice, to avoid summary judgment on the issue of priority. 37 C.F.R. § 1.617(a). As a preliminary matter we note that, although the board focused on the June 1983 to September 1983 lapse in work, and Griffith's reasons for this lapse, Griffith is burdened with establishing a prima facie case of reasonable diligence from immediately before Kanamaru's filing date of November 17, 1982, until Griffith's reduction to practice on January 11, 1984. 35 U.S.C. § 102(g); 37 C.F.R. § 1.617(a).

On appeal, Griffith presents two grounds intended to justify his inactivity on the aminocarnitine project between June 15, 1983, and September 13, 1983. The first is that, notwithstanding Cornell University's extraordinary endowment, it is reasonable, and as a policy matter desirable, for Cornell to require Griffith and other research scientists to obtain funding from outside the university. The second reason Griffith presents is that he reasonably waited for Ms. Debora Jenkins to matriculate in the Fall of 1983 to assist with the project. He had promised her she should have that task which she needed to qualify for her degree. We reject these arguments and conclude that Griffith has failed to establish grounds to excuse his inactivity prior to reduction to practice.

II

The reasonable diligence standard balances the interest in rewarding and encouraging invention with the public's interest in the earliest possible disclosure of innovation. * * * Griffith must account for the entire period from just before Kanamaru's filing date until his reduction to practice. * * * As one of our predecessor courts has noted:

> Public policy favors the early disclosure of inventions. This underlies the requirement for "reasonable diligence" in reducing an invention to practice, not unlike the requirement that, to avoid a holding of suppression or concealment, there be no unreasonable delay in filing an application once there has been a reduction to practice.

Naber v. Cricchi, 567 F.2d 382, 385 n. 5 (CCPA 1977), cert. denied, 439 U.S. 826 (1978) (citation omitted).

The board in this case was, but not properly, asked to pass judgment on the reasonableness of Cornell's policy regarding outside funding of research. The correct inquiry is rather whether it is reasonable for Cornell to require the public to wait for the innovation, given the well settled policy in favor of early disclosure. As the board notes, Chief Judge Markey has called early public disclosure the "linchpin of the patent system." *Horwath v. Lee*, 564 F.2d 948, 950 (CCPA 1977). A review of caselaw on excuses for inactivity in reduction to practice reveals a common thread that courts may consider the reasonable everyday problems and limitations encountered by an inventor. See, e.g., Bey v. Kollonitsch, 806 F.2d 1024 (Fed.Cir.1986) (delay in filing excused where attorney worked on a group of related applications and other applications contributed substantially to the preparation of Bey's application); Reed v. Tornqvist, 436 F.2d 501 (CCPA 1971) (concluding it is not unreasonable for inventor to delay completing a patent application until after returning from a three week vacation in Sweden, extended by illness of inventor's father); Keizer v. Bradley, 270 F.2d 396 (CCPA 1959) (delay excused where inventor, after producing a component for a color television, delayed filing to produce an appropriate receiver for testing the component); Courson v. O'Connor, 227 F. 890, 894 (7th Cir.1915) ("exercise of reasonable diligence * * * does not require an inventor to devote his entire time thereto, or to abandon his ordinary means of livelihood"); De Wallace v. Scott, 15 App.D.C. 157 (1899) (where applicant made bona fide attempts to perfect his invention, applicant's poor health, responsibility to feed his family, and daily job demands excused his delay in reducing his invention to practice); Texas Co. v. Globe Oil & Refining Co., 112 F.Supp. 455 (N.D. Ill.1953) (delay in filing application excused because of confusion relating to war).

Griffith argues that the admitted inactivity of three months between June 15, 1983, and September 13, 1983, which he attributes to Cornell's "reasonable" policy requiring outside funding and to Griffith's "reasonable" decision to delay until a graduate student arrived, falls within legal precedent excusing inactivity in the diligence context. We disagree. We first note that, in regard to waiting for a graduate student, Griffith does not even suggest that he faced a genuine shortage of personnel. He does not suggest that Ms. Jenkins was the only person capable of carrying on with the aminocarnitine experiment. We can see no application of precedent to suggest that the convenience of the timing of the semester schedule justifies a three-month delay for the purpose of reasonable diligence. Neither do we believe that this excuse, absent even a suggestion by Griffith that Jenkins was uniquely qualified to do his research, is reasonable.

Griffith's second contention that it was reasonable for Cornell to require outside funding, therefore causing a delay in order to apply for such funds, is also insufficient to excuse his inactivity. The crux of Griffith's argument is that outside funding is desirable as a form of peer review, or monitoring of the worthiness of a given project. He also suggests that, as a policy matter, universities should not be treated as businesses, which ultimately would detract from scholarly inquiry. Griffith states that these considerations, if accepted as valid, would fit within the scope of the caselaw excusing inactivity for "reasonable" delays in reduction to practice and filing.

These contentions on delay do not fit within the texture and scope of the precedent cited by the parties or discussed in this opinion. Griffith argues this case is controlled by the outcome of Litchfield v.

Eigen, 535 F.2d 72 (CCPA 1976). We disagree. In Litchfield, Judge Rich held that the inventors failed to establish due diligence because of their inactivity between April 1964 and September 1965. The court based this conclusion on the finding that the inventors possessed the capacity to test the invention and chose instead to test other compounds. Judge Rich did not reach the issue of the alleged budgetary limitations imposed by the sponsor and stated that the inventors failed to show any evidence of such financial limitations and that, therefore, the court could not consider this contention.

Griffith's excuses sound more in the nature of commercial development, not accepted as an excuse for delay, than the "hardship" cases most commonly found and discussed supra. Delays in reduction to practice caused by an inventor's efforts to refine an invention to the most marketable and profitable form have not been accepted as sufficient excuses for inactivity. D. Chisum, Patents § 10.07(2) at 10–122 & n. 4 (1986) (citations omitted). Griffith's case is analogous to that in Seeberger v. Dodge, 24 App.D.C. 476 (1905). In that case, the inventor was the first to conceive of an improvement in an escalator and was attempting to show diligence. The court noted:

> The testimony shows that he (Seeberger) was a man of means, and might have constructed an escalator had he undertaken to do so. Instead of this, his constant effort was to organize corporations, or to interest capital in other ways, for the purpose of engaging in the general manufacture of escalators.

Id. at 484–85.

The court held this unacceptable:

> One having the first complete conception of an invention cannot hold the field against all comers by diligent efforts, merely, to organize and procure sufficient capital to engage in the manufacture of his device or mechanism for commercial purposes. This is a different thing from diligence in actual reduction to practice.

Id. at 485 (citation omitted).

The comparison we draw is that Cornell University, like Seeberger, has made a clear decision against funding Griffith's project in order to avoid the risks and distractions, albeit different in each case, that would result from directly financing these inventions. Griffith has placed in the record, and relies on, an able article by President Bok of Harvard, Business and the Academy, *Harvard Magazine,* May–June 1981, 31. Bok is explaining the policy issues respecting academic funding of scientific research, for the benefit of Harvard's alumni who must, of course, make up by their contributions the University's annual deficit. While much academic research could produce a profit, pursuit of such profit may be business inappropriate for a university though it would be right and proper for a commercial organization. For example, it might produce conflicts between the roles of scientists as inventors and developers against their roles as members of the university faculty. However large the university's endowment may be, it may be better to enlist private funding and let this source of funds develop the commercial utilization of any invention as perhaps, the beneficial owner. If there is a patent, the source of funds may end up [as] assignee of the patent. It seems also implicit in this policy choice that faculty members may not be allowed single-minded pursuit of reduction to practice whenever they conceive some idea of value, and at times the rights of other inventors may obtain a priority that a single-minded pursuit would have averted. Bok says diligent reduction to practice, to satisfy the patent laws, may interfere with a faculty member's other duties. Bok is asking the approval of his alumni, not of the courts. The management of great universities is one thing, at least, the courts have not taken over and do not deem themselves qualified to undertake. Bok does not ask that the patent laws or other intellectual property law be skewed or slanted to enable the university to have its cake and eat it too, *i.e.*, to act in a noncommercial manner and yet preserve the pecuniary rewards of commercial exploitation for itself.

If, as we are asked to assume, Cornell also follows the policy Bok has so well articulated, it seems evident that Cornell has consciously chosen to assume the risk that priority in the invention might be lost to an outside inventor, yet, having chosen a noncommercial policy, it asks us to save it the property that would have inured to it if it had acted in single-minded pursuit of gain.

III

The board in this case considered primarily Griffith's contention that the Cornell policy was reasonable and therefore acceptable to excuse his delay in reduction to practice. Although we agree with the board's conclusion, it is appropriate to go further and consider other circumstances as they apply to the reasonable diligence analysis of 35 U.S.C. § 102(g). The record reveals that from the relevant period of November 17, 1982 (Kanamaru's filing date), to September 13, 1983 (when Griffith renewed his efforts towards reduction to practice), Griffith interrupted and often put aside the aminocarnitine project to work on other experiments. Between June 1982 and June 1983 Griffith admits that, at the request of the chairman of his department, he was primarily engaged in an unrelated research project on mitochondrial glutathione metabolism. Griffith also put aside the aminocarnitine experiment to work on a grant proposal on an unrelated project. Griffith's statement in the record that his unrelated grant application, if granted, might "support" a future grant request directed to the aminocarnitine project does not overcome the conclusion that he preferred one project over another and was not "continuously" or "reasonably" diligent. Griffith made only minimal efforts to secure funding directly for the aminocarnitine project.

The conclusion we reach from the record is that the aminocarnitine project was second and often third priority in laboratory research as well as the solicitation of funds. We agree that Griffith failed to establish a prima facie case of reasonable diligence or a legally sufficient excuse for inactivity to establish priority over Kanamaru.

Conclusion

Griffith has failed to establish a *prima facie* case of "reasonable diligence" to establish grounds for the award of priority as against Kanamaru's filing date.

Affirmed.

NOTES

1.   Gould v. Schawlow, 363 F.2d 908 (CCPA 1966), involved an interference on a patent claim for a laser, a device for generating coherent beams of light that has become important in such applications as the compact disc player, which uses a laser beam to read digital information encoded on the disc, or for optical communications, discussed infra page 1029 in Corning Glass Works v. Sumitomo Electric U.S.A., Inc. The senior applicants, Schawlow and Townes, with an application date of July 30, 1958, were an employee of Bell Telephone Laboratories and a consultant to the Laboratories who was also a Professor of Physics at Columbia University. The junior applicant, Gould, was a graduate student at Columbia who had conceived of the laser and made a notebook sketch of its key elements in November of 1957, prior to the Bell Telephone filing date. Gould lost, both on the ground that his notebook sketch was not a sufficiently clear conception and that he was not diligent. Gould's arguments that as a graduate student and later as a technical employee he was not in a position to reduce his invention to practice were rejected. The court pointed out that Gould could simply have filed for a patent without actually constructing the device, and thus obtained a constructive reduction to practice. Gould nevertheless persisted, and obtained some laser patents. See Patlex Corp. Inc. [the assignee of the Gould laser patents] v. Mossinghoff, 585 F.Supp. 713 (E.D. Pa.1983), and Bela A. Lengyel, Evolution of Masers and Lasers, 34 Am.J. Physics 903 (1966). Litigation over the Gould laser patents continues. See Gould v. Control Laser Corp., 866 F.2d 1391 (Fed.Cir.1989).

2.   Rebecca S. Eisenberg, Proprietary Rights and the Norms of Science in Biotechnology Research, 97 Yale L.J. 177 (1987), considers the relationship between the patent system and the norms of basic scientific research.

3.   Because it is impossible to foresee situations in which proof of conception, reasonable diligence and reduction to practice may be needed, the priority rules create incentives for some form of regular record-keeping in research laboratories. One common practice is to have each researcher keep a diary in which he records the results of each days work, and to have the entries witnessed and dated by another person.

PAULIK v. RIZKALLA

United States Court of Appeals, Federal Circuit, 1985.

760 F.2d 1270.

PAULINE NEWMAN, CIRCUIT JUDGE.

This appeal is from the decision of the United States Patent and Trademark Office Board of Patent Interferences (Board), awarding priority of invention to the senior party Nabil Rizkalla and Charles N. Winnick (Rizkalla), on the ground that the junior party and de facto first inventors Frank E. Paulik and Robert G. Schultz (Paulik) had suppressed or concealed the invention within the meaning of 35 U.S.C. § 102(g). We vacate this decision and remand to the Board.

I.

Rizkalla's patent application has the effective filing date of March 10, 1975, its parent application. Paulik's patent application was filed on June 30, 1975. The interference count is for a catalytic process for producing alkylidene diesters such as ethylidene diacetate, which is useful to prepare vinyl acetate and acetic acid. Paulik presented deposition testimony and exhibits in support of his claim to priority; Rizkalla chose to rely solely on his filing date.

The Board held and Rizkalla does not dispute that Paulik reduced the invention of the count to practice in November 1970 and again in April 1971. On about November 20, 1970 Paulik submitted a "Preliminary Disclosure of Invention" to the Patent Department of his assignee, the Monsanto Company. The disclosure was assigned a priority designation of "B", which Paulik states meant that the case would "be taken up in the ordinary course for review and filing."

Despite occasional prodding from the inventors, and periodic review by the patent staff and by company management, this disclosure had a lower priority than other patent work. Evidence of the demands of other projects on related technology was offered to justify the patent staff's delay in acting on this invention, along with evidence that the inventors and assignee continued to be interested in the technology and that the invention disclosure was retained in active status.

In January or February of 1975 the assignee's patent solicitor started to work toward the filing of the patent application; drafts of the application were prepared, and additional laboratory experiments were requested by the patent solicitor and were duly carried out by an inventor. The evidentiary sufficiency of these activities was challenged by Rizkalla, but the Board made no findings thereon, on the basis that these activities were not pertinent to the determination of priority. The Board held that "even if Paulik demonstrated continuous activity from prior to the Rizkalla effective filing date to his filing date * * * such would have no bearing on the question of priority in this case", and cited 35 U.S.C. § 102(g) as authority for the statement that "[w]hile diligence during the above noted period may be relied upon by one alleging prior conception and subsequent reduction to practice, it is of no significance in the case of the party who is not the last to reduce to practice". The Board thus denied Paulik the opportunity to antedate Rizkalla, for the reason that Paulik was not only the first to conceive but he was also the first to reduce to practice.

The Board then held that Paulik's four-year delay from reduction to practice to his filing date was prima facie suppression or concealment under the first clause of section 102(g), that since Paulik had reduced the invention to practice in 1971 and 1972 he was barred by the second clause of section 102(g) from proving reasonable diligence leading to his 1975 filing, and that in any event the intervening activities were insufficient to excuse the delay. The Board refused to consider Paulik's evidence of renewed patent-related activity.

II.

The Board's decision converted the case law's estoppel against reliance on Paulik's early work for priority purposes, into a forfeiture encompassing Paulik's later work, even if the later work commenced before the earliest activity of Rizkalla. According to this decision, once the inference of suppression or concealment is established, this inference cannot be overcome by the junior party to an interference. There is no statutory or judicial precedent that requires this result, and there is sound reason to reject it.

United States patent law embraces the principle that the patent right is granted to the first inventor rather than the first to file a patent application.[2] The law does not inquire as to the fits and starts by which an invention is made. The historic jurisprudence from which 35 U.S.C. § 102(g) flowed reminds us that "the mere lapse of time" will not prevent the inventor from receiving a patent. Mason v. Hepburn, 13 App.D.C. 86, 91, 1898 C.D. 510, 513 (1898). The sole exception to this principle resides in section 102(g) and the exigencies of the priority contest.

There is no impediment in the law to holding that a long period of inactivity need not be a fatal forfeiture, if the first inventor resumes work on the invention before the second inventor enters the field. We deem this result to be a fairer implementation of national patent policy, while in full accord with the letter and spirit of section 102(g).

The Board misapplied the rule that the first inventor does not have to show activity following reduction to practice to mean that the first inventor will not be allowed to show such activity. Such a showing may serve either of two purposes: to rebut an inference of abandonment, suppression, or concealment; or as evidence of renewed activity with respect to the invention. Otherwise, if an inventor were to set an

---

2. As observed by the Industrial Research Institute, a first-to-invent system "respects the value of the individual in American tradition and avoids inequities which can result from a 'race to the Patent Office'". Final Report of the Advisory Committee on Industrial Innovation, U.S. Dept. of Commerce, Sept. 1979, p. 174.

invention aside for "too long" and later resume work and diligently develop and seek to patent it, according to the Board he would always be worse off than if he never did the early work, even as against a much later entrant.

Such a restrictive rule would merely add to the burden of those charged with the nation's technological growth. Invention is not a neat process. The value of early work may not be recognized or, for many reasons, it may not become practically useful, until months or years later. Following the Board's decision, any "too long" delay would constitute a forfeiture fatal in a priority contest, even if terminated by extensive and productive work done long before the newcomer entered the field.

We do not suggest that the first inventor should be entitled to rely for priority purposes on his early reduction to practice if the intervening inactivity lasts "too long," as that principle has evolved in a century of judicial analysis. Precedent did not deal with the facts at bar. There is no authority that would estop Paulik from relying on his resumed activities in order to pre-date Rizkalla's earliest date. We hold that such resumed activity must be considered as evidence of priority of invention. Should Paulik demonstrate that he had renewed activity on the invention and that he proceeded diligently to filing his patent application, starting before the earliest date to which Rizkalla is entitled—all in accordance with established principles of interference practice—we hold that Paulik is not prejudiced by the fact that he had reduced the invention to practice some years earlier.

III.

This appeal presents a question not previously treated by this court or, indeed, in the historical jurisprudence on suppression or concealment. We take this opportunity to clarify an apparent misperception of certain opinions of our predecessor court which the Board has cited in support of its holding.

There is over a hundred years of judicial precedent on the issue of suppression or concealment due to prolonged delay in filing. From the earliest decisions, a distinction has been drawn between deliberate suppression or concealment of an invention, and the legal inference of suppression or concealment based on "too long" a delay in filing the patent application. Both types of situations were considered by the courts before the 1952 Patent Act, and both are encompassed in 35 U.S.C. § 102(g). The result is consistent over this entire period—loss of the first inventor's priority as against an intervening second inventor—and has consistently been based on equitable principles and public policy as applied to the facts of each case.

The earliest decisions dealt primarily with deliberate concealment. In 1858, the Supreme Court in Kendall v. Winsor, 62 U.S. (21 How.) 322, 328 (1858) held that an inventor who "designedly, and with the view of applying it indefinitely and exclusively for his own profit, withholds his invention from the public" impedes "the progress of science and the useful arts".

In Mason v. Hepburn, supra, the classical case on inferred as contrasted with deliberate suppression or concealment, Hepburn was granted a patent in September 1894. Spurred by this news Mason filed his patent application in December 1894. In an interference, Mason demonstrated that he had built a working model in 1887 but showed no activity during the seven years thereafter. The court held that although Mason may have negligently rather than willfully concealed his invention, the "indifference, supineness, or willful act" of a first inventor is the basis for "the equity" that favors the second inventor when that person made and disclosed the invention during the prolonged inactivity of the first inventor. 13 App.D.C. at 96.

* * *

The legislative history of section 102(g) makes clear that its purpose was not to change the law. As described in H.R.Rep. No. 1923, 82d Cong., 2d Sess. 17–18 (1951), section 102(g) "retains the present rules of [the case] law governing the determination of priority of invention". The pre-1952 cases all dealt with situations whereby a later inventor made the same invention during a period of either prolonged inactivity or deliberate concealment by the first inventor, after knowledge of which (usually, but not always, by the issuance of a patent to the second inventor) the first inventor was "spurred" into asserting patent rights, unsuccessfully.

The decisions after the 1952 Act followed a similar pattern, as the courts considered whether to extinguish a first inventor's priority under section 102(g). The cases show either intentional concealment or an unduly long delay after the first inventor's reduction to practice. Some cases excused the delay, and some did not. A few examples will illustrate the application of the statute.

In Gallagher v. Smith, 206 F.2d 939 (CCPA 1953), a seven-year delay (from 1938 to 1945) was excused in the absence of evidence of actual concealment or suppression, as against a later applicant who had a reduction to practice in 1943. Note that the applicant who had delayed was nonetheless the first to file. In Schnick v. Fenn, 277 F.2d 935 (CCPA 1960), a lapse of nineteen months was excused absent intentional concealment or suppression and in view of the mitigating circumstances of uncertain market demand for the invention. In Woofter v. Carlson, 367 F.2d 436 (CCPA 1966), an eight-year delay after Carlson's reduction to practice was not excused, on evidence that Woofter's entry during this period had spurred Carlson into filing. The court found that there was deliberate concealment, and held that "[u]nder these circumstances, [Carlson] has forfeited its right to a patent". 367 F.2d at 448.

In Brokaw v. Vogel, 429 F.2d 476 (CCPA 1970), Vogel filed a patent application in 1963, having reduced the invention to practice in 1957. Brokaw filed in 1959. The court observed that Vogel remained inactive until he learned of Brokaw's issued patent, and that "there is nothing to show that any step was ever taken by Vogel during that time to make the invention available to the public and nothing tending to excuse Vogel's inaction." 429 F.2d at 480. In Palmer v. Dudzik, 481 F.2d 1377 (CCPA 1973), a first inventor's willful concealment of his invention, which continued until news of the junior party's independent invention spurred him to action, required "forfeiture" of his right to the patent in favor of the later inventor, even though in this case the first inventor got to the Patent Office first.

Young v. Dworkin, 489 F.2d 1277 (CCPA 1974), held that a 27-month delay amounted to suppression. Young had refrained from filing a patent application until he had acquired the machines to practice his invention commercially. Focusing on the character of Young's activity between his reduction to practice and filing date, the court found that during Young's prolonged period of inactivity Dworkin conceived the invention and filed his patent application. In concurrence, Judge Rich observed that "it is not the time elapsed that is the controlling factor but the total conduct of the first inventor," adding "[i]t may also be a relative matter, taking into account what the later inventor is doing too." 489 F.2d at 1285.

In Peeler v. Miller, 535 F.2d 647 (CCPA 1976), relied on by the Board, Miller was inactive during the four-year period following his reduction to practice, and the proffered excuse (that work of higher priority was done in other areas) was found inadequate. As noted by the Board, there are many similarities with the case at bar. The difference, however, is significant: Peeler had entered the field and filed his patent application while Miller remained dormant; Rizkalla entered the field, according to the record before us, after Paulik had renewed activity on the invention.

In Horwath v. Lee, 564 F.2d 948 (CCPA 1977), the court found an equitable estoppel based on Horwath's "suppression or concealment" of the invention for 66 months. Horwath filed in December 1971, and traced his invention back to an invention disclosure drawn up in April 1967 for which research had begun in November 1965. Attempting to account for the delay between the invention disclosure and his patent application, Horwath presented evidence of research to perfect his invention in 1971, well after Lee had filed in 1969. The court found Horwath's excuse inadequate. The same distinction exists as in other cases: the second inventor filed while the first inventor slept.

In Shindelar v. Holdeman, 628 F.2d 1337, (CCPA 1980), cert. denied, 451 U.S. 984 (1981), also relied on by the Board, there was a delay of two years and five months between reduction to practice and filing. This was held to be too long as against the second inventor who was the first (by two days) to file a patent application. The court held that the filing delay, attributed solely to the attorney's workload, "raised an inference of suppression * * * which has not been rebutted". 628 F.2d at 1341. The opinion is silent on the question of renewed work by the first inventor before the second inventor entered the field. Although the Board appeared to consider this case controlling as applied to Paulik, we do not see this case as controlling a situation which was not before it. The *Shindelar* court's closing words are: "We reiterate that each case involving the issue of suppression or concealment must be considered on its own particular set of facts." 628 F.2d at 1343.

IV.

The decisions applying section 102(g) balanced the law and policy favoring the first person to make an invention, against equitable considerations when more than one person had made the same invention: in each case where the court deprived the de facto first inventor of the right to the patent, the second inventor had entered the field during a period of either inactivity or deliberate concealment by the first inventor. Often the first inventor had been spurred to file a patent application by news of the second inventor's activities. Although "spurring" is not necessary to a finding of suppression or concealment, see Young v. Dworkin, 489 F.2d at 1281 and citations therein, the courts' frequent references to spurring indicate their concern with this equitable factor.

Some decisions used the word "forfeiture" to describe the first inventor's loss of priority; but none interpreted section 102(g) as requiring an absolute forfeiture rather than requiring a balance of equities. In *Brokaw v. Vogel,* for example, the court said "the *Mason v. Hepburn* principle is not a forfeiture in the true sense; rather it is a rule according to which the patent right goes to the most deserving. Realistically, it is a forfeiture by the de facto first inventor of the right to rely on his earlier reduction to practice." 429 F.2d at 480. In *Young v. Dworkin* Judge Rich wrote "I cannot agree with the board that the question in this case is whether Young 'forfeited his *right to a patent*'. But for Dworkin's conflicting claim, Young forfeited nothing and would get a patent. All he *forfeited* * * * was the right to rely on his prior actual reduction to practice in a priority dispute."

In no case where the first inventor had waited "too long" did he end his period of inactivity before the second inventor appeared. We affirm the long-standing rule that too long a delay may bar the first inventor from reliance on an early reduction to practice in a priority contest. But we hold that the first inventor will not be barred from relying on later, resumed activity antedating an opponent's entry into the field, merely because the work done before the delay occurred was sufficient to amount to a reduction to practice.

This result furthers the basic purpose of the patent system. The exclusive right, constitutionally derived, was for the national purpose of advancing the useful arts—the process today called technological innovation. As implemented by the patent statute, the grant of the right to exclude carries the obligation to disclose the workings of the invention, thereby adding to the store of knowledge without diminishing the patent-supported incentive to innovate.

But the obligation to disclose is not the principal reason for a patent system; indeed, it is a rare invention that cannot be deciphered more readily from its commercial embodiment than from the printed patent. The reason for the patent system is to encourage innovation and its fruits: new jobs and new industries, new consumer goods and trade benefits. We must keep this purpose in plain view as we consider the consequences of interpretations of the patent law such as in the Board's decision.

A foreseeable consequence of the Board's ruling is to discourage inventors and their supporters from working on projects that had been "too long" set aside, because of the impossibility of relying, in a priority contest, on either their original work or their renewed work. This curious result is neither fair nor in the public interest. We do not see that the public interest is served by placing so severe a sanction on failure to file premature patent applications on immature inventions of unknown value. In reversing the Board's decision we do not hold that such inventions are necessarily entitled to the benefits of their earliest dates in a priority contest; we hold only that they are not barred from entitlement to their dates of renewed activity.

* * *

Having established the principle that Paulik, although not entitled to rely on his early work, is entitled to rely on his renewed activity, we vacate the decision of the Board and, in the interest of justice, remand to the PTO for new interference proceedings in accordance with this principle.

Vacated and remanded.

* * *

NOTES

1. There are reasons to apply for a patent other than to obtain an enforceable patent. Because a patent application is a constructive reduction to practice, an application can serve to defend against patent claims of others on the same technology. Thus a firm might decide to apply for a patent even though it has no desire to enforce patent rights. Section 157, added by the Patent Law Amendments of 1984, P.L. 98–622, now authorizes the PTO to publish a "statutory invention registration" which is not examined but has all the attributes of a patent, except that it does not confer any rights against infringement.

2. For an invention registration to work, it must properly disclose and claim the technology. Once this much work has been done, why shouldn't a firm let the patent office go ahead and examine the application? The PTO charges $400 for publication of a registration prior to action by the Examiner and $800 after action by the Examiner, 37 C.F.R. §§ 1.17(n), 1.17(o).

3. Can a person who has lost his right to obtain a patent either because of the § 102(b) time bar or because of § 102(g) abandonment enforce trade secret rights on the same subject matter under Kewanee v. Bicron, supra page 525?

No protection from the outside, you must maintain secrecy. Trade secret does not protect from indep observer/invention, patent does.

I. SPECIFICATION AND CLAIMS

Drafting a patent is one of the most challenging tasks a lawyer can face. He must draft to satisfy the requirements of 35 U.S.C. § 112. They are three:

1. There must be a written description of the invention, and of the manner and process of making and using it, in such full, clear concise, and exact terms as to enable any person skilled in the art to which it pertains to make and use the same.

[handwritten margin note: at the time of filing]

2. The patent must set forth the best mode contemplated by the inventor for carrying out his invention. Although no time is specifically designated, this is presumably the mode contemplated at the time of application.

[handwritten margin note: you don't have to disclose later improvements]

3. The patent must conclude with one or more claims particularly pointing out and distinctly claiming the subject matter which constitutes the invention. (The statute says "which the applicant regards as his invention," but it has always been held that the claim must cover the invention in fact, no matter what the good faith belief of the applicant.)

The first requirement is a considerable challenge to the art of clear and effective descriptive writing. If you don't think that is difficult, write a description of the physical structure of this book. A good patent description should convey to the reader a sense of full disclosure rather than evasive obfuscation. See generally, Arthur M. Smith, The Art of Writing Readable Patents (P.L.I.1958), which draws upon such authorities as U. S. Department of Health, Education and Welfare Training Manual No. 7, Getting Your Ideas Across Through Writing (U. S. Government Printing Office 1950), for the point that a good patent is a well written patent. The legal requirement of adequate description is not especially difficult to satisfy. Indeed, the same decisions which accord to the person skilled in the art considerable powers under section 103 would seem by implication to uphold highly technical descriptions under section 112. The custom is to err on the side of caution, writing the description so that it can be understood not only by one skilled in the art but by any person with a general technical background. This tends to make patent descriptions long and detailed and may even in some cases make them more difficult to understand. Alfred P. Orenzo, Insufficient Disclosure, Obviousness, and the Reasonable Man, 49 J.P.O.S. 387 (1967), criticizes this practice. But with the ultimate decision in the hands of a lay judge and a legal penalty for underdisclosure but not for overdisclosure, it takes considerable courage, if not foolishness, to depart from the practice.

The second requirement requires close coordination between the drafting patent attorney and the inventor and his company, if any. For instance if a patent attorney were to obtain information on the best mode from the client, spend three months preparing the application, and submit it while the client was busy finding an improved best mode, the patent could turn out to be invalid.

FLICK–REEDY CORP. v. HYDRO–LINE MFG. CO.
United States Court of Appeals, Seventh Circuit, 1965.
351 F.2d 546.

KILEY, CIRCUIT JUDGE.

Hydro-Line and Flick-Reedy are competitors in the manufacture and sale of precision, machine tool grade, air and hydraulic piston and cylinder devices, known in the trade as cylinders. The [patent] * * * in suit, owned by Flick-Reedy, [is] * * * a sealing arrangement to improve the pressure capacity of hydraulic cylinders by virtue of preventing the escape of fluid from the cylinders (2,842,284) * * *.

* * *

Patent No. 2,842,284

The district court's findings of fact 7 through 15, reported at 241 F.Supp. 127, 130–32, and which we adopt, describe the plaintiff's patented seal for use in preventing leakage between the end of a cylinder tube and the head. The findings of fact and the patent specifications and claims make clear that an essential element of the patent is the "sealing relation" between the outer machined surface of the reduced thickness at the end of the tube and the outer surface of the recessed groove in the head. This sealing relation is described in terms of "absolute concentricity," "zero clearance" and a "metal to metal contact provided between the head and the cylinder tube [which] performs the function of sealing against fluid leakage. * * *" The specifications state that the outer surface of the reduced thickness section is formed with a "special tool." This "special tool" is not disclosed or described in the specifications or claims.

Flick, the president of plaintiff and inventor of the seal, testified that the "special tool" was an "aid" in achieving the required concentricity and that he contemplated using the tool at the time the patent application was filed. When asked what the tool was, Flick stated

[W]e must use a mechanical tracer tool. I am sorry to have to tell you what it is. These sort of things cost us a lot of money to develop.

Any one of the four types, mechanical, air tracer, electronic tracer, or hydraulic tracer tool can be used.

He further told the court

Your Honor, there are times when you could apply for a patent, I believe, but the enforcement thereof, where it is a tool used for an exclusive purpose in a plant, the enforcement thereof would be most difficult, and you may elect to try to keep the information of a secret nature.

* * *

This is what we elected to do.

Flick also testified that he did not believe that mechanical tracer tools, which his company used, were well known for this purpose, and there was expert testimony that a person skilled in the art would not know from reading the patent specifications what was meant by the "special tool."

The district court concluded that the patent is invalid because plaintiff withheld specific information concerning the "special tool" used in finishing the metal surfaces, in violation of 35 U.S.C. § 112.

* * *

The Constitutional provision and implementing patent law are intended to reward with a seventeen-year monopoly an inventor who "refrains from keeping his invention a trade secret." * * * [cite]. The *quid pro quo* for the monopoly is disclosure which will enable those skilled in the art to practice the invention at the termination of the monopoly, and to "warn the industry concerned of the precise scope of the monopoly asserted." Id. To accept the monopoly and withhold the full disclosure of the "best mode contemplated by the inventor," which will result in a contribution to the common good upon expiration of the monopoly is the "selfish desire" against which 35 U.S.C. § 112 is directed. Application of Nelson, 280 F.2d 172, 184 (CCPA 1960). The record before us shows that the patent specifications disclosed neither what the special tool is nor where a description of it may be found in any prior art. * * *

We hold that the district court's findings on this point are not clearly erroneous and that its conclusion of invalidity because specific information about the "special tool" was withheld in violation of 35 U.S.C. § 112 is supported by substantial evidence. On this issue we affirm the judgment.

NOTES

1. McDougall, The Courts Are Telling Us: "Your Client's Best Mode Must Be Disclosed," 59 J.P.O.S. 321 (1977), reports that he could find no case prior to 1965 holding a patent invalid for failure to disclose the best mode. Since then there have been a number of cases. A recent case is Spectra-Physics, Inc. v. Coherent, Inc., 827 F.2d 1524 (Fed.Cir.1987).

2. Because the priority and time bar rules create incentives to apply for a patent before the invention has been commercialized, and because any commercial product will usually have to involve many patents, the best mode requirement does not enable a competitor to simply read the patents and go into business. By the time the patent expires some twenty years later, the best mode disclosure will be obsolete. What then, is the function of the best mode requirement? See Kitch, the Nature and Function of the Patent System, 20 J. of Law & Econ. 265, 287–88 (1977).

The third requirement of § 112, that the patent must conclude with one or more claims particularly pointing out and distinctly claiming the subject matter which constitutes the invention, is challenging. The claim must point out and define those elements of the thing described which constitute the invention—in the legal sense. The elements claimed must be patentable; but a claim that extends beyond patentable elements is invalid. The drafter must tread the line between the claim which is so narrow as to destroy the commercial value of the patent and the claim that is so broad as to be invalid. This he must do at a time when the commercial significance of the invention is probably not fully appreciated by his client and without the benefit of the exhaustive searches that will be conducted if the patent proves valuable and is challenged in litigation. Furthermore, he must draft the claim so as to satisfy the immediate demands of the patent office while at the same time keeping an eye on the unknown court that may someday try an infringement case.

The difficulty of drafting claims is ameliorated by provision for multiple claims. These can be used as a form of alternative pleading, enabling the drafter to prepare for different eventualities. The statute puts no limit on this practice, providing simply for "one or more" claims. There are, however, extra fees for more than 3 claims.

The drafter can take some solace from the fact that should he fail to successfully negotiate the maze there is a provision for reissue of a patent that "through error without any deceptive intention," is "deemed wholly or partly inoperative or invalid, by reason of the patentee claiming more or less than he had a right to claim in the patent." 35 U.S.C. §§ 251, 252. The reissued patent cannot claim matter not disclosed in the original application.

The patent specification is not under the statute required to disclose the features that make the invention non-obvious. Nevertheless, patent specifications frequently describe the prior art and the advantages afforded by the invention. In part this simplifies the problem of describing the invention. And in part it may be thought that it gives the patent a stronger "aura" of validity. The practice is a risky one because a subsequent infringement court may hold the applicant bound to the theories of non-obviousness disclosed by the specification. This is wrong, but the courts are disconcerted by the thought that an applicant can make a patentable invention without ever understanding why his invention was non-obvious. See Robert A. Choate, Invention and Unobviousness—"Afterthoughts"—Reliance on Features and Advantages Undisclosed at Original Filing, 49 J.Pat.Off.Soc'y. 619 (1967).

HALLIBURTON OIL WELL CEMENTING CO. v. WALKER

Supreme Court of the United States, 1946.
329 U.S. 1, 67 S.Ct. 6, 91 L.Ed. 3.

MR. JUSTICE BLACK delivered the opinion of the Court.

* * *

[Action for infringement of a patent on a device for measuring the depth of oil wells. Because of the machinery in and around the wells and the fact that some wells did not go straight down, it was impractical to measure their depth by simply lowering a line. It was important to know the depth of the well in order to properly place the pump in the well. The oil industry had made use of a sound echo device to measure the depth by measuring the elapsed time between a sound and its echo. But this method was inaccurate because sound in the wells did not travel at the uniform surface speed of 1100 feet per second. Walker, the inventor, undertook to] search for a method which would more accurately indicate the sound and pressure wave velocity in each well. Walker was familiar with the structure of oil wells. The oil flow pipe in a well, known as a tubing string, is jointed and where these joints occur there are collars or shoulders. There are also one or more relatively prominent projections on the oil flow pipe known as tubing catchers. In wells where the distance to the tubing catcher is known, Walker observed that the distance to the fluid surface could be measured by a simple time-distance proportion formula.[4] For those wells in which the distance to the tubing catcher was unknown, Walker also suggested another idea. The sections of tubing pipe used in a given oil well are generally of equal length. Therefore the shoulders in a given well ordinarily are at equal intervals from each other. But the section length and therefore the interval may vary from well to well. Walker concluded that he could measure the unknown distance to the tubing catcher if he could observe and record the shoulder echo waves. Thus multiplication of the number of shoulders observed by the known length of a pipe section would produce the distance to the tubing catcher. With this distance, he could solve the distance to the fluid surface by the same proportion formula used when the distance to the tubing catcher was a matter of record. The Lehr and Wyatt instrument could record all these echo waves. But the potential usefulness of the echoes from the shoulders and the tubing catcher which their machine recorded had not occurred to Lehr and Wyatt and consequently they had made no effort better to observe and record them. Walker's contribution which he claims to be invention was in effect to add to Lehr and Wyatt's apparatus a well-known device which would make the regularly appearing shoulder echo waves more prominent on the graph and easier to count.

The device added was a mechanical acoustical resonator. This was a short pipe which would receive wave impulses at the mouth of the well. Walker's testimony was, and his specifications state, that by

---

4. The known distance from well top to the tubing catcher is to the unknown distance from well top to the fluid surface as the time an echo requires to travel from the tubing catcher is to the time required for an echo to travel from the fluid surface.

Walker's patent emphasizes that his invention solves the velocity of sound waves in wells of various pressures in which sound did not travel at open-air or a uniform speed. Mathematically, of course, his determination of the distance by proportions determines the distance to the fluid surface directly without necessarily considering velocity in feet per second as a factor.

making the length of this tubal resonator one-third the length of the tubing joints, the resonator would serve as a tuner, adjusted to the frequency of the shoulder echo waves. It would simultaneously amplify these echo waves and eliminate unwanted echoes from other obstructions thus producing a clearer picture of the shoulder echo waves. His specifications show, attached to the tubal resonator, a coupler, the manipulation of which would adjust the length of the tube to one-third of the interval between shoulders in a particular well. His specifications and drawings also show the physical structure of a complete apparatus, designed to inject pressure impulses into a well, and to receive, note, record and time the impulse waves.

The District Court held the claims here in suit valid upon its finding that Walker's "apparatus differs from and is an improvement over the prior art in the incorporation in such apparatus of a tuned acoustical means which performs the function of a sound filter * * *" The Circuit Court of Appeals affirmed this holding, stating that the trial court had found "that the only part of this patent constituting invention over the prior art is the 'tuned acoustical means which performs the functions of a sound filter.'"

For our purpose in passing upon the sufficiency of the claims against prohibited indefiniteness we can accept without ratifying the findings of the lower court that the addition of "a tuned acoustical means" performing the "function of a sound filter" brought about a new patentable combination, even though it advanced only a narrow step beyond Lehr and Wyatt's old combination.[5] We must, however, determine whether, as petitioner charges, the claims here held valid run afoul of Rev.Stat. 4888 because they do not describe the invention but use "conveniently functional language at the exact point of novelty." General Electric Co. v. Wabash Appliance Corp., supra, at 371.

* * *

A claim typical of all of those held valid only describes the resonator and its relation with the rest of the apparatus as "means associated with said pressure responsive device for tuning said receiving means to the frequency of echoes from the tubing collars of said tubing sections to clearly distinguish the echoes from said couplings from each other."[7] The language of the claim thus describes this most crucial

---

5. See Hailes v. Van Wormer, 20 Wall. 353; Knapp v. Morss, 150 U.S. 221, 227–28; Textile Machine Works v. Louis Hirsch Textile Machines, Inc., 302 U.S. 490; Lincoln Engineering Co. v. Stewart-Warner Corp., 303 U.S. 545, 549–50.

7. Both parties have used Claim 1 as a typical example for purposes of argument throughout the litigation. Other claims need not be set out. Claim 1 is as follows:

"In an apparatus for determining the location of an obstruction in a well having therein a string of assembled tubing sections interconnected with each other by coupling collars, means communicating with said well for creating a pressure impulse in said well, echo receiving means including a pressure responsive device exposed to said well for receiving pressure impulses from the well and for measuring the lapse of time between the creation of the impulse and the arrival at said receiving means of the echo from said obstruction, and means associated with said pressure responsive device for tuning said receiving means to the frequency of echoes from the tubing collars of said tubing sec-

element in the "new" combination in terms of what it will do rather than in terms of its own physical characteristics or its arrangement in the new combination apparatus. We have held that a claim with such a description of a product is invalid as a violation of Rev.Stat. 4888. Holland Furniture Co. v. Perkins Glue Co., 277 U.S. 245, 256–57; General Electric Co. v. Wabash Appliance Corp., supra. We understand that the Circuit Court of Appeals held that the same rigid standards of description required for product claims is not required for a combination patent embodying old elements only. We have a different view.

* * *

Patents on machines which join old and well-known devices with the declared object of achieving new results, or patents which add an old element to improve a pre-existing combination, easily lend themselves to abuse. And to prevent extension of a patent's scope beyond what was actually invented, courts have viewed claims to combinations and improvements or additions to them with very close scrutiny.

* * *

This patent and the infringement proceedings brought under it illustrate the hazards of carving out an exception to the sweeping demand Congress made in [the statute] * * *. Neither in the specification, the drawing, nor in the claims here under consideration, was there any indication that the patentee contemplated any specific structural alternative for the acoustical resonator or for the resonator's relationship to the other parts of the machine. Petitioner was working in a field crowded almost, if not completely, to the point of exhaustion. In 1920, Tucker, in Patent No. 1,351,356, had shown a tuned acoustical resonator in a sound detecting device which measured distances. Lehr and Wyatt had provided for amplification of their waves. Sufficient amplification and exaggeration of *all* the different waves which Lehr and Wyatt recorded on their machine would have made it easy to distinguish the tubing catcher and regular shoulder waves from all others. For, even without this amplification, the echo waves from tubing collars could by proper magnification have been recorded and accurately counted, had Lehr and Wyatt recognized their importance in computing the velocity. Cf. General Electric Co. v. Jewel Incandescent Lamp Co., 326 U.S. 242.

Under these circumstances the broadness, ambiguity, and overhanging threat of the functional claim of Walker become apparent. What he claimed in the court below and what he claims here is that his patent bars anyone from using in an oil well any device heretofore or hereafter invented which combined with the Lehr and Wyatt machine performs the function of clearly and distinctly catching and recording echoes from tubing joints with regularity. Just how many different devices there are of various kinds and characters which would serve to emphasize these echoes, we do not know. The Halliburton device,

tions to clearly distinguish the echoes from
said couplings from each other."

alleged to infringe, employs an electric filter for this purpose. In this age of technological development there may be many other devices beyond our present information or indeed our imagination which will perform that function and yet fit these claims. And unless frightened from the course of experimentation by broad functional claims like these, inventive genius may evolve many more devices to accomplish the same purpose. See United Carbon Co. v. Binney & Smith Co., 317 U.S. 228, 236; Burr v. Duryee, 1 Wall. 531, 568; O'Reilly v. Morse, 15 How. 62, 112–13. Yet if Walker's blanket claims be valid, no device to clarify echo waves, now known or hereafter invented, whether the device be an actual equivalent of Walker's ingredient or not, could be used in a combination such as this, during the life of Walker's patent.

Had Walker accurately described the machine he claims to have invented, he would have had no such broad rights to bar the use of all devices now or hereafter known which could accent waves. For had he accurately described the resonator together with the Lehr and Wyatt apparatus, and sued for infringement, charging the use of something else used in combination to accent the waves, the alleged infringer could have prevailed if the substituted device (1) performed a substantially different function; (2) was not known at the date of Walker's patent as a proper substitute for the resonator; or (3) had been actually invented after the date of the patent. Fuller v. Yentzer, supra, at 296–97; Gill v. Wells, supra, at 29. Certainly, if we are to be consistent with Rev.Stat. 4888, [predecessor to § 112] a patentee cannot obtain greater coverage by failing to describe his invention than by describing it as the statute commands.

* * *

Reversed.

NOTES

1. General Electric Co. v. Wabash Corp., 304 U.S. 364 (1938), relied on in *Halliburton,* involved a patent on an improved tungsten filament for light bulbs. Tungsten filaments were subject to "offsetting" and "sagging" which reduced their useful life by causing premature burn outs. By use of an alkaline silicate the inventor was able to make a tungsten filament with larger, coarser grains which would not sag or offset in use. The claim in suit read:

"A filament for electric incandescent lamps or other devices, composed substantially of tungsten and made up mainly of a number of comparatively large grains of such size and contour as to prevent substantial sagging and offsetting during a normal or commercially useful life for such a lamp or other device."

The Court held the claim defective. "The claim uses indeterminate adjectives which describe the function of the grains to the exclusion of any structural definition, and thus falls within the condemnation of the doctrine that a patentee may not broaden his product claims by describing the product in terms of function. Claim 25 vividly illustrates the vice of a description in terms of function. 'As a description of the invention it is insufficient and if allowed would extend the monopoly beyond the invention.'" The Court of Appeals had held that "in view of the difficulty, if not impossibility, of describing adequately

a number of microscopic and heterogeneous shapes of crystals, it may be that
* * * [the inventor] made the best disclosure possible, * * *". The Court
answered, "It may be doubted whether one who discovers or invents a product
he knows to be new will ever find it impossible to describe some aspect of its
novelty."

The patent in the *Wabash* case also contained process claims on the method
for making the filament, but the plaintiff sued only on the product claims. At
the trial below the defendant refused to reveal the method by which it made its
filaments. 17 F.Supp. at 904. The district court, however, found that the
defendant's filament was identical to the plaintiff's filament. Id. at 906.

2. Could the patentee in the principal case have claimed a process for
measuring the depth of oil wells? O'Reilly v. Morse, 56 U.S. 62 (1853), supra
page 795 and Tilghman v. Proctor, 102 U.S. 707 (1880), supra page 801 are
pertinent here. Should the *O'Reilly* case have ever been read for anything
other than the proposition that a claim broader than the applicant's invention
is invalid?

3. The third paragraph of 112 states:

"An element in a claim for a combination may be expressed as a
means or step for performing a specified function without the recital of
structure, material, or acts in support thereof, and such claim shall be
construed to cover the corresponding structure, material, or acts described in the specification and equivalents thereof."

P.J. Federico, Commentary on the New Patent Act (printed in front of the
first volume of 35 U.S.C. in 1954) 25–26 (1954), explains:

"The last paragraph of § 112 relating to so-called functional
claims is new. It provides that an element of a claim for a combination (and a combination may be not only a combination of mechanical
elements, but also a combination of substances in a composition claim,
or steps in a process claim) may be expressed as a means or step for
performing a specified function, without the recital of structure, material or acts in support thereof. It is unquestionable that some measure
of greater liberality in the use of functional expressions in combination
claims is authorized than had been permitted by some court decisions,
and that decisions such as that in Halliburton Oil Well Cementing Co.
v. Walker, 329 U.S. 1 (1946), are modified or rendered obsolete, but the
exact limits of the enlargement remain to be determined. The language specifies 'an' element, which means 'any' element, and by this
language, as well as by application of the general rule that the singular
includes the plural, it follows that more than one of the elements of a
combination claim may be expressed as different 'means' plus statements of function. The language does not go so far as to permit a so-
called single means claim, that is a claim which recites merely one
means plus a statement of function and nothing else. Attempts to
evade this by adding purely nominal elements to such a claim will
undoubtedly be condemned. The paragraph ends by stating that such
a claim shall be construed to cover the corresponding structure, material, or acts described in the specification and equivalents thereof.
This relates primarily to the construction of such claims for the
purpose of determining when the claim is infringed (note the use of the
word 'cover'), and would not appear to have much, if any, applicability
in determining the patentability of such claims over the prior art, that

is, the Patent Office is not authorized to allow a claim which 'reads on' the prior art."

Does the third paragraph of § 112 by implication invalidate functional claims for all inventions other than those for combinations? What, for purposes of the paragraph, is a combination? See Application of Barr, 444 F.2d 588 (CCPA 1971).

4. Generally speaking, the longer a claim is the less it will cover. Each additional item included in the claim will be an item whose absence will keep something from being within the terms of the claim.

APPLICATION OF SWINEHART

United States Court of Customs and Patent Appeals, 1971.
439 F.2d 210.

BALDWIN, JUDGE.

This appeal is from the decision of the Patent Office Board of Appeals, adhered to on reconsideration, which affirmed the rejection of claim 24 in appellants' application as failing to meet the requirements of 35 U.S.C. § 112. The board reversed the rejection of two other claims.

THE INVENTION

The subject matter of the appealed claim is a composition of matter essentially made up of barium fluoride and calcium fluoride in approximately eutectic proportions. [A eutectic proportion is that proportion of the constituent materials which has a lower melting point than any other proportion of the same materials.] The record indicates, and appellants confirm, that "[e]utectic compositions of barium fluoride and calcium fluoride are well known in the prior art." However, appellants are apparently the first to discover that when crystalline forms of these two components are melted together in eutectic proportion and then resolidified by "conventional crystal-growing techniques," there results a multi-phase crystalline body characterized by an intimate matrix of large, visible crystals, which, unlike the prior art materials, does not cleave, is resistant to thermal shock and impact and approaches maximum density for the overall composition. In addition, and allegedly unexpectedly, these crystalline bodies "are capable of transmitting collimated light," especially in the infrared wave range.

The appealed claim recites:

24. A new composition of matter, transparent to infra-red rays and resistant to thermal shock, the same being a solidified melt of two components present in proportion approximately eutectic, one of said components being BaF_2 and the other being CaF_2.

According to their brief, "[t]he exact point of novelty between appellants' claimed composition and that of the prior art is transparency." [2]

2. We observe that the term "transparent", as indicated by its primary dictionary definition of "having the property of transmitting light without appreciable scatter-

THE GROUNDS FOR REJECTION

The examiner rejected claim 24 "for failing to particularly point out and distinctly claim the invention as required in 35 U.S.C. 112." His asserted reasons were as follows:

> Claim 24 is functional and fails to properly point out the invention. Applicants point out on page 2 of the specification, lines 24–27 that when the components are merely fused and cast as an integral body, said body is opaque. This claim in reciting "transparent to infrared rays" is thus improperly functional. *   *   * It should also be noted that this claim does not require more than one phase.

The board agreed, adding:

> Claim 24 stands rejected as improperly functional in that it distinguishes over the unsatisfactory material of appellants' figure 3 merely in the functional term "transparent to infrared rays." We agree with the Examiner in this respect, as transparency of the claimed material cannot be treated as an inherent, characteristic property, in view of the fact that the composition of appellants' Example V (figure 3) lacks this property, yet is made of the same materials as appellants' Example I. *   *   * This claim is not the type covered by a proper functional limitation pursuant to 35 U.S.C. 112, since the language in question does not define a means or a step, or a distinguishing ingredient.

OPINION

It is fairly safe to conclude from the language quoted above that the examiner and the board considered the use of functional language, per se, to render the instant claim indefinite. Appellants have apparently conceded that "functionality" is ordinarily equated with indefiniteness. They argue strenuously, however, that the disputed language here does not necessarily refer to a function of the recited composition or to a desired result but rather it defines a physical property. On the record produced in the Patent Office, therefore, it would appear that the single issue before us is whether the disputed language is in fact "functional". If this issue were determinative, appellants would fail since we have no doubt that such language is "functional" at least insofar as we interpret the meaning of that term. In any event, for reasons which will become clear as this opinion progresses, we find that issue to be not only *not* determinative of whether claim 24 satisfies the

ing so that bodies lying beyond are entirely visible," generally is taken to refer to those light waves which are visible to the human eye. The parties here seem to agree that in the claim before us the term is used in its less common sense of being "pervious to any specified form of radiation." Clearly the most important defining characteristic of the word, which is the same in either sense, is that the light is transmitted "without appreciable scattering." Ref: Webster's Third New International Dictionary (G & C Merriam Co., 1969).

requirements of 35 U.S.C. § 112 but also irrelevant in the analysis leading up to that determination.

We take the characterization "functional", as used by the Patent Office and argued by the parties, to indicate nothing more than the fact that an attempt is being made to define something (in this case, a composition) by what it *does* rather than by what it *is* (as evidenced by specific structure or material, for example). In our view, there is nothing intrinsically wrong with the use of such a technique in drafting patent claims.[3] Indeed we have even recognized in the past the practical *necessity* for the use of functional language. See, for example, In re Halleck, 421 F.2d 911 (CCPA 1970). We recognize that prior cases have hinted at a possible distinction in this area depending on the criticality of the particular point at which such language might appear.[4] Our study of these cases has satisfied us, however, that any concern over the use of functional language at the so-called "point of novelty" stems largely from the fear that an applicant will attempt to distinguish over a reference disclosure by emphasizing a property or function which may not be mentioned by the reference and thereby assert that his claimed subject matter is novel. Such a concern is not only irrelevant, it is misplaced. In the first place, it is elementary that the mere recitation of a newly discovered function or property, inherently possessed by things in the prior art, does not cause a claim drawn to those things to distinguish over the prior art. Additionally, where the Patent Office has reason to believe that a functional limitation asserted to be critical for establishing novelty in the claimed subject matter may, in fact, be an inherent characteristic of the prior art, it possesses the authority to require the applicant to prove that the subject matter shown to be in the prior art does not possess the characteristic relied on.

We are convinced that there is no support, either in the actual holdings of prior cases or in the statute, for the proposition, put forward here, that "functional" language, in and of itself, renders a claim improper. We have also found no prior decision of this or any other court which may be said to hold that there is some other ground for objecting to a claim on the basis of *any* language, "functional" or otherwise, beyond what is already sanctioned by the provisions of 35 U.S.C. § 112.

Assuming that an applicant is claiming what he regards as his invention, there are in reality only two basic grounds for rejecting a

---

3. We think our views herein are in accord with those of Congress as indicated by the language of the third paragraph of 35 U.S.C. § 112. * * *

4. The solicitor, it appears, would also treat the question of *what* is being defined as important. He distinguishes a case relied on by appellants as "irrelevant" since the functional term there permitted dealt with novel proportions in a composition whereas here the question is "whether novelty in structure can be precisely defined in wholly functional terms." Nevertheless, we are unable to see merit in any proposition which would require the denial of a claim *solely* because of the *type* of language used to define the subject matter for which patent protection is sought. * * *

claim under § 112. The first is that the language used is not precise and definite enough to provide a clear-cut indication of the scope of subject matter embraced by the claim. This ground finds its basis in the second paragraph of section 112, the rationale for which was discussed by us recently in In re Hammack, 427 F.2d 1378 (CCPA 1970). The second is that the language is so broad that it causes the claim to have a potential scope of protection beyond that which is justified by the specification disclosure. Cf. General Electric Co. v. Wabash Appliance Corp., 304 U.S. 364 (1938). This ground of rejection is now recognized as stemming from the requirements of the first paragraph of 35 U.S.C. § 112. The merits of the "functional" language in the claim before us must be tested in the light of these two requirements alone.

"Functional" terminology may render a claim quite broad. By its own literal terms a claim employing such language covers *any and all* embodiments which perform the recited function. Legitimate concern often properly exists, therefore, as to whether the scope of protection defined thereby is warranted by the scope of enablement indicated and provided by the description contained in the specification. This is not to say, however, that every claim containing "functional" terminology is broad. Indeed, in many cases it will be obvious that only a very limited group of objects will fall within the intended category. Such appears to be the case here, since we do not sense any concern by the Patent Office that appellants are claiming more than they are entitled to claim under the first paragraph of section 112. We need not, therefore, consider whether there are any problems with the appealed claim arising under that paragraph. It is clear that the arguments of the parties are concerned solely with whether the disputed language serves to define the subject matter for which protection is sought with the distinctness and particularity which are required by the second paragraph of section 112.

In the brief for the Patent Office, it has been asserted for the first time that

> the limits of appellants' invention clearly are not fixed by the expression "transparent to infrared rays." The expression is not defined, and in fact does not appear, in appellants' written description of their invention.

The solicitor points out that, in their specification, appellants demonstrate the novel aspect of their invention by setting out three charts depicting the percentage (as a function of wavelength) of infrared radiation transmitted through a 5mm thick "window" made from a eutectic composition of the components recited in the claim. One chart indicates that a fused and cast mixture of the two components transmits "substantially zero" collimated light in the infrared range. The other two charts indicate that when the fused mixture is "grown to form a crystal ingot", windows made therefrom transmit up to approximately 80% of infrared radiation depending on the particular wavelength of the radiation. What those charts also appear to indicate, however, is that the conditions used in preparing the product may affect to some extent both the percentage transmission and the band of wavelength transmitted. The solicitor argues that "transparency is a matter of degree" and complains that because the "less favorable conditions" which produce a less effective product are not specifically disclosed in the specification

> one would not know whether a product is "transparent to infrared rays", and therefore would infringe the claims, if the product transmits less infrared than is shown in Fig. 2.

Accepting the solicitor's argument as an attack on the definiteness of the disputed language in the claim before us, we must nevertheless disagree that the claim is rendered indefinite by that language. The record before us establishes that prior art compositions are substantially opaque to infrared rays. Appellants have produced a composition which is substantially transparent to such rays. Such a composition is conceded to be novel. It is true that the figures reproduced in the specification indicate that the degree of transparency varies depending on such factors as the conditions employed in producing the crystal, the thickness of the crystal and the particular wave length of the radiation transmitted. However, in all cases a *substantial* amount of infrared radiation is transmitted. We do not read appellants' disclosure as suggesting that only certain *degrees* of transparency to infrared are comprehended within the teaching there given. It follows that when appellants' claim is read in light of that disclosure the limits it purports to define are made sufficiently clear.

The decision of the board is reversed.

Reversed.

LANE, JUDGE (concurring).

I concur in the result reached by the principal opinion. While I do not necessarily disagree with the conclusions about functionality stated therein, I find it unnecessary in this case to make such conclusions.

Taking the language of the third paragraph of section 112 as a definition of the type of "functional" expressions which have long been troublesome in patent law, I find that such expressions are those which recite "a means or step for performing a specified function without the recital of structure, material, or acts in support thereof." An example of what is meant by "a specified function" is found in the Supreme Court's opinion in General Electric Co. v. Wabash Appliance Corp., 304 U.S. 364 (1938). In that case, offsetting and sagging of filaments in incandescent lamps had long been a problem in the art. The specification there described how to remedy those problems by regulating the size and shape of the grains of material making up the filaments. The claims contained the following expression, which was relied upon for novelty: "grains of such size and contour as to prevent substantial sagging and off-setting during a normal or commercially useful life for such a lamp." Id. at 368. The court stated:

A limited use of terms of effect or result, which accurately define the essential qualities of a product to one skilled in the art, may in some instances be permissible and even desirable, but a characteristic essential to novelty may not be distinguished from the old art solely by its tendency to remedy the problems in the art met by the patent.

Id. at 371. The court thus held, under the patent law then in effect, that certain kinds of functional expressions were impermissible at the point of novelty, specifically, those wherein the recited function is merely the solution of a problem in the art.

It cannot be the law that all functional terms are condemned when used to distinguish a claimed invention from the prior art. If this is the law, and it is carried to its logical conclusion, many nouns and adjectives would be condemned as functional, since they define in terms of use or effect. For example, a "door" is something used to close and open a passageway; a "nail" is an object used to hold two pieces of material together; a "black" material is one incapable of reflecting visible light. It is apparent to me that if functionality at the point of novelty is ever per se a ground for rejecting claims, it is not always so.

The kind of function recited in the product claim before us— transparent to infrared rays—is a physical characteristic of the composition of matter claimed. Moreover, no one has suggested a more distinct way of defining that composition, although it has been argued that the degree of transparency might be more precisely defined. I conclude that the recitation here is not the kind of claim functionality condemned by earlier cases but that it is a kind which is permitted.

It is true that all expressions in claims, functional or otherwise, must be definite in order to satisfy the second paragraph of 35 U.S.C. § 112. I am in agreement with the principal opinion that the expression here in issue is reasonably definite.

* * *

J. SCOPE OF PATENT RIGHTS

A patent confers the right to exclude others from making, using or selling the patented invention (see 35 U.S.C. § 271). The patented invention is that which is covered by the claims of the patent, that portion of the specification that points out and distinctly claims the subject matter (see 35 U.S.C. § 112).

The owner of a patent does not acquire by virtue of the ownership of the patent the right to practice the invention if doing so would otherwise be illegal. For instance, if practice of an invention would violate laws regulating pollution or involve the possession of an illegal substance, the patent offers no protection against such laws.

An illustration of this point is that an invention within the claims of one patent can also be within the claims of another patent and thus infringe the other patent. This may come about if the claim is for an improvement to the invention of the other patent. In this situation, the owner of the patent whose invention falls within the other patent cannot practice it without the consent of the owner of that other patent. In this situation, the other patent is said to "block" the patent. Indeed, if one patent contains a broad but commercially impracticable claim while the second contains a commercially viable implementation of the first, it may be impossible for either patent owner to market a successful product without the consent of the other.

An understanding of the scope of the right to exclude conferred by a particular claim is important to understanding the practical significance of the patent, and each step of the drafting and application process must be informed by an understanding of the practical value of the rights that particular claims will confer.

Infringement is defined in 35 U.S.C. § 271. Subsection (a) provides that "whoever makes, uses or sells any patented invention within the United States during the term of the patent therefor, infringes the patent."

A person infringes when he makes, uses or sells something that falls within the scope of the claims of the patent. The claims of the patent are like the boundary descriptions in a deed to real estate: they demarcate the subject matter as to which the owner of the patent has a right to exclude.

(1) MAKE, USE OR SELL

Not every use of a patent infringes, even uses of benefit to the user. For instance, examination and study of a patent is not infringement, even if the information obtained enables a person to make a successful non-infringing product. In Van Kannell Revolving Door Co. v. Revolving Door & Fixture Co., 293 Fed. 261 (S.D.N.Y.1920), the defendant had bid on a revolving door job whose bid specifications specified a door within the claims of the plaintiff's patent. After winning the bid, the defendant persuaded the customer that an equivalent but non-infringing design would be suitable, and completed the job. The patent owner sued claiming that submitting a bid that fell within the terms of the patent was infringement. Judge Learned Hand ruled that it was not.

> The defendant under these circumstances neither made, sold, nor used the patented door. Now a patent confers an exclusive right upon the patentee, limited in those terms. He may prevent anyone from making, selling, or using a structure embodying the invention, but the monopoly goes no further than that. It restrains everyone from the conduct so described, and it does not restrain him from anything else. If, therefore, anyone says to a possible customer of a patentee, "I will make the article myself; don't buy of the patentee," while he may be doing the patentee a wrong, and while equity will forbid his carrying out his promise, the promise itself is not part of the conduct which the patent forbids; it is not a "subtraction"

from the monopoly. If it injures the plaintiff, though never performed, perhaps it is a wrong, like a slander upon his title; but certainly it is not an infringement of the patent. Luten v. Town of Lee (D.C.) 206 Fed. 904. And while equity forbids the carrying out of the promise, equity does not thereby adjudge the promise to be a wrong, but only evidence of a proximate wrong; i.e., infringement. To procure an adjudication that the promise is a wrong, and its accompanying injunction, the plaintiff must rest his case, not upon any subtraction from the monopoly, but upon an injury analogous to injuries arising from similar conduct which affects the value of any kind of property.

On the other hand, use and use alone of an invention infringes. Thus in Aro Mg. Co. v. Convertible Top Co., 377 U.S. 476 (1964), the Court held that owners of Ford automobiles with convertible top designs that infringed the plaintiff's patent infringed that patent simply by owning and driving their cars. "Not only does [§ 271(a)] * * * explicitly regard an unauthorized user of a patented invention as an infringer, but it has often and clearly been held that unauthorized use, without more, constitutes infringement." 377 U.S. 476, 483.

Since there is no requirement that an infringer have any knowledge or even any reason to know that a patent is being infringed, it is possible to engage in extensive patent infringement without being aware that it is occurring. For instance if a firm itself designs and introduces a new product, it will be liable for infringement if any feature of that product infringes a valid patent. The only protection for the firm would be to pay for a patent search making use of the patents available in the patent office to determine whether or not any patents in force contain claims which encompass the product. Not only is such a search a demanding (and thus likely to be costly) professional task, but it may be technically impossible, since not all presently in-force patents can always be located in the patent office at any one time.

Where a product is purchased from another, the buyer can protect itself by obtaining a warranty of non-infringement. Section 2–312(3) of the Uniform Commercial Code provides:

"Unless otherwise agreed a seller who is a merchant regularly dealing in goods of the kind warrants that the goods shall be delivered free of the rightful claims of any third person by way of infringement or the like but a buyer who furnishes specifications to the seller must hold the seller harmless against any such claim which arises out of compliance with the specifications."

If the product turns out to be infringing, the buyer is subject to a suit for infringement, but can bring an action over against the seller for the amount of damages resulting from the infringement. Of course, if the seller becomes insolvent, the warranty may provide little or no protection.

ROCHE PRODUCTS, INC. v. BOLAR PHARMACEUTICAL CO.

United States Court of Appeals, Federal Circuit, 1984.
733 F.2d 858.

NICHOLS, SENIOR CIRCUIT JUDGE.

This is an appeal from a judgment entered on October 14, 1983, in which the United States District Court * * * for the Eastern District of New York held United States Patent No. 3,299,053 not infringed and denied relief. We reverse and remand.

I

At stake in this case is the length of time a pharmaceutical company which has a patent on the active ingredient in a drug can have exclusive access to the American market for that drug. Plaintiff-appellant Roche Products, Inc. (Roche), a large research-oriented pharmaceutical company, wanted the United States district court to enjoin Bolar Pharmaceutical Co., Inc. (Bolar), a manufacturer of generic drugs, from taking, during the life of a patent, the statutory and regulatory steps necessary to market, after the patent expired, a drug equivalent to a patented brand name drug. Roche argued that the use of a patented drug for federally mandated premarketing tests is a use in violation of the patent laws.

Roche was the assignee of the rights in U.S. Patent No. 3,299,053 (the '053 patent), which expired on January 17, 1984. The '053 patent, which was issued on January 17, 1967, is entitled "Novel 1 and/or 4–substituted alkyl 5–aromatic–3H–1, 4–benzodiazepines and benzodiazepine–2–ones." One of the chemical compounds claimed in the '053 patent is flurazepam hydrochloride (flurazepam hcl), the active ingredient in Roche's successful brand name prescription sleeping pill "Dalmane."

In early 1983, Bolar became interested in marketing, after the '053 patent expired, a generic drug equivalent to Dalmane. Because a generic drug's commercial success is related to how quickly it is brought on the market after a patent expires, and because approval for an equivalent of an established drug can take more than 2 years, Bolar, not waiting for the '053 patent to expire, immediately began its effort to obtain federal approval to market its generic version of Dalmane. In mid–1983, Bolar obtained from a foreign manufacturer 5 kilograms of flurazepam hcl to form into "dosage form capsules, to obtain stability data, dissolution rates, bioequivalency studies, and blood serum studies" necessary for a New Drug Application to the United States Food and Drug Administration (FDA).

* * *

The [district] court held that Bolar's use of the patented compound for federally mandated testing was not infringement of the patent in suit because Bolar's use was *de minimis* and experimental. * * *

use, make, or sell

II

The district court correctly recognized that the issue in this case is narrow: does the limited use of a patented drug for testing and investigation strictly related to FDA drug approval requirements during the last 6 months of the term of the patent constitute a use which, unless licensed, the patent statute makes actionable? The district court held that it does not. This was an error of law.

III

A

When Congress enacted the current revision of the Patent Laws of the United States, the Patent Act of 1952 * * * a statutory definition of patent infringement existed for the first time since section 5 of the Patent Act of 1793 was repealed in 1836. Title 35 U.S.C. § 271(a) * * *.

It is beyond argument that performance of only one of the three enumerated activities is patent infringement. It is well-established, in particular, that the use of a patented invention, without either manufacture or sale, is actionable. See Aro Manufacturing Co. v. Convertible Top Replacement Co., 377 U.S. 476, 484 (1964); * * *. Thus, the patentee does not need to have any evidence of damage or lost sales to bring an infringement action.

Section 271(a) prohibits, on its face, any and all uses of a patented invention. Of course, as Judge Learned Hand observed in Cabell v. Markham, 148 F.2d 737, 739 (2d Cir.), aff'd, 326 U.S. 404 (1945):

> "[I]t is true that the words used, even in their literal sense, are the primary, and ordinarily the most reliable, source of interpreting the meaning of any writing: be it a statute, a contract, or anything else. But it is one of the surest indexes of a mature and developed jurisprudence not to make a fortress out of the dictionary; but to remember that statutes always have some purpose or object to accomplish, whose sympathetic and imaginative discovery is the surest guide to their meaning."

Because Congress has never defined use, its meaning has become a matter of judicial interpretation. Although few cases discuss the question of whether a particular use constitutes an infringing use of a patented invention, they nevertheless convincingly lead to the conclusion that the word "use" in section 271(a) has never been taken to its utmost possible scope. See, e.g., Pitcairn v. United States, 547 F.2d 1106 (Ct.Cl.1976), cert. denied, 434 U.S. 1051 (1978) (experimental use may be a defense to infringement); United States v. Univis Lens Co., 316 U.S. 241 (1942) ("An incident to the purchase of any article, whether patented or unpatented, is the right to use and sell it, * * *." Id. at 249); General Electric Co. v. United States, 572 F.2d

745 (1978) ("[I]t can be properly assumed that as part of the bargain the seller of a device incorporating a patented combination * * * authorizes the buyer to continue to use the device so long as the latter can and does use the elements he purchased from the patentee or licensor." Id. at 784–85).

Bolar argues that its intended use of flurazepam hcl is excepted from the use prohibition. It claims two grounds for exception: the first ground is based on a liberal interpretation of the traditional experimental use exception; the second ground is that public policy favors generic drugs and thus mandates the creation of a new exception in order to allow FDA required drug testing. We discuss these arguments seriatim.

B

The so-called experimental use defense to liability for infringement generally is recognized as originating in an opinion written by Supreme Court Justice Story while on circuit in Massachusetts. In Whittemore v. Cutter, 29 Fed.Cas. 1120, 1121, (C.C.D.Mass.1813) (No. 17,600), Justice Story sought to justify a trial judge's instruction to a jury that an infringer must have an intent to use a patented invention for profit, stating:

> "[I]t could never have been the intention of the legislature to punish a man who constructed such a machine merely for philosophical experiments, or for the purpose of ascertaining the sufficiency of the machine to produce its described effects."

Despite skepticism, see, e.g., Byam v. Bullard, 4 Fed.Cas. 934 (C.C.D.Mass.1852) (No. 2,262) (opinion by Justice Curtis), Justice Story's seminal statement evolved until, by 1861, the law was "well-settled that an experiment with a patented article for the sole purpose of gratifying a philosophical taste, or curiosity, or for mere amusement is not an infringement of the rights of the patentee." Peppenhausen v. Falke, 19 Fed.Cas. 1048, 1049 (C.C.S.D.N.Y.1861) (No. 11,279). (For a detailed history and analysis of the experimental use exception, see Bee, Experimental Use as an Act of Patent Infringement, 39 J.Pat.Off.Soc'y 357 (1957).) Professor Robinson firmly entrenched the experimental use exception into the patent law when he wrote his famous treatise, W. Robinson, The Law of Patents for Useful Inventions § 898 (1890):

> "§ 898. No Act an Infringement unless it Affects the Pecuniary Interests of the Owner of the Patented Invention.
>
> "[T]he interest to be promoted by the wrongful employment of the invention must be hostile to the interest of the patentee. The interest of the patentee is represented by the emoluments which he does or might receive from the practice of the invention by himself or others. These, though not always taking the shape of money, are of a pecuniary charac-

ter, and their value is capable of estimation like other property. Hence acts of infringement must attack the right of the patentee to these emoluments, and either turn them aside into other channels or prevent them from accruing in favor of any one. An unauthorized sale of the invention is always such an act. But the manufacture or the use of the invention may be intended only for other purposes, and produce no pecuniary result. *Thus where it is made or used as an experiment, whether for the gratification of scientific tastes, or for curiosity, or for amusement, the interests of the patentee are not antagonized, the sole effect being of an intellectual character in the promotion of the employer's knowledge or the relaxation afforded to his mind.* But if the products of the experiment are sold, or used for the convenience of the experimentor, or if the experiments are conducted with a view to the adaptation of the invention to the experimentor's business, the acts of making or of use are violations of the rights of the inventor and infringements of his patent. In reference to such employments of a patented invention the law is diligent to protect the patentee, and even experimental uses will be sometimes enjoined though no injury may have resulted admitting of positive redress." [Emphasis supplied, footnotes omitted.]

The Court of Claims, whose precedents bind us, on several occasions has considered the defense of experimental use. * * * [cites]. Bolar concedes, as it must, that its intended use of flurazepam hcl does not fall within the "traditional limits" of the experimental use exception as established in these cases or those of other circuits. Its concession here is fatal. Despite Bolar's argument that its tests are "true scientific inquiries" to which a literal interpretation of the experimental use exception logically should extend, we hold the experimental use exception to be truly narrow, and we will not expand it under the present circumstances. Bolar's argument that the experimental use rule deserves a broad construction is not justified.

Pitcairn, the most persuasive of the Court of Claims cases concerning the experimental use defense, sets forth the law which must control the disposition of this case: "[t]ests, demonstrations, and experiments * * * [which] are in keeping with the legitimate business of the * * * [alleged infringer]" are infringements for which "[e]xperimental use is not a defense." 547 F.2d at 1125–1126. We have carefully reviewed each of the other Court of Claims cases, and although they contain some loose language on which Bolar relies, they are unpersuasive. * * *

Bolar's intended "experimental" use is solely for business reasons and not for amusement, to satisfy idle curiosity, or for strictly philosophical inquiry. Bolar's intended use of flurazepam hcl to derive FDA required test data is thus an infringement of the '053 patent. Bolar may intend to perform "experiments," but unlicensed experiments conducted with a view to the adaption of the patented invention to the experimentor's business is a violation of the rights of the patentee to exclude others from using his patented invention. It is obvious here that it is a misnomer to call the intended use *de minimis*. It is no trifle in its economic effect on the parties even if the quantity used is small. It is no dilettante affair such as Justice Story envisioned. We cannot construe the experimental use rule so broadly as to allow a violation of the patent laws in the guise of "scientific inquiry," when that inquiry has definite, cognizable, and not insubstantial commercial purposes.

* * *

The decision of the district court holding the '053 patent not infringed is reversed. The case is remanded with instructions to fashion an appropriate remedy.

NOTE

1. Congress rejected the *Bolar* result as applied to drugs by adding § 271(e) as part of the Drug Price Competition and Patent Term Restoration Act of 1984, P.L. 98–417. Under that statute, owners of patented drugs got the opportunity to extend the patent term to compensate for delays caused by the regulatory review of the Food and Drug Administration, while their potential "generic" competitors got the right to initiate regulatory testing and approval procedures prior to the expiration of the patent term. The interrelationship of the F.D.A. regulation and patent incentives was first analyzed in E.W. Kitch, "The Patent System and the New Drug Application: An Evaluation of the Incentives for Private Investment in New Drug Research and Marketing," in Landau (ed.), *Regulating New Drugs* (University of Chicago Center for Policy Study, 1973).

(2) WITHIN THE UNITED STATES

DEEPSOUTH PACKING CO. v. LAITRAM CORP.

Supreme Court of the United States, 1972.
406 U.S. 518, 92 S.Ct. 1700, 32 L.Ed.2d 273.

MR. JUSTICE WHITE delivered the opinion of the Court.

The United States District Court for the Eastern District of Louisiana has written:

"Shrimp, whether boiled, broiled, barbecued or fried, are a gustatory delight, but they did not evolve to satisfy man's palate. Like other crustaceans, they wear their skeletons outside their bodies in order to shield their savory pink and white flesh against predators, including man. They also carry their intestines, commonly called veins, in bags (or sand bags) that run the length of their bodies. For shrimp to be edible, it is necessary to remove their shells. In addition, if the vein is removed, shrimp become more pleasing to the fastidious as well as more palatable."

Such "gustatory" observations are rare even in those piscatorially favored federal courts blissfully situated on the Nation's Gulf Coast, but they are properly recited in this case. Petitioner and respondent both hold patents on machines that devein shrimp more cheaply and efficiently than competing machinery or hand labor can do the job. Extensive litigation below has established that respondent, the Laitram Corp., has the superior claim and that the distribution and use of petitioner Deepsouth's machinery in this country should be enjoined to prevent infringement of Laitram's patents. * * * We granted certiorari * * * to consider a related question: Is Deepsouth, barred from the American market by Laitram's patents, also foreclosed by the patent laws from exporting its deveiners, in less than fully assembled form, for use abroad?

I

A rudimentary understanding of the patents in dispute is a prerequisite to comprehending the legal issue presented. The District Court determined that the Laitram Corp. held two valid patents for machinery used in the process of deveining shrimp. One, granted in 1954, accorded Laitram rights over a "slitter" which exposed the veins of shrimp by using water pressure and gravity to force the shrimp down an inclined trough studded with razor blades. As the shrimp descend through the trough their backs are slit by the blades or other knife-like objects arranged in a zig-zag pattern. The second patent, granted in 1958, covers a "tumbler, 'a device to mechanically remove substantially all veins from shrimp whose backs have previously been slit,' " * * * by the machines described in the 1954 patent. This invention uses streams of water to carry slit shrimp into and then out of a revolving drum fabricated from commercial sheet metal. As shrimp pass through the drum the hooked "lips" of the punched metal, "projecting at an acute angle from the supporting member and having a smooth rounded free edge for engaging beneath the vein of a shrimp and for wedging the vein between the lip and the supporting member," * * * engage the veins and remove them.

Both the slitter and the tumbler are combination patents; that is,

> "[n]one of the parts referred to are new, and none are claimed as new; nor is any portion of the combination less than the whole claimed as new, or stated to produce any given result. The end in view is proposed to be accomplished by the union of all, arranged and combined together in the manner described. And this combination, composed of all the parts mentioned in the specification, and arranged with reference to each other, and to other parts of the (machine) in the manner therein described, is stated to be the improvement, and is the thing patented." Prouty v. Ruggles, 16 Pet. 336, 341, 10 L.Ed. 985 (1842).

The slitter's elements as recited in Laitram's patent claim were: an inclined trough, a "knife" (actually, knives) positioned in the trough, and a means (water sprayed from jets) to move the shrimp down the trough. The tumbler's elements include a "lip," a "support member," and a "means" (water thrust from jets). As is usual in combination patents, none of the elements in either of these patents were themselves patentable at the time of the patent, nor are they now. The means in both inventions, moving water, was and is, of course, commonplace. (It is not suggested that Deepsouth infringed Laitram's patents by its use of water jets.) The cutting instruments and inclined troughs used in slitters were and are commodities available for general use. The structure of the lip and support member in the tumbler were hardly novel: Laitram concedes that the inventors merely adapted punched metal sheets ordered from a commercial catalog in order to perfect their invention. The patents were warranted not by the novelty of their elements but by the novelty of the combination they represented. Invention was recognized because Laitram's assignors combined ordinary elements in an extraordinary way—a novel union of old means was designed to achieve new ends. Thus, for both inventions "the whole in some way exceed(ed) the sum of its parts." Great A. & P. Tea Co. v. Supermarket Equipment Corp., 340 U.S. 147, 152 (1950).

II

The lower court's decision that Laitram held valid combination patents entitled the corporation to the privileges bestowed by 35 U.S.C. § 154, the keystone provision of the patent code. "(F)or the term of seventeen years" from the date of the patent, Laitram had "the right to exclude others from making, using, or selling the invention throughout the United States * * *." The § 154 right in turn provides the basis for affording the patentee an injunction against direct, induced, and contributory infringement, 35 U.S.C. § 283, or an award of damages when such infringement has already occurred, 35 U.S.C. § 284. Infringement is defined by 35 U.S.C. § 271 * * *.

As a result of these provisions the judgment of Laitram's patent superiority forecloses Deepsouth and its customers from any future use (other than a use approved by Laitram or occurring after the Laitram patent has expired) of its deveiners "throughout the United States." The patent provisions taken in conjunction with the judgment below also entitle Laitram to the injunction it has received prohibiting Deepsouth from continuing to "make" or, once made, to "sell" deveiners "throughout the United States." Further, Laitram may recover damages for any past unauthorized use, sale, or making "throughout the United States." This much is not disputed.

But Deepsouth argues that it is not liable for every type of past sale and that a portion of its future business is salvageable. Section 154 and related provisions obviously are intended to grant a patentee a monopoly only over the United States market; they are not intended to grant a patentee the bonus of a favored position as a flagship company free of American competition in international commerce. Deepsouth, itself barred from using its deveining machines, or from inducing others to use them "throughout the United States," barred also from making and selling the machines in the United States, seeks to make the parts of deveining machines, to sell them to foreign buyers, and to have the buyers assemble the parts and use the machines abroad. Accordingly, Deepsouth seeks judicial approval, expressed through a modification or interpretation of the injunction against it, for continuing its practice of shipping deveining equipment to foreign customers in three separate boxes, each containing only parts of the 1¾–ton machines, yet the whole assemblable in less than one hour. The company contends that by this means both the "making" and the "use" of the machines occur abroad and Laitram's lawful monopoly over the making and use of the machines throughout the United States is not infringed.

Laitram counters that this course of conduct is based upon a hypertechnical reading of the patent code that, if tolerated, will deprive it of its right to the fruits of the inventive genius of its assignors. "The right to make can scarcely be made plainer by definition . . .," Bauer v. O'Donnell, 229 U.S. 1, 10 (1913). Deepsouth in all respects save final assembly of the parts "makes" the invention. It does so with the intent of having the foreign user effect the combination without Laitram's permission. Deepsouth sells these components as though they were the machines themselves; the act of assembly is regarded, indeed advertised, as of no importance.

The District Court, faced with this dispute, noted that three prior circuit courts had considered the meaning of "making" in this context and that all three had resolved the question favorably to Deepsouth's position. * * * The District Court held that its injunction should not be read as prohibiting export of the elements of a combination patent even when those elements could and predictably would be combined to form the whole.

> "It may be urged that . . . [this] result is not logical . . . But it is founded on twin notions that underlie the patent laws. One is that a combination patent protects only the combination. The other is that monopolies—even those conferred by patents—are not viewed with favor. These are logic enough." * * *

The Court of Appeals for the Fifth Circuit reversed, thus departing from the established rules of the Second, Third, and Seventh Circuits. In the Fifth Circuit panel's opinion, those courts that previously considered the question "worked themselves into * * * a conceptual box" by adopting "an artificial, technical construction" of the patent laws, a construction, moreover, which in the opinion of the panel, "[subverted] the Constitutional scheme of promoting 'the Progress of Science and useful Arts' " by allowing an intrusion on a patentee's rights, * * *, citing U.S. Const., Art. I, § 8.

III

We disagree with the Court of Appeals for the Fifth Circuit. Under the common law the inventor had no right to exclude others from making and using his invention. If Laitram has a right to suppress Deepsouth's export trade it must be derived from its patent grant, and thus from the patent statute. We find that 35 U.S.C. § 271, the provision of the patent laws on which Laitram relies, does not support its claim.

Certainly if Deepsouth's conduct were intended to lead to use of patented deveiners inside the United States its production and sales activity would be subject to injunction as an induced or contributory infringement. But it is established that there can be no contributory infringement without the fact or intention of a direct infringement.
* * *

The statute makes it clear that it is not an infringement to make or use a patented product outside of the United States. 35 U.S.C. § 271. * * *. Thus, in order to secure the injunction it seeks, Laitram must show a § 271(a) direct infringement by Deepsouth in the United States, that is, that Deepsouth "makes," "uses," or "sells" the patented product within the bounds of this country.

Laitram does not suggest that Deepsouth "uses" the machines. Its argument that Deepsouth sells the machines—based primarily on Deepsouth's sales rhetoric and related indicia such as price—cannot carry the day unless it can be shown that Deepsouth is selling the "patented invention." The sales question thus resolves itself into the question of manufacture: did Deepsouth "make" (and then sell) something cognizable under the patent law as the patented invention, or did it "make" (and then sell) something that fell short of infringement?

The Court of Appeals, believing that the word "makes" should be accorded "a construction in keeping with the ordinary meaning of that term," * * * held against Deepsouth on the theory that "makes" "means what it ordinarily connotes—the substantial manufacture of the constituent parts of the machine." * * * Passing the question of whether this definition more closely corresponds to the ordinary meaning of the term than that offered by Judge Swan in *Andrea* [Radio Corp. of America v. Andrea, 79 F.2d 626 (CA2 Cir.1935)] 35 years earlier (something is made when it reaches the state of final "operable" assembly), we find the Fifth Circuit's definition unacceptable because it collides head on with a line of decisions so firmly embedded in our patent law as to be unassailable absent a congressional recasting of the statute.

We cannot endorse the view that the "substantial manufacture of the constituent parts of [a] machine" constitutes direct infringement when we have so often held that a combination patent protects only against the operable assembly of the whole and not the manufacture of its parts. "For as we pointed out in Mercoid v. Mid–Continent Investment Co. [320 U.S. 661] a patent on a combination is a patent on the assembled or functioning whole, not on the separate parts." Mercoid Corp. v. Minneapolis–Honeywell Regulator Co., 320 U.S. 680, 684 (1944).

It was this basic tenet of the patent system that led Judge Swan to hold in the leading case, Radio Corp. of America v. Andrea, 79 F.2d 626 (CA2 1935), that unassembled export of the elements of an invention did not infringe the patent.

"[The] relationship is the essence of the patent.

". . . No wrong is done the patentee until the combination is formed. His monopoly does not cover the manufacture of sale of separate elements capable of being, but never actually, associated to form the invention. Only when such association is made is there a direct infringement of his monopoly, and not even then if it is done outside the territory for which the monopoly was granted." Id., at 628.

* * *

We reaffirm this conclusion today.

Reversed and remanded.

NOTE

1. Congress rejected the result in *Laitram.* See 35 U.S.C. § 271(f), added by Public Law 98–622 § 101, Nov. 8, 1984.

2. Doesn't Congress' rejection of *Laitram* favor foreign producers over U.S. producers? A foreign firm can still manufacture and ship the machine without infringing the U.S. patent (assuming that there is no applicable foreign patent) but a U.S. firm cannot. But if there is foreign competition, wouldn't we expect the U.S. patent owner to price its machines for export so as to meet that competition?

3. The limitation of infringement to acts performed within the United States is particularly important in the area of process claims. If one holds a patent claiming a product then any importation of that product into the United States will infringe. But the practice of a process patent outside the United States and importation of the resulting product into the United States does not infringe under § 271(a). This would be true even if the product could only be made through the use of the patented process. In 1988 Congress added § 271(g) which makes it an infringement of a U.S. patent to import into, or sell or use in, the United States a product manufactured by means of a process which if practiced in the United States would be patent infringement. Public Law 100–418 § 9003, Aug. 23, 1988. Note the limitations on § 271(g). What considerations justify them?

(3) WITHIN THE TERM OF THE PATENT

PAPER CONVERTING MACHINE CO. v. MAGNA–GRAPHICS CORP.

United States Court of Appeals, Federal Circuit, 1984.
745 F.2d 11.

NICHOLS, SENIOR CIRCUIT JUDGE.

This appeal is from a judgment of the United States District Court for the Eastern District of Wisconsin * * * entered on December 1, 1983, and awarding plaintiff Paper Converting Machine Company (Paper Converting) $893,064 as compensation for defendant Magna–Graphics Corporation's (Magna–Graphics) willful infringement of United States Patent No. Re. 28,353. We *affirm-in-part and vacate-in-part.*

I

Although the technology involved here is complex, the end product is one familiar to most Americans. The patented invention relates to a machine used to manufacture rolls of densely wound ("hard-wound") industrial toilet tissue and paper toweling. The machine, commonly known as an automatic rewinder, unwinds a paper web continuously under high tension at speeds up to 2,000 feet per minute from a large-diameter paper roll—known as the parent roll or bedroll—and simultaneously rewinds it onto paperboard cores to form individual consumer products.

Before the advent of automatic rewinders, toilet tissue and paper towel producers used "stop-start" rewinders. With these machines, the entire rewinding operation had to cease after a retail-sized "log" was finished so that a worker could place a new mandrel (the shaft for carrying the paperboard core) in the path of the paper web. In an effort to increase production, automatic rewinders were introduced in the early 1950's. These machines automatically moved a new mandrel into the path of the paper web while the machine was still winding the paper web onto another mandrel, and could operate at a steady pace at speeds up to about 1,200 feet per minute.

In 1962, Nystrand, Bradley, and Spencer invented the first successful "sequential" automatic rewinder, a machine which not only overcame previous speed limitations, but also could handle two-ply tissue. This rewinder simultaneously cut the paper web and impaled it on pins against the parent roll. Then, after a new mandrel was automatically moved into place, a "pusher" would move the paper web away from the parent roll and against a glue-covered paperboard core to begin winding a new paper log.

On April 20, 1965, United States Patent No. 3,179,348 (the '348 patent) issued, giving to Paper Converting (to whom rights in the invention had been assigned) patent protection for machines incorporating the sequential rewinding approach. On September 1, 1972, Paper Converting applied to have the claims of the '348 patent narrowed by reissue, and on March 4, 1975, United States Patent No. Re. 28,353 (the '353 patent) issued on this application. The '353 patent, like the original '348 patent on which it is based, received an expiration date of April 20, 1982. Claim 1 of the '353 patent defines the improvement in the web-winding apparatus as an improvement comprising:

"(C) means for transversely severing said web to provide a free leading edge on said web for approaching a mandrel on which said web is to be wound in said path, and

"(D) pin means extensibly mounted on said roll for maintaining a web portion spaced from said edge in contact with said roll, and pusher means extensibly mounted on said roll to urge said maintained web portion against an adjacent mandrel."

Paper Converting achieved widespread commercial success with its patented automatic rewinder. Although there are not many domestic producers of toilet tissue and paper toweling, Paper Converting has sold more than 500 machines embodying the invention.

In 1979, Paper Converting brought the present action against Magna–Graphics for infringement of the '353 patent. After a trial concerning only issues of liability, the district court held the '353 patent valid and found it willfully infringed * * *. It awarded treble damages, finding that Magna–Graphics had acted without the advice of counsel as to the change it made in its machines to avoid infringement. The Seventh Circuit affirmed * * *. The parties commendably raise no issues here which the Seventh Circuit has already decided as to Magna–Graphics' liability.

When the district court held the accounting for damages (after the Seventh Circuit had affirmed it on the liability portion of the case), it found that Magna–Graphics had made two sales of infringing rewinders and associated equipment: one to the Fort Howard Paper Company (Fort Howard) under circumstances to be described, and one to the Scott Paper Company (Scott). The court awarded to Paper Converting $112,163 for Magna–Graphics' sale to Scott, and $145,583 for Magna–Graphics' sale to Fort Howard. The court then trebled these damages, and added $119,826 as prejudgment interest on the untrebled award. This appeal is from the judgment awarding damages.

II

* * * Magna–Graphics contends that the district court erred in finding the sale, substantial manufacture, and delivery of the Fort Howard rewinder to be an infringement * * *.

III

A

Magna–Graphics first argues that it should bear no liability whatsoever for its manufacture, sale, or delivery of the Fort Howard rewinder because that machine was never *completed* during the life of the '353 patent. We disagree.

In early 1980 Fort Howard became interested in purchasing a new high-speed rewinder line. Both Paper Converting and Magna–Graphics offered bids. Because Magna–Graphics offered to provide an entire rewinder line for about 10 percent less than did Paper Converting, it won the contract. Delivery would have been before the '353 patent expired. Magna–Graphics began to build the contracted for machinery, but before it completed the rewinder, on February 26, 1981, the federal district court in Wisconsin determined that a similar Magna–Graphics' rewinder built for and sold to Scott infringed the '353 patent. The court enjoined Magna–Graphics from any future infringing activity.

Because at the time of the federal injunction the rewinder intended for Fort Howard was only 80 percent complete, Magna–Graphics sought a legal way to fulfill its contract with Fort Howard rather than abandon its machine. First, Magna–Graphics tried to change the construction of the rewinder so as to avoid infringement. It submitted to Paper Converting's counsel three drawings illustrating three proposed changes, and asked for an opinion as to whether the changes would avoid infringement. Paper Converting's counsel replied, however, that until a fully built and operating machine could be viewed, no opinion could be given. Magna–Graphics, believing such a course of action unfeasible because of the large risks in designing, engineering, and building a machine without knowing whether it would be considered an infringement, instead negotiated with Fort Howard to delay the final assembly and delivery of an otherwise infringing rewinder until after the '353 patent expired in April 1982.

Magna–Graphics thereafter continued to construct the Fort Howard machine, all the while staying in close consultation with its counsel. After finishing substantially all of the machine, Magna–Graphics tested it to ensure that its moving parts would function as intended at a rate of 1,600 feet of paper per minute. Although Magna–Graphics normally *fully* tested machines at its plant before shipment, to avoid infringement in this instance, Magna–Graphics ran its tests in two stages over a period of several weeks in July and August of 1981.

To understand Magna–Graphics' testing procedure, it is necessary to understand the automatic transfer operation of the patented machine. First, from within a 72–inch long "cutoff" roll, a 72–inch blade ejects to sever the continuous web of paper which is wound around the bedroll. Then, pins attached to the bedroll hold the severed edge of the web while pushers, also attached to the bedroll, transfer the edge of the web towards the mandrel (the roll on which the paperboard core is mounted).

In the first stage of its test, Magna–Graphics checked the bedroll to determine whether the pushers actuated properly. It installed on the bedroll two pusher pads instead of the thirty pads normally used in an operating machine. It greased the pads and operated the bedroll to determine whether the pads, when unlatched, would contact the core on the mandrel. (Magna–Graphics greased the pads so as to provide a visual indication that they had touched the core.) During this stage of tests, no cutoff blades or pins were installed.

In the second stage of the test, Magna–Graphics checked the cutoff roll to determine whether the cutting blade actuated as intended. It tested the knife actuating mechanism by installing into the cutoff roll a short 4–inch section of cutter blade rather than the 72–inch blade normally used. After taping a 4–inch wide piece of paper to the outer surface of the cutoff roll, Magna–Graphics operated the cutoff roll to determine whether the latch mechanism would eject the blade to cut the paper. During this phase of the testing, no pins or pusher pads were installed. At no time during the tests were the pins, pushers, and blade installed and operated together.

To further its scheme to avoid patent infringement, Magna–Graphics negotiated special shipment and assembly details with Fort Howard. Under the advice of counsel, Fort Howard and Magna–Graphics agreed that the rewinder's cutoff and transfer mechanism would not be finally assembled until April 22, 1982, two days after the expiration of the '353 patent. With this agreement in hand, Magna–Graphics shipped the basic rewinder machine to Fort Howard on September 17, 1981, and separately shipped the cutoff roll and bedroll on October 23, 1981. The rewinder machine was not assembled or installed at the Fort Howard plant until April 26, 1982.

B

With this case we are once again confronted with a situation which tests the temporal limits of the American patent grant. See Roche Products, Inc. v. Bolar Pharmaceutical Co., 733 F.2d 858 (Fed.Cir.1984). We must decide here the extent to which a competitor of a patentee can *manufacture* and test during the life of a patent a machine intended solely for post-patent use. Magna–Graphics asserts that no law prohibits it from soliciting orders for, *substantially* manufacturing, testing, or even delivering machinery which, if *completely* assembled during the patent term, would infringe. We notice, but Magna–Graphics adds that it is totally irrelevant, that Paper Converting has lost, during the term of its patent, a contract for the patented machine which it would have received but for the competitor's acts.

Clearly, any federal right which Paper Converting has to suppress Magna–Graphics' patent-term activities, or to receive damages for those activities, must be derived from its patent grant, and thus from the patent statutes. "Care should be taken not to extend by judicial construction the rights and privileges which it was the purpose of Congress to bestow." Bauer v. O'Donnell, 229 U.S. 1, 10 (1913).

* * *

Here, the dispositive issue is whether Magna–Graphics engaged in the making, use, or sale of something which the law recognizes as embodying an invention protected by a patent. Magna–Graphics relies on Deepsouth Packing Co. v. Laitram Corp., 406 U.S. 518 (1972).

* * *

Magna–Graphics' effort to apply Deepsouth as precedential runs into the obvious difficulty that the element of extraterritoriality is absent here, yet it obviously was of paramount importance to the Deepsouth Court. We must be cautious in extending five to four decisions by analogy * * *. The analysis of *where* infringement occurs is applicable, Magna–Graphics says, to determining *when* an infringement occurs, whether before or after a patent expires. We have not found any case that has so held, and are not cited to any. It does not at all necessarily follow, for the *Deepsouth* analysis is made to avert a result, extraterritoriality, that would not occur whatever analysis was made in the instant case.

Although in *Deepsouth* the Court at times used broad language in reaching its decision, it is clear that Deepsouth was intended to be narrowly construed as applicable only to the issue of the extraterritorial effect of the American patent law. The Court so implied not only in Deepsouth ("[A]t stake here is the right of American companies to compete with an American patent holder *in foreign markets. Our patent system makes no claim to extraterritorial effect,* * * * " 406 U.S. at 531 (emphasis added)), but in a subsequent decision as well ("The question under consideration [in *Deepsouth*] was whether a patent is infringed when unpatented elements are assembled into the combination *outside the United States.*" Dawson Chemical Co. v. Rohm & Haas Co., 448 U.S. 176, 216 (1980) (emphasis added)). Moreover, in Decca Limited v. United States, 544 F.2d 1070 (Ct.Cl.1976), the Court of Claims considered the worldwide system of electronic navigation aids called "Omega," which employs as a means of fixing the locations of ships and planes "master" and "slave" transmission stations, and receivers making computer printouts on board the ships and planes to be guided. The government relied on *Deepsouth* to establish that the involved patent, if enforced against it, would be given an extraterritorial application. The Court of Claims held that the application was not extraterritorial and therefore *Deepsouth* was not implicated. The Court of Claims viewed *Deepsouth* as simply and wholly a decision against extraterritorial application of United States patent laws. Id. at 1072–74.

While there is thus a horror of giving extraterritorial effect to United States patent protection, there is no corresponding horror of a valid United States patent giving economic benefits not cut off entirely on patent expiration. Thus, we hold that the expansive language used in *Deepsouth* is not controlling in the present case. The facts in *Deepsouth* are not the facts here. Because no other precedent controls our decision here, however, we nevertheless look to *Deepsouth* and elsewhere for guidance on the issue of whether what Magna–Graphics did is an infringement of the '353 patent.

A further examination of the *Deepsouth* opinion reveals that the Court stated what was for it a most unusual reliance on a precedent established in an inferior court, the case being Radio Corporation of America v. Andrea, 79 F.2d 626 (2d Cir.1935). The reason for this was the eminently logical one that when in 1952 the Congress recodified the patent law, and specifically § 271, the most relevant precedent was *Andrea* as to the legal effect of exporting, unassembled, components that if exported assembled would infringe a "combination patent." Presumably the Congress accepted and enacted Judge Swan's interpretation in *Andrea,* absent any relevant pronouncement by our highest court.

Judge Swan's opinion on the appeal from a preliminary injunction is, indeed, a rather dramatic application of the view of the law he announced. The patents related to radio receiving sets. The alleged infringer, Andrea, exported them complete except for vacuum tubes exported *in the same package,* but not in their sockets. All the buyer had to do to have a patented set was, therefore, to put the tube in the socket designed to receive it. Swan's opinion does not mention any horror of extraterritoriality. Rather, the analysis is that the sale in this condition, even to domestic users, is not a direct infringement, but is only a contributory infringement. Thus, the practical impact of the Swan opinion, but not its reasoning, is limited to export sales, where contributory infringement is not logically applicable. Swan notes, however, as possible direct infringement evidence, that the alleged infringer put the tubes in their sockets to test them, and the sets generally, and then disassembled for export, and the reversal leaves it open to the trial court to look into this.

The trial court thereafter made further findings and entered its final judgment (then called its decree) and the case came up again, same name, 90 F.2d 612 (2d Cir.1937). Where previously the panel had consisted of only Swan and the subsequently ill-famed Manton, this _bribery_ time Circuit Judge Chase was added and Manton authored the opinion. The matter of testing was now clarified, and it was also now clear to the panel:

> "The purchaser to connect the tube needs only insert it in the socket. No adjustment is required; no screw or nut need be tightened. Where the elements of an invention are thus sold in substantially unified and combined form, infringement may not be avoided by a separation or division of parts which leaves to the purchaser a simple task of integration. Otherwise a patentee would be denied adequate protection." (Id. at 613.)

The court further noted that in part the sets were fully assembled for testing in the United States and that the sales of the completed though partly disassembled sets were made in the United States. The main problem dealt with in the second *Andrea* opinion was what "implied license" the infringer acquired when it bought the tubes separately.

Swan dissented, saying the holding that the sale of the disassembled parts in this country was an infringement overruled the decision in 79 F.2d 626. This history was, of course, not overlooked in the Supreme Court * * *.

What are we to make of all this? It does seem as if the concept of an "operable assembly" put forward by Justice White in his majority opinion is probably something short of a full and complete assembly; thus, if the infringer makes an "operable assembly" of the components of the patented invention, sufficient for testing, it need not be the same thing as the complete and entire invention. The other thing is, if the

infringer has tested his embodiment of the invention sufficiently to
satisfy him, this may be a "use," because as held in *Roche Products,
Inc.*, "use" includes use for the purpose of testing. Apparently, this
was also a factor in the second *Andrea* decision, though given the
confusing way Manton put his opinion together, it is hard to be sure.
Swan also may be right that Manton is simply overruling the interlocutory 79 F.2d 626 decision. If so, apparently the Supreme Court majority liked the first holding better. That is, the part quoted above of the
second decision is not law. But there is no apparent difference between
Swan and the rest of the second panel as to the legal effect of testing
and sale.

In any case, we would not be justified in thinking Justice White
and the Supreme Court majority intended to hold, or to be understood
as holding, that the second *Andrea* decision in 90 F.2d 612, was not
before Congress just as much as the first *Andrea* decision in 79 F.2d
626, or was not just as much to be considered in interpreting § 271, as
reenacted in 1952.

* * *

It is undisputed that Magna–Graphics intended to finesse Paper
Converting out of the sale of a machine on which Paper Converting
held a valid patent during the life of that patent. Given the amount of
testing performed here, coupled with the sale and delivery during the
patent-term of a "completed" machine (completed by being ready for
assembly and with no useful noninfringing purpose), we are not persuaded that the district court committed clear error in finding that the
Magna–Graphics' machine infringed the '353 patent.

To reach a contrary result would emasculate the congressional
intent to prevent the making of a patented item during the patent's full
term of 17 years. If without fear of liability a competitor can assemble
a patented item past the point of testing, the last year of the patent
becomes worthless whenever it deals with a long lead-time article.
Nothing would prohibit the unscrupulous competitor from aggressively
marketing its own product and constructing it to all but the final
screws and bolts, as Magna–Graphics did here. We rejected any
reduction to the patent-term in Roche; we cannot allow the inconsistency in the patent law which would exist if we permitted it here. Magna–
Graphics built and tested a patented machine, albeit in a less than
preferred fashion. Because an "operable assembly" of components was
tested, this case is distinguishable from Interdent Corp. v. United
States, 531 F.2d 547, 552 (Ct.Cl.1976) (omission of a claimed element
from the patented combination avoids infringement) and Decca Ltd. v.
United States, 640 F.2d 1156, 1168 (Ct.Cl.1980) (infringement does not
occur until the combination has been constructed and available for use).
Where, as here, significant, unpatented assemblies of elements are
tested during the patent term, enabling the infringer to deliver the
patented combination in parts to the buyer, without testing the entire
combination together as was the infringer's usual practice, testing the

assemblies can be held to be in essence testing the patented combination and, hence, infringement.

That the machine was not operated in its optimum mode is inconsequential: imperfect practice of an invention does not avoid infringement. We affirm the district court's finding that "[d]uring the testing of the Fort Howard machine in July and August 1981, Magna–Graphics completed an operable assembly of the infringing rewinder."

* * *

The judgment of the district court awarding damages and prejudgment interest for Paper Converting's lost profits on two automatic rewinder lines is affirmed. The trebling of damages on the Fort Howard machine is vacated, and remanded for a determination of willfulness.

NIES, CIRCUIT JUDGE, dissenting-in-part.

I dissent from the majority's holding that Magna–Graphics' activities in connection with the Fort Howard machine constitute direct infringement of any claim of Paper Converting's patent. The majority's conclusion necessitates giving a meaning to "patented invention" contrary to the definition set forth by the Supreme Court in Deepsouth Packing Co. v. Laitram Corp., 406 U.S. 518 (1972).

I do not see in *Deepsouth* that the Supreme Court's only concern was the extraterritorial operation of our patent laws. The activities of Deepsouth under attack were all performed in the United States and were found not to result in direct or contributory infringement of the patent. That the activities of final assembly occurred abroad merely precluded a holding that Deepsouth's activities constituted contributory infringement. Contributory infringement cannot arise without a direct infringement. Mercoid Corp. v. Mid–Continent Investment Co., 320 U.S. 661, 677 (1944). The situation in *Deepsouth* is exactly comparable to the one at hand. That the activities of final assembly occurred after the patent expired precludes holding Magna–Graphics to be a contributory infringer, there being no direct infringement by another to which the charge can be appended.

Thus, we are back to the dispositive direct infringement issue in *Deepsouth*, which is the same as the issue here. What is the meaning of "patented invention" in 35 U.S.C. § 271(a)? The alleged infringer, in each case, made and sold something, but was it the "patented invention"?

* * *

Nothing in Justice White's opinion in *Deepsouth* indicates that the concept of an operable assembly is "probably something short of a full and complete assembly," as the majority states. The Court had before it the Fifth Circuit opinion which had analyzed just such less-than-full-assembly situations. Repeatedly, the Court emphasized that the "patented invention" means that all of its claimed elements must be united.

Thus, if the claimed invention comprises the elements A, B, C and D, it is only the combination in its entirety that is protected. The making of the lesser combination A, B and D falls short of direct infringement, even though the missing element C is also supplied by the alleged infringer.

* * *

Indeed, the *Deepsouth* decision is not without redeeming virtue. This is one of the few areas of patent law where a bright line can be, and has been, drawn. That consideration in itself has merit. A competitor should be able to look to the patent claims and know whether his activity infringes or not. Here, the majority provides no guidance to industry or the district courts. One cannot tell from the opinion whether testing and sales activity must also accompany substantial assembly, as it appears to hold, or whether simply substantially making the device preparatory to selling after the patent expires would be sufficient. Given the disjunctive language of the statute, no basis appears for "summing up" partial making with the testing of partial assemblies and with sales made by the alleged infringer. Those activities do not, in some nebulous way, supply the missing physical elements of the "patented invention."

* * *

(4) CONTRIBUTORY INFRINGEMENT

The courts have long recognized that someone who does not himself infringe may be liable because of actions which significantly contribute to the infringement of another. This doctrine has already been discussed in the *Laitram* decision, *supra* p. 994, when the court made the point that the purchasers who fully assembled and used the machine abroad would not be infringing, and thus providing them with the instruments to infringe was not contributory infringement. The doctrine is analogous to the general doctrine that one who aids or abets the commission of a tort will be liable as a tortfeasor.

Contributory infringement is codified in 35 U.S.C. § 271(b).

DAWSON CHEMICAL CO. v. ROHM AND HAAS CO.

Supreme Court of the United States, 1980.
448 U.S. 176, 100 S.Ct. 2601, 65 L.Ed.2d 696.

MR. JUSTICE BLACKMUN delivered the opinion of the Court.

This case presents an important question of statutory interpretation arising under the patent laws. The issue before us is whether the owner of a patent on a chemical process is guilty of patent misuse, and therefore is barred from seeking relief against contributory infringement of its patent rights, if it exploits the patent only in conjunction with the sale of an unpatented article that constitutes a material part of the invention and is not suited for commercial use outside the scope of the patent claims. The answer will determine whether respondent, the owner of a process patent on a chemical herbicide, may maintain an action for contributory infringement against other manufacturers of the chemical used in the process. To resolve this issue, we must construe the various provisions of 35 U.S.C. § 271, which Congress enacted in 1952 to codify certain aspects of the doctrines of contributory infringement and patent misuse that previously had been developed by the judiciary.

I

The doctrines of contributory infringement and patent misuse have long and interrelated histories. The idea that a patentee should be able to obtain relief against those whose acts facilitate infringement by others has been part of our law since Wallace v. Holmes, 29 F.Cas. 74 (No. 17,100) (CC Conn.1871). The idea that a patentee should be denied relief against infringers if he has attempted illegally to extend the scope of his patent monopoly is of somewhat more recent origin, but it goes back at least as far as Motion Picture Patents Co. v. Universal Film Mfg. Co., 243 U.S. 502. The two concepts, contributory infringement and patent misuse, often are juxtaposed, because both concern the relationship between a patented invention and unpatented articles or elements that are needed for the invention to be practiced.

Both doctrines originally were developed by the courts. But in its 1952 codification of the patent laws Congress endeavored, at least in part, to substitute statutory precepts for the general judicial rules that had governed prior to that time. Its efforts find expression in 35 U.S.C. § 271 * * *.

Of particular import to the present controversy are subsections (c) and (d) [of § 271]. The former defines conduct that constitutes contributory infringement; the latter specifies conduct of the patentee that is not to be deemed misuse.

A

The catalyst for this litigation is a chemical compound known to scientists as "3,4–dichloropropionanilide" and referred to in the chemical industry as "propanil." In the late 1950's, it was discovered that this compound had properties that made it useful as a selective, "post-emergence" herbicide particularly well suited for the cultivation of rice. If applied in the proper quantities, propanil kills weeds normally found in rice crops without adversely affecting the crops themselves. It thus permits spraying of general areas where the crops are already growing, and eliminates the necessity for hand weeding or flooding of the rice fields. Propanil is one of several herbicides that are commercially available for use in rice cultivation.

Efforts to obtain patent rights to propanil or its use as a herbicide have been continuous since the herbicidal qualities of the chemical first came to light. The initial contender for a patent monopoly for this chemical compound was the Monsanto Company. In 1957, Monsanto filed the first of three successive applications for a patent on propanil itself. After lengthy proceedings in the United States Patent Office, a patent, No. 3,382,280, finally was issued in 1968. It was declared invalid, however, when Monsanto sought to enforce it by suing Rohm and Haas Company (Rohm & Haas), a competing manufacturer, for direct infringement. * * * The District Court held that propanil had been implicitly revealed in prior art dating as far back as 1902, even though its use as a herbicide had been discovered only recently. * * * Monsanto subsequently dedicated the patent to the public, and it is not a party to the present suit.

Invalidation of the Monsanto patent cleared the way for Rohm & Haas, respondent here, to obtain a patent on the method of process for applying propanil. This is the patent on which the present lawsuit is founded. Rohm & Haas' efforts to obtain a propanil patent began in 1958. These efforts finally bore fruit when, on June 11, 1974, the United States Patent Office issued Patent No. 3,816,092 (the Wilson patent) to Harold F. Wilson and Dougal H. McRay. The patent contains several claims covering a method for applying propanil to inhibit the growth of undesirable plants in areas containing established crops.[2] Rohm & Haas has been the sole owner of the patent since its issuance.

Petitioners, too, are chemical manufacturers. They have manufactured and sold propanil for application to rice crops since before Rohm & Haas received its patent. They market the chemical in containers on which are printed directions for application in accordance with the method claimed in the Wilson patent. Petitioners did not cease manufacture and sale of propanil after that patent issued, despite knowledge that farmers purchasing their products would infringe on the patented method by applying the propanil to their crops. Accordingly, Rohm & Haas filed this suit, in the United States District Court for the Southern District of Texas, seeking injunctive relief against petitioners on the ground that their manufacture and sale of propanil interfered with its patent rights.

The complaint alleged not only that petitioners contributed to infringement by farmers who purchased and used petitioners' propanil, but also that they actually induced such infringement by instructing farmers how to apply the herbicide. See 35 U.S.C. §§ 271(b) and (c). Petitioners responded to the suit by requesting licenses to practice the patented method. When Rohm & Haas refused to grant such licenses, however, petitioners raised a defense of patent misuse and counterclaimed for alleged antitrust violations by respondent. The parties entered into a stipulation of facts, and petitioners moved for partial summary judgment. They argued that Rohm & Haas has misused its

---

2. The Wilson patent contains several claims relevant to this proceeding. Of these the following are illustrative: 1. "A method for selectively inhibiting growth of undesirable plants in an area containing growing undesirable plants in an established crop, which comprises applying to said area 3,4–dichloropropionanilide at a rate of application which inhibits growth of said undesirable plants and which does not adversely affect the growth of said established crop." 2. "The method according to claim 1 wherein the 3,4–dichloropropionanilide is applied in a composition comprising 3,4–dichloropropionanilide and an inert diluent therefor at a rate of between 0.5 and 6 pounds of 3,4–dichloropropionanilide per acre."

patent by conveying the right to practice the patented method only to purchasers of its own propanil.

The District Court granted summary judgment for petitioners. * * * It agreed that Rohm & Haas was barred from obtaining relief against infringers of its patent because it had attempted illegally to extend its patent monopoly. The District Court recognized that 35 U.S.C. § 271(d) specifies certain conduct which is not to be deemed patent misuse. The court ruled, however, that "[t]he language of § 271(d) simply does not encompass the totality of (Rohm & Haas') conduct in this case." * * * It held that respondent's refusal to grant licenses, other than the "implied" licenses conferred by operation of law upon purchasers of its propanil, constituted an attempt by means of a "tying" arrangement to effect a monopoly over an unpatented component of the process. The District Court concluded that this conduct would be deemed patent misuse under the judicial decisions that preceded § 271(d), and it held that "[n]either the legislative history nor the language of § 271 indicates that this rule has been modified."
* * *

The United States Court of Appeals for the Fifth Circuit reversed. * * * It emphasized the fact that propanil, in the terminology of the patent law, is a "nonstaple" article, that is, one that has no commercial use except in connection with respondent's patented invention. After a thorough review of the judicial developments preceding enactment of § 271, and a detailed examination of the legislative history of that provision, the court concluded that the legislation restored to the patentee protection against contributory infringement that decisions of this Court theretofore had undermined. To secure that result, Congress found it necessary to cut back on the doctrine of patent misuse. The Court of Appeals determined that, by specifying in § 271(d) conduct that is not to be deemed misuse, "Congress *did* clearly provide for a patentee's right to exclude others and reserve to itself, if it chooses, the right to sell nonstaples used substantially only in its invention." 599 F.2d, at 704 (emphasis in original). Since Rohm & Haas' conduct was designed to accomplish only what the statute contemplated, the court ruled that petitioners' misuse defense was of no avail.

We granted certiorari to forestall a possible conflict in the lower courts and to resolve an issue of prime importance in the administration of the patent law.

B

For present purposes certain material facts are not in dispute. First, the validity of the Wilson patent is not in question at this stage in the litigation. We therefore must assume that respondent is the lawful owner of the sole and exclusive right to use, or to license others to use, propanil as a herbicide on rice fields in accordance with the methods claimed in the Wilson patent. Second, petitioners do not dispute that their manufacture and sale of propanil together with instructions for use as a herbicide constitute contributory infringement of the Rohm & Haas patent. * * * Accordingly, they admit that propanil constitutes "a material part of [respondent's] invention," that it is "especially made or especially adapted for use in an infringement of [the] patent," and that it is "not a staple article or commodity of commerce suitable for substantial noninfringing use," all within the language of 35 U.S.C. § 271(c).[6] They also concede that they have produced and sold propanil with knowledge that it would be used in a manner infringing on respondent's patent rights. To put the same matter in slightly different terms, as the litigation now stands, petitioners admit commission of a tort and raise as their only defense to liability the contention that respondent, by engaging in patent misuse, comes into court with unclean hands.

As a result of these concessions, our chief focus of inquiry must be the scope of the doctrine of patent misuse in light of the limitations placed upon that doctrine by § 271(d). On this subject, as well, our task is guided by certain stipulations and concessions. The parties agree that Rohm & Haas makes and sells propanil; that it has refused to license petitioners or any others to do the same; that it has not granted express licenses either to retailers or to end users of the product; and that farmers who buy propanil from Rohm & Haas may use it, without fear of being sued for direct infringement, by virtue of an "implied license" they obtain when Rohm & Haas relinquishes its monopoly by selling the propanil. * * * The parties further agree that §§ 271(d)(1) and (3) permit respondent both to sell propanil itself and to sue others who sell the same product without a license, and that under § 271(d)(2) it would be free to demand royalties from others for the sale of propanil if it chose to do so.

The parties disagree over whether respondent has engaged in any additional conduct that amounts to patent misuse. Petitioners assert that there has been misuse because respondent has "tied" the sale of patent rights to the purchase of propanil, an unpatented and indeed unpatentable article, and because it has refused to grant licenses to other producers of the chemical compound. They argue that § 271(d) does not permit any sort of tying arrangement, and that resort to such a practice excludes respondent from the category of patentees "otherwise entitled to relief" within the meaning of § 271(d). Rohm & Haas, understandably, vigorously resists this characterization of its conduct. It argues that its acts have been only those that § 271(d), by express mandate, excepts from characterization as patent misuse. It further asserts that if this conduct results in an extension of the patent right to a control over an unpatented commodity, in this instance the extension has been given express statutory sanction.

6. We follow the practice of the Court of Appeals and the parties by using the term "nonstaple" throughout this opinion to refer to a component as defined in 35 U.S.C. § 271(c), the unlicensed sale of which would constitute contributory infringement. A "staple" component is one that does not fit this definition. We recognize that the terms "staple" and "nonstaple" have not always been defined precisely in this fashion.

II

*   *   *

As we have noted, the doctrine of contributory infringement had its genesis in an era of simpler and less subtle technology. Its basic elements are perhaps best explained with a classic example drawn from that era. In Wallace v. Holmes, 29 F.Cas. 74 (No. 17,100) (CC Conn. 1871), the patentee had invented a new burner for an oil lamp. In compliance with the technical rules of patent claiming, this invention was patented in a combination that also included the standard fuel reservoir, wick tube, and chimney necessary for a properly functioning lamp. After the patent issued, a competitor began to market a rival product including the novel burner but not the chimney. *   *   * Under the sometimes scholastic law of patents, this conduct did not amount to direct infringement, because the competitor had not replicated every single element of the patentee's claimed combination. Cf., e.g., Prouty v. Ruggles, 16 Pet. 336, 341, 10 L.Ed. 985 (1842). Yet the court held that there had been "palpable interference" with the patentee's legal rights, because purchasers would be certain to complete the combination, and hence the infringement, by adding the glass chimney. 29 F.Cas., at 80. The court permitted the patentee to enforce his rights against the competitor who brought about the infringement, rather than requiring the patentee to undertake the almost insuperable task of finding and suing all the innocent purchasers who technically were responsible for completing the infringement. Ibid. *   *   *

The Wallace case demonstrates, in a readily comprehensible setting, the reason for the contributory infringement doctrine. It exists to protect patent rights from subversion by those who, without directly infringing the patent themselves, engage in acts designed to facilitate infringement by others. This protection is of particular importance in situations, like the oil lamp case itself, where enforcement against direct infringers would be difficult, and where the technicalities of patent law make it relatively easy to profit from another's invention without risking a charge of direct infringement. *   *   *

Although the propriety of the decision in *Wallace v. Holmes* seldom has been challenged, the contributory infringement doctrine it spawned has not always enjoyed full adherence in other contexts. The difficulty that the doctrine has encountered stems not so much from rejection of its core concept as from a desire to delimit its outer contours. In time, concern for potential anticompetitive tendencies inherent in actions for contributory infringement led to retrenchment on the doctrine. The judicial history of contributory infringement thus may be said to be marked by a period of ascendancy, in which the doctrine was expanded to the point where it became subject to abuse, followed by a somewhat longer period of decline, in which the concept of patent misuse was developed as an increasingly stringent antidote to the perceived excesses of the earlier period.

The doctrine of contributory infringement was first addressed by this Court in Morgan Envelope Co. v. Albany Paper Co., 152 U.S. 425 (1894). That case was a suit by a manufacturer of a patented device for dispensing toilet paper against a supplier of paper rolls that fit the patented invention. The Court accepted the contributory infringement doctrine in theory but held that it could not be invoked against a supplier of perishable commodities used in a patented invention. The Court observed that a contrary outcome would give the patentee "the benefit of a patent" on ordinary articles of commerce, a result that it determined to be unjustified on the facts of that case. * * *

Despite this wary reception, contributory infringement actions continued to flourish in the lower courts. Eventually the doctrine gained more wholehearted acceptance here. In Leeds & Catlin Co. v. Victor Talking Machine Co., 213 U.S. 325 (1909), the Court upheld an injunction against contributory infringement by a manufacturer of phonograph discs specially designed for use in a patented disc-and-stylus combination. Although the disc itself was not patented, the Court noted that it was essential to the functioning of the patented combination, and that its method of interaction with the stylus was what "mark(ed) the advance upon the prior art." Id., at 330. It also stressed that the disc was capable of use only in the patented combination, there being no other commercially available stylus with which it would operate. The Court distinguished the result in Morgan Envelope on the broad grounds that "[n]ot one of the determining factors there stated exists in the case at bar," and it held that the attempt to link the two cases "is not only to confound essential distinctions made by the patent laws, but essential differences between entirely different things." 213 U.S., at 335.

The contributory infringement doctrine achieved its high-water mark with the decision in Henry v. A.B. Dick Co., 224 U.S. 1 (1912). In that case a divided Court extended contributory infringement principles to permit a conditional licensing arrangement whereby a manufacturer of a patented printing machine could require purchasers to obtain all supplies used in connection with the invention, including such staple items as paper and ink, exclusively from the patentee. The Court reasoned that the market for these supplies was created by the invention, and that sale of a license to use the patented product, like sale of other species of property, could be limited by whatever conditions the property owner wished to impose. Id., at 31–32. The A.B. Dick decision and its progeny in the lower courts led to a vast expansion in conditional licensing of patented goods and processes used to control markets for staple and nonstaple goods alike.

This was followed by what may be characterized through the lens of hindsight as an inevitable judicial reaction. In Motion Picture Patents Co. v. Universal Film Mfg. Co., 243 U.S. 502 (1917), the Court signalled a new trend that was to continue for years thereafter.[10] The

---

10. In addition to this judicial reaction, there was legislative reaction as well. In 1914, partly in response to the decision in Henry v. A.B. Dick Co., 224 U.S. 1 (1912), Congress enacted § 3 of the Clayton Act, 38 Stat. 731, 15 U.S.C. § 14. See Interna-

owner of a patent on projection equipment attempted to prevent competitors from selling film for use in the patented equipment by attaching to the projectors it sold a notice purporting to condition use of the machine on exclusive use of its film. The film previously had been patented but that patent had expired. The Court addressed the broad issue whether a patentee possessed the right to condition sale of a patented machine on the purchase of articles "which are no part of the patented machine, and which are not patented." Id., at 508. Relying upon the rule that the scope of a patent "must be limited to the invention described in the claims," id., at 511, the Court held that the attempted restriction on use of unpatented supplies was improper:

> "Such a restriction is invalid because such a film is obviously not any part of the invention of the patent in suit; because it is an attempt, without statutory warrant, to continue the patent monopoly in this particular character of film after it has expired, and because to enforce it would be to create a monopoly in the manufacture and use of moving picture films, wholly outside of the patent in suit and of the patent law as we have interpreted it." Id., at 518.

By this reasoning, the Court focused on the conduct of the patentee, not that of the alleged infringer. It noted that as a result of lower court decisions, conditional licensing arrangements had greatly increased, indeed, to the point where they threatened to become "perfect instrument[s] of favoritism and oppression." Id., at 515. The Court warned that approval of the licensing scheme under consideration would enable the patentee to "ruin anyone unfortunate enough to be dependent upon its confessedly important improvements for the doing of business." Ibid. This ruling was directly in conflict with Henry v. A.B. Dick Co., supra, and the Court expressly observed that that decision "must be regarded as overruled." 243 U.S., at 518.

The broad ramifications of the Motion Picture case apparently were not immediately comprehended, and in a series of decisions over the next three decades litigants tested its limits. In Carbice Corp. v. American Patents Corp., 283 U.S. 27 (1931), the Court denied relief to a patentee who, through its sole licensee, authorized use of a patented design for a refrigeration package only to purchasers from the licensee of solid carbon dioxide ("dry ice"), a refrigerant that the licensee manufactured. The refrigerant was a well-known and widely used staple article of commerce, and the patent in question claimed neither a machine for making it nor a process for using it. Id., at 29. The Court held that the patent holder and its licensee were attempting to exclude competitors in the refrigerant business from a portion of the market, and that this conduct constituted patent misuse. * * *

Although none of these decisions purported to cut back on the doctrine of contributory infringement itself, they were generally perceived as having that effect, and how far the developing doctrine of

tional Business Machines Corp. v. United
States, 298 U.S. 131, 137–138 (1936).

patent misuse might extend was a topic of some speculation among members of the patent bar. The Court's decisions had not yet addressed the status of contributory infringement or patent misuse with respect to nonstaple goods, and some courts and commentators apparently took the view that control of nonstaple items capable only of infringing use might not bar patent protection against contributory infringement. This view soon received a serious, if not fatal, blow from the Court's controversial decisions in Mercoid Corp. v. Mid–Continent Investment Co., 320 U.S. 661 (1944) (Mercoid I), and Mercoid Corp. v. Minneapolis–Honeywell Regulator Co., 320 U.S. 680 (1944) (Mercoid II). In these cases, the Court definitely held that any attempt to control the market for unpatented goods would constitute patent misuse, even if those goods had no use outside a patented invention. Because these cases served as the point of departure for congressional legislation, they merit more than passing citation.

Both cases involved a single patent that claimed a combination of elements for a furnace heating system. Mid–Continent was the owner of the patent, and Honeywell was its licensee. Although neither company made or installed the furnace system, Honeywell manufactured and sold stoker switches especially made for and essential to the system's operation. The right to build and use the system was granted to purchasers of the stoker switches, and royalties owed the patentee were calculated on the number of stoker switches sold. Mercoid manufactured and marketed a competing stoker switch that was designed to be used only in the patented combination. Mercoid had been offered a sublicense by the licensee but had refused to take one. It was sued for contributory infringement by both the patentee and the licensee, and it raised patent misuse as a defense.

In *Mercoid I* the Court barred the patentee from obtaining relief because it deemed the licensing arrangement with Honeywell to be an unlawful attempt to extend the patent monopoly. The opinion for the Court painted with a very broad brush. Prior patent misuse decisions had involved attempts "to secure a partial monopoly in supplies consumed . . . or unpatented materials employed" in connection with the practice of the invention. None, however, had involved an integral component necessary to the functioning of the patented system. 320 U.S., at 665. The Court refused, however, to infer any "difference in principle" from this distinction in fact. Ibid. Instead, it stated an expansive rule that apparently admitted no exception:

> "The necessities or convenience of the patentee do not justify any use of the monopoly of the patent to create another monopoly. The fact that the patentee has the power to refuse a license does not enable him to enlarge the monopoly of the patent by the expedient of attaching conditions to its use. . . . The method by which the monopoly is sought to be extended is immaterial. . . . When the patentee ties something else to his invention, he acts only by virtue of his right as the owner of property to make contracts concerning it and not

otherwise. He then is subject to all the limitations upon that right which the general law imposes upon such contracts. The contract is not saved by anything in the patent laws because it relates to the invention. If it were, the mere act of the patentee could make the distinctive claim of the patent attach to something which does not possess the quality of invention. Then the patent would be diverted from its statutory purpose and become a ready instrument for economic control in domains where the anti-trust acts or other laws not the patent statutes define the public policy." Id., at 666.

The Court recognized that its reasoning directly conflicted with *Leeds & Catlin Co. v. Victor Talking Machine Co.,* supra, and it registered disapproval, if not outright rejection, of that case. 320 U.S., . at 668. It also recognized that "[t]he result of this decision, together with those which have preceded it, is to limit substantially the doctrine of contributory infringement." Id., at 669. The Court commented, rather cryptically, that it would not "stop to consider" what "residuum" of the contributory infringement doctrine "may be left." Ibid.

*   *   *

What emerges from this review of judicial development is a fairly complicated picture, in which the rights and obligations of patentees as against contributory infringers have varied over time. We need not decide how respondent would have fared against a charge of patent misuse at any particular point prior to the enactment of 35 U.S.C. § 271. Nevertheless, certain inferences that are pertinent to the present inquiry may be drawn from these historical developments.

First, we agree with the Court of Appeals that the concepts of contributory infringement and patent misuse "rest on antithetical underpinnings." 599 F.2d at 697. The traditional remedy against contributory infringement is the injunction. And an inevitable concomitant of the right to enjoin another from contributory infringement is the capacity to suppress competition in an unpatented article of commerce. See, e.g., Thomson–Houston Electric Co. v. Kelsey Electric R. Specialty Co., 72 F. 1016, 1018–1019 (CC Conn.1896). Proponents of contributory infringement defend this result on the grounds that it is necessary for the protection of the patent right, and that the market for the unpatented article flows from the patentee's invention. They also observe that in many instances the article is "unpatented" only because of the technical rules of patent claiming, which require the placement of an invention in its context. Yet suppression of competition in unpatented goods is precisely what the opponents of patent misuse decry. If both the patent misuse and contributory infringement doctrines are to coexist, then, each must have some separate sphere of operation with which the other does not interfere.

Second, we find that the majority of cases in which the patent misuse doctrine was developed involved undoing the damage thought to have been done by *A.B. Dick.* The desire to extend patent protection to control of staple articles of commerce died slowly, and the ghost of the expansive contributory infringement era continued to haunt the courts. As a result, among the historical precedents in this Court, only the *Leeds & Catlin* and *Mercoid* cases bear significant factual similarity to the present controversy. Those cases involved questions of control over unpatented articles that were essential to the patented inventions, and that were unsuited for any commercial noninfringing use. In this case, we face similar questions in connection with a chemical, propanil, the herbicidal properties of which are essential to the advance on prior art disclosed by respondent's patented process. Like the record disc in *Leeds & Catlin* or the stoker switch in the *Mercoid* cases, and unlike the dry ice in *Carbice* * * *, propanil is a nonstaple commodity which has no use except through practice of the patented method. Accordingly, had the present case arisen prior to *Mercoid,* we believe it fair to say that it would have fallen close to the wavering line between legitimate protection against contributory infringement and illegitimate patent misuse.

III

The *Mercoid* decisions left in their wake some consternation among patent lawyers and a degree of confusion in the lower courts. Although some courts treated the *Mercoid* pronouncements as limited in effect to the specific kind of licensing arrangement at issue in those cases, others took a much more expansive view of the decision. Among the latter group, some courts held that even the filing of an action for contributory infringement, by threatening to deter competition in unpatented materials, could supply evidence of patent misuse. See, e.g., Stroco Products, Inc. v. Mullenbach, 67 USPQ 168, 170 (SD Cal.1944). This state of affairs made it difficult for patent lawyers to advise their clients on questions of contributory infringement and to render secure opinions on the validity of proposed licensing arrangements. Certain segments of the patent bar eventually decided to ask Congress for corrective legislation that would restore some scope to the contributory infringement doctrine. With great perseverance, they advanced their proposal in three successive Congresses before it eventually was enacted in 1952 as 35 U.S.C. § 271.

The critical inquiry in this case is how the enactment of § 271 affected the doctrines of contributory infringement and patent misuse. Viewed against the backdrop of judicial precedent, we believe that the language and structure of the statute lend significant support to Rhom & Haas' contention that, because § 271(d) immunizes its conduct from the charge of patent misuse, it should not be barred from seeking relief. The approach that Congress took toward the codification of contributory infringement and patent misuse reveals a compromise between those two doctrines and their competing policies that permits patentees to exercise control over nonstaple articles used in their inventions.

Section 271(c) identifies the basic dividing line between contributory infringement and patent misuse. It adopts a restrictive definition of contributory infringement that distinguishes between staple and non-staple articles of commerce. It also defines the class of nonstaple items narrowly. In essence, this provision places materials like the dry ice of the *Carbice* case outside the scope of the contributory infringement doctrine. As a result, it is no longer necessary to resort to the doctrine of patent misuse in order to deny patentees control over staple goods used in their inventions.

The limitations on contributory infringement written into § 271(c) are counterbalanced by limitations on patent misuse in § 271(d). Three species of conduct by patentees are expressly excluded from characterization as misuse. First, the patentee may "deriv[e] revenue" from acts that "would constitute contributory infringement" if "performed by another without his consent." This provision clearly signifies that a patentee may make and sell nonstaple goods used in connection with his invention. Second, the patentee may "licens[e] or authoriz[e] another to perform acts" which without such authorization would constitute contributory infringement. This provision's use in the disjunctive of the term "authoriz[e]" suggests that more than explicit licensing agreements is contemplated. Finally, the patentee may "enforce his patent rights against . . . contributory infringement." This provision plainly means that the patentee may bring suit without fear that his doing so will be regarded as an unlawful attempt to suppress competition. The statute explicitly states that a patentee may do "one or more" of these permitted acts, and it does not state that he must do any of them.

In our view, the provisions of § 271(d) effectively confer upon the patentee, as a lawful adjunct of his patent rights, a limited power to exclude others from competition in nonstaple goods. A patentee may sell a nonstaple article himself while enjoining others from marketing that same good without his authorization. By doing so, he is able to eliminate competitors and thereby to control the market for that product. Moreover, his power to demand royalties from others for the privilege of selling the nonstaple item itself implies that the patentee may control the market for the nonstaple good; otherwise, his "right" to sell licenses for the marketing of the nonstaple good would be meaningless, since no one would be willing to pay him for a superfluous authorization. *   *   *

Rohm & Haas' conduct is not dissimilar in either nature or effect from the conduct that is thus clearly embraced within § 271(d). It sells propanil; it authorizes others to use propanil; and it sues contributory infringers. These are all protected activities. Rohm & Haas does not license others to sell propanil, but nothing on the face of the statute requires it to do so. To be sure, the sum effect of Rohm & Haas' actions is to suppress competition in the market for an unpatented commodity. But as we have observed, in this its conduct is no different from that which the statute expressly protects.

The one aspect of Rohm & Haas' behavior that is not expressly covered by § 271(d) is its linkage of two protected activities—sale of propanil and authorization to practice the patented process—together in a single transaction. Petitioners vigorously argue that this linkage, which they characterize pejoratively as "tying," supplies the otherwise missing element of misuse. They fail, however, to identify any way in which this "tying" of two expressly protected activities results in any extension of control over unpatented materials beyond what § 271(d) already allows. Nevertheless, the language of § 271(d) does not explicitly resolve the question when linkage of this variety becomes patent misuse. In order to judge whether this method of exploiting the patent lies within or without the protection afforded by § 271(d), we must turn to the legislative history.

B

Petitioners argue that the legislative materials indicate at most a modest purpose for § 271. Relying mainly on the Committee Reports that accompanied the "Act to Revise and Codify the Patent Laws" (1952 Act), 66 Stat. 792, of which § 271 was a part, petitioners assert that the principal purpose of Congress was to "clarify" the law of contributory infringement as it had been developed by the courts, rather than to effect any significant substantive change. They note that the 1952 Act undertook the major task of codifying all the patent laws in a single title, and they argue that substantive changes from recodifications are not lightly to be inferred. * * * They further argue that, whatever the impact of § 271 in other respects, there is not the kind of "clear and certain signal from Congress" that should be required for an extension of patent privileges. See Deepsouth Packing Co. v. Laitram Corp., 406 U.S. 518, 531 (1972). We disagree with petitioners' assessment. In our view, the relevant legislative materials abundantly demonstrate an intent both to change the law and to expand significantly the ability of patentees to protect their rights against contributory infringement.

The 1952 Act was approved with virtually no floor debate. Only one exchange is relevant to the present inquiry. In response to a question whether the Act would effect any substantive changes, Senator McCarran, a spokesman for the legislation, commented that the Act "codif(ies) the patent laws." 98 Cong.Rec. 9323 (1952). He also submitted a statement, which explained that, although the general purpose of the Act was to clarify existing law, it also included several changes taken "[i]n view of decisions of the Supreme Court and others." Ibid. Perhaps because of the magnitude of the recodification effort, the Committee Reports accompanying the 1952 Act also gave relatively cursory attention to its features. Nevertheless, they did identify § 271 as one of the "major changes or innovations in the title." H.R.Rep. No. 1923, 82d Cong., 2d Sess., 5 (1952). In explaining the provisions of § 271, the Reports stated that they were intended "to codify in statutory form the principles of contributory infringement and at the same time (to) eliminate . . . doubt and confusion" that had resulted from "decisions of the courts in recent years." Id., at 9. The Reports also commented that §§ 271(b), (c), and (d) "have as their main purpose clarification and stabilization." Ibid.

These materials sufficiently demonstrate that the 1952 Act did include significant substantive changes, and that § 271 was one of them.

The principal sources for edification concerning the meaning and scope of § 271, however, are the extensive hearings that were held on the legislative proposals that led up to the final enactment. * * *

[The Court undertook an extended review of the legislative history, which it found consistent with the view that § 271 did effect a significant change in the law] * * *.

There is one factual difference between this case and *Mercoid:* the licensee in the *Mercoid* cases had offered a sublicense to the alleged contributory infringer, which offer had been refused. *Mercoid II,* 320 U.S., at 683. Seizing upon this difference, petitioners argue that respondent's unwillingness to offer similar licenses to its would-be competitors in the manufacture of propanil legally distinguishes this case and sets it outside § 271(d). To this argument, there are at least three responses. First, as we have noted, § 271(d) permits such licensing but does not require it. Accordingly, petitioners' suggestion would import into the statute a requirement that simply is not there. Second, petitioners have failed to adduce any evidence from the legislative history that the offering of a license to the alleged contributory infringer was a critical factor in inducing Congress to retreat from the result of the *Mercoid* decisions. Indeed, the *Leeds & Catlin* decision, which did not involve such an offer to license, was placed before Congress as an example of the kind of contributory infringement action the statute would allow. Third, petitioners' argument runs contrary to the long-settled view that the essence of a patent grant is the right to exclude others from profiting by the patented invention. 35 U.S.C. § 154 * * *. If petitioners' argument were accepted, it would force patentees either to grant licenses or to forfeit their statutory protection against contributory infringement. Compulsory licensing is a rarity in our patent system, and we decline to manufacture such a requirement out of § 271(d).

IV

Petitioners argue, finally, that the interpretation of § 271(d) which we have adopted is foreclosed by decisions of this Court following the passage of the 1952 Act. They assert that in subsequent cases the Court has continued to rely upon the *Mercoid* decisions, and that it has effectively construed § 271(d) to codify the result of those decisions, rather than to return the doctrine of patent misuse to some earlier stage of development. We disagree.

* * *

The only two decisions that touch at all closely upon the issues of statutory construction presented here are Aro Mfg. Co. v. Convertible Top Co., 365 U.S. 336 (1961) (Aro I), and Aro Mfg. Co. v. Convertible Top Co., 377 U.S. 476 (1964) (Aro II). These decisions emerged from a single case involving an action for contributory infringement based on the manufacture and sale of a specially cut fabric designed for use in a patented automobile convertible top combination. In neither case, however, did the Court directly address the question of § 271(d)'s effect on the law of patent misuse.

The controlling issue in *Aro I* was whether there had been any direct infringement of the patent. The Court held that purchasers of the specially cut fabric used it for "repair" rather than "reconstruction" of the patented combination; accordingly, under the patent law they were not guilty of infringement. 365 U.S., at 340, 346. Since there was no direct infringement by the purchasers, the Court held that there could be no contributory infringement by the manufacturer of the replacement tops. This conclusion rested in part on a holding that § 271(c) "made no change in the fundamental precept that there can be no contributory infringement in the absence of a direct infringement." Id., at 341. It in no way conflicts with our decision.

* * *

Aro II is a complicated decision in which the Court mustered different majorities in support of various aspects of its opinion. See 377 U.S., at 488, n. 8. After remand from *Aro I*, it became clear that the Court's decision in that case had not eliminated all possible grounds for a charge of contributory infringement. Certain convertible top combinations had been sold without valid license from the patentee. Because use of these tops involved direct infringement of the patent, there remained a question whether fabric supplied for their repair might constitute contributory infringement notwithstanding the Court's earlier decision.

Aro II decided several questions of statutory interpretation under § 271. First, it held that repair of an unlicensed combination was direct infringement under the law preceding enactment of § 271, and that the statute did not effect any change in this regard. 377 U.S., at 484. * * *

Second, the Court held that supplying replacement fabrics specially cut for use in the infringing repair constituted contributory infringement under § 271(c). The Court held that the specially cut fabrics, when installed in infringing equipment, qualified as nonstaple items within the language of § 271(c), and that supply of similar materials for infringing repair had been treated as contributory infringement under the judicial law that § 271(c) was designed to codify. 377 U.S., at 485–488. It also held that § 271(c) requires a showing that an alleged contributory infringer knew that the combination for which his component was especially designed was both patented and infringing. 377 U.S., at 488–491. We regard these holdings as fully consistent with our understanding of § 271(c). In any event, since petitioners have conceded contributory infringement for the purposes of this decision, the scope of that subsection is not directly before us.

Third, the Court held that the alleged contributory infringer could not avoid liability by reliance on the doctrine of the *Mercoid* decisions. Although those decisions had cast contributory infringement into some doubt, the Court held that § 271 was enacted "for the express purpose . . . of overruling any blanket invalidation of the (contributory infringement) doctrine that could be found in the *Mercoid* opinions." 377 U.S., at 492. Although our review of the legislative history finds a broader intent, it is not out of harmony with *Aro II*'s analysis. The Court explicitly noted that a defense of patent misuse had not been pressed. Id., at 491. Accordingly, its discussion of legislative history was limited to those materials supporting the observation, sufficient for purposes of the case, that any direct attack on the contributory infringement doctrine in its entirety would be contrary to the manifest purpose of § 271(c). Since the Court in *Aro II* was not faced with a patent misuse defense, it had no occasion to consider other evidence in the hearings relating to the scope of § 271(d).

* * *

Perhaps the quintessential difference between the *Aro* decisions and the present case is the difference between the primary-use market for a chemical process and the replacement market out of which the Aro litigation arose. The repair-reconstruction distinction and its legal consequences are determinative in the latter context, but are not controlling here. Instead, the staple-nonstaple distinction, which *Aro I* found irrelevant to the characterization of replacements, supplies the controlling benchmark. This distinction ensures that the patentee's right to prevent others from contributorily infringing his patent affects only the market for the invention itself. Because of this significant difference in legal context, we believe our interpretation of § 271(d) does not conflict with these decisions.

V

Since our present task is one of statutory construction, questions of public policy cannot be determinative of the outcome unless specific policy choices fairly can be attributed to Congress itself. In this instance, as we have already stated, Congress chose a compromise between competing policy interests. The policy of free competition runs deep in our law. It underlies both the doctrine of patent misuse and the general principle that the boundary of a patent monopoly is to be limited by the literal scope of the patent claims. But the policy of stimulating invention that underlies the entire patent system runs no less deep. And the doctrine of contributory infringement, which has been called "an expression both of law and morals," *Mercoid I,* 320 U.S., at 677 (Frankfurter J., dissenting), can be of crucial importance in ensuring that the endeavors and investments of the inventor do not go unrewarded.

It is perhaps, noteworthy that holders of "new use" patents on chemical processes were among those designated to Congress as intended beneficiaries of the protection against contributory infringement that § 271 was designed to restore. * * * We have been informed that the characteristics of practical chemical research are such that this form of patent protection is particularly important to inventors in that field. The number of chemicals either known to scientists or disclosed by existing research is vast. It grows constantly, as those engaging in "pure" research publish their discoveries.[23] The number of these chemicals that have known uses of commercial or social value, in contrast, is small. Development of new uses for existing chemicals is thus a major component of practical chemical research. It is extraordinarily expensive.[24] It may take years of unsuccessful testing before a chemical having a desired property is identified, and it may take several years of further testing before a proper and safe method for using that chemical is developed.[25]

Under the construction of § 271(d) that petitioners advance, the rewards available to those willing to undergo the time, expense, and interim frustration of such practical research would provide at best a dubious incentive. Others could await the results of the testing and then jump on the profit bandwagon by demanding licenses to sell the unpatented, nonstaple chemical used in the newly developed process. Refusal to accede to such a demand, if accompanied by any attempt to profit from the invention through sale of the unpatented chemical, would risk forfeiture of any patent protection whatsoever on a finding of patent misuse. As a result, noninventors would be almost assured of an opportunity to share in the spoils, even though they had contributed nothing to the discovery. The incentive to await the discoveries of others might well prove sweeter than the incentive to take the initiative oneself.

Whether such a regime would prove workable, as petitioners urge, or would lead to dire consequences, as respondent and several amici

23. As of March 1980, the Chemical Registry System maintained by the American Chemical Society listed in excess of 4,848,000 known chemical compounds. The list grows at a rate of about 350,000 per year. The Society estimates that the list comprises between 50% and 60% of all compounds that ever have been prepared. * * *

24. For example, the average cost of developing one new pharmaceutical drug has been estimated to run as high as $54 million. Hansen, The Pharmaceutical Development Process: Estimates of Development Costs and Times and the Effects of Proposed Regulatory Changes, in Issues in Pharmaceutical Economics 151, 180 (R. Chien ed. 1979).

25. See Wardell, The History of Drug Discovery, Development, and Regulation, in Issues in Pharmaceutical Economics 1, 8–10 (R. Chien ed. 1979) (describing modern techniques and testing requirements for development of pharmaceuticals). Although testing of chemicals destined for pharmaceutical use may be the most extensive, testing for environmental effects of chemicals used in industrial or agricultural settings also can be both expensive and prolonged. See A. Wechsler, J. Harrison, & J. Neumeyer, Evaluation of the Possible Impact of Pesticide Legislation on Research and Development Activities of Pesticide Manufacturers 18–52 (Environmental Protection Agency, Office of Pesticide Programs, pub. no. 540/9–75–018, 1975). See generally A. Baines, F. Bradbury, & C. Suckling, Research in the Chemical Industry 82–163 (1969).

insist, we need not predict. Nor do we need to determine whether the principles of free competition could justify such a result. Congress' enactment of § 271(d) resolved these issues in favor of a broader scope of patent protection. In accord with our understanding of that statute, we hold that Rohm & Haas has not engaged in patent misuse, either by its method of selling propanil, or by its refusal to license others to sell that commodity. The judgment of the Court of Appeals is therefore affirmed.

It is so ordered.

MR. JUSTICE WHITE, with whom MR. JUSTICE BRENNAN, MR. JUSTICE MARSHALL, and MR. JUSTICE STEVENS joined, dissented.

* * *

NOTES

1. The doctrine of patent misuse is closely related to the cases that have held that certain patent licensing practices can constitute unreasonable restraints of trade in violation of the antitrust laws. It is clear that any licensing practice that is an antitrust violation is also misuse. It is probably also true that any licensing practice that is patent misuse is at the least almost an antitrust violation. Because the doctrine of patent misuse is so closely related to antitrust law, it is not further examined here. The topic of antitrust constraints on patent licensing is left for the antitrust course, although it should be noted that any lawyer who handles a patent or technology licensing transaction must be sensitive to the antitrust doctrines.

2. As a matter of antitrust theory, contractual restrictions in relation to patents should be analyzed like any other contractual provision made in relation to a property right. However, patents have attracted special skepticism in antitrust cases because the judges have tended to view patents as monopolies. The *reductio ad absurbum* of course would be the idea that simply enforcing a patent is a violation of the antitrust laws, a position to which the Court came perilously close in *Mercoid* itself. In any case, the antitrust issues have had the practical consequence that many patent infringement complaints are met with an antitrust counterclaim, a move that greatly increases the costs of licensing and enforcing patents. Ironically, one safe way to proceed has always been to license the patent to no one, thus restricting its availability.

Antitrust hostility to patents has begun to recede in recent years. Section 271(d) enacted in 1952 appears to have been a precursor of a less hostile attitude, although one should note that as late as 1980 only five members of the Supreme Court were willing to venture the conclusion that § 271(d) means what it said. Congress has since used § 271(d) as a vehicle to further protect patents from antitrust hostility. See §§ 272(d)(4) and (5), added by P.L. 100–703, Nov. 19, 1988.

The view that patents are monopolies, although instinctively appealing, has been challenged by one of the present authors. See Edmund W. Kitch, Patents: Monopolies or Property Rights?, 8 Research in Law and Economics 31 (1986). There is a vast literature on patents and antitrust which can be accessed through any of the antitrust treatises. Ward S. Bowman, Jr., Patent and Antitrust Law: A Legal and Economic Appraisal (Chicago and London: Univ. of Chicago Press, 1973), is among the most thoughtful extended examinations of the subject.

(5) CONSTRUCTION OF THE CLAIMS

The scope of the patent is determined by the claims. These function like a boundary description in a real estate deed. They tell the world (and the courts) what is and what is not within a patent. The more elements that a claim contains the smaller its scope since only a product or process that has all of the elements required by the claim will infringe.

Thus a competitor confronted with a patent on a product can try to avoid the patent by changing any of the elements of the claimed product. This has confronted the courts with the need to distinguish between changes sufficiently material to avoid infringement and changes so insubstantial that the product infringes.

GRAVER TANK & MFG. CO. v. LINDE AIR PRODUCTS CO.

Supreme Court of the United States, 1950.
339 U.S. 605, 70 S.Ct. 854, 94 L.Ed. 1097.

MR. JUSTICE JACKSON delivered the opinion of the Court.

Linde Air Products Co., owner of the Jones patent for an electric welding process and for fluxes to be used therewith, brought an action for infringement against Lincoln and the two Graver companies. The trial court held four flux claims valid and infringed and certain other flux claims and all process claims invalid. * * * The Court of Appeals affirmed findings of validity and infringement as to the four flux claims but reversed the trial court and held valid the process claims and the remaining contested flux claims. * * * We granted certiorari * * * and reversed the judgment of the Court of Appeals insofar as it reversed that of the trial court, and reinstated the District Court decree. Rehearing was granted, limited to the question of infringement of the four valid flux claims and to the applicability of the doctrine of equivalents to findings of fact in this case.

* * *

In determining whether an accused device or composition infringes a valid patent, resort must be had in the first instance to the words of the claim. If accused matter falls clearly within the claim, infringement is made out and that is the end of it.

But courts have also recognized that to permit imitation of a patented invention which does not copy every literal detail would be to convert the protection of the patent grant into a hollow and useless thing. Such a limitation would leave room for—indeed encourage—the unscrupulous copyist to make unimportant and insubstantial changes and substitutions in the patent which, though adding nothing, would be enough to take the copied matter outside the claim, and hence outside the reach of law. One who seeks to pirate an invention, like one who seeks to pirate a copyrighted book or play, may be expected to introduce minor variations to conceal and shelter the piracy. Outright and forthright duplication is a dull and very rare type of infringement. To prohibit no other would place the inventor at the mercy of verbalism and would be subordinating substance to form. It would deprive him of the benefit of his invention and would foster concealment rather than disclosure of inventions, which is one of the primary purposes of the patent system.

The doctrine of equivalents evolved in response to this experience. The essence of the doctrine is that one may not practice a fraud on a patent. Originating almost a century ago in the case of Winans v. Denmead, 15 How. 330, 14 L.Ed. 717, it has been consistently applied by this Court and the lower federal courts, and continues today ready and available for utilization when the proper circumstances for its application arise. "To temper unsparing logic and prevent an infringer from stealing the benefit of the invention" a patentee may invoke this doctrine to proceed against the producer of a device "if it performs substantially the same function in substantially the same way to obtain the same result." Sanitary Refrigerator Co. v. Winters, 280 U.S. 30, 42. The theory on which it is founded is that "if two devices do the same work in substantially the same way, and accomplish substantially the same result, they are the same, even though they differ in name, form or shape." Union Paper–Bag Machine Co. v. Murphy, 97 U.S. 120, 125. The doctrine operates not only in favor of the patentee of a pioneer or primary invention, but also for the patentee of a secondary invention consisting of a combination of old ingredients which produce new and useful results * * * although the area of equivalence may vary under the circumstances. * * * The wholesome realism of this doctrine is not always applied in favor of a patentee but is sometimes used against him. Thus, where a device is so far changed in principle from a patented article that it performs the same or a similar function in a substantially different way, but nevertheless falls within the literal words of the claim, the doctrine of equivalents may be used to restrict the claim and defeat the patentee's action for infringement. Westinghouse v. Boyden Power Brake Co., 170 U.S. 537, 568. In its early development, the doctrine was usually applied in cases involving devices where there was equivalence in mechanical components. Subsequently, however, the same principles were also applied to compositions, where there was equivalence between chemical ingredients. Today the doctrine is applied to mechanical or chemical equivalents in compositions or devices. See discussions and cases collected in 3 Walker on Patents (Deller's ed. 1937) §§ 489–492; Ellis, Patent Claims (1949) §§ 59–60.

What constitutes equivalency must be determined against the context of the patent, the prior art, and the particular circumstances of the case. Equivalence, in the patent law, is not the prisoner of a formula and is not an absolute to be considered in a vacuum. It does not require complete identity for every purpose and in every respect. In determining equivalents, things equal to the same thing may not be equal to each other and, by the same token, things for most purposes different may sometimes be equivalents. Consideration must be given to the purpose for which an ingredient is used in a patent, the qualities it has when combined with the other ingredients, and the function which it is intended to perform. An important factor is whether persons reasonably skilled in the art would have known of the interchangeability of an ingredient not contained in the patent with one that was.

A finding of equivalence is a determination of fact. Proof can be made in any form: through testimony of experts or others versed in the technology; by documents, including texts and treatises; and, of course, by the disclosures of the prior art. Like any other issue of fact, final determination requires a balancing of credibility, persuasiveness and weight of evidence. It is to be decided by the trial court and that court's decision, under general principles of appellate review, should not be disturbed unless clearly erroneous. Particularly is this so in a field where so much depends upon familiarity with specific scientific problems and principles not usually contained in the general storehouse of knowledge and experience.

In the case before us, we have two electric welding compositions or fluxes: the patented composition, Unionmelt Grade 20, and the accused composition, Lincolnweld 660. The patent under which Unionmelt is made claims essentially a combination of alkaline earth metal silicate and calcium fluoride; Unionmelt actually contains, however, silicates of calcium and magnesium, two alkaline earth metal silicates. Lincolnweld's composition is similar to Unionmelt's, except that it substitutes silicates of calcium and manganese—the latter not an alkaline earth metal—for silicates of calcium and magnesium. In all other respects, the two compositions are alike. The mechanical methods in which these compositions are employed are similar. They are identical in operation and produce the same kind and quality of weld.

The question which thus emerges is whether the substitution of the manganese which is not an alkaline earth metal for the magnesium which is, under the circumstances of this case, and in view of the technology and the prior art, is a change of such substance as to make the doctrine of equivalents inapplicable; or conversely, whether under the circumstances the change was so insubstantial that the trial court's invocation of the doctrine of equivalents was justified.

Without attempting to be all-inclusive, we note the following evidence in the record: Chemists familiar with the two fluxes testified that manganese and magnesium were similar in many of their reactions. There is testimony by a metallurgist that alkaline earth metals are often found in manganese ores in their natural state and that they serve the same purpose in the fluxes; and a chemist testified that "in the sense of the patent" manganese could be included as an alkaline earth metal. Much of this testimony was corroborated by reference to recognized texts on inorganic chemistry. Particularly important, in addition, were the disclosures of the prior art, also contained in the record. The Miller patent, No. 1,754,566, which preceded the patent in suit, taught the use of manganese silicate in welding fluxes. Manganese was similarly disclosed in the Armor patent, No. 1,467,825, which also described a welding composition. And the record contains no evidence of any kind to show that Lincolnweld was developed as the result of independent research or experiments.

It is not for this Court to even essay an independent evaluation of this evidence. This is the function of the trial court. * * *

The trial judge found on the evidence before him that the Lincolnweld flux and the composition of the patent in suit are substantially identical in operation and in result. He found also that Lincolnweld is in all respects equivalent to Unionmelt for welding purposes. And he concluded that "for all practical purposes, manganese silicate can be efficiently and effectively substituted for calcium and magnesium silicates as the major constituent of the welding composition." These conclusions are adequately supported by the record; certainly they are not clearly erroneous.

It is difficult to conceive of a case more appropriate for application of the doctrine of equivalents. The disclosures of the prior art made clear that manganese silicate was a useful ingredient in welding compositions. Specialists familiar with the problems of welding compositions understood that manganese was equivalent to and could be substituted for magnesium in the composition of the patented flux and their observations were confirmed by the literature of chemistry. Without some explanation or indication that Lincolnweld was developed by independent research, the trial court could properly infer that the accused flux is the result of imitation rather than experimentation or invention. Though infringement was not literal, the changes which avoid literal infringement are colorable only. We conclude that the trial court's judgment of infringement respecting the four flux claims was proper, and we adhere to our prior decision on this aspect of the case.

Affirmed.

CORNING GLASS WORKS v. SUMITOMO ELECTRIC U.S.A., INC.

United States Court of Appeals, Federal Circuit, 1989.
868 F.2d 1251.

NIES, CIRCUIT JUDGE.

Sumitomo Electric U.S.A., Inc. [and other affiliated parties] * * * appeal from the judgment of the United States District Court for the Southern District of New York, 671 F.Supp. 1369 (S.D.N.Y.1987) (Conner, J.), holding Sumitomo liable for infringement of claims 1 and 2 of United States Patent No. 3,659,915 ('915) and claim 1 of United States Patent No. 3,884,550 ('550), all directed to the structure of optical waveguide fibers. On appeal, Sumitomo challenges the validity of both patents and the finding of infringement of the '915 patent by one of its accused products. * * * We affirm the judgment in all respects.

I. BACKGROUND

A. GENERAL TECHNOLOGY

The inventions involved in this case relate to optical waveguide fibers of the type now widely used for telecommunications, such as long-distance telephone transmissions. Such fibers were developed as a medium for guiding the coherent light of a laser a distance suitable for optical communications.

It had long been known that light could be guided through a transparent medium that was surrounded by another medium having a lower refractive index (RI). A glass fiber surrounded by air for example, will function as a conduit for light waves, because air has a lower RI than glass. To prevent scratches, imperfections, or foreign materials on the fiber surface from scattering light away from the fiber, glass fibers were clad with a glass layer having a lower RI. Before 1970, however, these glass-clad, glass-core fibers, referred to generally as "fiber optics," were capable of transmitting light of practical intensity only for very short distances due to high attenuation of the glass fibers then available. While suitable for illumination or for imaging systems, as in endoscopic probes, they could not be used for optical communications.

Another impediment to the use of conventional fiber optics for optical communications was the need that the fiber limit the transmitted light to preselected rays or "modes." In contrast, conventional fibers were designed to pass the maximum amount of incident light. The relatively large core diameter of conventional fibers permitted modes of light to enter the core over a fairly wide range of angles which, provided they entered at less than the critical angle, would be propagated along the fiber. Upon entering a fiber core, the light modes travel to the cladding and then back into the core, thus "bouncing" back and forth in a zig-zag path along the length of the fiber. The shallower the angle at which the modes enter the core, the less they will "bounce" and the sooner they will reach the receiving end of the fiber. When the number of modes are restricted, intelligibility of the information transmitted increases. The optimum restriction is achieved when only a single mode is transmitted, and by limiting the core diameter, that purpose is accomplished.

By the mid-1960's, worldwide efforts were ongoing to develop long-distance lightwave transmission capability. In particular, the British Post Office sought an optical waveguide with an attenuation of 20 db/km, the approximate transmission efficiency of the copper wire commonly used in telephone communications.

B. THE '915 INVENTION

Corning's work on optical waveguides began in 1966, when it was contacted by the British Post Office. Drs. Robert D. Maurer and Peter

C. Schultz, working at Corning, developed the world's first 20 db/km optical waveguide fiber by early 1970. That achievement was due, in part, to the development of a fiber with a pure fused silica cladding and a fused silica core containing approximately three percent by weight of titania as the dopant in the core.[2] It was also due to the careful selection of the core diameter and the RI differential between the core and the cladding.

Bell Laboratories confirmed the attenuation measurements of Corning's fibers and considered Corning's achievement an important breakthrough, making long-distance optical telecommunications possible. Dr. Maurer first publicly reported the achievement of a 20 db/km optical waveguide fiber at the Conference on Trunk Telecommunications by Guided Waves held in London, England. That announcement created enormous interest and was the subject of many articles in both technical and general publications. The inventors' advancement in technology won them accolades from various societies and institutes, for which they were presented with many prestigious awards and honors. In addition, the invention of the '915 patent has achieved impressive commercial success on a worldwide basis. The district court determined that "[t]he 915 patent clearly covers a basic, pioneering invention."

The '915 patent discloses a fused silica optical waveguide fiber capable of limiting the transmitted light to preselected modes for use in optical communication systems. Specifically, such a fiber is disclosed as having a doped fused, silica core and a fused silica cladding (doping optional), wherein the RI of the core is greater than that of the cladding. Prior to the filing date of the application for the '915 patent, the inventors had experimented with dopants which increased the RI of fused silica, e.g. titania, and the '915 specification mentions only such positive dopant materials. At the time the application was filed, the inventors did not know of specific dopants that would decrease the RI of fused silica, although it had been known in the art since 1954 that the introduction of fluorine decreases the RI of certain multicomponent glasses.

C. THE '550 INVENTION

Corning's titania-doped fibers required heat treatment to reduce attenuation to an acceptable level. An undesirable result of that treatment was a lowering of the mechanical strength of the fibers. Consequently, Corning sought to develop a low attenuation fiber which did not require heat treatment. In 1972, Drs. Maurer and Schultz found a solution in doping a fused silica core with germania, which also had the advantage of transmitting more light than using titania.

---

2. Dopants are chemicals added to another material (here, fused silica) to alter one or more of its properties (here, the RI).   The effect of the titania was to increase the RI of the core.

D. THE '454 INVENTION

Corning recognized that when optical waveguide fibers were produced by flame hydrolysis, they contained hydroxyl ions. The residual hydroxyl ions absorbed light at certain wavelengths used in optical communications and, if they remained, would increase the attenuation of the fiber at those wavelengths. Working at Corning, Dr. Robert D. DeLuca invented a process to overcome this inherent problem by introducing a chlorine-containing drying atmosphere into the furnace during the "consolidation" phase.

E. DISTRICT COURT

Corning is the assignee of the three patents at issue. Sumitomo * * * [is] engaged in the manufacture and sale of optical waveguide fibers. This appeal involves two suits which were consolidated: an action by [Sumitomo] * * * seeking a declaration of invalidity and noninfringement of Corning's '915 and '454 patents with a counterclaim by Corning alleging Sumitomo's * * * infringement of those patents, and a suit by Corning against Sumitomo * * * asserting infringement of the '915, '550, and '454 patents.

The trial court held, *inter alia,* that claims 1 and 2 of the '915 patent and claim 1 of the '550 patent were not invalid and were infringed by Sumitomo. It found no infringement of the '454 patent. These rulings are the subject of this appeal and cross-appeal.

II

VALIDITY AND INFRINGEMENT OF CLAIMS 1 AND 2 OF '915 PATENT

A

* * * [The court held that the '915 claims in issue were not anticipated by United Kingdom Patent No. 1,113,101 which disclosed an optical fiber not intended for use as an optical waveguide. In the course of the discussion, the court quoted claim 1 of the '915 patent:]

An optical waveguide comprising

(a) a cladding layer formed of a material selected from the group consisting of pure fused silica and fused silica to which a dopant material on at least an elemental basis has been added, and

(b) a core formed of fused silica to which a dopant material on at least an elemental basis has been added to a degree in excess of that of the cladding layer so that the index of refraction thereof is of a value greater than the index of refraction of said cladding layer, said core being formed of at least 85 percent by weight of fused silica and an effective amount up to 15 percent by weight of said dopant material.

B

The infringement issue on appeal involves only Sumitomo's S–3 fibers which were found to infringe under the doctrine of equivalents. A claim in a patent provides the metes and bounds of the right which the patent confers on the patentee to exclude others from making, using, or selling the protected invention. See Graver Tank & Mfg. Co. v. Linde Air Prods. Co., 339 U.S. 605, 607 (1950). As explained in Autogiro Co. of America v. United States, 384 F.2d 391 (Ct.Cl.1967):

> "The claims of the patent provide the concise formal definition of the invention. They are the numbered paragraphs which 'particularly [point] out and distinctly [claim] the subject matter which the applicant regards as his invention.' 35 U.S.C. section 112. It is to these wordings that one must look to determine whether there has been infringement."

384 F.2d at 395–96. "These wordings" of a claim describe and point out the invention by a series of limiting words or phrases (limitations). In the determination of infringement, the words of the claim must first be interpreted, id. at 396, and, as properly interpreted, they must be "read on" the accused structure to determine whether each of the limitations recited in the claim is present in the accused structure. Envirotech Corp. v. Al George, Inc., 730 F.2d 753, 758 (Fed. Cir.1984). However, to hold a patentee to the precise claim language in all cases could turn "the patent grant into a hollow and useless thing." Graver Tank, 339 U.S. at 607. * * * The district court found that [the test for infringement by equivalency announced in *Graver Tank*, supra page 1004 * * *] was met, stating:

> "Although fiber S–3 is not within the literal language of either claim 1 or 2 of the '915 patent, it performs substantially the same function in substantially the same way to obtain the same result as the optical waveguide fiber described in those claims of the '915 patent."

In the instant case, there is no dispute that the accused S–3 fiber performs substantially the same overall function to obtain the same overall result as the claimed invention. The question then is whether it does so in "substantially the same way." As stated in *Perkin Elmer Corp. v. Westinghouse Electric Corp.*:

> "Perkin–Elmer's repeated assertions that the claimed and accused devices perform substantially the same function and achieve substantially the same end result are not helpful. That circumstance is commonplace when the devices are sold in competition. That a claimed invention and an accused device may perform substantially the same function and may achieve the same result will not make the latter an infringement under the doctrine of equivalents where it performs the

function and achieves the result in a substantially different way. * * *"

822 F.2d 1528, 1531 n. 6 (Fed.Cir.1987).

The accused S–3 fibers are optical waveguides as defined in the claims at issue in that the fibers have the differential in RI between core and cladding and the structural dimensions necessary for the preselection of particular modes of light waves. Thus, these limitations of claim 1 which * * * are required by the preamble are met in the accused S–3 fibers. Also, there is no dispute over a literal reading of paragraph (a) on these fibers. Corning concedes, however, that all of the limitations of paragraph (b) do not literally read on the accused fibers. Although each claim limitation may not literally be found in the accused structure, the "substantially the same way" prong of the Graver Tank test is met if an equivalent of a recited limitation has been substituted in the accused device, see Graver Tank, 339 U.S. at 610. * * *

Applying these principles, the district court found that the accused S–3 fibers infringed the '915 claims. In so ruling, the district court recognized that the claim limitation calling for addition of a dopant to the core was not literally met in the accused S–3 fibers. Nevertheless, the court found that the substitution of "fluorine . . . dopant which negatively alters the index of refraction of fused silica in the cladding" equivalently met the limitation requiring the addition to the core of "a dopant which positively alters the index of refraction of fused silica."

Sumitomo alleges clear error in the court's finding of equivalency. Per Sumitomo, nothing was substituted in the core of the S–3 fiber for a dopant which performed the function of increasing the core's refractive index, and, therefore, "an element" required by the claim, namely, a doped core, is entirely missing. Sumitomo asserts, that where an element of a claim is entirely missing, there is no infringement. The premise on which Sumitomo relies, known as the "All Elements" rule, see 4 D. Chisum, Patents § 18.03(4) (1986), correctly states the law of this circuit adopted in banc in *Pennwalt*. See Pennwalt Corp., 833 F.2d at 935 (infringement requires that each element of a claim or its substantial equivalent be found in the accused device). However, we do not agree that an "element" of the claim is entirely "missing" from the S–3 fibers.

Sumitomo's analysis illustrates the confusion sometimes encountered because of misunderstanding or misleading uses of the term "element" in discussing claims. "Element" may be used to mean a single limitation, but it has also been used to mean a series of limitations which, taken together, make up a component of the claimed invention. In the All Elements rule, "element" is used in the sense of a limitation of a claim. See Julien v. Zeringue, 867 F.2d 1569, 1571 (Fed. 1989) ("If a claim *limitation* or its substantial equivalent is not present, there can be no infringement." (emphasis added)). Sumitomo's analysis is faulty in that it would require equivalency in components, that is, the substitution of something in the core for the absent dopant. However, the determination of equivalency is not subject to such a rigid formula. An equivalent must be found for every limitation of the claim somewhere in an accused device, but not necessarily in a corresponding component, although that is generally the case.

Corning urges that the question of equivalency here is a narrow one: Is the substitution of a negative dopant in the cladding equivalent to a positive dopant in the core? When the limitations of paragraph (b) are analyzed individually, the accused S–3 fibers literally meet the limitation that the fiber be composed of a core of fused silica as well as the limitation that "the index of refraction (of the core) is of a value greater than the index of refraction of said cladding layer." The question of equivalency then does center on the part of the claim following the word "core," namely, "to which a dopant material . . . has been added to a degree in excess of that of the cladding layer." If those limiting words are met equivalently, no "element," i.e., limitation, of the claim is missing.

* * *

This court has not set out in its precedent a definitive formula for determining equivalency between a required limitation or combination of limitations and what has been allegedly substituted therefor in the accused device. Nor do we propose to adopt one here. We note that the district court resolved the question by comparison of the function/way/result of the substitution with the function/way/result of the limitation in the context of the invention; that is, the court made a subsidiary analysis comparable to the overall function/way/result analysis mandated for determining infringement of the claim under the doctrine of equivalents. In particular, after explaining how the negative dopant of the S–3 fiber worked, it found:

> "[t]he use of fluorine as a [negative] dopant in the cladding thus performs substantially the same function in substantially the same way as the use of a [positive] dopant in the core to produce the same result of creating the refractive index differential between the core and cladding of the fiber which is necessary for the fiber to function as an optical waveguide."

The district court's "function/way/result" equivalency analysis with respect to a claim limitation appears to be a helpful way to approach the problem and entirely in accord with the analysis actually made in Graver Tank, 339 U.S. at 609–10. Support for this approach is found in our precedent. As one of our predecessor courts stated:

> "It is fundamental patent law that infringement is not avoided by substituting for an element in a claimed device another element which is its full equivalent, i.e., does substantially the same thing in substantially the same way to get substantially the same result. Equivalency is a question of fact and must be resolved in each instance by analyzing the function of the elements or parts concerned."

Tektronix, Inc. v. United States, 445 F.2d 323, 329 (Ct.Cl.1971). Although not stated exactly as above, this court has made that type of analysis repeatedly in determining whether a substitution was, in the context of the entire claim, an equivalent of a limitation. In *Atlas Powder* [Atlas Powder Co. v. E.I. du Pont De Nemours & Co., 750 F.2d 1569 (Fed.Cir.1984)], for example, the court used the following similar language to assess the equivalency of the substituted ingredient:

"Where, as here, the accused product avoids literal infringement by changing one ingredient of a claimed composition, it is appropriate for a court to consider in assessing equivalence whether the changed ingredient has the same purpose, quality, and function as the claimed ingredient."

750 F.2d at 1579–80. See also Perkin–Elmer Corp. v. Westinghouse Elec. Corp., 822 F.2d at 1531–35 (substituted loop-coupling not equivalent because it did not produce the same structural-functional-operational interrelationships achieved by tap-coupling specified in claim); Raytheon Co. v. Roper Corp., 724 F.2d 951, 962 (Fed.Cir.1983) (substituted hole in duct " 'performs substantially the same function in substantially the same way to obtain the same result' as . . . blower inlet" of the claim), cert. denied, 469 U.S. 835 (1984); Caterpillar Tractor Co. v. Berco, S.p.A., 714 F.2d 1110, 1115 (Fed.Cir.1983) (thinner driving flange in accused seal did not affect the mode of operation or result obtained by flange in claimed invention).

Finally, Sumitomo asserts that because the prior art, namely, United States Patent No. 3,320,114 (the Litton patent) teaches that a differential in the RI can be achieved between core and cladding in a fiber optic by negative doping of the cladding, Corning cannot assert equivalency between positive dopant in the core and negative dopant in the cladding. To do so, per Sumitomo, would "expan[d] the claim to encompass what was already in the public domain, *i.e.,* a fiber with a pure undoped core." Contrary to Sumitomo's argument, the substitution of an ingredient known to be an equivalent to that required by the claim presents a classic example for a finding of infringement under the doctrine of equivalents. Graver Tank, 339 U.S. at 609 (important factor [in determining equivalency] is whether persons reasonably skilled in the art would have known of the interchangeability). Nothing is taken from the "public domain" when the issue of equivalency is directed to a limitation only, in contrast to the entirety of the claimed invention. This is such a case. The Litton patent teaches nothing about optical waveguides. Thus, the finding of equivalency in the substitution of a negative dopant in the cladding takes nothing from the "public domain."

With respect to our standard of review, we are mindful that [*Graver Tank* says that a finding of equivalence is a determination of fact to be decided by the trial court] * * *.

In sum, we are unpersuaded of error either in the district court's understanding of the law; in its finding that adding negative dopant to the cladding is equivalent to adding positive dopant to the core in the context of the claimed invention; or in its finding that the S–3 fiber is an infringement of the inventions of claims 1 and 2 of the '915 patent.

* * *

The judgment of the district court is affirmed in all respects.

NOTES

1. The task of construing patent claims does not present the courts with problems any different than the problem of construing language in legislation or private contracts. In all of these contexts courts must confront arguments that they should construe the document based upon (1) the literal language, (2) the context in which the language appears, (3) the entire situation in which the language was drafted, and (4) in light of policy considerations extraneous to the particular document in issue. The problems of construction are not advanced by an overlay of specialized jargon such as "the doctrine of equivalents," which might be translated to mean: "the patent claim will be construed in a way that makes sense considering the patent and technological situation as a whole."

2. Mr. Justice Jackson's comment that the doctrine of equivalents may be applied against, as well as for, the patentee, supra page 1027, is a reference to decisions which find that a literal infringement is *not* infringement because the infringing device is really quite different. This is sometimes called "the reverse doctrine of equivalents."

3. The concept that "pioneer" or basic patents are entitled to broader protection, echoed in the *Graver* opinion supra page 1027, is an oft-repeated canon of claim construction.

4. Another doctrine of claim construction is file wrapper estoppel. The "file wrapper" is the jacket in which the records of the patent prosecution are kept. It includes the notations by the patent office examiner recording the progress of the prosecution. Typically, the process of prosecution is a dialog between the applicant and the examiner focused on narrowing the scope of the claims to entirely novel subject matter. The idea of file wrapper estoppel is that this prosecution history can be used like legislative history to assist in the construction of the claims that survive in the issued patent. File wrapper estoppel is encrusted with its own technicalities. See Chisum, *Patents* § 18.05.

5. Claim construction can present many difficult questions. In Pennwalt Corp. v. Durand–Wayland, Inc., 833 F.2d 931 (Fed.Cir.1987), cert. denied 108 S.Ct. 1226, 1474 (1988), the Federal Circuit sitting *en banc* split 7 to 4 on the question of whether a patent on a fruit sorting device which used hard wired circuits to identify particular sizes and colors of fruit was infringed by a device that used a general purpose microcomputer programmed to accomplish the same task. The court affirmed a district court judgment of no infringement. *Pennwalt* is analyzed in Martin J. Adelman & Gary L. Francione, The Doctrine of Equivalents in Patent Law: Questions that *Pennwalt* Did Not Answer, 137 Univ. of Penn.Law.Rev. 673 (1989).

(6) ABSENT EXHAUSTION OF THE RIGHT

KEELER v. STANDARD FOLDING–BED CO.

Supreme Court of the United States, 1895.
157 U.S. 659, 15 S.Ct. 738, 39 L.Ed. 848.

MR. JUSTICE SHIRAS delivered the opinion of the court.

* * * [The defendant purchased a carload of wardrobe bedsteads in the state of Michigan, brought them to Boston and are engaged in reselling them there. The wardrobe bedsteads were of a design covered by a patent. The plaintiff is the exclusive licensee of the patent for the state of Massachusetts. The firm that sold the bedsteads to the defendant is the exclusive licensee of the patent for the state of Michigan. The plaintiff sued defendant for infringement, and prevailed in the circuit court below.]

Where the patentee has not parted, by assignment, with any of his original rights, but chooses himself to make and vend a patented article of manufacture, it is obvious that a purchaser can use the article in any part of the United States, and, unless restrained by contract with the patentee, can sell or dispose of the same. It has passed outside of the monopoly, and is no longer under the peculiar protection granted to patented rights. As was said by Mr. Justice Clifford in Goodyear v. Rubber Co., 1 Cliff. 348, Fed.Cas. No. 5,557: "Having manufactured the material and sold it for a satisfactory compensation, whether as material or in the form of a manufactured article, the patentee, so far as that product of his invention is concerned, has enjoyed all the rights secured to him by his letters patent, and the manufactured article and the material of which it is composed go to the purchaser for a valuable consideration, discharged of all the rights of the patentee previously attached to it or impressed upon it by the act of congress under which the patent was granted."

Suppose, however, the patentee has exercised his statutory right of assigning by conveying to another an exclusive right under the patent to a specified part of the United States. What are the rights of a purchaser of patented articles from the patentee himself within the territory reserved to him? Does he thereby obtain an absolute property in the article, so that he can use and vend it in all parts of the United States, or, if he take the article into the assigned territory, must he again pay for the privilege of using and selling it? If, as is often the case, the patentee has divided the territory of the United States into 20 or more "specified parts," must a person who has bought and paid for the patented article in one part, from the vender having an exclusive right to make and vend therein, on removing from one part of the country to another, pay to the local assignee for the privilege of using and selling his property, or else be subjected to an action for damages as a wrongdoer? And is there any solid distinction to be made, in such a case, between the right to use and the right to sell? Can the owner of the patented article hold and deal with it the same as in case of any other description of property belonging to him, and, on his death, does it pass, with the rest of his personal estate, to his legal representatives, and thus, as a part of the assets to be administered, become liable to be sold?

These are questions which, although already in effect answered by this court in more cases than one, are now to be considered in the state of facts disclosed in this record.

* * *

* * * [In] Adams v. Burke, 17 Wall. 453 * * * Lockhart and Seelye owned, by assignment, all the right, title, and interest which the patentees had in a certain patented coffin lid, in a circular district of a diameter of 10 miles, whereof the city of Boston was the center. Adams, also by assignment, was the owner of all other rights under the patent. Burke, an undertaker, carried on his business at Natick, and within the territory covered by the patent as owned by Adams. To a bill for an infringement, filed by Adams in the circuit court of the United States for the district of Massachusetts, Burke pleaded that the patented coffins used by him in his business were purchased by him from Lockhart and Seelye, and were sold to him without condition or restriction.

The validity of this plea was sustained by the circuit court, and its decree dismissing the bill was affirmed by this court.

Mr. Justice Miller, in giving the opinion of the court, said: "In the essential nature of things, when the patentee, or the person having his right, sells a machine or instrument whose sole value is in its use, he receives in consideration for its use, and he parts with the right to restrict that use. The article, in the language of the court, passes without the limit of the monopoly; that is to say, the patentee or his assignee having in the act of sale received all the royalty or consideration which he claims for the use of his invention in that particular machine or instrument, it is open to the use of the purchaser without further restriction on account of the monopoly of the patentee. * * * A careful examination of the plea satisfies us that the defendant, who, as an undertaker, purchased each of these coffins, and used it in burying the body which he was employed to bury, acquired the right to this use of it, freed from any claim of the patentee, though purchased within the ten-mile circle and used without it."

It is obvious that necessarily the use made by Burke of these coffins involved a sale in every case. He did not put them to his personal use, unless we are permitted to suppose that he was himself buried in each one of the coffins. He bought the coffins for the purpose of selling them to others, and the legal significance of the decision upholding his defense is that a person who buys patented articles from a person who has a right to sell, though within a restricted territory, has a right to use and sell such articles in all and any part of the United States; that, when the royalty had once been paid to a party entitled to receive it, the patented article then becomes the absolute, unrestricted property of the purchaser, with the right to sell it as an essential incident of such ownership.

That this was the meaning of this decision not only appears from the language used, and from the necessary legal effect of the conclusion reached as between the parties, but from the dissenting opinion of Justice Bradley, whose reasoning went wholly upon the assumption that such was its meaning.

Boesch v. Graff, 133 U.S. 698, is cited by the defendant in error. But it is not out of line with the previous cases. The exact question presented was whether a dealer residing in the United States could purchase in another country articles patented there from a person authorized there to sell them, and import them to and sell them in the United States without the license or consent of the owners of the United States patent, and the court held that the sale of articles in the United States under a United States patent cannot be controlled by foreign laws. In this case neither the patentee nor any assignee had ever received any royalty or given any license to use the patented article in any part of the United States.

* * *

This brief history of the cases shows that in Wilson v. Rousseau, 4 How. 688, and cases following it, it was held that as between the owner of a patent, on the one side, and a purchaser of an article made under the patent, on the other, the payment of a royalty once, or, what is the same thing, the purchase of the article from one authorized by the patentee to sell it, emancipates such article from any further subjection to the patent throughout the entire life of the patent, even if the latter should be by law subsequently extended beyond the term existing at the time of the sale, and that, in respect of the time of enjoyment, by those decisions the right of the purchaser, his assigns or legal representatives, is clearly established to be entirely free from any further claim of the patentee or any assignee; that in Adams v. Burke, 17 Wall. 453, it was held that as respects the place of enjoyment, and as between the purchaser of patented articles in one specified part of the territory and the assignee of the patent of another part, the right once legitimately acquired to hold, use, and sell will protect such purchaser from any further subjection to the monopoly; that in Hobbie v. Jennison, 149 U.S. 355, it was held that, as between assignees of different parts of the territory, it is competent for one to sell the patented articles to persons who intend, with the knowledge of the vender, to take them for use into the territory of the other.

Upon the doctrine of these cases, we think it follows that one who buys patented articles of manufacture from one authorized to sell them becomes possessed of an absolute property in such articles, unrestricted in time or place. Whether a patentee may protect himself and his assignees by special contracts brought home to the purchasers is not a question before us, and upon which we express no opinion. It is, however, obvious that such a question would arise as a question of contract, and not as one under the inherent meaning and effect of the patent laws.

The conclusion reached does not deprive a patentee of his just rights, because no article can be unfettered from the claim of his monopoly without paying its tribute. The inconvenience and annoyance to the public that an opposite conclusion would occasion are too obvious to require illustration.

* * *

The decree of the court below is reversed, and the cause remanded, with directions to dismiss the bill.

Reversed.

NOTES

1. The issue addressed in *Keeler* is an issue of patent law. After an authorized first sale, the patent owner or his successors in interest cannot sue the purchaser for infringement, even if the sale was conditional. But the fact that the patent owner cannot sue the purchaser for infringement is separate from the question of whether he could sue the first seller both for breach of the licensing contract and for infringement itself, as well as sue a purchaser who knew of the license restriction for inducing a breach of contract.

2. A system of exclusive distribution territories can be created by contract. A licensee who had promised not to make sales outside a licensed territory and who did so would be violating the contract and subject to an action for breach of contract. Thus a company might be licensed to manufacture a product and to sell it to persons who are purchasing for their own use and who are resident in the state, and breach of the agreement might be enjoinable on the ground that the damages flowing from a breach would be difficult to prove and hence an inadequate remedy. Exclusive distribution arrangements such as these have frequently been challenged as unreasonable restraints of trade under the antitrust laws. In United States v. Arnold, Schwinn & Co., 388 U.S. 365 (1967), the Court held that a system of exclusive distribution territories created by a manufacturer through clauses in its dealer agreements was a *per se* violation of the Sherman antitrust act. *Schwinn* was overruled in Continental T.V., Inc. v. GTE Sylvania Inc., 433 U.S. 36 (1977), which held that such restraints were to be analyzed under a "rule of reason." Under the rule of reason, arrangements which serve legitimate commercial objectives of the contracting parties generally will be upheld. Although neither case involved a patented product, the same rule would seem to apply to distribution contracts for a patented as for an unpatented product.

In United States v. Studiengesellschaft Kohle, 670 F.2d 1122 (D.C.Cir.1981), the court followed *Continental T.V.* in using a rule of reason analysis to test the legality under the antitrust laws of restrictions in a license to practice a process patent which restricted the licensee to producing for its own use. The restrictions were upheld.

3. The owner of a patented machine acquired from the patentee or a licensee is entitled to use the machine, and that includes the right to make regular and necessary repairs. The owner, cannot, however, engage in a reconstruction, building a new machine from components obtained from the old one. The distinction between the permissible repair and the prohibited reconstruction is an issue in many reported cases. For instance in *Aro I* (Aro Mfg.

Co. v. Convertible Top Co., 365 U.S. 336 (1961)), discussed in the *Dawson* opinion, supra page 1022, the issue was whether replacing a worn out convertible top was a repair or a reconstruction of a patented combination claim on the fabric top and associated structure. The Court held that it was a repair. An example of a decision finding a reconstruction is Monroe Auto Equip. Co. v. Precision Rebuilders, Inc., 229 F.Supp. 347 (D.Kan.1964), which held that it was reconstruction to rebuild worn out shock absorbers.

MET–COIL SYSTEMS CORP. v. KORNERS UNLIMITED, INC.

United States Court of Appeals, Federal Circuit, 1986.
803 F.2d 684.

NIES, CIRCUIT JUDGE.

The determinative issue in this appeal is whether a patent owner's unrestricted sale of a machine useful only in practicing the claimed [process] inventions presumptively carries with it an implied license under the patent [to use components purchased from others required to practice the patented process]. The United States District Court for the Western District of Pennsylvania decided that legal issue in the affirmative. We affirm.

I.

Met–Coil Systems Corp. is the assignee of U.S. Patent No. 4,466,641, which claims an apparatus and method for connecting sections of metal ducts of the kind used in heating and air conditioning systems. Under the claimed inventions, the ends of the metal duct sections are bent to form integral flanges, specially shaped corner pieces are snapped in place, and the sections are bolted together. Met–Coil makes and sells roll-forming machines that its customers use to bend integral flanges in the ends of metal ducts so as to practice the claimed inventions. Met–Coil also sells the specially shaped corner pieces for use with the integral flanges. Korners Unlimited, Inc. makes corner pieces for use with Met–Coil's integral flanges and sells them to purchasers of Met–Coil's machines. Met–Coil sued Korners for inducing infringement of claims 1–12, 14–25 of its patent. Korners moved for summary judgment.

The basis of Korners' motion for summary judgment was that Met–Coil, by selling the roll-forming machine, granted an implied license under the patent to its customers. Because of that license, Korners contended, Met–Coil's customers cannot infringe the claims of the patent and, thus, Korners can neither induce infringement nor contributorily infringe. Met–Coil, on the other hand, contended that its sales of the machines do not confer an implied license under the patent upon its customers.

II.

The district court recognized that "[t]he integral flanges are an essential part of Met–Coil's patented duct connecting system" and that the "flanges have no use other than in the practice of the duct connecting system." Applying the holding of United States v. Univis Lens Co., 316 U.S. 241 (1942), to those facts, the court held that purchasers of Met–Coil's machines enjoyed an implied license under the patent.

In *Univis*, the patent covered multifocal eyeglass lenses, and the patent owner sold blank eyeglass lenses to its licensees. The Court held that the sale of the blanks carried a license to complete the lenses:

> "But in any case it is plain that where the sale of the blank is by the patentee or his licensee—here the Lens Company—to a finisher, the only use to which it could be put and the only object of the sale is to enable the latter to grind and polish it for use as a lens by the prospective wearer. An incident to the purchase of any article, whether patented or unpatented, is the right to use and sell it, and upon familiar principles the authorized sale of an article which is capable of use only in practicing the patent is a relinquishment of the patent monopoly with respect to the article sold. Leitch Mfg. Co. v. Barber Co., 302 U.S. 458, 460–61 (1938); B.B. Chemical Co. v. Ellis, 314 U.S. 495 (1942). Sale of a lens blank by the patentee or by his licensee is thus in itself both a complete transfer of ownership of the blank, which is within the protection of the patent law, and a license to practice the final stage of the patent procedure.

> ". . . (W)here one has sold an uncompleted article which, because it embodies essential features of his patented invention, is within the protection of his patented invention, and has destined the article to be finished by the purchaser in conformity to the patent, he has sold his invention so far as it is or may be embodied in that particular article. The reward he has demanded and received is for the article and the invention which it embodies and which his vendee is to practice upon it."

316 U.S. at 249–51. The trial court recognized that Univis was factually distinct from the instant case, but found the distinction to be of no effect:

> "It should be noted, however, that unlike Univis . . ., the practice of the final stage of Met–Coil's patented system requires not just "finishing" the element sold, i.e. forming the integral flanges, but also the purchase of an additional element of the patented system, i.e. the corner pieces. Met–Coil cites

no authority which suggests that this difference takes the present case out of the rule of Univis.

Met–Coil appealed the district court's judgment of noninfringement to this court.

III.

On appeal, Met–Coil urges that the district court erred in relying on *Univis.* To support that proposition, Met–Coil cites Bandag, Inc. v. Al Bolser's Tire Stores, Inc., 750 F.2d 903 (Fed.Cir.1984). In that case, the owner of a patent claiming a method for retreading tires sued a retreader who had purchased retreading equipment from a former licensee of the patent owner. This court set out two requirements for the grant of an implied license by virtue of a sale of nonpatented equipment used to practice a patented invention. First, the equipment involved must have no noninfringing uses. Id. at 924. In *Bandag,* the retreading equipment had noninfringing uses, so no license could be implied. To the contrary, Met–Coil's machines have no noninfringing use. Second, the circumstances of the sale must "plainly indicate that the grant of a license should be inferred." Id. at 925, quoting Hunt v. Armour & Co., 185 F.2d 722, 729 (7th Cir.1950). The circumstances of the sale in Bandag, purchase of the equipment from the former licensee of the patent owner, did not plainly indicate that the grant of a license should be inferred.

Met–Coil contends that this case does not meet the two-part test set out in *Bandag,* that is, although the machines sold have no noninfringing use, the circumstances do not plainly indicate that the grant of a license should be inferred. In this connection Met–Coil introduced certain written notices to customers with respect to the purchase of corner pieces from unlicensed sources.[4] Met–Coil relies on cases holding that no implied license arises where the original sale was accompanied by an express notice negating the grant of an implied license. Radio Corp. of America v. Andrea, 90 F.2d 612, 615 (2d Cir.1937); General Electric Co. v. Continental Lamp Works, Inc., 280 F. 846, 851 (2d Cir.1922). Those cases, however, are inapposite. Met–Coil does not assert that its customers were notified at the time of the sale of the machine. Rather, the customers were notified after they purchased the machine. The subsequent notices are not a part of the circumstances at the time of the sale, when the implied license would have arisen. After the fact notices are of no use in ascertaining the intent of Met–Coil and its customers at the time of the sales. * * *

Met–Coil urges that, even though it has not shown that the sales were accompanied by an express disclaimer of license, Korners has not met its burden of proof. As the alleged infringer, Korners has the

---

4. Met–Coil's subsidiary Iowa Precision Industries, Inc. sent a letter to owners of Lockformer machines and distributors of Iowa Precision's corner pieces, notifying them that "as long as you are a customer of ours, you are automatically licensed to use the (claimed invention) insofar as your use involves forming rolls and corners purchased from us but not from other unauthorized sources."

burden of showing the establishment of an implied license. Bandag, 750 F.2d at 924. We agree with the district court that Korners met that burden. A patent owner's unrestricted sales of a machine useful only in performing the claimed process and producing the claimed product "plainly indicate that the grant of a license should be inferred." Korners established a prima facie case, thereby shifting the burden of going forward to Met–Coil. Met–Coil offered nothing to carry its burden. Absent any circumstances tending to show the contrary, we see no error in the district court's holding that Met–Coil's customers enjoyed an implied license under the patent.[5]

The sole disputed issue decided by the trial court, the existence of an implied license, is a question of law. See Bandag, 750 F.2d at 926 ("the conclusion of the district court that an implied license of the Carver patent was extended to Bolser"); AMP, Inc. v. United States, 389 F.2d 448, 451 n. 3 (Ct.Cl.1968) ("the legal issue of implied license"). The parties raised no genuine issue of material fact. Because of our affirmance of the district court's holding that Met–Coil's customers enjoyed an implied license to practice the inventions claimed in Met–Coil's patent, there can be no direct infringement under the facts of this case. Absent direct infringement of the patent claims, there can be neither contributory infringement, Porter v. Farmers Supply Service, Inc., 790 F.2d 882, 884 (Fed.Cir.1986), nor inducement of infringement, Stukenborg v. Teledyne, Inc., 441 F.2d 1069, 1072 (9th Cir.1971). Therefore, Korners was entitled to summary judgment of noninfringement as a matter of law. Accordingly, we affirm the judgment of the district court.

Affirmed.

GENERAL TALKING PICTURES CORP. v. WESTERN ELECTRIC CO.

Supreme Court of the United States, 1938.
305 U.S. 124, 59 S.Ct. 116, 83 L.Ed. 81.

MR. JUSTICE BRANDEIS delivered the opinion of the Court.

In this case, we affirmed on May 2, 1938 (304 U.S. 175), the judgment of the Circuit Court of Appeals (2 Cir., 91 F.2d 922), which held that petitioner had infringed certain patents relating to vacuum tube amplifiers. On May 31st, we granted a rehearing, upon the following questions which had been presented by the petition for certiorari.

1. Can the owner of a patent, by means thereof, restrict the use made of a device manufactured under the patent, after the device has

5. Because our review is limited to the case before us, we emphasize that this case does not involve sales accompanied by a notice expressly precluding the grant of a license under the patent. Nor do we express any opinion on the legality of requiring the combined purchase of a machine and corner pieces. Moreover, our affirmance of the district court's holding that Met–Coil's customers enjoy an implied license prevents us from reaching the arguments raised by Met–Coil as to why Korners' sales are infringing.

passed into the hands of a purchaser in the ordinary channels of trade, and full consideration paid therefor?

2. Can a patent owner, merely by a "license notice" attached to a device made under the patent, and sold in the ordinary channels of trade, place an enforceable restriction on the purchaser thereof as to the use to which the purchaser may put the device?

Upon further hearing we are of opinion that neither question should be answered. For we find that, while the devices embody the inventions of the patents in suit, they were not manufactured or sold "under the patent[s]" and did not "pass into the hands of a purchaser in the ordinary channels of trade."

These are the relevant facts. Amplifiers embodying the invention here involved are useful in several distinct fields. Among these is (a) the commercial field of sound recording and reproducing, which embraces talking picture equipment for theatres, and (b) the private or home field, which embraces radio broadcast reception, radio amateur reception and radio experimental reception. For the commercial field exclusive licenses had been granted by the patent pool to Western Electric Company and Electrical Research Products, Inc. For the private or home field the patent pool granted non-exclusive licenses to about fifty manufacturers. Among these was American Transformer Company. It was licensed

"solely and only to the extent and for the uses hereinafter specified and defined * * * to manufacture * * *, and to sell * * * only for radio amateur reception, radio experimental reception and radio broadcast reception * * * licensed apparatus so manufactured by the Licensee. * * *"

The license provided further:

"Nothing herein contained shall be regarded as conferring upon the Licensee either expressly or by estoppel, implication or otherwise, a license to manufacture or sell, any apparatus except such as may be manufactured by the Licensee in accordance with the express provision of this Agreement."

Transformer Company, knowing that it had not been licensed to manufacture or to sell amplifiers for use in theatres as part of talking picture equipment, made for that commercial use the amplifiers in controversy and sold them to Pictures Corporation for that commercial use. Pictures Corporation ordered the amplifiers and purchased them knowing that Transformer Company had not been licensed to make or sell them for such use in theatres. Any use beyond the valid terms of a license is, of course, an infringement of a patent. Robinson on Patents, § 916. If where a patented invention is applicable to different uses, the owner of the patent may legally restrict a licensee to a particular field and exclude him from others, Transformer Company was guilty of an infringement when it made the amplifiers for, and sold them to, Pictures Corporation. And as Pictures Corporation ordered, purchased and leased them knowing the facts, it also was an infringer.

The question of law requiring decision is whether the restriction in the license is to be given effect. That a restrictive license is legal seems clear. Mitchell v. Hawley, 16 Wall. 544, 21 L.Ed. 322. As was said in United States v. General Electric Co., 272 U.S. 476, 489, the patentee may grant a license "upon any condition the performance of which is reasonably within the reward which the patentee by the grant of the patent is entitled to secure." The restriction here imposed is of that character. The practice of granting licenses for a restricted use is an old one, see Providence Rubber Company v. Goodyear, 9 Wall. 788, 799, 800, 19 L.Ed. 566; Gamewall Fire–Alarm Telegraph Co. v. Brooklyn, C.C., 14 F. 255. So far as appears, its legality has never been questioned. The parties stipulated that

> "it is common practice where a patented invention is applicable to different uses, to grant written licenses to manufacture under United States Letters Patents restricted to one or more of the several fields of use permitting the exclusive or non-exclusive use of the invention by the licensee in one field and excluding it in another field."

As the restriction was legal and the amplifiers were made and sold outside the scope of the license, the effect is precisely the same as if no license whatsoever had been granted to Transformer Company. And as Pictures Corporation knew the facts, it is in no better position than if it had manufactured the amplifiers itself without a license. It is liable because it has used the invention without license to do so.

We have consequently no occasion to consider what the rights of the parties would have been if the amplifier had been manufactured "under the patent" and "had passed into the hands of a purchaser in the ordinary channels of trade." Nor have we occasion to consider the effect of a "licensee's notice" which purports to restrict the use of articles lawfully sold.

Affirmed.

see Muncie Deer for opposite view (bad law!)

NOTES

1. Why did not the sale of the amplifiers by the Transformer Company "exhaust" the patent right so that the purchaser Talking Pictures Corporation was entitled to use them in any manner it wished? It is true that Pictures Corporation knew of the restriction, and thus might be liable for inducing Transformer Company to breach its contract with Western Electric, but the case involves only an action for patent infringement. In spite of the tension between *Talking Pictures* and *Keeler, Talking Pictures* continues to be regarded as good law in the lower courts.

2. One way to eliminate the tension is to read *Keeler* as resting only on a construction of an implied license, a result subject to change by a supervening explicit agreement with different terms. Note that the Federal Circuit in *Met–Coil* implies that an explicit contractual restriction might have been effective to change the result in that case. But such a construction is not consistent with the facts of *Keeler,* is it?

3. Does the notion that the patent owner is entitled to only one reward before the patent right is exhausted make any sense? Can a patent owner lease instead of sell machines, and set a lease royalty rate based on the duration of the lease or the number of times the machine is used? The answer is yes. But why isn't each lease payment beyond the first more than "one" reward? Isn't the answer that the scope of the reward turns on what the payer of the reward has bargained for?

4. Isn't the common sense concern of *Keeler* a concern about the position of innocent purchasers in a world where goods were frequently sold with limited licenses? But couldn't this problem be resolved by implying an unlimited license unless the purchaser has reasonable notice of a limited license? Would it be adequate notice to place a plate upon the machine or folding bed carrying the following legend: "Only the immediate purchaser from the original manufacturer or its licensees is licensed to use this [bed, machine, etc.]. Others may purchase licenses to use by writing to: [*here insert name and address of patentee*]." Would you buy something subject to such a restriction?

* * *

K. PROTECTION OF INVENTORS

ROBERTS v. SEARS, ROEBUCK AND CO.
United States Court of Appeals, Seventh Circuit, 1978.
573 F.2d 976, 197 USPQ 516.

SPRECHER, CIRCUIT JUDGE.

The major issues in this case are whether the district court properly declined to decide the validity of plaintiff's patent in a suit for fraud, breach of a confidential relationship and negligent misrepresentation in defendant's procurement of an assignment of plaintiff's patent rights and whether the district court properly concluded that plaintiff had elected his legal remedies and, therefore, was barred from seeking his equitable remedies of rescission and restitution.

I

This case involves the efforts of one of this nation's largest retail companies, Sears, Roebuck & Co. (Sears), to acquire through deceit the monetary benefits of an invention of a new type of socket wrench created by one of its sales clerks during his off-duty hours. That sales clerk, Peter M. Roberts (Plaintiff), initiated the unfortunate events that led to this appeal in 1963, when at the age of 18 he began work on a ratchet or socket wrench that would permit the easy removal of the sockets from the wrench. He, in fact, designed and constructed a prototype tool with a quick-release feature in it that succeeded in permitting its user to change sockets with one hand. Based on that prototype, plaintiff filed an application for a United States patent. In addition, since he was in the employ of Sears, a company that sold over a million wrenches per year, and since he had only a high school education and no business experience, he decided to show his invention to the manager of the Sears store in Gardner, Massachusetts where he worked. Plaintiff was persuaded to submit formally his invention as a suggestion to Sears. In May 1964, the prototype, along with a completed suggestion form, was sent to Sears' main office in Chicago, Illinois. Plaintiff, thereafter, left Sears' employ when his parents moved to Tennessee.

It was from this point on that Sears' conduct became the basis for the jury's determination that Sears appropriated the value of the plaintiff's invention by fraudulent means. Plaintiff's evidence proved that Sears took steps to ascertain the utility of the invention and that based on the information it acquired, Sears became convinced that the invention was in fact valuable. Sears had two sets of tests run on plaintiff's wrench by its custom manufacturer of wrenches, Moore Drop Forging Co. (Moore). The first test was conducted in July 1964, and it proved that the wrench operated normally and that the quick-release feature did not substantially weaken the structure of the wrench. The second test, conducted in May 1965, showed that actual mechanics liked the quick-release feature. Moore reported the results of these tests to Sears.

Based presumably on these tests, and the expert opinion of its senior tool buyer, Arthur Griesbaum, Sears in March 1965, had Moore design a fine-tooth wrench with the quick-release feature built into it. In addition, at about the same time, Sears put in motion plans to incorporate the quick-release feature into then-existing wrench models that constituted 74.27 percent of all the wrenches Sears sold. Thus, by early 1965, it was clear to Sears that this invention was very useful and probably would be quite profitable.

Sears also received reports from Moore regarding the manufacturing cost of plaintiff's quick-release feature. In the initial prototype built by Moore, the cost was 44 cents per unit. By June of 1965, Sears had received a report indicating that the cost could be reduced to 20 cents per unit. Thus, early in 1965, Sears learned that the feature was relatively inexpensive to manufacture.

Sears also took pains to ascertain the patentability of the quick-release feature. In April 1965, it received outside patent counsel's advice that there was "some basis for limited patentability" (defendant's Exhibit 9). It had previously learned in February 1965 from plaintiff's lawyer, Charles Fay, that he believed the invention was patentable based on a limited search. In addition, Sears was informed in early May 1965, by plaintiff's lawyer that a patent had been issued to plaintiff.[1]

With all of this information either available or soon to be available, Sears contacted plaintiff in January 1965, and began negotiations regarding the purchase of rights to use plaintiff's invention. During these negotiations, conducted with plaintiff's attorney, Sears' lawyer,

---

1. We might note here that Mr. Fay contacted Sears before informing plaintiff that a patent had issued. In addition, it was shown that Sears had contacted Mr. Fay during the period of these negotiations about doing some work for it and that he, in fact, did perform a couple of routine matters for Sears, thus raising some doubt about the independence of his advice to plaintiff.

Leonard Schram, made various representations to plaintiff that serve as the essential basis for plaintiff's complaint. In April 1965, in a letter seeking merely a license, Schram first told plaintiff that the invention was not new and that the claims in any patent that would be permitted would be "quite limited" (plaintiff's Exhibit 34). Second, Schram told plaintiff that the cost of the quick-release feature would be 40–50 cents. Third, he told plaintiff the feature would sell only to the extent it would be promoted and thus $10,000 was all that the feature was worth. Finally, and perhaps most ironically, Schram wrote to plaintiff that "[o]nce we have paid off the royalty expense, then we would probably take the amount previously allocated to said expense and use it for promotional expenses *if we desire to maintain sales on the item.*" (Emphasis added).

Based on this letter, plaintiff entered into the agreement on July 29, 1965, which provided for a two cent royalty per unit up to a maximum of $10,000 to be paid in return for a complete *assignment* of all of plaintiff's rights. In fact, for no extra charge, plaintiff's attorney gave Sears all of plaintiff's foreign patent rights. A provision was included in the contract regarding what would happen if Sears failed to sell 50,000 wrenches in a given year, thus reinforcing the impression that the wrenches might not sell very well. Also, a provision was inserted dealing with the contingency that a patent might not be issued, notwithstanding that Sears already knew, and plaintiff did not, that the patent had been granted.

By July, Sears knew that it planned to sell several hundred thousand wrenches with a cost per item increase of only 20 cents, that a patent had issued and that this product in all likelihood would have tremendous appeal with mechanics. Nonetheless, it entered into this agreement both having failed to disclose vital information about the product's appeal and structural utility and having made representations to plaintiff that were either false at the time they were made or became false without disclosure prior to the time of the signing of the contract.

Within days after the signing of the contract, Sears was manufacturing 44,000 of plaintiff's wrenches per week—all with plaintiff's patent number prominently stamped on them—and within three months, Sears was marketing them as a tremendous breakthrough. Within *nine months,* Sears had sold over 500,000 wrenches and paid plaintiff his maximum royalty thereby acquiring all of plaintiff's rights. Between 1965 and 1975, Sears sold in excess of 19 million wrenches, many at a premium of one to two dollars profit because no competition was able to market a comparable product for several years. To say the least, plaintiff's invention has been a commercial success.

Plaintiff, a Tennessee resident, filed suit against Sears, an Illinois Corporation, in federal district court in December 1969, based on diversity jurisdiction, seeking alternatively return of the patent and restitution or damages for fraud, breach of a confidential relationship and negligent misrepresentation. A jury trial was held from December 20, 1976, until January 18, 1977. During the trial, plaintiff basically proved the facts as presented above. Sears argued that it did not misrepresent any facts to plaintiff, that he had a lawyer and thus there was no confidential relationship and that the success of the wrenches was a function of advertising and the unforeseeable boom in do-it-yourself repairs, and thus Sears did not misrepresent the salability of plaintiff's wrenches. The jury was instructed on each of the three counts in plaintiff's complaint and told that it could award plaintiff profits for Counts I and II and could consider a reasonable royalty as a remedy for Count III. The jury apparently believed the plaintiff's evidence because it found Sears guilty on all three counts and entered judgment for one million dollars on each count, but the award was not cumulative.

Both parties filed post-trial motions. Sears filed for judgment NOV and plaintiff sought rescission of the contract and restitution. The district court denied both motions holding as to Sears' motion that the jury verdict was in accordance with the evidence and that the damages award was reasonable and holding as to plaintiff's motion that when he permitted the case to go to the jury he had elected his legal remedy and could not later also seek his equitable relief. Plaintiff appealed seeking equitable relief and Sears cross-appealed the one million dollar judgment against it. Since Sears' cross-appeal raises basic issues of liability, we will deal with it first. We will subsequently consider plaintiff's appeal on the issues of the appropriate remedy.

II

Sears' primary argument in its cross-appeal is that the district court erred in not determining conclusively the validity of plaintiff's patent as a precondition to trying plaintiff's claims for fraud, breach of a confidential relationship and misrepresentation. Relying on Lear, Inc. v. Adkins, 395 U.S. 653 (1969), Sears contends that if the district court had concluded that the patent was invalid, then plaintiff could not have been injured by any fraud Sears may have committed since it paid $10,000 for a "worthless" invention.

Sears' analysis, however, misconceives the Supreme Court's holding in Lear. There the Court held that a patent licensee was not estopped to contest the validity of the licensor's patent, and, in fact, was not required to pay the contractually-provided royalties for the license on the invalid patent during the pendency of the litigation. Contrary to Sears' implication, the Lear Court did not hold that the potentially invalid patent was worthless and thus the royalties offered in exchange for the right to use that patent would be unjustified. Instead, the Court explicitly recognized that there was significant economic value in the rights to an unchallenged patent. 395 U.S. at 669. In this regard the Court stated that "the existence of an unchallenged patent may deter others from attempting to compete with the licensee," thereby creating a monopoly in fact if not in law. Id.

Other courts have also acknowledged that significant economic value attaches to the rights to an uncontested patent. The Supreme Court recognized this recently in an opinion by Chief Justice Burger: "[E]ven though a discovery may not be patentable that does not 'destroy the value of the discovery * * *.'" Kewanee Oil Co. v. Bicron Corp., 416 U.S. 470, 482 (1974). Similarly, this court has held that "[w]hile there are paradoxical aspects of allowing recovery to arise from illegal interference with the sale of something which ultimately was proven to have no sales value, it cannot be said that there was no such value during the period of the presumptive validity of the patent." Moraine Products v. ICI America, Inc., 538 F.2d 134, 149 (7th Cir.1976).

The facts of this case, by themselves, make abundantly clear both that Sears believed that the uncontested patent had significant economic value as a deterrent to competitors and that the patent, in fact, did serve to deter competitors. Sears had the patent number stamped on all of its wrenches with plaintiff's quick-release feature, which presumably was done for the purpose of scaring off competitors. Also, Sears' competitors did not enter this lucrative market for several years after it became clear that this product had genuine sales appeal, which can only be explained by the existence of the patent.

It is at least somewhat disingenuous for Sears to argue before this court that plaintiff's patent was valueless when it made every effort in its marketing to exploit the economic value of the uncontested patent, received the benefits of a factual monopoly for several years because of that uncontested patent and to this day has refused to return the patent rights to plaintiff in return for the $10,000 originally paid to acquire these "valueless" rights. We, therefore, have little difficulty finding that Sears' deception caused plaintiff to be injured in fact.

The issue remains whether the public interest, recognized in Lear, in having patent validity challenged is of such significance that we should extend Lear to cover this case. The Lear Court held that a licensee should be permitted to contest the validity of a licensor's patent because "[l]icensees may often be the only individuals with enough economic incentive to challenge the patentability of an inventor's discovery." 395 U.S. at 670. Thus, the Court feared that if licensees "are muzzled, the public may continually be required to pay tribute to would-be monopolists without need or justification." Id.

We believe that the reasoning in Lear does not extend to this case for two reasons. First, we deal here with a complete assignment of plaintiff's patent rights to Sears. * * * Thus, the primary evil that the Court in Lear sought to end—that the public might have to pay tribute to a "would-be monopolist"—is completely irrelevant to this case. Plaintiff has no legal basis for exacting any "tribute" until the patent rights are returned to him. At that point in time, the patent's validity can be tested either in an infringement suit or after plaintiff enters into a licensing agreement. The public's interest would not be injured by our decision to bar Sears from contesting this patent at this time.

Second, and perhaps even more fundamentally, the Court's analysis in Lear initiated with an assessment of "the spirit of contract law, which seeks to balance the claims of promisor and promisee in accord with the requirements of *good faith*." 395 U.S. at 670 (emphasis added). Only after the Court satisfied itself that the equities were balanced on each side did it proceed to a consideration of the needs of patent law and the public interest. Sears' actions in this matter have violated completely the basic assumption in Lear that there was good faith in the dealings between the parties. There is no balance of equities between Sears and plaintiff in their contractual relations. For this court to employ the public interest in patent law to sanction Sears' conduct is unjustifiable. Certainly nothing in patent law requires this court to permit fraud to go unremedied. Cf. Kewanee Oil Co. v. Bicron Corp., 416 U.S. 470, 487 (1974) (nothing in patent law discourages states from preventing industrial espionage). We, therefore, hold that the district court properly concluded that Lear, Inc. v. Adkins, is no bar to plaintiff's recovery.

* * *

IV

Sears' final argument in its cross-appeal is that plaintiff failed to prove the existence of a confidential relationship between himself and Sears. In assessing that argument, we recognize at the outset that there are no hard and fast rules for determining whether a confidential relationship exists. See G. Bogert, The Law of Trusts and Trustees § 482 (2d ed. 1960). The trier of fact must examine all of the circumstances surrounding the relationship between the parties and determine whether "one person reposes trust and confidence in another who thereby gains a resulting influence and superiority over the first." Kester v. Crilly, 405 Ill. 425, 91 N.E.2d 419, 423 (1950).

Various factors have been recognized judicially as being of particular relevance to that inquiry. Among them are disparity of age, education and business experience between the parties. Melish v. Vogel, 35 Ill.App.3d 125, 343 N.E.2d 17, 26 (1975). Additional factors are the existence of an employment relationship and the exchange of confidential information from one party to the other. See Yamins v. Zeitz, 322 Mass. 268, 76 N.E.2d 769, 772 (1948). All five of those factors are present in this case. In addition, one of Sears' witnesses admitted that the company expected plaintiff to "believe" and to "rely" on various representations that Sears made to him (Tr. at 1981). Obviously, this question is best left to the trier of fact, and this court under any circumstances would hesitate to disturb the jury's findings. That hesitation is especially strong here where so many factors suggest that a confidential relationship in fact existed.

Sears argues, however, that there are two factors involved here that eliminate any possible confidential relationship. They are that plaintiff never proved that Sears had knowledge of the confidential relationship upon which plaintiff was relying and that plaintiff retained counsel to guide him, and therefore, did not rely on Sears. We find neither factor sufficient to justify overturning the jury's verdict on this issue.

* * *

V

Plaintiff, in his appeal, seeks review of the district court's decision that he elected his legal remedies by taking the case to the jury, and therefore, is barred from pursuing his equitable remedies of rescission and restitution. Plaintiff argues that the district court, as a court of equity, should have accepted the jury's liability determination, but should have disregarded its damages verdict and instead should have granted rescission and restitution.

* * *

The general rule as to when an election is necessary is that " 'a certain state of facts relied on as the basis of a certain remedy is inconsistent with, and repugnant to, another certain state of facts relied on as the basis of another remedy.' " Prudential Oil Corp. v. Phillips Petroleum Co., 418 F.Supp. 254, 257 (S.D.N.Y.1975). Here, the jury was instructed that plaintiff could receive profits for Counts I and II, fraud and breach of a confidential relationship. Apparently dissatisfied with the size of the jury verdict, plaintiff sought in a post-trial motion to have the court reconsider the evidence and award relief based on essentially the same standard the jury used. To have granted plaintiff's request would have been completely unfair to Sears. It might have been better for the court to require the plaintiff to elect his remedy expressly prior to instructing the jury, but plaintiff did not object to the court's procedure, and therefore, must have been satisfied to let the jury determine the appropriate award. Having let the case go to the jury, without getting the issue clarified, plaintiff should not be heard to complain about the outcome of that procedure.

With regard to an election between the profits awarded by the jury and return of the patent based on rescission, however, we see no basis for invoking the election of remedies doctrine. Based on the jury instruction, plaintiff will receive one million dollars as the measure of *past* profits earned by Sears up to the time of trial. That award, however, is not inconsistent with return of the patent so that plaintiff can receive the *future* benefits of the patent that Sears fraudulently acquired. There will be neither a double recovery nor a factual inconsistency between these remedies. See Prudential Oil Corp., supra at 257; G. Bogert, The Law of Trusts and Trustees § 946 (2d ed. 1962). Therefore, we conclude that going to the jury under a past profits instruction did not bar plaintiff from seeking rescission and thereby possibly recovering his patent. Whether rescission is appropriate, however, is an issue that should be decided in the first instance by the district court.

For the reasons stated above, we affirm the district court's judgment against Sears on all three counts in plaintiff's complaint and the court's decision not to alter plaintiff's monetary award, but reverse the court's determination that it lacked the power to award rescission and remand to the district court for a determination of whether rescission is appropriate under the facts of this case.

Affirmed in part; reversed in part; and remanded.

NOTES

1. Is the patent on the Roberts' socket wrench valid? If it is not valid, just what did Sears obtain from Roberts? As part of the relief in the litigation, Sears reassigned the patent to Roberts. Roberts then sued Sears for infringement for the period after the reassignment. The District Court held the patent valid, but the Seventh Circuit reversed. A panel held the patent invalid, 697 F.2d 796 (7th Cir.1983), but the court granted rehearing *en banc* and reversed, 723 F.2d 1324 (7th Cir.1983). The en banc court held that the instructions to the jury, which permitted it to decide the ultimate question of patent validity, were improper, and remanded the case for retrial. In the fall of 1988, the district court was making rulings preparatory to retrial.

2. Robert L. Gullette, State Legislation Governing Ownership Rights In Inventions Under Employee Invention Agreements, 62 J.P.O.S. 721 (1980), reports on recent statutes passed in a few states that limits the ability of employers by contract to require employees to assign to them rights in inventions made on their own time and without the use of the employer's facilities.

3. An independent inventor faces many problems before he can expect to benefit from his invention. He will not infrequently lack the resources to develop and market it. He may be wildly overoptimistic about its prospects. He may lack the cash to pay for expert advice. In recent years some firms have appeared that promoted themselves as invention developers but who in fact profited only from fees charged to hopeful inventors. See Paul Shemin, Idea Promotor Control: The Time Has Come, 60 J.P.O.S. 261 (1978); Robert J. Thomas, Invention Development Services and Inventors: Recent Inroads on Caveat Inventor, 60 J.P.O.S. 355 (1978). The F.T.C. has proceeded against some of these firms and some states have passed statutes regulating their disclosures to prospective clients and providing additional remedies in the event of fraud or deception.

*

SUPPLEMENT A

FEIST PUBLICATIONS, INC. v. RURAL TELEPHONE SERVICE CO., INC.

Supreme Court of the United States, 1991.
— U.S. —, 111 S.Ct. 1282, 112 L.Ed.2d 358.

JUSTICE O'CONNOR delivered the opinion of the Court.

This case requires us to clarify the extent of copyright protection available to telephone directory white pages.

I

Rural Telephone Service Company is a certified public utility that provides telephone service to several communities in northwest Kansas. It is subject to a state regulation that requires all telephone companies operating in Kansas to issue annually an updated telephone directory. Accordingly, as a condition of its monopoly franchise, Rural publishes a typical telephone directory, consisting of white pages and yellow pages. The white pages list in alphabetical order the names of Rural's subscribers, together with their towns and telephone numbers. The yellow pages list Rural's business subscribers alphabetically by category and feature classified advertisements of various sizes. Rural distributes its directory free of charge to its subscribers, but earns revenue by selling yellow pages advertisements.

Feist Publications, Inc., is a publishing company that specializes in area-wide telephone directories. Unlike a typical directory, which covers only a particular calling area, Feist's area-wide directories cover a much larger geographical range, reducing the need to call directory assistance or consult multiple directories. The Feist directory that is the subject of this litigation covers 11 different telephone service areas in 15 counties and contains 46,878 white pages listings—compared to Rural's approximately 7,700 listings. Like Rural's directory, Feist's is distributed free of charge and includes both white pages and yellow pages. Feist and Rural compete vigorously for yellow pages advertising.

As the sole provider of telephone service in its service area, Rural obtains subscriber information quite easily. Persons desiring telephone service must apply to Rural and provide their names and addresses; Rural then assigns them a telephone number. Feist is not a telephone company, let alone one with monopoly status, and therefore lacks independent access to any subscriber information. To obtain white pages listings for its area-wide directory, Feist approached each of the 11 telephone companies operating in northwest Kansas and offered to pay for the right to use its white pages listings.

1058 FEIST PUBLICATIONS v. RURAL TELEPHONE SERVICE CO.

Of the 11 telephone companies, only Rural refused to license its
listings to Feist. Rural's refusal created a problem for Feist, as omitting these listings would have left a gaping hole in its area-wide
directory, rendering it less attractive to potential yellow pages advertisers. In a decision subsequent to that which we review here, the District
Court determined that this was precisely the reason Rural refused to
license its listings. The refusal was motivated by an unlawful purpose
"to extend its monopoly in telephone service to a monopoly in yellow
pages advertising." Rural Telephone Service Co. v. Feist Publications,
Inc., 787 F.Supp. 610, 622 (Kan.1990).

Unable to license Rural's white pages listings, Feist used them
without Rural's consent. Feist began by removing several thousand
listings that fell outside the geographic range of its area-wide directory,
then hired personnel to investigate the 4,935 that remained. These
employees verified the data reported by Rural and sought to obtain
additional information. As a result, a typical Feist listing includes the
individual's street address, most of Rural's listings do not. Notwithstanding these additions, however, 1,309 of the 46,878 listings in Feist's
1983 directory were identical to listings in Rural's 1982–1983 white
pages. App. 54 (¶ 15–16), 57. Four of these were fictitious listings that
Rural had inserted into its directory to detect copying.

Rural sued for copyright infringement in the District Court for the
District of Kansas taking the position that Feist, in compiling its own
directory, could not use the information contained in Rural's white
pages. Rural asserted that Feist's employees were obliged to travel
door-to-door or conduct a telephone survey to discover the same information for themselves. Feist responded that such efforts were economically impractical and, in any event, unnecessary because the information copied was beyond the scope of copyright protection. The District
Court granted summary judgment to Rural, explaining that "[c]ourts
have consistently held that telephone directories are copyrightable"
and citing a string of lower court decisions. 663 F.Supp. 214, 218
(1987). In an unpublished opinion, the Court of Appeals for the Tenth
Circuit affirmed "for substantially the reasons given by the district
court." App. to Pet. for Cert. 4a, judgt. order reported at 916 F.2d 718
(1990). We granted certiorari, 498 U.S. ___, 111 S.Ct. 40, 112 L.Ed.2d
17 (1990), to determine whether the copyright in Rural's directory
protects the names, towns, and telephone numbers copied by Feist.

II

A

This case concerns the interaction of two well-established propositions. The first is that facts are not copyrightable; the other, that
compilations of facts generally are. Each of these propositions possesses an impeccable pedigree. That there can be no valid copyright in
facts is universally understood. The most fundamental axiom of copyright law is that "[n]o author may copyright his ideas or the facts he

narrates." Harper & Row, Publishers, Inc. v. Nation Enterprises, 471 U.S. 539, 556 (1985). Rural wisely concedes this point, noting in its brief that "[f]acts and discoveries, of course, are not themselves subject to copyright protection." Brief for Respondent 24. At the same time, however, it is beyond dispute that compilations of facts are within the subject matter of copyright. Compilations were expressly mentioned in the Copyright Act of 1909, and again in the Copyright Act of 1976.

There is an undeniable tension between these two propositions. Many compilations consist of nothing but raw data—i.e. wholly factual information not accompanied by any original written expression. On what basis may one claim a copyright in such a work? Common sense tells us that 100 uncopyrightable facts do not magically change their status when gathered together in one place. Yet copyright law seems to contemplate that compilations that consist exclusively of facts are potentially within its scope.

The key to resolving the tension lies in understanding why facts are not copyrightable. The *sine qua non* of copyright is originality. To qualify for copyright protection, a work must be original to the author. See *Harper & Row,* supra, at 547–549. Original as the term is used in copyright, means only that the work was independently created by the author (as opposed to copied from other works), and that it possesses at least some minimal degree of creativity. 1 M. Nimmer & D. Nimmer, Copyright §§ 2.01[A], [B] (1990) (hereinafter Nimmer). To be sure, the requisite level of creativity is extremely low, even a slight amount will suffice. The vast majority of works make the grade quite easily, as they possess some creative spark, "no matter how crude, humble or obvious" it might be. Id. § 1.08[C][1]. Originality does not signify novelty, a work may be original even though it closely resembles other works so long as the similarity is fortuitous, not the result of copying. To illustrate, assume that two poets, each ignorant of the other, compose identical poems. Neither work is novel, yet both are original and, hence, copyrightable. See Sheldon v. Metro–Goldwyn Pictures Corp., 81 F.2d 49, 54 (CA2 1936).

Originality is a constitutional requirement. The source of Congress' power to enact copyright laws is Article I, § 8, cl. 8, of the Constitution, which authorizes Congress to "secur[e] for limited Times to Authors . . . the exclusive Right to their respective Writings." In two decisions from the late 19th Century—The Trade–Mark Cases, 100 U.S. 82, 25 L.Ed. 550 (1879); and Burrow–Giles Lithographic Co. v. Sarony, 111 U.S. 53 (1884)—this Court defined the crucial terms "authors" and "writings." In so doing, the Court made it unmistakably clear that these terms presuppose a degree of originality.

In *The Trade–Mark Cases,* the Court addressed the constitutional scope of "writings." For a particular work to be classified "under the head of writings of authors," the Court determined, "originality is required." 100 U.S., at 94. The Court explained that originality requires independent creation plus a modicum of creativity: "[W]hile the word *writings* may be liberally construed, as it has been, to include original designs for engraving, prints, &c., it is only such as are *original*, and are founded in the creative powers of the mind. The writings, which are to be protected are *the fruits of intellectual labor,* embodied in the form of books, prints, engravings, and the like." Ibid. (emphasis in original).

In *Burrow–Giles,* the Court distilled the same requirement from the Constitution's use of the word "authors." The Court defined "author," in a constitutional sense, to mean "he to whom anything owes its origin; originator; maker." 111 U.S., at 58, 4 S.Ct., at 281 (internal quotations omitted). As in *The Trade–Mark Cases,* the Court emphasized the creative component of originality. It described copyright as being limited to "original intellectual conceptions of the author," ibid., and stressed the importance of requiring an author who accuses another of infringement to prove "the existence of those facts of originality, of intellectual production, of thought, and conception." Id., 111 U.S., at 59–60.

The originality requirement articulated in *The Trade–Mark Cases* and *Burrow–Giles* remains the touchstone of copyright protection today. See Goldstein v. California, 412 U.S. 546, 561–562 (1973). It is the very "premise of copyright law." Miller v. Universal City Studios, Inc., 650 F.2d 1365, 1368 (CA5 1981). Leading scholars agree on this point. As one pair of commentators succinctly puts it: "The originality requirement is *constitutionally mandated* for all works." Patterson & Joyce, Monopolizing the Law: The Scope of Copyright Protection for Law Reports and Statutory Compilations, 36 UCLA L.Rev. 719, 763, n. 155 (1989) (emphasis in original) (hereinafter Patterson & Joyce). Accord id., at 759–760, and n. 140. Nimmer § 1.06[A] ("originality is a statutory as well as a constitutional requirement"); id., § 1.08[C][1] ("a modicum of intellectual labor . . . clearly constitutes an essential constitutional element").

It is this bedrock principle of copyright that mandates the law's seemingly disparate treatment of facts and factual compilations. "No one may claim originality as to facts." Id., § 2.11[A], p. 2–157. This is because facts do not owe their origin to an act of authorship. The distinction is one between creation and discovery: the first person to find and report a particular fact has not created the fact he or she has merely discovered its existence. To borrow from *Burrow–Giles,* one who discovers a fact is not its "maker" or "originator." 111 U.S., at 58. "The discoverer merely finds and records." Nimmer § 2.03[E]. Census-takers, for example, do not "create" the population figures that emerge from their efforts; in a sense they copy these figures from the world around them. Denicola, Copyright in Collections of Facts: A Theory for the Protection of Nonfiction Literary Works, 81 Colum.L. Rev. 516, 525 (1981) (hereinafter Denicola). Census data therefore do not trigger copyright because these data are not "original" in the constitutional sense. Nimmer § 2.03[E]. The same is true of all facts—scientific, historical, biographical, and news of the day. "[T]hey may not be copyrighted and are part of the public domain available to every person." *Miller,* supra, at 1369.

Factual compilations, on the other hand, may possess the requisite originality. The compilation author typically chooses which facts to include, in what order to place them, and how to arrange the collected data so that they may be used effectively by readers. These choices as to selection and arrangement, so long as they are made independently by the compiler and entail a minimal degree of creativity, are sufficiently original that Congress may protect such compilations through the copyright laws. Nimmer §§ 2.11[D], 3.03; Denicola 523, n. 38. Thus, even a directory that contains absolutely no protectible written expression, only facts, meets the constitutional minimum for copyright protection if it features an original selection or arrangement. See *Harper & Row,* 471 U.S., at 547. Accord Nimmer § 3.03.

This protection is subject to an important limitation. The mere fact that a work is copyrighted does not mean that every element of the work may be protected. Originality remains the *sine qua non* of copyright, accordingly, copyright protection may extend only to those components of a work that are original to the author. Patterson & Joyce 800–802; Ginsburg, Creation and Commercial Value: Copyright Protection of Works of Information, 90 Colum.L.Rev. 1865, 1868, and n. 12 (1990) (hereinafter Ginsburg). Thus, if the compilation author clothes facts with an original collocation of words, he or she may be able to claim a copyright in this written expression. Others may copy the underlying facts from the publication, but not the precise words used to present them. In *Harper & Row,* for example, we explained that President Ford could not prevent others from copying bare historical facts from his autobiography, see 471 U.S., at 556–557, but that he could prevent others from copying his "subjective descriptions and portraits of public figures." Id., at 563. Where the compilation author adds no written expression but rather lets the facts speak for themselves, the expressive element is more elusive. The only conceivable expression is the manner in which the compiler has selected and arranged the facts. Thus, if the selection and arrangement are original, these elements of the work are eligible for copyright protection. See Patry, Copyright in Compilations of Facts (or Why the "White Pages" Are Not Copyrightable), 12 Com. & Law 37, 64 (Dec. 1990) (hereinafter Patry). No matter how original the format, however, the facts themselves do not become original through association. See Patterson & Joyce 776.

This inevitably means that the copyright in a factual compilation is thin. Notwithstanding a valid copyright, a subsequent compiler remains free to use the facts contained in another's publication to aid in preparing a competing work, so long as the competing work does not feature the same selection and arrangement. As one commentator explains it "[N]o matter how much original authorship the work displays, the facts and ideas it exposes are free for the taking. [T]he very same facts and ideas may be divorced from the context imposed by the author, and restated or reshuffled by second comers, even if the author was the first to discover the facts or to propose the ideas." Ginsburg 1868.

It may seem unfair that much of the fruit of the compiler's labor may be used by others without compensation. As Justice Brennan has correctly observed, however, this is not "some unforeseen byproduct of a statutory scheme." *Harper & Row,* 471 U.S., at 589 (dissenting opinion). It is, rather, "the essence of copyright," ibid., and a constitutional requirement. The primary objective of copyright is not to reward the labor of authors, but "[t]o promote the Progress of Science and useful Arts." Art. I, § 8, cl. 8. Accord Twentieth Century Music Corp. v. Aiken, 422 U.S. 151, 156 (1975). To this end, copyright assures authors the right to their original expression, but encourages others to build freely upon the ideas and information conveyed by a work. *Harper & Row,* supra, 471 U.S. at 556–557. This principle, known as the idea/expression or fact/expression dichotomy, applies to all works of authorship. As applied to a factual compilation, assuming the absence of original written expression, only the compiler's selection and arrangement may be protected; the raw facts may be copied at will. This result is neither unfair nor unfortunate. It is the means by which copyright advances the progress of science and art.

This Court has long recognized that the fact/expression dichotomy limits severely the scope of protection in fact-based works. More than a century ago, the Court observed: "The very object of publishing a book on science or the useful arts is to communicate to the world the useful knowledge which it contains. But this object would be frustrated if the knowledge could not be used without incurring the guilt of piracy of the book." Baker v. Selden, 101 U.S. 99, 103 (1880). We reiterated this point in *Harper & Row.*

"[N]o author may copyright facts or ideas. The copyright is limited to those aspects of the work—termed 'expression'—that display the stamp of the author's originality.

"[C]opyright does not prevent subsequent users from copying from a prior author's work those constituent elements that are not original— for example . . . facts, or materials in the public domain—as long as such use does not unfairly appropriate the author's original contributions." 471 U.S., at 547–548 (citation omitted).

This, then, resolves the doctrinal tension: Copyright treats facts and factual compilations in a wholly consistent manner. Facts, whether alone or as part of a compilation, are not original and therefore may not be copyrighted. A factual compilation is eligible for copyright if it features an original selection or arrangement of facts, but the copyright is limited to the particular selection or arrangement. In no event may copyright extend to the facts themselves.

B

As we have explained, originality is a constitutionally mandated prerequisite for copyright protection. The Court's decisions announcing this rule predate the Copyright Act of 1909, but ambiguous language in the 1909 Act caused some lower courts temporarily to lose sight of this requirement.

The 1909 Act embodied the originality requirement, but not as clearly as it might have. See Nimmer § 2.01. The subject matter of copyright was set out in § 3 and § 4 of the Act. Section 4 stated that copyright was available to "all the writings of an author." 35 Stat. 1076. By using the words "writings" and "author"—the same words used in Article I, § 8 of the Constitution and defined by the Court in *The Trade–Mark Cases* and *Burrow–Giles*—the statute necessarily incorporated the originality requirement articulated in the Court's decisions. It did so implicitly, however, thereby leaving room for error.

Section 3 was similarly ambiguous. It stated that the copyright in a work protected only "the copyrightable component parts of the work." It thus stated an important copyright principle, but failed to identify the specific characteristic—originality—that determined which component parts of a work were copyrightable and which were not.

Most courts construed the 1909 Act correctly, notwithstanding the less-than-perfect statutory language. They understood from this Court's decisions that there could be no copyright without originality. See Patterson & Joyce 760–761. As explained in the Nimmer treatise: "The 1909 Act neither defined originality, nor even expressly required that a work be 'original' in order to command protection. However, the courts uniformly inferred the requirement from the fact that copyright protection may only be claimed by 'authors'. . . . It was reasoned that since an author is 'the . . . creator, originator' it follows that a work is not the product of an author unless the work is original." Nimmer § 2.01 (footnotes omitted) (citing cases).

But some courts misunderstood the statute. See, e.g., Leon v. Pacific Telephone & Telegraph Co., 91 F.2d 484 (CA9 1937); Jeweler's Circular Publishing Co. v. Keystone Publishing Co., 281 F. 83 (CA2 1922). These courts ignored § 3 and § 4, focusing their attention instead on § 5 of the Act. Section 5, however, was purely technical in nature: it provided that a person seeking to register a work should indicate on the application the type of work, and it listed 14 categories under which the work might fall. One of these categories was "[b]ooks, including composite and cyclopaedic works, directories, gazetteers, and other compilations." § 5(a). Section 5 did not purport to say that all compilations were automatically copyrightable. Indeed, it expressly disclaimed any such function, pointing out that "the subject-matter of copyright [i]s defined in section four." Nevertheless, the fact that factual compilations were mentioned specifically in § 5 led some courts to infer erroneously that directories and the like were copyrightable *per se,* "without any further or precise showing of original—personal—authorship." Ginsburg 1895.

Making matters worse, these courts developed a new theory to justify the protection of factual compilations. Known alternatively as "sweat of the brow" or "industrious collection," the underlying notion was that copyright was a reward for the hard work that went into compiling facts. The classic formulation of the doctrine appeared in Jeweler's Circular Publishing Co., 281 F., at 88:

> "The right to copyright a book upon which one has expended labor in its preparation does not depend upon whether the materials which he has collected consist or not of matters which are publici juris, or whether such materials show literary skill *or originality,* either in thought or in language, or anything more than industrious collection. The man who goes through the streets of a town and puts down the names of each of the inhabitants, with their occupations and their street number, acquires material of which he is the author" (emphasis added).

The "sweat of the brow" doctrine had numerous flaws, the most glaring being that it extended copyright protection in a compilation beyond selection and arrangement—the compiler's original contributions—to the facts themselves. Under the doctrine, the only defense to infringement was independent creation. A subsequent compiler was "not entitled to take one word of information previously published," but rather had to "independently wor[k] out the matter for himself, so as to arrive at the same result from the same common sources of information." Id., at 88–89 (internal quotations omitted). "Sweat of the brow" courts thereby eschewed the most fundamental axiom of copyright law—that no one may copyright facts or ideas. See Miller v. Universal City Studios, Inc., 650 F.2d at 1372 (criticizing "sweat of the brow" courts because "ensur[ing] that later writers obtain the facts independently . . . is precisely the scope of protection given . . . copyrighted matter, and the law is clear that facts are not entitled to such protection").

Decisions of this Court applying the 1909 Act make clear that the statute did not permit the "sweat of the brow" approach. The best example is International News Service v. Associated Press, 248 U.S. 215 (1918). In that decision, the Court stated unambiguously that the 1909 Act conferred copyright protection only on those elements of a work that were original to the author. Associated Press had conceded taking news reported by International News Service and publishing it in its own newspapers. Recognizing that § 5 of the Act specifically mentioned "[p]eriodicals, including newspapers," § 5(b), the Court acknowledged that news articles were copyrightable. Id., at 234. It flatly rejected, however, the notion that the copyright in an article extended to the factual information it contained. "[T]he news element—the information respecting current events contained in the literary production—is not the creation of the writer, but is a report of matters that ordinarily are *publici juris;* it is the history of the day." Ibid.**

Without a doubt, the "sweat of the brow" doctrine flouted basic copyright principles. Throughout history, copyright law has "recognize[d] a greater need to disseminate factual works than works of fiction or fantasy." *Harper & Row,* 471 U.S., at 563. Accord Gorman, Fact or Fancy: The Implications for Copyright, 29 J. Copyright Soc. 560, 563 (1982). But "sweat of the brow" courts took a contrary view; they handed out proprietary interests in facts and declared that authors are absolutely precluded from saving time and effort by relying upon the facts contained in prior works. In truth, "[i]t is just such wasted effort that the proscription against the copyright of ideas and facts, . . . [is] designed to prevent." Rosemont Enterprises, Inc. v. Random House, Inc., 366 F.2d 303, 310 (CA2 1966), cert. denied 385 U.S. 1009 (1967). "Protection for the fruits of such research . . . may in certain circumstances be available under a theory of unfair competition. But to accord copyright protection on this basis alone distorts basic copyright principles in that it creates a monopoly in public domain materials without the necessary justification of protecting and encouraging the creation of 'writings' by 'authors.' " Nimmer § 3.04, p. 3–23 (footnote omitted).

C

"Sweat of the brow" decisions did not escape the attention of the Copyright Office. When Congress decided to overhaul the copyright statute and asked the Copyright Office to study existing problems, see Mills Music, Inc. v. Snyder, 469 U.S. 153, 159 (1985), the Copyright Office promptly recommended that Congress clear up the confusion in the lower courts as to the basic standards of copyrightability. The Register of Copyrights explained in his first report to Congress that "originality" was a "basic requisit[e]" of copyright under the 1909 Act, but that "the absence of any reference to [originality] in the statute seems to have led to misconceptions as to what is copyrightable matter." Report of the Register of Copyrights on the General Revision of the U.S. Copyright Law, 87th Cong., 1st Sess., p. 9 (H. Judiciary Comm. Print 1961). The Register suggested making the originality requirement explicit. Ibid.

Congress took the Register's advice. In enacting the Copyright Act of 1976, Congress dropped the reference to "all the writings of an author" and replaced it with the phrase "original works of authorship." 17 U.S.C. § 102(a). In making explicit the originality requirement, Congress announced that it was merely clarifying existing law: "The two fundamental criteria of copyright protection [are] originality and fixation in tangible form. . . . The phrase 'original works of authorship,' which is purposely left undefined, is intended to incorporate

** The Court ultimately rendered judgment for International News Service on noncopyright grounds that are not relevant here. See 248 U.S., at 235, 241–242.

without change *the standard of originality established by the courts under the present [1909] copyright statute.*" H.R.Rep. No. 94–1476, p. 51 (1976) (emphasis added) (hereinafter H.R.Rep.); S.Rep. No. 94–473, p. 50 (1975), U.S.Code Cong. & Admin.News 1976, pp. 5659, 5664 (emphasis added) (hereinafter S.Rep.). This sentiment was echoed by the Copyright Office. "Our intention here is to maintain the *established standards* of originality. . . ." Supplementary Report of the Register of Copyrights on the General Revision of U.S. Copyright Law, 89th Cong., 1st Sess., Part 6, p. 3 (H.Judiciary Comm.Print 1965) (emphasis added).

To ensure that the mistakes of the "sweat of the brow" courts would not be repeated, Congress took additional measures. For example, § 3 of the 1909 Act had stated that copyright protected only the "copyrightable component parts" of a work, but had not identified originality as the basis for distinguishing those component parts that were copyrightable from those that were not. The 1976 Act deleted this section and replaced it with § 102(b), which identifies specifically those elements of a work for which copyright is not available: "In no case does copyright protection for an original work of authorship extend to any idea, procedure, process, system, method of operation, concept, principle, or discovery, regardless of the form in which it is described, explained, illustrated, or embodied in such work." § 102(b) is universally understood to prohibit any copyright in facts. *Harper & Row,* supra, at 547, 556. Accord Nimmer § 2.03[E] (equating facts with "discoveries"). As with § 102(a), Congress emphasized that § 102(b) did not change the law, but merely clarified it. "Section 102(b) in no way enlarges or contracts the scope of copyright protection under the present law. Its purpose is to restate . . . that the basic dichotomy between expression and idea remains unchanged." H.R.Rep., at 57; S.Rep., at 54, U.S.Code Cong. & Admin.News 1976, p. 5670.

Congress took another step to minimize confusion by deleting the specific mention of "directories . . . and other compilations" in § 5 of the 1909 Act. As mentioned, this section had led some courts to conclude that directories were copyrightable *per se* and that every element of a directory was protected. In its place, Congress enacted two new provisions. First, to make clear that compilations were not copyrightable *per se,* Congress provided a definition of the term "compilation." Second, to make clear that the copyright in a compilation did not extend to the facts themselves, Congress enacted 17 U.S.C. § 103.

The definition of "compilation" is found in § 101 of the 1976 Act. It defines a "compilation" in the copyright sense as "a work formed by the collection and assembly of preexisting materials or of data *that* are selected, coordinated, or arranged *in such a way that* the resulting work as a whole constitutes an original work of authorship" (emphasis added).

The purpose of the statutory definition is to emphasize that collections of facts are not copyrightable *per se.* It conveys this message through its tripartite structure, as emphasized above by the italics.

The statute identifies three distinct elements and requires each to be met for a work to qualify as a copyrightable compilation: (1) the collection and assembly of pre-existing material, facts, or data; (2) the selection, coordination, or arrangement of those materials; and (3) the creation, by virtue of the particular selection, coordination, or arrangement, of an "original" work of authorship. "[T]his tripartite conjunctive structure is self-evident, and should be assumed to 'accurately express the legislative purpose.'" Patry 51, quoting *Mills Music,* 469 U.S., at 164.

At first glance, the first requirement does not seem to tell us much. It merely describes what one normally thinks of as a compilation—a collection of pre-existing material, facts, or data. What makes it significant is that it is not the *sole* requirement. It is not enough for copyright purposes that an author collects and assembles facts. To satisfy the statutory definition, the work must get over two additional hurdles. In this way, the plain language indicates that not every collection of facts receives copyright protection. Otherwise, there would be a period after "data."

The third requirement is also illuminating. It emphasizes that a compilation, like any other work, is copyrightable only if it satisfies the originality requirement ("an *original* work of authorship"). Although § 102 states plainly that the originality requirement applies to all works, the point was emphasized with regard to compilations to ensure that courts would not repeat the mistake of the "sweat of the brow" courts by concluding that fact-based works are treated differently and measured by some other standard. As Congress explained it, the goal was to "make plain that the criteria of copyrightable subject matter stated in section 102 apply with full force to works . . . containing preexisting material." H.R.Rep., at 57; S.Rep., at 55, U.S.Code Cong. & Admin.News 1976, p. 5670.

The key to the statutory definition is the second requirement. It instructs courts that, in determining whether a fact-based work is an original work of authorship, they should focus on the manner in which the collected facts have been selected, coordinated, and arranged. This is a straight-forward application of the originality requirement. Facts are never original, so the compilation author can claim originality, if at all, only in the way the facts are presented. To that end, the statute dictates that the principal focus should be on whether the selection, coordination, and arrangement are sufficiently original to merit protection.

Not every selection, coordination, or arrangement will pass muster. This is plain from the statute. It states that, to merit protection, the facts must be selected, coordinated, or arranged "in such a way" as to render the work as a whole original. This implies that some "ways" will trigger copyright, but that others will not. See Patry 57, and n. 76. Otherwise, the phrase "in such a way" is meaningless and Congress should have defined "compilation" simply as "a work formed by the collection and assembly of preexisting materials or data that are selected, coordinated, or arranged." That Congress did not do so is dispositive. In accordance with "the established principle that a court should give effect, if possible, to every clause and word of a statute," Moskal v. United States, 498 U.S. ___, ___, 111 S.Ct. 461, 466, 112 L.Ed. 2d 449 (1990) (internal quotations omitted), we conclude that the statute envisions that there will be some fact-based works in which the selection, coordination, and arrangement are not sufficiently original to trigger copyright protection.

As discussed earlier, however, the originality requirement is not particularly stringent. A compiler may settle upon a selection or arrangement that others have used; novelty is not required. Originality requires only that the author make the selection or arrangement independently (*i.e.*, without copying that selection or arrangement from another work), and that it display some minimal level of creativity. Presumably, the vast majority of compilations will pass this test, but not all will. There remains a narrow category of works in which the creative spark is utterly lacking or so trivial as to be virtually nonexistent. See generally Bleistein v. Donaldson Lithographing Co., 188 U.S. 239, 251 (1903) (referring to "the narrowest and most obvious limits"). Such works are incapable of sustaining a valid copyright. Nimmer § 2.01[B].

Even if a work qualifies as a copyrightable compilation, it receives only limited protection. This is the point of § 103 of the Act. Section 103 explains that "[t]he subject matter of copyright . . . includes compilations," § 103(a), but that copyright protects only the author's original contributions—not the facts or information conveyed:

> "The copyright in a compilation . . . extends only to the material contributed by the author of such work, as distinguished from the preexisting material employed in the work, and does not imply any exclusive right in the preexisting material." § 103(b).

As § 103 makes clear, copyright is not a tool by which a compilation author may keep others from using the facts or data he or she has collected. "The most important point here is one that is commonly misunderstood today: copyright . . . has no effect one way or the other on the copyright or public domain status of the preexisting material." H.R.Rep., at 57; S.Rep., at 55, U.S.Code Cong. & Admin. News 1976, p. 5670. The 1909 Act did not require, as "sweat of the brow" courts mistakenly assumed, that each subsequent compiler must start from scratch and is precluded from relying on research undertaken by another. See, e.g., *Jeweler's Circular Publishing Co.*, 281 F., at 88–89. Rather, the facts contained in existing works may be freely copied because copyright protects only the elements that owe their origin to the compiler—the selection, coordination, and arrangement of facts.

In summary, the 1976 revisions to the Copyright Act leave no doubt that originality, not "sweat of the brow," is the touchstone of copyright protection in directories and other fact-based works. Nor is there any doubt that the same was true under the 1909 Act. The 1976 revisions were a direct response to the Copyright Office's concern that many lower courts had misconstrued this basic principle, and Congress emphasized repeatedly that the purpose of the revisions was to clarify, not change, existing law. The revisions explain with painstaking clarity that copyright requires originality, § 102(a); that facts are never original, § 102(b); that the copyright in a compilation does not extend to the facts it contains, § 103(b); and that a compilation is copyrightable only to the extent that it features an original selection, coordination, or arrangement, § 101.

The 1976 revisions have proven largely successful in steering courts in the right direction. A good example is Miller v. Universal City Studios, Inc., 650 F.2d, at 1369–1370: "A copyright in a directory . . . is properly viewed as resting on the originality of the selection and arrangement of the factual material, rather than on the industriousness of the efforts to develop the information. Copyright protection does not extend to the facts themselves, and the mere use of information contained in a directory without a substantial copying of the format does not constitute infringement" (citation omitted). Additionally, the Second Circuit, which almost 70 years ago issued the classic formulation of the "sweat of the brow" doctrine in *Jeweler's Circular Publishing Co.*, has now fully repudiated the reasoning of that decision. See, e.g., Financial Information, Inc. v. Moody's Investors Service, Inc., 808 F.2d 204, 207 (CA2 1986), cert. denied, 484 U.S. 820 (1987); Financial Information, Inc. v. Moody's Investors Service, Inc., 751 F.2d 501, 510 (CA2 1984) (Newman, J., concurring); Hoehling v. Universal City Studios, Inc., 618 F.2d 972, 979 (CA2 1980). Even those scholars who believe that "industrious collection" should be rewarded seem to recognize that this is beyond the scope of existing copyright law. See Denicola 516 ("the very vocabulary of copyright is ill suited to analyzing property rights in works of non-fiction"); id., at 520–521, 525; Ginsburg 1867, 1870.

III

There is no doubt that Feist took from the white pages of Rural's directory a substantial amount of factual information. At a minimum, Feist copied the names, towns, and telephone numbers of 1,309 of Rural's subscribers. Not all copying, however, is copyright infringement. To establish infringement, two elements must be proven: (1) ownership of a valid copyright, and (2) copying of constituent elements of the work that are original. See *Harper & Row*, 471 U.S., at 548. The first element is not at issue here; Feist appears to concede that Rural's directory, considered as a whole, is subject to a valid copyright because it contains some foreword text, as well as original material in its yellow pages advertisements. See Brief for Petitioner 18; Pet. for Cert. 9.

The question is whether Rural has proved the second element. In other words, did Feist, by taking 1,309 names, towns, and telephone numbers from Rural's white pages, copy anything that was "original" to Rural? Certainly, the raw data does not satisfy the originality requirement. Rural may have been the first to discover and report the names, towns, and telephone numbers of its subscribers, but this data does not " 'ow[e] its origin' " to Rural. *Burrow–Giles,* 111 U.S., at 58. Rather, these bits of information are uncopyrightable facts; they existed before Rural reported them and would have continued to exist if Rural had never published a telephone directory. The originality requirement "rule[s] out protecting . . . names, addresses, and telephone numbers of which the plaintiff by no stretch of the imagination could be called the author." Patterson & Joyce 776.

Rural essentially concedes the point by referring to the names, towns, and telephone numbers as "preexisting material." Brief for Respondent 17. Section 103(b) states explicitly that the copyright in a compilation does not extend to "the preexisting material employed in the work."

The question that remains is whether Rural selected, coordinated, or arranged these uncopyrightable facts in an original way. As mentioned, originality is not a stringent standard; it does not require that facts be presented in an innovative or surprising way. It is equally true, however, that the selection and arrangement of facts cannot be so mechanical or routine as to require no creativity whatsoever. The standard of originality is low, but it does exist. See Patterson & Joyce 760, n. 144 ("While this requirement is sometimes characterized as modest, or a low threshold, it is not without effect") (internal quotations omitted; citations omitted). As this Court has explained, the Constitution mandates some minimal degree of creativity, see The Trade–Mark Cases, 100 U.S., at 94; and an author who claims infringement must prove "the existence of . . . intellectual production, of thought, and conception." *Burrow–Giles,* supra, 111 U.S., at 59–60.

The selection, coordination, and arrangement of Rural's white pages do not satisfy the minimum constitutional standards for copyright protection. As mentioned at the outset, Rural's white pages are entirely typical. Persons desiring telephone service in Rural's service area fill out an application and Rural issues them a telephone number. In preparing its white pages, Rural simply takes the data provided by its subscribers and lists it alphabetically by surname. The end product is a garden-variety white pages directory, devoid of even the slightest trace of creativity.

Rural's selection of listings could not be more obvious: it publishes the most basic information—name, town, and telephone number—about each person who applies to it for telephone service. This is "selection" of a sort, but it lacks the modicum of creativity necessary to transform mere selection into copyrightable expression. Rural expended sufficient effort to make the white pages directory useful, but insufficient creativity to make it original.

We note in passing that the selection featured in Rural's white pages may also fail the originality requirement for another reason. Feist points out that Rural did not truly "select" to publish the names and telephone numbers of its subscribers; rather, it was required to do so by the Kansas Corporation Commission as part of its monopoly franchise. See 737 F.Supp., at 612. Accordingly, one could plausibly conclude that this selection was dictated by state law, not by Rural.

Nor can Rural claim originality in its coordination and arrangement of facts. The white pages do nothing more than list Rural's subscribers in alphabetical order. This arrangement may, technically speaking, owe its origin to Rural; no one disputes that Rural undertook the task of alphabetizing the names itself. But there is nothing remotely creative about arranging names alphabetically in a white pages directory. It is an age-old practice, firmly rooted in tradition and so commonplace that it has come to be expected as a matter of course. See Brief for Information Industry Association et al. as *Amici Curiae* 10 (alphabetical arrangement "is universally observed in directories published by local exchange telephone companies"). It is not only unoriginal, it is practically inevitable. This time-honored tradition does not possess the minimal creative spark required by the Copyright Act and the Constitution.

We conclude that the names, towns, and telephone numbers copied by Feist were not original to Rural and therefore were not protected by the copyright in Rural's combined white and yellow pages directory. As a constitutional matter, copyright protects only those constituent elements of a work that possess more than a *de minimis* quantum of creativity. Rural's white pages, limited to basic subscriber information and arranged alphabetically, fall short of the mark. As a statutory matter, 17 U.S.C. § 101 does not afford protection from copying to a collection of facts that are selected, coordinated, and arranged in a way that utterly lacks originality. Given that some works must fail, we cannot imagine a more likely candidate. Indeed, were we to hold that Rural's white pages pass muster, it is hard to believe that any collection of facts could fail.

Because Rural's white pages lack the requisite originality, Feist's use of the listings cannot constitute infringement. This decision should not be construed as demeaning Rural's efforts in compiling its directory, but rather as making clear that copyright rewards originality, not effort. As this Court noted more than a century ago, " 'great praise may be due to the plaintiffs for their industry and enterprise in publishing this paper, yet the law does not contemplate their being rewarded in this way.' " *Baker v. Selden,* 101 U.S., at 105.

The judgment of the Court of Appeals is

Reversed.

Justice BLACKMUN concurs in the judgment.

*

INDEX